OLD ENGLISH SYNTAX

VOLUME II

SUBORDINATION, INDEPENDENT ELEMENTS, AND ELEMENT ORDER

The aim of this work is to chart the whole realm of the syntax of Old English. It adopts the formal descriptive approach and the traditional Latin-based grammar because, in the author's opinion, these remain the most serviceable for the study of Old English syntax. As far as is at present possible, Old English usage is described and differences between Old and Modern English noted, with special reference to those phenomena which are the seeds of characteristic Modern English idioms.

Volume I sets out the general principles of concord in Old English and examines the parts of speech, the elements of the simple sentence and the types of simple and multiple sentences, and the complex sentence (including sections on punctuation, subordination and hypotaxis, correlation and anticipation, and the order and arrangement of clauses). Volume II deals with subordinate clauses, independent elements, and element order. It also offers a discussion of particular problems related to poetry, although poetry as well as prose is used illustratively throughout the book.

Old English syntax has been much less intensively studied than the syntax of the classical languages. There are many difficulties in the way of making definitive statements. They include the absence of native informants and of a knowledge of intonation patterns, limitations in the size and range of the corpus, the difficulty in assigning definite dates and locations to texts, problems of punctuation, and the possibility of later scribal changes. Hence this book does not lay down 'rules' but rather offers suggestions, demonstrates, where appropriate, the possibility of different interpretations, summarizes the present state of knowledge about the phenomena discussed, and indicates possible lines of future research.

This is the first work of its kind to be published; it will provide an essential foundation for more accurate and detailed exploration of Old English and of the English language by new generations of scholars equipped with the full collections of *A Microfiche Concordance to Old English*.

OLD
ENGLISH
SYNTAX

BY

BRUCE MITCHELL

VOLUME II

SUBORDINATION, INDEPENDENT ELEMENTS,
AND ELEMENT ORDER

CLARENDON PRESS · OXFORD
1985

Oxford University Press, Walton Street, Oxford OX2 6DP

London New York Toronto
Delhi Bombay Calcutta Madras Karachi
Kuala Lumpur Singapore Hong Kong Tokyo
Nairobi Dar es Salaam Cape Town
Melbourne Auckland

and associated companies in
Beirut Berlin Ibadan Mexico City Nicosia

Oxford is a trade mark of Oxford University Press

Published in the United States
by Oxford University Press, New York

British Library Cataloguing in Publication Data
Mitchell, Bruce
Old English syntax.
1. Anglo-Saxon language——Syntax
I. Title
429'.5 PE131
ISBN 0-19-811944-5

Typeset by Joshua Associates, Oxford
Printed in Great Britain
at the Thetford Press

In Memoriam

ALISTAIR CAMPBELL

*who would have written
a better book*

ANGUS CAMERON

'dead ere his prime'

*Generous scholars and
good men*

Grateful acknowledgement is made to the
British Academy for a generous grant towards
the cost of printing this book

SUMMARY OF CONTENTS

VOLUME I

VOLUME II

CONTENTS OF VOLUME I

CONTENTS OF VOLUME II

CHAPTER VIII: OTHER SENTENCE ELEMENTS
AND PROBLEMS   905

ABBREVIATIONS AND SYMBOLS

LANGUAGES AND DIALECTS

Ecc.Lat.	Ecclesiastical Latin	NHG	New High German
Gmc.	Germanic	nW-S	non-West-Saxon
Goth.	Gothic	OE	Old English
IE	Indo-European	OFr.	Old French
Lat.	Latin	OFris.	Old Frisian
ME	Middle English	OHG	Old High German
Merc.	Mercian	ON	Old Norse
MnE	Modern English	OS	Old Saxon
MnFr.	Modern French	WGmc.	West Germanic
Nb.	Northumbrian	W-S	West-Saxon

Before the name of a language or dialect: e = Early; l = Late; pr/Pr = Primitive

GRAMMATICAL TERMS

a., acc.	accusative	m., masc.	masculine
adj.	adjective	n., neut.	neuter
adv.	adverb	n., nom.	nominative
art.	article	p., pl.	plural
aux.	auxiliary	part.	partitive
compar.	comparative	pass.	passive
conj.	conjunction	pers.	person
correl.	correlative	poss.	possessive
d., dat.	dative	prep.	preposition
def.	definite	pres.	present
dem.	demonstrative	pret.	preterite
f., fem.	feminine	pret.-pres.	preterite-present
g., gen.	genitive	pron.	pronoun
i., inst.	instrumental	ptc.	participle
imp.	imperative	refl.	reflexive
impers.	impersonal	rel.	relative
ind.	indicative	s., sg.	singular
indef.	indefinite	st.	strong
inf.	infinitive	subj.	subjunctive
infl.	inflected	super.	superlative
interj.	interjection	tr.	transitive
interr.	interrogative	vb.	verb
intr.	intransitive	wk.	weak

's' may be added where appropriate to form a plural

SYMBOLS INVOLVING LETTERS

C	Complement	P	*See* §1901
O	Object	Sc	*See* §1911
S	Subject	Sp	*See* §1901
V	Verb	(Sp)	*See* §1901
v	Auxiliary verb	Ss	*See* §1901
Vv	Infinitive or participle + auxiliary verb	(Ss)	*See* §1901
vV	Auxiliary verb + infinitive or participle		

OTHER SYMBOLS

>	gives, has given
<	derived from
*	a reconstructed form
☆	an emendation or a reconstructed group of words
|, ||	(in verse) the medial and end caesura respectively
. . .	(in quotations) word or words omitted
/	(in citation of forms) alternatives. Thus *mid þæm/þam/þan/þon/þi/þy þe* means that in this formula *mid* and *þe* can be separated by any one of the six given forms.
( )	(in citation of forms) optional elements. Thus *(sona) hraðe/hraþe (. . .) þæs (. . .) þe* means that this particular combination occurs either with or without initial *sona*, with the given alternative spellings, and with the elements together or separated by other speech elements: *hraðe þæs þe; hraðe . . . þæs þe; hraðe þæs . . . þe; hraðe . . . þæs . . . þe.*
×	(preceding a section number). See chapter XI (§§3977–4000) for an addition to this section.

OLD ENGLISH TEXTS: SHORT TITLES AND SYSTEM OF REFERENCE

The abbreviations for, and the method of reference to, OE texts are those proposed in 'Short titles of Old English texts', by Bruce Mitchell, Christopher Ball, and Angus Cameron (*ASE* 4 (1975), 207-21, and *ASE* 8 (1979), 331-3). These depend on 'A List of Old English Texts' by Angus Cameron (*Plan*, pp. 25-306). The whole basis of the system is that reference to Cameron's 'List'—which will form part of the first fascicle of the *DOE*—is inevitable for everything except the poetry and a few well-known prose texts. It is obviously impossible to reproduce all this material here. I can give only the short titles to the two groups excepted above, crave the reader's indulgence for the inevitable inconvenience, and at the same time warn him that, unless otherwise stated, I use the texts specified in Cameron's 'List' (1973), which sometimes differs from *The List of Texts* published in 1980 to accompany *A Microfiche Concordance to Old English*. But I can explain a few special points which may help him to recognize the short titles for some other prose texts.

Where necessary, a reference is made to a particular manuscript by the addition in brackets of the appropriate sigil, e.g. *Bede(T)*, or to a particular edition by the addition of (an obvious abbreviation for) the name of the editor.

Standard abbreviations are used for the books of the Bible and the reference is to chapter, or psalm, and verse.

For the Heptateuch and the Psalms respectively, reference to the manuscripts will be by means of the abbreviations set out by S. J. Crawford, *The Old English Version of the Heptateuch* (EETS 160), p. 1, and by C. and K. Sisam, *The Salisbury Psalter* (EETS 242), pp. ix–x. So *Ps(A)* = the Vespasian Psalter, *Ps(F)* = the Stowe Psalter, and *Ps(P)* = the prose psalms of the Paris Psalter.

For the gospels the following system will obtain:

Li	Lindisfarne Gospels
Ru1	Rushworth Gospels (Mercian)
Ru2	Rushworth Gospels (Northumbrian)
WS	West-Saxon Gospels
WSA	Cambridge, University Library, MS Ii. 2. 11
WSB	Oxford, Bodleian Library, MS Bodley 441
WSC	British Museum, MS Cotton Otho C. i
WSCp	Cambridge, Corpus Christi College, MS 140
WSH	Oxford, Bodleian Library, MS Hatton 38
WSR	British Museum, MS Royal 1. A. xiv

Thus *Matt(Li)* means the Lindisfarne version of St. Matthew and *Mark(WSH)* the West-Saxon version of St. Mark in Hatton 38.

The charters present a special problem because there is no one complete edition. For short charters the Sawyer numbers will suffice, but something more may be needed for longer ones. Where this is so, an editorial designation is added after the charter number according to the following system:

B	*Cartularium Saxonicum*, ed. W. de Gray Birch
BMFacs	*Facsimiles of Ancient Charters in the British Museum*, ed. E. A. Bond
H	*Select English Historical Documents of the Ninth and Tenth Centuries*, ed. F. E. Harmer
Ha	*Anglo-Saxon Writs*, ed. F. E. Harmer
K	*Codex Diplomaticus Ævi Saxonici*, ed. J. M. Kemble
N	*The Crawford Collection of Early Charters and Documents*, edd. A. S. Napier and W. H. Stevenson
OSFacs	*Facsimiles of Anglo-Saxon Manuscripts*, ed. W. B. Sanders
R	*Anglo-Saxon Charters*, ed. A. J. Robertson
W	*Anglo-Saxon Wills*, ed. D. Whitelock

and so on, as necessary. References such as *Ch* 1188 *H* 2. 11 (page 2, line 11, of Harmer's *Select Documents*) and *Ch* 1428 *Ha* 113. 40 (line 40 of charter 113 in Harmer's *Writs*) are thus possible. Unless otherwise stated, I use the most recent of the editions cited by Sawyer.

Legal references follow the system used by F. Liebermann in *Die Gesetze der Angelsachsen* (Halle, 1903–16). In volume iii of *Leechdoms* (*Lch* iii), I have followed the pagination of the Singer reprint (London, 1961), where *De Tonitru* begins at p. 224, and not that of the Rolls Series 35 (London, 1864–6) and the Kraus reprint (Wiesbaden, 1965), where *De Tonitru* begins at p. 280. Both versions have the same numbering until p. 159; after that, there is a discrepancy of 56 pages.

Roman numerals refer to volume numbers except in the abbreviations for the titles of those poems whose title includes a roman numeral. Arabic numerals are used for sequences of separate texts, such as the charters, homilies, riddles, and psalms.

For continuous prose texts references are by page and line. When a prose text consists of a number of separated items numbered continuously from beginning to end, the reference is given by piece and line number; an example is Pope's *Homilies of Ælfric* (EETS 259 and 260). When this is not possible—as in Napier's *Wulfstan*, where the line numbers begin afresh on each page, and in Morris's *Blickling Homilies*, where no line numbers are given—page and line numbers are used. (This explains why, in *Ch* 1188 *H* 2. 11 and *Ch* 1428 *Ha* 113. 40 above, 2 is a page number and 113 a charter number.) When numbering the lines in such texts, I have counted the headings which occur within the page. So my numbers may not always agree with those given by other scholars. I am particularly conscious of variations in the *Blickling Homilies*.

When a passage is referred to but not quoted, the reference is to the line number in which the passage containing the discussed phenomenon begins, unless the example has been quoted elsewhere to illustrate something different. In that event, the reference is to the line at which the quotation begins, and the section number in which it is to be found is given in brackets. When a particular word or phrase is singled out for comment, the reference is to the line in which it occurs, again provided that the passage has not been quoted elsewhere, in which case the procedure just outlined obtains.

The OE and Latin examples are printed without length marks and in general without editorial italics, brackets, and the like. I have occasionally permitted myself a silent emendation, e.g. in §2490, where I read *Bede(B)* 144. 21 *Is* instead of *S* (space).

Verse texts

With the exception of *Beowulf*, for which I use the text (but not the diacritics) of Klaeber 3, the poems are cited according to the lineation of The Anglo-Saxon Poetic Records or, in the case of the few poems not found there, according to the lineation of the editions specified in the list. With the charms, *Metres*, and riddles, the item number precedes the line number. In the Paris Psalter, of course, the reference is by psalm and verse. References consisting of a roman numeral followed by an arabic one are to volume and page number in The Anglo-Saxon Poetic Records:

Aldhelm	Aldhelm (vi. 97)
Alms	Alms-Giving (iii. 223)
And	Andreas (ii. 3)
Az	Azarias (iii. 88)
BDS	Bede's Death Song (vi. 107)
Beo	Beowulf (iv. 3)
Brun	Battle of Brunanburh (vi. 16)
BrussCr	Brussels Cross (vi. 115)
Cæd	Cædmon's Hymn (vi. 105)
Capt	Capture of the Five Boroughs (vi. 20)
CEdg	Coronation of Edgar (vi. 21)
ChristA	Christ (iii. 3), lines 1–439
ChristB	Christ (iii. 15), lines 440–866
ChristC	Christ (iii. 27), lines 867–1664

Cnut	Cnut's Song (*Liber Eliensis*, ed. E. O. Blake (R. Hist. Soc., Camden Soc. 3rd ser. 92) (London, 1962), 153)
CPEp	The Metrical Epilogue to the Pastoral Care (vi. 111)
CPPref	The Metrical Preface to the Pastoral Care (vi. 110)
Creed	Creed (vi. 78)
DAlf	Death of Alfred (vi. 24)
Dan	Daniel (i. 111)
DEdg	Death of Edgar (vi. 22)
DEdw	Death of Edward (vi. 25)
Deor	Deor (iii. 178)
Dream	Dream of the Rood (ii. 61)
Dur	Durham (vi. 27)
El	Elene (ii. 66)
Exhort	Exhortation to Christian Living (vi. 67)
Ex	Exodus (i. 91)
Fates	Fates of the Apostles (ii. 51)
Finn	Battle of Finnsburh (vi. 3)
Fort	Fortunes of Men (iii. 154)
FrCask	The Franks Casket (vi. 116)
GDPref	Metrical Preface to Gregory's Dialogues (vi. 112)
GenA	Genesis (i. 1), lines 1–234 and 852–2936
GenB	Genesis (i. 9), lines 235–851
Gifts	Gifts of Men (iii. 137)
Glor i	Gloria i (vi. 74)
Glor ii	Gloria ii (vi. 94)
Godric	Godric's Prayer (*EStudien*, 11 (1888), 423)
Grave	The Grave (*Erlanger Beiträge zur englischen Philologie*, 2 (1890), 11)
GuthA	Guthlac (iii. 49), lines 1–818
GuthB	Guthlac (iii. 72), lines 819–1379
Hell	Descent into Hell (iii. 219)
HomFr i	Homiletic Fragment i (ii. 59)
HomFr ii	Homiletic Fragment ii (iii. 224)
Husb	Husband's Message (iii. 225)
Instr.	Instructions for Christians (*Ang.* 82 (1964), 4)
JDay i	Judgement Day i (iii. 212)
JDay ii	Judgement Day ii (vi. 58)
Jud	Judith (iv. 99)
Jul	Juliana (iii. 113)
Kenelm	Distich on Kenelm (N. R. Ker, *Catalogue of Manuscripts Containing Anglo-Saxon* (Oxford, 1957), 124)
KtHy	Kentish Hymn (vi. 87)
KtPs	Psalm 50 (vi. 88)
LEProv	Latin-English Proverbs (vi. 109)
Loth	Distich on the Sons of Lothebrok (N. R. Ker, *Catalogue of Manuscripts Containing Anglo-Saxon* (Oxford, 1957), 124)
LPr i	Lord's Prayer i (iii. 223)
LPr ii	Lord's Prayer ii (vi. 70)
LPr iii	Lord's Prayer iii (vi. 77)
LRid	Leiden Riddle (vi. 109)
Mald	Battle of Maldon (vi. 7)

Max i	Maxims i (iii. 156)
Max ii	Maxims ii (vi. 55)
MCharm	Metrical Charms (vi. 116)
Men	Menologium (vi. 49)
MEp	Metrical Epilogue to MS 41 (vi. 113)
Met	Metres of Boethius (v. 153)
MRune	Rune Poem (vi. 28)
MSol	Solomon and Saturn (vi. 31)
OrW	Order of the World (iii. 163)
Pan	Panther (iii. 169)
Part	Partridge (iii. 174)
Pha	Pharaoh (iii. 223)
Phoen	Phoenix (iii. 94)
PPs	Metrical Psalms of the Paris Psalter (v. 3)
Pr	A Prayer (vi. 94)
Prec	Precepts (iii. 140)
ProvW	A Proverb from Winfrid's Time (vi. 57)
PsFr	Fragments of Psalms (vi. 80)
Res	Resignation (iii. 215)
Rid	Riddles (iii. 180, 224, 225, and 229)
Rim	Riming Poem (iii. 166)
Ruin	Ruin (iii. 227)
RuthCr	Ruthwell Cross (vi. 115)
Sat	Christ and Satan (i. 135)
Sea	Seafarer (iii. 143)
Seasons	Seasons for Fasting (vi. 98)
Soul i	Soul and Body i (ii. 54)
Soul ii	Soul and Body ii (iii. 174)
Summons	A Summons to Prayer (vi. 69)
Thureth	Thureth (vi. 97)
Vain	Vainglory (iii. 147)
WaldA	Waldere i (vi. 4)
WaldB	Waldere ii (vi. 5)
Wan	Wanderer (iii. 134)
Whale	Whale (iii. 171)
Wid	Widsith (iii. 149)
Wife	Wife's Lament (iii. 210)
Wulf	Wulf and Eadwacer (iii. 179)

Major prose texts

ÆCHom i, ii	*The Sermones Catholici* or *Homilies of Ælfric*, volumes i and ii, ed. B. Thorpe (London, 1844 and 1846)[1]
ÆGram	*Ælfrics Grammatik und Glossar*, ed. J. Zupitza (Berlin, 1880)
ÆHom	*The Homilies of Ælfric*, ed. J. C. Pope (EETS, 1967 and 1968)
ÆLS	*Ælfric's Lives of Saints*, ed. W. W. Skeat (EETS, 1881–1900)[2]

[1] I have used Thorpe's edition because the EETS edition is not yet complete (March, 1981).

[2] Here I now use Skeat's homily number and not the Cameron number; see *ASE* 8 (1979), 331. But there may still remain an occasional uncorrected reference with the Cameron number.

Alex	*Letter of Alexander the Great to Aristotle* in *Three Old English Prose Texts*, ed. S. Rypins (EETS, 1924)
ApT	*The Old English Apollonius of Tyre*, ed. P. Goolden (Oxford, 1958)
Bede	*The Old English Version of Bede's Ecclesiastical History of the English People*, ed. T. Miller (EETS, 1890-8)
BenR	*Die angelsächsischen Prosabearbeitungen der Benedictinerregel*, ed. A. Schröer (BASPr. ii, 1888)
BlHom	*The Blickling Homilies*, ed. R. Morris (EETS, 1874-80)
Bo	*King Alfred's Old English Version of Boethius*, De Consolatione Philosophiae, ed. W. J. Sedgefield (Oxford, 1899)
ByrM	*Byrhtferth's Manual*, ed. S. J. Crawford (EETS, 1929)
Ch	Charter. *See* p. xxxi
Chron	*The Anglo-Saxon Chronicle*[3]
CP	*King Alfred's West-Saxon Version of Gregory's Pastoral Care*, ed. H. Sweet (EETS, 1871)
GD	*Bischofs Wærferth von Worcester Übersetzung der Dialoge Gregors des Grossen*, ed. H. Hecht (BASPr. v, 1900)
Law	Law. *See* p. xxxi
Lch i, ii, iii	*Leechdoms, Wortcunning and Starcraft of Early England*, volumes i, ii, and iii, ed. O. Cockayne (London, 1864-6). *See* p. xxxi
Marv	*Wonders of the East* in *Three Old English Prose Texts*, ed. S. Rypins (EETS, 1924)
Or	*King Alfred's Orosius*, ed. H. Sweet (EETS, 1883)[4]
Solil	*König Alfreds des Grossen Bearbeitung der Soliloquien des Augustinus*, ed. W. Endter (BASPr. xi, 1922)
WHom	*The Homilies of Wulfstan*, ed. D. Bethurum (Oxford, 1957)

BOOKS AND PERIODICALS

The system of reference to books, periodicals, and the like, is explained in the introductory paragraphs to the Select Bibliography.

LATIN TEXTS

When the editor of an OE text provides a Latin original, I quote his Latin. The following separate editions of Latin texts have been used:

for *Bede, Bede's Ecclesiastical History of the English People*, edd. Bertram Colgrave and R. A. B. Mynors (Oxford, 1969);

for *Bo, Boethius, The Consolation of Philosophy with the English Translation of 'I.T.' (1609)*, rev. H. F. Stewart (Loeb Classical Library, 1953);

for *Cp, S. Gregorii Magni Regulæ Pastoralis Liber*, ed. H. R. Bramley (Oxford and London, 1874);

for *GD, Gregorii Magni Dialogi Libri IV*, ed. Umberto Moricca (Rome, 1924).

---

[3] Reference to Earle and Plummer by Chronicle letter, page and line, and annal, e.g. *ChronA* 94. 1 (905).

[4] My copy of *The Old English* Orosius, ed. J. Bately (EETS, 1980), reached me in December 1980. It was then more than I could face to change all the *Or* references.

VII

SUBORDINATE CLAUSES

A. INTRODUCTORY REMARKS

§1926. I have set out my reasons for retaining the traditional terminology in §§1633, 1876, and 1883-4. But (as would happen with any system) many problems of classification and terminology arise in the course of this chapter. Some are due to the difficulty of distinguishing principal from subordinate clauses already discussed in §1885. Others involve various types of subordinate clauses. Some of these must be discussed here.

§1927. As Jespersen points out (*Ess.*, §33. 4), MnE clauses such as 'Whoever says so [is a liar]' and 'Whatever I get [is at your disposal]' are in their entirety the subject of the sentence and can therefore be described as 'primaries'. Some authorities therefore classify them as noun (or substantive) clauses; see, for example, Curme 1931, pp. 181 ff. I concede that this is satisfactory for MnE. But the situation in OE is more complicated. It is true that *swa hwa swa* and *swa hwæt swa* can introduce only what I call 'indefinite adjective clauses'. But they sometimes refer to antecedents and 'postcedents'. Moreover, the OE relatives *se* and *þe*, alone and in combination, can introduce both definite and indefinite adjective clauses. Again, OE noun clauses introduced by *þæt* never stand at the beginning of their sentence, whereas *swa hwa swa* and *swa hwæt swa* frequently do. For these and similar reasons, it is more convenient to treat clauses introduced by *swa hwa swa*, *swa hwæt swa*, and the like, with adjective clauses (§§2363-73).

§1928. The presence of an ambiguous verb form—one in which singular and plural and/or indicative and subjunctive are not distinguished (§§18-22 and 601-1a)—often creates difficulty. Thus, we cannot be sure whether we have a purpose or result clause in *ÆCHom* i. 540. 23 *and [God] hi onlihte mid gife þæs Halgan Gastes swa þæt hi wiston þa towerdan ðing and mid witigendlicere gyddunge bododon*. This problem—which, as I show in §§2802-4, is often more terminological than real—can arise even when the verb is *magan*, e.g. *ÆCHom* i. 26. 7 *Ða worhte he fela wundra, þæt men mihton gelyfan þæt he wæs Godes Bearn*.

§1929. Many problems involve the word *þæt*. We can classify the *þæt* clause in *ÆCHom* i. 6. 24 *Gif þu ne gestentst þone unrihtwisan and hine ne manast þæt he fram his arleasnysse gecyrre and lybbe* . . . as noun or purpose; that in *ÆCHom* ii. 80. 12 *Ac þæra ealdfædera ceorung is to understandenne heora gnornung, þæt hi rihtlice for heofonan rice leofodon and swa ðeah mid langsumere elcunge hit underfengon* as noun or cause;[1] that in *ÆCHom* ii. 142. 2 *þa getimode his wife wyrs ðonne he beðorfte, þæt heo ðurh wodnysse micclum wæs gedreht* as noun or result; and that in *BlHom* 59. 33 *Hwylc man is þæt mæge ariman ealle þa sar 7 þa brocu þe se man to gesceapen is?* as adjective or result. One does not escape these frequently artificial difficulties by adopting other classifications. They either crop up again, perhaps in slightly different form, or are replaced by others; for examples see Campbell, *RES* 7 (1956), 64–8; Mitchell, *MÆ* 25 (1956), 36–40; Behre, p. 67; and Schwartz, 'Derivative Functions in Syntax', *Lang.* 44 (1968), 747–83. We must accept their existence, at the same time recognizing that OE *þæt* is more widely used than MnE 'that'; consider *ÆCHom* i. 2. 26 *For þisum antimbre ic gedyrstlæhte, on Gode truwiende, þæt ic ðas gesetnysse undergann* 'I dared to undertake this task'; *ÆCHom* i. 4. 27 *He neadað þurh yfelnysse þæt men sceolon bugan fram heora Scyppendes geleafan* 'He compels men to turn from belief in their Creator'; *ÆCHom* i. 274. 13 *gif we willað habban þa micclan geðincðe þæt we beon Godes bearn* 'if we wish to have the great honour of being God's children'; *ÆCHom* ii. 566. 2 *ðonne sind hi stunte þæt hi cepað þæs ydelan hlysan* 'foolish in heeding vain renown'; and *ÆCHom* ii. 140. 21 . . . *biddende æt ðam lareowe liðe miltsunge þæt hi his lare ær to lyt gymdon* 'asking their teacher's mercy for having previously paid too little attention to his teaching'; and the more frequent use in MnE of the accusative and infinitive to express a dependent command. As in MnE, both clauses and infinitives are possible with certain verbs or nouns; cf. *ÆCHom* ii. 398. 30 . . . *us is beboden þæt we sceolon forlætan þas eorðan* with *ÆCHom* ii. 398. 28 *forðan ðe us is beboden . . . ofsittan and fortredan ða gewilnigendlican lustas*; *ÆCHom* ii. 328. 7 *Cypmannum gedafenað þæt hi soðfæstnysse healdon* with *ÆCHom* ii. 318. 15 *Us gedafenað to donne dugeðe on sibbe*; *ÆCHom* i. 6. 17 . . . *þa mihte þæt he heofenlic fyr asendan mæge* with *ÆCHom* i. 588. 26 . . . *cwæð þæt he hæfde mihte his sawle to syllenne*; and the two clauses in *ÆCHom* ii. 106. 19 *forðan ðe God ne het us gewelgian ða hæbbendan, ac þæt we ða wædligendan gefultumedon.* Manabe, in 'Syntactic and Stylistic Analysis of Finite and Non-Finite Clauses in Four Texts of Alfred's

---

[1] Ericson writes on 'Noun Clauses in *because*' in *Ang.* 61 (1937), 112–13.

Time', *SEL* (Tokyo) (English Number, 1976), 87–103, offers some statistics on the comparative frequency of *þæt(te)* clauses, infinitives, participles, and verbal nouns, in a limited corpus of 'Alfredian' and eME prose and verse texts. 'The proportion of non-finite to finite clauses is much lower in the OE corpus of Alfred's time than in the early ME corpus (1 : 5 as against 1 : 2)' (p. 102). 'The higher frequency of participles as adjuncts in the OE corpus is to some extent accounted for by reference to "source conditioning" ', i.e. the influence of a Latin original (p. 103).

✕ §1930. The abbreviation *þ̄* is the cause of much difficulty. Klaeber's note on *Beo* 15 seems to suggest that it can stand for *þæt, þa,* or *þe* (but see §2135), and his note on *Beo* 1141 that it can stand for *þæt* or *þe*.[2] In favour of these propositions is the fact that such selective resolution enables us to solve not only these but also many other textual and syntactic difficulties, e.g. the problems of concord involving *þæt* in adjective clauses (§§2134–44) and that of *oþþe* 'until', which could be described as the result of scribal interchange rather than of analogy or the weakening of *þæt* to *þe̦* (§§2751 and 2755). The argument that it is unlikely that the same abbreviation could stand for three different things in the same manuscript is weakened, but not necessarily disposed of, by the fact (drawn to my attention by A. J. Bliss in a private communication, 1969) that in some fifteenth-century manuscripts *þi* can stand for 'thy' or 'they', for these two words are different parts of speech and have no syntactical functions in common. A stronger argument against Klaeber's suggestion is this. If *þ̄* were an accepted abbreviation for *þe*, one would on the law of averages expect to find it occurring in a certain number of situations where only *þe* is possible; a case in point would be **seþ̄* for *seþe*. I have so far found no such examples. So I agree with Krapp (*The Junius Manuscript*, p. xxii):

But when one recalls the almost unlimited opportunities the scribe had for writing the abbreviation for *þa, þe,* or other forms besides *þæt*, and did not do so, it is unreasonable to interpret the abbreviation in these few doubtful cases as meaning anything other than *þæt*. If *þæt* for the abbreviation seems at any time an inappropriate form, the difficulty must be surmounted by emendation, not by a special interpretation of the abbreviation.

[2] This is the tip of a big iceberg. For other examples see Ball's review of Carnicelli's edition of *Solil* (*MÆ* 39 (1970), 175). Kärre's suggestion (pp. 131–2) that in *Ch* 711 *þ̄* is used eight times for *þonne* can be dismissed. *þ̄ = þæt* is correctly used of the finishing points in the description of the boundaries, *þonne* for the starting points.

Anyone attempting a detailed investigation of the function of *þ̄* should note Robinson's comment (*Speculum*, 48 (1973), 451 fn. 31) that 'in addition to its normal function as a consonant sign *ð* is occasionally used as an abbreviation for *ða* . . . , for *ðis* . . . , and possibly for *ðæt* . . .'.

Even if we were to accept the hypothesis that *þ* may have stood for *þæt* or for *þe* in some rough manuscripts or working drafts, we would still, I think, have to follow this principle, for both wrong abbreviations and wrong resolutions are scribal errors. Mistakes such as *oðþ* for *oðþe* 'or' in *Dan* 321 and *þ þ* for *þæt þa* in *Dan* 327 are clearly the result of scribal somnolence; in both places he has written a possible OE sequence which is not acceptable in the context in question. Emendation in such situations is, of course, legitimate. But a passage so emended cannot provide syntactical evidence.

§1931. For lists of conjunctions and relative pronouns in, and/or for examples from, particular texts, see (in addition to 'the prose text dissertations' and 'the eighteen German dissertations') the works by Halfter, Kopas, Rübens, Schücking, and Steche. All the subordinate clauses in the poetry are listed in my unpublished Oxford D.Phil. thesis, 'Subordinate Clauses in Old English Poetry' (1959), of which there are copies in the Bodleian Library and in the libraries of the Australian National University and the University of Toronto. Neither time nor space permits my undertaking a similar task for the prose. The potential value of such a study has, however, been demonstrated; for one example, see the discussion by Liggins (1970, especially pp. 318-20) of the individual variations in the handling of subordinate clauses in the 'Alfredian' translations.

§1932. The rules for negatives set out in §§1595-632 are of general application in subordinate clauses. Any special problems are treated as they arise.

§1933. Problems of element order peculiar to the type of subordinate clause in question are dealt with in the appropriate section as need arises. To avoid tedious repetition, tendencies which apply, *mutatis mutandis*, to all types of subordinate clause are discussed in chapter IX. It follows that the sections devoted to the different types of subordinate clause contain no specific subdivision on element order.

§1934. The order and arrangement of clauses are dealt with as necessary. References to these discussions will be found in the General Index.

B. NOUN CLAUSES

1. DIRECT, NON-DEPENDENT, DEPENDENT, AND REPRESENTED, SPEECH

§1935. As pointed out in §1635, direct speech, as in MnE 'I said: "He did it" ', 'He said: "I am ill" ', and 'He asked: "Are you ill?" ', is a special form of non-dependent speech. The latter is discussed in chapter IV. Direct speech can usually be distinguished in OE from dependent (or indirect) speech, as in MnE 'I said that he did it', 'He said that he was ill', and 'He asked whether I was ill'. The former involves verbatim quotation of the words of a speaker, e.g. *CP* 101. 5 *Eft he cuæð be ðæm ilcan: Ðonne ic wæs mid Iudeum ic wæs suelc hie, CP* 49.7 . . . *7 cuæð: Eala eala eala Dryhten, ic eom cnioht; hwæt conn ic sprecan?*, and the examples cited in §1636. The latter involves the use of a noun clause, described in the *Report of the Joint Committee on Grammatical Terminology* (p. 13) as 'a part of a sentence equivalent to a Noun . . . and having a Subject and Predicate of its own . . .'. The sentence of which the noun clause is part is called the principal (or main) clause, but no implication concerning the respective importance of the contents of the two clauses is intended.

§1936. The subject of these two clauses may be the same, e.g. *ÆCHom* i. 4. 16 *And se gesewenlica deofol . . . cwyð þæt he sylf God beo*, or different, e.g. *ÆCHom* i. 282. 14 *be ðam cwæð se apostol þæt he wære his Fæder wuldres beorhtnys.* So we can distinguish 'the speaker' (which may mean the wisher, the questioner, the promiser, the exclaimer, or, for example in reports of Gospel statements, the original writer) from 'the performer', the subject of the noun clause; see §1995 fn. The writer—in this case Ælfric— is also involved. There is, of course, no implication that the non-dependent equivalent of the noun clause was necessarily ever spoken or written. But sometimes 'the reporter(s)' may come between the writer and the speaker. In *ÆCHom* i. 86. 31 . . . *and [Herodes] cwæð, 'Ic wat þæt ðis Iudeisce folc micclum blissigan wile mines deaðes'*, Herod is both reporter and speaker. But this is not true in *ÆCHom* i. 44. 32 *and ða leasan gewitan him on besædon, '. . . We gehyrdon hine secgan þæt Crist towyrpð þas stowe . . .'*, where Ælfric, the false witnesses, Stephen, and Christ, all play a part. This example underlines the dangers of explaining the mood of a particular verb in dependent speech by too easily attributing attitudes to those involved, for we could say that the indicative *towyrpð* reflects the certain belief of Ælfric and Stephen that the statement was true or the insistence of the false witnesses that what they thought to be a lie was true.

§1937. Noun clauses fall into two main divisions—those introduced by *þæt* or some other conjunction (see §§1956-61) and those beginning with an interrogative or exclamatory word. These two groups may each be divided—the first into dependent statements and dependent desires (a general term covering commands, requests, exhortations, entreaties, and wishes) and the second into dependent questions (further subdivided into *x*-questions and nexus questions; see §1640) and dependent exclamations. The term 'dependent speech' is used with general reference to these four groups.

§1938. The distinction between the two main groups is rarely in doubt, although some noun clauses which are questions in form are almost without interrogative force, e.g. *þæt* and *hu* sometimes appear in parallel clauses with no obvious distinction; see §1961. The line between dependent statements and desires cannot always be drawn with certainty, for an element of desire enters into many statements and some words may introduce either a dependent statement or a dependent desire. In examples like

Jul 307   Swylce ic Egias   eac gelærde
                   þæt he unsnytrum   Andreas het
                   ahon haligne   on heanne beam,

we have a desire which was actually realized. So the *þæt* clause could be called result. Dependent questions sometimes shade into adverb or adjective clauses of time, especially with *hwonne* (§§2775-83), and dependent questions and exclamations cannot always be distinguished.

§1939. Direct speech gives us the words of the speaker. These words may be reproduced in dependent speech when the introductory verb is in the present tense, e.g. *ÆCHom* i. 364. 23 *Ic ðe secge, þæt þu eart stænen and ofer ðysne stan ic timbrige mine cyrcan*, and even when it is past, e.g. *ÆCHom* i. 300. 10 *þa twegen englas sædon þæt Crist cymð swa swa he uppferde*. This retention of the words of the speaker occurs in several different situations in OE. The choice between direct and dependent speech is, of course, made by the writer. For an analysis of the principles which guided one Anglo-Saxon, see Waterhouse, 'Ælfric's use of discourse in some saints' lives', *ASE* 5 (1976), 83-103. In her conclusion (p. 103), she speaks of

Ælfric's exploitation of the double resources of discourse for his didactic ends, those of direct speech to give his 'good' characters, especially the central saint, dramatic impact and those of indirect speech, particularly through terms which the speakers themselves would not have used, to convey a moral judgement of the characters that are 'bad'.

§1940. First, in the Gospels the conj. *þæt* commonly introduces what is really direct speech under the influence of Latin *quia/quoniam*, which in turn is due to Greek ὅτι, e.g. *Matt(WSCp)* 16. 18 *7 ic secge þe þ þu eart Petrus 7 ofer þisne stan ic timbrige mine cyricean*, Latin *et ego dico tibi quia tu es Petrus et super hanc petram aedificabo ecclesiam meam*, Greek κἀγὼ δέ σοι λέγω, ὅτι σὺ εἶ Πέτρος, καὶ ἐπὶ ταύτῃ τῇ πέτρᾳ οἰκοδομήσω μου τὴν ἐκκλησίαν. As Gorrell (p. 350) points out, there are instances in which the conjunction appears in the OE but not in the Latin, e.g. *Matt(WSCp)* 27. 11 *þa cwæð se Hælend þ ðu segst*, Latin *Dicit ei Iesus tu dicis*.

§1941. Second, while Ælfric sometimes quotes without preamble from the Scriptures or the works of the Fathers, e.g. *ÆCHom* i. 220. 5 *'þa ða Crist bebyrged wæs . . .'* and *ÆCHom* i. 206. 8 *'Se Hælend ferde to ðære byrig Hierusalem . . .'*, he frequently prefaces such quotations with the conj. *þæt*, e.g. *ÆCHom* ii. 82. 7 and *ÆCHom* i. 618. 25 *Se witega cwæð, þæt se miccla Godes dæg is swiðe gehende and þearle swyft*—the same quotation appears in direct speech at *ÆCHom* i. 618. 13—and (with the inverted commas which Thorpe usually uses with this construction) *ÆCHom* i. 314. 3-15, *ÆCHom* i. 520. 14 *Paulus se Apostol cwæð þæt 'Crist is Godes Miht and Godes Wisdom'*, and (with the introductory verb in the present tense) *ÆCHom* i. 510. 22 *þis dægþerlice godspell cwyð þæt 'Drihtnes leorningcnihtas to him genealæhton, þus cweðende . . .'*. Similar variations after *Hit is awriten* will be found in *ÆCHom* ii. 336. 28 and *ÆCHom* ii. 338. 27. In these examples *þæt* has almost the value of the modern colon or inverted commas. Gorrell (pp. 350-1 and 482) sees the construction as the result of imitation of constructions with ὅτι or *quia* and of analogical extension. Delbrück (pp. 228-9) discusses similar phenomena in other Germanic languages and suggests that the construction may be of Germanic origin, representing the first stage in the development of dependent speech. See also Curme, *MLN* 24 (1909), 98, and Muxin, *UZLIJ* 3 (1956), 19 fn. 1.

§1942. Third, a perpetual or general truth is sometimes found with the present indicative when the introductory verb is in the past tense, e.g. *ÆCHom* i. 386. 33 . . . *and mid micelre bylde þam Iudeiscum bodade, þæt Crist, ðe hi wiðsocon, is ðæs Ælmihtigan Godes Sunu,* *ÆCHom* i. 446. 6 *Drihten cwæð ær his upstige þæt on his Fæder huse sindon fela wununga,* and *ÆCHom* i. 300. 10 *þa twegen englas sædon þæt Crist cymð swa swa he uppferde.* (The line between these examples and those quoted in the previous section is sometimes a fine one.) But this is not always true. We find a change of tense in *ÆCHom* i. 136. 14 *and se ealda man Symeon . . . geseah þone Hælend and hine georne gecneow þæt he wæs Godes Sunu,* a change of mood in at least the second noun clause in *ÆCHom* i. 284. 15 *Ne bepæce nan man hine sylfne, swa þæt he secge oððe gelyfe þæt ðry Godas syndon oððe ænig had on þære Halgan þrynnysse sy un-mihtigra þonne oðer*—on *syndon* as a subjunctive see §651—and a change of both mood and tense in *ÆCHom* i. 282. 14 *be ðam cwæð se apostol þæt he wære his Fæder wuldres beorhtnys.* Visser (ii, §§826–8) offers further examples and comments. But he fails to draw our attention to some changes in mood.

§1943. Fourth, this retention of the mood and tense of the non-dependent speech is not restricted to perpetual or general truths, e.g. *ÆCHom* i. 46. 2 *We gehyrdon hine secgan þæt Crist towyrpð þas stowe and towent ða gesetnysse ðe us Moyses tæhte, ÆCHom* i. 542. 19 *Eac he him behet mid soðfæstum behate þæt hi on ðam micclum dome ofer twelf domsetl sittende beoð . . . ,* and *ÆCHom* ii. 528. 29 *Gregorius . . . cwæð þæt ure Drihten us manað hwilon mid wordum, hwilon mid weorcum.* In the last example, we may have the actual words of the speaker; the distinction between this type and that dis-cussed in §1940 is also a fine one, seemingly dependent on whether we today can identify the source of the remark or not. For further examples (some with the subjunctive), see Visser, ii. 845. As Stead-man (*passim*) points out, this explains several apparent breaches of the 'rule' of sequence of tenses and eliminates some of the alleged examples of the 'historic present' in OE.

§1944. But more usually the form of words is different in depen-dent speech. In OE there may be changes not only in person, tense, and element order in questions (as in MnE), but also in mood and in element order in dependent statements and desires, e.g. *ÆCHom* i. 4. 16 *And se gesewenlica deofol . . . cwyð þæt he sylf God beo* and *ÆCHom* i. 190. 32 . . . *þæt hi cwædon þæt he God wære.* These changes are exemplified and discussed in more detail below.

§1945. There is in MnE and in some other languages another form of non-dependent speech, sometimes called *erlebte Rede,* 'hinted speech', or 'represented speech'; see Karpf in *NS* 36 (1928), 571–81, and *Ang.* 57 (1933), 225–76; Collinson, *TPS* 1941, p. 98; and Jespersen, *Phil. Gr.*, pp. 290 ff. Here the fact that a speech is being reported is made clear from the context and from changes in person and tense without direct subordination to a verb of speaking. The original element order is retained in questions: 'She laughed. She wasn't going to fall for that. Did he think she was going to marry him after what had happened? Was she really such a fool?' Visser (ii. 783–5) finds examples in English from the eighteenth century on. I dismiss the possibility that it occurred in OE in §1984. Some passages which may seem to approximate to it, e.g. *ÆCHom* i. 452. 9–16, *And* 795–9, and *El* 979–88, are examples of the partial transition from dependent to non-dependent speech to which I now turn, for in all of them a verb of speaking or commanding precedes.

§1946. There are occasional examples in which the transition occurs, sometimes violently, within a short sentence and we have what could be described as an intermingling of dependent and direct speech, since the words of the speaker are vividly presented. They include *ChronA* 48. 24 (755) *þa cuædon hie þæt hie hie þæs ne onmunden þon ma þe eowre geferan þe mid þam cyninge ofslægene wærun* (MS E has *heora* for *eowre*), *ÆCHom* i. 314. 24 *God cwæð þurh ðæs witegan muð þæt he wolde his Gast asendan ofer mennisc flæsc and manna bearn sceolon witigian and ic sylle mine forebeacn ufan of heofonum*, *PPs* 74. 4 and 5, and

Sat 670   Brohte him to bearme   brade stanas,
              bæd him for hungre   hlafas wyrcan—
              'gif þu swa micle   mihte hæbbe'.

Note also

El 157   Ða þæs fricggan ongan   folces aldor,
              sigerof cyning,   ofer sid weorod,
              wære þær ænig   yldra oððe gingra
              þe him to soðe   secggan meahte,
              galdrum cyðan,   hwæt se god wære,
              boldes brytta,   þe þis his beacen wæs
              þe me swa leoht oðywde   ond mine leode generede,
              tacna torhtost,   ond me tir forgeaf,
              wigsped wið wraðum,   þurh þæt wlitige treo,

where we have a question which is anticipated by the pronoun *þæs*, but has the order of the original non-dependent question, no introductory interrogative word, and changes from the mood, tense, and person, which would have been used by the speaker to those appropriate to dependent speech.

§ 1947. More common is a gradual and often partial transition from dependent to non-dependent speech as the introductory verb is left further and further behind. The best-known examples in OE are probably those in the account of the voyages of Ohthere and Wulfstan in *Or* 17. 1–21. 17, e.g. *Or* 19. 10 *He cwæð þæt nan man ne bude be norðan him . . . þyder he cwæð þæt man mihte geseglian on anum monðe . . . 7 ealle ða hwile he sceal seglian be lande* and *Or* 19. 32 *Wulfstan sæde þæt he gefore of Hæðum, þæt he wære on Truso on syfan dagum 7 nihtum, þæt þæt scip wæs ealne weg yrnende under segle. Weonoðland him wæs on steorbord . . . 7 þonne Burgenda land wæs us on bæcbord.* (Gorrell analyses this passage at p. 479.) But there are many others, including *ÆCHom* i. 596. 29–35. A few shorter but characteristic examples follow.

§ 1948. In *ÆCHom* i. 452. 12 . . . *cwæð þæt seo fyrd wicode wið ða ea Eufraten and seofon weardsetl wacodon ofer ðone casere. þa com ðær stæppende sum uncuð cempa . . .*, the first clause after *cwæð* is in dependent speech while the third has the element order of non-dependent narrative. The status of the *and* clause is arguable. In *ÆCHom* i. 488. 12 *Se wyrdwritere Iosephus awrat . . . þæt se wælhreowa Herodes lytle hwile æfter Iohannes deaðe rices weolde, ac wearð for his mandædum ærest his here on gefeohte ofslegen . . .*, we have a change from preterite subjunctive to preterite indicative. The subjunctive mood of dependent speech appears with the present tense of non-dependent speech in *ÆLS(J)* 5. 332 *Ure hælend lyfde þæt mann his life gebeorge*—MS *V* has the preterite *geburge*—and *Luke(WSCp)* 22. 32 *Ic gebæd for þe þ ðin geleafa ne geteorige.* We have the element order of non-dependent speech in *ÆCHom* i. 20. 12 *Nu smeagiað sume men hwanon him come sawul.* We have a change to the tense of non-dependent speech in *ÆCHom* i. 596. 30 . . . *cweðende þæt swa halig wer hangian ne sceolde . . . forðan ðe he ne geswicð soð to bodigenne*; to the person of non-dependent speech in *ÆLS* 2. 185 . . . *cwæð þæt heo eode to hyre licgendre on læces hiwe and hi wolde forlycgan gif heo þæt bysmor forberan wolde ac ic hrymde sona mid sarlicre stæmne oþþæt an minra wimmanna me wið hine ahredde*; and to the imperative mood of non-dependent speech in *ÆCHom* i. 334. 25 *Ic bidde eow, mine gebroðra, þæt ge beon gemyndige ðæs Lazares reste and ðæs rican wite and doð swa swa Crist sylf tæhte.* These few examples must suffice.[3]

[3] More will be found at Gorrell, pp. 477–82; Behre, pp. 71 and 76; and Visser, ii. 770–85. Moloney discusses some examples of the change from dependent to non-dependent speech in Ælfric's *Lives of the Saints* in *NQ* 224 (1979), 498–500. Heusler is not concerned with syntactical problems in 'Der Dialog in der altgermanischen erzählenden Dichtung', *ZfDA* 46 (1902), 189–284.

§1949. We have what we can clearly call direct speech if the exact words of the speaker are retained when a verb of speaking interrupts the speech, irrespective of its tense. Thus we find (with a noun subject) *Or* 42. 1 *Ic wat geare, cwæð Orosius, þæt ic his sceal her fela oferhebban* and *BlHom* 99. 12 *Ic eow halsige, cwæþ Agustinus, þæt ge gongan to byrgenne weligra manna*; (with a pronoun subject) *Bede* 410. 14 *Gea, cweð ic, þu eart min Bosel, Bede* 164. 3 *Me þynceð, broðor, cwæð he, þæt þu wære þæm ungelærdum monnum heardra, þonne hit riht wære . . .* , *BlHom* 171. 6 *Oþer is, ic cweþe, se æresta apostol, oþer se nehsta*, and *WHom* 2. 42 *ac secge þæt he secge, he cwæð, ne gelyfe ge him æfre* (Ogura 1979, pp. 5–6, notes that *Bede* generally has *cwæþ he, WHom he cwæþ*); and (with two subjects in apposition) *Bede* 144. 9 *Bi þisse mægðe geleafan, cwæð he Beda, me sægde sum arwyrðe mæssepreost. . . .* For more examples see § 1982. Ogura (1979, p. 6) quotes two with no expressed subject, viz. *Bede(T)* 192. 6 *Ic hæbbu, cwæð, þæs treowes dæl . . .* , where (according to Miller) MSS *O* and *Ca* have *cwæð/cū he* instead of the expected *ic*, and *BlHom* 225. 25 *Drihten, cwæð, gif ic nugit sie þinum folce nedþearflic . . .* , where the Vercelli version lacks the parenthetic insertion but Junius 86 has *cwæð he*. Gorrell (p. 353) says that 'instances of this usage are not numerous'. However, Ogura (1979, pp. 5–6 and 27), from her limited corpus, gives over one hundred, mostly from *Or, Bede,* and *WHom*. But writers of OE did not always retain the mood and/or tense of non-dependent speech when they interpolated a verb of saying; see § 1982.

§1950. The function of the noun clause in the sentence to which it belongs is discussed in detail in the appropriate sections. But it is important that the OE noun clause does not occupy first place in OE sentences as it does in MnE examples like 'That he is rich is true' and 'Why he did it is a mystery'. I have found no examples with a *þæt* clause in this position[4] and so far only two with a dependent question. They are *Bede* 270. 26 *Hwæðer he þæt bi him seolfum cwæde þe bi oðrum men hwelcum, þæt us is uncuð*, Latin *Quod utrum de se an de alio aliquo diceret, nobis manet incertum*, and *Bede* 178. 1 *Hwelc þæs cyninges geleafa ⁊ modes wilsumnis in God wære, þæt æfter his deaðe mid mægena wundrum wæs gecyðed*, Latin *Cuius quanta fides in Deum, quae deuotio mentis fuerit, etiam post mortem uirtutum miraculis claruit*. Both of these are unidiomatic imitations of the Latin.

---

[4] The *þæt* clause in *Res* 109 is not one; in my opinion, it is an exclamation to be taken with what goes before and perhaps *apo koinou* with *seo bot*.

2. DEPENDENT STATEMENTS AND DESIRES

a. Introductory Words

(1) *Governing words*

§1951. Dependent statements and desires may be dependent on a verb, a noun, an adjective, or a preposition, or may be anticipated by a pronoun or adverb. Examples will be found in the sections which follow. Certain words introduce only dependent desires, e.g. *biddan* 'to ask', *healsian* 'to beseech, entreat', *bena* 'petitioner', and *frymði* 'making request'. A few verbs with two distinct meanings can introduce either dependent desires or dependent statements, e.g. *beodan* and its compounds in *a-, be-,* and *ge-* 'to command' or 'to announce', and *unnan* 'to wish' or 'to grant'.[5]

§1952. Words which introduce dependent statements can imply the idea of saying, e.g. *andettan* 'to confess', *onsacan* 'to deny', *að* 'oath', and *geþafa* 'agreeing';[6] of thinking, e.g. *hycgan* 'to think' and *wen* 'expectation'; of asking or knowing, e.g. *geahsian* 'to learn by enquiry', *witan* 'to know', *tacen* 'sign', and *undyrne* 'manifest'; of giving or granting, e.g. *lætan* 'to allow', *leaf* 'permission', and *gifeðe* 'given, granted'; of obligation, e.g. *gedafenian* impers. 'to behove', *riht* 'right, duty', and *gerysne* 'proper'; of forgetting and remembering, e.g. *forgitan* 'to forget' and *gemyndig* 'mindful'; and of feeling, e.g. *ondrædan* 'to fear', *hreowan* impers. 'to distress, grieve', *þanc* 'thanks', and *orwena* 'despairing'. This list covers the main categories, but is not exhaustive. Problems of classification inevitably arise. We could say that the *þæt* clauses after *spanan* 'to persuade, allure' in *GenB* 575, 589, and 684, are noun clauses. But since the verb-forms in the *þæt* clauses are respectively subjunctive, indicative, and ambiguous, we could equally well say that we have clauses of purpose, result, and purpose or result, respectively.

§1953. Some maids of all work can introduce either dependent statements or dependent desires, e.g. *cyðan* 'to make known', *secgan* 'to say', and *wenan* 'to think'. These and many others, e.g. *ongietan*

---

[5] If we exclude forms of the second participle with *ge-*, we find (despite Standop, p. 44) that there is a generally observed distinction between *hatan* 'to command' and *gehatan* 'to promise'. A few exceptions will be found in BT(S), s.vv. The only one in the poetry is *hætsð* in *Jul* 53, where J. R. R. Tolkien suspected a verb connected with *hægtess(e), hætse, hæts* 'a witch, a Fury'. On the word as a form of *hatan*, see *OEG,* §§732 and 734, and Woolf's note to line 53 in her *Juliana* (London, 1955). See further Nagucka, 'Syntax and Semantics of *hatan* Compounds', *Kwartalnik Neofilologiczny*, 26 (1979), 19–28.

[6] See Ogura 1978 and 1979 for discussions of verbs of saying, with special reference to *cweþan* and *secgan*.

'to perceive' and *gemunan* 'to remember', can also introduce dependent questions. The relationship of these governing words to the
clauses which follow them is discussed in the appropriate sections
below.

§1954. Noun clauses can be governed not only by a finite verb
form, e.g. *ÆCHom* i. 6. 20 *Ure Drihten bebead his discipulum þæt
hi sceoldon læran and tæcan eallum þeodum ða ðing þe he sylf him
tæhte*, but also by a present participle, e.g. *ÆCHom* i. 596. 29 *þa
betwux ðisum eode eall þæt folc to Egeas botle, ealle samod clypigende
and cweðende þæt swa halig wer hangian ne sceolde*, or by an infinitive, e.g. *ÆCHom* i. 156. 22 *we sceolon hryman . . . to ðam Hælende
þæt he todræfe ða yfelan costnunga fram ure heortan, ÆCHom* i.
46. 2 *We gehyrdon hine secgan þæt Crist towyrpð þas stowe*, and
(I believe) *LS* 23. 108 *and fram þysum weorcum is to gelyfanne þæt
god Zosimus on þæt mynster gelædde* (but see §937). As already
noted, they may also be dependent on a noun, e.g. *ÆCHom* i. 22. 12
. . . *þonne beo ic gemyndig mines weddes þæt ic nelle heononforð
mancynn mid wætere adrencan*; or on an adjective, e.g. *ÆCHom* i.
54. 18 . . . *and þu þær gemyndig bist þæt ðin broðor hæfð sum ðing
ongean ðe* . . . ; be governed by a preposition, either directly, e.g.
ÆCHom ii. 96. 12 *Hwæt wille we furðor ymbe ðis smeagan, buton
þæt se hæfð þa mede ðe he geearnað . . . ?*, or in apposition with a
prepositional phrase, e.g. *ÆCHom* ii. 318. 7 and *ÆCHom* i. 94. 1
*And þæt tacn wæs ða swa micel on geleaffullum mannum, swa micel
swa nu is þæt halige fulluht, buton ðam anum þæt nan man ne mihte
Godes rice gefaran, ærðan þe se come þe ða ealdan æ sette*; or be
anticipated by a pronoun, e.g. *ÆCHom* ii. 122. 5 *Hit gedafenað þæt
Alleluia sy gesungen on ðam lande*, or by an adverb, e.g. *ÆCHom*
ii. 582. 33 *þæt andgit we understandað swa: þæt Godes huse gedafenað þæt his lof sy þærinne gesungen.*

§1955. Dependent statements and desires can of course perform
other functions in the sentence to which they belong. These are discussed and exemplified in §§1962-75.

(2) *Conjunctions*

§1956. The most common conjunction introducing noun clauses
containing statements and desires in prose of all periods and in the
poetry is *þæt*. Numerous examples have already been quoted. More
will be found in Wülfing (i. 73-101); Ropers (pp. 12-21); Jost
(1909, pp. 36-50); Visser (ii, §§863-75); and Behre, part II, chapters i, vii, and viii, *passim*. Gorrell (p. 345) and Mann (*Archiv*, 180

(1942), 88-9) agree that 'this conjunction was originally a demonstrative pronoun denoting the inner object of the principal sentence'
—*He geseah þæt. Hit wæs god.* See further Visser, ii, §826. *OED*
(s.v. *that*, conj.) does not demur. The subordinating particle *þe* is
sometimes added. The more common result is *þætte*, which appears
alongside *þæt* in certain texts (but not, as far as I have observed, in
Ælfric or Wulfstan), e.g. *Or* 58. 13 *Ic wene, cwæð Orosius, þæt nan
wis mon ne sie, buton he genoh geare wite þætte God þone ærestan
monn ryhtne 7 godne gesceop, BlHom* 27. 1 *Men þa leofestan, her
sagaþ Matheus se godspellere þætte Hælend wære læded on westen
7 þæt he wære costod from deofle,* and *Beo* 2913-27. BT (s.v.
þætte) records *þæt þe* in *CP* 105. 1 *Forðæm eac wæs ðæt ðe beforan ðæm temple stod æren ceac* and I have noted two examples
in the poetry, viz. *Met* 1. 30 and

And 1602   Nu is gesyne   ðæt þe soð meotud,
                cyning eallwihta,   cræftum wealdeð,
                se ðisne ar   hider on sende
                þeodum to helpe.

Beo 1846 may be a third. But *ðe* can be a personal pronoun.

§1957. The standard dictionaries (including *OED*, s.v. *The*, particle;
on this article, see Dobson, *NQ* 206 (1961), 408) and other writers
have suggested that *þe* sometimes introduces a noun clause. Most of
the proposed examples can be otherwise explained. Some, including
CP 55. 9 and *Beo* 1333, are adjective clauses. Others are causal, e.g.
GuthA 715 and *Phoen* 409. In *PPs* 117. 2 *þe* seems to be a literal
translation of *quoniam*, which can introduce a noun or a causal clause;
see Nunn, pp. 52-4. In *Or* 142. 12, *þe* has its regular subordinating
function (§2428) and *þæm gelicost . . . þe* means literally 'most like
to that, namely . . .'. Wülfing (ii. 101) cites *LawAf(E)* 7 [Liebermann,
p. 16] *Be ðon þe mon on cynges healle feohte.* But MS *G* has *þæt* for
þe. Such variations in prepositional formulae are common; see §1230.
In *LawA Gu* 4, Liebermann has the expected *þæt* in both manuscripts
rather than *þe*, which Wülfing (ii. 97) prints, following Schmid. We are,
I think, forced to conclude that *þe* did not introduce noun clauses in
OE. So, with most authorities, I accept the emendation of *þe* to *þæt* in

El 981   Sceoldon Romwarena
              ofer heanne holm   hlaford secean
              ond þam wiggende   wilspella mæst
              seolfum gesecgan,   þæt ðæt sigorbeacen
              þurh meotodes est   meted wære,
              funden in foldan. . . .

On *And* 1129 see §2324.

§1958. Whether *þæs þe* introduces noun clauses is a terminological problem. Most of the proposed examples involve a verb, noun, or adjective, which governs the genitive, such as *þancian, þanc,* or *fægen.* Since it is arguable whether the *þæt* clause in *Sat* 532 *þanceden þeodne þæt hit þus gelomp* is noun or cause, the same is (I suppose) true of the *þæs þe* clause in *Beo* 227 *Gode þancedon ‖ þæs þe him yþlade eaðe wurdon* and of similar clauses after *gefeon* (*GenA* 1468), *þanc* (*Sat* 549), and *fægen* (*Sol* 262. 34 *lyt monna weorð lange fægen ðæs ðe he oðerne bewrencð*). It is theoretically possible that in such examples *þæs þe* represents an original *þæt þe* attracted into the genitive. But the fact that *þæt þe* is so much less common than *þæt* in noun clauses (see §1956) whereas *þæs þe* is much more common than *þæs* in the clauses under discussion seems to rule out this explanation. It is more likely that in such examples as *Beo* 227 above, *þe* has its usual subordinating function (§2428) and *þæs þe* can be explained as the functional equivalent of MnE 'for that [thing], namely . . .'. This is an extension of Klaeber's view (*MP* 3 (1905-6), 253-5) that in *Beo* 2794 and *Beo* 1627 . . . *þeodnes gefegon, ‖ þæs þe hi hyne gesundne geseon moston, þæs þe* introduces clauses of 'an exegetical character' with an *apo koinou* use of the verb of the principal clause. This enables us to explain examples like *Dan* 678 *Ða wæs endedæg ‖ ðæs ðe Caldeas cyningdom ahton*; as Blackburn's note has it, 'the idiom here used is very common in OE. A sentence is given the construction of a noun, the case being indicated by *ðæs ðe, ðam ðe,* etc., at the beginning.' Further on *þæs þe* 'because', see §§3113-17.

§1959. Examples in which *þæs* could be said to introduce a noun clause are much less common than those with *þæs þe* and can be disposed of by similar arguments; consider *MSol* 131 *banan heardlice ‖ grimme ongieldað, ðæs hie oft gilp brecað* and *El* 961 *Gode þancode, ‖ wuldorcyninge, þæs hire se willa gelamp,* where *þæs*—whether it is the result of attraction or of reduction of the more common *þæs þe*—may have achieved the status of a causal conjunction; see §§3113-16. A comparison of *GD(C)* 24. 33 *Gode ic þanc secge þæs þu gefyldest þæt ic bebead* with *GD(H)* 24. 35 *Gode þanc þæt þu gefylldest þæt ic þe bebead,* could suggest that after words meaning 'thank' and the like, OE *þæs* and *þæt* varied in the same way as MnE 'because' and 'that'.

§1960. Other conjunctions sometimes occur where *þæt* could have been used. They include the prepositional formulae with *for,* e.g. *BlHom* 235. 13 *Drihten Hælende Crist þa wiste forðon þe se halga*

Andreas þa slep, where there may be influence from Latin *quoniam* 'since, that'—note *ÆHom* 6. 93 *Fæder, ic þancige þe, for ðam ðe þu me gehyrdest*, Latin *Pater gratias ago tibi quoniam audisti me*;[7] *swilce*, e.g. *ÆCHom* ii. 104. 8 *þu hiwast swilce þu ðinum cildum hit sparige* and *LS* 34. 93 . . . *þe wolde þincean færunga swilce ealle ða anlicnyssa ðe on þære byrig to godon geond ealle gesette wæron ðæt hi ealle ætgædere oncwædon* . . . , in both of which 'as if' would give good sense (but note that in the second the conjunction is repeated after an adjective clause (§1979), but by *þæt*, not *swilce*[8]); *þa*, e.g. *ÆCHom* i. 400. 25 *Ic geseah, ðurh Godes Gast, þa se ðegen alyhte of his cræte and eode togeanes ðe*; *gif*, e.g. *ÆCHom* i. 140. 29 *Gif ðu oncnæwst ðinne Drihten mid ðinum æhtum be ðinre mæðe, hit fremeð þe sylfum to ðam ecan life*; *þær*, e.g. *Matt(Ru)* 26. 24 *god him wære þær he akenned ne wære*, where *WSCp* has *þ*, *Li gif*, and the Latin *si*, and *Soul i* 76; and *þeah*, e.g. *ÆCHom* ii. 432. 2 *La hwæt fremað ðære burhware þeah ðe þæt port beo trumlice on ælce healfe getimbrod*. . . . Both *þeah* and *gif* appear in *ÆCHom* i. 476. 3. Variations between *þæt, gif*, and *þeah*, are particularly common with verbs or nouns meaning 'wonder', e.g. *ÆCHom* i. 226. 14 *Mare wundor wæs þæt he of deaðe aras þonne he cucu of ðære rode abræce*, *ÆCHom* i. 286. 26 *Hwylc wundor is gif se Ælmihtiga God is unasecgendlic* . . . , and *ÆCHom* ii. 186. 9 *Hwilc wundor wæs, ðeah se halga wer ealne middaneard ætforan him gesawe*. . . . There is no point in arguing about what these should be called. But a *þeah* clause may be in apposition with *hit*, e.g. *ÆLS* 2. 160 *Ic wene þæt hit ne sy unrihtwisnysse ætforan Gode þeah ðe þu wifes bruce and blysse on life*; see further Burnham, p. 27. Clauses with *þeah (þe)* for *þæt* are further discussed in §§3407-15 and 3674. Clauses governed by verbs of fearing are usually introduced by *þæt*, e.g. *CP* 73. 20 . . . *ond eac hwelc se bið ðe him ondrædan sceal ðæt he unmedome sie*, but *þy læs* 'lest' does occur, e.g. *CP* 461. 30 *Ac him is ðonne micel ðearf ðæt he hine hrædlice selfne gewundige mid ðy ege ðæt he him ondræde ðylæs he weorðe upahæfen for his wordum*, where the Latin has . . . *magna cura necesse est ut timoris laceratione se mordeat*, and *Bede* 294. 25 . . . *þa ongon þæs cynelecan modes monn him ondrædan, þonne he to deaðe cumende wære 7 mid micle sare wæced þy læs he owiht unwyrþes oðþe ungerisnes dyde mid his muþe, oðþe mid oðerra lima styrenesse*, Latin *Qui . . . timere coepit homo animi regalis, ne ad mortem ueniens tanto adfectus dolore*

[7] Gorrell, p. 351, gives more examples of the *for* formulae and of *swilce*. Visser (ii. 775-6) notes a comparable use of ME *for*.

[8] The syntax of this whole sentence as printed by Skeat is not clear. We can either emend *þe* to conj. *þæt* (see §1957) or take *þe* as the second person dative singular of the pronoun beginning a new sentence and introduced under the influence of *we* in line 90.

*aliquid indignum suae personae uel ore proferret uel aliorum motu
gereret membrorum.* Shearin (1903, p. 98 fn. 1) wrongly cites
GD(C) 106. 12 as an example of *þy læs* introducing 'an object clause
after *gyman*'; *þy læs* here is an adverb.

§1961. The interrogative *hu* also appears after words meaning 'wonder', e.g. *ÆCHom* i. 166. 32 *Nu wundrað gehwa hu se deofol dorste
genealæcan to ðam Hælende þæt he hine costnode; ac he ne dorste
Cristes fandian gif him alyfed nære* and *ÆCHom* i. 590. 23 *Ic wundrige
ðearle ðin, humeta þu sy to swa micelre stuntnysse gehworfen*, in
both of which *þæt* would have done, and *ÆCHom* i. 230. 10 *Nu
trahtnað se papa Gregorius ðis godspel and cwyð þæt gehwa wundrað
hu se Hælend become in to his apostolum, and wæron ðeahhwæðere
ða dura belocene*, where *hu* puts the emphasis on the manner of the
action. The two also fluctuate after other words. In examples like
ÆCHom ii. 12. 16 and *ÆCHom* ii. 486. 24 *þa ongunnon ða apostoli
hi to lærenne and to secgenne hu Adam for his ofergægednysse
wearð on deofles ðeowdome gebroht and þæt se mildheorta God
swaðeah forgeaf þam mannum þe hine ænne wurðiað þæt se deofol
him derian ne mæg*, where the two appear in parallel clauses, there
seems little point in the variation. The same is true of

PPs 106. 20   Forðon hi nu andettan   ecum drihtne
                 þæt he milde wearð   manna cynne

and

PPs 106. 30   Hi andettan   ealle drihtne
                 hu he milde wearð   manna cynne.

But such examples do not justify Gollancz and Schaar in translating
þæt as 'how' in *ChristA* 310. Gorrell (p. 449) writes that 'it will be
found that the two constructions are not used indiscriminately: *hu*
has a definite stylistic value; it is the concrete, vivid introduction as
opposed to the colorless *þæt*'. He particularly draws our attention to
its use in Alfred's preface to the *Cura Pastoralis*, quoting *CP* 3. 2–13
and *CP* 5. 8 *Ða ic ða ðis eall gemunde ða gemunde ic eac hu ic geseah,
ærðæmðe hit eall forhergod wære 7 forbærned, hu ða ciricean giond
eall Angelcynn stodon maðma 7 boca gefyldæ. . . .* But perhaps we
should add 'always' after 'not' and 'sometimes' after *hu*, in view of
some of the examples I have quoted.

b. The relationship of the noun clause to the sentence

§1962. We have defined a noun clause as 'a part of a sentence equivalent to a noun'. So it is not surprising that it has many of the functions

of a noun. Thus we may say that a noun clause can be the subject, object, or complement, of the verb of the principal clause; that it may be in apposition with, or dependent on, another element in the principal clause; or that it may appear alone with no principal clause expressed. Here, of course, we are concerned with *þæt* clauses.

§1963. Let us consider first the patterns in which the *þæt* clause can be described as the equivalent of a nominative, remembering that sentences in which a subject noun clause occupies first place, as in 'That he committed murder is impossible', do not occur in OE, despite Pilch's adaptation of *Sat* 140-1 (*Altenglische Grammatik* (Munich, 1970), 174); see §1950. We can start, if we wish, by saying that in *ÆCHom* i. 256. 32 *þam spedigum gedafenað þæt he spende and dæle*, *ÆCHom* ii. 122. 15 *Æfter ðisum gelamp þæt micel manncwealm becom ofer ðære Romaniscan leode,* and *ÆCHom* i. 60. 32 *Dyslic bið þæt hwa woruldlice speda forhogige for manna herunge* . . . , the *þæt* clause is the subject of the principal clause, and that in *ÆCHom* ii. 122. 5 *Hit gedafenað þæt Alleluia sy gesungen on ðam lande,* *ÆCHom* i. 562. 28 *þa gelamp hit þæt sume ða hæðenan wurdon mid andan getyrigde,* and *ÆCHom* i. 404. 7 *Hit nis na gedafenlic þæt we on ðisum halgan godspelle ealle ða sceamlican yrmðu gereccan,* it is in apposition with the pronoun subject *hit.* But since the presence or absence of a formal pronoun subject is often optional—note *ÆCHom* i. 234. 19 *Ne getimode þam apostole Thome unforsceawodlice . . . ac hit getimode þurh Godes forsceawunge* and see §§1031-5—it seems better to say that we have the same pattern without and with a formal pronoun subject. Trnka observes that in OE 'in agreement with Old German the impersonal verbs are complemented by the pronominal subject *hit,* if they are not connected with the dative of the indirect object . . . or preceded by an adverb . . .' (pp. 160-1). This is not true; exceptions involving *þæt* clauses will be found in *KtPs* 16, *And* 609, *Met* 26. 4, *GenA* 289, *Soul i* 35, and elsewhere. Both *þæt* and *þis* can also serve as formal subjects, e.g. *BlHom* 13. 19 *Wel þæt eac gedafenaþ þæt he to eorþan astige* . . . and *ÆCHom* ii. 556. 4 *Ðis gelimpð dæghwomlice on Godes gelaðunge þæt gehwilce ge-leaffulle . . . beoð gebrohte . . . to ðam incundum andgite.* . . .

§1964. So far we have seen examples with and without a formal neuter pronoun subject (*hit, þæt,* or *þis*) involving impersonal verbs and combinations of *beon/wesan* and an adjective. But similar variations occur with other combinations. With *beon/wesan* and a noun, we find no pronoun in *ÆCHom* ii. 192. 30-194. 9 and in *ÆCHom* ii. 284. 24 *Anfeald neod us is þæt we ða boclican lare mid carfullum*

mode smeagan. When a pronoun does occur, it may be neuter, as in
ÆCHom i. 42. 5 *forðan þe hit næs nan neod þam Ælmihtigum
Scyppende þæt he of wife acenned wære* and *ÆCHom* ii. 398. 32
*þis is swaðeah feawra manna dæd, þæt hi ealle eorðlice ðing sæmninga
forlætan magon,* or may take the gender of the noun, as in *ÆCHom*
ii. 422. 18 *Ic gelyfe and þes is min geleafa fram ðissere tide, þæt
Crist is þæs Lifigendan Godes Sunu* and *ÆCHom* i. 528. 31 *Seo is
soð lufu, þæt gehwa his freond lufie on gode and his feond for gode.*
Here too it is better to say that we have the same pattern without
and with a formal pronoun subject than to erect an artificial distinction by saying that in the first group the *þæt* clause is the complement and that in the second it is in apposition with the pronoun. It
could also, I suppose, be argued that in some examples it is in apposition with the noun.

§1965. Other patterns with which these variations can be observed
include *beon/wesan* and an inflected infinitive, e.g. *ÆCHom* ii. 210.
3 *Is eac to understandenne þæt þæt Egyptisce folc wearð mid tyn
witum geslagen* but *GD(H)* 146. 1 *ac la, ic þe bidde, cwyst þu,
hwæþer hit to gelyfenne sy, þæt þysum Godes ðeowan mihte symble
æt beon se witedomes gast . . . ?*; *beon/wesan* and a past participle
forming an impersonal passive, e.g. *ÆCHom* ii. 160. 17 *and him wæs
geðuht þæt seo cæppe hine atuge of ðam streame* but *ÆCHom* ii.
230. 13 . . . *þy læs ðe hit wære geðuht þæt he hi for his teonan wode
hete, na æfter soðum ðincge* and *ÆCHom* i. 268. 1 *Is hwæðere
getæht . . . þæt wise men sceolon settan steore dysigum mannum*
but *ÆCHom* ii. 338. 27 *Hit is awriten þæt se healica God hataô
unrihtwisra gife;*[9] and *beon/wesan* or *weorþan* alone, e.g. (with questions) *ÆCHom* i. 360. 1 *Hu mæg beon butan strece and neadunge
þæt gehwa mid clænnysse þæt gale gecynd þurh Godes gife gewylde?*
but *ÆCHom* i. 198. 27 *hu mæg hit ðonne gewurðan þæt ic butan
weres gemanan cennan scyle?* and *ÆCHom* i. 198. 25 *Hu mæg þæt
beon þæt ic cild hæbbe . . . ?*, and (with statements, especially in
Cura Pastoralis) *CP* 353. 17 *Be ðæm wæs eac ðætte Fines forseah his
neahgebura freondscipe* but *CP* 355. 5 *ðæt wæs ðæt ðu adydes ða
bearwas of Iudea londe.*[10] This last construction may explain or ex-
pand a preceding statement or word, e.g. *ÆCHom* i. 138. 27 *Eac swa
þa unclænan nytenu getacniað ure unclænan geþohtas and weorc,
ða we sceolon symle acwellan, oððe behwyrfan mid clænum; þæt is

---

[9] But Trnka (p. 161) is wrong when he claims that in the poetry 'the impersonal *passive*
constructions . . . are found only, if they are followed by dependent clauses'. Exceptions
will be found in *Dan* 454, *PPs* 102. 8, *PPs* 121. 1, and elsewhere.

[10] See Gorrell, pp. 406-9; Jost 1909, pp. 51-2; and Visser, ii, §852.

þæt we sceolon ure unclænnysse and ure yfelnesse symle adwæscan, and forlætan yfel, and don god[11] and *ÆLS* 16. 314 *An is temperantia þæt is gemetegung on englisc, þæt is þæt man beo gemetegod* . . . ;[12] may deny one possibility to establish another, e.g. *BlHom* 19. 32 *Næs þæt na þæt he nyste hwæt se blinda wolde* . . . *ah Drihten wile þæt hine mon bidde* . . . ; may introduce a dependent desire with the subjunctive, e.g. *ÆCHom* ii. 44. 34, or with **sculan*, e.g. *ÆCHom* i. 138. 27 above; or may give emphasis to what follows, e.g. *CP* 323. 13 . . . *gehieren hie ðone cwide ðe on Cristes bocum awriten is, ðæt is ðæt sio winestre hand ne scyle witan hwæt sio suiðre do.* For further examples of these types, which inevitably merge into one another, see Gorrell, pp. 407–9.

§1966. Formal grammarians could well debate whether the *þæt* clause in *ÆCHom* ii. 422. 18 *Ic gelyfe and þes is min geleafa fram ðissere tide þæt Crist is þæs lifigendan Godes Sunu* is accusative after *gelyfe* or nominative in apposition with *min geleafa.* Similarly, the *þæt* clause which follows *Met* 8. 39 *Eala, þær hit wurde oððe wolde god* is 'nominative' after *hit wurde* and 'accusative' after *wolde!* It is, of course, only a debating point. For the combination of a nominative noun or adjective and *beon/wesan*, or a verb of appearing, coming, or the like, is often the equivalent of a verb of saying, thinking, or the like, e.g. *ÆCHom* i. 196. 29 . . . *and wæs hyre gewita þæt heo mæden wæs, ÆCHom* i. 136. 9 . . . *ða com him andswaru fram þam Halgan Gaste þæt he ne sceolde deaðes onbyrigan* . . . , *ÆCHom* ii. 508. 30 *and næs him nan wen þæt he ahwar wende buton to ðam halgan*, and *ÆCHom* i. 414. 29 *Ac uton we beon carfulle, þæt ure tima mid ydelnysse us ne losige.*

§1967. And so we turn to the *þæt* clause as the object of an introductory finite verb—its most common function. A few examples must suffice: *ÆCHom* i. 86. 31 *Ic wat þæt ðis Iudeisce folc micclum blissigan wile mines deaðes, ÆCHom* i. 208. 27 *and beodað þæt hi healdon ealle ða beboda þe ic eow tæhte, ÆCHom* ii. 428. 19 *'God! ic ðancige ðe þæt ic ne eom na swilce oðre menn'*, and *ÆCHom* ii. 32. 32 . . . *and micclum fægnodon þæt heo wæs þam breðer gelic* . . . . There is no point in arguing about the 'case' of these clauses, for *witan* takes the accusative or genitive of the thing known, *beodan* the accusative, *þancian* the genitive, and *fægnian* the genitive or

---

[11] Cf. with this the absence of conj. *þæt* in the immediately preceding sentence *ÆCHom* i. 138. 25 *þæt is, we sceolon ure yfelnysse behreowsian*. . . .

[12] Cf. *ÆCHom* ii. 288. 18 and *ÆCHom* ii. 228. 33 *Twa bysmorlice word hi cwædon to Criste: an is þæt he wære Samaritanisc, oðer þæt he deofol on him hæfde.*

dative. The influence of the introductory word is, of course, apparent when an anticipatory pronoun is used, as in *ÆHom* 11. 266 *ac hi ðanciað þæs ðe swiðor heora Scyppende æfre, þæt he hi swa ahredde fram þam reðum witum*; see further §1892.

§1968. Combinations of a noun and a noun clause are common, but present certain problems. (On this see also §§2067-8.) Sometimes the noun is essential to sense and syntax, e.g. *ÆCHom* i. 316. 23 *Namon ða to ræde þæt him wærlicor wære þæt hi sumne dæl heora landes wurðes æthæfdon, ÆCHom* i. 324. 34 *Se Hælend ableow his Gast on his gingran, for ðære getacnunge þæt hi and ealle cristene men sceolon lufigan heora nehstan, ÆCHom* i. 190. 31 *þæt folc ne cuðe ðæra goda, þæt hi cwædon þæt he God wære . . .*, and *Beo* 681 *nat he þara goda, þæt he me ongean slea*. Sometimes the *þæt* elaborates or explains a noun which is syntactically superfluous, e.g. *ÆCHom* i. 22. 12 . . . *þonne beo ic gemyndig mines weddes þæt ic nelle heononforð mancynn mid wætere adrencan, ÆCHom* i. 30. 1 . . . *se Romanisca casere Octauianus sette gebann þæt wære on gewritum asett eall ymbhwyrft, ÆCHom* i. 90. 24 *and ic sette min wed . . . þæt ic beo ðin God and ðines ofspringes* (cf. *ÆCHom* ii. 542. 3 *Settað eornostlice on eowerum heortum þæt ge ne þurfon asmeagan hu ge andwyrdan sceolon), ÆCHom* ii. 468. 15 *God . . . him forgeaf ða gife þæt he awrat ða forman Cristes boc, ÆCHom* i. 372. 31 *Hælend him tæhte ðone regol, þæt hi sceoldon yfel mid gode forgyldan*, and *ÆCHom* i. 326. 18 . . . *he sceal gelyfan on ða Halgan Ðrynnysse, and on Soðe Annysse, þæt se Fæder, and his Sunu, and heora begra Gast syndon ðry on hadum, and an God untodæledlic, on anre Godcundnysse wunigende*. Examples like

Beo 1970   Higelace wæs
     sið Beowulfes   snude gecyðed,
     þæt ðær on worðig   wigendra hleo,
     lindgestealla   lifigende cwom,
     heaðolaces hal   to hofe gongan

offer a passive equivalent.

§1969. Sometimes the object of the principal clause appears as the subject of the noun clause, e.g. *ÆCHom* i. 588. 28 *Ic wundrige ðe snoterne wer, þæt ðu ðyssere lare fylian wylt* (cf. *Matt*(AV) 25. 24 Lord, I knew thee that thou art an hard man), *ÆCHom* i. 70. 5 *þa bædon ealle þa leodbisceopas ðone halgan apostol þæt he þa feorðan boc gesette*, and *ÆCHom* i. 16. 3 *He . . . het ða eorðan þæt heo sceolde forðlædan cuce nytenu*, or in some other case, e.g. *ÆCHom* ii. 452. 14 *Hwæt la, ne beheolde ðu minne ðeowan Iob, þæt his*

gelica nis on eorðan . . . ? A genitive, dative, or the object of a preposition, in the principal clause may appear in the *þæt* clause as subject,
e.g. *ÆCHom* i. 390. 4 *God Ælmihtig* . . . *geseah his geðanc, þæt he
ne ehte geleaffulra manna ðurh andan* . . . , *ÆCHom* i. 372. 31
(§1968), and *ÆCHom* i. 122. 24 *We sceolon rihtlice gelyfan on Crist
þæt he ure sawle fram synna fagnyssum gehælan mæge*, or as object,
e.g. *ÆCHom* i. 308. 10 *We rædað be ðam witegan Heliam, þæt
englas hine feredon on heofonlicum cræte* . . . and *ÆCHom* i. 516.
29 *God bebead his englum be ðe þæt hi ðe healdon.* . . .

§1970. A noun or pronoun and a noun clause joined by *ond* may
serve as nominatives to the same verb, e.g. *ÆCHom* ii. 590. 20 and
ÆCHom ii. 592. 4 *þa heafodleahtras sind mansliht, cyrcbræce, and
þæt man oðres mannes wif hæbbe, and leasgewitnyssa* . . . , or as
objects, e.g. *ÆCHom* i. 68. 23 *Symle ðu tæhtest mildheortnysse and
þæt man oðrum miltsode, ÆCHom* i. 588. 25 *and he on ær his
ðrowunge us foresæde and þæt he wolde on ðam þriddan dæge of
deaðe arisan*, and

PPs 144. 12   þæt þu cuð gedydest   ofer cneorisse,
                 þær synd manna bearn   manig ætsomne,
                 and þæt þin miht is   ofer middaneard
                 and þines rices   rædfæst wuldur.[13]

Other possibilities include that seen in *ÆCHom* ii. 58. 26 *Seðe nu
æfter gastlicum andgite understent be Adame, swa swa we cwædon,
and þæt se mægslaga Cain getacnode þæra Iudeiscra geleafleaste.* . . .

§1971. The non-expression of a verb in the principal clause gives
exclamatory force in examples like *ÆCHom* ii. 346. 27, *ÆCHom* ii.
428. 20, *ÆCHom* i. 596. 24 *Unriht wisdom, þæt se halga wer swa
ðrowode*, and *ÆCHom* ii. 186. 5 *Wunderlic gesihð þæt an deadlic
man mihte ealne middaneard oferseon.*

§1972. Noun clauses occasionally occur with no principal clause.
They are most common in chapter headings in *Cura Pastoralis* and
Bede and, Gorrell (p. 365) suggests, 'may be supposed to depend on
some such verb as *tacnian*'. This is possible; a modern reader may
well have in mind some such idea as 'The book shows . . .' when he
reads chapter headings like 'How the teacher is to be discreet in
silence and profitable in speech' and 'What kind of man ought to
rule'. These patterns occur in OE as the result of direct imitation of

---

[13] This is the ASPR punctuation. BASP has a comma after *PPs* 144. 11. The *þæt* clause
in *Dan* 330 may be explained in this way; see Mitchell 1959, p. 113.

a Latin original, e.g. *CP* 10. xv *Hu se lareow sceal bion gesceadwis on his swigean 7 nytwyrðe on his wordum*, Latin *Ut sit rector discretus in silentio, utilis in verbo*, and *CP* 10. x *Hwelc se bion sceal se to reccenddome cuman sceal*, Latin *Qualis quisque ad regimen venire debeat*. The same is true of the *þæt* clauses, e.g. *CP* 10. vii *Ðætte oft þæs lareowdomes þenung bið swiðe untælwierðelice gewilnod*, Latin *Quod nonnunquam praedicationis officium et nonnulli laudabiliter appetunt*. But the imitation of Latin is not always exact, as Gorrell (pp. 365–6) notes. In *CP* 10. xv above *sceal bion* represents Latin *sit*; in *Bede* 6. x *Ðæt ricsiendum Archadio Pelagius se Bryt wið Godes gife geleafan unrihtlice lare onfeng*, Latin *Vt Arcadio regnante Pelagius Bretto contra gratiam Dei superba bella susceperit*, we have an OE indicative representing a Latin subjunctive; and *ðætte* in *CP* 8. i *Ðætte unlærede ne dyrren underfon lareowdom* is not represented in Latin *Ne venire imperiti ad magisterium audeant*.

§1973. Latin influence, however, does not explain examples like *Or* 104. 1 and *Or* 104. 12 *Æfter þæm þe Romeburg getimbred wæs IIII hunde wintra 7 II, ðætte Cartaina þære burge ærendracan comon to Rome*. Perhaps some such expression as *hit gelamp* is to be understood here. Similar constructions are found in the poetry after expressions denoting lapse of time, e.g. *Men* 207 *þæs ymb feower niht ǁ þætte Martinus mære geleorde*, and (less frequently) in other contexts, e.g.

Dan 753   No þæt þin aldor   æfre wolde
              godes goldfatu   in gylp beran . . .

(see *OED*, s.v. *that*, conj., II. 2. b), *Sat* 377, and *Sat* 632 . . . *and no seoððan ǁ þæt hie up þonan æfre moton*. The difficult *þæt* in *Sea* 24 *ful oft þæt earn bigeal* may be another example. The subj. *beo* suggests that the *þæt* clause in *ÆCHom* i. 350. 4 is dependent on *cwæð* in line 1.

§1974. Dependent desires without a principal clause are not common. Indeed, according to Cook (*MLN* 10 (1895), 28), 'it is generally assumed that sentences of the form, "O that Ishmael might live before thee!" (Gen 17, 18), corresponding to Latin sentences beginning with *utinam*, do not exist in Old English, or at least that there is no clear evidence of their existence'. The earliest example in the *OED* (s.v. *that*, conj., II. 3. c) is from the thirteenth century and has the *present* subjunctive:[14] *A duc þer was . . . þat was traytour . . .*

---

[14] This is normal in Latin when the decision is in suspense (see GL, §§ 260–1) and appears in the Latin version of *Gen* 17. 18 *Utinam Ismael vivat coram te!*

þat God giue him ssame. But there are two parallels for this in OE poetry, viz.

LPr iii 3   þæt sy gehalgod,   hygecræftum fæst,
                 þin nama nu ða,   neriende Crist,
                 in urum ferhðlocan   fæste gestaðelod,

which is certified as a wish by the Latin *Sanctificetur nomen tuum*, and the ASPR punctuation of

MCharm 9. 10   þæt he næfre næbbe landes,   þæt he hit oðlæde,
                 ne foldan,   þæt hit oðferie,
                 ne husa,   þæt he hit oðhealde.[15]

Another possible example is the last clause in *BlHom* 15. 21 *Hælend . . . him tocwæþ 'Hwæt wilt þu þæt ic þe do?' Se blinda him ondswerede 7 cwæþ, 'Drihten, þæt ic mæge geseon'*, which is a reminiscence of *Mark(WSCp)* 10. 51 *lareow þ ic geseo*, Latin *rabboni ut uideam*. But it is perhaps more likely to be a noun clause dependent on [*ic wille*]—cf. *Bo* 57. 29 *Nis nan gesceaft gesceapen ðara þe ne wilnige þ hit þider cuman mæge*—or on [*do*]—cf. *ÆCHom* i. 158. 19 *La leof! do þæt ic mæge geseon*. On *Bo* 34. 6 see §1672.

§1975. It is possible that *LPr iii* 3 and *MCharm* 9. 10 (both quoted in §1974) are also dependent on an unexpressed principal clause; Magoun (*Archiv*, 171 (1937), 26) saw the latter as ' "[Gebe,] dass" usw.' Ælfric himself proposed a similar explanation for one OE equivalent of the Latin *utinam . . .* when he wrote *ÆGram* 125. 12 *utinam amarem deum, eala gif ic lufode god,*[16] *swylce ðu cweðe: forgeafe god, þæt ic hine lufode.*[17] He could, no doubt, have substituted *ic wisce* for *forgeafe god*, for this construction actually appears in *Gen* 17. 18 *Ic wisce þæt Ysmahel lybbe ætforan ðe* (translating Cook's own example *Utinam Ismael vivat coram te!*) and elsewhere, e.g.

PPs 118. 5   Ic þæs la wisce,   þæt wegas mine
                  on ðinum willan   weorþan gereahte,
                  þæt ic þin agen bebod   elne healde,

Latin *Utinam dirigantur viae meae, ad custodiendas justificationes tuas!*

---

[15] Here, as Dobbie acknowledges in his note, he follows a suggestion of Magoun. It is preferable to making *þæt he næfre næbbe landes* a purpose clause subordinate to the preceding series of commands.

[16] On constructions with *gif*, *þær*, or the inverted pattern VS, + pret. subj., expressing unrealized wishes, see §§1679–80, 3620, and 3682–3. These cannot properly be called dependent desires.

[17] The pret. subj. *forgeafe* here may be compared with that in *ÆCHom* i. 448. 34 *Se biscop him andwyrde, God forgeafe þæt ðu uðwitegunge beeodest.*

c. *The presence, repetition, or absence, of* þæt

§1976. When the dependent speech consists only of a simple sentence, *þæt*, if expressed, immediately precedes it, e.g. *ÆCHom* i. 86. 31 *Ic wat þæt ðis Iudeisce folc micclum blissigan wile mines deaðes*; on the absence of *þæt* see §§1981-91. When two or more noun clauses are in syndetic parataxis, *þæt* need not be repeated, e.g. *ÆCHom* ii. 110. 29 *ac him is neod þæt he his agene wodnysse tocnawe and mid geleafan æt Godes halgum þingunge bidde and mid micelre anrædnysse Drihtnes fet gesece*, *ÆCHom* ii. 218. 29 *Gifernys bið þæt se man ær timan hine gereordige oððe æt his mæle to micel ðicge*, and *ÆCHom* i. 128. 20, where we find the sequence . . . *þæt we . . . ne we . . . ac we.* . . . So it is arguable—but not important— whether the *ac* clause in

Beo 1522   Ða se gist onfand,
         þæt se beadoleoma   bitan nolde,
         aldre sceþðan,   ac seo ecg geswac
         ðeodne æt þearfe

is a principal clause or a noun clause, and whether *þæt* in *GenB* 386 is a demonstrative pronoun or a conjunction. But *þæt* is often repeated after *ond*, *ac*, and the like, for emphasis and/or contrast, e.g. *ÆCHom* i. 168. 8 *nu geðafode God þæt þæt heafod hine costnode and þæt ða limu hine ahengon*, *ÆCHom* i. 156. 20, and *ÆCHom* i. 512. 21 *Ne bebead he his gingrum þæt hi on lichaman cild wæron ac þæt hi heoldon bilewitra cildra unscæððignysse on heora þeawum*, or to mark off groups of noun clauses, e.g. *ÆCHom* ii. 590. 20. My examples suggest that *þæt* is repeated when the clauses are in asyndetic parataxis, e.g. *Or* 19. 32 *Wulfstan sæde þæt he gefore of Hæðum, þæt he wære on Truso on syfan dagum 7 nihtum, þæt þæt scip wæs ealne weg yrnende under segle*, *ÆCHom* ii. 18. 23, and the chiastic *ÆCHom* i. 108. 6. Its absence from the noun clauses in *ÆCHom* i. 134. 19 and *Beo* 1106 is explained by the intervention of the clauses of condition; see §§1987-9. The conj. *þæt* is not repeated when two noun clauses are contrasted by means of *þonne*; see §3232.

§1977. The existence of examples like *Or* 19. 32 (§1976) suggests that Andrew (*Postscript*, §32) overstates his case in claiming that 'there can be little doubt' that in sequences of two *þæt* clauses like that in

Beo 771   þa wæs wundor micel,   þæt se winsele
         wiðhæfde heaþodeorum,   þæt he on hrusan ne feol,
         fæger foldbold

'the second *þæt*-clause [is] not co-ordinate but subordinate to the first' and is a result clause, not a noun clause. Both interpretations are possible. For similar examples see *Beo* 1671 (noun or result clause?) and *Beo* 1085 (noun or purpose clause?).

× §1978. When the sentence in dependent speech is complex, the noun clause may precede or follow the subordinate clause or be interrupted by it. When the noun clause comes first, *þæt* is found immediately before it (as in the simple sentence), e.g. *ÆCHom* i. 128. 19 *Wel wat gehwa þæt cyning hæfð maran mihte þonne ænig hundredes ealdor*. When the noun clause follows the subordinate clause, 'that' usually precedes both clauses in MnE, e.g. 'He thought that, if he slew them all, the one whom he sought would not escape.' Gorrell (p. 347) remarks that this arrangement 'is naturally of frequent occurrence' in OE. This is not borne out by the facts. The solitary example he gives on p. 347—*CP* 85. 5—is not one. The one he quotes on p. 466—*Matt(WSCp)* 24. 43 *Witað þ gyf se hiredes ealdor wiste on hwylcere tide se þeof towerd wære, witodlice he wolde wacigean*—is the only one so far known to me in the prose and is influenced by the Latin *Illud autem scitote quoniam si. . . .* He says again (p. 466) that this arrangement is 'quite common'. The statistics he gives (pp. 466-7) do not support him. The 'two tendencies at work against the use' of this position he noted (p. 347) must have been stronger than he thought. There are none in the poetry. The regular arrangement in OE is for the subordinate clause to precede the whole noun clause including *þæt*, e.g. *Or* 210. 15 *7 gewearð þa senatos him betweonum, gif hie mon þriddan siþe oferwunne, þæt mon ealle Cartaina towurpe, ÆCHom* i. 82. 12 *ðohte gif he hi ealle ofsloge, þæt se an ne ætburste þe he sohte*, and *Beo* 1845. With this arrangement it is not always clear to us whether the subordinate clause belongs to the principal clause of the sentence rather than to the noun clause or whether it is used *apo koinou*, e.g. *Or* 20. 19 *7 þær is mid Estum ðeaw, þonne þær bið man dead, þæt he lið inne unforbærned . . . monað ge hwilum twegen, ÆCHom* i. 614. 5 *Swa eac ge magon witan, ðonne ge ðas foresædan tacna geseoð, þæt Godes rice genealæhð*, and *And* 271; cf. *ÆCHom* ii. 106. 30 *We willað eow geswutelian nu ærest, gif eower hwilc nyte hwæt mannes Bearn sy, þæt Crist sylf is mannes Bearn . . .*, where the *gif* clause belongs with the principal, not with the noun, clause. Less frequent, but also found in the prose, is *þæt* immediately preceding the subordinate clause and repeated before the noun clause, e.g. *CP* 220. 18 *Ac eft sint to manigenne ða geðyldegan ðætte, ðæt hie mid hiera wordum 7 mid hiera dædum forgiefað, ðæt hie ðæt eac on hiera ingeðonce forgifen* and *ÆCHom* i. 174. 26 . . . *he andwyrde ðam deofle and sealde us bysne mid his geðylde, þæt swa oft swa we fram ðwyrum mannum ænig ðing þrowiað, þæt we sceolon wendan ure mod to Godes lare.* . . . Gorrell (pp. 347–8) fails to distinguish this type from those which follow. For some comparable MnE examples, see H. W. Fowler, *A Dictionary of Modern English Usage* (Oxford, 1940), s.v. 'that', conj. 4. The only possible example of this type in the poetry is

Met 11. 15   . . . þa þa he wolde,   þæt þæt he wolde,
           swa lange swa he wolde,   þæt hit wesan sceolde,

where the first *þæt* of line 15 may be a conjunction parallel to *þæt* in line 16, but can be taken as the demonstrative antecedent of the *þæt* which immediately follows it.

§ 1979. When the subordinate clause falls within the noun clause, the pattern found in MnE is very common, e.g. *CP* 385. 19 *Hit is awriten on ðæm godspelle ðætte ure Hælend, ða he wæs twelfwintre, wurde beæftan his meder . . .* , *ÆCHom* ii. 62. 28 *Ge sceolon eac gelyfan þæt seo bletsung ðe God behet Abrahame gæð ofer us*, and *Beo* 442. But another (not unknown in MnE) is also found. This involves the repetition after the subordinate clause of the conj. *þæt* and of that part of the noun clause already expressed. The part of the noun clause most commonly repeated is the subject, e.g. *CP* 199. 16 *Forðæm hit is awriten ðætte Dauid, ða he ðone læppan forcorfenne hæfde, ðæt he sloge on his heortan*, *Bede* 80. 24 *Forþon seo æ bibead þæm aldan Godes folce, þætte se wer se ðe wære his wiife gemenged, þæt he sceolde wætre aðwegen 7 bebaðad beon*, *ÆCHom* i. 612. 19 *Ne gewurðe hit la, þæt ænig geleafful, seðe gewilnað God to geseonne, þæt he heofige for middangeardes hryrum*, and *Beo* 2864. On the ungrammatical *BlHom* 191. 36, see Gorrell, p. 397. Ælfric makes much use of this construction, which occurs most frequently with a subordinate adjective clause. Similar repetition after a long subject involving an adjective clause is found in *ÆCHom* i. 134. 3. But the repeated element need not be nominative. It is accusative in *ÆCHom* i. 158. 34 *Nu cweðe ic to ðam menn, þæt ða ðing þe he understynt and undergytan mæg, ne undergyt he na ða ðing þurh his lichaman ac þurh his sawle* (where the conj. *þæt* is not repeated) and is in a different case in *ÆCHom* i. 370. 16 . . . *þæt eal ðeodscipe gleawlice tocnawe, þæt swa hwa swa oðscyt fram annysse ðæs geleafan ðe Petrus ða andette Criste, þæt him ne bið getiðod naðor ne synna forgyfenys ne infær þæs heofenlican rices* and *Alex* 14. 2 *Het ic þa ælcne mon hine mid his wæpnum gegerwan 7 faran forð 7 þæt eac fæstlice bebead ðæt se mon se ne wære mid his wæpnum æfter fyrd wison gegered, þæt hine mon scolde mid wæpnum acwellan.* But see §2213.

§1980. The problem of combining a noun clause and an adjective clause has caused difficulty to Englishmen of all periods; see Jespersen, *Phil. Gr.*, pp. 349–51, and Visser, i, §547. Two OE patterns have already been exemplified in §1979—one (which is usual in MnE) in *ÆCHom* ii. 62. 68, the other in *ÆCHom* i. 612. 19 and (with the repeated element in a different case) *Alex* 14. 2. In a third—seen in *ÆCHom* ii. 54. 10 . . . *to ði þæt he wolde geswutelian þæt ða giftu beoð herigendlice, ðe for bearnteame beoð gefremode swiðor þonne for galnysse*—the adjective clause follows the noun clause and is separated from the antecedent; see §2289. Two others appear when the relative pronoun precedes the introductory verb. The first— described by Ardern (p. xxxiv) as 'a slightly incoherent formula'— is seen in *Bede* 280. 12 *Ðonne wæs Biise Eastengla biscop, þe we sægdon þætte in þæm foresprecenan seonoðe wære, CP(H)* 111. 20 (see below), *ÆCHom* i. 234. 2 *þam mannum he sceal don synna forgifenysse, þe he gesihð þæt beoð onbryrde ðurh Godes gife, ÆCHom* i. 464. 9, *ÆCHom* i. 484. 13, and *WHom* 6. 197 . . . *forðam þe we habbað gecnawen fela þæra fortacna þe Crist sylf foresæde þæt cuman scolde*; here the subject of the *þæt* clause is unexpressed and must be sought in the relative pronoun. There are no examples in the poetry. In the second, which is perhaps less common in the prose, but occurs occasionally in the poetry, the *þæt* clause contains an expressed subject. This subject may refer back to a nominative antecedent and its accompanying *þe*, and its omission would give us examples of the type just discussed, e.g. *Bede* 62. 4 *in þære cirican seo cwen gewunade hire gebiddan, þe we ær cwædon þæt heo cristen wære* and *ÆCHom* ii. 462. 21 *ac swaðeah se ðe hungre acwelð, we gelyfað þæt he gegæð Gode*; note *CP(C)* 110. 21 *Ac swæ he wierð self to ðæs onlicnesse þe awriten is ðæt he gesio ælce ofermetto*, where the antecedent of *þe* 'of whom' is *ðæs* and where MS *H* lacks the second *he*. Even more complicated patterns appear; consider *BlHom* 85. 16 *Wene we sy þis se þe we wendon þæt þurh his deaþ us sceolde beon eall middangeard underþeoded* '. . . through whose death we thought . . .', *GenA* 2040, and

Vain 37   . . .   *læteð inwitflan*
                    brecan þone burgweal   þe him bebead meotud
                    þæt he þæt wigsteal   wergan sceolde,

where *þe him* might mean 'to whom' or *þe* might refer to *þone burgweal*, with *þæt wigsteal* tautologic. In

Met 9. 61 　　　ðær wæs swiðe sweotol, 　þæt we sædon oft,
　　　　　　　　þæt se anwald ne deð 　awiht godes
　　　　　　　　gif se wel nele 　þe his geweald hafað,

the noun clause in line 62 is a second subject of *wæs*, the first being the adjective clause in line 61b, which is used as a primary (§1927). Further on these constructions see Wülfing, i. 414-16; Pogatscher, pp. 290-3; Curme, *JEGP* 11 (1912), 379-80; and Kellner, pp. 69-70. Curme denies that *þe* in these examples is a relative. The issue is terminological rather than syntactical. Wülfing (loc. cit.) took the construction with the pronoun to be the original. Pogatscher (op. cit.) argued the reverse, believing that *þæt* was originally the demonstrative object of a parenthetic verb of saying, knowing, or the like —'the man who (you know that) is dead'. Kock (p. 86) also disagreed with Wülfing.

§1981. We have already seen that the conj. *þæt* is not normally used to introduce direct speech; for exceptions involving quotations from the Scriptures and from the works of the Fathers, see §§1940-1. But its absence does not necessarily certify that we have direct speech. The element order, tense, mood, and/or person, may do so, e.g. *ÆCHom* i. 378. 3 *Nero cwæð, 'Hwæt is nu, Simon?', ÆCHom* i. 222. 26 *Se engel gehyrte ða wif, þus cweðende 'Ne beo ge afyrhte'*, and at least the clause governed by *cweðað* in *ÆCHom* i. 306. 21 *Ic secge eow, manega cweðað to me on ðam micclan dæge, Drihten, Drihten, la hu ne witegode we on ðinum naman . . . ?* But even these guides sometimes fail; thus in *ÆCHom* i. 304. 18 *Drihten cwæð, þa ðe gelyfað him fyligað þas tacnu*, the present tense is that of the general truth, the third person is original, and the order *him* VS would be possible in both non-dependent and dependent speech. The question arises 'Under what circumstances can we say that we have dependent speech without introductory *þæt*?' Gorrell (pp. 348-50 and 482) discusses this problem. However, his analysis is inadequate, for he failed to make several vital distinctions. See also Pogatscher, *Ang.* 23 (1900), 266-7; Johnsen, *EStudien*, 46 (1912), 6; Ellinger, *Ang.* 57 (1933), 78-109, and *EStudien*, 71 (1936-7), 73-82; and Bosker, *Neophil.* 31 (1947), 32. Kirch (*PMLA* 74 (1959), 506-7), discussing Jespersen's suggestion (*GS, §80*) that the absence of the conjunction 'that' in English may date from the Viking settlements and be due to Scandinavian influence, concludes that 'we cannot assume that this usage was introduced into English from Scandinavian'. Ulvestad, 'A Syntactical Problem in Old High German', *NM* 59 (1958), 211-19, deals with 'indirect discourse sentences containing object clauses without *dass* after negative verbs' in OHG. I have not found the presence or absence of a negative in the principal clause a relevant factor in OE.

§1982. The relevant examples fall into three groups. First, there are those involving the parenthetic use of expressions like *ic bidde* and *he cwæð*, already discussed in §1949. These are sometimes used in what is clearly direct speech, e.g. *ÆCHom* ii. 28. 34, *ÆCHom* i. 488. 19 *Augustinus se wisa us manað mid þisum wordum and cwyð 'Besceawiað, ic bidde eow, mine gebroðra, mid gleawnysse hu wræcfull ðis andwyrde lif is'*, and *BlHom* 171. 7 *Oþer is, ic cweþe, se æresta apostol,*[18] and sometimes in what is already dependent speech but becomes direct after the parenthesis, e.g. *ÆCHom* i. 294. 18 *and [se Hælend] bebead him þæt hi of ðære byrig Hierusalem ne gewiton, ac þæt hi ðær anbidedon his Fæder behates, he cwæð, þe ge of minum muðe gehyrdon*. But we also have examples in the early prose without the conj. *þæt* but with the subjunctive mood of dependent speech, e.g. *Bo* 78. 13 *Ge furðum þ, ic cweðe, sie sio soðe gesælð, Bo* 54. 8 *Ða getriewan friend þonne, ic secgge, sie ðæt deorwyrðeste ðing ealra þissa weoruldgesælða, CP* 423. 19 *Sio, he cwæð, wære on his limum*, and *CP* 389. 11 *Sio winestre hand Godes, he cwæð, wære under his heafde*. In *Bo* 78. 13 and *CP* 423. 19 the preceding passage is in dependent speech. But this is not so in the other two examples. I leave it to the reader to decide what to call these. I would not follow Ogura (1979, p. 8) in speaking of 'asyndeton or omission of conjunction *þæt*' in *CP* 389. 11 above or in *Bo* 116. 3, on which see §2037.

§1983. Second, there are those examples in which *þæt* is unexpressed immediately after a verb of saying, thinking, or the like. In some of these, the syntax suggests that we have genuine dependent speech. The subjects of the two clauses may be the same or different. The tense and person suggest dependent speech in *ÆLS* 3. 373 *and cwæð he wolde wiðsacan his criste* and *Beo* 199 *cwæð, he guðcyning || ofer swanrade secean wolde* (same subject); in *And* 1639 . . . *cwædon holdlice hyran woldon* (where the subject of *woldon* has to be inferred from the principal clause; see §1512); and in *BlHom* 131. 26 *Swa gemunde 7 wiste ure se heofonlica Fæder his þa leofan 7 þa gestreonfullan bearn afysed 7 on myclum ymbhygdum wæron*

---

[18] For more examples see §1949. The exact status of the oft-quoted *John(WSCp)* 21. 25 *Witodlice oðre manega þing synt þe se hælend worhte. Gif ða ealle awritene wæron ic wene ne mihte þes middaneard ealle þa bec befon* remains uncertain. The Latin has an accusative and infinitive. The OE element order is not decisive for direct speech, especially in the Gospels.

æfter him (see §1986) and *GenA* 1594 *cwæð, he wesan sceolde* ‖ *hean under heofnum, hleomaga þeow* (different subjects). The person suggests dependent speech in *Bede* 200. 25 *sægde he, he hit gehyrde from þæm seolfan Uttan mæssepreoste* (same subject), the tense in *GenB* 385 *swa ic wat, he minne hige cuðe* (different subjects). *BlHom* 143. 36 *7 wæs cweþende þis wæs se þridda dæg geworden on þæm heo gewat of lichoman fram us* is difficult. The apostles are *us*, the Virgin Mary *heo*, and the speaker apparently Peter. The pret. *wæs* suggests dependent speech, the 1st pers. pron. *us* non-dependent speech. The pret. ind. *gewat* is at odds with the fact that the Virgin Mary is still alive (*BlHom* 143. 33), but in accord with the statement that she has been set in Paradise (*BlHom* 143. 24). On this see Nellis, *NM* 81 (1980), 399–402. With one exception— *CP(H)* 111. 16 *ond wenð he sua micle ma wite ðonne oðre menn*, where MS *C* has *7 wenð ðæt*—all the examples known to me in which the subjunctive mood suggests dependent speech are in a passage of direct speech and have different subjects in the two clauses. In *Dan* 425 *cweðað, he sie ana ælmihtig god*, the introductory verb is *cweðan*. (But cf. *Beo* 92 *cwæð þæt se Ælmihtiga eorðan worhte*.) It is *wenan* in all the rest, viz. *Bo* 29. 28 *Wenst þu mæge seo wyrd þe gedon þ . . . ?*, *Bo* 63. 17 *. . . wenstu mæge his rice hine þær on londe wyrðne gedon?*, *CP* 405. 11 *Gif hwelc wif forlæt hiere ceorl 7 nimð hire oðerne, wenestu recce he hire æfre ma . . . ?*, and *BlHom* 85. 16 *Wene we sy þis se . . . ?* (On *BlHom* 181. 29 and *ÆCHom* i. 378. 4, see §1986 fn.) In these, *wen(e)stu* and *wene we* come close to being interrogative formulae like *cwyst ðu* and *cweðe ge* (see §§1649–50) and are followed by what could be non-dependent nexus questions. Although the element order argues for this—cf. *Bo* 20. 17 and *Bo* 30. 23 *Wenst þu þ sio menigo ðinra monna þe mæge don gesæligne?*—the subjunctive mood is a problem, for the indicative occurs with *wenan* in *Luke(WSCp)* 17. 9 *Wenst þu hæfð se þeowa ænigne þanc forþam ðe he dyde þ him beboden wæs . ne wene ic* and indeed is the norm in non-dependent nexus questions (including those introduced by *cwyst ðu* and *cweðe ge*) except those introduced by *hwæþer* with the order S(. . .)V; see §§1643–60. But it is probably due to the influence of *wenan*, which 'of all verbs introducing Indirect Discourse . . . is the most consistent in requiring the subjunctive of the dependent verb' (Gorrell, p. 384).

§1984. Some of the examples cited in the preceding section—and indeed in that which follows—may seem to some readers to come close to 'represented speech' (§1945). But they cannot be so taken because they are immediately preceded by a verb of saying and so are by definition excluded; see §1945. The phrase *oðre worde* in

Sat 224   Ða get ic furðor gefregen   feond ondetan;
                   wæs him eall ful strang wom and witu;   hæfdon wuldorcyning
                   for oferhigdum   anforlæten;
                   cwædon eft hraðe   oðre worde:
                   'Nu is gesene   þæt we syngodon
                   uppe on earde . . .'

might seem to suggest that lines 225-6 are in 'represented speech'. But even if we do not take them as a parenthetic aside by the poet, they are ruled out by the presence of *ondetan* in line 224.

§1985. There are in the poetry five certain examples in our second group (§1983) in which *þæt* is not expressed when the subject of the principal and the noun clause is the same. In all of them the introductory verb is *cwæð*. In four—*Beo* 199 *cwæð, he guðcyning* || *ofer swanrade secean wolde, Beo* 2939, *And* 1109, and *And* 1639 *cwædon, holdlice hyran woldon*—the verb of the noun clause is *wolde/woldon*. The fifth is *Beo* 1810 *cwæð, he þone guðwine godne tealde.* To these can be added *GenB* 276 *cwæð, him tweo þuhte . . .* , where *him* is the psychological subject of the noun clause. According to Andrew (*Postscript,* §34), this is the only context in the poetry in which absence of *þæt* is idiomatic: '. . . after quite different verbs and before clauses in which the subject is *not* the same . . . ðæt should be restored wherever it is missing.' Both his premises are wrong. We find unexpressed *þæt* in sentences in which the subjects are different after *cweþan* in

GenA 1592   þæt þam halgan wæs
                   sar on mode,   ongan þa his selfes bearn
                   wordum wyrgean,   cwæð, he wesan sceolde
                   hean under heofnum,   hleomaga þeow,
                   Cham on eorþan

and *Dan* 425 *cweðað, he sie ana ælmihtig god,*[19] and after other verbs in *Dan* 542 and *PPs* 77. 20 (*biddan*), *Jul* 301 (*secgan*), *GuthA* 468 (*willan*), and *GenB* 385 (*witan*). Andrew's insistence that in these examples and in similar ones in the next group, such as *Beo* 2207 (§1989), 'ðæt should be restored wherever it is missing' is completely misplaced.

§1986. The examples of the second group so far discussed are those in which the syntax suggests that we have dependent speech. But we

---

[19] These two examples suggest that it is unnecessary to accept the *þ* inserted by a late hand between *cwæð* and *se* in *GenB* 344 or to follow Sisam (pp. 58-9) in inserting *þæt* between *cweðað* and his acceptable *Godd life* in *Fast* 226.

frequently have what comes very close to direct speech. In most of these, the verbs are in the present tense. Thus we find (after *secgan*)

GenA 2393   Soð ic þe secge,   on þas sylfan tid
             of idese bið   eafora wæcned;

(after *witan*) *GenB* 551 *Ic wat, inc waldend god* || *abolgen wyrð*; (after *wenan*) *ÆCHom* i. 378. 4 *Ic wene wit sind oferswiðde*;[20] (after verbs of commanding or asking) *ÆCHom* i. 332. 12 *Ic bidde eow, men ða leofostan, ne forseo ge Godes ðearfan* and *ÆCHom* i. 434. 12 *Ic halsige ðe, Laurentius, ablin hwæthwega ðæra tintregena*; (after *geseon*) *PPs* 73. 18 *Geseoh þu nu sylfa, god, soð is gecyðed*; and (after an adjective) *And* 1562 *þæt is her swa cuð,* || *is hit mycle selre.* . . . There are also occasional examples in which at least one of the verbs has the past tense, e.g. *Luke(WSCp)* 7. 43 *þa andswarode Simon ic wene se ðe he mare forgef. Ða cwæð he rihte þu demdest,* Latin *respondens Simon dixit aestimo quia is cui plus donauit at ille dixit ei recte iudicasti,* and *ÆCHom* ii. 438. 26 *Soð þæt is, gesælige hi wæron.* In these examples, since the speaker used the preterite tense, it is arguable that we have direct speech. But, in a sentence like *BlHom* 131. 26 (§1983), the third person *his* and *him* and the preterite *wæron* certify that we have dependent speech.

§1987. The third group (§1982) comprises those examples in which a subordinate clause precedes what we would call a noun clause in dependent speech if it were introduced by *þæt*. Such subordinate clauses may, of course, belong to the principal, not to the noun, clause, e.g. *GenA* 2139, or may be used *apo koinou*, e.g. *Beo* 798. But there are many in which this intervening subordinate clause clearly does not go with the introductory clause. I start with examples from the prose in which it is one of condition. The mood and tense vary: present indicative of open condition in *CP* 383. 31 *Eac hie sint to manigenne ðæt hie geðencen, gif mon on niwne weall unadrugodne 7 unastiðodne micelne hrof 7 hefigne onsett, ðonne ne timbreð he no healle ac hryre* and *ÆCHom* i. 18. 2 *Nis hit na swa ðu segst ac God wat genoh geare, gif ge of ðam treowe geetað, þonne beoð eowere eagan geopenode*; preterite indicative of open condition in *Bo* 127. 7 *swa swa mon on ealdspellum sægð þ an nædre wære þe hæfde nigon heafdu 7 symle gif mon anra hwelc of aslog, þonne weoxon þær siofon on ðæm anum heafde* (here the relevant sentence

---

[20] In *BlHom* 181. 29 *ic wene wit syn oferswiþede*—a different version of the same conversation—*syn* can be taken as indicative, even though forms without -*d(on)* or -*t* are usually subjunctive in that text. But, as we have seen, *wene* could produce a subjunctive and *sind* in *ÆCHom* i. 378. 4 could be so taken.

is linked by *7* to a preceding noun clause introduced by *þ* and containing a preterite subjunctive); and preterite subjunctive of rejected condition in *CP* 311. 13 *Ongean ðæt ðonne is to cyðanne ðæm fæstendum, gif ðæs modes forhæfdnes ful oft mid ungeðylðe ne ascoke ða sibbe of ðæm sceate ðære smyltnesse, ðonne ne cuæde sanctus Petrus to his cnihtum sua sua he cuæð* . . . and *BlHom* 29. 4 *Geþencean we eac, gif oþer nyten wære to haligienne 7 geteod to þon ecan life, þonne onfenge he heora hiwe*. . . . In all of these, the mood and tense would be appropriate in both non-dependent and dependent speech—even in *Bo* 127. 7, where present indicative during the lifetime of the creature or preterite indicative after its death would be equally appropriate. Similarly, the element order in the apodosis is always VS, whether it is introduced by *þonne*, as in the examples quoted above, or not, as in *Bo* 17. 20 *Wite þu for soð, gif þ þine agne welan wæron þe þu mændest þ þu forlure, ne meahtest þu hi na forleosan*[21] and *ÆCHom* i. 220. 9 *We cweðað nu, gif hwa his lic forstæle, nolde he hine unscrydan*. This is not conclusive evidence that we have non-dependent speech—consider *Bo* 127. 5 *forðæm hit is þeaw þære spræce 7 þære ascungæ þte symle þonne ðær an tweo of adon bið, þonne bið þær unrim astyred* and *ÆCHom* i. 82. 1 *swa swa Moyses be ðam awrat þæt ne sceolde ateorian þæt Iudeisce cynecynn*—but is not incompatible with such a view.

§1988. Similar examples in which mood, tense, and element order, are compatible with direct or dependent speech occur in the prose with other types of subordinate clauses, including those introduced by *swa swa* in *CP* 407. 22 and *Bo* 120. 29 *7 ic þe secge giet swa swa he lengra bið swa hi bioð ungesæligran*; the *þa* clause in *Bede* 162. 21 *Secgað men, þa Oswald se cyning of Scotta ealonde biscopes bede* . . . *þa wæs him sended ærest oðer biscop reðes modes monn*; the *mid þy þe* clause in *BlHom* 237. 30 *þanon wæs geworden, mid þy þe hie me sendon on þis carcern, ic bæd urne Drihten þæt he hine æteowde*; and the *þonne* clause in *BlHom* 67. 8 *forþon þe hit wæs Iudisc þeaw, þonne heora ciningas hæfdon sige geworht on heora feondum, 7 hie wæron eft ham hweorfende, þonne eodan hie him togeanes mid blowendum palmtwigum, heora siges to wyorþmyndum*. I leave it to the reader to decide how to classify these examples.

---

[21] This is another instance of the difficulty of combining a noun clause and an adjective clause discussed in §1980. It is perhaps examples of this sort which prompted Gorrell's remark (p. 397) 'that there is a constant tendency to use this verb [*witan*] as a simple introductory expression like the Modern English "you know" '.

§ 1989. Those in the poetry—which I discuss in *NM* 69 (1968), 178-82—include

Vain 77

	Wite þe be þissum,
gif þu eaðmodne	eorl gemete,
þegn on þeode,	þam bið simle
gæst gegæderad	godes agen bearn
wilsum in worlde,	gif me se witega ne leag

and

ChristA 233

Ond þa sona gelomp,	þa hit swa sceolde,
leoma leohtade	leoda mægþum,
torht mid tunglum,	æfter þon tida bigong.

Taken in conjunction with those from the prose already discussed, they provide strong support for the acceptance of Sisam's reading (p. 51) of *Fast* 168-73 and for the dismissal of two observations concerning *Beo* 2200-14, viz. Hoop's suggestion (in his note on *Beo* 2207) that a lapse on the part of the poet produced a paratactic construction where we would expect hypotaxis and Andrew's claim (*Postscript*, § 34) that *þæt* 'should be restored' before *syððan* in *Beo* 2207; see § 1985. In this connection note the Wrenn–CH translation of this passage.

§ 1990. The absence of *þæt* and other elements in contracted noun clauses such as *ÆCHom* i. 78. 10 *He . . . befran hwær Cristes cenningstow wære. Hi sædon, on ðære Iudeiscan Bethleem* can be paralleled in all periods of English.

§ 1991. In an article which came to my attention when the preceding sections were ready for the press, Ogura (1979, pp. 8 and 28 n. 8) gives references to twenty-one sentences in which 'asyndeton or omission of conjunction *þæt* occurs'. Among them I detect examples of five of the seven OE constructions I have distinguished. The table which follows provides a convenient summary of these constructions.

No.	Description of construction	My reference	Ogura's examples
1	Verb of saying + what may be the exact words of the speaker, which may be in the present or the preterite tense.	§§ 1935 and 1986	*Bede* 188. 16 (also governed by the *cwæð* which follows); *BenR* 28. 20; *ÆLS* 31. 1399; and (from *WSCp*) *Matt* 23. 36, *Luke* 9. 27, and *John* 1. 51.

Table (*cont.*)

No.	Description of construction	My reference	Ogura's examples
2	Verb of saying + *þæt* + what may be the exact words of the speaker.	§§1940–1	None, by definition. But cf. *Luke(WSCp)* 4. 24 and 4. 25.
3	What may be the exact words of the speaker, with a parenthetic verb of saying.	§§1949 and 1982	*BlHom* 171. 6, *WHom* 3. 48, and *WHom* 3. 50.
4	Dependent speech with conjunction *þæt*; what may be the exact words of the speaker can appear.	§§1942–3	None, by definition.
5	Dependent speech with conjunction *þæt* unexpressed but with changes of person and/or mood and/or tense.	§1983	*Bede* 200. 25 and *BlHom* 143. 36 (see §1983).
6	Sentences in dependent speech with a parenthetic verb of saying.	§1982	*CP* 423. 19 and *Bo* 119. 7.
7	Sentences not in dependent speech with a parenthetic verb of saying and with person and/or mood and/or tense inappropriate to direct speech.	§1982	*CP* 389. 12 (I do not think this belongs under 6); *Bo* 54. 8, 114. 22, and 116. 3.

My insistence that the lines of demarcation are not definite is further justified by the fact that the remaining four of Ogura's examples —*BenR* 136. 20, *Matt(WSCp)* 16. 28, and *Luke(WSCp)* 4. 25 and 7. 26—may belong under 1 or 3 above, depending on whether we take the initial *soplice/witodlice* as part of the original speech or with the verb of saying; other such examples include *Luke(WSCp)* 7. 28. I have found no examples of represented speech (§1945), but there are examples of intermingling of dependent, non-dependent, and direct, speech (§§1946–8), phenomena not listed in the table.

d. Mood and the 'modal' auxiliaries

(1) *Introductory remarks*

§1992. The accusative and infinitive may be used in lieu of a *þæt* clause to express dependent statements and (more often) those dependent desires in which the speaker and performer are different (§1936); see §§3725-6. When they are the same, the simple infinitive is the alternative; cf. *WPol* 92. 113 . . . *we willað þæt he hit forgylde* with *WHom* 6. 191 . . . *gyf we sylfe þæs earnian willað*.

§1993. An imperative in non-dependent speech usually disappears in dependent speech, being replaced by the accusative and infinitive or by a *þæt* clause with the appropriate tense of the subjunctive. Its retention after *gemyne* in two oft-quoted *þæt* clauses in the prose —viz. *Bede(T)* 200. 4 *Ac gemyne þu þæt þu þisne ele þe ic þe nu sylle, synd* [MSS B, O, Ca *send*] *in þa sæ* and *Or* 242. 6 *gefera, gefera, gemyne þæt ðu ure gecwedrædenne 7 geferrædenne to longe ne oferbrec*—is used (not unreasonably) by Behre (p. 76) to justify retention of MS *weorð* in *Prec* 30 *Ræfn elne þis,* ‖ *þæt þu næfre fæcne weorðe* [so ASPR] *freonde þinum*. For examples in which the imperative appears in the second of two co-ordinate clauses see §2003.

§1994. A 'modal' auxiliary in non-dependent speech is retained in dependent speech with appropriate changes in mood and tense; cf. *John(WSCp)* 12. 21 *7 hi bædon hine and cwædon, Leof we wyllað geseon þone Hælend* with *ÆCHom* i. 136. 24 *Hit is awriten . . . þæt fela witegan and rihtwise men woldan geseon Cristes tocyme.*[22] But a 'modal' auxiliary may be imported to avoid possible ambiguity in the dependent speech; cf. *Matt(WSCp)* 27. 63 *Hlaford, we gemunon þ se swica sæde þa he on life wæs, Æfter þrym dagon ic arise* with *ÆCHom* i. 588. 25 *and he on ær his ðrowunge us foresæde and þæt he wolde on ðam þriddan dæge of deaðe arisan*. It would, however, be a singularly unprofitable exercise to attempt to distinguish examples on this basis, for we often have great difficulty in deciding the exact significance of any particular example of a 'modal' auxiliary, especially when the form is ambiguous. We have already seen this in §1009, where I passed to the lexicographers the complex semantic problems involved in the task. But I can offer a few observations on important tendencies and potential problems concerning the use of these auxiliaries in dependent speech.

§1995. Anyone attempting a full analysis will need to consider (among other factors) the meaning of the introductory verb, its person, mood, and tense, and the identity or non-identity of the speaker and

---

[22] No reliable distinction exists between indicative and subjunctive in the past tense of these verbs. In *willan* there is a distinction in the second person present singular and in the present plural; in *magan, *motan*, and *sculan*, in the present singular.

the performer, for these help to determine whether a 'modal' auxiliary is present or not, and, if so, which one. Thus (to cite one example), with verbs meaning 'to permit', where the speaker and performer[23] are different and the latter is dependent on the former, *motan 'to be allowed to' is very common. See further Gorrell, p. 457; Standop, pp. 41-6 and passim; and Ogawa, pp. 123-9. It will also be necessary to compare examples which are or seem to be parallel except that one has a simple verb-form and the other an auxiliary. Such comparison leads Standop (pp. 60-1) to suggest that magan expresses a different kind of uncertainty from the subjunctive of a simple verb.

§1996. In general, it can be said that the meaning of these verbs is much the same in dependent speech as in non-dependent speech; see §§1009-24 and the discussions which follow here on the various types of dependent speech. They are perhaps more likely to appear to be used in their modern weakened sense in dependent than in non-dependent speech. But consideration of individual examples often serves to reveal difference of opinion among modern scholars rather than truth about the situation in OE. There are certainly times when we can say with some assurance that the 'modal' auxiliary has (much of) its full force, e.g. ÆCHom i. 10. 33 . . . and cwæð þæt he mihte beon þam Ælmihtigum Gode gelic. But it is less easy to be certain about ÆCHom i. 558. 17 . . . and cwæð þæt hi sylfe eaðelice mihton to Godes miltsunge becuman, gif hi fram heora dwollicum biggengum eallunga gecyrdon. So disagreement is frequently the order of the day. Thus Gorrell (p. 457) says of magan and *motan that 'there is great irregularity in the employment of these auxiliaries; in most cases they appear to be used merely to form periphrases of the simple subjunctive'. In my opinion, this 'irregularity' is, to some extent at any rate, the result of the absence of native informants; Ogawa's analysis of noun clauses after volitional expressions in Orosius (passim) demonstrates how much can be achieved by the use of the methods outlined above and his conclusion (p. 137) that in such clauses 'the modal verbs . . . are not mere grammatical substitutes' is a warning against too easy acquiescence in the view that they are. So Behre's remark (p. 92 fn. 1) that 'the subjunctive of motan (magan) with the infinitive . . . in the 1st. pers. of the present [sc. singular] . . . is generally the only means of expressing the subjunctive mood' may be true only for modern scholars; are mæge and mote in

---

[23] The word 'performer' is used here without connotations of 'performative' in the sense adopted by J. L. Austin, How to Do Things with Words (Oxford, 1962), 6-7, or by Nagucka, Kwartalnik Neofilologiczny, 26 (1979), 19-28.

Sat 420   Nu ic þe halsige,   heofenrices weard,
                 for þan hirede   þe ðu hider læddest,
                 engla þreatas,   þæt ic up heonon
                 mæge and mote   mid minre mægðe

merely the equivalent of 'may rise' (see Standop, pp. 42-3 and 44)?

§1997. Similar differences arise with *willan* and **sculan*. I do not share Gorrell's confidence (p. 455) that 'the simple future character of the expression [*willað*] can hardly admit of any doubt' in *ÆCHom* ii. 482. 29 *and tomerigen, ymbe undern, cumað þine ærendracan ðe ðu asendest, and cyðað þe þæt ða Indiscan willað beon eowere gafolgylderas, and mid ealre sibbe eow underðeodan*; *cumað* is 'simple future' and *willað* must add some idea of volition, intention, or acquiescence. Nor do I believe, as he does (p. 452), that in *ÆCHom* i. 294. 1 *Eac we sceolon gelyfan þæt ælc lichama ðe sawle underfeng sceal arisan on domes dæge mid þam ylcum lichaman þe he nu hæfð, and sceal onfon edlean ealra his dæda: þonne habbað ða godan ece lif mid Gode, and he sylð þa mede ælcum be his geearnungum*, the phrase *sceal arisan* can be an example of 'the nearest approach to the modern periphrastic construction of the future' when *sceolon* implies obligation or necessity and *habbað* and *sylð* refer to the future. Such observations are common; see for example Schrader, pp. 73-5, and Gorrell, p. 409 and *passim*.

§1998. These facts and modern uncertainties about the significance of 'shall' and 'will' in some contexts warn us to avoid dogmatism about the exact status of the 'modal' auxiliaries in any particular example. But one thing is clear: as we might expect, they become more common in the prose during the OE period. Gorrell found little change in their frequency in the poetry of different periods and observed that 'the *Gospels*, in their almost entire neglect of the periphrastic forms, correspond to no other literary style' (p. 458). According to his statistics (pp. 457-8), 'the relative proportion of the subjunctive to the auxiliary forms in the former period ['Alfredian prose'] is as 3 to 1, while at the time of Ælfric the proportion is as 2 to 1'.[24] It seems very plausible to argue that such an increase in frequency of the auxiliaries would go *pari passu* with a weakening in their meaning towards that of the modern auxiliaries of tense and

[24] Yerkes (pp. 220-5) found the opposite tendency in Gregory's *Dialogues*. Of the forty-four examples in which one version has a 'modal' auxiliary and the other a simple finite verb, Wærferth's original has the auxiliary in thirty-five, the revision in only nine. But 'the reviser was led away from PresE in these examples because he chose for the most part to follow the Latin more closely' (p. 221). These two tendencies are frequently in conflict in the revision.

mood. But it remains unproven and I at any rate would be reluctant to lose the irony I detect in

Mald 29   Me sendon to þe   sæmen snelle
                   heton ðe secgan   þæt þu most sendan raðe
                   beagas wið gebeorge

by translating *þu most* as 'you must' rather than 'you are permitted'; see Standop, pp. 76–7, and Solo, *NM* 78 (1977), 225–7.

§1999. The problem of the 'modal' auxiliaries is linked with that of the indicative and subjunctive moods. An attempt is made in the sections which follow to outline the circumstances under which the indicative, the subjunctive, and the 'modal' auxiliaries, are used in the various kinds of dependent speech; to detect any preferences particular verbs or groups of verbs may have; and to consider whether any general principles governing their use become apparent. Those intending to go further should note the importance of distinguishing the *person* and *tense* as well as the *mood* of the introductory verb when giving statistics and of treating each verb or verb phrase separately within the sub-divisions outlined in §1952. The presence of a negative or a 'modal' auxiliary in the principal clause may also be important. So too may be the fact that the principal clause is a non-dependent question. Lexicographers should not overlook the evidence provided by the mood of the verb in dependent speech. Thus *þencan* seems to prefer the subjunctive, *geþencan* the indicative (Mitchell 1959, p. 702, and Faraci, *NM* 81 (1980), 382). Could this reflect a difference in meaning between *þencan* 'I think and offer it as an opinion' and *geþencan* 'I think it through and offer it as a fact or as a strong probability'?

§2000. Before starting my discussion, however, I will remind the reader of two things. The first is that such simplistic statements as those of Cook (p. 104) that 'certainty is rendered by the indicative' and of Mossé (1945, p. 159) that 'toutes les fois qu'il s'agit d'un fait, d'une constatation [statement], d'une réalité, on emploie l'indicatif' must be dismissed; see Muxin (pp. 5–26) and my §877, and consider in its context *ÆLS* 26. 256 *Nu is us gesæd þæt sum halig cyning is on eowrum earde Oswold gehaten*. Second, Behre's observation (p. 185) that 'in OE. as well as in other Old Germanic languages the "prospective" subjunctive does not exist' is true of the present subjunctive, which is not used as a substitute for the missing future indicative. But it cannot be denied that the OE preterite subjunctive had among its many functions a 'prospective' use. If, for example, the ambiguous form *neðdon* in

Beo 535   Wit þæt gecwædon   cnihtwesende
              ond gebeotedon   —wæron begen þa git
              on geogoðfeore—   þæt wit on garsecg ut
              aldrum neðdon,   ond þæt geæfndon swa

is taken as a preterite indicative, the time-reference must be to the past—'We . . . boasted that we had risked our lives . . .'—and not (as the context demands) to a future which is now past—'We . . . boasted that we would risk our lives . . .'. So the preterite subjunctive frequently refers to the future-in-the-past. As Frank (p. 79) has it, 'the preterite optative must have served regularly as the *only tense possible* [my italics] to express preterite-futures before the verbal auxilliaries [*sic*] appeared'.[25] Examples will be found in the sections which follow.

(2) *Dependent desires*

§ 2001. The term 'dependent desires' is clearly applicable to those clauses expressing commands, requests or entreaties, and wishes. An element of desire is also present in clauses expressing promises, precepts, or permissions. The speaker's purpose too is often, if not always, involved; hence many of these clauses come close to being final clauses.[26] Behre (pp. 71–83) discusses the varying nature of the subjunctive in different kinds of dependent desires.

§ 2002. The speaker and the performer (§ 1936) may be the same or different. When a speaker makes a wish, promise, or a request, on his own behalf, he may be the performer, e.g., with the reporter and the speaker the same, *ÆLS* 32. 74 *þæs ic gewilnige and gewisce mid mode þæt ic ana ne belife æfter minum leofum þegnum* and, with the reporter and the speaker different, *ÆCHom* i. 22. 8 *Ða behet God þæt he nolde næfre eft eal mancynn mid wætere acwellan* (on the use of *nolde* here see § 2012) and *ÆLS* 5. 335 *þa bæd Tiburtius þæt he beon moste mid þam papan*. But the two are usually different when requests, commands, precepts, or permissions, are involved, for one does not normally request, command, teach, or permit,

[25] See also Curme, *MLN* 24 (1909), 99. Visser's distinction (in the examples he quotes in ii, § 803) between *sohte, arærde,* and *eode,* as 'Modal Preterites' and *dydon* as an example of 'Non-modal preterites with futuric implication' is wrong. They are all ambiguous forms referring to the future-in-the-past.

[26] See further Standop, pp. 41–2. But I do not understand what he means by 'die konzessive Willensäußerung [expression of volition]: Einräumung [concession]' as a class distinct from 'die permissive Willensäußerung: Erlaubnis [permission]'. See Behre, p. 72 and *passim*.

oneself to do something. So we find, with the reporter and the speaker the same, *ÆHom* 3. 74 *and ic eac beode þam uplicum wolcnum þæt hi nænne renscur him on ne rinon* and, with the reporter and the speaker different, *ÆCHom* ii. 68. 7 *Petrus se apostol bead eac on his pistole ðeowum mannum þæt hi wæron heora hlaforde getreowe.* The two requests in *ÆCHom* i. 456. 30 *Ic bidde eow þæt ge hine geornlice biddon þæt he hider ne ge- wende* exemplify both these possibilities in turn. Both also exist in wishes and promises, e.g., with the reporter and the speaker the same, *John(WSCp)* 21. 22 *ic wylle þ he wunige ðus oð ic cume* and *ÆCHom* i. 426. 6 *Ic swerige . . . þæt þu scealt geoffrian* (on *scealt* see §§2012 and 2009), and, with the reporter and the speaker dif- ferent, *ÆCHom* i. 158. 16 *þeahhwæðere wile se goda God þæt we hine georne biddon* and *ÆCHom* i. 46. 11 . . . *hu se heofenlica God hine geceas him to geþoftan and him behet þæt ealle ðeoda on his ofspringe gebletsode wurdon* (where the ambiguous *wurdon* must be taken as subjunctive referring to the future-in-the-past). These dis- tinctions become important when we consider the choice of 'modal' auxiliaries in dependent desires.

§2003. The prevailing mood in dependent desires is naturally— I prefer this word to Traugott's 'by convention' (p. 100), which may imply 'by grammatical or structural rule' rather than by 'usual or nor- mal usage'—the subjunctive, not the indicative, since the equivalent mood in non-dependent speech is the imperative or the subjunctive, not the indicative; as Gorrell (p. 371) writes in another connection, the reference is 'not to an actual occurrence, but to an event which is to take place according to the will or design of the subject of [the] governing verb'. This equivalence of moods is made clear by examples in which a dependent desire with the subjunctive is followed by a co-ordinate clause with the imperative, e.g. *CP* 213. 14 *Ic eow healsige . . . ðæt ge no to hrædlice ne sien astyrede from gewitte, ne eow to suiðe ne ondrædað for nanes monnes wordum, ÆCHom* ii. 296. 2 *Ic ðe bebeode . . . þæt ðu gewite of ðyssere stowe and far to westene,* and

JDay ii 75   Ic lære þæt þu beo hrædra   mid hreowlicum tearum,
                      and þæt yrre forfoh   eces deman.

(For further examples see Gorrell, pp. 480-1.) The subjunctive is the norm whatever the sequence of tenses, e.g. (present + present = future) *ÆCHom* i. 8. 9 *Nu bidde ic and halsige on Godes naman, gif hwa þas boc awritan wylle, þæt he hi geornlice gerihte be þære bysene . . .* ; (past = perfect + present = future) *ÆCHom* i. 66. 29

Nu ic ageat mine tearas and for ðinre nytennysse geornlice bæd þæt þu of deaðe arise and þisum twam gebroðrum . . . cyðe hu micel wuldor hi forluron; and (past + past = future-in-the-past) *ÆCHom* i. 506. 31 . . . *and bædon þa Halgan þrynnysse þæt him wurde geswutelod sum gewiss beacn embe heora twynunge*. But, as we shall see, both the various 'modal' auxiliaries and the indicative have their place; the introductory verbs or verb phrases do not demand or automatically produce the subjunctive.

§2004. That the subjunctive is the natural mood for dependent desires is also demonstrated by its occurrence in dependent desires after neutral verbs which contain no element of volition and which are usually or frequently followed by the indicative, e.g. *ÆCHom* i. 568. 30 *Secgað eowrum hlaforde þæt he unforht sy, ÆCHom* i. 158. 19 *La leof, do þæt ic mæge geseon, ÆCHom* i. 564. 22 *þa wearð him geswutelod þæt he æt Gode abæde . . . , ÆCHom* i. 470. 11 *þa onwreah se apostol Bartholomeus be ðam geleaffullan cyninge Polimius þæt he biscophad underfenge*, and *LS* 34. 291 *Gyf ðin cynescipe swa cwyð, hit geworden bið sona þæt man heora magas gelangie*. . . .

§2005. Typical examples of commands, requests, wishes, and promises, with the subjunctive have been quoted in §§2002–3. We find precepts in *ÆCHom* i. 56. 20 *and ða yfelan we mynegiað þæt hi fram heora yfelnessum hrædlice gecyrron* and *ÆCHom* i. 538. 8 *Halige lareowas ræddon þæt seo geleaffulle gelaðung þisne dæg Eallum Halgum to wurþmynte mærsige . . .* , and permission in *ÆCHom* ii. 94. 25 *Gemænes hades preostum is alyfed . . . þæt hi syferlice sinscipes brucon* and *ÆCHom* ii. 40. 34 *Geðafa þæt ic beo gefullod*. . . .

§2006. It is important to note the various functions of the preterite subjunctive in dependent desires. It is regularly used with reference to the future-in-the-past, e.g. (in addition to many of the sentences quoted above) *ÆCHom* i. 42. 2 *Ac God asende his engel to Iosepe . . . and bead þæt he hire gymene hæfde and þæs cildes fosterfæder wære*, where the speaker's command refers to a future which is in the past for the reporter.

§2007. It is also used after an introductory *ic wolde* 'as a stylistic device for expressing a wish in a modest, courteous, or guarded manner' (Behre, p. 57)—cf. MnE 'Would you pass the salt, please?' Here the time reference is to the future for the speaker/reporter *ic* and for the performer, who is frequently *þu* but need not be. Examples include *Bo* 13. 10 *Ac ic wolde þæt þu me sædest hwæþer ðu wisse hwæt þu self wære*, *Or* 40. 23 *Ic wolde nu, cwæð Orosius, þæt me ða geandwyrdan þa þe secgað þæt þeos world sy nu wyrse* . . . , *CP* 9. 5 *forðy ic wolde ðætte hie ealneg æt ðære stowe wæren*, *And* 271, and

And 483   Wolde ic anes to ðe,
          cynerof hæleð,   cræftes neosan,
          ðæt ðu me getæhte,   nu þe tir cyning
          ond miht forgef,   manna scyppend,
          hu ðu wægflotan   wære bestemdon,
          sæhengeste,   sund wisige.

These examples predate those given in *OED*, s.v. *will* (v. 1) III. 36. Behre (p. 63) gives more from the poetry. Not all are unambiguous. Thus *El* 1079 may be taken as an impossible wish for the past.

§ 2008. For, as we have seen in §§ 1679-81, the preterite subjunctive may also be used to express wishes which are impossible or unrealized in the past, present, or future. So in

Met 8. 39   Eala, þær hit wurde   oððe wolde god
          þæt on eorðan nu   ussa tida
          geond þas widan weoruld   wæren æghwæs
          swelce under sunnan,

the *þæt* clause may imply a wish that something unrealized in the present may be realized in the future. In

Deor 24   Sæt secg monig   sorgum gebunden,
          wean on wenan,   wyscte geneahhe
          þæt þæs cynerices   ofercumen wære,

the wish expressed may be 'O that that kingdom would perish!' or 'O that that kingdom were no more!', and in

Beo 960   Uþe ic swiþor,
          þæt ðu hine selfne   geseon moste,
          feond on frætewum   fylwerigne!

modern scholars can debate whether the wish is unrealizable in the past ('O that you had been permitted to see him!') or in the present ('O that you were permitted to see him!'), or is a possibility in the future ('O that you might see him!'). The remaining possibility—that it expresses a wish impossible in the future—probably does not arise, since Hrothgar eventually does see Grendel's head. On the use of the preterite subjunctive with reference to past time in dependent statements, see §§ 2016-35.

§ 2009. We turn now to 'modal' auxiliaries in dependent desires. The difficulty of determining their exact significance, discussed in

§§1009-24, remains. But some tendencies may be observed. Which particular auxiliary is chosen will to some extent at any rate depend on the type of sentence; see Standop, p. 43. In commands, where the speaker is imposing an obligation on the performer, *sculan is naturally common, e.g. ÆCHom i. 16. 3 *He cwæð eft and het ða eorðan þæt heo sceolde forðlædan cuce nytenu* and ÆCHom ii. 68. 5 *Eft Crist bebead þæt gehwa sceolde agildan ðam casere þæt him gebyreð, and Gode þæt him gebyreð.* The latter example is immediately followed by ÆCHom ii. 68. 7 *Petrus se apostol bead eac on his pistole ðeowum mannum þæt hi wæron heora hlaforde getreowe.* . . . Similar fluctuation between a past subjunctive and *sceolde* appears in co-ordinate clauses after the same verb in ÆCHom i. 124. 5 *Seo ealde æ bebead þæt gehwilc hreoflig man gecome to þam sacerde and se sacerd sceolde hine fram mannum ascirian gif he soðlice hreoflig wære.* I find it hard to believe that a careful stylist like Ælfric used the two indiscriminately. When the indicative and the subjunctive of the 'modal' auxiliary differ in form, the indicative seems to be preferred, e.g. ÆLS 7. 79, ÆCHom ii. 604. 21 *Ðeahhwæðere we secgað her sceortlice be urum geleafan þæt ælc man seðe wile Gode gegan sceal gelyfan on ða Halgan Ðrynnysse*, and

Seasons 99   Swa he æt þæm setle   sylfa gedemde,
              sancte Petres   preostas syþþan
              lange lifes tyd   leordun þæt sylfe,
              þæt þu oþrum ne scealt   æfre filian.

Whether it is the 'rule' remains to be established. But an investigation of *sculan and the other auxiliaries with this question in mind might produce valuable evidence on their usage and meaning.

§2010. With requests, *motan is common when the speaker and the performer are the same, e.g. Or 64. 28 *mid þæm þe hie bædon þæt hie him fylstan mosten* . . . , ÆCHom i. 6. 10 . . . *hu se deofol dyde þa ða he bæd æt Gode þæt he moste fandian Iobes*, and

Beo 364   Hy benan synt,
          þæt hie, þeoden min,   wið þe moton
          wordum wrixlan;

for further examples see Standop, pp. 85-6. When the speaker and the performer are different, we very occasionally find *willan*, e.g. LS 34. 300 *we biddað þe, leof hlaford, þæt ðu gehyran wylle ure word*—'when [*willan* is] used there is generally implied a certain degree of deference to the will of the person addressed, almost equivalent to the modern phrase, "if you please" ' (Gorrell, p. 374)

—and *sculan*, e.g. *ÆCHom* i. 246. 3 *Hi wurpon ða tan betweox him, and bædon þæt God sceolde geswutulian hwanon him þæt ungelimp become*—according to Gorrell (p. 373), *sculan* here 'serves the purpose merely of a periphrasis of the subjunctive'.

§2011. The most common auxiliary in wishes is *motan*, e.g. *Or* 290. 20 *7 wilnedon to him þæt hie mosten on his rice mid friðe gesittan, ÆLS* 5. 401 . . . *wiscton þæt hi moston swa wunian oð ende*, and *GuthB* 1185. We occasionally find *magan*, e.g. *Bo* 57. 29 *Nis nan gesceaft gesceapen ðara þe ne wilnige þ hit þider cuman mæge þonan þe hit ær com; willan*, e.g.

Met 13. 68   Nis nu ofer eorðan   ænegu gesceaft
                þe ne wilnie   þæt hio wolde cuman
                to þam earde   þe hio of becom

(the change between the prose and metrical versions is noteworthy); and *sculan*, e.g.

GuthA 663   Wendun ge ond woldun   wiþerhycgende,
                þæt ge scyppende   sceoldan gelice
                wesan in wuldre.

In negated wishes *sculan* seems to imply a wish that something inevitable in certain circumstances will be averted, e.g. *ÆCHom* ii. 310. 4 *þa wiscte se biscop þæt se wælhreowa ne sceolde his sawle amyrran ðurh his mandædum* and

Met 21. 34   Nele se waldend   ðæt forweorðan scylen
                saula usse,   ac he hi selfa wile
                leoman onlihtan,   lifes wealdend.

§2012. In promises in which the speaker and the performer are the same, *willan* is common, e.g. *ChronC* 74. 8 (876) *and him þa aþas sworon . . . þæt hi hrædlice of his rice faran woldon* (*ChronA* has *foren*) and *ÆCHom* i. 22. 8 *Ða behet God þæt he nolde næfre eft eal mancynn mid wætere acwellan*. When they are different, we find *willan*, e.g. *CP* 387. 25 . . . *Ezechiel se witga . . . cwæð ðæt hie wolden weorðan forlorene*; *motan*, e.g. *ÆHom* 19. 248 *and Crist him sona behet þæt he cuman moste . . . mid him to ðam ecan wuldre*; and (more frequently) *sculan*, e.g. *ÆCHom* i. 426. 6 *Ic swerige . . . þæt þu scealt geoffrian oððe ic ðe mid mislicum pinungum acwelle* (note the indicative) and *ÆCHom* i. 204. 17 *God behet ðam heahfædere Abrahame þæt on his cynne sceolde beon gebletsod eal mancynn*.

§2013. We find the expected *sculan with precepts, e.g. ÆCHom i. 372. 30 cwæð þæt se Hælend him tæhte ðone regol, þæt hi sceoldon yfel mid gode forgyldan, and the expected *motan with permissions, e.g. ÆCHom ii. 216. 11 Hit wæs alyfed on ðære ealdan æ þæt gehwa moste his feond ofslean.

§2014. The appearance of the indicative after verbs and verb groups which imply some element of volition or purpose emphasizes the fact that the use of the moods in dependent desires is no matter of 'convention'. The indicative is used to emphasize the result, the actuality or certainty of the fulfilment of the command, wish, or promise. Typical examples are Or 262. 19 7 he bebead Tituse his suna þæt he towearp þæt templ on Hierusalem, Or 148. 3 7 under ðæm heo gelærde þone cyning þæt he hiene swa upp ahof. . . , BlHom 191. 13 Nu for feawum dagum me bædon 7 lærdon Romane þæt ic gewat heonan onweg, ÆCHom ii. 594. 14 Ic ðancige þam Ælmihtigum Scyppende mid ealre heortan þæt he me synfullum þæs geuðe þæt ic ðas twa bec . . . Angelcynne onwreah, ÆCHom i. 542. 19 Eac he him behet mid soðfæstum behate þæt hi on ðam micclum dome ofer twelf domsetl sittende beoð, to demenne eallum mannum . . . ,

Jul 307　　　　Swylce ic Egias　　eac gelærde
　　　　　　　　þæt he unsnytrum　　Andreas het
　　　　　　　　ahon haligne　　on heanne beam,

and Husb 11 Ic gehatan dear ‖ þæt þu þær tirfæste treowe findest. I prefer to take findest as an indicative here, although it is not certainly so; see §601a. But a good many of the examples cited by Visser (ii, §869) have ambiguous verb-forms which should be construed as subjunctives. Thus I would not regard befæstest in ÆCHom ii. 554. 8 as an indicative. The subjunctive is the norm after gedafenian (e.g. ÆCHom i. 380. 19). The indicative would imply that the idle servant entrusted the lord's money to the usurers—which is just what he did not do.

§2015. Space does not permit an examination of the preference of individual verbs for the subjunctive, the 'modal' auxiliaries, and the indicative. Valuable material will be found in Gorrell, pp. 352-410. See also Wülfing, ii. 73-101; Behre, pp. 71-99; Visser, ii, §§869-71; and, on the auxiliaries, Standop, pp. 41-6 (magan), 84-7 (*motan), 108-10 (*sculan), and 143-6 (willan), and Visser, iii, passim (see his table of contents).

(3) *Dependent statements*

§2016. As we have seen, the subjunctive is the usual and natural mood of dependent desires; the indicatives which do occur can be explained as departures from the norm. It is the view of some scholars that the subjunctive was also the usual and natural mood of dependent statements, at least after certain verbs such as those of reporting. Thus we read Hotz (p. 89) 'the subj. . . . . simply represents a statement as reported'; Gorrell (p. 352) '. . . the characteristic feature of Indirect Discourse in Anglo-Saxon [is] the use of the subjunctive as the exponent of a statement indirectly reported'; and Traugott (p. 100) 'In fact, reported speech is usually expressed in the subjunctive.' Behre (p. 209) speaks of examples in which the subjunctive 'acts practically as a kind of quotation mark in "Indirect Speech" ' —a function which (one could argue) had already been fulfilled by the conj. *þæt*. Faraci (*NM* 81 (1980), 378-84) criticizes these and other writers for not going far enough and claims that the subjunctive or, as she prefers, 'the modally marked form . . . in subordinate clauses . . . is merely a signal of subordination'. It is not clear whether this applies to all types of dependent speech including dependent desires and dependent questions and exclamations (which Faraci does not distinguish), but she does extend it to *ær* clauses, to clauses of concession, condition, and purpose, and even of result. The article concludes with this paragraph:

> To link meanings of doubt to the Old English modally marked verbs in dependent clauses is to ignore a valuable structure signal, misinterpret Old English passages, and foster the present day oversimplified notion that the marked verb form 'subjunctive' always means doubt or uncertainty.

Had the author read and understood all the 'literature', including my *Guide,* §156, she would have found that the over-simplification was begotten of misunderstanding.

§2017. For the writers whom Faraci dismisses so patronizingly and others whom she does not mention (including Muxin) showed the relevance of many more factors than 'doubt' and 'a valuable structure signal'. Muxin (*UZLIJ* 3 (1956), 5-26) after limiting dependent speech to clauses introduced by verbs of speaking or opining and excluding those after verbs of making known, revealing, seeing, and the like, produces the theory that the subjunctive is characteristic of dependent speech in the Old Germanic languages, that it had no modal character, and that it was originally merely an effective structural means of distinguishing dependent from non-dependent speech. But Muxin himself, who admits (as of course he has to) that the indicative does occur, sometimes suggests obligation, attraction, modal meaning, and reference to future time, as reasons for the subjunctive. There are others.

§ 2018. Here I can discuss only briefly these various factors; as with dependent desires, space does not permit a full treatment of the preferences of individual verbs. Valuable collections of material will be found in Gorrell (pp. 352–410) and Behre (pp. 217–24 and 235–7). All the examples in the poetry are listed in Mitchell 1959, pp. 695–754. Gorrell's treatment is inadequate in various ways. He fails to consider certain introductory verbs, including *willan* and those expressing emotion (on these, see Behre, pp. 225–37, and Visser, ii, § 872). He does not always sufficiently distinguish the usage after a present tense of an introductory verb from that after a past tense. He is not always sufficiently discriminating in his semantic grouping of introductory verbs. (Behre sometimes offends here.) He is sometimes too prone to take ambiguous forms as subjunctives, e.g. *ofslogon* in *ÆCHom* i. 168. 6 (p. 381), and does not distinguish ambiguous forms in his statistics. These are therefore only approximations. Similarly, the tables given by Faraci (my § 2016) do not distinguish present forms from preterite or ambiguous forms from unambiguous. Behre discusses the nature of the subjunctives after various introductory verbs at pp. 196–216 and 225–35. Ono, in *SEL* (Tokyo) (English Number, 1975), 33–60, discusses and gives the relative frequency of the various constructions which follow 'The Old English Verbs of Knowing' in a selected corpus of prose and poetry. The full figures for the poetry of noun clauses introduced by the verbs *witan* and *cunnan* are these:

Verb	*þæt* clauses	Dependent nexus questions	Dependent *x*-questions
witan	72	2	39
cunnan	3	1	17

As Ono (p. 38) notes, *cunnan* does not normally introduce *þæt* clauses. The three examples in the poetry—*Beo* 1181, *PPs* 55. 8, and *PPs* 118. 145—are all special cases.

§ 2019. The influence of the introductory verb is often said to be a determining factor in the choice of mood in a dependent statement; thus Gorrell (p. 440) has a category in which 'the Subjunctive [is] due to the nature of the governing verb'. Some tendencies can be distinguished which at first glance seem to support this view. Thus

verbs of direct perception and knowledge tend to take the indicative
and verbs of believing and thinking the subjunctive (see Frank, p. 69,
and Gorrell, pp. 440-1 and 443-4), while, among verbs of speaking,
cweðan seems to prefer the subjunctive, *cyðan* the indicative, and
secgan to occupy an intermediate position (see Gorrell, pp. 353-63).
But there are at least three reasons for describing this view as simplistic.[27]

§2020. First, even after those verbs which most consistently prefer
one mood, the other occurs. Thus *wenan*—'the most consistent in
requiring the subjunctive of the dependent verb' (Gorrell, p. 384)—
occasionally has the indicative, e.g. *ÆCHom* i. 396. 4 *Hwæt doð
ealle ðeoda middangeardes? Wenst ðu þæt hi beoð asyndrode fram
ðam dome?*, where the implication is 'Of course not!' (but cf. *ÆC
Hom* i. 424. 27-34),[28] and *gesweotolian*—'it sets forth the statement in a clear, objective manner, and hence the usual mood in the
dependent sentence is the indicative' (Gorrell, p. 366)—is found
with the subjunctive, e.g. *ÆCHom* i. 328. 25 *ac gif hit gylt nære,
þonne ne geswutulode þæt halige godspel swa gewislice be ðam
rican, þæt he wære mid purpuran and mid gode webbe geglencged*,
where there is no doubt that the gospel says that the rich man was
adorned with purple and fine linen. The only unambiguous subjunctive after *(ge)hyran* in the poetry (Mitchell 1959, p. 703) occurs in
Mald 117 *Gehyrde ic þæt Eadweard anne sloge*, where it is needed
for the metre.

§2021. Second, there are numerous verbs of which it cannot possibly be said that they demand or prefer one mood rather than the
other. One striking example must suffice. Ælfric frequently introduces statements from Holy Scripture with the verb-form *awrat*.
We find the subjunctive in *ÆCHom* i. 548. 11 and i. 308. 33, where
St. Matthew and St. Mark are the authorities; the indicative in
ÆCHom i. 314. 3 and i. 360. 30, where St. Luke and Isaiah are
quoted; and an ambiguous form in *ÆCHom* i. 438. 9, where St.
John is the source. (This ambiguity may exist only for modern
readers; it does not mean that Ælfric gives St. John a class II for

---

[27] Muxin (*UZLIJ* 3 (1956), 7-8) reports and with good reason attacks the view put forward by T. V. Stroeva, *Modal'nost' kosvennoj reči v nemeckom jazyke* (Leningrad, 1950)
that Old Germanic verbs of speech, communication, perception, and the like, can be divided
into two groups: first, those which always take the subjunctive, e.g. *cwepan*; and second, the
remainder, in which the subjunctive indicates doubt, the indicative certainty. Both these
points are taken up below.

[28] Gorrell's table (p. 387) shows few exceptions. But it is probably based on the assumption that all ambiguous verb forms are subjunctive.

reliability, as another theory to be discussed below might suggest.) Similar examples with other verbs abound. Thus we find *secgan* followed by the subjunctive and *cweþan* by the indicative in successive clauses in *ÆCHom* i. 100. 29, while *cyþan* has the preterite indicative in *ÆLS* 3. 262 but the preterite subjunctive in *ÆCHom* i. 128. 10. On the usage after the OHG cognates see Curme, *MLN* 24 (1909), 99. Of these three verbs, only *secgan* survives into present-day standard English. Ogura (1979, *passim*, especially pp. 11, 24, and 27) gives evidence to show that the specialization of *cweþan* in the 'quoth he/he quoth' function and its supersession by *secgan* in other uses was already well under way in OE.

§ 2022. Third, the theory that the introductory verb could automatically produce a certain mood in the verb of the dependent statement is too mechanistic. The fact that *cweðan* prefers the subjunctive and *cyðan* the indicative may reflect an original difference in meaning (see *Guide*, § 70) which may have survived into OE times. The possibility exists that the speaker's and/or the reporter's choice of introductory verb may have been influenced by the nuance he wished to convey and the mood he intended to use. To speak, as Gorrell (p. 442) does, of the 'inherent power' of a verb is to overlook, not only this possibility, but also the fact—which he himself recognized (pp. 389–90, 441, and elsewhere) —that a verb may have two different meanings, each with its own 'inherent power'. We must agree with Behre (p. 74) that 'a certain verb in the main clause does not cause or "govern" the subjunctive, and, when the subjunctive is used in the *þæt*-clause, the "introductory" or governing verb does not always determine the nature of the subjunctive'. Other factors— including the attitude of the speaker and/or the reporter—must be at work. The influence of the introductory verb cannot be described as purely mechanistic; it was chosen by the speaker or by the reporter. Changes of mood from subjunctive to indicative in successive clauses governed by the same introductory verb such as that in *ÆCHom* ii. 220. 12 *Se feorða leahtor is weamet, þæt se man nage his modes geweald, ac buton ælcere foresceawunge his yrsunge gefremað* are the result of the transition from dependent to non-dependent speech discussed in §§ 1945–8 which brought it about that the factors which produced the subjunctive were no longer felt.

§ 2023. Gorrell's threefold division of subjunctives in dependent speech (pp. 437–42) embraced (*a*) the subjunctive of simple report; (*b*) the subjunctive due to the nature of the governing verb—(1) expression of will, (2) design and uncertainty, (3) thinking and believing;

and (*c*) subjunctives due to other causes than the direct influence of
the governing verb, i.e. 'when moments of interrogation, negation,
condition, concession, and the like, enter into the expression'. But
since the factors listed under (*b*) and (*c*) all involve the speaker and/
or the reporter, I cannot accept that (*b*) is any more under 'the direct
influence of the governing verb' than (*c*). And, as Gorrell himself
admits (p. 438), the attitude of the speaker and/or the reporter is a
factor in (*a*). His division therefore cannot stand.

§2024. Since language is a human activity, it is not surprising that
the attitude of the speaker and/or the reporter—involving as it does
what is to be said and how it is to be said—is important in determining what mood is used. Various motives, conscious or unconscious,
have been detected. These must be discussed in turn.

§2025. A statement presented as true may be contrasted with one
presented as false or doubtful by the use of the indicative and subjunctive; see Gorrell, p. 355. Examples include *ÆCHom* i. 226. 17,
ÆCHom i. 372. 11 *Simon ða mid deofles cræfte dyde þæt ðæs
deadan lic styrigende wæs. þa wende þæt folc þæt he geedcucod
wære*, and *ÆCHom* i. 328. 18 *Ne sæde þæt halige godspel þæt se
rica reafere wære, ac wæs uncystig and modegode on his welum.* But
the indicative can be used of what is false or denied, e.g. *ÆCHom* i.
292. 25 *We sceolon gelyfan þæt ælces mannes sawul bið þurh God
gesceapen ac hwæðere heo ne bið na of Godes agenum gecynde* and
ÆCHom ii. 464. 33 *Ne cwæð he na þæt us beoð þa ateorigendlican
bigleofan forgyfene ac þærto geeacnode*, and the subjunctive of what
is true. Especially striking examples of this will be found in *ÆCHom*
i. 116. 8-27. Gorrell (p. 439) singled out *ÆCHom* i. 116. 18 . . . *and
wiðsocon þæt he deadlic flæsc underfenge* as an example in which
'the subjunctive expresses what is in the opinion of the speaker a
downright falsehood'. He conveniently failed to quote the first half
of the sentence *Sume gedwolan andetton þæt he soð God wære and
soð cyning*, where the subjunctive is used of what both Ælfric and
the speakers believed to be true. This is the third of three successive
sentences in which a confessed truth and a denied truth both have
the preterite subjunctive. The whole passage will repay careful study.
So too will *ÆCHom* i. 474. 4 *þa cwæð se Hælend þæt he nære for
his agenum synnum, ne for his maga, blind geboren, ac forði þæt
Godes wundor þurh hine geswutelod wære*, where *wære* in the first
þæt clause denotes a denied reason which is (given as) a true fact,
and *wære* in the second refers to the future-in-the-past.

§2026. Another motive assigned is the desire of the reporter 'to cast doubts on the truth of what was reportedly said' (Traugott, p. 100)[29] or 'to express himself non-committally as to the truth of what was said' (Visser, ii, §874) or to show that he 'does not give his warrant to the statement' (Gorrell, p. 439). Both Traugott and Gorrell quote *ÆCHom* i. 16. 19 *Nu cwædon gedwolmen þæt deofol gesceope sume gesceafta, ac hi leogað*. One might argue that Ælfric was casting more than doubt on the statement and was far from being non-committal. Other more convincing illustrations of what they suggest include some cited by Visser, e.g. *ÆLS* 6. 25 *þa nolde Maurus ðam mannum þæs tiðian, cwæð þæt seo dæd nære him gedafenlic* and others. But I cannot believe that Ælfric was expressing doubt in *ÆCHom* i. 452. 3 *He swor þæt he on æfnunge . . . witodlice hi gesawe* and there can be no question of Ælfric or Augustine wanting to express himself non-committally about Stephen's statement in *ÆCHom* i. 48. 9 *Se wisa Augustinus spræc ymbe ðas rædinge, and smeade hwi se halga cyðere Stephanus cwæde þæt he gesawe mannes bearn standan æt Godes swyðran, and nolde cweðan Godes bearn*. The fact that, of thirty-nine quotations in dependent statement in a portion of *Cura Pastoralis*, none had the indicative and that comparable figures for parts of *Blickling Homilies* and Ælfric's *Catholic Homilies* respectively were fifteen : one and fifteen : seventeen respectively (Gorrell, p. 361) does not support the propositions under discussion. And, as Behre (pp. 196–8) points out, they cannot be applied to sentences such as

Creed 49 Eac ic gelyfe   þæt syn leofe gode
þe þurh ænne geþanc   ealdor heriað,
heofona heahcyning   her for life,

in which one man is the speaker and the reporter and is making profession of his faith. Here *syn* may be indicative, not subjunctive, as Behre takes it; see §651. But I find Behre's explanation (pp. 203–4) for his subjunctive desperate; he argues that 'the speaker is here not concerned with expressing a first-hand and direct judgement: "they are dear to God". He is concerned with telling us that with regard to this truth he believes in it.' Against this, we can apply an argument Behre himself uses against another writer (p. 230)—that *ic gelyfe* has already told us this. I cannot myself distinguish between *ÆCHom* i. 532. 11 *Ic gelyfe þæt min Alysend leofað* and *ÆCHom* i. 446. 7 *soðlice we gelyfað þæt he nu todæg þa wynsumestan wununge his leofan meder forgeafe*. Visser's notion (ii, §873) that in examples

[29] She says this was the original use, on what evidence I cannot imagine. Frank's theory (discussed in §2032) seems a more likely one.

like *WHom* 7a. 24 *And we gelyfað þæt hine clæne mæden gebære,*
Sancta Maria . . . 'it might be assumed that *to believe* has the weakened
sense *to suppose*' casts a peculiar light on Wulfstan's Christianity.
The question 'Whose truth? Ælfric's, Andrew's, or Egeas's?' must
arise in *ÆCHom* i. 590. 23-32. There are similar examples.

§2027. We turn now to the influence of an imperative, subjunctive,
or modal verb, of a negative, or of a non-dependent question, in the
principal clause. Principal clauses with an imperative and the like
obviously involve an element of volition on the part of the speaker;
as Behre (pp. 75-6) points out, they are in this respect similar to
dependent commands such as

Dream 95   Nu ic þe hate,   hæleð min se leofa,
                þæt ðu þas gesyhðe   secge mannum,
                onwreoh wordum   þæt hit is wuldres beam,
                se ðe ælmihtig god   on þrowode. . . .

Examples in the prose include *BlHom* 45. 6 *Se biscop sceal* . . .
þrafian þa mæssepreostas mid lufe ge mid laþe þæt hie healdan
Godes æwe on riht, ÆCHom i. 372. 6 *Genealæcað ðære bære and*
gelyfað þæt ðæs bodung soð sy, ðe ðone deadan to life arærð, and
ÆCHom i. 56. 23 *Ondræde se goda þæt he fealle; hogige se yfela*
þæt he astande. But there are numerous exceptions. Thus we find
wite + indicative in *ÆCHom* i. 12. 19, i. 96. 2, i. 150. 26, i. 292. 22
Wite gehwa eac þæt nan man ne mot beon tuwa gefullod, and elsewhere. Other exceptions include *ÆCHom* i. 198. 14 *Gelyfað nu,*
þurh ðas word, þæt he is soð God of soðum Gode and *ÆCHom* i.
228. 20 *Ac uton we gelyfan þæt God Fæder wæs æfre butan an-*
ginne. . . . More will be found in the sections which follow.

§2028. Behre (pp. 80-1) cites *Gifts* 16 *Næfre god demeð* ‖ *þæt*
ænig eft þæs earm geweorðe as an example in which 'the subjunctive
is used of an action represented as not desired'. But the idea that
'when the thought concerns a negative, the complement is regularly
subjunctive' (Traugott, p. 101; cf. Gorrell, p. 398) cannot stand. The
indicative is common, whether the negative is in the principal clause,
e.g. *ÆCHom* i. 234. 19 *Ne getimode þam apostole Thome unfor-*
sceawodlice þæt he ungeleafful wæs Cristes æristes and *Sea* 66 *Ic*
gelyfe no ‖ *þæt him eorðwelan ece stondað*, or in the subordinate
clause, e.g. *ÆCHom* ii. 592. 20 *Wite gehwa cristenra manna, þæt nan*
man ne sceal sceattas niman for Godes cyrcan, ÆCHom ii. 18. 35
And wite þu gewiss þæt we næfre ne bugað to ðinum hæðenscipe,
and

Beo 433　　　　Hæbbe ic eac geahsod,　　þæt se æglæca
　　　　　　　for his wonhydum　　wæpna ne recceð.

Similarly Visser's idea (ii, §873) that in *John(WSCp)* 9. 18 *Ne ge-lyfdon þa Iudeas be him þ he blind wære 7 gesawe* . . . , Latin *non crediderunt ergo Iudaei de illo quia caecus fuisset et uidisset* . . . , the negative accounts for the subjunctive, which 'emphasizes the unbelief', is hard to sustain in view of the frequency of positive examples with the subjunctive after *gelyfan*, e.g. *ÆCHom* i. 446. 7 *soðlice we gelyfað þæt he nu todæg þa wynsumestan wununge his leofan meder forgeafe.* The presence of a negative with verbs express-ing doubt and uncertainty, says Gorrell (p. 394), 'not only eliminates the element of doubt, but changes the expression into a strong affir-mation. Hence, the usual mood in the dependent clause is the indica-tive', e.g. *ÆCHom* i. 480. 23 . . . *and for ðam deaðe ne geortruwað þæt ic God eom.* But again, as he himself admits, there are excep-tions, e.g. *ÆCHom* i. 160. 19 *Hu mæg þe nu twynian þæs ecan leohtes, ðeah hit ungesewenlic sy, þonne þu hæfst lif of ungesewen-licre sawle, and þe ne twynað nan ðing þæt þu sawle hæbbe, ðeah ðu hi geseon ne mage?*

§2029. The fact that a question asked by the speaker implies some doubt or perplexity on his part can explain subjunctives like those in *ÆCHom* i. 198. 25 *þa cwæð Maria to ðam engle, 'Hu mæg þæt beon þæt ic cild hæbbe, forðan ðe ic nanes weres ne bruce? Ic geteohode min lif on mægðhade to geendigenne: hu mæg hit ðonne gewurðan þæt ic, butan weres gemanan, cennan scyle?'* and in *ÆCHom* i. 230. 15 *Hwilc wundor is þæt se Hælend mid ecum lichaman come inn, belocenum durum* . . . ? But not all questions produce a subjunctive. We find the indicative after the very same question *Hwylc wundor is* . . . ? in *ÆCHom* i. 286. 26 *Hwylc wundor is gif se Ælmihtiga God is unasecgendlic and unbefangenlic* . . .?, where the question may be rhetorical; and after a negated question in *CP* 25. 18 *Hua nat ðæt ða wunda ðæs modes bioð digelran ðonne ða wunda ðæs lichaman?,* where the implication is 'Everybody knows . . .', and in *ÆCHom* i. 430. 11 *Ða cwæð Laurentius, 'Eala ge ungesæligan, ne undergyte ge þæt eowre gleda nane hætan minum lichaman ne gedoð, ac swiðor celinge?',* where the indicative emphasizes Lawrence's point: 'Of course they don't hurt me.'

§2030. So the presence of an imperative, a subjunctive, or a modal verb, of a negative, or of a non-dependent question, in a principal clause may mean that an environment exists in which the speaker and/or the reporter will use a subjunctive. On this subject see further

Nader, *Ang.* 11 (1888-9), 482; Henk, pp. 13-38; Vogt, *passim*; and
Behre, *passim*. Cf., however, Mourek, *passim*, and Glunz, p. 121.
That there is no automatic rule—mechanistic or psychological—is
shown by the following table, which gives the figures for all examples
of dependent speech (statement, desire, question, and exclamation)
in OE poetry:

Principal clause contains	percentage of examples in which the verb of the subordinate clause is		
	Indicative	Ambiguous	Subjunctive
Imperative	17+	47+	35+
Subjunctive	26	23	51
Modal Verb	36+	35+	28+
Negative	22	42+	35+
Interrogative	40	13	47

The fact that there is a higher percentage of such subjunctives in
noun clauses than in adjective clauses in the poetry (§§2386-415)
merely reflects the general situation in the two types of clause.

§2031. Some subjunctives can be explained by the fact that the
clause in dependent speech is subordinate to a clause expressing purpose, concession, condition, or the like, e.g. *BlHom* 191. 26 *Ic befæste þe nu þæt eowde þæt þu me sealdest þæt hie ne oncneowon
þæt hie buton me beon, þa þe habban*, WHom 1b. 30 *7 ðeah þæt
geweorðe þæt ure ænig þe nu leofað þonne ne libbe, þeah we agan
þearfe . . .* , and *ÆCHom* i. 148. 4 *Gif wife getimige þæt heo hire wer
forleose, ðonne nime heo bysne be ðisre wudewan*. But again the
attitude of the speaker and/or the reporter is clearly responsible. The
indicative does occur, e.g. *ÆCHom* i. 26. 7 *Ða worhte he fela wundra,
þæt men mihton gelyfan þæt he wæs Godes bearn* and *ÆCHom* i.
372. 23 *. . . arær nu ðisne cnapan, þæt ðis folc oncnawe þæt nan
God nys buton ðu ana.*

§2032. There are other factors which are not independent of the
speaker and/or the reporter, but which may affect his choice of
mood. One is whether the report is made in the present or in the
past. 'It is a well-known fact', says Frank (p. 78), 'that the optative
is more frequent after a leading verb in the past tense than after a
present.' (See also Curme, *MLN* 24 (1909), 97-100.) This variation
is illustrated by *ÆCHom* i. 190. 28-192. 2, which begins *þæt folc
cwæð ða be Criste, þæt he wære soð witega. Nu cweðe we be Criste,*

þæt he is ðæs lifigendan Godes Sunu . . . , and by the fact that all the indicative examples listed by Gorrell after *wenan* (p. 385) and *þincan* (p. 391) are in the present tense. More work is needed here; unfortunately Gorrell did not take the tense of the introductory verb into consideration when presenting his statistics, although Behre did. One reason for the greater frequency of the preterite subjunctive is, of course, that the preterite indicative cannot refer to the future-in-the-past, whereas the present indicative can refer to the future. Frank (*passim*, especially p. 79) suggests that the ancestors of verbs like *gelyfan* and *wenan* originally expressed desire or intention and so were followed by the preterite subjunctive referring (as only it could) to 'a time future to the past', and that this subjunctive remained idiomatic after the verbs had changed their meaning and were used with reference to 'narrated facts' of past time. Analogical extension of the preterite subjunctive expressing past time to other verbs followed. The theory has its attractions. But other factors will have to be borne in mind. They include the identity of the reporter and the meaning of the introductory verb. Behre (p. 208) points out that 'the indicative is generally used in *þæt*-clauses containing a statement made by the speaker [= my reporter] in present time'. This is natural enough. Behre (pp. 196 ff.) attempts to explain why the subjunctive appears in such examples. We have already seen that the subjunctive is the natural mood after verbs introducing dependent desires; in this connection Gorrell (pp. 359–60) notes that in the present tense *secgan* with the present indicative means 'to say', but with the present subjunctive 'to order' or the like—a sense in which it is rarely used in the past. Another illustration of the importance of the meaning of the introductory verb can be seen by comparing *ÆCHom* ii. 40. 34 *Geðafa þæt ic beo gefullod æt ðinum handum* . . . (where a desire or purpose for the future has the subjunctive and the indicative would be impossible) with *ÆCHom* ii. 594. 15 . . . *þæt he me synfullum þæs geuðe, þæt ic ðas twa bec* . . . *Angelcynne onwreah* (where a desire granted or a purpose fulfilled in the past has the indicative and the subjunctive would refer to the future-in-the-past).

§2033. Two other factors are the preferences of individual authors and changes in the language itself; as Behre (p. 211 fn. 2) puts it, 'allowance should always be made for the possibility that the writer does not avail himself of the means at his command for expressing every shade of thought that may be expressed by the subjunctive, and also for the decline in the subjunctive usage in the later period of OE'. The fact that 'Wulfstan is most consistent in the use of the subjunctive after *biddan*, while Ælfric shows a tendency to the use of the periphrastic forms' (Gorrell, p. 374) suggests personal prefer-ence. Gorrell (p. 355) draws our attention to the markedly higher percentage of subjunctives after *cweðan* in *Cura Pastoralis* than 'in later Anglo-Saxon' and says that this is 'in great measure due to the gradual disuse of the subjunctive in the later language'. But personal preference may complicate the situation. On Gorrell's figures (p. 357) there are twenty-nine subjunctives to one indicative after *cweðan* in *Cura Pastoralis*, twenty-one to two in *Blickling Homilies*, seventy-eight to forty-nine in Ælfric's *Catholic Homilies*, and ten to five in Wulfstan. These figures do not support the notion of a gradual change in the language uncomplicated by other factors. The influ-ence of a Latin original too may play a part. A comparison of sub-junctives and indicatives in the original and revised versions of Gregory's *Dialogues* reveals conflicting testimony. Thus, in *GD* 86. 24 (after *sæde*) and in *GD* 107. 2 (after *is awriten*) the revision and the Latin have the indicative where the original has the subjunctive. In *GD* 41. 29 (after *cwæð*) the revision has the indicative where the original and the Latin have the subjunctive. But in *GD* 134. 18 the original . . . *he cyðde þæt hit wæs him gesæd* is revised to what was rejected in the previous example, viz. *cwæð* + subjunctive—. . . *he cwæð þæt hit wære him gesæd*; the Latin versions vary between *fuisse* and *fuissit*. (For the material on which this analysis is based, see Yerkes, pp. 213–14.) But it is idle to deny that the subjunctive became less common during the OE period and that analogy and the ambiguous verb-forms played their part in the process.

§ 2034. So I may seem to be falling back on a statement which comes perilously close to enshrining the attitude condemned by Frank (p. 64) over seventy years ago: 'For a long time—and to a few conservatives the long time seems not yet ended—grammarians who dealt with Indo-European syntax were satisfied with the broad generalization that the optative mood in oratio oblique [*sic*] was the mood of "subjectivity".' But my statement is this:

The indicative is the norm when the content of the noun clause is presented as a fact, as certain, as true, or a result which has ac-tually followed or will follow, or, as Curme (*MLN* 24 (1909), 98–9) suggests, when an utterance in the past is not felt to be an indirect report, but is related vividly in 'the past indicative, the tense of direct narrative'.

The subjunctive is the norm when some mental attitude to the content of the noun clause is implied. One of the following ideas may be present: desire (exhortation, command, prohibition, wish), purpose, obligation, supposition, perplexity, suspicion, doubt, possibility, uncertainty, unreality, emotion (wonder, joy, grief, shame, hope, fear), concession, or condition, or the idea that, as Curme (ibid.) puts it, a narrator of past events 'may no longer feel directly related to the events and may consequently use the indirect form of statement, the subjunctive'.

The attitude may be that of what I call the speaker or of what I call the reporter (§1936). Even Curme's explanation is not entirely mechanistic; it involves some subjectivity, some involvement on the part of the speaker or the reporter. Gorrell (p. 390) remarks that 'the reality of the statement introduced by *þyncan* is dependent only upon the opinion of the object of *þyncan*'. But this does not mean that the attitude of the object of *þyncan* necessarily determines the mood of the *þæt* clause. It does in

GenA 169 Ne þuhte þa gerysne rodora wearde,
       þæt Adam leng ana wære
       neorxnawonges, niwre gesceafte,
       hyrde and healdend,

where the subjunctive represents the attitude of God: 'It is not fitting that Adam should any longer live by himself.' But it does not in

Wan 39   . . . ðonne sorg ond slæp somod ætgædre
       earmne anhogan oft gebindað,
       þinceð him on mode þæt he his mondryhten
       clyppe ond cysse, ond on cneo lecge
       honda ond heafod. . . .

Here the wanderer thinks these things are actually happening and would have used the indicative; the subjunctive is, as Behre (pp. 200-1) points out, 'used of a reported thought, belief, etc. that from the speaker's point of view is doubtful, false, or erroneous . . .'. Here the attitude of the reporter [Behre's speaker] is the vital one.

§2035. There are still many loose ends. Even if we accept Curme's view that the subjunctive is 'the indirect form of statement', we cannot be sure whether that was the original rule in Germanic, as he seems to suggest (*MLN* 24 (1909), 98), or whether it arose by analogy, as Frank would have it (my §2032). As we have seen, many other factors can play a part. But we cannot recreate the thought-processes of long-dead speakers and writers and we do not know what taboos and primitive fears may lie behind the use of the subjunctive. Hence I do not propose to pursue this topic further.

§2036. The use of the 'modal' auxiliaries in dependent desires—including promises, precepts, and permissions—has been discussed in §§ 2011-15. The main problem in dependent statements is the difficult one already mentioned in § 1009, viz. to what extent have these verbs lost their original meanings and moved along the road to their modern ones? As I said there, the problem is one for the lexicographers. But it must be remembered that the answers are not 'Completely' and 'All the way', as Standop (pp. 60-2) reminds us, quoting

Met 19. 34   Wenað samwise
            þæt hi on ðis lænan mægen   life findan
            soða gesælða,   þæt is selfa god

and *Bo* 39. 31 *ic wat þæt he mihte, gif he wolde* as sentences in which *magan* is no mere circumlocution for the subjunctive but is essential for the sense. Similar examples with other such verbs can, of course, be found very readily; they include *ÆCHom* i. 218. 1 *Se gewuna stent on Godes cyrcan, þurh lareowas geset, þæt gehwær on Godes gelaðunge se sacerd bletsian sceole palmtwigu on ðisum dæge, and hi swa gebletsode ðam folce dælan* and *ÆCHom* ii. 298. 30 *þa com seo burhwaru samod to ðam apostole, cwædon þæt hi woldon his lare gehyran.* On the 'modal' auxiliaries in dependent statement, see further Gorrell, *passim* and especially pp. 386, 409-10, 449-58, and 484; Behre, pp. 196-237; and Standop, pp. 60-2, 90-1, 115-17, and 153-4.

§ 2037. One use of **sculan* (which can be paralleled in other languages) calls for special mention. In both non-dependent and dependent speech, **sculan* can convey the idea that a statement is reported or is not vouched for by the speaker. The past tense is common. Thus, we find in non-dependent speech *Bo* 115. 27 *þa sceolde þæs Iobes fæder bion eac god, Bo* 116. 3 *Sio, hi sædon, sceolde bion swiðe drycræftigu*, and

Met 26. 51   Sceolde eac wesan   Apollines
            dohtor diorboren,   dysiges folces
            gumrinca gyden,

and in dependent speech *Bo* 102. 1 *Ða sædon hi þ ðæs hearperes wif sceolde acwelan ⁊ hire saule mon sceolde lædan to helle, ÆCHom* i. 486. 5 *Sume gedwolmenn cwædon þæt þæt heafod sceolde ablawan ðæs cyninges wif Herodiaden, HomU* 34. 197. 16 *and he ahefð hine sylfne ofer ealle, þa ðe hæðene men cwædon, þæt godas beon sceoldan on hæðene wisan*, and

Met 26. 73   Ða ongunnon wercan   werðeoda spell,
            sædon þæt hio sceolde   mid hire scinlace
            beornas forbredan. . . .

§2038. *OED* (s.v. *shall* B. II. 15) says that 'the corresponding use of *shall* (= G. *soll*, "is said to") is not evidenced in Eng., the OE instances alleged by Bosw.-Toller having apparently a different meaning'. The examples in question are both in *Lch* ii. 236. 13 *Be þære frecnan coþe þe se mon his utgang þurh ðone muð him fram weorpe sceal aspiwan. He sceal oft bealcettan . . .* (BT, s.v. *sculan* II. 13). Cockayne translated *sceal aspiwan . . . sceal oft bealcettan* as 'they say speweth' and 'they say oft belcheth'. I do not know what *OED*'s rather coy observation means. Cockayne and BT derive some support from *ÆCHom* ii. 572. 16 *Sume gedwolmen cwædon þæt seo halige Maria, Cristes modor, and sume oðre halgan sceolon hergian æfter ðam dome ða synfullan of ðam deofle, ælc his dæl*, where the reference is still to the future and Ælfric is denying the statement. In the light of *ÆCHom* i. 486. 5 (§2037), it is tempting to read *sceoldon*; Malcolm Godden (private communication) tells me that such errors are common. But all manuscripts have *sceolon*.

e. The 'expletive' negative

§2039. The two exchanges ' "It is true!" "I do not doubt that" ' and ' "It is not true!" "I do not doubt that" ' ought logically to produce a positive and a negative noun clause respectively, as in *Bo* 107. 6 *Forðæm hit is nan tweo þ ta goodan beoð symle waldende 7 þa yflan nabbað nænne anwald; forðy ða goodan ðæt god on riht secað 7 ða yflan on woh.* But in OE, when negated verbs (or nouns) expressing doubt govern a *þæt* clause, a negative which is not required by the sense sometimes appears in the *þæt* clause; cf. *Bo* 105. 30 *7 ic eac nauht ne tweoge ðæt ðu hit mæge gelæstan* with *Bo* 113. 21 *Forðæm ne þearf nænne wisne mon tweogan þ ða yflan næbben eac ecu edlean hiora yfles, GD* 305. 5 *Ne tweoge ic na, þæt hellefyr sy lichamlic* with *GD* 213. 20 *7 ne þuhte nanum men þæs tweo, þæt gif þæt stanclif feolle, þæt hit ne ofsloge þæt scræf . . .*, and *BlHom* 83. 9 . . . *7 secggean þæt nænigne tweogean ne þearf þæt seo wyrd on þas ondweardan tid geweorþan sceal . . .* with *BlHom* 65. 8 *forþon nis nan tweo þæt he forgifnesse syllan nelle þam þe hie geearnian willaþ.* Einenkel (*Ang.* 35 (1912), 206-8) gives more examples, reports that his attempt to trace the influence of Latin *non dubito quin* . . . proved fruitless, and concludes that a construction which permits an author to use either a positive or a negative can scarcely be the product of 'eine echt [genuinely] germanische Konstruktion'. Perhaps it was genuine Germanic confusion, for it is hard to see any logic in these variations. These superfluous negatives in the *þæt* clauses are 'expletive' in the sense that they are words 'inserted in a . . . sentence, to satisfy some grammatical or syntactical rule or custom, but the omission of which would not alter or affect the meaning of the . . . sentence' (PG, p. 70). Can the idiomatic piling up of negatives (§§ 1627-9) be a factor here?

§ 2040. The term 'expletive' is frequently extended to negatives in *þæt* clauses after verbs meaning 'to deny [something]', e.g. *LS* 8. 273 *He þa oðsoc þæt he hit nære*; 'to avoid [doing something]'—through doubt, fear, hesitation, or neglect—e.g. *CP* 37. 3 *Se ilca Dauid ðe forbær ðæt he ðone kyning ne yfelode*; and 'to forbid' or 'to prevent [someone doing something]', e.g. *ÆCHom* ii. 464. 16 *Hwi forgifð God þam wacum wyrtum swa fægerne wlite, and us forbyt þæt we ne sceolon hogian ymbe ure frætewunge . . . ?* The twenty or so OE verbs which, according to Joly (1972, p. 32), take this 'expletive' negative fall into one of these three groups. Some belong to more than one, e.g. *wiþsacan*, which can mean 'to deny' or 'to refuse'. All these verbs have in common that the state or action described in the *þæt* clause is from the speaker's point of view negative—in other words, there would be a negative in the non-dependent equivalent, as in *BlHom* 37. 15 *Ne gelyfe þæs nænig mon þæt him ne genihtsumige þæt fæsten to ecere hælo, buton he mid oþrum godum hit geece*, where denial is expressed by *Ne gelyfe* but the negative of the non-dependent statement ☆*Ne genihtsumaþ* . . . is retained. So I do not find it surprising that in a language in which multiple negation is idiomatic the negative idea implicit in the verb can, but—as the examples which follow show—need not, be repeated in the *þæt* clause. One can see that 'Don't do that! I forbid you' is logically 'I forbid you that you do that'. But one can equally see that the OE equivalent of the (to us) illogical 'I forbid you that you do not do that' would have been emphatic. So Einenkel (*Ang.* 35 (1912), 208) is probably right when he distinguishes these examples from those expressing doubt discussed in the previous section, for in them the speaker means 'I do not doubt that *x* is true'.

§ 2041. Again, while it is hard to see any logic in variations involving words expressing denial or hesitation, one can see how they might have arisen. Sequences such as 'He denied that. It was not so' carry with them an essential ambiguity, depending on whether 'that' refers to 'It' or to the sentence containing 'It'. Similarly, one can reasonably construe *CP* 379. 8 . . . *forðyðe he forwandode ðæt he swa ne dyde* . . . as '. . . because he hesitated, so that he did not do so'—cf. 'He hesitated. He did not do so'; note that a similar explanation can hold for *CP* 379. 14 . . . *forðæm ic næfre ne forwandode*

ðæt ic eow ne gecyðde eall Godes geðeaht. But if we think of þæt as
introducing a noun clause, we can see the logic of CP 379. 11 . . . swa
he læs wandade ðæt he hira unðeawas ofsloge, literally '. . . the less
he hesitated that he slew their vices' but better '. . . the less he hesitated to slay their vices'.

§2042. Joly (1972, p. 31), after quoting LS 8. 273, CP 37. 3 (both
in §2040), and CP 177. 13 7 ðeah for eaðmodnesse wandiað ðæt hi
hit ne sprecað, goes on to say that 'cette négation, dite "explétive",
a pour caractéristique de ne pas vraiment négativer la subordonnée
dans laquelle elle se trouve, ce qui apparaît dans les traductions en
anglais moderne' ['this negation, called expletive, has the characteristic of not really negating the subordinate clause in which it occurs,
a characteristic which is apparent in the translations into Modern
English']. There is no doubt that MnE dispenses with the negative in
such subordinate clauses. But since it also dispenses with multiple
negation as a means of emphasis, I doubt the relevance of this.

§2043. Whatever the logic of and explanation for these fluctuations,
they are idiomatic in OE, although examples with the 'expletive'
negative seem to be more common than those without. The normal
principles of mood obtain whether we have it or not. Thus, we find
denial in ÆCHom ii. 230. 1 þa wiðsoc Crist swiðe rihtlice þæt he
deofol on him næfde; ac he ne wiðsoc þæt he nære Samaritanisc
but ÆCHom i. 116. 16 ac hi wiðsocon þæt he God wære; failure to
act in CP 43. 6 . . . hwi forcwið ðonne se ðe him God suelce cræftas
giefð ðæt he ne fede his heorde but CP 49. 17 7 forðam he forcwæð
7 nolde ðæt hine mon sende to læranne, in CP 345. 9 . . . gif hie
ðurh ungemodnesse agiemeleasiað ðæt hie anmode beon nyllað on
ryhte 7 on gode but CP 427. 3 Hu mæg se bion orsorg ðære wrace
his scylda, se ðe nu agiemeleasað ðæt he hreowsige his synna?, and in
CP 49. 4 Oðer for ðæm ege, ðe he ondred ðæt he hit sua medomlice
don ne meahte, him wiðsoc but CP 107. 16 7 eft wið ða wiðerweardan ne ondræde he ðæt he begonge his ryhtwisnesse;[30] and prohibition in Or 262. 21 . . . 7 forbead þæt mon na ðær eft ne timbrede
but Or 254. 8 7 forbead þæt hiene mon god hete and in ÆCHom ii.
464. 16 Hwi forgifð God þam wacum wyrtum swa fægerne wlite and
us forbyt þæt we ne sceolon hogian ymbe ure frætewunge . . . ? but
BlHom 53. 27 Nis eow þonne forboden þætte æhta habban. . . .
Bacquet ('From Doubt to Negativity. Remarks on the Particle ne in

---

[30] Visser (ii, §872) observes that 'the French idiom of using a negative adverb before the
verb in the sub-clause (e.g. "je crains qu'il ne vienne") does not seem to have been adopted
by English writers . . .'. But it was also a native idiom.

Old English', *Studies in English Grammar*, edd. A. Joly and T. Fraser (Paris, 1975), 13-15 (translated by Denis Keen)) offers some comments on what he calls 'negativity through concordance' and concludes thus: 'It would be interesting to see how far there is a relation between this *ne* of concordance in Old English and the subjunctive mood.' It is, however, clear from the examples quoted above that the 'expletive' negative is not restricted to clauses whose verb is in the subjunctive.

§2044. The 'expletive' negative may occur in multiple form, e.g. *Or* 262. 21, *ÆCHom* ii. 464. 16 (both in §2043), and *ÆHom* 9. 182 *and him swiðe forbudon þæt hi nan ðing ne bodedon be þam Hælende nahwar.*

§2045. The presence or absence of a negative in the principal clause containing the verb of denying, failing to act, or prohibiting, does not seem to be a factor. Thus we find 'expletive' negatives in *ÆCHom* ii. 230. 1 *þa wiðsoc Crist . . . þæt he deofol on him næfde* and in *ÆCHom* ii. 230. 2 *ac he ne wiðsoc þæt he nære Samaritanisc*, but no negatives in *CP* 451. 1 *Ac hwæt wile ðæt nu beon weorca ðæt us on oðerre stowe forbiet ðæt we hit beforan mannum don . . . ?* and in *BlHom* 53. 27 *Nis eow þonne forboden þæt æhta habban. . . .*

§2046. For further examples see Einenkel, *Ang.* 35 (1912), 208; Bacquet, pp. 503-4; and BT(S), s.vv. Joly (1972, *passim*) discusses this phenomenon in various IE languages and attempts to explain it. That one explanation must cover all these languages is an assumption which I cannot pursue here.

3. DEPENDENT QUESTIONS AND EXCLAMATIONS

a. Introductory remarks

§2047. The inevitable problems of classification (some little more than terminological) arise here. The line between dependent *x*-questions and dependent exclamations is often hard to draw, especially when the governing verb is not specifically interrogative, e.g. *ÆCHom* i. 272. 21 *On ðam is geswutelod hu swiðe God lufað annysse and geþwærnysse on his folce* and *ÆCHom* i. 288. 1 *Hwæt wenst ðu hu miccle swiðor is Godes andweardnys and his miht and his neosung æghwær.* Element order does not help in distinguishing them and the introductory word too fails unless it is used only in questions. The seeds of ambiguity exist here; see *NM* 65 (1964),

140-1. But I have as yet noticed no serious problems arising in OE as a result.

§ 2048. As we have seen in §§ 1652 and 1670, we sometimes have to ask whether a question is non-dependent or dependent. But it is usually not difficult to decide. Normally dependent speech requires a governing verb and involves changes in one or more of mood, tense, person, and element order, e.g. *ÆCHom* i. 512. 7 . . . *and axodon ða ðone Hælend hwa wære fyrmest manna on heofonan rice* (*wære* certifies that Thorpe's punctuation of this as non-dependent is wrong), *ÆCHom* ii. 394. 15 . . . *and ðu axast hwa ðe hreopode* (cf. *ÆCHom* ii. 394. 13 *þa cwæð se Hælend, 'Hwa hreopode me?'*), and *ÆCHom* i. 246. 5 *Hi axodon hine hwæt he wære oððe hu he faran wolde.*

§ 2049. Another problem is that of deciding whether the OE interrogatives *hwa, hwæt,* and *hwelc,* or *hwær, hwonne,* and the like, ever introduce adjective or adverb clauses as opposed to dependent questions. Whether we answer 'Yes' or 'No' largely depends on how we define the terms and how we interpret the examples.

§ 2050. *Hwa, hwæt,* and *hwelc,* serve in OE as both interrogatives and indefinites. If—despite Kock (p. 58)—we follow Curme (1931, pp. 182-3) and others in classifying 'who' in 'I asked who did it' as interrogative and 'who' in 'I know who did it' as indefinite—cf. *ÆGram* 231. 9-232. 5—we can say that *hwa, hwæt,* and *hwelc,* serve both as interrogatives and as indefinite relatives in OE; note here *ÆGram* 116. 5-117. 2 and 112. 10-113. 20. I do not propose to pursue this problem in detail here. It is well aired (with reference to other discussions) by Karlberg (pp. 28-36), who produces the following table (p. 36) to illustrate the complexity of the relationships between different types of clauses introduced by *hwa, hwæt, hwelc,* and their descendants:

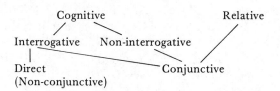

Cognitive sub-clauses connected with expressions involving some aspect of interrogation or desire to know may be called 'conjunctive questions'. These may be divided into 'indirect questions' (e.g. *Tell me who did it*) and 'reported questions' (e.g. *He asked who did it*).

§2051. A few examples will illustrate the problem. *ChronE* 219. 30 (1086) *7 se Xƥendom wæs swilc on his dæge ƥ ælc man hwæt his hade to belumpe folgade se ƥe wolde* is Karlberg's earliest example of what he calls (p. 42) 'simple independent relative *what*'. He goes on to observe that 'there may be hesitation whether to interpret *hwæt* as dependent on *folgade* (introducing an object-clause) or as a concessive relative (introducing an adverbial clause, ModE *whatever*)'. But if we take the *hwæt* clause as object of *folgade*, it remains an open question whether we call it a dependent question or an indefinite adjective clause used as a primary. Despite Johnsen (*Ang.* 37 (1913), 292-3), Visser (i, §411), Carnicelli (pp. 26-7), and others, I have not yet seen examples in which this choice does not in my opinion present itself.

§2052. The fact that *qua hora* is represented by *hwænne* in *Luke (WSCp)* 12. 39 *Witað ƥ gif se hiredes ealdor wiste hwænne se ƥeof cuman wolde* . . . , Latin *Hoc autem scitote quoniam si sciret pater familias qua hora fur ueniet* . . . , but by *ðætte tide ðe* in *Ru2* (where the lack of concord in gender testifies to the mechanical nature of the gloss) and that *quem* is represented by *hwæne* in *Luke(WSCp)* 12. 5 *Ic eow ætywe hwæne ge ondredon. adrædað ƥone ƥe anweald hæfð* . . . , Latin *ostendam autem uobis quem timeatis timete eum qui . . . habet potestatem* . . . (cf. *ÆCHom* ii. 542. 12), but by *ðone* in *Li* and *Ru2* demonstrates that the OE constructions were alternatives, not that they were identical; the variation between *hwæne* and *ƥone ƥe* in *Luke* 12. 5 above illustrates this. So in *ApT* 30. 23 . . . *ƥæt heo sylf geceose hwilcne eowerne*[31] *heo wille*, Latin . . . *ut ipsa sibi eligat quem uoluerit*, the translator has preferred *hwilcne* to *ƥone ƥe* as a rendering of the Latin *quem*, which he may have interpreted as an interrogative or as an indefinite relative. The terminological problem remains in examples of this sort, where the reference is to one of a number of possible persons or things.

§2053. But *hwa, hwæt,* and *hwelc*, are not used as definite relative pronouns with an antecedent in OE. Examples in which they appear to be so used are either imitations of a Latin original, e.g. *Luke (WSCp)* 6. 3 . . . *ne rædde ge ƥ hwæt david dyde* . . . , Latin . . . *nec hoc legistis quod fecit dauid* . . . (see *OED*, s.v. *what* C. I. 7), or examples of double objects, e.g. *ÆLS* 1. 127 . . . *swa hraðe heo mæg ƥa burh on hire geƥohte gescyppan hwylc heo bið*, *Deut* 31. 21 *ic wat soðlice ðæs folces geðanc, hwæt hi todæg don willað* . . . , and

---

[31] On *eowerne* see §301.

Met 10. 42   Hwa wat nu þæs wisan   Welandes ban,
on hwelcum hi hlæwa   hrusan þeccen?,

or of double subjects, e.g. *HomU* 27. 151. 13 *ac bið æt gode anum gelang eall, hwæt we gefaran sceolon.*

§ 2054. That a distinction existed between constructions with *hwa,* *hwæt,* and *hwelc,* and those involving *se* and/or *þe,* is clear from a comparison of

El 859   Ne meahte hire Iudas,   ne ful gere wiste,
sweotole gecyþan   be ðam sigebeame,
on hwylcne se hælend   ahafen wære,
sigebearn godes,

where we have the subjunctive, with

El 443   . . .   ond geflitu ræran
be ðam sigebeame   on þam soðcyning
ahangen wæs,   heofonrices weard,
eallre sybbe bearn,

where we have the indicative. I believe, with Gorrell (p. 417), that in examples like *Or* 24. 21 *Nu hæbbe we gesæd ymbe ealle Europe landgemæro hu hi tolicgað, Or* 250. 28 *nu ic wille eac forþ gesecgan hwelc mildsung 7 hwelc geþwærnes siþþan wæs* . . . , and *ÆCHom* i. 116. 31 *We habbað gesæd embe ðas þryfealdan lac, hu hi to Criste belimpað,* the

use of the indicative is to be explained by the fact that, though interrogative particles are here employed, the interrogative idea is at its lowest point and the dependent clause is no more than an expression of time, place, or manner, with reference to a known object. Indeed, in many cases, these constructions are on the border-line between indirect questions and adverbial or relative clauses, and frequently, when there is identity in the conjunctive particles of these two kinds of expressions, it is impossible to make any clear demarcation.

But this does not mean that *ÆCHom* ii. 282. 10 *Ac Drihten aras of deaðe gesund, buton ælcere forrotodnysse, and hi sceolon geseon æt ðam micclan dome hwæne hi gewundodon wælhreawlice on rode* (cf. *John* 19. 37) and *ÆCHom* ii. 388. 26 *Ne eom ic na scinnhiw, swa swa ge wenað: oncnawað þone þe ge geseoð* (no exact equivalent in *Matt* 14. 27 or *Mark* 6. 50) are identical. We must agree with Karlberg (p. 68):

As appears from this critical survey there are no instances of the *wh*-pronouns as clearly relative earlier than the 12th century, with one exception: *eall hwæt* (above, pp. 64, 63, 62).[32] On the other hand there are certainly quite a few cases

---

[32] Even these are late: 'Clearly relative *eall hwæt* occurs first in the glossed psalters F, 11th c., and J, 1050–1100 and in Boethius, MS B, *c.* 1100' (Karlberg, p. 64). The idiom does not of course persist into standard English.

which are suggestive of a relative interpretation, and it is seen that conditions existed for the cognitive pronouns to become relative, not only independent but also dependent relative pronouns.

It will be noticed that I do not ask the question 'What is the origin of the use of MnE "who" as an indefinite and definite relative pronoun?' That is outside the scope of this work. But it is clear from the preceding discussion that I accept the view that the interrogative use of OE *hwa* was an important factor. This must not be taken as implying that in my opinion the use of *hwa* as an indefinite pronoun 'anyone' and as part of the indefinite relative *swa hwa swa* played no part; see §2363 fn. 75.

§2055. *Mutatis mutandis*, the same conclusions are applicable to *hwær* (see Yamakawa 1971, pp. 18-19), *hwonne* (Yamakawa 1969, *passim* and p. 42), and the like. *Hwær* and *hwonne* too can be used as indefinites. They too can appear in syntactically inappropriate contexts under Latin influence, e.g. *John(Ru2)* 12. 26 *7 hwer am ic ðer 7 hera ðegn min bið*, Latin *et ubi sum ego illic et minister meus erit*, where *WSCp* has *þær þær* and *Li sua huer . . . ðer* for *ubi*, and *Mark(WSCp)* 8. 20 *And hwænne seofon hlafas feower þusendum 7 hu fela wyligena brytsyna ge namon?*, Latin *quando et septem panes in quattuor milia quot sportas fragmentorum tulistis?*, where *Li* has *huoenne ł ða*. They too can be used in double object constructions, e.g. *ÆCHom* i. 160. 33 *Deor habbað hola and fugelas habbað nest, hwær hi restað,*

El 673	þu scealt geagninga
	wisdom onwreon,　　swa gewritu secgaþ,
	æfter stedewange　　hwær seo stow sie
	Caluarie,

ÆHomM 11. 10 . . . *gif he wiste þone timan hwænne se ðeof come,* and

Wan 25	. . . sohte sele dreorig　　sinces bryttan,
	hwær ic feor oþþe neah　　findan meahte
	þone þe in meoduhealle　　min mine wisse,

where the possibility that *seledreorig* is a compound merely emphasizes that *hwær* is not a relative pronoun with antecedent *sele*. Other words such as *hwi* also appear in the double object construction, e.g. *ÆLS* 10. 135 *Ic axe þone intingan hwi þu me gelangodest.* Here too there are examples in which *hwær* and *hwonne* have been called 'indefinite relatives', e.g. *John(WSCp)* 20. 2 . . . *7 we nyton hwar hi hyne ledon*, Latin . . . *et nescimus ubi posuerunt eum*, and *Gen* 19. 33 *7 se fæder nyste hu he befeng on hi ne hwænne heo aras*, Latin

at ille non sensit, nec quando accubuit filia, nec quando surrexit.
To me these are dependent questions. Nor do I accept the claim that
OE *hwær, hwonne*, and the like, are used unambiguously as definite
relative adverbs referring to a definite antecedent or as conjunctions
introducing adverb clauses. None of the examples cited by Kock
(chapter iii) leads me to change these conclusions. See further
§§ 2494-507 and 2775-83.

b. Introductory words

(1) Governing words

§ 2056. What Gorrell (pp. 411-14) describes as 'verbs of inquiry'—
acsian, (be)frignan, fandian and its compounds, *cunnian, fricgean*,
and *hleotan*—naturally introduce dependent questions. Whether
the apparently similar clauses introduced by verbs of speaking (e.g.
cweðan, cyðan, and *secgan*), of thinking and believing (e.g. *þencan,
smeagan,* and *wenan*), and of perceiving or knowing (e.g. *ongietan,
geseon,* and *witan*), should also be called dependent questions has
just been discussed. For examples involving these and other verbs, see
Gorrell, pp. 414-37, and Karlberg, pp. 37-69, and the sections which
follow.

§ 2057. Impersonal verbs or verbs used impersonally may introduce
dependent questions, e.g. *Or* 182. 22 *Hu þyncð eow nu Romanum
hu seo sibb gefæstnad wære . . . ?, ÆCHom* i. 556. 14 . . . *ac us
twynað hwæðer ge magon maran deopnysse ðæron þearflice tocnawan,
Conf 1. 4* 411 *Her cyþ on hu seoc man mot his fæsten alesan,* and
Conf 3. 1(O) 44. 17 *Her segð hu se halga apostol Paulus lærð ælcum
mæssepreoste.* In

Rid 31. 18	Wrætlic me þinceð,
hu seo wiht mæge	wordum lacan
þurh fot neoþan,	frætwed hyrstum,

wrætlic me þinceð is the equivalent of *ic wundrige* or the like.

§ 2058. Dependent questions may also be governed by nouns, e.g.
(nexus) *ÆCHom* i. 506. 17 *þa wearð micel twynung . . . hwæðer hi
inneodon oððe hi halgian sceoldon* and *ÆCHom* i. 212. 10 *Swa eac
gehwilc man hæfð agenne cyre . . . hweðer he wille filian deofles
willan oððe wiðsacan,* and (x-questions) *ÆCHom* i. 98. 17 *ac we ne
gemetað nane geswutelunge on cristenum bocum hwi þes dæg to
geares anginne geteald sy* and *ÆCHom* i. 290. 7 . . . *and nam bysne
be mannum hu ælc sunu bið gingra þonne se fæder on ðisum life.*

Similar examples with adjectives include (nexus) *Or* 192. 4 *for þon þe hie wæron orwene hwæðer æfre Romane to heora anwealde becomen* and

GenA 2710   Ne wæs me on mode cuð,
             hwæðer on þyssum folce   frean ælmihtiges
             egesa wære,   þa ic her ærest com

(I have as yet found no such examples in Ælfric), and (*x*-questions) *ÆCHom* i. 52. 25 *Beoð gemyndige hwæt seo sylfe Soðfæstnys on ðam halgan godspelle behet* . . . and *ÆCHom* i. 440. 18 *Nis nanum deadlicum men cuð hu oððe on hwylcere tide hyre halga lichama þanon gebroden wære.* . . . For dependent questions in apposition with pronouns, see §§2064-5.

(2) *Conjunctions, pronouns, adjectives, and adverbs*

§2059. Dependent nexus questions are introduced by *gif* and *hwæþer* (alone and in combination), by *swa . . . swa* (see §2088), and after *reccan, nytan*, and words of similar meaning, by *þeah* (see §§3416-20). Two examples with initial verb are discussed in §2072. Care must be taken to distinguish nexus questions with *hwæþer* 'whether', e.g. *ÆCHom* i. 298. 10 *Se halga heap befran Crist hwæðer he wolde on ðam timan þisne middangeard geendian*, from *x*-questions with *hwæþer* 'which (of two)?', e.g. *ÆCHom* i. 256. 13 *Gif rice wif and earm acennað togædere, gangon hi aweig; nast ðu hwæðer bið þæs rican wifan cild, hwæðer þæs earman* (to take *hwæðer* as 'whether' would involve an anacoluthon) and *ÆCHom* ii. 252. 12 *þa befran Pilatus þæs folces menigu hwæðerne hi gecuron, Hælend oððe Barraban* (where case is decisive).[33] Whether a *gif* clause is interrogative or conditional is determined in MnE by intonation; see Collinson, *TPS* 1941, p. 60. This test is denied to us in examples like *ÆCHom* ii. 248. 16 *þa axode hine se ealdorbiscop, and mid aðe gehalsode, þæt he openlice sæde, gif he Godes Sunu soðlice wære, ÆCHom* ii. 490. 30 *We halsiað þe, on naman Hælendes Cristes, þæt ðu sprece and secge, gif ðes diacon þas unrihtwisnysse gefremode*, and

Beo 272   þu wast, gif hit is
             swa we soþlice   secgan hyrdon,
             þæt mid Scyldingum   sceaðona ic nat hwylc,
             deogol dædhata   deorcum nihtum
             eaweð þurh egsan   uncuðne nið,
             hynðu ond hrafyl.[34]

---

[33] On this distinction see further Nusser, pp. 160-4. But the more I ponder examples like *Or* 212. 13 and the *hwæðer* clause beginning at *LS* 34. 117, the harder I find it to be sure that we have one rather than the other.

[34] Toy, 'Whether and If', *SP* 28 (1931), 546-50, offers a few perfunctory comments on nexus questions in Latin, Greek, Gothic, English, and German.

§2060. Dependent *x*-questions are introduced by pronouns, adjectives, and adverbs. The pronouns are *hwa/hwæt* in the appropriate case, e.g. nom. *hwa* (*ÆCHom* i. 240. 21), acc. *hwæt* (*ÆCHom* i. 186. 5), acc. after a preposition *þurh hwæt* (*Beo* 3068), gen. *hwæs* (*ÆCHom* i. 474. 3), and dat. *hwam* (*ÆCHom* i. 66. 5). *Hwilc* appears independently (as a pronoun), e.g. nom. sg. *hwilc* (*ÆCHom* i. 580. 29) and nom. pl. *hwilce* (*ÆCHom* i. 114. 3), and dependently (as an adjective), e.g. nom. sg. *hwilc gast* (*ÆCHom* i. 324. 27), acc. sg. masc. *on hwilcne timan* (*ÆCHom* i. 82. 8), gen. sg. masc. *to hwilces timan* (*ÆCHom* i. 78. 18), dat. sg. fem. *on hwilcere tide* (*ÆCHom* i. 128. 11), and dat. pl. *mid hwilcum feondum* (*ÆCHom* i. 410. 9). The pronoun *hwæþer* has been exemplified in §2059.

§2061. As in MnE, the pronoun derives its case from the noun clause; in

And 1099   Leton him þa betweonum   taan wisian
                  hwylcne hira ærest   oðrum sceolde
                  to foddurþege   feores ongyldan,

hwylcne should strictly be *hwylc* and in *Matt(WSCp)* 16. 13 *7 ahsode hys leorningcnihtas hwæne secgeað menn þ sy mannes sunu*, Latin *et interrogabat discipulos suos dicens quem dicunt homines esse filium hominis*, and *Luke(Li)* 9. 18 *7 gefrægn ða ilco cuoeðende huælcne mec cuoeðas þ ic se ðas hergas*, Latin *et interrogauit illos dicens quem me dicunt esse turbae*, the changed OE constructions require nominative forms in place of the Latin-based *hwæne* and *huælcne*. The construction seen in the last two examples is still common.

§2062. The interrogative adverbs include *hwær* (*ÆCHom* i. 60. 22), *hwider* (*ÆCHom* i. 160. 27), *hwanon* (*ÆCHom* i. 12. 18), *hwonne* (*ÆHom* 18. 45), *hu* (*ÆCHom* i. 6. 10),[35] *humeta* (*ÆCHom* i. 486. 17), and the instr. sg. neut. of *hwæt*, e.g. *forhwy* (*Or* 162. 9) and *hwi* (*ÆCHom* i. 18. 12). We find *to hwæs* 'whither' in *Ex* 192.

§2063. Some of these words, e.g. *hwæt* and *hu*, can introduce dependent exclamations. As already noted, the boundaries are ill-defined. So comments which apply to dependent *x*-questions in the sections which follow are in general applicable to dependent exclamations as well.

---

[35] Wilbur, 'The Germanic Interrogatives of the *how* Type', *Word*, 19 (1963), 328-34, and Peeters, 'On "How" in Germanic', *Studia Linguistica*, 26 (1972), 116-19, are concerned with etymology and variant forms, not with syntax.

c. The relationship of the noun clause to the sentence

§2064. *Mutatis mutandis*, the principles enunciated in §§1962-75 for dependent statements and desires apply here. The minimum of examples will therefore be given unless a point of special interest arises. We find the dependent question as the equivalent of a nominative, either with a formal pronoun subject, e.g. *ÆCHom* i. 52. 30 *Ge gehyrað nu, mine gebroðra, þæt hit stent þurh Godes gyfe on urum agenum dihte hu us bið æt Gode gedemed*, or without one, e.g. *ÆCHom* i. 50. 35 *On ðyssere dæde is geswutelod hu micclum fremige þære soðan lufe gebed* and *ÆCHom* i. 386. 13 *þær ðe bið gesæd hwæt ðe gedafenige to donne.*

§2065. A dependent question may also serve as the direct object of a verb, e.g. *ÆCHom* ii. 244. 6 *þa befran Iudas gif he hit wære*, *ÆLS* 11. 293 *Nyte we hweþer se weardmann wære æfre gefullod*, *ÆCHom* i. 376. 27 *Sege me, Petrus, on sundorspræce hwæt ðu ðence*, and *ÆCHom* i. 460. 22 . . . *ic do þæt þu . . . gehyrst mid hwilcum cræfte he is geðuht þæt he untrumnysse gehæle*; or be in apposition with a pronoun in the accusative, e.g. *Or* 212. 14 *þeh þe Romane hæfden ær longsum gemot ymb þæt, hwæþer him rædlecre wære* . . . and *ÆCHom* i. 48. 15 *Eall ðæra Iudeiscra teona aras þurh þæt, hwi Drihten Crist, seðe æfter flæsce soðlice is mannes Sunu, eac swilce wære gecweden Godes Sunu*, or in another case, e.g. *ÆLS* 32. 211 *Men þa þæs wundrodon, hu þa weargas hangodon* and *GenB* 432 *Hycgað his ealle,* ‖ *hu ge hi beswicen.*

§2066. Gorrell (p. 426) notes that, when the introductory verb is *wenan*, the whole expression is frequently interrogative, e.g. *CP* 353. 10 *Ac hu wene we hu micel scyld ðæt sie ðæt monn aðreote ðære nætinge yfelra monna* . . . ? and *CP* 425. 1 *Wenstu, gif hwa oðrum hwæt gieldan sceal, hwæðer he hine mid ðy gehealdan mæge ðæt he him nauht mare on ne nime* . . . ? The construction in *CP* 281. 13 and *ÆCHom* i. 442. 8 . . . *hu miccle swiðor wenst þu þæt he nu todæg þæt heofonlice werod togeanes his agenre meder sendan wolde*, with a *þæt* which seems to us tautologic, should be compared with that discussed in §1980.

§2067. Combinations of a noun and a dependent question present similar problems to those which arise with a noun and a *þæt* clause (§§1968-70). Sometimes the noun is essential to sense and syntax, e.g. *ÆCHom* i. 408. 27 *forðan ðe heo micele sace wið hi sylfe hæfð hwi heo ða geniðerunge . . . nolde ær on life mid ænigre carfulnysse foresceawian.* Sometimes the clause is in apposition with and explains a noun which is syntactically superfluous, e.g. *ÆCHom* i. 82. 17 *Ac he cydde syððan his facenfullan syrewunge, hu he ymbe wolde gif he hine gemette* and *ÆCHom* i. 502. 23 *Hi ða heora biscop rædes befrunon, hwæt him be ðam to donne wære.* Sometimes we have the construction seen in 'Consider the lilies of the field, how they flourish', in which the subject of the dependent question appears in the principal clause as object of the verb, e.g. *ÆCHom* i. 286. 30 *Beheald þas sunnan, hu heage heo astihð, and hu heo asent hyre leoman geond ealne middangeard, and hu heo onliht ealle ðas eorðan þe mancynn on eardað*; as object of a preposition, e.g. *ÆCHom* i. 116. 31 *We habbað gesæd embe ðas þryfealdan lac, hu hi to Criste belimpað*; in an oblique case, e.g. *ÆCHom* i. 28. 26 *We wyllað to trymminge eowres geleafan eow gereccan þæs Hælendes acennednysse be ðære godspellican endebyrdnysse: hu he on ðysum dægðerlicum dæge on soðre menniscnysse acenned wæs on godcundnysse*; or represented by a possessive, e.g. the second clause in *ÆCHom* ii. 300. 1 . . . *þæt we þe ealle geseon and ðine stemne gehyron, hwilce cyðnysse ðu wilt cyðan be Criste.*

§ 2068. A noun clause dependent question may be used in coordination with any other element which can serve as a noun, e.g. *ÆCHom* ii. 500. 1 . . . *smeagende symle ymbe Godes cyrcan and hu he on westene wunian mihte, ÆCHom* i. 68. 23 *Symle ðu tæhtest mildheortnysse, and þæt man oðrum miltsode; and gif man oðrum miltsað, hu micele swiðor wile God miltsian and arian mannum his handgeweorce,* and *ÆCHom* ii. 506. 30 *Ða nyste heora nan his naman to secgenne, ne on hwæs timan he ðrowunge underhnige.*

§ 2069. As has been pointed out in § § 1652, 1658-9, and 1670, it is possible that we should understand some sort of a principal clause to govern questions such as those in *ÆCHom* i. 136. 30 *Hwæðer ic mote lybban oðþæt ic hine geseo?*,

Met 19. 5　　　Hwæðer ge willen　　on wuda secan
　　　　　　　　gold ðæt reade　　on grenum triowum?,

and

Met 10. 18　　　Eala, ofermodan,　　hwi eow a lyste
　　　　　　　　mid eowrum swiran　　selfra willum
　　　　　　　　þæt swære gioc　　symle underlutan?,

and exclamations like those in *ÆCHom* ii. 120. 26 *Walawa, þæt swa fægeres hiwes menn sindon ðam sweartan deofle underðeodde, ÆCHom* i. 40. 6 *Eala hu rihtlice hi andetton þone halgan geleafan mid þisum wordum . . . , Sat* 167 *Eala þæt ic eam ealles leas ecan dreames . . . , ChristA* 275, and *ChristC* 1459 *Hu þær wæs unefen racu unc gemæne!*

§2070. Chapter headings like *Or* 7. 1 *Hu Aurelius feng to Romana rice* and *GD(H)* 9. 26 *Be Libertine þam prafoste, hu he wearð of his horse aworpen* can be similarly explained; cf. those introduced by *þæt* discussed in §1972.

§2071. Contracted dependent questions occur, as in MnE, e.g. *ÆHom* 29. 40 . . . *wolde witan þurh hi hu him sceolde gelimpan, hwæðer þe lif þe deað, ÆCHom* i. 66. 3 . . . *þæt he hordað and nat hwam, ÆCHom* i. 184. 20 *His discipuli woldon eac þæt folc fedan, ac hi næfdon mid hwam,* and

Jul 699   Min sceal of lice
          sawul on siðfæt,   nat ic sylfa hwider,
          eardes uncyðgu.

d. The presence, absence, or repetition, of the interrogative word

§2072. An interrogative word is essential for *x*-questions, non-dependent and dependent, and is almost always present in dependent nexus questions. Examples like *ÆCHom* ii. 502. 26 *Ða befran se sceaða þe hine onsundron heold, hwæt he manna wære, oððe wære ofdræd* and

El 157   Ða þæs fricggan ongan   folces aldor,
                 sigerof cyning,   ofer sid weorod,
                 wære þær ænig   yldra oððe gingra
                 þe him to soðe   secggan meahte,
                 galdrum cyðan,   hwæt se god wære,
                 boldes brytta,

are rare. In them the element order of the non-dependent nexus question is retained, but the mood and tense have shifted.

§2073. The interrogative word is repeated when dependent nexus and *x*-questions are in asyndetic parataxis, e.g. *ÆCHom* i. 268. 11, *ÆCHom* i. 242. 27 *Ac behealde ge hwæðer ge sind Godes scep, hwæðer ge hine gyt oncneowon, hwæðer ge mid soðfæstnysse hine lufiað,* and *ÆCHom* i. 240. 20 *Nast ðu hwa bið hyra, hwa hyrde, ærðam ðe se wulf cume.*

§2074. It can be repeated when they are in syndetic parataxis, e.g. (*x*-questions) *ÆCHom* i. 240. 4 *Mid lare he sceal him tæcan, þæt hi cunnon hwæt deofol tæchð mannum to forwyrde, and hwæt God bebyt to gehealdenne, for begeate þæs ecan lifes, ÆCHom* i. 376. 26 *. . . ðonne secge he hwæt ic ðence oððe hwæt ic don wylle*, and *ÆCHom* i. 46. 13 (where we have the verb *geniwode* governing the noun *gemynd*, three *hu* clauses, and a *be* phrase, all joined by *and*), and (nexus questions) *Bede* 86. 22 *Ac þonne gena is se seolfa geþoht to asmeagenne, hwæðer he geeode þe mid scynisse þe mid lustful-nisse, oððe hwæþer þonne gena, þæt mare is, mid gyfunge þære synne, Solil* 44. 20, *Solil* 52. 5 (where *hwæðer/hweðer* appears three times), *John(WSCp)* 7. 17, *ÆCHom* i. 480. 7 (where *gyf* is repeated after *oððe* in a chiasmus; see §2084), and *Gen* 43. 27 *Iosep . . . axode hi hwæþer heora fæder wære hal þe hi him foresædon oþþe hwæðer he leofode.*

§2075. But the conjunction need not be repeated in a dependent question which is in syndetic parataxis. Examples involving *x*-questions include *ÆCHom* i. 376. 31 *Sege nu, Simon, hwæt ic ðohte, oððe cwæde, oþþe gedyde* and *ÆCHom* i. 502. 16 *. . . and he ða mid graman wearð astyred, hwi se fearr angenga his heorde forsawe, and gebende his bogan, and mid geættrode flan hine ofsceotan wolde. Hu* is not repeated in *ÆCHom* i. 230. 10 *Nu trahtnað se papa Gregorius ðis godspel, and cwyð, þæt gehwa wundrað hu se Hælend become in to his apostolum, and wæron ðeah hwæðere ða dura belocene* because the second *and* clause is concessive. In *ÆCHom* i. 438. 3 *Soðlice fram anginne þæs halgan godspelles ge geleornodon hu se heahengel Gabriel þam eadigan mædene Marian þæs heofonlican Æðelinges acennednysse gecydde, and þæs Hælendes wundra, and þære gesæligan Godes cennestran þenunge, and hyre lifes dæda on þam feower godspellicum bocum geswutollice oncneowon*, the *hu* clause ends at *gecydde*, but a momentary confusion may overtake the modern reader. For examples of nexus questions in syndetic parataxis in which *gif* and *hwæþer* are not repeated, see §§2083 and 2086.

§2076. Clauses introduced by different interrogatives can of course be in either asyndetic or syndetic parataxis, e.g. *ÆCHom* i. 168. 13 *þa smeade se deofol hwæt he wære; hwæðer he wære Godes Sunu, seðe manncynne behaten wæs, ÆCHom* i. 246. 5 *Hi axodon hine hwæt he wære oððe hu he faran wolde, ÆCHom* i. 440. 18 *Nis nanum deadlicum men cuð hu oððe on hwylcere tide . . . oððe hwider . . . oððe hwæðer heo of deaðe arise*, and *ÆCHom* i. 558. 13, where we have a *hwæt* clause, a *hwær* clause, and two nouns, all joined by *and*. The parallelism in *ÆCHom* i. 54. 31 *Eala ðu mann, þu sceawast hwæt ðin broðor þe dyde and þu ne sceawast hwæt ðu Gode gedydest* is typical of Ælfric.

§2077. When two or more dependent questions are paratactically related, the verb need not be expressed in the second and subsequent questions, e.g. *ÆCHom* ii. 372. 30 *on handum and on eallum lichaman we habbað hrepunge, þæt we magon gefredan hwæt bið heard, hwæt hnesce, hwæt smeðe, hwæt unsmeðe, and swa gehwæt, ÆCHom* i. 20. 12 (§2086), and *ÆCHom* i. 268. 11 *Deofol mot ælces mannes afandigan, hwæðer he aht sy oððe naht.* In *ÆCHom* i. 440. 18 (§2076) the same clause is introduced by *hu oððe on hwylcere tide.* . . .

e. Mood and the 'modal' auxiliaries

§2078. Gorrell's statement (p. 444) is a useful introduction:

There is great irregularity in the use of mood [in the Indirect Interrogative Sentence]. When the dependent clause is truly interrogative in character, the subjunctive is employed; in a large number of instances, however, the descriptive rather than the interrogative idea is present and hence in mood they do not differ from the corresponding declarative sentences; yet, in some cases, the interrogative construction of the dependent clause calls for the subjunctive, though there is little or no trace of any distinct interrogative idea. The broad statement may therefore be made that the employment of the subjunctive in the Indirect Interrogative Sentence is somewhat more extensive than in the Indirect Declarative Sentence.

To this may be added Behre's observation (p. 252): 'As to OE. dependent questions in general, it is worth noting that the frequent use of the subjunctive contrasts with its rare occurrence in independent questions.'

§2079. Here again space does not permit consideration of the preference of individual verbs for one mood or 'modal' auxiliary rather than another. Wülfing (ii. 167-72), Gorrell (pp. 411-37), and Behre (pp. 258-69), offer valuable material, and my thesis lists all the dependent questions/exclamations in OE poetry with the governing word and the mood of the verb in the dependent clause (Mitchell 1959, Noun Clause Appendices). But some observations are made in the sections which follow. They can be supplemented by reference to Gorrell (pp. 444-9) and to Behre (pp. 238-58), who discusses both the use and the nature of the subjunctive in dependent questions/exclamations. In general it may be said that those factors which affect the mood of the verb in dependent statements and desires exercise a similar influence here; see §§1992-2038.

§2080. At the same time one has to bear in mind that because we are not native informants we cannot understand or explain every variation; some will seem to us capricious. So we must be cautious of erecting 'rules' and of expecting them to operate consistently. It is possible to explain the indicative in *Beo* 162 *men ne cunnon,* || *hwyder helrunan hwyrftum scriþað* by reference to Ardern's theory (p. xxxvi) that 'the indicative is fairly common . . . in a question as to some *circumstance* of an event that is not itself questioned'. But if we accept this, we can ask why we have the subjunctive and then the indicative in

MSol 426   Full oft ic frode menn   fyrn gehyrde
                  secggan and swerian   ymb sume wisan,
                  hwæðer wære twegra   butan tweon strengra,
                  wyrd ðe warnung,   ðonne hie winnað oft
                  mid hira ðreamedlan,   hwæðerne aðreoteð ær,

where it seems logical to argue that, if one wearies before the other, one must be stronger and where the poet goes on to explain that *wyrd* can be moderated.

§2081. The 'modal' auxiliaries appear in dependent questions and exclamations in contexts which suggest that they have lost their full force and are used in the same way as their modern equivalents, e.g. *ÆCHom* i. 232. 19 *Ac we sceolon geleornian on mannum hu we magon becuman to Godes lufe* (Thorpe 'may come'), *ÆCHom* i. 214. 31 . . . *and syrwedon mid micelre smeaunge hu hi mihton hine to deaðe gebringan* (Thorpe 'might bring'), *ÆCHom* i. 86. 2 . . . *and eac geswutelode on hwilcum suslum he moste æfter forðsiðe ecelice cwylmian* (Thorpe 'must suffer'), *ÆCHom* i. 220. 22 . . . *and hi ge- wissode to ðære lare and to ðam geleafan hu hi eallum mancynne tæcan sceoldon* (Thorpe 'should teach'), and *ÆCHom* i. 566. 28 *Oft hwonlice gelyfede menn smeagað mid heora stuntan gesceade hwi se Ælmihtiga God æfre geðafian wolde þæt* . . . (Thorpe 'would per- mit'). But examples like *ÆCHom* ii. 268. 7 *Nu smeadon gehwilce men oft, and gyt gelome smeagað, hu se hlaf, þe bið of corne ge- gearcod, and ðurh fyres hætan abacen, mage beon awend to Cristes lichaman; oððe þæt win, ðe bið of manegum berium awrungen, weorðe awend, þurh ænigre bletsunge to Drihtnes blode* and *ÆCHom* i. 506. 17 *þa wearð micel twynung betwux ðære burhware be ðære cyrcan, hwæðer hi inn eodon, oððe hi halgian sceoldon,* with their fluctuations between a subjunctive and a periphrasis with *magan* or **sculan*, argue against too easy an acceptance of the apparent equa- tion. So too do examples in which the 'modal' auxiliaries have some- thing approaching their full meaning. Typical are *CP* 163. 1 (*mæg*),

ÆCHom i. 556. 14 . . . *ac us twynað hwæðer ge magon maran deop-nysse ðæron þearflice tocnawan,* CP 409. 2 *Ðæm monnum is gecyðed hwelce stowe hi moton habban beforan urum fæder . . . , ÆCHom* ii. 250. 4 *Ac se mildheorta Crist wolde him æteowian on his agenum gylte hu he oðrum sceolde mannum gemiltsian on mislicum gyltum,* and *ÆCHom* ii. 30. 7 *þa gemette heo ænne deofol on mannes hiwe, se befran, hwider heo wolde. þæt earme wif andwyrde, and cwæð, þæt heo wolde to cyrcan gan, and þone sunu ðe hi tirigde awyrian.* For the reasons given in §1009, the point cannot be pursued here. On the use of the 'modal' auxiliaries in dependent questions, see Standop, pp. 57-60 (*magan*), 90 (**motan*), 115 (**sculan*), and 152-3 (*willan*).

§ 2082. I discuss some problems of mood in dependent questions and exclamations in the poetry in *NM* 68 (1967), 139-49.

f. Dependent nexus questions

§ 2083. In what Jespersen (*Ess.*, p. 304) calls 'simple' nexus ques-tions, e.g. *ÆCHom* i. 46. 7 *Is hit swa hi secgað?* and *ÆCHom* i. 268. 14 *Swa swa man afandað gold on fyre, swa afandað God þæs mannes mod on mislicum fandungum, hwæðer he anræde sy,* the negative alter-native is implied. But it can be expressed, e.g. *Matt(WSCp)* 22. 17 *Ys hyt alyfed þ man casere gaful sylle þe na?, Coll* 283 *Anra gehwylc wat gif he beswuncgen wæs oððe na, Solil* 56. 10, CP 361. 7 . . . *7 huru ðær ðær hie nyton hwæðer sio sibb betre betwux gefæstnod bið ðe ne bið,* and *ÆCHom* i. 268. 11 *Deofol mot ælces mannes afandigan hwæðer he aht sy oððe naht.* (So Gorrell's observation (p. 446) that 'when an alternative is expressed or implied the sub-junctive is always found' makes no sense and is not borne out by the facts.) This is one type of 'disjunctive' nexus question. In the other, two distinct possibilities are stated and we can choose one or neither, e.g. *ÆCHom* i. 480. 6 *Eart ðu se ðe toweard is oþþe we oðres and-bidian sceolon?* and *ÆCHom* i. 506. 17 (§ 2081).

§ 2084. Typical dependent nexus questions introduced by *gif* in-clude (simple) *ÆCHom* ii. 244. 6 *þa befran Iudas gif he hit wære* and *Beo* 1319 *frægn gif him wære* || *æfter neodlaðum niht getæse,* and (disjunctive) the last example in this section and *ÆCHom* i. 480. 7 *Swilce he cwæde, Geswutela me, gyf ðu sylf wylle nyðer astigan to hellwarum for manna alysednysse, swa swa ðu woldest acenned beon for manna alysednysse; oððe gif ic sceole cyðan ðinne tocyme hellwarum, swa swa ic middangearde þe toweardne bodade, geswutela*. There are no examples of the latter with *gif* in the poetry. The mood is usually subjunctive. The indicatives in *CP* 157. 15 *Gif sio ðonne ontyned við, ðonne mæg mon geseon gif ðær hwelc dieglu scond inne við, sua se witga dyde* and *ÆCHom* i. 380. 12 *Ic wylle geseon gif ðu ðas behat mid weorcum gefylst* may be explained as due to the speaker's choice of *geseon* (see Gorrell, pp. 432-3) if we do not take the *gif* clauses as conditional. This escape is not available in *Coll* 283 *Anra gehwylc wat gif he beswuncgen wæs oþþe na*—one of the very few dependent nexus questions I have noted with the preterite indicative; note Latin *erat* and see § 2085.

§ 2085. We find the conj. *hwæþer* introducing dependent 'simple' nexus questions in *ÆCHom* i. 268. 14 *Swa swa man afandað gold on fyre, swa afandað God þæs mannes mod on mislicum fandungum, hwæðer he anræde sy, ÆCHom* i. 298. 10 *Se halga heap befran Crist, hwæðer he wolde on ðam timan þisne middangeard geendian, ÆLS* 11. 293 *Nyte we hweþer se weardmann wære æfre gefullod*, and *And* 129 *Woldon cunnian hwæðer cwice lifdon. . . .* Again, the usual mood is the subjunctive—see further *Bo* 45. 8, *Bede* 384. 23, and *ÆHom* 5. 68—but the indicative occasionally occurs, e.g. *ÆCHom* ii. 414. 19 *We sceolon geseon hwæðer ðin Iacobus ðe alyst fram ðisum bendum* (where the governing verb is again *geseon*), *ÆCHom* ii. 228. 21 . . . *ðonne tocnæwð he hwæðer he is fram Gode* (where Gorrell (p. 445) sees 'complete knowledge of a fact'; *Coll* 283 (§ 2084) could belong here too), and *ÆCHom* i. 532. 25 *forðan þe he nat hwæðer he wurðe is into þam ecan rice* and

Beo 1355　　　　　　　　　　　　no hie fæder cunnon,
　　　　　hwæþer him ænig wæs　　ær acenned
　　　　　dyrnra gasta

(in both of which Gorrell, p. 445, detects 'absolute ignorance').

§ 2086. We turn now to dependent disjunctive nexus questions in which the alternatives are expressed by the use of the patterns *hwæþer (. . .) (þe) . . . þe*[36] or *hwæþer . . . oþþe*; these are more common than those involving repetition of *hwæþer* quoted in §§ 2073-4. The alternatives offered may be nouns or their equivalents, e.g. *CP* 427. 31 . . . *ða hi ne scrifon hwæðer hit wære ðe dæg ðe niht, Solil* 3. 1 *þa andswarode me sum ðing, ic nat hwæt, hweðer þe ic sylf þe oðer þing*, and *ÆCHom* i. 268. 11 *Deofol mot ælces mannes afandigan, hwæðer he aht sy oððe naht*; adjectives, e.g. *ÆCHom* ii. 120. 22 *Eft*

---

[36] See Nusser, pp. 160-4, for a variety of sentences involving *hwæþer* pronoun and *hwæþer* conjunction. For some difficult examples, see § 1873.

ða Gregorius befran hwæðer þæs landes folc cristen wære ðe hæðen and ÆCHom i. 236. 32 Hwæt sceole we smeagan embe ða oðre þe gewitað to ðam ecum forwyrde, hwæðer hi alefede beon oððe limlease, þonne hi beoð on ecere susle wunigende?; phrases, e.g. ÆCHom i. 20. 12 Nu smeagiað sume men hwanon him come sawul, hwæþer ðe of þam fæder, þe of þære meder and ÆCHom i. 618. 31 . . . and on ure geendunge us欸 bið gedemed, hwæðer we on reste oþþe on wite ðone gemænelican dom anbidian sceolon; adverbs or prepositions, e.g. Bede 128. 19 Ða frægn he hine . . . hwæðer he þe ute þe inne wære and Solil 3. 2 ne þæt nat hwæðer hit wæs innan me ðe utan . . . ; infinitives or infinitive groups, e.g. ÆCHom i. 212. 10 Swa eac gehwilc man hæfð agenne cyre, ærðam þe he syngige, hweðer he wille filian deofles willan, oððe wiðsacan and ÆHom 10. 49 God sylf afandað ælces mannes heortan, hwæðer se mann wylle his wununge habban oþþe leahtras lufian, þe Gode misliciað; and clauses, e.g. Bede 96. 15 Eft he frægn hwæðer þa ilcan londleode cristne wæron þe hi þa gen in hæðennesse gedwolan lifden and ÆCHom i. 268. 11 Deofol mot ælces mannes afandigan . . . hwæðer he God mid inweardlicre heortan lufige oððe he mid hiwunge fare. It will be seen that once again the subjunctive is the norm. We have the pret. ind. wæs in Solil 3. 2 above, where 'absolute ignorance' (Gorrell, p. 445) can again be held responsible, and ÆCHom i. 242. 27 Ac behealde ge hwæðer ge sind Godes scep, hwæðer ge hine gyt oncneowon, hwæðer ge mid soðfæstnysse hine lufiað, where the indicatives after the imperative may involve 'a tacit assumption of the reality of the contents of the clause'—an explanation proposed by Gorrell (p. 445) for the gif clause in ÆCHom ii. 228. 20 Smeage nu gehwa on his mode, gif ðas beboda and oðre þillice habbað ænigne stede on his heortan, ðonne tocnæwð he hwæðer he is fram Gode, which he takes as dependent question but which may be conditional.

§2087. There are only four 'disjunctive' nexus questions in the poetry. One is GenB 531; see §3416. The other three involve hwæþer . . . þe; they are ChristC 1305 (present indicative after Ne mæg . . . geseon), ChristC 1329 (present subjunctive after We . . . ne magun . . . þurhwlitan)—it is hard to explain this variation—and ChristC 1549 (present subjunctive in a 'subjunctive' context).

§2088. There are a few examples in the prose in which swa . . . swa appears in what can be described as dependent nexus questions; they include LS 34. 306 . . . ne we be him naþor nyton swa hi ðær libban swa hi ðær deade ligcon and ÆCHom i. 292. 31 ac God . . . læt hi habban agenne cyre swa heo syngige swa heo synna forbuge. The verb is subjunctive. The latter can be compared with *ÆCHom* i. 212. 10 (§2086).

§2089. On *þeah (þe)* 'whether' introducing dependent nexus questions, see §§3416–20.

§2090. What are in effect nexus questions can be asked by presenting the alternatives in clauses subordinate to an *x*-question, e.g. *ÆCHom* i. 424. 3 *Gif hit riht sy þæt we to deoflum us gebiddon swiðor þonne to ðam Ælmihtigan Gode, deme ge hwa þæs wurð-myntes wurðe sy, se ðe geworht is, oððe se ðe ealle ðing gesceop.*

g. Dependent x-questions and exclamations

§2091. Examples of both these constructions have already been quoted in the preceding sections. More will be found in Gorrell (pp. 411–37), Wülfing (i. 424–37 and ii. 167–72), Behre (pp. 258–69), and Visser, ii, §875). In the sections which follow I content myself with quoting a few more to illustrate the various interrogative and exclamatory words and phrases and the variations of mood which occur. As with dependent statements and desires (see §§1992–2038), there are no 'rules' which can explain the latter.

§2092. Verbs of asking and enquiring usually take the subjunctive, e.g. (with a pronoun) *ÆCHom* i. 474. 2 *ðaða his leorningcnihtas hine axodon for hwæs synnum se mann wurde swa blind acenned* and *ÆCHom* i. 168. 15 . . . *cwæð þa on his geðance þæt he fandian wolde hwæt he wære*; (with an adjective) *ÆCHom* i. 128. 11 *He ða befran on hwilcere tide he gewyrpte* (ambiguous preterite which is almost certainly subjunctive); and (with an adverb) *ÆCHom* i. 18. 12 *þa com God and axode hwi he his bebod tobræce* and *ÆCHom* i. 78. 11 . . . *and befran hwær Cristes cenningstow wære*. No example with the indicative has as yet been noted in the prose. The only one in the poetry is

ChristA 92   Fricgað þurh fyrwet   hu ic fæmnan had,
                mund minne geheold,   ond eac modor gewearð
                mære meotudes suna,

where the indicative after an imperative emphasizes the Virgin Mary's triumphant affirmation of the Virgin Birth; there is really no question. The questions in *JDay ii* 65 and *MSol* 371 are rightly punctuated in ASPR vi as non-dependent. 'Modal' auxiliaries, of course, occur where appropriate, e.g. *ÆCHom* i. 14. 22 . . . *and axode*

Adam hu heo hatan sceolde and *ÆCHom* ii. 30. 7 *þa gemette heo ænne deofol on mannes hiwe, se befran, hwider heo wolde. þæt earme wif andwyrde, and cwæð, þæt heo wolde to cyrcan gan.* . . .

§ 2093. Verbs of saying show much the same tendencies as they do when governing dependent statements. *Cweðan* rarely occurs except as a sort of interrogative particle representing Latin *num(quid)*; see §§ 1649-50. After other verbs of saying, we find the indicative in *ÆCHom* i. 116. 31 *We habbað gesæd embe ðas þryfealdan lac, hu hi to Criste belimpað: we willað eac secgan hu hi to us belimpað æfter ðeawlicum andgite, ÆCHom* i. 324. 26 *Ælces mannes weorc cyðað hwilc gast hine wissað, ÆCHom* i. 608. 13 *He geswutelode hu fela ðrowunga forestæppað þyssere worulde geendunge* . . . , and *ÆCHom* i. 336. 12 *þa wearð his abbude geswutelod hwæne he bær,* and the subjunctive in *Bede* 90. 29 *Ac se ælmihti God wolde gecyþan hwylcre gearnunge se halga wer wære, ÆCHom* i. 386. 13 *þær ðe bið gesæd hwæt ðe gedafenige to donne, LS* 34. 115, *ÆCHom* i. 50. 35 *On ðyssere dæde is geswutelod hu micclum fremige þære soðan lufe gebed,* and *ÆCHom* i. 246. 3 *Hi wurpon ða tan betweox him, and bædon þæt God sceolde geswutulian hwanon him þæt ungelimp become.* The 'modal' auxiliaries can be exemplified by *ÆCHom* i. 82. 17 (§ 2067).

§ 2094. Verbs of thinking and the like prefer the subjunctive, e.g. *ÆCHom* i. 92. 30 *Wen is þæt eower sum nyte hwæt sy ymbsnidennys, ÆCHom* ii. 124. 14 *Hogiað forði hwilc se becume ætforan gesihðe þæs strecan Deman* . . . , *ÆCHom* i. 12. 18 *Nu þencð menig man and smeað hwanon deofol come, ÆCHom* i. 168. 13 *þa smeade se deofol hwæt he wære, ÆCHom* i. 78. 34 *soðlice toweard is þæt Herodes smeað hu he þæt cild fordo* (where there is an element of purpose), and *ÆCHom* i. 340. 20 *þis is to smeagenne hwi sy mare bliss be gecyrredum synfullum.* The indicative sometimes appears, e.g. *ÆCHom* i. 308. 19 *Us is to smeagenne hu seo clænnys wæs ðeonde geond þa geferedan ðenas.* This, according to Gorrell (p. 425), is because 'the attention is directed to an event which has actually taken place or whose reality is unquestioned'.

§ 2095. Verbs of perceiving prefer the indicative, e.g. *ÆCHom* i. 272. 29 *We magon geseon on urum agenum lichaman hu ælc lim oðrum þenað* and *BlHom* 19. 10 *Gehyran we nu forhwon se blinda leoht onfeng.* But the subjunctive is found, e.g. *ÆCHom* i. 280. 8 *Uton nu gehyran be ðan Halgan Gaste hwæt he sy*—the contrast between this and the previous example is interesting—and *ÆCHom* i. 580. 27 *Zacheus . . . wolde geseon hwilc he wære.*

§2096. As *BlHom* 19. 10 and *ÆCHom* i. 280. 8 (both in §2095) suggest, there is no automatic rule that demands a subjunctive in the dependent clause when the principal clause contains a 'volitional expression'—an imperative, a jussive subjunctive, a form of the verb **sculan*, or *uton* + infinitive. Thus we find the subjunctive in *ÆCHom* i. 160. 27 *Uton behealdan hwider Crist gange, ÆCHom* i. 614. 1 *Understandað nu hwilc sy on weges geswince to ateorigenne, and ðeah nelle þone weg geendigan,* and *ÆCHom* i. 280. 8 *Uton nu gehyran be ðan Halgan Gaste hwæt he sy,* but the indicative in *ÆCHom* i. 286. 30 *Beheald þas sunnan, hu heage heo astihð, and hu heo asent hyre leoman geond ealne middangeard, and hu heo onliht ealle ðas eorðan þe mancynn on eardað* and *ÆCHom* i. 578. 15 *Smeagað nu hu Drihten mancynne ætbræd wuldor.* . . .

§2097. That there is no automatic rule which produces a subjunctive in the dependent question when there is a negative in the principal clause can be seen by comparing *ÆCHom* i. 410. 7 *and hi mid mænigfealdum ðreatungum geangsumiað, þæt heo on ðam forðsiðe oncnawe mid hwilcum feondum heo ymbset bið, and ðeah nan ut fær ne gemet, hu heo ðam feondlicum gastum oðfleon mage* with *ÆCHom* i. 588. 7 *Romanisce ealdras gyt ne oncneowon Godes soðfæstnysse, hu Godes Sunu to mannum com, and tæhte þæt þas deofolgyld, þe ge begað, ne synd na godas* . . . and by noting that the indicative is common after both *witan,* e.g. *ÆCHom* i. 114. 3 *ac he wat swaðeah on ær hwilce þurh agenne willan syngian willað, ÆCHom* i. 158. 14 *Eower heofenlica Fæder wat hwæs ge behofiað, ÆCHom* i. 112. 24 *Georne wiste se Ælmihtiga Scyppend* . . . *hwæt toweard wæs,* and *ÆCHom* i. 588. 17 *Eala gif ðu witan woldest þære halgan rode gerynu, mid hu sceadwisre lufe manncynna Ealdor, for ure edstaðelunge þære rode gealgan underfeng, na geneadod, ac sylfwilles,* and *ne witan,* e.g. *ÆCHom* i. 66. 5 *and nat hwam he hit gegaderað, ÆCHom* i. 532. 25 *forðan þe he nat hwæðer he wurðe is into þam ecan rice, ÆCHom* i. 22. 24 *and heora nan nyste hwæt oðer cwæð,* and *ÆCHom* i. 316. 29 *þaða he bebyrged wæs, þa com his wif Saphira, and nyste hu hire were gelumpen wæs.* But the subjunctive also occurs after both, e.g. *ÆCHom* i. 336. 23 *Gif ic wiste hwæt he wære, ic wolde licgan æt his fotum* (rejected condition) and *ÆCHom* ii. 306. 8 *Ða nyste heo gewiss hwilc wære Cristes rod ærðan ðe he mid tacnum hi geswutelode.* See further Gorrell, pp. 429-31.

§2098. Again, there is no automatic rule of attraction; compare *ÆCHom* i. 404. 27 *Gif þu wistest hwæt þe toweard is, þonne weope ðu mid me* with *ÆCHom* i. 336. 23 (§2097) and *ÆCHom* i. 588. 17

(§2097) with *ÆCHom* i. 452. 24 *Gif hwa smeage hu ðis gewurde
. . .* , and consider *ÆCHom* i. 410. 7 (§2097).

§2099. The principles governing the use of the moods in dependent questions are very similar to those which operate in dependent
statements. 'When the interrogative idea is prominent in the dependent clause the subjunctive is used, irrespective of the character of
the governing verb' (Gorrell, p. 446); it 'denote[s] the content of the
question as having been submitted to the reflection or meditation of
the speaker or of some other person' (Behre, p. 257). 'The indicative
is used in indirect questions presented to the hearer in a first-hand
and direct manner without any implication of an attitude of reflection or meditation on the part of the speaker or of some other
person towards the content of the dependent interrogative clause'
(Behre, p. 258). Further on these points, see the items cited in
§§1992-2038.

4. MOOD IN SUBORDINATE CLAUSES IN DEPENDENT SPEECH

§2100. In general the mood appropriate to the type of subordinate
clause is retained in dependent speech, even when the verb of the
noun clause is subjunctive; there is no rule in OE like that in Latin
which requires all verbs in subordinate clauses in *oratio obliqua* to be
subjunctive (GL, p. 414)—even, *pace* Callaway (1931, p. 123), in
temporal clauses. A few typical examples must suffice: *ÆCHom* i.
402. 6 *Gregorius se trahtnere cwæð þæt se Hælend beweope ðære
ceastre toworpennysse ðe gelamp æfter his ðrowunge*, *ÆCHom* i.
302. 34 *Hwæt fremað þe þæt ðu hæbbe geleafan gif ðu næfst ða
godan weorc?*, and *ÆCHom* i. 580. 26 *Ic wene þæt þas word ne sind
eow full cuðe, gif we hi openlicor eow ne onwreoð*, where the present
tense of *wenan* (a verb which prefers the subjunctive) allows retention of the indicative in both clauses in what is very close to non-
dependent speech.

§2101. When a subjunctive occurs in dependent speech in a subordinate clause which normally has the indicative, a reason can usually be
found. Thus, in the well-known sentence in which Alfred announces
his policy about the teaching of English and Latin (*CP* 7. 6-15), the
subjunctives *sien* (line 7) and *hæbben* (line 11) can be explained as
generic—'of such a sort that . . .'—whereas the indicative *is* (line
10) refers to a well-defined group. But if *mægen* (line 8) is indeed
subjunctive, as *magon* (line 9) would suggest, I am hard put to explain

it. The possibility of 'attraction' must be admitted here; Visser's condemnation of Brook (ii, §887) is not supported by *GenA* 2212 and
is (I am inclined to think) too whole-hearted. But (despite the ASPR
note) we need not import this notion to explain *eardien* in *GuthA* 54
Dryhten sceawað ‖ *hwær þa eardien þe his æ healden*; there is a prevailing atmosphere of uncertainty about the sentence as far as the
speaker is concerned and again a generic reference—'. . . men of
such a sort that they respect God's laws'. The indicative may, as the
ASPR note suggests, be more usual in such contexts. But the subjunctive is rightly allowed to stand. This is one of the only three
present subjunctives in a subordinate clause in dependent speech in
OE poetry; see further *Neophil.* 49 (1965), 49. Finally, in *ÆCHom*
ii. 338. 33 *Se awyrigeda gast andwyrde, God gecwæð þæt ælc synn
ðe nære ofer eorðan gebet, sceolde beon on ðissere worulde gedemed*,
the subj. *nære* is used because the adjective clause implies a condition
—'if each sin were not atoned for . . .'.

§2102. This problem will be discussed in more detail in the course
of this chapter as need arises; see the General Index. Gorrell (pp. 458-
69) has some valuable comments.

C. ADJECTIVE CLAUSES

1. INTRODUCTORY REMARKS

§2103. The traditional definition of an adjective clause is expressed
by the Joint Committee (p. 13)—'a part of a sentence equivalent to
a[n] . . . Adjective . . . and having a Subject and a Predicate of its
own . . .'. Such clauses, says Onions (p. 70), may be 'introduced by
Relative Pronouns . . . , Relative Adjectives . . . , or Relative Adverbs
. . . , referring to a noun or noun-equivalent called the Antecedent,
expressed or implied in the Principal Clause'. The use of the word
'implied' is explained by the fact that Onions later (p. 74) describes
'To help who want, to forward who excel' as exemplifying 'omission
of the antecedent'; 'who', he says, is for 'those who'. Similarly, 'Who
steals my purse steals trash' is often said to exemplify 'omission' of
'he'. Jespersen (*Phil. Gr.*, p. 104) describes this as 'one of the numerous uncalled-for fictions which have vitiated and complicated grammar without contributing to a real understanding of the facts of
language'. Such a clause as 'Who steals my purse' can be described
as a noun clause—cf. 'The man steals trash'—or as an adjective
clause used as a primary; see Jespersen, *Phil. Gr.*, pp. 103-7. For

the reasons given in §1927, I discuss the various OE equivalents of such clauses in the sections which follow; these 'indefinite adjective clauses' involve not only the relatives *se* and *þe* alone or together, but also combinations such as *swa hwa swa* and *swa hwelc swa*.

§2104. 'Definite adjective clauses'—those referring to a specific antecedent—are introduced by *se* and *þe* alone or in combination and by the 'relative adverbs' defined in §2384. When *se* and/or *þe* are used in sentences in which both the principal and the adjective clause require the same case, there are three possibilities. Thus in *ÆCHom* i. 54. 1 *forðan ðe se apostol Paulus ne bið geligenod, þe cwæð* . . . we could have *se cwæð* or *seþe cwæð*, and in *ÆCHom* i. 54. 30 *Ne mæg ic minne feond lufian ðone ðe ic dæghwonlice wælhreowne togeanes me geseo, ðone ðe* could be replaced by *ðone* or by *ðe*. When the two clauses require different cases, there are four possibilities. Thus in *ÆCHom* i. 34. 30 *Se Ælmihtiga Godes Sunu, ðe heofenas befon ne mihton, wæs geled on nearuwre binne* the indeclinable *ðe* could be replaced by *þone, þone þe*, or *se þe*, and in *ÆCHom* i. 30. 18 *efne ic eow bodige micelne gefean, þe becymð eallum folce* we could have *se, se þe*, or *þone þe*, instead of *þe*. These variations are discussed in detail below. However, it can be said that the form of the relative pronoun is not a reliable criterion for the relative dating of OE literature; see Amos, pp. 129–31 and 169.

§2105. Problems of classification inevitably arise. When *se* is used alone, it is sometimes difficult or indeed impossible to decide whether it is a demonstrative or a relative; see §§2109–21. The form *þæt* causes many problems; see the Index of Words, s.v. A particularly vexed one is whether *þæt(te)* is an indeclinable relative pronoun or a conjunction in sentences such as *BlHom* 247. 24 *Min Drihten Hælend Crist, send þinne þone Halgan Gast, þæt awecce ealle þa þe on þisse wætere syndon*. On this see §§2139–43 and 2886.

§2106. Difficulties arising with *þe* can be illustrated by a consideration of the possible interpretations of *Mald* 189–90, which I discuss in *Neophil.* 49 (1965), 48, and of *Beo* 1435 *he on holme wæs* ǁ *sundes þe sænra, ðe hyne swylt fornam*, where we can explain *þe* . . . *ðe* as instrumentals expressing proportion, can take *ðe hyne* as relative 'whom', or can translate *ðe* as 'because' or even 'when' with *þe* as an instrumental of cause 'on that [account], for that [reason]'. The pseudo-pronoun *swa* is discussed in §§2379–82.

§2107. The exact status of *þæt* and *þe* has been the subject of much discussion. In essence, the question is whether they are relative

pronouns or subordinating particles. Geoghegan (p. 56) gives recent
and convenient expression to the latter view:

Clearly then, Middle English *that* [as in ME *þis beoð þe wepnen þat me wurst
wundeð*] is not the reflex of the Old English demonstrative pronoun *þæt*, which
remained as the only demonstrative pronoun (besides *this*, which is from another
paradigm), but of the coalescence of the two subordinating particles *þe* and *þæt*
when morphological, phonological, and syntactic changes elsewhere in the system caused a surface confusion of the particle *þe* with the article *þe* (< *se*).

It is true that both *þæt* and *þe* serve as 'subordinating particles' or
conjunctions in OE and that *þæt* functions as a demonstrative. But
I cannot see any point in denying that both also serve as relative
pronouns, whatever origin we may care to assume for them. I discuss this problem for *þæt* in §§1956 and 2126-33 and for *þe* in
§§2427-30.

§2108. Adjective clauses may express cause (see Liggins 1955,
pp. 398-437); concession (see Burnham, pp. 67-73, and Quirk,
pp. 98-101 and 103-8); or condition (see Liebermann, *Archiv*, 118
(1907), 384, and Gehse, pp. 53-4, and note the almost anacoluthic
examples like *ÆCHom* i. 516. 21 *Se ðe eow hrepað, hit bið me swa
egle swilce he hreppe mines eagan seo* discussed in §2213).[37] See
also the General Index.

[37] Collections of examples of OE adjective clauses will be found in Wülfing, i, §§275-
307; Grossmann; Anklam; Bacquet, pp. 278-376; and the dissertations on individual texts.
See also my article 'Adjective Clauses in Old English Poetry', *Ang.* 81 (1963), 299-322.

H. Johansen, *Zur Entwicklungsgeschichte der altgermanischen Relativsatzkonstruktionen*
(Copenhagen, 1935), offers a comparative study of the development of relative constructions in the Germanic languages, based on a limited selection of texts.

Kivimaa (pp. 27-9) offers some useful 'notes on common Germanic features in relatives',
with references to discussions on them and on the possible origin of adjective clauses. But
her statistics fail to make some necessary distinctions; see her pp. 34 and 37-9.

I do not share what O'Neil (p. 207) calls 'the sense we have when looking back at these
early stages of Old English that anything is possible in the grammar of relative clauses; etc.'.
But I do note that one pattern which he says does not occur (p. 203, lines 25-7) does in fact
occur at least once—in the familiar, but unidiomatic, *CP* 5. 3. Whether—in view of his use
of the word 'crucially'—this destroys his case, I cannot tell.

Dowsing's limited corpus, which strangely includes *ÆLS* but not *ÆCHom*, and/or her
faulty observation must cast doubt on some of her findings. These include (*a*) p. 291, lines
6-7: but cf. *ÆCHom* i. 170. 6 (§2124); (*b*) p. 292, lines 15-16: but cf. *ÆCHom* i. 90. 28
and *WHom* 6. 167, which is in her corpus (§2124); (*c*) p. 296, lines 3-6: but cf. *ÆLS*
15. 117 (§2124) and *WHom* 6. 66, which she actually quotes (p. 295); (*d*) p. 297, lines
25-6: *þæt* is certainly the 'rule' after *eall* (§2263), but the structure quoted is not 'usual';
(*e*) p. 299, lines 5-6: but see §2216. She uses the term 'correlation' (pp. 294, 295-6, and
299-300) in a sense which I do not find helpful.

I do not understand much of Hallander's remarks about 'Old English relative constructions'
in *SN* 50 (1978), 141 fn. 21, and I disagree with what I can understand.

The sections which follow were completed before Georges Bourcier, *Les Propositions
relatives en vieil-anglais* (Paris, 1977), came into my hands. For better or for worse, they
have not been altered as a result of my reading of that book. I give my reasons for this attitude in a review in *MÆ* 48 (1979), 121-2.

2. *SE, SEO, ÞÆT*, IN DEFINITE ADJECTIVE CLAUSES

a. The ambiguous demonstrative/relative

§2109. Campbell (*OEG*, §710) observes that 'the lack of a relative pronoun in OE is largely made up for by the use of *se* either alone or followed by the particle *þe* (which shows it to be relatival, not demonstrative in function)'.[38] The last clause clearly—and rightly —implies that, when any form of *se* is used alone in examples like *ÆCHom* i. 254. 18 *Se man hæfð gold, þæt is god be his mæðe: he hæfð land and welan, þa sint gode* and *ÆCHom* i. 44. 1 *We sceolon geefenlæcan þysum hyrdum, and wuldrian and herian urne Drihten on eallum ðam ðingum þe he for ure lufe gefremode, us to alysednysse and to ecere blisse, ðam sy wuldor and lof mid ðam Ælmihtigum Fæder, on annysse þæs Halgan Gastes, on ealra worulda woruld. Amen*, we cannot be sure—lacking as we do a knowledge of the intonation patterns—whether it is a demonstrative or a relative.[39] Inconsistencies in the editorial punctuation of what may appear to be parallel clauses demonstrate the problem; consider *Bede* 236. 13 *In þæm wæs Æðelhere Annan broðor Eastengla cyninges, se æfter him to rice feng: se wæs ordfruma þæs gefeohtes, ÆCHom* i. 116. 35 *Mid store bið geswutelod halig gebed, be ðam sang se sealmscop, 'Drihten, sy min gebed asend swa swa byrnende stor on ðinre gesihðe.' þurh myrran is gehiwod cwelmbærnys ures flæsces; be ðam cweð seo halige gelaðung, 'Mine handa drypton myrran'*, and the treatment given by the various editors and translators to *Beo* 1351-5, 2409-13, and 2610-19.

§2110. Whether we decide to take such ambiguous pronouns as demonstrative or relative is obviously not without influence on our literary judgment. Various possible criteria have been proposed. Despite Bock (1887, p. 22), Grossmann (p. 51), Andrew (*SS*, §§41-55), and others, I do not regard element order as decisive; the fact that we have SV and not S . . . V in *ChronA* 46. 26 (755) . . . *he wolde adræfan anne æþeling se was Cyneheard haten* does not certify

---

[38] Despite Heltveit (*NJL* 31 (1977), 81), this is not all that Campbell had to say about OE relative pronouns; he discussed *þe* in fn. 3 to *OEG*, §710.

[39] The problem is usually confined to the independent use. But it can be detected in sentences in which *se* is used dependently, e.g. *ÆCHom* i. 90. 15 *þa wæs his nama geciged Iesus, þæt is Hælend, ðam naman he wæs gehaten fram ðam engle* (Thorpe 'by which name'); *ÆCHom* ii. 188. 9 . . . *to þam mynstre ðe we hatað Florege, on ðære stowe his ban restað* . . . (Thorpe 'in which place'); and *ÆCHom* ii. 228. 30 *Samaria hatte an burh, ða burh forsawon þa Iudeiscan* . . . (Thorpe 'which city'). Rübens (p. 37) detects the same difficulty in examples involving *þær* and *þanon*; see §§2444-9.

that *se* is a demonstrative. Here I agree with Rübens (p. 35) and Anklam (p. 37). Dowsing (p. 297) notes that in her limited corpus of late prose texts adjective clauses introduced by *þæt* normally have S . . . V, those introduced by *se* normally have SV. This point demands further investigation. But I cannot emulate the confidence with which Dowsing (p. 298 and *passim*) assigns stress to *se* and lack of stress to *þæt*.

§2111. Metre was extensively used by Andrew (*SS* and *Postscript, passim*) to buttress his theories; cf. Grossmann, pp. 47-9. But it too must be dismissed. Samuels (*MÆ* 18 (1949), 60-4) clearly and convincingly exposed the flaws in Andrew's arguments and I do not see how any modern scholar can use metre as the basis for conclusions firm enough to be accepted as definitive.[40]

§2112. The punctuation of the manuscripts does not help us to solve the problem: it is not always consistent, its purpose is not always obvious, and the distinction between the various marks of punctuation cannot be determined with sufficient accuracy to be decisive. The tests I have carried out only confirm that the problem of the ambiguous demonstrative/relative is a reality for modern scholars. A few examples based on a comparison of the punctuation of two manuscripts of the *Catholic Homilies* and of Thorpe's edition must suffice here. Thorpe prints *ÆCHom* i. 116. 35 as I have quoted it in §2109. The manuscript he is following (Cambridge University Library Gg. 3.28) has a *punctus* (.) after both *gebed* and *flæsces*. So it is hard to see why he prints a comma and then a semi-colon; this is closer to the punctuation of British Library Royal 7C. xii, which has a *punctus* after *gebed* but a *punctus elevatus* (⁏) after *flæsces*. But this contrast is not sufficient to establish that the first *be ðam* is relative and the second demonstrative, for (as Harlow (p. 14) points out), the *elevatus* frequently occurs before clauses which modern scholars at any rate would unhesitatingly classify as subordinate. Thorpe prints *ÆCHom* i. 254. 18 *Se man hæfð gold, þæt is god be his mæðe: he hæfð land and welan, þa sint gode.* The Cambridge manuscript has nothing after *gold* and a *punctus* after *welan*, while the Royal has an *elevatus* after *gold* and nothing after *welan*. It is hard to believe that Ælfric intended the clauses which follow these words to be taken differently. The problem appears in a different

---

[40] The reader will find that Andrew is mentioned frequently in the sections which follow, sometimes with approbation, sometimes with criticism. This is because he is in my opinion a very important and very stimulating writer whose work, though often reaching wrong conclusions, deserves more attention than it has so far received. See further Mitchell 1959, p. 200, and §§2448 and 2536-8 below.

form when we consider Thorpe's *ÆCHom* i. 342. 34 *Throni sind þrymsetl, þa beoð gefyllede mid swa micelre gife ðære Ælmihtigan Godcundnysse, þæt se Eallwealdenda God on him wunað, and ðurh hi his domas tosceat*, where in both manuscripts a *punctus* precedes *þa*, which here must introduce a limiting adjective clause—the thrones of Ninus of Assyria and of Alexander of Macedon were not *throni* in Ælfric's sense.

§2113. Andrew (*SS, §48*) proposes a Draconian solution: 'No part of the demonstrative pronoun *se seo þæt* other than the neuter nominative can stand at the head of a sentence except as antecedent, and any supposed instance to the contrary is really a relative pronoun.' He extends this rule to *Beowulf* in *Postscript* (pp. 32–8). But it cannot be allowed to stand either for prose or for poetry. The reasons are not far to seek.

§2114. Andrew—like Wülfing (i. 395) before him—accepts the proposition that where the Latin original has a relative pronoun, the OE version must have one too. Sprockel (p. 170) says that 'since this conclusion [the rule quoted above] was based on a careful investigation of several texts translated from Latin, it seems that we must take it seriously'. The reverse is in fact true. As Rynell (p. 23) points out, this method

overlooks the obvious fact that two languages may be at different stages of development, one being largely hypotactic, the other paratactic, in structure; naturally, a translator had to avail himself first and foremost of the means of expression which his own language placed at his disposal, even if he was to some extent influenced by the foreign constructions in his original.

These remarks are confirmed by a comparison of the Latin and the OE versions of the Psalms. Thus, in *PPs* 102. 3 and 102. 5, OE *he* represents Latin *qui*; in *PPs* 56. 3, an OE *þe* clause represents a Latin clause co-ordinate with the principal clause; and the Latin *qui* of *Ps* 102. 4 is represented in the Paris Psalter by *he* and in the Benedictine Fragments by *se*. Such variations could be multiplied—see *PPs* 145. 5 and 6 and *PPs* 146. 3 and 4—but they are not necessarily a reflection on the OE writer. As Vleeskruyer (p. 190) puts it in his note to *LS* 3. 19 ff. (*St Chad*), 'the translators, whose word-for-word method is closely akin to the glossator's practice, probably did not always fail to perceive and fathom the more complex sentence-structure of their originals, but had yet to devise means of reproducing it in their own idiom'. The fact that, when comparing the Latin and OE versions of a sentence from Bede, Andrew (*SS, §108*) could say that 'this helpless repetition [in the OE] is astonishing when we compare the variety of the Latin original' should have warned him that the resources of the two languages were different.

§2115. Here, as elsewhere, Andrew's practice reflects his belief that hypotaxis is necessarily superior to parataxis—a belief strikingly illustrated by his rhetorical question about *Beo* 461-9: 'Can anyone believe that such a string of emphatic demonstrative sentences truly represents the genius of OE poetry?' (*SS*, §112). It may have arisen because he was 'a slave to his modern linguistic instinct' (Rynell, p. 22) or because he was well-versed in the classics (Mossé, *PB* 45 (1949), 171). But whatever the reason, the result is that wherever MnE punctuation can make a sentence periodic rather than paratactic, Andrew finds reason for adopting that punctuation. To do this, he has to turn himself into a prescriptive grammarian for OE— emending boldly, e.g. in *Beo* 348 (*Postscript*, §38), but not always consistently, e.g. his two attempts to improve the manuscript reading at *Beo* 194 (*SS*, §§52 and 110, but *Postscript*, §101), on the dubious assumption that his 'rules' are right and the manuscripts are wrong; note his wholesale removal of *þara* before *þe* in *Beowulf* (*SS*, §§122-4).

§2116. All this is bad enough. But there is an inherent improbability in his rule that initial *se, seo, ðæt,* can stand only as a relative or antecedent when it is considered in the light of his claim that 'internally, in *Beowulf* as in prose (*SS*, §51), the demonstrative is freely used in the oblique cases of all numbers and genders' (*Postscript*, §40). According to Andrew (*SS*, §45), those who think that initial *se* can be a demonstrative have 'a difficult semantic problem to solve, viz., what is the difference in meaning between *se* and *he*?' But the same question might be asked of *se* and *he, þone* and *hine, þæs* and *his*, and so on, when they are used internally. Samuels (*MÆ* 18 (1949), 62) has pointed out that similar sequences to *se . . . he* in MnE ('This man . . . ; he') and in NHG (*Der . . . ; er*) seem to cause no difficulty. Such sequences are easily found in OE; consider sentences such as *Or* 40. 15 *þa þis gedon wæs, þa gyt lyfedan ða gebroðra. Se yldra wæs haten Danaus, þe þæs yfeles ordfruma wæs. Se wearð of his rice adræfed, 7 on Arge þæt land he fleonde becom; 7 his se cyning þær Tenelaus mildelice onfeng, ÆCHom* ii. 114. 20 *Ic hæbbe oðre scep, þa ðe ne sind of ðyssere eowde, and ða ic sceal lædan, and hi gehyrað mine stemne,* and

GenA 1476   þa gyt se eadega wer
              ymb wucan þriddan   wilde culufran

> ane sende.   Seo eft ne com
> to lide fleogan,   ac heo land begeat,
> grene bearwas.

We are not obliged to follow Andrew in disposing of these three examples by omitting the first *and* in *ÆCHom* ii. 114. 20[41] and by taking *se, ða,* and *seo,* in their turn as relatives. It is no more surprising to have a personal pronoun after a demonstrative than after a relative, and, if we take *se* as a demonstrative in

ÆCHom ii. 596. 12   Ic gelyfe on God, Fæder Ælmihtigne, Scyppend heofenan and eorðan; and ic gelyfe on Hælend Crist, his ancennedan Sunu, urne Drihten, se wæs geeacnod of ðam Halgan Gaste, and acenned of Marian þam mædene, geðrowod under ðam Pontiscan Pilate, on rode ahangen, he wæs dead and bebyrged, and he niðer astah to helle, and he aras of deaðe on ðam ðriddan dæge, and he astah up to heofenum . . . ,

it could (contrary to Andrew, *Postscript,* §47(4)) carry more emphasis than the personal pronouns in the sequence *he . . . he . . . he . . . he . . .* which follows; cf.

GuthA 398   He wæs þeara sum;
> ne won he æfter worulde,   ac he in wuldre ahof
> modes wynne.   Hwylc wæs mara þonne *se*?

§2117. The answer to another of Andrew's questions is twofold: 'the editors may fairly be asked why the supposed demonstrative *se* never occurs except where there is an obvious antecedent' (*Postscript,* §35). First, it occasionally seems to do so, e.g. *ÆCHom* ii. 344. 17 *Furseus oncneow sona ða sawle; se wæs his tunman ær on life,* where the fact that *se* is masculine seems to me to rule out the possibility that it is a relative with antecedent *ða sawle,* and *GuthA* 1 *Se bið gefeana fægrast þonne hy æt frymðe gemetað,* ‖ *engel ond seo eadge sawl!* Second, as Samuels (*MÆ* 18 (1949), 62) observes, 'that *se* should always have an obvious antecedent is not surprising (cf., apart from purely deictic uses, Mn.E. "this")', a view which echoes the comment in

ÆGram 98. 22   Is se ys subjunctivum, þæt ys, underðeodendlic oþðe relativum, þæt ys, edlesendlic, forðan ðe he ne mæg beon æfter rihte gecweden, buton þæt andgyt beo ærfore sæd; swa eac on engliscre spræce ne cweð nan man se, buton he ær sum ðingc be ðam men spræce. *Aeneas fuit filius Veneris; is est, qui vicit Turnum,* Eneas wæs Veneres sunu; se oferswiðde Turnum.

---

[41] This is one of Andrew's favourite devices (*SS*, §44). He uses it to turn *se* into a relative in *Bede* 382. 3 *Wæs in ðæm mynstre sum geong monn, ðam unwlitig swylce 7 atolic his eagan breg wyrde 7 wemde. 7 se dæghwamlice wæs weaxende, 7 ðæs eagan forwyrde tobeotode. Teoleden his læcas 7 ðone swylce mid sealfum 7 mid beþinge geðwænan woldon; ac hie ne mehton* without noticing that it is impossible to do the same for *ðone.*

So Andrew's rule for distinguishing demonstrative from relative *se* must be rejected.

§2118. Sprockel (pp. 170-1) claims that 'in a few cases we can be certain [that *se* is a relative] without applying Andrew's main rule'. He gives in fact three situations. The first is 'when the clause introduced by a *se*-form is interpolated', e.g. *ChronA* 22. 21 (616) *On þyses cinges dagum Laurentius erceб se was on Cent æfter Agustine forþferde.* . . . Wülfing (i. 395), Grossmann (pp. 46-7), and Anklam (p. 37), anticipated him here. Dowsing (p. 296) makes the same point. But we cannot be certain that *se* in such contexts is a relative in a language so given to parenthesis as OE; in examples like *ChronA* 22. 21—and indeed in many others—the intonation may have varied from reader to reader; see §§2109-10 and 2423. The second is 'when what precedes is not a clause', e.g. *ChronA* 76. 5 (878) *7 Sumursætna se dæl se þær niehst wæs.* This we can probably accept. The third—'when the *se*-form introduces a clearly restrictive clause'—is at first glance compelling and the balance of probabilities suggests its acceptance. But I cannot believe that *se* in *Or* 76. 31 *Seo cwen het þa бæm cyninge þæt heafod of aceorfan, 7 beweorpan on anne cylle, se wæs afylled monnes blodes* and *seo* in *ÆCHom* i. 24. 21 *Бa æt nextan, þa se tima com þe God foresceawode, þa asende he his engel Gabrihel to anum mædene of þam cynne, seo wæs Maria gehaten* were pronounced by all Anglo-Saxons who read them with the intonation appropriate to a MnE relative pronoun. Everything with an antecedent is not necessarily a relative. To these we can add, with Grossmann (p. 46) a fourth situation, seen in examples such as *Beo* 1977 *Gesæt þa wið sylfne se ба sæcce genæs,* || *mæg wið mæge*, where *se* is used without a correlative or an antecedent but with definite (not indefinite) reference.

§2119. But sometimes it seems obligatory to take initial *se, seo, бæt*, as demonstrative. There are sentences in which the demonstrative repeats the antecedent, either in the same case, e.g. *Bo* 19. 31 *forбæm se se бe hine forþencб se biб ormod, ac se se бe hine sceamaб se biб on hreowsunga* and *ÆCHom* i. 50. 7 *Бone deaб soбlice þe se Hælend gemedemode for mannum þrowian, бone ageaf Stephanus fyrmest manna þam Hælende*, or in a different case proper to the principal clause—thereby involving a form of anacoluthia—e.g. *Or* 22. 22 *þa land þe man hæt Gallia Bellica, be eastan þæm is sio ea þe man hæt Rin* and *ÆCHom* i. 250. 4 *Ælc бæra бe geornlice bitt and þære bene ne geswicб, þam getiбaб God þæs ecan lifes.* Such examples modify rather than contradict Andrew's 'rule'. But there are also sentences in which *se* follows *ond*, e.g. *ÆCHom* ii. 58. 21 *Crist gewat on ðære rode and his side wearð mid spere geopenad, and of ðære fleowon þa gerynu þe his gelaðung wearð mid gesceapen him to clænre bryde*, where it is difficult to adopt Andrew's solution of omitting *and*.

§2120. Stylistic considerations too confirm that Andrew's 'rule' is not valid. There are certainly prose examples in which (as Wülfing (i. 395) suggested) not to take *se* as a relative would make an unacceptably awkward sentence, e.g. *ÆCHom* ii. 598. 7 *And ic gelyfe on ðone Halgan Gast, ðone Liffæstendan God, se gæð of ðam Fæder and of ðam Suna, and se is mid ðam Fæder and mid þam Suna gebeden and gewuldrod, and se spræc þurh witegan*, or would destroy the sense, e.g. *ÆCHom* i. 342. 34 *Throni sind þrymsetl, þa beoð gefyllede mid swa micelre gife ðære Ælmihtigan Godcundnysse, þæt se Eallwealdenda God on him wunað and ðurh hi his domas tosceat.* On the other hand, there are prose examples in which awkwardness would result from taking *se* as a relative, e.g. *Or* 192. 17 *Gemong ðæm gewinnum þa twegen Scipian, þe þa wæron consulas 7 eac gebroðor, hie wæron on Ispanium mid firde, 7 gefuhton wið Hasterbale, Hannibales fædran, 7 hiene ofslogon, 7 his folces XXX M sume ofslogon sume gefengon. Se wæs eac Pena oþer cyning* and *ÆCHom* ii. 476. 16–22, or in which a rhetorical effect would be lost, e.g. *ÆCHom* ii. 58. 21 (§2119) and *ÆCHom* i. 538. 23–9.

§2121. So it is with the poetry. If Andrew were right, the Heathobard episode could not be regarded as beginning at *Beo* 2024b and *GuthA* 1 could not be the beginning of a poem or of a major division of a poem. To take the demonstrative as a relative would weaken the dramatic force of many passages, e.g. in *ChristC* 923 and *Met* 11. 2. At times the cure would be worse than the disease, for the rule would seem to require such passages as *GenA* 215–24 and *El* 737–49 to be read as one sentence. To misquote Andrew (*SS*, §112), can anyone believe that such a string of relative clauses truly represents the genius of OE poetry? We can confidently strike the shackles imposed by Andrew's 'rule' from both OE prose and poetry.

b. *All forms of* se *except* þæt

§2122. I have dismissed Andrew's 'rule' and most of the proposed tests for distinguishing demonstrative and relative uses of *se* in the preceding sections. I have suggested in §1686 that the term 'ambiguous demonstrative/relative' should not be taken as implying that the choice is simply between a subordinate clause and an independent sentence in the modern sense of the words. None the less, there are many OE examples in which—while it must remain a matter of doubt whether all Anglo-Saxons would have read or spoken them in the same way—it seems reasonable to claim that forms of *se*—in all possible genders, cases, and numbers—are used as relatives. These are exemplified below, apart from *þæt*—on which see §§2124-5 and 2134-44. We find nominative forms in *CP* 35. 24 *Se ilca se monegum yfelum wið hine selfne forworhtum ær gearode, he wearð eft sua ungemetlice grædig ðæs godan deaþes*, *ÆCHom* i. 30. 5 *þa ferde Ioseph, Cristes fosterfæder, fram Galileiscum earde, of ðære byrig Nazareð, to Iudeiscre byrig, seo wæs Dauides, and wæs geciged Bethleem*, and *Beo* 113 . . . *swylce gigantas þa wið Gode wunnon*; accusative forms in *Or* 8. 2 . . . *Oceanus . . . þone man garsecg hateð*, *ÆCHom* i. 138. 28 . . . *ure unclænan geþohtas and weorc, ða we sceolon symle acwellan*, and

> *Beo* 2020   Hwilum for duguðe   dohtor Hroðgares
>   eorlum on ende   ealuwæge bær,
>   þa ic Freaware   fletsittende
>   nemnan hyrde   . . . ;

genitive forms in *Bede* 342. 25 . . . *to neata scipene, þara heord him wæs þære neahte beboden*, *ÆCHom* i. 98. 4 . . . *Sarra . . . ðære dohtra ge sind* . . . , and

> *Jul* 182   meotud moncynnes,   in þæs meahtum sind
>   a butan ende   ealle gesceafta;

and dative forms in *Bede* 26. 27 . . . *fif Moyses boca ðam seo godcunde æ awriten is*, *ÆCHom* i. 280. 15 . . . *and of ðam Suna, þam he is gelic and efenece*, and *GenA* 228 . . . *seo æftre Ethiopia . . . þære is Geon noma*. For examples involving prepositions see §§2231-48.[42] In the prose the pronoun is occasionally doubled after an already expressed antecedent, e.g. *CP* 57. 5 *Ðonne he to fundað, he ondræt ðæt he ne mote to cuman, ond sona swa he to ðære are cymð, swa ðyncð him ðæt se hie him niedscylde sceolde se se hie him sealde*, *CP* 301. 26 *Sume, ða ða wenað ðæt hie eaðmode sien, hii doð for ege ðone weorðscipe mannum ðe hie Gode don scoldon*, *ÆCHom* i. 10. 5 *He gesceop gesceafta þaða he wolde* (where *þaða* could mean 'when'), and *ÆCHom* i. 138. 7 *Ne sohte Crist na ða modigan, þa þa micele beoð on hyra geþance* (where the present tense certifies that

---

[42] In view of the examples from Ælfric already quoted and the many like them, I do not understand why Pope (*Ælfric*, ii. 909) says that 'the particle *þe* is sometimes omitted'; his examples are *ÆHom* 1. 66, 1. 74, and 2. 213.

þa þa cannot mean 'when'). This may be for emphasis—'he who
. . .' and 'those who . . .'. For doubled *se* with combinations of *se* and
þe see §§2164-5 and 2192. Bourcier (pp. 32 and 72 n. 32) dismisses
both types as 'probablement le fruit d'erreurs scribales'. This may be
Procrustean. But cf. §2149.

§2123. In all these examples, *se* agrees with its antecedent in number and gender, but takes its case from the adjective clause. For
exceptions, see §§2338-62. Examples like

PPs 118. 21   þu oferhydige   ealle þreadest,
                þa þu awyrgde   wistest gearuwe
                and þine bebodu   efnan noldan,

in which *þa* serves first as an accusative and then as a nominative, are
rare. On indefinite *se* with no antecedent, see §2216.

c. þæt

§2124. We can begin by observing that the neut. sg. nom. and acc.
þæt is used as a relative in the same way as other forms of *se* and
that, *mutatis mutandis*, the remarks made in §§2122-3 apply. When
þæt refers to a specific neuter antecedent—either a noun or a pronoun—it takes its case from the adjective clause. We find nom. *þæt*
in *WHom* 6. 167 *Đurh ælc þing seo menniscnes adreah þæt hyre to
gebyrede* and *ÆCHom* i. 282. 1 . . . *and he is of ðam Fæder eal þæt
he is,* and acc. *þæt,* which is more common, in *ÆCHom* i. 50. 11
*Stephanus is Grecisc nama, þæt is on Leden Coronatus, þæt we
cweðað on Englisc, Gewuldorbeagod, ÆCHom* i. 90. 28 *Đis is min
wed, þæt ge healdan sceolon betwux me and eow, ÆCHom* i. 236. 8
*Ac we cweðað þærtogeanes þæt God is Ælmihtig and mæg eal þæt
he wile, ÆCHom* i. 14. 8 *Hwæt mæg hit þonne beon þæt þu forgan
sceole?, ÆCHom* i. 8. 14 *forþi sceal gehwa gerihtlæcan þæt þæt he
ær to woge gebigde* (on this combination see further §2129), and
ÆCHom i. 170. 6 *Næs þæt na awriten be Criste þæt he ða sæde.* . . .
In these last two examples, the first *þæt* is the antecedent, the
second the relative pronoun. But *þæt þæt* occasionally occurs in the
prose in sentences which contain an expressed antecedent or 'postcedent' other than the first *þæt* of the two, e.g. *CP* 233. 11 *forðæm
butan tweon ðæt bið ure ðæt ðæt we lufigeað on oðrum monnum
. . . , ÆCHom* i. 242. 15 *þæt þæt losode þæt ic wylle secan and
ongean lædan; þæt þæt alefed wæs, þæt ic gehæle, ÆCHom* ii. 442.
32 *þæt þæt Maria dyde, to ðam we hopiað,* and *ÆCHom* i. 158. 33
Hu mæg ic gewilnian ðæs gastlican leohtes, þæt þæt ic geseon ne

mæg? Here too the repetition gives emphasis. The varying agreement of the elements in the last two examples is noteworthy. Johnsen (*EStudien*, 46 (1912-13), 7) quotes six examples of *þæt þæt* from *ÆLS*—one with antecedent *hit* (*ÆLS* 15. 117), one with antecedent *þis* (*ÆLS* 4. 51), and four with 'postcedent' *þæt* (*ÆLS* 7. 234 (two examples), *ÆLS* 11. 351, and *ÆLS* 31. 84 (cf. *ÆCHom* i. 258. 4)).

§2125. *þæt* may refer back to a whole sentence, e.g. *Bede* 444. 24 *7 he monige forð acigde butan yldincge þæt hi heora mandæda hreowe dydon, þæt ic eac swylce wisce forð swa on leornunge ura stafa* and *ÆCHom* i. 448. 11 *Soðlice Maria is se mæsta frofer and fultum cristenra manna, þæt is forwel oft geswutelod, swa swa we on bocum rædað.* (So too may *þætte*, e.g. *Bede(T)* 118. 9 *ond untrum ongon þurh his gebed þa frecenisse þæs fyres onweg adrifan, þætte ær seo trume hond strongra monna þurh micel gewin don ne meahte;* MS *B* has *þ.*) Here *þæt* may be demonstrative rather than relative; as Andrew (*Postscript*, p. 35) remarks, 'the neuter nominative *ðæt* in the sentence-form *ðæt is* may, like *se*, be either the demonstrative antecedent or the relative'. But one can scarcely take seriously his subsequent claims (*Postscript*, pp. 35-6 and 38) that

most frequently, however, in this sentence-form, *ðæt* is a demonstrative of *general* reference as in Mod E. . . . *Ðæt* cannot therefore be used, in a mere statement of identity, to refer to a person, as it is in

      B 348 *Wulfgar maþelode   —þæt wæs Wendla leod;*

here, if the pronoun is intended as a demonstrative, it should be *he* . . . ; if as a relative, an idiomatic form of it after a proper noun both in prose and verse is *ðe,* . . . and '*þæt*' in 348 probably stands for '*ðe*' . . .

and that 'this neuter demonstrative never has reference to a specific noun, but only to an action or event implied in the preceding sentence'. These remarks must be dismissed in the light of examples such as *Beo* 11 *þæt wæs god cyning!*,

GenA 2100   Him ferede mid
      Solomia   sinces hyrde;
      þæt wæs se mæra   Melchisedec,
      leoda bisceop,

Mald 74   Het þa hæleða hleo   healdan þa bricge
      wigan wigheardne,   se wæs haten Wulfstan,
      cafne mid his cynne,   þæt wæs Ceolan sunu . . . ,

and

Dream 65   Ongunnon him þa moldern wyrcan
      beornas on banan gesyhðe;   curfon hie ðæt of beorhtan stane,
      gesetton hie ðæron sigora wealdend.

See further §2267.

d. *þæt, þæt þæt, þæt þe, and þætte, meaning 'what(ever)'*

§2126. Strictly speaking, *þæt þe* and *þætte* should appear in the sections which deal with combinations of *se* and *þe*. *þæt þæt* has already been exemplified in §2124. But these uses of *þæt* and of the listed combinations are best discussed together, for—as will be seen from some of the examples to be cited—they seem to be interchangeable in the sense 'what(ever)' (relative, not interrogative). This is also true when they are used as simple relatives 'which, that', referring to a specific antecedent. A typical example is *GD* 174. 9, where MS *C* has . . . *eall þæt þe beneoþan Gode wæs*, MS *O eall þæt beneoþan Gode wæs*, and MS *H eall þæt þæt beneoðan Gode ys.*

§2127. *þæt* commonly means 'what(ever)'. Frequently both clauses require the same case or—to put it perhaps more accurately—*þæt* is (*a*) the subject or complement of a clause which serves as the subject or complement of the sentence, as in *Bede(O)* 80. 8 *Nalæs þæt* [MS *T þætte*] *ingangeð on muð mannan besmiteð, Coll* 242 7 *beo þæt þu eart, Met* 13. 80 . . . *and eac wesan þæt hio æror wæs*, and *Rid* 37. 3 . . . *ond micel hæfde* ‖ *gefered þæt hit felde*; or is (*b*) the object of a clause which serves as the object of the sentence, e.g. *Or* 78. 3 . . . *se* . . . *gedyde þæt nan hæþen cyning ær gedon ne dorste, ÆCHom* i. 14. 7 . . . *buton þu do þæt ic þe hate and forgang þæt ic þe forbeode*, and *Mald* 289 *he hæfde ðeah geforþod þæt he his frean gehet.*

§2128. But this is not always true. *þæt* may be (*c*) the subject of a clause which is the object of the sentence, e.g. *CP* 367. 8 . . . *forðæmðe ealle ða geleaffullan bodiað be Gode ðæt* [MSS *C ðætte*] *soð is, ÆLS* 14. 3 *Nu wille we eow secgan þæt soð is be ðam, Dan* 119 *No he gemunde þæt him meted wæs*, and *ChristC* 1105 . . . *geseoð him to bealwe þæt him betst bicwom*; or (*d*) the object of a clause which is the subject of the sentence, e.g. *Bede* 470. 11 . . . *me is eallinga lytel* 7 *medmicel gesewen þæt ic ær ðyssum cuðe* 7 *ongeat, WHom(EI)* 20. 37 *Ac soð is þæt ic secge, MSol* 253 *Soð is ðæt ðu sagast*, and *Beo* 1748 *þinceð him to lytel þæt he lange heold.*

§2129. I turn now to the various combinations. We have *þæt* . . . *þæt* relative + 'postcedent' in *ÆCHom* i. 66. 2 *witodlice þæt he for gytsunge uncyste nanum oðrum syllan ne mæg, þæt he hordað and nat hwam.* According to Grossmann (p. 39), *was* 'what' is expressed through *þæt* . . . *þæt* in *CP* 310. 4 . . . *ða he* . . . *ðæt gebiecnede ðæt ða giet diegle wæs* and in *Or* 58. 7 *Nu is hit scortlice ymbe þæt gesægd þætte* [sic] *ær gewearð ær Romeburg getimbred wære.* Formally, however, we must describe the relationship as one of antecedent + relative. The same is, I believe, true of *þæt þæt* as in *CP* 169. 3 . . . *ðonne he for Godes lufum 7 for Godes ege deð ðæt ðæt he deð* and *ÆCHom* i. 8. 14 *forþi sceal gehwa gerihtlæcan þæt þæt he ær to woge gebigde*; cf. §2161. We may also have antecedent *þæt* + relative *þe* in the examples which follow, in which it is convenient to translate *þæt þe* or *þætte* as 'what'. These fall into the same four groups as those introduced by *þæt*. Corresponding to (*a*) we have *BlHom* 11. 14 *On hire wæs gefylled þætte on Cantica Canticorum wæs gesungen* and *Coll* 243 . . . *wesan . . . þæt þe he wesan sceal*; to (*b*) *CP(C)* 56. 4 *ðonne he hæfð ðætte* [MS *H ðæt*] *he habban wolde, he bið swiðe ðriste*; to (*c*)—this is the commonest pattern in my collections—*Or* 86. 15, *CP* 328. 17 *Wa ðæm þe . . . gemanigfaldað ðætte his ne bið, ÆCHom* i. 582. 6 *Ic com to secenne and to gehælenne þæt þe on mancynne losode, Prec* 4 *Do a þætte duge . . .* , and *PPs* 60. 6 *Hwylc seceð þæt þe soðfæst byð?* (where the metre argues for antecedent + relative); and to (*d*) ☆*Ac soð is þætte ic secge*; I have as yet noted no actual examples. *Bede* 340. 14 *Ða onget heo ge in þæm swefne ge on hire modes gesyhðe hire æteawed weosan, þætte heo geseah* belongs formally to group (*b*), semantically to group (*d*), since *þætte* is the subject of the accusative and infinitive construction. But in view of the interchangeability of *þæt, þæt þe,* and *þætte,* attested by the variant readings cited, we can (if we wish) interpret the last two as relative combinations rather than as antecedent + relative.

§2130. The modern scholar can find the same problem in other combinations involving *se* and *þe*. *Seþe* can sometimes be translated 'he who' or 'whoever'; see §2204. Does *mid ðam ðe* in *CP* 45. 4 . . . *forðonðe he nyle giefan ðæt him God geaf 7 helpan ðæs folces mid ðam ðe he his healp* mean 'with what', or 'with that with which'? Does *þam ðe* in

Beo 3053　　　. . . þæt ðam hringsele　　hrinan ne moste
　　　　　　　　gumena ænig,　　nefne God sylfa,
　　　　　　　　sigora Soðcyning　　sealde þam ðe he wolde
　　　　　　　　—he is manna gehyld—　　hord openian,
　　　　　　　　efne swa hwylcum manna,　　swa him gemet ðuhte

mean 'to whom' or 'to that [man] to whom'? See also §§2160-2. I see little profit in pursuing such questions.

§2131. Sometimes the concord shows that *ðæt ðe* is not a relative referring to an apparent antecedent but an emphatic demonstrative

+ relative *þe*, e.g. *CP* 105. 1 *Forðæm eac wæs ðæt ðe beforan ðæm temple stod æren ceac onuppan twelf ærenum oxum* (where *æren ceac* (masc.) is in epexegetic apposition with what precedes) and *ÆCHom* ii. 264. 23 *Sume ðas race we habbað getrahtnod on oðre stowe, sume we willað nu geopenian, þæt þe belimpð to ðam halgan husle* (where the same relationship exists between *sume* and the last clause). On the other hand, the noteworthy variation in *Coll* 242 7 *beo þæt þu eart; forþam micel hynð* 7 *sceamu hyt is menn nellan wesan þæt þæt he ys* 7 *þæt þe he wesan sceal*, where *þæt, þæt þæt*, and *þæt þe*, all represent Latin *quod*, suggests that there was sometimes little real distinction between these forms. But some of the variations involving the various patterns discussed here can be accounted for by a desire for emphasis; compare *John(WSCp)* 3. 6 *Ðæt þe acenned is of flæsce þ is flæsc* 7 *þ þe of gaste is acenned þ is gast* with *John(Li)* 3. 6 *þ acenned is ł bið of lichoma lichoma is* 7 *þte acenned bið ł is of gaste gast* and consider *ÆCHom* i. 254. 23 *He gewanode þæt he forlætan sceal, and þæt bið geiht þæt þæt he habban sceal on ecnysse.* For further examples, see Visser, i. 546-50.

§2132. *þæt(te)* may also be translated 'what' in the formulae *þæt mare is* and *þætte læsse wæs*, e.g. *Bede* 86. 22 *Ac þonne gena is se seolfa geþoht to asmeagenne, hwæðer he geeode þe mid scynisse þe mid lustfulnisse, oððe hwæþer þonne gena, þæt mare is, mid gyfunge þære synne, Or* 106. 33 7 *eac self sæde þæt seo dæd his nære, ne eac beon ne mehte nanes eorðlices monnes, þætte ealre worolde swelce sibbe bringan mehte, þætte twa þeoda ær habban ne mehton, ne, ðætte læsse wæs, twa gemægþa*, and *ÆCHom* i. 244. 12 *On ðisum dagum we sceolon gebiddan ure eorðlicra wæstma genihtsumnysse, and us sylfum gesundfulnysse and sibbe, and, þæt gyt mare is, ure synna forgyfenysse.*

§2133. On *þæs* 'what(ever)'—as possibly in *þæs we gesioð* in *Bo(C)* 128. 18 below—see §2316. The combination *þæs þe* often appears as the genitive of *þæt þe* 'what(ever)'. Sometimes the genitive is the appropriate case for both clauses, e.g. *ÆCHom* i. 248. 32 *and him getiðað þæs ðe he bitt* and *ÆCHom* ii. 448. 19 *and ic ðearfum ne forwyrnde þæs ðe hi gyrndon.* But it may be the case of the principal clause, e.g. *Bo(C)* 128. 18 *Ac þ þ we wyrd hatað, þ bið Godes weorc þ he ælce dæg wyrcð, ægþer ge þæs we gesioð ge þæs þe us ungesewenlic bið* (where, as I construe it, the fourth *þ* introduces a noun clause, despite MS *B þe*; see §1957), or that of the subordinate clause, e.g. *ÆCHom* i. 450. 6 *Eala ðu casere, soðlice we budon ðe ðæs ðe we sylfe brucað. . . .* In *Bo(C)* 128. 18 *þe* could be inserted after *þæs* and both occurrences of *þæs þe* taken as examples of *þæs* antecedent + *þe* relative. But since *beodan* is not recorded with the genitive, this interpretation is not possible in *ÆCHom* i. 450. 6. On this problem, cf. §§2129-31.

e. *þæt: problems of concord and function*[43]

✕ §2134. In matters of concord, *þæt* appears to be the most consistent offender in adjective clauses. However, I believe that in general scholars have been too ready to accept the verdict of Kellner (p. 205)—'as early as the time of Alfred the Great, the neuter *þæt* seems to become indifferent to gender and number'—and that of Ardern (p. xxxiv), who, throwing caution to the winds, says that *þæt* is 'an indeclinable particle, used in every respect like *þe*'. McIntosh (p. 81 fn. 21) comes nearer to the true situation when he speaks more cautiously of 'occasional examples in O.E. of what appears to be, or could easily grow into, a relative *þæt* after masculine and feminine antecedents'. He could perhaps have added plural antecedents. Indeed, examples like *Or* 256. 11 *Wyrþigre wrace hie forwurdon ða, cwæð Orosius, þæt þa heora synna sceoldon hreowsian 7 dædbote don swiþor þonne heora plegan began* . . . and

PPs 121. 1   Ic on ðyssum eom   eallum bliðe,
                 þæt me cuðlice to   acweden syndon . . . ,

Latin *Laetatus sum in his, quae dicta sunt mihi*, are less easily explained than those with what appear to be masculine and feminine antecedents, e.g. *Or* 86. 30, *CP* 9. 14, *CP(H)* 189. 21, and *BlHom* 3. 1, all of which are discussed in §§2135-6.

§2135. Wrenn may have overstated his case in remarking that *þæt* in

Beo 14   fyrenðearfe ongeat,
         þæt hie ær drugon   aldorlease
         lange hwile

'must here be the conjunction'. But I believe that it is; see §§3119-20. For, as I see it, most of the apparent examples of relative *þæt* showing lack of concord—including those cited by Wülfing (i, §§284-5)—can be otherwise explained.[44] In *CP* 9. 14 . . . *heht him*

---

[43] It is only fair to remark that some of the points made in the sections which follow have been made independently by Kivimaa (pp. 39-46).

[44] Swanton, in his note to *Dream* 2, objects that Scragg's suggestion (*NQ* 213 (1968), 166-8) that we follow Bouterwek and Kemble and read *þæt* rather than *hwæt* for MS *hæt* in *Dream* 2 'would lack agreement of gender (masc. *cyst* [*sic*, but '*cyst* f.' appears in his Glossary], neut. *þæt*)'. But *þæt* could agree with *swefn* (neut.).

swelcra ma brengan bi ðære bisene, ðæt he his biscepum sendan meahte, ðæt is a conjunction introducing a clause of purpose or result. In *CP(H)* 189. 21 . . . *ðæt hi magon eac be ðisse bisene ongietan ðæt him is to gecueden: Bearn, beo ge underðiodde eowrum ieldrum magum on Dryhtne*, the second *ðæt* in my opinion means 'what'; cf. the Latin *Nam, quod intelligi et figuraliter potest, illis dicitur: Filii, obedite parentibus vestris in Domino.*[45] In *BlHom* 3. 1 *Ond wæs se dom oncyrred Euan ungesælignesse þæt hire wæs to gecweden þæt heo cende on sare 7 on unrotnesse þa hire bearn*, where both *þæt* clauses are noun clauses, the first is in apposition with *se dom. ÆCHom* i. 276. 21 *forði ælc edwist þætte God nys, þæt is gesceaft; and þæt þe gesceaft nis, þæt is God* means 'therefore every substance—that which is not God—that is a creation; and that which is not a creation, that is God'. In *ÆCHom* i. 518. 1 *Nis hit na Petrus þæt ðær cnucað, þæt* refers back to *hit*. Johnsen (*Ang.* 37 (1913), 291) is wrong when he says that 'in *se man þe . . . þe* was sometimes replaced by *þæt: Se man þ æwe brycð . . .*'. Raith (BASPr. xiii) has the correct reading: *Conf 3. 1* 77. 8 *Se man þe æwe brycð, fæste vii ger iii dagas on wucan*. However, these and other OE uses of *þæt* demonstrate that the use of MnE 'that' as what is generally said to be a relative was by the time of the Norman Conquest inevitable. All are exemplified here, except for those involving *þæt* + a postposition; on these see §§2236-43.

§2136. We can begin with the exclamatory and explanatory uses. These shade into one another, but can be seen in examples like *Beo* 11 *þæt wæs god cyning!*, *GuthA* 18 *Ðæt sind þa getimbru þe no tydriað . . .*—Kivimaa (p. 40) suggests that the 'collective force' in examples like this may have helped to extend the use of relative *þæt* with plural antecedents—*ÆCHom* i. 8. 24 *An angin is ealra þinga, þæt is God Ælmihtig*, and *CP* 29. 12 *Soðlice ða eagan ðæt beoð ða lareowas 7 se hrygc ðæt sint ða hieremenn. Or* 86. 30 *7 hie benoman heora heafodstedes þæt hie Capitoliam heton* and *Or* 240. 32 may belong here. The parenthetic exclamatory use of *þæt is*, discussed in §§323-7, does, and might explain apparent examples of relative *þæt* like *CP* 443. 5 *Ðone Nazareniscan Hælend*—*ðæt wæs afandon wer betwux eow on mægenum 7 tacnum 7 foretacnum ða worhte Dryhten ðurh hine ongemang eow*—*ðone ge beswicon ðurh unryhtwisra monna honda . . .* (my punctuation). Examples include

---

[45] In both these examples, I disagree with Sweet's EETS note (p. 483) on *CP* 189. 21. In the second example, MS *C* has *þe* for *ðæt*. So here I am forced to assert that the scribe of *C* made the same mistake as Sweet, either because he misunderstood the Latin or because he was careless in copying. It is worthy of note that in the first example the EETS translation contradicts Sweet's note and takes *ðæt* as a conjunction.

Bede 360. 13 *opðæt heora riht cyning Wihtred, þæt wæs Ecgbyrhtes sunu, wæs in rice gestrongad*, those from Ælfric quoted in §§323-7, *Ex* 183, and

Seasons 28 . . . and þonne offredan unmæne neat
     þæt is lamb oþþe styrc, leofum to tacne
     þe for worulde wæs womma bedæled.

§2137. Other constructions which may have contributed to the modern use of *þæt* as a relative include the 'It's time that I went' construction seen in *Bede* 262. 26 *þa cwom his tid þæt he scolde of middangearde to Drihtne feran* and elsewhere—note the variation between *ðe* and *ðæt* in *CP* 121. 14 *Ðonne cymð his hlaford on ðæm dæge ðe he ne wenð ond on ða tiid ðæt he hine ær nat*; the interchangeability of *þe* and *þæt* in such prepositional formulae as *forþon þe* and *forþon þæt*; and examples like

PPs 143. 4 Hwæt is se manna, mihtig drihten,
     þe þu him cuðlice cyþan woldest,
     oððe mannes sunu, þæt hit gemet wære,
     þæt þu him aht wið æfre hæfdest?,

where *þe* in line 2 and *þæt* in line 4 both represent *quoniam* in the Latin *Domine, quid est homo, quoniam innotuisti ei? aut filius hominis, quoniam reputas eum?* (though this may be a symptom rather than a cause).

§2138. There is also the possibility that *þæt* occurred more frequently as a relative than other forms of *se*. *þæt*—not *þe*—is the norm after the antecedent *eal* in examples like *Or* 38. 8 . . . *þæt he ægþer sloh ge ða menn ge ða nytenu ge eall þæt on þæm lande wæs weaxendes 7 growendes*. The combination *se (seo)* + noun + relative *se (seo)* could occur only when both antecedent and relative were nominative, but with *þæt* + noun + relative *þæt* both antecedent and relative could be nominative or accusative, giving four possibilities. Theoretically, therefore, the latter could be expected to be more common, though there are of course many imponderables and further work will be necessary before we can be certain. But my figures show that in the poetry the percentage of examples with the relative *se, seo, þæt* after the combination *se, seo, þæt* + noun is highest when the noun is neuter singular.[46] Moreover, according to McIntosh (p. 81), the pattern *þæt* + noun + *þæt* is more common in the prose; he tells us that in 'Alfredian' English '. . . and in later Old

---

[46] It is true that *þe* is the preferred relative in these situations; see §2253. But this does not affect the argument here.

English, the *neuter* antecedent "demonstrative" or "demonstrative + noun" often, though by no means regularly, uses a relative *þæt*. Thus the type *se mann se* is very rare, whereas *þæt iegland þæt* is not. . . .' To all this can be added the fact that in the poetry the declined relative *se, seo, þæt* is always more common with neuter singular antecedents than with masculine and feminine singular antecedents. (The figures for the poetry referred to here are based on Mitchell 1959, pp. 146 ff.)

§2139. Finally, I turn to clauses in which *þæt(te)* might be a relative pronoun offending against the rules of concord or a conjunction introducing a purpose or result clause with unexpressed subject. These occur in prose and poetry of all periods. The verb in the *þæt(te)* clause may be indicative (or an ambiguous form which is to be taken as an indicative), e.g. *Bede* 108. 26 *Wæs he se ðridda cyning in Ongolþeode cyningum þæt allum suðmægþum weold* (cf. *Bede* 108. 31 *fifta Eadwine Norðanhymbra cyning, se hæfde rice ofer ealle Breotone . . .*), *BlHom* 65. 30 . . . *hu se mildheorta Drihten . . . hine sylfne geeaþmedde þæt of hehþe þæs fæderlican þrymmes to eorþan astag,*

Beo 565   ac on mergenne   mecum wunde
                be yðlafe   uppe lægon,
                sweordum aswefede,   þæt syðþan na
                ymb brontne ford   brimliðende
                lade ne letton,

and

Rid 40. 68   nis zefferus,   se swifta wind,
                þæt swa fromlice mæg   feran æghwær,

or subjunctive (or an ambiguous equivalent), e.g. *Bede* 128. 25 *Ac gesaga me hwylce mede þu wille syllan þam men, gif hwylc sy, þætte þec from þissum nearonessum alyse . . . , BlHom* 247. 24 *Min Drihten Hælend Crist, send þinne þone Halgan Gast, þæt awecce ealle þa þe on þisse wætere syndon . . . ,*

Ex 508   forðam þæs heriges   ham eft ne com
                ealles ungrundes   ænig to lafe
                þætte sið heora   secgan moste . . . ,

and

El 406   Ge nu hraðe gangað,
                sundor asecaþ   þa ðe snyttro mid eow,
                mægn ond modcræft,   mæste hæbben,
                þæt me þinga gehwylc   þriste gecyðan,
                untraglice,   þe ic him to sece.

§2140. Clauses of this sort are especially common with principal clauses which contain a rhetorical question demanding the answer 'No', e.g. *Or* 50. 13 *Hwa is þætte ariman mæge hwæt þær moncynnes forwearð on ægðere hand . . . ?, BlHom* 59. 33 *Hwylc man is þæt mæge ariman ealle þa sar ⁊ þa brocu þe se man to gesceapen is?,* HomU 26. 140. 3 *Nu, leofan men, hwa is æfre þæt hæbbe swa hearde heortan . . . ?,* and *Met* 28. 18 *Hwa is on weorulde þæt ne wafige . . . ?,* or a negative statement which in effect answers such a question, e.g. *Bede* 92. 7 *Ne wæs æfre ænig cyninga ne aldormonna þætte ma heora londa utamærde . . . , BlHom* 103. 19 *⁊ hwæþre nis nænig man þæt asecggan mæge þa miltsa . . . ,* and *Beo* 1366 *No þæs frod leofað ‖ gumena bearna, þæt þone grund wite,* which Glunz described once as an adjective clause and twice as a consecutive clause; see Behre, p. 293 fn. 1. Pogatscher (pp. 265–73) and Callaway (1933, pp. 21–4) offer more examples; Shearin (1903, pp. 85–7) discusses eleven instances from the prose with the subjunctive or an ambiguous equivalent and adds three from the poetry (1909, p. 244); and Visser (ii. 936) offers three *þæt* clauses with the subjunctive which follow a *gif* clause, viz. *HomU* 44. 284. 9 *gyf þæt þonne hwylc mon sy þæt him on his mode to earfoðe þince þæt he on ælce tid swa forwernedlice lyfige, tylige he þonne huru þæt . . .* (where the first *þæt* clause must be consecutive, not adjective), *HomU* 47. 301. 30 *and gif hwa sy þæt he nu gyt ne cunne, he hit leornige swyþe georne* (where we also have a consecutive *þæt* clause), and *HomU* 26. 136. 11 *and gyf hwylc man sy þæt ne cunne his pater noster and his credan, beo he swyðe geornlice embe þæt he hit leornige* (where the question is open).

§2141. Is this a genuine OE construction? A comparison of

Met 28. 5   Hwa is moncynnes
           þæt ne wundrie   ymb þas wlitegan tungl,
           hu hy sume habbað   swiðe micle
           scyrtran ymbehwerft,   sume scriðað leng
           utan ymb eall ðis?

with

Met 28. 1   Hwa is on eorðan   nu unlærdra
           þe ne wundrige   wolcna færeldes,
           rodres swifto,   ryne tunglo,
           hu hy ælce dæge   utan ymbhwerfeð
           eallne middangeard?

may suggest the possibility of scribal confusion of *þ* and *þe*. This could have arisen by careless copying or because *þ* in an earlier manuscript was used as an abbreviation for both *þæt* and *þe*; Woolf's note on

Jul 510

	Ne wæs ænig þara
þæt me þus þriste,	swa þu nu þa,
halig mid hondum,	hrinan dorste ...

reads '*þæt* (MS *þ̄*). The neuter pronoun is loosely used here for the masculine. Possibly the original reading here was *þe*, which in an earlier MS was written as *þ̄*, an abbreviation only used for *þæt* in the *Exeter Book*, and which should therefore have been expanded; cf. also l. 519.' If this is so, there was only one construction—an adjective clause introduced by *þe* standing as subject. I find it hard to accept this explanation. In my opinion the *þæt* clause with unexpressed subject is too common to be explained away as the result of scribal confusion and the notion that the same abbreviation could mean two things in the same manuscript seems unlikely; see §1930. It seems even more unlikely that a scribe would write *þæt* in full throughout a manuscript and use *þ̄* for *þe*, which is shorter than *þæt* and perhaps easier to write than *þ̄*.

§2142. The probability of this explanation is not increased by the fact that it cannot hold for those examples in which we have *þætte*, e.g. *Bede* 128. 25 (§2139), *Or* 50. 13 (§2140), and *Ex* 508 (§2139), or for the rarer examples with *þæt þe/ðe* such as *Or* 42. 6 *Hwa is þæt þe eall ða yfel þe hi donde wæron asecgean mæge oððe areccean?* and *Sat* 17 *Hwa is þæt ðe cunne || orðonc clene nymðe ece god?* These would have to be explained as the result of analogy, which is of course possible since *þæt, þætte,* and *þæt þe,* are interchangeable in other situations.

§2143. If we accept the construction with *þæt* as genuine, do we explain *þæt* as a relative with lack of concord or as a conjunction? The controversy is a long-standing one. As Pogatscher (pp. 275-6) points out, Wülfing, Plummer, and Trautmann, took the former view; Klinghardt, Lohmann, and Einenkel, the latter. Shearin (1903, pp. 85-7) preferred the former. 'Der treffliche Grein' had a foot in both camps. Since then writers and editors have continued to differ. Evidence for a firm decision is lacking. The fact that sometimes, e.g. in *Exod* 32. 1 *Aris 7 wyrce us godas þæt faran beforan us*, Latin *Surge, fac nobis deos, qui nos præcedant*, and *Deut* 1. 22 *Vton sendan sceaweras, ðæt sceawion ðæt land*, Latin *Mittamus uiros qui considerent terram*, the idiom represents a Latin adjective clause does not prove that *þæt* is a relative, despite Shearin (loc. cit. and 1909, p. 244). Equally, the idiomatic demonstrative use seen in

PPs 83. 5   þæt byð eadig wer,   se þe him oðerne
                fultum ne seceð   nymþe fælne god

and

PPs 126. 6   þæt bið eadig wer,   se ðe a þenceð
                 þæt he his lust on ðon   leofne gefylle

cannot be used to prove that *þæt* can be used as a relative pronoun without regard to gender or number; see §§2125 and 2136. The possibility that we have an unexpressed subject here is established by examples like *BlHom* 53. 27 *Nis eow þonne forboden þætte æhta habban* (cf. *BlHom* 55. 2 . . . *us gedafenaþ þæt we gehyron þa word* . . .), *ÆCHom* i. 88. 8 *Æt nextan, ðaða he gefredde his deaðes nealæcunge, þa het he him his seax aræcan to screadigenne ænne æppel, and hine sylfne hetelice ðyde, þæt him on acwehte* (cf. *ÆCHom* i. 100. 23 *Sind eac manega mid swa micclum gedwylde befangene, þæt hi cepað be ðam monan heora fær*), and *Beo* 299 *swylcum gifeþe bið, ‖ þæt þone hilderæs hal gedigeð* (cf. *Beo* 555 *hwæþre me gyfeþe wearð, ‖ þæt ic aglæcan orde geræhte*). In none of these can *þæt* be a relative; in the first of each pair the subject is unexpressed. (On this see further §1510 and Pogatscher, pp. 276-7.) Indeed, we sometimes find a *þæt* clause with an unexpressed subject followed by a *þæt* clause with an expressed subject, e.g. *BlHom* 247. 24 *Min Drihten Hælend Crist, send þinne þone Halgan Gast, þæt awecce ealle þa þe on þisse wætere syndon, þæt hie geliefon on þinne naman* and *HomU* 26. 140. 3 *Nu, leofan men, hwa is æfre, þæt hæbbe swa hearde heortan þæt he ne mæge him ondrædon þa toweardan witu?* Such variations suggest that final and consecutive *þæt* clauses with unexpressed subjects were idiomatic. So too were *þæt* clauses with a pronoun object unexpressed, e.g. *Exod* 10. 25 *Wilt ðu us syllan ofrunge þæt we bringon urum gode?* and *Num* 11. 13 *Hwanan sceolde me cuman flæsc ðæt ic sylle ðison folce?*; see §1572. Kock (p. 32) says that 'when *þæt* . . . followed on an indefinite, negative or int[errogative] expression, it was perhaps originally a conj. . . . which gradually was identified with the rel.'. I incline to this view. Such identification would be helped by the existence of the idiom with *þe* and a subsequent further blurring in the minds of those Anglo-Saxons who used the constructions. That the two idioms seen in *Met* 28. 1 and *Met* 28. 5 were interchangeable to the scribe is a possible explanation of that variation. It might explain also the fact that the same writers sometimes used the *þæt* clause with an unexpressed subject, sometimes that with an expressed subject, and the fact that the subject is sometimes expressed, sometimes un-expressed, in different manuscript versions of the same sentence; see Pogatscher, p. 277. Another pointer may be the fact that, as far as I have observed, Ælfric does not use the *þæt* clause with unexpressed subject which could be taken as an adjective clause; as a grammarian, he might have avoided a construction which was ambivalent.[47] While I do not accept Kruisinga's verdict (*EStudies*, 6 (1924), 144) that 'the Present English relative *that* is and always has been a conjunc-tion', I agree with Kivimaa (pp. 43-4) that the appropriate way to end this discussion is to quote Shearin (1903, p. 86): 'Further study of the phenomenon in all subordinate clauses in Old English might show that the Modern English relative pronoun *that*, standing for all genders, numbers and cases, was materially influenced by the analogy of the conjunction *ðæt*.'

§2144. Unfortunately this cannot be my last word. Dowsing (p. 300) has now claimed that '*þæt* as a relative pronoun was not inflected in the late Old English material investigated'. Properly analysed, her texts demonstrate the opposite: that *þæt* was still part of a well-preserved demonstrative/relative declension. She says (p. 291) that 'unlike *þæt* antecedent *se* is used in the plural, and oblique forms other than the accusative also occur'. This is only true by virtue of her fn. 5 (p. 290): 'As *se* and *seo* behave in the same way syntacti-cally, they will be treated together and referred to as *se*. Unless otherwise stated *se* refers to the singular and plural, all cases of *se* and *seo*. *þæt* refers to the nominative/accusative singular neuter *þæt* only.' This is illogical. With such a definition, it is inevitable that 'the use of *se* admits of far more variety than the corresponding use of *þæt*' (Dowsing, p. 293). For it allows her to say that we have *se* in *ÆLS* 6. 182 *þu eart soðlice Maure . þæs mæran Benedictes folgere on wundrum . be ðam we for wel oft gehyrdon þyllice gereccan*—which she does (p. 293)—but not *þæt* in *ÆHom* 3. 86 *and seo winwringe getacnode þæt weofud þær wiðinnan, on þam man offrode Gode on ða ealdan wisan mænigfealde lac*—a possibility which escapes her. So she seems to be surprised (p. 300) by the fact that 'in none of the examples from the present material does *þæt* occur in a case other than the nominative and accusative'. By her definition (p. 290 fn. 5, above), we have to add the words 'singular neuter'. I would not describe this as 'non-inflection of *þæt*' (p. 300) or as 'partial isolation of a single form, *þæt*' (p. 301). I would say that one could not have a better description of the part played by

---

[47] *Gen* 33. 15 *Ic bidde ðe þæt ðu nyme þe ladmenn of minum geferum ðæt þe wegas wission* comes from a portion of the translation not attributed to Ælfric.

þæt in 'the paradigm to which it originally belonged' (p. 301)—and to which it still belonged.

3. *þE* IN DEFINITE ADJECTIVE CLAUSES

§2145. This indeclinable particle functions as what is traditionally called a relative pronoun referring to antecedents of all numbers and genders and is found representing all cases in both prose and poetry. The inverted spelling *þy* is occasionally found, e.g. in *Met* 22. 10, where it is allowed to stand in ASPR, and *Jul* 467, where it is emended to *þe*.

§2146. *þe* most commonly serves as either the subject of the principal clause, e.g. *Or* 76. 33 *þu þe þyrstende wære monnes blodes xxx wintra, drync nu þine fylle, ÆCHom* i. 18. 33 . . . *mid þam deofle ðe hine forlærde, ÆCHom* i. 18. 21 . . . *þæt hi wæron ða deadlice þe mihton beon undeadlice . . .* , and *Beo* 191 *wæs þæt gewin to swyð,* || *laþ ond longsum, þe on ða leode becom*, or its object, e.g. *Or* 19. 22 . . . *to þæm porte þe mon hæt æt Hæþum, ÆCHom* i. 14. 32 *And he beheold þa ealle his weorc ðe he geworhte*, and

Beo 354   ond þe þa andsware   ædre gecyðan,
                 ðe me se goda   agifan þenceð.

§2147. But it may stand for the genitive, e.g. *Or* 20. 9 . . . *of ðæm mere ðe Truso standeð in staðe, Or* 136. 33 . . . *under þæm twæm consulum þe oðer wæs haten Fauius, CP* 147. 16 . . . *ðæt he sie wiðerwinna on ðære diegelnesse his geðohtes ðæs ðe he bið gesewen ðeow on his ðenunge '. . . of that one whose . . .', ÆCHom* ii. 254. 16 *and him budon drincan gebitrodne windrenc, ac he hit asceaf sona fram his muðe; nolde his onbyrian for ðære biternysse. þes gebiteroda drenc hæfde getacnunge his deaðes biternysse, ðe he ða onbyrigde,*[48] and

Pan 1   Monge sindon   geond middangeard
                 unrimu cynn   þe we æþelu ne magon
                 ryhte areccan   ne rim witan,

or the dative/instrumental, e.g. *Or* 118. 27 . . . *he sealde his dohtor Alexandre þæm cyninge his agnum mæge, þe he ær Æpira rice geseald hæfde, Or* 158. 25 *Ac siþþan hi þa gesawan, hie hie gegremedan, þæt hie þa wæron swiþe sleande þe hie fylstan sceoldon* (where I take each *þa* as a demonstrative), *ÆCHom* ii. 534. 24 . . . *æt ðam*

---

[48] The verb *onbyrgan* can take the accusative or the genitive. The use of *his* (after *nolde*) suggests that *ðe* stands for the genitive. But one cannot be sure; see § 1240.

mannum . . . þe he ða heofenlican myrhðe bodað, and *El* 717 . . . *on þa dune up ðe dryhten ær* || *ahangen wæs*. Liggins (1970, p. 319) observes that *þe* equals the genitive and dative more often in *Orosius* than in the other 'Alfredian' texts. On *þe* with postpositions, see §§ 2231-5.

§2148. *þe* may stand for different cases when repeated in successive clauses, e.g. *Ch* 1507 *H* 18. 16 . . . *7 þam mannum þe me folgiað, þe ic nu on Eastertidum feoh sealde, twa hund punda agyfe man him 7 dæle man him betweoh*, and even when not repeated, e.g. *Solil* 13. 15 . . . *oððe þam freondum þe ic lufige and me lufiað, ÆCHom* i. 40. 5 *Uton gefaran to Bethleem and geseon þæt word þe geworden is and God us geswutelode*, and

PsFr 24. 6   Ne gemynega þu me   minra fyrena
                gramra to georne,   þe ic geong dyde
                and me uncuðe   æghwær wæron.

§2149. Doubled *þe* occasionally occurs in the prose, e.g. *Bede(Ca)* 98. 27 *Utan biddan ælmihtine god þe ðe eardian deð þa anmodan in his fæder huse* (MS *O* has *þe þe*, but MSS *T* and *B* have *se ðe*), *Bo* 67. 26 *ðe þe wille fullice anweald agan, he sceal tiligan ærest þ he hæbbe anweald his agenes modes* (Sedgefield emends to *se þe*), *BlHom* 159. 8 . . . *mid eallum þæm cynne þe þe him ondrædaþ*, and *Exod* 3. 8 *on þæt land þe þe flewð meolce 7 hunie*. The occasional occurrence of doubled *se* (§2122) can lend these examples only dubious support. Dittography or late confusion of forms is more probably involved; see Carnicelli's note (p. 55) on *Solil* 13. 4-5. Cf. §2122.

§2150. Like the neut. *þæt, þe* can mean 'what', e.g. *Bo* 106. 8 . . . *þ ðu mæge ðy bet gelefan ðe ic ðe . . . recce* and *ÆCHom* i. 462. 31 *and forði ic sprece ðe he me het*. In *BlHom* 81. 33 *We þonne synt þe þær æfter fylgeaþ*, it serves as antecedent and relative in a definite adjective clause. Further on the uses of indefinite *ðe* with no antecedent, see §§ 2322-5.

§2151. The origin of *þe* and its exact status in OE are vexed questions. That it goes back to a locative adverb *þai* has been suggested by Neckel (p. 60). Examples like *ChronA* 78. 25 (885) . . . *þy geare þe sio sunne apiestrode* and *ChronA* 91. 3 (897) . . . *on ða healfe þæs deopes ðe ða Deniscan scipu aseten wæron* could be cited to demonstrate the possibility of this. Sprockel (pp. 167-8) thinks that it comes from *þær*—'as usual semantic weakening was followed by phonetic reduction'—and suggests the following stages: (1) dem. *se*, (2) relative *se*, (3) relative *se* strengthened by *þær*, (4) *seþe*, (5) *þe*. As Kock (p. 57) pointed out in 1897, other writers, including Nader, Klinghardt, and Sweet, had flirted with this idea. He did not think much of it:

I have before me over a hundred other ex:s with *þær* after a rel., but in no single instance do I feel inclined to declare unreservedly, that *þær* is entirely 'pleonastic', or that it is used for the sole purpose of distinguishing the rel. *se* etc. from the dem. To me it seems as though *þær* had always retained at least some part of its original local (or temporal) signification.

There are other reasons for objecting to Sprockel's sequence; see §§2160-2 and 2173.

§2152. Curme (*JEGP* 10 (1911), 335-56), arguing that *þe* may still be adverbial in OE, suggests that the demonstrative/relative ambiguity seen in *se* (§§2109-21) extends to *þe* and to combinations of *se* and *þe*. This position (which he develops further in *JEGP* 11 (1912), 10-29, 180-204, and 355-80) is in marked contrast to that adopted by Andrew (*SS*, chapter v). Sprockel (p. 169) claims that 'when *þe* is not part of a sentence, but only serves as a connective, it should be regarded as a conjunction'; his examples include *ChronA* 78. 25 and 91. 3 (§2151), *ChronA* 85. 22 (894) *þa besæt sio fierd hie þær utan þa hwile þe hie þær lengest mete hæfdon*, and similar sentences, in all of which *þe* is the functional equivalent of a dative. To Sprockel (pp. 168-9), *þe* is a relative when it is the equivalent of a nominative, e.g. *ChronA* 12. 23 (457) . . . *in þære stowe þe is gecueden Crecgan-ford*, or accusative, e.g. *ChronA* 64. 21 (851) . . . *þæt mæste wæl . . . þe we secgan hierdon*, or is used with a preposition, e.g. *ChronA* 80. 7 (885) . . . *þære rode dæl þe Crist on þrowude*. The distinction seems a fine one, especially when we remember that, if *secgan* in *ChronA* 64. 21 were regarded as taking the genitive (see §1092), we should presumably have to classify *þe* in that example as a conjunction. We can certainly argue that if we are to have a term to cover all the uses of indeclinable *þe* in OE, it might be better to call it a conjunction rather than an indeclinable relative. But pedagogically at any rate it is convenient to distinguish *þe* indeclinable relative, as in *ChronA* 12. 23 and 80. 7 above, where *þe* must be represented in the translation, from *þe* subordinating particle, as in *CP* 31. 6 *Ðeah ðæt folc ðyrste ðære lare, hie hie ne magon drincan, ac hio bið gedrefed mid ðam ðe ða lareowas oðer doð oðer hie lærað*, where *ðe* is not only untranslatable but can be dispensed with; cf. *ÆLS* 24. 135 *and*

mid ðam he ineode þa aras se cyning.[49] The fact that an example like
ChronA 85. 22 above could fall into either group, depending on
whether *þa hwile þe* was apprehended as the equivalent of MnE
'during the time in which' or of OE *þenden* and MnE 'while', is no
reason for pretending that the distinction does not exist.

4. COMBINATIONS OF *SE* AND *þE* IN DEFINITE ADJECTIVE CLAUSES

a. Introductory remarks

§2153. A demonstrative often serves as the only possible antecedent to *þe* functioning alone as a relative pronoun. The two can be
separated by other elements, e.g. *Or* 84. 34 *Uton nu brucan þisses
undernmetes swa þa sculon þe hiora æfengifl on helle gefeccean
sculon, ÆCHom* i. 234. 4 *and þam he sceal aheardian þe nane
behreowsunge nabbað heora misdæda*, and *Beo* 3007 (§2175), or
can be together, e.g. *Or* 10. 20 . . . *betux þære ie Indus 7 þære þe
be westan hiere is, Tigris hatte, ÆCHom* i. 106. 15 *Se Hælend
bodade on his tocyme sibbe us ðe feorran wæron, and sibbe þam ðe
gehende wæron*, and *Jul* 111 and *Beo* 3033 (both in §2175). In the
poetry the separation can be by line or half-line boundaries, e.g. *El*
294 and *Sat* 364 (again both in §2175), *PPs* 60. 6 *Hwylc seceð
þæt | þe soðfæst byð?*, and

ChristC 1199   Hwæs weneð se   þe mid gewitte nyle
                 gemunan þa mildan   meotudes lare . . . ?

§2154. The *se* element may be in the case appropriate to both
clauses, e.g. *Or* 84. 34 (§2153), or in that appropriate to the principal clause, e.g. *Or* 10. 20 (§2153). On examples in which it is appropriate to the adjective clause see §§2326–7. The last arrangement
appears in *ÆHom(CH)* 6. 10 *la leof hlaford, þone þe þu lufast /
lufodest ys nu geuntrumod*. But in MS *F þone* is altered to *se*, the
case required by the principal clause. The reference of these clauses
may be indefinite, i.e. to any one member of a group, or to a specific
individual; see §§2201–5.

§2155. But there are sentences in which a combination of *se* and *þe*
has another antecedent and so can be said to perform the relative

---

[49] The fact that *þe* can be dispensed with in this way seems to me an argument against
Curme's proposition that it was adverbial in OE. As I see it, a possible chain of development
for the formulae with *mid* is from *mid þæm* adverb + *þe* subordinating particle to *mid þæm
þe* subordinating conjunction to *mid þæm* subordinating conjunction. I cannot see how this
development could have taken place if *þe* had been an adverb. Nor do I see how *þe* in the
divided prepositional formulae (§2420) can be adverbial. See further §§2427–30.

function. (I note with regret that I failed in my D.Phil. thesis (Mitchell 1959) to distinguish examples of this sort from those discussed in the two preceding sections.) Theoretically *seþe* should be the perfect OE relative—with *þe* telling us that the ambiguous *se* is relative, not demonstrative, and *se* telling us the case of the indeclinable *þe*. Unfortunately it does not work that way, for the *se* element can have the case of either the *adjective* clause or the *principal* clause. So *þone þe* can mean 'whom', as in

Beo 1296	Se wæs Hroþgare hæleþa leofost
	on gesiðes had be sæm tweonum,
	rice randwiga, þone ðe heo on ræste abreat,
	blædfæstne beorn,

where *Se . . . rice randwiga*, is the antecedent and *þone* has the case of the adjective clause, or 'who', as in

Beo 3002	. . . syððan hie gefricgeað frean userne
	ealdorleasne, þone ðe ær geheold
	wið hettendum hord ond rice . . . ,

where *ðe* serves as subject of the adjective clause and *þone* agrees with the antecedent *frean userne* in the principal clause and can, according to Traugott (p. 103 fn. 17), 'be called an emphatic demonstrative followed by the indeclinable *þe*'. (Note, however, that *þone* in *Beo* 3003b does not carry metrical stress according to the traditional rules of scansion.) I distinguish these as the *'seþe* and *se'þe* relatives respectively.

§2156. The distinction between these two cannot always be made with certainty. In examples like

Beo 102	wæs se grimma gæst Grendel haten,
	mære mearcstapa, se þe moras heold,
	fen ond fæsten,

both clauses require the same case, the meaning is crystal clear, and the only 'ambiguity'—which is for the grammatical classifier—is easily solved by designating such a combination the *seþe* relative. If we were able to recapture the intonation patterns of OE, we might find that all the examples belonged to either the *'seþe* or the *se'þe* group or that some fell into one category, some into the other. The point is largely academic, but see §2178. This group consists mostly of examples in the nominative singular, e.g. *Or* 5. 20 *Hu Lucinius se consul, se þe eac wæs Romano ieldesta biscep, for mid fierde angean Aristonocuse þæm cyninge, ÆCHom* i. 24. 3 . . . *and wæs se soða Scyppend, seðe ana is God, forsewen and geunwurþod*, and

Beo 86   Ða se ellengæst   earfoðlice
               þrage geþolode,   se þe in þystrum bad;

in the nominative plural, e.g. *Bede* 30. 4 *þæt to tacne is, þæt sume
menn gesawon ða þe wæron fram nædran geslegene, þæt . . .* ,
ÆCHom i. 24. 12 *and of þam cynne comon ealle heahfæderas and
witegan, þa ðe cyðdon Cristes tocyme to þisum life,* and

Beo 377   Ðonne sægdon þæt   sæliþende,
               þa ðe gifsceattas   Geata fyredon . . . ;

in the accusative plural, e.g. *Bede* 4. 29 . . . *þa dæda his lifes . . .
sumu ða þe ic sylf ongitan mihte þurh swiðe getreowra manna gesægene, ic toycte, ÆCHom* i. 74. 34 *Nu ic ðe betæce, Drihten! þine
bearn, ða ðe þin gelaðung, mæden and moder, þurh wæter and þone
Halgan Gast, ðe gestrynde,* and

Prec 72   Ac læt þinne sefan healdan
               forð fyrngewritu   ond frean domas,
               þa þe her on mægðe gehwære   men forlætaþ
               swiþor asigan,   þonne him sy sylfum ryht;

with nominative *þætte/þæt þe,* e.g. *CP* 55. 14 *Hu ðæt mod ðætte
wilnað for oðre beon lihð him selfum, ÆCHom* i. 276. 21 *forði ælc
edwist þætte God nys, þæt is gesceaft* (the only example I have
noted of relative *þætte* in *ÆCHom*—*ÆCHom* i. 276. 21 *and þæt þe
gesceaft nis, þæt is God* immediately follows it), and

PPs 118. 176   Ic gedwelede   swa þæt dysige scep,
               þætte forweorðan   wolde huru;

or with *þætte/þæt þe* accusative, e.g. *Solil* 60. 8 *ic wundrige hwi ðu
swa swiðe georne* [verb] *and swa gewislice þæt to witanne, þætte
nefre nan man . . . witan ne myhte, Gen* 21. 7 *Hwa wolde gelyfan
þæt Sarra lecgan sceolde cild to hyre breoste to gesoce on ylde, þæt
ðe heo Abrahame on hys ylde acende?,* and

ChristC 1585   . . . þæt he ne forleose   on þas lænan tid
               his dreames blæd   ond his dagena rim,
               ond his weorces wlite   ond wuldres lean,
               þætte heofones cyning   on þa halgan tid
               soðfæst syleð   to sigorleanum
               þam þe him on gæstum   georne hyrað.

§2157. All the examples of the *sepe* relative so far quoted have been
in sentences in which both the principal and the adjective clause
require the same case. But since *þa* can be nominative or accusative
plural and *þæt* nominative or accusative singular neuter, there are

examples in which the two clauses require the same *form* but different *cases*. Thus we find *þa þe* with the sequence principal clause nominative-adjective clause accusative in *Bede* 466. 21 *ge eac, þa ðe hi iu cuðan 7 mid langre gymeleasnesse ealdian ongunnon, þa eft mid his lare on ðone ærran steall geedniwode wæron, ÆCHom* ii. 296. 20 *and ic dyde eow witan, ðurh Drihtnes mihte, þæt ðas deofolgild eow sind derigendlice, ða ðe ge mid ydelnysse oð þis wurðodon,* and

El 894   Ða wæs þam folce   on ferhðsefan,
         ingemynde,   swa him a scyle,
         wundor þa þe worhte   weoroda dryhten
         to feorhnere   fira cynne,
         lifes lattiow,

but with the sequence principal clause accusative-adjective clause nominative in *Bede* 466. 14 *Swylce he eac husulfatu 7 leohtfatu 7 monig oðer þysses gemetes, þa ðe to Godes huses frætwednesse belimpað, he geornfullice gegearwode, ÆCHom* i. 114. 6 *and he hatað ealle ða ðe unrihtwisnysse wyrcað,* and

El 153   Heht þa wigena weard   þa wisestan
         snude to sionoðe,   þa þe snyttro cræft
         þurh fyrngewrito   gefrigen hæfdon,
         heoldon higeþancum   hæleða rædas.

Similarly, we find *þætte/þæt þe* with the sequence nominative-accusative in *Bede(Ca)* 78. 19 *7 geþenc, broðor þu leofesta, þ eall þ ðe we þrowiað on þyssum deadlican untrumnysse is . . . rihte Godes dome geendebyrded* and

GuthB 980   Bryþen wæs ongunnen
         þætte Adame   Eue gebyrmde
         æt fruman worulde,

but with the sequence accusative-nominative in *CP* 351. 25 *Hwæt mæg bion dyslicre ðonne hwa lufige hwelcre wuhte spor on ðæm duste 7 ne lufige ðæt ðætte ðæt spor worhte?,* the first *þæt ðe* clause in *ÆCHom* i. 158. 26 (§2161), and

Jul 1   Hwæt! We ðæt hyrdon   hæleð eahtian,
         deman dædhwate,   þætte in dagum gelamp
         Maximianes. . . .

In *Luke(Li)* 2. 15 *7 gesea woe ðis word þte aworden wæs ðætte dyde se drihten . . .* we have the sequence accusative-nominative-accusative. The modern scholar may be tempted to argue that the *se* element in all these examples must belong either to the principal clause (*se'þe*) or to the adjective clause ('*seþe*) and that the intonation of the Anglo-Saxon speaker would have determined the issue for each example. But in view of the remarks made in §§2156 and 2178, we can, I think, reasonably solve the insoluble by assigning them to the *sepe* group, which is further discussed (with examples involving other cases) in §§2178-9.

§2158. There are, however, occasional examples in which the two clauses (may) require different cases and the *se* element can be taken as part of the principal clause or as part of the adjective clause, thereby giving different meanings to the sentence. In *ÆCHom* i. 230. 12 *Nu cwyð eft se halga Gregorius, þæt Cristes lichama com inn, beclysedum durum, seðe wearð acenned of ðam mædene Marian beclysedum innoðe*, it is not clear whether we have the *'sepe* relative referring to *Cristes* or the *sepe* relative referring to *lichama*; in *ÆCHom* i. 32. 5 *Mine gebroðra þa leofostan, ure Hælend, Godes Sunu, euenece and gelic his Fæder, seðe mid him wæs æfre buton anginne, gemedemode hine sylfne . . .* , *seðe* could refer to *ure Hælend* (*sepe*) or to *his Fæder* (*'sepe*); and in

Beo 2291   Swa mæg unfæge   eaðe gedigan
                 wean ond wræcsið   se ðe Waldendes
                 hyldo gehealdeþ!

we may take *hyldo* as accusative, in which case the relative pronoun is nominative (the *sepe* type 'that one who'), or as nominative, with the relative combination meaning 'that one whom' (the *se'pe* type). But even here, the effect on the meaning is negligible. It is not worth erecting a fourth class for examples like these. They belong to one of the three classes already distinguished. Which one must depend upon the individual reader's interpretation. But Anklam's claim (p. 30) that 'in einer großen Anzahl von Fällen scheint *se ðe* aus Gründen der Deutlichkeit gewählt zu sein' ['in a great number of instances, *se ðe* appears to be chosen for the sake of clearness'] is mistaken. 'Clearness' is just what combinations of *se* and *þe* do not give —to modern readers at least. We can see this when we consider the manuscript reading of

Dan 141   Ne ge mætinge   mine ne cunnon,
                 þa þe me for werode   wisdom bereð.

Here Krapp emends by reading *Nu* for *Ne* and *berað* for *bereð* to give a nominative plural form of the *sepe* type 'you who . . .'. But, as Farrell points out in his note, the manuscript reading can be retained by taking *þa* as accusative singular feminine and *þe* as nominative singular feminine, so giving a *se'þe* relative: 'nor do you know my dream, which brings wisdom to me before the assembly'.

✕ §2159. Those familiar with my article in *Ang.* 81 (1963), 298-322, and with my *Guide*, §§162-3, will notice that I have modified the system of classification used there, which first saw what can scarcely be called the light of day in my D.Phil. thesis. The equivalences are

Number	Old System	New System	Definition
1.	*seþe*	*'seþe*	The *se* element is in the case of the adjective clause
2.	*se'þe*	*se'þe*	The *se* element is in the case of the principal clause
3.	*seþe* or *se'þe*	(*a*) *seþe*	The *se* element is in the case appropriate to both clauses
		(*b*) No symbol	The two clauses require different cases, but the *se* element can be taken with either (§2158)

These three groups can be subsumed under the general title 'the compound relatives'. Two manufactured examples will point the difference between types 3(*a*) and 3(*b*). In ☆*Ic eom se mann se þe þinne wifmann cyste*, there is no ambiguity of sense and we have the *seþe* relative. In ☆*Ic eom se mann se þe þin wif cyste, þin wif* may be nominative ('that one whom' *se'þe*) or accusative ('that one who' *seþe*). Without intonation patterns, the classification of the relative and the meaning of the sentence are in doubt. We find types 2, 1, and 3(*a*) (in that order)—*þara þe, seþe*, and *seþe*—in *Or* 248. 23-9, where the changes in number are noteworthy.

§2160. No criterion other than case for distinguishing the three types of compound relatives seems satisfactory. The intonation patterns are unavailable; see below. Metre and line division I cannot accept as decisive. Andrew (*SS*, pp. 102 and 105, and *Postscript*, p. 41) seems to suggest that a possible criterion is whether the two components are written together or separately—hence he distinguishes the *seþe* (my *'seþe*) and *se þe* (my *se'þe*) types. This is not satisfactory. At best, it is a mechanical test and a study of word-division generally in OE manuscripts inspires no confidence in its reliability. See further *Ang.* 81 (1963), 299. Sprockel (p. 169) agrees that in examples like *ChronA* 102. 7 (921) . . . *7 ofslogon þone cyning* . . . *7 ealle þa þe þær binnan wæron* 'there is some reason for doubt as to whether *þa* is an antecedent or *þa þe* the relative pronoun' but goes on to assert that the construction in *ChronA* 72. 32 (874) . . . *7 he gearo wære mid him selfum 7 on allum þam þe him læstan woldon*, 'where inflected *allum þam* shows clearly that *þam* cannot belong to the relative clause, seems to solve the problem in favour of considering the *se-* form as the antecedent even when *ealle* precedes'. But one could argue the opposite by drawing the analogy with examples like

Met 29. 67   Ac se milda metod   monna bearnum
                      on eorðan fet   eall þætte groweð,

Or 260. 4 *Oðsace nu, cwæð Orosius, se se þe wille* . . . , *ÆCHom* i. 26. 27 *forði he com to us þæt he wolde for us deað þrowian, and swa eal mancynn þa ðe gelyfað mid his agenum deaðe alysan fram hellewite*, and

El 282   Ða wæs gesamnod   of sidwegum
                  mægen unlytel,   þa ðe Moyses æ
                  reccan cuðon.

§2161. It is true that in examples like *ÆCHom* i. 76. 2 *Onfoh me to minum gebroðrum mid ðam ðe ðu come* and *ÆCHom* i. 314. 17 *And ure ælc gehyrde hu hi spræcon urum gereordum on ðam ðe we acennede wæron*, where a preposition intervenes between the antecedent and a relative which it governs, we can say with some confidence that the *se* element belongs both logically and rhythmically to the adjective clause and that we have the *'seþe* relative. But the question must be asked whether even case itself can always be decisive in determining the exact function of the *se* element in any one compound relative. We may agree that in the *'seþe* type it belongs grammatically to the adjective clause; in the *se'þe* type to the principal clause; and in the *seþe* type to either or both. But in the absence of intonation patterns we cannot be sure that this was the sole or vital criterion. Detailed study of the punctuation of the manuscripts may throw further light on the problem. Thus Harlow, who writes on punctuation in some manuscripts of Ælfric but does not distinguish the *'seþe* and *se'þe* relatives, remarks (p. 10) that

. . . *se ðe* clauses strongly favour punctuation [before the *se* element]. . . . Although this might be so because the majority are descriptive, even the restrictive clauses introduced by *se ðe* are usually punctuated. . . . Perhaps when punctuation came before *se ðe* it was felt as 'he who' or 'that which' would be in modern English, the *se* element acting as a demonstrative pronoun in apposition to the antecedent, and *þe* as a relative pronoun proper. This use of *se ðe* would then be the equivalent, in the third person, of the use of *þu ðe, we þe*, &c., to introduce a relative clause in the second or first person. . . .

This explanation could hold for the *se'þe* and the *seþe* types, but is more difficult to accept for the *'seþe* type, where the *se* element is in the case of the adjective clause and therefore (it seems reasonable to argue) belongs to it rhythmically; cf. the examples with *þe ic* and *þe we* quoted in §2181. It is not difficult to extend the same conclusion to the *seþe* type; see further §2178. But some scholars have felt —the word seems more appropriate here than 'thought'—that even in the *se'þe* type the *se* element also belongs rhythmically to the adjective clause. Klinghardt (p. 196) argued that in such examples the pronoun belongs 'rhythmisch zum Attributivsatze, logisch und formell zum Hauptsatze', and Ardern (p. xxxiv) writes that 'in spite of its Case-form, the Pronoun appears to be "felt" as part of the Relative sign'. These opinions in a way conflict with that quoted above from Harlow, who (as already noted) did not distinguish the *se'þe* and *'seþe* types. Another observation of his (p. 19 fn. 1) comes closer to the view of Klinghardt and Ardern: 'The later scribes do very rarely insert a point between a contiguous *se* and *ðe*, but R and C offer strong evidence that Ælfric intended these words to be closely linked in the contexts where he used them, just as they are in a conjunctional phrase like *for þan ðe*.' But an example like *ÆCHom* i. 158. 26 *ac uton biddan leoht æt urum Drihtne: na þæt leoht ðe bið geendod, þe bið mid þære nihte todræfed, þæt ðe is gemæne us and nytenum; ac uton biddan þæs leohtes þe we magon mid englum anum geseon, þæt ðe næfre ne bið geendod* points in the opposite direction. For here, despite the fact that the antecedent of the first *þæt ðe* is accusative and the antecedent of the second *þæt ðe* is genitive, I feel that Ælfric intended the two adjective clauses to be parallel—'thát which . . .'. If we argue that because of the difference in case the second *þæt ðe* must be an example of the *'seþe* relative, we would seem bound to conclude that *þæt þæt* is a relative, not an antecedent + a relative, in *ÆCHom* i. 158. 33 and *ÆCHom* ii. 442. 32, both in §2124. I find it hard to accept this.

§2162. But it is impossible for a modern writer to adjudicate here. Different speakers may have given different intonation to the same example or the same speaker may have given different utterance to examples which seem identical to us. It follows that suggestions like that of R. Huchon (*Histoire de la langue anglaise*, i (Paris, 1923),

216)—*se þe* is used in preference to *þe* when 'l'antécédent est empreint d'une certaine solennité'—and of Kivimaa (p. 45)—*seþe* is used 'more markedly showing reverence than does *se*'—can be little more than expressions of personal opinion.

§2163. The method of classification I propose seems preferable— on pedagogical grounds at least—to Traugott's suggestion (pp. 103-4) that the OE relatives are *þe, se*, and 'a third very rare relative' which she exemplifies by *Or* 260. 4 *Oðsace nu, cwæð Orosius, se se þe wille oþþe se þe dyrre, þæt þæt angin nære gestilled for þæs cristendomes Gode* . . . and which Bourcier (pp. 32 and 72 n. 32) says is 'probablement le fruit d'erreurs scribales'; see §2122. Her system takes no cognizance of the *'seþe* type and so fails to alert the student to the fact that *ðam ðe*, which means 'to those who' in *ÆCHom* ii. 322. 13 *Wa ðam ðe talað* . . . *yfel to gode*, means 'to whom' in *ÆCHom* i. 330. 26 *and he ða ðone wolde habban him to mundboran, þam ðe he nolde ær his cruman syllan* and in *ÆCHom* ii. 304. 18 . . . *þæt seo swiðre ne wurde æfre gewemmed ðurh readum blode Romaniscre leode, ðam ðe he geuðe ælcere dugeðe* . . . , and leaves him unprepared for such variations as *Bede* 230. 11 . . . *in heora dæghwamlicum gebeodum, þa ðe in þære stowe Drihtne þeowdon* 'of them who . . .' (*'seþe*) but *Bede* 376. 2 . . . *ealle ða hrægl, þa ðe he mid gegearwad wæs* 'with which' (*se'þe*; see §2232 and fn.);

El 302   Ge to deaþe þone
         deman ongunnon,   se ðe of deaðe sylf
         woruld awehte   on wera corþre
         in þæt ærre lif   eowres cynnes

'who' (*'seþe*) but

Dream 97   . . .   þæt hit is wuldres beam,
       se ðe ælmihtig god   on þrowode
       for mancynnes   manegum synnum

'on which' (*se'þe*); *ÆCHom* i. 464. 28 *An Ælmihtig God is, ðone ðe Bartholomeus bodað* 'whom' (*'seþe*) but *ÆCHom* i. 192. 23 . . . *þæt he wolde mancynn ahreddan þurh ðone þe he ealle gesceafta mid geworhte* 'through him with whom' and *ÆCHom* ii. 434. 12 *and ic herode and wuldrode þone ðe leofað on ecnysse* 'him who' (both antecedent demonstrative + *þe*); and *ÆCHom* i. 560. 20 . . . *to sumum westene, on þam þe cristene menn for geleafan fordemde wræc siðedon* 'in(to) which' (*'seþe*) but *ÆCHom* i. 314. 9 *and hi* . . . *ongunnon to sprecenne mid mislicum gereordum be ðam þe se Halga*

Gast him tæhte 'about that which' (antecedent demonstrative + *þe* or 'according as' prepositional formula), *ÆCHom* i. 42. 16 . . . *be ðam ðe ða hyrdas sædon* 'about that which', and *ÆCHom* ii. 480. 4 *þis fyr sceal gecyrran to þam ðe hit asende* 'to him who' (both antecedent demonstrative + *þe*).

§ 2164. *Or* 260. 4 *Oðsace nu, cwæð Orosius, se se þe wille*, which has been quoted in § 2163 as exemplifying 'a third very rare relative' (Traugott, p. 103 fn. 1), can be described as one manifestation of a tendency to repeat *se* when it is in the case of the principal clause. It may, of course, be in the case of the adjective clause as well, as it is in *Or* 260. 4. But this is not essential; note *Solil* 5. 11, quoted in § 2165. See further Liggins 1970, p. 316. This repetition, which is more common in early than in late prose and occurs only occasionally in the poetry, e.g. *Wid* 132, takes various forms.

§ 2165. It occurs with both forms of *se* together, e.g. *Or* 260. 4 (§ 2163), *Or* 248. 10 . . . *þæt on his dagum sceolde weorþan geboren se se þe leohtra is 7 scinendra þonne sio sunne þa wære, CP* 261. 18 *Se se ðe deadum monnum lif gearuwað* . . . *he becom to deaðe*, and *Solil* 5. 11 *þu þe nelt þe eallunga geeowian openlice nanum oðrum buton þam þam þe geclænsode beoð on heora mode*; with the two forms separated, e.g. *Or(C)* 250. 23 *þa wearð se geboren se þe þa sibbe brohte eallre worolde, CP* 279. 19 *Se gemetgað irre, se ðe ðone disigan hætt geswugian*, and *CP* 279. 17 *Ðæt is ðonne se ðe his tungan ne gemidlað, se towierpð anmodnesse*; and with three *se* forms, one alone and two together, e.g. *CP* 62. 8 *Oððe hu dear se gripan* . . . *se se þe hiene selfne hiwcuðne ne ongit Gode* . . . ? and *CP* 279. 16 *Ac se se ðe ðone wer bricð* . . . *se bið fruma ðæs geflites*. The use of *þæs* . . . *þe* and *ðæs* . . . *þæs ðe* in *ÆCHom* ii. 528. 2 *and se bitt on ðæs Hælendes naman, seþe þæs bitt ðe belimpð to soðre hæle. Gif hwa ðæs bitt þæs ðe him ne fremað, ne bitt he on ðæs Hælendes naman* is interesting. Other possible arrangements include the sequence *se þe* . . . *7 se se þe* . . . *he* in *CP* 49. 23-51. 4. See further Kivimaa, p. 33. On the repetition of *se* when *þe* is not used, see § 2122.

§ 2166. The comparative frequency of *se*, *þe*, and the compound relatives, remains to be established. Any figures must, of course, be approximate because of the ambiguous demonstrative/relative (§§ 2109-21), compound relatives of type 3(*b*) (§ 2159), and other problems of classification. My (approximate) percentages for the poetry are *se* 31, *þe* 35, *se'þe* 12, *'seþe* 2.5, and *seþe* 19.5. (These are subject to the reservation made in §2155.) The following table, covering the first twenty homilies in *ÆCHom* i, has been supplied to me by Lee Little of Western Kentucky University:

Type of relative		Number of examples	Approximate percentage
se		99	12.6
þe with antecedent other than *se*		442	56. 2
se + *þe* with *se* the only possible antecedent	= *'seþe*	3	.4
	= *se'þe*	18	2.3
	= *seþe*[50]	80	10. 2
'seþe		35	4.4
se'þe		5	.6
seþe		104	13. 2
Total		786	99.9

§2167. These figures compel three comments. First is the fact that while the combined figure for *se* and *þe* remains much the same—66 per cent in the poetry against 68. 8 in the selection from Ælfric—*þe* is much more frequent in Ælfric. Further study of the form of the antecedents is necessary before the significance of this can be assessed. Second, the comparative percentages for combinations of *se* and *þe* (with and without any antecedent other than the *se* element)—34 for the poetry, 31 for Ælfric—lend little support to van der Laan's assertion (*Neophil.* 14 (1929), 34) that 'an extensive use is made of this compound relative in poetry owing to its high phonetic value'. But obviously more work is needed before it can be dismissed. Third, it is clear from the table which follows that in combinations of *se* and *þe* in Ælfric, the *se* element is normally in the case required by the adjective clause.

[50] I do not now use these symbols for those combinations in which *se* is the only possible antecedent; see §2155. But I trust the reader will forgive me for using them as a convenient shorthand for purposes of comparison in this table and that which follows.

se element in case of	Type of relative	Number of examples		Total
		No possible antecedent other than *se*	Another antecedent	
adjective clause	(=) *'seþe*	3	35	38
adjective and principal clauses	(=) *seþe*	80	104	184
principal clause	(=) *se'þe*[51]	18	5	23
Total		101	144	245

This means that in 222 examples out of 245 (almost exactly 90 per cent), the *se* element tells us the case of the relative pronoun. The comparative figure for the poetry is only 65 per cent. This might suggest that the compound relative was becoming less ambiguous or more 'efficient'—see §§2172-3—as it became moribund. But it is hard to reconcile this idea with the already-noted fact that in the portion of Ælfric under discussion *þe*—which does not tell the case of the relative pronoun—is almost five times more common than *se* —which does. Again more work is needed.

§2168. I give my reasons for rejecting Andrew's claim that the compound relatives in *Beowulf* are intruders in *Ang.* 81 (1963), 299. It can, however, be noted here that an observation he makes at *Postscript*, p. 40, lacks a basis of research: 'Our text of *Beowulf* shows both a mixture of types and a syntactical licence in the use of them to which there is no parallel in any prose work.' There is room for more work here. But see §2251.

§2169. How did these compound relatives arise? I am unable to accept Noack's proposition (p. 16) that there was a development by which relative *se* > *seþe* > *þe*, despite Sprockel's support for it (pp. 167-8); see §2151. The sequence seems more likely to be first, *þe* enclitic and *se* demonstrative, and later relative too, in use side by side; second, *se'þe*; third *'seþe*, through examples in which both clauses required the same case, i.e. my *seþe* type. This sequence is not contradicted by the evidence of the Parker Chronicle, where both the *se'þe* and the *seþe* relatives occur before 891, i.e. in the portion written by the first scribe—*se'þe* appears in *ChronA* 66. 17 (855)

[51] See the previous footnote.

and 72. 33 (874), *seþe* in 6. 20 (46), 8. 7 (81), and 60. 26 (827), where it introduces a limiting clause—but (as far as I have observed) the *'seþe* form does not appear until 124. 3 (984). (For further examples see Rübens, pp. 46-7, and Sprockel, pp. 97-8, 112-13, and 170.) Andrew (*SS*, §119) makes what is in effect the same suggestion: 'Is it not possible that in a sentence like *Preostas þa ðe Læden cunnon* (= priests [those] that know Latin) the *ðá ðe* was misread as *ðaðe* and then the *seðe* form (= *ðe*) became general for all cases of the pronoun?' But the word 'misread' implies a strange conception; it would seem more natural to suggest that the construction spread from the spoken to the written language rather than in the opposite direction.

§2170. The suggestion that the *se'þe* form was the first of the compound relatives to appear may derive some support from a comparison of the examples of 'partitive apposition' cited in §1455 with the examples of the *se'þe* relative like *ÆCHom* i. 30. 26 *and on eorðan sibb mannum þam ðe beoð godes willan*, where the last five words may originally have been in partitive apposition with *mannum*: 'and peace on earth to men, to thóse who are of good will'. The same interpretation could stand for examples with *þa þe* like *ÆCHom* i. 24. 12 *and of þam cynne comon ealle heahfæderas and witegan, þa ðe cyðdon Cristes tocyme to þisum life* and (despite the change in number) *ÆCHom* i. 26. 27 *forði he com to us þæt he wolde for us deað þrowian, and swa eal mancynn þa ðe gelyfað mid his agenum deaðe alysan fram hellewite*; in these *þa* is probably emphatic 'thóse (who)' and so part of the principal clause, thereby giving us what is in effect the *se'þe* relative in both sentences. See further Mitchell 1964a, pp. 138-40.

§2171. Compound relatives also occur when the adjective clause is indefinite; see §§2201-25.

b. *'Seþe*

§2172. Here the *se* element is in the case of the adjective clause. How logical and efficient it would have been if this had been the only way to express the relative pronoun in OE is neatly demonstrated by the sequence *ðam ðe* 'whom' (*seþe*) ... *seðe* 'who' (*'seþe*) in *ÆCHom* i. 470. 19 *We magon niman bysne be ðære apostolican lare, þæt nan cristen mann ne sceal his hæle gefeccan buton æt ðam*

Ælmihtigan Scyppende, ðam ðe gehyrsumiað lif and deað, untrumnys and gesundfulnys, seðe cwæð on his godspelle, þæt an lytel fugel ne befylð on deað butan Godes dihte. The *'seþe* pattern occurs in prose and poetry of all periods and is used with antecedents of both numbers and all genders and in all cases, e.g. (masc. dat. sg. + acc.) *Bede* 222. 23 . . . *þæt heo ne woldon heora Gode hyran, þone þe heo gelyfden*; (pl. gen. + nom.) *Bede* 4. 26 . . . *ac mid gesægene unrim geleaffulra witena, þa þe þa ðing wiston*; (fem. acc. sg. + gen. pl.) *Bede* 56. 4 . . . *þonne heo þa elreordan þeode . . . þara þe heo furðum gereorde ne cuþon, gesecan scolde*; (masc. dat. sg. after preposition + dat. + nom.) *ÆCHom* i. 470. 19 above; (fem. acc. sg. + dat. after preposition) *ÆCHom* ii. 30. 31 *and dæghwomlice ge-neosodon ða halgan cyrcan, on þære ðe wæs þæs wuldorfullan Stephanes gemynd*; (neut. dat. sg. + nom.) *ÆCHom* ii. 192. 7 . . . *to godan lande and bradum, þæt ðe fleowð mid meolce and mid hunige*; (masc. dat. sg. + nom.)

GenA 1993
                þær wæs eaðfynde
    eorle orlegceap,   se ðe ær ne wæs
    niðes genihtsum;

and (neut. acc. sg. + gen.)

ChristC 1476   ac forgield me þin lif,   þæs þe ic iu þe min
                þurh woruldwite   weorð gesealde.

§ 2173. The *'seþe* relative is unusual in OE poetry, comprising as it does only some 2.5 per cent of all occurrences of the relative pro-noun. I have not found its equivalent in the *Heliand*. My impression is that it is less common in the earlier prose than in Ælfric. But full statistics for the prose are not available. To ascertain them might be a useful test of Jespersen's theory of efficiency in the development of language, for, if the theory is right, one would expect the *'seþe* relative to become progressively more common than the *se'þe* rela-tive as the OE language developed. On this point see also § § 2166-7.

§ 2174. On *'seþe* in indefinite adjective clauses, see § § 2209, 2211, 2215, 2223, and 2225.

c. Se'þe

§ 2175. Here the *se* element is in the case of the principal clause. As I have already observed in § 2166 fn., I do not now describe as *se'þe* relatives those combinations of *se* and *þe* in which the *se* element is

the sole antecedent. The following series from the poetry is interesting:

Beo 3007   Nu is ofost betost,
            þæt we þeodcyning   þær sceawian,
            ond þone gebringan,   þe us beagas geaf,
            on adfære;

El 294   . . .   þa ge wergdon þane
            þe eow of wergðe   þurh his wuldres miht,
            fram ligcwale,   lysan þohte,
            of hæftnede;

Sat 364   . . . and wel is þam   ðe þæt wyrcan mot;

Jul 111   . . . lufige mid lacum   þone þe leoht gescop . . . ;

Beo 3033   Fundon ða on sande   sawulleasne
            hlimbed healdan   þone þe him hringas geaf
            ærran mælum;

and

Beo 3002   . . . syððan hie gefricgeað   frean userne
            ealdorleasne,   þone ðe ær geheold
            wið hettendum   hord ond rice. . . .

In these examples, the *se* element begins by being an antecedent
separated from the particle *þe*, but gradually becomes more closely
linked with it, although always retaining the case of the principal
clause. *Beo* 3002, where the antecedent is *frean userne*, clearly
exemplifies the *se'þe* type. In *Beo* 3033 the status of *sawulleasne*
and therefore of *þone þe* is arguable—'. . . found that one lifeless
who . . .' (demonstrative antecedent + *þe*) or '. . . found the lifeless
one, that one who . . .' (*se'þe*)?

§ 2176. The *se'þe* relative is found in prose and poetry of all periods.
Examples with antecedent and relative together include *Bede* 330. 19
. . . *fore generednisse heora freonda þara ðe of weorulde geleordon,*
GD 202. 3 *hi adulfon gehwylcne dæl þæs wyrtgeardes þæs þe þær ær*
undolfen wæs (where *þæs* certifies that—as the context makes clear
—none of the garden had previously been dug), *Ps(P)* 9. 11 *heriað*
forði Drihten, þone ðe eardað on Sion, Lch ii. 26. 22 *genim grenne*
finul gedo on wæter xxx nihta on ænne croccan þone þe sie gepicod
utan, ÆCHom i. 30. 26 . . . *and on eorðan sibb mannum, þam ðe*
beoð godes willan,

Beo 2249   guðdeað fornam,
            feorhbealo frecne,   fyra gehwylcne
            leoda minra   þara ðe þis lif ofgeaf,

and

ChristC 1635   Hyra blæd leofað
æt domdæge,   agan dream mid gode
liþes lifes,   þæs þe alyfed biþ
haligra gehwam   on heofonrice.

But the antecedent and *se'þe* may be separated, e.g. *Bede* 174. 14 *Ond monige þara broðra þæs ylcan mynstres þara þe in oðrum husum wæron, sægdon þæt heo swutolice engla song geherdon, þone þe in Ps(P)* 14. 5 . . . *and se þe þone rihtwisan weorþað þone þe Godes ege hæfð, ÆCHom* i. 204. 5 *Fela riccra manna geðeoð Gode, þæra ðe swa doð swa swa hit awriten is, Beo* 97 . . . *lif eac gesceop* ‖ *cynna gehwylcum þara ðe cwice hwyrfaþ*, and *ðara þe* in

ChristA 46   . . .   þa se waldend cwom,
se þe reorda gehwæs   ryne gemiclað
ðara þe geneahhe   noman scyppendes
þurh horscne had   hergan willað.

§ 2177. I discuss the function of the *se* element in the *se'þe* relative in § 2161. On *se'þe* in indefinite adjective clauses see §§ 2212 and 2218.

d. Seþe

§ 2178. The *seþe* type has already been discussed and exemplified in §§ 2156–7. The important thing is that both clauses require the same form of *se* and, apart from the examples involving *þa þe* and *þætte/ þæt þe* which are discussed in § 2157, the same case. Typical examples are *Or* 178. 20 . . . *þæt se wære leoda cyning se þe ær wæs folce þeow, ÆCHom* i. 230. 15 *Hwilc wundor is þæt se Hælend mid ecum lichaman come inn, belocenum durum, seðe mid deadlicum lichaman wearð acenned of beclysedum innoðe þæs mædenes?*, and

Beo 229   þa of wealle geseah   weard Scildinga,
se þe holmclifu   healdan scolde,
beran ofer bolcan   beorhte randas,
fyrdsearu fuslicu.

In these three examples *seþe* can be taken at its face value and translated 'who'. But we cannot be sure whether the *se* element was stressed and *þe* unstressed 'that one who'; whether the two formed an unstressed combination equivalent to MnE 'who'; or whether there was some intermediate stage not known in MnE; cf. § 2536.[52]

---

[52] This uncertainty was my reason for using the now-abandoned symbol *seþe* or *se'þe* for this type. It accurately represented the dilemma of the grammarian in classifying these examples, but stressed their grammatical ambiguity at the expense of their fundamental semantic unambiguity.

The vast majority of examples have nom. sg. masc. *se þe*; nom. sg. fem. *seo þe*, e.g. *Or* 74. 22 *Seo ilce burg Babylonia, seo ðe mæst wæs 7 ærest ealra burga, seo is nu læst 7 westast, ÆCHom* i. 84. 2 *Eadig is heora yld, seo ðe þa gyt ne mihte Crist andettan, and moste for Criste þrowian*, and

> *Beo* 1443   scolde herebyrne   hondum gebroden,
>   sid ond searofah   sund cunnian,
>   seo ðe bancofan   beorgan cuþe . . . ;

or *þa þe* or *þætte/þæt þe*, both of which are exemplified in §2157. Notorious examples involving lack of concord such as *Beo* 1343 *seo hand . . . ‖ se þe* (but here we might have a triumph of sex over gender), *Beo* 1886 *yldo . . . ‖ se þe*, and

> *Beo* 1258   Grendles modor,
>   ides aglæcwif   yrmþe gemunde,
>   se þe wæteregesan   wunian scolde,
>   cealde streamas . . . ,

also belong here. See further §2358.

§2179. The *seþe* relative occasionally occurs in forms and cases other than those already exemplified. Here I am particularly conscious of the incompleteness of my collections. But I note acc. sg. masc. *þone þe* in *Bede* 56. 6 *Ond þa sona sendon Agustinum to þæm papan, þone þe him to biscope gecoren hæfde, ÆCHom* i. 54. 30 *Ne mæg ic minne feond lufian, ðone ðe ic dæghwonlice wælhreowne togeanes me geseo*, and

> *Beo* 1053   ond þone ænne heht
>   golde forgyldan   þone ðe Grendel ær
>   mane acwealde;

acc. sg. fem. *þa þe* in *Or* 234. 23 *7 eft hie him sendon ane tunecan ongean þa þe hie to geheton* and *ÆHomM* 15. 322 . . . *and on me gefylde his mildheortnysse þa þe he behet Israheles hirede*; gen. sg. *þæs þe* in *GenB* 401 *Ne gelyfe ic me nu þæs leohtes furðor þæs þe he him þenceð lange niotan, ‖ þæs eades mid his engla cræfte* (*neotan* can take the genitive as well as the accusative and dative); sg. fem. *þære þe* in *ÆLS* 31. 1326 *Mid þære ylcan hæse he afligde þa scealfran mid þære þe he deofla adræfde of mannum*; dat. sg. *þæm þe* in *ÆCHom* i. 470. 19 *We magon niman bysne be ðære apostolican lare, þæt nan cristen mann ne sceal his hæle gefeccan buton æt ðam Ælmihtigan Scyppende, ðam ðe gehyrsumiað lif and deað* . . . ; gen. pl. *þara þe* in

Beo 877   . . .   wide siðas,
                    þara þe gumena bearn   gearwe ne wiston,
                    fæhðe ond fyrena,   . . .

and

GenA 2040   He þær wigena fand,
                    æscberendra,   XVIII
                    and CCC eac   þeodenholdra,
                    þara þe he wiste   þæt meahte wel æghwylc
                    on fyrd wegan   fealwe linde

(*witan* can take the genitive as well as the accusative); and dat. pl.
þam þe in *GD(C)* 1. 5 . . . *þætte us, þam þe God swa micle heanesse
worldgeþingða forgifen hafað, is seo mæste ðearf* . . . (MS *H* retains
the same construction) and

Dan 33   þa wearð reðemod   rices ðeoden
                    unhold þeodum   þam þe æhte geaf.

I have little doubt that there are more examples for subsequent workers to find. Here I am in the dilemma explained in the penultimate
paragraph of my Introduction.

5. COMBINATIONS OF *SE*, *ÞE*, OR THE COMPOUND
RELATIVE, AND A PERSONAL PRONOUN, IN DEFINITE
ADJECTIVE CLAUSES

a. þe + *personal pronoun*

§2180. The indeclinable particle *þe* can be accompanied by a personal
pronoun in the person and number appropriate to the antecedent but
in the case appropriate to the adjective clause. The combination may
be governed by a preposition. The personal pronoun is usually found
next to *þe*; for exceptions see §§2186-8. The combination occurs
sporadically with the other relatives (see below), but it is only with
þe that all three persons of the pronoun are found. Examples follow.
I discuss some from the poetry in more detail in *RES* 15 (1964),
135-7 and 137-8.

§2181. I have found very few examples in which *þe* + a first person
pronoun serves a relative function. The pronoun is, of course, the
antecedent in sentences such as *ÆCHom* i. 612. 30 *we soðlice, ðe
þæs heofonlican eðles gefean eallunga oncneowon, sceolon anmodlice
to ðam onettan,* while *þe* in *BlHom* 81. 33 *We þonne synt þe þær
æfter fylgeaþ* has to do duty as antecedent and relative 'those who'.
In *Bede* 486. 11 . . . *þæt ic þe be syndrigum mægþum oððe þam*

heorum stowum, þa þe ic gemyndewyrðe 7 þam bigengum þoncwyrþe gelyfde, geornlice ic tilode to awritenne, þæt ic mid eallum þone wæstm arfæstre þingunge gemette, ic, the antecedent of *þe,* is repeated in *ic tilode;* see §1503. Possible examples are *Luke(WSCp)* 1. 19 *Ic eom Gabriel ic þe stande beforan gode* and *ÆCHom* i. 180. 17 *nu sceole we ure gymeleaste on þysne timan geinnian, and lybban Gode, we ðe oðrum timan us sylfum leofodon*—in both of which we have the equivalent of the *seþe* relative—and *BlHom* 81. 21 *Hæl us on eorþan we þe synt on lichomum lifgende* and *ÆCHom* ii. 376. 11 *ac ða gyt wæs ure rymet æmtig, we ðe of eallum middanearde to ðære feorme cumað*—in both of which *we* has the case of the adjective clause and can be compared with the *se* element in the *'seþe* relative, as Harlow (p. 10) points out. In the two examples in the poetry—*Rid* 12. 13 *Saga hwæt ic hatte,* ‖ *þe ic lifgende lond reafige* (cf. *Rid* 1. 14 *Saga hwa mec þecce,* ‖ *oþþe hu ic hatte, þe þa hlæst bere*) and

ChristA 22   Huru we for þearfe   þas word sprecað,
              ...   ...
              ...   þe we in carcerne
              sittað sorgende—

the personal pronoun follows *þe* and so can scarcely be taken as an antecedent. This is, however, possible in the prose examples; see §§2157 and 2161.

§2182. Kock (p. 79) draws our attention to examples such as *LawAfElPro Ic eom dryhten ðin God. Ic ðe utgelædde of Egipta lande,* Latin *Ego sum Dominus Deus tuus qui eduxi te de terra Egypti,* in which a Latin relative is represented in OE with a repeated *Ic* with no relative particle.

§2183. When the second person pronoun is used with *þe* to form a relative combination, *þu þe* and *ge þe* occur with such regularity that apparent examples with *þe þu* and *þe ge* must be suspect. The point is neatly illustrated by *ÆCHom* i. 538. 1 *Læd us, Ælmihtig God, to getele ðinra gecorenra halgena, inn to þære ecan blisse ðines rices, þe þu gearcodest fram frymðe middangeardes þe lufigendum, þu ðe leofast and rixast mid þam Ecan Fæder and Halgum Gaste on ealra worulda woruld,* where we have *þe þu* 'which Thou' followed by *þu ðe* 'Thou who'; see further *Ang.* 81 (1963), 305. In the vast majority of the examples I have noticed, the case of the principal clause is nominative or vocative and that of the adjective clause nominative; *þu þe* and *ge þe* are therefore the equivalent of the *seþe* relative. The personal pronoun is, of course, the antecedent in examples like *ÆCHom* ii. 20. 34 *þu eart mære and micel ðe wundra wyrcst* and *BlHom* 191. 36 *7 wite ge eac þe Godes frynd synd þæt . . .* and part of it in examples like *ÆCHom* ii. 264. 33 *þu Godes Lamb, ðe ætbretst middaneardes synna, gemiltsa us.* The examples which follow are typical of the relative use of *þu þe* and *ge þe* in both prose and poetry: *Or* 76. 33 *þu þe þyrstende wære monnes blodes xxx wintra, drync nu þine fylle, CP* 76. 2 *Doð eow clæne, ge þe beroð Godes fatu, ÆCHom* i. 76. 4 *þu eart Crist, ðæs lifigendan Godes Sunu, þu þe be ðines Fæder hæse middangeard gehældest and us ðone Halgan Gast asendest, ÆCHom* i. 348. 20 *Drihten, ðu ðe sitst ofer cherubin, geswutela ðe sylfne,*

Met 4. 53   Eala min drihten,   ðu þe ealle ofersihst
             worulde gesceafta,   wlit nu on moncyn
             mildum eagum,

and

PPs 134. 2   Ge þe on godes huse   gleawe standað
             and on cafertunum   Cristes huses
             þæs godan godes   gearwe syndan,
       3   Lofiað ge drihten   . . . .[53]

✕ §2184. There are occasional examples in the prose in which *þe þu* might mean 'thou who', e.g. *LS* 34. 586 *Sege us hwæt manna þu sy oþþe hwanon þu cumen sy þe þu þus eald feoh gemettest and þus ealde penegas hider brohtest.* Despite Liggins (1955, p. 402), I regard *þe* here as causal. I know of no examples in either prose or poetry in which *þe ge* can be taken as 'you who'. There are only two possible examples of *þe þu* 'thou who' in the poetry, viz.

KtHy 7   We ðe heriað   halgum stefnum
          . . .   . . .
          ðe ðu, god dryhten,   gastes mæhtum
          hafest on gewealdum   hiofen and eorðan
          an ece feder,   ælmehtig god

and

KtHy 22   Ðu eart heofenlic lioht   and ðæt halige lamb,
          ðe ðu manscilde   middangeardes
          for þinre arfestnesse   ealle towurpe. . . .

[53] There are more exceptions to Schrader's 'rule' (p. 52)—that the pronoun appears *in* [my italics] the relative clause only when it does not appear in the principal clause—than the two he cites, viz. *ÆCHom* ii. 600. 5 and 10. They include *ÆCHom* ii. 600. 24 as well as *ÆCHom* i. 348. 20 and *PPs* 134. 2-3, both quoted above.

This may be a Kentish peculiarity. But we could explain *ðe* in both these examples as 'because'. Even if we do accept *ðe ðu* as a relative combination, we do not need to follow GK (p. 703) in the view that *þe* in

Creed 1   Ælmihtig fæder   up on rodore
           þe ða sciran gesceaft   sceope and worhtest . . .

equals *þe þu*; *þe* can stand alone and, if we were to supply a personal pronoun, it should precede *þe*. See further Mitchell 1963*c*, pp. 305-6. The strength of the preference for *þu þe* is demonstrated by examples like *ÆCHom* i. 348. 20 (§ 2183),

PPs 79. 2   Ðu ðe sylfa nu   sittest ofer cherubin,
           æteow fore Effraim   eac Mannasse
           and Beniamin,   nu we biddað þe,

and

PPs 122. 1   To þe ic mine eagan hof,   ece drihten,
           þu þe heofonhamas   healdest and wealdest,

where *þu* has the case required by the adjective clause and *þu þe* is the equivalent of the *'seþe* relative. Klinghardt (pp. 195-6) suggests that the order *þu þe* or *ge þe* was preferred for reasons of euphony. Another factor may be the predominance of examples in which the *þu* or *ge* could be felt as a vocative in the principal clause; note, for example, *PPs* 134. 2 (§ 2183). *þu þe* appears even in *Gen* 48. 15 *Drihten, þu þe mine fæderas on þinre sihðe eodon*, Latin *Deus, in cuius conspectu ambulaverunt patres mei*, where *þu þe* is the equivalent of a *se'þe* relative, since *þu* has the case of the principal clause and *þe* . . . *on þinre*—a combination of *þe* and a possessive—renders *in cuius*. The intervention of the noun subject is noteworthy; cf. § 2187.

§ 2185. The third person pronoun usually follows *þe* immediately, e.g. *Or* 130. 34 *Chalisten þone Philosofum he ofslog, his emnscolere, ðe hi ætgædere gelærede wæron æt Aristotolese, Or* 102. 24 *7 ic gehwam wille þærto tæcan þe hiene his lyst ma to witanne, Mart* 2 118. 3 *On þone ilcan dæg bið þære fæmnan tid þe hire noma wæs Sancta Anatolia, BlHom* 47. 6 *forþon þe hi habbaþ manega saula on heora gewaldum þe him wile git God miltsian,* and *Sea* 12 *þæt se mon ne wat* ǁ *þe him on foldan fægrost limpeð.* In *CP* 27. 4 . . . *forðon licet suiðe monig ðæt he æwfæsð lareow sie, ðe he wilnað micle woroldare habban*, where the Latin offers no help, *ðe he* may mean 'who' or *ðe* can be taken as 'because'; cf. *KtHy* 7 and *KtHy* 22 (both in § 2184) and *BlHom* 69. 12 *He wæs eac se wyresta gitsere, þe he gesealde wiþ feo heofeones Hlaford 7 ealles middangeardes.*

§2186. But if the personal pronoun which combines with *þe* is in an oblique case and the subject of the adjective clause is a pronoun, the latter may intervene in both prose and poetry, e.g. *Or* 80. 19 *Ac gesette þa men on ænne truman þe mon hiora mægas ær on ðæm londe slog*, *Bo* 125. 5 *7 se yfela þe mon his yfel gestioran ne mæg bið symle wites wyrþe*, *Gen* 45. 8 . . . *ac þurh God, þe ic þurh hys willan hider asend wæs*, *Num* 1. 4-5 *ða ealdras beoð mid inc mid heora hiredum, ðe ðis synd heora naman* . . . (where the verb too intervenes), *El* 161 . . . *hwæt se god wære, ‖ boldes brytta, þe þis his beacen wæs*, and

Wan 9

                      Nis nu cwicra nan
    þe ic him modsefan   minne durre
    sweotule asecgan.

§2187. In the prose a noun subject may also intervene, e.g. *Or* 14. 9 . . . *oþ Armenia beorgas, þe þa landleode hi hatað Parcoadras*, *ChronA* 78. 26 (885) *se wæs Karles sunu þe Æþelwulf Westseaxna cyning his dohtor hæfde him to cuene* (this seems to be the only example of *þe* and a personal pronoun in *ChronA*), *Gen* 48. 15 (§2184), and *HomU* 35. 211. 12 . . . *Iordanis seo ea þe Crist wæs on hire gefullad*. This does not occur in the poetry. But we may note

GuthA 715

    Ic þæt gefremme,   þær se freond wunað
    on þære socne,   þe ic þa sibbe wið hine
    healdan wille,   nu ic his helpan mot,
    þæt ge min onsynn   oft sceawiað,

where both *ic* and a noun object intervene if *þe* . . . *wið hine* is a relative combination, but where *þe* may introduce a causal clause. We find a negative, a noun object, and a verb, intervening in

ChristC 1095

    . . . þær he leoflice   lifes ceapode,
    þeoden moncynne,   on þam dæge,
    mid þy weorðe,   þe no wom dyde
    his lichoma   leahtra firena,
    mid þy usic alysde

if we follow Gollancz in translating '. . . He whose body wrought no crime . . .'. This seems plausible and avoids the need for emendation.

§2188. When two or more clauses joined by *and* contain the relative combination *þe* + personal pronoun, *þe* (as far as I have observed) appears only in the first. When the clauses require the same case, the personal pronoun may occur in all of them, e.g.

El 725

    Dryhten hælend,   þu ðe ahst doma geweald,
    ond þu geworhtest   þurh þines wuldres miht

heofon ond eorðan   ond holmþræce,
sæs sidne fæðm,   samod ealle gesceaft,
ond þu amæte   mundum þinum
ealne ymbhwyrft   ond uprador,
ond þu sylf sitest,   sigora waldend,
ofer þam æðelestan   engelcynne . . . ,

or only in the first, e.g. *ÆCHom* i. 76. 4 and *PPs* 134. 2–3 (§2183),
or only in the second, e.g. *CP* 304. 6 . . . *se ilca Moyses ðe God self
lærde 7 hine lædde ðurh ðæt westen . . . , ÆCHom* i. 474. 19, and
ÆCHom ii. 90. 23 *Ælc ðæra ðe gehyrð þæt heofenlice word and he
hit ne understent, ðonne cymð se yfela and gelæhð hit.*

§2189. When there is a change of case, it can be signalled by using
the personal pronoun in all the clauses, e.g.

PPs 93. 11   þæt bið eadig mann,   þe þu hine, ece god,
on þinre soðre æ   sylfa getyhtest
and hine þeodscipe   ðinne lærest
and him yfele dagas   ealle gebeorgest . . . ,

or only in the second, e.g. *ÆCHom* i. 492. 1 and *ÆCHom* ii. 582. 22
. . . *se is Hælend Crist, þe us ealle gehylt and ure nan hine healdan
ne þearf.* The personal pronoun may occur only in the first clause,
the change of person not being signalled, e.g. *Lev* 11. 2–3 *Secgað
Israhela bearnum, ðæt hi eton þa nytenu ðe heora clawa todælede
beoð 7 ceowað,* Latin *Dicite filiis Israel, Omne quod habet diuisam
ungulam et ruminat in pecoribus, comedetis,* where the sequence is
ðe heora 'whose', *and* 'and [who]', and

PPs 145. 4   þonne bið eadig   þe him æror wæs
Iacobes god   geara fultumiend,
and ær his hiht on god   hæfde fæste,

where the second clause requires a nominative ['who'] which has to
be supplied from *þe him* 'whom'. In *CP* 181. 23 *Waa ieow welegum,
ðe iower lufu eall 7 eower tohopa is on eowrum woruldwelum, 7 ne
giemað ðæs ecan gefean . . .* we have *ðe iower* 'whose' . . . *7 eower*
'whose'. . . *7 ne giemað* 'and [who] care not'. . . . Cf. §2148.

§2190. When a relative combination of *þe* + personal pronoun is
governed by a preposition, the preposition immediately precedes the
personal pronoun, e.g. *LawIIAs* 25. 1 . . . *ond se biscop amonige þa
oferhyrnesse æt þam gerefan þe hit on his folgoþe sy* and *LawIIAs*
26 *buton he hæbbe ðæs biscopes gewitnesse ðe he on his scriftscire
sy.* Examples already quoted include *Gen* 48. 15 (§2184), *Gen* 45. 8
(§2186), *HomU* 35. 211. 12 (§2187), and *GuthA* 715 (§2187).

ChronC 141. 24 (1011) *7 hi þær in to comon þurh syruwrencas for-þon Ælmær hi becyrde þe se arcb Ælfeah ær generede æt his life* is not one, since *life* is dative, not accusative. The phrase *æt his life*—and the corresponding *his life* in *ChronE* 141. 24 (1011) *7 hi þær in to comon þurh syrewrenceas forþon Ælmær hi becyrde Cantwara-burh þe se arcb Ælfeah ær generede his life*—are datives of respect '. . . whom Ælfeah had spared in respect of his life'.

b. Seþe + *personal pronoun and* 'seþe + *personal pronoun*

§2191. I have found no examples of the combination 'seþe + personal pronoun. This is not surprising; the personal pronoun would be tautologic with 'seþe, in which the *se* element itself has the case of the adjective clause. This can be seen in the occasional examples in which a *seþe* combination is followed by a personal pronoun, e.g. *Bede(Ca)* 42. 3 . . . *þa wæron forðgongende þa cristenan men 7 ða geleafsuman, þa þe hi ær . . . on wudum . . . hi hyddon 7 digledon,* where MS *B* has *þa ðe ær.* In *CP* 295. 18 *Hwæs onlicnesse hæfde Assael ða buton ðara ðe hiera hatheortnes hie suiðe hrædlice on færspild gelæd?,* where both clauses require the genitive plural, we have demonstrative antecedent *ðara* and the relative combination *ðe* + personal pronoun in the genitive. In *ÆCHom* ii. 582. 22 *Soðlice se ðe ealle þa gebytlu hylt and hine nan ne berð, se is Hælend Crist,* we have two co-ordinate relative clauses, the first with the nom. *seþe* 'who' (*seþe* type) and the second with *and hine* 'and whom', with the pers. pron. *hine* denoting the change of case; cf. §2189. *BlHom* 7. 5 *forþon he me mycel dyde se þe mihtig is 7 his noma halig* at first glance shows a similar pattern. But here the co-ordinate clause goes with the principal, not with the adjective, clause: 'and holy is His name'. For more examples see Wülfing, i, §290.

c. Se'þe + *personal pronoun*

§2192. With the possible exception of *ChristA* 30 (§2194), all the examples in which a combination of *se* in the case of the principal clause + *þe* is followed by a personal pronoun in the case of the adjective clause involve the third person pronoun. This is not surprising when we consider that dem. *se* means 'that one'.[54] But most of them have the demonstrative which immediately precedes *þe* as the sole antecedent and therefore belong to the demonstrative antecedent + *þe* + personal pronoun group. Examples include *Or* 84. 11,

---

[54] See however §2260, where a few examples of relative *se* with first or second person pronoun antecedents are discussed.

Bede 376. 23, *Bo* 4. 33 *Hu se Wisdom lærde þone þe he wolde wæstmbære land sawan þ he atuhge of ærest þa þornas, CP* 43. 6 . . . *hwi forcwið ðonne se ðe him God suelce cræftas giefð ðæt he ne fede his heorde, Deut* 1. 13 *Ceosað eow wise men of eowrum cynne 7 gleawe 7 ða ðe heora drohtnung si afandod*, and *Beo* 440 *ðær gelyfan sceal* || *Dryhtnes dome se þe hine dead nimeð.*[55] There are a few examples with two demonstrative antecedents, e.g. *CP* 67. 24 *Se ðonne bið siwenige se ðe his 7git bið to ðon beorhte scinende ðæt* . . . , *CP* 73. 10 (§2193), *CP* 73. 17 *forðæm hit is wen ðæt se ne mæge oðerra monna scylda ofaðuean se se ðe hine ðonne giet his agena onherigeað*, and

Wid 131	Swa ic þæt symle onfond on þære feringe,
	þæt se biþ leofast londbuendum
	se þe him god syleð gumena rice
	to gehealdenne, þenden he her leofað

(cf. §2122), and a few with an antecedent additional to a demonstrative, e.g. *Dream* 85 . . . *ond ic hælan mæg* || *æghwylcne anra, þara þe him bið egesa to me* and *GDPref* 8 *þæt mæg se mon begytan, se þe his modgeðanc* || *æltowe byþ*. These can be classified as examples of *se'þe* + personal pronoun. But it is less important to distinguish between examples like *Beo* 440 and *Dream* 85, in both of which the *se* element has the case of the principal clause and is followed by *þe* + personal pronoun as a relative combination in the case of the adjective clause, than it is to distinguish between *Beo* 440 and *Dream* 85 on the one hand and examples like *Beo* 1624 *sælace gefeah,* || *mægenbyrþenne þara þe he him mid hæfde*, where both the personal pronouns are completely independent of *þe*; see further §2199.

§2193.   In all the preceding examples, the personal pronoun which is associated with *þe* follows it immediately. The rare exceptions include *CP* 73. 10 *Se bið eac eallenga healede se se ðe eall his mod bið aflogen to gæglbærnesse* and, of course, those examples in which the personal pronoun occurs alone after *and* to signal the case of a co-ordinate relative clause, e.g. *se þe hine . . . and hine . . . and on his* in

PPs 64. 4	He weorðeð eadig, se þe hine ece god
	cystum geceoseð and hine clæne hafað,
	and on his earduncgstowum eardað syððan.

[55] Curme (*JEGP* 10 (1911), 340 ff.), basing much of his argument on modern parallels of dubious relevance, claims that in *Beo* 440 and the like we have not adjective clauses but clauses which are 'asyndetic without a relative'. The problem is terminological rather than syntactical; as Curme himself admits, it cannot be resolved by syntactical criteria.

In

GDPref 8   þæt mæg se mon begytan,   se þe his modgeðanc
              æltowe byþ,   and þonne þurh his ingehygd
              to þissa haligra   helpe geliefeð,
              ond hiora bisene fulgað,   swa þeos boc sagað,

subjects for *geliefeð* and *fulgað* have to be understood from the combination *se þe his*.

§2194. The Exeter Book reads

ChristA 30   . . . gedo usic þæs wyrðe,   þe he to wuldre forlet,
              þa þe heanlice   hweorfan sceoldan
              to þis enge lond,   eðle bescyrede.

Pope (*ASE* 9 (1980), 149-54) makes an attractive case for the emendation *þa we* in line 31. But, if we take the manuscript reading *þa þe*
as a relative referring back to *usic*, we can justify the unusual use of
a relative compound of *se* and *þe* referring back to a first or second
person pronoun antecedent by reference to *ChristA* 18 (§2360) and
can translate '. . . may make us—people who have had to turn away
abjectly into this narrow land, bereft of home—thus worthy, us
whom he admitted to glory'. The poet could have written *þe we* (as
in *ChristA* 25) instead of *þa þe*. But *þa* could be said to have a
generalizing force which is brought out in the translation by the
word 'people'.

d. Se + *personal pronoun*

§2195. There are some examples in which *þæt* + personal pronoun
has been explained as a relative combination. Kock (p. 78) speaks of
'combinations like *þæt he* = *qui*' in examples like *Or* 21. 13 *7 þær is
mid Estum an mægð þæt hi magon cyle gewyrcan* and

Dan 188   þær þry wæron   on þæs þeodnes byrig,
              eorlas Israela,   þæt hie a noldon
              hyra þeodnes dom   þafigan onginnan. . . .

Visser (i, §75) adds

GuthB 923   Nænig forþum wæs,
              þæt he æwiscmod   eft siðade,
              hean, hyhta leas. . . .

In my opinion, *þæt* in these and similar examples is better taken as
a conjunction; see §§2134-44.

§2196. I have noted no examples in the prose of a form of *se* other than *þæt* combining with a personal pronoun to form what might be a relative combination, except *Bede* 374. 15 *Ðæt wolde ða openlicor æteawan seo godcunde arfæstnes, in hu myclum wuldre se Dryhtnes wer Cuðbyrht æfter his deaðe lifde; þæs his lif ær ðam deaðe mid healicum tacnum heofenlicra wundra openade 7 æteawde*, where all manuscripts agree in representing Latin *cuius . . . uita* by *þæs his lif*. But the translator may have intended a new sentence—the one Latin period covering *Bede* 374. 15-24 is represented by three sentences in the translation even if *þæs his* is a relative—and may have written *þæt his lif*; for this construction see §107. There are, however, a few in the poetry. I have discussed these in *Ang.* 81 (1963), 304-5, and *RES* 15 (1964), 134-5.

§2197. We occasionally find *se* taken up by the personal pronoun in the second of two co-ordinate adjective clauses, e.g. *Mart 2* 60. 4 *On þone þrio ond twentegðan dæg þæs monðes bið sancte Iorius tid þæs æðelan weres, þone Datianus se casere seofon gear mid unasæcgendlicum witum hine þreade þæt he Criste wiðsoce ond he næfre hine ofersuiðan meahte*, *ÆGram* 92. 4 *Pronomen ys naman speliend, an dæl ledenspræce se byð underfangen for agenum naman and he underfehð hadas mid fulre gewissunge*, and

El 926   . . .   ic awecce wið ðe
                 oðerne cyning,   se ehteð þin
                 ond he forlæteð   lare þine
                 ond manþeawum   minum folgaþ,
                 ond þec þonne sendeð   in þa sweartestan
                 ond þa wyrrestan   witebrogan . . .

(where, however, *he* does not appear in the third and fourth adjective clauses).

e. General remarks

§2198. The relative combination seen in OE *þe* + personal pronoun —indeclinable particle followed by pronoun showing the case relation—is not restricted to OE; see Jespersen *MnEG* iii. 109-10. It is, however, not common in OE. In the poetry it is found in only some five per cent of *þe* clauses.[56] It is even less common in the prose. Mossé (1945, p. 157) suggests that it was archaic. Its occasional occurrence in Ælfric perhaps argues against this.

---

[56] In OS poetry, it is still more rare, being found (as far as I know) only with the third person pronoun. See Sehrt, p. 592.

§2199. What is odd is the sporadic occurrence of a construction which, according to Wülfing (i, §296), removes ambiguity by using the personal pronoun to make clear the case for which the indeclinable *þe* stands—an observation which appears to be confirmed by the fact that the combination does not occur at all with the *'seþe* relative, in which the *se* element itself has the case of the adjective clause (§2191). But to some extent this removal of ambiguity is illusory, for there are numerous examples in which the immediate sequence *þe* + personal pronoun is not a relative combination. A few examples from Ælfric in which the personal pronoun is independent of *þe* will suffice to illustrate the trap: *ÆHom* 5. 27 . . . *and þam ne þyrst on ecnysse þe of þam wætere drincð þe ic him sylle* '. . . which I give him'; *ÆCHom* ii. 362. 13 . . . *þæt he forgife ece lif ðam eallum ðe ðu him forgeafe* '. . . whom Thou hast given him'; *þone ðe hi* 'whom they' in *ÆCHom* i. 300. 17, below; and *ÆCHom* i. 460. 33 . . . *and ne mæg nateshwon andwyrdan ðam þe him to gebiddað* '. . . those who pray to him'. I am inclined to think that Thorpe fell into this trap when he translated *ÆCHom* i. 300. 17 *Ne geseoð þa arleasan Cristes wuldor, ðe hine ær on life forsawon, ac hi geseoð þonne egefulne þone ðe hi eadmodne forhygedon* 'The impious will not see the glory of Christ, whom they had before despised in life, but they will then see him awful whom humble they had contemned.' It seems to me better to take the first *ðe* as a nominative referring to *þa arleasan* and to translate 'the impious . . . who had despised Him'; Thorpe's interpretation involves an unexpressed subject—a construction which, though possible, seems unlikely here in view of the presence of nom. *hi* 'they' in the second adjective clause. We can perhaps conclude by quoting *Ps(P)* 31. 1 *Eadige beoð þa þe him beoð heora unrihtwisnesse forgifene and heora synna beoð behelede*, Latin *Beati, quorum remissae sunt iniquitates, et quorum tecta sunt peccata*, which poses a nice problem—*þe him* 'to whom' or *þe . . . heora* 'whose'? See §2192.

§2200. The use of this construction may be dictated by stylistic, rhythmic, or metrical, considerations, or by a desire for emphasis. It is interesting to speculate on the reason for its use in

PPs 117. 21   þone sylfan stan   þe hine swyðe ær
               wyrhtan awurpan,   nu se geworden is
               hwommona heagost,

where the antecedent appears first in the case of the adjective clause, is picked up by *hine* in the same case, and is then repeated by *se* in the case of the principal clause.

6. INDEFINITE ADJECTIVE CLAUSES INVOLVING
SE AND/OR *þE*

a. *Introductory remarks*

§2201. In MnE, sentences containing an indefinite adjective clause take various forms. There are those in which the adjective clause is used as what Jespersen calls a 'primary' (see §2103) and in which one word serves as both antecedent and relative, e.g. 'Who steals my purse steals trash' and 'Whoever did that was wrong'. In these the adjective clause comes first if it is the subject of the principal clause. The same is true in examples like 'Whoever did it, he will die', which involve what is to modern speakers a tautologic 'postcedent'. Patterns of this sort are very common in OE prose. So too are those like 'The law will punish whoever offends' and 'He did what(ever) he could', in which the adjective clause is the object of the principal clause.

§2202. But an adjective clause serving as subject of the principal clause may follow part or all of the principal clause in examples in which an antecedent is expressed, e.g. 'He who speaks thus will die' and 'He will die who speaks thus'. Here we can substitute 'The man' or 'Anyone' for 'He'. Similarly, we find 'The law will punish him who offends' and 'He did that which he could'. In examples like these, the adjective clause could (I suppose) be called 'definite' in that it refers to an antecedent. But the fact that the reference of the whole sentence is not to one particular individual and the way in which these constructions are handled in OE make it convenient for us to consider them together. There is a clear difference between the examples dealt with here and those like the following, in which the reference is to one specific individual: *ÆCHom* i. 50. 5 *and se ðe wæs leorningcniht on hade ongann wesan lareow on martyrdome* (Stephen), *ÆCHom* i. 226. 13 *Ac se ðe nolde of ðære rode abrecan, se aras of ðære byrgene* (Christ), *ÆCHom* i. 254. 9 *Se ðe æfre is god, he brincð us yfele to godum mannum* (God), and

Beo 788   Heold hine fæste
                    se þe manna wæs   mægene strengest
                    on þæm dæge   þysses lifes

(Beowulf).

§2203. Here we are concerned only with *se* and *þe* used alone or in combination to introduce indefinite adjective clauses. There are, of course, other possibilities, as we see from *ÆCHom* i. 156. 1–9, where we find *se man þe, se ðe*, and *swa hwa swa. Mutatis mutandis*, the remarks made about definite adjective clauses introduced by *se* and *þe*, alone and in combination, hold for indefinite clauses with antecedents such as *se man, ælc*, and the like. But see further §§ 2214–15, 2225, and 2377. On *swa hwa swa* and similar combinations, see §§ 2363–73.

§ 2204. In OE, as in MnE, three points demand attention: the form of the relative, the presence or absence of an antecedent, and the relative position of the two clauses. But since it is often impossible for us to decide whether the *se* element in a combination of *se* and *þe* is the antecedent or part of the relative, we must beware of equating OE and MnE patterns too rigidly. Thus, there is no point in arguing whether in *LawAbt* 53 *Se þe earm þurhstinð, vi scillingum gebete* we have the equivalent of 'Whoever . . .' or of 'He who . . .', although both Carkeet and Dowsing seem confident it is the latter. Carkeet translates *se þe* as 'he who' (1977, p. 177) and 'him who' (p. 182) and Dowsing (p. 291) writes '*se* ‖ *ðe*'.

§ 2205. In the sections which follow, a major distinction is made between sentences in which both the principal and the adjective clause require the same case and those in which they require different cases. It has already been pointed out in § 2157 that, since *þa* may be nominative or accusative plural, four different sequences may be detected when a clause introduced by *þa þe* refers back to a plural antecedent. To avoid much repetition, it is convenient to state here that the same four sequences occur when plural *þa þe* is used alone with no possible antecedent other than the *þa*. So we find both clauses requiring the nominative in *ÆCHom* i. 130. 23 *þurh eastdæl magon beon getacnode þa ðe on geogoðe to Gode bugað*; both clauses requiring the accusative in *ÆLS* 5. 19 *ac he wolde gehyrtan ða þe se hæðena casere dæghwamlice acwealde*; the principal clause requiring the nominative and the adjective clause the accusative in *LawGer* 7 . . . *gyf hine magan wyldan ða ðe he scolde wealdan*; and the principal clause requiring the accusative and the adjective clause the nominative in *ÆCHom* ii. 20. 5 *and se lig sloh ut of ðam ofne feorr up and forbærnde to deaðe ða ðe hi inn awurpon*. The same holds for clauses introduced by *þæt þe/þætte* 'what(ever)'; see §§ 2126–33.

b. *The adjective clause precedes the principal clause and*
both clauses require the same case

(1) Se *or* þe *alone or with a personal or demonstrative pronoun*
in the principal clause

§2206. It is not surprising that there are few examples of this pattern. Relative þe is unlikely to begin a sentence and initial se 'whoever' could be confused with dem. se. It does, however, occur in *CP*
55. 1 *Se ðonne for ðære gewilnunge swelcra weorca biscopdom ne*
secð, he bið ðonne him self gewita ðæt he wilnað him selfum gielpes.
Or should we detect here the ambiguous demonstrative/relative?

(2) *Combinations of* se *and* þe *alone*

§2207. This pattern occurs spasmodically in the prose, e.g. *LawAbt*
50 *Se þe cinban forslæhð, mid xx scillingum forgelde, ÆCHom* i. 28.
13 *and ða ðe his beboda eallunga forseoð beoð on helle besencte*, and
ChronE 232. 35 (1096) *7 þa þe mid him ferdon þone winter on Puille*
wunedon. The preferred equivalent in the poetry is the pattern seen
in *Beo* 1003 *fremme se þe wille.* Here of course we cannot decide
whether se belongs to the adjective clause (cf. MnE 'whoever') or to
the principal clause (cf. MnE 'he who' and 'those who').

(3) *Combinations of* se *and* þe *with a personal or demonstrative*
pronoun in the principal clause

§2208. These patterns occur in prose of all periods. We find 'postcedent' he in *Bede* 2. 9 *7 se ðe hit gehyreð, he flyhð þæt 7 on-*
scunaþ, ÆCHom i. 326. 8 *Se ðe ne lufað his broðor ðone ðe he*
gesihð, hu mæg he lufian God þone þe he ne gesihð lichamlice?, and
(with *se se ðe*) *CP* 49. 24 *7 se se ðe wolde ðæt hine mon sende, he*
geseah ær hine clænsian.... 'Postcedent' se appears in *Bede* 70. 15,
CP 279. 17 *Ðæt is ðonne se ðe his tungan ne gemidlað, se towierpð*
anmodnesse, ÆCHom i. 232. 32 *and ðam ðe ge ofteoð þa forgife-*
nysse, ðam bið oftogen, and (with *se se ðe*) *CP* 279. 16 *Ac se se ðe*
ðone wer bricð 7 ðæt wæter utforlæt, se bið fruma ðæs geflites.
They appear in successive clauses in *ÆCHom* i. 300. 28 *seðe gelyfð*
and bið gefullod, se bið gehealden; se ðe ne gelyfð, he bið genyðerod.
Here again we cannot be sure whether we have s<u> </u>þe (cf. MnE 'whoever') or se'þe (MnE 'he who'), except perhaps in those examples with
doubled se before þe. There are occasional examples in the poetry,
including

PPs 93. 9   Se ðe ærest ealdum   earan worhte,
                hu se oferhleoður   æfre wurde?,

PPs 124. 1   þa þe on drihten heora   dædum getreowað,
                     hi beoð on Sionbeorge   swyþe gelice,

and

Met 16. 1   Se þe wille anwald agon,   ðonne sceal he ærest tilian
                     þæt he his selfes   on sefan age
                     anwald innan. . . .

c. The adjective clause precedes the principal clause and the two clauses require different cases

(1) Se, þe, *or* se *in the case of the adjective clause* + þe, *alone*

§2209. These relatives can—in theory at any rate—be in or represent only one case in any one sentence. So when one of them appears in an example like *Bede(O)* 58. 6 *7 se þe him hyrsum beon wolde, buton tweon he gehet ecne gefean on heofonum*, the possibility of 'ellipsis' arises; *Bede(B)* 58. 6 in fact has *him* after *gehet*. I therefore postpone treatment of possible examples until §§2315-27.

(2) Se *or* þe *with a personal or demonstrative pronoun in the principal clause*

§2210. I have noted this pattern spasmodically with *se*, e.g. *CP(H)* 31. 22 *Se ðonne to halgum hade becymð . . . betre him wære ðæt . . .*—MSS *C* have þe after *ðonne*—and *CP* 55. 1 *Se ðonne for ðære gewilnunge swelcra weorca biscopdom ne secð, he bið ðonne him self gewita ðæt he wilnað him selfum gielpes.*

(3) Se *in the case of the adjective clause* + þe *with a personal or demonstrative pronoun in the principal clause*

§2211. This pattern, which I have observed in early and late prose, presents no real difficulty. We can produce anacoluthia (§3878) by taking the *se* element as antecedent—'He who . . . to him . . .'. This is unnecessary; but see §§2204 and 2213. Examples include (with a personal pronoun) *CP* 85. 21 *Ða ðe hine onfengon he salde him anwald . . .*, *Bede* 78. 15 . . . *forhwon þonne, se þe blodryne þrowað monaðaðle, ne alefað hire in Drihtnes cirican gongan?*, *ÆCHom* i. 212. 2 *Se ðe gewemð Godes tempel, God hine fordeð*, and *ÆCHom* i. 368. 24 *Se ðe ne bytlað of ðam grundwealle, his weorc hryst to micclum lyre*, and (with a demonstrative) *ÆCHom* i. 6. 5 *þa ðe his leasungum gelyfað, þam he arað.*

(4) Se *in the case of the principal clause* + þe

§2212. I have so far noted no examples of the type ☆*se þe se Hælend Crist lufað, (he) sceal Crist lufian.* In *ÆHom(F)* 6. 10 *La leof hlaford, se þe þu lufast ys nu geuntrumod*—where MSS *C* and *H* have *þone* for *se*—the reference is not indefinite but to Lazarus; see §2154.

d. The adjective clause precedes the principal clause and se + þe is the equivalent of 'if anyone'

§2213. Strictly speaking we have anacoluthia in examples like *ÆCHom* i. 390. 14 *Se ðe eow hrepað, hit me bið swa egle swylce he hreppe ða seo mines eagan.* But indefinite adjective clauses and conditional clauses are very similar in semantic value; cf. *ÆCHom* ii. 90. 23 *Ælc ðæra ðe gehyrð þæt heofenlice word and he hit ne understent, ðonne cymð se yfela and gelæhð hit*, note the variation in *LawAbt* 17 *Gif man in mannes tun ærest geirneþ, vi scillingum gebete; se þe æfter irneþ, iii scillingas; siððan gehwylc scilling*, and see further §§2108, 2372, 3699-702, and 3882-3.

e. Only an antecedent precedes the adjective clause

(1) *Both clauses require the same case*

§2214. As already noted, the patterns discussed in §§2207 and 2208 could be included here. Apart from them, we find sentences with no 'postcedent' in the principal clause, e.g. *Matt(WSCp)* 7. 24 *Eornustlice ælc þæra þe ðas mine word gehyrð 7 þa wyrcð byþ gelic þam wisan were se hys hus ofer stan getimbrode*[57] and *ÆCHom* i. 362. 20 *Ælc ðæra ðe hine onhefð bið geeadmet;*[58] with a 'post-cedent' demonstrative, e.g. *Matt(WSCp)* 7. 26 *7 ælc þæra þe gehyrþ ðas mine word 7 þa ne wyrcð se byþ gelic þam dysigan men þe getimbrode hys hus ofer sandceosel*; and (more commonly) with a 'postcedent' personal pronoun, e.g. *ÆCHom* i. 260. 14 *And se man ðe Gode gecwemð, he bið Godes bearn, ÆCHom* ii. 540. 1 *and we mennisce men, þe on eallum woruldþingum syngiað, on eallum ðingum we beoð eft gewitnode*, and *ÆCHom* ii. 228. 8 *Ælc ðæra ðe synne wyrcð, he bið þonne ðære synne ðeow.* Clauses in which the antecedent + the adjective clause is the object of the sentence also

---

[57] This and the other examples with *ælc þæra þe* are quoted here because (despite the intervention of gen. pl. *þæra*) the antecedent *ælc* and the relative *þe* are both nominative and the whole expression could be replaced by *se (man) þe* or *ælc man (se) þe*; cf. *ÆCHom* i. 66. 4 (§2222).

[58] The fact that this sentence goes on *and se ðe hine geeadmet bið geuferod* illustrates both the point made in the first sentence of this paragraph and that made in fn. 57.

occur, e.g. *Josh* 1. 3 and *John(WSCp)* 12. 50 *þa þing þe ic sprece, ic sprece*. . . . The equivalents of these occur in MnE without 'postcedents' and are similar in meaning to sentences containing 'whoever' or 'what-(ever)'. Compare *ÆCHom* i. 528. 35 (§2371) and *Num* 23. 26.

(2) *The two clauses require different cases*

§2215. As I have pointed out in §2211, it is unnecessary to import the idea of anacoluthia into sentences like *ÆCHom* i. 212. 2 *Se ðe gewemð Godes tempel, God hine forðeð* by taking *se* as antecedent 'He' or 'that (one)'. But it is certainly possible, for the idea cannot be avoided when we consider examples like *ÆCHom* ii. 528. 9 *Eft, se man ðe went his earan þæt he ne gehyre Godes æ, his gebed bið Gode andsæte, ÆCHom* i. 512. 2 . . . *ga to ðære sæ and wurpe ut ðinne angel and þone fisc ðe hine hraðost forswelhð, geopena his muð, ÆCHom* i. 250. 4 *Ælc ðæra ðe geornlice bitt and þære bene ne geswicð, þam getiðað God þæs ecan lifes, ÆCHom* i. 214. 19 *and ealle ða wundra þe he worhte, on eallum he herede and wuldrode his Fæder naman*, and *ÆHom* 5. 143 and 5. 144 (both in §900).

f. The adjective clause follows (part of) the principal clause and both clauses require the same case

(1) Se *or* þe *alone*

§2216. Here one word functions as both antecedent and relative. This is not a common pattern. However, examples which refer to persons include (with *se*) *LawAf* 19. 1 *Gif hi hie ne gesamnien, gielde se ðæs wæpnes onlah þæs weres ðriddan dæl 7 þæs wites ðriddan dæl, Beo* 142 *heold hyne syðþan || fyr ond fæstor se þæm feonde ætwand, El* 1201, and

Rid 55. 14		Nu me þisses gieddes
	ondsware ywe,	se hine on mede
	wordum secgan	hu se wudu hatte,

and (with *þe*) *LS* 34. 147 *and her on gehendnysse syndon þe þine deorlingas beon sceoldon, HomU* 21. 4. 11 *and þær wurdan hale þe ær wæran limmlaman, ChronC* 162. 13 (1042) *Her gefor Harðacnut . . . 7 he færinga feoll to þære eorðan . . . 7 hine gelæhton ðe þar neh wæron*, and

Beo 138	þa wæs eaðfynde	þe him elles hwær
	gerumlicor	ræste sohte,
	bed æfter burum.	

On *Max i* 183 see Mitchell 1964a, pp. 131–2.

§2217. On *þæt* 'what(ever)', see §§2126–33.

(2) *Combinations of* se *and* þe *alone*

§2218. Here, as in §2207, we cannot decide whether *se* belongs to the principal or to the adjective clause. Examples include *Bede(Ca)* 158. 30 ... *forðon þe munecas wæron þa þe hider coman to læranne, ÆCHom* i. 8. 3 *ac God geswutelað his wundra þurh ðone þe he wile, Beo* 1003 *fremme se þe wille, Rid* 59. 15 *Ræde, se þe wille* || . . . , and *And* 161 *þa wæs gemyndig se ðe middangeard* || *gestaðelode.* . . . The examples with plural *þa þe* in §2205, in which both clauses require the same *case* (as opposed to the same *form*), are relevant here.

§2219. On *þætte, þæt þe*, and *þæs þe*, 'whatever', see §§2126-33.

(3) Se *or* þe *preceded by a personal or demonstrative pronoun antecedent*

§2220. Three examples of this pattern will suffice: *Or* 21. 3 *7 se nimð þone læstan dæl se nyhst þæm tune þæt feoh geærneð, Or* 88. 4 *7 þær wurdon mid hungre acwealde, þær heora þa ne gehulpe þa þær æt ham wæron*, and *Exod* 21. 19 . . . *he bið unscyldig þe hine sloh.*

(4) *Combinations of* se *and* þe *preceded by a personal or demonstrative pronoun antecedent*

§2221. Again, it is sufficient to exemplify this pattern: *CP* 279. 13 *Se forlæt ut ðæt wæter, se ðe his tungan stemne on unnyttum wordum lætt toflowan, CP* 41. 6 *ðylæs ða gongen on sua frecne stige, ða ðe ne magon uncwaciende gestondan on emnum felda, Deut* 27. 20 *Sy se awyrged se ðe hæme mid his fæder wife, LawAf* 12 *Ac gif he hire ne recce, se ðe hie bohte* . . . , and

Sat 303   Forþon se bið eadig   se ðe æfre wile
                  man oferhycgen,   meotode cweman,
                  synne adwæscan.

We find *se* . . . *se se þe* in *CP* 62. 8 *Oððe hu dear se gripan on ða scire ðæt he ærendige oðrum monnum to Gode, se se þe hiene selfne hiwcuðne ne ongit Gode ðurh his lifes geearnunga?*; cf. §2122.

(5) Se, þe, *or combinations of* se *and* þe, *preceded by other antecedents*

§2222. The examples which follow are to be compared with those in §2214: *CP* 9. 15 *forðæm hi his sume ðorfton, ða ðe Lædenspræce læste cuðon, Or* 20. 36 *ðonne cymeð se man se þæt swiftoste hors hafað to þæm ærestan dæle, Deut* 27. 17 *Beo se man awyrged ðe ne arwurðað his fæder 7 his modor, Deut* 27. 22 *Sy ðe man awyrged se ðe hæme wið his swustor, ÆCHom* i. 66. 4 *On idel bið ælc man gedrefed seðe hordað . . . , ÆCHom* i. 14. 32,

Beo 3071	. . . þæt se secg wære	synnum scildig,
	hergum geheaðerod,	hellbendum fæst,
	wommum gewitnad,	se ðone wong strude . . . ,

and

Dream 112	Frineð he for þære mænige	hwær se man sie,
	se ðe for dryhtnes naman	deaðes wolde
	biteres onbyrigan,	swa he ær on ðam beame dyde.

> g. *The adjective clause follows (part of) the principal clause*
> *and the two clauses require different cases*

(1) Se, þe, *or se in the case of the adjective clause* + þe, *alone*

§2223. Here too, as in the examples discussed in §2209, the possibility of 'ellipsis' presents itself. So I discuss these examples in §§2315-27.

(2) Se, þe, *or se in the case of the adjective clause* + þe, *with*
a personal or demonstrative pronoun in the principal clause

§2224. A few examples of these patterns will suffice. *Law ICn(Ld)* 7 . . . *ne on his mæges lafe se swa neah sib wære,* where the other manuscripts have þe, *Bede* 230. 10 . . . *þæt he meahte swiðe gefultumed beon in heora dæghwamlicum gebeodum þa ðe in þære stowe Drihtne þeowdon, ÆCHom* i. 6. 3 *þa ofslihð se deofol ðe him wiðstandað* (where I follow Thorpe in taking *þa* as a demonstrative) *and hi þonne farað . . . to heofenan rice, ÆCHom* ii. 368. 6 *Ne bidde ic na for ðisum anum, ac eac swilce for ða ðe on me gelyfað þurh heora word* (but see §§1186 and 2205), and

Beo 183		Wa bið þæm ðe sceal
	þurh sliðne nið	sawle bescufan
	in fyres fæþm,	frofre ne wenan,
	wihte gewendan!

(3) Se, þe, *or se in the case of the adjective clause* + þe, *preceded*
by other antecedents

§2225. The examples which follow are to be compared with those in §§2214 and 2222: *Or* 176. 19 . . . *mid þæm þæt hie mæst eall ut awurpon þæt ðæron wæs, CP* 75. 11 *he sceal bion for eaðmodnesse hira gefera ælces ðara ðe wel doo* (in this and the following example I take the relative as *þe*; see §2214 fn. 57),

Beo 1460

næfre hit æt hilde ne swac
manna ængum   þara þe hit mid mundum bewand,
se ðe gryresiðas   gegan dorste,
folcstede fara,

and

PPs 60. 4   yrfe þu sealdest   anra gehwylcum
se þe naman ðinne   þurh neod forhtað.

7. RELATIVE PRONOUNS AND PARTITIVE GENITIVES

§2226. The relative *þæt(te)* sometimes governs or appears to govern a partitive genitive. In examples such as *Or* 32. 19 *7 swa þeah þæt þær to lafe wearð þara Thelescisa hi hiora lond ofgeafan, CP* 75. 20 . . . *forðæm ðæt he mæge adrygean of oðra monna heortan ðæt ðæron fules sie*, and *CP* 191. 5 *Eac sculun wietan ða ofer oðre gesettan ðæt ðæt hie unaliefedes ðurhteoð . . . sua manegra wieta hie beoð wyrðe*, where there is no expressed antecedent, *þæt* means 'what' and we have to say that the genitives are dependent on it. The same is probably true in *CP* 195. 20 *Sua hit is cynn ðætte ða sien ðe fore oðre beon sculon . . . 7 ðætte tælwyrðes on him sie, ðæt hie ðæt tælen* '. . . and what is blameworthy in them, that they blame that'; the last *þæt* is more likely to be an emphatic recapitulatory demonstrative than an antecedent and we can scarcely separate *ðætte* and argue whether *tælwyrðes* is dependent on *ðæt* or *te/þe*.

§2227. But in *CP* 213. 7 *ða ongon he æresð herigean on him ðæt ðæt he fæsðrædes wiste, CP* 61. 14 *Ne sceal he naht unaliefedes don, ac ðæt ðætte oðre menn unaliefedes dot he sceal wepan*, and

Met 20. 117   Ne þincð me þæt wundur   wuhte þe læsse
þæt ðios eorðe mæg   and egorstream,
swa ceald gesceaft,   cræfta nane
ealles adwæscan   þæt þæt him on innan sticað
fyres gefeged   mid frean cræfte,

ðæt ðæt(te) means 'that which', we have antecedent + relative, and it is arguable which of the two governs the partitive genitive. The same question arises with the sequence *eal þæt* in examples like *Or* 18. 25 *Eal þæt his man aþer oððe ettan oððe erian mæg, þæt lið wið ða sæ* (cf. *CP* 195. 20 in §2226), *Or* 38. 8 . . . *þæt he ægþer sloh ge ða menn ge ða nytenu ge eall þæt on þæm lande wæs weaxendes*

7 growendes, CP 155. 11 . . . *ðætte him bið eall cuð ðæt hie unaliefedes ðenceað,* and

Jud 338   . . .   ond eal þæt se rinca baldor
                     swiðmod sinces ahte   oððe sundoryrfes,
                     beaga ond beorhtra maðma. . . .

For more examples see Wülfing, i, § 286, and Shipley, pp. 92–3.

§ 2228. The same problem also arises in examples like

ChristC 1032   Hafað eall on him
                     þæs þe he on foldan   in fyrndagum,
                     godes oþþe gales,   on his gæste gehlod . . .

and

PPs 75. 4   ne þær wiht fundan,   þa þe welan sohtan,
                     þæs þe hi on handum   hæfdan godes.

But here the solution is perhaps less in doubt. Shipley (p. 92) writes
of *ChristC* 1032:

To make *godes* depend on *þe* would surely force the construction; the natural
relation is *eall godes oððe gales, þæs þe* (*þæs þe* rel.). The closeness of the relation between *eall* and a following rel., would tend to effect the transfer of a
limiting gen. after the rel. clause or within it,—positions familiar even in Modern
English.

I agree, with the reservation that, if *þæs þe* were genitive only in anticipation of *godes oþþe gales,* the latter could be dependent on the
former; cf. here § 457. Evidence has been given in § 1921a for the
proposition that elements belonging to the principal clause could in
OE find themselves in the subordinate clause. However, the distinction is of grammatical rather than of semantic importance, for,
whichever view we adopt, the natural translation of

JDay ii 135   Ðonne eallum beoð   ealra gesweotolude
                     digle geþancas   on þære dægtide,
                     eal þæt seo heorte   hearmes geþohte
                     oððe seo tunge   to teonan geclypede
                     oþþe mannes hand   manes gefremede
                     on þystrum scræfum   þinga on eorðan;
                     eal þæt hwæne sceamode   scylda on worulde,
                     þæt he ænigum men   ypte oððe cyðde,
                     þonne bið eallum   open ætsomne,
                     gelice alyfed   þæt man lange hæl

is 'all the evil that . . . all the wickedness that . . . all the sins that
. . .'.

§2229. A similar situation occasionally arises with combinations of *se* and *þe* other than *þætte*, e.g. *ÆCHom* i. 352. 15 *Iohannes eac be Godes dihte fullode ða ðe him to comon ðæra Iudeiscra ðeoda*, which may mean 'whoever of the Jews . . .' or 'those of the Jews who . . .'; with *þe* alone, e.g.

GenA 2372   ...   heht þæt segn wegan
          heah gehwilcne   þe his hina wæs
          wæpnedcynnes,

PPs 89. 11, *ChristC* 1322 . . . *þone lytlan fyrst þe her lifes sy*, and

Jud 48   ...   þæt se bealofulla
      mihte wlitan þurh,   wigena baldor,
      on æghwylcne   þe ðær inne com
      hæleða bearna . . . ;

and with forms of *se* other than *þæt*, e.g.

GenA 2142   ...   nis woruldfeoh,
      þe ic me agan wille,
      sceat ne scilling,   þæs ic on sceotendum,
      þeoden mæra,   þines ahredde,
      æðelinga helm

and

GenB 618   Gif giet þurh cuscne siodo
      læst mina lara,   þonne gife ic him þæs leohtes genog
      þæs ic þe swa godes   gegired hæbbe.

In

GenB 435   Se þe þæt gelæsteð,   him bið lean gearo
      æfter to aldre,   þæs we her inne magon
      on þyssum fyre forð   fremena gewinnan,

fremena might be dependent on *lean*, but is more likely to go with *þæs*—'a reward for what of benefits . . .' or 'a reward (consisting) of what of benefits . . .'. These last three examples are further discussed in §§2317, 2313, and 2316, respectively.

§2230. It is possible to take *of heora cynne* with *ealle* in *ÆCHom* i. 216. 28 *and seo godcundnys wæs on ðære hwile on helle, and gewrað þone ealdan deofol, and him of anam Adam, þone frum-sceapenan man, and his wif Euan, and ealle ða ðe of heora cynne Gode ær gecwemdon* and to translate 'all those from their race who had pleased God'. But 'all those who from their race had pleased God' is equally acceptable.

8. RELATIVE PRONOUNS, PREPOSITIONS, AND POSTPOSITIONS

a. The norms

§2231. Certain theoretical problems which arise here and also in sentences not involving relative pronouns are discussed in §§1060-80. However, we can summarize the 'rules' given in §§1062 and 1079 thus: in both prose and poetry, the relatives *se* and *'seþe* are in general preceded by prepositions, while the relatives *þe* and *se'þe* are followed by postpositions (for this term see §§1062 and 1076). The nom. and acc. sg. neut. *þæt* requires special attention; see §§2236-43. On the placing of prepositions in relation to the other elements in the clause, see §§1154-76.

§2232. One example of each pattern from the prose and from the poetry must suffice: *(se,* excluding *þæt) ÆCHom* ii. 292. 9 *þæt fyr getacnode ðone Halgan Gast, ðurh ðone we beoð gehalgode* and

Ex 572

> ealle him brimu blodige þuhton,   Gesawon hie þær weallas standan,
> þurh þa heora beadosearo wægon;

('seþe, excluding *þætte* and *þæt þe) ÆCHom* i. 346. 11 *Hwæt sind þas buton ðrymsetl heora Scyppendes, on ðam ðe he wunigende mannum demð?* and

PPs 143. 10   . . . mid tyn strengum   getogen hearpe,
> on þære þe ic þe singe   swiþe geneahhe;

(þe) ÆCHom i. 14. 10 *and mid þære eaðelican gehyrsumnysse þu geearnast heofenan rices myrhðu and þone stede þe se deofol of afeoll* and

GenA 961

> Gesæton þa æfter synne   sorgfulre land,
> eard and eðyl   unspedigran
> fremena gehwilcre   þonne se frumstol wæs
> þe hie æfter dæde of   adrifen wurdon;

and *(se'þe) Bede(T)* 376. 2 *Swylce eac ealle ða hrægl þa ðe he mid gegearwad wæs, nales ðæt an þæt hie ungewemmed wæron ah swylce eac . . .* and

Dream 97

> . . . onwreoh wordum   þæt hit is wuldres beam,
> se ðe ælmihtig god   on þrowode
> for mancynnes   manegum synnum.[59]

---

[59] *Se'þe* examples are not common. I have found none in Ælfric's *Catholic Homilies.* However, the example in *Dream* 97 seems certain and I believe that *þa* in *þa ðe* in *Bede(T)* 376. 2 is nominative with *ða hrægl*, not accusative with *mid*; that would require **ða hrægl*

§2233. That *se'þe* follows the same rule as *þe* is not surprising, since —grammatically at any rate; see §2161—only the *þe* element belongs to the adjective clause. But the necessity of distinguishing the *se'þe* relatives (where an antecedent other than the *se* element is involved) from those examples in which the demonstrative as sole antecedent is followed by the relative *þe* is clearly apparent here; consider *ÆCHom* ii. 306. 21 *Cristene men sceolon soðlice abugan to gehalgodre rode, on ðæs Hælendes naman, forðan ðe we nabbað ða ðe he on ðrowade* (where *þe* is governed by a postposition), *ÆCHom* ii. 480. 4 *þis fyr sceal gecyrran to þam ðe hit asende* (where the demonstrative is governed by a preposition), and *ÆCHom* i. 192. 23 *. . . þæt he wolde mancynn ahreddan þurh ðone þe he ealle gesceafta mid geworhte, ðurh his agen Bearn* (where the two elements are governed by *þurh* and *mid* respectively).

§2234. When a relative combination of *þe* + a personal pronoun is governed by a preposition, the preposition immediately precedes the personal pronoun; for examples see §2190.

§2235. The relative *þe* is often found as a dative of place or time without a postposition after an antecedent which is governed by a preposition, e.g. *Or* 5. 30 *. . . on þæm fiftan geare þe Marius wæs consul* (see further Liggins 1970, p. 316), *ChronA* 91. 3 (897) *þreo asæton on ða healfe þæs deopes ðe ða Deniscan scipu aseten wæron, ÆCHom* i. 98. 32 *. . . on þam dæge þe þæt Ebreisce folc heora geares getel onginnað;* cf. (with the accusative) *Beo* 2399 *. . . oð ðone anne dæg,* ‖ *þe he wið þam wyrme gewegan sceolde.* But a postposition is occasionally found in such contexts, e.g. *ÆCHom* i. 28. 10 *. . . mid þam ylcan lichaman þe he on þrowode* and *ChristC* 1075 *. . . of þam eðle þe hi on lifdon* (where the preposition and the postposition are different) and *ÆCHom* i. 246. 12 *God . . . abær hine to ðam lande þe he to sceolde, PPs* 141. 4 *On þyssum grenan wege, þe ic gange on . . . ,* and

Jud 125   þa seo snotere mægð   snude gebrohte
                þæs herewæðan   heafod swa blodig
                on ðam fætelse   þe hyre foregenga,
                blachleor ides,   hyra begea nest,
                ðeawum geðungen,   þyder on lædde,

mid þa ðe. . . . The Latin (442. 31) has *sed et uestimenta omnia, quibus indutum erat, non solum intemerata uerum etiam . . . parebant,* which may account for what I regard as MS *C*'s ungrammatical *eall þa hrægl þæm þe he mid gegearwed wæs,* with the preposition after the *'seþe* relative. In this connection it is worth noting that MS *O* has *eall þa hrægl þa. þe . . .* (one erasure) and MS *B þa hrægl þe. . . .* MS *Ca* has *eall ða hrægel þa ðe,* so agreeing (in the essentials) with MS *O* and with MS *T.*

(where they are the same). However, I would not follow Grossmann (p. 18) or Anklam (pp. 19 ff.) in speaking of repetition ('Wieder-holung') of prepositions in examples like the last three or Wülfing (i, §300) in suggesting that a preposition is not repeated in *Or* 5. 30 (above) and the like. Nor would it be helpful to speak of 'omission' of *of* governing *þe* in *Or* 72. 13 . . . *7 eac þa geata þe hie ut of Rome-byrig to þæm gefeohte ferdon*; here *of* seems almost to be used *apo koinou* with both *þe* and *Romebyrig*. For *þe* as a dative in other con-texts, see §§2147-8.

b. þæt, þæt þe, *and* þætte

§2236. In MnE, relative 'that' is followed by postpositions, e.g. 'This is the book that I told you about'. A preference for the post-position is already apparent with OE *þæt* when it is used as a relative.

§2237. There are occasional examples in the prose and poetry in which *þæt, þæt þe*, and *þætte*, behave like *se* and *'seþe* in being pre-ceded by prepositions, e.g. *Or* 86. 15 *swa ic eac ealles þises mid-dangeardes na maran dæles ne angite buton ðætte on twam on-wealdum gewearð, on þæm ærestan 7 on ðæm siþemestan, ÆCHom* ii. 364. 14 . . . *fram ðam godcundum worde ðurh þæt ðe ealle þing sind geworhte, ChronA* 206. 8 (1070) *þa þa hi þyder comon 7 umbe oþer þing gesprecon hæfdon umbe þ hi sprecan woldon . . . , ChristC* 1299 *synbyrþenne, ‖ firenweorc berað, on þæt þa folc seoð*, and

PPs 106. 19   He him wisfæstlic   word onsende,
                 þurh þæt hi hrædlice   hælde wæron
                 and of heora forwyrde   wurdan generede.

§2238. But the pattern *þæt* . . . postposition dominates. There are occasional examples in which the syntax suggests that *þæt* introduces a clause of purpose, e.g. *LawAf* 19 *Gif hwa his wæpnes oðrum onlæne þæt he mon mid ofslea* . . . and *CP* 467. 23 *Ac ic ðe bidde ðæt ðu me on ðæm scipgebroce ðisses andweardan lifes sum bred geræce ðinra gebeda, ðæt ic mæge on sittan oð ic to londe cume*, in which *mid* and *on* can be taken as adverbs and in both of which the verb of the *þæt* clause is subjunctive, and *Bede* 320. 3 *þa heht heo sume broðor faran 7 þone stan secan þæt mon meahte þa ðruh of geheawan 7 gewyrcan*, where *þæt* obviously cannot agree with *þone stan*, though the Latin . . . *lapidem de quo* . . . has a relative pronoun, which might account for MS *B*'s *þe*. There are more in which the word in post-position may be taken as an adverb and the *þæt* clause as final, e.g. *Or* 80. 7 and *Or* 286. 9 *Æfter þæm he gegaderade fierd*

. . . 7 bebead, þonne he eft wære eastane hamweard, þæt mon hæfde anfiteatrum geworht æt Hierusalem, þæt he mehte Godes þeowas on don, þæt hie dior þærinne abite. But in the latter the Latin has a relative *ampitheatrum . . . in quo.* In most examples, however, this solution is not possible either because of the run of the sentence alone, e.g. *Solil* 26. 10 . . . *gyf ic geseo and habbe þæt ðæt ic æfter swince,* or because of this and because the verb is indicative, e.g. *CP* 331. 24 *Ðæt ierfe ðæt ge ærest æfter hiegiað, æt siðesðan hit við bedæled ælcre bledsunge* and *CP* 331. 18 . . . *he forgiet ðæt grin ðæt he mid awierged wirð;* cf. *CP* 331. 20 7 *he ne geliefð ðæs grines ðe he mid gebrogden wyrð.*

§2239. Those sentences in which *þæt* serves or seems to serve as a relative governed by a postposition may be divided into four groups: those in which the antecedent of *þæt* is a noun, e.g. *CP* 331. 24 and *CP* 331. 18 (both in §2238), *Or* 202. 2 7 *locian hwæþer he þæt land gecneowe þæt hie toweard wæron,* and *CP* 419. 31 . . . *ðonne hi ðæt yfel mid ondetnesse him of aweorpað ðætte hira modes innað yfele 7 hefiglice mid gefylled wæs;* those in which a demonstrative antecedent *þæt* is separated from the relative, e.g. *WHom* 13. 78 7 *se ðe þæt deð þæt ic ymbe spece;* those in which we have *þæt þæt* 'that which', e.g. *Solil* 26. 10 (§2238) and *CP* 449. 14 *Hie sellað wið to lytlum weorðe ðæt ðæt hie meahton hefonrice mid gebycggan;* and those in which *þæt* serves as both antecedent and relative, e.g. *Bo* 120. 19 *Ac ic ondræde þ ic forlæte þ wyt ær æfter spyredon.* More examples are quoted in the sections which follow.

§2240. Disagreements of gender like those in *Bede* 320. 3 (§2238) are rare; the neuter form is almost always appropriate in the context. But *þæt* frequently seems to be used without regard to the case which the word in post-position usually governs when used as a preposition. This fact has led to the suggestion that *þæt* was used carelessly (Wülfing, ii, §615) or that it was already felt as 'un terme invariable' (Bacquet, p. 346 fn. 3). The evidence for these propositions is not as overwhelming as might at first sight appear. We can find support for the sequences acc. *þæt . . . æfter* as in *Bo* 120. 19 (§2239; see §1179); acc. *þæt . . . mid* as in *CP* 331. 18 (§2238; see §1195); acc. *þæt . . . on* with *on* denoting rest in a place as in *Or* 286. 9 (§2238) and *Max i* 133 *þæt is rice god* ‖ *. . .* ‖ *se us eal forgeaf þæt we on lifgaþ* (see §1177(4)); and acc. *þæt . . . to* as in *CP* 351. 7 . . . *sua him læs licað ðæt ðæt hie to gelaðode sindon* (see §1215). But to the best of my knowledge acc. *þæt . . . of* as in *Bede* 320. 3 (§2238) and *Or* 80. 7 7 *ealles his heres wæs swelc ungemet*

*þæt mon eaðe cweþan mehte ðæt hit wundor wære, hwær hie landes
hæfden þæt hie mehten an gewician, oþþe wæteres þæt hie mehten
him þurst of adrincan* remains without the support of any examples
in which *of* takes the accusative.

§ 2241. It would of course be easy to suggest that *þæt* is an error for
þe, perhaps through mistaken resolution of *þ*. (I have already rejected
the idea that *þ* could actually signify *þe*; see § 1930.) It is true that
in some examples the manuscripts fluctuate between *þæt* and *þe*, e.g.
CP(H) 197. 13 . . . *bi ðæm scræfe ðæt he oninnan wæs* (where MSS
C have *ðe*) and *Bede(T)* 384. 26 . . . *ðæt ealond . . . ðæt we ær ut of
gongende wæron* (where MS *B* and *C* have *þ*, MS *Ca* has *ðe*, and MS
O has *þ* altered to *þe*). In the light of these fluctuations and of those
seen in examples like *CP* 331. 18 and *CP* 331. 20 (§ 2238) and
ÆHom 5. 256 *þa heahfæderas and þa witegan þe embe þone Hælend
cyddon, þa wæron þa sæderas þe seowon Godes lare, and þæt gelyfede folc þe þa gelyfde on God wæs þæt gerip soðlice þæt Crist
embe sæde* . . . , it is perhaps tempting to dispose of the examples of
relative *þæt* + postposition by emendation to *þe*. But in view of their
number—in my collection of examples, which is not complete for
the prose, sentences involving relative *þæt* + a postposition are more
common than those involving preposition + relative *þæt* in early and
late prose and in the poetry—and of the fact that the idiom is now
the established one, this temptation must be rejected.

§ 2242. Perhaps when we look at the examples involving the sequence
þæt . . . of in § 2240 and at others like *ÆCHom* i. 446. 20 *þurh ure
ealdan modor Euan us wearð heofonan rices geat belocen, and eft
ðurh Marian hit is us geopenod, þurh þæt heo sylf nu to dæg wuldor-
fullice inn ferde*, we may be inclined to argue that even when we
have to take *þæt* as a relative, the element in post-position is an
adverb. Be that as it may—and the problem has already been aired
in § 1080—we are bound to see in these examples forerunners of
the modern use. It is, however, interesting to note that the OE examples are more numerous in the early prose (see Wülfing, ii. 311
and 418, and van der Gaaf, *EStudies*, 12 (1930), 5) than in the later
prose, where (like Anklam, pp. 44-6, 49-50, and 53) I have found
none in Ælfric's *Catholic Homilies* or *Lives of the Saints*. The only
example in Ælfric so far known to me is in *ÆHom* 5. 256 (§ 2241).
There are occasional examples in Wulfstan, e.g. *WHom* 13. 78
(§ 2239) and *WHom* 13. 16 *His wylla is þæt we . . . þæt geearnian
þæt we to gelaðode syn*; in the later *Chronicle*, e.g. *ChronD* 147. 20
(1016) *7 slogon eall þ hi to comon*; and in the later *Laws*, e.g.

LawIICn 23 . . . *hwanan him come þæt him man æt befehþ.* But on Anklam's figures (ibid.) they become more frequent in eME texts such as homilies, the *Ormulum*, and the *Ancrene Wisse.* The apparent decline in lOE is odd. But the construction is continuously if sporadically attested in OE prose. Perhaps it was a colloquial or non-standard one which offended Ælfric's grammatical sensibilities.

§2243. Examples from the poetry not already quoted are to be found in *Dan* 418, *ChristA* 326, *PPs* 88. 3, *Met* 28. 79, and perhaps *ChristC* 1282, *Jud* 46, and *Beo* 1140 (see Mitchell 1968*c*, p. 295).

c. *Other exceptions*

(1) *Forms of* se *other than* þæt + *postposition*

§2244. The only example of this pattern which has so far come to my notice is

Rid 6.6   Hwilum ic monigra   mod arete,
                   hwilum ic frefre   þa ic ær winne on
                   feorran swiþe.

This is, however, a special case, for *þa* does duty as both antecedent and relative—see further §§2216 and 2319-21—and *on* could not precede *þa*, since it governs the relative only.

(2) *Preposition* + *þe?*

§2245. There are occasional examples in the prose and one in the poetry in which *þe* seems to be preceded by a preposition. However, in all those in my collections, *þe* can be taken as the 2nd pers. pron. 'thee'. Three of them come from one passage in *Solil*, viz. *Solil* 5. 19 *Ðe ic bydde, drihten, þu þe æart seo hehsten soðfæstnesse and for þe hyt is soð æall þætte soð is. Ic þe bydde, drihten, ðu þe æart se hehstan wysdom and þurh þe sint wyse æalle þa þe wyse sint. Ic þe bidde þe, drihten, þu þe æart riht lif and þurh þe lybbað æall þa þe lybbað.* In all three the Latin has relative pronouns in the formula *in quo et a quo et per quem.* A fourth example occurs in the same paragraph, viz. *Solil* 6. 5 *Ðu þe æart þæt andgitlice leoht, þurh þe man ongit,* which represents the same Latin formula. Bacquet's suggestion (p. 347 fn. 2) that in the last *þe* may be for *þæt* need not detain us, as the emendation is impossible in the first three. Carnicelli (pp. 27-8) argues that because the Latin has a relative it is better to take *þe* as a relative rather than as a personal pronoun. This argument, which enshrines an old fallacy, can carry no weight here because the formula *in quo et a quo et per quem* occurs in the original of the two sentences which come between the first three and the last one quoted above, viz. *Solil* 6. 2 *þu eart seo hehste gesælð and for þe sint geselige æalle þa þe geselige synt. þu æart þæt hehste god and se hehsta wlite and þurh þe is god and wlitig eall þætte god ys and wlityg.* Here *þe* in *for þe* and *þurh þe* cannot be a relative.

§2246. I take *þe* as a personal pronoun preceded by a preposition in all these. The absence of any examples in which *þe* is preceded by a preposition when it is an unambiguous relative argues in my favour. *Solil* 6. 5 can be compared with

PPs 122. 1   To þe ic mine eagan hof,   ece drihten,
                        þu þe heofonhamas   healdest and wealdest.

In both of these, *þu þe* is the equivalent of the *'seþe* relative; see §2184. In *Solil* 5. 19, we have not repetition of relative *þe* but the idiomatic use of the personal pronoun after *and* to indicate a change of case in the relative pronoun; see §2189. Carnicelli's observation (p. 27) that in these 'a relative pronoun makes the sentence more coherent' misses the point; in examples like these, *þe* is the personal pronoun and yet (as it were) also the relative. Other examples in the prose, such as *BlHom* 9. 3, *BlHom* 191. 26 *Ic befæste þe nu þæt eowde þæt þu me sealdest þæt hie ne oncneowon þæt hie buton me beon, þa þe habban. þurh þe ic þys eowde styran 7 rihtan, nu ne mæg,* where the Latin has *per quem,* and *ÆCHom* i. 420. 10 *þu dumba deofolgyld, þurh ðe forleosað earme menn þæt ece lif*—are comparable with *Solil* 6. 5 (§2245). I suspect that in all these examples the intonation would have decided for the personal pronoun. The reason why relative *þe* was not preceded by a preposition is probably that it was not strong enough to carry the necessary stress and had to pick up the antecedent (either immediately or at the end of the principal clause) without the intervention of a preposition.

§2247. The sole example in the poetry—

ChristA 328   þu eart þæt wealldor,   þurh þe waldend frea
                        æne on þas eorðan   ut siðade—

has produced the same difference of opinion. GK (p. 701) takes it as relative, Cook in his edition as a personal pronoun. I agree with Cook.

§2248. Apart from examples like these, the possibility of confusion between the relative *þe* and the pers. pron. *þe* rarely arises. The relative and the personal pronoun can fluctuate in sentences which are in asyndetic parataxis, e.g. *ÆCHom* i. 66. 25 *Eala ðu cniht, ðe þurh*

ðines flæsces lust hrædlice ðine sawle forlure; eala þu cniht, þu ne
cuðest ðinne Scyppend; þu ne cuðest manna Hælend; þu ne cuðest
ðone soðan freond. . . . In *OrW* 6, *þe* may be the latter or may with
the preceding *þa* form a *'seþe* relative. In

MSol 232   hafað tungena gehwylc   XX orda,
             hafað orda gehwylc   engles snytro,
             ðara ðe wile anra hwylc   uppe bringan,
             ðæt ðu ðære gyldnan gesiehst   Hierusalem
             weallas blican . . . ,

Menner glosses *ðe* first as a relative (p. 160) and then as a personal
pronoun (p. 164). He was (I suspect) right the second time, with
ðara an ambiguous demonstrative/relative and/or forming a unit with
anra. But in *GenA* 1341, *þe* is perhaps more likely to be a relative.
See §2313.

9. THE ANTECEDENT AND THE RELATIVE PRONOUN

a. The form of the antecedent

§2249. As in MnE, the following words may serve as antecedents:
nouns of any sort (including proper nouns), either alone or qualified
by a demonstrative and/or adjective(s); personal pronouns; demonstratives; possessives; indefinites; numerals; superlatives; and sentences
or clauses.

§2250. Attempts have been made to produce statistics showing the
relationship between the form of the antecedent and that of the
relative. Thus Anklam (pp. 70-1) produced tables in which he distinguished noun and pronoun antecedents in his limited corpus of
later OE and eME texts and gave the number of examples in which
these were followed by *se, þe*, and combinations of *se* and *þe*, in the
various cases and the two numbers. This division was too blunt,
neglecting as it did not only the distinctions in antecedents made in
§2249, including the important consideration whether the noun
antecedent was used alone, with a demonstrative or possessive, or
with an indefinite, but also gender and the distinction between the
'seþe and *se'þe* relatives. In my 1959 thesis (pp. 146-59), I attempted
an analysis for the poetry in which I made the distinctions noted
above but neglected to distinguish the case of the relative pronoun;
see *Ang.* 81 (1963), 311-13 for a summary of my results. Kivimaa
says that *þe* is 'used with antecedents of all kinds' (pp. 30 and 35)
and is preferred to *þa* in the plural (pp. 32 and 36); refers to a reluctance to use *se* with inanimate antecedents (pp. 31 and 35-6); and

notes that the compound relatives rarely occur with inanimate nouns (pp. 33 and 36)—a point also made for Ælfric by Anklam (p. 30). Future workers in OE will need to distinguish animate from inanimate antecedents, bearing in mind both Kivimaa's observation (p. 38) that *þe* is more common in Wulfstan's *Homilies* than in those of Ælfric and McIntosh's examination of the relatives *þe* and *þat* in eME (McIntosh, *passim*). So more work is necessary if the differences in the usage of the early and the late prose and of the poetry are to be established; see McIntosh, pp. 79-80 and fn. 19.

§2251. The extent to which this task could be pursued with profit is as yet uncertain. As will become clear in the sections which follow, there are so many possible factors and so many limitations to our knowledge that full statistics are likely to be overwhelming, subjectively uncertain, and nugatory in that in essence they will demonstrate only what we know already, viz. that *se*, *þe*, and combinations of the two, ultimately disappeared from the language apart from MnE 'that'.[60] Moreover, I am convinced that there are in neither OE prose nor OE poetry 'rules' which enable us to determine the form of the relative once we know that of the antecedent. Andrew (*Postscript*, §45) observes that 'our text of *Beowulf* shows both a mixture of types and a syntactical licence in the use of them to which there is no parallel in any prose work'. I doubt whether any Anglo-Saxon speaker would have agreed and I think that a detailed examination of prose texts would reveal similar 'mixture' and 'licence' once due allowance is made for the demands of metre; consider the variation in the forms of the relative in *CP* 295. 4-8, *Solil* 1. 1-25, *BlHom* 71. 2-17,[61] *ÆCHom* i. 20. 13-20, 32. 21-4, 282. 7-11 (repeated with minor variations at *ÆCHom* ii. 606. 9-14), and *ÆCHom* ii. 556. 11-22, and compare *ÆCHom* i. 54. 5-8 with *ÆCHom* i. 512. 28-34 and *ÆCHom* i. 88. 17 *soðlice hi sind forð-farene, ðaðe ymbe þæs cildes feorh syrwdon* with *ÆCHom* i. 88. 27 *þa sind forðfarene, þe embe ðæs cildes feorh syrwdon*. These must be my excuses for not fully pursuing the relationship between the form of the antecedent and that of the relative. However, it is

---

[60] The history of *þe* and *þæt* has been discussed by McIntosh (pp. 73-87); Stevick (*EStudies*, 46 (1965), 29-36); Kivimaa, *passim*; and Jack (*EStudies*, 56 (1975), 100-7). Kivimaa (pp. 29-39 and 44) has some useful comments on combinations of relative pronouns and antecedents in her texts—selections from *CP*, *Or*, *Chron*, *ÆCHom*, and *WHom*. But her statistics can be disregarded. Not only are they based on selections, they are 'estimated' and 'have no absolute value' (Kivimaa, p. 8) and do not distinguish *'seþe* and *se'þe* (p. 9).

[61] The sequence *seo se* in *BlHom* 71. 10 is, however, suspect and should probably be *seo þe* rather than *seo seo*.

possible to distinguish certain tendencies and to isolate certain factors as important.

b. Factors affecting the form of the relative

(1) The form of the antecedent

§2252. The observations which follow are based on a limited sampling of the prose (see §§2166-7 and 2250-1) and a full examination of the poetry.

§2253. The first of the tendencies referred to in §2251 is this: when the antecedent is a noun qualified by a demonstrative or possessive, *þe* seems to be preferred as a relative to *se, seo, þæt*, e.g. *CP* 295. 4 *Forðæm ðæt wif ðe Abigall hatte . . . , CP* 3. 4 *7 hu ða kyningas ðe ðone onwald hæfdon ðæs folces on ðam dagum Gode 7 his ærendwrecum hersumedon, ÆCHom* i. 2. 23 . . . *buton þam mannum anum ðe þæt Leden cuðon and buton þam bocum ðe Ælfred cyning snoterlice awende of Ledene on Englisc . . .* , and

Beo 2711   Ða sio wund ongon,
          þe him se eorðdraca   ær geworhte
          swelan ond swellan.

This tendency is least noticeable when the antecedent is neuter singular nominative or accusative; see §2138. See also Kivimaa, pp. 30 and 35; Mitchell 1964a, p. 131; and Bourcier, p. 303, where the suggestion is made that in Ælfric the sequence *se* + noun + *se* is limited to descriptive clauses (§§2271-2), e.g. *ÆCHom* i. 4. 14 *þonne cymð se Antecrist, se bið mennisc mann and soð deofol*, where *se*—and not enclitic *þe*—could give the intonation appropriate in the MnE equivalent.

§2254. A similar preference for *þe* is apparent when a noun antecedent is qualified by *(n)an, (n)ænig, manig, eall, oðer, gehwilc*, or *æghwilc*. Here it is least obvious when the antecedent is plural, in which event combinations of *se* and *þe* are more common.

§2255. However, when the antecedent is a noun by itself or a noun qualified by an 'adjective proper' (§97), the relative *se* is preferred in the singular, though again the compound relative is more common in the plural. As McIntosh (p. 79) has it, 'if the antecedent is . . . what I shall refer to, because of the absence of any demonstrative element, as "indefinite", we have one of the situations in which the declined relative is preferred to *þe*'.

§ 2256. Case does not seem to be the determining factor, for all the relatives occur in all cases with the three types of antecedents so far discussed. Perhaps we have here another example of the unconscious tendency to eliminate unnecessary distinctions. In the first two groups, the gender and number of the antecedent and therefore of the relative is more likely to have been indicated than in those examples in the third group in which a noun occurs alone or with a strong form of an adjective in the nominative. So the use of the relative *se* may to that extent have been felt as tautologic in the first two groups and *þe* consequently preferred, though to be sure it did not make clear the case of the relative pronoun.

§ 2257. Andrew (*Postscript*, p. 42) assures us that 'in *Beowulf*, as in prose, *ðe* is idiomatic after . . . proper nouns'. This is not true for the poetry or the prose. In the poetry, *se* appears as the relative after some forty-five per cent of those proper nouns which are so qualified, *þe* after thirty-six per cent; combinations of *se* and *þe* in which the *se* element is in the case of the adjective clause account for the remaining examples. As far as I noted, the prose also shows a preference for *se*. McIntosh (pp. 80-1) tells us that 'it is certainly true to say that in Alfred's period the declined relative is far commoner after personal names than *þe* is, and that it remains common even in late Old English prose, where *þe* is to some extent replacing *se, seo, þæt*' and Kivimaa (p. 44) says that 'the one restriction the present writer noticed in the use of *þe* is a reluctance to employ it with personal names, unless they are preceded by the article and after an adjectival adjunct also; but even in this instance there are exceptions'. So we do not have to eliminate *se* before *þe* in *Beo* 506 *Eart þu se Beowulf se þe wið Brecan wunne* in the belief that '*Maldon* has the right form after a proper noun with the article' in *Mald* 325 *Næs þæt na se Godric þe ða guðe forbeah* (Andrew, *SS*, pp. 107-9). These are the only examples in the poetry of *se* + proper noun + relative pronoun.

§ 2258. As antecedent, the personal pronoun is found in both numbers and in all persons and cases. Thus *hiora* is the antecedent in

PPs 68. 4   Hiora is mycle ma   þonne ic me hæbbe
             on heafde nu   hæra feaxes,
             þe me earwunga   ealle feogeað.

§ 2259. The particle *þe* has as antecedent personal pronouns of all numbers and both genders. Some problems associated with the first and second person pronouns are discussed in § § 2180-200. The third person pronoun presents no difficulties.

§2260. It is scarcely surprising that *se*—with its strong suggestion of the third person 'that one'—is rarely found with first and second person pronoun antecedents. There are no examples in the poetry and those referred to by Kock (p. 80) are the result of mechanical glossing; they include *Ps(A)* 16. 7 *Gewundra mildheornisse ðine, se hale gedoest ða gehyhtendan in ðec*, Latin *Mirifica misericordias tuas, qui saluos facis sperantes in te*, where the antecedent is not expressed. The compound relatives, which include a *se* element, show a marked preference for third person antecedents in the poetry, where there are only six exceptions in forty-five examples—*Sat* 556, *PPs* 89. 14, and *PPs* 102. 13 (first person plural); *Dan* 142 (if we retain the ASPR emendation; but see Farrell's note) and *PPs* 121. 6 (second person plural); and *ChristA* 18 (§2360). My limited collections from the prose include only the two examples noted by Wülfing (i, §297): *Ps(P)* 4. 1 *forðam þu eart se ðe me gerihtwisast*, where there is no relative in the Latin, and *Ps(P)* 21. 8 *Drihten, þu eart se þe me gelæddest of minre modor innoðe*, Latin *Quoniam tu es qui abstraxisti me de ventre*. If Andrew had restricted his observation that 'in *Beowulf*, as in prose, *ðe* is idiomatic after personal pronouns' (*Postscript*, p. 42) to the first and second person pronouns, we could have accepted it. But, as it stands, it does not hold for the poetry— the respective percentages are *þe* 36, *se* 12+, and the compound relatives 51+—or, on the basis of the evidence I have so far collected and of McIntosh's observations (p. 82), for the prose.

§2261. The problem of deciding whether a demonstrative *se* which immediately precedes *þe* is (part of) the antecedent has been discussed in §§2153-79. But when a demonstrative is separated by other sentence elements from an adjective clause which qualifies it, that demonstrative may be reasonably taken as the antecedent or, if it follows the adjective clause, as in *ÆCHom* i. 6. 5 below, the 'postcedent'. Thus, we find, with relative *þe, Or* 158. 26 . . . *þæt hie þa wæron swiþe sleande þe hie fylstan sceoldon* . . . and *ÆCHom* i. 326. 32 . . . *he bið, swa swa se apostol cwæð, þam gelic þe deofolgyld begæð*; with relative *se, Or* 21. 3 *7 se nimð þone læstan dæl se nyhst þæm tune þæt feoh geærneð* and *ÆCHom* i. 48. 22 . . . *and seo heofenlice soðfæstnyss be ðam cydde gecyðnysse þone seo eorðlice arleasnyss huxlice tælde*; with relative *se'þe, GuthA* 538 *is þæs gen fela || to secgenne, þæs þe he sylfa adreag* . . . (I have so far observed no such examples in the prose); with relative '*seþe, Or* 268. 20 . . . *7 eac þæt ælc þara moste cristendome onfon se þe wolde* and *ÆCHom* i. 6. 5 *þa ðe his leasungum gelyfað, þam he arað*; and, with relative *seþe, Or* 178. 20 . . . *þæt se wære leoda cyning se þe ær wæs folce þeow* and *WHom* 7. 113 *7 se bið swyðe clæne ælcere synne, se ðe þæne bryne ðurhfærð unbesencged.* Similar patterns occur in the poetry. Examples (with the approximate percentages of occurrences in poetry in brackets after each relative) include:

þe (42),

GenB 644   . . . *þe þæt laðe treow*
     on his bogum bær,   *bitre gefylled;*
     þæt wæs deaðes beam   *þe him drihten forbead;*

se'þe (4),

ChristC 1204   *Swa þam bið grorne*   *on þam grimman dæge*
     domes þæs miclan,   *þam þe dryhtnes sceal,*
     deaðfirenum forden,   *dolg sceawian,*
     wunde ond wite;

'seþe (3),

El 302   *Ge to deaþe þone*
     deman ongunnon,   *se ðe of deaðe sylf*
     woruld awehte   *on wera corþre*
     in þæt ærre lif   *eowres cynnes;*

seþe (19),

Jul 1   *Hwæt! We ðæt hyrdon*   *hæleð eahtian,*
     deman dædhwate,   *þætte in dagum gelamp*
     Maximianes,   *se geond middangeard,*
     arleas cyning,   *eahtnysse ahof* . . . ;

and *se* (32),

Beo 1455   *Næs þæt þonne mætost*   *mægenfultuma,*
     þæt him on ðearfe lah   *ðyle Hroðgares*

and

El 465   *Se is niða gehwam*
     unasecgendlic,   *þone sylf ne mæg*
     on moldwege   *man aspyrigean.*

§2262. Examples in which *þes* serves as (part of) an antecedent include *CP(C)* 2 (heading) *Ðis is seo forespræc hu S. Gregorius ðas boc gedihte þe man Pastoralem nemnað, ÆLS* 4. 51 *Gefæstna þis, Hælend, þæt þæt ðu on us gewyrcst, Sat* 252 *þis is idel gylp ‖ þæt we ær drugon ealle hwile,* and

El 902   *Hwæt is þis, la, manna*   *þe minne eft*
     þurh fyrngeflit   *folgaþ wyrdeð* . . . ?

Some at least of these examples illustrate Wülfing's observation (i, §262) that dem. *þes* points to a relative pronoun more emphatically than dem. *se*.

§ 2263. Antecedent *(n)an, (n)ænig, ælc, æghwa, æghwilc, gehwa, gehwilc, fela, manig, sum*, and *oþer*, prefer *þe* or the compound relatives to *se*—the respective percentages for the group in the poetry are 41, 40, and 19. *Eall* shows similar tendencies when used in the plural. But when *eall* is used with a relative in the nominative or accusative, that relative is almost invariably *þæt* in both prose (see McIntosh, p. 82 fn. 25) and poetry. The exceptions so far known to me include the variations *eall þæt, eall þæt þe*, and *eall þæt þæt*, in *GD* 174. 9 (for *þæt þæt* see § 2124), the noteworthy *ChronE* 174. 23 (1048) *eall þ æfre betst wæs*, the sequence *eall þætte* in

Met 29. 67   Ac se milda metod   monna bearnum
                on eorðan fet   eall þætte groweð,
                wæstmas on weorolde,

the easily explained lack of concord of 'postcedent' *eall* in

ChristC 1180   þa þe æþelast sind   eorðan gecynda,
                  ond heofones eac   heahgetimbro,
                  eall fore þam anum   unrot gewearð,
                  forhtafongen,

and

Met 20. 34   us is utan cymen   eall þa we habbað
                gooda on grundum   from gode selfum,

where *eall* may be neuter plural or *þa* may take its number from *gooda* but where *þe*, proposed by Grein, Assmann, and Krämer, is (I should say) impossible. There are three examples in the poetry of the *se'þe* relative in the sequence *eall(es) þæs þe*, viz. *ChristC* 1032, *Fort* 97, and *JDay i* 40.

§ 2264. In the poetry and in my limited collections from the prose, numerals prefer relative *se*. But *þe* appears in examples like

GuthA 709   Eom ic þara twelfa sum   þe he getreoweste
               under monnes hiw   mode gelufade,

where we have *se* + a numeral used as a noun; see § 548.

§ 2265. In the poetry limiting adjective clauses qualifying an antecedent which is or contains a superlative are introduced by *se'þe*, e.g.

Dan 691   þæt wæs þara fæstna   folcum cuðost,
             mæst and mærost   þara þe men bun,
             Babilon burga . . . ,

and *þe*, e.g.

GenB 626   þa gieng to Adame   idesa scenost,
                  wifa wlitegost   þe on woruld come.

(I have noted a similar example in the prose, viz. *WHom* 18. 20 *And þæt wæs þæt mæreste hus þe on eorðan geworht wurde.*) *Se* is found only in descriptive clauses, e.g.

Phoen 395   . . . ond hi þa gesette   on þone selestan
                   foldan sceata,   þone fira bearn
                   nemnað neorxnawong. . . .

But we also find *þe* in

ChristB 517   We mid þyslice   þreate willað
                   ofer heofona gehlidu   hlaford fergan
                   to þære beorhtan byrg   mid þas bliðan gedryht,
                   ealra sigebearna   þæt seleste
                   ond æþeleste,   þe ge her on stariað
                   ond in frofre geseoð   frætwum blican.

On the difference in mood see §2403. Andrew's claim (*SS*, p. 107), that 'after a superlative the simple relative *ðe* is the norm' rests on unjustified omission of *þara* in the *þara ðe* examples; his objections to the singular verb after *þara þe* are invalid (see §§2343-50) and it is doubtful whether the second of the two constructions which he says 'we cannot mix' (*SS*, p. 106) in fact existed, despite Gehse (pp. 70-7).

§2266. Occasionally, as in *Or* 74. 22 *Seo ilce burg Babylonia, seo ðe mæst wæs 7 ærest ealra burga, seo is nu læst 7 westast, GuthA* 709 (§2264), and

Beo 205   Hæfde se goda   Geata leoda
                 cempan gecorone   þara þe he cenoste
                 findan mihte,

a superlative is found in the adjective clause. But it is certainly not part of the antecedent in the first two examples and need not be taken as part of it in the third. Cf. here §1921a.

§2267. Andrew (*Postscript*, pp. 34-5) quotes

Beo 587   . . . þeah ðu þinum broðrum   to banan wurde,
                 heafodmægum; þæs þu in helle scealt
                 werhðo dreogan,   þeah þin wit duge,

Beo 2477   . . .   ac ymb Hreosnabeorh
                  eatolne inwitscear   oft gefremedon.
                  þæt mægwine   mine gewræcan . . . ,

and

Beo 2628   Ne gemealt him se modsefa,   ne his mæges laf
                    gewac æt wige;   þæt se wyrm onfand,
                    syððan hie togædre   gegan hæfdon,

and observes that

the neuter relative in 588, 2479 and 2629 is idiomatic *without* antecedent, in Old as in Modern English, when referring to the action predicated in the preceding sentence: 'for which (i.e. the slaying of thy brother) thou shalt suffer damnation in hell', 'all which (i.e. the malicious slaying) my kinsmen-friends avenged', 'which (= as) the worm discovered' (in 2479 *ðæt* might perhaps be taken as the consecutive conjunction). All the exx. in this section thus conform strictly to the prose rule, if the pronouns are taken as relatives.

This interpretation, though always possible and sometimes convenient, can lead to a forced and unnatural translation; 'that' or 'for that' is sometimes more natural. Here again we see the ambiguous demonstrative/relative. The same difficulty is apparent when a clause which may refer to the sentence occurs internally, e.g.

Met 9. 53   Eala, gif he wolde,   ðæt he wel meahte,
                    þæt unriht him   eaðe forbiodan,

where *ðæt he wel meahte* can be taken as an adjective or as a parenthetic clause. But *ðæt* may well mean 'what' in this sentence. Noack (pp. 11–12) and Flamme (p. 28) err in including in this group examples like

Beo 1465   Huru ne gemunde   mago Ecglafes
                    eafoþes cræftig   þæt he ær gespræc
                    wine druncen

and *BlHom* 11. 14 *On hire wæs gefylled þætte on Cantica Canticorum wæs gesungen*, where *þæt(te)* means 'what'; see § 2129. Further on *þæt* referring to a sentence, see § 2125.

§ 2268. Kock (p. 43) says that 'I have found no ex. where the ant. of *þe* is . . . a whole clause'. Possible examples include

Beo 2135   Ic ða ðæs wælmes,   þe is wide cuð,
                    grimne gryrelicne   grundhyrde fond,

where the translation 'as is widely known' is convenient (but see § 3369), and (less likely)

Mald 189   he gehleop þone eoh   þe ahte his hlaford,
                    on þam gerædum   þe hit riht ne wæs,

where other explanations are possible; see §§ 2106, 3369, and 3428.

§2269. *Swa* and *þæs þe* can also introduce clauses which refer to a sentence or an idea already expressed; for examples see §§3264-5 and 3350-1.

§2270. In *Ang.* 81 (1963), 313, I summarized the main tendencies in the poetry as follows:

þe follows an antecedent which consists of, or includes some form of, the demonstratives *se* and *þes*, or of the possessive adjective;

þe follows personal pronouns and other pronouns except *eall* in the neuter singular;

se follows nouns not qualified by a demonstrative or by a possessive adjective, and also the pronoun *eall* in the neuter singular.

The compound relative (663 examples against 690 of *þe* and 602 of *se*) occurs in all the contexts noted above. It is least common after noun antecedents qualified by a demonstrative and most common (51%) after the personal pronoun. Throughout it is more common after plural than after singular antecedents.

But they remain tendencies and cannot be made into 'rules'. I have already pointed out that more work is needed to establish the prose usages. However, as far as I have observed, the tendencies noted above are also apparent in early and late prose. Here Andrew (*SS*, pp. 101-5) has some valuable observations. But they must not be accepted without being checked; see §2283.

(2) *The function of the adjective clause*

§2271. According to Andrew (*SS*, pp. 35 and 109-10), the form of the relative pronoun in OE prose largely depends on the function of the adjective clause it introduces:

The simplest OE relative pronouns are *þe* and *se*, *þe* being used when the clause has the function of a limiting or distinguishing adjective and *se* when it has the function of a descriptive adjective, e.g. Se casere *þe* wæs Claudius haten 'the Emperor called Claudius', Se casere, *se* wæs Claudius haten 'the Emperor, who was called C.' In the first sentence the relative clause distinguishes one particular emperor from others, in the second it adds a descriptive detail to a noun already sufficiently defined by the context. Both kinds of clause may qualify the same noun, e.g. *Hom.* I. 100. 4 Se eahtateoða dæg *þæs* monðes *þe* we hatað Martius *þone* ge hatað Hlyda 'the 18th day of the month that we call March, which you call Hlyda'

and

    (i) in a limiting relative clause, the relative pronoun is normally *ðe*, as always in *ASC*, though pleonastic *seðe* is found occasionally in late prose but is not always well certified;

    (ii) in a descriptive relative clause, there are three forms of the relative pronoun (*a*) unstressed *se*, as always with one exception in *ASC* and predominantly

in *Orosius* and *Bede*; (*b*) unstressed *seðe* (= *se* with a relative suffix, cf. ModE
'who that' 'when that') as in Ælfric, *CP*, and WS *Gospels*; in the oblique cases
it is only used with any consistency in the Durham Book; (*c*) epexegetic *se ðe*,
where *se* is the stressed antecedent in apposition to a preceding noun; it occurs
sporadically in all texts but predominantly only in the Rushworth *St Matthew*.
There are good grounds for supposing that *ðe* and *se* were the earliest forms,
that, outside Northumbrian, *seðe* (= *se* or *ðe*) was West-Saxon and late, and that
seðe forms in *Beowulf* and some prose writings are due to the scribe.

He qualified (or contradicted) these 'rules' by observations such as
'the regular form of the limiting relative without antecedent was *se*'
(*SS*, p. 108) and 'in *Beowulf*, as in prose, *ðe* is idiomatic after personal pronouns or proper nouns' (*Postscript*, p. 42), and did not
extend them to *Beowulf* or the poetry because he could not—'our
text of *Beowulf* shows both a mixture of types and a syntactical
licence in the use of them to which there is no parallel in any prose
work' (*Postscript*, p. 40). Here again we see him as the prescriptive
grammarian, erecting what are admittedly tendencies into 'rules'
which form the basis of the emendations by which he establishes the
'rules'.

§2272. Such clear-cut distinctions are in themselves to be suspected.
Sometimes we do indeed distinguish by intonation or punctuation
between limiting and descriptive clauses, e.g. 'The soldiers who were
tired lay down' but 'The soldiers, who were tired, lay down'. That
the limiting clause also describes is no reason for rejecting the distinction, though it might be a reason for preferring 'non-limiting' to the
traditional term 'descriptive'. But often we neither know nor care
whether we are limiting or describing: we are simply using a syntactic device in which it is enough to connect the qualifying clause to
the main noun, the qualification itself being of a neutral sort, neither
specifically limiting nor specifically descriptive, e.g. 'The mother who
suckled the child also mourned', 'A waiter who was pouring wine
suddenly fell down dead', and 'Deliver me, O Lord, from the malice
of my enemies who fight against me'. In addition, we have sentences
such as 'I knocked at the door of the Lord Chief Justice, who opened
it himself' (where the adjective clause is 'continuative' or 'connecting', the relative being the equivalent of 'and' and a demonstrative
or a personal pronoun) and 1 Pet 1. 12 '. . . but unto us they did
minister the things, which are now reported unto you by them . . . ;
which things the angels desire to look into.'

§2273. The first three types clearly existed in OE prose and poetry,
e.g. (limiting) *Bede* 32. 13 . . . *of þære byrig ðe Lepti hatte*, *ÆCHom*
i. 2. 23 . . . *buton þam mannum anum ðe þæt Leden cuðon*, and

GenA 1279   . . . cwæð þæt he wolde   for wera synnum
                   eall aæðan   þæt on eorðan wæs;

(descriptive) *Bede* 4. 11 . . . *Danieles þæs arwurðan Westseaxna
biscopes, se nu gyt lifigende is, ÆCHom* i. 24. 11 . . . *þæt Ebreisce
folc, þe God lufode,* and

GenA 231   þridda is Tigris,   seo wið þeodscipe,
                  ea inflede,   Assirie belið;

and (neither specifically limiting nor descriptive) *Bede* 26. 27 . . . *fif
Moyses boca, ðam seo godcunde æ awriten is, ÆCHom* i. 90. 3 . . .
þam Ælmihtigan to wurðmynte, seþe leofað and rixað a butan ende,
and *Sat* 619 *þonne stondað þa forworhtan, þa ðe firnedon.*

§2274. Something similar to the continuative adjective clause exists
in OE. But it takes a different form; as Reuter points out (pp. 6–9),
there can be no exact equivalents because *hwa* and *hwelc* are not
used as relatives in OE. Possible examples are seen in sentences like
Bede 220. 11 *þa wæs gecoren sexta ærcebiscop Deosdedit to þæm
seðle Contwara burge, se wæs of Westseaxna þeode; þane cwom
þider to halgianne Itthamar se biscop þære cirican æt Hrofesceastre,*
where *þane* is represented in the Latin by *quem; Bede* 226. 25 *Seo
ærre stow is in Pente stæðe þære ea, oðer is in Temese stæðe. In
þæm he gesomnode micel weorod Cristes þeowa . . . ,* where *In þæm*
renders Latin *In quibus; ÆCHom* i. 22. 6 *Wearð þa ælc þing cuces
adrenct, buton þam ðe binnon þam arce wæron; of þam wearð eft
geedstaðelod eall middangeard; ÆCHom* i. 348. 1 *Micel getel is ðæra
haligra gasta þe on Godes rice eardiað, be ðam cwæð se witega Daniel
. . . ,* cited by Reuter (p. 9); and

GenA 163   Geseah þa lifes weard
                 drige stowe,   dugoða hyrde,
                 wide æteowde,   þa se wuldorcyning
                 eorðan nemde,

which represents *Gen* 1. 10 *Et vocavit Deus aridam Terram.* But in
these examples, as the different punctuations adopted by the editors
testify, we have to do with the ambiguous demonstrative/relative,
which Andrew failed to recognize; see §§2109–21. That *se* in
examples like these was probably felt as a demonstrative rather than
a relative is suggested by the frequent appearance of the *punctus
elevatus,* which 'is not a normal substitute for the point; it falls at
a comparatively stronger break . . . before the pronoun *se,* which
often begins a clause with the value of modern English "continuative"
who' (Harlow, p. 14).

§2275. The ambiguous demonstrative/relative may also appear in examples like *Bede* 442. 9 *Ic seolfa cuðe sumne broðar, ðone ic wolde ðæt ic næfre cuðe, ðæs noman ic eac swylce genemnan mæg* . . . and *ÆCHom* ii. 38. 9 *þaða he geðogen wæs, þa com him to Godes bebod, þæt he sceolde faran to mannum, and bodian fulluht on synna forgifenysse, and sceolde fullian þæt folc ðe him to come mid his agenum fulluhte, on ðam fulluhte næs nan synne forgifenyss*, which Thorpe translates '. . . with his own baptism, in which baptism there was no forgiveness of sin'; cf. 1 Pet 1. 12 (§2272). Reuter (pp. 8-9) adds examples with compound relatives, e.g. *CP* 69. 4 *Swa sindon wel monege ðara ðe gewundiað hiera mod mid ðæm weorcum ðisses flæsclican lifes, ða ðe meahton smealice 7 scearplice mid hiera 7gite ryht geseon, ac mid ðæm gewunan ðara wona weorca ðæt mod bið adimmod* and *ÆCHom* i. 470. 20 . . . *æt ðam Ælmihtigan Scyppende, ðam ðe gehyrsumiað lif and deað, untrumnys and gesundfulnys, seðe cwæð on his godspelle, þæt an lytel fugel ne befylð on deað butan Godes dihte*, and with *þe*, e.g. *Bede* 292. 14 *þonne is sum wundor hælo, þe us nis to forlætenne, þe seo ilce booc sagað, þætte æt liictune geworden wære Gode þære leofan gesomnunge*. The presence of *þe* probably certifies that these are adjective clauses. That they are continuative seems less certain; see §§2295-6.

§2276. As Reuter points out (pp. 7-8), examples like *Matt(WSCp)* 12. 39 *He andswarode hym 7 cwæð*, Latin *Qui respondens ait illis*, suggest that the continuative adjective clause was not natural to OE; *Matt(Li)* 12. 39 *Seðe onduarde cueð to ðæm ł him*, Latin *Qui respondens ait illis*, is a mechanical gloss.

§2277. There is no doubt that the first distinction made by Andrew —*þe* in limiting, *se* in descriptive, adjective clauses—often works. The following examples testify this: *CP* 295. 4 *Forðæm ðæt wif ðe Abigall hatte suiðe herigendlice forsuigode ðæt dysig hiere fordruncnan hlafordes, se wæs haten Nabal*, *ÆCHom* i. 32. 17 *He wæs acenned on þæs caseres dagum þe wæs Octauianus gehaten, se gerymde Romana rice* . . . , *ÆCHom* ii. 164. 13 *Benedictus þa ferde to ðam munte þe is gecweden Casinum, se astihð up ðreo mila on heannysse*,

Beo 191

wæs þæt gewin to swyð,
laþ ond longsum, þe on ða leode becom,
nydwracu niþgrim, nihtbealwa mæst,

and

Beo 1427 . . . swylce on næshleoðum nicras licgean,
ða on undernmæl oft bewitigað

> sorhfulne sið   on seglrade,
> wyrmas ond wildeor.

I do not have complete figures for the prose. But in the poetry clauses introduced by *þe* are predominantly limiting and the most common relative in descriptive clauses is *se*. To this extent Andrew's first 'rule' (my §2271) has a basis in fact.

§2278. But there are many examples in both prose and poetry which run counter to it. Thus *þe* does not introduce a limiting clause in *Or* 120. 33... *þone cyning his fæder þe þær æt ham wæs, ÆCHom* i. 34. 30 *Se Ælmihtiga Godes Sunu, ðe heofenas befon ne mihton, wæs geled on nearuwre binne . . . , ÆCHom* i. 290. 30, *ÆCHom* ii. 444. 13,

GenB 259 Ac he awende hit him to wyrsan þinge,   ongan him winn upahebban
          wið þone hehstan heofnes waldend,   þe siteð on þam halgan stole,

and

Dream 135   ond ic wene me
          daga gehwylce   hwænne me dryhtnes rod,
          þe ic her on eorðan   ær sceawode,
          on þysson lænan   life gefetige. . . .

Limiting clauses introduced by *se* include *Or* 1. 6 *Hu þæt heofenisce fyr forbærnde þæt lond on þæm wæron þa twa byrig on getimbred, Sodome 7 Gomorre, Or* 18. 25 *Eal þæt his man aþer oððe ettan oððe erian mæg þæt lið wið ða sæ, ÆCHom* ii. 296. 27 . . . *to anre byrig seo is Geropolis geciged* (cf. *ÆCHom* ii. 296. 32 . . . *on ðære ylcan byrig þe we ær namodon*), *ÆCHom* i. 236. 9 . . . *God is Ælmihtig and mæg eal þæt he wile, Beo* 142 *heold hyne syðþan ‖ fyr ond fæstor se þæm feonde ætwand* (cf.

Beo 138   þa wæs eaðfynde   þe him elles hwær
          gerumlicor   ræste sohte,
          bed æfter burum . . .),

and

And 1623   Het þa onsunde   ealle arisan
          geonge of greote,   þa ær geofon cwealde

(cf.

And 1613   Sende þa his bene   fore bearn godes,
          bæd haligne   helpe gefremman
          gumena geogoðe,   þe on geofene ær
          þurh flodes fæðm   feorh gesealdon).

Both parts of the 'rule' are broken in *ÆCHom* i. 24. 10 *þa gestrynde he sunu se wæs gehaten Eber, of þam asprang þæt Ebreisce folc, þe God lufode.*

§2279. The table given in §2283 demonstrates that the first 'rule' postulated by Andrew does not hold for OE poetry. What I believe to be the situation in both the prose and the poetry is neatly summed up by McIntosh (p. 79 fn. 19): 'I am unable to agree with Andrew . . . that in Old English *þe* invariably introduces a restrictive, *se* etc. invariably a non-restrictive clause, though it so happens that this is often the case.' Harlow, who points out at pp. 6–7 that in the Ælfric manuscripts with which he was concerned there is 'generally no punctuation . . . before a restrictive relative *þe* clause . . . but some punctuation is found . . . before many descriptive relative *þe* clauses', is obviously unable to agree with Andrew either. He has an even more important observation at p. 19 fn. 1: 'Thus the pronoun *se* in a relative function is heavily punctuated, except in the neuter *þæt*, which has no punctuation or at most only a point. . . . *þe* is strongly enclitic, rarely enduring any punctuation before it, unless it is already separated from its antecedent.' Encouraged by these remarks and remembering the strong tendency for an antecedent consisting of a demonstrative (+ an adjective) + a noun to be followed by the relative *þe*, we can perhaps indulge in a moment's speculation. Originally *þe* was enclitic and *se*—initially as a demonstrative and then as a relative—non-enclitic; cf. §2169. This would mean that originally *þe* clauses were or tended to be limiting, while *se* clauses were or tended to be descriptive. This situation obtains in examples like *CP* 169. 22 . . . *7 hat wyrcean twegen stengas of ðæm treowe ðe is haten sethim, ðæt ne wyrð næfre forrotad, ÆCHom* i. 100. 4 *Se eahte-teoða dæg þæs monðes þe we hatað Martius, ðone ge hatað Hlyda* . . . , and *ÆCHom* ii. 352. 19 *Seo micele byrnende dene, þe ðu ærest gesawe, is witnungstow, on ðære beoð manna sawla gewitnode.* . . . But the distinction between enclitic *þe* and non-enclitic *se* was the primary one and that between limiting *þe* and descriptive *se* was derivative, secondary, and less well established. Andrew's mistake was to put the cart before the horse by elevating the secondary distinction into the primary one. That even the primary distinction weakened to become merely a tendency is suggested (for me at any rate) by reading aloud the last batch of examples quoted and by variations like *ChronA* (827) 60. 30 *siexta wæs Oswald se æfter him ricsode* but *ChronE* 61. 28 *sixta wæs Oswald þe æfter him rixade* and *GD(C)* 20. 18 . . . *se abbud se æfter þæs arwurðan Honorates forðfore heold 7 hæfde þone ræcenddom 7 hlaforddom þæs mynstres*

... but *GD(H)* 20. 18 ... *se abbod þe æfter þæs arwurðan Honorates forðfore heold þæs mynstres reccendom. . . .* (Yerkes (pp. 158-9) notes twenty-five examples in which the reviser of *GD* replaced *se* by *þe* and five in which he replaced *þe* by *se*.) It is strikingly confirmed by examples like *ÆCHom* i. 248. 21 *Se hiredes ealdor þe wæs on his reste gebroht mid his cildum is Crist, þe sitt on heofonum mid his apostolum and mid martyrum and mid eallum þam halgum þe he on ðisum life gefette*, where *þe* seems to me to introduce clauses which are respectively limiting, descriptive, and not specifically one or the other. This weakening may have been due in part at any rate to the intrusion of the compound relatives into the domain of simple *þe* and *se* which I discuss in §§2169-70; note the variations given in §2282.

§ 2280. As we have seen in §2271, Andrew (*SS*, pp. 109-10) goes on to include the compound relatives in his 'rules': 'pleonastic *seðe*' is occasionally found in limiting clauses in late prose, while 'unstressed *seðe*' and 'epexegetic *se ðe*' [my *se'þe*] occur alongside *se* in descriptive clauses.[62] That these 'rules'—which in part at any rate depend on emendations made in the belief that the 'rules' are right—do not hold for the early or late prose or for the poetry is sufficiently demonstrated by the examples quoted in the next two sections.[63]

§ 2281. First, we find *'seþe* introducing limiting clauses in *Bede* 78. 15 . . . *forhwon þonne, se þe blodryne þrowað monaðaðle, ne alefað hire in Drihtnes cirican gongan?, Bede* 274. 10 . . . *þæt heo eac swylce for hine, se ðe him þa stowe gesealde, a þa stondendan munecas þær to Drihtne cleopodon 7 for hine þingodon, ÆCHom* ii. 30. 31 . . . *and dæghwomlice geneosodon ða halgan cyrcan, on þære ðe wæs þæs wuldorfullan Stephanes gemynd*, and

Beo 1341   . . . *þæs þe þincean mæg   þegne monegum*
                     se þe æfter sincgyfan   on sefan greoteþ;

se'þe introducing limiting clauses in *Bede* 330. 19 . . . *fore generednisse heora freonda þara ðe of weorulde geleordon, ÆCHom* i. 30. 25

---

[62] I have to admit that I do not understand the difference between 'pleonastic *seðe*' ('in which *ðe* is a suffix to the unstressed relative *se*' (*SS*, §117) and which, on the evidence Andrew supplies in *SS*, §119, does not seem to be restricted to late prose) and 'unstressed *seðe*'.

[63] For the poetry see again the table given in §2283. Harlow (p. 10) speaks of restrictive and descriptive *se ðe* clauses, but does not distinguish the *se'þe* and *'seþe* types. McIntosh (p. 79 fn. 15) deliberately eschewed consideration of them, presumably because he thought that they were not relevant to the problem with which he was primarily concerned.

Sy wuldor Gode on heannyssum and on eorðan sibb mannum þam ðe beoð godes willan, and

Beo 2293   Hordweard sohte
                georne æfter grunde,   wolde guman findan,
                þone þe him on sweofote   sare geteode;

and *sepe* introducing limiting clauses in *CP* 7. 6 *Forðy me ðyncð betre, gif iow swæ ðyncð, ðæt we eac sumæ bec, ða ðe niedbeðearfosta sien eallum monnum to wiotonne, ðæt we ða on ðæt geðiode wenden ðe we ealle gecnawan mægen,* ÆCHom i. 114. 6 *and he hatað ealle ða ðe unrihtwisnysse wyrcað,* ÆCHom ii. 328. 22 *ðone ðe Drihten lufað, þone he ðreað,* and *Beo* 506 *Eart þu se Beowulf se þe wið Brecan wunne . . . ?*

§2282. Second, we find *se, þe,* and the compound relatives, in both prose and poetry in what seem to us similar contexts. Examples include: *Bede* 2. 2 7 *ic ðe sende þæt spell þæt ic niwan awrat be Angelþeode 7 Seaxum . . . , Bede(Ca)* 38. 18 *þa ðis wundor ða geseah betwuh oðre se sylfa cwellere ðe hine slean sceolde . . . ,* and *Bede(B)* 38. 18 *ða þis wundor þa geseah se cwellere se ðe hine slean sceolde . . . ;* ÆCHom i. 282. 7 *Seo sunne ðe ofer us scinð is lichamlic gesceaft, and hæfð swa ðeah ðreo agennyssa on hire: an is seo lichamlice edwist, þæt is ðære sunnan trendel; oðer is se leoma oððe beorhtnys æfre of ðære sunnan, seoðe onliht ealne middangeard; þridde is seo hætu, þe mid þam leoman cymð to us;*

PPs 101. 4   Ic eom hege gelic,   þam þe hraðe weornað . . . ,

PPs 101. 5   Ic geworden eom   pellicane gelic,
                se on westene wunað,

and

PPs 101. 5   . . . ic genemned eam   nihthrefne gelic,
                þe on scræfe eardað . . . ;

Pr 11   Se byð earming   þe on eorðan her
                dæiges and nihtes   deofle campað . . .

and

Pr 16   Se byð eadig,   se þe on eorðan her
                dæiges and nyhtes   drihtne hyræð . . . ;

and

PPs 134. 11   Wæs Seon efne   sum þara kynincga,
                and Og kyning,   se þe æror wæs
                on Basane   breme and mære

and

PPs 135. 21   And Og swylce,   þe æror wæs
                   swyþe breme cyning   on Basane.

Andrew's theories derive no support from Old Saxon; see Mitchell
1959, pp. 129–30 and 187, and *Ang.* 81 (1963), 299.

§2283. The table which follows gives the situation in OE poetry.
The number of examples cannot be exact, for some clauses may be
taken as noun, some as adverb, rather than as adjective. The ambiguous examples are accounted for in part by the existence of clauses
which are neither specifically limiting nor specifically descriptive,
and in part by the absence of the guides of punctuation and intonation. The percentages are approximate and *must be interpreted in the
light of the fact that I classified over two-thirds of the clauses as
limiting.*

Relative	Number of Clauses	Percentage of Clauses		
		Limiting	Descriptive	Ambiguous
þe	690	85	5	10
se	602	38	41	21
'seþe	49	70	10	20
se'þe[64]	236	96	2	2
seþe	378	76	8	16

It is clear that *þe* tends to introduce limiting clauses and that the
most common relative in descriptive clauses is *se*. But *se* is almost as
common in limiting as in descriptive clauses and clauses introduced
by the compound relatives are predominantly limiting. So Andrew's
claim (*SS*, p. 109) that 'in a limiting relative clause, the relative pronoun is normally *ðe*' is a misstatement. I cannot delay here in order
to produce full figures for the prose! But my impression is that the
situation there is much the same as in the poetry. One thing, however, is certain: as I state in §2270, Andrew's 'rules' are no more
than tendencies.

(3) *Intonation and metre*

§2284. It is clear from the preceding discussion that modern syntacticians cannot discover any system which governed the choice

---

[64] Some of these consist of combinations of *se* as sole antecedent + *þe*. These I would
now classify as *þe* clauses; see §2166 fn.

between *se, þe*, and the compound relatives, in the extant prose or poetry. As we have seen, it is possible that there was originally a simple system involving enclitic *þe* and non-enclitic *se*, that it was no longer operative in the extant texts, and that its breakdown presaged the complete disappearance in ME of the OE relative system.

§2285. But there is another possibility: that a system based on phonetic, stylistic, or rhetorical, criteria does lie behind the fluctuations which seem pointless to us. Van der Laan (*Neophil.* 14 (1929), 41) suggests that 'the form of the O.E. relative pronoun in a large measure depended on the stress-quality of the antecedent'. Harlow, in showing 'that the decision to punctuate depends also on other factors, some clearly rhetorical' (p. 7), isolates and illustrates (pp. 7–11) the following factors, which may have influenced not only punctuation but also the form of the relative:

(*a*) the length of the clause—this must be to help in oral delivery; (*b*) variation in the type of word or expression used to connect clauses; (*c*) the relative importance of a group of clauses—this is primarily a matter of grammatical structure, but is also influenced by rhetorical considerations; (*d*) the overall rhythm of the sentence—this is a purely rhetorical matter.

§2286. These articles are salutary reminders of the importance of intonation to OE syntactical studies. But it is a clue denied to modern students, who have to bear in mind that different speakers may have given different intonation to the same example or that the same speaker may have given different utterance to examples which seem identical to us. So once again we cannot lay down 'rules'; cf. §§2161-2. I do not propose to speculate further here. Those wishing to do so will find material in van der Laan, *Neophil.* 14 (1929), 27–41; Wrenn, *PBA* 32 (1946), 278-80; *Postscript*, p. 104; Samuels, *MÆ* 18 (1949), 62; and Rynell, pp. 18-19.

§2287. Metrical considerations must sometimes at any rate have affected the choice of the relative in the poetry; consider the variations quoted in §2175 and see, in addition to the standard works on metre, Grossmann, pp. 87-92. This topic cannot be pursued here. However, future workers must take cognizance of Whitman, 'Constraints on the Use of the Relative Pronoun Forms in *Beowulf*', *TSLL* 21 (1979), 1-16, though they should not follow him in failing to distinguish *'sepe, se'þe*, and *sepe*; should consider carefully his conception of what constitutes an antecedent, especially in relation to examples like *Beo* 90b (p. 1) and 2864b (p. 12) and to *Beo* 3034b and 2295a (p. 13); and should weigh carefully the exceptions he admits (pp. 4-6) to his general principle that half-lines containing an initial monosyllabic relative or conjunction and an immediately following stressed syllable are avoided where possible. None the less, this is an important article in which Whitman demonstrates clearly that metrical considerations sometimes play what is perhaps a primary part in determining the form of the relative in *Beowulf*, but that syntactic considerations are usually relevant also. Yet there remains an element of free choice. Thus, if we consider only *seþe* relatives with an expressed antecedent, Whitman's conclusions suggest that *seþe* is metrically essential in *Beo* 103b but that *þe* for *seþe* would have been acceptable in *Beo* 506b and 87b; see Whitman, pp. 3 and 12, and compare *Beo* 500a and 2258b. Whitman also suggests that the principle stated above has implications for the choice between using and not using 'the definite article' and for choosing between such alternatives as *þæt* or *þætte* and *þeah* or *þeah þe*.

c. The position of the adjective clause in relation to the antecedent

(1) The adjective clause follows its antecedent

§2288. The OE adjective clause normally comes after its antecedent. It is commonly found in the position usual in MnE, viz. immediately after the antecedent or separated from it by a word or phrase which qualifies it.[65] The antecedent may, of course, be at the beginning of its own clause, or somewhere within it, e.g. *Or* 12. 16 *Seo Ægyptus þe us near is, be norþan hire is þæt land Palastine*, *ÆCHom* ii. 8. 33 *Se ylca Godes Sunu, seðe ealle ðing gesceop, he eac gesceop his agene moder*—on such repetition of the antecedent, see §1893—*Bede* 54. 24 *Ðæs caseres rices ðy teoðan geare Gregorius se halga wer, se wæs on lare 7 on dæde se hehsta, feng to biscophade . . . , Bede*

---

[65] There is room for more work here. I have to confess that I have no statistics to support the impression which led me to write 'commonly'. O'Neil (p. 199) says that 'the most striking characteristic of the relative clause—indeed, of all subordinate clauses—in Old English has gone undiscussed and thus unaccounted for: the fact that such clauses are (almost) always at the margins of the main clause, (almost) never flanked by material from the main clause'. I believe this assertion to be far too sweeping. Carkeet, who begins by attacking 'descriptivist studies of Old English (OE) syntax' and users of percentages but ends by describing and using percentages, says that 'Old English shows a marked aversion to sentence-internal relative clauses' (1977, pp. 173-4). This seems to me a somewhat extreme way of describing a phenomenon which occurs in twenty-nine per cent of adjective clauses in his prose corpus (p. 178) and (it would appear from his figures) in seventy per cent of adjective clauses in *Beowulf*—111 examples out of 155 (p. 180). Such percentages in any event cannot be exact. They are likely to be affected (for example) by the point I make in §2204; by Latin influence, e.g. *Bede* 44. 31 (Carkeet 1977, pp. 180-1); and by the fact that in some contexts, e.g. *Beo* 506 *Eart þu se Beowulf se þe wið Brecan wunne?*, the 'sentence-internal relative clause' is impossible. See further D. Yerkes, *Syntax and Style in Old English* (Binghamton, N.Y., 1982), 96.

34. 14 *Ða gelamp þæt he sumne Godes mann preosthades, se wæs ða*
reþan ehteras fleonde, on gestliðnysse onfeng, ÆCHom i. 24. 3 . . .
and wæs se soða Scyppend, seðe ana is God, forsewen and geunwurþod,
and

Beo 229   þa of wealle geseah   weard Scildinga,
                 se þe holmclifu   healdan scolde,
                 beran ofer bolcan   beorhte randas,

or at its end, e.g. *Bede* 4. 11 *Danieles þæs arwurðan Westseaxna*
biscopes, se nu gyt lifigende is, Or 12. 29 . . . *wið þone Readan Sæ*,
þe ic ær beforan sæde, ÆCHom i. 76. 2 *Onfoh me to minum ge-*
broðrum mid ðam ðe ðu come, and

Beo 377   Ðonne sægdon þæt   sæliþende,
                 þa ðe gifsceattas   Geata fyredon
                 þyder to þance. . . .

Harlow (p. 8) notes that in some Ælfric manuscripts 'relative clauses
which are placed between the subject and predicate of the principal
sentence are usually punctuated after the relative clause, but not
before it'.

§ 2289. But in OE the relative is frequently separated from the antecedent and the word or phrase which qualifies it. The result is a pattern which is usually avoided in MnE, e.g. *Or* 19. 9 *Ohthere sæde þæt*
sio scir hatte Halgoland þe he on bude, CP 7. 17 . . . *ða ongan ic . . .*
ða boc wendan on Englisc ðe is genemned on Læden Pastoralis, CP
301. 26 *hii doð for ege ðone weorðscipe mannum ðe hie Gode don*
scoldon, ÆCHom i. 98. 4 *Swa swa Sarra gehyrsumode Abrahame,*
and hine hlaford het, ðære dohtra ge sind, wel donde and na on-
drædende ænige gedrefednysse, ÆCHom i. 464. 28 *An Ælmihtig*
God is, ðone ðe Bartholomeus bodað, ÆCHom i. 262. 25 *Nis þæt na*
swa to understandenne, swylce Godes nama ne sy genoh halig, seðe
æfre wæs halig (where *seðe*, which Thorpe takes as referring to
Godes, may refer to *nama*), *Beo* 97 . . . *lif eac gesceop || cynna ge-*
hwylcum þara ðe cwice hwyrfaþ (a common pattern in the poetry),

Beo 205   Hæfde se goda   Geata leoda
                 cempan gecorone   þara þe he cenoste
                 findan mihte,

Beo 309   þæt wæs foremærost   foldbuendum
                 receda under roderum,   on þæm se rica bad,

Beo 2020   Hwilum for duguðe   dohtor Hroðgares
                 eorlum on ende   ealuwæge bær,

          þa ic Freaware   fletsittende
          nemnan hyrde,

and

GenA 2107   Wæs ðu gewurðod   on wera rime
               for þæs eagum   þe ðe æsca tir
               æt guðe forgeaf!

As will be apparent, the separating element may be anything from
a single word, as in *CP* 301. 26 and *GenA* 2107, to the whole predicate of the principal clause, as in *ÆCHom* i. 98. 4 and *Beo* 309. We
even find another clause intervening, e.g.

Beo 2999   þæt ys sio fæhðo   ond se feondscipe,
               wælnið wera,   ðæs ðe ic [wen] hafo,
               þe us seceað to   Sweona leoda. . . .

§ 2290. Zuck (p. 89) points out that frequently 'the elements separating the relative and its antecedent can not be modified by the relative, either because the elements do not agree with the relative in
number and gender, or because they are verbs or adverbs and can
never be modified by relatives'. Harlow (p. 12) remarks that even
limiting adjective clauses can be punctuated before *þe* 'especially when
other words, such as an adverbial phrase or even the main verb, stand
between the antecedent and the relative pronoun'. Such clues will
often remove uncertainty about the reference of an adjective clause.
But ambiguity can arise.

§ 2291. Sometimes it is not clear which word is the antecedent. The
gender of the relative may point to the nearest of a group of nouns in
apposition or co-ordination, e.g. *ÆCHom* i. 282. 9 *oðer is se leoma
oððe beorhtnys æfre of ðære sunnan, seoðe onliht ealne middangeard*
(where the context makes it clear that the antecedent is not *sunnan*)
and

Beo 2749   . . .   þæt ic ðy seft mæge
          æfter maððumwelan   min alætan
          lif ond leodscipe,   þone ic longe heold,

or (in the poetry at any rate[66]) to the first noun in the group, e.g.

GenA 228   þonne seo æftre   Ethiopia
           land and liodgeard   beligeð uton
          ginne rice,   þære is Geon noma

[66] It is probably the third rather than the first in *ÆCHom* i. 288. 23 *An sawul is, and an
lif, and an edwist, seoðe hæfð þas ðreo ðing on hire.* . . .

and, as Robinson has shown—see my §46—

Beo 67   Him on mod bearn,
         þæt healreced   hatan wolde,
         medoærn micel   men gewyrcean
         þone yldo bearn   æfre gefrunon. . . .

There is of course no ambiguity about the meaning in these examples.
There can be argument about the grammatical antecedent in examples
like *WPol* 127. 183 *þæt is laðlic lif þæt hi swa maciað* and *Dan* 277
þæt wæs wuldres god ‖ *þe hie generede wið þam niðhete*, but it
makes little real difference whether we translate the latter ‘It was the
God of glory who saved them’ or ‘He who saved them was the God
of glory’.

§2292. When the clause belongs to one antecedent rather than
another, the context usually makes it clear. Nobody is likely to
entertain for one second the idea that *Englisc* is the antecedent of
the *ðe* clause in *CP* 7. 17 . . . *ða ongan ic ongemang oðrum mislicum
7 manigfealdum bisgum ðisses kynerices ða boc wendan on Englisc
ðe is genemned on Læden Pastoralis*. Nor is there doubt that *he* is the
antecedent in both *ÆCHom* i. 278. 17 *He is ðæs Fæder Wisdom and
his Word and his Miht, þurh ðone se Fæder gesceop ealle ðing and
gefadode* and

Sat 258   God seolfa him
         rice haldeð.   He is ana cyning,
         þe us eorre gewearð,   ece drihten,
         meotod mihtum swið.

§2293. But there are occasional examples in which there is some
uncertainty. In *Bede* 56. 6 *Ond þa sona sendon Agustinum to þæm
papan, þone þe him to biscope gecoren hæfde* . . . , the absence of
the subject pronouns combines with the separation of antecedent
and relative to produce momentary ambiguity. In *ÆCHom* i. 262. 25
. . . *Godes nama . . . seðe* . . . (§2289), both God and His name are
holy, and in *ÆCHom* i. 230. 13 . . . *Cristes lichama . . . seðe* (§2158),
both Christ and His body were born of the Virgin Mary. This sort of
ambiguity is common and may seem trifling. But it troubled at least
one Anglo-Saxon, for Timmer (1939, pp. 56–7) gives several examples
in which the reviser of *GD* altered the position of a genitive phrase so
that antecedent and relative could be together rather than separate.
They include *GD(H)* 137. 1 . . . *butan þæs mannes gast þe on him
sylfum byð?*, where MS *C* has . . . *se gast ðæs mannes þe* . . . , and
GD(H) 17. 4 . . . *mid hæse þæs abbodes þe wæs þæs mynstres hyrde*

..., where MS *C* has ... *mid þæs abbudes hæse* ... without a *þe* clause; on this point see further §2296. In *ÆCHom* ii. 24. 16 *Eucharius hatte sum mæssepreost, on þam lande þe is gehaten Hispania, se wæs ðearle geswenct mid langsumum broce*, it is clear from the context that the priest and not the land is afflicted with disease, even if we entertain the possibility that *Hispania*, unlike *land*, was masculine. In *Beo* 2291 (§2158) the ambiguity lies in the form of the relative, not in its possible separation from one of the possible antecedents. So, while separation of antecedent and relative may sometimes be the cause of momentary uncertainty—semantic or grammatical— it rarely, if ever, produces lasting ambiguity.

§2294. According to Carkeet (1976, pp. 44–7),

Old English exhibits a rather strong stylistic constraint mitigating against sentences in which a relative clause intervenes between constituents of the main clause. This constraint is not at all uncommon in language. . . . But the Old English (OE) tendency to avoid sentences like (1a) [The waiter gave the customer who was visibly hungover Post Toasties] is much stronger than in Modern English, so much stronger, in fact, as to suggest that the difference between the two systems is one of kind and not just one of degree.

The basis for this assertion is the existence of 'stylistic options systematically exploited by OE writers to achieve a reuniting of constituents of one clause that threaten to be separated by an intervening clause'. One is repetition of the antecedent, as in *Or* 42. 2 *7 þa spell þe ic secge ic hi sceal gescyrtan*; see §1893. Another—'extraposition' —is exemplified only by *Or* 19. 9 (§2289). But here the antecedent is *sio scir*, not *Halgoland*, and is separated from the adjective clause. 'Another rule inverts the verb phrase and the subject when the subject is modified by a relative clause, thereby bringing the relative clause to the end of the sentence.' This is exemplified by *Solil* 12. 11 *gef ðe þurh treowa findon þa ðe þe findon, sile me þa treowa*. The fourth is the splitting of groups seen in *ÆLS* 14. 145 *Eac swylce þa sacerdas suncon forð mid and sume ða hæðenan þe þær gehende stodon*. Carkeet goes on (p. 46): 'In every case the derived pattern is highly marked when one ignores the relative clause. That is, subjects are not normally repeated in Old English, nor is there normally inversion of subjects and verb phrases, nor are conjoined subjects normally split apart.' As a study of the relevant sections of this book will show, these assertions are false. None of the phenomena described by Carkeet and exemplified above is restricted to contexts involving adjective clauses in particular or subordinate clauses in general. His suggestion (p. 44) that the difference here between OE and MnE 'is one of kind and not just of degree' seems to me contradicted by his own observations (p. 47) on the differences between OE, ME, and MnE, and by the evidence presented by Yerkes which I discuss in §2297.

§2295. Separation of antecedent and relative was one of the factors which led Reuter (pp. 8-9) to see in examples like *ChronE* 7. 25 (47) *þa feng Nero to rice æfter Claudie se æt nextan forlet Brytene igland for his uncafscipe* something akin to the MnE continuative clause introduced by 'who' or 'which'. 'This', he observes, 'is particularly the case in asyndetically coordinated relative clauses', citing among others *CP* 69. 4 and *ÆCHom* i. 470. 20 (both in §2275). But in translating these examples, we would not replace the second relative with 'and they' or 'and he'; we would insert 'and' before the relative and read 'and who' in both examples. So I do not class these clauses as continuative. Nor, I think, would Kock, who says (p. 88) that 'when, in OE or ME, two rel. clauses have the same ant., there was usually no conj. between them. . . . Less frequent were rel. clauses united by a coordinate conj.' See further §§2328-37. The insertion of a conjunction is, of course, impossible in those examples in which a non-limiting clause is preceded by the antecedent and a limiting clause qualifying it, e.g. *Bede* 40. 22 . . . *neah ðære ceastre ðe Romane heton Uerolamium, seo nu fram Angelðeode Werlameceaster oþþe Wæclingaceaster is nemned* and *ÆCHom* i. 100. 4 *Se eahteteoða dæg þæs monðes þe we hata ð Martius, ðone ge hata ð Hlyda, wæs se forma dæg ðyssere worulde*; see further §§2271-83.

§2296. There is even less reason for seeing *ChronE* 7. 25 (47)—the first example in §2295—as a continuative adjective clause. Rather we see both an instance of what was originally at any rate two sentences, the second introduced by dem. *se*—'Then after Claudius, Nero succeeded to the throne. That [man] finally abandoned the island of Britain because of his sloth'—and also an explanation for the frequency of such separation in OE: it goes back to a stage in which the language was paratactic. The demands of metre may be a partial explanation of the phenomenon in the poetry. But it is a feature of the language. Schwarz (*Lang.* 44 (1968), 752-4) draws our attention to the similarity between the separation of a limiting clause from its antecedent, as in *CP* 301. 26 (§2289), and the separation of a genitive phrase from its governing noun, as in *CP* 3. 5 . . . *ða kyningas ðe ðone onwald hæfdon ðæs folces.* . . . We may perhaps see in these two forms of separation a manifestation of the same feeling which led to repetition of subjects or objects (§§1503-5 and 1570-1) and the splitting of groups (§§1464-72).

§ 2297. The suggestion that this separation of antecedent and adjective clause is a relic of an earlier paratactic stage of the language is in accordance with the evidence presented by Yerkes (pp. 259–63), which confirms the observations of Timmer cited in § 2293 and shows clearly that the reviser of *GD* had a strong preference for the MnE practice of placing antecedent and relative together.[67] I quote here from Yerkes's conclusions (p. 259):

In fifty-eight examples an adjective clause lies further from its antecedent in Wærferth than in the revision. The reverse obtains in only six examples. . . . The revision therefore usually agrees with normal PresE and places the adjective clause adjacent to its antecedent. The Latin supports the revision here in less than half of the examples. . . . The adjective clause lies adjacent to its antecedent in Wærferth in all six of the examples. . . . The adjective clause lies adjacent to its antecedent in the revision in all but three of the other fifty-eight examples. . . .

Whether the separation of antecedent and relative was in general less common in the later than in the earlier prose remains to be established. Anyone pursuing the topic will need to take into account the grammatical relationship between the antecedent and the relative and the form of the adjective clause; see Carkeet, 1976, pp. 46 and 57, and 1977, pp. 179–80.

§ 2298. Qualifiers of the antecedent such as adjectives, nouns and pronouns in the genitive, and genitive phrases, are usually found in the principal clause. Exceptions are discussed in § § 1921a and 2227–30.

(2) *The adjective clause precedes its principal clause or its 'postcedent'*

§ 2299. When the adjective clause precedes its principal clause, it is normally indefinite; see § § 2206–13. The reader will recall that such clauses can, but need not be, followed by a 'postcedent' in the principal clause, e.g. *ÆCHom* i. 300. 28 *seðe gelyfð and bið gefullod, se*

---

[67] It follows therefore that I do not accept these comments made by Carkeet (1977) about the attitude of OE writers to 'sentence-internal relative clauses': 'marked aversion' (p. 174), 'seem to go out of their way to avoid' (p. 174), 'appears to have been deliberately avoided' (p. 178)—cf. 'deliberately chosen' (p. 177)—'do not like' and 'work very hard to achieve a paraphrase' (p. 187). Nor would I describe the chiastic sentence he quotes from *Ch* 1460 as 'pointlessly complex' or 'a mere response to the threat of sentence-internal relative clauses' (p. 182). Is *this* the secret of Ælfric's style?

It is interesting that O'Neil, who starts from the same alleged phenomenon as Carkeet 1977—that 'Old English shows a marked aversion to sentence-internal relative clauses' (Carkeet 1977, p. 174)—reaches a conclusion which seems almost antithetic to that adopted by Carkeet (1976 and 1977) but very similar to mine, viz. that 'it is possible in fact that there were *no* relative clauses at all in the Germanic language(s) that preceded in time those earliest recorded Germanic languages . . . and . . . it follows in this line of speculation that there were no dependent clauses at all in the older common language(s)' (p. 207).

biδ gehealden; se δe ne gelyfδ, he biδ genyδerod, but *ÆCHom* i. 28.
13 *and δa δe his beboda eallunga forseoδ beoδ on helle besencte.*

§2300. But there are some adjective clauses which have specific reference and stand at the beginning of the sentence. Most of them are
introduced by the *sepe* relative—in which *se* may be taken as the antecedent; see §2178—and are followed by 'postcedent' *se* or *he*, e.g.
CP 261. 14 *Se δe us oferdrencδ mid δæs ecan lifes liδe, he gefandode
geallan biternesse* . . . , *ÆCHom* i. 226. 13 *Ac se δe nolde of δære
rode abrecan, se aras of δære byrgene*, and *ÆCHom* i. 254. 9 *Se δe
æfre is god, he brincδ us yfele to godum mannum, gif we bugaδ fram
yfele and doδ god*, where the references are to Christ, Christ, and
God, respectively. *Se* appears without a 'postcedent' in *GD(O)* 107.
34, but MS *C* has 'postcedent' *he* and MS *H* has *se þe*; see §2319.

§2301. Examples in which the 'postcedent' is something other than
a personal or demonstrative pronoun are rare. *GD(H)* 60. 20 *Eall þæt
ure alysend dyde þurh his menniscean lichaman, eall þæt he gegearwode us on gebysnunge godes weorces* does not strictly belong here
because the adjective clause is preceded by the antecedent *eall* which
is repeated after the adjective clause. In

PPs 51. 8   forþan þu eart se gooda,   gleaw on gesyhδe,
                     þe þinne held curan,   þara haligra,

we have a typical example of the clumsy workmanship of the poet of
the *Paris Psalter* rather than a convincing parallel for

Beo 1133   . . .   oþ δæt oþer com
                    gear in geardas,   swa nu gyt deδ,
                    þa δe syngales   sele bewitiaδ,
                    wuldortorhtan weder,

where *þa* seems to be explained by 'postcedent' (or appositive?)
wuldortorhtan weder, so making lines 1135a–36b a variant of *gear*.
A closer parallel is provided by

PPs 134. 22   þa þe him ondræden   drihtnes egsan,
                    bletsien drihten   beornas ealle.

10. APPARENT ABSENCE OF ANTECEDENT OR RELATIVE PRONOUN

a. Introductory remarks

§2302. I deliberately use this non-committal heading in the hope of
clarifying it as I write. The unsatisfactory terms 'ellipsis', 'omission

of the relative', and 'omission of the antecedent', have been used to cover a variety of constructions. In 1894, Wülfing (i. 420-1) wrote that much had already been written 'über die Auslassung des relativen Fürwortes' and that the opinion of the various writers diverged widely. Over fifty years later, Bosker (*Neophil.* 31 (1947), 32) spoke of 'ellipsis-mania'. Undoubtedly there are cases of scribal error. The different readings of MSS *O* and *B* in *Bede* 58. 6 may be a case in point; see §2209. Endter is probably right to insert *þe* in *Solil* 52. 14 *Forðam þes nis nan tweo þæt ælc þincg þara* [*þe*] *ys hwærhwugu is* and MS *D* has *þe* after *þæs*, where we find

Brun(A) 47   mid heora herelafum   hlehhan ne þorftun
                þæt heo beaduweorca   beteran wurdun
                on campstede   cumbolgehnastes,
                garmittinge,   gumena gemotes,
                wæpengewrixles,   þæs hi on wælfelda
                wiþ Eadweardes   afaran plegodan.

(In this particular example *þæs* or *þæs þe* can be taken as a conjunction 'when' (§2685) or 'because' (§3113) rather than as a relative.) But there is more to it than scribal error. Here I try to arrange the bones which strew this oft-fought-over battlefield in some sort of order.[68]

§2303. Among the most obvious reasons for the confusion apparent in many writings on this subject is the failure of scholars to distinguish sentences in which there is an expressed antecedent from those in which one word does duty as both antecedent and relative and to distinguish definite from indefinite clauses. The latter distinction cannot always be made with certainty—see §§2129-33 and 2204—but the attempt to make it is sometimes rewarding. The possibility of *apo koinou* constructions, of asyndetic parataxis, of lack of concord in case, and of 'attraction', must also be remembered.

---

[68] Wülfing (i. 420-1) gives an excellent review of the writings up to 1894 concerning these phenomena in the English language. His failure to mention L. Tobler, 'Über Auslassung und Vertretung des Pronomen relativum', *Germania*, 17 (1872), 257-94, is noteworthy. Tobler made some of the points I make here about OE and covered other Germanic languages. See Visser, i. 550, for a list of subsequent writings on 'the absence of the relative object-pronoun'. The list in Visser, i. 14-15, covers all types of 'no subject' constructions.

b. Apparent absence of a relative pronoun in a definite adjective clause referring to an expressed antecedent other than part of the demonstrative se[69]

(1) *Introductory remarks*

§2304. The major distinction here is one of case; cf. MnE 'There's a man at the door wants to see you', where the expressed relative would be 'who', with 'This is the man I saw' and 'This is the man I gave the book to', where the expressed relative would be 'whom'. In OE, of course, we would distinguish the first 'whom' as accusative and the second as dative. Jespersen (*Ess.*, §34. 3) called these 'contact-clauses'. Visser (i, §§18 and 627) uses the term *apo koinou* of both types and also calls the latter the 'zero-construction'. Terasawa (pp. 129–30) prefers to follow Jespersen, for what seem to me sound reasons. For other possibilities, see Meritt, p. 18. But what to call them is not the most important problem. What does matter is the relationship between the two elements of the sentence and when, if ever, emendation is necessary in OE examples.[70]

(2) *The adjective clause requires the nominative case*

§2305. This phenomenon manifests itself most frequently in OE with forms of the verb *hatan* 'to be named', viz. *hatte, hatton*, e.g. *Or* 10. 20 . . . *betux þære ie Indus 7 þære þe be westan hiere is, Tigris hatte, Or* 70. 8 . . . *under þæm twæm consulum, Tita 7 Publia hatton, HomNap* 98. 14 *an deofles man wæs hwilan on Rome, Simon hatte*, and *Gen* 29. 29 *7 se fæder hyre sealde ane ðeowene, Bala hatte* (not by Ælfric), and *is/wæs (ge)haten*, e.g. *Bede* 134. 11 *Him þa andswarode his ealdorbisceop, Cefi wæs haten, ÆLet* 4. 302 *His ginsta sunu buton anum, wæs Ioseph gehaten, wearð ðær hlaford on Egipta lande* . . . , and

GenA 1159   þa wearð on eðle   eafora feded,
            mago Cainanes,   Malalehel wæs haten.

But the relative pronoun does appear with these forms, e.g. *CP* 445. 34 . . . *on ðæm bocum ðe hatton Apocalipsin, ChronA* 46. 26 (755) . . . *anne æþeling se was Cyneheard haten*, and *ÆHom* 27. 17 and 1. 174 (both in §1475). Further on naming constructions, see §§1473–81.

---

[69] Visser's 'rule' about the priority of pronouns over nouns as antecedents in these constructions (i. 536) can be dismissed. The two constructions must be regarded as different.

[70] Curme (*JEGP* 10 (1911), 335 ff.) discusses these constructions in OE without making the situation any clearer to me. Kirch (*PMLA* 74 (1959), 503–6) disproves Jespersen's suggestion (*GS*, §80) that such constructions may have been due to Scandinavian influence.

§2306. Indisputable examples involving other verbs are few. They include (with the verb 'to be') *ChronA* 92. 14 (901) *7 on þys ilcan gere forðferde Æþered, wæs on Defenum ealdormon, Bede* 184. 7, *ChronA* 94. 20 (906) *Her on þys geare gefor Ælfred, wæs æt Baðum gerefa* (MS *A* adds *se* above the line before *wæs* in the second *Chronicle* example and the later MS *B* inserts *se* in both of them and in similar examples from the later *Chronicle* cited by Anklam (pp. 6–7)); (with the verb *belifan*) *ÆCHom* ii. 348. 20 *Ða licmenn ða ealle mid fyrhðe fornumene, flugon aweg, buton þam wife anum, þe hine swiðost lufode, belaf þær afyrht*; and (twice with *nele*; cf. §§1690 and 1923) *Jul* 382–97.

§2307. Editors sometimes eliminate examples by inserting a relative pronoun, e.g. *þa þe* in *Bede* 70. 24 and *þe* in *And* 717, *Rid* 40. 58 and 105 (cf. the ASPR notes on *Rid* 37. 4 and *Met* 13. 20), and *Res* 2. The scribal addition of *þe* in *And* 101 and *PPs* 80. 10 and the variant readings at *Brun* 51 lend some plausibility to these emendations. Others can be differently explained, e.g. *Beo* 286 and *GenA* 2893 (both quoted by Visser, i. 12), and others are the result of misunderstanding of the text, e.g. *Or* 70. 8 (cited by Bacquet, p. 365).

§2308. It may be noted that all the possible examples discussed here could be eliminated by editorial insertion of *þe* or some other relative.

§2309. Meritt (pp. 90–109) makes the fact that we find both sentences with *þe* and sentences without *þe* grounds for refusing *apo koinou* status to examples like *Or* 70. 8 (§2305) and *ChronA* 94. 20 (§2306); in such examples, he argues (p. 95), the second element is an 'attributive clause [which] was distinctly felt to be subordinate' and 'the two parts were not felt to be independent parts expressed one after the other'. But the fact that two constructions are, or appear to be, interchangeable does not certify that they are syntactically identical. My own feeling, at least about examples like 'There's a man at the door wants to see you', is that the two elements are equal in weight, that there is no sense of a missing 'who', and that its insertion completely changes the relationship.

(3) *The adjective clause requires the accusative or the dative case*

§2310. Here again some of the alleged examples are the result of misunderstanding the text, e.g. *ChronA* 94. 5 (905) (see Blain, p. 21, and Visser, i. 537) and *Or* 86. 3 (see Bacquet, p. 365, and my §3221). Some can be eliminated by repunctuation to give a new sentence, e.g. *Bede* 426. 2, *BlHom* 9. 35, and *ÆCHom* i. 100. 13.

§ 2311. As in the previous group, all the possible examples can be eliminated by the insertion of *þe* or some other relative. Sometimes this has the authority of a variant reading, e.g. *ChronA* 42. 22 (722), *Bede(Ca)* 66. 1, *GD(H)* 106. 30, and *LawIICn* 8. 2. Sometimes it does not, e.g. *ChronE* 115. 25 (963), *LawRect* 20. 2, *PPs* 72. 12, *PPs* 73. 3, *Ch* 1501 *gange þ land on Boccinge into Cristes circean þam hirede for uncera saule 7 for mines fæder þe hit ær begeat eall buton anre hide ic gean into þære cyrcean þam preoste þe þar gode þeowaþ*, *Marv* 60. 9 *Ðonne is oþer stow elreordge men beoð on*, and

Beo 1173   Beo wið Geatas glæd,   geofena gemyndig,
                nean ond feorran   þu nu hafast.

HomU 45. 291. 16 (§ 2316) may belong here.

(4) *Conclusion*

§ 2312. At present the attitudes of editors towards the examples discussed are inconsistent; cf.

And 717   Ðis is anlicnes   engelcynna
               þæs bremestan   mid þam burgwarum
               in þære ceastre is,

where the ASPR editors insert *þe*, with

PPs 72. 12   Gif ic sylf cwæde   and sæcge eac,
               swa þe bearn weorðað   geboren syþþan,
               þa ylcan ic   ær foreteode,

where, despite the Latin *Si dicebam: Narrabo sic: ecce natio filiorum tuorum, quibus disposui*, they do not. However, I cannot suggest any principles for their guidance and cannot subscribe wholeheartedly to Meritt's conclusion (p. 95):

In all the Old Germanic languages, wherever it occurs, the attributive-clause construction may in some instances be due to the omission of the relative and in some instances it may continue an early asyndetic means of joining before the use of relatives; but its occurrence always along with similar expressions where a kind of relative is used justifies one in holding that the construction was always one of hypotaxis. And in this it is distinguished from asyndetic parataxis, which bears some similarity to ἀπὸ κοινοῦ.

It contains an element of self-contradiction, it relies on the argument that (apparent) interchangeability certifies syntactical identity, and it (like me) offers editors no practical help.

c. Apparent absence of a relative pronoun in a definite adjective clause referring to an expressed antecedent which ends with part of the demonstrative se *in the case appropriate to the principal clause*

§2313. The distinction between this pattern and the preceding one is made clear in the respective headings. But here too the (apparent) syntactical irregularity can be corrected by inserting *þe* after the demonstrative element. The adjective clause may require the nominative, e.g.

Beo 2196   Him wæs bam samod
          on ðam leodscipe   lond gecynde,
          eard eðelriht,   oðrum swiðor
          side rice   þam ðær selra wæs

and

ChristC 918   He bið þam yflum   egeslic ond grimlic
          to geseonne,   synnegum monnum,
          þam þær mid firenum cumað,   forð forworhte;

the accusative, e.g. *LawIICn(A)* 39. 1 *7 binnan ðrittigum nihtan aginne bote ægðer ge wið Godd ge wið menn be eallum þam he age* (where the other manuscripts have *þe* or *ðe* after *þam*), *GenA* 2118 *. . . and halegu treow, ‖ seo þu wið rodora weard rihte healdest,*

El 1193   Bið þæt beacen gode
          halig nemned,   ond se hwæteadig,
          wigge weorðod,   se þæt wicg byrð,

and

KtPs 4   Wæs he under hiofenum   hearpera mærost
          ðara we an folcum   gefrigen hæbben;

or the dative, e.g. *Ch* 1510 *7 ic biddo higon for Godes lufe ðæt se monn se higon londes unnen to brucanne ða ilcan wisan leste on swæsendum to minre tide* and

GenB 618   Gif giet þurh cuscne siodo
          læst mina lara,   þonne gife ic him þæs leohtes genog
          þæs ic þe swa godes   gegired hæbbe.

The other examples in the poetry are *GenA* 1428, *OrW* 9, *Res* 24 and 68, *PPs* 77. 13, and possibly *Brun(A)* 47 (see §2302). On two examples in which *þe* follows the demonstrative but may be taken as a personal pronoun—*GenA* 1341 and *MSol* 234—see §2248.

§2314. In some of these examples, e.g. *LawIICn(A)* 39. 1, the insertion of *þe* seems inevitable; cf. *GD(C)* 37. 10 *he cymð æfter me, se þu secest* with *GD(H)* 37. 11 *he cymð nu æfter me, se þe þu secst.* In others, e.g. *KtPs* 4, it seems to offer the best solution. But in those like *GenA* 2118 and *El* 1193, the possibility exists that a form of the relative *se* has been attracted into the case appropriate to the principal clause. However, Campbell (*JEGP* 37 (1938), 140) sees *Ch* 1510 (§2313) as an example in which the *se* of the compound relative has been 'attracted to the case of the antecedent, of which it is then an emphatic repetition' (so producing what I call the *se'þe* relative) and 'the particle *þe* is omitted'.

d. A form of se alone does duty as antecedent and relative

(1) þæt

§2315. The neut. *þæt* often does duty as both antecedent and relative. It is sometimes difficult or impossible to decide whether it is definite (MnE 'what') or indefinite (MnE 'whatever'). Both clauses usually require the same case, e.g. (nominative) *Bede(Ca)* 78. 35 *7 oft butan synne bið don þ of synne cymeð* (some MSS *þte*) and *Coll* 242 *7 beo þæt þu eart* and (accusative) *CP* 201. 6 *Wið God ge doð ðæt ge dooð* and

Beo 1465   Huru ne gemunde   mago Ecglafes
                    eafoþes cræftig,   þæt he ær gespræc
                    wine druncen. . . .

But there are occasional examples in which this is not so, including *Bede(Ca)* 66. 13 *þ ofer si 7 to lafe, sellað ælmessan 7 eow beoð ealle clæne* (some MSS *þte*)—cf. Pope's 'To help who want, to forward who excel'—and *Bede* 80. 20 . . . *forhwon þonne þæt wiif þæt heo clæne mode of gecynde þrowað sceal hire in unclænnesse geteled beon?*—cf. Byron's 'Whom the gods love die young'. See further §§2127-8.

(2) þæs *(neuter)*

§2316. Many of the alleged examples of an absent antecedent or relative involve *þæs* used as both antecedent and relative. Sometimes it is the genitive of *þæt* 'what(ever)' used correctly with no possibility of ellipsis or omission. This is certainly true in those examples in which the genitive is an appropriate case for both clauses, e.g. *Max i* 103 *a mon sceal seþeah leofes wenan,* ‖ *gebidan þæs he gebædan ne mæg,* HomU 45. 291. 16 *and [þu scealt] ðonne mid þinre anre sawle riht agildon alra ðinga gehwylces, þæs ðu ær mid þinum licaman fremedest godes oððe yfeles,*[71]

---

[71] The genitive is found after both *ongildan* and (in *Or* 168. 17) *fremman*; see the List of Verbal Rections. But *þæs* may here agree with *gehwylces*—in which case the example belongs in §2311—rather than being independent 'for each of all things, for what of good and evil you formerly did with your body'.

GenA 2811
    Forðon ðe giena speow
    þæs þu wið freond oððe feond   fremman ongunne
    wordum oððe dædum,

and

GenB 435   Se þe þæt gelæsteð,   him bið lean gearo
    æfter to aldre,   þæs we her inne magon
    on þyssum fyre forð   fremena gewinnan.

GK (p. 696. 4) postulates ellipsis of the relative *þe* in the last example; but see §2229. It can be inserted in the other examples too; cf. *ÆCHom* i. 248. 32 and *ÆCHom* ii. 448. 19 (both in §2133). But this is not necessary; like *þæt* 'what' and *þætte* or *þæt ðe* 'what', *þæs* and *þæs ðe* are alternatives. So a case can be made for reading either *þæs* or *hwæs* for MS *wæs* in *And* 145, despite Brooks's note; see Samuels, *RES* 14 (1963), 176.

§2317. Examples in which *þæs* is the form appropriate for only the principal clause include those in which the principal clause requires a partitive genitive, e.g. *BlHom* 25. 1 *Hwæt wille we on domes dæg forþberan þæs we for urum drihtne arefnedon, nu he swa mycel for ure lufan geþrowode?* and

El 565   Heo wæron stearce,   stane heardran,
    noldon þæt geryne   rihte cyðan,
    ne hire andsware   ænige secgan,
    torngeniðlan,   þæs hio him to sohte,

and those in which the verb of the principal clause governs the genitive, e.g. *GD(C)* 20. 5 *me lysteþ wel þæs þu sagast,*

Rid 41. 6   Ne magon we her in eorþan   owiht lifgan,
    nymðe we brucen   þæs þa bearn doð,

and possibly

Beo 1397   Ahleop ða se gomela,   Gode þancode,
    mihtigan Drihtne,   þæs se man gespræc.

But if *secgan* and *sprecan* do take the genitive (see the List of Verbal Rections), *GD(C)* 20. 5 and *Beo* 1397 could belong in the previous section. Here again the (apparent) irregularities can be corrected by inserting *þe* after *þæs*. Sometimes this has been done by an Anglo-Saxon; cf. *GD(C)* 20. 5 above with *GD(H)* 20. 5 *wel me licað þæs þe þu sægst*. Sometimes one is tempted to do it, e.g. in *Bo(C)* 128. 18 (see §2133) and in *Solil* 36. 1 *ne gebelge ic me nawiht wið þe, ac fagnige þæs þu cwyst*, which is to be compared with *Solil* 32. 15 *Ac ic bidde gyt þæs þe þu me ær gehete* and *Solil* 34. 12 *Ic eom geþafa þæs þe þu me segst.* The case required by the adjective clause may be nominative, as in

GenB 481

Sceolde on wite a
mid swate and mid sorgum   siððan libban,
swa hwa swa gebyrgde   þæs on þam beame geweox,

or the accusative as in *GenA* 2142 (§2229), *Soul i* 147, *Met* 28. 67, and *El* 565 above. It is probably a matter of chance that my collections do not contain an example in which the adjective clause requires the dative.

§2318. The remaining possibility is for *þæs* to be the form appropriate to the subordinate clause only. So far the only examples I have found are *Or* 126. 29 . . . *7 sæde hu he him an his gewill beforan þam folce ondwyrdan sceolde þæs he hiene ascade* and

Max i 97   . . .   ond heo hine in laðaþ,
wæsceð his warig hrægl   ond him syleþ wæde niwe,
liþ him on londe   þæs his lufu bædeð,

which Mackie (EETS, OS 194) translated '. . . grants him on the land what his love requires', thereby anticipating my translation in *RES* 15 (1964), 129–30. In these two examples, the insertion of *þe* achieves nothing.

(3) *Other forms of* se
§2319. Examples in which both clauses require the same case and a masculine or feminine form of *se* used alone as both antecedent and relative means (or seems to mean) 'whoever' have been discussed in §§2206 and 2216. There are, however, occasional examples in both prose and poetry in which this pattern occurs when the reference is to a specific individual or group of individuals, e.g. *GD(C)* 89. 14 *þa semninga se þær forðfered wæs onfeng his sawle* and *GD(O)* 107. 34 *witodlice se þa swin fedde gefeoll under hine sylfne* —MS *C* has *he* before *gefeoll* in the second example and MS *H* has *se þe* for *se* in both; see §2300—

Beo 1977   Gesæt þa wið sylfne   se ða sæcce genæs,
mæg wið mæge,   syððan mandryhten
þurh hleoðorcwyde   holdne gegrette,
meaglum wordum,

and *MSol* 460 *Ðæt sindon ða usic feohtað on.*

§2320. There are also, in both prose and poetry, sporadic examples in which a form of *se* other than *þæt* or neut. *þæs* appears alone as both antecedent and relative in the case appropriate to the principal

clause only. The adjective clause may require the nominative, e.g.
Solil 52. 14 *Forðam þes nis nan tweo þæt ælc þing þara ys hwærhwugu is*, *GenA* 1757 *lisse selle*, ‖ *wilna wæstme þam þe wurðiað*
(where *þe* is (or appears to be) the personal pronoun), *Beo* 2779,
GenA 2295, and *ChristA* 141, and

Rid 55. 5   . . . ond rode tacn,   þæs us to roderum up
                hlædre rærde,   ær he helwara
                burg abræce;

the accusative, e.g. *Bo* 112. 6 *ac þa unrihtwisan cyngas ne magon nan
god don, forþam ic þe nu sæde*; or the dative, e.g. *GenA* 857 *wiste
forworhte þa he ær wlite sealde*. The adjective clause may refer to
one specific person, e.g. Christ in *Rid* 55. 5, or may be indefinite,
e.g. *GenA* 857. Here again we can regularize the syntax by inserting
þe. But see Mitchell 1964a, pp. 131–2.

§2321. Examples in which *se* serves as both antecedent and relative
and has the case appropriate to the adjective clause only are few and
doubtful. *Ps(A)* 64. 5 *Eadig ðone ðu gecure* is a direct imitation of
the Latin *Beatus quem elegisti*. Krapp emends *þa* to *þam* to turn
GenA 857 (§2320) into one. Similarly Andrew (*Postscript*, p. 49)
reads *þam* for *þa* in *Beo* 402 *Snyredon ætsomne þa secg wisode*.
There is one in the ASPR version of

And 1320   Hafast nu þe anum   eall getihhad
             land ond leode,   swa dyde lareow þin.
             Cyneþrym ahof,   þam wæs Crist nama,
             ofer middangeard,   þynden hit meahte swa,

where in his 1906 edition Krapp (following Cosijn) provides a nominative antecedent for the adjective clause by omitting the full stop
after *þin* and treating line 1322a as parenthetical. But we can accept
these by explaining them as examples in which the pronoun antecedent of the principal clause is unexpressed. Again we may compare
MnE 'Whom the gods love die young'. Here again the insertion of *þe*
does not solve the problem.

      e. þe, *alone or with the personal pronoun, does duty as
                antecedent and relative*

§2322. *þe* may stand alone as antecedent and relative when both
clauses require the nominative, e.g. *LS* 34. 147 *and her on gehendnysse syndon þe þine deorlingas beon sceoldon* and *GuthA* 298
Sindon wærlogan þe þa wic bugað, or the accusative, e.g. *Bo* 106. 8
. . . *þ ðu mæge ðy bet gelefan ðe ic ðe oðre hwile recce be ðæm*

oðrum, oðre hwile be ðæm oðrum and *ÆCHom* i. 462. 31 *and forði ic sprece ðe he me het*, or when the two clauses require different cases. In all the examples of this last sort I have noted, the adjective clause requires the nominative. But the principal clause may require the accusative, e.g. *Dan* 443 *Hæfde on þam wundre gewurðod ðe þa gewyrhto ahton;*[72] the genitive, e.g. *PPs* 67. 23 and

PPs 118. 63   Ic eom dælneomend   þe heom ondrædað þe
                  and þine halige bebodu   healdað georne;

or the dative, e.g. *Rid* 50. 9 and

PPs 145. 6   He his soðfæst word   swylce gehealdeð,
                 and on worulde his   wise domas
                 deð gedefe   þe her deorce ær
                 teonan manige   torne geþoledan.

The reference of the adjective clause is indefinite in all the examples I have noted and plural in most; those with the singular include *Beo* 138, *Max i* 169, and *Rid* 50. 9, all quoted in §§2323–4.

§2323. In these examples the (apparent) syntactical irregularity can be corrected by inserting before *þe* the form of *se* appropriate to the principal clause; cf. the variations in *LawICn* 20. 1, where MS G reads *forþam byð witodlice God hold þe byð his hlaforde rihtlice hold* whereas the other manuscripts have *ðam/þam* before *þe*, and note that Holthausen supplies *þam* before *þe* in *Rid* 50. 9 *Leanað grimme* ‖ *þe hine wloncne weorþan læteð* and that Grein, Assmann, and Krapp, all supply *þara* before *þe* in

PPs 67. 21   Hwæðere wealdend god   wiðhycgendra
                 heafdas feonda   her gescæneð,
                 and he tofylleð   feaxes scadan
                 þara þe her on scyldum   swærum eodon.

Here again we see editorial inconsistency.

§2324.

And 1129   Ne mihte earmsceapen   are findan,
               freoðe æt þam folce,   þe him feores wolde,
               ealdres geunnan

has long been a source of difficulty. Krapp, in his 1906 edition and in ASPR, followed Pogatscher (*Ang.* 23 (1901), 272) in taking the *þe* clause as an explanatory noun clause. But I do not accept that *þe* can introduce a noun clause; see §1957. Grein (*Dichtungen der Angelsachsen*, iii. 2) took *þe* as a relative pronoun with *folce* as its

---

[72] *PPs* 56. 3 appears to have two such examples. But *þe* in line 2 represents Latin *et*. *Ps(A)* 56. 3 and other versions have the expected *7*.

antecedent. Brooks in his edition rightly objected that this would require Ettmüller's *nolde* and concluded that 'it seems that Krapp is right in taking *þe* as the conjunction, understanding *folc* as the unexpressed subject'. In my thesis (Mitchell 1959, p. 169), I quoted

Beo 138   þa wæs eaðfynde   þe him elles hwær
                   gerumlicor   ræste sohte . . .

as an example in which *þe* stands for both antecedent and relative, and went on '*And* 1129 could be included here, taking *findan apo koinou*'. In both of these *þe* must be taken as singular. But they are not parallel in case, for in *Beo* 138 both clauses require the nominative, whereas in *And* 1129 the sequence is accusative + nominative. There are, however, other examples in the poetry in which *þe* serves as a singular when the two clauses require different cases; they include *Rid* 50. 9 (§2323) and

Max i 169   Longað þonne þy læs   þe him con leoþa worn,
                   oþþe mid hondum con   hearpan gretan,

in which the sequence is respectively dative + nominative and accusative + nominative; see further Mitchell 1964*a*, p. 137. So what Samuels (*RES* 14 (1963), 176 fn. 1) saw as 'the possibility that *findan* . . . *þe* [in *And* 1129 above] means "find (anyone) who . . ." ' is to my mind a certainty.

§2325. In

PPs 145. 4   þonne bið eadig   þe him æror wæs
                   Iacobes god   geara fultumiend . . . ,

þe him serves as both antecedent and relative in a sentence in which the principal clause requires the nominative and the adjective clause the dative. Again we can compare MnE 'Whom the gods love die young' and again we note that the personal pronoun seems to remove a possible ambiguity. But when we compare *Beo* 138 (§2324), *PPs* 118. 63 (§2322), and *Max i* 169 (§2324)—in none of which the personal pronoun is in the case represented by *þe*—we see that (for modern scholars at any rate) the ambiguity exists until we have done our parsing. The same is true of

PPs 93. 11   þæt bið eadig mann   þe þu hine, ece god,
                   on þinre soðre æ   sylfa getyhtest,

where *þæt* provides the antecedent missing in *PPs* 145. 4. On this problem see further §§2198-9.

f. Combinations of se and þe

§2326. Here the possibility of 'omission' or non-expression of an antecedent can arise only when the two clauses require different cases and the *se* element is in the case of the adjective clause—in other words, when we have the *'seþe* relative alone. For in examples in which both clauses require the same case, e.g. *Beo* 603 *Gæþ eft se þe mot* ‖ *to medo modig*—see §2204—or in which the *se* element has the case appropriate to the principal clause only, e.g.

Beo 3033   Fundon ða on sande   sawulleasne
                  hlimbed healdan   þone þe him hringas geaf
                  ærran mælum—

see §§2153-4—the *se* element can be taken as the antecedent.

§2327. The two possible examples known to me can be eliminated by adopting an alternative manuscript reading. They are (with reference to no specific individual) *Bede(O)* 58. 6 *7 se þe him hyrsum beon wolde, buton tweon he gehet ecne gefean on heofonum*, where MS *B* inserts *him* after *gehet*, and (with reference to Lazarus) *ÆHom (C, H)* 6. 10 *La leof hlaford, þone þe þu lufast ys nu geuntrumod*, where MS *F* has *se þe*.

g. Expression or non-expression of the relative in co-ordinate adjective clauses

§2328. The relative pronoun does not normally appear in the second of two adjective clauses joined by *and, ac, ne, oþþe*, or the like, when the reference is to the same antecedent and both clauses require the same case, e.g. *CP* 5. 19 . . . *ðara godena wiotona ðe giu wæron giond Angelcynn, 7 ða bec eallæ befullan geliornod hæfdon*, *BlHom* 19. 32 *Næs þæt na þæt he nyste hwæt se blinda wolde, se ealle þing wat 7 him leoht forgeaf, ÆCHom* i. 342. 2 *Maran lufe nimð se heretoga on gefeohte to ðam cempan, þe æfter fleame his wiðerwinnan ðegenlice oferwinð, þonne to ðam þe mid fleame ne ætwand, ne ðeah on nanum gecampe naht ðegenlices ne gefremode, ÆGram* 84. 2 *and ælc þæra ðinga þe man wihð on wægan oððe met on fate . . . , ÆGram* 84. 8 *Sume naman synd eac þe nabbað anfeald getel ac beoð æfre menigfealdlice gecwedene*, and

GenA 2807   Sweotol is and gesene   þæt þe soð metod
                  on gesiððe is,   swegles aldor,
                  se ðe sigor seleð   snytru mihtum
                  and þin mod trymeð,
                  godcundum gifum.

§2329. However, the relative pronoun need not be expressed in the second adjective clause even when there is a change of case. In such examples the same *form* of the relative is usually appropriate, e.g. after *7* in *Bede* 466. 20 *7 he gehwæðer ge þa cyricsangas lærde, þe hi ær ne cuðan, ge eac, þa ðe hi iu cuðan 7 mid langre gymeleasnesse ealdian ongunnon, þa eft mid his lare on ðone ærran steall geedniwode wæron, Solil* 13. 15 . . . *þam freondum þe ic lufige and me luf[i]að,* and *HomU* 34. 195. 15 *Ealle þa stowa þe se soða Crist lufode and oftost on wunode, þa he towyrpð.* However, in *Bede(Ca)* 222. 22 *7 cwæð þ hi fracuðe 7 earme wære þæt hi ne woldan heora Gode hyron þone ðe hi gescop 7 hi on gelyfdon, þone* does not suit the principal clause or the first of the subordinate clauses. But it fits the subordinate clause in *T*'s reading—. . . *þæt heo ne woldon heora Gode hyran, þone þe heo gelyfden.* In *ÆCHom* i. 182. 25 *Seo sæ þe se Hælend oferferde getacnað þas andweardan woruld, to ðære com Crist and oferferde; þæt is, he com to ðisre worulde on menniscnysse, and ðis lif oferferde, to ðære* does not fit the second clause. *Bede* 222. 20 *Ac gen ma þætte he forseah 7 on hete hæfde þa men, þe he onget, þæt heo on Cristes geleafan gelærde wæron, 7 þa weorc þæs geleafan habban ne woldon* exemplifies the combination of noun and adjective clauses discussed in §1980.

§2330. But the relative pronoun can appear (in the same or in a different form) to signal a change of reference or case in the second clause, e.g. *Or* 10. 19 *Of þære ie Indus, þe be westan eallum þæm lande ligeð, betux þære ie Indus 7 þære þe be westan hiere is, Tigris hatte* . . . , *BlHom* 71. 9 *Seo menigo þe þær beforan ferde 7 seo se þær æfter fylgde, ealle hie cegdon* . . . , *ÆCHom* i. 214. 3 *þæt folc ðe Criste beforan stop and þæt ðe him fyligde, ealle hi sungon* . . . , and *ÆLS* 21. 388 *þa cwæð þæt wif him to þæt hit wære Swyðun se ðe hine lærde mid þære halgan lare and þone ðe he geseah on ðære cyrcan swa fægerne,* and (after *ge eac*) *Bede* 466. 20 (§2329).

§2331. It can, however, be expressed in the second clause even when there is no change of reference or case, e.g. *Solil* 45. 7 *Ælc þara þe hys wilnað and þe hys geornful byð, he hym mæg cuman to, ÆCHom* i. 354. 7 *Se dæg bið gemyndig Godes ðeowum ðe ða halgan, æfter gewunnenum sige, asende to ecere myrhðe fram eallum gedreccednyssum, and se is heora soðe acennednys, ÆCHom* i. 366. 32 *Se is lybbende God þe hæfð lif and wununge ðurh hine sylfne, butan anginne, and seðe ealle gesceafta þurh his agen Bearn, þæt is, his Wisdom, gesceop,* and *ÆCHom* i. 492. 14 *Se mann ðe tosæwð ungeþwærnysse betwux cristenum mannum, oððe seðe sprecð unrihtwisnysse on heannysse ðurh his muðes geat, he bið dead geferod.* In

ÆCHom ii. 140. 18 *ac ðæs halgan andwerdnyss eaðelice acwencte þæs deofles dyderunge, þe hi dwollice filigdon, and ðæs lifes word lythwon gymdon*, something seems to have gone wrong; *and* introduces what is in effect a result clause.

§ 2332. The personal pronoun can appear in the second clause in lieu of a relative pronoun, whether there is a change of case or not. For details see § § 2180-200. The variation in *Bede(T)* 442. 5 *þa beoð eadge þe heora wonnesse forlætne beoð 7 þara þe synna bewrigene beoð* is noteworthy.

§ 2333. When two adjective clauses are in asyndetic parataxis in the prose, the relative is expressed in both, e.g. *CP* 155. 20 *Ða creopendan wuhta beinnan ðam wage getacniað ða ingeðoncas ðe wealcað in ðæs monnes mode, ðe æfre willað licgean on ðæm eorðlicum gewilnungum* and *ÆCHom* i. 350. 24 *Geleaffullum mannum mæg beon micel truwa and hopa to ðam menniscum Gode Criste, seðe is urc Mundbora and Dema, seðe leofað and rixað mid Fæder . . .* , where both clauses require the same case, and *Or* 14. 6 *þæt is þonne of þæm beorgum þe mon hæt Caucasus, þe we ær beforan sædon, þa þe be norþan India sindon* and *ÆCHom* i. 348. 1 *Micel getel is ðæra haligra gasta, þe on Godes rice eardiað, be ðam cwæð se witega Daniel . . .* , where the clauses require different cases. I have so far found no exceptions in the prose.

§ 2334. But in the poetry the relative pronoun can be expressed in both clauses, e.g.

Beo 2041   þonne cwið æt beore   se ðe beah gesyhð,
                 eald æscwiga,   se ðe eall geman . . .

and

Met 10. 48   Hwær is eac se wisa   and se weorðgeorna
                 and se fæstræda   folces hyrde,
                 se wæs uðwita   ælces ðinges,
                 cene and cræftig,   ðæm wæs Caton nama?,

but need not appear in the second, e.g.

Beo 2982   Ða wæron monige,   þe his mæg wriðon,
                 ricone arærdon,   ða him gerymed wearð,
                 þæt hie wælstowe   wealdan moston

and

ChristA 18   Eala þu reccend   ond þu riht cyning,
                 se þe locan healdeð,   lif ontyneð. . . .

§2335. As in MnE, asyndetic and syndetic parataxis are not mutually exclusive, e.g.

GenA 2643   Hwæt, þu æfre,   engla þeoden,
               þurh þin yrre wilt   aldre lætan,
               heah beheowan,   þæne þe her leofað
               rihtum þeawum,   bið on ræde fæst,
               modgeþance,   and him miltse
               to þe seceð?

and

JDay ii 129   þænne bið geban micel,   and aboden þider
               eal Adames cnosl   eorðbuendra
               þe on foldan wearð   feded æfre
               oððe modar gebær   to manlican,
               oþþe þa þe wæron   oððe woldon beon
               oþþe towearde   geteald wæron awiht.

§2336. We must of course distinguish the pattern P | Sp | Ss seen in

Dan 476   forþam he is ana   ece drihten,
           dema ælmihtig,   se ðe him dom forgeaf,
           spowende sped,   þam þe his spel berað

from P | Sp | Sc seen in

ChristC 1156   Eft lifgende   up astodan
              þa þe heo ær fæste   bifen hæfde,
              deade bibyrgde,   þe dryhtnes bibod
              heoldon on hreþre;

see further §§1901 and 1911.

§2337. The problem of the ambiguous demonstrative/relative (see
§§2109-21) sometimes arises here. Thus in both ÆCHom i. 354. 7
*Se dæg bið gemyndig Godes ðeowum ðe ða halgan, æfter gewun-
nenum sige, asende to ecere myrhðe fram eallum gedreccednyssum,
and se heora soðe acennednys* and ÆCHom i. 550. 29 *ac ða beoð
eadige, ðe heora synna bewepað, forðan þe se Halga Gast hi gefrefrað,
seðe deð forgyfenysse ealra synna, se is gehaten Paraclitus, þæt is,
Frefrigend* . . . , the last *se* may be demonstrative—'and that is their
true birth' and 'He (That One) is called Paraclete . . .'.

11. CONCORD

a. The normal agreements

§2338. As is pointed out in §45, relative pronouns normally agree
with their antecedents in number and gender, but take their case

from the adjective clause. 'The so-called "case-law" (Kasus-Regel) which supposes that in some earlier period the relative pronoun showed the same case as its antecedent' (van der Laan, *Neophil.* 14 (1929), 36) by definition was not valid in OE. Whether it ever was is a topic which will not be pursued here. The relatives cannot strictly be said to have any person in themselves except for those which include part of the personal pronoun (see §§2180-200). But *se* carries with it a strong suggestion of the third person and only exceptionally is found with first and second person antecedents (see §2260).

§2339. The verb of the adjective clause naturally takes its number and person from its subject. When this is the relative pronoun, they are derived from the antecedent, which may or may not be the subject of the principal clause.

§2340. There are exceptions to all these agreements. Some have been emended by editors, others have not. Thus Krapp in ASPR emends

PPs 108. 19   Wese he hrægle gelic   þe her hraðe ealdað
                  and gyrdelse   se ðe hine man gelome gyrt

by omitting *se* but retains the manuscript reading in *Ex* 380 *þæt is se Abraham se him engla god ‖ naman niwan asceop*, where, according to Blackburn, *se him* is probably an error for *þe him*. But see §2196. The relative *þæt* presents special problems; see §§2134-44 and the Index of Words and Phrases.

b. Case

§2341. The problems which arise here have already been discussed. Those involving indefinite adjective clauses are treated in §§2201-25 and 2363-73, the rest in §§2302-37.

c. Number

§2342. Here three elements are involved—the antecedent, the relative, and (if the relative is the subject of its clause[73]) the verb of the adjective clause. Each one of these may be the odd man out. But this is not the best way of classifying examples with (apparently) faulty concord in number.

[73] This point was not taken by all the writers mentioned in the next footnote.

§2343. The most discussed group is probably that containing the combination *þara þe* with *þe* as subject of the adjective clause.[74] Here the verb of that clause is sometimes singular, sometimes plural. Shipley (pp. 94-5) summed up thus:

The relative combination *þara þe* has generally been imperfectly understood. The entire subject has been reviewed by E. A. Kock (The English Relative Pronouns, Lund, 1897). The fact that the verb with *þara þe* is sometimes sing. and sometimes plur., is accounted for by the dependence or non-dependence of *þara þe* on some non-plur. expression, such as *ænig, ælc*. In the former case the verb of the relative clause is sing. or plur.; in the latter always plur. Kock considers that the fluctuation between sing. and plur. was originally owing to whether the *ænig* or the *þara* had the stronger force and accentuation.

This statement describes the usual situation; Visser's observation (i, §110) that 'the Old English relative *þara þe* (= of those who, of those which) being plural . . . is usually construed with a plural verb form' completely misses the mark. But Shipley's statement requires qualification.

§2344. First, then, for examples in which *þara þe* is not dependent on a 'non-plur.'—dare we say 'singular'?—expression. Here the verb of the adjective clause is plural, e.g. *Bede* 330. 19 . . . *fore generednisse heora freonda þara ðe of weorulde geleordon*, *CP* 205. 14 *Gemunað eowerra foregengena, ðara ðe eow bodedon Godes word* . . . , *ÆCHom* ii. 94. 21 *þæt is ðæs gehadodan mannes clænnyss, þæra ðe Gode þeniað* . . . , and

GuthA 153   He gecostad wearð
    in gemyndigra monna tidum,
    ðara þe nu gena þurh gæstlicu
    wundor hine weorðiað ond his wisdomes
    hlisan healdað. . . .

We need not regard as exceptions sporadic examples like

Rid 28. 7   Dream bið in innan
    cwicra wihta, clengeð, lengeð,
    þara þe ær lifgende longe hwile
    wilna bruceð ond no wið spriceð,
    ond þonne æfter deaþe deman onginneð,
    meldan mislice

and

Pr 3   Ic wat mine saule synnum forwundod;
    gehæl þu hy, heofena drihten,

[74] See (*inter alios*) Hotz, pp. 85-7; Nader, *Ang.* 11 (1888-9), 474-7; Wülfing, ii, §§416-19; Kock, pp. 19-25; Shipley, pp. 94-5; Klaeber, *MP* 3 (1905-6), 260; Grossmann, pp. 56-61; Anklam, pp. 83-4; Wagner, pp. 70-1; Bauch, pp. 54-7; Trnka, p. 162; Gehse, pp. 70-7; Woolf, *MLQ* 4 (1943), 50-1; and Andrew, *SS*, pp. 105-7, and *Postscript*, pp. 126-7.

and gelacna þu hy,   lifes ealdor,
forþan ðu eðest miht   ealra læca
ðæra þe gewurde   side oððe wyde,

in which the verb of the adjective clause appears to be singular when *þara þe* is not dependent on a singular expression, for both *-eþ* and *-e* may be plural endings; see §§18–20.

§2345. I turn now to examples in which *þara þe* is dependent on a singular expression. This may be a singular noun, e.g.

Rid 5. 10   Næfre læcecynn
on folcstede   findan meahte,
þara þe mid wyrtum   wunde gehælde . . . ,

or a singular superlative or indefinite. The superlative may have a demonstrative + a noun in agreement, e.g.

ChristA 275   Eala þu mæra   middangeardes
seo clæneste   cwen ofer eorþan
þara þe gewurde   to widan feore . . . ,

or may be accompanied by a genitive plural of a noun, e.g.

El 1221   . . .   þæt hie weorðeden
mode ond mægene   þone mæran dæg,
heortan gehigdum,   in ðam sio halige rod
gemeted wæs,   mærost beama
þara þe of eorðan   up aweoxe,
geloden under leafum

(where there is no demonstrative with the superlative) and

Beo 2381   hæfdon hy forhealden   helm Scylfinga,
þone selestan   sæcyninga
þara ðe in Swiorice   sinc brytnade,
mærne þeoden

and

Ex 362   Niwe flodas   Noe oferlað,
þrymfæst þeoden,   mid his þrim sunum,
þone deopestan   drencefloda
þara ðe gewurde   on woruldrice

(where the superlative is accompanied by a demonstrative). All the examples in these categories known to me are in the poetry and all have a preterite form in *-e* which either is or must be taken as a subjunctive; see §2403. There is no point in arguing whether these forms are singular or plural; see again §§18–20.

§2346. Detectable difference in number after *þara þe* when *þe* is subject is limited in my collections to examples in which *þara* is dependent on a form of *æghwylc, ælc, gehwylc, manig, nan, sum*, or the like—the so-called 'indefinites'; see §241. In these, as Wülfing (i, §303) rightly remarks, the verb in the adjective clause is more often singular than plural. But Wülfing's examples need more careful classification.

§2347. We need first to eliminate examples such as *Bede* 174. 14 *Ond monige þara broðra þæs ylcan mynstres þara þe in oðrum husum wæron, sægdon . . .* , *CP* 69. 4 *Swa sindon wel monege ðara ðe gewundiað hiera mod mid ðæm weorcum ðisses flæsclican lifes . . .* , *Ps(P)* 3. 1 *Eala Drihten, hwi synt swa manige minra feonda þara þe me swencað?*, and *Ps(P)* 34. 3 *Geteoh þin sweord and cum ongean hy and beluc heora wegas mid þinum sweorde þara þe min ehtað*, Latin *Effunde frameam et conclude adversus eos qui me persequuntur*, in which the adjective clause naturally has a plural verb after a plural indefinite and *þara þe*.

§2348. There are no certain examples of this sort in the poetry. At first glance,

El 969   . . . mære morgenspel   manigum on andan
                   þara þe dryhtnes æ   dyrnan woldon,

with its plural verb, seems to be one. But *manigum* may be singular; cf.

Dan 492   . . . oðþæt hine mid nyde   nyðor asette
                   metod ælmihtig,   swa he manegum deð
                   þara þe þurh oferhyd   up astigeð,

where the adjective clause has what appears to be a singular verb. (But note MS *bereð*, which must be plural, in *Dan* 142.) These two examples typify the second group we must eliminate, viz. that in which we have *þara þe* dependent on a form of an indefinite which may be singular or plural. Other examples in this second group include (with a singular verb) *Bo* 59. 19 *7 swaðeah hi hit gehatað ælcum ðara þe hi hæfð*, *WHom* 13. 18 . . . *þæt is heofona rice ðæt he hæfð gegearwod ælcum þæra þe his willan gewyrcð her on worulde*, and

Beo 1050   Ða gyt æghwylcum   eorla drihten
                   þara þe mid Beowulfe   brimlade teah,
                   on þære medubence   maþðum gesealde . . . ;

(with a plural verb) *Or* 152. 15 . . . *þeh heora na ma ne lifde þara þe Alexandres folgeras wæron, Ps(P)* 24. 8 *Ealle Godes wegas syndon mildheortnes and rihtwisnes ælcum þæra þe his æ secað and his bebodu lufiað, Ps(P)* 36. 8 *ne bysna þe be nanum þæra þe yfel don, Beo* 97... *lif eac gesceop* || *cynna gehwylcum þara ðe cwice hwyrfaþ*, and

Brun 24

heardes hondplegan　　Myrce ne wyrndon
þæra þe mid Anlafe　　hæleþa nanum
on lides bosme　　　　ofer æra gebland
fæge to gefeohte;　　　land gesohtun,

and (with a verb form which may be ambiguous), *CP* 173. 7 *Bioð simle gearwe to læranne 7 to forgiefanne ælcum ðara ðe iow ryhtlice bidde ymbe ðone tohopan ðe ge habbað on eow* and *CP* 325. 22 *Sele ælcum ðara ðe ðe bidde.*

§2349. We are now left with the significant examples—those in which *þara þe* depends on an unambiguously singular form of an indefinite. A noun in the genitive plural may, but need not, precede or follow *þara*. Here the verb is usually singular, e.g. *Bo* 93. 26 *ælc þara gesceafta þe sawle hæfð* . . . , *CP* 299. 12 *Ælc ðara ðe bið geeaðmed, he bið upahæfen, Ps(P)* 3 (Introduction) *swa deþ ælc þæra manna þe þisne sealm singð, Ps(P)* 9. 11 *Forðam þu ne forlætst nanne þara þe ðe secð, LS* 34. 635 . . . *wolde georne sumne man gecnawan oþþe broðor oððe mæg oþþe sumne þara þe him ær cuð wæs geond þa byrig* . . . , *ÆCHom* i. 362. 20 *Ælc ðæra ðe hine onhefð bið geeadmet* . . . , and *ÆCHom* ii. 228. 8 *Ælc ðæra ðe synne wyrcð, he bið þonne ðære synne ðeow*, or ambiguous in number, e.g. *Or* 248. 23 *þridde wæs þæt he bebead þæt ælc þara þe on elðeodignesse wære, come to his agnum earde, WHom* 7. 84 . . . *cwæð þæt ælc ðæra þe on rihtan geleafan þurhwunode 7 fulluht underfenge gehealden wurde wið deofles dare*, and

Beo 2733

　　　　　　　　　　　næs se folccyning,
ymbesittendra　　　ænig ðara,
þe mec guðwinum　　gretan dorste,
egesan ðeon.

There are in my collections not many examples in which we have an unambiguous singular form of an indefinite followed by *þara þe* and an unambiguously plural verb in the adjective clause. They include *Or* 94. 7 *Ne þara nanne yflian noldan þe to ðæm Godes huse oðflugon, ÆCHom* i. 582. 23 *Swa hwa swa sylð ceald wæter drincan anum þurstigan menn ðæra ðe on me gelyfað, ne bið his med forloren,*

Dan 63 . . . oðþæt hie burga gehwone abrocen hæfdon
þara þe þam folce to friðe stodon,

and

El 1286 þonne on þreo dæleð
in fyres feng folc anra gehwylc,
þara þe gewurdon on widan feore
ofer sidne grund.

But my collections are not complete. In

Beo 2249 guðdeað fornam,
feorhbealo frecne fyra gehwylcne
leoda minra þara ðe þis lif ofgeaf,
gesawon seledream,

we have a singular and then a plural. This demonstrates what Kock
of course realized: that, while his explanation of the origin of these
fluctuations—viz. that after expressions like *ælc þara þe* the verb
was singular when *ælc* carried the emphasis and plural when *þara* carried it (Kock, pp. 19-25)—is plausible and satisfying, it cannot
explain those which actually occur in OE. As he says (p. 19), 'afterwards analogies, as usual, played an important part'.

§2350. In apparent ignorance of much that has been previously
written on this subject, and without a complete investigation, Andrew
(*SS*, pp. 105-7, and *Postscript*, pp. 126-8) argues unconvincingly
against accepting the singular verb in such contexts as idiomatic OE.
Some of his comments on individual passages seem unnecessarily perverse and the fact that half the clauses he discusses show 'false concord' and that three-quarters of them are 'syntactically irregular in
one way or another' should have led Andrew to question his ideas of
'falseness' and 'irregularity'. Further, he argues in a circle. Only 'if
we remove the *þara*' from the great majority of examples is it true
that 'after a superlative the simple relative *ðe* is the norm'. Yet this
claim is used to justify the 'removal' of *þara* in other contexts. On
the evidence provided, emendation on the scale suggested by Andrew
is quite unjustified. I do not believe that it can ever be justified. The
fact that these and other pronouns which he would remove rarely
offend against Kuhn's Law is another argument against the suggestion that they are scribal insertions.

§2351. That the idea of the several individuals in the group often
triumphs over the idea of the one group and so produces a plural
verb after a collective noun in the same or in a subsequent clause

has already been exemplified in §§81-6. A few examples involving collective antecedents of adjective clauses follow: (with a singular verb) *Or* 112. 24 . . . *mid þæm folce þe hiene ær fultumes bæd, Or* 210. 11 . . . *þæt him nan folc ne getruwade þe him underþeow wæs,* WHom 6. 124 . . . *eal þæt Iudeisce folc þe þa on life wæs* . . . ; (with a verb ambiguous in number) *ÆCHom* i. 580. 29 *ac he ne mihte for ðære menigu ðe him mid ferde* and

Met 26. 60	Cuð wæs sona
	eallre þære mænige þe hire mid wunode
	æþelinges sið;

and (with a plural verb) *Or* 116. 1 *Philippuse geþuhte æfter þæm þæt he an land ne mehte þæm folce mid gifan gecweman þe him an simbel wæron mid winnende, ÆCHom* i. 348. 23 . . . *betwux ðam werode ðe sind throni gecigede,* and *ÆCHom* i. 212. 19 *þæt folc ðe heora reaf wurpon.* . . . Sometimes a collective noun is followed by a plural relative. In this event, the verb of the adjective clause is usually plural, as in *ÆCHom* ii. 12. 27 *and þurh Crist is eal mancynn gebletsod, þa ðe rihtlice gelyfað* (though here we probably have a partitive adjective clause; see §1455), *ChronE* 139. 5 (1009) . . . *7 þet folc þa þe on ðam scipe wæron* . . . , *ChronE* 147. 10 (1016) *þa cydde mann þam cyninge þ hine mann beswicon wolde, þa þe him on fultume beon sceoldon,* and

El 282	Ða wæs gesamnod of sidwegum
	mægen unlytel, þa ðe Moyses æ
	reccan cuðon.

So the singular verb in *ÆCHom* i. 182. 22 *þæt folc ða ðe ðis tacen geseah cwæð þæt Crist wære soð witega* . . . is unexpected.

§2352. An indefinite adjective clause introduced by a singular relative may also be said to have collective force; hence the change in number in examples like *Or* 94. 22 *Æfter þæm þe Læcedemonie hæfdon Perse oft oferwunnen, þa gebudon him Perse þæt hie hæfden III winter sibbe wiþ hie, se þe þæt wolde, 7 se þe þæt nolde, þæt hie wolden þa mid gefeohte gesecan* and *Or* 248. 25 *7 se þe þæt nolde, he bebead þæt mon þa ealle sloge.*

§2353. It has been pointed out in §30 that two or more singular subjects joined by *and* may have a singular verb when they are thought of as a unit. This idea may account for the singular relatives in

PPs 80. 15	He hi fedde mid fætre lynde,
	hwæte and hunige, þæt him halig god
	sealde of stane, oþþæt hi sæde wæron,

where *þæt* has the gender of *hunige*, and in

GenB 802   Nu slit me hunger and þurst
           bitre on breostum,   þæs wit begra ær
           wæron orsorge   on ealle tid,

where the OS version

Gen 12   Nu thuingit mi giu hungar endi thurst,
           bitter balouuerk,   thero uuaron uuit er beðero tuom

has the plural. The Anglo-Saxon poets may have been thinking of 'fat, wheat, and honey' as 'food' and 'hunger and thirst' as 'lack of sustenance'. In

Met 21. 31   Ac þæt is wundorlic   wlite and beorhtnes
               þe wuhta gehwæs   wlite geberhteð,
               and æfter þæm   eallum wealdeð,

the verbs *geberhteð* and *wealdeð* may take their number from *þæt*, from *wlite and beorhtnes* as a single idea, or may be plural; see §§ 18-20.

§ 2354. The possibility that forms like *him* and *þam*, which can be singular or plural, may produce a change in number has been discussed in § 77. The same applies to forms in *-um* like *ælcum*; see § 2348. Such ambiguity may explain the singular verb in the adjective clause in

Sat 242   God seolfa wæs
           eallum andfeng   þe ðær up becom,
           and hine on eorðan   ær gelefde

and the change to *hit* in the noun clause in

Met 13. 51   Swa bið eallum treowum   þe him on æðele bið
               þæt hit on holte   hyhst geweaxe

and may account for the plural forms in the last clauses in

And 889   þam bið wræcsið witod,   wite geopenad,
           þe þara gefeana sceal   fremde weorðan,
           hean hwearfian,   þonne heonon gangaþ

and

PPs 118. 165   þam bið sib mycel   þe him þenceð
               þæt hi naman þinne   neode lufien.

§ 2355. In general, then, apparent breaches of concord in number can usually be explained. There is no need for us to accept Stoelke's verdict (p. 47) that 'auch bei relativem Subjekt im Plural steht das Prädikat oft im Singular' ['even when a relative subject is in the plural the predicate is often in the singular']. All his examples except one involve *mæge*, preterite forms in *-e*, or present indicative forms in *-eþ* or (for *-ian* verbs) *-aþ*; on these see §§18–20. The exception is

GenB 595   þæt is micel wundor
             þæt hit ece god   æfre wolde
             þeoden þolian,   þæt wurde þegn swa monig
             forlædd be þam lygenum   þe for þam larum com.

R. K. Gordon, who translated this '. . . that so many men should be led astray by lies when they sought for instruction', presumably thought that *þe* introduced, not a temporal clause 'when', but an adjective clause qualifying *þegn*. The singular *com* is consistent with this. C. W. Kennedy's prose translation—'. . . tricked with lies by one who brought such counsel'—does impossible violence to the OE. But in his verse translation he has '. . . tricked with lies that came as good counsel'. The word *for* can bear this sense of 'instead of, in place of', e.g. *Bede* 146. 12 *Betweoh ðas ðing ða wæs Iustus se ærcebiscop gelæded to þæm heofonlecan rice þy feorðan dæge iduum Novembrium. Ond Honorius wæs haten se ðe for hine to biscope gecoren wæs.* But if *þam lygenum* is the antecedent, we should expect ☆*comon* in the adjective clause, because there is no intervening element between antecedent, relative, and verb. We can hardly compare it with *Or* 120. 14 *7 eower Romana brocu þe ge ðær ealneg drifað, næs buton þrie dagas*, where *brocu* is plural but may have turned into a singular notion 'misery, trouble' in the translator's mind.

d. Gender

§2356. Lack of agreement in gender is sometimes due to the triumph of natural over grammatical gender, e.g. *Luke(WSCp)* 13. 11 *þa wæs þar sum wif seo hæfde untrumnesse gast ehtatyne gear,*

And 565   Synnige ne mihton
             oncnawan þæt cynebearn,   se ðe acenned wearð
             to hleo ond to hroðre   hæleða cynne,
             eallum eorðwarum,

and

Met 30. 17   Ðæt is sio soðe   sunne mid rihte,
             be ðæm we magon singan   swylc butan lease,

where the sun is Almighty God. The same explanation can be applied to examples with indefinite *seþe*, e.g. *Bede* 78. 15 . . . *forhwon þonne, se þe blodryne þrowað monaðaðle, ne alefað hire in Drihtnes cirican gongan?*; cf.

Rid 25. 9
                  Feleþ sona
    mines gemotes,   se þe mec nearwað,
    wif wundenlocc,

where the ASPR emendation of *se* to *seo* is officious.

§ 2357. In *CP* 235. 6 . . . *7 se anda ða ðe he hæfde to his breðer . . . se anda wearð to sæde ðæs broðurslæges*, *ða* may be the adverb rather than the accusative singular feminine of the demonstrative. But this somewhat desperate solution is not available in *Sat* 36 *Hwær com engla ðrym,* ‖ *ða þe we on heofnum habban sceoldan?*, where Krapp omits *ða* in ASPR. The gender of the relative *þæne* in

Men 11
    And þæs embe fif niht   þætte fulwihttiid
    eces drihtnes   to us cymeð,
    þæne twelfta dæg   tireadige,
    hæleð heaðurofe,   hatað on Brytene,
    in foldan her

is probably due to attraction; *dæg*, the nearest noun to the relative, is masculine and, although not its antecedent, goes with the relative and so may have influenced its gender.

§ 2358. The well-known passages from *Beowulf* in which a feminine noun is followed by *seþe* (lines 1260, 1344, 1887, 2685) or *se* (line 2421) have not been satisfactorily explained. Andrew's solution—to drop *se* and read *þe* alone in all five passages—is based on the faulty observation that 'the erring word in all of them' is *seþe* and is accordingly ruled out by *se* in line 2421; see *Postscript*, p. 62. A triumph of sex over gender can be seen in the sequences *seo hand/sio hand . . . se þe/se ðe* in *Beo* 1343-4 and 2684-5, where the reference is to Æschere and Beowulf respectively. But this solution fails in the other three examples. See also § 2178. For more examples of *se/seo* confusion, see Mōri 1980 (my § 55), pp. 4-5 and 7.

e. Person

§ 2359. The person of the verb in the adjective clause, like its number, can, of course, be influenced by the relative and/or the antecedent only when the relative is its subject. Problems of agreement can arise only when the principal clause contains nominative elements (including the vocative use of the nominative) in different persons, as in MnE 'I am/You are the man who sings in the choir'. So in OE we naturally find the verb in the first or second person in those examples in which no third person element intervenes between a first or second person pronoun in the principal clause and the relative. These last two elements may be together, e.g. *Or* 76. 33 *þu þe þyrstende wære monnes blodes XXX wintra, drync nu þine fylle,*

Rid 12. 13   Saga hwæt ic hatte,
            þe ic lifgende   lond reafige
            ond æfter deaþe   dryhtum þeowige,

and *LPr i* 1 *Ælmihtig fæder, þu þe on heofonum eardast,* || *geweorðad wuldres dreame,* or separated, e.g. *Rid* 27. 15 *Frige hwæt ic hatte,* || *ðe on eorþan swa esnas binde* . . . ,

Creed 1   Ælmihtig fæder   up on rodore,
            þe ða sciran gesceaft   sceope and worhtest
            and eorðan wang   ealne gesettest,
            ic þe ecne god   ænne gecenne,
            lustum gelyfe,

and

ChristA 412   þu, gebletsad leofa,
            þe in dryhtnes noman   dugeþum cwome
            heanum to hroþre.

§2360. When a third person element intervenes between a first or second person pronoun and the relative (of which the third person element may be a part), there are two possibilities. We find the first —the verb of the adjective clause in the third person—in *ByrM* 198. 8 *Ic eom angin þe sprycð eow,* Latin *Ego principium qui et loquor uobis, ÆLS* 21. 294 *Ge magon to soðum witan þæt ic Swyðun eom se ðe wundra wyrcð, ÆCHom* i. 480. 6 *Eart ðu se ðe toweard is . . . ?,* and

ChristA 18   Eala þu reccend   ond þu riht cyning,
            se þe locan healdeð,   lif ontyneð,
            eadgan upwegas,   oþrum forwyrneð
            wlitigan wilsiþes,   gif his weorc ne deag.

§2361. The second possibility—the verb of the adjective clause in the first or second person—appears in *Ps(P)* 4. 1 *forðam þu eart se ðe me gerihtwisast, Ps(P)* 21. 8 *Drihten, þu eart se þe me gelæddest of minre modor innoðe,*

ChristA 239   þu eart seo snyttro   þe þas sidan gesceaft
            mid þi waldende   worhtes ealle,

and

PPs 76. 11   þu eart ana god,   þe æghwylc miht
                       wundor gewyrcean   on woruldlife.

Luke(WSCp) 1. 19 *Ic eom Gabriel ic þe stande beforan Gode* does
not belong here, since *ic* is repeated before the relative; cf. *ÆCHom*
i. 76. 4 *þu eart Crist, ðæs lifigendan Godes Sunu, þu þe be ðines
Fæder hæse middangeard gehældest, and us ðone Halgan Gast
asendest*, where *þu* similarly intervenes.

§ 2362. In the absence of full collections from the prose, I am unable to say which (if either) of these two patterns is more common.
Despite my confidence in *Ang*. 81 (1963), 315, and *RES* 15 (1964),
134, it is not clear which we have in *Beo* 506 *Eart þu se Beowulf se
þe wið Brecan wunne . . . ?*; *wunne* may be second person singular
preterite indicative or, since the question is rhetorical, second or
third person singular preterite subjunctive; see § 2406 and cf. *PPs*
59. 9 *Ac ne eart þu se sylfa god ðe us swa drife?*

12. OTHER RELATIVES

a. Swa hwa/hwæt/hwæþer/hwelc swa

§ 2363. The use of *se, þe,* and the compound relatives, in indefinite
adjective clauses has been discussed in §§ 2201-25. Such clauses can
also be introduced by the combinations *swa hwa swa, swa hwæt swa,
swa hwæþer swa*, and *swa hwelc swa*. Like *hwa* and *hwæt*, the first
two are used independently only, i.e. as pronouns. Like *hwæþer* and
hwelc, the last two may be used both independently and dependently, i.e. as pronouns and adjectives.[75] Examples follow: (*swa hwa
swa*) *Bo* 51. 28 *Swa hwa swa wille sawan westmbære land, atio ærest*

---

[75] This is not the place for a detailed discussion on the origin of these formulae. *OED*
(s.v. *whoso*) has the note: 'ME *wha swa, hwa se*, reduced form of OE *swa hwa swa*, generalized form of *hwa* who.' This seems to imply that *hwa* came first. If this is so, the question
is: Was it *hwa* interrogative or *hwa* indefinite? Opinions are divided. There is a lengthy discussion by Johnsen in *Ang*. 37 (1913), 281-302. The references are often inadequate or
inaccurate, the interpretation of examples not always reliable, the arguments sometimes
tenuous, and the whole article seems to me coloured by Johnsen's apparent determination
to deny the possibility that the interrogative use of *hwa* played any part in the development
of MnE 'who' as an indefinite and a definite relative pronoun. His view seems to be that the
essential stages are first, *hwa* indefinite 'anyone'; second, *swa hwa swa* indefinite relative
'whoever'; third, *hwa* relative pronoun. I have no doubt that the wearing down of *swa hwa
swa* played its part. But, as is clear from §§ 2049-54, I also believe that the interrogative
uses of *hwa* were important factors. So I can find no enthusiasm for discussions about which
of these uses is the sole source. This is not a case of parthenogenesis.

of ða þornas..., *ÆCHom* i. 156. 6 *Swa hwa swa oncnæwð þa blind-nysse his modes, clypige he mid inweardre heortan...*, and

GenB 481

                          Sceolde on wite a
      mid swate and mid sorgum   siððan libban,
      swa hwa swa gebyrgde   þæs on þam beame geweox;

(*swa hwæt swa*) *Bede* 94. 21 *7 he mid dede gefylde swa hwæt swa he mid worde lærde*, *Bo* 112. 2 ... *ðonne onginð him leogan se tohopa þære wræce 7 swa hwæs swa his irsung wilnað, þonne gehet him þæs his reccelest, ÆCHom* i. 248. 29 *Swa hwæt swa man eaðelice begyt, þæt ne bið na swa deorwyrðe swa þæt þæt earfoðlice bið begyten*, and

GenB 755

                    Swa hwæt swa wit her morðres þoliað,
      hit is nu Adame   eall forgolden
      mid hearran hete   and mid hæleða forlore ... ;

(*swa hwæþer swa* independent) *Bo* 91. 19 *Nim ðonne swa wuda swa wyrt, swa hwæðer swa þu wille...*, *ÆLS* 17. 256 ... *swa god swa yfel, swa hwæðer swa he begæð, HomU* 27. 145. 12 *and beoð þonne mid urum sawlum ece symle earme oððe eadige, swa hwæðer swa we her on worulde ær urum endedæge geearniað*, and

LPr ii 96

      þonne bið egsa   geond ealle world,
      þar man us tyhhað on dæg   twegen eardas,
      drihtenes are   oððe deofles þeowet,
      swa hwaðer we geearniað   her on life,
      þa hwile þe ure mihta   mæste wæron;[76]

(*swa hwæþer swa* dependent) *ChronA* 84. 27 (894) *þa foron hie siþþan æfter þæm wealda hloþum 7 flocradum bi swa hwaþerre efes swa hit þonne fierdleas wæs* and

Beo 685

                    ond siþðan witig God
      on swa hwæþere hond   halig Dryhten
      mærðo deme,   swa him gemet þince;

(*swa hwelc swa* independent) *Bede(T)* 98. 31 *ond þurh swa hwelces bene swa he gehæled sy, þisses geleafa 7 wyrcnis seo* [MS *Ca si*] *lefed God* [MS *Ca gode*] *onfenge 7 allum to fylgenne, ÆCHom* ii.

---

[76] Burnham (pp. 38–42 and 125) classifies as disjunctive concessions examples like *Bo* 110. 26 *forðæm ðæt is se betsta anwald þ mon mæge 7 wille wel don, swa læssan spedum swa maran, swæðer he hæbbe* and *ÆGram* 19. 11 *hie coruus ðes hremn, swa hwæðer swa hit byð, swa he, swa heo.* One can see the point. None the less, in these two examples and in those like them quoted above, *swa hwæþer swa* or *swæþer* means 'whichever'. But this is not true in *HomU* 34. 201. 10 *swa hweðer swa he bið ofslagen þurh miht ures drihtnes agenes bebodes oððe Michael godes heahengel hine ofslea, þurh ðæs lifigendan godes miht he bið ofslagen and na þurh nanes engles mihte.* See further §§1826 and 3463.

228. 30 *Samaria hatte an burh, ða burh forsawon þa Iudeiscan to ðan swiðe, þæt swa hwilcne swa hi to hospe habban woldon, ðonne cwædon hi be ðam þæt he wære Samaritanisc, ÆCHom* ii. 246. 11 *Swa hwilcne swa ic cysse, cepað his sona,* and

Beo 942 　　　　　　　　　　　　Hwæt, þæt secgan mæg
　　　　efne swa hwylc mægþa　　swa ðone magan cende
　　　　æfter gumcynnum,　　　gyf heo gyt lyfað,
　　　　þæt hyre Ealdmetod　　este wære
　　　　bearngebyrdo;

and (*swa hwelc swa* dependent) *Or* 50. 16 *þeah swa hwelcne mon swa lyste þæt witan, ræde on his bocum hwelce ungetina . . . ,* *ÆCHom* i. 94. 12 *Swa hwylc hysecild swa ne bið ymbsniden on þam fylmene his flæsces his sawul losað,* and

Part 5　　　In swa hwylce tiid　　swa ge mid treowe to me
　　　　on hyge hweorfað,　　ond ge hellfirena
　　　　sweartra geswicað,　　swa ic symle to eow
　　　　mid siblufan　　sona gecyrre
　　　　þurh milde mod.

To these can be added examples with *swæþer*, e.g. *CP* 85. 14 *7 ge-ðence he simle, sie sua æðele sua unæðele suæðer he sie, ða æðelu ðære æfterran acennesse* and *BenR* 110. 6 . . . *þæt hig ðurh gode geearnunga furðor beon gemedemod, beon swæðer hig beon, swa sacerdhades swa clerichades.* . . .

§2364. Some observations may now be made. When *swa hwæþer swa* and *swa hwelc swa* are used adjectivally, the noun always appears before the second *swa*. Apart from this, the elements are usually together, but may be separated by the appearance before the second *swa* of a partitive genitive, as in *CP* 234. 10, *ÆHom* 13. 215, *Beo* 3051, and *Beo* 942 (§2363). This is quite common. But a partitive genitive often follows the second *swa* in the prose, e.g. *CP* 203. 10 *On ðæm medwisan is to trymmanne swa hwæt sua hie ongietan mægen ðæs godcundan wisdomes* and *ÆCHom* ii. 90. 18 *and forði swa hwæt swa ðæs godan sædes on swylcum wege befylð, bið mid yfelum geðohtum oftreden, and ðurh deoflum gelæht.* Other elements which occasionally precede the second *swa* include an adverb, e.g. *CP* 193. 19 *Sua hwa ðonne sua his lif to biesene bið oðrum monnum geset, ne sceal he no ðæt an don ðæt he ana wacie*; a governing noun, e.g. *Bede* 98. 31 (§2363); and a subject, object, and verb, as in *Beo* 685 (§2363).

§2365. These combinations can of course be used in all cases, e.g. (nominative) *Bo* 51. 28 (for this and the next seven examples see

§2363), *ÆCHom* i. 94. 12, and *GenB* 481; (accusative) *Or* 50. 16, *ÆCHom* i. 248. 29, and *GenB* 755; (genitive) *Bede(T)* 98. 31, *Bo* 112. 2, *ÆCHom* i. 318. 28, *ÆCHom* i. 480. 32 . . . *and se fæder ða mid aðe behet þæt he wolde hire forgyfan swa hwæs swa heo gewilnode*, and *ÆCHom* ii. 308. 18 . . . *gif he him ne sæde swa hwæs swa he axode* (there are none in the poetry); and (dative), e.g. *ÆCHom* ii. 274. 3 *Swa hwam swa ðyrste, cume to me and drince, Beo* 3051, and

PPs 137. 4   Swa hwylce daga   ic þe deorne cige,
               gehyr me hwætlice,   and me hraðe gedo
               micle mine sawle   on þines mægenes sped.

They can also be governed by prepositions, e.g. *Bede* 160. 26 . . . *on swa hwilcre stowe swa hi coman, ÆCHom* ii. 474. 2 *And to swa hwilcere leode swa we cumað . . . , ÆCHom* ii. 534. 7 *On swa hwilcum huse swa ge incumað . . . , Beo* 685 (§2363), and *Part* 5 (§2363).

§2366. There are very occasional examples in which the first *swa* is unexpressed, e.g. *GD(O)* 327. 26 *hwæt swa þin hand mage wyrcan, wyrce arudlice*, where MS *C* has the expected *swa hwæt swa; Bo(C)* 109. 17 *hwa swa*, where MS *B* has *swa hwa swa; ChronE* 37. 1 (675) *7 hwa swa hit tobreceð, þa wurðe he amansumed 7 aniðrod mid Iudas* (this is a Peterborough addition and therefore late); and

GenB 554   . . .   þæt git ne læstan wel
               hwilc ærende swa   he easten hider
               on þysne sið sendeð.

For more examples see Johnsen, *Ang.* 37 (1913), 286, and Bødtker 1910, p. 13.

§2367. Absence of the second *swa* is somewhat more common. The most noteworthy example is *ÆGram* 114. 7 *eft quisquis, swa hwa, quaequae, swa hwylc, quodquod, swa hwylc*, for Ælfric always uses both *swas* in *ÆCHom* and (as far as I have so far observed) rarely fails to do so elsewhere. Other examples—apart from glosses such as *Ps(A)* 137. 4 *in swe hwelcum dege*—include *Bede(Ca)* 204. 31 . . . *7 þa ðonne swa hwylcum seocum men þearf wæs* . . . (see EETS, OS 110, p. 224), *ÆLS* 34. 193 *and swa hwæs he gewilnode him ne forwyrnde God, HomU* 21. 5. 13, *LPr ii* 96 (§2363), and *PPs* 137. 4 (§2365).[77]

---

[77] For more examples see *ArPrGl* 1 (Logeman) 119. 69; Johnsen, *Ang.* 37 (1913), 282-6; and Bødtker 1910, pp. 13-14. We do not need to follow Johnsen (*EStudien*, 46 (1912-13), 4) in including here *BlHom* 53. 17; see BT, s.v. *sam-hwilc*. Johnsen discusses other combinations which occur in the glosses, viz. *se/seðe swa hwelc* and *swa hwelc se/seðe/þæt/þe*, in *Ang.* 37 (1913), 286-91. These, I think, belong to the lexicographer.

§2368. Sporadic examples with three *swas* have been noted. They include *Bede* 258. 22 *ond swa hwelce men swa swa wilnadon þæt heo in halgum leorningum tyde wæron* . . . , *BenRGl* 68. 8 *swa swa hwæt fram leornincnihtum swa bið agyld*, Latin *quicquid a discipulis delinquitur*, and *Part* 5 (§2363). We also have *GD(C)* 78. 3 *ac swa swilce swa hit mihte, hit slat 7 wundode heora limu mid bitum*, where MS *H* has *ac swa hwylce swa*. . . .

§2369. There are also sporadic examples in which *oþþe* or *þe* replaces *swa*, e.g. *LawRect* 5. 3 *7 gyf he wel gelend bið, he sceal beon gehorsad þæt he mæge to hlafordes seame þæt syllan oððe sylf lædan, swæðer him man tæce*, *LPr ii* 96 (§2363), and *ÆGram* 243. 14 *hic miluus, þes glida, swa hwæðer swa hit sy, he þe heo*. See further Nusser, pp. 189–90.

§2370. The indefinite clause may occur initially, e.g. *Bo* 51. 28, *ÆCHom* i. 156. 6, and *GenB* 755 (all in §2363), or may follow (part of) the principal clause, e.g. *Bede* 94. 21, *HomU* 27. 145. 12, and *GenB* 481 (all in §2363). In the latter event, we occasionally find an antecedent—usually *eall*—in the principal clause, e.g. *GD(C)* 79. 30 *soðlice eall swa hwæt swa he gewilnode æt Gode þam ælmihtigan, efne swa he his bæd* . . . (where MS *H* has *soðlice swa hwæt swa*), *BlHom* 9. 11 *7 he forgifeþ eall swa hwæt swa þes middangeard ær wiþ hine æbyligða geworhte*, *ÆCHom* i. 528. 28 *Ðeah se mann hæbbe fullne geleafan, and ælmessan wyrce, and fela to gode gedo, eal him bið ydel, swa hwæt swa he deð, buton he hæbbe soþe lufe to Gode and to eallum cristenum mannum* (where *eal* may be used *apo koinou*), and

GenB 438   Sittan læte ic hine wið me sylfne,   swa hwa swa þæt secgan cymeð
                on þas hatan helle,   þæt hie heofoncyninges
                unwurðlice   wordum and dædum
                lare * * *

Johnsen (*Ang.* 37 (1913), 294–300) quotes and discusses more examples with antecedent *eall*, in which combination he claims (p. 300) *swa hwæt swa* 'was on a fair way to become a definite relative'.

§2371. Examples of 'postcedents'—usually a demonstrative or a personal pronoun—are more common. Thus we find, with both clauses requiring the same case, *Bo* 70. 3 . . . *swa hwa swa* . . . *he* . . . , *Bo* 112. 2 (§2363), *Bede* 350. 27 *Swa hwæt swa* . . . *þæt* . . . , *ÆC Hom* i. 162. 21 *Swa hwa swa* . . . *se* . . . , *ÆCHom* i. 52. 35 . . . *swa hwæt swa* . . . *eal* . . . *hit*, and *ÆCHom* i. 528. 35 *and swa hwylcne swa he gemet butan soþre lufe, ðæne he befrinð mid graman.* There are no examples of this sort in the poetry. Examples with the two clauses requiring different cases include *CP* 73. 15 *Sua hwelc ðonne sua ðissa uncysta hwelcre underðieded bið, him bið forboden ðæt he offrige Gode hlaf, BlHom* 49. 17 . . . *7 swa hwylcne swa he on eorþan alysde, þæt se wære on heofonum onlysed, Gen* 9. 6 *Swa hwa swa agyt ðæs mannes blod, his blod byð agoten,* and four examples in §2363, viz. *ÆCHom* i. 248. 29, *ÆCHom* ii. 228. 30 and 246. 11, and *GenB* 755.

§2372. The fact that conditional and indefinite adjective clauses have very similar semantic value has already been exemplified in §2213. It is apparent also in examples like *ÆCHom* ii. 588. 23 *Swa hwa swa getimbrað, ofer ðisum grundwealle, gold, oððe seolfor, oððe deorwurðe stanas, oþþe treowa, streaw oþþe ceaf, anes gehwilces mannes weorc bið swutel*; cf. 1 *Cor* 3. 12 *Si quis autem superaedificat super fundamentum hoc aurum, argentum, lapides pretiosos, ligna, foenum, stipulam,* [13] *Unius cuiusque opus manifestum erit.* But strictly speaking, the OE version is anacoluthic; we should require *his* instead of *anes gehwilces mannes* to give us the construction seen in the examples in the preceding section and in *ÆCHom* ii. 468. 32 *Ic stande æt ðære dura cnucigende, and swa hwa swa mine stemne gehyrð, and ða duru me geopenað, ic gange in to him, and mid him gereordige and he mid me.*

§2373. I have quoted or referred to all the examples of *swa hwa/ hwæt/hwæþer/hwelc swa* in the poetry, where these combinations are much less common than in the prose, probably for metrical reasons. There are three in *Beo*, four in *GenB*, and one each in *Part, PPs*, and *LPr* ii. It seems better to classify *Finn* 26 *Ðe is gyt her witod* ‖ *swæþer ðu sylf to me secean wylle* as dependent question. I do not have full collections for the prose. But Kivimaa (pp. 33, 45, and 46) speaks of the 'awkwardness' and hence the 'unpopularity' and sparing use of these combinations in her corpus.

b. Swelc

§2374. *Swelc* 'such as, whatever'[78] is occasionally used alone, combining both antecedent and relative, e.g. *CP* 101. 5 *Ðonne ic wæs mid Iudeum ic wæs suelc hie,*

---

[78] *Swelc/swilc/swylc* sometimes represents Goth. *swaleiks*, sometimes a contraction of *swa hwilc.* See Kock, p. 48, and *OEG*, §720. Einenkel's note 'Swelc > such' (*Ang.* 26 (1903), 561–6) has nothing for the student of OE syntax beyond a few OE examples.

Phoen 236   ðonne furþor gin
         wridað on wynnum,   þæt he bið wæstmum gelic
         ealdum earne,   and æfter þon
         feþrum gefrætwad,   swylc he æt frymðe wæs,
         beorht geblowen,

and

PsFr 19. 9   Do, drihten, cyng   dædum halne
         and us eac gehyr   holdum mode,
         swylce we ðe daga,   drihten, cigen.

§2375. It is more frequent in a correlative use *swelc* (. . .) *swelc* 'such as . . . such', e.g. *CP* 133. 6 *Suelc ðæt folc bið, suelc bið se sacerd. Ðonne bið se sacerd suelc suelc ðæt folc bið ðonne he ðæt ilce deð ðæt hie doð*, *Or* 74. 7 . . . *to gesecgenne hu ænig mon mehte swelce burg gewyrcan swelce sio wæs*, *BlHom* 59. 28 *Eal swylce seo lange mettrumnes biþ þæs seocan mannes . . . swylc is þæt lif þysses middangeardes*, *ÆCHom* i. 2. 31 *Ðonne beoð swilce gedreccednyssa swilce næron næfre . . .* ,

Beo 1246   Wæs þeaw hyra,
         þæt hie oft wæron   an wig gearwe,
         ge æt ham ge on herge,   ge gehwæþer þara
         efne swylce mæla,   swylce hira mandryhtne
         þearf gesælde,

and *Beo* 1328 *Swylc scolde eorl wesan, || æþeling ærgod, swylc Æschere wæs*. It will be noted that the first *swelc* may be used independently, either alone or with a partitive genitive, or dependently.

§2376. *Swelc* is also found occasionally with antecedents other than *swelc*, e.g. *Bede* 328. 6 *Ond hine ascode hwæðer he ða alysendlecan rune cuðe, 7 þa stafas mid him awritene hæfde, be swylcum men leas spel secgað 7 spreocað*, *Or* 202. 3 *þa sæde he him þæt he gesawe ane tobrocene byrgenne, swelce hiera þeaw wæs þæt mon ricum monnum bufan eorðan of stanum worhte*, *Notes* 26. 3 *Na hyrde we to soðe siþþan seccgan þ on ðære ealdan æ ænig wurde hus aræred swylic þ mære wæs*,

Beo 71   . . . ond þær on innan   eall gedælan
         geongum ond ealdum,   swylc him God sealde,
         buton folcscare   ond feorum gumena,

Met 26. 85   Cnihtas wurdon,
         ealde ge giunge,   ealle forhwerfde
         to sumum diore,   swelcum he æror
         on his lifdagum   gelicost wæs . . . ,

and perhaps

Beo 296   . . .   oþ ðæt eft byreð
                  ofer lagustreamas   leofne mannan
                  wudu wundenhals   to Wedermearce,
                  godfremmendra   swylcum gifeþe bið,
                  þæt þone hilderæs   hal gedigeð,

where *swylcum* may be demonstrative rather than relative. In such
contexts too, *swelc* means 'whatever' and 'such as' and does not seem
to be used as a mere substitute for the simple relative. The ASPR
note on

Beo 1154   Sceotend Scyldinga   to scypon feredon
                  eal ingesteald   eorðcyninges,
                  swylce hie æt Finnes ham   findan meahton
                  sigla searogimma

reads: 'Trautmann and Holthausen emend to *swylc*, to secure agreement with the neuter *ingesteald*. But the plural *swylce* may have
been suggested by the collective sense of *eal ingesteald*.' But it is not
necessary to assume that there is any discrepancy in concord. The
swylce clause is more likely to be a direct object of *feredon* in loose
apposition with, rather than in strict dependence on, *eal ingesteald.*

§2377. However, antecedent *swelc* is sometimes qualified or accompanied by what appears to be a normal adjective clause, e.g. *Ch* 1482
*7 ic bidde 7 bebeode swælc monn se ðæt min lond hebbe ðæt he
ælce gere agefe ðem higum æt Folcanstane L ambra maltes . . . ,
Ch* 1482 *7 swælc monn se ðe to minum ærfe foe, ðonne gedele he
ælcum mæssepreoste binnan Cent mancus goldes . . . ,* and perhaps
ÆLSPr 59 *An woruldcynincg hæfð fela þegna and mislice wicneras.
He ne mæg beon wurðful cynincg butan he hæbbe þa geþincðe þe
him gebyriað and swylce þeningmen þe þeawfæstnysse him gebeodon,*
where, however, *swylce* may mean 'also' (but scarcely 'as it were', as
Skeat has it); by a *swa* clause, e.g. *ÆLS* 29. 262 . . . *þa com þær
heofonlic leoht ofer ealle þa meniu swilc swa hi ær ne gesawon* and
ÆCHom ii. 162. 17 . . . *Florentius, se wolde habban swilcne hlisan
swa Benedictus*; by a *swilce swa* clause, e.g. *ÆHom* 12. 5 *ne mæg nan
mann soðlice swylce tacna wyrcan swilce swa ðu wyrcst, buton God
beo mid him* (on *(swilce) swa* clauses see further §§3325–6 and
3330); by a *þær* clause, e.g. *ÆCHom* ii. 162. 24 . . . *and bebead him,
on Godes naman, þæt he ðone cwelmbæran hlaf aweg bære, and on
swilcere stowe awurpe, ðær hine nan man findan ne mihte*; by a
hwelc clause, e.g. *Or* 48. 4 *Hit is scondlic, cwæð Orosius, ymb swelc
to sprecanne hwelc hit þa wæs . . .* ; by a noun clause in apposition,

e.g. *Or* 40. 27 *Hwær is nu on ænigan cristendome betuh him sylfum þæt mon him þurfe swilc ondrædan, þæt hine mon ænigum godum blote?*, *ChristA* 78, and (despite Wülfing (i, §270, Anm.)) *Bo* 21. 14; or by a result clause, e.g. *Or* 80. 7 *7 ealles his heres wæs swelc ungemet þæt mon eaðe cweþan mehte ðæt hit wundor wære . . .* and *WHom* 5. 90 *. . . þonne God geþafað þæt he mot on his agenum halgum swylc wundor gewyrcan þæt Enoh 7 Elias þurh þone þeodfeond gemartrode weorðaþ.*

§2378. Sometimes the form *swelce* can be taken either as a pronoun agreeing with an antecedent or as a conjunction 'as, like' (see §§3323 and 3327), e.g. *Or* 68. 25 *þa he ðæt secgean nolde, þa acsedon hie hine hu fela þær swelcerra manna wære swelce he wæs* (where *swelce* may be plural in agreement with the antecedent *swelcerra manna*), *WHom* 3. 57 *In diebus illis erit tribulatio talis qualis non fuit ab initio mundi nec postea erit. Ðæt is on Englisc þæt swylc yrmð 7 earfoðnes bið þonne on worulde swylce æfre ær næs ne eft ne geweorþeð* (where *swylce* may agree with nom. sg. fem. *earfoðnes*), and

Sea 82	næron nu cyningas	ne caseras
	ne goldgiefan	swylce iu wæron,
	þonne hi mæst mid him	mærþa gefremedon
	ond on dryhtlicestum	dome lifdon.

Sometimes, however, it appears that *swelce* must be a conjunction because the pronoun would require some other form, e.g. *CP* 64. 24 *Ðin nosu is swelc swelce se torr on Libano ðæm munte* and *ÆLS* 3. 502 *Eala þu Effrem eall swylc is Basilius swylce þes fyrena swer* (in which we should expect *swelc* if it were the pronoun); *Bo* 63. 21 *Wære se mon on swelcum lande swelce he wære . . .* (where *swelcum* would be the expected form); and *Bo* 117. 4 *ac gif ic hæfde swilcne anwald swilce se ælmihtiga God hæfð . . .* and *Beo* 756 *ne wæs his drohtoð þær ‖ swylce he on ealderdagum ær gemette* (where *swilcne* would be needed). Some of the examples Wülfing (i, §271) cites as belonging to this second group seem to me to belong to the ambiguous first one, e.g. *Or* 40. 29 *oððe hwær syndon ure godas þe swylcra mana gyrnen swilce hiora wæron?*

c. Swa?

§2379. *Swa* is sometimes translated 'which', e.g. by Morris in *BlHom* 17. 3 *. . . he him gehet his æriste, swa he þa mid soðe gefylde gelice swa he ær þa þrowunge dyde* and by Wrenn–CH in *Beo* 2331 *breost innan weoll ‖ þeostrum geþoncum, swa him geþywe ne wæs,*

and *swa* (. . . *swa*) clauses often seem to have almost the same function and meaning as adjective clauses; cf. *BlHom* 53. 4 *7 swa feala
earmra manna swa on þæs rican neaweste 7 þæs welegan sweltaþ 7
he him nele syllan his teoþungsceatta dæl, þonne bið he ealra þara
manna deaþes sceldig* with *BlHom* 53. 2 *Soþ is þæt ic eow secgge,
swa hwylc man swa nele Drihten lufian 7 his æhta for his naman
dælan, þonne genimeþ hi Drihten mid mycclum teonan on him* and
BlHom 53. 10 *Se mon se þe wile þone heofonlican gefean begytan,
agife he symle mid rihte þone teoþan sceat Gode*, and then

GenA 1314	Noe fremede swa hine nergend heht,
	hyrde þam halgan heofoncyninge,
	ongan ofostlice þæt hof wyrcan,
	micle merecieste

with

Ex 558	wile nu gelæstan þæt he lange gehet
	mid aðsware, engla drihten,
	in fyrndagum fæderyncynne. . . .

But, similar though they may be to adjective clauses (see Behre,
pp. 278-9), these *swa* clauses, like their MnE equivalents, are comparative; to translate *swa* as 'which' in contexts where it can be so
translated implies acceptance of the view that *swa* is a relative pronoun. This idea has often been expressed, e.g. by Blackburn (in the
glossary to his edition of *Exodus and Daniel*); by Thomas (*MLR* 12
(1917), 343); by Curme, who asserts that 'the literal meaning of this
expression [*swa hwa swa*] is "that that one that" ' (*JEGP* 11 (1912),
369), though he does not justify this remarkable claim and elsewhere
speaks of 'the demonstrative adverbs *swa—swa*' (ibid., p. 195); by
Dekker, who tells us that '*swa* contained a pronominal element as
early as Beo', which seems to belie his title 'The pseudo-pronoun
"so" ' (*Neophil.* 23 (1938), 144); and by other writers whose views
I have attacked in the places listed in §2381 fn. See also Kock
(pp. 50-1); but note his later views in *Ang.* 42 (1918), 102-3, and cf.
Ericson, *JEGP* 30 (1931), 16.

§2380. In my opinion *swa*, like its common Germanic ancestor (see
Small 1924, p. 148), is by usage an adverb rather than a pronoun.[79]
It can hardly be seriously suggested that *swa* is the subject of *gelamp*
in

[79] Johnsen's claim (*Ang.* 38 (1914), 97) that 'the original sense and function of *swa* was
also that of a local-demonstrative adverb' reflects again the undue preoccupation with the
Charters apparent in connection with his similar claim for *þonne*; see Small 1924, pp. 95-
100, and Sturtevant, *MLN* 40 (1925), 496.

Beo 1251   Sum sare angeald
                  æfenræste,   swa him ful oft gelamp,
                  siþðan goldsele   Grendel warode . . .

or the object of *bæd* in

Beo 28   hi hyne þa ætbæron   to brimes faroðe,
                  swæse gesiþas,   swa he selfa bæd,
                  þenden wordum weold   wine Scyldinga. . . .

Examples like *Gen* 41. 13 *7 he sæde unc eal swa swa hit syððan aeode*, Latin *Audiuimus quidquid postea rei probauit eventus*, merely prove that there is more than one way of translating Latin *quidquid*. Contrasted examples like *BlHom* 67. 12 *Wel þæt gedafenode þæt Drihten swa dyde on þa gelicnesse* but *BlHom* 41. 6 *7 gif we þæt nu ne doþ* and *BlHom* 15. 34 *forðon he þis dyde* . . . , and like *GenA* 1314 but *Ex* 558 (both in §2379), prove that *swa* and a demonstrative or relative were sometimes interchangeable, not that they were identical. It is perhaps examples like these which prompted the unsupported observations by Clarke in *YWES* 1931, p. 67. More examples are given by Dekker, *Neophil.* 23 (1938), 136-8.

§2381. I do not propose to pursue this topic here. I have given elsewhere[80] my reasons for agreeing with Ericson when he says (1931, p. 19):

Certain it is that translators of Old English as well as later grammarians have been too quick to label *swa* a pronoun, either relative or demonstrative. In that matter it is better to be a 'fundamentalist', harking back to Ælfric's dictum [*ÆGram* 229. 10]
      Sume [adverbia] syndon similitudinis, ða getacniað gelicnysse. Sic swa, sicut swaswa. Sicut fecisti swa swa ðu dydest. . . .
The most one can say safely is, that certain cases [*sic*] of *swa* are used with more or less pronominal force; outside of these, and they are not numerous, the *swa* pronoun in Old English is not to be found;

and again (Ericson 1932, p. 27):

Careful investigation must convince any scholar that examples of indisputable pronominal *swa* are seldom met with. Old English lexicographers and translators have been too ready to render these pseudo-substantives as pronouns. Many of them give the clearest possible meaning if taken in the usual modal sense.

Small (*MLN* 49 (1934), 537-9) agrees. Many of the apparent examples of pronominal *swa* are satisfactorily explained by Ericson (*JEGP* 30 (1931), 6-20) and Kock (*Ang.* 42 (1918), 101-3). Thus

---

[80] *Ang.* 81 (1963), 300; *RES* 15 (1964), 140; *NM* 70 (1969), 75-8; and §1567. Dekker (*Neophil.* 23 (1938), 134-45) discusses the question in relation to all periods of English.

the seemingly clear case of the use of *swa* as a relative pronoun in

El 643   Hu is þæt geworden   on þysse werþeode
               þæt ge swa monigfeald   on gemynd witon,
               alra tacna gehwylc   swa Troiana
               þurh gefeoht fremedon?

proves on examination not to be so; if a comma is inserted after *gehwylc* in line 645, it becomes clear that *swa* introduces a comparative clause.

§2382. It is interesting to note that Ericson, in accounting for the origin of the construction in which *swa* appears to be used as a relative pronoun (1931, pp. 8–9), gives much the same explanations as those given in *OED* (s.v. *as* VI. 24) for similar MnE constructions with 'as'. See also Curme, *JEGP* 11 (1912), 377, and Jespersen *Ess.*, pp. 364–5. My insistence that *swa* is not pronominal in OE may seem a terminological trifle. Reference to my articles will show that this is not so. The belief that *swa* is pronominal has often led to mistranslation.

d. Loc(a) hwa/hwæt/hwæþer/hwelc

§2383. These combinations appear sporadically in the later prose as indefinite relatives. Examples include *HomU* 46. 294. 32 *and loca hwa þære mihte age, he mot gehæftne man alysan, ÆGram* 58. 11 *hic et hæc et hoc uetus, loc hwæt eald sy, ÆCHom* ii. 576. 10 *Bide me loce hwæs ðu wille and ic ðe sylle, ChronE* 237. 18 (1101)... *7 loc hweðer þæra gebroðra oðerne oferbide wære yrfeweard ealles Englalandes 7 eac Normandiges*, and *HomU* 46. 295. 3 *and loca hwylc cristen man sy ungesibsum, man ah on þam dæge hine to gesibsumianne*. We also find *loc(a) hu/hwær/hwider/hwonne*; on these see the Index of Words and Phrases. There are no examples in the poetry. For more examples of these combinations in all periods of English and for discussions on their origin, see BTS, s.v. *loc, loca*; *OED*, s.v. *look* I. 4b; Cook, *MLN* 31 (1916), 442; Lotspeich, *JEGP* 37 (1938), 1–2; Eccles, *JEGP* 42 (1943), 386–400; Liggins 1955, p. 411; Penttilä, pp. 136–40; Prins, *EStudies*, 43 (1962), 165–9; and Yamakawa 1969, pp. 19–20. The type 'See where . . .' discussed by F. Karpf in *Jespersen Gram. Misc.*, pp. 253–60, is different. Sentences like *CP* 49. 9 *Loca nu hu ungelic spræc eode of ðissa tuega monna muðe* do not exemplify the formula. But they may be factors in its development.

e. Relative adverbs

§2384. Clauses in which local and temporal conjunctions refer back to an antecedent and so introduce what are technically adjective clauses are discussed in the appropriate sections in this chapter; see the Index of Words and Phrases.

f. Hwa, hwæt, hwelc, hwær, hwonne, and the like?

§2385. There is no doubt that in OE these words are frequently used in clauses which lie on the borderline between dependent question and adverb or adjective clauses with sometimes indefinite, sometimes definite, reference. But there is in my opinion nothing to be gained by insisting that they are used in OE as conjunctions or relative pronouns. See further §§2050-4 and 2363 fn. 75.

13. MOOD AND TENSE

a. Introductory remarks

§2386. The prevailing mood in adjective clauses in OE is the indicative. Understandably (I hope), I do not have full figures for the prose. But in the poetry, the indicative occurs in almost sixty per cent of the examples. Less than five per cent have the subjunctive. The remainder have a form which is ambiguous for mood. There is no good reason for supposing that the proportion of indicatives to subjunctives within this group is significantly different from that in the unambiguous examples. The preoccupation with the subjunctive apparent in the titles and contents of many works on OE syntax—and indeed in these sections—is understandable and perhaps inevitable. But it should not blind us to these facts.

§2387. When a subjunctive occurs in an OE adjective clause, its *raison d'être* should be sought in the attitude of the speaker; as the following sections show, the comparative figures of indicative and subjunctive are sufficient to demolish completely the view that the subjunctive is present in obedience to some 'law of symmetry'.[81] The belief in such laws no doubt arises from observation of the fact that in certain contexts a speaker tends to use the subjunctive, but it proves to be based on a study of selected examples.[82]

---

[81] Hotz, p. 61. See Mourek, p. 122; Glunz, p. 67; Behre, pp. 182-3 and *passim*; Wilde, p. 376; and Cobb, p. 43.

[82] See Hotz, p. 61, and Vogt, pp. 46-9. Cf., however, Mourek, *passim*, especially pp. 121-2.

§ 2388. Since so much has been written about the subjunctive and 'its real nature', it seems worth saying that, in many of the examples discussed in this chapter, a perfectly natural translation and probably a fairly accurate impression of the state of the speaker's mind can be obtained by the somewhat obvious expedient of translating the OE subjunctive by a MnE subjunctive or subjunctive-equivalent. In this connection

And 544

                                       Nænig manna is
under heofonhwealfe,   hæleða cynnes,
ðætte areccan mæg   oððe rim wite
hu ðrymlice,   þeoda baldor,
gasta geocend,   þine gife dælest

is perhaps not without interest.

§ 2389. In the discussion of those contexts in which the subjunctive is sometimes said to occur by 'rule', Behre's system of classification has been adopted; it is on the whole adequate and simple and covers the important points noted by Wülfing (ii, §§ 475-8), Anklam (pp. 127-30), Glunz (*passim*), and Wilde (*passim*). At the same time, it must be borne in mind that the system is only a guide and that the categories often overlap. See Glunz, p. 67; Behre, p. 181; and such examples as *Bede* 486. 7, *Ps(P)* 13. 3, *Alex* 14. 2, *GenA* 1335, *And* 943, and *ChristA* 230.

§ 2390. Standop discusses the use of the 'modal' auxiliaries in adjective clauses at pp. 62-5 (*magan*), 91-2 (**motan*), 117 (**sculan*), and 155 (*willan*).

b. The adjective clause is connected with a principal clause containing a 'volitional expression'

§ 2391. Behre's term 'volitional expression' (p. 182) comprises an imperative, a subjunctive expressing a desire, purpose, or the like, or a form of **sculan*. When one of these appears in a principal clause, the verb of a dependent adjective clause may be in the subjunctive, often in marked contrast to the indicative of a Latin source, though occasionally a subjunctive is due to Latin influence, as in *Matt(WSCp)* 21. 41 *He forðeð þa yfelan mid yfele 7 gesett hys wingerd myd oþrum tilion þe him hys wæstm hyra tidon agyfon*, Latin *illi malos male perdet et uineam locabit aliis agricolis qui reddant ei fructum temporibus suis*. Examples include: (with an imperative) *Bede* 66. 12 *Quod superest, date elemosynam et ecce omnia munda sunt vobis:* *ðætte ofer seo 7 to lafe, sellað ælmesse, 7 eow beoð eal clæno,*

Matt(WSCp) 5. 42 *Syle þam ðe þe bidde*, Latin *qui petit a te da ei*, *LS* 4. 76. 14 *drihten min god syle gode mede þam þe mine þrowunga awrite*,

El 372

Nu ge raþe gangaþ
ond findaþ gen   þa þe fyrngewritu
þurh snyttro cræft   selest cunnen,
æriht eower . . . ,

and

Exhort 16   Wyrc þæt þu wyrce,   word oððe dæda,
hafa metodes ege   on gemang symle;

(with a subjunctive expressing purpose or desire) *Bede* 2. 10 *Forþon hit is god godne to herianne 7 yfelne to leanne þæt se geðeo se þe hit gehyre* (different construction in the Latin), *Bede* 82. 30 *Qui se continere non potest, habeat uxorem suam, se ðe hine ahabban ne mæg, hæbbe his wiif, ÆCHom* i. 56. 24 *Se ðe yfel sy geefenlæce he Paules gecyrrednysse; se ðe god sy þurhwunige he on godnysse mid Stephane, ÆCHom* i. 160. 29 *Se ðe me þenige, fylige he me, Rid* 67. 15 *Secge se þe cunne,* ‖ *wisfæstra hwylc, hwæt seo wiht sy,* and *And* 1164 *Ne hele se ðe hæbbe holde lare,* ‖ *on sefan snyttro;* and (with a form of **sculan*) *LawAf(E)El* 14 *Se ðe slea his fæder oððe his modor se sceal deaðe sweltan.* The term 'volitional expression' can reasonably be extended to cover phrases like *gearwe sindon* in

And 1368   Secgas mine
to þam guðplegan   gearwe sindon,
þa þe æninga   ellenweorcum
unfyrn faca   feorh ætþringan;

see Behre, p. 190. But I do not follow Behre (p. 193) in extending his definition (p. 182) by the inclusion of examples in dependent speech; on these see §§2410–13.

§2392. The present subjunctive is predictably the norm in adjective clauses with the subjunctive in these contexts. That the preterite subjunctive may occur when necessary is adequately attested by the long sequence in *WHom* 10c. 122–38, which begins *And se ðe wære gitsiende oðra manna þinga 7 æhta, weorðe of his agenan rihte begytenan ælmesgyfa georne. Se þe wære gifre, weorðe se syfre; 7 se ðe wære galsere on fulan forligere, weorðe se clænsere his agenre sawle.*

§2393. The so-called 'permissive' clause belongs here. It usually occurs with the present subjunctive in both clauses, e.g. *Bo* 112. 19

*wyrce hwa þ ðæt he wyrce oððe do þ he do, a he hæfð þ þ he ge-
earnað, WHom(EI)* 20. 49 *And þæs we habbað ealle þurh Godes
yrre bysmor gelome, gecnawe se ðe cunne,* and

Beo 1002   No þæt yðe byð
          to befleonne   —fremme se þe wille—,
          ac gesecan sceal   sawlberendra
          nyde genydde,   niþða bearna,
          grundbuendra   gearwe stowe,
          þær his lichoma   legerbedde fæst
          swefeþ æfter symle.

But the preterite subjunctive does occur in the prose, e.g. *Bo* 63. 21
*Wære se mon on swelcum lande swelce he wære þe hi ahte, ðonne
wære his wela 7 his weorðscipe mid him, WHom* 17. 16, and *Ch*
1150 . . . *geafe se ðe his geafe.* Further on this type, see §§3451-6.

§2394. But in adjective clauses after volitional expressions non-
subjunctive verbs are much more common than subjunctive verbs.
The approximate figures for the poetry are subjunctive twenty per
cent, indicative forty per cent, and forms ambiguous for mood forty
per cent. This demonstrates quite clearly that in OE poetry there is
no 'law of symmetry' and that an imperative, a subjunctive, or the
verb **sculan,* in a principal clause does not of itself cause the verb of
an adjective clause to be subjunctive. I do not have full figures for
the prose, but believe that the same is true there.

§2395. The presence of **sculan* is much less likely to produce a subjunctive than that of an imperative or subjunctive; consider *CP* 75.
11 *he sceal bion for eaðmodnesse hira gefera ælces ðara ðe wel doo;
he sceal bion stræc wið ða ðe ðær agyltað,* where the subjunctive in
the first adjective clause is probably due to the generic idea ('. . .
each of those of such a sort that he does well'), which is not present
in the second, *Beo* 440 *ðær gelyfan sceal ‖ Dryhtnes dome se þe hine
deað nimeð,* and

Seasons 200   Gyf se sacerd hine   sylfne ne cunne
          þurh dryhtnes ege   dugeþum healdan,
          nu þa, folces mann,   fyrna ne gyme
          þe gehalgod mann   her gefremme,
          ac þu lare scealt   lustum fremman
          ryhthicgennde   þe he to ræde tæchð,

where we can detect a difference in the speaker's attitude—there is
doubt or uncertainty about the priest's sins ('whatever they may be')
but his teaching is clear and certain.

§2396. But even an imperative or a subjunctive does not demand a subjunctive in an adjective clause, e.g. *ÆCHom* i. 156. 6 *Swa hwa swa oncnæwð þa blindnysse his modes, clypige he mid inweardre heortan.* We find a subjunctive immediately followed by an indicative after an imperative in *BlHom* 99. 5 *Men þa leofostan, geþenceaþ þæt ge gelomlice winnað 7 a embe þæt sorgiað þæt we urne lichoman gefyllan 7 gefrætwiað* (but the last clause may be noun rather than adjective, as Morris has it). The fluctuations after a subjunctive verb in *Deut* 27 are noteworthy: *Deut* 27. 20 *Sy se awyrged se ðe hæme mid his fæder wife* and *Deut* 27. 21 *Beo se man awyrged ðe hæme wið nyten* but *Deut* 27. 16 *Beo se man awyrged ðe ne arwurðað his fæder 7 his modor* and *Deut* 27. 26 *Beo se awyrged ðe ne wunað on ðisse æ.* The presence of a negative in the adjective clauses with the indicative does not, I believe, explain them; cf. *WHom* 7a. 18 *And se ðe þurh Ledenspræce rihtne geleafan understandan ne cunne, geleornige huru on Englisc. . . .* Exceptions in the poetry include examples with both present and preterite indicative, e.g.

GuthA 255	Gewitað nu, awyrgde, werigmode, from þissum earde þe ge her on stondað, fleoð on feorweg,

PPs 89. 14	Do us þa þine swiðran hand, drihten, cuðe, þam þe on snytrum syn swyðe getyde, and þa heora heortan healdað clæne

(where *syn* is probably to be taken as indicative; see §651),

MCharm 1. 75	Ful æcer fodres fira cinne, beorhtblowende, þu gebletsod weorþ þæs haligan noman þe ðas heofon gesceop and ðas eorþan þe we on lifiaþ,

and

ChristA 74	. . . arece us þæt geryne þæt þe of roderum cwom, hu þu eacnunge æfre onfenge bearnes þurh gebyrde.

The reason why the indicative is preferred to the subjunctive in the adjective clauses in these sentences is clear enough; there is no doubt in the author's mind nor is any wish implied by him about the contents of those clauses.

§2397. Some interesting variations are to be found in the Laws. The code of Æthelbert has two relevant examples—*LawAbt* 50 *Se þe cinban forslæhð, mid xx scillingum forgelde* and *LawAbt* 53 *Se þe earm þurhstinð, vi scillingum gebete*—in both of which the adjective clause has an indicative and the principal clause a subjunctive expressing a wish. The code of Alfred prefers the subjunctive when the principal clause contains a subjunctive or *sceal*, e.g. *LawAfEl(E)* 13 *Se mon se ðe his gewealdes monnan ofslea, swelte se deaðe* and *LawAfEl(E)* 14 *Se ðe slea his fæder oððe his modor, se sceal deaðe sweltan*, and even in *LawAfEl(E)* 17 *Se ðe slea his agenne þeowne esne . . . ne bið he ealles swa scyldig*, where the principal clause has the indicative. The code of Ine has the subjunctive with the subjunctive in *LawIne(E)* 66 *Se ðe hæbbe þreora hida, tæcne oþres healfes*, but the indicative with *sceal* and *mot* in *LawIne(E)* 65 *Se ðe hæfð x hida, se sceal tæcnan vi hida gesettes landes* and *LawIne(E)* 16 *Se ðe ðeof ofslihð, se mot gecyðan mid aðe þæt he hine synnigne ofsloge*. Other manuscripts have *mæg* for *mæge* in *LawIne(E)* 33 *Cyninges horswealh, se ðe him mæge geærendian, ðæs wergield bið CC scill.*, with *bið* in the principal clause. There is room for further study of these and other variations in the various codes of Laws. But they seem explicable only in terms of individual preferences. Visser (ii, § 876) somewhat misrepresents the situation by quoting only the adjective clauses in the examples he selects from the codes of Ine and Alfred. For similar variations in *gif* clauses see § § 3560–82.

§ 2398. The significance of those subjunctives which do occur in adjective clauses after volitional expressions has been summarized by Behre (p. 183) in the following terms:

. . . the subjunctive is used in relative clauses connected with an expression of volition to denote a volitional attitude on the part of the speaker towards the content of the dependent clause. As a matter of fact, the speaker has adopted an attitude of volition towards the content of the whole sentence, an attitude that is manifested in the main clause by an expression of exhortation, command, wish, concession, etc.

Visser (ii. 858) suggests other states of mind, such as doubt and uncertainty: when 'the modally marked [= subjunctive] form is used in attributive clauses, it expresses the speaker's reserve as to the possibility of the fulfilment of the condition in the clause. When this reserve is absent a modally zero [= indicative] form is used.' I have to confess that I become almost schizophrenic when I try to apply these explanations to the examples cited above and in § 3701. Space compels me to stop here, with the observation that in my collections the subjunctive is less frequent than the indicative, except in some of the legal codes.

*c. The adjective clause has as (part of) its antecedent an
indefinite such as* æghwylc, ælc, eall, gehwylc, *and the like*

§ 2399. Wülfing (ii, §§ 475-8) does not mention this group and, like
Anklam (pp. 128-9), I have noted no examples in the prose in which
an indefinite by itself in a principal clause is accompanied by an
adjective clause with a subjunctive verb. In all the possible prose
examples known to me, the indefinite is accompanied by another
of the elements discussed in these sections, e.g. (by an imperative)
CP 325. 22 *Sele ælcum ðara ðe ðe bidde*; (by a subjunctive) *Bo*
89. 5 *ælc þara ðe freo sie fundige to þam goode*; (by a form of
*sculan) *CP* 75. 11 *he sceal bion for eaðmodnesse hira gefera ælces
ðara ðe wel doo*; (by a negative) *Bede* 246. 19 *Ne wæs in þa tiid
ænig biscop buton þam Wine in alre Breotene þara þe rihtlice gehalgad wære*; (by a rhetorical question) *Gen* 41. 38 *Hwar magon we
findan swilcne man þe mid Godes gyfe sy swa afilled?*; and (by a subjunctive in dependent speech) *Or* 248. 23 *þridde wæs þæt he bebead
þæt ælc þara þe on elðeodignesse wære come to his agnum earde. . . .*

§ 2400. The only possible example in the poetry in which an indefinite in a principal clause unaccompanied by any other relevant element is connected with an adjective clause containing a subjunctive
verb is

PPs 102. 6　　Hafast þu milde mod,　　mihta strange,
　　　　　　　　drihten, domas　　eallum þe deope her
　　　　　　　　and ful treaflice　　teonan þolian.

Here the manuscript has *poliaðn*. I am inclined to think that the
scribe was right the first time and made the alteration after a casual
glance at *teonan*. But see § 2402. The subjunctive *wisien* in

PPs 148. 11　　Eorðcyningas eac　　ealle swylce
　　　　　　　　þe folcum her　　fore wisien
　　　　　　　　and ealdormen　　ahwær syndan,
　　　　　　　　and ealle þe þas eorþan　　ahwær demeð

is due to the imperative *do* in *PPs* 148. 10, the influence of which
seems to evaporate and so allow *syndan* (but see § 651) and *demeð*
for *demað*. All the other examples cited by Behre (pp. 193-4 and
195) either have a verb form which is ambiguous for mood, e.g.

GenA 1530　　Ælc hafað magwlite　　metodes and engla
　　　　　　　　þara þe healdan wile　　halige þeawas

and

ChristC 1064   . . . ond se hearda dæg   ond seo hea rod,
                ryht aræred   rices to beacne,
                folcdryht wera   biforan bonnað,
                sawla gehwylce   þara þe sið oþþe ær
                on lichoman   leoþum onfengen,

or contain one of the elements already discussed, e.g.

MCharm 11. 1   Ic me on þisse gyrde beluce   and on godes helde bebeode
                wið þane sara stice,   wið þane sara slege,
                wið þane grymma gryre,
                wið ðane micela egsa   þe bið eghwam lað,
                and wið eal þæt lað   þe in to land fare,

where (as Behre (p. 194) points out) 'volition is suggested in the main clause by the verb *bebeode*'.

§2401. A few typical examples with the indicative from prose and poetry follow: *CP* 299. 12 *Ælc ðara ðe bið geeaðmed, he bið upahæfen. . . . Ælc ðara ðe hine selfne upahefeð, he wierð gehined*, *ÆCHom* i. 54. 7 *Ælc ðæra þe his broðor hatað is manslaga*, *ÆLS* 11. 294 *ac we witon swa þeah hwæt wise lareowas sædan þæt ælc ðæra þe bið acweald for cristes geleafan bið soðlice gefullod þonne he swylt for gode*, *GenA* 2550 *Lig eall fornam* || *þæt he grenes fond goldburgum in*,

GenA 1521   Ælc hine selfa   ærest begrindeð
                gastes dugeðum   þæra þe mid gares orde
                oðrum aldor oðþringeð,

and

ChristA 430   þæt is healic ræd
                monna gehwylcum   þe gemynd hafað,
                þæt he symle oftost   ond inlocast
                ond geornlicost   god weorþige.

§2402. According to Behre (pp. 187-8), 'the subjunctive is here concessive and at the same time used as a stylistic means of emphasizing the general character of the relative clause. Ultimately, in this construction, too, it is an expression of volition manifesting itself in the relative clause as challenge.' He sees the implication of *PPs* 102. 6 (§2400) as 'let them here deeply and grievously suffer injury!' If we wished to retain *þolian*, we could emphasize the generic nature of the adjective clause by translating '. . . for all of such a sort that they here deeply and very grievously suffer injury'. Behre goes on to say that 'the indicative is most frequently found [sc. is the usual mood] in relative clauses after indefinite pronouns'. This in my opinion is an understatement. I do not accept that the influence of an indefinite alone in the principal clause could produce a subjunctive in an accompanying adjective clause.

d. The adjective clause has a superlative as (part of) its antecedent

§2403. It has already been noted in §2265 that limiting clauses in this category are introduced by se'þe, e.g.

ChristA 275 Eala þu mæra middangeardes
       seo clæneste cwen ofer eorþan
       þara þe gewurde to widan feore . . .

and

Rid 39. 13 . . .   ac gewritu secgað
      þæt seo sy earmost ealra wihta,
      þara þe æfter gecyndum cenned wære,

or þe, e.g. WHom 18. 20 And þæt wæs þæt mæreste hus þe on eorðan geworht wurde and

Rid 84. 29   fromast ond swiþost,
      gifrost ond grædgost grundbedd trideþ,
      þæs þe under lyfte aloden wurde
      ond ælda bearn eagum sawe . . . ,

whereas we find se and þe in non-limiting clauses like

Phoen 395 . . . ond hi þa gesette on þone selestan
      foldan sceata, þone fira bearn
      nemnað neorxnawong . . .

and ChristB 517 (§2265). There is a more significant and obvious difference: the limiting clauses have the subjunctive mood and the non-limiting the indicative.[83] This, as Hotz (p. 86) points out, is proof that the superlative does not cause the subjunctive. Here too it seems that in a certain context—in this case a superlative followed by a limiting clause—the speaker felt the need of the subjunctive. Hotz (p. 85) explains this in the following words: 'Thus the nature of the subj. after the superlative is to imply, that not only the facts of which we are aware, but all similar facts which might happen or have happened are comprised.' This seems to mean much the same as

---

[83] I have noted no examples in OE prose or poetry of the construction postulated by Andrew (SS, p. 106): 'hreowa tornost þara þe hine lange begeaton (indic.)', although the indicative is found in Old Saxon under certain conditions; see Behaghel, Die Modi im Heliand (Paderborn, 1876), 33-4, Die Syntax des Heliand (Wien, 1897), 308, and DS iii. 619; and Behre, p. 190.

Behre's observation (p. 188) that the subjunctive in these examples
has a 'concessive-generalizing force' and is illuminated by J. R. R.
Tolkien's translation (in a lecture) of

Ex 362   Niwe flodas   Noe oferlað,
                þrymfæst þeoden,   mid his þrim sunum,
                þone deopestan   drencefloda
                þara ðe gewurde   on woruldrice

as '. . . the deepest deluge that could ever have been'. See further
Behre, pp. 188-90. But I detect an element of unreality here.

e. The adjective clause is connected with a principal clause containing a negative expression or a question

§2404. When accompanied by an adjective clause, negated indicatives and rhetorical questions are often merely different ways of expressing the same idea; compare

Max ii 63   Næni eft cymeð
                hider under hrofas,   þe þæt her for soð
                mannum secge   hwylc sy meotodes gesceaft,
                sigefolca gesetu,   þær he sylfa wunað

with

Met 28. 1   Hwa is on eorðan   nu unlærdra
                þe ne wundrige   wolcna færeldes,
                rodres swifto,   ryne tunglo,
                hu hy ælce dæge   utan ymbhwerfeð
                eallne middangeard?[84]

As these examples suggest, the subjunctive is used in adjective clauses
dependent on such expressions when the action or situation described
is regarded as uncertain, surprising, unreal, or impossible.

§2405. Other examples in which a negated indicative—the term
embraces negated ambiguous verb-forms which are to be taken as
indicatives and also virtual negatives such as *feawa* in *Matt(WSCp)*
7. 14 and *fea ænig* in *Rid* 60. 3 (both quoted below)—is accompanied
by an adjective clause with a verb in the subjunctive include *Bo* 57.
29 *Nis nan gesceaft gesceapen ðara þe ne wilnige þ hit þider cuman
mæge þonan þe hit ær com*, *Matt(WSCp)* 7. 14 *7 swyþe feawa synt
þe þone weg findon* (cf. *Matt(WSCp)* 7. 13 *7 swyþe manega synt þe
þurh þone weg farað*), *ÆCHom* ii. 400. 26 . . . *ac þær næs nan mann*

[84] On the close relationship between examples like *Met* 28. 1 and those like *Met* 28. 18
Hwa is on weorulde þæt ne wafige . . . , see §§2139-43.

ðe þone hlaf him betwynan tobræce, *WHom* 4. 24 *Forðam nis nan man þæt ne sy synful,* ApT 36. 15 *Mid þam þe ic becom to fullon andgite, þa næs nan cræft ðe wære fram cynegum began oððe fram æðelum mannum þe ic ne cuðe,*

ChristA 241   Forþon nis ænig þæs horsc,   ne þæs hygecræftig,
                      þe þin fromcyn mæge   fira bearnum
                      sweotule geseþan,

Rid 60. 3   fea ænig wæs
                monna cynnes,   þæt minne þær
                on anæde   eard beheolde,

and

Met 8. 33   Næs ðeos eorðe besmiten   awer þa geta
                beornes blode   þe hine bill rude,
                ne furðum wundne wer   weoruldbuende
                gesawan under sunnan.

§2406. Examples with a rhetorical question and a subjunctive in the adjective clause include *CP* 411. 25 *Hwa is nu ðæra ðe gesceadwis sie 7 to ðæm gleaw sie ðæt he swelces hwæt tocnawan cunne, ðætte nyte ðætte on gimma gecynde carbunculus bið diorra ðonne iacinctus?,* Matt(WSCp) 12. 11 *Hwylc man ys of eow þe hæbbe an sceap 7 gyf þ̄ afylð restedagum on pytt hu ne nymð he þ̄ 7 hefþ hyt upp?,* Latin *Quis erit ex uobis homo qui habeat ouem unam et si ceciderit haec sabbatis in foueam nonne tenebit et leuabit eam?,* ApT 10. 6 *Oððe hwæt is manna þe nyte þæt þeos ceasterwaru on heafe wunað . . . ?,*

MSol 477   Is ðonne on ðisse foldan   fira ænig
                eorðan cynnes,   ðara ðe man age,
                ðe deað abæde . . . ?

(cf. Menner's reading—*MSol* 467 in his edition), and *Met* 28. 1 (§2404). The only example I have so far noted with a verb in the preterite tense is

PPs 143. 4   Hwæt is se manna,   mihtig drihten,
                þe þu him cuðlice   cyþan woldest,
                oððe mannes sunu,   þæt hit gemet wære,
                þæt þu him aht wið   æfre hæfdest?,

where *woldest* is to be taken as subjunctive; see §601a. But *ÆLS* 34. 154 *Hwa com þanon hider þe mihte us secgan gif hit swa wære?* may be another.

§2407. But when the content of the adjective clause is something which has happened, is happening, or will happen, and not something presented as uncertain, surprising, unreal, or impossible, the indicative is quite regular even when the principal clause contains a negated indicative (as defined in §2405) or a rhetorical question. Examples with negated indicatives include *Bo* 62. 29 *þæt ne magon don þa ðe þone anweald habbað þisse worulde*, *Bede* 80. 8 *Nales þætte in-gongeð in muð monnan besmiteð*, *ÆLS* 9. 75 *Ne synd ge þe þær sprecað*, *WHom* 7. 102 *Heora lif nis naht buton seo mæste yrmð þe æfre gewarð*,

Beo 1465   Huru ne gemunde   mago Ecglafes
              eafoþes cræftig,   þæt he ær gespræc
              wine druncen,

and

ChristA 351   Næs ænig þa giet   engel geworden,
                 ne þæs miclan   mægenþrymmes nan
                 ðe in roderum up   rice biwitigað. . . .

See further Behre, p. 295, and *Guide*, §165. 2.

§2408. Behre (p. 296) rightly points out that 'the indicative is used with reference to facts after questions that are not rhetorical'. This is true of examples like *Bede* 68. 22 *Hwæðer moton twegen æwe gebroðor twa geswustor in gesinscipe onfon þa ðe beoð feorr heora cneorisse from him acende?*, *ÆCHom* i. 78. 6 *Hwær is Iudeiscra leoda cyning seðe acenned is?*,

GenA 2890   Wit her fyr and sweord,   frea min, habbað;
               hwær is þæt tiber,   þæt þu torht gode
               to þam brynegielde   bringan þencest?,

and

El 902   Hwæt is þis, la, manna,   þe minne eft
            þurh fyrngeflit   folgaþ wyrdeð,
            iceð ealdne nið,   æhta strudeð?

But the indicative appears in adjective clauses after questions which seem to me undoubtedly rhetorical, e.g. *Bo* 46. 21 *Oððe hwær is nu se foremæra 7 se aræda Romwara heretoga, se wæs haten Brutus . . . ?*, *CP* 161. 8 *Hwæt tacnað ðonne Ezechhiel se witga buton ða lareowas, to ðæm is gecueden . . . ?*, *Bo* 59. 8 *hu ne bið ælc mon genog earm þæs ðe he næfð, þonne hit hine lyst habban?*, *Ps(P)* 11. 4, *ÆCHom* i. 314. 17 *La hu, ne sind þas ðe her sprecað Galileisce?*,

ÆCHom i. 326. 8 *Se ðe ne lufað his broðor, ðone ðe he gesihð, hu mæg he lufian God, þone þe he ne gesihð lichamlice?*, and (despite Behre (p. 296), who cites the second half of this example to illustrate his statement with which this paragraph begins)

Met 10. 44   Hwær is nu se rica   Romana wita,
and se aroda,   þe we ymb sprecað,
hiora heretoga,   se gehaten wæs
mid þæm burgwarum   Brutus nemned?
Hwær is eac se wisa   and se weorðgeorna
and se fæstræda   folces hyrde,
se wæs uðwita   ælces ðinges,
cene and cræftig,   ðæm wæs Caton nama?

Here too the content of the adjective clause is presented as simple fact.

§2409. The basic situation, then, is clear: the subjunctive appears in these two contexts when the content of the adjective clause is presented as being influenced by the attitude of someone involved (see §1936) or as unreal or impossible, the indicative when it is presented as something which has happened, is happening, or will happen. Behre (pp. 292–306) endorses this view—with one (to me important) omission; see §2414—and endeavours to explain the nature of these subjunctives. At p. 298 he says:

From examples of this kind we can draw the conclusion that the subjunctive as occurring in consecutive and relative clauses after negative and interrogative expressions does not express unreality or negation but an attitude of rejection, disapproval, or surprise generally towards an assumed event, sometimes also towards a fact (= the meditative-polemic subjunctive). The subjunctive as used in this manner has parallels in *þæt*-clauses after verbs of thinking and saying and in indirect questions;

and at p. 304:

The constitutive factor, then, that determines the use of the subjunctive in consecutive and relative clauses after negative and interrogative expressions is an attitude of meditation or reflection on the part of the speaker generally towards an assumed event, sometimes also towards a fact. As pointed out above, the meditative subjunctive (in the wide sense of this term) may, according to the situation, have an emotional (polemic), sometimes an optative or a preceptive tone.

I do not propose to discuss the nature of the subjunctive. But I have found no evidence—and Behre offers none—for his use of the repeated phrase 'sometimes also towards a fact' in connection with adjective clauses. On its validity for consecutive clauses, see §2997.

f. The adjective clause is in dependent speech

§2410. The prevailing mood in adjective clauses in dependent speech is the indicative even when the verb of the noun clause is subjunctive. The approximate figures for the poetry are indicative forty-two per cent, subjunctive eight per cent, and forms ambiguous for mood fifty per cent. Three typical examples of the indicative will suffice: (dependent statement) *Or* 178. 19 *þa ondwyrde he him, 7 cwæð þæt hit na geweorþan sceolde þæt se wære leoda cyning se þe ær wæs folce þeow*; (dependent question/exclamation) *ÆLS* 34. 244 *Fyr me forbærne gif ic ne buge to Criste siþþan ic geseo hu eowre sawla farað to þam oþrum life þe ge embe sprecað* (where the principal clause of the whole complex contains a volitional expression); and (dependent desire) *Bede* 108. 2 *Wrat he 7 sende ærendgewrit to him: bæd heo 7 halsade, þæt heo in annesse sibbe 7 in gehælde rihtra Eastrana geþwærede mid þa Cristes cirican, seo geond ealne middangeard togoten is.*

§2411. Examples with the subjunctive in an adjective clause in dependent statement include *CP* 383. 7 *Ðæt is ðonne ðæt mon ierne from geate to oðrum, ðæt he ierne ðreatigende from ðara unðeawa ælcum to oðrum, ðe deað mæge ingan on ðæs monnes mod, Alex* 17. 4 . . . *7 cwædon þ we fundon sumne swiðe micelne mere in þæm wære fersc wæter 7 swete genog,*

Beo 3069   Swa hit oð domes dæg   diope benemdon
               þeodnas mære,   þa ðæt þær dydon,
               þæt se secg wære   synnum scildig,
               hergum geheaðerod,   hellbendum fæst,
               wommum gewitnad,   se ðone wong strude . . . ,

and

GenB 529   he cwæð þæt þa sweartan helle
               healdan sceolde   se ðe bi his heortan wuht
               laðes gelæde.

In the last three of these, the preterite subjunctive refers to the future-in-the-past and so reflects an element of uncertainty or the like on the part of the speaker and/or the reporter. There is something hypothetical too about the present subjunctive in *CP* 383. 7. Similar explanations can usually be found for such subjunctives when they do occur. But the possibility of attraction does sometimes arise; see §2101.

§2412. The subjunctive is found in an adjective clause in dependent question/exclamation in examples like *Bo* 6. 16 . . . *7 hu mon sceolde*

ælcne mon hatan be þam deore þe he gelicost wære, Ps(P) 13. 3
Drihten locað of heofenum ofer manna bearn, and hawað hwæðer
he geseo ænigne þæra þe hine sece oþþe hine ongite,

GenA 1026

      forþon ic lastas sceal
wean on wenum wide lecgan,
hwonne me gemitte manscyldigne,
se me feor oððe neah fæhðe gemonige,
broðorcwealmes,

El 414

  . . . sohton searoþancum, hwæt sio syn wære
þe hie on þam folce gefremed hæfdon
wið þam casere, þe him sio cwen wite,

ChristC 1316 Ne þæt ænig mæg oþrum gesecgan
mid hu micle elne æghwylc wille
þurh ealle list lifes tiligan,
feores forhtlice, forð aðolian,
synrust þwean ond hine sylfne þrean,
ond þæt wom ærran wunde hælan,
þone lytlan fyrst þe her lifes sy,

and *GuthA* 54 *Dryhten sceawað ‖ hwær þa eardien þe his æ healden.*
Behre (pp. 303-4 and 306) describes these subjunctives as 'chiefly
meditative' but also as implying 'an emotional element'. This, I assume, can be taken as covering the element of uncertainty seen in all
these examples, as well as the generic or indefinite idea which can
also be detected in some of them, e.g. *Bo* 6. 16 '. . . by the name of
whichever animal he was most like' and *GuthA* 54 '. . . men of such
a sort that they respect God's laws'. See further Mitchell 1965*a*,
p. 49, and §2101.

§2413. The following are typical of those adjective clauses in dependent desires which have the subjunctive: *Bede* 374. 27 . . . *7 het ðæt
hie þæt dydon ðy dæge þe his gemynddæg wære 7 his forðfor, Bede*
388. 9 *Mid ðy he ða sumre tiide in foreword Eastorfæsten ðider
cuom to wunienne, ða heht he his geferan, ðæt hio sohton sumne
earmne ðearfan, se ðe wære micelre untrumnisse 7 woedelnisse
hefigad . . . , WPol* 179. 4 *And we lærað þæt preosta gehwilc to
sinoðe hæbbe his cleric and gefædne man to cnihte and nænigne
unwitan þe disig lufige, Alex* 14. 2 *Het ic þa ælcne mon hine mid his
wæpnum gegerwan 7 faran forð 7 þæt eac fæstlice bebead ðæt se
mon se ne wære mid his wæpnum æfter fyrd wison gegered þæt hine
mon scolde mid wæpnum acwellan,* the first adjective clause in

Dan 448 Gebead þa se bræsna Babilone weard
swiðmod sinum leodum, þæt se wære his aldre scyldig,
se ðæs onsoce þætte soð wære
mære mihta waldend, se hie of þam morðre alysde,

and

El 1204   þa seo cwen ongan
              læran leofra heap   þæt hie lufan dryhtnes,
              ond sybbe swa same   sylfra betweonum,
              freondræddenne   fæste gelæston
              leahtorlease   in hira lifes tid,
              ond þæs latteowes   larum hyrdon,
              cristenum þeawum,   þe him Cyriacus
              bude, boca gleaw.

Behre (p. 193) groups the last two examples and several others from
the poetry—I would exclude *MCharm* 1. 59—among examples
whose 'main clause contains a subjunctive of volition'. There is certainly an element of desire affecting the content of some of these
adjective clauses, e.g. in *Alex* 14. 2, where the speaker does not want
anyone to be unarmed, and in *Dan* 448, where Nebuchadnezzar
wishes God to be honoured. But a generic element can also be detected in these and in some of the other examples, including *Bede*
388. 9. An element of uncertainty is also present in those in which
the reference is to the future-in-the-past. However, *Bede* 374. 27
presents difficulties. The element of desire here is associated with
the proposed action rather than with the identity of the day, which
could scarcely have been in doubt. Bede wrote . . . *iussitque ut die
depositionis eius hoc facere meminissent* without any suggestion that
he or bishop Eadberht was ignorant of the date of Cuthbert's death.
It is hard to believe that the translator was.

g. General remarks

§ 2414. Two important facts emerge. First, that the indicative and
not the subjunctive is the predominant mood in adjective clauses in
OE. Second, that while the subjunctive can often be explained in
terms of the attitude of the speaker and/or of the reporter (but see
§ 1936), there are examples in which the reason for it lies buried
with these individuals. Some of these have already been discussed.
Others include *Bede* 280. 3 and *Bede* 444. 23 (see Wülfing, ii, § 478,
but note the variations in the manuscripts), *Marv* 63. 10 . . . *7 on
þære ilcan stowe is æt sunnan upgange setl quietus þæs stillestan
bisceopes se nænine operne mete ne þige buton sæ ostrum 7 be þam
he lifede, ÆLS* 36. 326 *and heardmod bið se man þe ne mage þysum
gelyfan* (though a generic or indefinite element may be detected
here), and the three examples from the poetry which I discuss in
Neophil. 49 (1965), 50. But, unlike Behre (my § 2409), I cannot
eliminate unreality or impossibility as factors; see, for example,
§§ 2403 and 2404.

§2415. In *Ch* 1482 *H* 4. 15 *Gif him elles hwæt sæleð, ðonne ann ic his minra swæstarsuna swælcum se hit geðian wile 7 him gifeðe bið*, the form *wile* is ambiguous for mood, for 3rd pers. sg. *wille* and *wile* occur in almost identical contexts in the same document at *H* 3. 9 and *H* 3. 12. So Harmer may be right to take the two clauses which follow *swælcum se* as co-ordinate and to translate '. . . to whichever of my sister's sons is willing to receive it and succeeds in getting it'. But it seems to me more likely that *7 him gifeðe bið* is independent and means 'and it will be granted to him', i.e. 'it will become his own property'. (I now note that I was anticipated in this suggestion by Thorpe, *Dip. Ang.*, p. 472.)

D. ADVERB CLAUSES: INTRODUCTORY REMARKS

1. TYPES OF CLAUSES

§2416. As usual, I adopt the conventional classification, which distinguishes eight types of adverb clause—place, time, purpose, result, cause, comparison, concession, and condition.

§2417. But there is, of course, considerable overlap. Clauses of time can shade into purpose, result, cause, concession, and condition. *þær* can be translated 'when' and 'if' as well as 'where'. Clauses introduced by *swa* are not necessarily clauses of comparison. Small (1924, pp. 133-54) has some valuable comments on these variations. I discuss them as they become relevant; see the Indexes.

2. THE AMBIGUOUS ADVERB/CONJUNCTIONS

§2418. Just as *se* can serve as both a demonstrative and a relative (§§2109-21), so certain words can serve as both adverbs and conjunctions. They include *ær, nu, þær, þanon, þider, þa, þeah, þonne, siþþan*, and *swa*. Frequently it cannot be determined which we have. The problem is discussed as it becomes relevant. But see initially the discussions in §§1931, 2444-9, and 2536-60.

3. TYPES OF CONJUNCTIONS

a. Non-prepositional conjunctions

§2419. These can be divided into three groups, viz. simple (or one-word) conjunctions, e.g. *þæt* 'so that'; grouped conjunctions, e.g. *swa þæt* and *þæs þe* 'so that'; and divided conjunctions, e.g. *swa . . . þæt* 'so . . . that' in *ÆLS* 32. 16 *He wæs eadmod and geþungen and swa anræde þurhwunode þæt he nolde abugan to bysmorfullum leahtrum.*

b. Prepositional conjunctions

§2420. I use this term to denote conjunctions which consist of a preposition + an oblique case of the demonstrative *se* (+ *þe* or *þæt*). They can be divided into grouped prepositional conjunctions, e.g. *forþon* in *BlHom* 49. 11 *Moyses onfeng scinendum wuldorhelme, forþon he symle þa nyrugde þe God oferhogodan, forþon þe* in *BlHom* 25. 20 *Eadige beoþ þa þe nu wepað, forþon þe hi beoþ eft afrefrede, forði þe* in *ÆCHom* i. 8. 25 *he is ordfruma, forði þe he wæs æfre,* and *forði þæt* in *ÆCHom* i. 184. 29 *ac ðæs wundredon men, na forði þæt hit mare wundor wære ac forði þæt hit wæs ungewunelic*; and divided prepositional conjunctions, e.g. *forðon . . . þe* in *BlHom* 17. 29 *7 forðon God to us niþer astahg þe he wolde þæt we wæron upahafene to his godcundnesse* and *forði . . . þæt* in *ÆCHom* i. 26. 27 *forði he com to us þæt he wolde for us deað þrowian.*

4. THE ORIGIN OF THE CONJUNCTIONS

§2421. Enough material exists for a monograph on this subject. For reasons of space, I am unable to attempt a full treatment here. I have discussed elsewhere some aspects of the problem, with special reference to the 1976 paper by Carkeet (see Mitchell, at press (*c*)) and disagree with what is said by O'Neil (p. 205, lines 18–30): *nu* and *þæs* can introduce causal clauses (see §§3097–106 and 3113–16); for equivalents of *þenden* see §§2626–53; and on the function of *þe* see §§2427–8. But a few general points must be made.

§2422. Looked at as they appear in the language, OE conjunctions can be divided into several groups. First, there are the 'one-word' conjunctions which have their origin in one word or which appear to be one word and are not immediately recognizable as combinations. These include what Braunmüller (pp. 104–5 and 107–9) calls 'genuine proto-Germanic conjunctions', 'conjunctions directly derived from pronouns and other deictic items', and 'conjunctions derived from enclitic particles plus other predications'. His examples include, respectively, (the equivalents of) OE *and* and *gif, þa* and *þæt,* and *þeah.* The demonstrative origin of conjunctions such as *þæs* and *þy* is undoubted. That of *þær, þa, þonne,* and others, is fairly widely accepted; see such authorities as *OED*. A demonstrative origin would be in accordance with the conventional view that words like *þær, þæs, þeah*, and the like, were first used as adverbs and then developed into conjunctions, either alone, in doubled form, or with *þe* or *þæt*; see §§2423-6. We do not have to postulate a long period of time between parataxis and hypotaxis. But if, as seems almost beyond dispute (see §§1956 and 2109), the conjunction *þæt* introducing noun clauses and the relative *se* introducing adjective clauses were originally demonstratives in simple sentences, it seems reasonable to believe that those conjunctions which were originally demonstratives passed through an intermediate stage in which they were adverbs which could introduce or be used within simple sentences.

§2423. I believe that in OE 'phonological differentiation' existed between demonstrative *þæt* and conjunction *þæt*, despite Braunmüller (p. 112), between demonstrative *se* and relative *se*, and between adverbs such as *ær, nu, swa, þær, þanon, þider, þa, þeah*, and *þonne*, and conjunctions of the same spelling. But in the absence of intonation patterns and native informants, we are frequently unable to decide which we have. On the possibility that there may have been an intermediate stage, or intermediate stages, between the two in OE, see initially §2536.

§2424. Means of avoiding much, though not all, of this ambiguity arose. Some of these words appear in doubled form in the work of some writers. So, for example, *swa swa* is usually a conjunction. Some appear in combination with *þe*, e.g. *þæt þe* or *þætte*. Some are recorded with both. The forms *þa þa* and *þær þær* are much more common than *þa þe* and *þær þe*. But *þider þe* appears more often than *þider þider* in my collections and I have so far recorded *þanon þe* but not *þanon þanon*. Simple *þonne* is preferred to *þonne þe* and *þonne þonne*, but the latter two do appear. Rhythm may be a factor here, the tendency perhaps being to double monosyllables and to add *þe* to dissyllables. However, the presence of *þe* is not absolute proof that we have the conjunction rather than the adverb; as Baker (*Speculum*, 55 (1980), 25-6 and 33) points out, conjunctions such as *for þæm (þe)* and *þeah (þe)* are subject to scribal omission or insertion of *þe* and are therefore not 'very stable'. The addition of *þæt* sometimes denotes a difference in function; compare *swa*, which is primarily comparative when used as a conjunction, with *swa þæt*, which is primarily final or consecutive. But this is not always so. Thus *oþ* and *oþ þæt* can both be conjunctions and *gyf þæt* appears in *HomU* 44. 284. 9, predating *OED*'s *ȝiff þatt* from *Orrmulum*.

These topics are discussed in §§2437-3721 below as they become relevant; see the Indexes. But the use of words such as *þa . . . þa* in what appear to be correlative pairs does not certify that one of the clauses must be subordinate; consider the conventional, but not necessarily 'correct', punctuation of

Beo 126   Ða wæs on uhtan   mid ærdæge
                   Grendles guðcræft   gumum undyrne;
                   þa wæs æfter wiste   wop up ahafen,
                   micel morgensweg.

§2425. The second group of OE conjunctions (§2422) comprises those which consist of an oblique case of the demonstrative *se* and a noun, to which may be added *þe* or *þæt*. We cannot be sure that combinations like *ChronE* 79. 26 (885) *þy geare þe, Or* 226. 17 *þære ilcan niht þe*, and *ÆCHom* ii. 186. 22 *þæs geares ðe*, were ever more than temporal phrases qualified by what was in origin, or became felt as, an adjective clause; see §2428. It seems to me unlikely that they ever became conjunctions. It is, however, certain that such a transition took place in the ancestor of MnE 'while', which started off in the same way—consider *ChronE* 129. 16 (994) *7 man gislade þa hwile in to þam scipum*—and appears in the following forms: *Or* 212. 26 *þa hwile . . . þe* (the sole recorded example in which the two elements are separated), *BlHom* 175. 2 *þa hwile þe, Lch* iii. 2. 6 *þa hwile*, and *ChronE* 252. 34 (1123) *ða hwile þ*. The form with *þ* or *þæt* is recorded only in post-Conquest texts and *wile* is first recorded in eME *ChronE* 264. 25 (1137). But exactly when this transition from temporal phrase + *þe* clause to conjunction occurred cannot be determined.

§2426. The formula *on þære hwile þe*, recorded in *Or* 130. 9 and 170. 12, is probably no more to be taken as a conjunction than MnE 'during the time that', but it provides a convenient means of transition to the third group of OE conjunctions, viz. combinations involving prepositions. These consist of a preposition followed by the appropriate case of the neuter demonstrative *þæt*, with the possible addition of *þe* or *þæt*, which may immediately follow the demonstrative (grouped formulae) or be separated from it (divided formulae). So we find (with the accusative) *oþ þæt, þurh þæt þe*, and *wiþ þæt . . . þæt*; (with the genitive) *to þæs, to þæs þe/þæt*, and *to þæs . . . þe/þæt*; and (with the dative/instrumental *þæm, þam, þon, þy*, and other spellings) *forþon, forþon þe/þæt*, and *forþon . . . þe/þæt*. Combinations involving *æfter*, e.g. *æfter þæm (þe)*, and *ær*, e.g. *ær þæm (þe)*, and the conjunction *siþþan*—*siþþan þe* has not yet been recorded—may belong here. But they may be comparative rather than prepositional formulae; see the Indexes and Mitchell, at press (c). On the possibility that the formulae with *to* 'at first . . . were followed by a clause' and so were (presumably) conjunctions before they were adverbs, see §1136 fn. 264.

§2427. The question naturally arises whether a distinction can be drawn between *þe* and *þæt* in the combinations discussed in the last two sections and in others like them. It seems to me reasonable to postulate that originally the two were quite distinct and that *þæt* was a conjunction introducing what we would describe as a noun clause in apposition with a preceding object governed by a preposition. This object could be either a demonstrative used independently, as in *Or* 54. 18 *7 mid ungemetlicre pinunge he wæs þæt folc cwielmende, to ðon þæt hie him anbugen*, or a demonstrative + noun, as in *Or* 52. 32 *7 he Cirus Persea cyning hæfde þriddan dæl his firde beæftan him, on þæt gerad, gif ænig wære þe fyr fluge þe on ðæm gefeohte wæs þonne to þæm folce þe þær beæftan wæs, þæt hine mon sloge swa raðe swa mon hiora fiend wolde*. Here I differ from Benham (pp. 218-19): 'as in the case of purpose phrases, the word following the pronoun is *ðæt*, which, in the original composition of the phrase, was a demonstrative pronoun in relative function introducing an adjective clause'.[85] For I cannot myself see how the *þæt* clauses in the two examples quoted above can be described as 'adjective clauses' in the sense in which I use the term. That the apparent agreement in *on þæt gerad . . . þæt* in *Or* 52. 32 above is illusory is clear from the appearance of formulae like *ÆCHom* ii. 534. 35 *for ðam intingan þæt* and *WHom* 6. 156 *to þam þingum þæt*.

§2428. The original function of *þe* is even less certain. In my *Guide* (p. 88), I wrote of the formula *for þæm þe* 'because' that 'we can call *þe* (if we wish) a subordinating particle. This is the general function of *þe* and its use as a relative pronoun is probably a special adaptation. . . . We can perhaps get nearest to its original force by translating it as "namely" '; on this, see Small 1924, pp. 148-52; 1926, pp. 312-13; and 1930, pp. 381-3. Carkeet (1976, p. 56) objects that this 'demands that we assign a brand new property to *þe*, that of "subordinating particle" . . . , whereas the hypothesis proposed in this paper is based on the independently motivated and universally accepted view of *þe* as a relative pronoun'. I do not accept the phrases

---

[85] Shearin (1903, p. 58) also used the word 'relative': 'Old English *ðæt* . . . [was] originally a pronominal neuter accusative used with relative force as a conjunction.' But he defined the clause introduced by *þæt* as a 'substantive clause' (p. 63).

'brand new' and 'universally accepted' and still hold to my view that the general function of *þe* was that of a subordinating particle.[86] Even if we accept Carkeet's complicated hypothesis, it can explain only some prepositional formulae with *þe* and the appearance of *þe* 'relative pronoun' in a few non-prepositional formulae such as *þær þe, þa þe,* and *þonne þe,* in which *þe* is the exception rather than the rule (see §1889) and is therefore more likely to be a later accretion than a fundamental and integral element. It cannot explain the prepositional formulae with *þæt* and cannot explain the appearance of *þe* in *þeah þe, þæt þe* conj.—which Benham (p. 207) thinks may be 'the parent form from which *ðæt* [conjunction] is descended' (a doubtful proposition; see Kivimaa, p. 161)—*þætte, þy læs þe, þon ma þe,* and the like, or how *þe* in these groups can function as a 'relative pronoun'. But the hypothesis that *þe* was a subordinating particle explains these and also its use as a relative. As I suggested in *Guide* (§169), it also explains the presence of *þe* in prepositional formulae like *for þæm þe,* where it is hard to see how *þe* could ever have meant 'which'—either with or without a noun before it—but easy to see how it could have meant something like 'namely'. If we accept that the use of *þe* had its origin in formulae like *þa hwile þe* and *☆æfter þæm timan þe,* we can accept Kivimaa's proposition (pp. 162 and 164-5) that it was originally of 'relatival nature' and that its presence in formulae like *þeah þe* and *for þæm þe* was due to analogical use after 'its full values' had 'faded'. But it seems more plausible to me to argue that in *þa hwile þe, for þæm þe,* and *þeah þe,* it was originally a subordinating particle and that in *þa hwile þe* it was subsequently interpreted as a relative '[during] the time in which'; see Mann, *Archiv,* 180 (1942), 91-2, and the quotation from *Guide* (p. 88) with which I began this section.

§2429. But, in either event, the formulae with *þæt* and those with *þe* would be different in origin. This is in fact suggested by Adams (p. 109) as a possible explanation for the solitary example he found of *æfter þæm þæt* conjunction 'after' (*Or* 212. 28 but see §2657):

---

[86] The idea that *þe* is a particle which is not used solely in clauses which we think of as 'adjective clauses' did not originate with me. For example, *OED* speaks of '†The, *particle (conj., adv.), relative pron.*' *OED* and I are not alone; see Kivimaa, p. 160. But other writers, including Kivimaa, have taken the view that *þe* was in origin a relative; see Kivimaa, pp. 160-7, who distinguishes 'an adverbial relative' *þe* from a 'pronominal' one (p. 162). Geoghegan, who shows some unfamiliarity with OE, takes a view contrary to that of Carkeet. She speaks of 'the Old English subordinating particle *þe*' (pp. 31 and 50) and says that 'the word *þe* can in no way be considered a pronoun' (p. 43). We can, I believe, safely occupy the middle ground between these two extremes.

The use of *ðæt* in this way is unusual, but may be regarded as one of the early stages in its progress toward its present regular relative use. Beside the more common *oð ðæt* we find *oððe*, so that in some connections the demonstrative and the relative were felt to be closely related, even in OE. Or *ðæt* may be regarded as the demonstrative introducing a substantive clause in apposition with *ðæm*.

But Adams's first explanation opens up another possibility, viz. that in all these formulae, *þe*—not *þæt*—was the original and that *þæt* came in only because the originally distinct *þe* and *þæt* became to some extent interchangeable, first perhaps by phonetic weakening of *þæt* to *þe*, as suggested for example by Adams for *oþþæt* and *oþþe*, and then by analogy.

§2430. This is undoubtedly a plausible and possible chain of events. But I do not accept it. The fact that Adams found so few temporal prepositional formulae with *þæt*[87] means that he was on firm ground when he put forward the idea that they were the result of later confusion. A similar preference for *þe* is apparent in the figures for grouped formulae with *for* in causal clauses in early prose cited by van Dam—166 with *for þæm/þam/þan þe* but four with *for þæm þæt(te)* (pp. 44-5) and 335 with *for þon þe* but three with *for þon þæt(te)* (pp. 52-3). The case for believing that in these two constructions the formula with *þe* was the original and the sporadic examples with *þæt* are intruders is strong. But the reverse is true in clauses of purpose and result. *þæt*, not *þe*, is the norm when formulae with *for* introduce clauses of purpose; see §§2911-16 and 3041-70. Shearin (1903, pp. 63-8 and 78) notes only one example of a grouped *to* formula with dative/instrumental + *þe* in purpose clauses against 269 with *þæt* or (rarely) *þætte*. Even this has *þæt* on the testimony of Liebermann: *LawAfEl(EGH)* 13 *aluc ðu hine from minum weofode to þam þæt he deaðe swelte*. In clauses of result, Benham (pp. 218 and 228) mentions none with *þe* against 202 with *þæt* or (rarely) *þætte*. Neither formula with *to* occurs in the poetry. Here the presumption must be that the formula with *þæt* was the original (*þæt* being an essential element) and that *þe* is the intruder. So the proposition that formulae with *þæt* and formulae with *þe* arose independently but later became confused as a result of phonetic reduction and analogy seems established. Further on the possibility of interchange of function between *þæt* and *þe*, see Kivimaa, pp. 148-67. Her table on p. 161 is of special interest.

---

[87] See his appendices I and V. Excluding *oþþæt* and its variants, there are only ten examples: two with *æfter*, one with *fram*, three with *mid*, and four with *to*. They are distributed thus: *Alex* (1), *Chron* 1127 (1), *Lch* iii (1), *LS* 10 *Guthlac* (4), and *Or* (3). The solitary *to ð* in *ChronE* 264. 13 (1137) is a ME ghost; Clark reads *it ð* [*at*].

§2431. There are other types of OE conjunctions. Formulae which certainly involve a comparative include *no ðy ær, þon ma þe*, and *þy læs (þe)*. Formulae with *loc(a)*, e.g. *loc(a) hwær* and *loc(a) hwonne*, and with *(swa . . .) swa*, e.g. *swa hwær swa* and *sona swa*, are also noteworthy. The list is not complete. But it does illustrate the variety of OE conjunctions—a variety which suggests to me that we are unlikely to find one sequence which will explain the origin of all, or even nearly all, of them. Yet the belief that conjunctions such as *þær, þa, þonne*, and *þeah, þa hwile (þe)*, and *forþon (þe)*, were originally adverbs in simple sentences is satisfying, and will not surprise those who, like me, accept Small's proposition (1924, p. 125) that 'it may be laid down as a general principle that in the progress of language parataxis precedes hypotaxis', or who, like Mann (*Archiv*, 180 (1942), 88), believe that 'wenn wir nach der Entstehung der Konjunktionen forschen, also nach den Hilfsmitteln, die einen Nebensatz dem Hauptsatz unterordnen, müssen wir von der Erkenntnis ausgehen, dass sich die moderne Sprachform der Unterordnung aus der der Beiordnung (Asyndese–verbundene Parataxe–Hypotaxe) entwickelt hat'. (For a translation see §1688.)

§2432. For further comments on the possible origin of the various groups of OE conjunctions distinguished above, see the Indexes. In Mitchell, at press (*c*), I express my marked disagreement with many of Carkeet's claims about the origin of OE conjunctions and with many of the remarks about the OE correlative system on which he bases them.

5. MOOD

§2433. The nature and the origin of the subjunctive in OE are subjects which cannot be given full consideration in this work; see §878. But we cannot altogether avoid discussing the questions why and under what circumstances the subjunctive occurs in adverb clauses.

§2434. One explanation—that designated by Callaway (1931, pp. 18-19) 'the Erdmann–Bernhardt theory of mood-syntax'—is that the nature of the principal clause is the primary factor. This has been adopted, with more or less conviction, by many scholars, including Hotz, Wülfing, and Adams. I have already shown that there is no automatic rule that the verb of a noun clause containing a dependent statement, desire, or question, or the verb of a subordinate clause in dependent speech, must be in the subjunctive; see §§2014-15, 2032-5, and 2100-2. It is clear that what Campbell (*RES* 7

(1956), 65) has described as 'perhaps the most far-reaching rule of OE. syntax—viz. that relative clauses (including clauses of time and place), clauses of result, *swa* clauses, and clauses expressing real positive conditions take the subjunctive when the principal clause contains an imperative, a subjunctive, or a negated indicative' is (as his statement implies) by no means universal. Exceptions in adjective clauses have already been discussed; see §§2386–415. They also occur in all types of adverb clauses mentioned above; for references see the General Index.

§2435. Behre agrees that there are no automatic laws of symmetry; to him (p. 296) 'the function of the subjunctive in OE. is not to represent an event as simply assumed or imagined but to express a particular mental attitude towards an event, whether this event be assumed or real'. This is a salutary observation in that it directs our attention to the fact that human beings were involved in all the OE writings and utterances which survive. But we have to remember that there may be up to four, viz. the writer, the reporter, the speaker, and the performer; see §1936. So there are dangers in too easily attributing a particular 'attitude' to one of them; see further §§874–8. Campbell's refreshing reminder of 'the highly rectional syntactic state of OE.' (*RES* 7 (1956), 65) is a valuable antidote here.

§2436. These points will be taken up where necessary as I deal with the different types of adverb clauses. But, as far as possible, I shall avoid theoretical discussion and shall content myself with attempting to establish the facts, with drawing any conclusions which can be drawn, and with adumbrating possibilities.

E. CLAUSES OF PLACE

1. INTRODUCTORY REMARKS

§2437. Clauses of place, or local clauses, are conventionally divided into those referring to place where, place whither, and place whence. Klaeber (1929, *passim*) distinguishes place where (*absoluter Typus*) from the other two (*Richtungstypus*), the former involving rest in a place, the latter motion to or from a place, but not unnaturally finds the distinction not always easy to make—consider *ÆCHom* i. 372. 4 *þa gelamp hit þæt man ferede anre wuduwan suna lic ðær Petrus bodigende wæs*—and is forced to recognize a *Mischtypus* to cope with examples like Stevenson's 'I . . . walked right up to the man where he stood', *ÆCHom* i. 162. 9 . . . *oðþæt he com to his leorningcnihtum ðær ðær hi wæron on rewute*, *ÆCHom* ii. 32. 6 . . . *and hi urnon to me, an æfter anum, ðær ic inne sæt ða gearo to ganne*, and

Jul 89   Eode þa fromlice   fæmnan to spræce,
             anræd ond yreþweorg,   yrre gebolgen,
             þær he glædmode   geonge wiste
             wic weardian.

Burkhart (pp. 5–7) divides place where into three (Immediacy, Semi-Immediacy, and Non-Immediacy)—a classification of value to him in his study of prepositions—and is content to group the remaining types under the concepts of indefinite place and of 'motion in space in any one of a number of different relationships to place *here* and place *there*'.

§ 2438. The distinction between definite and indefinite clauses of place is of course a valid one—cf. *Beo* 356 *Hwearf þa hrædlice þær Hroðgar sæt* with *Beo* 1394 . . . *ga þær he wille*. But, although it is not always clear-cut, e.g. *ÆCHom* ii. 368. 11 *Fæder min, ic wille þæt ða þe ðu me forgeafe beon mid me ðær ðær ic beo* and

PPs 88. 6   þu bist gewuldrad god,   þær bið wisra geðeaht
             and haligra   heah gemetincg,

it may involve clauses denoting place where, place whither, and place whence. So our study of place 'indefinite in location' (Burkhart's fifth group) must embrace not only rest in, but also motion to or from, such a place.

§ 2439. A distinction may also be made between adjective and adverb clauses of place, e.g.

Beo 691   Nænig heora þohte,   þæt he þanon scolde
             eft eardlufan   æfre gesecean,
             folc oþðe freoburh,   þær he afeded wæs,

and *Beo* 286 *Weard maþelode ðær on wicge sæt*. But again the distinction is not always clear-cut, e.g. in *ÆCHom* i. 86. 19 *þaða he mid swiðlicum luste his lifes gewilnode, þa het he hine ferigan ofer ða ea Iordanen, ðær þær wæron gehæfde hate baðu, þe wæron halwende gecwedene adligendum lichaman*, where *ða ea Iordanen* may be taken as the antecedent of the *ðær þær* clause or *ðær þær* may introduce an adverb clause,[88] and

---

[88] It is possible that *þær* is here expletive or introductory and that Thorpe's translation 'where there were hot baths' is absolutely literal. On this see §§ 1491–7.

Sat 588 Leaðað us þider to leohte þurh his læcedom,
þær we moton seolfe sittan mid drihtne . . . ,

where the *þær* clause may qualify *leohte* or may be parallel to *to leohte* with the verb taken *apo koinou*. If we take them as adverb clauses, we face again the 'definite or indefinite?' dilemma. In

GenA 2704 Forðon ic wigsmiðum wordum sægde
þæt Sarra min sweostor wære
æghwær eorðan þær wit earda leas
mid wealandum winnan sceoldon,

the choice is between a definite adjective clause or an indefinite adverb clause.

§2440. In view of all this and of other phenomena apparent in OE clauses of place, it seems best to distinguish as far as possible definite clauses from indefinite clauses and then to divide these two groups according to the introductory conjunction or formula. The other distinctions can be made as the need arises.

§2441. The 'theological *þær*-clause' used by Schaar (pp. 304–9) as a criterion of authorship is not a separate grammatical category—its examples belong to one of the types discussed above—but is distinguished by its subject-matter.

§2442. Several problems remain. One—that of the ambiguous adverb/conjunction—is treated separately in §§2444–9. Another is the suggestion advanced by Burkhart (pp. 19–21 and 261) that *þær, swa hwær swa*, and *þider*, can introduce noun clauses. When a local clause is used as what he calls a 'predicate nominative', e.g. *Bo* 20. 21 *Oððe gif hit on ænegum ænige hwile fæstlice wunað, se deaþ hit huru aferreð þ hit bion ne mæg þær hit ær wæs* and *Bo* 17. 18 *Ælc soþ wela 7 soþ weorþscipe sindan mine agne þeowas, 7 swa hwær swa ic beo hie bioð mid me*, the problem is terminological, for it can be argued that the clauses introduced by *þær* and *swa hwær swa* are used as what Jespersen called 'primaries'. On this see §1927. But those in which the clause of place appears to be the object of a verb like *getæcan* and *getacnian* are less easily dismissed, e.g. *Solil* 11. 12 *and getæc me þider ic me beseon sceolde to þe, þad ic þe þær gehawian mæge*, Latin *Dic mihi qua attendam, ut aspiciam te*, and

Res 10 Getacna me, tungla hyrde,
þær selast sy sawle minre
to gemearcenne meotudes willan,
þæt ic þe geþeo þinga gehwylce. . . .

In the former, *þider* may be explained as a careless rendering of Latin *qua*; cf. such glosses as *ðer vel huer* for *ubi* discussed in §2501. BTS (s.v. *getacnian* II b) and Mackie, who in his EETS edition translates 'Signify to me, Shepherd of the stars, where it may be best . . .', agree with Burkhart about the latter. The lexicographers will have to decide whether it is possible to translate 'Show me to the place where . . .'; here we can perhaps compare

Fates 9   Halgan heape   hlyt wisode
              þær hie dryhtnes æ   deman sceoldon,
              reccan fore rincum.

But we may have to do with noun clauses. If so, they are aberrant examples, unrecorded by *OED* and perhaps due to the confusion between *þær/þider* and *hwær/hwider* discussed in §2501.

§2443. In

MSol 207   Wat ic ðæt wæron Caldeas
             guðe ðæs gielpne   and ðæs goldwlonce,
             mærða ðæs modige,   ðær to ðam moning gelomp
             suð ymbe Sanere feld

and

PPs 104. 39   Sealde þam leodum   landes anweald
              on agene æht   oðre þeode
             and hi folca gewinn   fremdra gesæton.
        40   þær hi heoldan   halige domas
             and his soðfæst word   swylce georne,
             and his æbebod   awa to feore

(where *þær* represents the *ut* of a Latin purpose clause), it is possible to read *þæt* for *þær*. Emendation might be justified by a comparison of

Rid 30a. 5   Ful oft mec gesiþas   sendað æfter hondum,
             þæt mec weras ond wif   wlonce cyssað

with the corresponding passage in *Rid* 30b, where we find *þær* for *þæt*. But the local clauses give good sense. The same is true in *GenA* 2837, where the editors emend *þær* to *þæt*. See further Mitchell 1964a, p. 141.

2. THE AMBIGUOUS ADVERB/CONJUNCTIONS

§2444. It is not always possible to say with certainty whether clauses introduced by words such as *þær*, *þa*, and *þonne*, are principal or subordinate. The problem arises more often in the poetry, where the element order is a less certain guide than it is in the prose; see §§2536-60. There is, of course, no doubt that we have the adverb *þær* in examples like *ÆCHom* i. 182. 27, *ÆCHom* i. 188. 9, *ÆCHom* i. 182. 14 *þa cwæð se Hælend, Doð þæt þæt folc sitte. And þær wæs micel gærs on ðære stowe* . . . , and *ÆCHom* ii. 42. 16 *þær stod se Sunu on ðære menniscnysse, and se Fæder clypode of heofonum, and se Halga Gast niðer astah to Criste. þær wæs ða eal seo Halige Ðrynnys, seoðe is an God untodæledlic.* However, Rübens (p. 37) found ambiguity in examples like *ChronA* 16. 1 (519) *7 þy ilcan geare hie fuhton wiþ Brettas þær mon nu nemneþ Cerdices ford* and *ChronA* 16. 17 (547) *Her Ida feng to rice þonon Norþanhymbra cynecyn onwoc*, and Thorpe translates that portion of the Creed which reads *ÆCHom* ii. 596. 18 . . . *and sitt nu æt swiðran Godes Ælmihtiges Fæder, þanon he wyle cuman to demenne ægðer ge ðam cucum ge ðam deadum* as '. . . thence he will come to doom both the quick and the dead'. While it may be said that in these examples the element order points strongly to the presumption that the *þær* and *þanon* clauses are subordinate, it is dangerous to be too confident; see §§2518-27.

§2445. The same is even more true in the poetry. Schaar (pp. 119-20) professed to have found a solution:

How do we know the difference between coordination and subordination? In most cases the context, easily enough, answers this question, but sometimes it is hard to say whether a certain word introduces a main clause or a sub-clause. This is especially true of *þær*. In this chapter we shall try to overcome this difficulty by regarding a *þær*-clause as part of a complex series when it is to be found in a system of sub-clauses. Such a *þær*-clause may naturally be considered a relative sub-clause.

Rynell (pp. 19-20) objects to this. The main difficulty, as I see it, can be demonstrated from

Beo 3166   forleton eorla gestreon   eorðan healdan,
             gold on greote,   þær hit nu gen lifað
             eldum swa unnyt,   swa hit æror wæs,

where the *þær* clause does not have to be taken as subordinate. Schaar's criterion—like some theories of art—is ultimately only the rationalization of personal opinions; it cannot be decisive in doubtful cases. There is, of course, nothing to prevent editors punctuating such clauses as subordinate. What is objectionable is insistence that they cannot be principal clauses. Emerson (*MP* 23 (1925-6), 395-9) avoided this trap when discussing the punctuation of *þær* and *þanon* clauses in *Beowulf*—unlike Andrew (see §§2446-7). How much personal opinion comes into it can be illustrated from

Beo 461
                                    ða hine Wedera cyn
                for herebrogan   habban ne mihte.
                þanon he gesohte   Suð-Dena folc
                ofer yða gewealc,   Ar-Scyldinga;
                ða ic furþum weold folce Deniga
                ond on geogoðe heold   ginne rice,
                hordburh hæleþa;   ða wæs Heregar dead,
                min yldra mæg   unlifigende,
                bearn Healfdenes;   se wæs betera ðonne ic!

This is Klaeber's punctuation. Both Emerson and Andrew prefer a more periodic interpretation. But Emerson sees the principal clause as the first *ða* clause—'Then, for fear of war, the Weder people were not able to harbor him, whence he sought the Danish folk over the welling of the waves . . .'—whereas to Andrew (*SS*, §112) the principal clause is that beginning with *þanon*—'When the Weder-folk through fear of war might hold him not, thence sought he the South-Dane people . . .'; on this see §2446. If we accept (as I do) Campbell's view (1970, p. 95) 'that such passages were open to personal interpretation, and that reciters would indicate their view of the passage by intonation', we can agree that both may be right.

§2446. However, Andrew's rules concerning element order as a criterion for determining whether a *þær* clause in the poetry is principal or subordinate—conveniently summarized in *SS*, §§19 and 34 —are particularly open to attack. Like many of his conclusions, they are often based on faulty premises, e.g. his belief in the existence of rigid 'rules', and faulty method, e.g. undue reliance on Latin originals[89] or unjustified use of metrical criteria, and their application involves great, sometimes almost impossible, violence to the poetry, as in

Dream 33
                                    Geseah ic þa frean mancynnes
                efstan elne mycle   þæt he me wolde on gestigan.
                þær ic þa ne dorste ofer dryhtnes word
                bugan oððe berstan, þa ic bifian geseah
                eorðan sceatas,

---

[89] Andrew (*SS*, §§20, 24, and elsewhere) relies on the status of clauses in the original Latin for establishing that of the OE equivalents; see further §2114. It is therefore unfortunate that he failed to take cognizance of the fact that in *PPs* 75. 3, 77. 44, 79. 9, 131. 18, and elsewhere, a Latin principal clause is represented by a *þær* or *þanon* clause which, according to his rules, must be subordinate. (It seems only fair to add that in a personal letter written in 1950, Andrew (then in his eighty-fourth year) told me that all his collections from the poetry were destroyed by a V2 in September 1944.)

where he would have to take the *þær* clause as subordinate. Similar examples will be found in *Beo* 771-7 (where an obvious correlation would be destroyed), *Dan* 185-92 (where the rhetorical sweep of the poem would be upset), and *Brun* 10-20 (where an intolerable hiatus would be involved). I also detect in his 'rules' an internal inconsistency in that one might expect that rules which are valid for clauses introduced by *þær, þonne,* and *þa,* would also hold for *þanon* and *þider* clauses. Andrew fails to consider this possibility. This may be simply an omission. But one becomes suspicious when one considers examples (I quote from Klaeber) like

Beo 518

	þa hine on morgentid
on Heaþo-Ræmes	holm up ætbær;
ðonon he gesohte	swæsne eþel,
leof his leodum,	lond Brondinga,
freoðoburh fægere,	þær he folc ahte,
burh ond beagas,	

where Andrew (*SS,* § 16) takes the *ðonon* clause as principal. The same is true in *Beo* 461 (§ 2445). One of his 'rules' (*SS,* §§ 19 and 34) is that sentences of the form *þa/þonne/þær he com* 'are, both in prose and verse, always subordinate clauses'. Here Andrew was (or should have been) in a difficult situation. The pattern *þanon he gesohte* should be subordinate. But if it is, neither *Beo* 461-9 nor 518-23 can be one periodic sentence, as Andrew would have us believe, for there is no clause in either which, according to his rules, must not be subordinate, except those beginning *ða wæs* in *Beo* 467 and *se wæs* in *Beo* 469. And they will not do.

§ 2447. The fact that many of Andrew's rules can be shown to be impossibly rigid (see the General Index) has unfortunately meant that recent editors of OE texts have often given them scant consideration and have neglected what is good in them. The edition of *The Wanderer* by Dunning and Bliss is an honourable exception here; see pp. 14 ff. and note especially their observation (p. 15) that Andrew's 'statement of these principles is more dogmatic than we should find acceptable—his "certainly" is our "probably", his "always" our "normally" '. But it is not clear on what principle Irving takes the *þær* clauses in *Ex* 16 and 24 as principal when Krapp punctuates them as subordinate and the editions of *Beowulf* by Dobbie and by Wrenn do not take account of Andrew's pertinent criticisms of the conventional punctuation. Editorial inconsistencies like that revealed by a comparison of

GenA 1931

	Wunode siððan
be Iordane	geara mænego.

> þær folcstede   fægre wæron,
> men arlease,   metode laðe

with

> *GenA* 1844   þa com ellenrof   eorl siðian,
> Abraham mid æhtum   on Egypte,
> þær him folcweras   fremde wæron,
> wine uncuðe

abound. Such inconsistencies and our ultimate inability to be certain whether we have parataxis or hypotaxis must reinforce Amos's conclusions (p. 140) that 'the use of paratactic or hypotactic sentence structure makes a poor chronological test' and that 'an author's sentence structure does not provide a reliable indication of the date of his work'.

§2448. Indeed, it is over fifty years since Emerson (*MP* 23 (1925-6), 393-405) drew our attention to marked editorial inconsistencies in the punctuation of *Beowulf*. But even his alterations to the traditional punctuation of *þær* and *þanon* clauses were limited to subordinating them to a preceding clause. This seems to be the only possibility consistently considered by most editors. As a result, it is rare to find in the existing editions of OE poems a subordinate clause introduced by *þær*, *þanon*, or *þider*, anywhere but after its principal clause. There are occasional examples in which one is so punctuated that it appears within the principal clause, e.g.

> *Dan* 345   þa wæs on þam ofne,   þær se engel becwom,
> windig and wynsum,   wedere gelicost
> þonne hit on sumeres tid   sended weorðeð
> dropena drearung   on dæges hwile,
> wearmlic wolcna scur

and

> *Rid* 56. 10   Ic lafe geseah
> minum hlaforde,   þær hæleð druncon,
> þara flana geweorc,   on flet beran.

But in these no other punctuation is really possible. There are even a few with a subordinate clause at the beginning of the sentence, e.g. *Dan* 503, *PPs* 70. 20, and

> *Jul* 364   þær ic hine finde   ferð staþelian
> to godes willan,   ic beo gearo sona
> þæt ic him monigfealde   modes gælsan
> ongean bere   grimra geþonca,
> dyrnra gedwilda,   þurh gedwolena rim.

To what extent this rarity of initial position of these subordinate clauses represents actual OE usage is a matter of doubt. But the possibility exists that the number of examples could be increased by repunctuation; consider *And* 1049-53 and *ChristC* 1081-4 as well as the examples discussed by Andrew (*Postscript*, §23) to illustrate his claim that 'the superstition, which disallows subordination in a clause preceding the principal sentence . . . evidently extends to ðær'. Unfortunately, this criticism has remained almost unheeded. I am not saying that it ought always to be accepted. But it ought sometimes to be considered. This holds for clauses introduced by *þa, þonne*, and the like; on these see §§2536-8.

§2449. Attempts to use the position of a clause as a criterion for deciding whether it is principal or subordinate usually beg this question. In any case, they have met with little real success; see Schaar, pp. 119-20, Rynell, pp. 19-20, Quirk, pp. 26-8, and the General Index.

3. CLAUSES INTRODUCED BY *þÆR, þÆR þÆR*, AND *þÆR þE*

a. Definite *þær* (*þær*) clauses

§2450. The conjunction which most frequently introduces local clauses is *þær* or one of its variants *þar, þara*, or *þer*. It may occur alone or in the doubled form *þær þær*. It usually means 'where' or 'to where, whither'. Occasionally it may seem to a modern reader to mean 'from where, whence', e.g. *ÆLS* 26. 200 *Eac swilce þær he feol on þam gefeohte ofslagen, men namon ða eorðan to adligum mannum, Beo* 286 *Weard maþelode, ðær on wicge sæt*, and

And 305   Him þa beorna breogo,   þær he on bolcan sæt,
                   ofer waroða geweorp   wiðþingode.

But the first of these can be viewed as an example of Klaeber's *Mischtypus* (see §2437) and Klaeber himself (1929, p. 10) sees examples like the last two as *absoluter Typus*, 'place where'. This is plausible, since speaking need not have involved motion for the Anglo-Saxon mind, though Klaeber (1929, p. 9) thinks that looking at something does involve motion.

§2451. When *þær* denotes rest in a definite place, it may introduce clauses with an antecedent (adjective clauses), e.g. *Or* 58. 28 *An wæs Babylonicum, þær Ninus ricsade; þæt oðer wæs Creca, þær Alexander*

ricsade; þridda wæs Affricanum, þær Ptolome ricsedon, ÆCHom i.
42. 26 *þa geseah heo þæt cild licgan on binne, ðær se oxa and se assa
gewunelice fodan secað, ÆCHom* i. 536. 14 *On ðære bytminge wæs
se arc rum, þær ða reðan deor wunedon* (where antecedent and relative are separated; see §§2288-97), and

Beo 691   Nænig heora þohte,   þæt he þanon scolde
                 eft eardlufan   æfre gesecean,
                 folc oþðe freoburh,   þær he afeded wæs,

or clauses without an antecedent (adverb clauses), e.g. *Or* 8. 30
*7 þære Affrica norþwestgemere is æt þæm ilcan Wendelsæ þe of
ðæm garsecge scyt ðær Ercoles syla stondað, ÆCHom* i. 132. 18 . . .
*swa swa Crist on his godspelle cwæð, þær næfre heora wyrm ne
swylt, ne heora fyr ne bið adwæsced*, and

Beo 775   þær fram sylle abeag
            medubenc monig   mine gefræge
            golde geregnad,   þær þa graman wunnon.

§2452. Examples in which *þær* clauses denote motion to a definite
place include both adjective clauses, e.g. *Bede(T)* 154. 19 *Is seo stow
gen to dæge æteawed . . . þær se Oswald to þissum gefeohte cwom,
Luke(Li)* 12. 33 . . . *in heofnum ðer ðeaf ne geneoleceð*, Latin . . . *in
caelis quo fur non appropriat*, and

ChristA 434   He him þære lisse   lean forgildeð,
                 se gehalgoda   hælend sylfa,
                 efne in þam eðle   þær he ær ne cwom,

and adverb clauses, e.g. *CP* 255. 22 *Baloham ðonne fulgeorne feran
wolde ðær hine mon bæd* (not indefinite; see *Num* 23. 20), *Bo* 71.
12 *7 he nænne ne mæg gebringan þær he him gehet, þ is æt þæm
hehstan goode, ÆCHom* ii. 416. 11 *þu asendest us þær we wæron
ontende*, and

Dream 139   . . . ond me þonne gebringe   þær is blis mycel,
                 dream on heofonum,   þær is dryhtnes folc
                 geseted to symle,   þær is singal blis. . . .

§2453. Doubled *þær* is less common than *þær* in the prose, except
perhaps in Ælfric, and occurs only once in the poetry, in

Met 7. 11   Ne mæg eac fira nan
           wisdom timbran   þær ðær woruldgitsung
           beorg oferbrædeð.

A few prose examples in which it refers to a definite place will suffice here: (adjective clauses) *Or* 22. 28 *Be suðan Narbonense is se*

Wendelsæ, þær þær Rodan seo ea utscyt (?'from which'), *ÆCHom* i. 350. 5 . . . *fram ðam micclan huse, þær ðær gehwilc onfehð wununge be his geearnungum* and *ÆCHom* ii. 44. 4 . . . *and þæt hus eall ge-fylde mid fyre, ðær ðær hi inne sæton, swilce hit eal burne* (both place in which, but with separation of antecedent and relative in the second example), and *ÆCHom* ii. 370. 4 . . . *to ðam heofonlican eðle, þær ðær næfre ær ne becom nan ðing ðæs gecyndes* (place to which); and (adverb clauses) *Solil* 9. 17 . . . *swa þat heora ægðer byð eft emme þat þæt hyt ær wæs and þær þær hyt ær wes* and *ÆCHom* ii. 514. 18 *Hit gelamp hwilon þæt an wod man gesæt þær ðær se eadiga wer hine ær gereste.* Harlow (p. 9) notes that in the Ælfric manuscripts with which he was concerned, doubled conjunctions like *þær þær* are preceded by a mark of punctuation in thirty-three of forty-five examples. On the origin and history of subordinate *þær* clauses, see Curme, *JEGP* 10 (1911), 335–77 (*passim*); Klaeber 1929, pp. 17–22; and Burkhart, p. 206 fn. 1, where Curme 1931, p. 263, is quoted.

b. *Indefinite þær (þær) clauses*

§2454. Here we are of course concerned only with adverb clauses. Examples with *þær* include those referring to an indefinite place in which, e.g. *CP* 263. 24 *Ðær se Dryhtnes gast is, ðær is freodoom, ÆCHom* i. 38. 12 *Ðas word geswuteliað þæt ðær wunað Godes sibb þær se goda willa bið, ÆCHom* ii. 244. 15, and

And 1401   Næfre ic geferde   mid frean willan
              under heofonhwealfe   heardran drohtnoð,
              þær ic dryhtnes æ   deman sceolde,

and an indefinite place to which, e.g. *Bede* 144. 31 . . . *ac eac swylce in sibbe tiide, þær he rad betweoh his hamum oðþe be tunum mid his þegnum . . . , John(WSCp)* 21. 18 *þa þu gingra wære, þu gyrdest þe 7 eodest þær þu woldyst,*

Beo 1392   no he on helm losaþ,
              ne on foldan fæþm,   ne on fyrgenholt,
              ne on gyfenes grund,   ga þær he wille!,

and *GuthA* 290 *Ongin þe generes wilnian, ‖ far þær ðu freonda wene, gif ðu þines feores recce.*

§2455. Typical examples with *þær þær* include *Solil* 67. 8 *and þeah heo scyneð swiðe beorhte þær þer heo bið* ('wherever'), *ÆCHom* ii. 558. 1 *ðonne sceal se, þær ðær he mæg, earmum ðingian to ðam rican* ... ('wherever'), *John(WSCp)* 12. 26 *7 min þen bið þær þær ic eom* ('wherever'), and *ChronA* 96. 9 (911) ... *7 þæt hie mehten faran unbefohtene þær þær hie wolden* ('whithersoever'). *Alc* 105. 23 *þa unclæne gastes byð simle þider baldeste, þær þær heo geseoð oferætes 7 druncanysse oft rædlice begangen* seems to belong to the *Mischtypus*. There are no examples in the poetry. The fact that *þær þær* can occur in definite as well as in indefinite clauses (§2450) reduces the validity of Yamakawa's observation (1971, p. 9) about 'the appropriateness of the double determinative form for intensive or general indication of place'.

c. *þær þe clauses*

§2456. This is not a common combination. I have found a few examples in the early prose, e.g. *Bede(T)* 78. 34 *Forðon þara godra mooda 7 monna þeaw bið, þæt heo þær hwilum synne ongeotað, þær þe syn ne bið* (the other manuscripts also have *þær þe/ðe*), *Bede(Ca)* 154. 19 *Is seo stow gyt to dæg ætywed ... ðær þe Oswald to ðyssum gefeohte com* (but other manuscripts have *þær Oswald* or *þær se Oswald*), *GD(C)* 108. 31 *þæs þe ic wene, Petrus, þær þe beoþ to aberene 7 geþyldelice to adreoganne þa yflan men, þær hi sume beoð gode onfundene 7 gemette*, and *GD(C)* 109. 2 *ac þær þe eallum gemete se wæstm wana byð on þam godum mannum, þær æt nehstan byð unnyt gewinn 7 idel on þam yflan mannum* (there is a gap here in MS *H*). There are two examples in the poetry, viz.

Dan 626   þa he eft onhwearf
                 wodan gewittes,   þær þe he ær wide bær
                 herewosan hige,   heortan getenge

and

Sat 637   ... hu hie him on edwit   oft asettað
                 swarte suslbonan,   stæleð feondas
                 fæhðe and firne,   þær ðe hie freodrihten,
                 ecne anwaldan,   oft forgeaton ... ,

where the *þær ðe* clause may be an adjective clause of place, but may express cause; see §§2464-5. Ure (*The Benedictine Office* (Edinburgh, 1957), 104) would add a third by reading *þar þe* for *þar we* in

LPr ii 27   Cum nu and mildsa,   mihta waldend,
                 and us þin rice alyf,   rihtwis dema,
                 earda selost   and ece lif,
                 þar we sibbe and lufe   samod gemetað,
                 eagena beorhtnysse   and ealle mirhðe,

> þar bið gehyred   þin halige lof
> and þin micele miht,   mannum to frofre,
> swa þu, engla god,   eallum blissast.

§2457. I have noted no examples in the later prose. So it may be more than chance or personal preference that, as pointed out above, MS *H* has *þær þær* where *GD(C)* 108. 31 has *þær þe*.

d. *þær with prepositions and postpositions*

§2458. *þær* is frequently followed by what may be called a postposition, both in adverbial combinations such as *þær on* and *þær to* and when used as a relative adverb or conjunction; see §§1060-80 and Mitchell 1978*a*, pp. 240-57, for a fuller discussion. Examples with *þær* as a relative adverb or conjunction include *Or* 36. 9 . . . *Parnasus, þær se cyning Theuhale on ricsode, Or* 134. 32 . . . *þa for he to oðre byrg, þær Ambira se cyning on wunode, ÆCHom* i. 78. 23 . . . *bufon ðam gesthuse þær þæt cild on wunode, ÆCHom* ii. 6. 26 . . . *forði þæt he wolde us to his rice gebringan þær we to gesceapene wæron,*

PPs 103. 24	His is mycel sæ and on gemærum wid, þær is unrim on ealra cwycra mycelra and mætra,
LPr ii 39	Swa þin heahsetl is heah and mære, fæger and wurðlic, swa þin fæder worhte, æþele and ece, þar ðu on sittest on sinre swiðran healf,

and

ChristB 494	Cyning ure gewat þurh þæs temples hrof þær hy to segun, þa þe leofes þa gen last weardedun on þam þingstede, þegnas gecorene.

Burkhart (*passim*) gives more examples with *on, to*, and other postpositions.

§2459. The combination *to þær* occasionally means 'to where', e.g. *ÆLS* 26. 165 . . . *and rad mid werode to þær his broðor heafod stod on stacan gefæstnod* and *Judg* 7. 19 *7 ferde nihtes to þær heora fynd wicodon*. These are not exceptions to the tendencies noted in §1079, since *to* goes with the verb of the principal clause and *þær* (. . .) *to* would be impossible.

e. *Other uses of* þær (þær)

(1) *Introducing temporal clauses*

§ 2460. Like Latin *ubi*, *þær (þær)* is often used in a temporal sense 'when, while'. One cannot of course always distinguish with certainty between the local and temporal uses. Thus, we may argue whether *þær* introduces an adjective clause of place or an adverb clause of time in

Beo 506   Eart þu se Beowulf,   se þe wið Brecan wunne,
                   on sidne sæ   ymb sund flite,
                   ðær git for wlence   wada cunnedon
                   ond for dolgilpe   on deop wæter
                   aldrum neþdon?

or whether it introduces an adverb clause of place or time in

Beo 2484   þa ic on morgne gefrægn   mæg oðerne
                   billes ecgum   on bonan stælan,
                   þær Ongenþeow   Eofores niosað.

§ 2461. But we may see adjective clauses referring to a definite time in *Mart 2* 188. 11 *ond sume dæge þær heo hy gebæd heo onsende hyre gast to Gode*, *ÆLS* 31. 1038 *Eft on sumne sæl þær Martinus siðode mid his geferum . . .* , and

Creed 55   . . . and ic þone ærest   ealra getreowe,
                   flæsces on foldan   on þa forhtan tid,
                   þær ðu ece lif   eallum dælest,
                   swa her manna gehwylc   metode gecwemað;

adverb clauses referring to a definite time in *CP* 451. 5 *Ac ðær ðær us God forbead ðæt we ure ryhtwisnesse beforan monnum dyden, he us gecyðde forhwy he hit forbead, ða he cwæð, ðylæs hi eow herigen*, Latin *Nam cum nos . . . Dominus prohiberet . . .* , *ÆCHom* ii. 146. 15 *For nahte bið geteald anes geares lust, þær ðær se swearta deað onsigende bið*, and

ChristC 892   þæt bið foretacna mæst
                   þara þe ær oþþe sið   æfre gewurde
                   monnum oþywed,   þær gemengde beoð
                   onhælo gelac   engla ond deofla,
                   beorhtra ond blacra;

and indefinite clauses of time in *CP* 455. 3 *Ðæt bið eac swiðe hefig broc ðæm lareowe ðæt he scyle on gemænre lare, ðær ðær he eall folc ætsomne lærð, ða lare findan ðe hi ealle behofigen*, *WHom* 16b. 21 . . . *ac clummiað mid ceaflum þar hi scoldan clipian*, and

Exhort 4   . . .   and wæccan lufa
                on hyge halgum   on þas hwilwendan tid,
                bliðe mode,   and gebedum filige
                oftost symle   þær þu ana sy.

§2462. The fact that *þær* can mean 'where' or 'while' permits re-punctuation to make the *þær* clause subordinate in such examples as

ChristC 1081   þær him sylfe geseoð   sorga mæste,
                synfa men,   sarigferðe.
                Ne bið him to are   þæt þær fore ellþeodum
                usses dryhtnes rod   ondweard stondeð;

see §§2448-9. Further on the temporal use of *þær*, see Adams, pp. 56-9; Schücking, p. 55; Callaway 1931, pp. 86-7, 102, and 113; Böhme, pp. 24-6; Small 1924, p. 140; Klaeber (ed.), *Beowulf*, glossary, s.v. *þær*; Andrew, *SS*, p. 24, and *Postscript*, p. 21; and, for a useful examination of the problem, Möllmer, pp. 33-5.

§2463. For possible examples of *þonne* and *þa* correlative with the conj. *þær* see §2515.

(2) *Introducing clauses with an element of cause*

§2464. An element of cause can be detected in some clauses introduced by *þær*, e.g. *CP* 355. 3 *7 mid ðæm ðu geearnode Godes irre ðær ða godan weorc ær næren on ðe mette*, where the EETS translation has 'because' for *þær*, *ÆCHom* i. 38. 12 *Ðas word geswuteliað þæt ðær wunað Godes sibb þær se goda willa bið*, *PPs* 63. 5, *GuthA* 773, and

PPs 58. 9   Ic mine strengðe on ðe   strange gehealde,
                forðon þu me god eart   geara andfencgea,
                and mildheortnes   mines drihtnes
                me fægere becom,   þær me wæs freondes þearf.

In *PPs* 117. 12 the Roman Psalter has *et*, the Gallic *quia*, where the OE has *þær*. Another possible example from the poetry is

Rid 30a. 7   þonne ic mec onhæbbe,   ond hi onhnigaþ to me
                monige mid miltse,   þær ic monnum sceal
                ycan upcyme   eadignesse,

where *Rid* 30b has *swa* instead of *þær*. *Sat* 637, with *þær þe*, has been discussed in §2456. For further examples from the prose, see Liggins 1955, pp. 425-8.

§2465. This almost causal force of *þær* can perhaps be seen as an extension of the temporal use discussed in §§2460-3, an extension which overtakes other temporal conjunctions; consider *PPs* 58. 9 (§2464).

(3) *Introducing clauses with an element of concession*

§2466. Burnham (pp. 78-9), Andrew (*Postscript*, p. 22), and Quirk (pp. 114-15), note that clauses of place introduced by *þær (þær)* may shade into the concessive. There is room for difference of opinion concerning individual sentences, but examples in which some element of concession may be detected include *CP* 463. 1 . . . *ðætte ðær ðær he oðer(ra) monna wunda lacnað, he self ne weorðe aðunden on upahæfennesse for ðære giemeleste his hælo, GD* 91. 11 *þær Paulus ne mihte mid scipe faran, þær Petrus eode mid drigum fotum, ByrM* 96. 3 *Se ðe his agene spræce awyrt, he wyrcð barbarismum; swylce he cweðe, þu sot þær he sceolde cweðan, þu sott, El* 1260, and

ChristC 1492   . . .   þa mec þin wea swiþast
               æt heortan gehreaw,   þa ic þec from helle ateah,
               þær þu hit wolde sylfa   siþþan gehealdan.

But I prefer to take the last example as conditional; see §3619. Andrew (*Postscript*, p. 22) suggests repunctuation in

Beo 1269   þær him aglæca   ætgræpe wearð;
             hwæþre he gemunde   mægenes strenge,
             gimfæste gife,   ðe him God sealde,
             ond him to Anwaldan   are gelyfde,
             frofre ond fultum

and

Beo 1470   þær he dome forleas,
             ellenmærðum.   Ne wæs þæm oðrum swa,
             syðþan he hine to guðe   gegyred hæfde

to make the initial *þær* clause subordinate, translating respectively 'Even when . . .' and 'Whereas . . .'.

§2467. On the pattern seen in *Beo* 1394 *ga þær he wille*, see §§3451-6.

(4) *Introducing independent wishes and conditional clauses*

§2468. On these see §§1679-81 and 3615-25.

4. CLAUSES INTRODUCED BY *ÞANON (ÞE)*

§2469. When used as a conjunction, *þanon* may introduce clauses referring to a definite place, or an indefinite place, from which, in both the prose and the poetry. *þanon þe* is similarly used, but only in the prose. Definite clauses of place are found with an antecedent (adjective clauses), e.g. *Bede* 352. 3 . . . *in Hibernia Scotta ealond þonon he ær cwom, Bede* 46. 6 . . . *on þæs sæs waroþe to suðdæle, þanon ðe hi sciphere on becom, BlHom* 115. 33 . . . *he eft to þæm fæderlican setle eode, þonon he næfre onweg ne gewat þurh his þa ecean godcundnesse, BlHom* 9. 25 . . . *on ða uplican ricu, þonon þe he ær sended wæs,*

Fates 30   He in Effessia   ealle þrage
                leode lærde,   þanon lifes weg
                siðe gesohte . . . ,

and (if we repunctuate)

El 346   He on gesyhðe wæs,
           mægena wealdend,   min on þa swiðran,
           þrymmes hyrde.   þanon ic ne wende
           æfre to aldre   onsion mine;

or without an antecedent (adverb clauses), e.g. *Bo* 5. 4 . . . *7 hu ælc gesceaft . . . wilnað þ hit cume þider ðonan þe hit ær com, Bo* 57. 29 *Nis nan gesceaft gesceapen ðara þe ne wilnige þ hit þider cuman mæge þonan þe hit ær com, ÆCHom* ii. 132. 3 *ondræd ðe swaðeah þæt ðin mod ne beo ahafen mid dyrstignysse on ðam tacnum þe God ðurh ðe gefremað, and þu ðonon on idelum wuldre befealle wiðinnan, þonon ðe ðu wiðutan on wurðmynte ahafen bist*—Thorpe translates *þonon ðe* 'because', but the idea of place, of falling from the heights of worldly glory to the depths of inner vainglory, is certainly present —and (the only such example in the poetry)

Fates 59   Sweordræs fornam
           þurh hæðene hand,   þær se halga gecrang,
           wund for weorudum,   þonon wuldres leoht
           sawle gesohte   sigores to leane.

Liggins (1955, pp. 429-30) quotes other sentences in which *þanon (þe)* acquires almost causal force.

§ 2470. Indefinite adverb clauses introduced by *þanon (þe)* do not occur in the poetry and are not common in the prose. They may be exemplified by *CP* 463. 20 *Astig eft ofdune ðonan ðe ðu wenst ðæt ðu wlitegost sie* and *Ch* 959 . . . *butan ða munekes of xþes circean 7 heore is þ scip 7 si ouerfæreld þare hæuene 7 si tolne of ealle scipen bi þas ðe hit beo 7 cume ðanon þe hit cume þe to þare ilicare hæuene æt Sandwic cumð.*

5. CLAUSES INTRODUCED BY *þIDER (þE)*

§2471. When used as a conjunction, *þider* may introduce clauses referring to a definite place, or an indefinite place, to which, in both the prose and the poetry. *þider þe* is similarly used, but only in the prose. Definite clauses of place are found with an antecedent (adjective clauses) *BlHom* 125. 29 . . . *up to heofenum . . . þider hie witon þæt he Drihten mid lichoman astag, Luke(WSCp)* 12. 33 . . . *on heofenum þyder ðeof ne genealæcð*, Latin . . . *in caelis quo fur non appropriat, ÆCHom* ii. 536. 25 *gelæde us to ðam ecan life ðider ðe he us gelaðode*, and

PPs 67. 26   Bebeod þinum mægene;   þu eart mihtig god;
                and þin weorc on us   mid wisdome
                getryme on þinum temple   tidum gehalgod;
                þæt ys on Hierusalem,   þyder ðe gyfe lædað
                of feorwegum   foldan kynincgas,

or without an antecedent (adverb clauses), e.g. *Solil* 58. 19 *Ac ic wolde þæt wit fengen eft þider wit ær weron,. CP* 65. 16 *ðonne ne magon ðider fullice becuman ða stæpas ðæs weorces ðieder ðe he wilnað, Bede* 444. 15 *7 þider þe he sylfa toweard wæs æfter deaþe, þider he his eagan sende ær his deaðe, þæt he þy bliþelicor þrowade, John(WSCp)* 8. 21 *ne mage ge cuman þyder ic fare* (but see §2472), *ÆCHom* i. 52. 5 *þider ðe Stephanus forestop . . . ðider folgode Paulus*, and

GuthA 6   Nu þu most feran   þider þu fundadest
             longe ond gelome.   Ic þec lædan sceal.

§2472. Indefinite adverb clauses introduced by *þider (þe)* include *Bo* 140. 1 *ac ic bio swiðe swiðe gefægen gif þu me lædst þider ic ðe bidde, GD(C)* 25. 1 *far nu þider þe þu wille—MS H* has *swa hwider swa—Ch* 1487 *ga hyt for uncra begra sawle þider him leouest sy, John(WSCp)* 13. 36 *Simon Petrus cwæð to him Drihten hwyder gæst þu? Se Hælend him andswarode 7 cwæð Ne miht þu me fylian þyder ic nu fare* (but this and *John(WSCp)* 8. 21 (§2471) may be taken as definite or indefinite),

Met 13. 1   Ic wille mid giddum   get gecyðan
               hu se ælmihtga   ealla gesceafta
               bryrð mid his bridlum,   begð ðider he wile,

and

Met 26. 118   . . . and þæt ingeþonc   ælces monnes
                 þone lichoman   lit þider hit wile.

§2473. Liggins (1955, p. 429) draws our attention to the presence of a causal element in some clauses introduced by *þider (þe)*, including *Or* 236. 17 *7 raðe þæs þe þa senatus gehierdon þæt Marius to Rome nealæcte, hie ealle ut aflugon on Creca lond æfter Sillan 7 æfter Pompeiuse, þider hi þa mid firde gefaren wæron.*

6. RELATIVE PRONOUNS

§2474. It follows from the fact that *þær* can introduce adjective clauses of place that relative pronouns and *þær* can be used interchangeably in this function. We may compare *Bede* 178. 3 . . . *in þære stowe þe he for his eðle mid his leodum compade* with *Bede* 154. 19 . . . *seo stow . . . þær se Oswald to þissum gefeohte cwom*; *ÆCHom* i. 460. 16 *forðan ðe we gewilniað þæt we rice beon on his rice, on ðam næfð adl, ne untrumnyss, ne unrotnyss, ne deað, nænne stede, ac þær is ece gesælð and eadignys, gefea butan ende mid ecum welum* (is *þær* a conjunction 'where' or introductory adverb 'there'?) with *ÆCHom* i. 154. 1 *And hi ða comon to ðære stowe þær se blinda man sæt be ðam wege* and *ÆCHom* ii. 162. 25 . . . *and on swilcere stowe awurpe ðær hine nan man findan ne mihte*; and the variant readings in

Dur(C) 18   Eardiæð æt ðem eadige   in in ðem minstre
              unarimeda   reliquia,
              ðe monia wundrum gewurðað   . . . ,

where the ASPR text prefers MS *H*'s *ðær* to MS *C*'s *ðe*. We find the two side by side in *ÆCHom* ii. 156. 1 . . . *to anre westenre stowe, þe is Sublacus gecweden, feowertig mila fram Romebyrig, þær hine afedde sum eawfæst munuc, Romanus hatte, þreo gear* and we may note that in

PPs 77. 67   . . . ac he geceas Iudan him   geswæs frumcynn
              on Sione byrig,   þær him wæs symble leof

OE *þær* represents *quem* of the Latin *Sed elegit tribum Juda, montem Sion, quem dilexit.*

§2475. The combination *æghwonan þe* 'wherever' in *Bede* 304. 11 *Ða gesomnodon þa bisceopes men þa ælnet æghwonan þe hie meahton* is worthy of note. In *CP* 308. 2 *Ðy mon sceal fæsðne weal wyrcean, ðy mon ær gehawige ðæt se grund fæsð sie, ðær mon ðone grundweall onlecgge, ðy . . . ðy* can be taken as 'in that place/there . . . in that place/where . . .'. But see BTS, s.v. *se* V. 5 ('where condition is marked: *then . . . when . . . Ðy (tunc) . . . ðy (cum) . . .*'), and Visser, ii. 882 fn. 1.

7. *ÞÆS ÞE, TO ÞÆS (ÞE),* AND *WIÞ ÞÆS ÞÆT*

§2476. The adverbial use of *þæs* and *to þæs* 'to that (point, extent)' is well attested, especially in the poetry, e.g.

Sea 39   Forþon nis þæs modwlonc   mon ofer eorþan,
                 ne his gifena þæs god,   ne in geoguþe to þæs hwæt,
                 ne in his dædum to þæs deor,   ne him his dryten to þæs hold,
                 þæt he a his sæfore   sorge næbbe,
                 to hwon hine dryhten   gedon wille,

and (with *to þæs* 'there, thither' correlative with a local conjunction) *Sat* 529 *To ðæs gingran þider || ealle urnon þær se eca wæs* and

Dan 41   To þæs witgan foron,
        Caldea cyn,   to ceastre forð,
        þær Israela   æhta wæron,
        bewrigene mid weorcum.

There are occasional examples in the poetry in which *þæs þe* and *to þæs (þe)* are used as conjunctions in the sense 'to the point where, whither' or 'as far as'. They include

ChristA 71   Eala wifa wynn   geond wuldres þrym,
               fæmne freolicast   ofer ealne foldan sceat
               þæs þe æfre sundbuend   secgan hyrdon . . .

(where the genders make it difficult to take *þæs þe* as a relative, the only possible grammatical antecedent being *wifa*);

Rid 84. 28   hio biþ eadgum leof,   earmum getæse,
               freolic, sellic;   fromast ond swiþost,
               gifrost ond grædgost   grundbedd trideþ,
               þæs þe under lyfte   aloden wurde
               ond ælda bearn   eagum sawe . . .

(where *þæs þe* might mean 'of what');

And 1068   To þam fæstenne
        wærleasra werod   wæpnum comon,
        hæðne hildfrecan,   to þæs þa hæftas ær
        under hlinscuwan   hearm þrowedon;

Beo 714, *Beo* 1966, *And* 1058; and

Beo 2409   He ofer willan giong
        to ðæs ðe he eorðsele   anne wisse,
        hlæw under hrusan   holmwylme neh,
        yðgewinne.

On *Beo* 1584 see Mitchell 1975a, pp. 22-3.

§2477. *þæs wide . . . swa* in

Pan 4   þæs wide sind   geond world innan
             fugla ond deora   foldhrerendra

> wornas widsceope,   swa wæter bibugeð
> þisne beorhtan bosm . . .

can be seen as a correlative combination; cf. the patterns discussed
in §2488. But the *swa* clause can be explained as a worn-down correlative clause; see §§2489-93.

§2478. As far as I know, *wiþ þæs* did not achieve adverbial status,
but examples like *Bo* 25. 16 *Ac ic eow mæg mid feawum wordum
gereccan hwæt se hrof is ealra gesælða; wið þas ic wat þu wilt higian
þon ær þe ðu hine ongitest* show that it could have done. However,
in *Bo* 139. 24 *Me wære leofre þ ic onette wið þæs þ ic þe moste
gelæstan þ ic þe ær gehet, wið þæs þ* means 'towards the point that'
and so 'with a view to, so that'.

8. *ÞÆT*

§2479. The idiomatic *þæt* clause in

Beo 1361	Nis þæt feor heonon
	milgemearces, þæt se mere standeð;
	ofer þæm hongiað hrinde bearwas,
	wudu wyrtum fæst wæter oferhelmað

should be compared with the similar temporal clauses discussed in
§§2784-8.

§2480. On examples such as *Ch* 1305 *Ðis synd þa landgemæra to
þordune ondlong amman broces þ hit sticað in þidelan ondlong
þidelan þ hit cymð to oredeshamme* and

Beo 356	Hwearf þa hrædlice þær Hroðgar sæt
	eald ond anhar mid his eorla gedriht;
	eode ellenrof, þæt he for eaxlum gestod
	Deniga frean,

in which *þæt* comes close to expressing a local or temporal limit, see
§§2745-6. The origin of this usage is perhaps to be found in the idea
of result which is also present and the *þæt* clauses can be construed
as consecutive.

9. *OÞ, OÞÞE, OÞÞÆT*

§2481. Clauses introduced by one of these may express a limit
which is local rather than or as well as temporal, e.g. *Ch* 1513 . . .

þonne on þane gemænan garan beuton þæm dic of [for *oþ*] *þæt eft geð inna þet read geat* and

Jud 138   Hie ða beahhrodene
                feðelaste   forð onettan,
                oð hie glædmode   gegan hæfdon
                to ðam wealgate.

On these, see further §§2743-59.

10. *SWA* ALONE AND IN COMBINATION

a. Swa hwær swa

§2482. *Swa hwær swa* does not occur in the poetry, perhaps for metrical reasons, but is found in the prose introducing indefinite adverb clauses of place. Examples include (with the local clause in first position) *ÆCHom* i. 284. 2 *Swa hwær swa heora an bið, þær hi beoð ealle ðry, æfre an God untodæledlic* and *ÆCHom* ii. 196. 10 *swa hwær swa hit ætstod, þær hi wicodon* (Liggins (1955, p. 429) detects a causal element in these two examples) and (with the principal clause first) *ÆCHom* ii. 194. 32 *Æfter ðisum him com bigleofa of heofenum, swa hwær swa hi wicodon geond þæt westen* and *ÆCHom* ii. 212. 31 . . . *and hi inn eodon swa hwær swa hi stodon.*

§2483. The second *swa* is sometimes not expressed, e.g. *ChronF* 128. 2 (994) *⁊ þ mæste yfel worhton þe æfre æni here mihte on eallon ðingan, swa hwar hi ferdon,* and sometimes doubled, e.g. *ÆLS* 31. 425 . . . *and Martinus æfre swa hwær swa he þa deofolgild to wearp swa worhte he cyrcan.*

§2484. The prevailing mood is the indicative, but the subjunctive sometimes occurs in the contexts outlined in §2509, e.g. *BenRW* 41. 16 *oðöo swa hwar swa heo sy sittende, standende, odðo gangende, æfre beo hniwiende mid hyre heafede.*

b. Swa hwider swa

§2485. Like *Swa hwær swa, swa hwider swa* does not occur in the poetry. Examples from the prose include (with the local clause first) *ÆLS* 26. 268 *and swa hwider swa he com he cydde þas wundra* and *ÆCHom* i. 348. 14 *and swa hwider swa se stowlica engel flihð, he bið befangen mid his andwerdnysse* and (with the principal clause first) *ÆCHom* i. 88. 34 *Hi sind ða ðe Criste folgiað on hwitum gyrlum, swa hwider swa he gæð* and *ÆCHom* ii. 504. 1 . . . *sæde þæt he wolde his wiðerwinna beon on eallum his færelde, swa hwider swa he ferde.*

§ 2486. We occasionally find *swa hwider*, e.g. *GD* 295. 21 *swa hwider se lichama byþ, þider beoð gesomnode þa earnas*, and *hwider swa*, e.g. *Matt(R)* 8. 19 *ic wille folgian þe hwider swa þu ganges* ɫ *gæst.*

§ 2487. The mood in *swa hwider swa* clauses is the indicative, but the subjunctive can appear in one of the contexts outlined in § 2509, e.g. *Bede* 262. 1 *þa nedde se ærcebiscop hine swiðe, þæt he ridan scolde swa hwyder swa ðæs þearf wære* and *ÆCHom* ii. 416. 30 *Far ðe frig swa hwider swa ðu wille.*

c. Swa . . . swa

§ 2488. Other combinations with *swa . . . swa* include *swa hwæþer . . . swa*, e.g. *ChronA* 84. 27 (894) *þa foron hie siþþan æfter þæm wealda hloþum 7 flocradum bi swa hwaþerre efes swa hit þonne fierdleas wæs*; *swa hwelc . . . swa*, e.g. *Mart* 2 116. 8 *ond on swa hwelcre stowe swa min þrowung awriten sy ond man þa mærsige, afyrr þu, drihten, from þære stowe blindnesse ond helto*; *swa feor . . . swa*, e.g. *ChronE* 141. 7 (1010) *þa hi swa feor gegan hæfdon swa hi þa woldon, þa comon hi to ðam middan wintra to scipon* and *ChronE* 145. 27 (1014) . . . *com þet mycele sæflod geond wide þisne eard 7 ærn swa feor up swa næfre ær ne dyde*; and *(swa) wide swa (swa)*, e.g. *ChronE* 143. 5 (1012) *þa toferde se here wide swa he ær gegaderod wæs,*

GenA 2554
```
                          Bearwas wurdon
          to axan and to yslan,    eorðan wæstma,
          efne swa wide    swa ða witelac
          reðe geræhton    rum land wera,
```

and

Met 16. 11
```
          . . . efne swa wide    swa swa westmest nu
          an iglond ligð    ut on garsecg. . . .
```

d. Swa (. . .) (swa) *in 'worn-down correlative clauses'*

§ 2489. Kock (*Ang.* 42 (1918), 102-3) is in basic agreement with Ericson (*EStudien*, 65 (1931), 343-50, and 1932, pp. 48-50), who explained certain clauses with *swa, swa swa*, or *swa . . . swa*, as 'worn-down correlative clauses' in which these conjunctions have the same sense as *swa hwær swa* in *Matt(WSCp)* 24. 28 *Swa hwær swa hold byþ, þæder beoð earnas gegaderude* or as *swa wide swa* in

And 332   Farað nu geond ealle   eorðan sceatas
emne swa wide   swa wæter bebugeð,
oððe stedewangas   stræte gelicgaþ.[90]

The translation 'wherever' is obligatory or much to be preferred in some, e.g. *ÆLet 4* 74. 1252 *Of þam iungum cnihtum þe comon of ðam hungre, on eallum þam lande hi alæddon aweg to wircenne godeweb, swa swa hi wæron getogene, And 1229, And 1441,* and

And 1581   Smeolt wæs se sigewang,   symble wæs dryge
folde fram flode,   swa his fot gestop.

In others the sense 'as far as' seems appropriate, e.g. *Bede* 480. 20 *þas þing by stære Ongelþiode cirican on Brytene, swa swa geo of manna gewritum oððe of ealdra gesegene oððe of minre sylfre cyþeþe ic gewitan mihte, mid Dryhtnes fultume gedyde ic Beda . . . , Or 17. 15,* and *Or 17. 19 þa siglde he þonan suðryhte be lande swa swa he mehte on fif dagum gesiglan.*

§2490. But in many of the examples, any of the translations 'wherever', 'as far as', or 'as widely as', will do. They include (with *swa*) *Bede* 260. 27 *þegnade Wilferð biscop þone biscophad in Eofor-wicceastre 7 eac swylce in eallum Norðanhymbrum ge eac in Peohtum, swa Osweoes rice wæs þæs cyninges, GenA 2212, El 967,* and

Beo 90   Sægde se þe cuþe
frumsceaft fira   feorran reccan,
cwæð þæt se Ælmihtiga   eorðan worh(te),
wlitebeorhtne wang,   swa wæter bebugeð . . . ;

(with *swa swa*) *Bede(B)* 144. 21 *Is þ sægd þ in ða tid swa micel sibb wære on Brytene æghwæðer ymb swa swa Eadwines rice wære . . . , Met 9. 38,* and

Met 16. 8   þeah him eall sie
þes middangeard,   swa swa merestreamas
utan belicgað,   on æht gifen . . . ;

and (with *swa . . . swa*)

GenA 2204   Ic þe wære nu,
mago Ebrea,   mine selle,
þæt sceal fromcynne   folde þine,

---

[90] See also Burkhart (pp. 22-3) and Glogauer (pp. 37-8, where *hwær* in the heading is presumably an error for *þær*). I list all the possible examples in the poetry in my thesis (Mitchell 1959, p. 772).

>   sidland manig,   geseted wurðan,
>   eorðan sceatas   oð Eufraten,
>   and from Egypta   eðelmearce
>   swa mid niðas   swa Nilus sceadeð
>   and eft Wendelsæ   wide rice.

§2491. That Kock and Ericson were right to attribute these meanings to these conjunctions is demonstrated by the fact that the Latin
equivalent of *Bede* 260. 27 (§2490) is . . . *Uilfrido administrante
episcopatum Eboracensis ecclesiae necnon et omnium Nordanhymbrorum sed et Pictorum, quousque rex Osuiu imperium protendere
poterat* and that

PPs 102. 12   Swa þas foldan   fæðme bewindeð
                 þes eastrodor   and æfter west,
                 he betweonan þam   teonan and unriht
                 us fram afyrde   æghwær symble

represents Latin *Ps* 102. 12 *Quantum distat oriens ab occasu: elonga-
uit a nobis iniquitates nostras.* However, in some at least of the alleged
examples, the *swa* clause may be one of simple comparison; consider
MSol 185, *Wid* 41,

Beo 2606   Gemunde ða ða are,   þe he him ær forgeaf,
                wicstede weligne   Wægmundinga,
                folcrihta gehwylc,   swa his fæder ahte

(understanding a pronoun object in the *swa* clause), and

JDay i 12   bið eal þes ginna grund   gleda gefylled,
                reþra bronda,   swa nu rixiað
                gromhydge guman. . . .

Quirk (pp. 109-10) does not mention the possibility that *swa* may
mean 'as far as' when discussing this passage. Note also the different
translations by Garmonsway of *swa* in *DEdw* 9 and *Capt* 1.

§2492. Hoops (*Beowulfstudien*, pp. 15-17), while accepting the
equation suggested by Kock and Ericson, denies that *swa* in such
examples is a worn-down correlative. For him *swa wide swa, swa
hwær swa*, and *(swa) sona swa* (§§2697-9), are extensions of a single
swa, the object of such extensions being to strengthen the expression. As a possible point of departure, he suggests the use of *swa* in
the meaning *so wie, in dem Masse wie* 'as . . . as, in the measure/
proportion as' (a sense which appears in all three extensions), with
swa swa as an intermediate stage. This series might illustrate his theory:

Rid 21. 1   Neb is min niþerweard;   neol ic fere
                ond be grunde græfe,   geonge swa me wisað
                har holtes feond,

Met 9. 38   Wiold emne swa þeah
    ealles þisses mæran   middangeardes,
    swa swa lyft and lagu   land ymbclyppað,
    garsecg embegyrt   gumena rice,
    secgea sitlu,   suð, east and west,
    oð ða norðmestan   næssan on eorðan,

and *swa wide swa swa* in *Met* 16. 11 (§ 2488). Hoops cites in support
of his theory the fact that in the poetry *swa* is more common in such
clauses than the expanded conjunctions, but this may only prove
that *swa* was more amenable to the discipline of the alliterative line
than *swa wide swa* and the like.

§ 2493. There are occasional sentences in which *swa (swa)* means
'where' as opposed to 'wherever', e.g. *Bede* 428. 23 *þa cerde he ða
sona on ða swiðran hond, 7 mec ongon lædan suðeast on ðon roðor,
swa swa on wintre sunne upp gongeð*, Latin . . . *qui mox conuersus
ad dextrum iter quasi contra ortum solis brumalem me ducere
coepit, Bede* 424. 19, and

GenA 1668   þæs þe hie gesohton   Sennera feld,
    swa þa foremeahtige   folces ræswan,
    þa yldestan   oft and gelome
    liðsum gewunedon. . . .

In view of the two examples from *Bede* and of the variations *Rid*
30a. 8 *þær/Rid* 30b. 8 *swa* discussed in § 2464, we are not bound to
accept Braasch's suggestion (p. 120, s.v. *swa* 2b) that *swa* in *GenA*
1668 above is causal.

11. *HWÆR, HWANON, AND HWIDER*

§ 2494. Are *hwær, hwanon*, and *hwider*, used to introduce adjective
or adverb clauses in OE? Or, to put it another way, are clauses introduced by these words always interrogative? Various writers who will
be mentioned below have answered these questions 'Yes' and 'No'
respectively with regard to individual examples. This is, of course,
only one aspect of a larger problem which concerns all OE words
which can be used as interrogatives or indefinites; see § § 2049-55
and the Indexes. As far as I know, Yamakawa 1971 is the only study
devoted to *hwær, hwider*, and *hwanon*, though reference to the last
two is inevitably occasional because there are so few examples. This
is also true here. But, *mutatis mutandis*, the same conclusions apply
to them as apply to *hwær*. (Yamakawa also studies words meaning
'when' (Yamakawa 1969) and deals with the later history of the

derivatives of *þær* and *hwær* in *The Hitotsubashi Journal of Arts and Sciences*, 14 (1973), 1-44.)

§ 2495. My answers to the questions asked in § 2494 tend to be respectively 'No' and 'Yes'. In the late prose it is clear that the use of *hwær*, *hwanon*, and *hwider*, to introduce adjective and adverb clauses is inevitable. But I believe that the clauses they introduce are dependent questions rather than adjective and adverb clauses and that those writers who argue to the contrary are misinterpreting the evidence except perhaps in one or two very late examples; see again §§ 2049-55. The contrast between the relative adverb *þær* and the interrogative *hwær* is starkly illustrated in *ÆCHom* i. 452. 1 *þa eode se bisceop into ðære oðre cyrcan, þær se martyr inne læig, and befran ðone cyrcweard hwær ðæs halgan wæpnu wæron.*

§ 2496. As I see them, the proposed examples of *hwær* relative adverb or conjunction fall into six main groups: (*a*) those in which *hwær* clearly introduces a dependent question; (*b*) and (*c*) those in which *hwær* begins to shade into a conjunction and a relative adverb respectively; (*d*) those which depend on a mistaken use of the evidence of the glosses; (*e*) and (*f*) those introduced by *loc(a) hwær* and *swa hwær swa* respectively. Space does not permit me to quote or refer to all the examples given by the various writers. But those which do not fall readily into one of these six groups are dealt with individually in §§ 2504-5.

§ 2497. The group (*a*) examples must be subdivided. First, there are those in which the *hwær* clause is the direct object of a verb or verb equivalent (i.e. a verb + an adjective or a noun) which can—and in my opinion does—introduce a dependent question. Here I include *Bo* 46. 25 *7 nan mon nat hwær hi nu sint* (Bacquet, p. 363), *ÆCHom* i. 60. 21 *On ðam oðrum dæge eode se apostol be ðære stræt, þa ofseah he hwær sum uðwita lædde twegen gebroðru* (Yamakawa 1971, p. 10), *Prov 1 Warn* 4. 23 *uncuð hware hwa oðres beðurfe*, *Sea* 117 *Uton we hycgan hwær we ham agen*, and *Wife* 7 *hæfde ic uhtceare* ‖ *hwær min leodfruma londes wære*. These are clearly not adverb clauses of place. I do not see how they can even be said to be transitional examples; there can be no doubt that in the last sentence, the wife is not in the same place as the husband.[91] The same is true of the sentences in the second type of group (*a*) examples, viz. those

[91] Visser (ii, § 895) indiscriminately cites clauses introduced by *þær* and *hwær*. But all his *hwær* examples are dependent questions. I think he is aware of this. But his method of presentation is likely to mislead the unwary.

in which the *hwær* clause is the second direct object of a verb, e.g. *Gen* 37. 16 *Ic sece mine gebroðru, hwar hig healdon heora heorda*, Latin *Indica mihi ubi pascant greges*; of a verb + a preposition, e.g. *Or* 144. 33 *Æfter þæm Antigones 7 Perðica gebeotedan . . . 7 longe ymb þæt siredon hwær hie hie gemetan wolden*; or of a verb equivalent, e.g.

El 426   Nu is þearf mycel
        þæt we fæstlice   ferhð staðelien,
        þæt we ðæs morðres meldan ne weorðen
        hwær þæt halige trio beheled wurde
        æfter wigþræce.

In these (all of which are taken from Yamakawa 1971, p. 11), the noun/pronoun object of the verb (equivalent) could not be taken as the antecedent of an adjective clause introduced by *hwær*; on this point see further §2500.

§2498. Group (*b*) examples—those in which *hwær* begins to shade into a conjunction introducing an adverb clause—must also be subdivided. First, there are sentences in which the *hwær* clause is the object of a verb which can introduce a dependent question, e.g. *ChronA* 89. 10 (896) *þa sume dæge rad se cyng up be þære eæ 7 gehawade hwær mon mehte þa ea forwyrcan* . . . (Yamakawa 1971, p. 10) and *LS* 34. 264 . . . *þa het se casere georne smeagan hwær mann æfre þa halgan geaxian mihte* (Johnsen, *Ang.* 37 (1913), 293-4, and Yamakawa 1971, pp. 17-18). The first example differs from *Wife* 7 and the like (§2497) in that the place where King Alfred did his reconnoitring and the place where the river was eventually blockaded are the same. Hence I classify this as a transitional example. But it remains a dependent question. The second is transitional by virtue of *æfre*. Johnsen (loc. cit.) claims that *hwær . . . æfre* is an indefinite relative and the EETS translation reads '. . . then the emperor bade search diligently wherever they could hear of the Saints'. This is obviously wrong, for the context makes it clear that they heard nothing. So *hwær . . . æfre* means 'where on earth'. Yamakawa (loc. cit.) compares *LS* 34. 267 *ðær man gengde geond eall abutan þone portweall man scrutnode on ælcere stowe þær man hi æfre geaxian cuðe*. This merely demonstrates that *hwær* still introduces dependent questions and *þær* adjective clauses of place.

§2499. The second subdivision of group (*b*) examples comprises those in which the introductory verb is *habban/nabban*, e.g. *Matt (WSCp)* 8. 20 *Foxas habbað holu 7 heofenan fuglas nest. Soþlice mannes sunu næfð hwær he hys heafod ahylde* (Yamakawa 1971,

p. 13), a sentence from BT, s.v. *hwanan, Ða næfde he hwanon he his wer agulde* (Kock, p. 75),[92] and *ÆCHom* i. 160. 34 *and ic næbbe hwider ic ahylde min heafod* (Yamakawa 1971, p. 13). But here again the interrogative element is predominant. Karlberg (p. 51) makes this point well. He says that 'Lat. *habere* could be coloured with the notion of *scire*'. He cites *Solil* 14. 11 *Ac seige nu hwæs þu earnodest oððe hwæt þu habban woldest!*, Latin *Quid ergo scire vis?*, in support of the proposition that 'this relation "have : know" is also clear in OE' and concludes that 'the construction can be regarded as a formalized cognitive phrase'. See also Behre, p. 244.

§2500. It is also necessary to subdivide the sentences in group (*c*) —those in which *hwær* begins to shade into a relative adverb. First, there are those in which a noun/pronoun and a *hwær* clause are the direct objects of a verb which can introduce a dependent question and which is used *apo koinou*. Examples include the ASPR reading of

Wan 23   . . .   ond ic hean þonan
          wod wintercearig   ofer waþema gebind,
          sohte sele dreorig   sinces bryttan,
          hwær ic feor oþþe neah   findan meahte
          þone þe in meoduhealle   min mine wisse

(Yamakawa 1971, p. 11; if we read *seledreorig* this belongs in group (*a*); see *Guide,* §159); *ÆCHom* i. 160. 33 *Deor habbað hola, and fugelas habbað nest, hwær hi restað* (Kivimaa, p. 37, and Yamakawa 1971, p. 13); *ÆLS* 16. 157 *Foxas habbað holu and fugelas habbað nest and ic næbbe wununge hwider ic min heafod ahyldan mæge*; and *Mart 2* 196. 24 *ond þa æfter fif ond fiftegum geara godes engel getæhte sumum geleaffullum wife . . . þa stowe hwær se lichoma wæs* (Burkhart, p. 22). Second, there are those in which a noun/pronoun and a *hwær* clause are used in a similar way, but have some other function in the sentence, e.g. that of subjects, as in *Or* 38. 34 *þæt tacn nugyt is orgyte on þæs sæs staðe, hwær þara wigwægna hweol on gongende wæron* (Wülfing, ii, §430; Bacquet, p. 364; Burkhart, p. 87; Kivimaa, p. 35; and Yamakawa 1971, p. 13. Here the *hwær* clause is parallel to *þæt tacn* and is not dependent on *staðe* or *þæs sæs*), or objects of a preposition, as in

El 673   þu scealt geagninga
          wisdom onwreon,   swa gewritu secgaþ,
          æfter stedewange   hwær seo stow sie
          Caluarie . . .

[92] This seems to be a conflation from Thorpe, *Dip. Ang.* 207. 33-6. Thorpe reports that he was unable to find the manuscript. I have not succeeded in tracing the charter in Sawyer.

(Yamakawa 1971, p. 11). Despite Yamakawa (1971, p. 12), these examples differ from those in group (a) (second type) like *Gen* 37. 16 (§2497) in that here there is a possible antecedent and the *hwær* clause could be parsed as an adjective clause of place. I agree with Yamakawa (private communication) that 'a transitional stage in the development can be actually demonstrated by these examples'. However, it is hard to say without a native informant how far along the road these and others like them are.

§2501. We turn now to the examples from the glosses, which comprise my group (d). The only ones from OE quoted by *OED*, s.vv. *where* II Relative and conjunctive uses and *whither* II Relative uses, are from the Lindisfarne Gospels—*ðer uel huer/huoer* for *ubi* in *Matt* 6. 21 and *John* 11. 32 and *huidir* for *ubi* in *John* 21. 18, where *WSCp* has *þær*. Burkhart (p. 22) quotes *Ps(E)* 131. 7 *we gebiddæþ on stowe hwer stodon fet his*, Latin *adoravimus in loco ubi steterunt pedes eius*, and claims this as an example of *hwær* introducing an adjective clause, even while he draws our attention in a footnote to the fact that in *Ps(A)* 131. 7 we read . . . *in stowe ðer*. He adduces similar variations with *hwanon/þonan* (p. 228). Yamakawa (1971, pp. 15-16) too quotes similar variations involving *hwær/ðær/swa hwær swa*. All these authorities seem to agree with Johnsen (*Ang.* 37 (1913), 300-1), who says of the Lindisfarne variations that '*þær* being the older and traditional equivalent of *ubi* is placed first, the newer and better one, *hwær*, is given last'. But these glosses do not necessarily equate *ðær* and *hwær*. They rather certify that two functions of Latin *ubi* were distinguished in OE. It could perhaps be further deduced that the confusion between them already existed, but this is by no means certain. In my opinion Yamakawa (1971, p. 19) puts it somewhat too strongly when he writes: 'It cannot be overlooked, on the other hand, that, as is proved by the variant renderings in the quotations from the Lindisfarne Gospels, the influence by the Latin interrogative-indefinite *ubi* is a good deal responsible for the development of OE *hwær* as definite relative or subordinate conjunction.'

§2502. In group (e) we have examples with *loc(a) hwær*. This combination usually means 'wherever', e.g. *BenR* 82. 15 *sitte hig loca hwær se ealdor him tæce oððe hate*, *ChronF* 130. 25 (995) *⁊ het hi faran loc whar hi woldon*, *ByrM* 182. 28 *þys taken hatte crisimon ⁊ man hyt mæg settan to tacne, loca hwær se writere wylle*, and *LawIICn* 80. 1 *⁊ forga ælc man minne huntnoð, loce hwær ic hit gefriðod wylle habban, be fullan wite*, but sometimes may have its

literal meaning, e.g. *Lch* iii. 142. 15 *Loca hwær þ blod utwealle.*
Gif þu þa stowe geracen mægen, gif þat blod of þara ceolan utwealle,
nym cole. . . . Yamakawa (1971, p. 14), after quoting *ChronF* 130.
25 (995) above, rightly remarks that 'the presence of this usage
illustrates the potentiality of indefinite-interrogative *hwær* to be
developed into a relative or subordinate conjunction'. But *hwær*
is still interrogative. The same is true with examples of *loc(a) hwider*
'withersoever', e.g. *RegCGl* 571 *þænne gan hi loce hwyder gan hi*
habban singende antefnas, where the Latin has *tunc uadant quo ire*
habent canentes antiphonas.

§2503. The group (*f*) examples—those with *swa hwær swa*—have
already been discussed in §§2482-4. Yamakawa (1971, pp. 16-17)
quotes examples from the Gospels and other texts and concludes
that 'from these instances we may safely infer that the use of an
indefinite relative, so far as *hwær* is concerned, has been well enough
established in Old English'. But examples with *swa hwær swa* do not
prove anything about the use of *hwær* as a relative or a conjunction.

§2504. I turn now to those individual examples in which *hwær*, or
hwanon, or *hwider*, seems to some scholars to be used with no interrogative force as a conjunction or relative adverb. There is one in the
poetry, viz.

> *GuthA* 22   þider soðfæstra   sawla motun
> cuman æfter cwealme,   þa þe her Cristes æ
> læraÐ ond læstaÐ,   ond his lof ræraÐ;
> oferwinnaÐ þa awyrgdan gæstas,   bigytaÐ him wuldres ræste,
> hwider sceal þæs monnes   mod astigan,
> ær oþþe æfter,   þonne he his ænne her
> gæst bigonge,   þæt se gode mote,
> womma clæne,   in geweald cuman.

The ASPR note reads: 'The edd. take *hwider* as an interrogative,
placing a question mark after *cuman*, l. 29. But *hwider* is better
taken as a relative "to which".' Schaar (pp. 78-9) prefers a comma
after *ræraÐ*, with *þider* . . . *hwider* (introducing an adverb clause)
used correlatively. It is possible that from a formal grammatical viewpoint, *hwider* introduces a dependent question parallel to *ræste*; cf.
the ASPR reading of *Wan* 23 (§2500). In translating *GuthA* 22 into
MnE, however, the ASPR version seems the best way out. This is
clearly a transitional example. Liggins (1955, p. 429) sees a causal
element in the third *hwær* clause in *Lch* ii. 260. 14 *Be þisum tacnum*
þu meaht hwær se man to lacnianne sie ongitan hwær ne sie. hwær
mon unsofte getilaÐ on forewearde þa adle þonne þ sar ærest gestihÐ

on þa sculdru 7 on þa breost. Sona sceal mon blod of ædre lætan.
(I give Cockayne's punctuation of this tenth-century example.) However, I am inclined to take the three *hwær* clauses as parallel dependent questions on *ongitan*—for the change in mood see §2080—
and to link the *þonne* clause—which, the order SV suggests, is subordinate—with the clause which follows.

§2505. There remains a prose example quoted by Burkhart (p. 25
fn. 3) from the twelfth-century manuscript Cotton Vespasian D xiv.
(I disregard examples from what are now accepted without dispute
as ME texts.) This is the second *hwar* clause in *Nic(C)* 81. 27 *þa
cwæð ic to him 'Æteowe me þa byrigeles hwar ic þe leigde'. Se
Hælend me þa beo þære rihthand genam 7 me at lædde hwar ic hine
byrede 7 syððen he lædde me to Barimathia, to minre agenre rice,*
which, for the obvious reason that *lædan* does not introduce dependent questions, cannot be interrogative—unlike the first, which
belongs to the first sub-division of group (*c*) above. But there is no
equivalent in either *Nic(A)* or *Nic(B)* for the words *hwar ic hine
byrede 7 syððan he lædde*. So this example provides no evidence for
OE usage. But it seems to suggest that *hwær* did introduce adverb
clauses of place in the twelfth century.

§2506. So I return to my original proposition (§§2494-5) that
even in late OE the difference between the interrogative *hwær* and
the conjunction and relative adverb *þær* was still real, even though
its disappearance was inevitable. Here I agree with Yamakawa (1971,
p. 18): 'we cannot say that *hwær* has been fully developed into a
relative adverb referring to an antecedent of a definite local signification'. I do not think there is anything in *ÆGram* 224. 12-225. 5 or
231. 9-232. 2 to contradict this.

§2507. Yamakawa (1971, p. 1) tells us that '*there* maintained its
longer resistance against *where* than *then* or *tho* did against *when*,
though on the other hand the incipient phenomena of *hwær* in the
subordinating function can be attested to in Old English texts, probably to a greater extent than the case of *hwonne*', and concludes
(1971, p. 18), that 'there are some data convincing enough to cor-
roborate Johnsen's assertion [*Ang*. 37 (1913), 300] that *hwær* is the
first indefinite relative in Old English that has begun to be used as
a definite relative'. Everything in these two quotations except the
principal clause in the first depends on the evidence of the glosses
and so in my opinion must be dismissed. That '*there* maintained its
longer resistance against *where* than *then* or *tho* did against *when*'

is in accordance with my view that '*hwonne* has advanced further than the other interrogatives along the road which was to lead to their modern use as both interrogatives and conjunctions or relatives' (*Neophil.* 49 (1965), 160); see further §§2775-83. But since we are not native informants, we must not make too much of what must after all be largely a matter of subjective impression. The important point has long been clear: both *hwær* and *hwonne* were acquiring new roles in the OE period.

12. MOOD

§2508. The prevailing mood in both definite and indefinite clauses of place in OE prose and poetry is the indicative. Numerous examples have already been quoted. This is true even when the principal clause contains an imperative, e.g. *ÆCHom* i. 464. 24 . . . *and far to westene, þær nan fugel ne flyhð* and

Sat 616   Ge sind wilcuman!   Gað in wuldres leoht
             to heofona rice,   þær ge habbað
             a to aldre   ece reste;

a subjunctive, e.g. *LawIICn* 24. 3 *And us ne þingð na riht þæt ænig man agnian sceole þær gewitnesse byð*,

Beo 3105   Sie sio bær gearo,
             ædre geæfned,   þonne we ut cymen,
             ond þonne geferian   frean userne,
             leofne mannan   þær he longe sceal
             on ðæs Waldendes   wære geþolian,

and

Sat 286   gearwian us togenes   grene stræte
             up to englum,   þær is se ælmihtiga god;

uton, e.g. *Sat* 216 *Uta cerran þider* ‖ *þær he sylfa sit, sigora waldend*; a form of **sculan*, e.g. *ÆCHom* ii. 558. 1 *ðonne sceal se, þær ðær he mæg, earmum ðingian to ðam rican* and

And 174   Ðu scealt feran   ond frið lædan,
             siðe gesecan,   þær sylfætan
             eard weardigað,   eðel healdaþ
             morðorcræftum;

or a negated indicative, e.g. *ÆCHom* i. 604. 26 *Ne bið nan ðing digle þær ðær druncennys rixað* and

Beo 1377   Eard git ne const,
             frecne stowe,   ðær þu findan miht
             sinnigne secg;

and when the clause of place is in dependent speech, e.g. *ÆCHom* ii. 132. 3 (where the verb governing the noun clause is imperative), *ÆCHom* ii. 558. 17 *Is nu forði gehwilcum men to hogienne þæt he ydel ne cume his Drihtne togeanes on ðam gemænelicum æriste, þær we ealle beoð gegaderode þe her lif underfengon*, and

Max ii 63   Næni eft cymeð
    hider under hrofas,   þe þæt her for soð
    mannum secge   hwylc sy meotodes gesceaft,
    sigefolca gesetu,   þær he sylfa wunað.

§2509. I have so far noted no examples in Ælfric's writings in which any of these phenomena is accompanied by a clause of place with a subjunctive verb. There are, however, sporadic examples elsewhere. They include (with an imperative) *Lch* ii. 118. 16 *þonne þu hit smyrian wille þær sio adl sie, fylge him mid þisse sealfe* and

GenA 2723   Wuna mid usic   and þe wic geceos
    on þissum lande   þær þe leofost sie;

(with a jussive subjunctive) *LawHl* 12 *Gif man oþrum steop asette ðær mæn drincen buton scylde, an eald riht scll' agelde þam þe þæt flet age . . .* , *WHom* 10a. 18 *Forbugan sacu sylfe swa hi geornost magon 7 ðær oðre men sace onginnan, sehtan hi georne*, and

Met 7. 31   . . .   wyrce him siððan
    his modes hus,   þær he mæge findan
    eaðmetta stan   unigmet fæstne,
    grundweal gearone;

(with a subjunctive in a purpose clause) *CP* 443. 35 *forðæm we ceorfað heah treowu on holte ðæt we hi eft uparæren on ðæm botle ðær ðær we timbran willen*; (after a form of **sculan*) *CP* 308. 2 *Ðy mon sceal fæsðne weal wyrcean, ðy mon ær gehawige ðæt se grund fæsð sie, ðær mon ðone grundweall onlecgge*; and (with the local clause in dependent speech or in the accusative and infinitive construction) *CP* 5. 1, *Bede* 260. 32 . . . *heht hine Theodor biscop ridan, þær him se weg lengra gelumpe*, *Or* 18. 31 *7 norðeweard he cwæð, þær hit smalost wære, þæt hit mihte beon þreora mila brad to þæm more*, *BlHom* 193. 6 *Sume men wæron þe sægdon þæt hine wulfas abiton 7 fræton, þær he mid cyle 7 mid hungre on wudum dwolgende astifod læge*, and (the only such example in the poetry)

Ex 269   Ic on beteran ræd,
    þæt ge gewurðien   wuldres aldor,
    and eow liffrean   lissa bidde,
    sigora gesynto,   þær ge siðien.

The subjunctive after *willan* in *LS* 7. 129 *ac ic wille faran to wera mynstre þær nan man min ne wene* is noteworthy.

§2510. Two patterns demand special comment. One is the so-called 'challenge construction' seen in examples like *Bede* 386. 1 *Cærde we usic ðider we cærde, gemætton we usic æghwonon geliice storme* (where the verbs are in the past tense) and *BlHom* 129. 33 *for þon æghwylc man, sy þær eorðan þær he sy, þurh gode dæda Gode lician sceal, ThCap 1 474 ne forlæte he hit ne fullie, sy þonon þe hit sy,* and

Beo 1392   Ic hit þe gehate: no he on helm losaþ,
         ne on foldan fæþm,   ne on fyrgenholt,
         ne on gyfenes grund,   ga þær he wille!

(where the verbs are in the present tense). In these the clause of place and its accompanying principal clause combine to form what can be called an indefinite concessive-equivalent clause of place. On these see further §§3451-6. The important thing here is that in these constructions the verbs in both clauses are overwhelmingly subjunctive.

§2511. The second pattern is that in which the principal clause contains a negated indicative. This, according to the 'rule' proposed by Campbell and quoted in §2512, is one of the situations in which a clause of place takes the subjunctive. But here the 'rule', which was stated briefly for review purposes, needs elaboration. In examples like *ÆCHom* i. 604. 26 *Ne bið nan ðing digle þær ðær druncennys rixað,* which could be translated 'Everything is revealed where drunkenness reigns', the verb in the clause of place is indicative. This is true of all the examples in the poetry and of all those I have noted in the prose. None of them contains the generic idea seen in examples like *WHom* 4. 24 *Forðam nis nan man þæt ne sy synful.* Examples like ☆*Nis nan stow þær Crist ne rixige* are theoretically possible. So far, however, I have not found any.

§2512. Campbell, in his review of Quirk (*RES* 7 (1956), 65), spoke of what he called 'perhaps the most far-reaching rule of OE syntax— viz. that relative clauses (including clauses of time and place), clauses of result, *swa* clauses, and clauses expressing real positive conditions take the subjunctive when the principal clause contains an imperative, a subjunctive, or a negated indicative'. It is clear, however, that this 'rule' does not reach very far into clauses of place. Its sporadic application is clear in examples like *LawHl* 13 *Gif man wæpn abregde þær mæn drincen 7 ðær man nan yfel ne deþ, scilling þan þe þæt flet age* and *CP* 463. 3 . . . *ðæt he hine selfne ne forlæte ðær he oðerra freonda tilige 7 him self ne afealle ðær ðær he oðre tiolað to ræranne*, where we have the subjunctive and then the indicative in what seem to be parallel clauses. I give the full figures for the poetry in my thesis (Mitchell 1959, pp. 261-5). On the nature of the subjunctive in local clauses, see Vogt, p. 38, and Behre, pp. 278-9.

§2513. With rare exceptions such as *LS* 7. 129 *ac ic wille faran to wera mynstre þær nan man min ne wene*, where (as the context shows) the reference is to a specific monastery, all the clauses of place with the subjunctive in both prose and poetry are or can be explained as indefinite. But it would be wrong to formulate a rule that definite clauses take the indicative ('There it is') and indefinite clauses the subjunctive ('There it may be'). As we have seen, the vast majority of all local clauses in OE—definite and indefinite—have the indicative. Where the subjunctive does occur, it is due, not to the nature of the local clause, but to special factors in the context in which it occurs.

13. CORRELATION AND CLAUSE ORDER

§2514. Conjunctions such as *þær (þær)* can of course appear without a correlative adverb, e.g. *ÆCHom* ii. 104. 29 *Ne behyde ge eowerne goldhord on eorðan þær ðær omm and moððan hit awestað, and ðeofas adelfað and forstelað; ac hordiað eowerne goldhord on heofenum, þær ne cymð to ne om ne moððe, ne þeofas ne delfað ne ne ætbredað*. When a correlative adverb is present, it need not be in initial position in its clause, e.g. *ÆCHom* ii. 64. 29 . . . *forðan ðe we tocnawað urne cyning Crist and his rice and ure rice ðær awritene, þær we ær swilce be oðrum mannum gereccednysse ræddon*. But it frequently is, e.g. (with the principal clause, which may be in dependent speech, first) *Bo* 90. 6 (§2516) and *ÆCHom* i. 38. 12 *Ðas word geswuteliað þæt ðær wunað Godes sibbe, þær se goda willa bið*, and (with the principal clause second) *ÆCHom* i. 132. 28 . . . *þonne understande he þisne drihtenlican cwyde, þæt þær bið soð ærist, ðær ðær beoð wepende eagan and cearcigende teð* and *ÆCHom* ii. 386. 24 *þær þær ic sylf beo, þær bið min ðen*. The principal clause usually follows the subordinate clause in correlated sentences in the prose. On Carkeet's claim (1976, p. 52) that it does so 'almost exclusively', see Mitchell, at press (*c*). On the order in the poetry see ibid. and §§2448-9.

§2515. Most of the examples cited in these sections involve correlative *þær* because most of the local clauses in OE are introduced by *þær*. But examples with correlative *þanon* and correlative *þider* do occur and some are quoted. *þær, þider*, and *þanon*, can also occur in correlation with words other than themselves when the sense or the preference of the author requires. So we find *gehwær þær* in *ÆCHom* i. 292. 15, *hider . . . þær* in *PPs* 72. 8, *swa hwar swa . . . þar* in *Exod* 10. 23, *þider þær* in *Sat* 216, *þiderweard þær* in *Met* 20. 159, *þider . . . þær þær* in *Alc* 105. 23 (§2455), *þider (. . .) þonan ðe* in *Bo* 5. 4 and 57. 29 (both in §2469), and *to þæs . . . þær* in *Dan* 41 (§2476). Whether *þa . . . þær* in *PPs* 106. 6 and *Ðær . . . þonne* in *PPs* 70. 20 are correlative is a matter of terminology.

§2516. It is clear from the examples of clauses of place so far quoted that when the adverb and the conjunction are distinguished in form, the conjunctions are *þær þær*, not *þær þe*, but *þanon þe* and *þider þe*, not *þanon þanon* and *þider þider*, e.g. *Bo* 90. 6 *Ic ðe tæhte þa þ þær wære ðæt hehstæ god þær þær þa good ealle gegadrade bioð* and *ÆCHom* ii. 104. 32 *Soðlice ðær ðær þin goldhord is, þær bið þin heorte* but *CP* 391. 12 . . . *7 ðonon ðe hi utan bioð ahæfene, ðanon hie bioð innan afeallene, ÆCHom* ii. 132. 5 *and þu ðonon on idelum wuldre befealle wiðinnan, þonon ðe ðu wiðutan on wurð-mynte ahafen bist, CP* 65. 16 *ðonne ne magon ðider fullice becuman ða stæpas ðæs weorces ðieder ðe he wilnað*, and *ÆCHom* i. 52. 5 *þider ðe Stephanus forestop . . . ðider folgode Paulus*. There are very occasional examples of *þider þider*, e.g. *Bo* 108. 3 *Ongit nu hu un-mehtige þa yflan men bioð, nu hi ne magon cuman ðider ðider ða ungewittigan gesceafta wilniað to tocumanne*, but I have noted none with *þider . . . þider þider, þanon þanon*, or *þanon . . . þanon þanon*. This may be the result of faulty observation on my part. On *þær þe* see §§2456-7.

§2517. We have already seen in §§2444-5 that a single *þær* appear-ing as the first element in its clause without a correlative can be ambiguous in examples like *ÆCHom* i. 130. 28 *þa rican bearn beoð aworpene into ðam yttrum ðeostrum, þær bið wop and toða gebitt* and *ÆCHom* i. 130. 32 *and he awyrpð hi on ða yttran þeostru, ðær bið wop and toða gebitt*, which Thorpe translates '. . . into utter darkness, there shall be weeping and gnashing of teeth' and '. . . into utter darkness, where there is weeping and gnashing of teeth' respec-tively, and *ÆCHom* ii. 348. 8 . . . *on oðre stowe bebyriged; þær beoð æteowde his geearnunga þurh wundrum*, where Thorpe (despite his semi-colon) translates *þær* as 'where'. On these, which can be com-pared with *ÆCHom* i. 130. 20 *þurh ða twegen dælas, eastdæl and westdæl, sind getacnode ða feower hwemmas ealles middangeardes, of þam beoð gegaderode Godes gecorenan of ælcere mægðe*, where the *of þam* clause has VS, see §2525.

§2518. The fact that the adverb and conjunction are different in form in the six examples quoted in the first sentence in §2516 means of course that the problem of the ambiguous adverb/conjunction does not arise in them. But the fact that in the examples involving *þær* and *þider* the principal clauses have the order VS and the subordinate clauses S(. . .)V demonstrates the well-known truth that element order can also serve as a guide. This is not so in the two sentences involving *þanon* because in them the presence of *ond* produces the order S(. . .)V in the principal clause, so giving it an order similar to that in the subordinate clause. The reliability of element order as a guide has already been discussed for the poetry in §§2445–7 and the warning has been given in §2444 that 'it is dangerous to be too confident' about its reliability in the prose. Andrew (*SS*, §34) lays it down that, in the prose, clauses with *þær* S(. . .)V must be subordinate and clauses with *þær* VS 'which are admittedly principal sentences as a rule' can be subordinate. Let us start by considering the situation in Ælfric.

§2519. We frequently find that when two correlative clauses are introduced by *þær*, the principal clause has VS and the subordinate S(. . .)V, e.g. *ÆCHom* i. 288. 25 *forði þær þæt gemynd bið þær bið þæt andgit and se willa* and (with *þær þær* in the subordinate clause) *ÆCHom* ii. 386. 24 *þær þær ic sylf beo, þær bið min ðen*. Sentences with only one *þær* clause which has VS in what the context shows is a principal clause include *ÆCHom* i. 132. 20 *þær beoð þonne geferlæhte on anre susle, þa þe on life on mandædum geðeodde wæron* and *ÆCHom* i. 132. 25 *þær bið wop and toða gebitt, forðan ðe ða eagan tyrað on ðam micclum bryne*, while a single *þær* (*þær*) clause which seems clearly subordinate has S(. . .)V in *ÆCHom* i. 62. 24 *þa becom se apostol æt sumum sæle to þære byrig Pergamum, þær ða foresædan cnihtas iu ær eardodon* and *ÆCHom* ii. 104. 29 *Ne behyde ge eowerne goldhord on eorðan þær ðær omm and moððan hit awestað*.

§2520. But this distinction can break down. Principal clauses frequently lose the order SV under the influence of *ond*, e.g. the sentences with *þanon* in §2516, *ÆLS* 31. 323 . . . *and þær nan man næfde nan þing synderlices*, and *ÆLS* 31. 334 . . . *and þær hnesce gewæda wæron to læhtre getealde*, but need not, e.g. *ÆCHom* i. 182. 14 *And þær wæs micel gærs on ðære stowe*.

§2521. But Ælfric has SV in some *þær* clauses not influenced by *ond* which seem to be principal, e.g. *ÆCHom* ii. 442. 32 *þæt þæt Martha dyde, þær we sind; þæt þæt Maria dyde, to ðam we hopiað* and *ÆC Hom* ii. 556. 18 *Se unholda ðeowa wearð ða aworpen on þam yttrum þeostrum, forðan ðe he ðolode ðurh wite þa yttran blindnysse seðe ær, ðurh his gylt, on ðam inrum þeostrum befeoll. Ðær he ðolað neadunge þeostra ðurh wrace, seðe ær lustlice forbær his unlustes þeostra* (on these see §2525) and VS in some subordinate clauses. This latter fact, I would urge, is proved by its appearance in clauses introduced by *þær þær*, since such doubling is one of Ælfric's favourite ways of indicating subordination. Examples include both adjective clauses of place, e.g. *ÆCHom* ii. 370. 3 *On ðam dæge abær se Ælmihtiga Godes Sunu urne lichaman to ðam heofonlican eðle, þær ðær næfre ær ne becom nan ðing ðæs gecyndes* and *ÆCHom* ii. 294. 17 *Ða gelæhton hine þa hæðenan, and gelæddon to heora deofolgylde, þær ðær wæs an ormæte draca*, and adverb clauses of place, e.g. *ÆCHom* i. 132. 28 . . . *þonne understande he þisne drihtenlican cwyde, þæt þær bið soð ærist, ðær ðær beoð wepende eagan and cearcigende teð* and *ÆCHom* i. 532. 4 *Gif hwam twynige be æriste, þonne mæg he understandan on þisum godspelle, þæt þær bið soð ærist þær ðær beoð eagan and teð*. So it seems reasonable to argue that similar clauses with *þær* VS can be subordinate; possible examples include *ÆCHom* ii. 104. 31 *ac hordiað eowerne goldhord on heofenum, þær ne cymð to ne om ne moððe* (where *ne* brings the verb before the subject) and *ÆCHom* ii. 152. 27 *His lic wearð bebyrged on Lindisfarneiscre cyrcan, þær wurdon geworhte wundra forwel fela ðurh geearnungum his eadigan lifes*. On the absence from my Ælfric collections of examples like ✩*þær is þin goldhord þær bið þin heorte*, see §§2525 and 2526.

§2522. In texts other than those by Ælfric we also find occasional examples with VS in what can be taken as subordinate clauses. They include *Bo* 7. 19 *Sende þa digellice ærendgewritu to þam kasere to Constentinopolim, þær is Creca heahburg 7 heora cynestol, forþam se kasere wæs heora ealdhlafordcynnes* and *Or* 34. 27 *On ðære ylcan tide ricsade Baleus se cyning in Assirin, þær ær wæs Ninus*, which can be compared with *Or* 28. 5 *7 þone westsceatan man hæt Libeum; þær is seo burh neah þe man hæt Libeum*. Andrew (*SS*, §24) cites the last of these as an example in which *þær* must mean 'where' because the Latin has *ubi*. Sweet's semi-colon, which is inconsistent with his comma in *Or* 34. 27 above, implies the contrary view. I see in these three examples the ambiguous adverb/conjunction discussed in §§2444-9 and accept the probability that different readers gave different intonation to such sentences.

§2523. Andrew (*SS*, §24) would similarly see *þær* V(. . .)S in sub-ordinate clauses in *Bede* 324. 9, *Or* 104. 7, and *Or* 160. 4, in all of which the Latin has *ubi*. Space does not permit me to quote these passages in full. But in all three Andrew's punctuation produces an unacceptably complicated construction. Here at any rate we can believe that the order VS demonstrates that we have principal clauses. I am inclined to think the same of the last three examples which Andrew quotes in *SS*, §20, viz. *Or* 14. 10, 138. 12, and 176. 16.

§2524. Andrew (*SS*, §21) quotes four examples from texts out-side Ælfric with SV in what the editors punctuate as principal clauses, but which he says are subordinate. In some, his explanations seem reasonable without compelling acceptance. For *CP* 115. 20 *He cuæð to him ðæt he wære his gelica: ðær he gecyðde his eaðmodnesse*, he suggests the meaning 'whereby he showed his humility'. In *ChronA* 22. 6 (607) *þar man sloh eac cc preosta*, he suggests scribal omis-sion of an *7* which would account for the order SV. This solution may have been a better one for *ChronA* 18. 15 (565) . . . *and heora cyng him gesealde þæt igland þe man Ii nemnað. þar syndon fif hida þæs ðe man seggað. þar se Columban getimbrade mynster* than his suggestion that 'we have an obvious antecedent to *þar* in *þæt igland þe man Ii nemnað* just [!] before'. The fourth example is *Matt (WSCp)* 18. 20 *Ðær twegen oððe þry synt on minum naman ge-gaderode, þær ic eom on hyra midlene*, Latin *ubi enim sunt duo uel tres congregati in nomine meo ibi sum in medio eorum*. Here both clauses in the OE have SV, which in the absence of a doubled con-junction *þær þær* would create real ambiguity if it were regularly used. Andrew says that 'there can be little doubt that in the English a conjunction [equivalent to Lat. *enim*] has been omitted which would make the order normal'. *Ac* could account for the order and sometimes has a causal sense; see §1770. But it does not fit this context. *Forþon*, which occurs in *Matt(Li)* 18. 20, might suit the context, but is unlikely to produce SV; consider *ÆCHom* i. 288. 25 *forði þær þæt gemynd bið, þær bið þæt andgit and se willa*. I am inclined to think that in *Matt(WSCp)* 18. 20 the natural gloss *ic eom* for Lat. *sum* became fossilized as the text was quoted but produced no serious ambiguity because the text was so well known.

§2525. Here again, I have to confess that my collections are not complete and that there is room for further work. I have no doubt that future investigators will find more exceptions or apparent exceptions to the strong tendency for prose clauses with *þær* VS to be principal and clauses with *þær* S(. . .)V to be subordinate. So I would warn them against the danger of erecting these tendencies into rules. A great stylist like Ælfric was the master of his medium. He uses the regular SV followed by VS in *ÆCHom* i. 52. 5 *þider ðe Stephanus forestop, mid Saules stanum oftorfod, ðider folgode Paulus gefultum-od þurh Stephanes gebedu* to create a balanced yet doubly chiastic sentence; see *Guide*, § 150. But he is ready to depart from this norm when it suits him for rhythmic, stylistic, or pedagogic, reasons *provided significant ambiguity does not result*. The desire to avoid such ambiguity accounts for his reluctance to use the *þær* SV *þær* SV pattern seen in *Matt(WSCp)* 18. 20 (§ 2524) or the *þær* VS *þær* VS pattern; see § 2521. But he is prepared to use SV in a principal clause in *ÆCHom* ii. 442. 32 (§ 2521) to achieve parallelism and in *ÆCHom* ii. 556. 18 (§ 2521) to achieve parallelism and to stress the relationship between *he* and *seðe* which would have been less obvious had he written ☆*Ðær ðolað he. . . .* (I do not think that he wanted the *Ðær* clause to be subordinate to *þeostrum*.) He is also prepared to use VS in subordinate clauses which are clearly marked by initial *þær þær*; see § 2521. But no ambiguity of meaning arises with the ambiguous adverb/conjunction discussed in § 2517. In such situations Ælfric was probably content to leave it to his Anglo-Saxon readers to decide whether *þær* meant 'there' or 'where'; cf. Campbell's remark about the poetry quoted in § 2445.

§ 2526. None the less, a modern reader or translator will need to have good reason for taking a clause with *þær* SV in the prose as principal or with *þær* VS as subordinate. Thorpe was wrong to translate *ÆCHom* i. 38. 12 *Ðas word geswuteliað þæt ðær wunað Godes sibb þær se goda willa bið* as 'These words manifest that where the peace of God dwelleth, there is good will.' Andrew (*SS*, § 109) was wrong to tack *ÆCHom* i. 52. 7 *þær nis Paulus gescynd þurh Stephanes slege, ac Stephanus gladað on Paules gefærrædene; forðan þe seo soðe lufu on heora ægðrum blissað* on to *ÆCHom* i. 52. 5 (§ 2525) in order to make a single period of the two. He was also wrong to insist (*SS*, § 21) that *ond* must be missing before *þær* in *ÆCHom* i. 386. 11 *Ic eom se Hælend þe ðu ehtst: ac aris nu, and far forð to ðære byrig; þær ðe bið gesæd hwæt ðe gedafenige to donne* because *Acts* 9. 6 reads *et ibi dicetur tibi . . .* and because *and* appears before *ðær* in *ÆCHom* i. 124. 22 *Ga inn to ðære ceastre and ðær þe bið gesæd hwæt þe gedafenað to donne*. The sweep of the two OE sentences is completely different and I find it hard to believe that Ælfric would have written *ond* before *þær* in *ÆCHom* i. 386. 11. The only example Burkhart (p. 206) quotes to illustrate a group of 109 examples of *þær* translating *ubi* or *ibi* in which, he claims, the

'interpretation either *there* or *where*' is possible is *John(WSCp)* 4. 46
7 he com eft to Chanaa Galilee þær he worhte þæt win of wætere,
Latin *uenerat ergo iterum in Cana Galilaeae ubi fecit aquam uinum*.
An example with VS would have been more convincing.

§2527. In the poetry, there is more room for doubt; see §§2445-7.
So, as Yamakawa (1971, pp. 7-9) points out, *þær* in

Sea 1   Mæg ic be me sylfum   soðgied wrecan,
                 siþas secgan,   hu ic geswincdagum
                 earfoðhwile   oft þrowade,
                 bitre breostceare   gebiden hæbbe,
                 gecunnad in ceole   cearselda fela,
                 atol yþa gewealc,   þær mec oft bigeat
                 nearo nihtwaco   æt nacan stefnan,
                 þonne he be clifum cnossað

may mean 'there' or 'where'. But I cannot myself see why he does
not allow the same ambiguity in

Sea 23   Stormas þær stanclifu beotan,   þær him stearn oncwæð
                 isigfeþera;   ful oft þæt earn bigeal,
                 urigfeþra;   ne ænig hleomæga
                 feasceaftig ferð   frefran meahte,

where he takes the second *þær* as 'where'.

§2528. Similar problems arise in clauses introduced by *þa* and
þonne; see §§2543-60.

14. CO-ORDINATION

§2529. Clauses of place occur in both asyndetic and syndetic parataxis. Examples of the former include (with the subordinating conjunction not repeated)

Beo 2047   Meaht ðu, min wine,   mece gecnawan,
                 þone þin fæder   to gefeohte bær
                 under heregriman   hindeman siðe,
                 dyre iren,   þær hyne Dene slogon,
                 weoldon wælstowe . . . ,

(with the conjunction repeated)

Fates 117   . . . þæt we þæs botles   brucan motan,
                 hames in hehðo,   þær is hihta mæst,
                 þær cyning engla   clænum gildeð
                 lean unhwilen,

and (with different conjunctions) *ÆHom* 6. 43 . . . *and comon on þone feorðan dæg þæs þe he bebyrged wæs to Bethanian wic, þær he bebyrged wæs, þanon wæron to Ierusalem fiftene furlang.* Examples of syndetic parataxis include (with the conjunction not repeated) *ÆCHom* i. 464. 24 . . . *and far to westene, þær nan fugel ne flyhð ne yrðling ne erað ne mannes stemn ne swegð, Sat* 24, and

Beo 1512   Ða se eorl ongeat,
             þæt he in niðsele   nathwylcum wæs,
             þær him nænig wæter   wihte ne sceþede,
             ne him for hrofsele   hrinan ne mehte
             færgripe flodes,

and (with the conjunction repeated) *ÆCHom* i. 298. 22 . . . *and ða bec þurhwuniað on cristenre ðeode, ægðer ge ðær þær ða apostoli lichamlice bodedon, ge þær ðær hi na ne becomon.*

F. CLAUSES OF TIME

1. INTRODUCTORY REMARKS

§2530. The most common method of classifying temporal clauses is that adopted by Wülfing (ii, 103–22 and 685), Adams (p. 9), Möllmer (pp. vii–viii), and others. This divides them into six groups, viz. clauses denoting time when, immediate sequence, and duration; clauses determining the time of an action by reference to a preceding and to a subsequent action; and finally, clauses indicating the time of the termination of the action of the main clause. These headings are a roundabout—and potentially confusing (see §3155)—way of saying that adverb clauses of time can be introduced by conjunctions meaning 'when', 'as soon as', 'while', 'after', 'before', and 'until'. In practice, this is more useful than Callaway's threefold division according to whether the action is antecedent to, subsequent to, or contemporaneous with, that of the main clause (Callaway 1931, *passim*) —which (Behre, p. 164, observes) 'lead[s], if taken seriously, to a false conception of the subjunctive in temporal clauses in OE'. The sixfold classification involves some repetition. As Adams (p. 10) puts it, 'there are many cases in which *ða* might be translated *while* or *after*, just as the modern English *when* is often used to introduce clauses which logically bear such relations to the main clause; but whatever may be the different meanings which might be assigned to the particle, they certainly have no influence on its syntax'. I can, however, see no practical alternative to it.

§2531. Adams (for the prose) and Möllmer (for prose and poetry) give statistics and examples. It must, however, be said that Adams's collections are not complete, even for the texts in his corpus; that he does not always give references for the number of examples he claims to have found; and that, since he classifies -*on* as preterite indicative and -*en* as preterite subjunctive, there are more examples in which the mood of the verb is ambiguous than he says there are. Liggins (1970, *passim* and fn. 12) offers comments on, and gives tables (based on Adams) for the use of temporal conjunctions in 'Alfredian' prose. My D.Phil. thesis lists all the examples in the poetry. I must leave it to someone else to produce tables for all OE texts based on full concordances. But until this is done, the work by Adams will remain an indispensable source of examples which Möllmer and Visser (ii, §879) occasionally augment. Space does not permit me to reproduce everything they say which is worthy of note. But I have attempted to include what is important and to supplement and qualify their work when necessary throughout my discussion of temporal clauses.

§2532. Johnsen (*Ang.* 38 (1914), 83–100, and 39 (1916), 101–20) found a local-demonstrative adverbial origin for a large number of adverbs and conjunctions of time, including *æfter þæm þe, ær, forþ þæt* 'until', *oð* alone and in combination with *þæt* and/or *þe, siþþan, sona, þæs þe, þæt* 'until', *þa, þe* 'when' (but see §§2594-6), and *þonne*. These articles display singlemindedness, but in general do not carry conviction. Reference is made to them in the appropriate section when necessary.

§2533. Since the saying *post hoc ergo propter hoc* is sometimes true, temporal clauses sometimes acquire a causal colouring. Examples are given in the sections which follow, but fuller treatments will be found in Liggins 1955 and van Dam. Elements of concession and condition may also be detected in temporal clauses; see the General Index. It may, however, be said that the idea of time is rarely—if ever—completely eliminated; see, for example, Adams, p. 11, and Liggins 1955, pp. 310-15 and 544. This is in my opinion true even of *þa* in *CP* 401. 24 and *Or* 48. 14 (despite van Dam, p. 66)[93] and of *siþþan* in *Bo* 104. 28, *CP* 465. 17, and *ÆLS* 25. 76 (despite Liggins 1955, p. 310).

[93] There seems to be something wrong in *Or* 48. 14. The sense is incomplete when compared with the Latin. If *þa* is a subordinating conjunction and *þe* is allowed to stand, there is no principal clause in the OE sentence. In van Dam's third example, *Bede* 86. 4 (pp. 66-7), MS *B* has the correct reading *gescead þ*; *þa* is due to the Latin *discretio quae*.

§2534. The use of temporal adverbs in non-dependent clauses is discussed in the sections which follow. Two co-ordinate clauses may be related temporally, e.g. *ChronA* 78. 5 (883) *Her for se here up on Scald to Cundoþ 7 þær sæt an gear*, where the first clause could be replaced by a subordinate *þa* clause, and

And 629　　　Hwæt frinest ðu me,　　frea leofesta,
　　　　　　　wordum wrætlicum,　　ond þe wyrda gehwære
　　　　　　　þurh snyttra cræft　　soð oncnawest?

where *ond* could almost be translated 'when'. Participial and absolute constructions can also express time; see again the General Index.

§2535. On the use of 'modal' auxiliaries in temporal clauses see Standop, pp. 53-5 (*magan*), 89 (**motan*), 114 (**sculan*), and 151 (*willan*).

2. THE AMBIGUOUS ADVERB/CONJUNCTIONS

§2536. It is sometimes difficult to decide whether clauses introduced by *þa* and *þonne* and (less frequently) by *ær*, *nu*, and *siþþan*—all of which can serve as both adverbs or conjunctions—are principal or subordinate. *Mutatis mutandis*, the points made in §§2444-9 about clauses introduced by *þær* are relevant here. First, the difficulty arises less frequently in the prose than in the poetry because element order is more regular in the former. On this see §§2539-60. Second, the use of modern punctuation forces editors into unnecessary decisions on this point. Campbell (1970, p. 95), after asking whether *Ða* in

Beo 917　　　　　　　　　　　　Ða wæs morgenleoht
　　　　　　　scofen ond scynded.　　Eode scealc monig
　　　　　　　swiðhicgende　　to sele þam hean
　　　　　　　searowundor seon

was to be translated 'Then' or 'When' observed: 'I think that such passages were open to personal interpretation, and that reciters would indicate their view of the passage by intonation.' This is perceptive and I accept without hesitation the idea that a choice existed. But I feel—and I use the word deliberately—that Campbell may have presented that choice in starker terms than the actual situation warranted and that there may have been an intermediate stage between 'Then' and 'When'. I pursue this question at greater length in *NQ* 223 (1978), 390-4, and in *RES* 31 (1980), 395-412. Third, the 'curious superstition' which permits the subordination of a temporal clause in poetry only when it follows the principal clause is apparent in the treatment of *þa* and *þonne* clauses; see Andrew, *Postscript*, pp. vii–viii, 4–5, 9, and 20, and my §§1898–9. That Andrew has a point which deserves investigation is suggested by the following entries from a table given by Möllmer (pp. 9–10) to show the position of *þa* clauses in their sentences:

Text	after principal clause	within principal clause	before principal clause
Beowulf	28	8	1
Genesis *A* and *B*	41	10	5
A-S Chronicle	14	1	98

An illustration of the effect of this 'superstition' can be gained from a consideration of Klaeber's punctuation of

Beo 321   Guðbyrne scan
        heard hondlocen,   hringiren scir
        song in searwum,   þa hie to sele furðum
        in hyra gryregeatwum   gangan cwomon.
        Setton sæmeþe   side scyldas,
        rondas regnhearde   wið þæs recedes weal;
        bugon þa to bence,——   byrnan hringdon,
        guðsearo gumena;   garas stodon,
        sæmanna searo   samod ætgædere,
        æscholt ufan græg;   wæs se irenþreat
        wæpnum gewurþad,

where Andrew (*SS*, p. 76, and *Postscript*, pp. 50 and 90)—rightly in my opinion—attached the *þa* clause to what follows. His translation reads: 'as soon as they had reached the hall [and], sea-wearied men, had set their broad shields against the wall, [they bowed to the bench]'. I prefer to take *setton* and *bugon* as the verbs of two principal clauses in asyndetic parataxis and to punctuate lines 323b–27a as a parenthesis within the verse paragraph; note the parallelism of the verbs *song* and *hringdon*. Another illustration is to be found in

Beo 1465   Huru ne gemunde   mago Ecglafes
        eafoþes cræftig,   þæt he ær gespræc
        wine druncen,   þa he þæs wæpnes onlah
        selran sweordfrecan;   selfa ne dorste
        under yða gewin   aldre geneþan,
        drihtscype dreogan;   þær he dome forleas,
        ellenmærðum.

If we follow Carleton Brown (*PMLA* 53 (1938), 915) in putting the semi-colon after *druncen*, we change the emphasis: cowardice was primarily responsible for Unferth's action. Andrew (*SS*, p. 76, and

Postscript, p. 54) takes *onlah* and *dorste* as parallel, translating 'When he lent his weapon to a better swordsman [and] did not dare himself to hazard his life, then he lost glory. . . .' But my own inclination here is to take the *þa* clause *apo koinou* as an element in the verse paragraph; see §3799.

§2537. But it would be worse than foolish to assert that Möllmer's table and examples like the last two prove that the editors of *Beowulf*, *Genesis A*, and *Genesis B*, mispunctuated. The interpretation of the examples is a matter of opinion and the table could equally well reflect a real difference between the syntax of these poems and of the *Chronicle* which the editors correctly interpreted. Samuels, in his reviews of *Postscript* (*MÆ* 18 (1949), 60–4) and of Brooks's *Andreas* (*RES* 14 (1963), 175–7), touched on this problem and gave some reasons for the view that what Andrew objected to was more than a 'curious superstition', reasons which he generously elaborated in private communications in 1978. First, he suggested, 'there is, in Germanic alliterative verse, an undoubted preference for postmodification (and parataxis where relevant)' (p. 176). We may see here the influence of what Heusler termed *Zeilenstil*: 'in the early tradition the beginning of both sentence and whole-line coincided', whereas *Bogen-* or *Hakenstil*, in which sentences often begin in *b*-lines, is later (p. 61). If this is so, 'it must follow that all subordinate clauses starting in the second half-line must, originally in the tradition at least, be regarded as "trailing" . . . and not anticipatory or periodic. That, at least, would account for the preferences of earlier editors, especially the German ones; and it is certainly somewhat firmer than a mere "curious superstition"' (private communication). However, this would not apply to examples like

Beo 126   Ða wæs on uhtan   mid ærdæge
                 Grendles guðcræft   gumum undyrne;
                 þa wæs æfter wiste   wop up ahafen,
                 micel morgensweg,

where both clauses or sentences start at the beginning of a line and the sequence 'when . . . then' could have developed as the language moved from parataxis to hypotaxis; see Stanley, *CB*, pp. 120–2, and my §2424. Second, this punctuation could reflect a natural tendency in native English prose and poetry towards a loose or 'trailing' sentence structure as opposed to the periodic 'When . . . then' seen in much OE prose, which could have developed under the influence of Latin authors and/or rhetorical handbooks. (I would add a native movement towards hypotaxis as a possible contributory factor.) The traditional punctuation would then presuppose or assume that this was not extended to the poetry, possibly for the very reason that it was felt to be 'prosaic'. Third, Samuels anticipated Enkvist and Foster (see § 2554)—but not, of course, Andrew; see § 2546—in the suggestion that *þa* is frequently a resumptive or narrative connecting particle. So, he argued, when it 'stands second and is enclitic, it is difficult to see how it could retain the full adverbial force required for correlation' (p. 61).

§ 2538. I make no attempt to prove that Andrew was right or wrong. But I do assert that the continuing failure or refusal of editors of OE poems to consider the problem he raised is a neglect of editorial responsibility. A striking demonstration will be found in the inconsistency of the punctuation of *þa* clauses in the ASPR text of *Maldon* (published after *SS* but before *Postscript*); for examples compare *Mald* 5 with *Mald* 143 and *Mald* 84 with *Mald* 260. Sweet, *R*. 15 (published in 1967, well after both), agrees in essentials with ASPR.

§ 2539. In the prose, element order is a valuable guide in determining whether a clause introduced by an adverb/conjunction is principal or subordinate. What are generally regarded as unambiguous patterns are Conj. S(. . .)V, adv. VS, e.g. *ÆCHom* ii. 166. 18 *ac ær se ærendraca mihte to ðam gebroðrum becuman, ær hæfde se deofol towend þone weall, ÆCHom* i. 304. 29 *syððan se geleafa sprang geond ealne middangeard, siððan geswicon ða wundra, BlHom* 219. 17 *Ða he þa hwile on ðæm gebede wæs, þa færinga wearð se deada man cwic eft,* and (with doubled ða in the subordinate clause) *ÆCHom* i. 10. 28 *Ðaða hi ealle hæfdon þysne ræd betwux him gefæstnod, þa becom Godes grama ofer hi ealle,* and (less frequent) Adv. VS, conj. S(. . .)V, e.g. *ÆCHom* i. 30. 10 *Ða gelamp hit, þaða hi on þære byrig Bethleem wicodon, þæt hire tima wæs gefylled . . .* and *BlHom* 175. 12 *nu is min yfel twyfeald, nu Paulus þæt ilce læreþ.* The different arrangements with clauses introduced by *þa* sometimes reflect a difference in the time-reference of the verb of the subordinate clause; see § 3201. These arrangements are, however, unusual with *ær, nu,* and *siþþan,* for SV is not infrequently found in sentences introduced by these words when they are used adverbially, e.g. *ÆCHom* ii. 376. 15 *Ær he het faran to strætum and to wicum. . . . Nu he het faran to wegum and to hegum . . .* and *ÆCHom* ii. 484. 2 *Ic hate healdan hi and eow, oðþæt heora sagu afandod sy; siððan we witon hwilce we sceolon gearwurðian, hwilce fordeman.*

§ 2540. The subject usually precedes the verb in both principal and subordinate clauses introduced by *ær*. But I have found no examples involving real ambiguity. The context is often decisive. But there are grammatical clues. First, the adv. *ær* in initial position and the conj. *ær* are not often used correlatively. The adverb may be used internally, e.g. *ÆCHom* ii. 140. 1 [*God*], *seðe giu ær Elian afedde þurh ðone sweartan hremm, ær he to heofonan siðode*, and/or may be correlative with *ærþæm (þe)*, e.g. *BlHom* 169. 24 . . . *buton þæt he ær eode beforan Criste ærðæm þe he beforan him sylfan gangan mihte* and *Mart 2* 172. 1 *ær ic me sylfne ofslea mid mine sweorde, ærðon ic sende mine hond on þas fæmnan*. Second, the subordinate clause frequently has the subjunctive, e.g. *ÆCHom* ii. 252. 34 *ær hi sind gebundene, ær hi beon geborene* and (with both mood and element order significant) *ChronC* 186. 4 (1055) *ac ær þær wære ænig spere gescoten ær fleah ðæt Englisce folc*. A third possible clue is that an *ær* clause with the order S . . . V is very likely to be subordinate, as in *ÆCHom* ii. 140. 1 above. I have, however, noted no examples of *ær* . . . *ær* sequences in which this alone is decisive.

§2541. The only ambiguity I have detected in the pattern *nu . . . nu* —in which there is of course a strong causal element—is the grammatical one of deciding whether we have two independent clauses or one principal and one subordinate. This problem arises in *Or* 14. 5 *Nu hæbbe we awriten þære Asian suþdæl; nu wille we fon to hire norðdæle*, Latin *Et quoniam meridianam partem Asiae descripsimus; superest ut ab oriente ad septentrionem pars, quae restat, expediatur*, and in *Or* 14. 26 *Nu hæbbe we scortlice gesæd ymbe Asia londgemæro; nu wille we ymbe Europe londgemære areccean* . . . , Latin *Expliciti sunt quam brevissime fines Asiae; nunc Europam . . . stylo pervagabor*. Andrew (*SS*, §36) claims that in *Or* 14. 5 (not, as he wrongly says, *Or* 14. 26) 'the Latin (*Quoniam descripsimus*) certifies the first sentence as subordinate'. If this were a valid argument, then the Latin would certify that both sentences in *Or* 14. 26 are principal clauses, whereas Andrew gives the translation 'Now that we have briefly spoken about Asia we will go on to describe the boundaries of Europe.' This further illustrates the dangers of believing that the Latin original can be decisive. Campbell (1970, p. 96) translates the first sentence in *Or* 14. 26 'Now that we have briefly told . . .' and explains it as an example of analogical extension of the order VS to a subordinate clause with a pronominal subject under the influence of the law of sentence-particles. This may be so. In my opinion, however, the possibility remains that in these examples we have two simple sentences in parataxis. But if we decide that we have a complex sentence, the context will tell us that in each example the first clause is subordinate. Other guides include the position of the adverb, the tense of the verb, and clause or element order. In my opinion, it is not certain whether we have a subordinate *nu* clause in the following sentences: *CP* 311. 17 *Nu ge habbað geleafan, wyrceað nu god weorc*, *CP* 377. 21 *Nu ðonne, nu ða lichomlican læcas ðus scyldige gerehte sint, nu is to ongietanne æt hu micelre scylde ða beoð befangne* . . . , *Or* 110. 9 *Nu ic þyses Alexandres her gemyndgade, cwæð Orosius, nu ic wille eac þæs maran Alexandres gemunende beon* . . . , and *LS* 8. 360 *Nu ic hæbbe eall þis gesæd swa hit gelamp, nu bidde ic ðe*. . . . But if we do, there is no doubt about its identity.

§2542. *Mutatis mutandis*, the remarks made above about *nu* clauses hold for *siþþan* clauses. Consider the following examples: *Or* 90. 8 *Ac siþþan hie on Sicilium wunnon, hie eac siþþan betweonum him selfum winnende wæron* (position of adverb), *Bo* 129. 1 *Siððan we hit hatað wyrd siððan hit geworht bið; ær hit wæs Godes foreþanc* (element order, context, and tense), *ÆCHom* i. 108. 32 *ac syððan hi comon to Iudeiscum earde, syððan he wæs heora latteow* (context), *ÆCHom* i. 460. 24 *Se awyrigeda deofol, siððan he ðone frumsceapenan mann beswac, syððan he hæfde anweald on ungelyfedum mannum* . . . (sentence arrangement and element order), and of course *ÆCHom* i. 304. 29 (§2539) (element order).

§2543. With *þa* and *þonne*, however, the pattern Conj. S(. . .)V, adv. VS is well established in the prose of all periods, e.g. (with *þa*) *ChronA* 2. 11 (—), *ChronA* 87. 6 (894), *ChronD* 112. 29 (948), *ChronE* 133. 4 (999), *ChronE* 180. 3 (1052), *ChronE* 207. 7 (1070), and *ChronE* 245. 7 (1114) *Ða he to him com, þa neodde he him to þam biscoprice of Hrofeceastre*, and (with *þonne*) *Or* 21. 6, *BlHom* 17. 23, *ÆCHom* i. 210. 6 and 7, and *ChronE* 220. 10 (1086) *7 þonne se cyng wæs on Normandige, þonne wæs he mægest on þisum lande*. As already noted, Adv. VS, conj. S(. . .)V is less frequent. But see §1879.

§2544. When we come to consider the relationship between two successive *þa/þonne* clauses, we meet two problems. First, can a clause with *þa/þonne* VS be subordinate? The answer must, I think, be a matter of opinion. Rübens (pp. 38-9) argues that the first *þa* clause in *ChronA* 48. 11 (755) *Ða on morgenne gehierdun þæt þæs cyninges þegnas þe him be æftan wærun þæt se cyning ofslægen wæs, þa ridon hie þider* is subordinate to the second, thereby producing the only correlative *þa* . . . *þa* pattern in this annal and one which is irregular in that both clauses have VS. Whitelock (Sweet, *R.* 15, 2. 25) puts a full stop after *wæs*, thereby making two simple sentences out of what Rübens (loc. cit.) rightly said is the only sequence in this annal where two *þa* clauses follow one another without the interposition of *7*. That the order VS does occur in subordinate *þa* and *þonne* clauses has been strongly urged by Andrew. He argues (*SS*, §§ 11–13, 24, and 109) that in sequences of *þa* VS *þa* VS like those in *Bede* 118. 6, *Bede* 166. 28, *Or* 156. 29, and *Or* 234. 20 *Æfter þæm hiene mon het casere. þa bæd he þæt mon þone triumphan him ongean brohte. þa sende him mon ane blace hacelan angean, him on bismer, for triumphan*, 'there can be little doubt that the first sentence . . . should be taken as a temporal clause' (*SS*, § 11). His reason is that the Latin originals have subordinate *cum* clauses. But this is far from conclusive. These originals will be found respectively at *Bede* 156. 25, *Bede* 232. 8, *Or* 157. 23, and *Or* 235. 16. But a study of them demonstrates that we have no reason for believing that subordinate *cum* clauses must always be represented by subordinate *þa* clauses. The parallels are not always exact. In *Or* 234. 20, above, the Latin has *Cumque ab exercitu Imperator adpellatus esset, Romamque nuncios de victoria misisset. . . .* Andrew quotes this as '*cum nuncios de victoria misisset*'. Such selective and misleading quotation is, I fear, the norm rather than the exception. Although Andrew repeats that 'there can be little doubt', even this reservation soon disappears, for he goes on to claim that 'such passages establish quite clearly the *þa com he* type of subordinate clause as a genuine OE idiom' in which 'the juxtaposition usually demands correlation' (*SS*, § 12). This applies to biblical passages such as *Exod* 2. 12 *Ða beseah he hine ymbutan hider 7 ðyder, 7 geseah þæt þær nan man gehende næs; þa ofsloh he þone Egyptiscan 7 behydde hine on þam sande* and *Matt* 8. 18 (§ 2545) and 'especially to examples from the mature prose of Ælfric and his school' (*SS*, § 12) such as *ÆCHom* ii. 310. 1 *þa befran se arleasa casere, hwi he suwade. þa sæde se halga, þæt he spræce to Criste.*[94] In *SS*, § 38, he finds *þa* used as what he calls a ' "continuative" conjunction' in examples like *Or* 174. 2, where he misquotes and truncates the OE, and *ÆCHom* ii. 28. 21 *þa wicode heo be wege wið þære ea þe is gehaten Bagrade, and on ærnemerien siðode, swa swa heo gemynt hæfde. Ða geseah heo licgan ðone hring on ðam wege ætforan . . .* , where he would replace the full stop after *hæfde* with a comma and translate '. . . at daybreak she continued her journey as she had intended, when she saw the ring lying . . .'. It is, however, worth noting that in *ÆCHom*

---

[94] Andrew also takes *Gen(L)* 32. 25 *þa geseah he* as a subordinate clause without noting that MS *C* has *ða he geseah* (*SS*, § 11). In *SS*, § 9, however, he does make use of the alternative reading *Or(C)* 284. 33 *þa gefor he* because he does not want to accept *Or(L)* 284. 33 *þa he gefor*. It has to be said that such selective inconsistency is not uncommon in his work.

ii. 28. 16-25 there are no fewer than five clauses with *þa* VS, all punctuated by Thorpe as principal clauses. It is not immediately clear why Andrew links the *Ða geseah heo* clause with the preceding sentence and does not take it as a subordinate clause correlative with the following *þa wende heo*, thereby bringing it into line with *ÆCHom* ii. 310. 1, above. We cannot accurately represent with modern punctuation the way Ælfric intended *ÆCHom* ii. 28. 16-25 to be read. The intonation may well have varied from reader to reader. The same is true of *ÆCHom* i. 60. 21 *On ðam oðrum dæge eode se apostol be ðære stræt, þa ofseah he hwær sum uðwita lædde twegen gebroðru* . . . , which Andrew (replacing the colon Thorpe does not have after *stræt* by the comma which he does) translates 'On the second day he was going along the street when he saw . . .'. This is certainly possible. But Ælfric may have intended a longer pause after *stræt*, for the complex goes on until line 26. See further Mitchell 1980*a*, p. 392.

§2545. Campbell (1970, pp. 95-6), arguing that element order in OE prose was influenced by that of poetry, accepts as subordinate such clauses as the first in *Matt(WSCp)* 8. 18 *Ða geseah se hælend mycle menigeo ymbutan hyne. þa het he hig faran ofer þone muþan*, Latin *uidens autem Jesus turbas multas circum se iussit ire trans fretum*; cf. *ÆCHom* i. 478. 33. Like Andrew, he notes that the corresponding clause in the Latin is subordinate. But this element order, unusual in a subordinate clause, is due in his opinion to the fact that the writer desired to keep the verb unaccented and so was forced to put it immediately after *þa* instead of after the noun subject to avoid offending against the law of sentence-particles which obtained in the poetry. Again, we must accept this as a possibility. The fact that Campbell claims that *geseah* in *Matt* 8. 18 is unstressed whereas Andrew (*SS*, §11) says that it is stressed emphasizes the danger of imagining that one is a native informant of OE.

§2546. What, then, are we to make of those passages in which two successive clauses introduced by *þa* or *þonne* have the order VS? That both can be principal clauses is clear from passages like *ÆCHom* i. 452. 9-21 (*þa æfter ðrim dagum com. . . . þa com ðær stæppende sum uncuð cempa. . . . þa bead se bisceop . . .*) and *ÆCHom* ii. 52. 3-10 (*Ðonne andwyrt se godfæder. . . . þonne axað he eft. . . . þonne hæfð he wiðsacen . . . deofle. . . . Ðonne axað he gyt . . .* ; I cannot follow Andrew (*SS*, §24) when he suggests that this last clause may be subordinate). So the assumption accepted by Rübens and Andrew that two successive *þa/þonne* clauses must be correlative whatever the element order is untenable. (For another possible reason for rejecting this assumption, see Enkvist, *NM* 73 (1972), 96 fn. 1.) But it is also clear that a *þa/þonne* clause with VS can often be taken as subordinate by a modern reader. Were they so intended by the author or translator? Most of us will probably feel bound to answer 'Yes' at times. How often is a matter of choice, not principle. I believe that we have here further evidence for the proposition that in OE at any rate there was at least one intermediate stage between hypotaxis and parataxis and that the use of modern punctuation forces us into unnecessarily rigid distinctions. I suggest that in *ÆCHom* ii. 190. 1-6 the clauses beginning *ða gesette God . . .* and *ða awende Crist . . .* were taken as principal by some readers and subordinate by others; cf. Campbell's remarks on *Beo* 917 which I discuss in §2536. The same can be said of at least some of those examples in which Andrew construed *þa* as a ' "continuative" conjunction'; see *SS,* §38, and *Postscript,* §4, and my §2554. In *ÆCHom* i. 22. 10 *Ic wylle settan min wedd betwux me and eow to þisum behate; þæt is, þonne ic oferteo heofenas mid wolcnum, þonne bið æteowod min renboga betwux þam wolcnum, þonne beo ic gemyndig mines weddes, þæt ic nelle heonforð mancynn mid wætere adrencan,* the second *þonne* clause is used *apo koinou*; it is in a sense a principal clause to the first and a subordinate clause to the third clause introduced by *þonne.* The variations in the element order in the clauses containing *þa* in *ÆCHom* i. 168. 13-22 are for the modern scholar minatory rather than instructive. As the doubled conjunction and the element order show, *ðaða Crist hingrode . . .* is subordinate to and correlative with *ða wende se deofol. . . . Cwæð þa on his geðance . . .* may be a principal clause—in which case *þa smeade se deofol . . .* could be taken as subordinate to it—or, in the absence of a subject, may be semi-subordinate to *þa smeade se deofol . . .* taken as a principal clause. (A striking parallel will be found in *ÆCHom* ii. 418. 31-5.) *Ða fæste Crist . . .* could be taken as subordinate to and correlative with *ða on eallum þam fyrste ne cwæð se deofol. . . .* But if it is subordinate, why not ✩*þa þa Crist fæste . . .* ? (The same applies to *þa smeade se deofol . . .* above.) Such examples could be multiplied; consider *ÆCHom* i. 16. 27-18. 5 and *ÆCHom* ii. 150. 21-9. For more on this problem, see Mitchell 1980*a.*

§2547. The second of the two questions referred to in §2544 is this: Can a principal clause introduced by *þa* or *þonne* have the order SV or the order S . . . V?[95] Andrew (*SS,* §10) says that, in the prose,

---

[95] Clauses in which *þa* or *þonne* follows conjunctions like *ac, forþæm,* and *ond,* or interjections like *efne* and *hwæt,* must be considered separately, because of the possible influence

sentences of the type *þa he com*—a formula which, it would seem
from *SS*, §§ 1-5, can sometimes embrace both these orders; see
§ 2556 fn. 99—are 'unambiguously subordinate'. He extends this
conclusion to the pattern *þonne he stod* in *SS*, § 24. In my opinion,
he is too dogmatic.

§ 2548. 'The supposed instances' to the contrary (*SS*, § 10) which he
dismisses on his way to this conclusion (*SS*, chapters ii and iii) fall
into two different groups. First there are those in which a *þa/þonne*
S(. . .)V clause can be explained as subordinate to and correlative
with another clause. In some of these, Andrew's repunctuation almost
certainly gives the right syntax, e.g. *ChronA* 86. 3 (894), *ChronA*
87. 4 (894), *Or* 46. 7, *Gen* 31. 21 *þa he ferde mid þam ðingum ðe
hys on riht wæron.* [22] *þa cydde man Labane on þam ðriddan
dæge þæt Iacob wæs asceacen*, Latin *Cumque abiisset tam ipse quam
omnia quae iuris sui erant, nunciatum est Laban die tertio quod
fugeret Iacob*, and *ÆCHom* i. 172. 20 . . . *þonne bið he deofles
ðeowa, þonne he deofle gecwemð and þone forsihð ðe hine geworhte.*
Or(C) 284. 32 *þa he þæt geacsade 7 him ongeanweard wæs, þa gefor
he on þæm færelte*, where MS *L* has *þa he gefor* (see § 2544 fn.),
belongs here. So too may *ÆCHom* ii. 212. 19 and *ÆCHom* i. 418.
20 *Ða se eadiga Laurentius ðwoh heora ealra fet, and ða wudewan
fram hefigtimum heafodece gehælde. Eac sum ymesene man mid
wope his fet gesohte, biddende his hæle*, in which Andrew takes as
one sentence what Thorpe took as two. But some readers may prefer
Thorpe's version when they see these passages in context. There is
more room for disagreement when other examples are considered.
No doubt it was lack of space that forced Andrew to present many
passages in truncated versions. But this method had the for him
happy result of making many of his proposed correlations more convincing in his pages than they are in context. Examples include *Bede*
36. 33-38. 5, *Or* 62. 3-8, *BlHom* 225. 9-16, and *LS* 34. 526-30
(Andrew, *SS*, § 7, omits the initial *and* in this example), in all of
which the impact of the passage is weakened by the correlation.

§ 2549. The second group consists of examples from *Bede* in which
an OE clause with S(. . .)V must be principal not because the Latin
equivalent has a principal clause (as it usually does), but because of
the run of the OE sentence. Andrew points out that these can all be
regularized by assuming scribal corruption and/or the literal glossing

---

of these words on the element order; see § 3889 and compare, for example, *ÆCHom* ii.
32. 2 *Efne ða he aras* . . . with *ÆCHom* ii. 182. 28 *Efne ða on æfnunge, ðaða hi æt gereorde
sæton, cwæð þæt halige mæden to hire arwurðfullan breðer*. . . .

which is not uncommon in *Bede*. Thus we may have scribal insertion of unidiomatic *þa* at the beginning of the principal clause in *Bede(T)* 360. 12 *þa he ða forðferde, þa ðæt rice þa sum fæc tide tweonde cyningas 7 fremde forluron 7 towurpun*, where MS *Ca* has *7 he ða forðferde, ðæt rice ða . . .* (is *7* in error for *þa?*); misreading of *þa* for *þā* = *þam* where the Latin has *Quibus* in *Bede* 102. 20 *þa se Godes wer Scs Agustinus is sægd þæt he beotigende forecwæde . . .* and of *ða* for *ðæt* in *Bede(T)* 400. 26 *þa gelomp mid þa godcundan fore-seonnesse þære synne to witnunge minre unhersumnesse; ða ic hreowsende wæs ða ic mid ðy heafde 7 mid honda com on ðone stan dryfan*, where MSS *O* and *Ca* both have *. . . hreosende wæs, þ ic com . . .*, the former with erasure of *a*; literal glossing of *et* by *7* and then scribal substitution of *þa* for *7* (perhaps exemplified in *Bede(Ca)* 360. 12 above) in *Bede(T)* 252. 1 *þa þis þa þus gedon wæs, þa se biscop 7 heora lareowas gefeonde 7 blissigende ham hwurfon*, Latin *Quibus ita gestis, et ipsi sacerdotes doctoresque eorum domum rediere laetantes*, where MS *Ca* has *. . . gedon wæs, 7 se bisceop . . .* ; and scribal inversion in *Bede(O)* 444. 8 *þa he þa þus spræc, þa he butan hælo wegnyste of worulde gewat*, where MS *B* has *. . . spræc, he ða butan. . . .* Andrew proposes similar solutions for examples from other texts. These include *ChronE* 51. 16 (762) *þa man ge-halgode Pyhtwine to ƀ* and *CP* 161. 10, where Andrew suggests that *7* has been omitted before *þa* and *ðonne* respectively; *Mark(WSCp)* 14. 10 *Ða Iudas Scarioth þ is wiþersaca an of þam twelfum ferde to þam heahsacerdum . . .*, where the Latin begins *Et* and *Li* has *7*; and *ÆCHom* i. 152. 25 *þa eal þæt folc þe þæt wundor geseh, herede God mid micelre onbryrdnysse*, where the Gospel original (*Luke* 18. 43) begins with *Et* in the Latin and with *and/7* in the OE ver-sions. My difficulty in accepting this proposition is that (as I point out in §1723), *and þa* and *and þonne* are to the best of my know-ledge followed by the order VS, not S(. . .)V. There is room for further work here. But Andrew's citation (*SS*, §9) of the *Chronicle* entry for 755 in connection with *ChronE* 51. 16 (762) above is dis-ingenuous; there is not one example in it of the order *7 þa* S(. . .)V. So those not willing to accept *ChronE* 51. 16 (762), *ChronA* 62. 17 (835) *þa he þæt hierde 7 mid fierde ferde 7 him wiþ feaht æt Hengestdune . . .* (an example overlooked by Andrew), and the like, as genuine OE idiom will do better to explain them as examples of scribal inversion of verb and subject rather than as examples of 'omission' of *7*. See § 3922.

§ 2550. We must admit that such scribal errors are sometimes pos-sible. But I find it hard to believe that, whenever we have in the prose a clause with *þa/þonne* S(. . .)V which must be a principal clause, there must be a scribal error. Stylistic, rhythmic, and/or pedagogic, considerations may be relevant. Waterhouse (1978, pp. 46–53) discusses some examples from *ÆLS*. I offer a few from *ÆCHom*. In *ÆCHom* i. 144. 14 *þa Maria, þæt halige mæden, and þæs cildes fostorfæder, Ioseph, wæron ofwundrode þæra worda þe se ealda Symeon clypode be ðam cilde. And se Symeon him ða sealde bletsunge* . . . , we can produce one sentence by omitting *And*. But the ideas make more impact in two separate sentences and the unusual element order could be due to a desire 'to keep the subject distinct from the predicate and to avoid separating the verb from the predicate by a long subject, as would occur if subject and verb were inverted', as Barrett (p. 9) wrote of *ÆCHom* i. 62. 17-20 and *ÆLS* 21. 139-46.[96] This excellent suggestion explains other examples, e.g. *ÆCHom* ii. 156. 8-12 and ii. 260. 28-31. A desire to retain the parallelism of the Latin original *Prov* 1. 28 *Tunc invocabunt me et non exaudiam; mane consurgent et non invenient me*—which Andrew (*SS*, §23) does not quote—may account for *ÆCHom* ii. 378. 2 *þonne hi clypiað to me, and ic hi ne gehyre; hi arisað on ærnemerigen ac hi ne gemetað me*. Andrew (*SS*, §8) explains the *þa* clause in *ÆCHom* i. 26. 29 *He nolde geniman us neadunge of deofles anwealde, buton he hit forwyrhte; þa he hit forwyrhte genoh swiðe, þaða he gehwette and tihte ðæra Iudeiscra manna heortan to Cristes slege* as causal 'since he did indeed forfeit it altogether when . . .'. But this does not make sense. Barrett (pp. 8-9) rejects it and also the possibilities that the scribe misread *7* as *þa* or that he miscopied ☆*þa forwyrhte he hit* or that *þa* introduces a modal clause. Perhaps Ælfric deliberately repeated *he hit forwyrhte* for stylistic or pedagogic effect. There are, to be sure, other ways—which may seem more idiomatic to us—in which he could have handled these last two examples. But we have the evidence of the manuscripts, which agree on the essentials in both passages.

§2551. Similar examples will be found in translations still attributed to Alfred: *CP* 375. 8, *CP* 385. 5 *Ðonne we sittað innan ceastre, ðonne we us betynað binnan ðæm locum ures modes, ðylæs we for dolspræce to widgangule weorðen. Ac eft ðonne we fullgearowode weorðað mid ðæm godcundan cræfte, ðonne bio we of ðære ceastre ut afærene, ðæt is of urum agnum ingeðonce, oðre men to læranne*, and possibly *Solil* 33. 13, where Endter's punctuation should be compared with that printed by Carnicelli (70. 24).

[96] Barrett, however, errs when he says that 'in the second case there is no other clause which could possibly be taken as a main clause'. We could obtain a strained correlation by putting a comma at the end of line 142, where Barrett's quotation ends.

§2552. There are other sequences in the prose in which I cannot see any real alternative to taking a *þa* or *þonne* clause with S(. . .)V as principal. They include *ÆCHom* i. 498. 13–18 and i. 610. 23–30. I am at present forced to concede the possibility that in the prose *þa/ þonne* VS sometimes occurs in what can be taken as a subordinate clause—here I agree with Andrew (*SS,* §§13 and 19 (iii))—and that *þa/þonne* S(. . .)V sometimes occurs in what can be taken as a principal clause—here I disagree with Andrew (*SS,* §§13 and 19 (i)). So I do not claim that the patterns Adv. VS, conj. S(. . .)V, and Conj. S(. . .)V, adv. VS are the inviolable rule for *þa* and *þonne*. Waterhouse (1978, p. 54) says that more such problems appear in *ÆLS* 31 (Martin) than elsewhere in *ÆLS* and discusses some of them (1978, pp. 54–62).

§2553. But these formulae must be restated more generally. If anything other than an adverb (phrase) of time intervenes between *þa/ þonne* and the verb, e.g. expletive *þær,* direct object, indirect object, or a prepositional phrase other than one of time, we do not have *þa/ þonne* VS. Miyabe (p. 29) is (I believe) wrong when he cites *CP* 183. 17 . . . *ðonne hine ne magon ða welan forwlencean* as an example, for pron.OVS is better taken as a variant of SVO; see §§3918–20 and 3929. Rewritten as Adv. VS, conj. . . . V(. . .) and as Conj. . . . V(. . .), adv. VS, the formulae are extremely useful guides. They make it easy, for example, to split open the well-known but difficult passage about Cædmon in *Bede* 342. 20 (§2562) and I remain convinced (despite Whitelock, Sweet, *R.* 15, 35. 34, and Earle and Plummer) that we do not want a full stop or semi-colon after *woldon* in *ChronA* 84. 33 (894) *ne com se here oftor eall ute of þæm setum þonne tuwwa. oþre siþe þa hie ærest to londe comon, ær sio fierd gesamnod wære, oþre siþe þa hie of þæm setum faran woldon; þa hie gefengon micle herehyð, 7 þa woldon ferian norþ weardes ofer Temese in on East Seaxe ongean þa scipu,* where the manuscript has no punctuation after *woldon* but a slightly heavy, but not capital (Malcolm Parkes tells me), *þ* in *þa* and where the closest MnE to that *þa* is probably 'for'. We may have here another illustration of the stage between parataxis and hypotaxis discussed in §2536.

§2554. But, even as restated, these formulae must not be pressed too far, for grammatical analysis is no more than a means to an end. Two recent studies on *þa* illustrate this. Enkvist (*NM* 73 (1972), 90–6), in an article entitled 'Old English adverbial *þa*—an action marker?', analyses the use of *þa* in *Beowulf*, claims that 'a sweep over a sample of Old English poetry and prose seems to support rather than contradict the view that one of the functions of adverbial *þa* is to mark actions and sequences of actions', and in a final footnote urges the dangers of rigid application of the rules proposed by Andrew. Foster (*NM* 76 (1975), 404-14), writing on 'The use of *þa* in Old and Middle English narratives',[97] suggests (with analyses of two passages by Ælfric)

that many Old English narrative passages are composed of strings of largely independent units marked and coordinated by *þa*, which is used here as an infinitely repeatable marker of temporal sequentiality and carries little or no information about the grammatical relation of clauses. Each of these *þa*-headed discourse units is composed of one or more independent clauses. Within each unit, there may be found both coordination and subordination, and even cases of subordination by the *þa . . . þa* 'when . . . then' construction. These passages, then, can be examined from a broader perspective than the level of grammatical relations, namely that of the organization of narrative material.

Waterhouse (1978, pp. 41-2) criticizes these two studies—which were to some extent anticipated by Andrew and by Samuels; see §2537—and I do not agree with all the details they contain. But both are salutary in that they reveal the dangers of rigid grammatical analyses based on the assumption that the rhythm and flow of OE prose or poetry can be adequately conveyed by MnE punctuation.

§2555. So far, however, we have considered the validity of Andrew's rules for temporal clauses in the prose only. Those he proposes for the poetry are equally Draconian and cannot be accepted. *Mutatis mutandis*, many of the observations made in §§2446-7 and 2518 about clauses introduced by *þær* apply here.

§2556. Andrew's rules for *þa* and *þonne* (and also for *þær*) in the poetry are based on the assumptions that when they are used as initial adverbs, *þa* and *þonne* must carry metrical stress (*SS*, §14, and *Postscript*, p. 3 and §13); that verbs like *wæs*, *wearþ*, and *sceal*, were always unstressed after *þa* (*SS*, §28); and that verbs like *com* in *þa com* were always stressed (*Postscript*, §11).[98] They can be summarized as follows. In principal clauses, the adverb can take second place after the verb (*Com þa*)—if the subject is unchanged, it is frequently unexpressed in clauses of this type—or after a pronoun in the nominative or in another case (*He þa, Him þa*); see *SS*,

---

[97] I understand that his failure to mention Enkvist's article is due to the fact that the two articles were at press together.

[98] I do not accept these assumptions. But the point cannot be pursued here. See, in addition to the standard works on metre, Schücking, pp. 108-16; Magoun, *NM* 56 (1955), 81-2; Cable, *JEGP* 69 (1970), 81-8; Stanley, *Ang.* 93 (1975), 307-34; and Cosmos, *TSLL* 18 (1976), 306-28. This list is far from exhaustive.

§§ 15-16, and *Postscript,* § 12. Another possible form of principal clause is what he characterizes as *þa wæs he,* i.e. the order Adv. VS with what he assumes to be an unstressed verb. But this, he says, can also appear in a subordinate clause; see *SS,* §§ 19, 28, and 32, and *Postscript,* §§ 15 and 24. I agree that clauses of this type are ambiguous, though not for Andrew's reasons. But I cannot accept his proposition that all other clauses introduced by *þa, þonne,* or *þær,* in the poetry are unambiguously subordinate, whether they have Adv. V(. . .)S with what he assumes to be a stressed verb (*þa com he;* see *SS,* §§ 19 and 28-32, and *Postscript,* §§ 11 and 18) or Adv. S(. . .)V (*þa he com;*[99] see *SS,* §§ 16, 25, and 27, and *Postscript,* §§ 3-8).

§ 2557. A valuable summary of Andrew's conclusions, together with some cogent reasons for not accepting them *in toto,* will be found in Dunning and Bliss, pp. 14-16. These include the observations that 'Andrew's views on Old English metre, to which he constantly appeals, are too eccentric to command acceptance' and that 'he is much too ready to remove by emendation all the instances in which the texts do not conform to his hypotheses'. There are other defects. His examples are carefully selected, e.g. he does not mention in either of his books *Beo* 730a or *Beo* 1522b, which according to his rules must be subordinate but can scarcely be so taken. Many of the examples he quotes are judiciously censored, with the result that interpretations which seem plausible as he presents them frequently prove on examination of the full text to involve an intolerable hiatus; consider his treatment of *GuthA* 1-5 (*SS,* § 31), where he conveniently forgets another 'rule' which would make *Se* in *GuthA* 1 a relative pronoun (*SS,* § 48, and *Postscript,* §§ 35-6). Such inconsistencies are not uncommon. The argument used in *SS,* § 16—'unless it can be shown that poetic usage differed from that of prose'—cuts little ice when one finds that differences are said to exist in §§ 19(iii) and (iv). On theoretical grounds, it is not clear why 'rules' which apply to *þa, þonne,* and *þær,* should not apply to *nu* (*SS,* § 92(*l*)) and *þanon* (§§ 2445-6) or, despite *SS,* § 13, why the three syntactically significant orders—SV, S . . . V, and VS—should not occur in both principal and subordinate clauses introduced by *þa, þonne,* and *þær,* when they occur (in both prose and poetry) in clauses with initial S or V which must be principal and in clauses which must be subordinate; see §§ 3900-2.

---

[99] Andrew's use of an intransitive verb means that in his summaries, for example those in *SS,* §§ 19 and 34, it is not clear whether *þa he com* refers only to Adv. SV (his 'common order') or to Adv. S . . . V (his 'conjunctive order') as well; see § 2547. Cable (*JEGP* 69 (1970), 82), does not mention the former type; see § 2558.

§ 2558. Even Andrew himself is forced to admit exceptions, e.g. *And* 415 and *And* 537 (*SS*, § 14), in both of which a clause introduced by *þa* comes between two passages of non-dependent speech and must be principal. There are other examples of this kind, e.g. *El* 462, *ChristA* 195, *GuthB* 1224, and (with *þonne*) *ChristC* 1515. I divide the remaining exceptions—which are much more numerous than Andrew admits—into four groups. First, there are the correlative pairs, both of which must, according to Andrew's rules, be subordinate, e.g.

> *GenA* 1598   þa nyttade   Noe siððan
>   mid sunum sinum   sidan rices
>   ðreohund wintra   þisses lifes,
>   freomen æfter flode,   and fiftig eac, þa he forð gewat,

> *Beo* 1104   gyf þonne Frysna hwylc   frecnan spræce
>   ðæs morþorhetes   myndgiend wære,
>   þonne hit sweordes ecg   syððan scolde,

and *GenB* 430 *Gif hie brecað his gebodscipe, þonne he him abolgen wurðeþ*. Second, there are examples where sense and context demand a principal clause and *þonne* translates Latin *tunc*, e.g. *PPs* 88. 17 and 125. 3. Third, there is the pattern *Ða ic . . . gefrægn* seen in

> *Beo* 2752   Ða ic snude gefrægn   sunu Wihstanes
>   æfter wordcwydum   wundum dryhtne
>   hyran heaðosiocum,   hringnet beran,
>   brogdne beadusercean   under beorges hrof.
>   Geseah ða sigehreðig,   þa he bi sesse geong,
>   magoþegn modig   maððumsigla fealo . . . ,

where Andrew's rule forces him into what seems to me an anachronistic interpretation: 'When (as I heard the tale) W.'s son quickly obeyed his wounded lord, then saw he many a costly jewel'; see *SS*, § 101. The last group is made up of examples in which there are literary objections to Andrew's interpretation, e.g. the *þa* clauses in *Beo* 710, *Finn* 13, and *Mald* 89, and the *þonne* clauses in *ChristC* 1634, *Whale* 56, *MSol* 30, and *Men* 37. Here, as in most of his work, we see Andrew's determination to eliminate parataxis from OE poetry whenever he could by producing correlative pairs; see § 1686. A notably contrary view is expressed by Cable (*JEGP* 69 (1970), 81–8), who attacks Andrew without mentioning *Postscript*, concluding (p. 88) that his own approach 'suggests that there are fewer subordinating conjunctions in *Beowulf* than Andrew finds and that the style is largely paratactic'. I cannot accept his assumption (p. 82) 'that the syntax and meter of clauses introduced by *þa* in *Beowulf* are evident from the word order' and do not believe that he himself accepts it. He uses 'suggests', not 'proves', in the first quotation above and accepts that 'there is general agreement' that the patterns V *þa* . . . N [N seems to stand for Noun] and *þa* N . . . V 'usually contain adverbs and conjunctions respectively'. The main point of his article is to deny Andrew's distinction between the *þa wæs* and the *þa com* types and to claim that in what he characterizes as the *þa* V . . . N structure, *þa* receives metrical stress only when there is more than one unstressed syllable between *þa* and the first alliterating syllable in the half-line. So he reads *Beo* 467b *ðǎ wǽs Héregǎr déad* but *Beo* 607a *þá wǽs ǒn sálǔm.* But it is not clear whether his conclusion is that clauses of this type are always principal.

§2559. The danger of concentrating (as Andrew does) on sequences of two *þa/þonne* clauses is that it leads to a neglect of larger rhetorical patterns involving a series of *þa/þonne* clauses. This has already been demonstrated for the prose in §§2546 and 2554, and can be further illustrated by Miller's mistaken idea that a new sentence begins after *beboden* in *Bede* 342. 26; see Yamakawa 1969, pp. 12–13. Macrae-Gibson (*NM* 74 (1973), 84) has pointed out that the substitution of a full stop for the comma after *mæg* and of a comma for the full stop after *onconn* in

Rim 70 Me þæt wyrd gewæf, ond gewyrht forgeaf,
    þæt ic grofe græf, ond þæt grimme græf
    flean flæsce ne mæg, þonne flanhred dæg
    nydgrapum nimeþ, þonne seo neaht becymeð
    seo me eðles ofonn ond mec her eardes onconn.
    þonne lichoma ligeð, lima wyrm friteþ, . . .

produces a more satisfying reading: 'when death . . . , then the night . . . , then the body . . .'. Similarly, we could replace the semi-colon after *weleras* with a comma in

Whale 51 þonne hine on holme hungor bysgað
    ond þone aglæcan ætes lysteþ,
    ðonne se mereweard muð ontyneð,
    wide weleras; cymeð wynsum stenc
    of his innoþe. . . .

But here too we meet the possibility of different interpretations by different reciters. Thus a comma could be substituted for the full stop after *gefremman* in

Beo 2444 Swa bið geomorlic gomelum ceorle
    to gebidanne, þæt his byre ride
    giong on galgan; þonne he gyd wrece,
    sarigne sang, þonne his sunu hangað
    hrefne to hroðre, ond he him helpe ne mæg

eald ond infrod   ænige gefremman.
Symble bið gemyndgad   morna gehwylce
eaforan ellorsið.

How to read such passages was probably a matter of personal choice then and remains so today.

§2560. Thus, as I said in *NM* 69 (1968), 190-1, it seems clear to me that element order is not conclusive in the poetry, that it cannot be used to prove that a certain clause must be subordinate and another principal. But this, of course, does not stop an editor from suggesting that a poet may deliberately have arranged his clauses so that those with S(. . .)V were subordinate and those with VS were principal. Nor does it mean that such a suggestion is wrong; it merely means that it cannot be proved right.

3. CONJUNCTIONS MEANING 'WHEN'

a. Introductory remarks

§2561. Adams, whose particular concern was with the prose, discusses the conjunctions which introduce clauses denoting time when (pp. 10-62) and gives references to all the examples he found (pp. 162-95). The most common ones are *þa, þonne*, and combinations involving them. These, along with *nu* (alone and in combination), *þe*, certain prepositional formulae, and noun phrases of time + *þe* such as *þy geare þe*, are discussed in the sections which follow. On *hwonne* and combinations involving *þæt(te)*, see §§2775-83 and 2784-8 respectively. Other conjunctions introducing clauses in which the idea of time when has been detected are listed in §§2608-9. Liggins (1970, pp. 291-4)—using Adams as a base—tabulates and discusses the use of some of these conjunctions in the 'Alfredian' texts.

b. The meanings of þa and þonne

§2562. It is a syntactical commonplace that, whereas *þa* conjunction is the equivalent of Modern German *als*, being used only with the preterite indicative of a completed act in the past or of a series now regarded as a single act, *þonne* is the equivalent of *wenn*, being used frequentatively in the past, present, and future, and of a single act yet to be completed at some indefinite time. The *locus classicus* for the distinction between *þa* and *þonne* in the past is, of course, this passage in Bede's account of the poet Cædmon:

Bede 342. 20   Ond he forþon oft in gebeorscipe, þonne þær wæs blisse intinga
gedemed, þæt heo ealle scalde þurh endebyrdnesse be hearpan singan, þonne he
geseah þa hearpan him nealecan, þonne aras he for scome from þæm symble 7
ham eode to his huse. þa he þæt þa sumre tide dyde, þæt he forlet þæt hus þæs
gebeorscipes, 7 ut wæs gongende to neata scipene, þara heord him wæs þære
neahte beboden, þa he ða þær in gelimplicre tide his leomu on reste gesette 7
onslepte, þa stod him sum mon æt þurh swefn 7 hine halette 7 grette 7 hine be
his noman nemnde: Cædmon, sing me hwæthwugu.

Here the phrases *oft . . . þonne* and *þa . . . sumre tide* point the distinction, which is also apparent in *ÆCHom* ii. 266. 15 *Ðæt Israhela
folc ætt þæs lambes flæsc on heora Eastertide, þaþa hi ahredde
wurdon, and we ðicgað nu gastlice Cristes lichaman, and his blod
drincað, þonne we mid soðum geleafan þæt halige husel ðicgað* and
ÆGram 132. 18 *cum ament, þonne hi lufiað . . . cum amarem, þa ða
ic lufode.* As Kivimaa (p. 159) and Yamakawa (1969, pp. 11–12)
point out, this distinction accounts for the preponderance of *þonne*
over *þa* in *CP* and of *þa* over *þonne* in *Or* and *Chron.* BT (s.v. *þanne*)
and Andrew (*SS,* § 22) were content to leave the problem there.
(Adams's statement (p. 18) is uncharacteristically inadequate.) But
there is more to be said.

§ 2563. *þonne* with a preterite indicative implies that the series of
actions is complete, as in *Bede* 342. 20 above. With a present tense, it
is sometimes difficult to decide whether *þonne* refers to a single act
or is used frequentatively, e.g.

Beo 20   Swa sceal geong guma   gode gewyrcean,
                 fromum feohgiftum   on fæder bearme,
                 þæt hine on ylde   eft gewunigen
                 wilgesiþas,   þonne wig cume,
                 leode gelæsten.

(On the subjunctive *cume* see § 2625.) But this is true of MnE 'whenever'. *þa* may refer to a momentary action, as in *Bede* 342. 20
(§ 2562), or to one which continued for a longer period of time, e.g.
BlHom 131. 29 *Se Halga Gast hie æghwylc god lærde 7 him æghwylc
yfel bewerede, swa he Drihten ondweardlice spræc to his gingrum þa
he on lichoman wæs* and

Soul i 22   Hwæt, ðu huru wyrma gyfl
                 lyt geþohtest,   þa ðu lustgryrum eallum
                 ful geeodest,   hu ðu on eorðan scealt
                 wyrmum to wiste!

In this last example we come close to having a series of completed
acts viewed as one. But see § 2566.

§ 2564. Exceptions to the rule that *þa* takes only the preterite indicative are rare. Adams (p. 12), after examining some 3,300 *þa* clauses in OE prose, 'noticed only seventeen instances in which either the present tense or the optative mode appears'. But these can all be discounted. Most of them have ambiguous verb-forms and should be taken as preterite indicatives. The subj. *bede/bæde* in *Bede* 162. 21 is probably due to the combined influence of the Latin *postulasset* and of the fact that it is in dependent speech. The rest occur in texts which are either late and corrupt or are really Middle, not Old, English. In the poetry, apparent exceptions are even rarer. A verb has probably been lost in *And* 829. *Funde* in *Wife* 18 is, of course, an indicative. And we can say that the present indicatives in *Beo* 1428, *ChristC* 958, *Phoen* 66 and 466 (despite Blake's glossary), and *Met* 28. 24, certify that *þa* is a relative (or demonstrative) and not a temporal conjunction.[100] I discuss three more difficult examples—*Bede* (*T*) 86. 3 (where MS *B* has *þ* and the Latin *quae*), *LS* 23. 551, and *PPs* 143. 12—in *Neophil.* 49 (1965), 46–7.[101] The fact that we have *ðaða*, not *ðonne*, in *CP* 5. 5 rules out the conditional interpretation which appears in the EETS translation; see Mitchell 1963*b*, p. 327.

§ 2565. *þonne* presents more difficulties. The clauses with the preterite indicative which have already been discussed must be distinguished from those with the preterite subjunctive. In the latter, the time-reference is not to the past, but to the future-in-the-past. The subjunctive expresses the uncertainty inherent in the idea of indefinite time in the future, which inevitably shades into condition. The reference may be to a single act which was completed later in the past, e.g. *Or* 176. 1 *7 bebead þæm twam folcum, þonne he self mid þæm fyrmestan dæle wið þæs æftemestan fluge, þæt hie þonne on Reguluses fird on twa healfa þwyres on fore*, *Bede* 156. 20, *BlHom* 15. 34, *GuthA* 440, and

Dan 510   Het þæt treow ceorfan
        and þa wildan deor   on weg fleon,
        swylce eac þa fugolas,   þonne his fyll come;

to a single act yet to be completed, e.g. *ÆCHom* ii. 512. 29 *Ne sæde ure Hælend þæt he swa wolde beon mid purpuran gehiwod, oþþe mid helme scinende, þonne he eft come mid engla ðrymme*; or to a series of acts, e.g. *Bede* 196. 6 and *Or* 54. 23 *He þa swa dyde, 7*

---

[100] It is not always possible, however, to decide whether *þa* is a relative or a temporal conjunction when the verb has a preterite indicative or an ambiguous preterite form; consider, for example, *Beo* 402, *GenA* 1796, and *PPs* 148. 5. In *ChristA* 31 it is possible to keep the manuscript reading and to explain the *þaþe* clause as adjective qualifying *usic*; see § 2194.

[101] See further Adams, pp. 142–3; Böhme, pp. 16–17; Wülfing, ii. 103 ff.; Wilde, pp. 331 and 365–6; and Möllmer, p. 106.

*geworhte anes fearres anlicnesse of are, to ðon, þonne hit hat wære,
7 mon þa earman men oninnan don wolde, hu se hlynn mæst wære,
þonne hie þæt susl þæron þrowiende wæron.* GenB 467–76, the third
of the examples in the poetry of *þonne* with a verb which is (to be
taken as) subjunctive, probably belongs here too; the reference is
general, not to one specific individual.

§2566. Sometimes *þonne* appears with (what is to be taken as) a
preterite indicative when the reference is to a series of repeated or
habitual deeds which is now complete and/or to a continuing state.
These are in a sense frequentative, even though *þonne* cannot be
translated 'whenever'. Examples include *Or* 40. 23 and *Or* 50. 1 *Hu
wene ge hwelce sibbe þa weras hæfden ær þæm cristendome, þonne
heora wif swa monigfeald yfel donde wæron on þiosan middangearde?*
—in both these, the verb is *donde wæron*—*CP* 427. 29 *Gif Sodome
hira synna hælen, ðonne ne syngodon hi na butan ege, ac hi forleton
eallinga ðone bridels ðæs eges, ða hi ne scrifon hwæðer hit wære ðe
dæg ðe niht, ðonne ðonne hi syngodon,* and

Beo 2633   Ic ðæt mæl geman,   þær we medu þegun,
                  þonne we geheton   ussum hlaforde
                  in biorsele,   ðe us ðas beagas geaf,
                  þæt we him ða guðgetawa   gyldan woldon. . . .

But cf. *Soul i* 22, discussed in §2563. Sometimes a causal explanation is also possible, e.g. *Or* 52. 10, *Bede* 20. 18 *Ðæt ða benda sumes
gehæftes tolysede wæron, þonne for him mæssan sungene wæron,*
Latin *Vt uincula cuiusdam captiui, cum pro eo missae cantarentur,
soluta sint,* and *ÆCHom* i. 22. 31 (§2567).

§2567. But there are examples in which *þonne* clearly introduces
a clause describing a single act which had been completed in the past
when it was related. In some of these, *þonne* carries something close
to a causal implication 'because, since, seeing that'. Examples include
Or 42. 32 *þonne þa Lapithe gesawon Thesali þæt folc of hiora horsum
beon feohtende wið hie, þonne heton hi hie Centauri, ÆCHom* i.
22. 31 *Eft ðonne hi deade wæron, þonne cwædon þa cucan þæt hi
wæron godas* (but see §2566), *ÆCHom* i. 102. 10 *Wa ðam men þe
bricð Godes gesceafta . . . þonne se ðeoda lareow cwæð, Paulus . . .*
(but we could just as easily have had *cwið* here), *ÆCHom* ii. 64. 4,
ÆLS 28. 117 *Hwæt wille we furðor secgan hu se unsæliga casere his
fyrdinge geendode þonne he forferde on ende?, ÆLS* 31. 72,[102] and

---

[102] I received a sharp reminder of how much work I have not done when I read Waterhouse's observation (1978, p. 188) that Ælfric has *þonne* in *ÆLS* 31. 74 but *ðaða* in the
corresponding passage in *ÆCHom* ii. 500. 30. It is interesting to note that the respective
translations have 'since' and 'when'.

perhaps *Sat* 320, where, however, *þonne* may mean 'then'; see §2556. Liggins (1955, p. 266) cites nine temporal/causal *þonne* clauses referring to the past in which a 'perfect meaning' is the only satisfactory one. They include *CP* 409. 21 *7 eac cyðde hu wærlice hi hine healdan scolden, ðonne hie hine underfangen hæfden* and *ÆLS* 31. 881 *Hi wendon þæt he wære witodlice forbærnd on swa langsumum bryne þonne þæt bræstligende fyr on slæpe hi awrehte.*

§2568. Other examples, however, have proved more difficult to explain as causal or as referring to a series of repeated acts. Möllmer (pp. 24-5) offers a list. In some of those he proposes, *þonne* can be taken as an adverb. They include *Beo* 1121 and *Beo* 1143 (where, however, I prefer 'whenever' without accepting Andrew's explanation in *Postscript,* §19). See further §2572. Some are definitely frequentative, e.g. *ChronE* 141. 19 (1011) *ac þonne hi mæst to yfele gedon hæfdon, þonne nam man grið 7 frið wið hi.* Some can, with varying degrees of acceptability, be explained as frequentative, e.g. *Beo* 2880, *Sat* 78, 80, and 163, and

ChristC 1163   Hwæt, eac sæ cyðde
          hwa hine gesette   on sidne grund,
          tirmeahtig cyning;   forþon he hine tredne him
          ongean gyrede,   þonne god wolde
          ofer sine yðe gan.

Other examples (not all from Möllmer) which seem to be frequentative are *Or* 186. 18 *Swa þonne he to ðæm syndrigum stane com, þonne het he hiene mid fyre onhætan 7 siþþan mid mattucun heawan,* where—as the Latin *invias rupes* shows—more than one rock is involved, and *Exod* 34. 33 *7 þonne he wið hig gesprecen hæfde, he heng hrægl beforan his neb;* cf. *Exod* 34. 34 and 35, which are not in the OE version. However, I find it hard to see how *þonne* in *GenB* 522-31 can be frequentative—*Adam maðelode . . . ‖ . . . 'þonne ic sigedrihten ‖ . . . mæðlan gehyrde ‖ . . . ‖ . . . and me þas bryd forgeaf ‖ . . . ‖ . . . he cwæð þæt . . .'.* There are also three examples in *GD* in which the revised MS *H* has *þonne* when the reference is to a single act in the past and MSS *C* and *O* have *þa, ða,* or *þa þa;* see *GD(C)* 16. 23, 33. 21, and 61. 33. There is an element of cause in *GD* 33. 21, but not in the others. The Latin cannot explain these changes. They may be manifestations of a falling-together of *þa* and *þonne* postulated by Möllmer (p. 25). The Kirkdale Sundial's *ORM GAMAL SVNA BOHTE SCS GREGORIVS MINSTER ÐONNE HIT WES ÆL TOBROCAN . . .* (where the reference is to a continuous state) may be relevant here. There is room for more work on this when full collections are available.

§2569. Are the beginnings of a falling-together of *þa* and *þonne* apparent in their use as adverbs or is the distinction made in §2562 preserved in the adverbs, as Andrew (*SS*, §22) claims? The adverb *þa* is usually used of the past in contrast to the present. This contrast is made explicit in examples like *Or* 86. 10 *gif hie þonne soð ne sædon, þonne næron naþer gode, ne þa ne nu*, where *þonne* is used, not temporally, but 'marking a consequence dependent upon a hypothesis' (BT, s.v. *þanne* A. VI; see §2571), and *ÆCHom* ii. 378. 11 *ac hit mæg eow nu fremian swa micclum swa hit ða mihte*. Enkvist (*NM* 73 (1972), 94), having in mind 'the Romance distinction between narrative tenses such as the *passé simple* and descriptive tenses such as the *imparfait*', is 'tempted to suggest that Old English employed adverbial *þa* in a function related to that of the French *passé simple*'. This would accord with the use of *þa* as a conjunction referring to a single completed act in the past. But we have already seen (§2563) that *þa* conjunction can be used of a long-continuing state and examples like *ChronA* 48. 26 (755) *7 hie þa ymb þa gatu feohtende wæron oþþæt hie þær inne fulgon* are not in accord with Enkvist's suggestion. Adverbial *þa* is used without reference to the past in what seem to me the peculiar combinations *nuþa*, e.g. *ÆCHom* i. 182. 29 . . . *forðon ðe he astah up to heofenum and þær sitt nuða mid his halgum, Beo* 657 . . . *buton þe nu ða*, and *And* 489 *Ic wæs on gifeðe iu ond nu þa* ‖ *syxtyne siðum*, and *nu . . . þa*, e.g. *ÆCHom* i. 202. 8 *Nu com ða seo eadige Maria to his huse. And* 489 presents a striking contrast to

Rid 71. 2   Staþol wæs iu þa
      wyrta wlitetorhtra;   nu eom wraþra laf,
      fyres ond feole. . . .

But, to the best of my present knowledge—and understandably in view of its subsequent disappearance and replacement by *þonne* and/ or its descendants—*þa* is not used alone as an adverb with reference to the present or future; in my opinion the tense of the verbs and the presence of *þonne* certify that *þa* is the demonstrative antecedent of *þe* in *ÆCHom* i. 6. 3 *þa ofsliho se deofol ðe him wiðstandað, and hi þonne farað mid halgum martyrdome to heofenan rice.*

§2570. *þonne* often refers to the future in contrast to the present, as in *BlHom* 15. 7 *Nu we faraþ to Gerusalem 7 þonne beoð gefylde ealle þa halgan gewreotu þe be mannes suna awritene wæron. . . .* But, as a glance at the entries in the standard dictionaries will show, it has senses other than the purely temporal in which it is used when the reference is to the past. Particularly noteworthy here is its appearance where *ac* would serve, e.g. *Bede* 280. 12 *Đonne wæs Büse Eastengla biscop, þe we sægdon þætte in þæm foresprecenan seonoðe wære; wæs he Bonefatius æfterfylgend þæs biscopes*, Latin *Bisi autem episcopus Orientalium Anglorum, qui in praefata synodo fuisse perhibetur, ipse erat successor Bonifatii*, the first *þonne* in *ÆCHom* i. 134. 18 . . . *þæt is feowertig daga, gif hit hysecild wære: gif hit þonne mædencild wære, þonne sceolde heo forhabban fram ingange Godes huses hundehtatig daga*, and

GenB 467   Oðer wæs swa wynlic,   wlitig and scene,
                liðe and lofsum,   þæt wæs lifes beam;
                . . .   . . .
                þonne wæs se oðer   eallenga sweart,
                dim and þystre;   þæt wæs deaðes beam,
                se bær bitres fela.

On this, see Andrew, *SS*, §22; Glogauer, p. 26; and Small 1924, pp. 75-6.

§2571. *þonne* is frequently used correlatively with *gif* when the reference is to the present or future, e.g. (with initial *þonne*) *ÆHom* 4. 252 *Gif ðas heafodleahtras habbað stede on þam menn, þonne næfþ Godes gast nane wununge on him*, (with medial *þonne*) *ÆHom* 4. 21 *Gif se sceocca soðlice is on him sylfum todæled, hu mæg þonne standan his rice staþolfæst?*, and (with final *þonne*) *ÆHom* 4. 25 . . . *and gif ic on his naman adræfe deofla of mannum, on hwæs naman adræfaþ eowre suna þonne?*, or when verbs in the preterite subjunctive are used in rejected or imaginary conditions, e.g. *CP* 217. 21 *forðæm, gif se weobud ufan hol nære 7 ðær wind to come, ðonne tostencte he ða lac, ÆCHom* i. 140. 1, *ÆCHom* i. 404. 27 *Gif þu wistest hwæt þe toweard is, þonne weope ðu mid me, ÆCHom* ii. 106. 4 *Gif ealle menn on worulde rice wæron, þonne næfde seo mildheortnyss nænne stede, Beo* 1104, and

GenB 409   Gif ic ænegum þægne   þeodenmadmas
                geara forgeafe,   þenden we on þan godan rice
                gesælige sæton   and hæfdon ure setla geweald,
                þonne he me na on leofran tid   leanum ne meahte
                mine gife gyldan. . . .

But correlative *gif . . . þonne* occasionally occurs when the verbs are in (what must be taken as) the preterite indicative, e.g. *Or* 86. 10 (§2569), *Bo* 127. 9 *7 symle gif mon anra hwelc of aslog, þonne weoxon þær siofon on ðæm anum heafde, Bede* 268. 18 *Gif þonne swiðra wind aras, þonne tynde he his bec 7 forþleat in his ondwlitan, ÆCHom* i. 560. 10 . . . *oððe gif heora hwylc ðwyrode, þonne wearð se mid swa micelre fyrhte fornumen þæt he ðærrihte his andweard-*

nysse forfleah, and (here I disagree with Thorpe) *ÆCHom* ii. 514. 14
*Gif him ænig heafodman hwilces þinges forwyrnde, ðonne wende he
to Gode mid gewunelicum gebedum.* . . .

§2572. There are also examples in which *þonne* is used without correlative *gif* when the reference is to the past. These include *ChronA*
84. 27 (894) *þa foron hie siþþan æfter þæm wealda hloþum 7
flocradum bi swa hwaþerre efes swa hit þonne fierdleas wæs* (where
we have adv. *þa* . . . adv. *þonne*), *Or* 142. 26 *Swa þonne dyde Ptholo-
meus, Alexandres þegna an, þa he togædere gesweop ealle Egyptum
7 Arabia* and *Ch* 1507 *Ha* 18. 30 *þonne hæfde ic ær on oðre wisan
awriten ymbe min yrfe þa ic hæfde mare feoh 7 ma maga* (adv.
þonne . . . conj. *þa*), *Beo* 377 (but Andrew (*SS*, §30, and *Postscript*,
§18) takes *þonne* as a causal conjunction), and

El 481		
	þa siððan wæs	
of rode ahæfen	rodera wealdend,	
. . .	. . .	
. . .	ond þa þy þriddan dæg	
ealles leohtes leoht	lifgende aras,	
. . .	. . .	
. . .	þonne broðor þin	
onfeng æfter fyrste	fulwihtes bæð,	
leohtne geleafan.	þa for lufan dryhtnes	
Stephanus wæs	stanum worpod.	

So the suggestion that *þonne* might mean 'then' in *Beo* 1121 (§2568)
and in *Sat* 320 (§2567) remains a possibility. That precursors of the
later disappearance of *þa* and of the assumption of its temporal adverbial role by (a descendant of) *þonne* should occur in OE need cause
no surprise. A possible source of the confusion may be examples like
those in *BlHom* 39. 28 and *BlHom* 39. 26 *Hwylc beren mænde he
þonne elles buton heofona rice?*, where *þonne* marks 'a conclusion,
inference or result based on a previous statement' (BT, s.v. *þanne* A.
V). Liggins (1955, pp. 225 and 230) notes two interesting examples:
ða conj. . . . *þonne* adv. in *BlHom* 169. 10 and *þaþa* conj. . . . *þonne*
adv. in *LS* 34. 123. In both of these, *þonne* could be translated 'in
consequence, therefore' or 'then'.

c. þa, *alone and in combination*

§2573. As we have already seen in §2562, *þa* is habitually used
with reference to acts completed in the past. It usually introduces
adverb clauses—examples will be found below—but there are very
occasional *þa* clauses which could be classified as adjective clauses,

e.g. *ChronF* 126. 24 (992) *7 on ðare nihte ða hi scolde an morgen togædere cuman se sylfa Ælfric scoc fram ðare fyrde* (but *ChronE* 127. 14 (992) has *7 þa on þere nihte ðe . . . ða sceoc he . . .*), *ÆCHom* i. 508. 32 *. . . ac on dægrede, þa Godes þeowas þærbinnan Godes lof singað*, *ÆCHom* ii. 156. 21 *On sumum dæge, þaða he ana wæs, þa com him to se costere*, *Beo* 510, and *Ex* 47 *Dæg wæs mære* ǁ *ofer middangeard þa seo mengeo for*. But *þe*, not *þa*, is the word which usually appears with nouns of time in temporal collocations, both in prepositional phrases, e.g. *ChronE* 127. 14 (992) above and *ÆCHom* i. 286. 23 *. . . ac on ðære tide þe ðu his neb gesihst, þu ne gesihst na his hricg*, and in non-prepositional phrases, e.g. *Or* 226. 17 *Ac þære ilcan niht þe mon on dæg hæfde þa burg mid stacum gemearcod . . .* and *ÆCHom* ii. 186. 22 *þæs geares ðe he gewat he cyðde his forðsið on ær. . . .* It would be a pointless terminological exercise to argue whether the *þa* clauses are adjective or adverb in *ChronA* 84. 33 (894) *Ne com se here oftor eall ute of þæm setum þonne tuwwa, oþre siþe þa hie ærest to londe comon . . . oþre siþe þa hie of þæm setum faran woldon . . .* or whether we have adverb or noun clauses introduced by *þa* in *ÆCHom* i. 400. 25 *Ic geseah, ðurh Godes Gast, þa se ðegen alyhte of his cræte* (where Thorpe translates 'I saw . . . that . . .') and in *ChristB* 720 *Wæs se forma hlyp þa he on fæmnan astag*, ǁ *mægeð unmæle* and the similar examples which follow in lines 720–38a.

§2574. *þa* may be used without correlative *þa* in both prose and poetry as an adverb, e.g. *ChronA* 70. 12 (871), *ÆCHom* i. 6. 11 *He gemacode ða þæt fyr come ufan swilce of heofenum*, and *Beo* 720 *Com þa to recede rinc siðian*, or as a conjunction, e.g. *Or* 44. 17, *ÆCHom* i. 42. 2 *Ac God asende his engel to Iosepe ða Maria eacnigende wæs*, and *Beo* 539 *Hæfdon swurd nacod, þa wit on sund reon,* ǁ *heard on handa*. The adverb *þa* sometimes appears in a subordinate *þa* clause but not in the principal clause, e.g. *Or* 68. 29 *þa þæt þa Porsenna gehierde, he ðæt setl 7 þæt gewin mid ealle forlet. . . .* I have not as yet found this pattern in Ælfric.

§2575. The doubled form *þaþa* often introduces a subordinate clause without an accompanying *þa* in the principal clause in the prose, e.g. *ChronA* 87. 2 (894) *7 eft oþre siþe he wæs on hergað gelend on þæt ilce rice þaþa mon his geweorc abræc* and *ÆCHom* i. 24. 26 *Ðaða hire tima com, heo acende*. The four examples of *þaþa* in the poetry—*Met* 8. 6, 11. 15, 26. 21, and *CEdg* 15 *swa neah wæs sigora frean* ǁ *ðusend aurnen, ða þa ðis gelamp*—are all without *þa* in the principal clause and are found, according to Böhme (p. 15), in poetry which carries 'den Stempel des Verfalls' ['the stamp of decay'].[103] That Adams (p. 17) is right in suggesting that 'probably one of the ða's was originally an adverb, and the other a conjunction' is demonstrated by examples like *ÆCHom* ii. 382. 29 *Ða mid þam ðe he swiðost motode . . . þa stop him to Godes engel*. The doubled form *þaþa*—much used by Ælfric—certainly became a means of distinguishing the subordinate from the principal clause in correlative sequences. But whether it ever 'came to be used for *ða*, without any difference in meaning' (Adams, p. 17) or whether it always carried the sense 'Then when' (or 'When then') cannot be determined. However, some of the correlative uses cited below support Adams. So too perhaps does the use of *þaþa* and *þa* to introduce successive subordinate clauses in (for example) *Or* 102. 1.

§ 2576. Correlation has already been discussed in connection with element order and the ambiguous adverb/conjunction in §§ 2543–60. Space does not permit complete illustration of the various ways in which the adverb *þa* and the conjunction *þa(þa)* are used correlatively. I give here one example of the combinations which occur most commonly in the prose, with the reminder that the subordinate clause may precede or (less frequently) follow the principal clause (§ 2543). We have *þa . . . þa . . .* , as in *ÆCHom* i. 184. 5 *þa se Hælend gesæt up on ðære dune, ða ahof he up his eagan*;[104] *þaþa . . . þa . . .* , as in *ÆCHom* i. 10. 28 *Ðaða hi ealle hæfdon þysne ræd betwux him gefæstnod, þa becom Godes grama ofer hi ealle*; *þa* (conj.) *. . . þa* (adv.) *. . . þa* (adv.) *. . .* , as in *BlHom* 175. 4 *þa Neron þa þæt geseah, þa wende he þæt hit Godes Sunu wære*; and *þa* (adv.) *. . . þa* (conj.) *. . . þa* (adv.) *. . .* , as in *ÆCHom* i. 24. 21 *Ða æt nextan, þa se tima com þe God foresceawode, þa asende he his engel Gabrihel. . . .* Adams (p. 17) claimed to have found the sequence *þaþa* (adv.) *. . . þaþa* (conj.) in *GD* 330. 13, but this is not supported by Hecht's report of the readings of the manuscripts, which gives *þa . . . þaþa* (MS *C*) and *þa . . . þa* (MS *O*). Waterhouse (1978, p. 221) notes the absence in *ÆLS* of a correlative adv. *þa* in subordinate clauses modified by a temporal *þa* clause.

§ 2577. The adverb *þa* need not occupy initial position in the principal clause, e.g. *BlHom* 79. 7 *þa he þa geseah þæt hie nænige bote ne hreowe don noldan . . . Drihten þa sende on hie maran wræce . . .* , *ÆCHom* ii. 350. 15 *Se engel me lædde ða furðor to anre þeostorfulre*

---

[103] Möllmer (p. 16) repeats this phrase word for word. Such repetition happens more than once.

[104] Thorpe sees an example of this kind in *ÆCHom* i. 38. 22, but the first *þa* is missing.

stowe, and *ÆLS* 18. 233 *Sende ða to hæðengilde.* . . . For references
to more examples of all these types, see Adams, pp. 162-77. Suggestive observations on the preferences of different authors will be
found in Adams, pp. 15-18; Pope, *Ælfric*, i. 102; Liggins 1970, pp.
292-3; Foster, *NM* 76 (1975), 410; and Waterhouse 1978, pp. 42-5,
where we are told that 'there are four main types of sentence-opening
pattern' in *ÆLS*, viz. *þa* VS (*ÆLS* 2. 66); S *þa* V (*ÆLS* 2. 92); SV
þa (*ÆLS* 2. 28); and V *þa*, with unexpressed subject (*ÆLS* 2. 181).
There is room for more work here.

§2578. The only one of these combinations found in the poetry is
þa . . . *þa* . . . , as in

Beo 138   þa wæs eaðfynde   þe him elles hwær
                gerumlicor   ræste sohte,
                bed æfter burum,   ða him gebeacnod wæs,
                gesægd soðlice   sweotolan tacne
                healðegnes hete,

where the problem of the ambiguous adverb/conjunction does not
in my opinion arise. But cf. *Beo* 126 (§2537).

§2579. Like MnE 'when', the conj. *þa(þa)* may denote the point of
time at which the action of the principal clause occurs ('when'), e.g.
ÆCHom i. 24. 21 (§2576) and

Beo 419   selfe ofersawon,   ða ic of searwum cwom,
                fah from feondum,   þær ic fife geband,
                yðde eotena cyn,

or after which it occurs ('after'), e.g. *ÆCHom* i. 10. 28 (§2576),

GenA 1143   Him æfter heold,   þa he of worulde gewat
                Enos yrfe,   siððan eorðe swealh
                sædberendes   Sethes lice,

and

Mald 22   þa he hæfde þæt folc   fægere getrymmed,
                he lihte þa mid leodon   þær him leofost wæs,
                þær he his heorðwerod   holdost wiste;

in the second group the verb in the *þa(þa)* clause is always pluperfect
in meaning and may be so in form. A subordinate *þa(þa)* clause may
also fix the temporal limits within which the action of the principal
clause occurs ('while'), e.g. *ÆCHom* i. 30. 10 *Ða gelamp hit, þaða hi
on þære byrig Bethleem wicodon, þæt hire tima wæs gefylled* . . .
and *Beo* 539 *Hæfdon swurd nacod, þa wit on sund reon,* ‖ *heard on*

handa. These different meanings do not affect the syntax of the *þa(þa)* clauses or of the sentences. Nor does the fact that *þa(þa)* clauses may convey the idea of cause, e.g. *ÆCHom* i. 86. 19 *þaða he mid swiðlicum luste his lifes gewilnode, þa het he hine ferigan ofer ða ea Iordanen* and

Beo 199   cwæð, he guðcyning
       ofer swanrade   secean wolde,
       mærne þeoden,   þa him wæs manna þearf,[105]

or the idea of concession, e.g. *ÆCHom* i. 140. 9 *na þæt an þæt he wolde mann beon for us, ðaða he God wæs, ac eac swylce he wolde beon þearfa for us ðaða he rice wæs* and

Dream 35   þær ic þa ne dorste   ofer dryhtnes word
                bugan oððe berstan,   þa ic bifian geseah
                eorðan sceatas.[106]

Adams (p. 11) compares these uses of *þa* with similar ones of Latin *cum.*[107] An element of hypothesis can be detected in the *ðaða* clause in *ÆCHom* i. 50. 22 *and betwux ðæra stana hryre, ðaða gehwa mihte his leofostan frynd forgytan, ða betæhte he his fynd Gode.* But it is not the equivalent of a conditional clause. Various writers have followed BT (s.v. *þa* III. a(3)) in suggesting that we have *þa* 'marking condition *when, if*' in *ÆCHom* i. 478. 8 *ac hit wæs swa gewunelic on ðam timan þæt rice menn sceopon heora bearnum naman be him sylfum, þæt hit wære geðuht þæs ðe mare gemynd þæs fæder, ðaða se sunu, his yrfenuma, wæs geciged þæs fæder naman.* However, while the difference between 'when', 'if', and 'because', in this context is very small, Ælfric did use *þa* and not *gif*. Mather does not mention the conditional use of *þa* and there are (I believe) no examples in the poetry; in view of §2652 and of *Beo* 718-19 and 734-6, it is my opinion that Swanton is both misleading and quite wrong when he translates *Beo* 706 *þa Metod nolde* as 'if Providence did not wish it'. In any event, as Adams (p. 11) says, 'in OE the causal or concessive or conditional notion never became so strong as to exclude that of time'.

---

[105] See further van Dam, pp. 66-8, and Liggins 1970, p. 300.

[106] See further Burnham, pp. 75-7, and Quirk, pp. 112-13. Quirk says that there are ten examples in the poetry of subordinate *þa* clauses 'used concessively', but gives references to only seven. Of these *ChristA* 31 depends on an emendation which is not essential, *ChristC* 1157 is an adjective clause introduced by *þaþe*, and in *GenA* 2300 *efne þa* might mean 'just when' rather than 'even when'. Small (1924, p. 143) adds *Mald* 276. He has a case. But one could also argue for a causal interpretation. On the concessive use of the adv. *þa*, alone and with *gyt*, see Böhme, pp. 17-18; Adams, pp. 99-100; and Quirk, pp. 63-7 and 68-9.

[107] See further Böhme, p. 17; Möllmer, pp. 18-19; Schücking, pp. 6-8 and 18-19; Small 1924, pp. 142-3; Sturtevant, *MLN* 40 (1925), 499; and Liggins 1955, pp. 222-49.

§2580. The combination *þa þe* 'when' occurs occasionally in the prose, e.g. *CP(H)* 53. 19 *On ða tiid wæs to herigeanne ðæt mon wilnode biscephades, ða ðe nan twio næs ðæt he ðurh ðone sceolde cuman to hefegum martyrdome* (where, even if we do not emend in the light of MS *C*'s *þa þa*, it is better to take *ða ðe* as causal 'for', 'because', than to link it with *on ða tiid*), *BlHom* 163. 15 *7 þa þe æghwylc mennisc leahter on þæm eadigan Sancte Iohanne cennendum gestilled wæs . . . þa sona seo unwæstmfæstnes fram him fleah*, and *ÆCHom* i. 484. 11 *Witodlice Herodes, ðaðe he nolde . . . þone unclænan sinscipe awendan, ða wearð he to manslihte befeallen*. See further Adams, pp. 23–4 and 186. There are other examples with variants like those in *CP* 53. 19, e.g. *GD(C)* 330. 17 *þa þa* but *GD(O)* 330. 17 *þa ðe*, and *ÆLS(E)* 31. 26 *þa þe* but *ÆLS(K)* 31. 26 *þa ða*. The suspicion that all these might be scribal errors for *þa þa* is not lessened by the fact that four of the seven examples of temporal/causal *þa (. . .) þe* listed by Liggins (1955, p. 232) have variant readings *þa (. . .) þa*. There are no examples in the poetry; Blackburn's attempt to find one in *Ex* 501 has been silently but rightly rejected by subsequent editors. The absence of *þa þe* from the poetry, as Möllmer points out (pp. 17–18), argues against the suggestion made by Adams (p. 23) that *þa þe* was the original form and *þa* a reduction. Möllmer (ibid.) and Böhme (p. 15) believe the opposite. See further §§ 2422–4 and 2431–2.

§2581. As noted in §2564, the verb in *þa* clauses is in the preterite indicative. Problems of mood do not arise.

d. *þonne, alone and in combination*

§2582. As we have already seen (§2562), *þonne*—also spelt *þanne* and *þænne* (eleventh century?), *þenne* (twelfth century?), *þone, þane, þon*, and (of course) with initial *ð*[108]—means 'whenever', being used frequentatively in the past (but see §§ 2567–9), but of both single and repeated actions in the present, future, and future-in-the-past. It usually introduces adverb clauses—on these see below— but there are occasional *þonne* clauses which can be described as adjective, e.g. *John(WSCp)* 9. 4 *Niht cymþ þonne nan man wyrcan ne mæg, Soul* ii 83 *. . . on þam miclan dæge þonne eallum monnum beoð ‖ wunde onwrigene*, and *Met* 22. 23 *. . . on sumera, þonne swegles gim, ‖ hador heofontungol, hlutrost scineð*.

---

[108] For spellings of *þonne* 'than', see §3205. Full details of these variants must await *DOE*.

§2583. *þonne* may be used without correlative *þonne* as both an adverb, e.g. *ÆCHom* i. 4. 14 *þonne cymð se Antecrist, se bið mennisc mann and soð deofol* (see §§2569-72), and a conjunction, e.g. *ÆCHom* i. 20. 18 *and he lætt hi habban agenne cyre þonne hi geweaxene beoð, swa swa Adam hæfde.* Doubled *þonne*—which does not occur in the poetry and, according to Adams (p. 185), is found only in *Bo* and *CP* (but add *Matt(Ru)* 6. 6) in the prose—occasionally introduces a subordinate clause without an accompanying *þonne* in the principal clause, e.g. *CP* 167. 7 *Ac sio æcs wint of ðam hielfe, 7 eac us of ðære honda, ðonne ðonne sio lar wint on reðnesse suiður ðonne mon niede scyle.* As Adams (p. 23) says, 'originally, in all probability, one element was felt as an adverb, the other as a conjunction; but it is impossible to determine which is which'. It is also impossible to determine whether the Anglo-Saxons would have agreed with his next sentence: 'To all intents and purposes, the two form one conjunction, not differing in meaning or use from the simple *ðonne*.'

§2584. Correlation has already been discussed in §§2543-60. I give here examples of the possible combinations, with the reminder that the subordinate clause may precede or (less frequently) follow the principal clause. The prevailing sequence is *þonne . . . þonne . . .*, e.g. ('when . . . then') *ÆCHom* i. 210. 6 *þonne we sind gelaðode, þonne sind we untigede* and ('then . . . when') *ÆCHom* i. 322. 14 *þonne byrnð seo eorðe, þonne ðæs eorðlican mannes heorte bið ontend to Godes lufe*; for more examples see Adams, pp. 177-85. The others are *þonne þonne . . . þonne . . .*—according to Adams, p. 185, this appears only in *CP*—e.g. *CP* 243. 23 *Ac ðæt is ðeah syndrig yfel twiefaldra monna ðætte, ðonne ðonne hie oðre menn mid hira lote bismriað, ðonne gielpað hie 7 fægeniað ðæs*, and *þonne . . . þonne . . . þonne . . .*, e.g. *CP* 185. 10 *Ðonne mon ðonne ongiete ðæt he ryhte gedemed hæbbe, 7 he wene ðæt he ryht be oðrum gedemed hæbbe, ðonne secge him mon suiðe gedæftelice. . . .* Of this last, Adams (p. 186) notes only eight examples—six in *Bo* and one each in *Sol* and *CP*. The adverb need not occur initially in the principal clause, e.g. *ÆCHom* i. 54. 20 *and ðonne ðu eft cymst to ðam weofode, geoffra ðonne ðine lac* and *ÆHom* 4. 21 and 4. 25, both in §2571. See further Adams, pp. 18-23, and Liggins 1970, p. 293.

§2585. Of these patterns, only *þonne . . . þonne* occurs in the poetry, e.g.

Beo 484   Ðonne wæs þeos medoheal   on morgentid,
                 drihtsele dreorfah,   þonne dæg lixte,

eal bencþelu   blode bestymed,
heall heorudreore.

The sequence *þa . . . þonne* in

Dan 345   þa wæs on þam ofne,   þær se engel becwom,
windig and wynsum,   wedere gelicost
þonne hit on sumeres tid   sended weorðeð
dropena drearung   on dæges hwile,
wearmlic wolcna scur

is not surprising in view of the tenses involved.

§2586. The subordinate clause introduced by *þonne* may refer to
the point of time at which the action of the principal clause occurs,
e.g. *ÆCHom* ii. 512. 29 *Ne sæde ure Hælend þæt he swa wolde beon
mid purpuran gehiwod . . . þonne he eft come mid engla ðrymme* and
Beo 3105, or after which it occurs, e.g. *ÆCHom* i. 536. 31 *On ðisum
andweardan life sind þa gecorenan feawa geðuhte ongean getel þæra
wiðercorenra, ac þonne hi to ðam ecan life gegaderode beoð, heora
tel bið swa menigfeald, þæt hit oferstihð, be ðæs witegan cwyde,
sandceosles gerim* and *Beo* 2741, or may fix the temporal limits
within which that action occurs, e.g. *ÆCHom* ii. 342. 33 *Ðonne ðu
on digelnysse beo, heald þonne geornlice Godes beboda; and eft,
ðonne þu ut færst, betwux mannum, far for heora sawla hælu, na for
woruldlicum gestreonum* and *Beo* 932.

§2587. Clauses introduced by *þonne* may contain an element of
cause, e.g. *ChronE* 135. 15 (1003) *Ðonne se heretoga wacað þonne
bið eall se here swiðe gehindred* and *Jul* 695; of concession, e.g.
ÆCHom i. 462. 27 *And menn us wurðiað for godas, þonne we soðlice deoflu sind* and *Rid* 37. 5; or of condition, e.g. *ÆCHom* ii. 210.
34 *Turtlan we offriað, gif we on clænnysse wuniað. Þeorfe hlafas
we bringað Gode to lace, ðonne we buton yfelnysse beorman on
ðeorfnysse syfernysse and soðfæstnysse farað* (where *gif* and *þonne*
seem interchangeable) and *Beo* 572 *Wyrd oft nereð ‖ unfægne eorl,
þonne his ellen deah* (cf. *And* 460 . . . *gif his ellen deah*). But in
these, as in similar examples with *þa* (§2579), *þonne* seems to retain
some temporal significance.[109]

[109] See further (on cause) Liggins 1955, pp. 249–81; (on concession) Burnham, p. 77,
Quirk, pp. 112–14 (he cites only four of the ten examples he says exist. Of these, *Met* 21.
25 is clearly comparative, not temporal/concessive, and *JDay i* 76 could be comparative),
and Campbell, *RES* 7 (1956), 67–8; and (on condition) Glogauer, p. 27, Small 1924, pp. 74–
5, Möllmer, pp. 27–8, and §§3695–7.

§ 2588. There are three recorded examples of *þonne þe* in the prose, viz. *GD* 206. 26, *Bede* 350. 23, and *ÆCHom* i. 48. 12. The only possible example in the poetry is

Sat 149　　　Ealle we syndon　　ungelice
　　　　　　　þonne þe we iu in heofonum　　hæfdon ærror
　　　　　　　wlite and weorðmynt.

I take *þonne þe* here to mean 'when', comparing the sequence *gelicost efne þonne* in

Dan 273　　　Him þær on ofne　　owiht ne derede,
　　　　　　　ac wæs þær inne　　ealles gelicost
　　　　　　　efne þonne on sumera　　sunne scineð,
　　　　　　　and deaw dryge　　on dæge weorðeð,
　　　　　　　winde geondsawen

and reminding the reader of Clubb's note: 'Thorpe renders the anacoluthon satisfactorily: "unlike to what we were when we, etc.".' The difficulty is not solved by explaining *þonne þe* as 'than when'. For the preterite *hæfdon*, compare *Beo* 2633 and the similar examples discussed in § 2567.

§ 2589. Adams notes three examples of the sequence *þonecan þe* 'whenever', viz. *Bo* 44. 7, 58. 2, and 61. 5 (pp. 48-9), and one of *þonne ær þe*, viz. *Bo* 49. 27 (pp. 51-2).

§ 2590. On mood in temporal clauses introduced by *þonne*, see §§ 2610-25.

e. Nu, nu . . . þæt, *and* nu þæt

§ 2591. The conj. *nu* is well established as a causal conjunction; see §§ 3097-106. Adams (pp. 61-2), followed by van Dam (p. xii), rejects the suggestion that it is ever used in a purely temporal sense in either prose or poetry. I agree with this verdict. For *Bo* 80. 22 *Wundorlice cræfte þu hit hæfst gesceapen þæt þ fyr ne forbærnð þ wæter 7 þa eorþan nu hit gemenged is wið ægðer* he suggests the translations 'although' or 'now that' for *nu*.

§ 2592. I have found no examples of the sequence *nu . . . þæt* in the sense 'now that' in the prose or poetry. For my reasons for rejecting Gordon's suggestion that we have an example in *Sea* 33, see *NM* 69 (1968), 59-63. On the possibility that we have an example in *Bede (B)* 486. 3, see Robinson, *SP* 78 (1981), 15.

§2593. The *OED* has no examples of 'now that' before 1530. There may, however, be two examples in OE poetry, viz. *Met* 8. 42 and

Met 10. 57   Ac hit is wyrse nu
                    þæt geond þas eorðan   æghwær sindon
                    hiora gelican   hwon ymbspræce,
                    sume openlice   ealle forgitene,
                    þæt hi se hlisa   hiwcuðe ne mæg
                    foremære weras   forð gebrengan.

The translation 'because' for *þæt* would fit these sentences very well, but the evidence for this sense is flimsy; see §§3118-27. To take *þæt* as introducing a noun clause in apposition to *hit* is very strained. So 'now that' seems the most convincing possibility. See §2784.

f. þe

§2594. Adams (p. 28) claims that ten examples in the prose establish 'beyond doubt the fact that *ðe* is used as a temporal conjunction in OE prose'. He gives references to nine of these on p. 186. The tenth is *Law VIAs* 2 (Adams, pp. 104-5, and Callaway 1931, pp. 26-7).[110] It is true that 'when' gives good sense in many of these. But the fact that most of them can be otherwise explained weakens their collective force. In *Bede* 240. 6 the temporal conjunction is *ða*; see Miller's introduction, pp. xxix-xxxi. In *Or* 148. 32 *þy swiþor . . . þe* forms a causal/comparative sequence; see Johnsen, *Ang.* 38 (1914), 85, van Dam, p. 72, and §3138. In *CP* 73. 8 *Ðonan . . . ðe* can be taken together in the sense 'from that place from which'. *Ðe he* in *CP* 85. 21 and *þe hie* in *Or* 2.6 and *BlHom* 129. 25 could all mean 'who'. In the last two at any rate *þe* could mean 'because'; cf. Möllmer, p. 35. In *Solil* 8. 1 too *þe* could be the relative '. . . death from which . . .'. Adams (pp. 104-5) is himself doubtful about *Law VIAs* 2, where *þæs* may have dropped out before *þe*—the Latin has *postquam*—and *HomS* 22. 114, where *þe* could be the relative; on these, see §2667. This leaves only *GD* 273. 16 *Eac me sæde, Petrus, sum swyþe æwfæst wer 7 getreowe, 7 ic þa gyt wæs wuniende ealling in þam mynstre þe he me þis cyðde þæt sume dæge men wæron on scipfærelde of Siccilia þam ealande secende Romesbyrig.* Even here *þe* could be the relative. The Latin has *Quidam autem religiosus adque fidelissimus vir adhuc mihi in monasterio posito narravit quod. . . .* But even if we take *þe* to mean 'when' in this last example, we have only one swallow and so no summer.

---

[110] Johnsen (*Ang.* 38 (1914), 85-6)—firmly astride his hobby horse—claims that 'the notion of place is still present' in some of these examples. On them, see also Möllmer, pp. 35-6; van Dam, pp. 72-4; and Liggins 1955, pp. 142-3, 145, and 325. Dodd (p. 205) glosses *þe/ðe* as 'when'. But his examples involve *þa hwile þe*.

§2595. The situation is very similar in the poetry. Adams (p. 29) found no examples. In *PPs* 118. 84 *þe* is the relative. In *Beo* 1436, *ðe* can be taken alone as a relative or can be combined with the immediately preceding *þe sænra* to form a causal/comparative combination. According to Small (*PMLA* 45 (1930), 369), the context 'seems decidedly to call for the temporal shade of meaning'. There is no doubt an element of time implied, but this does not make it necessary to translate *þe* as 'when'. On *þonne þe* in *Sat* 149 see §2588. But here too we have a swallow:

Beo 999

> hrof ana genæs
> ealles ansund, þe se aglæca
> fyrendædum fag on fleam gewand,
> aldres orwena,

where *þe* clearly seems to mean 'when'; see Schücking, p. 7, and Möllmer, p. 36. It would be cowardly, though not impossible, to call scribal error to our rescue here. Adams's suggestion (p. 28) that *þe* in similar examples in the prose could be a weakening of *þa* is syntactically possible here, since *gewand* is preterite. But it seems phonetically unlikely. This idea may lie behind BT's suggestion (s.v. *belimpan* II) that we read *Beo* 2468b *ða* [sic] *him sio sar belamp* 'when that pain befell him' for the manuscript *þe him sio sar belamp*. But this and the alternative possibility that *þe* means 'when' both appear to founder on the fact that the noun *sar* is neuter. It could, however, be argued that *Beo* 2468b is evidence that *sar* could also be feminine; compare §§62-5.

§2596. Thus, although the temporal use of *þe* is not established beyond all doubt, as Adams claimed, it cannot perhaps be entirely dismissed. If we accept that it can mean 'when', it is not clear whether *þe* would be the indeclinable particle or a form of the instrumental *þy/þi*, which is established as a causal conjunction; see §§3128-47.

g. Prepositional formulae

(1) *Those with a demonstrative + a noun (. . .) (+ þe)*

§2597. Formulae of this sort are found sporadically in the prose at the head of clauses denoting time when. Typical examples include *GD(C)* 29. 28 . . . *7 sona ongæt þæt seo Godes fæmne wæs gehæled in þa ylcan tide þe se Godes þeow cyrde* (MS *H* has *on þære ylcan tide þe*), *Lch* i. 256. 12 . . . *7 to ðam timan ðe se fefor to ðam men genealæcean wylle, smyre hyne þærmid*, and *ÆCHom* ii. 356. 8 . . . *and wæron forði þa gebytlu on ðam dæge swiðost geworhte ðe he ða ælmessan gewunelice dælde*. I have recorded no examples in the poetry. Despite Whitman (Adams, p. 34), *þe* in *ChristC* 1097 is best taken with *his lichoma* 'whose body'. Adams (pp. 32-4 and 188-9) gives more examples from the prose. We have here a terminological problem: are these combinations to be described as temporal formulae or does *þe* introduce an adjective clause qualifying the noun? The combination *in swa hwylce tiid swa* is of course a different pattern; see §2795.

§2598. As far as I have observed, *BlHom* 133. 12 *Mid þon dæge wæs gefylled se dæg þe is nemned Pentecosten . . . þa wæron ealle þa apostolas wunigende on anre stowe* is unique in two respects: it is the only example involving *mid* and a noun and it is the only example involving a noun without a following *þe*.

(2) Those with mid + *a demonstrative (+* þe/þæt*)*

§2599. In these combinations, *mid* is followed by the dative or instrumental of *se*, which occurs in the following spellings in the prose: *þam*, *þæm* (according to Adams, p. 37, only in *Or* and *CP*), *þan*, *þon*, *þy* (the preferred form in *Bede*; see Liggins 1970, p. 292), *þi, ty*, and *te*, and of course with initial *ð*. In my opinion, both *þe* and *þæt* in these formulae are subordinating particles; see §§2425-30. Adams (appendix V, p. 243) gives references to numerous examples. As far as I know, the form *mittes*—which Adams (p. 46) says 'is derived probably from *mid* and *ðys*, the instrumental of *ðes*'—occurs only in *LS* 3 (*Chad*); see Vleeskruyer's edition, s.v. *mid*. According to Adams (p. 37), the primary sense of the formula is 'when'. At pp. 36-48 and 189-93, he records some 220 examples of the formula without *þe*, some 150 examples with *þe*, and three with *þæt*. Visser (ii. 872-3) adds a few more with *þæt* from *CP*. We can add *CP* 210. 19 *7 ðætte eft sien hira scylða geðreade mid ðam ðæt we hie tælen*.

§2600. Not all such sequences are temporal conjunctions. Visser (ii. 872) errs by including *CP* 293. 22 . . . *mid ðy ðæt we hie forbugen . . .* '. . . by avoiding them . . .'. Here *þæt* introduces a noun clause in apposition with the preceding demonstrative. In *ÆCHom* ii. 44. 18 . . . *ac he com ofer Criste on culfran hiwe, forði þæt he wolde getacnian mid þam þæt Crist wæs on ðære menniscnysse swiðe liðe and unhearmgeorn* 'because he wished thereby to betoken that . . .', *mid þam* picks up the preceding *ac* clause. When the sequence involves *þe*, the demonstrative may be the antecedent of an adjective clause introduced by *þe* or may form a relative pronoun with *þe*; see §§2153-5 and 2604.

§2601. But, when used temporally, a formula with *mid* can mean not only 'when', e.g. *Bede* 234. 6 *Forðon mid þy he micelre tide æfter lifde 7 georne halig gewreotu leornade 7 smeade, þa æt nyhstan onget he 7 geleornade in gaste, þæt he ne wæs mid wætre fulwihtes bæðes Gode to bearne acenned*, Latin *Nam cum multo post haec tempore uiueret, et scripturis legendis operam daret, tandem didicit se aqua baptismatis non esse regeneratum*, and *Bede* 304. 25 *Mid ðy he þa se bisceop þa stowe onfeng, þa gestaþelode he þær mynster*, Latin *Hunc ergo locum cum accepisset episcopus Uilfrid, fundauit ibi monasterium*, and 'whenever', e.g. *Or* 106. 15 (§2603); but also 'while', e.g. *Bede* 34. 15 *And mid þy ðe he hine þa geseah on singalum gebedum 7 wæccum dæges 7 nihtes beon abysgadne, þa wæs he semninga mid þam godcundan gyfe gesawen 7 gemildsad*, Latin *Quem dum orationibus continuis ac uigiliis die noctuque studere conspiceret, subito diuina gratio respectus exemplum fidei ac pietatis illius coepit aemulari . . . ;*[111] 'after', e.g. *Bede* 366. 12 *7 þa mid þy ðe ða feond onweg gewitone wæron, þa gesohte he him nearo wic 7 wununesse . . .* , Latin *Cum autem ipse sibi ibidem expulsis hostibus mansionem angustam circumuallante aggere et domus in ea necessarias iuuante fratrum manu . . . construxisset . . .* ; and (with correlative *færlice, hraþe, hrædlice, sona*, and the like) 'as soon as', e.g. *Bede* 186. 5 *þa heo þa mid þa cyste in þone cafertun eode þæs huses, þe se feondseoca mon in þræsted wæs, þa geswigade he semninga 7 his heafod onhylde, swa swa he slapan wolde, 7 his leomu in stilnesse gesette*, Latin *Et cum illa adferens, quae iussa est, intraret atrium domus, in cuius interioribus daemoniosus torquebatur, conticuit ille subito, et quasi in somnum laxatus deposuit caput membra in quietem omnia conposuit*. See further Adams, pp. 96-9 and 207-8 ('while'), and pp. 78-80 and 201-2 ('as soon as'). From the fact that these formulae usually represent a Latin *cum* or (less frequently, according to Adams, pp. 41 and 96, and Liggins 1955, p. 295) *dum*, Möllmer (p. 43) suggests that they are literary rather than colloquial. Their extreme rarity in the poetry is probably metrical. The fact that they represent *cum* more often than *dum* also supports Adams's conviction (p. 37) that 'the primary use of the conjunctions with *mid* is to introduce a clause indicating *time when*'. Further discussion must await full collections.

§2602. Of the patterns recorded by Adams (pp. 189-93) as occurring in the prose in the sense 'when', only three are represented by

---

[111] Adams's suggestion (p. 97) that in *Gen* 18. 9 '*mid ðam ðe* indicates the equal duration of the activity of the two clauses' is based on what seems to me on the evidence of the Latin an unacceptable punctuation.

more than ten examples: *mid þy/þi* (207), e.g. *Bede* 102. 30 *Mid þy he þæt feoht ongon, þa geseah he Æðelfrið se cyning heora sacerdas . . . sundor stondan ungewæpnade* and *BlHom* 237. 15 *Mid þi he þis cwæð, Drihten Hælend Crist, he astah on heofonas*; *mid þam/ þæm þe* (81), e.g. *Or* 104. 15 *Mid þæm þe þa ærendracan to Rome comon, þa com eac mid him seo ofermæte heardsælnesse* and *ÆCHom* i. 60. 11 *Mid þam ðe se apostol Iohannes stop into ðære byrig Ephesum, þa bær man him togeanes anre wydewan lic to byrigenne*; and *mid þy/þi þe* (57), e.g. *Bede* 168. 26 *Mid þy þe he eft Cænwalh on his rice geseted wæs, þa com in Westseaxe sum biscop of Ibernia* and *BlHom* 237. 17 *Mid þi þe hie comon to þæs carcernes dyru, hie þær gemetton seofon hyrdas standan.* This order of preference is not disturbed if we add the examples in which the formula is taken by Adams to mean 'as soon as' (pp. 201-2) and 'while' (pp. 207-8). The combined figures there are *mid þy/þi* 29, *mid þam þe* 30, and *mid þy/þi þe* 26. Material for those wishing to discover the preferences of individual prose writers will be found in Adams (for page references see his appendix V, p. 243) and Liggins 1970, p. 293.

§ 2603. Clauses introduced by these combinations show a marked tendency to occupy initial position in the sentence. They are found without a correlative adverb, e.g. *Bede* 28. 18 *Mid þy Peohtas wif næfdon, bædon him fram Scottum, Bede* 142. 28, and *ÆCHom* i. 126. 27 *Soðlice he geswutelode micele eadmodnysse mid þam ðe he cwæð 'Drihten . . .'*, or with one, e.g. (*swa*) *Or* 188. 8 *Mid þæm þe Hannibal to ðæm londe becom, swa gewicade he an anre diegelre stowe neah þæm oþrum folce*, (*þonne* with the present tense) *Bede* 88. 2 *Mid þy þonne se lichoma onginneð lustfullian, þonne onginneð þær seo syn acenned beon*, (*þonne* with the past tense (despite Adams, p. 44) because *mid þæm þe* means 'whenever') *Or* 106. 15 *7 mið þæm þe hie þara dura hwelce opene gesawon, þonne tugon hie heora hrægl bufan cneow 7 giredon hie to wige*, (*mid þy*) *CP* 55. 11 *Mid ðy ðe he sceolde his gestreon toweorpan, mid ðy he hie gadrað*, (*mid þam*) *ÆCHom* i. 122. 33 *Mid þam ðe he forbead þam gehæledum hreoflian þæt he hit nanum men ne cydde, mid þam he sealde us bysne þæt we ne sceolon na widmærsian ure weldæda . . .*, and (*þa*) *ÆCHom* i. 60. 11 *Mid þam ðe se apostol Iohannes stop into ðære byrig Ephesum, þa bær man him togeanes anre wydewan lic to byrigenne; hire nama wæs Drusiana.* The adverbs *þa* and *þonne* may also occur in the subordinate clause, either without a correlative in the principal clause, e.g. *Bede* 112. 7 *Mid þy heo þa gesegon þone biscop mæssan onsymbelnesse mærsian in Godes cirican 7 þæm folce husl syllan, wæron heo mid elreorde dysignesse onblawne* and *BlHom*

249. 18 *Mid þi þe þa wæron gefyllede seofon dagas swa swa him Drihten bebead, he ferde of Marmadonia ceastre efstende to his discipulum*, or with one, e.g. *Bede* 88. 2, above, and *LS* 7. 62 *Mid þy þa Eufrosina þone munuc þær wiste, þa gecigde heo hine to hire.* . . .

§2604. Despite Adams (p. 38) and Möllmer (p. 43), the formula does occur in the poetry. I have noted two examples, viz.

MSol 484   se sceall behealdan   hu his hyge [. . .
                . . .]dig growan   in godes willan,
                murnan metodes ðrym,   mid ðy ðe hit dæg bið

and (with a causal element, as the correlative *forðon* shows)

ChristC 1425   Mid þy ic þe wolde cwealm afyrran,
        hat helle bealu,   þæt þu moste halig scinan
        eadig on þam ecan life,   forðon ic þæt earfeþe wonn.

There may be a third in *Whale* 44, but I think that here *mid þam* is more likely to mean 'with whom' or (as Mackie has it) 'with these'; cf. *ÆCHom* i. 76. 2 *Onfoh me to minum gebroðrum mid ðam ðe ðu come and me gelaðodest*, where there is no doubt that *mid ðam ðe* means 'with whom'. On ambiguities of this sort, see further §§2152 and 2600.

§2605. On mood in these clauses, see §§2610-25.

(3) Those with wiþ

§2606. Hittle (p. 165) quotes several examples from the *Leechdoms* in which *wiþ* + a demonstrative + *þe* might mean 'when' or 'if'; *Lch* iii. 102. 2 *wið þam þe se streng under þare tunga toswollen byð* is typical. But, translating literally, we could explain *wið þam þe* as meaning 'against that, namely'; cf. *Lch* ii. 180. 9 *Wiþ sarum magan wegbrædan seaw 7 eced do on clað, lege on* and *Lch* ii. 190. 1 *Við spiwþan 7 wið þon þe him mete under ne gewunige, genim sinfullan.* . . . The combination *wið þæt* in *Lch* iii. 92. 10 *Wið þæt þæs mannes heafod clæppitað 7 to ealre þare clænsunge þas heafodes* could also be taken literally.

h. Demonstrative + *a noun* + *(. . .)* þe

§2607. Combinations of this sort are found—less frequently than the prepositional formulae with nouns discussed in §§2597-8—at the head of clauses which denote the time at which the action of the principal clause took place. Typical examples are *Or* 226. 17 *Ac þære*

ilcan niht þe mon on dæg hæfde þa burg mid stacum gemearcod . . .
wulfas atugan þa stacan up, GD 306. 14 . . . hi onfundon 7 geacsodon
þæt þy ylcan dæge þeodric se cyning wæs dead þe hit gecyþed wæs
7 geeowed þam Godes þeowe be his ænde 7 wite, ÆCHom ii. 186.
22 þæs geares ðe he gewat, he cyðde his forðsið on ær sumum his
leorningcnihtum, and

ChristC 1152   Hwæt, eac scyldge men
                gesegon to soðe,   þy sylfan dæge
                þe on þrowade,   þeodwundor micel,
                þætte eorðe ageaf   þa hyre on lægun.

For further examples see Adams, pp. 35-6 and 189. Here again we
have the terminological problem of deciding whether to call these
combinations temporal formulae or to say that *þe* introduces an
adjective clause qualifying the noun.

j. Other conjunctions

§2608. Adams (pp. 54-62 and 194-5) detects a temporal element in
some clauses introduced by *swa þæt* (see further Johnsen, *Ang.* 38
(1914), 99-100); by *þær* and *þær þær* (see §§2460-3); by *swa hwær*
swa (see also Liggins 1955, p. 429); by *loc(a) hwær* and *loc(a) hwonne*;
and by *gif*. See also Möllmer, pp. 9-46, where examples from prose
and poetry are given. Liggins (1955, pp. 429-30) adds *þanon, þider,*
and *swa hwider swa*. On the possibility that *hwonne* and *swa* may
mean 'when', see §§2775-83 and 2692-6 respectively. I reject completely the notion that *swa* can mean 'as when' in *Wan* 43; see §3285,
NM 69 (1968), 182-7, and *ASE* 4 (1975), 11 and 25-8. On *þonne ær*
þe, see §2712.

§2609. Ælfric uses *þæt* in *ÆCHom* ii. 220. 15 *Se fifta leahtor is*
unrotnys ðissere worulde, þæt se man geunrotsige ongean God for
ungelimpum ðises andwerdan lifes, but prefers *þonne* for obvious
reasons of euphony in *ÆCHom* ii. 220. 26 *Se seofoða heafodleahter*
is gehaten idelwuldor, þæt is gylp oððe getot, þonne se man gewilnað
þæt he hlisful sy. . . . Such variations do not prove that *þæt* means
'when'. So I know of no justification for Strunk's suggestion (adopted
by Woolf) that *þæt* means 'when' in

Jul 688   Ungelice wæs
                læded lofsongum   lic haligre
                micle mægne   to moldgræfe,
                þæt hy hit gebrohton   burgum in innan,
                sidfolc micel.

It introduces a clause of result which shades into a clause of time 'until'; see §2745.

k. Mood

§2610. The prevailing mood in clauses introduced by the conjunctions meaning 'when' which are discussed in the preceding sections is the indicative. Enough examples to demonstrate this have already been quoted. Clauses introduced by *þa* have the preterite indicative only, never the subjunctive mood or the present tense; see §§2562-4. With the other conjunctions, both tenses and both moods may occur.

§2611. Here, as I point out in §§2433-6, we are less concerned with the different theories which attempt to explain the presence of the subjunctive in these temporal clauses than with the circumstances under which it occurs. Adams (pp. 142-3) remarks that

when the optative does appear, it is due usually to some peculiarity of the main clause, and not to the time-relation of the two clauses. The most common cause for the use of the optative is an imperative in the main clause, though often it appears in clauses belonging to indirect questions, in object-clauses introduced by *ðæt*, or is due to attraction. In most of these cases the action of the temporal clause belongs to the future, and always has a doubtful or hypothetical character. Sometimes it is difficult to assign a definite reason for the mode; it seems to be the result of the general, indefinite character of the sentence in which it appears.

'An imperative in the main clause' may be taken to include a jussive subjunctive or part of the verb **sculan* and 'attraction' implies the influence of the attitude of mind of a person using a subjunctive in clauses of purpose, concession, and the like.

§2612. Callaway (1931, p. 90), after referring to Adams's statement and to similar views expressed by Wülfing and Fleischhauer, objects: 'Again I am forced to the conclusion that these scholars have unduly weighted the influence of the governing clause upon the mood of the dependent temporal clause; that a frequent coincidence has been elevated into a cause.' He has some justification for this; as we shall see below, the presence in the principal clause of one of the factors listed above does not always produce a subjunctive in the temporal clause. But Callaway's own work here is not without flaws. His table (1931, p. 92) seems to me of little value without a corresponding table showing the number of indicatives in clauses with an imperative or the like in the principal clause. Behre (pp. 157-8) notes that it includes a number of examples in which the verb is not unambiguously subjunctive and also *hwonne* clauses, which do not properly belong here; see §§2775-83. So Callaway's list of alleged exceptions to Adams's 'rules' is larger than it should be. And, as Behre (p. 158) adds: 'Apart from the unsatisfactory cases mentioned, Callaway's lists of examples of the subjunctive in temporal non-*ær* clauses consist chiefly of temporal clauses connected with a main clause of volition, or, this not being the case, temporal clauses in which the subjunctive corresponds to a subjunctive in a Latin text.'

§2613. On the basis of these sometimes dubious exceptions, Callaway rightly rejected the Erdmann–Bernhardt theory (see §2434) that the nature of the principal clause has almost everything to do with the subjunctive in the subordinate clause. He also—and quite rightly—rejected Mourek's theory (p. 123) that 'die Qualität des Hauptsatzes hat mit dem Modus des Nebensatzes nichts zu schaffen' ['the nature of the principal clause has nothing to do with the mood of the subordinate'], with the observation (1931, p. 91) that 'the truth seems to lie midway between these two extremes'. His own conclusion (1931, p. 119) was 'that the chief factor in the employment of the subjunctive is to be found in the nature of the dependent clause rather than in that of the governing clause. Another factor, one that has not hitherto been suggested, I think, is the influence of the Latin original.' I am not sure that the opposition between the 'nature of the main clause' theory and the 'nature of the dependent clause' theory is as stark as Callaway's condemnation of the former sometimes makes it seem. His own summary of the Erdmann–Bernhardt theory (1931, p. 18) includes the words '*primarily* by the nature of the main clause, only *secondarily* by the nature of the dependent clause' and that of his own theory (1931, p. 111) reads '. . . to me it seems that the *chief* cause is to be found *rather* in the ideal nature of the dependent temporal clause' [my italics]. Is this much more than saying the same thing with different emphasis?

§2614. Callaway was further criticized by Behre (p. 164):

To sum up, the subjunctive is used in temporal non-*ær* clauses to express an attitude of volition on the part of the speaker towards the content of the temporal clause, an attitude that is generally manifested in the main clause by a particular expression of volition (exhortation, wish, challenge, or precept). The volitional subjunctive in temporal clauses of the types discussed above is chiefly of an optative or a concessive nature. Hence it follows that the time-relation indicated by the temporal conjunction does not determine the modal use in the temporal clause. The term 'Temporal Subjunctive', used in the title of Callaway's recent book referred to above, is therefore misleading. His subdivisions: 'The

Subjunctive of Antecedent Action', 'the Subjunctive of Subsequent Action', etc., lead, if taken seriously, to a false conception of the subjunctive in temporal clauses in OE.

I agree. In my opinion Callaway's 'subjunctive of contemporaneous action' is neither a separate category nor something which explains all the subjunctives in clauses introduced by conjunctions meaning 'when' which Callaway lists (1931, p. 83). These subjunctives express different things or (we could say) are triggered by different attitudes in the mind of one of the individuals involved in producing the sentence in the form in which it reaches us.

§2615. On the basis of my own full statistics for the poetry of the subjunctives in the temporal clauses under discussion and of the statistics given by Adams for the prose, my present conclusion is that we can cut down the fence and occupy both positions by saying that in general the presence in the principal clause of one of the factors defined by Adams is likely to be accompanied by a dependent temporal clause with what Callaway (1931, p. 75) describes as an 'ideal nature' or that, in the words of Behre (p. 156), 'in this class of temporal clauses the subjunctive . . . occurs when the temporal clause is connected with an expression of volition in the main clause'. (For his definition of 'an expression of volition', see my §2391; it does not include dependent desires.) Möllmer (pp. 104-6) is in basic agreement. But there are exceptions.

§2616. A few typical examples of the various situations in which the subjunctive occurs and some contrasting ones with the indicative follow; for more, see Visser, ii, §879. We find that an imperative in the principal clause is usually accompanied by a subjunctive in the temporal clause, e.g. *Solil* 4. 6 *and þonne þu ðe gebeden hæbbe, awrit þonne þæt gebed*, *BlHom* 139. 13 *Mid þy þe þu me hate of minum lichoman gewitan, þonne onfoh þu minre sawle*, *ÆCHom* i. 180. 6 *þonne ðu nacodne geseo, scryd hine*, and

Beo 1178   . . .   ond þinum magum læf
                   folc ond rice,   þonne ðu forð scyle,
                   metodsceaft seon.

But the indicative occasionally occurs, e.g. *Josh* 8. 7 *Ðonne fare ge to, mid ðam ðe we fleonde beoð* and

PPs 82. 12   Gedo þæt hiora ansyn   awa sceamige,
                   þonne hi naman þinne   neode seceað.

Note also the fluctuation in the following example: *ÆCHom* ii. 342. 33 *Ðonne ðu on digelnysse beo, heald þonne geornlice Godes beboda;*

*and eft, ðonne þu utfærst, betwux mannum, far for heora sawla hælu,
na for woruldlicum gestreonum* and compare *Matt(WSCp)* 6. 5 with
Luke(WSCp) 6. 22 and 11. 2. Similarly, with a jussive subjunctive in
the principal clause, we usually find a subjunctive in the temporal
clause, e.g. *CP* 25. 2 *7 ðonne he god weorc wyrce, gemyne he ðæs
yfeles ðe he worhte, BlHom* 241. 22 *And mid þi þe he dead sie, uton
we dælan his lichaman urum burhleodum*, and *Beo* 3105 *Sie sio bær
gearo, || ædre geæfned, þonne we ut cymen*. But the indicative
appears, for example, in *CP* 85. 11 *Be ðæm geðence se sacerd, ðonne
he oðre men healice lærð, ðæt he . . .* and

Beo 2446   þonne he gyd wrece,
         sarigne sang,   þonne his sunu hangað
         hrefne to hroðre. . . .

Here again we have fluctuations; consider *BenR* 85. 17 . . . *þæt is,
þænne hy behofiað, sy him gefultumad*, where other manuscripts
read *behofian* or *behofien*. According to Fleischhauer (p. 81), the
mood in *þonne* clauses accompanied by an imperative or jussive subjunctive is indicative if the two actions are simultaneous and subjunctive if the action of the *þonne* clause precedes that of the principal
clause. I agree with Liggins (1955, p. 278) in dismissing this theory.

§2617. Behre (p. 156) includes 'a *sceal*-construction' in his list of
'volitional expressions' which tend to be accompanied by a subjunctive in the temporal clause. This sometimes happens, e.g. *MSol* 166
. . . *ac symle he sceal singan, ðonne he his sweord geteo, || Pater
Noster.* . . . But exceptions are more common, e.g.

Beo 1534   Swa sceal man don,
            þonne he æt guðe   gegan þenceð
            longsumne lof

and

MSol 377   Heo ðæs afran sceall   oft and gelome
            grimme greotan,   ðonne he geong færeð. . . .

A noteworthy fluctuation occurs in

El 1175   þæt manigum sceall
            geond middangeard   mære weorðan,
            þonne æt sæcce mid þy   oferswiðan mæge
            feonda gehwylcne,   þonne fyrdhwate
            on twa healfe   tohtan secaþ,
            sweordgeniðlan,   þær hie ymb sige winnað,
            wrað wið wraðum.

§2618. The uncertainty surrounding an unfulfilled desire often
produces a subjunctive in a temporal clause subordinate to a clause

of purpose, e.g. *Or 54. 23, Bede 418. 27 Ond somod he willnade from him onfon þera eadigra apastola reliquias 7 Cristes martira, þæt mid þy he diofolgeld towurpe 7 cirican timbrede 7 rærde in þære ðiode þe he lærde, ðæt he ðer gearwe hefde haligra reliquias in to settenne . . . , WHom 8c. 174 Ac utan don swa us ðearf is, helpan ure sylfra, 7 ðæs huru efstan, nu we fyrst habbað þa hwile ðe God wile, þe læs ðe we forweorðan þonne we læst wenan*, and (with an element of purpose in an *oðþæt* clause which is followed by a *þonne* clause with the subjunctive) *Dan* 513. But here too there are indicatives, e.g. *CP* 463. 1, where we have two temporal *ðær ðær* clauses with the indicative and one *ðær* clause with the subjunctive, and

LPr ii 84   Forgif us ure synna,   þæt us ne scamige eft,
           drihten ure,   þonne þu on dome sitst
           and ealle men   up arisað
           þe fram wife and fram were   wurdon acænned.

A generic result clause with the subjunctive is followed by an indicative *þonne* clause in *Hell* 64. Contrasting examples in which a temporal clause is dependent upon a concessive clause include (with the subjunctive) *Bede 76. 10 Forþon þeah þe heo in þa ilcan tiid, þe heo acenned hæbbe, Gode þoncunge to donne in circan gonge, ne bið heo mid nænige synne byrðenne ahefigad* and (with the indicative)

Met 7. 49   . . . þeah hine se wind   woruldearfoða
           swiðe swence,   and hine singale
           gemen gæle,   þonne him grimme on
           woruldsælða wind   wraðe blaweð,
           þeah þe hine ealneg   se ymbhoga
           ðyssa woruldsælða   wraðe drecce.

§ 2619. Liggins (1955, pp. 276-7) concludes that in 'temporal/causal' *þonne* clauses the subjunctive 'is probably best explained as due primarily to the meaning of indefinite time. . . . Subjectiveness, particularly in the form of a wish, is often important also, but it is *additional to* the determining element, the indefinite temporal and conditional sense.' Clauses involving a hypothesis are discussed in the next section. But it must be said that the subjunctive is no more the 'rule' in temporal/causal clauses than it is in temporal clauses; the idea of causality alone does not affect the mood of the verb.

§ 2620. Temporal clauses sometimes shade into clauses of condition. But this does not necessarily mean that the verb of the temporal clause will be subjunctive; consider *ÆCHom i. 66. 5 Witodlice ne bið he þæra æhta hlaford, þonne he hi dælan ne mæg; ac he bið þæra æhta ðeowa, þonne he him eallunga þeowað* and *Beo 572 Wyrd oft nereð* || *unfægne eorl þonne his ellen deah.* But some subjunctives in temporal clauses can be said to be due to the hypothetical nature of the clause or sentence, e.g. *GD* 261. 9, where we have one *þonne* clause with the subjunctive followed by two with the indicative—cf. §§1947-8—and two examples noted by Adams (p. 145), viz. *HomU* 27. 147. 23 and *HomU* 32. 189. 3 *and uton gecnawan hu læne and hu lyðre þis lif is on to getruwianne and hu oft hit wurð radost forloren and forlæten þonne hit wære leofost gehealden.* On this see further Liggins 1955, pp. 271-9.

§2621. We must, then, admit the existence of sufficient exceptions to demonstrate that the presence in a principal clause of one of the elements discussed above does not always 'cause' a subjunctive in a subordinated temporal clause. But it is very rare for a subjunctive to occur in such a clause when none of these elements is present. There are no real exceptions in Callaway's lists (1931, pp. 82-9); see §2612. Two difficult examples in the poetry are *Met* 13. 77 (where, as Behre (p. 157) suggests, the influence of the prose original may be responsible) and

Men 29

	Swylce eac is wide cuð
ymb III and twa	þeodum gewelhwær
his cyme kalend	ceorlum and eorlum
(butan þænne bises	geboden weorðe
feorðan geare;	þænne he furðor cymeð
ufor anre niht	us to tune),

(where the influence of *butan* may have produced an exaggerated degree of hypothesis in the poet's mind).

§2622. I have so far found no evidence to support the theory (Mourek, p. 123; Campbell, *RES* 7 (1956), 65) that a negated indicative or a rhetorical question in the principal clause is automatically followed by a subjunctive in the temporal clause; see (*inter alia*) §2690. Examples in which it does not work include *CP* 344. 14, *Beo* 2451 and 2741, and *Met* 19. 10, 19. 15, and 28. 41. But we do find a subjunctive in the *ða hwile ðe* clause in *CP* 43. 10 *Hwæt is ðonne betere ða hwile ðe we libben, ðonne we ures flæsces lustum ne libben, ac ðæs bebodum ðe for us dead wæs ⁊ eft aras?*

§2623. Both Callaway (1931, p. 119) and Behre (p. 158) have spoken of the possible influence of a subjunctive in a Latin original on the mood of an OE temporal clause. (Both these statements are quoted in §§2612-13.) This influence, if it exists at all, is very slight, as Callaway (1931, pp. 93, 96, and 98) admits. 'But', he goes on (1931, p. 98), 'the independence of the Old English translators is, perhaps, more decisively shown by the fact that, in far the majority of examples, the Latin circumstantial subjunctive with *cum* is rendered by an indicative with *ðonne* or *ða*.' Those wishing to pursue this matter should consult initially Callaway 1931, pp. 93-104.

§2624. As was pointed out in §§2100-2, there is no rule in OE that a subordinate clause in dependent speech must have the subjunctive. Thus we find temporal clauses with the indicative in dependent speech in *CP* 271. 10, *CP* 307. 7 (*ða he cuæð*), *CP* 455. 3 (*ðær ðær he . . . lærð*), and *CP* 455. 1 *Ymbe ðæt hu mon ænne mon scyndan scyle, ðonne he yfle costunga monega ðrowað*—to mention only a few examples from one prose text—and in *Beo* 3062 (*þonne leng ne mæg* ‖ *mon . . . buan*), *Rid* 3. 72, *Vain* 13, and

PPs 83. 11   Forþon god lufað   geornast ealles,
                    þæt man si mildheort   mode soðfæst,
                    þonne him god gyfeð   gyfe and wuldur.

So we cannot accept Callaway's observation (1931, p. 123) that 'indirect discourse seems to demand the subjunctive in the subordinate temporal clause'.

§2625. The subjunctive does, however, occur in temporal clauses in dependent speech when the reference is to the future-in-the-past and/ or when an element of desire or hypothesis is involved. A few typical examples follow: *CP* 307. 10, *Bede* 156. 20, *Bede* 76. 5 *Ðu frugne eac swylce, þonne wiif cennende wære, æfter hu feola daga heo moste in circan gongan*, *BlHom* 45. 12 *forþon se goda lareow sægde, þonne se mæssepreost oþþe se biscop wære gelæded on ece forwyrd, þæt hi þonne ne mihtan nawþer ne him sylfum, ne þære heorde þe hi ær Gode healdan sceoldan, nænige gode beon*, *Beo* 3174, *MSol* 168, and

Beo 20   Swa sceal geong guma   gode gewyrcean,
               fromum feohgiftum   on fæder bearme,
               þæt hine on ylde   eft gewunigen
               wilgesiþas,   þonne wig cume,
               leode gelæsten.

More examples will be found in §2565.

4. CONJUNCTIONS MEANING 'WHILE'

a. Introductory remarks

§2626. It has already been noted that the following conjunctions may introduce clauses fixing the temporal limits of the action of the principal clause: *þa* (§2579), *þonne* (§2586), and the formulae with *mid* (§2601). But there are conjunctions for which this is the primary function; they include *þa hwile (þe)*, *þenden*, and *swa lange swa*. The action of the principal clause may be a momentary one, e.g. *Or* 124. 10 *7 siþþan he gegaderode fird wið Perse, 7 þa hwile þe he hie gaderade, he ofslog ealle his mægas þe he geræcan mehte*, or may be of extended duration, occupying the whole period of time denoted by the subordinate clause, e.g. *ChronA* 89. 8 (896) *þa þæs on hær-fæste þa wicode se cyng on neaweste þare byrig þa hwile þe hie hira corn gerypon*, or some lesser period, e.g. *ChronA* 104. 8 (923)... *7 het oþre fierd eac of Miercna þeode þa hwile þe he þær sæt gefaran Mameceaster on Norþhymbrum.*

§2627. Among the 'Alfredian' texts, *Bede* stands out by preferring *mid þy (þe)* to *þa hwile þe*; see Liggins 1970, pp. 295-6, where the occurrences are given as twenty-four and one respectively. Adams's figures (pp. 203-8) suggest that the reverse is true for *Chron* and Wulfstan.[112] Ælfric shows a slight preference for *þa hwile þe*, but the number of examples is small. See also Möllmer, pp. 53-63. On mood, see §§2648-53.

b. Combinations involving the noun hwil

§2628. This formula has its origin in an accusative of duration of time—as in *ChronE* 129. 16 (994) *7 man gislade þa hwile in to þam scipum* and

Jud 212	Stopon heaðorincas,
...	þa ðe hwile ær
elðeodigra	edwit þoledon—

to which was added the particle *þe* either in its subordinating or in its relative use; see §§2425-8. So originally it meant 'during that time namely *or* in which'; 'during those times . . .' seems less likely. But examples like *ChronE* 264. 25 (1137) *7 ð lastede þa xix wintre wile Stephne was king* demonstrate that, as we should expect, it gradually became a formulaic conjunction. I incline to agree with Mann (*Archiv*, 180 (1942), 91-2) when he suggests that the two clauses were originally in parataxis, with *þa hwile* belonging to the principal clause. As Möllmer (p. 56) observes, the sole recorded example in which *þa hwile* and *þe* are separated—*Or* 212. 25 *Ic nat eac, cwæð he, hu nyt*

---

[112] But Adams was using Napier's edition. Thus, he comments on p. 84 on the frequent use by Wulfstan of *magan* and **motan* in *þa hwile þe* clauses. But the two examples he cites are from *HomU* 27. The point needs further investigation.

ic þa hwile beo þe ic þas word sprece—establishes the latter fact. Further on the origin of the formula, see Small 1924, pp. 134-6 and 150-2. Johnsen (*Ang.* 39 (1916), 118-19) manages to produce a local origin for it.

§2629. The formula is the exception in the poetry, where *þenden* is preferred; see §2635. There are only seven examples of *þa hwile þe* (*Mald* 14, 83, 235, and 272; *DAlf* 21; *LPr ii* 100; and *MCharm* 11. 42) and one of *þa hwile* (*JDay ii* 83)—all in ASPR vi. Möllmer's suggestion (pp. 54 and 56) that the retention of the older *þenden* when it was replaced in the prose by *þa hwile þe* reflects the conservatism of the poetry is plausible; note the marginal gloss *þa hwile* for *ðenden* at *GenB* 245, which I discuss in *NM* 70 (1969), 70-2. But the metrical difficulties presented by *þa hwile þe* should not be overlooked; thus *þa hwile þe* in *Bo* 49. 27 is replaced by *þenden* in *Met* 11. 72.

§2630. In the prose, *þa hwile þe* is almost the rule, whether the time-reference is to the past, present, or future, e.g. *Matt(WSCp)* 5. 25 *Beo þu onbugende þinum wiðerwinnan hraðe þa hwile þe ðu eart on wege mid him* and *BlHom* 175. 2 *7 þa þa hwile þe he þær stod, he wearþ færinga geong cniht 7 sona eft eald man* 'while . . .'; *BlHom* 101. 8 *Forðon, men ða leofestan, don we soþe hreowe 7 bote ure synna þa hwile þe we on þyssum life syn* 'as long as . . .'; and *ChronA* 85. 22 (894) *þa besæt sio fierd hie þærutan þa hwile þe hie þær lengest mete hæfdon*, where the adverb *lengest* emphasizes the sense 'as long as'. We occasionally find correlative *þa hwile*, e.g. *Or* 72. 22 *Cirus, Persa cyning, þe we ær beforan sægdon, þa hwile ðe Sabini 7 Romane wunnon on þæm westdæle, þa hwile wonn he ægþer ge on Sciþþie ge on Indie* and *ÆCHom* i. 10. 35 *and þa hwile þe he smeade hu he mihte dælan rice wið God, þa hwile gearcode se Ælmihtiga Scyppend him and his geferum helle wite*—with the adverb on both occasions followed by the order VS. But more common are *þa*, as in *ChronA* 89. 8 (896) (§2626) and *BlHom* 175. 2 above, and *þonne*, as in *Ch* 1446 . . . *7 him bebead Mired bisceop bebod on Godes ealmihtiges noman 7 on þære halgan þrinesse, þæt ða hwile þe ænig man wære on hira mægðe þe godcundes hades beon walde 7 þæs wyrðe wære, þæt he þonne fenge to þam lande æt Soppanbyrg*, where the time-reference is to the future-in-the-past. Adams (p. 83) notes *ealle þa hwile þe* in *Or* 20. 25 and *þa ane hwile þe* in *Ps(P)* 48. 18.

§2631. The phrase *on þære hwile þe* occurs in *Or* 130. 9 and 170. 12; the combination *þa hwile þæt* in *ChronE* 252. 34 and 253. 1, both in the entry for 1123. We can safely follow Adams (p. 83) in dismissing variants like *þa hwila þe* (*ChronD* 149. 30 (1016), *þa hwile þa* (*Lch* ii. 120. 15), and *þe hwile þe* (*Lch* iii. 120. 6), as scribal errors or late weakenings.

§2632. As in the poetry, *þa hwile* is rare. Examples include *Bede (Ca)* 188. 4, where MS *O* has *þenden* and MS *T þendæn*; *Solil* 48. 14, where Endter inserts *þe*; *Lch* iii. 2. 6; and *Lch* iii. 122. 18, where we have *ðe hwyle*. For more see Adams, pp. 85-6.

§2633. Liggins (1955, pp. 324-5) detects a causal element in a few examples, including *CP* 295. 3 *Ac ðæt mod, ða hwile ðe hit bið oferdruncen ðæs ierres, eal ðæt him mon ryhtes sægð, hit ðyncð him woh* and *ÆHex* 425 . . . *ne him nan gesceaft næfre ne derode ða hwile ðe he gehyrsumode his Scyppende on riht.*

c. þenden

§2634. Adams gives only seven examples of *þenden* from the prose (p. 206)—variant spellings include *ðende* (*Matt(Li)* 26. 6), *þendæn* (*Bede(T)* 188. 4), and (from the poetry) *þynden* (*And* 1323), *þendon* (*And* 1713), and *þendan* (*ChristB* 590)—against 273 of *þa hwile þe* and its variants (pp. 203-5). Typical examples are *Bede(T)* 188. 4, where MS *Ca* has *þa hwile*, *LawAf* 40. 1 *Gif ðisses hwæt gelimpe ðenden fyrd ut sie oððe in lenctenfæsten, hit sie twybote*, and *Mart 2* 40. 11 *ond wit sceolon a beon mid þe þenden þu leofast.*

§2635. The reverse is true in the poetry—eight examples of *þa hwile (þe)* (see §2629) against some seventy-five of *þenden*. The last number cannot be exact, for *þenden* can serve as an adverb, e.g. *Beo* 1018 *nalles facenstafas* || *þeod-Scyldingas þenden fremedon.* So the problem of the ambiguous adverb/conjunction sometimes arises, e.g. in

Beo 2417   Gesæt ða on næsse   niðheard cyning;
                 þenden hælo abead   heorðgeneatum,
                 goldwine Geata;

see further §2418. On the retention of *þenden* in the poetry after it had become obsolete in (we can reasonably assume) the spoken language and in the prose, see §2629.

§2636. Like *þa hwile þe*, *þenden* may mean 'while', e.g. *LawAf* 40. 1 (§2634) and

Beo 3024   ac se wonna hrefn
       fus ofer fægum   fela reordian,
       earne secgan,   hu him æt æte speow,
       þenden he wið wulf   wæl reafode,

or 'as long as', e.g. *Mart 2* 40. 11 (§ 2634) and, with the adverb *a*,

Beo 283   oððe a syþðan   earfoðþrage,
       þreanyd þolað,   þenden þær wunað
       on heahstede   husa selest.

In the latter sense, Möllmer (p. 54) observes, it frequently refers to the duration of life, e.g. *Beo* 57 *heold þenden lifde* ‖ *gamol ond guðreouw glæde Scyldingas*, or to the duration of the world, e.g. *GenA* 1542 . . . *þenden woruld standeð*.

§ 2637. Several writers have pointed out that, with a slight change in emphasis, a word meaning 'while' can easily come to convey the idea of 'until'. Both Möllmer (p. 55) and Glogauer (pp. 32–3) cite *Max i* 181 *Hy twegen sceolon tæfle ymbsittan, þenden him hyra torn to-glide*. . . . Glogauer also mentions *WaldA* 23 and *Ex* 255 (suggested by Heusler; I share Glogauer's doubts). But in these and other proposed examples, the translation 'while' is adequate. The same transition is, of course, possible in MnE

> And he sang as he watched and waited while his billy boiled:
> 'You'll come a-waltzing Matilda with me.'

Indeed, some performers sing 'till', not 'while'.

§ 2638. Examples referring to past, present, and future, have already been cited. On mood, see §§ 2648–53.

d. *Combinations involving* swa

§ 2639. The most common pattern in the prose is *swa lange swa*, e.g. *Bede* 436. 1 *7 hiene in ðæm streame sæncte 7 defde, swa longe swæ he gesegen wæs þæt he aræfnan meahte* and *ÆCHom* i. 54. 13 *forðan ðe swa lange swa he hylt ðone sweartan nið on his heortan, ne mæg he mid nanum ðinge þone mildheortan God gegladian*. This formula, which occurs only twice in the poetry—in *Met* 11. 16 and

Met 20. 243   Wunedon ætsomne
       efen swa lange   swa him lyfed wæs
       from þæm ælmihtigan . . .—

is in origin comparative and probably arose from constructions like that seen in *ÆCHom* i. 178. 13 *Eac se witega Elias fæste ealswa lange eac þurh Godes mihte*, where *swa Moyses* can be supplied from the preceding sentence. We find the adverb group and the conjunction used correlatively, e.g. *Or* 274. 10 *swa longe swa seo ehtnes wæs þara cristenra monna, swa longe him wæs ungemetlic moncwealm getenge* and *ÆCHom* ii. 108. 28 *Soð ic eow secge, swa lange swa ge forwyrndon anum of ðisum lytlum, and noldon him on minum naman tiðian, swa lange ge me sylfum his forwyrndon.* The formula is divided in *ÆCHom* ii. 230. 34 . . . *and swa lange leofode on ðisum deadlicum life swa he sylf wolde.* In *Ps(A)* 103. 31 (33) *swe longe* glosses *quamdiu.* For further examples see Adams, pp. 88–91 and 205–6, and Möllmer, pp. 59–61.

§2640. Liggins (1955, p. 324) observes that Ælfric prefers *swa lange swa* to *þa hwile þe* 'if there is more than a faint shade of cause'. The examples in *ÆCHom* do not altogether support this; they range from those in which there is no causal element at all, e.g. *ÆCHom* i. 526. 33 *Mine gebroþra, gif ge gode sind, þonne sceole ge emlice wiþercorenra manna yfelnysse forberan, swa lange swa ge on þisum andweardan life wuniað*, to those in which *swa lange swa* means 'inasmuch as, because', e.g. *ÆCHom* ii. 108. 28 (§2639) and *ÆCHom* ii. 108. 15 *Soð ic eow secge, swa lange swa ge dydon anum þisum læstan on minum naman, ge hit dydon me sylfum*, which are quotations of *Matt* 25. 4 and 25. 40 respectively, in both of which the Latin has *quamdiu* and *WSCp swa lange swa*. See further Adams, pp. 88–90, and note that Liggins detects a causal element in the *ða hwile ðe* clause in *ÆHex* 425; see my §2633.

§2641. Other patterns involving *swa* noted by Adams (pp. 88–92 and 205–6) in the prose—† indicates that he recorded only one example—include †*swa . . . lengost* (*ChronE* 159. 19 (1036)); †*swa mænige dagas swa* (*LS* 23. 392); †*swylce hwile swa* (*Lch* iii. 112. 17); and possibly *swa lange þæt*. But, as Adams (p. 91) points out in connection with *ChronE* 250. 34 (1122), this last combination may introduce clauses of result. The same is certainly true in two examples which he overlooked—*ÆCHom* i. 402. 33 *and hi wurdon ða utan ymbsette mid Romaniscum here swa lange þæt ðær fela ðusenda mid hungre wurdon acwealde* and *ÆCHom* ii. 156. 27 *þa beðohte he hine sylfne . . . and wylode hine sylfne on ðam þiccum bremlum . . . swa lange þæt he eall toclifrod aras.*

§2642. Adams (p. 99) translates *swa swa* in *ChronE* 136. 13 (1006) . . . *hergodon 7 bærndon 7 slogon swa swa hi ferdon* as 'while'. I prefer 'wherever'; see §2489. It is possible to translate *swa* in *And*

1288 'as long as', but this sense is unattested; see § 3673. *GenB* 307 —on which see Timmer's edition, p. 38—is not relevant here.

e. Other combinations

§ 2643. It will suffice to record these combinations with a reference to one example, which is marked † if it is the only one known to me. They fall into four groups. First, we have *þa giet þa* (*GD* 167. 11)— this combination means 'when' in *Or* 136. 11, where we have *þa giet þa . . . þa giet*—and *þa gen þa* (†*BlHom* 165. 17). Johnsen (*Ang.* 39 (1916), 116-17) says that these combinations are of local origin and are adverbial in all the examples quoted by Adams (pp. 99-100). I disagree with both these statements. It is true that *þa gen/giet þa* can be used adverbially; see *ÆLS* 32. 123 (§ 2645). But, as the correlation in *Or* 136. 11 above shows, it can also be used as a conjunction.

§ 2644. Second are two noun phrases without a preposition. The first, like *þa hwile þe*, has the accusative—*þa þrage þe* (†*Lch* ii. 284. 14)—and the second has the dative plural—*ðæm timum ðe* (†*CP* 253. 10). The third group comprises prepositional phrases which include a noun of time. Adams (pp. 95-6) notes four patterns: *in þære tide þe* (†*Bede* 128. 18), *binnon ðam fyrste ðe* (†*ÆCHom* ii. 150. 1), *on his dagum þe* (†*LS* 34. 477), and *geond twentig wintra fyrst þe* (†*ÆLS* 31. 1223). To these can be added *on þæm dagum þe* (†*Or* 180. 21; see Adams, p. 93).

§ 2645. In the fourth group we have prepositional formulae without a noun of the pattern seen in *ÆLS* 32. 123 *Betwux þam þe he clypode to Criste þagit þa tugon þa hæþenan þone halgan to slæge*; cf. the adverbial use of *betwux ðam* in *ÆCHom* i. 428. 1 *þa betwux ðam brohte se gelyfeda cempa Romanus ceac fulne wæteres*. The prepositions noted in such patterns are *betweoh* (†*Bede* 360. 10), *betwux* (*ÆLS* 32. 123), *amang* (*ChronE* 169. 3 (1046)), *gemang* (*Or* 160. 6), *onmang* (*LS* 34. 246), *ongemang* (*CP* 339. 24), *on* (*ChronD* 169. 28 (1050); Kivimaa (p. 153) suggests *CP* 123. 1 as an example, but the combination may mean literally 'in that, namely'), and *under* (†*Or* 30. 5).

§ 2646. Of uncertain origin is *þa lange þe* 'while, as long as' in *Lch* iii. 114. 18 *7 do þus þa lange þe hit beþurfe*; see Adams, p. 88, and Johnsen, *Ang.* 39 (1916), 111-12.

§ 2647. For further examples and discussion of the combinations listed above, see Adams, pp. 87-100, and Liggins 1970, pp. 295-6.

f. Mood

§2648. *Mutatis mutandis*, the remarks made in §§2610-25 apply here: the indicative is the prevailing mood in clauses denoting duration of time (for examples see the preceding sections); the subjunctive is rare in both prose and poetry; Adams and Callaway differ, not about the circumstances in which the subjunctive occurs, but about how best to explain why it occurs.

§2649. In the poetry, the only unambiguous subjunctives in clauses denoting duration of time are accompanied by governing clauses containing an imperative, a subjunctive, or a form of **sculan*, e.g. *Beo* 1224 *Wes þenden þu lifige,* || *æþeling, eadig!*, ChristB 771 *Utan us beorgan þa,* || *þenden we on eorðan eard weardien*, ChristC 1578, *PPs* 105. 5,

JDay ii 82   Nu þu scealt greotan,   tearas geotan,
                    þa hwile tima sy   and tid wopes,

and (with the temporal clause subordinate to a dependent desire)

Mald 233   Us is eallum þearf
                    þæt ure æghwylc   oþerne bylde
                    wigan to wige,   þa hwile þe he wæpen mæge
                    habban and healdan,   heardne mece,
                    gar and godswurd.

But an indicative sometimes occurs in company with a form of **sculan*, e.g. *Beo* 2497, *GenA* 931, and

GenA 906   þu scealt wideferhð   werig þinum
                    breostum bearm tredan   bradre eorðan,
                    faran feðeleas,   þenden þe feorh wunað,
                    gast on innan.

§2650. The subjunctive is not limited to these contexts in the prose. But it does occur in them. Thus, we find, with a principal clause containing an imperative, a subjunctive, or a form of **sculan*, *Solil* 14. 3 *and geclænsa me ða hwile ðe ic on þisse worulde si*, *BlHom* 101. 8 *Forðon, men ða leofestan, don we soþe hreowe 7 bote ure synna, þa hwile þe we on þyssum life syn*, *Deut* 4. 9 *ne cuman eow ðas word of gemynde swa lange swa ge libbon*, ChronE 163. 10 (1041) *healde þa hwile þe him God unne*, and *Lch BM Harley* 585, f. 151ʳ, *þas gebedu þriwa man sceal singan ælc þriwa on þysne drænc 7 þæs mannes oruð eallinga on þone wætan þa hwile þe he hit singe*. (This is quoted from BASPr. vi. 134. 18. Cockayne omitted it, presumably by oversight, in *Lch* iii. 27.) But the indicative occasionally appears in these circumstances, e.g. *Matt(WSCp)* 5. 25 *Beo þu onbugende þinum wiðerwinnan hraðe þa hwile þe ðu eart on wege mid him, John (WSCp)* 12. 35 *gaþ þa hwile þe ge leoht habbað*, where MSS *A*, *B*, and *C*, have the subj. *habbon*, and *BlHom* 35. 34 *7 swa we sceolan þa hwile þe we lifgaþ her on worlde.*

§2651. The mere fact that a temporal clause is in dependent speech does not mean that the verb must be subjunctive; consider *Bo* 26. 13 *þi ic wundrige hwi men sien swa ungesceadwise þ hi wenen þætte þis andwearde lif mæge þone monnan don gesæligne þa hwile þe he leofað* and *Ch* 1483 *And ic an þat Athelfled bruke þe lond þer wile þe hire lef beth.* However, the subjunctive is common when the noun clause is a dependent desire, e.g. (with the present tense) *CP* 6. 6, where (as Wülfing (ii. 112) rightly remarks) the whole sentence contains a wish, and *Solil* 13. 18 *forðam ic þe bydde þæt þu me simle lere þa hwile þe ic on þisum lycuman and þisse weorulde sie*, and (with the preterite subjunctive referring to the future-in-the-past) *Ch* 1441 *Ða wilnede Æþelwald swa þeh to þam biscope 7 to þam higen þæt heo him mildemode alefdan þæt he his moste brucan ða hwile ðe he wære* and *Ch* 1446 . . . *7 him bebead Mired bisceop bebod on Godes ealmihtiges noman 7 on þære halgan þrinesse, þæt ða hwile þe ænig man wære on hira mægðe þe godcundes hades beon walde 7 þæs wyrðe wære, þæt he þonne fenge to þam lande æt Soppanbyrg.* But even here there are occasional exceptions, e.g. *Solil* 32. 11 *Ac he deð swiðe disiglice, gyf he wilnað þæt he hi eallunga ongyte þa hwile þe he in þisse worlde byð.*

§2652. Sometimes the subjunctive in a clause expressing duration of time can be attributed to an element of indefiniteness and/or hypothesis in the temporal clause and/or in the whole period, e.g. *LawAf* 40. 1 (§2634), *CP* 63. 18 *Ac pinsige ælc mon hiene selfne georne, ðylæs he durre underfon ðone lareowdom ðæs folces ða hwile ðe him ænig unðeaw on ricsige, Solil* 1. 15, and *LS* 35. 121, where the reference is to the future-in-the-past and where we can reasonably supply *þæt* after *behet* 'promised', so solving Adams's problem (p. 149). *LS* 10. 165. 79 *Min bearn, nelt þu beon gemyndig; þas þing þe ic ær nolde nænigum woruldmen secgan þa hwile þe ic lifigende wære, ic hit þe wylle nu onwreon and gecyþan* also puzzled Adams (p. 149). Guthlac is, of course, still alive, but is very close to death. Perhaps this uncertainty and the presence of the adverb *ær* may account for the subjunctive, the implication being 'before I was ready to die'; see §2732.

§2653. On this topic see further Wülfing, ii. 110–12; Adams, pp. 148-9; Callaway 1931, pp. 72–82; Möllmer, pp. 107–8; Behre, pp. 163–4; and Visser, ii, §879.

5. CONJUNCTIONS MEANING 'AFTER' OR 'SINCE'

a. Introductory remarks

§2654. The three most common conjunctions are the formulae with *æfter*, which occur only in the prose, *siþþan*, and *þæs þe*. The word *æfter* is used as a preposition and an adverb, but is never found alone as a conjunction; this rules out the Bright/ASPR emendation of *sunnan* to *sunne* in *Ex* 109. Conjunctions meaning 'after' or 'since' are discussed by Adams (pp. 100–15) and Möllmer (pp. 63–75). Liggins (1970, p. 296) gives a table showing the number of these three conjunctions in 'Alfredian' prose and offers comments on variations in usage. The most important of these are taken up in the sections which follow. On mood, see §§2687–90.

§2655. Like those meaning 'when', temporal conjunctions meaning 'after' and 'since' easily acquire a causal connotation. This point too is taken up as it becomes relevant.

b. Combinations involving æfter

§2656. In these combinations, which occur only in the prose, *æfter* is followed by the dative or instrumental of *se*, which occurs in the spellings *þam, þæm, þan*, and *þon*, and with initial *ð*. The meaning is 'after'. It indicates that the action of the principal clause occurs after that of the subordinate, with no reference to the beginning point of the action of the principal clause and no implication about the closeness in time between the two actions unless *sona* or some such adverb is used; see §§2708–11. For examples with an element of cause, see §3155.

§2657. Adams (pp. 211–13) records 191 examples of the formula with *þe* (for examples see below) and two without it, viz. *Ps(A)* 126. 3 (2), where *efter ðon* glosses *postquam*, and *Bede(T)* 326. 9 *Ond æfter þon he hine gereste medmicel fæc, ða ahof hine up*, where MSS *O* and *Ca* agree with *T* in omitting *þe*, but MS *B* has it. Möllmer (p. 72) adds *Bede(T)* 356. 8 *æfter ðon*, where none of the manuscripts has *þe*. There is one late instance of *æfter þæt*, viz. *Lch* iii. 132. 30 *7 æfter þ seo blodlæse si gefylled, þu hine scealt scearpigean*;

for ME examples see *MED*, s.v. *after* conj. 1(*b*). Adams (p. 213) and Visser (ii. 868) take *æfter þæm þæt* in *Or* 212. 27 *Hit biþ eac georn-lic þæt mon heardlice gnide þone hnescestan mealmstan æfter þæm þæt he þence þone soelestan hwetstan on to geræceanne* as a temporal conjunction 'after'. But the subj. *þence* rules this out. BTS (s.v. *æfter* A. I(7)) suggests 'according as', but this makes no sense to me. Kivimaa (p. 152) suggests that '*æfter þæm* may be adverbial and *þæt* final'. The clause certainly expresses purpose, but *æfter þæm þæt* may mean something like 'to the end that'. Wülfing (ii. 114) clearly errs in assigning the sense 'after' to *æfter þon þætte* in *Bede* 28. 7 *þa gelamp æfter þon þætte Peahte ðeod com of Scyððia lande. . . .* In my opinion, the same is also true of *æfter þon þæt* in *Bede* 40. 24 *Ða wæs sona æfter þon þæt smyltnes com cristenra tida, þæt ðær wæs cyrice geworht . . .* ; in both *æfter þon* means 'after' (adv.) and *þæt(te)* introduces a noun clause. Cf. *BlHom* 121. 5 (§2660).

§2658. As already noted in §2654, *æfter* is not used as a conjunction in OE. In common with Adams, I have so far not noted any examples of this formula in the divided form ☆*æfter þæm/þon...þe*.

§2659. Of Adams's 191 examples of the formula with *þe*, one hundred occur in *Orosius*, all with *æfter þæm þe*. Of these, seventy-seven have the formula seen in *Or* 160. 16 *Æfter þæm þe Romeburg getimbred wæs feower hunde wintrum 7 LXXVII, gewurdon on Rome þa yfelan wundor* and two—*Or* 270. 5 and 278. 6—have *Æfter þæm þe Romeburg wæs getimbred* (Liggins 1970, p. 296). Möllmer (pp. 69–70), who gives the total as eighty, tells us that the formula corresponds to *post urbem conditam* twice (*Or* 68. 4 and 86. 19) and to *ab urbe condita* seventy-six times (e.g. *Or* 90. 22). Bede prefers the instrumental *æfter þon þe*. Ælfric has *æfter ðam ðe* in *ÆCHom* i. 478. 14 *þa wearð he hreowlice and hrædlice dead æfter ðam ðe he ða cild acwealde for Cristes acennednysse*, but *æfter þan þe* in *ÆCHom* i. 90. 13 *Æfter þan ðe wæron gefyllede ehta dagas Drihtnes acennednysse þæt he ymbsniden wære, þa wæs his nama geciged Iesus*. Neither Adams nor Dodd records any examples of the formula in Wulfstan.

§2660. We find the formula used correlatively, e.g. (with *þa* in the principal clause) *Or* 92. 7 *þa on ðæm ilcan dæge æfter þæm þe hie þiss gesprecen hæfdon, fuhton Gallie on þa burg* and the two examples from *ÆCHom* in §2659; (with *þa* also in the temporal clause) *HomS* 22. 169 *Æfter þan þe se hælend þa hæfde heora fet geþwagen, þa onfeng he eft his hrægle . . .* ; (with *seoþþan*) *BlHom* 79. 1 *Swa*

*swa hit seoþþan gelamp xl wintra æfter þon ðe hie Crist on rode
ahengon*; and (with *sona . . . þa . . . æfter þon*) *BlHom* 121. 5 *Swa we
leorniaþ þæt sona æfter þon þe Drihten on heofenas astag, 7 hie mid
Halgan Gaste getrymede wæron, þa wæs æfter þon þæt hie þysne
middangeard on twelf tanum tohluton.*

§2661. Adams (p. 105) tells us that

in origin, *æfter* is the comparative of the adverb *af*, meaning *from*, originally
local in signification. It means, therefore, in the sphere of time *later*. Its use as
a preposition came doubtless from its use in comparisons, and naturally it required the dative case. The step from preposition to conjunction is easy. Of
course, *ðe* is the relative.

But I cannot see any sense in which *þe* in examples like *Or* 160. 1
*Æfter þæm þe Tarentine geacsedan þæt Pirrus dead wæs, þa sendon
hie on Affrice to Cartaginenses æfter fultume* can be the relative unless we are postulating omission of a noun such as *timan* or *fyrste*;
cf. *ÆCHom* i. 134. 21 . . . *and æfter ðam fyrste gan mid lace to
Godes huse* and see Mitchell, at press (*c*). In my opinion, it functions as a subordinating particle; see §2428. On the instrumental
þon/þan expressing comparison see §3245. Further on the 'local
origin' of the formula, see Johnsen, *Ang.* 39 (1916), 109-11. Möllmer (p. 70) says that *æfter þæm þe* was originally an imitation of
Latin *postquam* which spread from there into the colloquial speech
and (he quite wrongly adds) into the poetry.

§2662. As Möllmer (pp. 71-2) points out, the usual tenses in clauses
introduced by the formulae with *æfter* are the preterite and the pluperfect. But we find the present, as in *Matt(WSCp)* 26. 32 *Witodlice
æfter þam þe ic of deaþe arise, ic cume to eow on Galilea* and *ÆLS*
36. 25 (in both of which the reference is to the future), and the perfect, as in *CP* 405. 21 . . . *nu sio Godes miltsung is swa micul ofer ða
dysegan, ðæt hiene na ne aðriet ðæt he hi to him ne laðige æfter
ðæm ðe hie gesyngod habbað.*

c. Prepositional formulae involving nouns of time

§2663. These fall into two groups—those in which the temporal
relationship 'after' is clearly indicated by the connective and those in
which it 'must be gathered from the context' (Adams, p. 112).

§2664. Clauses introduced by formulae of the first type denote the
time of the beginning of the action of the main clause. The prepositions are *fram* and *of*; the nouns are *dæg, gear, tid,* and *tima,* in the

dative case. Typical examples are *Or* 62. 15 *From þæm geare þe heo getimbred wearð, wæs hire anwald M wintra 7 C 7 LX 7 folnæh feower, Bede* 52. 8 *is þæt land ðe Angulus is nemned, betwyh Geatum 7 Seaxum; is sæd of þære tide þe hi ðanon gewiton oð to dæge, þæt hit weste wunige, ÆCHom* i. 462. 29 *Fram ðam dæge þe his apostol Bartholomeus hider com, ic eom mid byrnendum racenteagum ðearle fornumen,* and *WHom* 18. 78 *And of þam timan ærest þe se man fulluht underfehð, him wunað on se Halga Gast.* For more, see Adams, pp. 113–15.

§ 2665. The second group are formulae with *on* + a demonstrative, a numeral, and *gear* or *monaþ*, all in the dative case, + *þe*. The four examples noted by Adams (pp. 112–13) are *Ch* 1317, *Num* 1. 1, *Exod* 19. 1 *On ðam ðriddan monðe þe Israhela folc ferde of Egypta lande, hi ferdon to Sinai westene,* and *VSal* 1. 130 *And hyt wæs þa on þam ehtoðan geare þe se mycla hungor heom on becom þæt hig for þære hlafleaste þa eorðan æton.* On these Adams (p. 112) writes:

> The time-relation is not evident from the connective itself, but must be gathered from the context. One would like to think that *ðæs* has dropped out in all the cases, but that is rather too violent a method of dealing with the question.
>   Probably the examples were not felt as *after*-clauses at all, though logically they are. The clauses introduced by *ðe* may be considered relative adjective clauses depending on the noun of time; just as we might say, translating HL. 185. 131 [= *VSal* 1. 130, above], 'It was then in the eighth year that the great famine came upon them, that, etc.'

The same remarks hold for similar formulae without prepositions discussed in § 2686.

d. Siþþan

§ 2666. Three possible origins for *siþþan* have been advanced. Adams (pp. 100–1) argues against Sweet's explanation that it is compounded of the preposition *siþ* and its object in the dative—'*ðæm* does not become *ðan* until the later period of OE., and we have *siððan* in the earliest texts'—and prefers to see it as a combination of comp. adv. *siþ* 'later' (*OEG,* § 673) and *þan* 'the instrumental in a phrase of comparison'. Despite Johnsen's objections and his claim that '*siððan* is a juxtaposition of the two local adverbs *sið* and *ðan*' (*Ang.* 39 (1916), 106–9), Adams is probably right. See further Small 1930, p. 389 fn. 21, and Mitchell, at press (*c*). As an adverb and a conjunction, it appears in many different spellings. Variants of *-i-* include *e, eo, ie, io,* and *y*; of *-þþ- þð, ðþ, ð,* and *ðð*; and of *-an a, e, en,* and *on*; see Adams, p. 102, GK, p. 608, and Johnsen, *Ang.* 39 (1916), 108.

Adams (p. 211) also records one example of *sið*—in *Ch* 1440. In one or other of these forms, *sippan* is the most common conjunction meaning 'after' in both prose and poetry.

§2667. In the prose Adams (pp. 209-11) records 244 examples of *sippan*, used either alone without any correlative, e.g. *Or* 17. 23 *Ne mette he ær nan gebun land, sippan he from his agnum ham for* and *ÆCHom* i. 6. 15 *forðan þe he sylf næs on heofonum, syððan he for his modignysse of aworpen wæs*, or with correlative *þa*, e.g. *ChronE* 47. 7 (745) *Her Daniel forðferde. þa wæs xlvi wintra agan syððan he onfeng biscopdome* and *Alex* 20. 8 *sioðþan hie þa wyrmas hæfdon ondruncen þæs wætres, þa gewiton hie þonon*; and twenty-two examples of correlative *sippan . . . sippan*, as in *Or* 62. 33 . . . *hwelc mildsung sippan wæs sippan se cristendom wæs* and *ÆCHom* i. 108. 32 *ac syððan hi comon to Iudeiscum earde, syððan he wæs heora latteow*. In *LawVIAs* 2 7 *forgyldon þæt yrfe þe syððan genumen wære, þe we þæt feoh scuton*, Latin *et persoluamus pecus illud/ omne pecus quod captum fuerit/est, postquam pecuniam nostram contulerimus*, and *HomS* 22. 114 *Geearnode he þy syððan þe he drihten heora ealra modgeðances cunnode*, there are good reasons for not taking *syððan . . . þe* and *syððan þe* as unique instances of temporal conjunctions; see §2594. *Bede* prefers *þæs þe* to *sippan* (twenty-four examples to eight), *Or* prefers *sippan* to *þæs þe* (twenty-eight examples to fifteen); see Liggins 1970, p. 296. On the evidence presented by Adams (pp. 209-14), Ælfric and Wulfstan also prefer *sippan*.

§2668. In the poetry too, *sippan* is found with no correlative adverb, e.g.

Beo 129   Mære þeoden,
                 æþeling ærgod,   unbliðe sæt,
                 þolode ðryðswyð   þegnsorge dreah,
                 syðþan hie þæs laðan   last sceawedon,
                 wergan gastes,

or with a correlative adverb, which may be *sippan* itself, e.g.

Beo 2200   Eft þæt geiode   ufaran dogrum
                 hildehlæmmum,   syððan Hygelac læg,
                 . . .   .
                 syððan Beowulfe   brade rice
                 on hand gehwearf,

þa, e.g.

Beo 115   Gewat ða neosian,   syþðan niht becom,
                 hean huses,   hu hit Hring-Dene
                 æfter beorþege   gebun hæfdon,

þonne, e.g.

GenA 1824   Siððan Egypte   eagum moton
                  on þinne wlite wlitan   wlance monige,
                  þonne æðelinga   eorlas wenað . . . ,

or *eft*, e.g.

Beo 2387   ond him eft gewat   Ongenðioes bearn
                 hames niosan   syððan Heardred læg. . . .

§2669. It is impossible to give an exact number for the occurrences of the conjunction *siþþan* in the poetry because of the presence of ambiguous adverb/conjunctions. This problem arises occasionally in the prose, e.g. *ÆCHom* i. 72. 21, where *sealde, gewæpnode, halsode*, and *gedranc*, could all be taken as pluperfect and a comma could replace the full stop after *gedranc*. But it is much more common in the poetry. There are no criteria by which we can decide beyond doubt whether initial *siþþan* is an adverb or a conjunction in certain sentences. Sometimes the context will help. The Latin original sometimes suggests that *siþþan* is an adverb, e.g.

PPs 103. 21   Syþþan up cumeð   æðele sunne,
                 hi of siðum eft   gesamniað
                 and hi on holum   hydað hi georne,

Latin *Ortus est sol, et congregati sunt: et in cubilibus suis se collocabunt*, at others that it is a conjunction, e.g. (despite the ASPR punctuation reproduced here)

PPs 70. 10   Cweþað cuðlice: 'Wuton cunnian,
                 hwænne hine god læte   swa swa gymeleasne;
                 þonne we hine forgripen   and his geara ehtan;
                 syþþan he ne hæbbe   helpend ænne',

Latin *Dicentes: Deus dereliquit eum: persequimini et comprehendite eum, quia non est qui eripiat*. But it often fails, e.g. in *PPs* 106. 39, and is in any case a dangerous guide. Andrew does not claim that element order is a criterion here, as he does for *þa* and *þonne*; see §§2539-60. But he does try to establish the validity of metrical criteria (see, for example, *Postscript*, p. 27) which have been effectively dismissed by Samuels (*MÆ* 18 (1949), 62-4). Ambiguity therefore exists in such examples as *JDay* i 114,

Ex 144   Ealles þæs forgeton   siððan grame wurdon
               Egypta cyn   ymbe antwig;
               ða heo his mægwinum   morðor fremedon,
               wroht berenedon,   wære fræton,

where a full stop may be placed after *forgeton* and *siððan . . . ða* taken as 'then . . . when',

GenA 2854   Siððan þu gestigest   steape dune,
                      hrincg þæs hean landes,   þe ic þe heonon getæce,
                      up þinum agnum fotum,   þær þu scealt ad gegærwan . . . ,

where either *siððan* or *þær* may be a conjunction or where both may be adverbs, as Holthausen's punctuation suggests, and

Ex 224   Siððan hie getealdon   wið þam teonhete
                    on þam forðherge   feðan twelfe
                    moderofra;   mægen wæs onhrered,

where Blackburn has a comma after line 226a and where it is difficult to reconcile Irving's punctuation with his glossary. Compare also the handling by various editors of *Beo* 470, *Beo* 847, *Dan* 659, and *Sat* 447, and see Schücking, pp. 117–20.

§2670. Van Draat (*EStudien*, 32 (1903), 372) observes bluntly that 'Old English does not know the conjunction *since* in the sense of "seeing that".' Adams (p. 103) tells us that

in Modern English, *since* has passed very largely over to the causal signification. This is natural enough, for an event which precedes another is often its cause; but it is noteworthy that in OE *syððan* rarely or never has this meaning. I quote an example in which the two meanings seem about equally present: *ÆLS* 25. 74 *Fela wæron forbodene godes folce on ðære æ þe nu syndon clæne æfter Cristes tocyme siððan Paulus cwæð to þam cristenum ðus. . . .*

For Möllmer (p. 68) a causal connotation is certain in

Beo 884   Sigemunde gesprong
                æfter deaðdæge   dom unlytel,
                syþðan wiges heard   wyrm acwealde,
                hordes hyrde,

for van Dam (pp. 63–4) in *Or* 156. 11 *þa, siþþan he irre wæs 7 gewundod, he ofslog micel þæs folces. . . .* Liggins, who claims an earlier date for causal *siþþan* than had hitherto been proposed (1955, p. 544), notes (1955, pp. 310–15) that the earliest examples of the causal meaning of 'since' date from the mid-fifteenth century, but finds more examples than the solitary one noted by Adams of 'temporal/causal' *siþþan* in OE prose. She admits, however, that the temporal sense is dominant in all but three, viz. *ÆLS* 25. 74 above, *Bo* 104. 26 *Ac ic þe wille nu giet getæcan ðone weg . . . siððan ðu ongitst þurh mine lare hwæt sio soðe gesælð bið*, where *siððan* represents Latin *quoniam*, and 'probably' *CP* 465. 17 *Ac siððan he ongeat*

*ðæt he wæs aðunden on upahæfennesse for his godan weorcum, ða
gecyðde he swiðe hræðe æfter ðæm hwæt he siððan dreag*, where the
Latin has *quia*. This last example in particular illustrates our dilemma.
I do not see how any modern reader can be sure how much causality
is implied in it or in sentences like *Or* 62. 33 and *ÆCHom* i. 6. 15
(both in §2667) or on what grounds it could be claimed that *siþðan*
is temporal 'after' and *þæs þe* causal 'because' (as Klaeber glosses it)
—and not vice versa—in

Beo 104   fifelcynnes eard
          wonsæli wer   weardode hwile,
          siþðan him Scyppend   forscrifen hæfde
          in Caines cynne—   þone cwealm gewræc
          ece Drihten,   þæs þe he Abel slog.

Even a native speaker of MnE might have difficulty in deciding
whether the sentence 'I haven't been to the Trout Inn since Tom left
for Australia' implies that Tom stimulated the speaker's interest in
beer or simply refers to two unconnected events which happen to
coincide in time. I shall return to this problem.

§2671. Adams observes that '*siððan* is used indifferently to express
the relations *ex quo* and *postquam*' (p. 101); it differs from *æfter
þæm þe* in that the latter 'never has reference to the beginning-point
of an action' (p. 105). But difficulties arise. First, *ex quo*—or at any
rate its English equivalent 'from the time that'—embraces two distinct situations. I can say 'I haven't stopped working from the time
that I got up'; here the action of the principal clause is still continuing and 'from the time that' can be replaced by 'since' but not by
'after'. But I can also say 'I didn't stop working from the time that
I got up until I went to bed', where the action of the principal clause
is completed and 'from the time that' can be replaced by 'after' but
not by 'since'. Previous discussions on *siþþan* have not made this
distinction explicit.[113] Yet it exists in OE. Thus we find *siþþan* 'from
the time that, since' but not 'after' in *Solil* 64. 8 *me ðincð nu þæt þu
hæbbe genoh swetole gesæd þæt ælces mannes sawl nu si and a beo
and a were syððan god ærest þone forman man gescop, BlHom* 23. 3
*we synd on þisse worlde ælþeodige 7 swa wæron siþþon se æresta
ealdor þisses menniscan cynnes Godes bebodu abræc, BlHom* 187. 2
*Manige gear syndon agan nu seoþþan ure bisceopas geond eal Romana
rice an to me gewreoto sende*, and

GenB 611   þu meaht nu þe self geseon,   swa ic hit þe secgan ne þearf,
          Eue seo gode,   þæt þe is ungelic

[113] Van Draat (*EStudien*, 32 (1901), 371-88) glimpsed the truth; see especially pp. 372-
3 and 375. But he was concerned with MnE 'since' and so did not pursue the point.

wlite and wæstmas,   siððan þu minum wordum getruwodest,
læstes mine lare.

In these examples the preterite verb-forms in the principal clauses
serve as perfects. But we find *siþþan* 'from the time that, after' but
not 'since' in *Or* 90. 8 *Ac siþþan hie on Sicilium wunnon, hie eac
siþþan betweonum him selfum winnende wæron, oþ þæt Darius,
Persa cyning, Læcedemonium on fultume wearð wið þæm Athenienses, for þæm gewinnum his ieldrena, ÆCHom* i. 108. 31 *Ne glad he
ealne weig him ætforan, ac syððan hi comon to Iudeiscum earde,
syððan he wæs heora latteow, oð þæt he bufan Cristes gesthuse
ætstod*, and

Brun 10   Hettend crungun,
                Sceotta leoda   and scipflotan
                fæge feollan,   feld dænnede
                secga swate,   siðþan sunne up
                on morgentid,   mære tungol,
                glad ofer grundas,   godes condel beorht,
                eces drihtnes,   oð sio æþele gesceaft
                sah to setle.

In these the fact that the action of the principal clause is finished is
clearly shown by the *oþ/oð (þæt)* clauses.

§2672. Second, is Adams right when he implies that *siþþan* can be
used in the sense 'after' in contexts where it has no reference to the
beginning-point of the action of the principal clause and therefore
cannot be translated 'from the time that'? There are some examples
in which the answer is doubtful, e.g. *Or* 30. 26, *BlHom* 111. 31
*Hwæt biþ hit la elles buton flæsc seoððan se ecea dæl ofbiþ, þæt is
seo sawl?, ÆCHom* i. 38. 16, *ChronE* 143. 18 (1013) *Syððan he
undergeat þet eall folc him to gebogen wæs, þa bead he þ man sceolde
his here metian 7 horsian*, and

Beo 833   þæt wæs tacen sweotol,
                syþðan hildedeor   hond alegde,
                earm ond eaxle   —þær wæs eal geador
                Grendles grape—   under geapne hrof.

We may think that the action of these principal clauses immediately
followed or dated from that of the *siþþan* clauses, but we have to
concede that the author did not make it explicit. But in the following examples this possibility does not arise and *siþþan* means 'after',
not 'from the time that': *Or* 178. 2 *Ac siþþan Metellus þa elpendas
ofercom, siþþan he hæfde eac raðe þæt oþer folc gefliemed* (see
Liggins 1970, p. 296, for more information about the situation in

the 'Alfredian' texts), *Mark(WSCp)* 1. 14 *Syððan Iohannes geseald wæs com se Hælend on Galileam*, Latin *Postquam autem traditus est Iohannes uenit Ihs in Galilaeam*, where *Li* has *æfter ðon* and *Ru1 æfter þon*, Gen 18. 12 *Syððan ic ealdode 7 min hlaford geripod ys, sceal ic nu æniges lustes gyman?*, Latin *Postquam consenui et dominus meus uetulus est, uoluptati operam dabo?*, Beo 4, and

GenA 2882 Wit eft cumað,
      siððan wit ærende   uncer twega
      gastcyninge   agifen habbað.

§2673. I turn now to a third question. We have established that *siþþan* may mean not only 'since' and 'from the time that' with reference to the time at which the action of the principal clause began but also 'after' with no such reference, despite van Draat (*EStudien*, 32 (1903), 371). Can it have any other meanings? We find combinations like *sona (. . .) siþþan* and *siþþan (. . .) ærest* meaning 'as soon as'; see §2710. But 'from the time that' and 'as soon as' are very close in meaning and Möllmer (p. 66) detects the latter sense in examples like *Bede* 164. 2 *Ða sæt he Aidan in þæm gemote betweoh oðrum weotum, cwæð to þam biscope, siðþan he his word gehyrde . . .*, *ChronE* 143. 18 (1013) (§2672), and

Beo 603 Gæþ eft se þe mot
      to medo modig,   siþþan morgenleoht
      ofer ylda bearn   oþres dogores,
      sunne sweglwered   suþan scineð!

There is room for difference of opinion here, as in the other examples in the group to which *ChronE* 143. 18 (1013) belongs.

§2674. It is a matter of semantic indifference whether we translate the subordinate clause in *ÆCHom* i. 304. 29 *syððan se geleafa sprang geond ealne middangeard, siððan geswicon ða wundra* by 'When faith had sprung up' or 'After faith sprang up' and the *syðþan* clause in

Dream 1 Hwæt! Ic swefna cyst   secgan wylle,
      hwæt me gemætte   to midre nihte,
      syðþan reordberend   reste wunedon!

by 'when men were at rest' or 'after men had sought their beds'; we do not need to follow Glogauer (pp. 28-9) in taking *syðþan* to mean *þenden* in the second example. But, as Möllmer (p. 67) points out, *siþþan* seems to mean 'when', not 'after', in

Beo 1202 þone hring hæfde   Higelac Geata,
      nefa Swertinges   nyhstan siðe,

> siðþan he under segne   sinc ealgode,
> wælreaf werede

and

Beo 2354

>   No þæt læsest wæs
> hondgemota,   þær mon Hygelac sloh,
> syððan Geata cyning   guðe ræsum,
> freawine folca   Freslondum on,
> Hreðles eafora   hiorodryncum swealt,
> bille gebeaten.

Neither Adams nor BT(S) mentions this possibility and I have as yet noted no similar examples in the prose. There is work for the lexicographers here.

§2675. The last question to arise is whether a study of the syntax can help us to distinguish these various meanings. BT (s.v. *siððan* II conj.) makes this distinction: '(1) where the tense of the verb in the clause introduced by *siððan* is past, in the other present, *since* . . . (2) where the tense is the same in each clause, *after* . . .'. This is satisfactory up to a point. Pattern (1) can be illustrated by *Mark(WSCp)* 9. 21 *Hu lang tid is syððan him þis gebyrede?*, Latin *quantum temporis est ex quo hoc ei accidit?*, and *GenB* 611 (§2671), pattern (2) by *Mark(WSCp)* 1. 14 and *GenA* 2882 (both in §2672). But it will not do, as some of BT's own citations show. It rightly says that in *Luke (WSCp)* 7. 45 *Coss þu me ne sealdest. þeos syððan ic ineode ne geswac þ heo mine fet ne cyste, syððan* means 'since'. But this does not conform to the definition it gives for pattern (1), since both verbs are preterite. The point, of course, is that *ineode* refers to an action completed in the past whereas *geswac . . . cyste* refer to one action begun in the past and continuing in the present; the combination serves as a perfect tense 'has not stopped kissing my feet'. The same is true of *BlHom* 23. 3 (§2671), of which BT presents a telescoped version; although the tenses of *wæron* and *abræc* are the same, the meaning is not 'We were exiles after our first ancestor broke God's commands' but 'We are exiles and have been since Adam broke God's commands'. This use of the OE preterite as a perfect is well authenticated, but to call it a 'present tense' is to make the term too elastic.[114]

§2676. Wattie (p. 127) observes that 'the special force of the perfect tense is not so much to indicate a completed action as to imply that this particular happening of the past has a bearing on the present'. So we can say that in some of the examples quoted above the *siþþan*

---

[114] Van Draat makes the same point in *EStudien*, 32 (1903), 371. But see fn. 115 to §2678.

clause expresses both the point of time at which the action of the principal clause began and the cause of, or reason for, that action. For example, *BlHom* 23. 3 in effect implies two statements: 'We have been exiles since Adam broke God's commands' and 'We are exiles because Adam broke God's commands'. But this relationship of cause and effect between the two clauses does not always exist; in *Luke(WSCp)* 7. 45 (§ 2675), Christ's entry was the opportunity for, but not the cause of, Mary's action. With this in mind, we can restate BT's divisions in terms of the distinction made in § 2671:

siþþan conj.—primarily temporal but often with some suggestion of a causal relationship, (1) where the action of the principal clause is conceived as having been completed—*after*; (2) where the action of the principal clause is conceived as still going on—*since*.

§ 2677. Some illustrative examples have already been given in the last two sections. A few more will not be out of place: (*siþþan* 'after') *Or* 90. 8, *ÆCHom* i. 108. 31, *Brun* 10 (all in § 2671), and *ÆCHom* i. 212. 8 *ac siððan he to cyninge gehalgod bið, þonne hæfð he anweald ofer þæt folc*; (*siþþan* 'since') *Solil* 64. 8, *BlHom* 187. 2, *GenB* 611 (all in § 2671), *Bo* 20. 1 *Gif þu nu gemunan wilt ealra ðara arwyrðnessa þe ðu for þisse weorulde hæfdest siððan ðu ærest geboren wære oð ðisne dæg* . . . , and *WHom* 6. 199 *He sæde þæt æfter þisum fæce gewurðan sceall swa egeslic tima swa æfre ær næs syððan þeos woruld gewearð.*

§ 2678. But even the rule given above cannot eliminate all ambiguities, for sometimes it is not clear whether a preterite tense is to be taken as a simple past tense or as a perfect or pluperfect. Thus *Or* 17. 23 *Ne mette he ær nan gebun land siþþan he from his agnum ham for* can be translated, with *ær* . . . *mette* taken as a pluperfect, 'He had not met any inhabited land since he left his own home' or, with *ær* implying 'until he reached the inhabited land he now saw', 'He did not see any inhabited land after he left his own home until . . .'. Liggins (1970, p. 298), after discussing some examples in *Or* in which *siþþan* 'appear[s] to be interchangeable with *æfter þæm þe*', remarks that 'we even find' *Or* 254. 3 . . . *on þæm twæm 7 on feowerteogþan geare þæs þe Agustus ricsade, þæt wæs siþþan Romeburg getimbred wæs VII C wintra 7 LII.* But there is no guarantee that *siþþan* must mean 'after' here. I am not convinced that it is impossible to translate '. . . in the forty-second year of the reign of Augustus, that was 752 years since Rome had been built'; the variation from the usual formula *æfter þæm þe* may be significant. Thorpe translates *ÆCHom* i. 6. 15 *forðan þe he sylf næs on heofonum syððan he for his modignysse of aworpen wæs* 'for he himself [the devil] was not in heaven after that he, for his pride, had been cast out'. I would prefer 'for the devil has not been in heaven since he was thrown out for his pride'. A similar instance will be found in *ÆCHom* ii. 450. 31. My last example must be

Beo 2628 Ne gemealt him se modsefa, ne his mæges laf
       gewac æt wige; þæt se wyrm onfand,
       syððan hie togædre gegan hæfdon,

which does not fit BT's rule quoted in §2675. The tenses are different, yet *siþþan* appears to mean 'after'. Only if both verbs are taken as pluperfect can it be translated 'since'.[115]

e. þæs (. . .) (þe)

§2679. The prevailing form of this conjunction is *þæs þe*, which is exemplified below. But even *þæs þe* is not common in the poetry or in the prose, except in *Chron, Bede,* and *Or*; see my D.Phil. thesis, p. 792, and Adams, pp. 213-14.

§2680. The only example of *þæs* noted by Adams (p. 111) in the prose is *Bede(T)* 108. 22 *þæt wæs ymb an 7 twentig wintra þæs Agustinus mid his geferum to læranne Ongolþeode sended wæs,* where all other manuscripts have *þæs þe/ðe.* In the poetry *þæs* appears in *GenB* 570 (?result; see §2873), *Sat* 576 (?cause), *Brun (ABC)* 51 (where MS *D* has *þæs þe*; see §2302), and

GuthB 1134 Wæron feowere ða forð gewitene
       dagas on rime, þæs se dryhtnes þegn
       on elne bad, adle gebysgad,
       sarum geswenced.

Two examples of *þæs* . . . *þe* are known to me, viz. *LS* 10. 168. 143 . . . *þæt þy ylcan dæge þæs ymbe twelf monað þe seo forðfore þæs eadigan weres wæs, hi þa þa byrgene untyndon,* where (according to Adams, p. 111) 'it would seem that *ymbe twelf monað* is, as it were,

---

[115] As I have already noted, some of the points made above were made by van Draat in *EStudien*, 32 (1903), 371-88. This article was not known to me when I presented my unpublished dissertation on 'Adverb Clauses in Old English Prose' for the degree of Master of Arts in the University of Melbourne in November 1951, which forms the basis of my discussion here. In particular, my redrafting of BT's article on *siþþan* in §2676 is quoted from p. 86 of that dissertation.

an afterthought, and is inserted parenthetically between the parts of the connective', and

ChristB 464   ... ærþon up stige   ancenned sunu,
                   efenece bearn,   agnum fæder,
                   þæs ymb feowertig   þe he of foldan ær
                   from deaðe aras,   dagena rimes,

where there are metrical reasons for the separation of *þæs* and *þe*.

§ 2681. Clauses introduced by *þæs (þe)* fall into three groups. First, there are those which are dependent on an expression of time and in which *þæs þe* can be explained as the genitive of the *se'þe* relative, e.g. *ChronA* 66. 12 (855) *7 ymb ii gear þæs ðe he on Francum com he gefor*, *ChronA* 88. 12 (894) *7 þæt wæs ymb twelf monað þæs þe hie ær hider ofer sæ comon*, *ÆCHom* ii. 196. 19 *Ða on ðam fifteo- goðan dæge ðæs ðe hi fram Egypta lande ferdon, wearð Godes wuldor gesewen on ðam westene* . . . (the only example in *ÆCHom*), and

Jud 12   þæt wæs þy feorðan dogore
                   þæs ðe Iudith hyne,   gleaw on geðonce,
                   ides ælfscinu,   ærest gesohte.

Liggins (1970, pp. 296-7) analyses in some detail the variations in this type in the 'Alfredian' texts. Here belong the two examples with *þæs . . . þe* in § 2680. Second, there are those which occur with an expression of time, but in which the gender of that expression makes it unlikely that *þæs þe* is a relative, e.g. *Bede* 332. 27 *Ac heo nales æfter micelre tide þæs þæ þæt mynster getimbred wæs gewat to þære ceastre* . . . , *ChronE* 135. 31 (1004) *7 se here com þa to þeod- forda binnon iii wuca þæs þe hi ær gehergodon Norðwic*, and

GenA 2768   Hine Abraham on   mid his agene hand
                   beacen sette,   swa him bebead metod,
                   wuldortorht ymb wucan,   þæs þe hine on woruld
                   to moncynne   modor brohte.

(I have to use the word 'unlikely' rather than 'impossible' because of examples like

Thureth 5   Gemyndi is he   mihta gehwylcre
                   þæs þe he on foldan   gefremian mæg. . . .

But *þæs* may be directly dependent on *gemyndi*.) Third, there are those in which there is no preceding expression of time which can serve as an antecedent, e.g. *Bede* 42. 3 *And þæs ðe þa seo costnung ðære ehtnesse gestilled wæs, þa wæron forðgongende þa cristenan*

men 7 ða geleafsuman, ChronC 105. 26 (918) *Ac swiðe hrædlice þæs
ðe hi þæs* [MS *D þus*] *geworden hæfde, heo gefor . . .* , and

GuthB 1052   Hreþer innan swearc,
        hyge hreowcearig,   þæs þe his hlaford geseah
        ellorfusne.

§2682. How did these uses of *þæs þe* originate if, as I suggest in
Mitchell, at press (*c*), Carkeet is wrong when he claims (1976, p. 53)
that *þæs þe* 'can be derived from *þæs* + NOUN OF TIME + RELA-
TIVE PRONOUN, as in attested OE *þæs geares þe* "in the year
when" '? I agree with Adams (p. 111) in rejecting the notion that it
'arose from the partitive use: *Or* 212. 13 *þa wæs þæt þridde gewin
geendad Punica 7 Romana on þæm feorþan geare þæs þe hit ær ongunnen wæs*' and disagree with Johnsen (*Ang.* 38 (1914), 100) when
he writes: 'I should suppose that *ðæs ðe* is originally a juxtaposition
of the two local-demonstrative adverbs'; if this were right, one would
expect *þæs þe* to mean 'whence', not 'when' or 'after'. The first
group of examples—those in which *þæs þe* can be taken as the genitive of the *se'þe* relative—correspond to examples like *ChronA* 72. 9
(871) *7 þæs ymb anne monaþ gefeaht Ælfred cyning wiþ alne þone
here* and *ChronA* 2. 7 (—) *Ond þæs ymb vi gear þæs þe hie up
cuomon geeodon West Seaxna rice*—where *þæs* can be taken as the
genitive singular of the demonstrative *se* referring back to *monaþ*
(m.) and *gear* (n.) respectively: 'after one month/six years from that
one'. The second group of examples—in which the possible antecedent for *þæs þe* is feminine—are comparable with *ChronA* 70. 11
(871) *Her cuom se here to Readingum on West Seaxe 7 þæs ymb
iiii niht ridon ii eorlas up* and *ChronA* 70. 14 (871) *þæs ymb iii niht
Æþered cyning 7 Ælfred his broþur þær micle fierd to Readingum
gelæddon*—where *þæs* does not agree with *niht* (f.). (Despite *ChronA*
74. 11 (876) *nihtes, niht* seems to have remained feminine in its
other uses, e.g. *ChronE* 65. 28 (852) *ane næht* and *ChronE* 127. 14
(992) *on þere nihte ðe.*) The third group of examples—in which *þæs
þe* has no possible antecedent and therefore can only be taken as
a conjunction—correspond to examples like *Or* 12. 20 *þeah sume
men secgen þæt hire æwielme sie on westende Affrica neh þam
beorge Athlans, 7 þonne fol raðe þæs sie east irnende on þæt sond*
and *Bo* 50. 9 . . . *þ ic his wæs swiðe wafiende . . . 7 þa fulhræðe ðæs
ic cleopode to him . . .*—in which *þæs* has no possible antecedent
and therefore can only be taken as an adverb.

§2683. It would seem reasonable to postulate that adv. *þæs* arose
from dem. *þæs* expressing time (cf. *ChronA* 72. 12 (871) *þæs geares*).

Whether *þæs þe* arose from *þæs þe* referring back to a masculine or neuter antecedent or from adv. *þæs* + *þe* (see Adams, pp. 110-11) need not be debated. I would suggest that both developments took place. In either event, I believe that here again *þe* was originally the subordinating particle and that in examples of the first type discussed above, it may subsequently have been felt as the relative. I concede neither the need for, nor the likelihood of, the development postulated by Carkeet.

§2684. Examples in which *þæs þe* is used correlatively include (with *þæs*) *ChronA* 2. 7 (§2682) and *Bede* 486. 20 *þæs ymbe syx gear þæs þe hi upp coman, geeodan Westseaxna rice*, and (with *þa*) *Or* 212. 13 (§2682), *Bede* 42. 3 and *ÆCHom* ii. 196. 19 (both in §2681), and

GenA 1438   Let þa ymb worn daga
    þæs þe heah hlioðo horde onfengon
    and æðelum eac eorðan tudres
    sunu Lameches sweartne fleogan
    hrefn ofer heahflod of huse ut.

§2685. When used with reference to time, *þæs þe* may mean 'after, from when', e.g. *Bede* 486. 20, *ÆCHom* ii. 196. 19, and *GenA* 1438 (§§2684, 2681, and 2684, respectively) or 'when, after', e.g. *Bede* 42. 3 and *GuthB* 1052 (both in §2681). In

Fort 58   Sum sceal on geoguþe mid godes meahtum
    his earfoðsiþ ealne forspildan,
    ond on yldo eft eadig weorþan,
    wunian wyndagum ond welan þicgan,
    maþmas ond meoduful mægburge on,
    þæs þe ænig fira mæge forð gehealdan,

þæs þe means 'to the extent that' or 'as far as' rather than 'as long as' and in *GuthB* 1134 (§2680) *þæs* can be translated 'while' but retains the basic sense 'from when'. Further on temporal *þæs* (*þe*) in the poetry, see Sorg, pp. 62-4, and Mitchell 1959, pp. 301-3. On *þæs* (*þe*) expressing cause, see §§3113-17.

f. Noun phrases

§2686. Adams (p. 113) notes three examples in which a combination of a demonstrative, a numeral, and a noun of time (all in the genitive or instrumental), + *þe*, introduce clauses denoting time after. They are *Bede* 30. 20 *7 þy syxtan monðe þe he hider com, he eft to Rome hwearf*, *ChronE* 119. 7 (972) . . . *on v idus Mai þe xiii geare þe he to rice feng*, and *ChronE* 235. 18 (1100) *þ wæs þæs þreotteðan geares þe he rice onfeng*. The remarks by Adams quoted in §2665 about similar formulae with prepositions apply here.

g. Mood

§2687. The prevailing mood in clauses introduced by conjunctions meaning 'after' or 'since' is the indicative. The subjunctive is found in concurrence with one of the phenomena already discussed in §§2610-25. *Mutatis mutandis*, the remarks made there apply here. Thus we find the subjunctive in a temporal clause accompanied by an imperative, a jussive subjunctive, or a form of **sculan*, in the principal clause, e.g.

GuthB 1175   Beo þu on sið gearu,
                    siþþan lic ond leomu   ond þes lifes gæst
                    asundrien   somwist hyra
                    þurh feorggedal,

Solil 46. 3 *Siððam he þonne þat gelæornod hæbbe þæt his eagan nanwiht þæt fyr ne onscyniað, hawie þonne on steorran and on monan*, and *Lch* iii. 132. 30 *7 æfter þ seo blodlæse si gefylled, þu hine scealt scearpigean*. Uncertainty surrounding an unfulfilled desire, purpose, or hypothesis, creates an environment suitable for a subjunctive in *Or* 296. 9 *7 þohte, siþþan þæt folc oferfunden wære, þæt hie siþþan wolde eall þæt he wolde*, *Gen* 22. 9 . . . *7 he ðær . . . þone wudu gelogode, swa swa he hyt wolde habban to hys suna bærnette syððan he ofslagen wurde*, and

Husb 20   heht nu sylfa þe
                    lustum læran,   þæt þu lagu drefde,
                    siþþan þu gehyrde   on hliþes oran
                    galan geomorne   geac on bearwe

—in these the reference is to the future-in-the-past[116]—and *CP* 445. 32 *hit is awriten ðæt him wære betere ðæt hi no soðfæstnesse weg ne ongeaten, ðonne hi underbæc gecerden, siððan hi hine ongeaten*, where we have something approaching a rejected or imaginary condition.

§2688. All the examples cited by Visser (ii, §879) and by Callaway (1931), pp. 15-18) fit into one of these categories. In his table (1931,

---

[116] This seems to be the point made by Muxin about *siþþan* clauses in *UZLGU* 262, vyp. 50 (1958), 158. But without more examples than he gives it is hard to be certain. See also Furkert, p. 23.

p. 20) the latter claims that there are fourteen exceptions. I have not been able to trace all these.[117] Examples which Callaway might have reckoned among his exceptions include *Or* 212. 27 (see §2657); *CP* 341. 15 *Siððan hie ðonne ðæt geleornod hæbben, ðonne sint hie siððan to læranne hu hie scilen mildheortlice dælan ðæt ðæt hie ofer ðæt habbað ðe hie hiora gitsunge mid gestillan sculon* (where *sint hie to læranne* expresses a desire or purpose and there is a strong hypothetical flavour running through the whole passage);

Beo 2884

    Nu sceal sincþego   ond swyrdgifu,
    eall eðelwyn   eowrum cynne,
    lufen alicgean;   londrihtes mot
    þære mægburge   monna æghwylc
    idel hweorfan,   syððan æðelingas
    feorran gefricgean   fleam eowerne,
    domleasan dæd

(where the subjunctive follows *sceal* and *mot*); and

GuthA 205

    wæron teonsmiðas   tornes fulle,
    cwædon þæt him Guðlac   eac gode sylfum
    earfeþa mæst   ana gefremede,
    siþþan he for wlence   on westenne
    beorgas bræce . . .

(where the introductory verb is *cweþan* (see §2022) and the subj. *bræce* might reflect the poet's disbelief in the specific claim made by the evildoers). At the moment, I must assume that all Callaway's so-called exceptions can be explained within the categories discussed in §§2610–25 and must conclude that the imposition of a 'Subjunctive of Antecedent Action' (Callaway 1931, p. 26) on OE is unnecessary and unhelpful.

§2689. Despite Adams (p. 108), *GD* 305. 16 *æfter þon þe þu swa earfoðlice 7 gewinfullice ongeate 7 gelyfdest, ic gelyfe þæt hit sy ræd, þæt* . . . is not an exception; *ongeate* is indicative. But there are exceptions which show that these 'rules' are not inviolate. For reasons of space, I quote only three typical examples:

OrW 80

    . . . oþþe hwa þæs leohtes   londbuende
    brucan mote,   siþþan heo ofer brim hweorfeð

(indicative after a subjunctive);

----

[117] According to Callaway's table, there are fifty-one 'after' clauses with the subjunctive in his lists. Adams (pp. 209–14) gives thirty-six from the prose. He omits *Or* 296. 9 and *BenR* 67. 3. I find eight in the poetry plus the dubious *Jud* 189 (where *sende* may be an ambiguous preterite rather than a present subjunctive). This gives forty-seven. So there are four of Callaway's examples unidentified if we assume that his collections and mine are otherwise identical. I would willingly have traded full references in contexts such as these for the elaborate—and to me useless—'synoptic tables' included as end-papers in his book.

Beo 1782   Ga nu to setle,   symbelwynne dreoh
                wiggeweorþad;   unc sceal worn fela
                maþma gemænra,   siþðan morgen bið

(indicative after *sceal*); and *CP* 405. 21 (§2662) (indicative in dependent speech).

§2690. Similarly, there is no 'rule' that a negated indicative or a rhetorical question in the principal clause requires a subjunctive in an accompanying temporal clause; consider *BlHom* 111. 27-33.

6. CONJUNCTIONS MEANING 'AS SOON AS'

a. Introductory remarks

§2691. No OE conjunction means 'as soon as' in its own right. What we have are combinations of a conjunction which means 'as', 'when', or 'after', and an adverb which means 'immediately' or 'soon'. These combinations may be used with or without another adverb. To save space, I have exemplified this systematically only for *sona swa*; see §2699. The most common patterns involve *swa* and *sona*—191 of Adams's 369 examples (p. 195)—or *þæs þe* and adverbs such as *hrædlice, hraþe*, and *sona*—seventy of Adams's examples. Other typical combinations include *sona þa, færlice mid þam þe, swiþe hraþe æfter þon þe*, and *hrædlice siþþan*. For obvious reasons of space, I do not quote, or even give references to, examples of all possible combinations. The discussion which follows can be supplemented from Adams, pp. 62-82 and 195-203; Ericson 1932, pp. 49-50; Möllmer, pp. 46-53; and Liggins 1955, pp. 317-22 (where she detects a causal element in some clauses introduced by conjunctions meaning 'as soon as'), and 1970, pp. 293-5. On mood, see §§2713-15.

b. Swa

§2692. There is marked difference of opinion about the meanings which *swa* may have when it is (or seems to be) used as a temporal conjunction. BT (s.v. *swa* V. 8) gives the meaning 'temporal, *as, when*' and BTS adds '*as soon as*'. Campbell (*RES* 7 (1956), 67 fn. 4) writes that 'normally, *swa* is used of time only as an equivalent of *sona swa* . . . but this would be forced in *Gen* 552'. Adams lists twelve examples from the prose in which, in his opinion, *swa* denotes time when (p. 193) and eight in which it denotes immediate sequence (p. 198). Möllmer (pp. 39-41) similarly distinguishes sentences in which *swa* means 'when, as' (contemporaneous) and those in which it means 'as soon as' (immediate sequence), with examples from prose and poetry. I have listed what I consider to be the possible examples in the poetry in Mitchell 1959, pp. 321-5 and 790. Despite Gradon (*Elene*, glossary, s.v. *swa*), I prefer to take the *swa* clauses in *El* 87 and 100 as comparative. Dunning and Bliss (pp. 32-6) propose a few more examples as the result of repunctuation.

§2693. It is impossible to quote and discuss here all the suggested examples. That such a process would lead to any indisputable conclusions is unlikely. Adams (p. 193) gives *GD(H)* 29. 12 *Swa þe halga wer þis gehyrde, þa smercode he*, Latin *quo audito vir sanctus dedignando subrisit*, as an example of *swa* 'when'. But we have *sona swa* in *GD(C, O)* 29. 13 *Sona swa se halga man þas ærendu gehyrde, þa hloh he*. As noted above, Campbell thought that 'as soon as' for *swa* would be forced in

GenB 551   Ic wat, inc waldend god
abolgen wyrð,   swa ic him þisne bodscipe
selfa secge,   þonne ic of þys siðe cume
ofer langne weg,   þæt git ne læstan wel
hwilc ærende swa   he easten hider
on þysne sið sendeð.

Yet Möllmer (pp. 40-1) cites only this, *Sat* 527, and *Met* 13. 54, as examples of *swa* 'as soon as' in poetry. We can perhaps agree that *swa* is less likely to mean 'as soon as' in *Or* 198. 23 *þa geacsedon þa consulas þæt ær, ær Hannibal, 7 him ongean comon, swa he þa muntas oferfaren hæfde, 7 þær hæfdon longsum gefeoht, ær þara folca aþer fluge*, where the Latin has *cum*, *ChronF* 130. 36 (995) *7 swa þu ham cume, do into þinan mynstre þas ylcan hadesmenn . . .*, *HomU* 37. 233. 12 *and swa hy us eac lædað into cyrican, þonne lærð us godes engel stilnesse and gemetlice spræce*,

Beo 879   . . .   buton Fitela mid hine,
þonne he swulces hwæt   secgan wolde,
eam his nefan,   swa hie a wæron
æt niða gehwam   nydgesteallan,

and

Jul 253   Wes þu on ofeste,   swa he þec ut heonan
lædan hate,   þæt þu lac hraþe
onsecge sigortifre,   ær þec swylt nime,
deað fore duguðe,

where the Latin has *cum te de carcere iusserit egredi . . .*, than it is in *Bo* 145. 24 *Ac sio gesihð æt frumcerre, swa þa eagan on besioð, hi*

*ongitað ealle þone andwlitan ðæs lichoman, LS 7. 89 and swa he
þone munuc geseah, þa axode he hine to hwi he come,* and

Sat 524	þa ic gongan gefregn	gingran ætsomne
	ealle to Galileam;	hæfdon gastes bled,
	ongeton haligne	godes sunu
	swa heo gesegon	hwær sunu meotodes
	þa on upp gestod,	ece drihten,
	god in Galileam.	

But it will be a bold man who will unhesitatingly assign to one category or the other examples like *BenR* 90. 8 *Ða þe on ytinge farað
ahwyder, niman him brec of hrægelhuse, eft swa hig cumon ham of
ðam færelde, betæcan him gewahsene, GD(H)* 29. 12 (above), *GenB*
551 (above), and

Beo 1666		þa þæt hildebil
	forbarn brogdenmæl,	swa þæt blod gesprang,
	hatost heaþoswata.	

§ 2694. An additional complication is that in a good many of the
proposed examples *swa* need not mean either 'when' or 'as soon as'.
As Liggins (1970, p. 294) notes for *Or* 198. 23 and Andrew (*SS*,
pp. 75 and 98) for *Beo* 879 (both in § 2693), *swa* may have a causal
sense. A modal interpretation 'as' is sometimes possible, e.g. in *Lch*
ii. 306. 30 *do eft on þ ilce fæt, nytta swa þe þearf sie,* in line 2 of

PPs 101. 9	Dagas mine gedruran	swa se deorca scua,
	and ic hege gelic,	swa hit hraðe weornað,

where the Latin has *sicut,* and in

And 928	... ðæt ðu on feorwegas	feran ne cuðe
	ne in þa ceastre	becuman mehte,
	þing gehegan	þreora nihta
	fyrstgemearces,	swa ic þe feran het
	ofer wega gewinn.	

At times, *swa* may be taken as an adverb 'thus', e.g. *Sat* 14 (despite
Möllmer, pp. 39–40) and *Wid* 50 and 135 (despite Kemp Malone's
note and his gloss, 'when'). Adams (p. 193) assigns the meaning 'when'
to the first *swa* in *Or* 198. 6 *Æfter þæm Fauius Maximus se consul
for mid sciphere to Tarentan þære byrg, swa Hannibal nyste, 7 þa
burg on niht abræc, swa þa nyston þe þærinne wæron . . . ,* but does
not record the second. However, the meanings are respectively 'without Hannibal knowing' and 'without those who were within knowing'; see § 1924. On the possibility of *swa* meaning 'if', see § 3673.
But a hard core of examples remains in which *swa* is best taken as
either 'when' or 'as soon as'. Visser (ii, § 879) adds *Bede* 270. 2.

§2695. The examples of 'swa as a temporal adverb'—a usage not recognized by the standard dictionaries—given by Ericson (1932, pp. 74-6) are of interest here. They include nine equivalents of 'the Pepysean, "And *so* to bed" ' in *Bede*, e.g. *Bede* 44. 19 *7 swa mid mycele sige ham foran*, and five in which *swa* is 'the latter arm of a temporal correlation'—with *mid þy* in *Bede(B)* 182. 18; with *mid þæm þe* in *Or* 188. 8; with *raðe þæs þe* in *Or* 170. 4; with *swa* in *Or* 172. 8 *Swa þæt þa se oðer consul gehierde Diulius, swa gefor he to ðæm iglonde mid xxx scipun*; and with *þa þa* in *GD* 216. 16 *7 þa þa he lange hwile gnad, swa se deada man onfeng his sawle 7 aganode 7 his eagan untynde 7 þa him sylf upp sæt.* (These are, of course, in addition to the examples of *swa* correlative with *sona swa* discussed in Ericson 1932, p. 49, and in §2699.) Ericson takes *swa* as 'then' in all these and translates *Swa . . . swa* in *Or* 172. 8 as 'When . . . then'. The sense 'immediately' would fit some of them, but is manifestly impossible in *GD* 216. 16. Neither Ericson nor I found any examples in the poetry.

§2696. Different opinions have been expressed about the origin of the temporal use of *swa*. Adams (pp. 52-3) and Small (1924, pp. 136-8) see it as an extension of the modal use. Ericson (1932, pp. 48-50) explained it as a worn-down form of *sona swa*; see also *EStudien*, 65 (1930-1), 347-9. Möllmer (pp. 38-9), urging as an argument against Ericson the presence of temporal *swa* in the earliest poetry, suggests that *sona swa* developed from an adverbial use of *swa*. Hoops (AF 74 (1932), 15-17) also thinks *swa* was the starting-point; for a summary of his argument see §2492. Johnsen (*Ang.* 38 (1914), 97-8) claims that 'the original function of *swa* was local, not comparative; and the temporal sense starts from this concrete, local-demonstrative meaning'. The argument cannot be pursued here.

c. *Combinations of* sona *and* swa

§2697. Immediate sequence is most commonly denoted in OE by a combination of *sona* and *swa*. This is true even in the poetry, where we find *sona swa* alone only in *DAlf* 19 *Sona swa he lende, on scype man hine blende* (1036) and three times with supporting adverbs— *Phoen* 120 (*swa*), *Met* 8. 1 (*þa siððan*), and *MCharm* 3. 12 (*þa*), and the combination *Swa . . . sona* twice—in *PPs* 108. 25 and *PPs* 111. 9 *Swa þæt synfull gesyhð, sona yrsað . . .* , Latin *Peccator videbit et irascetur. . . .* For the rest there are a few examples of *swa* alone (§§2693-4) and in combination with other adverbs (§2700). I turn now to the prose.

§2698. Adams (pp. 62–3) says:

In origin the construction was probably modal. We have seen that the *swa*-clause modal easily passes over to temporal use. The *sona swa*-clause differs from this only in that an adverb has been introduced to emphasize the temporal nature of the clause, to indicate more exactly the time-relation of the two clauses. Originally *sona* belonged to the main clause, as will appear from the examples which follow, but the combination came to be felt as a simple conjunction. . . .

In support of this he quotes *Bede* 46. 19 *7 hi wæron sona deade, swa hi eorðan gesohtan* and *ÆLS* 26. 210 *and hit sona aras swa hit hrepode þa stowe*. See further Adams, p. 67, and *CP* 419. 10.

§2699. The most common combination in the prose is *sona swa*, which may occur without a correlative adverb, e.g. *Or* 78. 22 *Sona swa Atheniense wiston þæt Darius hie mid gefeohte secan wolde, hie acuron endlefan þusend monna* . . . and *ÆLS* 7. 145 . . . *swa þæt þæs mædenes fex befeng hi eall abutan sona swa þa cwelleras hire claðas of abrudon*, or with one, e.g. *Or* 96. 14 *Sona swa þara Læcedemonia ladteow wiste þæt he wið þa twegen heras sceolde, him þa rædlecre geþuhte þæt he wið operne frið gename, BlHom* 173. 33 *þa sona swa þæt word becom to Nerone þæm casere, þa heht he Simon þone dry infeccan beforan hine*, and *ChronE* 131. 14 (998) *ac sona swa hi to gædere gan sceoldan, þonne wearð þær æfre þurh sum þing fleam astiht*. Other arrangements include *sona swa . . . swa* as in *Bede* 30. 2 *sona swa hi ðæs landes lyft gestuncan, swa swulton hi* and *ÆHomM* 15. 245 *Sona swa he beseah on hire scinendan nebbwlite, swa wearð he gegripen mid ðære galnysse his unstæððigan heortan*—Adams (p. 65) sees *sona swa . . . swa* as an intermediate stage between *sona . . . swa* and *sona swa*; *sona swa . . . sona* as in *ÆLS* 13. 21 *and sona swa his earmas for unmihte aslacodon, sona sloh Amalech and sige hæfde on him;swa . . . sona* as in *BenR* 126. 20 *Swa se cuma cnocige, oþþe se þearfa clypige, he sona cweþe 'Gode þanc'*; *swa sona swa* only (according to Adams, p. 67) in *ÆLS* 37. 184 *secgað me swa sona swa ge oncnawaþ þæt he cucu ne byð*; and *sona swa swa* only (according to Adams, pp. 67–8) in *GD(C)* 214. 12 *Sona swa swa Martinus gehyrde Benedictus word, he tobræc hraðe þone fotcops*, where the second *swa* may be an accidental repetition, since MS *O* has only *sona swa*. Adams (pp. 81–2) finally notes that in *LS* 10 (*Guthlac*) the combination *næs eac nænig hwil to þam sona* occurs once (*LS* 10. 145. 22) and the combination *næs þa nænig hwil to þan/þon sona swa* three times (*LS* 10. 144. 15, 148. 7, and 154. 1 *Næs þa nænig hwil to þon sona swa he mid þan hrægle swa miccles weres gegyred wæs, þa ne mihte þæt þæt sar aberan*).

d. Other combinations involving swa

§2700. In the poetry we find patterns such as *instæpes . . . swa* in

El 127   Flugon instæpes
        Huna leode,   swa þæt halige treo
        aræran heht   Romwara cyning,
        heaðofremmende;

swa . . . sniome in *PPs* 113. 3 *Swa heo sæ geseah, he hio sniome fleah,*
Latin *Mare vidit et fugit; swa . . . furðum* in *PPs* 105. 33 and

PPs 138. 11   onfenge me fægere,   swa ic furðum wæs
        of modur hrife   minre acenned,

Latin *suscepisti me de utero matris meae*; and *ða . . . swa* in

GuthB 1108   Aras ða eorla wynn
        heard hygesnottor,   swa he hraþost meahte,
        meðe for ðam miclan bysgum.

§2701. For the prose, I list the combinations noted by Adams (pp.
68-74 and 198-9) and give the reference to one example, which is
marked † if it is the only one he records: *on an . . . swa* (*WHom*
6. 159); *swa ær swa* (*ÆLS* 16. 317); *swa hraðe swa* (*ÆCHom* i. 584.
21); *swa . . . raðost* (*ChronA* 94. 1 (905)); *swa ricene swa* (†*ÆCHom*
i. 86. 34); *swa . . . swa* (*Or* 172. 8); and *þærrihte swa* (†*ÆCHom* ii.
80. 3). I agree with Adams (p. 74) in dismissing *BlHom* 185. 5 *swa
swiþe swa . . . swa swiþe*, despite Morris's translation. Johnsen (*Ang.*
39 (1916)) finds a local origin for *on an . . . swa* (p. 116) and for
þærrihte swa (pp. 114-15).

e. Sona 'as soon as'?

§2702. The possibility that *sona* may serve alone as a conjunction
'as soon as' has been suggested by BTS (s.v. *sona* III) for *LS* 23. 451
*ac sona ic halige fæmne þines suna rode geseo, ic mid þam wiðsace
þissere worulde* (where we could translate 'But immediately I see . . .'
without being forced to describe 'immediately' as a conjunction); by
Liggins (1955, p. 317) for *Lch* ii. 82. 21 *gif þa omihtan wannan þing
oþþe þa readan syn utan cumen of wundum oþþe of sniþingum oððe
of slegum sona þu þa þing lacna mid scearpinge 7 onlegena beres
æfter þære wisan þe læcas cunnan wel þu hit betst* (where the imperative *lacna* suggests that *sona* is an adverb); and by Schücking
(p. 106 and *Britannica*, pp. 85-8) for certain examples in *Beowulf*,

including *Beo* 743 (where this interpretation inartistically destroys the paratactic sweep of *Beo* 739-49),

Beo 750   Sona þæt onfunde   fyrena hyrde,
            þæt he ne mette   middangeardes,
            eorþan sceata   on elran men
            mundgripe maran;   he on mode wearð
            forht on ferhðe

(where it is more tolerable, but open to the same objection), and

Beo 1792   Geat unigmetes wel,
            rofne randwigan   restan lyste;
            sona him seleþegn   siðes wergum,
            feorrancundum   forð wisade . . .

(where it could be argued that the desire to sleep led Beowulf to call for the chamberlain). The idea has its attractions. As I have said in §2536, I do not believe that the choice in such circumstances is only between a principal and a subordinate clause in the modern sense of these terms. But it is a fact that *sona* can be taken as an adverb in all the cited examples and it is my opinion that it is better so taken. I accept Klaeber's verdict (*Ang. B.* 52 (1941), 216) on Schücking's *Britannica* article: 'Die sorgsame Untersuchung endigte mit einem *non liquet*; doch könnte man in dem negativen Urteil sogar noch weiter gehen' ['The careful study concluded with a *non liquet*, but it would be possible to take the negative conclusion even further'].

f. Combinations involving þa

§2703. In the prose, *sona* is the adverb most usually found with *þa*. The five examples noted by Adams (pp. 81 and 202) display the following patterns: *sona þa . . . þa* (*GD(H)*) 31. 8, 57. 30, and 143. 6; *GD(C)* has *sona swa* in all these), *ða sona þa* (*ÆLS* 31. 522), and *þa sona þa . . . þa* (*BlHom* 177. 35). Möllmer (p. 51) adds *þa sona þa þa* (*GD* 343. 15). A possible example of *sona . . . þa* in the poetry is

PPs 148. 5   Forðon he sylfa cwæð,   sona wærun
            wræclice geworht   wætera ðryþe,
            and gesceapene wærun,   þa he sylfa het,

Latin *Quia ipse dixit et facta sunt; ipse mandavit et creata sunt.* But it is possible to take *þa* as a relative pronoun with *ðryþe* as antecedent.

§2704. In the poetry, the combination *þa . . . furþum* is most frequent. It appears, for example, in *Beo* 465 and

Beo 321

Guðbyrne scan
heard hondlocen, hringiren scir
song in searwum, þa hie to sele furðum
in hyra gryregeatwum gangan cwomon.

Adams does not record it in the prose, but it appears in *Bo* 103. 12 *Ða he furðum on ðæt leoht com, ða beseah he hine underbæc wið ðæs wifes.*

§2705. Möllmer (p. 53) adds *uneaþe . . . þa* in *Gen* 27. 30 *Vneaðe Isaac geendode þas spræce þa Iacob ut eode; ða com Esau of huntoðe,* Latin *Vix Isaac sermonem impleuerat: et egresso Iacob foras, uenit Esau.*

§2706. We find *þa . . . ærest* in

Mald 5

þa þæt Offan mæg ærest onfunde,
þæt se eorl nolde yrhðo geþolian,
he let him þa of handon leofne fleogan
hafoc wið þæs holtes, and to þære hilde stop.

With this ASPR punctuation, *þa* is a conjunction. But some editors have a semi-colon after *geþolian* and so take *þa* as an adverb; see Gordon's note.

g. Combinations involving the formulae with mid

§2707. These are limited to the prose. With *sona*, we find *sona mid þam/þan/þy þe*, e.g. *ÆLS* 22. 150 *and he wearð hal sona mid þam ðe he clypode Cristes naman him to fultume; sona . . . mid þam þe,* e.g. *Or* 274. 3 *7 sona gedyde sweotol tacn þæt he Philippus ær besierede mid þæm þe he het cristenra monna ehtan*; and *mid þam þe . . . sona,* e.g. *GD(H)* 46. 27 *mid þam þe se Godes wer Constantius þa þis gehyrde, he sona swiðe bliðe forlet þa leohtfatu. . . .* Other combinations recorded by Adams (pp. 79–80 and 201–2) are *mid þam/þy/þi þe . . . færinga/hrædlice/hraþe/semninga,* e.g. *BlHom* 245. 14 *Mid þi þe he þæt gehyrde, hraþe he þa aras gesund* and *færlice mid ðam ðe* in *ÆCHom* i. 430. 31 *þa færlice mid ðam ðe he gesæt, comon ðæs caseres cempan.* We have *mid þe swa* in *LS* 3. 24 *7 mid þe swa he geherde þa eadmodnisse his andsware, þa cweð he. . . .*

h. Combinations involving conjunctions meaning 'after'

§2708. Three conjunctions are involved: *þæs (. . .) (þe)*, *siþþan*, and prepositional formulae with *æfter*. Here I restrict myself to listing the combinations with the reference to one example, which is marked † if it is the only one recorded by Adams. Combinations with *þæs (. . .) (þe)* are most common in *Bede*. Adams (pp. 74-6 and 199-200) records *sona (. . .) þæs þe (Bede* 326. 22); *sona þæs þe . . . sona (Bede* 394. 1); *sona ærest þæs þe (†Bede* 200. 9); *sona hraþe þæs þe (†Bede* 98. 7); *þæs þe . . . sona instepe (†Bede* 402. 33); and *þæs þe . . . hraþe (Bede* 162. 6).

§2709. Adams (pp. 74-7 and 199-201) notes the appearance in other texts of *sona þæs (ChronD* 199. 25 (1066)); *sona from fruman þæs þe (†LS* 10. 118. 16); *(h)raþe þæs þe (Or* 160. 3); *swiþe hraþe þæs þe (†Bo* 133. 23); *swiþe hrædlice þæs þe (†ChronC* 105. 25 (918)); *(h)raþe . . . þæs þe (BlHom* 27. 21 and *ChronD* 188. 21 (1057)—scarcely poetry, despite Adams, p. 76); *(h)raþe þæs . . . þe (Or* 168. 26); *forraðe þæs ðe (†ChB* 639); and *instepes þæs þe (†Bl Hom* 35. 5). I have recorded no such combinations in the poetry.

§2710. Combinations with *siþþan* include *hrædlice siþþan (†ÆC Hom* ii. 136. 22); *swiþe hraþe siþþan (†CP* 465. 22); *siþþan . . . raþe (†Or* 178. 3); *sona siþþan (Bede* 132. 4); and *sona (. . .) siþþan (Æ Let* 5. 35 and *Beo* 721). Again Adams notes no examples with *furþum*, but we find in the poetry *siþþan furþum (Jul* 497) and *siþþan . . . furþum (GenA* 2380). Adams does not record *siþþan (. . .) ærest* in the prose. But it occurs in the poetry meaning 'as soon as', e.g. *GenA* 2775 and

Beo 1945   ealodrincende   oðer sædan,
               þæt hio leodbealewa   læs gefremede,
               inwitniða,   syððan ærest wearð
               gyfen goldhroden   geongum cempan,
               æðelum diore. . . .

But (despite Möllmer, p. 47), it is obvious that this is not its meaning in

Beo 4   Oft Scyld Scefing   sceaþena þreatum,
               monegum mægþum   meodosetla ofteah,
               egsode eorlas,   syððan ærest wearð
               feasceaft funden.

We also find *siþþan . . . edre*, as in

El 1000   Secgas ne gældon
               syððan andsware   edre gehyrdon,
               æðelinges word.

§2711. There are a few examples in the prose with the *æfter* formulae: *sona æfter þam/þon þe (BlHom* 121. 6); *æfter þon þe . . . sona*

(*GD* 260. 15); *swiþe hraþe æfter þon þe* (†*GD* 297. 13); and *naht longe æfter þam* (†*Mart* 2 110. 2). As noted in § 2656, these formulae do not occur in the poetry.

j. þon(ne) ær þe

§ 2712. Adams (pp. 51-2) tentatively included *þonne ær þe* in *Bo* 49. 27 *Ac þonne ær þe he þ gewealdleðer forlæt þara bridla . . . þonne forlætað hi þa sibbe . . .* among his conjunctions meaning 'whenever' but took *þon ær þe* in *Bo* 25. 16 *Ac ic eow mæg mid feawum wordum gereccan hwæt se hrof is ealra gesælða; wið þas ic wat þu wilt higian þon ær þe ðu hine ongitest* and *CP* 331. 2 *Ðu cuist nu ðæt* [MSS *C ðu*] *wille geswican ðon* [MSS *C ðonne*] *ær ðe ðu genoh hæbbe* to mean 'as soon as' (pp. 72-3). In so doing, he rejected Wülfing's inclusion (ii. 116-19) of the formula among conjunctions meaning 'before', but overlooked Klaeber's observation (*MLN* 18 (1903), 242-3) that it meant 'as soon as' in both the *Boethius* examples; Klaeber compared *swa ær swa* in *Bede* 248. 25. Johnsen (*Ang.* 39 (1916), 112-14) grouped the three examples together and gave the meaning 'as soon as' for all three. Klaeber did the same in *Ang.* 40 (1916), 503-4, where he compared *þon(ne) ær þe* with *hwonne ær*; see § 2778. Adams, Johnsen, and Klaeber, all discuss possible origins for *þon(ne) ær þe*. So too does Small (*PMLA* 45 (1930), 390 fn. 24); he proposes the meaning 'even before' for *Bo* 25. 16, his only example. Callaway (1931, pp. 17-18) also discusses these three examples without commenting on the subj. *hæbbe* in *CP* 331. 2. It follows the verb *cweþan* in a context involving uncertainty and hypothesis; see § 2714.

k. Mood

§ 2713. Not surprisingly, the prevailing mood in clauses denoting immediate sequence is the indicative. Adams records only twenty-five clauses with the subjunctive out of the 369 he cites from the prose (pp. 195-203); they include most of those quoted by Callaway (1931, pp. 16-18). But even in some of these the verb-form is ambiguous, e.g. *ðu . . . forlete* in *CP* 465. 22, and in *BlHom* 111. 29 *sona syþþan* is an adverb. However, all the clauses with an unambiguous subjunctive fit into one of the categories discussed in §§ 2610-25.

§ 2714. We have an imperative or a jussive subjunctive in the principal clause in examples like *BenR* 101. 7 *Sona swa he þæt gewrit uppan ðam altare alecge, beginne þis fers and ðus cweþe . . .* and

BlHom 37. 20 *Brec þinne hlaf þearfendum mannum, 7 sona swa þu geseo nacodne wædlan, þonne gegyre þu hine, 7 ne forseoh þu næfre þine gecynd*. Those which do not fall into this group are subordinate clauses in dependent speech. As we have already seen, this in itself does not account for the subjunctive. In *Bede* 190. 13 *Ða he þa geseah þæt he wæs neah deaðe, þa ongon he forhtian 7 him ondrædon, þæt he, sona þæs þe he dead wære, fore geearnungum his synna to helle locum gelæded beon sceolde*, the reference is to the future-in-the-past. In

GD 317. 4   Witodlice, Petrus, se Illiricianus me sæde, þæt se Petrus sylfa him sæde, þæt hine sylfne gestode his lichaman mettrumness, 7 he wurde forþfered, ær he æfre þa westenu gesohte. 7 he sæde, þæt sona swa he wære of þam lichaman atogen, þæt he gesawe helle witu 7 unarimendlice stowa þara ligea. 7 eac he cyðde, þæt he gesawe sume þa rican men þissere worulde . . .

we have a notable series of unvouched-for statements, 'He said that he said . . . And he said . . .'. Even *cyþan*, with its strong preference for the indicative (§2022), is followed by the subjunctive. In *LS* 34. 793 . . . *and ic bidde þinne þrymfullan cynescype þæt þu to us cume swa þu raþost mæge*, the *þæt* clause is one of dependent desire and so involves an element of uncertainty. These examples are typical; see further Adams, pp. 147-8, and Visser, ii, §879.

§2715. Only one of the clauses in the poetry which I have classified as denoting immediate sequence has the subjunctive, viz. *Jul* 253 (§2693). Here the OE principal clause contains a subjunctive and the Latin equivalent of the temporal clause has a subjunctive *cum* clause.

7. CONJUNCTIONS MEANING 'BEFORE'

a. Introductory remarks

§2716. *Ær* is by origin a comparative adverb of time, 'earlier, sooner'; consider *Bede* 438. 21 *Ær hwene ðu come, eode inn on þis hus to me twegen geonge men . . .* 'A little before you came . . .'. In OE it is used not only as an adverb but also as a preposition and a conjunction. But, as Adams (p. 116) observes, it is difficult to say which of the last two arose first, since we find both *ær* and *ær þam/ þon (þe)* as conjunctions in early texts.

§2717. I have discussed the various theories concerning the origin of the use of *ær* and *ær þæm/þon (þe)* as conjunctions in Mitchell, at press (c). As I see it, the probability is that conj. *ær* arose directly from adv. *ær* and that the combinations arose independently. Whether *ær* in the combinations is a preposition governing the dative/instrumental or a comparative adverb followed by a dative/instrumental case of comparison (§3261) is arguable. Small (*PMLA* 45 (1930), 390-1) assumes without justification that *ær þon þe* was the original form—it occurs once in the poetry (*Jud* 252 *ærðon ðe*) and, according to Adams (pp. 215-20), only forty-three times in the prose (less than one-third in the 'Alfredian' texts) against *ær ðam ðe* (124) and *ær ðan ðe* (133, over 100 from Ælfric)—and suggests as its 'basic meaning' 'earlier than that, that' or 'earlier than that, namely'. Behre (p. 169) offers a perhaps unconscious modification of this theory. Behaghel (*DS* iii, §925)—followed by Möllmer (pp. 76-7)—explains *þon* as a form of the temporal adv. *þonne* and suggests that *er than* (OE *ær þonne/þon*) was originally used after a positive principal clause in a paratactic combination which can be represented by MnE 'I go before. Then he may come.' Johnsen (*Ang.* 39 (1916), 117-18) claims that both *ær* and *þon* were originally 'local demonstrative adverbs'. Space forbids further discussion here.

§2718. Detailed studies of the distribution within the different texts of the various forms of the conjunctions involving *ær* must await full collections. Some comments on the prose will be found in Adams (pp. 115-25), Kivimaa (p. 152), and Liggins 1970 (pp. 298-9). Of the ninety-five examples I noted in the poetry, sixty-eight had *ær* and the remainder *ærþon* (written as one word or two and with *ð* instead of *þ*), except for *ærþan* (*El* 1083), *ær þan* (*And* 1031), *ærðæm* (*Met* 5. 45), *ær ðam* (*Dan* 587), *ær þy* (*GenA* 2766), and *ærðon ðe* (*Jud* 252). The doubled form *ær ær* does not occur in the poetry. So Small's remark (*PMLA* 45 (1930), 390)—'Although *ær* alone is occasionally used as a subordinate conjunction, the usual forms are *ær þon þe* and *ær þam þe*'—is not true for the poetry. Since Adams records 298 examples of *ær* in the prose against fifty-two with *ær* + demonstrative and 300 with *ær* + demonstrative + *þe*, it does not hold for the prose either. Indeed, Adams (p. 116) remarks of the prose that 'the simple *ær* is the most common of the connectives of the *ær*-class in all the texts, save in the writings of Ælfric, in which *ær ðan ðe* predominates'. On mood, see §§2731-42.

b. Ær, ær ær, and ær . . . ær

§2719. *Ær* is used as an adverb, both alone, e.g. *ÆCHom* ii. 564. 14 *Geot ðu ðone ele ær, geot ðu siððan, æfre he oferswið þone oðerne wætan*, and with *on*, e.g. *ÆCHom* ii. 158. 26 *Ne sæde ic eow on ær þæt me and eow ne mihte gewurðan?*; as a preposition, e.g. *ÆHom* 1. 447 *ær Cristes þrowunge*; and as a conjunction, both with the verb of its clause unexpressed, e.g. *Or* 198. 23 *þa geacsedon þa consulas þæt ær, ær Hannibal, 7 him ongean comon* . . . and *ÆCHom* i. 290. 6 . . . *and cwæð þæt se Fæder wære ær se Sunu and nam bysne be mannum* . . . , and with it expressed.

§2720. In its purely temporal functions, *ær* (alone or in combination) usually means 'before' when used with a positive principal clause, e.g. *Bo* 144. 28 . . . *swa swa good scipstiora ongit micelne wind on hreore sæ ær ær hit geweorðe*, *ÆCHom* i. 54. 23 *and þu scealt be Godes tæcunge hine gegladian ær ðu ðine lac geoffrige*, and *Beo* 2018 *oft hio beahwriðan* ‖ *secge sealde ær hie to setle geong*, but may shade into 'until', e.g. *GD* 274. 2 *7 ic þa gyt wæs wuniende in minum mynstre ær ic þas biscopscire underfengce*, *ÆCHom* ii. 96. 6 *Se apostol Petrus hæfde wif and cild, and eac sume ða oðre apostolas, ær hi to Cristes lareowdome gecyrdon*, and *Beo* 264 *gebad wintra worn ær he on weg hwurfe*, ‖ *gamol of geardum*. The latter shade of meaning is more common after a negative principal clause, e.g. *Bede* 186. 27 *7 geseoh þæt þu ut þonon ne gonge ær seo aðl from þe gewiten sy*, *HomU* 38. 243. 18 . . . *ne wyrð hit æfre ful god ær on þisse ðeode ær man aweodige þa unriht and þa manweorc* . . . , *Matt (WSCp)* 5. 26 *Ne gæst þu þanone ær ðu agylde þone ytemestan feorðlingc*, Latin *Non exies inde donec reddas nouissimum quadrantem*, and *JDay* i 71 *Ne con he þæs brogan dæl*, ‖ *yfles ondgiet, ær hit hine on fealleð*.

§2721. But *ær* may have other senses. Glogauer (pp. 19–20) distinguishes between

And 1435

       Soð þæt gecyðeð
 mænig æt meðle on þam myclan dæge,
 þæt ðæt geweorðeð, þæt ðeos wlitige gesceaft,
 heofon ond eorðe, hreosaþ togadore,
 ær awæged sie worda ænig
 þe ic þurh minne muð meðlan onginne,

where no element of wish exists and where *ær* means 'with greater probability than'—cf. *Matt(WSCp)* 24. 35 *Heofene 7 eorþe gewitað witodlice mine word ne gewitað*, Latin *caelum et terra transibunt uerba uero mea non praeteribunt*—and examples like

Beo 251

       Nu ic eower sceal
 frumcyn witan, ær ge fyr heonan
 leassceaweras on land Dena
 furþur feran,

in which an element of wishing is present and in which *ær* means 'rather than'; cf. *Bo* 22. 31 . . . *forðæm mænegum men is leofre þæt*

he ær self swelte ær he gesio his wif 7 his bearn sweltende. As Glogauer notes, an element of purpose may be detected in sentences
belonging to the second group; the same is true in *CP* 141.
8 *sua
sindon ða loccas to sparienne ðæm sacerde ðæt hi ða hyd behelien, 7
ðeah ðæt he hie forceorfe ær, ær hie on ða eagan feallen,* Latin . . . *et
[capilli] resecantur ne oculos claudant,* and

GenA 2470　　　　　　　Ic eow sylle þa,
　　　ær ge sceonde　　wið gesceapu fremmen,
　　　ungifre yfel　　　ylda bearnum.

Behre (pp. 60 and 173) notes that *ær* translates *nisi* in *Bo* 25. 2 *Ne
nanwuht ne bið yfel ær mon wene þ hit yfel sie,* Latin *adeo nihil est
miserum nisi cum putes,* and shades from 'until' into 'unless' in examples like

GuthB 1221　　　　　　　　Huru, ic giet ne wat,
　　　ær þu me, frea min,　　furþor cyðe
　　　þurh cwide þinne,　　　hwonan his cyme sindon.

§2722. The conj. *ær* occurs alone—examples have already been
quoted—and in correlative combinations of which the following are
typical: *ær ær* (not found in the poetry), e.g. *Or* 198. 23 and *Bo*
144. 28 (§§2719 and 2720 respectively); *ær . . . ær,* e.g. *Or* 58. 7 *Nu
is hit scortlice ymbe þæt gesægd þætte ær gewearð ær Romeburg getimbred wære,* HomU 38. 243. 18 (§2720), and *Beo* 1368; *æror . . .
ær,* e.g. *ÆLS* 31. 918 *Martinus him cwæð to þæt he ne mihte na gan
æror to cyrcan ær se þearfa wære gescryd;* and *þa . . . ær,* e.g.

Beo 675　　　Gespræc þa se goda　　gylpworda sum,
　　　Beowulf Geata,　　　ær he on bed stige.

c. Ær + dative/instrumental of þæt (+ þe)

§2723. The following combinations are listed by Adams (pp. 217–
20) as occurring as conjunctions in the prose: *ær þam/þæm/þan/þon
þe* and *ær þam/þæm/þan/þon.* The usual alternation between *þ* and *ð*
of course obtains. For the combinations found in the poetry see
§2718. A typical adverbial use will be found in *ÆCHom* i. 356. 34
. . . *þæt he soð God wæs seðe wæs ærðan witega geðuht.*

§2724. These formulae are used with the same meanings as *ær:*
'before', e.g. *Bede* 282. 9 *þes halga wer, ær þon þe he biscop geworden wære, tu æðele mynster he getimbrede* and *ÆCHom* ii. 576.
21 *Nu forgife ic ðe eac wise heortan to ðan swiðe, þæt nan eorðlic
man næs ðin gelica ærðan þe ðu wære, ne eac æfter þe ne bið* (where

—even though it shades into 'until'—'before' is required to stress the contrast with 'after'); 'before, until', e.g. *Matt(WSCp)* 5. 18, where *ærþam* twice translates Latin *donec*, and *ÆCHom* ii. 134. 19 *ac hi ealle ne mihton mid heora frofre his dreorignysse adwæscan ærðan þe Cuðberhtus hit mid arfæstum cossum gegladode*; possibly 'with greater probability than', but I have as yet found no convincing examples; and (with an element of purpose) 'rather than', e.g. *ÆLS* 12. 178 . . . *swa swa we on bocum rædað be sumum treowfæstum wife þe wolde hire lif forlætan ærþanþe heo luge* and

And 1029   Swylce se halga   in þam hearmlocan
                     his god grette   ond him geoce bæd,
                     hælend helpe,   ær þan hra crunge
                     fore hæðenra   hildeþrymme. . . .

§2725. The adv. *ær* is occasionally found in the principal clause in correlation with one of these formulae, e.g. *CP* 385. 17 *ðeah ðe he self gegyltan ne meahte, nolde he ðeah ær bodian ða giefe ðæs fulfremedan lifes, ærðæmðe he self wære fulfremedre ielde, BlHom* 165. 31 . . . *7 hine ær monnum gecyþan 7 gesecgan teolode ærþon þe he sylfa lifde 7 mennisc leoht gesawe*, and *GD* 200. 21 *Witodlice nyste man ær hwylcum naman se ælþeodiga man genemned wæs ær þon se awyrgda gast . . . his naman acleopode*. Adams found no examples in which the correlative adverb is *ærþam, ærþon*, or the like. Nor have I, so far.

d. Ær þonne

§2726. In examples like *John(WSCp)* 1. 15 *Se ðe to cumenne is æfter me wæs geworden beforan me, forðam he wæs ær þonne ic* and

Beo 1180   Ic minne can
                 glædne Hroþulf,   þæt he þa geogoðe wile
                 arum healdan,   gyf þu ær þonne he,
                 wine Scildinga,   worold oflætest,

ær þonne is followed by a nominative and means 'earlier than'. It seems to carry the same meaning in *Lch* i. 360. 19 *Gif þu gesyxt wulfes spor ær þonne hyne, ne gesceþþeð he . . .* , where *hyne* is the second object of *gesyxt*.

§2727. Adams (p. 125) has recorded three prose examples in which the clause following *ær þonne* contains a verb, viz. *Bo* 117. 25 *Ic wene ðeah þ him losige se anwald ær þonne þu wolde oððe hi wenen, Lch* iii. 22. 3 . . . *syle wearm etan 7 on ufan drincon þriwa on dæg ær þonne he ete*, and *Bede(Ca)* 76. 27 *To hyre gerestscipe þonne hire wer ne sceal gangan ær ðonne þ acennede bearn from milcum awened sy*, where MS *T* has *ær þon*, *B ær ðon þe*, and *O ær þon þe*. At p. 220 he adds *HomU* 35. 221. 30. *Ær þonne* is not found in the poetry. On the suggestion that the formulae discussed in §§2723-5 had their origin in *ær þonne*, see §2717.

§2728. Behaghel (*DS* iii, §925) and Möllmer (pp. 76-7) both take *þonne* as a temporal adv. 'then'. Adams (p. 125) observes that '*ðonne* is regularly used in comparisons, and it is not surprising that we find it used with *ær*[,] the conjunction [*þonne*], strengthening, as it were, the comparative force of *ær*'. (My additions make clearer what I take to be his meaning.) I do not propose to adjudicate here; as the *OED* (s.v. *than* conj.) has it, the 'employment [of the adv. of time] as the connective particle after a comparative (= L. *quam*, F. *que*) is a pre-English development, existing already in WGer. . . . How the conjunctive use arose out of the adv. of time is obscure.'

e. Ær + a demonstrative + a noun of time + þe

§2729. Adams (p. 126) records two such examples: *Matt(WSCp)* 26. 29 *ær þam dæge þe* and *HomU* 24 *ær þam byre þe*.

f. Combinations involving toforan *and* foran to

§2730. Adams (pp. 126-7) quotes the four examples he found with this comment: 'It is noteworthy that we never find *beforan* so used.' All are in comparatively late texts. They are *Lch* i. 160. 22 *toforan þam þe*, *Lch* i. 206. 2 *toforan þam timan þe*, and *WHom* 2. 51 and 5. 101, both *foran to þam timan þe*. The last two clumsy circumlocutions remind me of the intolerable 'at this point in time'.

g. Mood

§2731. Let us start with some facts. Adams (p. 115) defines the clauses we are discussing as 'clauses determining the time of an action by reference to a subsequent action'—the word 'subsequent' could be replaced by 'coming' or 'future'—and tells us (pp. 151-2) that

all the instances of the indicative with *ær*, or any other connective of this class, occur in statements of fact in past time.

. . . The use of the indicative with *ær* is rare enough to have led even so capable a scholar as Mr. Sweet [*An Anglo-Saxon Reader*, Oxford, 1876, p. xcv] into such a statement as this: 'The conjunction *ær* is always followed by the subjunctive, even in simple statements [of facts].' However, about one-fourth of the total number of clauses I have noted have the indicative.

Four points need to be made here. First, some of Adams's 'indicative' verb-forms are in fact ambiguous; see §2531. Second, all verbs in the past tense in *ær* clauses[118] refer to what is the future-in-the-past from the point of view of the principal clause. Third, by the fourth edition of his *Reader* (1884)—if not before—Sweet's statement read 'The conjunction *ær* is generally followed by the subjunctive, even in simple statements of facts' (p. xcvii). Fourth, there are a few *ær* clauses with the present indicative in both prose and poetry. The references to the four examples in the poetry are given in the table in §2733. Those in the prose include (with positive principal clauses) *Bo* 25. 18, *CP* 215. 11, and *Matt(WSCp)* 6. 8 *Soðlice eower fæder wat hwæt eow þearf ys ær þam þe ge hyne biddað*; and (with negative principal clauses) *Bo* 12. 3, *Bo* 124. 7, *CP* 197. 23, *Solil* 60. 13, *Luke(WSCp)* 22. 34, *John(WSCp)* 13. 38, and *ÆCHom* i. 614. 34 *þas word spræc Drihten to Iudeiscre mægðe, and heora cynn ne gewit þurh ateorunge, ærðan ðe þes middangeard geendað.*

§2732. It is clear that Sweet was right when he said that 'the conjunction *ær* is generally followed by the subjunctive'. Can any principals be deduced to explain this and to account for the examples with the indicative? According to Behaghel (*DS* iii, §§925 and 1274–80) and Möllmer (pp. 99–104), the present subjunctive was natural after a positive principal clause referring to present time, while the indicative was natural after a negative principal clause referring either to the past or present. Analogical preterite subjunctives after positive principal clauses then arose. Thus (it is argued) the rule 'positive + subjunctive, negative + indicative' came into existence. Examples to the contrary are explained as 'Auflösungen der alten Regel' ['breakdowns [sc. neutralization of the force] of the old rule']. Campbell makes an interesting point here when he speaks in *RES* 7 (1956), 65, of

what is perhaps the most far-reaching rule of OE. syntax—viz. that relative clauses (including clauses of time and place), clauses of result, *swa* clauses, and clauses expressing real positive conditions take the subjunctive when the principal clause contains an imperative, a subjunctive, or a negated indicative. . . .

Conversely, comparative clauses with *þonne*, and temporal clauses with *ær*, take the subjunctive only after a positive indicative principal clause. Exceptions are largely due to the use of familiar sentence-patterns in positions not syntactically justified. . . .

[118] In this discussion, '*ær* clauses' serves as a convenient shorthand for clauses introduced by *ær* or by any of the formulae with *ær*. Similarly, *ær* includes the formulae.

'The old rule' still seems to work sometimes even in late OE; consider *ÆCHom* ii. 364. 22 *Seo Godcundnys wæs mid ðam Fæder
ærðan ðe middaneard gewurde æfre ælmihtig; and seo menniscnys
næs ærðan ðe he hi genam of ðam mædene Marian* and compare
Luke(WSCp) 22. 34 *ne cræwþ se hana todæg ær þu me ætsæcst,*
Latin *non cantabit hodie gallus donec ter abneges nosse me,* with
Luke(WSCp) 22. 61 . . . *þ ðu min ætsæcst þriwa todæg ær se hana
crawe,* Latin . . . *priusquam gallus cantet ter me negabis,* and

Seasons 106   and hit ærest ongan   eorl se goda,
                  mære Moyses,   ær he on munt styge

with

Seasons 128   Uton þæt gerine   rihte gehicgan,
                  þæt se mæra þegen   mihta ne hæfde
                  to astigenne   stæppon on ypplen
                  ær him þæt symbel wearþ   seald fram engle.

But the fact that, while (according to Campbell) it 'is perhaps the
most far-reaching rule of OE syntax', there are 'exceptions' is true
even of early OE; consider

CP 385. 13   For ðissum ilcan ðingum wæs ðætte ure Aliesend, ðeah he on hefenum sie Scieppend 7 engla lareow, nolde he ðeah on eorðan bion monna
lareow, ær he wæs ðritiges geara eald, forðæmðe he wolde ðæm fortruwodum
monnum andrysno halwendes eges on gebrengean; ðeah ðe he self gegyltan ne
meahte, nolde he ðeah ær bodian ða giefe ðæs fulfremedan lifes, ærðæmðe he
self wære fulfremedre ielde

and compare

GenA 20   Elles ne ongunnon
             ræran on roderum   nymþe riht and soþ,
             ærðon engla weard   for oferhygde
             dwæl on gedwilde

with

GenA 2531   Ne moton wyt
             on wærlogum   wrecan torn godes,
             swebban synnig cynn,   ær ðon þu on Sægor þin
             bearn gelæde   and bryd somed.

§2733. The table which follows gives details of all the *ær* clauses in
the poetry and of those from *Chron, CP,* and *ÆCHom* i (based on
Adams's lists, with some supplementation from mine; time does not
permit me to offer full details for the prose). It demonstrates that—
as its advocates have to admit—'the old rule' is not universally valid
for OE.

| Text | Principal clause is | Verb of ær (+) clause is | | | | | | |
| | | Indicative | | Subjunctive | | Ambiguous | | |
		Pres.	Pret.	Pres.	Pret.	Pres.	Pret.	Total
Chron. to 1121	Positive	0	2 (164. 3, 253. 16)	0	16 (86. 29, 100. 14, etc.)	0	18	36
	Negative	0	0	0	2 (84. 35, 240. 6)	0	2	4
CP	Positive	1 (215. 15)	0	17 (141. 10, 157. 20, etc.)	1 (5. 9)	2	5	26
	Negative	1 (199. 1)	2 (385. 15, 393. 16)	5 (331. 20, 431. 4, etc.)	1 (385. 17)	0	0	9
ÆCHom i	Positive	0	0	5 (2. 29, 54. 24, etc.)	12 (90. 16, 92. 21, etc.)	0	3	20
	Negative	1 (616. 1)	7 (26. 2, 40. 23, etc.)	1 (240. 21)	4 (94. 3, 94. 26, etc.)	0	1	14
Prose total	Positive	1	2	22	29	2	26	82
	Negative	2	9	6	7	0	3	27
Poetry —the whole corpus	Positive	2 (*Sat* 708, *Rim* 80[119])	3 (*Beo* 2019, *El* 1245, *Rid* 65. 2)	25 (*Beo* 252, *El* 447, etc.)	21 (*Beo* 264, *Beo* 676, etc.)	2	16	69
	Negative	2 (*JDay i* 72, *Met* 29. 11)	9 (*GenA* 22, *Sat* 407, etc.)	15 (*GenA* 2533, *El* 1083, etc.)	0	0	0	26

§2734. It is neither possible nor desirable to rehearse here the numerous discussions about the validity or otherwise of 'the old rule' for the Germanic languages in general or for OE in particular.

[119] This may be a principal clause, with *ær* an adverb.

Those interested should consult in the first instance Hotz, pp. 76-83; Adams, p. 153; Diekhoff, *JEGP* 11 (1912), 173-9; Behaghel, *DS* iii, §§925 and 1274-80; Möllmer, pp. 99-104; and Behre, pp. 164-74, where there is a discussion on the function and nature of various sub-junctives. Brook (p. 91) seems to accept Sweet's first statement (§2731): 'The subjunctive is used in subordinate clauses . . . in adver-bial clauses of time: *ær ðæm ðe hit eall forhergod wære*, "before it was all ravaged".' Behre's statement (p. 164) is more cautious: 'Having approached the subject-material of OE. without any preconceived ideas, one may lay it down that the use of the subjunctive is practi-cally the rule in such *ær*-clauses as are dependent on affirmative main clauses, whereas in those dependent on negative main clauses the indicative is very often used.' His first observation is in close con-formity with the facts displayed in my Table. The second less so: a negative *ær* clause is followed by an indicative in no examples against two with the subjunctive in *Chron*, in three against six with the subjunctive in *CP*, in eight against five with the subjunctive in *ÆCHom* i, and in eleven against fifteen with the subjunctive in the poetry. So 'very often' is not quite the phrase, especially for the poetry—which was Behre's province. The distribution of the 109 examples in the prose and the ninety-five from the poetry given in the Table shows remarkable similarity except in one respect—the complete absence from the poetry of the preterite subjunctive after negative principal clauses, which contrasts with the presence of seven such examples in the selected prose. Here the poetry follows 'the old rule'. But elsewhere there are exceptions. So it must remain doubtful whether it ever existed. I end the discussion with Adams's statement (p. 151): 'That the indicative is not found merely after a negative main clause hardly needs statement; but the principal seems to obtain in the other Germanic dialects, and has been sup-posed to exist for OE.'

§2735. For advocates of 'the old rule', the exceptions were (as we have seen) explained as the result of analogy. Analogy too was held responsible by Adams (pp. 150-1) for examples with the subjunctive which he could not otherwise explain:

Probably originally this mode was used because of the element of uncertainty which attaches to an event still in the future. But the use of the optative became conventional in such clauses, and is used even in statements relating to past events, the reality of which could not be a matter of doubt, and which could not be influenced by any feeling of optativity.

Thus the use of the optative in this sentence, of which sort there are many in *Or*, must be purely conventional: *Or* 40. 11 Ær ðam ðe Romeburh getimbred *wære* syx hund wintran 7 fif, in Egyptum wearð on anre niht fiftig manna of-slegen, ealle fram hiora agnum sunum.

§2736. Callaway (1931, pp. 29–54) distinguishes 'the Logical Sub-junctive of Subsequent Action' from the 'Illogical'. The latter refers 'to a past action or event about the certainty of which to the modern mind there is no doubt, and in which we should expect to find the indicative mood' (1931, p. 52); *Or* 40. 11, just quoted, will serve as an example. The former is detected 'when the dependent temporal clause refers to a future and contingent action' (1931, p. 29). Most of the examples of the 'logical' subjunctive are in the present tense, as in *Bede* 186. 27 *7 geseoh þæt þu ut þonon ne gonge, ær seo aðl from þe gewiten sy*. But Callaway (1931, p. 33) quotes six examples of 'future preterite subjunctives denoting a contingent or hypothetical action' which he describes as 'Logical'. Five of these—including *Bede* 438. 5 *þa wæs se cyng inngongende to him, forðon he hiene swiðe lufode, trymede hiene 7 lærde, þæt he ða get hreowe 7 ondet-nesse dyde his synna, ær ðon he swulte*—are in sentences expressing a dependent desire. The sixth is

Beo 262   Wæs min fæder   folcum gecyþed,
                 æþele ordfruma,   Ecgþeow haten;
                 gebad wintra worn,   ær he on weg hwurfe,
                 gamol of geardum.

How this differs from *Mart* 2 146. 6 *ond Decius se casere awedde; ond he clypode ær he swulte ond cwæð* . . . and from

Beo 675   Gespræc þa se goda   gylpworda sum,
                 Beowulf Geata,   ær he on bed stige—

both of which are quoted (1931, p. 40) as examples of the 'Illogical' subjunctive—I do not understand. At the moment, I am inclined to think that Callaway's distinction—which is used by Liggins (1970, p. 301): '*Or* is the only one [of the 'Alfredian' texts] to insert any significant number of such examples in the "illogical" preterite tense'—is merely an elaborate way of saying what I have already quoted in §2735 from Adams (pp. 150–1). Indeed, Callaway himself says (1931, p. 42): 'As to the Illogical Subjunctive of Subsequent Action, with Professor Adams I believe that analogy was an impor-tant factor in setting up the type.' But I deprecate the word 'Illogi-cal'. It seems to me possible to argue that it is just as logical to use the preterite subjunctive because the action or event in the *ær* clause was in the future(-in-the-past) in relation to that of the principal clause (see §2731) as it is to use the preterite indicative because the

action or event in the *ær* clause is in the past from the point of view
of those speaking or writing after its occurrence.

§2737. Callaway (1931, p. 42) claims that 'occasionally the [Illogi-
cal] subjunctive is due to the influence of the Latin original'; he
instances *Gen* 48. 5 *Witodlice þine twegen suna, ða þe acennede
wæron on Egypta lande ær þam ic hyder come, hi beoþ mine . . .* and
John(WSCp) 20. 1 *Witodlice on anon restedæge seo magdalenisce
Maria com on mergen ær hit leoht wære to þære byrgenne . . .* ,
'where we find, respectively, *antequam* and *cum* with a subjunctive';
on this topic see further Callaway 1931, pp. 34-9 and 45.

§2738. I propose not to discuss the question whether the nature of
the principal clause or of the subordinate clause is uppermost in
deciding the mood of the verb in *ær* clauses. Callaway (1931, pp. 30,
34, and 41-4) has some observations on it, with references to the
views of earlier writers. In my opinion, it is essentially a non-question;
see §§2611-13. But one point should be made. Some of the subjunctives in *ær* clauses occur in the conditions discussed in §§2649-52.
Thus, we have a principal clause containing a volitional expression in
CP 349. 12 *læt inc geseman ær ðu ðin lac bringe*; a dependent desire
in *CP* 371. 1 *hie sint to manigenne ðæt hie hie selfe ongieten on ðæm
halgum gewritum, ærðæmðe hie oðre læren . . .* ; a rhetorical question and *sculon* in *CP* 433. 23 *Hwæt elles getacnað se hea torr on
Libano buton ðone hean foreðonc 7 ða gesceadwisnesse ðara godena
monna, ða sculon ongietan ða costunga 7 ðæt gefeoht, ærðæmðe
hit cume, ðæt hi mægen ðy fæstor gestondan, ðonne hit cume?*;
a dependent question and a clause of purpose in *ChronE* 137. 19
(1006) *Agan se cyng georne to smeagenne wið his witan hwet heom
eallum rædlicost þuhte þ man þisum earde gebeorgan mihte ær he
mid ealle fordon wurðe*; and a *þeah* clause in *CP* 443. 35 *forðæm we
ceorfað heah treowu on holte ðæt we hi eft uparæren on ðæm botle,
ðær ðær we timbran willen, ðeah we hi for hrædlice to ðæm weorce
don ne mægen for grennesse, ærðæmðe hi adrugien.* But, as we have
already seen, many subjunctives occur in clauses where no such explanation is possible. Typical examples include *ChronA* 86. 28 (894)
hæfdon hi hiora onfangen ær Hæsten to Beamfleote come, CP 157.
19 *Sua ðu meaht ælcne unðeaw on ðæm menn æresð be sumum
tacnum ongietan, hwæs ðu wenan scealt, ær he hit mid wordum oððe
mid weorcum cyðe, ÆCHom* i. 2. 29 *and beoð fela frecednyssa on
mancynne ærðan þe se ende becume*, and *Beo* 675. (This example is
a very popular one. It has already been quoted and discussed in
§2736. But see further Behre (pp. 169-71 and 189-90) and Klaeber
(*Archiv*, 168 (1935), 106-7).)

§2739. For Muxin (*UZLGU* 262, vyp. 50 (1958), 155–61), there is nothing illogical about the use of moods in *ær* clauses. He claims that Western scholars have been too prone to detect 'original absolute meanings' for the subjunctive and to argue that occurrences of the subjunctive where such a meaning could not be divined were the result of analogy. So he attacks Adams's statement (p. 151) that 'the feeling of the reality of the action of the *ær*-clause is, in these cases [statements of fact in past time], so strong that it led to the use of the indicative rather than the conventional optative' by pointing to instances like *Or* 40. 11 (§2735) and, in effect, asking what event could be more 'real' than the foundation of Rome. He also argues against Callaway's explanation, urging that he ascribes to the Anglo-Saxons, in comparison with other linguistic groups, a greater ability to doubt and a greater inclination to be cautious; see Callaway 1931, p. 43. Muxin sees a perfectly clear-cut distinction. The past indicative is used only to express an action which *directly* follows the action of the main clause, in the same narrative plane. Both actions are links in the same chain of events, the action of the temporal clause forming an intermediate link between the action of the principal clause and the actions narrated in subsequent clauses. As examples, he instances the *ær þon* clause in *Or* 108. 28 *7 þæt longe donde wæron ær þæt folc wiste hwonan þæt yfel come—buton þæt hie sædon þæt hit ufane of ðære lyfte come —ær þon hit þurh ænne þeowne mon geypped wearð. þa wæron ealle þa wif beforan Romana witan gelaðede* and *ÆLS* 18. 5 *ac ofer Israhela folc þe on God belyfde næs nan eorðlic cynincg ærðan þe Saul swa swa hi sylfe gecuron ofer hi cynerice underfencg.* The preterite subjunctive, however, expresses an action which does not follow immediately from the action of the principal clause. It is not an intermediate link in a chain of events. It is separated from the action of the principal clause by a definite interval of time. In other words, says Muxin, the action of the temporal clause refers to the future in relation to the time of the action expressed by the verb of the principal clause (future-in-the-past). Examples are *Or* 28. 25 *Ær ðæm ðe Romeburh getimbred wære þrim hund wintra 7 þusend wintra, Ninus, Asyria kyning, ongan manna ærest ricsian on ðysum middangearde* and *LS* 8. 391 *þa gelamp hit þæt se casere Traianus wæs forðfaren ær þam Eustachius of þam gefeohte come. . . .* Thus, he claims, the preterite subjunctive in *ær* clauses is a means of defining more precisely the temporal relationship of the action of the subordinate clause to the action expressed by the verb of the principal clause.

§2740. Present subjunctive forms in *ær* clauses have the same function. They denote future actions and are used regardless of how the speaker views the action—as doubtful, impracticable, or inevitable, e.g. *CP* 433. 27 *Forðæmðe ælc here hæfð ðy læssan cræft ðonne he cymð, gif hine mon ær wat, ær he cume.* Present indicative forms, on the other hand, like past indicative forms, are used when the action of the temporal clause follows directly on the action expressed by the verb of the principal clause. His example is *Bo* 25. 18 *wið þas ic wat þu wilt higian þon ær þe ðu hine ongitest.* But here *þon ær þe* may mean 'as soon as'; see §§2712 and 2741.

§2741. This theory demands and deserves more consideration than I can give it at the moment. It can be conceded that Muxin's examples can be seen as illustrating his point. (This is true of *Bo* 25. 18 even if we take *þon ær þe* to mean 'as soon as', for Muxin extends his theory to clauses introduced by *siþþan* 'after' and other conjunctions; see §2687 fn.) So perhaps do some of those I have already quoted, including *GenA* 20 and 2531 (§2732). But there are others which do not support or conform to his theory. They include (with the indicative) *Matt(WSCp)* 6. 8, *ÆCHom* i. 614. 34 (both in §2731), and

JDay i 71   Ne con he þæs brogan dæl,
        yfles ondgiet,   ær hit hine on fealleð.
        He þæt þonne onfindeð,   þonne se fær cymeþ . . . ,

and (with the subjunctive) *ChronA* 86. 28 (894) and *John(WSCp)* 20. 1 (§§2738 and 2737 respectively), and

Beo 675   Gespræc þa se goda   gylpworda sum,
        Beowulf Geata,   ær he on bed stige:
        '. . .   . . ,'
        Hylde hine þa heaþodeor,   hleorbolster onfeng
        eorles andwlitan. . . .

My doubts are not quenched by a consideration of some of the contrasted examples I quote in §2732. So I remain to be convinced about the rightness of Muxin's view.

§2742. I leave this problem with one final comment. To some, the subjunctive after *ær* is conventional and the use of the indicative represents a triumph of meaning over form. To others, the fluctuations between the two moods reflect the attitudes of different speakers and/or reporters; such scholars may, but need not, subscribe to the theory that positive principal clauses once demanded a subjunctive verb in the *ær* clause, negative principal clauses an indicative verb. Whichever view we favour, we will (I think) find it hard to follow Muxin in denying that analogy played a part in producing the fluctuations we find in the OE monuments and even harder to claim that one theory satisfactorily explains them all.

8. CONJUNCTIONS MEANING 'UNTIL'

a. Introductory remarks

§2743. The most common OE conjunctions meaning 'until' are *oð þæt* and *oð*. Other combinations, some involving *oð*, occur less frequently. The prevailing mood in clauses they govern is the indicative; see §§2761-74. *Hwonne* can sometimes be translated 'until'. But this usage is restricted to contexts in which there appears the idea of delay in achieving something, usually something wished for. The verb of the *hwonne* clause is prevailingly subjunctive and *hwonne* is, in my opinion, still essentially an interrogative. See §§2775-83. It is not, however, true that *hwonne* is used in these contexts to the exclusion of *oð (þæt)*; consider *Bede* 254. 30 *þa wæs he ærest to subdiacone gehalgad 7 þa baad feower monað oððæt him feax geweoxe* (subjunctive mood in *oð þæt* clause) and *ÆCHom* i. 94. 5 *ac gehwylce halgan andbidodon on Abrahames wununge buton tintregum, þeah on helle wite, oðþæt se Alysend com . . .* (indicative mood).

§2744. The form which was to replace *oð (þæt)* first appears in eME as *til—ChronE* 263. 31 (1137) . . . *7 dide ælle in prisun til hi iafen up here castles* and *ChronE* 267. 27 (1140) . . . *for he besæt heom til hi aiauen up here castles.*

§2745. It is, of course, a commonplace that temporal clauses 'indicating the time of the termination of the action of the main clause' (Adams, p. vii) shade into clauses of result, and vice versa; note that, where *ChronA* has *ð he*—on erasure and in a later hand—in *ChronA* 92. 5 (901) *þa rad se cyning mid firde ð he gewicode æt Baddan byrig* and *ChronB* has *þ he*, *ChronC* has *oð he* and *ChronD oððe he*, and compare

Beo 144 Swa rixode ond wið rihte wan,
       ana wið eallum, oð þæt idel stod
       husa selest

with

Beo 1537 Gefeng þa be eaxle —nalas for fæhðe mearn—
       Guð-Geata leod Grendles modor;
       brægd þa beadwe heard, þa he gebolgen wæs,
       feorhgeniðlan, þæt heo on flet gebeah.

There are, as Adams (p. 136) points out, occasional *þæt* clauses in which it is hard to 'see that there is any connotation of result at all', e.g. *ChronE* 213. 4 (1076) *7 þa Bryttas hine heoldon þ se cyng com of Francland*, where the meaning seems to be 'until'. But, as we see from examples like *Or* 178. 23 *þa forcurfon hie him þa twa ædran on twa healfa þara eagena, þæt he æfter þæm slapan ne mehte, oþ he swa searigende his lif forlet* and

Beo 64	þa wæs Hroðgare heresped gyfen,
	wiges weorðmynd, þæt him his winemagas
	georne hyrdon, oðð þæt seo geogoð geweox,
	magodriht micel,

oð (þæt) and *þæt* are not always interchangeable; cf. Benham, p. 204.

§2746. Both *oð (þæt)* and *þæt* often imply a local rather than a temporal limit in the *Charters*, e.g. *Ch* 298 . . . *ðonne up on afene oð ðæt ðe se alda suinhaga utscioteð to afene* and *Ch* 1305 *Ðis synd þa landgemæra to þordune ondlong amman broces þ hit sticað in pidelan ondlong pidelan þ hit cymð to oredeshamme . . .*—here there is little, if any, idea of result—and elsewhere, e.g. *ChronE* 190. 20 (1064) . . . *7 he for suð . . . oð he com to Hamtune, ChronE* 143. 12 (1013) . . . *7 wende swyðe raðe abutan East Englum . . . 7 swa uppweard andlang Trentan þet he com to Gegnes burh,*

And 1058	Gewat him þa Andreas inn on ceastre
	glædmod gangan, to þæs ðe he gramra gemot,
	fara folcmægen, gefrægen hæfde,
	oððæt he gemette be mearcpaðe
	standan stræte neah stapul ærenne,

and

Beo 356	Hwearf þa hrædlice þær Hroðgar sæt
	eald ond anhar mid his eorla gedriht;
	eode ellenrof, þæt he for eaxlum gestod
	Deniga frean; cuþe he duguðe þeaw.

As Johnsen (*Ang.* 38 (1914), 99–100) points out, this is also true of occasional *swa þæt* clauses in the *Charters*, e.g. *Ch* 179 *And swa west ofer þa saltstræte to þæs wudes efese west swa þæt hit cumeð to þære hwitan dic.*

§2747. Johnsen (*Ang.* 38 (1914), 86–92) draws our attention to what certainly do look like adverbial uses of 'local-demonstrative *þæt*' in the *Charters*, e.g. *Ch* 254 . . . *þurh þone more to wiðig slede þæt to brocenan beorge swa to wudu forda þ to Lulles beorge. . . .* He uses these as evidence against the theory that the temporal use of *þæt* developed from its consecutive use—a theory which he confidently attributes to Adams, with (as far as I can see) little justification; see Adams, pp. 136-7—and found himself 'not in doubt that *þæt* employed as a conjunction of time must be explained as a further development of *þæt* when used as a local-demonstrative adverb'. He extends this argument to *swa þæt* (ibid., pp. 99–100). These questions cannot be pursued here. But see § 2828.

§ 2748. An *oð (þæt)* clause sometimes contains an element of purpose, e.g. *Bede* 254. 30 (§ 2743), *Matt(WSCp)* 18. 30 *He þa nolde ac ferde 7 wearp hyne on cweartern oððæt he him eall agefe*, and

PPs 67. 22   Of Basan, cwæð   bealde drihten,
                 ic me on sæ deopre   sniome onwende,
                 oþþæt þin fot weorðe   fæste on blode,

where the Latin has . . . *ut intingatur pes tuus in sanguine*. As Visser (ii. 877) rightly says, the problem of the ambiguous purpose/result clause (§§ 2802-4) arises in examples like *Lch* iii. 74. 15 . . . *7 geote þonne on oþer fæt 7 hlade eft oþre* . . . *7 do swa þ þu hæbbe þreo* and (we may add)

Jul 284   Forfoh þone frætgan   ond fæste geheald,
              oþþæt he his siðfæt   secge mid ryhte,
              ealne from orde,   hwæt his æþelu syn.

§ 2749. Mention has already been made in § 2637 of the fact that a word meaning 'while' can easily come to convey the idea of 'until'. The reverse tendency has been noted by GK (s.v. *oð þæt* 2) and by Glogauer (p. 31) for the *oððæt* clause in *And* 826 (where the possibility of dittography makes the passage suspect) and by Kershaw in her note on

Ruin 6   Eorðgrap hafað
             waldend wyrhtan   forweorone, geleorene,
             heardgripe hrusan,   oþ hund cnea
             werþeoda gewitan.

Her translation of *oþ* as 'while' is possible, but the normal 'until' gives satisfactory sense.

§ 2750. According to Quirk (pp. 112-14), two *oð þæt* clauses in OE poetry are used concessively, one in *Deor* and one in the *Riddles*. The latter cannot be identified (for Quirk does not give references here), but the former must be

Deor 38   Ahte ic fela wintra   folgað tilne,
              holdne hlaford,   oþþæt Heorrenda nu,

leoðcræftig monn   londryht geþah,
þæt me eorla hleo   ær gesealde.

Burnham reports no such examples in the prose.

b. Oð (þæt/þæt þe/þætte/þe)

§2751. *Oð*, either alone or in combination with *þæt* and/or *þe*, is the regular OE conjunction meaning 'until'. Of the possible combinations, *oð þæt* is the most common. The variant spellings show the usual fluctuation between *þ* and *ð* and between *æ* and *e*. The two elements may be written together or separately. We find *oð þæs* in *Bede(T)* 332. 8. But, despite Johnsen's ingenious defence of this form (*Ang.* 39 (1916), 101-2), I am inclined to agree with Adams (p. 128) that it is 'a mere scribal error'; MSS *B*, *O*, and *Ca*, agree on *oð þæt þe*, with variations in the spelling. Adams (p. 133) records a few late spellings of *of* for *oð*. The following table is based on Adams's figures for the prose (pp. 221-7) and mine for the poetry:

Conjunction	Prose	Poetry
oð þæt	701	200[120]
oð	224	16
oð þæt þe/þætte	9	0
oð . . . þæt þe/þætte	0	0
oððe	9	2[121]

The only prose texts which show a marked preference for *oð* are *Or* (seventy-one examples of *oð* against eleven of the remaining forms) and the *Charters* (fifty-eight against twenty-one). *Bede* has no examples of *oð* against thirty-four, *CP* fourteen of *oð* against twenty-eight, and *Chron* twenty-two of *oð* against thirty-five. Ælfric prefers *oð þæt*, avoiding *oð þætte*—see Adams, p. 130, and Kivimaa, pp. 163-4—and using *oð* only once in *ÆCHom*, viz. in *ÆCHom* ii. 166. 20 *þa het Benedictus beran þa tocwysedan lima on anum hwitle into his gebedhuse, and beclysedre dura anrædlice on his gebedum læg, oð þæt tocwysede cild, þurh Godes mihte, geedcucode: wunderlic ðing*, where (we can surmise) he wished to avoid *oð þæt þæt*. Kivimaa (p. 158) reports that in *WHom* the ratio between *oð þæt* and *oð* 'is about . . . 1 : 2'.

§2752. Typical examples of the various forms are (*oð*) *Or* 294. 3 *7 siþþan for ofer þa muntas, oþ he com to Aquilegia*; (*oð þæt*) *Or*

---

[120] Including three or four dubious examples.
[121] *PPs* 139. 11 and *Beo* 649.

102. 29 *7 seo eorþe swa giniende bad, oþ þæt Marcus, þe oþre noman hatte Curtius, mid horse 7 mid wæpnum þæroninnan besceat*; (*oð þe*) *Or* 20. 30 *Alecgað hit ðonne forhwæga on anre mile þone mæstan dæl fram þæm tune, þonne oðerne, ðonne þæne þriddan, oþ þe hyt eall aled bið on þære anre mile*; (*oð þætte*) *Or* 66. 25 *Ac þa cyningas þe æfter Romuluse ricsedon wæron forcuðran 7 eargran þonne he wære . . . oð þætte Tarcuinius . . . ealra þara Romana wif* [ð*a*] *þe he mehte he to geligre geniedde*; and (*oð þæt þe*) *Bede* 260. 13 *He ða eac in Cent mæssepreostas 7 diaconas hadode, oðþæt þe Theodor ærcebiscop to his seðle cwom.* We find correlative *oð þæt . . . oð þæt* in *Bede* 474. 17 *Ond he blissade in þon, þæt he oð þæt in lichoman gehealden wæs, oð þæt he geseah þa his geherend þone Eastordæg onfon. . . .*

§2753. Shades of meaning other than the temporal have already been discussed in §§2745-50. Adams (p. vii and *passim*) described clauses introduced by *oþ* and its variants as 'clauses indicating the time of the termination of the action of the main clause'. They frequently have this function, as well as that of introducing a new happening or marking a transition in the narrative, e.g. *Or* 294. 3 and *Or* 102. 29 (both in §2752), *ÆCHom* i. 78. 21 *þa tungelwitegan ferdon æfter þæs cyninges spræce, and efne ða se steorra, þe hi on eastdæle gesawon, glad him beforan, oð þæt he gestod bufon ðam gesthuse, þær þæt cild on wunode, Beo* 1127, and

Beo 99   Swa ða drihtguman   dreamum lifdon,
                       eadiglice,   oð ðæt an ongan
                       fyrene fremman   feond on helle.

Similar examples in which both limits are defined include *Or* 90. 8 *Ac siþþan hie on Sicilium wunnon, hie eac siþþan betweonum him selfum winnende wæron, oþ þæt Darius, Persa cyning, Læcedemonium on fultume wearð wið þæm Athenienses, for þæm gewinnum his ieldrena, ÆCHom* i. 108. 31 *Ne glad he ealne weig him ætforan, ac syððan hi comon to Iudeiscum earde, syððan he wæs heora latteow, oð þæt he bufan Cristes gesthuse ætstod, Brun* 10, and

PPs 112. 3   Fram upgange   æryst sunnan
                           oðþæt heo wende   on westrodur
                           ge sculon dryhtnes naman   dædum herigean.

§2754. But there are in the poetry examples in which there is a transition in the narrative with no implication that the action of the main clause is completed, e.g.

Beo 53
>Ða wæs on burgum   Beowulf Scyldinga,
>leof leodcyning   longe þrage
>folcum gefræge   —fæder ellor hwearf,
>aldor of earde—,   oþ þæt him eft onwoc
>heah Healfdene

and

Beo 217
>Gewat þa ofer wægholm   winde gefysed
>flota famiheals   fugle gelicost,
>oð þæt ymb antid   oþres dogores
>wundenstefna   gewaden hæfde,
>þæt ða liðende   land gesawon,
>brimclifu blican,   beorgas steape,
>side sænæssas.

We also find *oð þæt* beginning a new fit, e.g. in *Beo* 1735 and

GenA 1245
>   Ða giet wæs Sethes cynn,
>leofes leodfruman   on lufan swiðe
>drihtne dyre   and domeadig,
>oðþæt bearn godes   bryda ongunnon
>on Caines   cynne secan,
>wergum folce,   and him þær wif curon
>ofer metodes est   monna eaforan,
>scyldfulra mægð   scyne and fægere.

Hence there arises the much-canvassed possibility that *oð þæt* is used adverbially with some such sense as 'and then' or 'at length'.[122] Examples which have been adduced to support it include *Bede* 332. 17 *þær bysene heo wæs inhyrgende in foresetenesse elþeodgunge, 7 eal ger in þære foresprecenan mægðe Eastengla hæfd wæs, oð þæt heo eft from Aidane þæm biscope wæs ham gelaðad 7 gesponen*, where *oð þæt* represents *deinde* of Latin *Cuius aemulata exemplum, et ipsa proposito peregrinandi annum totum in praefata prouincia retenta est; deinde ab Aidano episcopo patriam reuocata, accepit locum unius familiae . . .* , *Bede* 474. 17 (§ 2752),

GenA 1851
>   Hie þæt cuð dydon
>heora folcfrean   þæt fægerro lyt
>for æðelinge   idesa sunnon,
>ac hie Sarran   swiðor micle,
>wynsumne wlite   wordum heredon,
>oðþæt he lædan heht   leoflic wif to
>his selfes sele,

---

[122] It is unlikely that the few late examples of *oð þæt* for *oð* preposition, such as *ChronE* 237. 22 (1101) *And se eorl syððan oð ðet ofer sc̃e Michaeles mæsse her on lande wunode* and those noted by Johnsen (*Ang.* 38 (1914), 94), are relevant here.

where we find *et* corresponding to *oðþæt* in *Gen* 12. 15—but there is, of course, no 'rule' that a translator cannot have a subordinate clause if his original does not—and

Dan 733   Ne mihton arædan   runcræftige men
                 engles ærendbec,   æðelinga cyn,
                 oðþæt Daniel com,   drihtne gecoren,
                 snotor and soðfæst,   in þæt seld gangan,

where the *oðþæt* clause marks a transition or new development in the narrative without implying that the action of the principal clause is completed. As Möllmer (p. 89) puts it, 'die Handlung des *oþ þæt*-Satzes trägt eine neue Vorstellung in die Erzählung hinein, so daß der Temporalsatz psychologisch als Hauptsatz anzusehen ist' ['the action of the *oþ þæt* clause introduces a new idea into the narrative, so that the temporal clause should psychologically be regarded as a main clause']. In my full discussion of this problem (*NQ* 223 (1978), 390-4), I add *CorpGl* (ed. W. M. Lindsay) 60 *eatenus*: *oð ðaet*—Plezia's *Lexicon* has s.v. *eatenus, ea tenus* adv. II *de tempore* = 1. *usque, ad hoc tempus*. 2. *tunc*—as additional evidence in favour of the proposition that *oð þæt* could be used adverbially, but go on to suggest that there are dangers in assuming that all usages of *oð þæt* can be rigidly classified as either 'adverb' or 'conjunction', for there may well have been an intermediate stage between the two in OE.

§2755. Such an adverbial use of *oð þæt* would give a source for the conjunctions discussed above: *oð* prep. > *oð þæt* prep. + dem. > *oð þæt* adv. > *oð þæt* conj. > *oð* conj.[123] In view of the absence of *oð þæt . . . þe* and the rarity of *oð þæt þe/þætte*, it seems likely that the latter was a later development from *oð þæt* conj., as Möllmer (pp. 88-9) suggests, rather than an essential stage in its development, as Small (1924, pp. 152-3) has it.[124] Whether we follow Adams (pp. 130-1), who prefers to explain *oððe* as *oð* + *ðe*, or Möllmer (p. 87), who sees it as a weakening of *oð þæt*, must be a matter of opinion.

§2756. All these theories see conj. *oð* as the last stage in the development. But Johnsen (*Ang.* 38 (1914), 92-5) suggests that *oð* came first as a development of *oð* local 'adverb denoting limit in space' and that *oðþæt*, *oðþæt þe*, and *oðþe*, are later developments in which

---

[123] See further Adams, pp. 127 and 131, and Kivimaa, pp. 163-4. Kivimaa (p. 158) writes: 'If the conjunction *oþ* is originally a preposition, it is the only one to become a conjunction in OE, excepting an isolated occurrence or two, such as *wiþ* in *Lindisfarne Glosses*'; on this see §2760. But we also find conj. *for* in late OE; see §3037. On *ær* see §2717.

[124] For Behaghel (*DS* iii. 134-5), the intermediate stage would presumably have been *⁎oð* (prep.) + *þæt* (dem.) + *þæt* (conj.).

þæt was originally a 'local-demonstrative adverb' and *þe* a 'local-demonstrative particle'. I give my reasons for preferring Möllmer's view at greater length in *NQ* 223 (1978), 390-4.

c. Combinations of swa lange/swiþe + oð (þæt) or + þæt

§2757. These are exemplified and discussed by Adams (pp. 133-6 and 226-7) and by Ericson (1932, pp. 70-1). It will suffice to list the various patterns, with a reference to one example: *swa lange oð* (*Bo* 121. 20); *swa lange oð þæt* (*ÆCHom* i. 232. 7: this pattern, not recorded by Adams, is wrongly said by Möllmer (p. 93) to occur in *ChronE* 180. 7 (1052) *Đa wiðlæg se cyng sume hwile þeah swa lange oð þet folc þe mid þam eorle wes wearð swiðe astyred ongean þone cyng*); *swa lange . . . oð þæt* (*ÆCHom* i. 304. 25); *swa lange þæt* (*ChronE* 117. 24 (963)); and *swa lange . . . þæt* (*ChronE* 178. 1 (1052), the only example found by Adams (p. 235)).

§2758. Johnsen (*Ang.* 38 (1914), 97) asserts that the combination *swa lange þæt* 'must, to begin with, have been a purely local one' and argues that those like *swa lange (. . .) oð (þæt)* are later contaminations. Adams (pp. 134-6) does not commit himself to any theory about which came first, but sees all the patterns discussed above as the product of confusion between the ideas of result and time. He detects a similar confusion in the examples of *swa swiðe (. . .) oð þæt* which appear in *HomU* 35. 206. 21, *GD* 220. 7, and *GD* 248. 21 *witodlice hit gelamp þæt þa yþa . . . wæron upp ahafene for þara winda mycelnessum swa swiðe oð þæt of þam scipe wæron þa næglas forlorene.*

d. Oð + an accusative noun phrase + þe/þæt/þonne

§2759. Most of these combinations are given by Adams (pp. 139-40 and 228). Again it will suffice to list them and to give the reference to one example: *oð þone byre þe* (*LS* 8. 336); *oð þone dæg þe* (*Luke* (*WSCp*) 1. 20); *oð þone dæg þonne* (*Mark(WSCp)* 14. 25); *oð þone fyrst þe* (*ChronD* 99. 29 (915)); *oð ða tide þe* (*Bede* 42. 12); *(swa lange) oð þone timan þe* (*ChronE* 142. 10 (1011)); and *oð ðone first þæt* (*Bo* 116. 10). The only examples in the poetry are *oð ðone anne dæg ∥ þe* (*Beo* 2399) and *oð þone dæg þe* (*PPs* 60. 5).

e. Other words and combinations

§2760. I list these in alphabetical order, with references to at least one example and to discussions other than those by Adams (pp. 138-

42 and 228-9): *fort(e)* (*Lch* iii. 102. 17 and 130. 15); *(swa lange)*
fortþan (*Lch* iii. 88. 23); *forð þæt* (*ChronD* 167. 35 (1050); see
Möllmer, p. 97, and Johnsen, *Ang.* 38 (1914), 95-7); *ongean þæt*
(*Gen* 43. 25); *þe gyt þe* (*ChronE* 246. 36 (1116); see Kivimaa, p. 153);
(næs long) to þon (. . .) þæt (*Alex* 12. 4 and *Beo* 2591); *(næs nan/*
nænig hwil) to þam/þan/þon þæt (*LS* 10. 139. 3)—on these last two
patterns see §§ 2784-5; *to þæm dæge þe* (*LS* 34. 487 . . . *of ðam*
dæge þe ða halgan slepon to ðam dæge þe hi eft awocon—despite
Adams (p. 228), the same formula in *ÆCHom* ii. 288. 7 means 'on
the day when'); and finally *wiþ* glossing *donec* (*Matt(Li)* 10. 23 and
17. 9). The ind. *onginnað* suggests to me that *for þat* means 'until' in
Solil 10. 4 . . . *and cumað oððer grenu, wexað and growað and ripiað,*
for þat hy eft onginnað searian.

f. Mood

§2761. The unnatural rigidity of Callaway's threefold division of
subjunctives in temporal clauses has already been discussed in §2614.
But it is very apparent here, for he puts 'until' clauses into his third
group—'the subjunctive denoting an action contemporaneous with
that of the main clause'—along with conjunctions meaning 'when',
'while', and the like. Logically, they would seem to belong with
conjunctions meaning 'before', which are in his second group and
have 'the subjunctive denoting an action subsequent to that of the
main clause'. In practice, however, Callaway's division has this to be
said for it, that clauses introduced by *oð (þæt)* and the like have
more in common with those in his third group in that they do not
present the problems of mood which arise with clauses introduced
by *ær* and its compounds. But they demand separate consideration.

§2762. Let us first have some facts. Unlike *hwonne* (§§ 2775-83),
oþ alone and in combination prefers the indicative. Adams's figures
for the prose—always inflated as far as the subjunctive is concerned
because he takes some ambiguous forms as unambiguously subjunctive; see §2531—are 226 subjunctives out of the 984 examples he
cites at pp. 221-7. In the poetry only fourteen out of some 220
clauses have an unambiguous subjunctive.

§2763. The use of the moods is not mechanical. In historical texts,
where the emphasis is on the fact that both clauses refer to completed acts or events in the past, as in *ChronA* 46. 21 (755) *7 he*
hæfde þa [Hamtunscire] oþ he ofslog þone aldormon þe him lengest
wunode, the verbs are overwhelmingly indicative: *Chron* has no

subjunctive in sixty-one examples, *Or* one in eighty-two. The exception is *Or* 114. 30 . . . *7 him bebead þæt hie ðæt lond hergiende wæron oþ hie hit awesten*, where *awesten* (though strictly ambiguous in form) is clearly a subjunctive expressing the ideas of wish and purpose inherent in the dependent desire introduced by *bebead*. The same ideas of purpose and/or desire are also apparent in exhortations, commands, and purpose clauses, and it is in texts which by their nature are likely to contain many examples of these four constructions that the subjunctive is most frequently used: *Laws* fourteen out of fourteen examples, *BenR* ten out of ten, and *Lch* eighty-two out of eighty-seven. In these sentences, the emphasis is on the fact that the action of the *oð (þæt)* clause has not yet taken place, but is something which is wished for or planned. In such contexts the subjunctive is the only possible mood in the preterite, where its reference is to the future-in-the-past (see § 2000) and is the natural one in the present. This contrast is well brought out in *CP* 425. 14 *7 swa swa we sigon ær on ðæt unaliefede, oððæt we afeollon, swa we sculon nu forberan ðæt aliefede, oððæt we arisen*, where what I take to be the pret. ind. *afeollon* contrasts with the pres. subj. *arisen*.

§ 2764. Two important points are made by Adams (pp. 155–8) about the use of 'modal' auxiliaries in the clauses under discussion. First, there is the general infrequency of these auxiliaries in temporal clauses; Adams found about 450 in the 8,000 or more clauses which he studied, whereas Shearin (1903, p. 100) found some 480 in his 3,000 clauses of purpose. Second, he remarks on p. 156, 'none of these auxiliaries is ever used in temporal clauses as mere substitutes for the optative. They preserve their primary meaning, and themselves take the optative under the same circumstances that lead to its use in the case of any other verb.' As I suggest in *Neophil.* 49 (1965), 45, the same is true in the poetry.

§ 2765. All the *oð (þæt)* clauses quoted from the prose by Wülfing (ii. 121–2), Adams (pp. 153–5), and Callaway (1931, pp. 55–8), fall into one of the categories already discussed in §§ 2610–25 for clauses introduced by conjunctions meaning 'when'. We find a present subjunctive with an imperative in the principal clause in *CP* 385. 4 *Sittað eow nu giet innan ceastre oððæt ge weorðen fullgearowode mid ðæm gæsðlican cræfte* and *ÆCHom* i. 252. 7 *strece ðærto þinne hiht and anbida oðþæt ðu hi hæbbe*; with a jussive subjunctive in the principal clause in *CP(C)* 290. 1 *Leornien hiene þa manðwæran 7 lufien oððæt hie hiene hæbben* and *ÆCHom* i. 126. 1 . . . *he hæbbe wununge betwux cristenum mannum oð þæt he full hal sy on his drohtnungum*; and with a form of **sculan* in the principal clause in *CP* 61. 20 *He sceal geleornian ðæt he gewunige to singallecum gebedum oð he ongite ðæt he mæge abiddan æt Gode . . .* and *ÆCHom* i. 218. 8 *Nu sceole we healdan urne palm oðþæt se sangere onginne ðone offringsang.* These examples can be contrasted with *Or* 19. 16 *þonne is þis land oð he cymð to Scirincges heale* and *BlHom* 21. 28 *ac sona he molsnaþ 7 wyrþ to þære ilcan eorþan þe he ær of gesceapen wæs oþþæt Drihten cymeþ on domes dæg*, where the emphasis is on the fact and there is no suggestion of desire, doubt, hypothesis, or purpose.

§2766. We also find the present subjunctive after a dependent desire, e.g. *CP* 7. 6, *CP* 447. 6 *Swa eac se ðe forlæt ðone cele ungetreownesse, 7 wyrð wlacra treowa, 7 nyle ðonne ðæt wlæce oferwinnan, 7 wearmian oð he wealle*, and *BlHom* 145. 2 *Broþor þa leofestan, ic eow bidde ealle þa þe on þisse stowe syndon þæt ge wacian mid me 7 we bærnan gastlico leohtfato oþþæt Drihten hider cume*; after a purpose clause, e.g. *CP* 457. 6, *CP* 373. 15 *Ðæt is ðonne ðæt mon his wætru utlæte, ðæt se lareow mid ðy cræfte his lareowdomes utane on oðre menn giote, oððæt hie innan gelærede weorðen*, and perhaps *Mark (WSCp)* 6. 45 *Ða sona he nydde his leorningcnihtas on scyp stigan þ hi him beforan foron ofer þæne muþan to Bethsaida oþ he þ folc forlete* (where, however, the *þ* clause may be one of result, with the purpose confined to the *oþ* clause); and sometimes after questions, e.g. *ÆC Hom* i. 136. 30 *Hwæðer ic mote lybban oðþæt ic hine geseo?* (I take *geseo* as subjunctive) and *ÆCHom* ii. 50. 23 *forðan ðe hit bið twylic, hwæðer hit on life aðolige oðþæt hit þam lareowe mid geleafan andwyrdan mage.* In *oð (þæt)* clauses in these contexts, we can detect (in varying degrees) elements of indefinite futurity, hypothesis, uncertainty, desire, and/or purpose. One or more of these elements may be adduced to explain subjunctives in *oð (þæt)* clauses after principal or other clauses containing an indicative verb, which may be negated, e.g. *CP* 457. 15 *Ne gaderað he no mid ðy unðeawas, ac tilað ðæs gewundedan werpe ðe he bewitan sceal, oððæt he hine fullice gehælan mæge* (I do not think the presence of *sceal* a factor here; we could just as easily have had *bewiteþ* and the adjective clause is restrictive) and *ÆCHom* ii. 200. 1 *An strica oððe an stæf ðære ealdan æ ne bið forgæged oðþæt hi ealle gefyllede beon*, or not, e.g. *ÆCHom* ii. 214. 29 *. . . and hi symle geedlæcað, oðþæt seo geendung eallum mannum becume* and *ÆCHom* i. 266. 35 *and eow ðær deofol getintregað, oðþæt ge habban ealle eowre gyltas geðrowade, oðþæt ge cumon to anum feorðlincge.*

§2767. As already noted, the preterite indicative occurs when the writer or speaker is referring to the contents of the *oð (þæt)* clause as something which took place in the past, as in *ChronA* 46. 21 (755) (§2763), *Or* 60. 14 *7 hit fela wintra siþþan on þæm stod, oð ðæt Arbatus, Meþa ealdormon, Sardanopolum Babylonia cyning ofslog*, and *ÆCHom* i. 94. 14 *þis tacen stod on Godes folce oð þæt Crist sylf com*. But the equally logical way of viewing the contents of the *oð (þæt)* clause—viz. as something which at the time of the action or event described in the principal clause was still to happen in the future—is apparent in those clauses with the preterite subjunctive. With this expression of the future-in-the-past there may be associated (again in varying degrees) elements of desire, hypothesis, purpose, and/or uncertainty. So the preterite subjunctive occurs in *oð (þæt)* clauses which are subordinate to noun clauses of dependent desire or to accusative and infinitive constructions after verbs of commanding and the like, e.g. *Or* 114. 30 (§2763) and *ÆCHom* ii. 312. 9 *þis wearð ða gecyd þam casere sona, and he wearð geangsumod mid ormætum graman, and het beheafdian ða halgan preostas, and ðæs papan lima gelome prician, oðþæt he swulte ðurh swylcum pinungum*; in *oð (þæt)* clauses expressing purpose, e.g. *Bede* 254. 31 . . . *7 þa baad feower monað oððæt him feax geweoxe þæt he to preoste bescoren beon meahte* and *Matt(WSCp)* 18. 30 *He þa nolde ac ferde and wearp hyne on cweartern oððæt he him eall agefe*; and in *oð (þæt)* clauses expressing uncertainty about the exact time of an event whose occurrence is (believed to be) beyond doubt, e.g. *Bede* 268. 6 *Is þæt hwelc wundor, þeah ðe he þone dæg his deaðes oðþe ma þone Drihtnes dæg bliðe gesege, þone he symle sorgende bad, oð þæt he cwome?*—note the rhetorical question, the *þeah ðe* clause (see §1960), and the verb *bad*!—and *ÆCHom* i. 82. 1 *swa swa Moyses be ðam awrat, þæt ne sceolde ateorian þæt Iudeisce cynecynn, oþþæt Crist sylf come*.

§2768. In the poetry the prevailing mood in some 220 *oð (þæt)* clauses is the indicative. All the fourteen unambiguous subjunctives have the present tense, but the ambiguous preterite form *becwoman* represents *irent* in

PPs 106. 6 Hi þa gelædde lifes ealdor,
        þær hi on rihtne weg ricene eodan,
        oðþæt hi cuðlice on becwoman
        to hiora cestre eardungstowe,

Latin *Ps* 106. 7 *Et deduxit eos in viam rectam ut irent in civitatem habitationis*, where the translator shows his independence of the

Latin by using *oðþæt* rather than *þæt* for *ut* and where *becwoman* can be taken as a subjunctive expressing purpose. I give my reasons for taking *gewitan* as a preterite indicative functioning as a future perfect 'shall have passed away' in

Ruin 6
           Eorðgrap hafað
    waldend wyrhtan   forweorone, geleorene,
    heardgripe hrusan,   oþ hund cnea
    werþeoda gewitan

in *Neophil.* 49 (1965), 44-6. There are no examples in the poetry in which a negated indicative is followed by a subjunctive in an *oð* (*þæt*) clause. For contrary examples see *Beo* 1735 and *Dan* 733.

§2769. Eleven of the fourteen present subjunctives—for full details see Appendix 'Time 6' in my D.Phil. thesis—are accompanied by a principal clause containing a volitional expression. They include (with an imperative) *PPs* 56. 1, where two co-ordinate causal clauses intervene, and

Sat 700   Grip wið þæs grundes;   gang þonne swa
                oððæt þu þone ymbhwyrft   alne cunne;

(with a jussive subjunctive)

PPs 129. 6   Fram þære mæran   mergentide
               oðþæt æfen cume   ylda bearnum,
               Israhelas on drihten   a getreowen;

(with a form of **sculan*)

Wan 70   Beorn sceal gebidan,   þonne he beot spriceð,
              oþþæt collenferð   cunne gearwe
              hwider hreþra gehygd   hweorfan wille

and

PPs 112. 3   Fram upgange   æryst sunnan
               oðþæt heo wende   on westrodur
               ge sculon dryhtnes naman   dædum herigean,

which should be compared with

PPs 106. 3   Fram uppgange   æryst sunnan
               oþþæt heo gewiteð   on westrodur
               and fram sæ norðan   swycedan geond westen;
               ne meahton ceastre weg   cuðne mittan,
               þe hi eardunge   on genaman,

where there is no volitional expression in the principal clause; and (with an accusative and infinitive followed by the present subjunctive)

Dan 513　　Het þonne besnædan　　seolfes blædum,
　　　　　　　twigum and telgum,　　and þeh tacen wesan,
　　　　　　　wunian wyrtruman　　þæs wudubeames
　　　　　　　eorðan fæstne,　　oðþæt eft cyme
　　　　　　　grene bleda,　　þonne god sylle.

But **sculan* is not always followed by a subjunctive *oð (þæt)* clause;
see *GenA* 1762, *Fort* 33 and 85, and *Finn* 28.

§2770. The three remaining examples are *PPs* 67. 22, where the
Latin has *ut* + subjunctive, and *PPs* 122. 3 and 141. 9, where the
Latin has *donec* + subjunctive. The Latin may have had some influ-
ence here. But all three contain elements of purpose and futurity and
the translator's subjunctives are acceptable as idiomatic OE. So
Behre's conclusion (p. 162) for the poetry is right:

The occurrence of the subjunctive in *oðþæt*-clauses may be briefly summarized
thus: It is used, as in other temporal clauses of class I, in connection with a main
clause containing an expression of volition. In other connections it occurs chiefly
in direct translation of a Latin subjunctive. There is consequently no justification for Callaway's statement that the employment of the subjunctive in OE.
oðþæt-clauses is wholly due to Latin influence.

§2771. It holds for the prose too. On the question of Latin influence the reader should consult Callaway 1931, pp. 61-6 and 120;
Liggins 1970, p. 301; and Behre, pp. 162-3. There he will find that
there are few exceptions to the statement that Latin subjunctives in
clauses introduced by *donec* and similar conjunctions meaning 'until'
are represented by subjunctives in the OE translations. Arguing from
this and from the non-occurrence or rarity of the subjunctive in
'until' clauses in texts such as *Chron* and *Beo* which are not dependent on a Latin original, Callaway (1931, p. 61) reprimands Adams
and others for not mentioning Latin influence and goes on (1931, p.
120) to conclude that 'the Subjunctive with particles meaning "until"
(especially with *oð* and *oð ðæt*) was probably not a native English
idiom'. I hope that my preceding discussion has made clear both the
fact that, and the reasons why, I agree with Behre (p. 163): 'Latin
influence has no doubt contributed to the extension of the subjunctive usage in *oðþæt*-clauses. On the other hand, the ready adaptation
of the mood in *oðþæt*-clauses to the Latin subjunctive cannot be explained as simply due to mechanical imitation but rather as due to
a tendency in the OE. language itself.' All the categories I have
erected to explain the present and preterite subjunctives in *oð (þæt)*
clauses—whether in translated or non-translated texts—concern the
attitudes of those involved in the situation and/or of those describing

it. This blanket explanation covers the once popular term 'the principle of attraction', which is mentioned by Adams (p. 153) and
which I take in §2611 to refer to the influence of the attitude of
mind of a person using a subjunctive in clauses of purpose, concession, and the like. There is nothing mechanistic about the use of the
subjunctive in *oð (þæt)* clauses.

§2772. Little more need be said about the 'reasons' for the appearance of the subjunctive in these clauses. Callaway (1931, pp. 58-60)
launches another attack on 'the Erdmann–Bernhardt theory of
mood-syntax'; see §§2612-13 for my fuller discussion of this. I cannot, I fear, understand his table (1931, p. 60). Anyone reading the
remarks by Hotz, Adams, and Fleischhauer, which he quotes or
refers to will, in my opinion, be compelled to agree that, here at any
rate, Callaway is attacking a windmill of his own erection. None of
these writers makes the claim that the influence of the principal
clause is the sole factor. Hotz (pp. 37-8) twice mentions 'intention-
ality'. Adams (p. 157) attributes some influence to 'the general indefinite character of the sentence'. And Fleischhauer, in nine lines
quoted by Callaway (1931, p. 59), twice speaks of the whole sentence (main clause and subordinate clause): 'der ganze Satz (Haupt-
und Nebensatz)'. We need not pursue this idle controversy.

§2773. Other discussions on this subject include those by Möllmer
(pp. 109-12) and by Muxin (*UZLGU* 262, vyp. 50 (1958), 158).
I am unable to follow the latter in extending to *oð (þæt)* clauses his
theory about the significance of the variation between subjunctive
and indicative which I discuss in detail for *ær* clauses in §§2739-42.

§2774. The remarks made here about *oð (þæt)* clauses apply, *mutatis mutandis*, to other conjunctions meaning 'until' exemplified by
Adams (pp. 227-9) and discussed by me in the preceding sections of
this sub-chapter.

9. HWONNE

§2775. *Hwonne* (also spelt *hwanne* and *hwænne*) was in OE primarily an interrogative, translating *quando* (not *cum*), and an indefinite
adverb 'at some time'. As Ælfric puts it in

ÆGram 231.9   INTERROGATIVA synd axigendlice. *cur*, hwi, *quare*, for hwi,
quam ob rem, for hwi oððe for ði, *ubi*, hwar, *unde*, hwanon, *quo*, hwyder,
quando, hwænne. sume ðas habbað þryfealde getacnunge. gyf ic cweðe *ubi
posuisti meum librum?*, hwar ledest ðu mine boc?, þonne is se *ubi* INTERRO-

GATIVVM, þæt is axigendlic. gyf ic cweðe *tu scis, ubi tuus liber est*, ðu wast,
hwar þin boc is, ðonne byð se *ubi* RELATIVVM, þæt is edlesendlic, þæt is
ongeancyrrendlic. gyf ic cweðe *nescio, ubi inueniam meum librum*, nat ic, hwar
ic finde mine boc, þonne byð se *ubi* INFINITIVVM, þæt is ungeendigendlic.
quando uenisti?, hwanne com ðu?, is INTERROGATIVVM. *quando eram
iuuenis*, ða ða ic wæs iung, is RELATIVVM. *quando ero doctus*, hwænne beo ic
gelæred, is INFINITIVVM: *quandoque*, on sumne sæl.

In MnE, of course, its descendant 'when' is an interrogative, a conjunction introducing adverb clauses of time, and a relative adverb
introducing adjective clauses of time. The best way to approach its
use in OE seems to be to ask what stage of development *hwonne* had
reached.

§2776. As I have already said in §§2052-5, *hwonne* can be explained as an interrogative in all the OE examples—in both native
texts and those based on a Latin original, and in both prose and
poetry—in which it is said to be a definite relative 'when', a conjunction of time 'when' or 'until', or an indefinite 'whenever'. So we
can confirm and extend Möllmer's dictum (p. 116): 'Der Vergleich
der ae. Denkmäler mit den lat. Vorlagen gibt Gewißheit darüber, daß
ae. *hwonne* . . . noch nicht bewußt als temporale Konjunktion ge-
braucht wird' ['The comparison of OE texts with their Latin sources
gives confirmation that OE *hwonne* . . . is not yet being used as a
temporal conjunction'].

§2777. It is true that *hwonne* with a subjunctive verb can often be
translated 'until'. But this usage is restricted to contexts in which
there is an idea of delay in achieving something. Usually it is something wished for, but not always; see §2781. So we find (after *bidan*)
Bede 440. 15 *7 ða dioflu gearwe bidað hwonne heo mec gegrypen 7
to helle locum gelæde, Bede* 178. 22 . . . *7 þær hwile bad hwonne his
horse bet wurde oðþe he hit þær dead forlete*, BlHom 109. 32 *ah he
þær on moldan gemolsnaþ 7 þær wyrde bideþ, hwonne se ælmihtiga
God wille þisse worlde ende gewyricean*, and

ChristA 146   Nu hie softe þæs
           bidon in bendum   hwonne bearn godes
           cwome to cearigum;

(with *þyncan (to) lang*) GD 245. 7 . . . *forþon þe hire þynceð lang
seo ylding 7 seo uferung hwænne heo cume to Gode, ÆCHom* i.
140. 19 *and ðincð him to lang hwænne he beo genumen of ðyses
lifes earfoðnyssum*, HomU 37. 236. 10 *swa oft swa he þærinne wæs,
him þuhte æfre to lang hwonne he moste beon ymbe þæs lichaman*

oferfylle, and *Mald* 66 *To lang hit him þuhte* ‖ *hwænne hi togædere garas beron*; (with *beon lang*) *CP* 121. 11 *Hit bið long hwonne se hlaford cume*; (with *langian*) *BlHom* 227. 1 *ah hine ðæs heardost langode hwanne he of ðisse worlde moste*; and (with *wenan*)

ChristA 25   . . .   þe we in carcerne
            sittað sorgende,   sunnan wenað,
            hwonne us liffrea   leoht ontyne,
            weorðe ussum mode   to mundboran,
            ond þæt tydre gewitt   tire bewinde. . . .

But since the prevailing mood in these examples is the subjunctive (§2780), since *hwonne* is not used in other contexts as the equivalent of *oðþæt* 'until' (§2743), and since MnE 'when' does not mean 'until', the presumption is strong that Ælfric would have been happy to quote any of these examples to illustrate his dictum *hwonne is interrogativum*. His statement quoted in §2775 is in my opinion a warning that where it is possible to take *hwonne*, *hwær*, and the like, as interrogatives, that is how native informants of OE—not, like modern scholars, wise after the event—would have taken it.

§2778. This possibility exists, I believe, not only in those examples in which *hwonne* seems to mean 'until', but also in those in which it comes close to being a relative adverb 'when', e.g. *CP* 227. 11 . . . *7 bit ðære tide hwonne he ðæs wierðe sie ðæt he hine besuican mote*, *Exod* 8. 9 *þa cwæð Moyses to Pharaone: Gesete me andagan hwænne ðu wille þæt ic for þe gebidde*, and

Rid 31. 12   . . . siteð æt symble,   sæles bideþ,
            hwonne ær heo cræft hyre   cyþan mote
            werum on wonge,[125]

or a temporal conjunction 'when' or 'whenever', e.g. *CP* 51. 4 *Ac forðæmðe hit swa earfoðe is ænegum menn to witanne hwonne he geclænsod sie, he mæg ðy orsorglicor forbugan ða ðegnunga*, *BlHom* 97. 24 *Swa eac monegum men genihtsumað þisse worlde gestreon æt his ende, þeah hwæþere he sceal winnan 7 sorgian, hwonne se dæg cume þæt he sceole þæs ealles idel hweorfan . . .* , *Gen* 19. 35 *7 se fæder nyste hu he befeng on hi ne hwænne heo aras, for his druncennysse*, and

GenA 2602   Ne wiste blondenfeax
            hwonne him fæmnan to bryde   him bu wæron,
            on ferhðcofan   fæste genearwod
            mode and gemynde,   þæt he mægða sið
            wine druncen   gewitan ne meahte.

[125] Here, as in *Ps(P)* 40. 5 *Hwonne ær he beo dead . . . ?*, Latin *Quando morietur . . . ?*, *ær* is the adverb. See Klaeber, *Ang.* 40 (1916), 503-4.

§ 2779. But it cannot be *proved* that *hwonne* is consciously used in any of these senses in OE. The prevailing mood in the clauses it introduces is the subjunctive (§ 2780) and its interrogative function can still to some extent at least be detected; see Yamakawa 1969, p. 16. I have as yet found no real exceptions to this observation. It holds for *ChronA* 158. 3 (1031) . . . *swa þ loc whenne þ flod byþ ealra hehst* . . ., where *whenne* interrogative combines with *loc* imperative to form a conjunction which means 'whenever' and is followed by the indicative, and for *WHom* 2. 62 *And ðy man sceal wacigean 7 warnian symle þæt man geara weorðe huru to ðam dome, weald hwænne he us to cyme*, where *weald* imperative + *hwænne* interrogative is followed by the subjunctive. It holds too for four examples I discuss elsewhere—*Mark* 8. 19 (§ 2780) and *GenA* 1263, *Max i* 103, and *Seasons* 222 (*Neophil.* 49 (1965), 157-60)—and for

Sat 619   þonne stondað þa forworhtan,   þa ðe firnedon;
                beoð beofigende   hwonne him bearn godes
                deman wille   þurh his dæda sped,

where we can either accept the interpretation seen in Clubb's translation 'They shall tremble for fear of the time when the Son of God will judge them' or believe that the alteration of *þonne* to *hwonne* in the manuscript was made by a later scribe to whom *hwonne* meant 'when', conjunction of time.

§ 2780. The prevailing mood in *hwonne* clauses is the subjunctive. The only unambiguous indicatives known to me in the prose are in glosses such as *Luke(Li)* 17. 20 *gefrognen wæs ðonne* . . . *huoenne cymmeð ric godes*, Latin *Interrogatus autem* . . . *quando uenit regnum dei*, where *Ru2* has *hwenne cymeð* but *WSCp hwænne* . . . *come* and *WSH hwanne* . . . *come*, and all versions of what appears in *Mark (WSCp)* 8. 19 as *hwænne ic bræc fif hlafas 7 twegen fixas 7 hu fela wyligena ge namon fulle*, Latin *quando quinque panes fregi in quinque milia et quot cophinos fragmentorum plenos sustulistis*, where (I would argue) mechanical glossing is apparent even in the W-S versions. The only indicative in the poetry occurs in the much-discussed

Ex 248   Fana up gerad,
            beama beorhtost;   bidon ealle þa gen
            hwonne siðboda   sæstreamum neah
            leoht ofer lindum   lyftedoras bræc,

where the manuscript has *rad* (248) and *buton* (249). Bright (*MLN* 27 (1912), 16-17), argued against Cosijn's emendation to *bræce* (251), 'for the people were still in doubt and despair "until the time when" (*hwonne*) the light of the guide "broke" thru the obstructions of the sky. The contrasted subjunctive after *hwonne* is fittingly employed in *neosan come* (475).' Krapp (it would appear, for his style here, as often, approaches the Delphic), Irving, and Lucas, all accept Bright's suggestion. Irving paraphrases it thus: 'The Israelites were not waiting *for* the pillar to move; they were waiting (in despair) when suddenly the pillar moved.' Lucas repeats Irving's first clause and goes on 'but were still waiting *when* it moved, and the indicative is appropriate, though *þa* would be more usual to convey this sense'. I would be inclined to say that *þa* would be required and cannot see why the subjunctive would be any less appropriate here than it is in *Ex* 475, where the poet is writing with fierce actuality of the drowning of the Egyptians in the Red Sea. I have no solution to this problem. But I must remind the reader that the solution favoured by the editors involves the acceptance of Grein's *bidon* for MS *buton* and the assumption that, while (in Lucas's words) 'emendation to the subj. *bræce* (so Grein) is not acceptable because it would produce an otherwise unknown metrical type, 3A, and Cosijn thought *bræc* to be "licentia poetica metri causa" (*PBB* 20 (1895), 100)', it is apparently quite acceptable to produce an otherwise unknown syntactical type by assuming that the mere substitution of *bidon* for *buton* has solved what may be a deep-seated corruption. I fear that I am still unable to understand why metrical 'rules' produced by modern scholars should override syntactical facts. I raised the metrical problem in *ASE* 4 (1975), 12–13. I accept the rebuke of Bliss (private communication, Jan. 1976) and of Hoad (*RES* 28 (1977), 193–4) that I overstated the number of acceptable half-lines in *Beowulf* which do not conform to any recognized type. But I do not accept that my argument has been answered. We are still left with four half-lines in *Beowulf* —2435b, 2717b, 2093a, and 3056a—where textual corruption is not obviously involved and which have in common 'their refusal to conform to any recognized type'; see Bliss 1958, §87. So, if four acceptable half-lines do not 'conform to any recognized type', why is the statement that emendation 'would produce an otherwise unknown metrical type' sufficient grounds for rejecting an editor's emendation? I accept that I am metrically sceptical and probably naïve. But I have so far failed to get what I think is a straight answer to a straight question.

§2781. The liking of *hwonne* for the subjunctive is in marked contrast to temporal conjunctions meaning 'when' or 'until', which show a strong preference for the indicative except under the special circumstances discussed in §§2610-25 and 2761-74. Behre (p. 249) tells us that

in a number of indirect questions the meditative subjunctive has also an optative tone. This is especially true of *hwonne*-clauses. . . . In the *hwonne*-clauses quoted above [*Dream* 136, and *ChristA* 25 and 146 (both in §2777)] the subjunctive is used to express a volitional attitude on the part of the speaker, but, also, as is the case in other indirect questions, an attitude of reflection, consideration, or meditation toward the content of the dependent clause. In some clauses introduced by *hwonne* the subjunctive does not contain any optative element, e.g.

GenA 2276   Nu sceal tearighleor
          on westenne   witodes bidan,
          hwonne of heortan   hunger oððe wulf
          sawle and sorge   somed abregde.

. . . In such cases the subjunctive is used to express an attitude of reflection or meditation, often with an emotional tone. There is no reason, then, from a modal point of view, for separating dependent clauses introduced by the interrogative-temporal connective *hwonne* from indirect questions.

This statement is much more acceptable to me than Muxin's attempt (*UZLGU* 262, vyp. 50 (1958), 158) to extend to *hwonne* the theory which he propounded for *ær* and which I discuss in §§2739-42.

§2782. In my opinion it is impossible to sustain the claim that *hwonne* was already in OE a relative adverb or a purely temporal conjunction. But it is equally impossible to deny that *hwonne* had already made a considerable advance along the road which was to lead to its use in these two capacities while remaining an interrogative; see the examples quoted and discussed by Möllmer (pp. 28-32), myself (*Neophil.* 49 (1965), 157-60), and Yamakawa (1969, pp. 15-20). The reasons for this development, which is shared by other interrogatives, are discussed in §§2050-5. In the absence of the clues which a knowledge of the intonation patterns would supply, we cannot really advance beyond the only statement we have from a native informant—that of Ælfric already quoted in §2775.

§2783. In *Neophil.* 49 (1965), 160, I suggested that *hwonne* had advanced further along this road than the other OE interrogatives. In contrast, Yamakawa (1971, p. 1) argues that 'the incipient phenomena of *hwær* in the subordinating function can be attested to in Old English texts, probably to a greater extent than the case of *hwonne*'. The fact that whereas *swa hwær swa* 'wherever' is common in OE, *swa hwonne swa* 'whenever' is extremely rare (see §§2482-4 and 2790) may be added to the reasons I give in §§2494-507 for preferring my own interpretation of the evidence.

10. A NOUN OR ADVERB (PHRASE) OF TIME
+ þÆT(TE)

§2784. The formulae in this category can be divided into two groups. First, there are the ancestors of such MnE constructions as 'It is/was time that he went', 'It is different now that I am old', 'It was long ago that I saw him', and 'It was long after that he died'. OE examples include *CP* 459. 33 *Nu us is tima ðæt we onwæcnen of slæpe* and

GuthB 1295

Tid is þæt þu fere,
ond þa ærendu   eal biþence,
ofestum læde,   swa ic þe ær bibead,
lac to leofre,

where, unlike the MnE equivalents, the *þæt* clause has its verb in the present tense; *ÆCHom* i. 90. 13 *Æfter þan ðe wæron gefyllede ehta dagas Drihtnes acennednysse þæt he ymbsniden wære* . . . , *ÆLS* 31. 915 *þa æfter lytlum fyrste com se ercediacon and cwæð þæt hit tima wære þæt he into cyrcan eode*, and *Mald* 104 *Wæs seo tid cumen ‖ þæt þær fæge men feallan sceoldon* (where number and/or gender and case at least suggest that *þæt* is not a relative pronoun); *Met* 8. 42 *nu ‖ þæt* and

Met 10. 57

Ac hit is wyrse nu
þæt geond þas eorðan   æghwær sindon
hiora gelican   hwon ymbspræce . . . ;[126]

Beo 932

Ðæt wæs ungeara,   þæt ic ænigra me
weana ne wende   to widan feore
bote gebidan

and

Dream 28

þæt wæs geara iu,   (ic þæt gyta geman),
þæt ic wæs aheawen   holtes on ende,
astyred of stefne minum;[127]

and

Soul i 5

Lang bið syððan
þæt se gast nimeð   æt gode sylfum
swa wite swa wuldor,   swa him on worulde ær
efne þæt eorðfæt   ær geworhte

[126] These are two possible examples of the type 'It is now that I must see him'. *OED* has no examples of 'now that' before 1530. I give my reasons for rejecting the proposition that *nu* . . . *þæt* in *Sea* 33-4 means 'now that' in *NM* 69 (1968), 59-63. See §§2592-3.

[127] These can be compared with the example cited by *OED*, s.v. *that* rel. pron. B. II. 7. c.

and

El 432   Ne bið lang ofer ðæt
                   þæt Israhela   æðelu moten
                   ofer middangeard   ma ricsian,
                   æcræft eorla. . . .

§2785. The second group consists of patterns which do not survive
into MnE. Those I have so far noted are the *þæt is/wæs þonne þæt*
formula seen in *BlHom* 19. 13 *þæt is þonne þæt we sceolan beon
gelærede mid þysse bysene . . .* and *BlHom* 9. 32 *þæt wæs þonne
þæt se wuldorcyning on middangeard cwom forþ of þæm innoþe
þære a clænan fæmnan;*[128] sequences with a noun meaning 'delay'
+ *þæt* in which *þæt* can conveniently be translated 'before' or 'until',
as in *Bede* 60. 30 *Ne wæs þa elding þætte monige gelefdon 7 geful-
wade wæron* and *And* 1522 *Næs þa wordlatu wihte þon mare* ‖ *þæt
se stan togan;* the formula seen in *LS* 10. 139. 3 *Næs þa nan hwil to
þam þæt he geseah ealra wihta and wildeora and wurma hiw in
cuman to him;* and that seen in *Beo* 2591 and

Beo 2845   Næs ða lang to ðon,
                   þæt ða hildlatan   holt ofgefan,
                   tydre treowlogan   tyne ætsomne. . . .

(On the last two patterns see further §2760.) However we interpret
it (see §186), we must also include here the much-discussed

Beo 83   ne wæs hit lenge þa gen,
                   þæt se ecghete   aþumsweoran
                   æfter wælniðe   wæcnan scolde.

§2786. The manuscript reading of

And 185   Nu bið fore þreo niht   þæt he on þære þeode sceal
                   fore hæðenra   handgewinne
                   þurh gares gripe   gast onsendan,
                   ellorfusne,   butan ðu ær cyme

could perhaps be taken as idiomatic OE, with *fore* as a preposition
and the translation 'It will be before three nights . . .', and compared
with *ChronE* 150. 6 (1016) *7 þa wæs ymbe twa niht þ se cyning
gewende ofer æt Brentforda* and with *El* 432 (§2784). But this does
not square with the prose version in *BlHom* 237. 26 *Nu þry dagas to
lafe syndon þæt hie þe willaþ acwellan.* The use of *bið* rather than
is argues against Krapp's ASPR translation of the manuscript reading: 'It is now three days before . . .'. Several editors follow Cosijn in

---

[128] I have so far found no examples of the type 'It was then that I went'. As far as I can
see, it is not exemplified in *OED*, s.vv. *that* rel. pron., *that* conj., or *then*.

reading *ofer* for the first *fore* and translating 'It will be after three days that . . .'; compare *Beo* 1762 *eft sona bið, ‖ þæt þec adl oððe ecg eafoþes getwæfeð*. Another possibility is to omit the first *fore* as the result of dittography. This would give a construction similar to that seen in *Bede* 60. 30 and *And* 1522, both in §2785, and a sense similar to that in *BlHom* 237. 26 above: 'Now it will be three days before/until . . .'.

§2787. As we have seen, the verb of the *þæt* clause is sometimes indicative, sometimes subjunctive. But since the present tense is used with reference to the present, even the examples with the subjunctive do not cast any light on the idiomatic use in MnE of what Visser (ii, §816) calls 'the modal preterite' in examples like 'It's time that I went'. The fuller study of the examples in the prose which is necessary to correct the inadequacies of *OED* may throw light on this problem. But I doubt it.

§2788. Constructions other than a *þæt* clause can, of course, follow a noun meaning 'time'. As in MnE, such nouns can be qualified by clauses introduced by a relative pronoun (§2607) or by a temporal conjunction (§2384), or can be defined by an infinitive, e.g. *ÆCHom* i. 602. 10 *Mine gebroðra, wite ge þæt nu is tima us of slæpe to arisenne* and *Beo* 316 *Mæl is me to feran*, or by a phrase, e.g. *ÆCHom* ii. 568. 18 *Nis nan gesceaft þe cunne ðone timan þyssere worulde geendunge buton Gode anum*. On *þæt* 'until' see §§2745-6.

11. CONJUNCTIONS INTRODUCING FREQUENTATIVE TEMPORAL CLAUSES

a. þonne

§2789. This—the most common OE conjunction introducing temporal clauses which refer to repeated acts in the past, present, or future—is discussed in §§2582-90.

b. Hwonne *and* swa hwonne swa

§2790. On *hwonne* see §§2775-83. The ancestor of the now-obsolete 'whenso' has been found only once in OE prose—in *CP* 389. 35 *Ond eac forðæm ðætte hie ðy fæsðlicor 7 ðy untweogendlicor gelifden ðara ecena ðinga, swa hwanne swa him ða gehete . . .*—and does not occur in the poetry.

c. Swa oft (. . .) swa

§2791. Adams (pp. 29–30 and 187) records seventy-seven examples of *swa oft swa* in the prose, including (without correlative *swa* in the main clause) *CP* 167. 4 *To wuda we gað mid urum freondum sua oft sua we sceawiað ura hieremonna unðeawas* and *ÆCHom* ii. 444. 3 *Witodlice swa oft swa we ymbe oðra manna neode hogiað, we geefenlæcað Marthan* and (with *swa* in the main clause) *Or* 142. 5 *Swa oft swa Galli wið Romanum wunnan, swa wurdon Romane gecnysede* and *ÆLS* 31. 1200 *and swa oft swa he þyder ferde swa forhtodon þa deofla on gewitseocum mannum*, and two of *swa oft . . . swa*, viz. *Or* 274. 23 and *CP* 273. 12 *forðæm hit gewitt sua oft fram us sua us unnytte geðohtas to cumað.* . . . Neither of these combinations occurs in the poetry.

§2792. Adams (pp. 31 and 188) records two examples of *swa oft swa . . . oftost*, viz. *HomU* 37. 234. 11 and *HomU* 27. 143. 10 . . . and *þæt we swuteliað swa oft swa we oftost pater noster singað*.

d. Swa . . . oftost

§2793. This combination is recorded five times in the prose by Adams (pp. 30–1 and 187). The most famous example is *CP* 5. 1 *7 forðon ic ðe bebiode . . . ðæt ðu ðe ðissa woruldðinga to ðæm geæmetige swæ ðu oftost mæge.* . . . It also occurs in

Met 22. 8   Sece þæt siððan   on his sefan innan,
                  and forlæte an,   swa he oftost mæge,
                  ælcne ymbhogan   ðy him unnet sie. . . .

e. Combinations involving a noun of time

§2794. Two combinations are each recorded twice by Adams (pp. 50–1 and 193) for the prose, viz. *on swa hwilcum dæge swa* in *Gen* 2. 17 and *Gen* 3. 5 *Ac God wat soðlice ðæt eowre eagan beoð geopenode on swa hwylcum dæge swa ge etað of ðam treowe*—in both verses the Latin has *in quocumque die*—and *swa hwilce dæge swa* in *ChronA* 72. 30 (874) *7 he him aþas swor . . . þæt he him gearo wære swa hwelce dæge swa hie hit habban wolden* and, translating *quocumque die*, *Exod* 10. 28.

§2795. In the poetry we find *in swa hwylce tiid swa . . . swa* in *Part* 5 and *swa hwylce daga*, representing *in quacumque die*, in *PPs* 137. 4.

f. Mood

§2796. *Mutatis mutandis*, the remarks made in §§2610-25 apply here.

12. CLAUSE ORDER AND CORRELATION

§2797. Temporal clauses may precede, follow, or occur within, the principal clause, except for *oð (þæt)* clauses. Adams (p. 127), writing of the prose, says that 'the fact that the *oð ðæt*-clause always follows its main clause is another evidence of its affinity to the result-clause, that being the regular order for such clauses'. I have found no initial or medial *oð (þæt)* clauses in the prose. Verse examples like *PPs* 112. 3 (§2753) and

PPs 106. 3   Fram uppgange   æryst sunnan
                 oþþæt heo gewiteð   on westrodur
                 and fram sæ norðan   swycedan geond westen;
                 ne meahton ceastre weg   cuðne mittan,
                 þe hi eardunge   on genaman

are not really exceptions. I have not the space to attempt a full treatment or to give full statistics on the position of the various types of temporal clauses within the sentence and must content myself with a few illustrative examples. Liggins (1970, pp. 291-301) offers comments on the position of the different types of temporal clauses in their sentences in 'Alfredian' prose. Those attempting a full study of the topic will find some valuable material in Waterhouse 1978, *passim*. Factors of importance include clause length and whether the temporal clause is subordinate to a principal clause or to a subordinate clause; see Waterhouse 1978, pp. 250-1, where we read that 'in the interests of clarity a temporal almost always follows a subordinate HC [Head Clause]'.

§2798. In sentences in which there is no adverb in the principal clause correlative with the temporal conjunction, we find the temporal clause before the principal clause, e.g. *Or* 32. 16 *Ær ðæm ðe Romeburh getimbred wære þusend wintra 7 hundsyfantig, Thelescises 7 Ciarsathi þa leode betuh him gewin up hofon*, *ÆCHom* i. 16. 10 *þaða he worhte ðone mann Adam, he ne cwæð na* . . . , and *Exod* 34. 33 *7 þonne he wið hig gesprecen hæfde, he heng hrægl beforan his neb*—on the reluctance of editors to admit this arrangement in the poetry see §§2536-8—and after it, e.g. *BlHom* 41. 29 *myccle bliþre bið seo sawl þæs mannes, þonne hire man þa ælmessan fore dæleþ, Matt(WSCp)* 5. 25 *Beo þu onbugende þinum wiðerwinnan hraðe þa hwile þe ðu eart on wege mid him*, and

Dream 150   Se sunu wæs sigorfæst   on þam siðfate,
               mihtig ond spedig,   þa he mid manigeo com,
               gasta weorode. . . .

§2799. Carkeet (p. 55) states that 'the correlative adverb occurs almost exclusively only in those main clauses which follow temporal clauses, and it only rarely occurs in those main clauses which precede temporal clauses'. There is room for more work here, with special reference to the position of the adverb—initial or medial— in the principal clause. But my present impression is that Carkeet puts the position too strongly.[129] It is true that the arrangement which he says occurs 'almost exclusively' is very common in the prose—I exclude the poetry from the discussion because of the problems discussed in §§2536-8 and 2555-60—both when the adverb and the conjunction are the same, e.g. *Or* 106. 20 *Ac þa þa Octauianus se casere to rice feng, þa wurdon Ianas dura betyneda, 7 wearð sibb 7 friþ ofer ealne middangeard* and *ÆCHom* i. 10. 28 *Ðaða hi ealle hæfdon þysne ræd betwux him gefæstnod, þa becom Godes grama ofer hi ealle*, or different, e.g. *Or* 160. 1 *Æfter þæm þe Tarentine geacsedan þæt Pirrus dead wæs, þa sendon hie on Affrice to Cartaginenses æfter fultume, BlHom* 133. 12, and *ÆCHom* i. 90. 13 *Æfter þan ðe wæron gefyllede ehta dagas Drihtnes acennednysse þæt he ymbsniden wære, þa wæs his nama geciged Iesus. . . .* The reader will easily find more examples. But the reverse pattern occurs (it seems to me) more often than 'rarely'. Examples include (with the adverb and the conjunction the same) *CP* 5. 5 *Geðenc hwelc witu us ða becomon for ðisse worulde, ða ða we hit nohwæðer ne selfe ne lufodon, Bo* 8. 9 *Me ablendan þas ungetreowan woruldsælþa . . . 7 me þa bereafodon ælcere lustbærnesse þa ða ic him æfre betst truwode, Or* 62. 33 *. . . hwelc mildsung siþþan wæs, siþþan se cristendom wæs, CP* 141. 9 *7 ðeah ðæt he hie forceorfe ær, ær hie on ða eagan feallen, CP* 325. 17 *Forðy mon scel ær geðencean, ær he hwæt selle, CP* 385. 17, *ÆCHom* i. 24. 21 *Ða æt nextan, þa se tima com þe God foresceawode, þa asende he his engel Gabrihel to anum mædene of þam cynne, seo wæs Maria gehaten*, and *ÆCHom* i. 30. 10 *Ða gelamp hit, þaða hi on þære byrig Bethleem wicodon, þæt hire tima wæs gefylled þæt heo cennan sceolde*, and (with the adverb and the conjunction different) *Bo* 13. 22, *Bede* 46. 19 *7 hi wæron sona deade, swa hi eorðan gesohtan, BlHom* 79. 1, *ÆLS* 26. 210 *and hit*

---

[129] On his use of this statement and others to establish a theory explaining the origin of the OE conjunctions, see Mitchell, at press (c).

sona aras swa hit hrepode þa stowe, Exod 16. 1 *þa ferdon hi ðanon on ðam fiftigoðan dæge þæs æftran monðes ðæs ðe hi ut ferdon of Egypta lande*, and perhaps *ChronE* 47. 7 (745) *Her Daniel forðferde. þa wæs xlvi wintra agan syððan he onfeng biscopdome*, where *þa* may be a conjunction. But a large number of these exceptions would disappear if Carkeet's observation were qualified by limiting it to sentences in which the correlative adverb is the same as the conjunction and has initial position in the principal clause.

§2800. The following will serve as examples of temporal clauses which occur within the principal clause: *CP* 385. 19 *Hit is awriten on ðæm godspelle ðætte ure Hælend, ða he wæs twelfwintre, wurde beæftan his meder 7 his mægum innan ðære ceastre Hierusalem, LS* 35. 118 *He þa se ealda, sona swa he þæt gehyrde, blissode and god herode,*

Beo 2977   Let se hearda   Higelaces þegn
                      bradne mece,   þa his broðor læg,
                      ealdsweord eotonisc   entiscne helm
                      brecan ofer bordweal,

and (with part of the principal clause repeated after the temporal clause) *Bede* 282. 9 *þes halga wer, ær þon þe he biscop geworden wære, tu æðele mynster he getimbrede . . .* and *ÆCHom* i. 484. 11 *Witodlice Herodes, ðaðe he nolde, þurh Iohannes mynegunge, þone unclænan sinscipe awendan, ða wearð he to manslihte befeallen.* We find a principal clause between two temporal clauses—in imitation of the Latin—in *Matt(WSCp)* 5. 18 *ærþam gewite heofon 7 eorðe an i oððe an prica ne gewit fram þære æ ærþam ealle þing gewurðan.*

13. CO-ORDINATION

§2801. *Mutatis mutandis*, the remarks made about clauses of place in §2529 apply here. To save space, I propose not to quote examples.

G. CLAUSES OF PURPOSE AND RESULT

1. INTRODUCTORY REMARKS

a. Reasons for treating clauses of purpose and result together

§2802. There are good grounds for treating clauses of purpose and result together. First, as GL (§543) tells us,

Sentences of Design are commonly called Final Sentences. Sentences of Tendency are commonly called Consecutive Sentences. Both contemplate the end —the one, as an aim; the other, as a consequence. . . . It is to be remarked that the difference between Final and Consecutive often consists only in the point of view. What is final from the point of view of the doer is consecutive from the point of view of the spectator.

See further Callaway 1933, pp. 1–4.

§2803. Second, OE scholars make the basic distinction between them by the mechanical and circular test of mood, on the assumption that the subjunctive implies that the aim has not been attained and therefore the clause is one of purpose whereas the indicative implies that the aim has been attained and therefore the clause is one of result. Allowance is, of course, made for examples like *ÆCHom* ii. 432. 2 *La hwæt fremað ðære burhware þeah ðe þæt port beo trumlice on ælce healfe getimbrod, gif ðær bið an hwem open forlæten, þæt se onwinnenda here þurh ðam infær hæbbe?* and

GuthB 865   Nænig monna wæs
of þam sigetudre   siþþan æfre
godes willan þæs georn,   ne gynnwised,
þæt he bibugan mæge   þone bitran drync
þone Eue fyrn   Adame geaf,

where, as Onions (p. 56) puts it, the result is 'merely *contemplated* or *in prospect*, and not . . . a fact', and like

PsFr 50. 12   Ne awyrp þu me,   wuldres ealdor,
fram ðinre ansyne   æfre to feore,
ne huru on weg aber   þone halgan gast,
þæt he me færinga   fremde wyrðe,

where the context and the absence of a negative in the *þæt* clause certify that the subj. *wyrðe* expresses a contingency, a contemplated (and feared) result, and not a purpose. This classification by mood, impossible in Latin, where all these clauses take the subjunctive, is probably justified by a comparison with MnE and by the fact that, apart from the odd exceptions discussed in §2984, *þy læs (þe)*, which introduces clauses of purpose only, takes only the subjunctive. But (as I have shown in *Neophil.* 49 (1965), 51–5) it has led some writers to adopt indefensible positions; on this, see further Standop, pp. 30–41. Moreover, it often fails because many OE verb forms are ambiguous for mood; consider *ÆCHom* i. 394. 10 *Soðlice ða hæðenan uðwitan fela ðinga forleton, swa swa dyde Socrates, seðe ealle his æhta behwyrfde wið anum gyldenum wecge, and syððan awearp ðone wecg on widre sæ, þæt seo gitsung ðæra æhta his willan ne hremde, and abrude fram ðære woruldlican lare ðe he lufode*, where *hremde* could be taken as indicative expressing result if *abrude* were not unambiguously subjunctive, and the examples discussed by Benham (pp. 209-10) and by Callaway (1933, p. 16).[130] It sometimes fails even when the mood is unambiguously subjunctive. Behre (p. 100) demonstrates this when he quotes

And 1212   Cyð þe sylfne,
            herd hige þinne,   heortan staðola,
            þæt hie min on ðe   mægen oncnawan

to illustrate his remark that 'in clauses of purpose (final clauses) the subjunctive is used to express a volitional attitude towards a verbal activity conceived of as the intended result of a preceding action'. Even if we take *findest* as an unambiguous indicative in a consecutive clause after the imperatives in

Husb 26   Ongin mere secan,   mæwes eþel,
            onsite sænacan,   þæt þu suð heonan
            ofer merelade   monnan findest,
            þær se þeoden is   þin on wenum,

it is only an isolated example (see §2992) and does not certify that, because we do not have *oncnawað* in *And* 1214, we cannot say that the *þæt* clause might be consecutive. See further §§2991-2.

§2804. So we come to our third reason for taking OE clauses of purpose and result together, viz. that—with the major exception of *þy læs (þe)*—they are introduced by the same conjunctions. This means that there are many occasions on which we have no way of deciding whether a clause is one of purpose or result: the conjunction fits either, both may have a verb negated by *ne*,[131] the form of the verb is not necessarily decisive even if it is unambiguous, we cannot reconstruct the intonation patterns, and the context permits either interpretation. A few typical examples from the poetry follow, to supplement those quoted in §1928 and those already discussed in §2803: (with ambiguous verb forms) *Beo* 3051, *GenA* 1841, *GuthA* 412,

PPs 118. 112   Ahylde ic mine heortan   holde mode,
            þæt ic þin soðfæst weorc   symble worhte,

[130] Noteworthy lack of concern for the existence of ambiguous verb-forms is shown by Shearin (1903, pp. 99-123, and 1909, pp. 247-50); Benham (pp. 232-7); and Mann (pp. 40-9). See further §§601-1a and Mitchell 1979*b*, pp. 537-8.

[131] When using Latin originals, the modern scholar must remember that in ecclesiastical Latin *ut non* may occur in both final and consecutive clauses; see Nunn, pp. 79 and 81. Benham (p. 210) overlooked this in his rather bizarre comments on *Matt(WSCp)* 7. 1, which provide a good illustration of the problem of classification I am discussing.

Latin *Inclinavi cor meum ad faciendas justificationes tuas in æter-num* . . . , where *worhte* could be translated 'have done' or 'might do', and

Jud 46   þær wæs eallgylden
              fleohnet fæger   ymbe þæs folctogan
              bed ahongen,   þæt se bealofulla
              mihte wlitan þurh . . . ;

(with an indicative form of *magan*)

And 859   We ðe, Andreas,   eaðe gecyðað
              sið userne,   þæt ðu sylfa miht
              ongitan gleawlice   gastgehygdum,

which should be compared with

PPs 68. 23   Syn hiora eagan   eac adimmad,
              þæt hi geseon ne magon   syþþan awiht,

where *magon* + infinitive represents the simple subjunctive of the Latin *Obscurentur oculi eorum, ne videant*; and (in dependent speech)

El 426   Nu is þearf mycel
              þæt we fæstlice   ferhð staðelien,
              þæt we ðæs morðres   meldan ne weorðen
              hwær þæt halige trio   beheled wurde
              æfter wigþræce . . . ,

where, if the second *þæt* clause is not taken as a second noun clause, it may be either purpose or result. These problems, however, are often more terminological than real. They also involve personal and varying reactions. On the whole question see (*inter alios*) Hotz, pp. 33-7; Schücking, p. 26; Vogt, *passim*; Glunz, pp. 31-7; Callaway 1933, pp. 1-5; Mann, pp. 1-5; and Behre, pp. 100-10. So, by taking clauses of purpose and result together, I hope to avoid repetition and to follow Ælfric (*ÆLS Pref* 26) in writing more briefly *ne fastidiosis ingeratur tedium . . . ; et non semper breuitas sermonem deturpat sed multotiens honestiorem reddit*. Those seeking more examples than I can give will find them in Shearin 1903 and 1909 (for purpose), and in Benham, Ericson 1932, pp. 65-73, and Callaway 1933 (for result). Mann's work is very often derivative. The studies by Shearin and by Benham cannot be trusted. Their figures must be viewed with suspicion because of the difficulties of classification discussed above, because neither takes cognizance of ambiguous verb-forms, and because they are not always accurate on their own terms. As Liggins (1970, pp. 306-8) remarks—in the course of a discussion about the varying preferences shown by the different 'Alfredian' texts in the use of final and consecutive conjunctions—Shearin's 'figures are far from accurate, with errors of both omission and inclusion' and Benham's work 'is notably unreliable'. I have made some silent corrections, have sometimes amended their figures, and have endeavoured to reveal the grosser errors. But I have not been able to spare the time for the complete reworking of OE final and consecutive clauses which is so obviously necessary and will be possible with the aid of full collections. So I have occasionally used the suspect figures provided by Shearin and Benham where the picture they give seems to me a reasonable—or not too distorted—representation of OE usage.

b. Other clauses involving elements of purpose and result

§2805. Other problems of classification and interpretation arise. Most authorities agree in taking as noun, rather than purpose and/or result, clauses which are the object of a verb, e.g. *Or 44. 17 7 þa hie hamweard wendon be westan þære ie Eufrate, ealle Asiam hie genieddon þæt hie him gafol guldon* and *Or 52. 3 He angan sierwan mid þæm folce þe he ofer wæs hu he hiene beswican mehte* (see Shearin 1903, pp. 55-6 and 87-9; Shearin 1909, pp. 244-5; and Benham, pp. 203-4);[132] examples like *Bo 101. 22 Hit gelamp gio ðætte an hearpere wæs on ðære ðiode ðe Ðracia hatte, sio wæs on Creca rice*, where (as Benham, p. 203, has it) 'the clause beginning with *ðætte is* the event, not a consequence of the event'; and clauses which are dependent on an adjective, e.g. *Solil 4. 13 . . . þæt ic si wurðe þæt ðu me for ðinre mildheortnesse alyse and gefreolsige* (see Benham, p. 204). See further §1929.

§2806. I have already discussed in §§2139-43 examples like

PPs 101. 20   Cumað folc syððan   feorran togædere
                    and ricu eac,   þæt hraðe drihtne
                    ful holdlice   hyran syþþan,

where the Roman Psalter has *ut* but Shearin (1909, p. 244) rather woollily detects 'a sort of compromise between the purely adverbial final clause of Old English and the relative adjective-clause of purpose in the Latin originals', and *BlHom 65. 3 7 se Alysend þysses menniscan cynnes hine sylfne geeaþmedde þæt of hehþe þæs fæderlican þrymmes to eorþan astag*, in which some take *þæt* as a conjunc-

---

[132] This view is supported by Harlow's observations (*RES* 10 (1959), 6 and 8) that in his Ælfric manuscripts 'there is generally no punctuation before an objectival noun clause', whereas '*þæt* expressing consequence or purpose is normally punctuated . . . and thus stands in strong contrast . . . with *þæt* introducing a noun clause'. This provides another instance of the loss inflicted by modern editorial suppression of the manuscript punctuation; see further Mitchell 1980a, pp. 386-7.

tion introducing a consecutive clause with unexpressed subject, while others see it as a relative pronoun with faulty concord; see §§ 2139-43. But there are clauses which, though they must be formally classified as adjective, contain an element of purpose. Shearin (1903, p. 81) tells us that

> the relative clause of purpose, then, is limited in the Germanic field and seems to be due to Latin influence. Even in Old English, the branch of early Germanic that allows it perhaps most frequently, it is felt as unidiomatic. This is shown by the great number of Latin relative clauses of purpose which find expression in the Old English translation, not by the Old English relative clause, but by the native purely adverbial clause.

Bede 62. 30 . . . *7 sona sende ærendwrecan to Rome, þæt wæs Laurentius mæssepreost 7 Petrus munuc, þæt heo scoldan secgan 7 cyþan þam eadigan biscope Scē Gregorii, þætte Ongelþeod hæfde onfongen Cristes geleafan 7 þætte he to biscope gehalgad wære*, Latin *reuersusque Brittaniam misit continuo Romam Laurentium presbyterum et Petrum monachum, qui beato pontifici Gregorio gentem Anglorum fidem Christi suscepisse ac se episcopum factum esse referrent*, will serve as an example of the latter phenomenon.[133] He then goes on (1903, pp. 82-5) to list forty-seven prose examples of OE adjective clauses with relative pronouns other than *þæt* which contain the idea of purpose. Not all need be so taken, e.g. *ÆCHom* i. 44. 28 *þa setton hi lease gewitan, ðe hine forlugon and cwædon þæt he tallice word spræce* . . . , where the ambiguous verb-forms permit the *ðe* clause to be taken as expressing result or purpose; *ÆCHom* ii. 76. 5 *Witodlice næs nan heahfæder, ne nan witega asend to hæðenum folce, þe heora gedwyld beloge, ær Drihtnes tocyme þurh his menniscnysse*, where the *þe* clause is equivalent to a consecutive clause expressing a tendency rather than to a final clause (see § 2992); and the five examples with the indicative mood (see § 2985). Less dubious examples include *Bede* 72. 15 *Ac þe sculon of Gallia rice biscopas cuman, þa þe æt biscopes halgunge in witscipe stonde*, Latin *Nam quando de Gallis episcopi ueniunt, qui in ordinatione episcopi testes adsistant?*[134] and *Bede* 120. 24 *Ond æfter þon þe heo ær funden hæfdon, wæs gehalgod to biscope Gode se leofa wer Scs Paulinus, se mid heo feran scolde* . . . , Latin . . . *et iuxta quod dispositum fuerat,*

---

[133] Here, where the Latin and the OE differ, Shearin can reasonably claim independence of Latin influence. Elsewhere (1903, pp. 85-6) he puts *Num* 11. 13 and *John(WSCp)* 14. 16 —in both of which the Latin has *ut* and the OE *þæt*—among examples of 'Đæt as an Apparent Relative Pronoun Introducing a Purpose Clause . . . apparently independent of Latin influence'. I cannot see the logic of this.

[134] At first glance, this may seem to be another example of interrogative *ac* in *Bede*; see Mitchell, *NM* 78 (1977), 98-100. But the translator has greatly abbreviated the Latin here. So, while the OE adjective clause translates the Latin adjective clause, the OE sentence is in my opinion a statement, not a question. Here I agree with Miller.

ordinatur episcopus uir Deo dilectus Paulinus, qui cum illa ueniret,
in both of which the Latin and the OE have an adjective clause with
a nominative relative; *Bede* 158. 9 *bæd he þæt heo him biscop on-*
sende, þæs lare 7 þegnunge Ongolþeode, þe rehte, þæs Drihtenlecan
geleafan gife leornade, Latin . . . *petens ut sibi mitteretur antistes*
cuius doctrina ac ministerio gens quam regebat Anglorum dominicae
fidei et dona disceret, where the relevant relative pronouns are genitive; and *Bede* 194. 26 *þær . . . wæs mynster getimbred in þæm for*
æghwæðres cyninges sawle alesnesse . . . dæghwamlice Drihtne bene
7 gebedo borene beon scoldon, Latin *ubi . . . monasterium construc-*
tum est in quo pro utriusque regis . . . animae redemtione cotidie
Domino preces offerri deberent. Examples with no (obvious) Latin
source include *Lch* ii. 210. 1 *siþþan óslege* [*sic*] *þe þa wunde clæn-*
sien and *ÆCHom* ii. 122. 8 . . . *and hine bæd þæt he Angelcynne*
sume lareowas asende ðe hi to Criste gebigdon.

§2807. Benham includes the relative pronoun in his list of connectives which introduce result clauses in the prose (p. 206) and gives
examples (pp. 211–13). They include *Bede* 86. 11–18, where only
the second adjective clause is represented in the Latin (100. 3), *Bede*
14. 32 . . . *7 eac him gehalgodne ele sealde, mid þam hi þone storm*
gestildon, Latin . . . *et oleum sanctum quo hanc sedarent dederit*,
and *ÆCHom* ii. 40. 8 *Iohannes cwæð be Criste þæt he wære Godes*
Lamb seðe ætbrude middaneardes synna. Personally, I find some of
Benham's examples strained. But the point cannot be pursued here.

§2808. I turn now to the poetry. Behre (p. 190) tells us that he has
'not found any instance of the subjunctive used to express purpose in
a relative clause, the main clause of which does not contain an expression of volition'; at p. 183 he cites as an example the second
adjective clause in

El 313   Gangaþ nu snude,   snyttro geþencaþ,
               weras wisfæste,   wordes cræftige,
               þa ðe eowre æ   æðelum cræftige
               on ferhðsefan   fyrmest hæbben,
               þa me soðlice   secgan cunnon,
               ondsware cyðan   for eowic forð
               tacna gehwylces   þe ic him to sece.

None of the examples of 'The Relative Adjective-Clause of Purpose'
in Shearin's collection (1909, p. 244) contradicts this claim. *El* 372
and *El* 406 belong with *El* 313. On *PPs* 101. 20 see §2806. The *þæt*
clause in

PPs 142. 9   Do me wegas wise   þæt ic wite gearwe
                on hwylcne ic gange   gleawe mode

is a straightforward clause of purpose; the translator has expanded the Latin *notam mihi fac uiam in qua ambulem*. That in *Jul* 30 can be taken as a noun clause on *hogde*, while the *þa* clause in

Dan 25   Oft he þam leodum   to lare sende,
             heofonrices weard,   halige gastas,
             þa þam werude   wisdom budon

could be a simple adjective clause with *budon* indicative. Two other examples not cited by Shearin—

Dan 315   þu him þæt gehete   þurh hleoðorcwyde,
             þæt þu hyra frumcyn   in fyrndagum
             ican wolde,   þætte æfter him
             on cneorissum   cenned wurde . . .

and the parallel passage in

Az 32   þu him gehete   þurh hleoþorcwidas
           þæt þu hyra fromcynn   on fyrndagum
           ycan wolde,   þæt hit æfter him
           on cyneryce   cenned wurde,
           yced on eorþan . . .—

illustrate the absurdity of pressing formal classification too far. In both, the subjunctive *wurde* refers to the future-in-the-past and is subjunctive because of this and of the general context. The *þæt(te)* clause in which it stands could therefore be classified as an adjective clause on *frumcyn*, a noun clause on *gehete* parallel to the preceding one, a final clause (God's purpose), or a consecutive clause (an undoubted happening in the future).

§2809. A consecutive element is present in some adjective clauses in the poetry, e.g.

Az 158   Forþon us onsende   sigora waldend
            engel to are,   se þe us bearg
            fyr ond feondas,   ond mid fiþrum bewreah
            wið brynebrogan,

as it was in the prose; see §2807. It was of the prose examples that Benham (p. 211) wrote: 'these relative clauses are naturally adjective clauses'. This is equally true of *Az* 158 and of all the examples of adjective clauses of purpose discussed above.

§2810. An element of result is frequently detected in temporal clauses with the indicative introduced by *oð (þæt)*; see §2745 and Benham, pp. 213–14, 217–18, and 224.[135] Similarly, there is an

[135] Benham is inconsistent in his treatment of *oð (þæt)* clauses. A study of prose texts other than *Orosius* does not support his contention (pp. 213–14) that '*oð* is used to introduce

element of purpose in *oð (þæt)* clauses with the subjunctive; see §2748, Shearin 1909, p. 243, and Hotz, pp. 37-9. Glogauer (p. 29) tentatively equates *siððan* with final *þæt* in

GenA 2379   he him þæs worhte to,
   siððan he on fære furðum meahte
   his waldendes   willan fremman.

§2811. Consecutive elements may be detected in comparative clauses such as *CP* 351. 6 . . . *forðæm swa him ðios stillnes 7 ðios ieðnes ma licað, sua him læs licað ðæt ðæt hie to gelaðode sindon*, *GD* 121. 11 *ac swa myccle ma he aræfnede æfter þon hefigran gewin, swa myccle swa he ma gemette 7 onfand þone lareow selfne þæs bealwes openlice feohtendne ongæn hine*, and *CP* 207. 4 *Ðone scamleasan mon mæg ðy bet gebetan ðe hine mon suiður ðreað 7 sciend*; see Benham, pp. 204-5 and 222-4; Callaway 1933, pp. 15-16; Quirk, p. 110; Čerepanov;[136] and Visser, ii, §891. Indeed, Benham (p. 204) says of result clauses that 'there is no doubt that they begin in relative clauses of comparison'. I often wish that I could offer such certainty to the reader.

§2812. The idea of purpose may sometimes be detected in causal clauses (see §3089); in concessive clauses, e.g.

JDay i 109   Næfre mon þæs hlude horn aþyteð
      ne byman ablaweþ, þæt ne sy seo beorhte stefn
      ofer ealne middangeard monnum hludre,
      waldendes word

(see Quirk, pp. 94-8); and in *gif* clauses, e.g. *Bede* 58. 20 *Warnode he him þy læs hie on hwylc hus to him ineodan; breac ealdre healsunge, gif hie hwylcne drycræft hæfdon þæt hi hine oferswiðan 7 beswican sceolden* and *LS* 23. 732 *and he geornlice mid his eagena scearpnyssum hawigende ge on þa swiðran healfe ge on þa wynstran swa swa se gleawesta hunta gif he þær mihte þæs sweteste wildeor gegripan*, where (despite Shearin 1903, p. 90) we probably have a dependent question rather than a conditional clause; cf. *Ps(P)* 13. 3 *Drihten . . .*

result clauses in *Or* only'; it would seem that he read the *oð* clauses in *Or* through result-coloured spectacles. Why, for example, take *Or* 66. 21 as consecutive but not *ChronA* 48. 10 (755)? Even within *Or* itself he is not consistent; *Or* 44. 20 has as good a claim to be consecutive as *Or* 66. 21. Moreover, he recorded eight examples in *CP* and two in *Chron* (p. 214).

[136] A. M. Čerepanov, 'Sojuzy pridatočnogo predloženija sledstvija v drevneanglijskom jazyke', *Učenye zapiski Leningradskogo gosudarstvennogo pedagogičeskogo Instituta A. I. Gercena*, 272, Leningrad (1965), 188-92. The author includes *swa efne* and *swilc . . . swilce* among conjunctions which introduce consecutive clauses. He is acquainted with Benham, cites a few examples from *CP, Bede, Chron*, and *ÆLS*, but has nothing new to say.

hawað hwæðer he geseo ænigne þæra þe hine sece and see further
Mather, pp. 58–9.

c. *The conjunctions*

§2813. Benham (pp. 205–6) distinguishes simple consecutive conjunctions (e.g. *þæt*) from grouped (e.g. *swa þæt* and *to þon þæt*) and
divided (e.g. *swa . . . þæt* and *to þon . . . þæt*) and treats the three
groups separately. A similar division could be made of final conjunctions. The terms are useful. But the interests of brevity seem better
served by taking simple conjunctions alone, dividing the remainder
according to the elements which make them up, and then subdividing
them into grouped and divided. Before doing so, however, it will be
useful to recall the usage in MnE. In clauses of purpose we regularly
use the simple and the grouped connectives—'He came late, that/so
that/to the end that all men might wonder why'—but only exceptionally, if at all, the divided connectives; even if someone were to
say 'He came so/to that extent late, that all men might wonder why',
the elements would not combine to form divided final connectives
'so/to that extent . . . that', although they would in a sentence like
'To this end He came, that He might save Mankind'. In clauses of
result, the patterns 'so that' and 'so . . . that' are the norm. The
simple connective 'that' is not used at all—OE *þæt* clauses are frequently rendered by MnE infinitives; see §1929 and consider *John
(WSCp)* 1. 12 *Soðlice swa hwylce swa hyne underfengon. he sealde
him anweald þ hi wæron godes bearn þam ðe gelyfað on his naman*,
the paraphrase of it in *GD* 161. 22 *swa manige swa hine onfengcon,
he sealde þam mihte þæt hi wæron Godes bearn*, and the examples
discussed in §2922—and the prepositional formulae only for special
effect; one does not normally use the patterns 'He came late, to the
extent that all men wondered why' or 'He came to that extent late,
that all men wondered why'.

§2814. The most common final conjunction in both OE prose and
poetry is *þæt*. *þæt*, *swa þæt(te)*, and *swa . . . þæt(te)*, all occur frequently in consecutive clauses in the prose, but *þæt* predominates in
the poetry. The exact figures given by Shearin and Benham are suspect; see §2804. But they will serve as some sort of a pointer. Shearin
listed 2,463 final clauses with *þæt* out of 3,000 in the prose (1903,
p. 58) and 168 out of 259 in the poetry (1909, p. 242). Benham's
figures for consecutive clauses in the prose were *þæt(te)* 561 (p. 206),
swa þæt(te) 533 (p. 215), *swa . . . þæt* 595 (p. 221), and grouped
and divided prepositional formulae 202 (pp. 218 and 228). The

situation is different in consecutive clauses in the poetry; I found
þæt predominant and the prepositional formulae very rare (§ 2895).
Metrical convenience is no doubt at least partly responsible for the
popularity of *þæt* in both types of clause in the poetry. The Table
of Contents lists the other conjunctions which are used in OE final
and consecutive clauses.

§2815. Mann (pp. 5–17) sees the origin of subordinate final and
consecutive clauses in sentences like

Beo 2312   Ða se gæst ongan   gledum spiwan,
                    beorht hofu bærnan—   bryneleoma stod
                    eldum on andan,

where the second of the two sentences in asyndetic parataxis expresses the result of the first, and my repunctuated version of

GenA 2723   Wuna mid usic   and þe wic geceos
                    on þissum lande   þær þe leofost sie
                    eðelstowe,   þe ic agan sceal.
                    Wes us fæle freond.   We ðe feoh syllað,

where *Wes us fæle freond* expresses the purpose of *ic* and the condition required for the fulfilment of the result *We ðe feoh syllað*. What
Mann sees as the second stage comes when two clauses or sentences
are in syndetic parataxis, e.g.

And 729   Nu ic bebeode   beacen ætywan,
                    wundor geweorðan   on wera gemange,
                    ðæt þeos onlicnes   eorðan sece,
                    wlitig of wage,   ond word sprece,
                    secge soðcwidum,   (þy sceolon gelyfan
                    eorlas on cyððe),   hwæt min æðelo sien

and

Beo 587   . . . þeah ðu þinum broðrum   to banan wurde,
                    heafodmægum;   þæs þu in helle scealt
                    werhðo dreogan,   þeah þin wit duge,

where the pronouns *þy* and *þæs* respectively clarify the relationship
between two independent sentences. Then, he argues, *þy* and *þæs*
lost their expressiveness and were replaced by *þæt*—'. . . werden
allgemein durch das neutrale *þæt* desselben Pronomens ersetzt' (p. 13)
—which then became a conjunction. Not all will wish to accept the
general line of development from parataxis to hypotaxis; see, for
example, Hill in *Language*, 28 (1952), 534. But even those who do
will find it hard to accept—or even to understand—the details of
Mann's proposed development. He does not, of course, imply that

the first two stages disappear. Nor must we think of the three stages as necessarily being in a direct line of descent. But the comparative scarcity of *þy* and *þæs* as adverbs, which Mann himself notes (p. 12), and their even greater rarity as final or consecutive conjunctions, suggest that the part played by examples like *And* 734 and *Beo* 587 was less than he seems to imply. The development of *þæt* was in my opinion quite independent of *þy* and *þæs*; see §2828.

§2816. The views that Mann expresses on the origin of the divided formula *swa . . . þæt* (pp. 17–20) and *to* + demonstrative + . . . *þæt* (pp. 20–5) are perhaps somewhat surprising when compared with his general theory. On the whole, he seems to regard them as later developments from *þæt* final and consecutive conjunction, suggesting that in a period when a demand for clear and logical expression of ideas and closer union of sentences was making itself felt, the ambiguity of *þæt* as a clause-introducer led the speaker or writer to place a demonstrative element in the principal clause. When—in what he sees as the next stage—the elements of the divided formulae were subsequently placed together to make the group formulae, as in *ÆCHom* ii. 134. 23 *Æfter ðisum wearð þæs eadigan Cuðberhtes cneow mid heardum geswelle alefed, swa þæt he mid criccum his feðunge underwreðode*, the demonstrative element lost its force and *swa þæt* (and the other grouped formulae) became mere equivalents of *þæt*. This, argues Mann, is shown by the existence of the pattern *swa . . . swa þæt*, e.g. *ÆCHom* ii. 120. 3 *Swa fulfremedlice he drohtnode on anginne his gecyrrednysse swa þæt he mihte ða gyu beon geteald on fulfremedra halgena getele*. See further §§2842–3 and Benham, p. 214. Mann could with equal plausibility have argued—and indeed he sometimes seems to flirt with this view (pp. 18, 22–3, 24–5)—that the divided formulae arose quite naturally from a stage seen perhaps in examples like

GenB 655   Adam, frea min,   þis ofet is swa swete,
                  bliðe on breostum,   and þes boda sciene,
                  godes engel god,   ic on his gearwan geseo
                  þæt he is ærendsecg   uncres hearran,
                  hefoncyninges

and

El 703   Is þes hæft to ðan strang,
        þreanyd þæs þearl   ond þes þroht to ðæs heard
        dogorrimum.   Ic adreogan ne mæg,
        ne leng helan   be ðam lifes treo . . . ;

a stage in which a demonstrative element in the first of two independent sentences pointed to the second and helped to make clear the relationship between the two. The development to *swa þæt* and the like might then have followed as Mann suggests. But to Ericson (1932, p. 65) 'the earliest form is in *swa*-alone. . . . In the later literature *þæt* or some other element was added to the *swa*.' This suggests the possibility that *swa þæt* and *swa . . . þæt* arose independently, the former from examples like

Finn 41   Hig fuhton fif dagas   swa hyra nan ne feol
                 drihtgesiða,   ac hig ða duru heoldon

(where a colon after *swa* might represent the original relationship) through an intermediate stage possibly represented by

PPs 107. 10   Hwæt, þu eart se sylfa god,   þe us synnige iu
                 adrife fram dome;   ne do þu æfre swa,
                 þæt þu of urum mægene   mod acyrre,

and the latter from examples like *GenB* 655, above. The rarity of *swa þæt* in the poetry, and the absence of *to þon (. . .) þæt* therefrom, could be used as arguments in this discussion, but they are probably irrelevant. Even if we accept that the language of some poetry represents an earlier stage than that of the prose (see Mann, pp. 6–8), it is not a sure guide to the usage of early colloquial speech or of early written prose. Space does not permit further examination of Mann's theories (to which he gives briefer expression in *Archiv*, 180 (1942), 89–91), although it may be said that he glosses over the differences between final and consecutive clauses rather too easily and seems at times to present the process as somewhat more conscious than it is likely to have been. I can find no satisfaction in Johnsen's theory (*Ang.* 38 (1914), 99–100) that *swa þæt*, like almost everything else, is a combination of two local-demonstrative adverbs.

d. Whose purpose?

§2817. Attempts to answer this question will sometimes resolve difficulties of classification. Thus, we can decide that the second *þæt* clause in

Jul 307   Swylce ic Egias   eac gelærde
                 þæt he unsnytrum   Andreas het
                 ahon haligne   on heanne beam,
                 þæt he of galgan his   gæst onsende
                 in wuldres wlite

is one of result, for it can scarcely have been the intention of either the devil or Egias to send Andreas into glory everlasting. Sometimes it may reveal difficulties. Thus, it is perhaps dangerous to conclude that, because a corslet is not conscious, the *þæt* clause in

Beo 1443   scolde herebyrne   hondum gebroden,
                   sid ond searofah   sund cunnian,
                   seo ðe bancofan   beorgan cuþe,
                   þæt him hildegrap   hreþre ne mihte,
                   eorres inwitfeng   aldre gesceþðan

is unambiguously consecutive, for we may here be dealing with the purpose of its maker or wearer or even that of the corslet itself—the armour and the sword Hrunting, which loses *dom* (*Beo* 1518-28), almost become thanes of Beowulf. On this, see Schücking, p. 26, and Standop, pp. 34-5. 'Whose purpose?' is a question raised by Shearin in his sections on mood (1903, pp. 99-123, and 1909, pp. 247-50) and by Standop in his discussion of **sculan* (pp. 104-8). I find the latter's observations—which are naturally limited to clauses containing a form of **sculan*—somewhat confusing. For example, his comment (p. 106) that in a sentence like *ÆCHom* i. 230. 7 *þas wundra sind awritene to ði þæt ge sceolon gelyfan þæt se Hælend is Godes Sunu, and ge sceolon habban þæt ece lif þurh ðone geleafan* 'Urheber des Zwanges ist ein Dritter, gewöhnlich das logische Subj. des übergeordneten Satzes' ['the author/source of the compulsion is a third, commonly the logical subject of the principal clause'] will not do. There are (or may be) involved first, the subject of the purpose clause (*ge*); second, the wonders (which I include for the sake of completeness); third, the scribe; fourth, Ælfric; and fifth, the inspirer of Ælfric—Æþelweard (*ÆCHom* i. 8. 18) and/or Almighty God (*ÆCHom* i. 2. 17). None the less I acknowledge a debt to Standop. Shearin's comments are more widely based and therefore more helpful. But I prefer to make my own path.

§2818. Space does not permit a highway. But some relevant considerations follow. When the governing clause contains an active verb-form other than a volitional expression, the subject of which is the same as that of the purpose clause, the purpose is one intended by that subject when the verb of the purpose clause is a simple verb, e.g. *BlHom* 73. 9 *Martha onfeng Crist on hire hus þæt heo him þegnode*; a form of *magan*, e.g. *ÆCHom* i. 580. 30 *þa forarn he ðam Hælende and stah uppon an treow þæt he hine geseon mihte*; or a form of *willan*, e.g. *ÆCHom* i. 94. 17 *He cwæð þæt he ne come to ðy þæt he wolde þa ealdan æ towurpan ac gefyllan*. The extent to which some higher authority is involved in examples such as these is arguable. But God or Christ does seem to be behind the subject of the purpose clause when it is the logical subject of an impersonal verb in the governing clause in *BlHom* 63. 32 *forþon us syndon nu to bebeorhgenne þa myccllan synna, þæt we þe eþelicor þa medmycclan gebetan magon, Bede* 270. 2 (where the purpose clause is in dependent speech), and the like.

§2819. When the governing clause contains a non-dependent command or wish uttered by the subject of the purpose clause, the purpose is one intended by that subject, although it can also be seen as the purpose of the person commanded or asked, e.g. *Solil* 11. 10 *Ac gehæl mine eahgan and untyn, þæt ic mage geseon þine wundru . . . and sile me wisdom, þæt ic mage þe ongytan and getæc me þider ic me beseon sceolde to þe, það ic þe þær gehawian mæge.* But when the governing clause contains a non-dependent command or wish directed to the subject of the purpose clause, the purpose is that of the speaker, although it may also be seen as that of someone else, for example of Augustinus and of God himself in *Solil* 4. 5 *Wilna ðe to gode hælend modes and lichaman, þæt ðu mage þurh ða hele begitan þæt ðæt þu wilnast and þonne þu ðe gebeden hæbbe, awrit þonne þæt gebed þi læs þu hit forgyte. . . .*

§2820. The purpose is primarily that of someone other than the subject of the purpose clause when the verb of that clause is a form of **sculan*, e.g. *ÆCHom* i. 238. 29 *Ælc bisceop and ælc lareow is to hyrde gesett Godes folce þæt hi sceolon þæt folc wið ðone wulf gescyldan* and *ÆCHom* i. 34. 1 *Ealle ðeoda þa ferdon þæt ælc synderlice be him sylfum cennan sceolde, on ðære byrig þe he to hyrde.* When it is a form of **motan*, as in *ÆCHom* i. 178. 10 *Moyses se heretoga fæste eac feowertig daga and feowertig nihta, to ði þæt he moste underfon Godes æ; ac he ne fæste na þurh his agene mihte, ac þurh Godes*, much depends on whether we take that form to express ability or permission.

§2821. When both clauses have the same subject but the verb of the governing clause is passive, that subject is not normally the initiator of the action, whether the verb of the final clause is a simple verb, e.g. *Bede* 120. 24 *Ond æfter þon þe heo ær funden hæfdon, wæs gehalgod to biscope Gode se leofa wer Scs Paulinus, se mid heo feran scolde, to ðon þæt he þa fæmnan 7 hire geferan æghwæðer ge mid þa mærsunge heofonlicra geryna ge mid his dæghwamlicre lare trymede . . .* and *CP* 29. 9 *Sien hira eagan aðistrode ðæt hi ne geseon;* a form of **motan*, e.g. *ÆCHom* i. 84. 1 *Gesælige hi wurdon geborene þæt hi moston for his intingan deað þrowian;* or a form of **sculan*, e.g. *VSal 1 31 and ic wæs æfter asend þæt ic sceolde to þam casere cuman Tiberie.*

§2822. When the subjects are different and the verb of the governing clause is active, the purpose is not that of the subject of the
purpose clause. The subject of the governing clause may be the initiator of the action, e.g. (with a simple verb) *Or* 46. 11 *7 þæm mæden-
cildum hie fortendun þæt swiðre breost foran þæt hit weaxan ne
sceolde, þæt hie hæfden þy strengran scyte*, and (with a form of
*sculan) *Or* 80. 26 *He het þa þæt fæste lond utan ymbfaran, þæt
him mon sceolde an ma healfa on feohtan þonne on ane.* Sometimes,
however, the subject of the governing clause is only the last agent in
a chain of purpose, e.g. *BlHom* 111. 2 *ac we sceolan us geearnian þa
siblecan wæra Godes 7 manna, 7 þone rihtan geleafan fæste staðelian
on urum heortum þæt he ðær wunian mæge 7 mote, 7 þær growan
7 blowan* (where God may be seen as the ultimate initiator); *Ch*
1084 *7 ic bidde eow eallan þ ge beon Baldewine abbe on fultume þ
he mote beon ælc þæra gerihta wurðe* (where *ic* is King Edward); and
ÆLS 27. 202 *Ac he . . . ablende þone deman þurh godes mihte þæt
menn mihton tocnawon hu mildheort se hælend is* (where 'God
moves in a mysterious way, His wonders to perform'). A general
sense of obligation or propriety deriving from God or some other
authority can also be involved, e.g. *Bede* 2. 10 *Forþon hit is god
godne to herianne 7 yfelne to leanne þæt se geðeo se þe hit gehyre.*

§2823. When the subjects are different and the verb of the governing clause is passive, the purpose is not that of its subject, e.g. *Bede*
288. 3 *þære sweostor mægen þæt æfter þæs apostolis cwide in untrymnesse gefremed wære, wæs heo semninga gehrinen mid hefigre
untrymnesse lichoman . . .* and *ÆCHom* i. 230. 7 (§2817). *BlHom*
15. 9 *7 he [Crist] bið geseald hæþnum mannum þæt hie hine
bysmrian* is perhaps a special case.

§2824. There is more to be said here, but space and fear of en-
croaching on the realm of the lexicographer demand that I go no
further, except to say that, with Standop (p. 38), I find Behre's
observation (p. 109) too vague to be of value: 'The circumlocution
with *motan, magan*, or *cunnan* may be employed for the simple subjunctive to emphasize the optative element of the subjunctive in
clauses of purpose.' Those wishing to pursue this subject should consult Shearin 1903, pp. 101–15, and 1909, pp. 247–9, and Standop,
pp. 30–41 (*magan*), 82–4 (*motan), 104–8 (*sculan), and 141–3
(*willan*). Other problems concerning *magan* and *willan* are discussed
in §§2974–5a and 2976–80 respectively.

2. CLAUSES INTRODUCED BY *þÆT* AND *þÆTTE*

§2825. *þæt*—also spelt *þat* and *þet* and with initial *ð*—is the most common conjunction in final clauses in prose of all periods and in poetry. The only 'Alfredian' prose text in which this is not true seems to be Gregory's *Dialogues*, in which, according to Liggins (1970, p. 307), *to þon þæt* appears almost three times as often as *þæt*. Final *þæt* appears in both native and translated texts. In the *Paris Psalter*, for example, OE *þæt* clauses represent a Latin *ut* clause in *PPs* 59. 4, a Latin principal clause in *PPs* 82. 4, and the Latin infinitive used of purpose in *PPs* 95. 12. On OE *þæt* clauses of purpose representing a Latin relative clause see §2806; for *þæt . . . ne* translating Latin *ne* see *PPs* 68. 23 and §2963. Typical examples of OE final *þæt* clauses with the subjunctive include (with time-reference to the future) *Or* 60. 8 *þæt ic wille eac gescadwislecor gesecgean þæt hit mon geornor ongietan mæge*, *ÆCHom* i. 20. 34 *Ic gegaderige in to þe of deorcynne and of fugelcynne symble gemacan, þæt hi eft to fostre beon*, and

PPs 75. 6   ðonne to dome   drihten ariseð,
              þæt he on eorðan do   ealle hale
              þe he mildheorte   meteð and findeð,

and (with time-reference to the future-in-the-past) *Or* 4. 2 *⁊ hu Punice gesetton eft þone ealdan Hannibalan þæt he mid scipum wiþ Romane wunne*, *ÆCHom* i. 34. 28 *He wæs mid wacum cildclaðum bewæfed, þæt he us forgeafe ða undeadlican tunecan, þe we forluron on ðæs frumsceapenan mannes forgægednysse*, and

PPs 105. 19   forðon he him his yrre   of acyrde,
              þæt he hi ne towurpe   geond werþeoda.

§2826. *þæt* is also the most common consecutive conjunction in OE poetry, but—despite Andrew (*Postscript*, §31)—is used with almost the same frequency as *swa þæt(te)* and *swa . . . þæt* in the prose; see §2814 for Benham's figures. The slight decline in the frequency of consecutive *þæt* in the OE period detected by Benham (p. 209) is in accord with the complete disappearance in MnE of simple 'that' as a consecutive conjunction. Like final *þæt*, consecutive *þæt* occurs in both native and translated texts. In *Exodus*, for example, OE *þæt* clauses represent a Latin *ut* clause in *Exod* 9. 4, a Latin principal clause in *Exod* 8. 31, and a Latin *et* clause in *Exod* 9. 7. But, according to Benham, *þæt* is more frequent in simple plain historical or narrative prose than in prose which is homiletic or persuasive. Typical examples of OE consecutive *þæt* clauses with the indicative include (with the present tense) *Or* 76. 1 *ac heo for hiere cristendome nugiet is gescild, ðæt ægþer ge hio self ge hiere anweald is ma hreosende for ealddome þonne of æniges cyninges niede,* *ÆCHom* ii. 486. 29 *Nu sind ge ðurh deofl bepæhte, þæt ge gelyfað on ydelum anlicnyssum, and forlætað eowerne Scyppend,*

PPs 111. 7　　Byð his heorte gearo　　hyhte to drihtne
　　　　　　　　getrymed and getyhted,　　þæt him teonan ne mæg
　　　　　　　　fæcne ætfæstan　　feonda ænig,

and

PPs 68. 3　　þær ic werigmod　　wann and cleopode,
　　　　　　　　þæt me grame syndan　　goman hase

(where the sequence of tenses can cause no offence; see Benham, pp. 237–9, and §§859–64), and (with the preterite tense) *Or* 38. 7 *þæt syfeðe wæs þæt þær com hagol se wæs wið fyre gemenged, þæt he ægþer sloh ge ða menn ge ða nytenu,* *ÆCHom* ii. 156. 8 *þa sume dæge se niðfulla deofol . . . wearp ða ænne stan to ðære bellan, þæt heo eall tosprang,* and

PPs 117. 13　　Ic wæs hearde cnyssed　　and ic me helpe fand,
　　　　　　　　þæt ic fæste ne feoll　　ac ic me frofre begeat. . . .

The problems posed by ambiguous verb-forms are discussed in §§2803 and 2969–99, but can be illustrated by *Or* 38. 28 *7 beforan Moyse 7 hys folce he ðone Readan Sæ on twelf wegas adrigde, þæt hi drigan fotan þæne sæ oferferdon,* which Shearin (1903, p. 131) takes as final, but which could easily be taken as consecutive.

§2827. Schücking (§16) proposed a threefold division for the type of consecutive clauses exemplified in the preceding section, viz. *þæt* clauses which follow a principal clause containing an indicative (or ambiguous for indicative) verb-form. First, there were those which express a logical and actual (as opposed to hypothetical) result of the principal clause, e.g.

Beo 1900　　He þæm batwearde　　bunden golde
　　　　　　　　swurd gesealde,　　þæt he syðþan wæs
　　　　　　　　on meodubence　　maþme þy weorþra,
　　　　　　　　yrfelafe;

second, those which serve to explain the principal clause (see below); and third, those which follow a verb of motion. Within the third type, Andrew (*Postscript*, §31) distinguished those which follow a verb of motion, e.g. *Beo* 358 *eode ellenrof, þæt he for eaxlum gestod* (where *þæt* comes close to meaning 'until'; see §§2745-7), from those which follow a verb of assailing, e.g.

Beo 1539　　　　brægd þa beadwe heard,　　þa he gebolgen wæs,
　　　　　　　　feorhgeniðlan,　　þæt heo on flet gebeah,

and suggested the translation 'and' for *þæt* in both. The existence of Schücking's second group was also noted by Klaeber when he wrote that *þæt* is sometimes 'used to indicate vaguely some other kind of relation' (Klaeber, 3, glossary, s.v. *þæt* conj.; see also *MP* 3 (1905-6), 463-4). The two examples Schücking and Klaeber have in common are

Beo 2802　　　　Hatað heaðomære　　hlæw gewyrcean
　　　　　　　　beorhtne æfter bæle　　æt brimes nosan;
　　　　　　　　se scel to gemyndum　　minum leodum
　　　　　　　　heah hlifian　　on Hronesnæsse,
　　　　　　　　þæt hit sæliðend　　syððan hatan
　　　　　　　　Biowulfes biorh . . . ,

which can be taken as result or purpose, and

Beo 2697　　　　Ne hedde he þæs heafolan,　　ac sio hand gebarn
　　　　　　　　modiges mannes,　　þær he his mæges healp,
　　　　　　　　þæt he þone niðgæst　　nioðor hwene sloh . . . ,

where the *þæt* clause can be taken as consecutive or as loosely explaining *healp*: '. . . he helped his kinsman by striking the vengeful stranger a little lower down . . .'. Most of the other examples suggested by Schücking can be taken as noun and/or purpose and/or result clauses. The existence of these types is worth noting. But we need not press the distinction too far.

§2828. It was of examples like those in Schücking's third group that Johnsen (*Ang.* 38 (1914), 88) wrote: 'I am myself not in doubt that *þæt* employed as a conjunction of time must be explained as a further development of *þæt* when used as a local-demonstrative adverb'; see §2747. Even if we accept this as a possible factor in the development of *þæt* conj., it cannot explain all its uses. A more generally applicable theory is suggested by the difficulties of classification discussed in §§2802-4. If we accept that demonstrative *þæt* came into use as a conjunction first with verbs of speaking, thinking, and the like—'We all know that; he once lived here' > 'We all know that he once lived here'; see *OED*, s.v. *that* conj. I. 1—we can follow Mann (pp. 3-5, 13-17, and 53, and also *Archiv*, 180 (1942), 89-90) and see *þæt* spreading into final and consecutive sentences, perhaps through examples like

GenB 527 . . .   and me warnian het
    þæt ic on þone deaðes beam bedroren ne wurde,
    beswicen to swiðe . . .

and

Jul 293   Ða gen ic Herode
    in hyge bisweop þæt he Iohannes bibead
    heafde biheawan . . . ,

in both of which the *þæt* clause could be described as a noun clause, but has a strong element of purpose and result respectively. This theory seems incompatible with Benham's suggestion (p. 207) that 'ðætte is the parent form from which ðæt descended'—a suggestion not accepted by Shearin (1903, pp. 59-60) or, not surprisingly, by Mann (pp. 15-16).

§ 2829. But when *þæt* introduces a clause with a subjunctive—as opposed to indicative (§ 2827)—verb, that clause may express a contemplated or contingent result—as opposed to an actual or certain result—rather than a purpose. The most convincing of the twenty-one examples cited by Callaway (1933, pp. 18-20) include *CP* 387. 13 *7 ðylæs hie gedwelle sio gehydnes 7 ða getæsu ðe hie on ðæm wege habbað, ðæt hie forgieten hwider hie scylen, Luke(WSCp)* 23. 22 *ne mette ic nan þing yfeles on þissum men þ he si deaþes scyldig*, and *ÆCHom* i. 514. 18 *Se æswicað oðrum þe hine on Godes dæle beswicð, þæt his sawul forloren beo.* But I am not sure that I can entirely eliminate the idea of purpose from the last example or from others quoted by Callaway, including *CP* 333. 8, *LawAf* 75 *Gif mon ða greatan sinwe forslea, gif hie mon gelacnian mæge þæt hio hal sie, geselle xii scill to bote*, and *BenR* 75. 5 *. . . tæce him man oþer weorc þæt he ealles unnyt ne beo.* If we eliminate these and similar examples, along with the noun clauses and those in which Callaway himself admits the possibility of a final interpretation, few of the twenty-one remain. Since, as Callaway himself stresses (1933, p. 4 and *passim*), classification is an extremely personal business, the reader will have to study Callaway's examples for himself. But my own conclusion is this. Even without making the not unnatural assumption that Callaway chose to quote the most favourable examples, I cannot, on the basis of those he did quote, accept his startling claim (1933, p. 17) that 'in Consecutive Clauses introduced by Single Particles, the Subjunctive is much more frequent than the Indicative'. As he himself admits (1933, p. 27) there is a marked discrepancy between his figures and those given by Benham. On this question see further §§ 2989-90.

§2830. On examples like *BlHom* 59. 33 *Hwylc man is þæt mæge ariman ealle þa sar . . . ?* and *BlHom* 103. 19 . . . *7 hwæþre nis nænig man þæt asecggan mæge þa miltsa . . .* , see §§2139-43 and 2886.

§2831. *þætte* is not common in final or consecutive clauses in the prose. The following table of occurrences is based on the not completely trustworthy figures of Shearin (1903, pp. 59-61) and Benham (pp. 206-8; I silently correct his addition):

Type of Clause	Early prose	Gospels: *Li* and *Ru*	Late prose
Purpose	28	15	0
Result	15	4	0

Mann (pp. 16-17) adds a few more examples from the early prose. The absence of *þætte* in late prose here is reminiscent of its absence from noun clauses in Ælfric and Wulfstan; see §1956. Typical examples from the early prose are (final) *Or* 64. 10 *ac Romane mid hiora cristnan cyninge Gode þowiende wæron, þætte he him for þæm ægþres geuþe, ge hiora cyninges ge heora anwaldes* and *CP* 219. 6 *Đæt tacnað ðæt ðæt geðyld sceal gehealdan ðara gecorenra monna mod, ðætte hit ne astyrige se wind ðære ungeðylde*; (consecutive expressing an actual result) *Or* 188. 10 *7 sum his folc sende gind þæt lond to bærnanne 7 to hergenne, þætte se consul wæs wenende þæt eall þæt folc wære gind þæt lond tobræd* and *CP* 283. 1 *Forðæm, ðonne we forslawiað ðone gecopestan timan, ðætte we ðonne ne beoð onælde mid ðære lustbærnesse ures modes, ðonne bistilð sio slæwð on us*; and (consecutive expressing a contemplated result) *CP* 363. 18 . . . *ðætte hie ðurh ða menniscan sibbe mægen astigan to ðære godcundan sibbe . . . ðætte hie ðonne gemonnðwærige sio lufu 7 sio geferræden hiora niehstena 7 hie to beteran gebrenge. Mutatis mutandis*, the remarks about mood made in §2829 apply to *þætte* clauses as well as to *þæt* clauses.

§2832. Shearin (1909, p. 242) tells us that *þætte* 'is not found as a final connective in the poetry'. A possible example is

KtPs 130　　　Gedoo nu fræmsume　　frofre ðine
　　　　　　　　to ðinum godan　　gastes willan,
　　　　　　　　ðætte Sione dun　　sigefest weorðe,
　　　　　　　　and weallas Sion　　wynfeste getremed,
　　　　　　　　Hierusolime,　　god lifiende,

which represents the Latin *Benigne fac, Domine, in bona uoluntate tua Sion: ut aedificentur muri Hierusalem*. But this may be taken as a result expressed as a tendency; see §2829 and note that *Ps(I)* has 7, representing Latin *et* for *ut*. The *þætte* clause in *Met* 20. 70, where the verb is *dorste*, may similarly be taken as final or consecutive. So I have to modify Shearin's remark by reading 'an unambiguously' for 'a'. However, *þætte* does occasionally introduce a result clause in the poetry. Unambiguous examples include

Dan 158   Ða eode Daniel,   þa dæg lyhte,
              swefen reccan   sinum frean,
              sægde him wislice   wereda gesceafte,
              þætte sona ongeat   swiðmod cyning
              ord and ende   þæs þe him ywed wæs,

GuthB 985 (the first *þætte* clause; on the second see §§2139-43), and

Whale 54   cymeð wynsum stenc
              of his innoþe,   þætte oþre þurh þone,
              sæfisca cynn,   beswicen weorðaþ,
              swimmað sundhwate   þær se sweta stenc
              ut gewiteð.

§2833. According to Shearin (1903, p. 61), 'rhetorically considered, *ðætte* seems to be used to introduce a clause with more emphasis than does the simple *ðæt*'; he compares it in this respect with the formulae involving *to* (1903, p. 67) and *for* (1903, p. 72). Adams (p. 129) found no support for this claim in the temporal clauses he examined. Benham (pp. 207-8) found it 'absurd'—'. . . in the works where *ðætte* occurs 99 out of every 100 sentences are long and involved, and if *ðætte* is used in one place, why not in all? Again, are but 25 [*sic*; but see the Table in §2831] sentences out of 3,000 to be considered emphatic?' Benham (ibid.) also dismissed Shearin's assertion (1903, p. 62) that *ðætte* introduces 'A. A complex or involved purpose clause' or 'B. A purpose clause following a complex or involved main clause' with a question: 'But does not this classification cover about all the sentences in the work of Alfred and his circle?' One must side with the critics against Shearin. Liggins (1970, pp. 307-8) shows that other considerations may have influenced the choice of connective; they include the weight of the element (be it subject, object, or prepositional phrase) which immediately follows it.

3. CLAUSES INTRODUCED BY COMBINATIONS OF *SWA* AND/OR *SWILC* + *þÆT(TE)*

a. Introductory remarks

§2834. Here we find the grouped conjunction *swa þæt(te)*, the divided conjunction *swa . . . þæt(te)*, and (occasionally) *swilc (. . .)*

þæt(te), and (also occasionally) the combinations *swa . . . swa þæt(te)* and *swilc . . . swa þæt(te)*. Wülfing (ii. 155) does not list any of these among conjunctions which introduce a clause of purpose. Originally (I suppose) *þæt(te)* introduced a clause explanatory of the preceding *swa* or *swilc*; see further §2889.

b. Swa þæt(te)

§2835. *Swa þæt* is the only one of those combinations just mentioned which Shearin classifies as a final conjunction. 'Very rarely', he says (1903, p. 89), 'the result formula *swa ðæt . . .* introduce[s] a clause containing something of final intent.' He quotes four examples of '*swa ðæt*: purpose blending with result' from *ÆCHom* (1903, pp. 89-90)—and that was all; no more from the prose, none from the poetry. Mann (p. 19) reports this without comment. Although the use of *swa þæt* does not prove that the clause is consecutive, there can be no doubt that it rarely introduces a clause which is unambiguously final. But I would say that it did in those two of Shearin's four examples in which the principal clause has an ambiguous verb-form which is to be taken as indicative and the *swa þæt* clause has the subjunctive, viz. *ÆCHom* i. 596. 10 *Orsorh and blissigende ic cume to ðe, swa þæt ðu me blissigende underfo, ðæs leorningcniht ðe on ðe hangode*, where Andrew is addressing the Cross as he approaches it, and *ÆCHom* ii. 252. 21 *Ða het Pilatus ðone Hælend beswingan, and betæhte hine ða to heora benum, swa þæt he wælhreawlice wurde ahangen*, where Christ has not yet been crucified. The other two can, as Shearin says, be taken as purpose or contemplated result. They are (with *uton* in the principal clause) *ÆCHom* i. 604. 5 *Uton awurpan þeostra weorc, and beon ymbscrydde mid leohtes wæpnum, swa þæt we on dæge arwurðlice faron* and (with *gedafenað*) *ÆCHom* ii. 546. 8 *Ac us gedafenað þæt we mid wacelum eagum þas ðreo gemetu behealdon, swa þæt we nateshwon ne ceorion ongean Godes swinglum. . . .* As we see in §§2829 and 2991-2, it is impossible for a modern scholar to draw a firm line, for it depends on the point of view he adopts.

✕ §2836. I cannot, however, understand why Shearin listed only these four examples. Without venturing outside *ÆCHom* i, I find others. To be compared with *ÆCHom* i. 596. 10 and *ÆCHom* ii. 252. 21 (both in §2835) and (I think) taken as final is *ÆCHom* i. 360. 14 *Oðer forhæfednysse cynn is deorwurðre and healicre, ðeah seo oðer god sy: styran his modes styrunge mid singalre gemetfæstnysse, and campian dæghwamlice wið leahtras, and hine sylfne ðreagian mid styrnysse ðære gastlican steore, swa þæt he ða reðan deor eahta heafodleahtra swilce mid isenum midlum gewylde*. But I have to admit that Benham (p. 242) takes this as consecutive, along with *ÆCHom* i. 268. 1, in which I sometimes see purpose, sometimes contemplated result. So perhaps these two examples should be compared with *ÆCHom* i. 604. 5 (§ 2835) and *ÆCHom* ii. 546. 8 (§ 2835). So too should *ÆCHom* i. 602. 2 (identical except for spelling with *ÆCHom* i. 604. 5), *ÆCHom* i. 604. 29, and *ÆCHom* i. 604. 13 *Mid ðam wæpnum we sceolon beon ymbscrydde, swa þæt we on dæge arwurðlice faron*. Thus, I also cannot understand why Benham (p. 242) listed only the two examples already referred to out of the nine mentioned in this section.

§ 2837. I have divided Shearin's examples into two categories—first, those in which the *swa þæt* clause can be taken as final, and second, those with a volitional expression or a verb expressing obligation in the principal clause in which the *swa þæt* clause can be taken as purpose or contemplated result. There are two more categories which in my opinion he should have considered. The third (numbering consecutively) consists of *swa þæt* clauses such as those in *ÆC Hom* i. 540. 22 *hi wæron Godes gesprecan, and þam he æteowde his digelnysse, and hi onlihte mid gife þæs Halgan Gastes, swa þæt hi wiston þa towerdan ðing, and mid witigendlicere gyddunge bododon* and *ÆCHom* i. 542. 6 . . . *and hi mid rihtum geleafan and soðre lare geteah, and eallum ðeodum to lareowum gesette, swa þæt se sweg heora bodunge ferde geond ealle eorðan, and heora word becomon to gemærum ealles ymbhwyrftes*, in which an ambiguous preterite verb-form can be taken as either a subjunctive expressing an event in the past as a purpose or a contemplated result or as an indicative expressing it as a result; cf. *ÆCHom* ii. 492. 4 *Æfter ðison gelamp þæt ðæs cyninges mæg, Nicanor, wearð gescoten mid anre fla on ðam cneowe æt sumon gefeohte, swa þæt nan man hi ne mihte of ðam bane ateon*, where the context is decisive for result. The fourth category consists of *swa þæt* clauses which I would classify as explanatory, and not as final or consecutive; typical examples are *ÆCHom* i. 114. 27 . . . *ac geearnige swiðor Godes mildheortnysse, swa þæt he wende his agenne cyre to his Scyppendes gehyrsumnysse and bebodum* 'by turning . . .', *ÆCHom* i. 134. 14 . . . *þæt ælc wif ðe cild gebære sceolde gebidan feowertig daga æfter þære cenninge, swa þæt heo ne come into Godes temple* 'without coming . . .', and *ÆCHom* i. 258. 26 *Crist is Godes Sunu, swa þæt se Fæder hine gestrynde of him sylfum, butan ælcere meder* 'in that, seeing that . . .'.

§2838. These four categories are not peculiar to *ÆCHom* i. The first is exemplified in *ChronE* 30. 23 (656) *Ic Wulfere gife to dæi Scē Petre 7 þone abbode Saxulf . . . ealle þa landes þa þær abuton liggeð ða of mine kynerice sindon freolice swa ðet nan man na haue þær nan onsting buton seo abbot 7 se muneces*; the second in *Bo* 103. 14 *Ðas leasan spell lærað gehwylcne mon ðara ðe wilnað helle ðiostro to flionne 7 to ðæs soðan godes liohte to cumanne, þ he hine ne besio to his ealdan yflum, swa ðæt he hi eft swa fullice fullfremme swa he hi ær dyde*; the third in *ChronE* 53. 8 (777) *. . . 7 seo kyning freode þa þ mynstre Wocingas wið cining . . . 7 wið ealle men swa þ nan man ne hafde þær nan onsting buton S. Peter 7 þone að* (cf. *ChronE* 30. 23, above) and *ChronA* 84. 31 (894) *hæfde se cyning his fierd on tu tonumen, swa þæt hie wæron simle healfe æt ham, healfe ute*; and the fourth in *Solil* 63. 6 *and ðu wast æac genoh geare þæt he nane gesceafta ne forlet eallunga gewitan swa þæt hy to nawuihte weorðe* 'by becoming nothing' and *ChronE* 23. 17 (616) *Æfter him feng Eadbold to rice his sunu se forlet his fulluht 7 lifode on heðenum þeawe swa þ he heafde his feder lafe to wife* 'by having . . .'. Such examples could be multiplied in the prose. Space forbids. But final *swa þæt* is very rare in the prose and—in this Shearin and I agree—does not occur in the poetry.

§2839. I turn now to *swa þæt(te)* in consecutive clauses. Benham (p. 215) records 533 examples in the prose. Many of these express an actual or certain result. Typical of those with *swa þætte*—twelve examples, including four with *swæ*, in *Li* and *Ru* and seventeen elsewhere, nearly all in 'Alfredian' prose[137]—are *Or* 172. 2 *þæt gefremede Diulius hiora consul, þæt þæt angin wearð tidlice þurhtogen, swa þætte æfter siextegum daga þæs þe ðæt timber acorfen wæs, þær wæron XXX 7 C gearora ge mid mæste ge mid segle* and *BlHom* 145. 29 *7 þær wæs swiþe swete stenc swa þætte ealle þa slepan þe þær wæron*. The rest of the 533 examples display *swa þæt* in its various spellings. According to Benham's figures (pp. 215 and 241–3), it is most common in *Chron, GD*, Ælfric, and in the Homilies attributed by Napier to Wulfstan. The following will serve as examples expressing actual result: (with present indicative) *Bede* 28. 30 *Hibernia Scotta ealond . . . on smyltnysse lyfta is betere mycle þonne Breotone land swa þæt ðær seldon snau leng ligeð þonne ðry dagas*, *ÆCHom* i. 54. 2, and *ÆCHom* ii. 8. 6 *. . . ac seo Godcundnys is ymbscryd mid þære menniscnysse, swa þæt ðær nys naðor gemencgednys ne todal*, and

---

[137] In *Bede(T)* 120. 2, where MSS *B, O*, and *Ca*, have *swa þ, swa þætte* probably introduces a consecutive clause. Miller's insertion of *þæt* is based on Latin *ita ut quod*. But the translator probably misunderstood. Schipper's texts (p. 142) make sense.

(with preterite indicative) *Bede* 378. 19 *Ða he ða eft ham hwearf, þa wearð he semninga on middum þæm siðfæte mid hefigre aðle gehrinen 7 gestonden, swa þæt he hreas 7 feoll on eorðan 7 long fæc forðheald licgende wæs, ÆCHom* i. 10. 20, and *ÆCHom* i. 86. 16 *Hine gedrehte singal slæpleast, swa þæt he þurhwacole niht buton slæpe adreah.* On explanatory *swa þæt* clauses see §§2837-8, and on those with a temporal element §2608.

§2840. But *swa þæt(te)* clauses with the subjunctive may express a contemplated or contingent result, e.g. *Bo* 108. 22 *Hu ne cwæde þu ær þ se wære an feðe mihtigost se þe meahte gan, þeah he wolde, oð ðisse eorþan ende, swa þte nan dæl þisse eorþan ofer þ nære?*, *ChronE* 37. 21 (675) *Ðas landes ic gife Scē Peter . . . swa þ nan min æftergengles þær nan þing of ne nime*, and *ÆCHom* i. 284. 15 *Ne bepæce nan man hine sylfne swa þæt he secge oððe gelyfe þæt ðry Godas syndon.* Callaway (1933, pp. 6-7) says that ninety-one of his consecutive *swa þæt(te)* clauses belong to this group. See further §§2989-90.

§2841. According to Benham (p. 214), 'there are three sentences in OE prose, where the *swa* of the connective is distinctly felt as belonging to the main clause'. They are *ÆGenPref* 98, *WHom* 9. 94 (note *gelærð swa þæt* (96) but *gelærð . . . þæt* (98-9)), and *Gen* 31. 26 *Hwi dydest ðu swa þæt ðu ætlæddest me mine dohtra swylce hyt gehergode hæftlingas wæron?* It is possible to see *þæt* in all these as a conjunction introducing what is formally a noun clause; cf. *ÆCHom* i. 402. 30, *ÆCHom* i. 448. 26 *þa gelamp hit swa þæt Basilius wearð to biscope gecoren*, and *ÆCHom* ii. 8. 24 *Seo oðer gesceapennys wæs swa þæt God gesceop Euan of hire weres sidan*, and consider the bracketed note after *WHom* 9. 94, above. They may represent an intermediate stage.

§2842. Consecutive *swa þæt* is rare in the poetry. It occurs in the combination *swa . . . swa þæt* in

Pr 51
    Ðyn mægen ys swa mære,   mihtig drihten,
    swa þæt ænig ne wat   eorðbuende
    þa deopnesse   drihtnes mihta,
    ne þæt ænig ne wat   engla hades
    þa heahnisse   heofena kyninges,

where the co-ordinate clause after *ne* is introduced by *þæt* alone. All the other possible examples known to me can be otherwise explained. In *Sat* 23 and *PPs* 107. 10 *ne do þu æfre swa,* ‖ *þæt þu of urum mægene mod acyrre, þæt* may introduce a noun clause; see §2841.

Ericson (1932, p. 67) is clearly wrong in listing the clauses beginning in *Beo* 1667 and *And* 1288 as examples; in both the conjunction is *swa*. He could be right about the clauses beginning in *And*
260 and *Whale* 11, but in both of these *þæt* could be a demonstrative anticipating the noun clause which follows and *swa* alone could
be the conjunction. *þæt* could also be a demonstrative in *Ex* 377
(with *Swa* meaning 'Thus'); in *El* 128 (with *swa* a temporal conjunction in the combination *instæpes . . . swa*); and in *Rid* 33. 11 and
84. 33 (with *swa* meaning 'as'). This completes the list of possible
examples of consecutive *swa þæt* in the poetry.

§2843. The pattern *swa . . . swa þæt* noted in *Pr* 51 (§2842) occurs
occasionally in the prose, e.g. *GD* 241. 28 and *ÆCHom* ii. 120. 3
*Swa fulfremedlice he drohtnode on anginne his gecyrrednysse swa
þæt he mihte ða gyu beon geteald on fulfremedra halgena getele*; see
further Benham, pp. 224 and 245, and Ericson 1932, p. 70. *Swa . . .
swa þætte* appears in *Or* 186. 33 and *Or* 252. 23 and *swilc . . . swa
þæt* in *Nic(A)* 494. 4 *uton eac nu gan 7 we magon heora byrgena
opene fyndan 7 hig synd on þære ceastre arymathia samod gebyd-
dende 7 wyð nanne man sprecende 7 swylce swigean healdende swa
þ hig wyð nanne man ne sprecað.*[138]

c. Swa . . . þæt(te)

§2844. The combination 'so . . . that' does not introduce clauses of
purpose in MnE; see §2813. So it is perhaps not surprising that
neither Wülfing nor Shearin lists *swa . . . þæt(te)* among OE final
conjunctions. A few possible examples merit discussion. But in my
opinion the presence of *swa . . . þæt(te)* strongly suggests, if it does
not certify, that we should look for another interpretation.

§2845. In *Bo* 57. 31 *Ac ælc gesceaft hwearfað on hire selfre swa
swa hweol; 7 to þam heo swa hwearfað þ heo eft cume þær heo ær
wæs* and the corresponding

Met 13. 73   Nis nu ofer eorðan   ænegu gesceaft
              þe ne hwearfige,   swa swa hweol deð,
              on hire selfre.   Forðon hio swa hwearfað,
              þæt hio eft cume   þær hio æror wæs,

we have a contemplated result. Sedgefield correctly translates the
prose '. . . and turneth in such a way as to come back to its starting-

---

[138] Despite Benham (p. 226) and Mann (p. 20), *ÆCHom* ii. 514. 1 is not an example. As
BT (s.v. *cliwen*) and Thorpe correctly have it, *swilce* is an adverb 'as it were'; it cannot agree
with *clywen* (neut.).

point'. Hotz (p. 37) states that the subjunctive never expressed result in OE and says of *cume* in *Met* 13. 76 that 'the subj. appears . . . consecutive in our eyes, but final according to the conception of an Anglo-Saxon'. This is too metaphysical for me.

§2846. Similarly, I believe, we have a contemplated or intended result, not purpose, in examples like *ÆCHom* i. 84. 29 *ac heo nele swa beon gefrefrod, þæt hi eft to woruldlicum gecampe gehwyrfon, þa þe æne mid sygefæstum deaðe middangeard oferswiðdon, ÆCHom* i. 318. 14 *Hit getimode æfter Noes flode, þæt entas woldon aræran ane burh, and ænne stypel swa heahne, þæt his hrof astige oð heofon,*

PPs 60. 6   Swa ic naman ðinum   neode singe,
                  þæt ic min gehat   her agylde
                  of dæge on dæg,   swa hit gedefe wese,

Latin *Sic psallam nomini tuo Deus in saeculum saeculi: ut reddam uota mea de die in diem, PPs* 118. 31, and

Seasons 140   uton fæstan swa   fyrene dædum
                on forhæfenesse   her for life,
                þæt we þæs muntes mægen   mærþa gestigan
                swa se ealda dyde   Elias iu.

In examples like

Beo 3069   Swa hit oð domes dæg   diope benemdon
             þeodnas mære,   þa ðæt þær dydon,
             þæt se secg wære   synnum scildig,
             hergum geheaðerod,   hellbendum fæst,
             wommum gewitnad,   se ðone wong strude

and

GuthA 670   Swa nu awa sceal
         wesan wideferh,   þæt ge wærnysse
         brynewylm hæbben,   nales bletsunga,

the impression that we have *swa . . . þæt* may be illusory; *þæt* could introduce a noun clause and *swa* be an independent adverb. On the former, see Mitchell, at press (*b*).

§2847. The use of *swa . . . þæt(te)* in unambiguously consecutive clauses is, however, well attested. As noted in §2814, it is the most common conjunction in OE prose; Benham found 595 examples of *swa . . . þæt* and thirty, all in 'Alfredian' prose, of *swa . . . þætte* (pp. 221 and 243-5). The use of this pattern, like that of MnE 'so . . . that', allows special emphasis to be placed on the word or words in the principal clause which are most closely connected with the clause of result. The element carrying this emphasis may be an adjective or participle, e.g. *ÆCHom* i. 14. 13 *And þa wæs Adam swa wis þæt God gelædde to him nytenu and deorcynn . . .* and *ÆCHom* i. 332. 21 *Eac ða halgan beoð mid heora Scyppendes rihtwisnysse swa afyllede, þæt hi nateshwon ne besargiað ðæra wiðercorenra yrmðe*; an adjective + a noun, e.g. *ÆCHom* i. 4. 32 *forþan ðe on ðam timan bið swa micel yfelnyss and þwyrnys betwux mancynne þæt hi wel wyrðe beoð þære deoflican ehtnysse*; an adverb, e.g. *ÆCHom* i. 402. 33 *and hi wurdon ða utan ymbsette mid Romaniscum here swa lange þæt ðær fela ðusenda mid hungre wurdon acwealde* and *LS* 23. 28 *Swa soðlice he wæs fulfremod on eallum munuclicum þeawum þæt wel oft munecas of feorrum stowum and of mynstrum to him comon . . .* ; an adverb (phrase) + an adjective or participle, e.g. *ÆCHom* i. 70. 8 *and he æfter ðam fæstene wearð swa miclum mid Godes gaste afylled, þæt he ealle Godes englas, and ealle gesceafta, mid heahlicum mode oferstah, ÆCHom* i. 456. 8 *Eower god is swa fæste mid isenum racenteagum gewriðen þæt he ne gedyrstlæcð þæt he furðon orðige oððe sprece,* and *ÆCHom* i. 514. 34 *þeos woruld is swa mid gedwyldum afylled, þæt heo ne mæg beon butan æswicungum*; or a verb, either as the sole element between *swa* and *þæt*, e.g. *ÆCHom* i. 414. 32 *þu, Ælmihtiga Drihten, gemiltsa us synfullum, and urne forðsið swa gefada, þæt we, gebettum synnum, æfter ðisum frecenfullum life, ðinum halgum geferlæhte beon moton* (here the boundary between purpose and hoped-for result is a fine one), or accompanied by other elements, e.g. *ÆCHom* i. 272. 15 *Crist gesette þis gebed, and swa beleac mid feawum wordum, þæt ealle ure neoda, ægðer ge gastlice ge lichamlice, ðæron sind belocene* and *ÆCHom* i. 528. 15 *Swa swiþe lufode God þysne middangeard þæt he his ancennedan Sunu sealde for us.*

§ 2848. Most of the examples just cited express actual result. But, as already noted in § § 2845-6, a contemplated or contingent result can be expressed, e.g. *ChronE* 116. 16 (963) *And ic gife þone tun . . . swa freolice þ ne king ne ƀ ne eorl . . . ne haue þær nane hæse* and *ÆCHom* i. 22. 18 *Ða cwædon hi betwux him þæt hi woldon wyrcan ane burh, and ænne stypel binnon þære byrig, swa heahne þæt his hrof astige up to heofenum.* Callaway (1933, pp. 6-7) records that 206 of the *swa . . . þæt(te)* consecutive clauses he noted belonged here. On this see further § § 2989-90.

§ 2849. The sentences quoted in the preceding sections will serve as examples of consecutive *swa . . . þæt.* Typical of those with *swa . . . þætte* are (actual or certain results) *Or* 44. 29 *þa wurdon hiora wif swa sarige on hiora mode 7 swa swiðlice gedrefed . . . þætte hie wæpna naman* and *CP* 109. 24 *For ðiosum ðonne oft gebyreð ðæt se reccere . . . wierð aðunden on ofermetto ðonne he sua suiðe oðre oferhlifað ðætte ealle licggeað under his willan . . .* , and (with the subjunctive expressing a contemplated result) *CP* 317. 5 *Ac sua he sceal etan ðætte hine sio gewilnung ðære gifernesse of his modes fæsðrædnesse ne gebrienge. . . .*

§2850. As with *swa þæt* (§§2837–8), we find sentences in which *swa . . . þæt* is followed by an explanatory clause, e.g. *ÆCHom* i. 138. 34, *ÆCHom* i. 262. 27, and *ÆCHom* i. 262. 34 *ac hit is swa to understandenne, þæt his rice beo ofer us and he on us rixige.*

§2851. There are some twenty-five *swa . . . þæt* consecutive clauses in the poetry[139] compared with some 240 introduced by simple *þæt*. Eleven of these twenty-five occur in the prose-based *Meters*. So too does the only *swa . . . þætte* clause, viz.

Met 11. 40   Swa hit nu fagað,   frean ealdgeweorc,
                  þætte winnende   wiðerweard gesceaft
                  fæste sibbe   forð anhealdað.

(In *Pan* 20, we have correlative *swa . . . swa* followed by consecutive *þætte*.) But none of the nineteen examples of consecutive *þæs . . . þæt* occurs in the *Meters*; on this, see §§2877–8.

§2852. Typical examples of consecutive *swa . . . þæt* clauses are, with the *swa* element emphasizing an adjective,

GenB 564   þonne wurðað þin eagan swa leoht
                  þæt þu meaht swa wide   ofer woruld ealle
                  geseon siððan . . . ;

a participle,

Phoen 147   Swa gedemed is
                  bearwes bigengan,   þæt he þær brucan mot
                  wonges mid willum . . . ;

an adjective + a noun,

PPs 147. 9   Ne dyde he ahwær swa   eldran cynne
                  þæt he him his domas   digle gecydde;

---

[139] These are the twenty-four examples listed in Appendix 'Result 4' of my D.Phil. thesis plus *Met* 13. 73; see §2845. Exactness is not possible. Sometimes—for example in *Met* 20. 9 —we can say that *swa* and *þæt* do not go together even though the clause which follows them is consecutive. But there are ambiguous examples. Thus *swa* and *þæt* may or may not go together in *Beo* 1769, in *Whale* 31, and in *Whale* 62. Sometimes editorial punctuation may affect the situation. Thus, if we put a full stop instead of a comma after *freawrasnum* in *Beo* 1451, a consecutive *swa . . . þæt* would appear.

an adverb,

Met 20. 161   þu gestaðoladest   þurh þa strongan meaht,
               weroda wuldorcyning,   wundorlice
               eorðan swa fæste   þæt hio on ænige
               healfe ne heldeð;

and a verb,

Met 29. 6   Swa hi gewenede   wuldres aldor
             æt frumsceafte   þæt sio fyrene ne mot
             sunne gesecan   snawcealdes weg,
             monan gemæro.

All these examples express an actual result or one which is regarded as certain to occur. Occasionally, as in

Met 22. 49   Nis þeah ænig man   þætte ealles swa
              þæs geradscipes   swa bereafod sie
              þæt he andsware   ænige ne cunne
              findan on ferhðe,   gif he frugnen bið,

we have a contemplated result. But the latter is more usually found with *þæs . . . þæt* in the poetry; see §§ 2877-8.

d. Swa . . . þe?

§ 2853. Benham (p. 221) writes of *LS* 34. 707 *hi wæron swa ær geo on ealdum dagum swa ðæt nis nan swa eald man þe hi nu on þisne timan mage geþencan* . . . that 'its interest lies in the fact that *ðe* is there substituted for *ðæt* as the second part of the connective'. If this is so, I would be inclined to regard it as a scribal error. But we could say that *þe* introduces an adjective clause. See §§ 2139-43 and, for similar variations after *to þæs*, § 2892.

e. Swilc (. . .) þæt(te)

§ 2854. These combinations appear very occasionally in the prose. I cannot accept some of the examples proposed by Benham (pp. 225-6 and 246) and by Mann (p. 20). It will suffice to quote *BenR* 126. 17 *seo ripung his gestæþþignesse sy swylc þæt hine ne worian ne scriðan ne lyste, CP* 435. 25 . . . *se ðe hine upahefeð on ða ofermetto swelcre unryhtwisnesse ðætte he fullfremme hwelc yfel huru ðurh geðeaht, Or* 122. 25 *Se ilca Papirius wæs æfter þæm gefeohte mid Romanum swelces domes beled þæt hie hiene to ðon gecoren hæfdon þæt he mid gefeohte mehte þæm maran Alexandre wiþstondan, Bo* 145. 7 *Swilc is se wisdom þ hine ne mæg nan mon of þisse weorulde ongitan swilcne swylce he is, ChronE* 219. 30 (1086) (§2051), and *HomU* 40. 273. 23 . . . *þonne god geþafað þæt he mot on his agenum halgum swylc wundor gewyrcean þæt Enoh and Elias þurh þone þeodfeond gemartirode weorðað.* . . . Callaway (1933, pp. 9-10) offers more examples.

§2855. Examples from the poetry like *And* 29 and

And 25

	Swelc wæs þeaw hira
þæt hie æghwylcne	ellðeodigra
dydan him to mose	meteþearfendum,
þara þe þæt ealand	utan sohte

are perhaps slightly different in kind; in them the *þæt* clause can be taken as a consecutive or as a noun clause. But cf. *HomU* 40. 273. 23 (§2854).

§2856. According to Benham (p. 226), *swylce . . . þær* in *GD(C)* 118. 23 *nim þisne hlaf 7 aweorp hine on swylce stowe þær he næfre ne mage beon gefunden fram nanum men* 'is a condensation for *swilce . . . ðæt ðær*, in which *ðær* is the ordinary local connective, but also has absorbed the consecutive *ðæt*'. This seems an unnecessary complication; see §§2450-3.

4. CLAUSES INTRODUCED BY *SWA, SWA SWA,* AND *SWA . . . SWA*

§2857. Neither Wülfing, Shearin, nor Mann, has suggested that *swa*, or *swa swa*, or *swa . . . swa*, introduces final clauses. The three *swa* examples from the poetry hesitatingly suggested by Glogauer (pp. 36-7) are unconvincing. In *Jul* 253 *swa* corresponds to Latin *cum*; see §2693. In *KtPs* 117 it corresponds to Latin *et* and means 'thus'. In *And* 972 it could be said to introduce a consecutive clause; see below. But it is perhaps more likely to introduce a comparative clause or to mean 'wherever', 'as far as', or 'as widely as'; see §2490. In the last two of these three, the verb in the *swa* clause is indicative. In the first it is subjunctive after the imperative *wes*. So the mood tells against Glogauer. In examples like

Beo 435   ic þæt þonne forhicge,   swa me Higelac sie,
                min mondrihten   modes bliðe,
                þæt ic sweord bere . . .

and

Jul 80   Ic þæt geswerge   þurh soð godu,
                swa ic are æt him   æfre finde . . . ,

swa is best taken as asseverative; cf. MnE 'So help me God' and see Behre, pp. 285-6 and 290, and Ericson 1932, pp. 80-1. Some of the possible examples of consecutive *swa* discussed below can be taken as final, e.g.

El 1289

	Soðfæste bioð
yfemest in þam ade,	eadigra gedryht,
duguð domgeorne,	swa hie adreogan magon
ond butan earfeðum	eaðe geþolian,
modigra mægen.	

But in the absence of firm examples, it would seem perverse to do so. Ericson (1932, p. 73) classifies as a purpose clause

Prec 86

	Hæle sceal wisfæst
ond gemetlice,	modes snottor,
gleaw in gehygdum,	georn wisdomes,
swa he wið ælda mæg	eades hleotan.

But here *swa* can be taken as an adverb or as a consecutive conjunction; *mæg* is not an auxiliary expressing the subjunctive.

§2858. Whether or not *swa (swa)* can be described as a consecutive conjunction is one facet of the general problem 'Parataxis or hypotaxis?'—a problem which arises very frequently with *swa*. Wülfing did not recognize it as such. Benham (p. 213), in discussing *swa*, says: 'Its use in Gothic without *þatei* to express result, its presence in so many Old English connectives of result, and its persistence in so many idioms of popular language in place of *that*, have led me to think that probably *swa* alone or doubled, as is usual in Gothic, was the primitive form of consecutive connective in Germanic.' Ericson (1932, p. 65) is in general agreement—'. . . the earliest form [of result clauses] is in *swa*-alone, since that form is used almost exclusively in the Cædmonian and Cynewulvian poetry'. He goes on 'It was a loose construction, something like our latter-day, "It was raining, *so* I put on my coat".'

§2859. Clauses in which *swa (swa)* can be taken as a consecutive conjunction must be divided into two groups—those without a negative and those with one. The first group is small. Of possible examples with *swa*, I reject *Bede* 92. 4 (proposed in BT, s.v. *swa* V(2)) for reasons given in §2874, and *GD* 318. 26 (proposed in BTS, s.v. *swa* V. 2) because *swa* translates Latin *sicut*. In *Or* 40. 33 *7 þære þeode operne naman ascop be him syluum, swa hi mon syððan het Persi*, Latin *et victor nomen subjectae genti dedit: namque a Perseo Persae sunt vocati*, *Prec* 86 (see §2857), and

GenB 384   Mid þy me god hafað
              gehæfted be þam healse,   swa ic wat he minne hige cuðe;
              and þæt wiste eac   weroda drihten,
              þæt sceolde unc Adame   yfele gewurðan
              ymb þæt heofonrice,   þær ic ahte minra handa geweald,

swa can be taken as an adverb 'so, thus, therefore'. Such examples
could be multiplied; see Ericson 1932, p. 65. In *Lch* i. 354. 5 *wyrc
swa hit man gehal forswelgan mæge* (Benham, p. 213),

PPs 92. 3   And þa ymbhwyrft   eorþan getrymede,
                   swa folde stod   fæste syþþan,

Latin *Etenim firmavit orbem terrae, qui non commovebitur*, and
similar examples, we can again take *swa* as an adverb 'so, thus'. But
if we do take it as a conjunction, the clause can be one of comparison and *swa* can be translated 'as' rather than 'so that'. The same
possibilities exist in *Or* 168. 11 *þa sendon hie þider Amilchor, heora
þone gleawestan mon, þæt he Alexandres wisan besceawade, swa he
hit him eft ham bebead on anum brede awriten, 7 siþþan hit awriten
wæs, he hit oferworhte mid weaxe*. (The change from *þæt* to *swa*
does not necessarily certify a change in meaning; see §2869.) So we
must not protest too much, for the relationship certainly shades into
one of result in all these examples with *swa*. Whether the idiom was
closer to MnE 'It was raining so; I put on my coat' or 'It was raining,
so I put on my coat' must be for the reader to decide. If we take
wære as a preterite subjunctive singular—as I believe we must—and
not as a preterite indicative plural (see §19) in *LS* 35. 215 *And in
minum geferscipe wæron weras and wif, and þær wæs ealdra manna
and iungra and lytelra cilda, swa þær wære hundsiofontig* (cited by
Ericson (1932, p. 65)), *swa* does not really mean 'so that'. This
example demonstrates the kind of comparative clause which led to
the use of *swa* in the sense 'as if'; see §3380.

§2860. I turn now to two positive *swa swa* clauses. In *CP* 141. 2,
classified as consecutive by Callaway (1933, p. 76), the first *sua sua*
clause is one of comparison, correlative with the preceding *sua*, and
the second *sua sua* clause—the one in question—seems to me a
clumsy parallel to it rather than a clause of result. Cockayne translates *swa swa* in *Lch* ii. 250. 26 *gebeat oþþe gegnið to duste swa swa
þreo cucles mæl sien oððe ma* (Benham, p. 218) as 'so that'. We
could translate 'so as' and thus convey the element of comparison
which is involved. We can certainly see *swa (swa)* shading into a consecutive conjunction in these positive clauses. But I can find no
reason for insisting that it is one in the same sense as *swa þæt*. It is

true that we read in the Litany 'That it may please thee to give and preserve to our use the kindly fruits of the earth, so as in due time we may enjoy them'. But there may be a subtle difference between 'so as' and 'so that' in this context; the former could imply 'such fruits as we may enjoy'—'Not thistles, O Lord, but grapes and cherries'. See, however, §2869.

§2861. But most of the alleged examples of consecutive *swa* occur in negative clauses. If we look at a sentence like

> *GenA* 901 ... and þa reafode, swa hit riht ne wæs,
> beam on bearwe and þa blæda æt,

we can see that, while the *swa* clause is basically comparative and means 'as was not right, in a way which was not right', it can easily be viewed as consecutive 'in such a way that it was not right' or as concessive 'though it was not right'. Such extensions do not necessarily depend on *swa* being a conjunction, for in examples like

> *Finn* 41 Hig fuhton fif dagas, swa hyra nan ne feol
> drihtgesiða, ac hig ða duru heoldon,

swa could originally have been an adverb ('they fought for five days thus: none fell . . .') and a consecutive implication ('so that none fell . . .') or an adversative one ('yet none fell . . .') could have followed, while in

> *Beo* 2005 ic ðæt eall gewræc
> swa begylpan ne þearf Grendeles maga
> ænig ofer eorðan uhthlem þone,

the adverbial and consecutive interpretations are possible, but not the adversative or concessive. In my opinion, the adverbial use of *swa* is the original from which the other functions stem.

§2862. *Mutatis mutandis*, these remarks apply to all the examples of consecutive *swa* clauses with a negated verb proposed by BT(S) (s.v. *swa* V. 2), Benham (p. 213), Ericson (1932, p. 65), and Callaway (1933, p. 18). Perhaps the most common pattern is that with the verb *nytan*, e.g. *LawIne* 7 *Gif hwa stalie swa his wife nyte 7 his bearn, geselle lx scill to wite*, *Or* 198. 6 *Æfter þæm Fauius Maximus se consul for mid sciphere to Tarentan þære byrg, swa Hannibal nyste, 7 þa burg on niht abræc, swa þa nyston þe þærinne wæron, 7 Hannibales latteow ofslog Cartalon, 7 xxx m mid him*, *LS* 34. 332 *þa spræcon hi him betweonan swa hit nan man nyste butan him sylfon þæt hi woldon ðisra haligra martyra martyrrace awritan*, and

And 260   Him ða ondswarode   ælmihti god,
                  swa þæt ne wiste,   se ðe þæs wordes bad,
                  hwæt se manna wæs   meðelhegendra,
                  þe he þær on waroðe   wiðþingode,

where I agree with Schaar (p. 51) in taking *swa* as the conjunction and *þæt* as a demonstrative anticipating the *hwæt* clause. In all these examples, the *swa* clauses can conveniently be translated 'without (x) knowing' or '(x) not knowing'. A similar example with *swa swa* appears in *CP* 301. 24 . . . *ðæt is ðæt sume menn onderfoð eaðmodnesse hiw, sume oformodnesse, sua sua hie nyton.* But other verbs of course occur, e.g. *Or* 296. 33 *7 sona þæs on þæm þriddan dæge hie aforan ut of þære byrig hiora agnum willan, swa þær ne wearð nan hus hiora willum forbærned, Mart 2* 128. 27 . . . *ond læg fif dagas beforan þæs mynstres geate swa he ne æt ne ne dranc, ac he bæd ingonges* (where the *ac* clause both emphasizes and explains the negative result or state; cf. *Az* 59, *Az* 186, and *Finn* 41 (§2861)), *ApT* 20. 11 *he rædlice sloh swa he hine næfre feallan ne let,* and

Seasons 108   he þæt fæsten heold   feowertig daga
                  and nyhta samod,   swa he nahtes anbat
                  ær he þa deoran æ   dryhtnes anfenge.

The only negative example with *swa swa* listed by Callaway (1933, p. 7)—*CP* 199. 10—belongs here. Benham (p. 218) proposes only *ChronA* 88. 19 (895) . . . *þa foron hie ofer Norðhymbra lond 7 Eastengla swa swa sio fird hie geræcan ne mehte,* which could be similarly explained. But here *swa swa* might mean 'wherever'; see §2489. Ericson (1932, p. 73) adds *ÆLet* 4. 1268 *7 þa halgan lareowas . . . tæhton þæt man drince swa swa him ne derede.*

§2863. Examples of this sort with a concessive element are further discussed in §§3476-80. But what has been said here and what is said there confirms the accuracy of Burnham's observation (pp. 14-15): 'As a rule, however, in both prose and verse the Old English construction with *swa* is somewhat ill-defined. . . . *Swa* must be interpreted in these cases as a rather characterless connective, shading into concession, result, or manner, as the case may be, and, with the negative, corresponding to Modern English "without," "not being." '

§2864. Turning to *swa . . . swa* clauses in the prose, we find that Benham (pp. 222 and 245) lists ten examples in which (he says) '*swa . . . swa = swa . . . ðæt*', and that Callaway (1933, pp. 6-7 and 76) has nineteen examples in which correlative *swa . . . swa* is 'used to introduce the dependent consecutive subjunctive'. Only two references appear in both lists, viz. *CP* 455. 28 (where Callaway rightly finds two examples) and *CP* 189. 9. Ericson (1932, pp. 72-3) gives three of these twenty-seven examples and adds five more, with the comment that 'in this type, *swa* replaces *þæt*'. These thirty-two sentences can conveniently be divided into four groups.

§2865. The first consists of three examples in which the verb of the subordinate clause is the present indicative of a verb other than a 'modal' auxiliary. These are *Lch* i. 166. 16, *CP* 431. 18 *Swa bið ðæt mod slæpende gewundad swa hit ne gefret, ðonne hit bið to gimeleas his agenra ðearfa*, and *Or* 134. 14 *7 hie his siþþan wæran swa swiðe ehtende swa hit is ungeliefedlic to secganne*, Latin . . . *incredibile dictu est*. In all these *swa . . . swa* can be translated 'so . . . that', expressing an actual or certain result. But a strong element of comparison can be detected.

§2866. In the last example, the meaning would not have been very different if we had had ☆*swa nan man geliefan ne mæg* or ☆*swa we geliefan ne magon*. This formula—with a negated indicative present tense of *magan* or its equivalent—is characteristic of four of the five sentences in the second group, viz. *GD(C)* 5. 27 (§2869), *ÆLet* 4. 492, *ÆCHom* i. 538. 14 *Ic geseah swa micele menigu swa nan man geryman ne mæg*, and *ÆCHom* ii. 578. 13 *Ðis weorc wæs swa gefadod mid deorwurðum stanum and readum golde, swa we eow reccan ne magon*. The fifth—*Bede* 48. 25 *Æfter þyssum com god gear, 7 swa eac micel genihtsumnys wæstma on Breotone lond, swa nænig æfteryldo syððan gemunan mæg*—differs only in the absence of *ne* before *mæg*. The last of the sentences in §2865 seems to me applicable here also, even though the result is negative; we could have had ☆*swa hit is uneaþelic to gerymenne/to reccenne* in *ÆCHom* i. 538. 14 and *ÆCHom* ii. 578. 13 without a change in meaning.

§2867. The third group contrasts with the second in that the six examples which comprise it have a positive *swa* clause whose verb is either pres. ind. *mæg* or pres. subj. *mæge*. Of these, the two in *Or* 18. 33 *7 se mor syðþan, on sumum stowum, swa brad swa man mæg on twam wucum oferferan; 7 on sumum stowum swa brad swa man mæg on syx dagum oferferan* have *mæg*. The other four have *mæge*. They are *CP* 61. 18, *CP* 119. 4, and the two in *CP* 455. 28 *Forðæm is ðæm læce swiðe geornlice to giemanne ðæt he swa strangne læcedom selle ðæm seocan, swa he mæge ða mettrymnesse mid geflieman, 7 eft swa liðne swa se tydra lichoma mæge astandan*. These too can be taken as consecutive clauses, those with the indicative expressing a result which is actual or certain, those with the subjunctive one which is contemplated or contingent. But here too a strong

element of comparison remains; it is interesting that in *CP* 455. 28
the EETS translation has 'so . . . as' for the first *swa . . . swa* and 'so
. . . that' for the second.

§ 2868. The remaining eighteen examples comprise the fourth group.
Twelve of these occur in *CP* 453. 17–35; see § 2869. In all eighteen,
the verb of the subordinate clause is a negated subjunctive of a
simple verb; typical examples are *CP* 189. 9 *Ðonne is micel ðearf,
ðonne him mon ðissa tuega hwæðer ondrætt suiður ðonne oðer, 7
wið ðæt wienð, ðæt he sua suiðe wið ðæt winne sua he on ðæt oðer
ne befealle, ðe he him ær læs ondred, BenR* 63. 18 . . . *stande se eaca
on ðæs abbodes dome þæt þonne swa sy foresceawod swa þær næfre
oferfyl ne filige,* and *Lch* ii. 254. 12 *Is hwæþere swa to lætanne swa
þ liflice mægen ne aspringe.* These obviously have much in common
with the examples discussed in § § 3476–80. The presence of the first
swa can be dispensed with if the translator wishes to use either 'without (*x*)' or '(*x*) not' + a present participle. But here again, as in the
first three groups, *swa . . . swa* can be translated 'so . . . that' or 'so
. . . as' expressing a contemplated or contingent result; here again,
the element of comparison remains strong. So it is not unreasonable
to say of all four groups that the line between the examples which
make them up and the comparative clauses with *swa . . . swa* and *þe
. . . þe* discussed by Benham (pp. 222–4) remains a fine one; consider, for example, *Bede* 48. 25 (§ 2866) and *Or* 18. 33 (§ 2867) and
note the seemingly arbitrary way in which the collections of Benham,
Callaway (even though he was collecting only subjunctives), and Ericson, fail to overlap. No doubt we would have had more than thirty-
two examples if a fourth scholar had written on the topic.

§ 2869. I have to confess that I started this discussion almost obsti-
nately determined to deny all validity to Benham's equation '*swa swa
= swa ðæt*'. But one noteworthy passage compelled my surrender.
This is to be found in *CP* 453. 17–35. In it there are fourteen clauses
which the EETS translator rendered by the formula 'without' +
present participle; the Latin equivalent is *sic . . . ut . . . non* or *sic . . .
ne*. The first and last of these 'without' formulae translate *swa . . .
þæt*, the intermediate twelve *swa . . . swa*! So I really could not continue to believe that the change from *þæt* to *swa* in *Or* 168. 11
(§ 2859) necessarily certified a change in meaning or continue to
insist that anything more than personal preference was necessarily
involved in the variation between *swa . . . swa* in *GD(C)* 5. 27 *7 hit
þonne se þoden 7 se storm on sæ adrifeð swa feorr swa he æt nyhstan
nænig land geseon ne mæg* and *swa . . . þæt* in *GD(H)* 5. 25 *7 hit
þonne se þoden 7 se storm ut adrifað swa feor þæt hy æt necstan ne*

magon nan land geseon. Once again, then, I endorse a verdict by Ericson—this time his observation (1932, p. 72) that 'in this type *swa* replaces *þæt*. Such clauses lean toward the notion of comparison, the same way as that in New English of expressing result by "so — as" where "so that" would be more common.'[140]

§2870. The two possible examples in the poetry are

Beo 1046	Swa manlice mære þeoden,
	hordweard hæleþa heaþoræsas geald
	mearum ond madmum, swa hy næfre man lyhð,
	se þe secgan wile soð æfter rihte,

which can be compared with the first group of *swa . . . swa* examples, and

Jud 67		Gefeol ða wine swa druncen
	se rica on his reste middan,	swa he nyste ræda nanne
	on gewitlocan,	

where GK and the Sweet *Reader* both take the *swa* in *Jud* 68 to mean 'as if'. But there was clearly no pretence about it. The comparison here is with *And* 260 and the other examples with *nytan* in §§1924 and 2862, and with the *swa . . . swa* examples in §§2868–9.

5. CLAUSES INTRODUCED BY *ÞÆS*, ALONE OR IN COMBINATION WITH *ÞÆT* OR *ÞE*

§2871. Shearin makes no mention of *þæs*, alone or in combination, as a final conjunction. It does not appear in Wülfing's lists of conjunctions introducing final or consecutive clauses, or in Mann's. Benham (pp. 218 and 224) noted two examples of *swa . . . þæs þe* preceding what seem to be consecutive clauses. I discuss below these two and a few other possible examples of final and consecutive clauses introduced by *þæs (. . .) (þæt/þe)*.

§2872. I agree with Wülfing and Shearin in not recording *þæs* as a final conjunction. But what seems to be an indisputable example of *þæs þe* appears in *ApT* 18. 5 *gemildsa me nacodum, forlidenum, næs na of earmlicum birdum geborenum, and ðæs ðe ðu gearo forwite hwam ðu gemiltsige, ic eom Apollonius se tirisca ealdorman,* Latin *et ut scias cui miserearis, ego sum Tyrius Apollonius, patriae meae princeps.* I have found nothing similar in the poetry.

---

[140] Ericson (1932, p. 71), however, errs in claiming to have found an example of *swa . . . ðaða* 'so . . . that' in *ÆCHom* ii. 452. 9; *ðaða* + pret. ind. *forlet* means 'when' (so Thorpe) or 'seeing that'.

§2873. The nearest approach to a consecutive clause introduced by *þæs* I have found in prose and poetry is

GenB 570   Gif þu him to soðe sægst   hwylce þu selfa hæfst
                bisne on breostum,   þæs þu gebod godes
                lare læstes,   he þone laðan strið,
                yfel andwyrde   an forlæteð
                on breostcofan. . . .

Here the *þæs* clause could be temporal; see §2680.

§2874. As to *þæs þe* consecutive clauses in the prose, I cannot add to Benham's two examples of *swa . . . þæs þe* (pp. 218 and 224): *Bede* 92. 4 *Se me allum Ongolcynnum 7 aldormonnum Bretta þeode fornom 7 forhergade, swa efne þæs ðe meahte wiðmeten beon Saule iu cyninge Israhela þeode* (BT errs in recording this s.v. *swa* V(2): 'adverbial conjunction . . . expressing an actual or possible result') and *Lch* i. 212. 14 *swa andweard heo ys þæs þe is sæd of ðam þe his afandedon þ heo þy ylcan dæge þa stanas forbrycð*. The only other possible instance I have noted is in the poetry, viz.

Seasons 216   Hwæt! Hi leaslice   leogan ongynnað
                and þone tæppere   tyhtaþ gelome,
                secgaþ þæt he synleas   syllan mote
                ostran to æte   and æþele wyn
                emb morgentyd,   þæs þe me þingeð
                þæt hund and wulf   healdað þa ilcan
                wisan on worulde. . . .

But here *þæs þe* may introduce a comparative clause.

§2875. Mann's suggestion (pp. 8–13) that the use of *þæs* seen in such examples as

El 207   . . .   swa se ealda feond
                forlærde ligesearwum,   leode fortyhte,
                Iudea cyn,   þæt hie god sylfne
                ahengon, herga fruman.   þæs hie in hynðum sculon
                to widan feore   wergðu dreogan!

formed a bridge between paratactic and hypotactic final and consecutive clauses would be more convincing if *þæs (þe)* regularly introduced such clauses. But it does not. On adv. *þæs* see further §§2422 and 3115 and cf. §2815.

§2876. In the poetry, where adv. *þæs* sometimes appears for adv. *swa* (§1141) and in the three examples in the prose discussed in §2878, *þæs . . . þæt* is an alternative to *swa . . . þæt*. Since there are no certain examples of *swa . . . þæt* introducing final clauses (§2844), it is perhaps not surprising that *þæs . . . þæt* does not serve as a final conjunction; in examples like

GenA 2030

> bæd him þræcrofe
> þa rincas þæs   ræd ahicgan,
> þæt his hyldemæg   ahreded wurde,
> beorn mid bryde,

the *þæt* clause is more naturally taken as noun, explanatory of *þæs*. The same explanation is available in examples like *GenA* 2581 and

And 307

> Hu gewearð þe þæs,   wine leofesta,
> ðæt ðu sæbeorgas   secan woldes . . . ?,

where a consecutive interpretation would be strained; cf. §2841.

§2877. But apart from these, there are nineteen examples in the poetry which I have construed as consecutive clauses introduced by *þæs . . . þæt*; they are listed in Appendix 'Result 6' of my D.Phil. thesis and are exemplified below. The two tables which follow show the uses of *swa . . . þæt(te)* and *þæs . . . þæt* in consecutive clauses in the poetry.

Table 1

Serial	After a principal clause containing	Number of examples with	
		swa . . . þæt(te)	*þæs . . . þæt*
1	a rhetorical question	1 (*JDay* ii 213; a dependent question)	3 (*And* 1372; *Rid* 1.1; *JDay* i 30)
2	a negated indicative	1 (*Sat* 348 *swa . . . swa . . . þæs swa . . . þæt*)	13 (exemplified below)
3	a negated ambiguous verb-form	1 (*PPs* 147. 9; Latin suggests actual result)	—
4	an imperative	—	—
5	a subjunctive	2 (*Met* 22. 49;[141] *MCharm* 12. 11)	1 (*Ex* 439)[141]
6	none of these and therefore usually a simple statement	20 (exemplified in §2847)	2 (*ChristC* 1472;[142] *Jul* 372)
Total		25	19

[141] These two examples also involve a negative.

[142] In my opinion, the context clearly certifies that this question is not rhetorical, but genuine.

Table 2

The consecutive clause contains	*swa . . . þæt(te)*	*þæs . . . þæt*
an actual result (serials 3 and 6)	21	2
a contemplated result, a result regarded as a tendency (serials 1, 2, 4, and 5)	4	17
Total	25	19

§2878. We see from Table 2 that five out of every six *swa . . . þæt* clauses in the poetry contain a result which has occurred or is regarded as certain to occur. In the prose, the figure is very roughly two of every three.[143] Seventeen out of nineteen *þæs . . . þæt* clauses in the poetry contain a contemplated result, a result expressed as a tendency.[144] The same is true of the three *þæs . . . þæt* clauses in the prose known to me; see below. Most of the *þæs . . . þæt* examples follow a principal clause containing a negated indicative, e.g.

JDay i 109   Næfre mon þæs hlude   horn aþyteð
                  ne byman ablaweþ,   þæt ne sy seo beorhte stefn
                  ofer ealne middangeard   monnum hludre,
                  waldendes word,

GuthB 865   Nænig monna wæs
                  of þam sigetudre   siþþan æfre
                  godes willan þæs georn,   ne gynnwised,
                  þæt he bibugan mæge   þone bitran drync . . . ,

and two examples from the prose. The first is *Bo(C)* 75. 4 . . . *forðæm ic wat þ nan nis þæs welig þ he sumes eacan ne þyrfe*, where MS B has *swa welig þ*. Benham (p. 230) sees this as due to omission—presumably scribal—of *to*. There may be something in this, since *to þæs . . . þæt* appears in *Bo* 53. 5 and elsewhere in the early prose; see §2909. The second is *HomU* 32. 184. 18 *la hwæt, þonne þam synfullum þinceð þæt nan wiht ne sy þæs hates ne þæs cealdes . . . þæt hig þonne mihte fram ures drihtnes lufan asceadan*. In this example, as in *Beo* 1366 *No þæs frod leofað* ‖ *gumena bearna, þæt þone grund*

---

[143] A figure reached by comparing unlike with unlike. Benham notes 595 *swa . . . þæt* (p. 221) and 30 *swa . . . þætte* (p. 245) clauses. Callaway (1933, pp. 8–9) notes 192 *swa . . . þæt* and 14 *swa . . . þætte* clauses in which result is expressed as a tendency. This gives totals of 625 and 206 respectively.

[144] Despite Callaway (1933, p. 10) *þæt* in *GenB* 833 introduces what is grammatically a noun clause dependent on *gesawe* in line 830 rather than a clause expressing a contemplated result; see Mitchell 1980a, p. 408.

wite, þæt may be taken as a relative pronoun with faulty concord; see §§2139-43. But a rhetorical question—the virtual equivalent of a negative; see §2404—sometimes occurs, e.g. *And* 1372,

JDay i 30   Hwa is þonne þæs ferðgleaw,   oþþe þæs fela cunne,
                   þæt æfre mæge heofona   heahþu gereccan,
                   swa georne þone godes dæl,   swa he gearo stondeð
                   clænum heortum,   þam þe þisne cwide willað
                   ondrædan þus deopne?,

and the third instance from the prose, viz. *Exod* 10. 10 *Hu mage ge ðæs frymdige beon, ge ðe mine ðeowas syndon, ðæt ge sceolan faran fram me mid eallum eowrum cynne 7 eowrum Gode offrian?* The only remaining example of *þæs . . . þæt* worthy of special note is

Ex 439   . . . nymðe hwylc þæs snottor   in sefan weorðe
                þæt he ana mæge   ealle geriman
                stanas on eorðan,   steorran on heofonum
                sæbeorga sand,   sealte yða,

where we have a negated subjunctive in a conditional clause in dependent speech. In non-dependent speech we should have had the equivalent of 'There is no man so wise that he . . .' (cf. *GuthB* 865 above) or of a rhetorical question (cf. *JDay i* 30 above). Quirk (pp. 94-8) explains these constructions as 'indefinite concessions of degree'. For my comments see *MÆ* 25 (1956), 38-9.

§2879. It is possible to take *þæs . . . þe* in

ChristA 241   Forþon nis ænig þæs horsc,   ne þæs hygecræftig,
                þe þin fromcyn mæge   fira bearnum
                sweotule geseþan

as a consecutive conjunction like *þæs . . . þæt*, with the subject of the consecutive clause unexpressed. For the reasons given in §§2139-43 and 2885-6, I prefer to take *þe* as a relative pronoun.

6. CLAUSES INTRODUCED BY OTHER COMBINATIONS INVOLVING *þÆT*

§2880. Here it will suffice to list and give examples. In final clauses we find *ði . . . þæt* in *ÆCHom* i. 248. 27 and *ÆCHom* i. 456. 12 *He is freond þæs Ælmihtigan Godes, and ði he com to ðyssere scire þæt he aidlige ealle ða hæðengyld þe ðas Indiscan wurðiað* and *þæt . . . þy* in *GD* 153. 26 *ac þæt se man mage swa fela of eorðan gefremman, þy com to eorðan of heofonum se scyppend heofones 7 eorðan*; see Shearin 1903, p. 59.

§2881. The following combinations have been noted in consecutive clauses: *þus þ* in *Mark(Ru)* 1. 45, *ðus þte* in *Mark(Li)* 1. 45, and *ðus ł suæ þte* in *Mark(Li)* 4. 32 (Benham, pp. 215 and 222); *þus . . . þ* in *Alex* 20. 5 *þas ðing we þus drugon þ we swa wið þam wyrmum fuhtan 7 wunnan huru twa tida þære nihte* (Benham, p. 225); *þus . . . þæt* in

Met 20. 204	Hwæt, þu ða saule,	sigora waldend,
	þeoda þrymcyning,	þus gesceope,
	þæt hio hwearfode	on hire selfre
	hire utan ymb;	

and *þyllic . . . þæt* in *ÆCHom* i. 406. 20 and *ÆLS* 1. 92 . . . *and seo an sawul is æðelboren þe ðonne lufað þe heo fram com . þe hi þyllice gesceop þæt heo on hire andgyte habban mihte godes anlicnesse and gelicnesse.*

§2882. Benham (pp. 226–7) sees *se, seo, þæt* as 'a qualitative, demonstrative adjective instead of a simple demonstrative' in examples like *Or* 40. 3 *On þære tide wæs sio ofermycelo hæto on ealre worulde: nales þæt an þæt men wæron miclum geswencte, ac eac ealle nytenu swyðe neah forwurdon*, *CP* 389. 14 *Sio swiðre hand hine ðonne beclipð, ðonne ðonne he hine gehielt on ðæm willan ðæt he mid ealre estfulnesse lufað ðæt ece lif*, *ÆCHom* ii. 564. 29 *forðan ðe hi hæfdon þæt gode ingehyd on heora heortan þæt hi woldon Gode anum gecweman*, *WHom* 8c. 6 . . . *gyf he þære ylde 7 ðæs andgytes hæfð þæt he hit understandan mæg*, and *HomU* 27. 147. 20 . . . *forðam þe þær ys seo bliss and þæt wuldor þæt nan eorðlic mann ne can ne ne mæg mid his wordum areccan and asecgan þa wynsumnysse and blisse þæs heofonlican lifes.* One can see the point. But Benham's view is, I believe, anachronistic, for he has failed to recognize that in the examples he cites there are two important differences of idiom between OE and MnE. First, MnE usually dispenses with the OE demonstrative before an abstract noun (§54); *Bo* 50. 26 *þa cwæð se Wisdom* and *Bo* 51. 16 *Ða cwæð þ Mod* are rendered 'Then Wisdom said' and 'Then Mind said'. Second, OE *þæt* can introduce consecutive clauses without a preceding adverb whereas MnE 'that' cannot. So the last two sentences quoted above can be translated '. . . if he has years and understanding so that he can comprehend it' and '. . . there is glory and gladness so/such that no earthly man . . .'. The only one of Benham's examples in which the demonstrative precedes what might not be an abstract noun is *VSal 1* 226 *þæt ic wat þæt ða ic on þære mænige wæs þæs folces þæt ic him to cuman ne myhte . . . ic wæs þa sona hal geworden. . . .* Here we can translate '. . . when I was in the crowd, so that I could not get to him . . .'. So I can

see no need to follow Benham in erecting the category of 'the qualitative demonstrative'.

§2883. On examples with *to* + adjective/adverb + *þæt*, see §§
2921-3.

7. CLAUSES INTRODUCED BY *þE* AND/OR *þY*

§2884. I agree with Shearin (1903, pp. 60-1) in finding in the prose
no clauses introduced by the indeclinable *þe* or by the instr. sg. neut.
þy which must be taken as clauses of purpose. Shearin (ibid. and
1909, pp. 242-3) cites one from the poetry, viz.

> *Beo* 240   Hwæt, ic hwile wæs
> endesæta,   ægwearde heold,
> þe on land Dena   laðra nænig
> mid scipherge   sceðþan ne meahte.

Klaeber glosses *þe* as the indeclinable particle. But it could be a form
of *þy* 'by which', referring back, not to *ægwearde* (fem.) but to the
whole principal clause. If this is so, it is parallel to

> *KtPs* 49   ...   ic ðe, gasta breogo,
> helende Crist,   helpe bidde,
> ðæt me forgefene   gastes wunde
> an forðgesceaft   feran mote,
> þy ðine wordcwidas   weorðan gefelde,
> ðæt ðu ne wilnast   weora æniges deað.

But we could take *þe* and *þy* in these examples as demonstrative 'by
that' rather than relative 'by which'; compare *ðy* in

> *Beo* 1270   hwæþre he gemunde   mægenes strenge,
> gimfæste gife,   ðe him God sealde,
> ond him to Anwaldan   are gelyfde,
> frofre ond fultum;   ðy he þone feond ofercwom,
> gehnægde helle gast

and contrast Klaeber's comma after *heold* in *Beo* 241 with his semi-
colon after *fultum* in *Beo* 1273. Mann (pp. 8-13 and *Archiv*, 180
(1942), 89-90) sees examples like *Beo* 1270 above as another of the
bridges between paratactic and hypotactic final and consecutive
clauses. The scarcity of *þy* (*þe*) as a conjunction introducing such
clauses (§2815) is against this view, which is perhaps more applicable
to the causal use of *þy* discussed in §§3128-47. Despite Furkert
(p. 27), *þe* in *GuthA* 458 is probably the indeclinable particle.

§2885. I do not think that it was as 'easy for ðe to become a consecutive connective' as does Benham (p. 207) and would take þe in his three proposed prose examples as a relative pronoun or as an example of the confusion between þæt and þe discussed in §§2427-30. They are *BenRW* 97. 11, *ÆCHom* i. 454. 18 *On ðam deofolgylde wunade swilc deofol ðe to mannum þurh ða anlicnysse spræc, and gehælde untruman*, and *LS* 34. 708 . . . *swa ðæt nis nan swa eald man þe hi nu on þisne timan mage geþencan*. . . . Mann (p. 17) quotes the same three examples without acknowledgement, but adds that in them *þe* is the result of the disappearance of the *þæt* of *þætte*. As far as I can understand him, Benham is not to blame for this astonishing suggestion, even though he fails to distinguish indeclinable *þe* from instr. sg. neut. *þy* (pp. 206-7) and does not make clear to me which of the two he sees in the three examples noted above. 'Presumably', says Callaway (1933, p. 26), 'he construes *þe* in these instances as a relative pronoun rather than a conjunction'. This is probably so, for Benham says of ðe . . . ðe that 'this ðe is for ðy, instrumental of *se, seo, ðæt*' (p. 223). But if it is, there is little point in calling *þe* 'a consecutive connective'. In *Solil* 1. 5 *ne com ic naþer mid anre byrðene ham, þe me ne lyste ealne þane wude ham brengan, þe* is best taken as causal; see Callaway 1933, pp. 25-6.

§2886. So I do not take *þe* as a consecutive conjunction in these sentences. I adopt the same view for similar examples in the poetry. In *MSol* 421 and

GuthB 923   Nænig forþum wæs,
        þæt he æwiscmod   eft siðade,
        hean, hyhta leas

we have consecutive clauses introduced by the conjunction *þæt* with an expressed subject. I follow Pogatscher (pp. 269-72) and Behre (pp. 292-3) in explaining the *þæt* clauses in examples like

Jul 510   Ne wæs ænig þara
        þæt me þus þriste,   swa þu nu þa,
        halig mid hondum,   hrinan dorste

and

Met 28. 5   Hwa is moncynnes
        þæt ne wundrie   ymb þas wlitegan tungl,
        hu hy sume habbað   swiðe micle
        scyrtran ymbehwerft,   sume scriðað leng
        utan ymb eall ðis?

as consecutive with unexpressed subject rather than adjective with lack of concord. But in

Max ii 63   Næni eft cymeð
          hider under hrofas,   þe þæt her for soð
          mannum secge   hwylc sy meotodes gesceaft,
          sigefolca gesetu,   þær he sylfa wunað

and

Met 28. 1   Hwa is on eorðan   nu unlærdra
          þe ne wundrige   wolcna færeldes . . . ?

(as in Benham's three prose examples), *þe* seems best taken with Behre (pp. 309 and 311) as a relative pronoun. See further § § 2139–43, where I conclude that adjective clauses and consecutive clauses were both idiomatic in such contexts. Indeed Callaway (1933, p. 26 n. 4) refers to three passages in which we have one and then the other; they include *GD* 320. 2 *witodlice, Petrus, nis nænig man þe hine cuðe þæt he nyte þæt he swylc wæs* and

PPs 143. 4   Hwæt is se manna,   mihtig drihten,
          þe þu him cuðlice   cyþan woldest,
          oððe mannes sunu,   þæt hit gemet wære,
          þæt þu him aht wið   æfre hæfdest?

§ 2887. As Mann (p. 13) points out, *ðy ðe* does seem to introduce a consecutive clause expressing a tendency in *CP* 65. 8 . . . *ðonne he næfre ne gesiehð mid his modes eagum ðæt towearde leoht, ðy ðe he hit lufige* '. . . so as to love it . . .'. As yet I have noted no more such examples.

§ 2888. On clauses involving correlative *þe . . . þe* (= *þy . . . þy*), some of which Benham (pp. 223–4) takes as consecutive, see § § 3137–43 and 3334–46.

8. CLAUSES INTRODUCED BY PREPOSITIONAL
FORMULAE

a. Introductory remarks

§ 2889. These combinations do not differ in character from *swa (. . .) þæt* and *þæs (. . .) þæt*; note the sequences *swa . . . swa . . . þæs swa . . . þæt* in *Sat* 348 and *þæs . . . þæs . . . to þæs . . . to þæs . . . to þæs . . . þæt* in *Sea* 39. They are all found in both grouped and divided forms and they all consist of adverbs or adverb phrases—as a consideration of

El 958   . . . ond þa wundrade ymb þæs weres snyttro,
       hu he swa geleafful on swa lytlum fæce
       ond swa uncyðig æfre wurde,
       gleawnesse þurhgoten

and

El 703   Is þes hæft to ðan strang,
    þreanyd þæs þearl ond þes þroht to ðæs heard
    dogorrimum

will demonstrate—with an added *þæt* or (very occasionally) *þe* clause which is in a sense explanatory. According to Mann (pp. 22-3 and 24-5), the development was from two paratactic sentences to a sentence containing a divided formula. Subsequently (he argues) what he sees as the less emphatic grouped formulae developed.

§ 2890. While Shearin's figures for final clauses in the prose are far from accurate, partly because of carelessness and partly because of the personal element necessarily involved in all classification (especially here with the *for* formulae), they provide us with the conspectus given in the table in § 2891.[145] Benham's figures for the divided prepositional formulae (pp. 228-30) are also untrustworthy, but the number of examples did not surprise me, for anyone familiar with OE prose will readily accept that these formulae are used much more frequently in consecutive clauses in OE than in MnE. Typical examples from Ælfric in which most speakers of MnE would use 'so' include *ÆCHom* i. 114. 26 *to ðan arleas þæt*, *ÆCHom* i. 32. 19 *to ðan swiðe þæt*, *ÆCHom* ii. 436. 1 *to ðan swiðe afyrht þæt*, *ÆCHom* i. 140. 3 *to ðam unspedig wære þæt*, *ÆCHom* ii. 350. 16 *to ðan swiðe mid þiccum þeostrum oferþeht þæt*, and *ÆCHom* ii. 418. 12 *To ðan swiðe ic geoffrige Gode soðe behreowsunge þæt*. . . . (Here it is interesting to note that *swa . . . þæt* in *GD(C)* 18. 12 is replaced by *to þam . . . þæt* in *GD(H)* 18. 12.) But the surprise which Benham's

[145] It would appear—though he does not say so—that the number of occurrences Shearin gives (1903, pp. 64-8) was meant to include both the grouped and divided *to* formulae. So I have deducted from them his figures for the divided formulae (1903, pp. 78-9) to produce the figures for the grouped formulae shown in the table. It must, however, be said that Shearin (1903, p. 2) was too modest when he spoke of 'a few minor incongruities' between the figures he gives in the body of the work, the Index Lists, and the chart (appendix I). A comparison between the figures for the *to* formulae given at Shearin 1903, pp. 64-8, and those in his appendix III will reveal major incongruities. Some texts said in one place to have examples do not appear in the other. The respective totals for formulae with *þon/ þan* are 144 against 126, with *þi/þy* sixty-one against forty-six, and with *þam/þæm* sixty-four against fifty-seven. On the evidence of my own collections, even a conflation of all his lists would not produce one which was complete.

figures for the grouped formulae with *to* + the dative/instrumental of the demonstrative (pp. 218–20) caused me, proved on investigation to be justified. The table which follows shows the actual distribution of his sixty-six examples. (To save space, *þ* and *ð* are not distinguished in this or in the next table.)

Formula	Benham's total of allegedly grouped formulae	I exclude	Grouped formulae		Divided formulae	My total
			Early texts	later texts		
to þæm/þam + þæt	10		2 (*Bo* 55. 21; *CP* 319. 17)	1 (*WHom* 9. 108)	7	10
to þon + þæt	35	2^{146}	24	1 (*Lch* ii. 208. 11)	8	33
to þan + þæt	21	1^{147}		1 (*ÆCHom* i. 36. 32)	19	20
Total	66	3	26	3	34	63

§2891. I have incorporated these corrected figures into the table which follows. But we must note that only twenty-nine of the sixty-three examples are actually grouped formulae and that twenty-six of these occur in early texts. This, together with the details given in the last sentence in §2896, the fact that in *GD(H)* 18. 10 and 37. 27 the reviser has *to þam . . . þæt* where *GD(C)* 18. 9 and 37. 28 had *to þon þæt*, and that *to þon þæt* in *GD(C)* 51. 14 is replaced by *swa þæt* in *GD(H)* 51. 13, suggests that the grouped formulae with *to*—exceptional in MnE consecutive clauses even if we accept 'to that extent that' and the like as their equivalents—were losing their popularity in OE consecutive clauses. There is room for more work on this. But here, with its admitted imperfections, is the promised table of final and consecutive prepositional formulae in the prose.

[146] From Benham's appendix 1. E (p. 243), I exclude *BH* = *Bede* 230. 23 (wrong reference) and his *Lch* i. 134. 31 = 134. 28 (§2900), where *to þy þ* introduces a clause which can be taken as final. It is not listed in Shearin 1903, appendix III. B, but may be the example from *Lch* i listed in Shearin 1903, p. 66. Other of Benham's examples can also be taken as final, e.g. *GD* 339. 19 and *ÆCHom* i. 36. 32 (§2901).

[147] Appendix 1. F (Benham, p. 243) has only twenty examples, despite Benham's figure of twenty-one (p. 220).

Components	Grouped formulae		Divided formulae	
	Purpose	Result	Purpose	Result
to þon/þan + þæt(te)	134	26	10	86
to þi/þy + þæt	55	1[148]	6	
to þæm/þam + þæt	51	3	13	61
to þæs + þæt				21
to þam + þe (see §2892)	1			
for þon + þæt/þe	3		1	
for þi/þy + þæt	3		13	
for þæm/þam + þæt	17		4	
for þæm/þon + þe	2			
wiþ þon + þe	2			
wiþ þæm/þam + þe	4			
wiþ þæt + þæt			1	
wiþ þæs + þæt	1			
be þæm + þæt	2			
on þæm/þon + þæt	2			1
Total	277	30	48	169

On formulae with preposition + *þæt*, see §§2924–7. Examples with a noun after the demonstrative are discussed as they become relevant.

§2892. A few general considerations arise. First, we may note that in the *to* formulae, the last element is *þæt*, not *þe*. Shearin (1903, p. 78) recorded one example with *þe*, but was misled by Schmid, *Die Gesetze der Angelsachsen* (Leipzig, 1858) (p. 60); according to Liebermann all manuscripts have *þæt* in *LawAfEl* 13 . . . *aluc ðu hine from minum weofode to þam þæt he deaðe swelte.* In sentences like *ÆCHom* ii. 480. 4 *þis fyr sceal gecyrran to þam ðe hit asende* and *ÆLS* 32. 60 *and cwæþ þæt him ræd þuhte þæt he to þam gebuge þe him bead Hinguar*, we have antecedent + relative. Spasmodic examples with *þætte* appear in the early prose. They include *CP(C)* 20. 22 *to þæm þætte*, *CP(H)* 21. 22 *to ðæm ðætte* (repeated at *CP(H)* 453. 6), *Bede* 74. 8 *to ðon þætte*, *Bede* 288. 6 and 296. 29 *to þon þætte*, and *Bede* 386. 12 *to þon ðætte*. In view of these facts, I cannot understand what Benham (pp. 218–19) means when he says that 'in the original composition of the phrase, [*þæt*] was a demonstrative pronoun in relative function introducing an *adjective* clause' [my italics]. Here I agree with Shearin (1903, p. 63)—cf. MnE 'to the end that'—and would extend his verdict to the formulae when they

---

[148] This is *Lch* i. 134. 28, on which see §2900.

are used with consecutive clauses: 'Here the purport of purpose lies in the preposition, which with its object forms a *phrase* of finality; while the *ðæt* introduces what, strictly analyzed, is a substantive clause explanatory of this object.'

§2893. Second, the rarity (if not the complete absence; see §2844) of *swa . . . þæt(te)* in clauses of purpose in OE prose and a consideration of MnE usage will make less surprising the fact that, on the evidence of the table, the grouped formulae are more common than the divided ones in final clauses; the proportion is 5.8 : 1. But in consecutive clauses—again not surprisingly—the reverse is true both with the *swa* formulae—*swa . . . þæt(te)* 595, *swa þæt(te)* 533; see §2814—and with the prepositional formulae, where the preference for the divided is a proportion of 5.6 : 1; see further §2891. Kivimaa's statement about the grouped formulae (p. 155)—'according to Benham (pp. 219-20) this [consecutive] meaning is not common'— somewhat misreports Benham but reflects the situation, especially in the later prose.

§2894. Third, we may note from the figures given above that *swa . . . þæt(te)* is more common in consecutive clauses than the divided prepositional formulae in a proportion slightly in excess of 3.5 : 1 (595 against 169 examples). Here we have a foreshadowing of the dominance of 'so . . . that' over 'to that extent . . . that' or the like in MnE. Further work will certainly alter the figures and proportions given in the last few sections. But my own impression is that it will confirm the general tendencies to which I have drawn attention.

§2895. If we exclude *oþþæt* in *PPs* 67. 22, which translates Latin *ut* (Shearin 1909, p. 243), on the grounds that it is a temporal conjunction (§2745), there are no examples of grouped prepositional formulae introducing final or consecutive clauses in the poetry. The divided formulae do not introduce final clauses. But we find consecutive clauses introduced by *to þon/ðon . . . þæt* in *Beo* 1876, *Rid* 40. 16, *Met* 28. 76; by *efne to þon . . . þæt* in *Met* 20. 153; and by *to ðam . . . þæt* in

Jud 275   þa wearð sið ond late   sum to ðam arod
                   þara beadorinca,   þæt he in þæt burgeteld
                   niðheard neðde,   swa hyne nyd fordraf.

This last example neatly illustrates how *þæt* may originally have introduced a noun clause (§2892). Indeed March (p. 206) translated it thus in 1873: '. . . ready for this, that he ventured . . .'. Other divided formulae occur in the poetry; on the four examples with *to þæs . . . þæt*, see §2906, and on *to . . . þæt*, §§2921-3.

§2896. According to Mann (pp. 20-1), the infrequency of preposi-tional formulae in final and consecutive clauses in the poetry reflects a fundamental difference between poetry, which he compares in this respect with everyday speech, and prose, which, being more formal and logical, naturally (he argues) makes more use of anticipatory elements in principal clauses to achieve closer connection and to ensure clarity. Shearin (1903, p. 68) holds a similar view: 'Therefore, in long, involved sentences we often find the emphatic *to-* formulae employed to mark interclausal relations that would not appear so boldly and clearly, if only the usual, less emphatic *ðæt* were used.' We can accept this and extend it to consecutive clauses, with one caveat: the distinction between 'the emphatic *to-* formulae' and 'the less emphatic *ðæt*' need not, I think, always exist. Shearin himself in fact recognizes this. 'Rhetorically considered', he says (1903, pp. 67-8), 'the compound *to-* formulae . . . denote greater emphasis upon the purpose idea than would be felt with the simple *ðæt*. E.g. *John* 1. 31 *ic com and fullode on wætere to ðæm ðæt he wære geswutelod on Israhela folce* (= *sed ut manifestaretur in Israhel propterea veni ego in aqua baptizans*). . . . Note here the emphatic *propterea . . . ut . . .* of the original.' But after only one paragraph he goes on (1903, p. 68): 'However . . . often the *to-* formulae are hardly to be differen-tiated from the simple *ðæt* in force, as in *Dial* 180. 6 *syle me on ðeowdome for hine, ðæt ðu ðinne sunu eft onfo* compared with the almost juxtaposed id. 180. 12 *ne tweo ðu na ðæt ðu sylle ðisne biscop on ðeowdome to ðon ðæt ðu ðinne sunu eft onfo*.' However, the fact that two different writers are concerned weakens Benham's argument (p. 229) that the presence of *to þon . . . þæt* in *GD(C)* 115. 26 and 155. 31, where MS *H* has *þæt* and an inflected infinitive respectively, 'seems to militate against Shearin's theory that the prepositional formulas are used for rhetorical emphasis'.

> *b.* To + *dative/instrumental of a demonstrative + (. . .)* þæt

§2897. Variations in the form of the demonstrative seem to be largely a matter of the date of the text and/or of the personal prefer-ences of the author or scribe. One would not expect them to have any effect on the meaning or function of the formulae. But note the discussion in §§2899-900. More detailed information about the distribution of the forms discussed below will be found in Shearin 1903, pp. 63-8 and 78-80, and Benham, pp. 218-20 and 228-30. But, as I have already said, their work needs checking.

§2898. I begin by quoting a few typical examples of these formulae. We have final clauses in *Or* 60. 12 *þa hiene mon ofslog, þa feng Sameramis his cwen to þæm rice, 7 getimbrede þa burg Babylonie, to þon þæt heo wære heafod ealra Asiria, Or* 264. 11 *7 he bebead þæt mon acwealde eall Dauides cynn, to þon, gif Crist geboren nære þa giet, þæt he na siþþan geboren ne wurde, ÆCHom* i. 34. 13 *Crist wolde on ytinge beon acenned, to ði þæt he wurde his ehterum bedigelod, ÆCHom* i. 598. 5 *Gif ðu to ði come þæt þu me alyse, nelle ic beon alysed lybbende heonon, ÆCHom* i. 592. 18 *Beoð swyðor gearwe to ðam þæt ge ðurh hwilwendlice gedreccednysse becumon to ðam ecum gefean,* and *ÆCHom* i. 614. 8 *To ðam he wext þæt he fealle,* and consecutive clauses in *Or* 56. 31 *Se heora cyning ongan ða singan 7 giddian, 7 mid þæm scopleoðe heora mod swiðe getrymede, to þon þæt hie cwædon þæt hie Mesiana folce wiðstondan mehten, Or* 216. 9 *Æfter þæm his weorod weox to þon swiþe þæt he monega land forhergeade, ÆCHom* i. 524. 9 *Se færð to his tune and forsihð Godes gearcunge, seðe ungemetlice eorðlice teolunge begæð to ðan swiðe, þæt he his Godes dæl forgymeleasað, ÆCHom* i. 558. 2 *þa wæs he ðeonde on gastlicere lare and gecneordnysse to ðan swiðe, þæt se apostol Petrus hine geceas to papan Romaniscre ðeode æfter his dæge, ÆCHom* i. 522. 27 *þa sind gemæste mid gife þæs Halgan Gastes to ðam swiðe þæt hi wilniað þæs upplican færeldes mid fyðerum gastlicere drohtnunge,* and *ÆCHom* i. 114. 25 *Ne sy nan man to ðan arleas þæt he Adam wyrige oððe Euan* (where we have the subjunctive of contingent result).

§2899. Shearin does not distinguish *to þon* and *to þan*. (Here again *þ* includes *ð*.) But on the evidence of Wülfing (ii, §§461-4), Benham, and my own collections, *to þon* is preferred in early texts and *to þan* in later. There are occasional exceptions, e.g. *Bede(Ca)* 52. 17 *to þan swiðe þæt* but *ThCap 1* 479. 33 *to þon swiðe þ. To þon* is especially common in *GD(C)*—but it is often replaced by *to þam* in *GD(H)*; see Benham, p. 219—and in *Or*, where, according to Liggins (1970, pp. 306-7), it is the only form found.

§2900. In *ÆCHom*, we find clauses of purpose with *to ðam þæt* in *ÆCHom* i. 592. 18 and *to ðam . . . þæt* in *ÆCHom* i. 614. 8 and there are clauses of result introduced by *to ðam . . . þæt* in *ÆCHom* i. 140. 3, 372. 1, 508. 30, and 522. 27, and in *ÆCHom* ii. 126. 18; some of these have been quoted in §2898. But Ælfric regularly uses *to þi/þy (. . .) þæt* to introduce clauses of purpose and *to þan . . . þæt* to introduce clauses of result; for examples see §2898. Indeed, as far as I have observed, *to þi* and its less common variant *to þy* occur only in the later prose and almost invariably in clauses which are unambiguously final, not consecutive. Possible examples of grouped formulae which could be taken as consecutive are (with a subjunctive verb) *Lch* i. 134. 28 *gemæncg eac hunig þærto hyt fremað swa some witodlice dimgendum eagum to þy þ seo beorhtnys agyfen sy* and (with an indicative verb) *ÆCHom* ii. 14. 8 *Ic eom cumen to ðe, Danihel, to ði þæt ic sceal ðe tæcan, and þu understand mine spræce, and understand þas gesihðe.* But both contain a strong element of purpose; see §§2890 (fn. 146) and 2983. Whether the presence of *to þi/þy* certifies them as clauses of purpose must await full collections. The fact that the clauses with *wolde* discussed in §§2976–80 are introduced (apparently indifferently) by *þæt, forði/ ðy þæt, forði/ðy . . . þæt, to ði/ðy þæt,* and *to ði/ðy . . . þæt,* will be relevant.

§2901. *ÆCHom* i. 36. 32 . . . *and þancian ðam Hælende þæt he gemedemode hine sylfne to ðan þæt he dælnimend wære ure deadlicnysse* . . . presents a problem. My inclination is to classify it as a clause of purpose. We do not have *to ði þæt,* which is the preferred grouped formula in the text for such clauses. But we have a grouped formula in a late text and the subjunctive mood—features which point to a purpose clause and which are not represented in Thorpe's translation: '. . . and to thank the Saviour that he so humbled himself that he was the partaker of our mortality . . .'. The pattern with a divided formula presented by Thorpe does occur in OE in both final and consecutive clauses, e.g. *ÆCHom* i. 82. 22 *ac to ði he com þæt he wolde his heofenlice rice geleaffullum mannum forgyfan* and *GD(H)* 18. 9 . . . *gif he to þam gedyrstlæhte þæt he þæs ungewunelican þinges to Gode gewilnode,* and should not be imported here.

§2902. According to Benham (pp. 219 and 228) *to þæm* is early usage, *to þam* late. Shearin does not distinguish the two. It is impossible to check his figures completely. He says (1903, pp. 66–7) that there are sixty-four examples—fifty *to þam,* fourteen *to þæm,* but gives references to only fifty-seven (1903, p. 136). But the fact that all the examples from *Bo* and *CP* have *to þæm* supports Benham's conclusion.

§2903. Shearin (1903, pp. 65–7) records the following unusual variations: *Ch* 98 *to ðon þæti, Ch* 1443 *to ðæn ðæt, GD* 100. 3 *to þisum . . . þæt, WHom* 9. 142 (and twice elsewhere) *to ðam anum þæt,* and *WHom* 17. 24 *to þam sylfan . . . þæt.* But, as I show in *NQ* 208 (1963), 326, we do not have *to ðæm . . . swæ* in *CP* 5. 3. On *to þæs . . . þe* see §2905.

§2904. There is no need for a special section dealing with mood in final and consecutive clauses introduced by prepositional formulae. The general treatment will be found in §§2969-99. Any other necessary points are made in the sections which follow here.

c. To þæs . . . þæt

§2905. As far as I have observed, this formula occurs only in the divided form and only in consecutive clauses. We can eliminate two prose examples proposed by Benham (pp. 230 and 246)—*Bo* 75. 4, where MS *C* has *þæs . . . þ* and MS *B swa . . . þ* (but see §2878), and *BlHom* 5. 27 . . . *ge þæt wite wæs to þæs strang þæt æghwylc man sceolde mid sare on þas world cuman*, where the *þæt* clause explains *þæt wite*. We can also eliminate examples with *to þæs . . . þe* such as the last clause in *BlHom* 117. 25 *We leorniaþ þæt seo tid sie to þæs degol þæt nære næfre nænig to þæs halig mon on þissum middangearde ne furþum nænig on heofonum, þe þæt æfre wiste*. . . (on the *to þæs . . . þæt* clause see §2907) and (the only such example in the poetry)

> *ChristA* 219   Nis ænig nu   eorl under lyfte,
> secg searoþoncol,   to þæs swiðe gleaw
> þe þæt asecgan mæge   sundbuendum,
> areccan mid ryhte . . . ,

where the *þe* clauses can be taken as adjective; cf. *ChristA* 241 (§2879). This is another manifestation of the problem discussed in §§2139-43.

§2906. This leaves nineteen of Benham's twenty-one *to þæs . . . þæt* examples. We can add *Bede* 28. 10 and *BlHom* 223. 23 (Benham recorded only one of the two examples in this sentence) and the four examples from the poetry, which are cited below. There are doubtless more. But within these twenty-five, we must distinguish several different patterns. First there is that seen in *Bo* 53. 5, *Solil* 44. 17, *BlHom* 111. 22 (where *forlæteð* is better taken as the verb of a principal clause and not as a parallel to *ne cume*), *BlHom* 223. 23, *HomS* 22. 151 *Hwæt, we witan þæt ne bið ænig man to ðæs clæne aðwægen þæt he þæs hwæðere næbbe þearfe þæt he hine eft þwea*, and

> *Sea* 39   Forþon nis þæs modwlonc   mon ofer eorþan,
> ne his gifena þæs god,   ne in geoguþe to þæs hwæt,
> ne in his dædum to þæs deor,   ne him his dryhten to þæs hold,
> þæt he a his sæfore   sorge næbbe,
> to hwon hine dryhten   gedon wille

(note the variation *þæs . . . to þæs*). All these have a negated principal clause, the same subject in both clauses, and a negative and the
present subjunctive of contingent or contemplated result in the *þæt*
clause. All of them could be re-expressed as a simple sentence beginning with 'Every', e.g. *Bo* 53. 5 *Nis nan to ðæs lytel æwylm þ he þa
sæ ne gesece* 'Every river seeks the sea'. Similar to these, but without
a negative in the *þæt* clause, are *BlHom* 127. 16, *Solil* 35. 11 *næfð
nan man to þæs hal eagan þæt he ænige hwile mage locigan ongean
þas sunnan þe we hær geseoð*, both of which can be paraphrased as
'Nobody can . . .', and *HomS* 22. 64 *Nis æniges mannes modgeðanc
to ðæs deagol þæt hit him behyded sy* 'Nobody's thoughts can be
hidden from God'. Another example,

MCharm 1. 64   Nu ic bidde ðone waldend,   se ðe ðas woruld gesceop,
             þæt ne sy nan to þæs cwidol wif   ne to þæs cræftig man
             þæt awendan ne mæge   word þus gecwedene,

where the subject of the *þæt* clause is unexpressed (§1512) and the
clause contains an expletive negative (§§2039-46), logically belongs
here: 'I pray that nobody may be able . . .'. A third group of like
general application, with negatives in both clauses but with different
subjects in the two clauses, comprises *Soul i* 97 and the parallel

Soul ii 90   þonne ne bið nænig to þæs lytel lið   on lime geweaxen,
             þæt þu ne scyle for æghwylc   anra onsundran
             ryht agieldan,   ðonne reþe bið
             dryhten æt dome,

which can be rendered 'Every joint will have to be paid for by you'.

§2907. All the examples so far cited have the present subjunctive
expressing a contemplated or contingent result. The same is true of
CP 345. 7 *Ða ungesibsuman sint to manigenne ðæt hie gewisslice
wieten ðæt hie na on to ðæs manegum goodum cræftum ne beoð,
ðæt hie æfre mægen gæsðlice beon . . .* , where the idea is that 'Nobody who is quarrelsome can be spiritual . . .'. But in *BlHom* 117. 25
(§2905), we have a positive statement followed by a preterite subjunctive expressing impossibility in the past, present, and future; see
§2008.

§2908. The remaining eleven examples—all from the prose—have
a result which is a fact rather than a tendency. We have a positive
actual result after a positive statement in *LS* 10. 142. 23, *BlHom*
213. 31, *BlHom* 225. 27, and *Alex* 34. 5 . . . *7 to þæs unheorlic
se wind geweox þ he þara ura getelda monige afylde*; after a negative

statement in *Bede(Ca)* 28. 10; and after a dependent question in *Bede(T)* 114. 29. The other five state a negative actual result after a positive statement: *Bede(T)* 366. 17, *BlHom* 221. 33, *BlHom* 223. 21, *BlHom* 227. 2, and *Alex* 27. 9 *7 him sæde þ he forealdod wære 7 to þæs eald wære þ he ne mihte elcor gewearmigan buton æt fyre.*

§2909. Now we have already seen in §2877 that in the poetry twenty-one out of twenty-five consecutive clauses introduced by *swa . . . þæt(te)* contain an actual result and seventeen out of nineteen introduced by *þæs . . . þæt* contain a contemplated or contingent result, as do the three *þæs . . . þæt* consecutive clauses known to me in the prose (§2878). This leads me to suggest that initially *(to) þæs . . . þæt* may have introduced clauses of contingent result (as opposed to *to þon/þan/þæm/þam . . . þæt* actual result; see §2891) and that its use in clauses of actual result was due to a natural enough confusion. (Imagine trying to teach the 'rule' *to þæs . . . þæt* contingent result, *to þon . . . þæt* actual result, to a class of young Beowulfs.) The suggestion derives some support from the fact that *to þæs . . . þæt* is not only uncommon, but also seems to be early. (This, along with the absence of *to þæs þæt*, may support Mann's theory that the divided formulae came before the grouped ones; see §2816.) Of the twenty-one examples in the prose, seven are in 'Alfredian' texts, only five occur in later texts—none in Ælfric or Wulfstan—and nine occur in *BlHom*, where they can be viewed as another manifestation of the archaizing tendencies of this collection. The distribution of the *BlHom* examples, shown in tabular form, is interesting:

	to þæs . . . þæt		Is *to þon . . . þæt* used of actual result?
	Contingent result	Actual result	
BlHom 10	1	—	Yes
BlHom 11	2	—	Yes
BlHom 18	1	5	Yes

So, in *BlHom* 10 and 11 the suggested distinction obtains; only in *BlHom* 18 do we have exceptions. As we have already seen in §689, the various homilies are not necessarily syntactically homogeneous.

§2910. I cannot explain how such a distinction could have arisen. But if we accept that it existed, we will find evidence that analogy was at work in *BlHom* 18; in the *þæs . . . þæt/swa . . . þæt* variation in *Bo* 75. 4 noted in §2878; in the examples in the poetry with *þæs*

. . . *þæt* and *swa* . . . *þæt(te)* in §2877 which do not conform; and in the eleven prose examples cited in §2908 in which *to þæs* . . . *þæt* introduces an actual result. There are three of these in *Bede*, but MS *B* has *swa* for *to þæs* in *Bede(Ca)* 28. 10 and *to ðam* for *to ðæs* in *Bede(T)* 114. 29 and 366. 17. Three occur in later texts and, as already noted, the other five are in *BlHom* 18. With so few examples, it is impossible to reach a firm conclusion. But the evidence presented is not incompatible with the suggestion that *to þæs* . . . *þæt* initially expressed contingent result and *to* + dat./instr. of dem. + . . . *þæt* actual result and that such a pointless distinction was soon eliminated. There is room for more work here.

   d. For + *dative/instrumental of a demonstrative* + (. . .) *þæt/þe*

§2911. 'Since', says Shearin (1903, p. 42), 'the reason, or motive, of an action considered objectively becomes the end, or purpose, of that action, we find *for* used with the dative to form a phrase of finality.' He illustrates this by two sentences from Ælfric, in whose work 'this passing of *for* of cause into *for* of purpose is found . . . most frequently': *ÆCHom* i. 534. 1 *He leofode on mynstre for neode swiðor þonne for beterunge*, which Thorpe translates 'He lived in the monastery rather from necessity than for bettering' and in which, says Shearin, 'the first phrase is causal, and the second final' and *ÆCHom* ii. 324. 10 *Ne gesceop se Ælmihtiga God men for galnysse, ac þæt hi gestrynon mid gesceade heora team*, where we have purpose expressed first by a *for* phrase and then by a *þæt* clause co-ordinated by *ac*. So it is not surprising to find various writers detecting at least an element of purpose in clauses introduced by prepositional formulae with *for*. Apart from those with forms of *willan* discussed in §§2976–80, the examples seem to be restricted to the prose. I have found none in the poetry, although

Met 17. 28   Forðæm hine anæþelað   ælmihtig god,
               þæt he unæþele   a forð þanan
               wyrð on weorulde,   to wuldre ne cymð,

where the *þæt* clause is one of result, not purpose, illustrates Shearin's point (1903, pp. 69–70) that when the two elements of the formula are separated it is difficult to decide whether we have a formula or whether the *for* + demonstrative element merely means 'therefore'. It must, I think, be a matter of opinion whether this choice presents itself in all such final clauses; consider *ÆCHom* i. 592. 31 (§2913), *ÆCHom* i. 606. 26, and *LS* 10. 164. 58 . . . *þonne far þu to minre swustor and hyre secge þæt ic forþon her on middanearde hire ansyne fleah and hi geseon nolde þæt wyt eft on heofonum beforan godes ansyne unc eft gesawon.* But in *ÆCHom* ii. 534. 30 *Ne sceal se goda bydel forði bodian þæt he her hwilwendlice mede underfo, ac forði bigleofan of ðære bodunge niman, þæt he æt ðære bodunge ne ateorige* the final rather than illative idea does seem uppermost.

§2912. An element of purpose is most frequently detected in clauses introduced by formulae whose last element is *þæt*. Indeed, Kivimaa (p. 157) tells us that 'the functions of the conjunctive phrases with *for* can roughly be outlined so that in the texts that reflect genuine OE usage, the combinations with *þe* express cause and those with *þæt* purpose, except when *þæt* is apparently used for emphasis in causal phrases, as in Ælfric's writings'. The proffered exceptions to this are few. Shearin (1903, p. 71) says that the formulae without *þæt* or *þe* do not introduce clauses of purpose. Fleischhauer (p. 29) proposes as an example *CP* 209. 21 . . . *ðæt we him sume opene scylde, ðe ær ðurhtogen wære, healfunga oðwieten, ðæt hie forðæm scamige, forðæm of ðære scylde ðe he hine ðonne bereccan ne mæge, he ongiete ða he ðonne deð. . . .* Van Dam (p. 42) accepts this. Liggins (1955, pp. 89-90) says that 'there is no other evidence that *forþæm* is used as a conjunction of purpose', but remains puzzled by the subjunctive, which can reasonably be explained as final. Examples with *þe* are also rare. The variation between *forðæmþe* and *for ðæm ðæt* in the manuscript readings of *CP* 203. 24 is noted by Shearin (1903, p. 78), van Dam (p. 47), and Liggins (1955, p. 214). Shearin (ibid.) cites *ÆLS* 4. 330 *and eode mid his wife aweg to his huse for þan þe he ne mihte geseon hu his sunu forburne*, where the translation 'because he was not able . . .' is certainly possible; van Dam (p. 54) *GD* 174. 24 *ac forþon þe þu þas sweotollice minum 7gytum ingute, ic þe bidde nu gyt þæt þu eft gehweorfe to ændebyrdnesse þissere gesægne*; and Liggins (1955, pp. 214-15) *BlHom* 147. 10 *7 ic þe bidde for þinum naman þæt þu gehwyrfe on me ealle eaþmodnesse þinra beboda, forþon þe ic mæg don þine gife*; on this see §2975. Van Dam (pp. 44-5) claims that *for þæm þæt(te)* is 'found to express purpose only' except in *GD(O)* 314. 4 *ga swiðe hraþe 7 sæge Stephane þæm gerefan þæt he cume recene forðam þæt his scip is nu gearu*, where MS *C* has *forþon þæt scip is gearu*—in both of which I take *þæt* as demonstrative; see §107—and in three examples from *ChronE*, viz. *ChronE* 23. 21 (616), where MS *A* has *for ðan ðe*; *ChronE* 29. 10 (654), which is from a Peterborough interpolation; and *ChronE* 81. 18 (887), where MS *A* has *forþæm*. Liggins (1955, pp. 117-19) listed sixteen examples in which *for þæm þæt* expressed cause, six with variants without *þæt* in other manuscripts, and added (1955, pp. 134-7) twenty-three introduced by *for þy/þi þæt*, ten from Ælfric and thirteen from *ChronE*, nine of which are in Continuations 1 and 2. On these, see §§3046-53. It must be said that there is room for difference of opinion on the classification of some of these and of some other examples of the formulae with *þæt*; note van Dam's disagreement (pp. 44-5) with Wülfing (ii, §§446 and 447) over *CP* 76. 7 (where the subjunctive seems decisive for purpose) and *CP* 210. 14. But on the evidence presented by Shearin (1903, pp. 68-73 and 78), van Dam (pp. 40-57), and Liggins (1955, *passim*), Kivimaa's statement of the situation is basically sound for the grouped formulae.

§2913. It is also basically sound for divided *for* formulae, although here too there is sometimes room for difference of interpretation. I discuss the examples in which divided formulae with *þæt* introduce clauses which are or can be taken as causal in §§3067-70. Typical examples of its use in final clauses include *CP* 205. 16 *Forðon he ðus cuæð ðæt he ða lotwrenceas oferwunne 7 oferreahte*, *CP* 423. 20 *Forðæm wæs sanctus Paulus gecostod mid his modes untrumnesse ðæt he ongeate his synna . . .* , Latin *Qui profecto idcirco tentatur ut in bono robustius ex ipsa infirmitatis suae cognitione solidetur*, *GD* 335. 8, *ÆCHom* i. 592. 31 *Forði ic ðreatige ðe to ura goda offrunge, þæt ðis folc ðe ðu bepæhtest forleton ða idelnysse ðinre lare, þæt hi urum godum geoffrian magon ðancwurðe onsægednysse* (but *forði* here may mean 'therefore'; see §§2911, 3013, and 3058), and *ÆCHom* ii. 534. 30 (§2911). More examples may be gleaned from Shearin 1903, pp. 69-73, and van Dam, p. 71. See also Liggins 1955, p. 164. *Mutatis mutandis*, the remarks made in §§2915-16 about mood in grouped formulae with *þæt* apply here.

§2914. Typical examples of grouped formulae with *þæt* introducing a clause with at least an element of purpose include *CP* 151. 12 *Monige sint, swa swa we ær cuædon, ðe mon sceal wærlice licettan, 7 ðeahhwæðre eft cyðan, forðæm ðæt hie ongieten ðæt hie mon tæle . . .* (the Latin has *ut*), *Bo* 133. 19 *Oft eac becymð se anwald þisse worulde to swiðe goodum monnum forðæm þ se anwald þara yfelana weorðe toworpen* (the Latin again has *ut*), and *ÆCHom* ii. 534. 33 *Soðlice swa hwa swa bodað forði þæt he her oððe mede oððe herunge underfo, buton twyn he bescyrað hine sylfne fram ðære ecan mede*. But we must not cast our net too enthusiastically. Despite Shearin (1903, p. 71), who was obviously influenced by Thorpe's translation, *ÆCHom* i. 162. 25 *Se weig seðe læt to heofenan rice is forði nearu and sticol, forði þæt we sceolon mid earfoðnysse geearnian urne eðel* is probably causal—'because we must . . .'. To take both subordinate clauses in *ÆCHom* i. 296. 24 *He gereordode hine æfter his æriste, na forði þæt he syððan eorðlices bigleofan behofode, ac to ði þæt he geswutelode his soðan lichaman* as final (as Shearin (1903, p. 71) does) or as causal (as Thorpe does in his translation) is to blur what I take to be a real distinction. (Liggins (1955, p. 136) independently takes the same view as I do of these last two clauses.) Examples with *wolde*, such as *ÆCHom* ii. 44. 18 . . . *ac he com ofer Criste on culfran hiwe forði þæt he wolde getacnian mid þam þæt Crist wæs on ðære menniscnysse swiðe liðe and unhearmgeorn*, are a special case. As Liggins (1955, p. 208) says: 'Most of the causal conjunctions are regularly associated with *willan* (usually with the past tense). The intention of the clause is almost that of purpose, but the grammatical function remains a causal one.' On such clauses, see §§2976-80.

§2915. The syntax of final clauses introduced by the *for* formulae differs from that of clauses expressing cause only in the fact that the former regularly have the subjunctive whereas in the latter the subjunctive is restricted to those clauses which express a suggested or rejected—as opposed to an accepted—reason; consider *ÆCHom* i. 184. 29 *ac ðæs wundredon men, na forði þæt hit mare wundor wære, ac forði þæt hit wæs ungewunelic* and see §§3174-9. Thus, I am inclined to agree with Liggins (1955, p. 136) that *forði þæt* in *ÆCHom* i. 474. 4 *þa cwæð se Hælend, þæt he nære for his agenum synnum, ne for his maga, blind geboren, ac forði þæt Godes wundor þurh hine geswutelod wære*, is 'a purely final conjunction', although we could, I suppose, call it causal by translating *wære* 'was to be'.

§2916. Liggins (1955, p. 118) accepts the view that *forþæm þæt* final clauses take a subjunctive (equivalent), but goes on to observe (1955, p. 137) that 'the subjunctive mood apparently is never found in a positive causal clause introduced by *forþy þæt*, but both indicative and subjunctive moods regularly occur when it is used as a conjunction of purpose'. I would not put it this way myself; see §§2981-8. For the reasons given there, I would emend *Solil* 66. 7 *þincð* to *þince* as a dittography of *Solil* 66. 6 *þincð* to give three final clauses with the subjunctive *þince*—one introduced by *Solil* 65. 29 *þæt* and two introduced by *forðam þæt*, viz. *Solil* 66. 3 and 66. 7.

e. *Other prepositions + a demonstrative + (. . .) þæt/þe*

§2917. Shearin (1903, pp. 73-7) records the following formulae as introducing clauses with an element of purpose in the prose: *be ðæm*

þ in *Bo* 108. 1 and 132. 4; *on ðæm ðæt* in *CP* 236. 7, where the indicative verb suggests that the *ðæt* clause is explanatory, and *on ðæm*
[MS *H ðæn*] *ðæt* in *CP* 250. 4, where the verb is subjunctive; *wið*
þæs þ—the primary idea here is of motion—in *Bo* 139. 24; *wið þæt*
. . . *þæt*—here too the *þæt* clause can be described as explanatory—
in *Solil* 68. 21; and *wið þæm/þam/þon þe* in *Bede* 126. 19, where the
Latin has *pro nece* and where one of the usual senses of this formula
—'on condition that'—almost fits, *CP* 254. 8 (but MS *H wið ðæm*
ðæt), *HomU* 29. 173. 23, *HomU* 31. 181. 30, *HomU* 45. 290. 8, and
Lch ii. 156. 5 *Wiþ þon þe hær ne weaxe æmettan ægru genim gnid*
smit on þa stowe ne cymð þær næfre ænig feax up. There are no
such examples in the poetry.

§2918. So far, I have (like Benham) found only prepositional formulae with *to* + a demonstrative + (. . .) *þæt* introducing consecutive clauses in the prose. If we take *æfter þon* as temporal in

GuthB 1178   Fys æfter þon
      þæt þu gesecge   sweostor minre,
      þære leofestan,   on longne weg
      to þam fægran gefean forðsið minne,
      on ecne eard . . .

and *forðæm* as 'therefore' in *Met* 17. 28 (§2911), the same is true in
the poetry.

f. Prepositional formulae with a demonstrative + a noun

§2919. There are very few of these. In clauses of purpose, we find
to þam þingum þæt, e.g. *WHom* 6. 155 . . . *þa þa he asende his agen*
bearn of heofonum . . . to þam þingum þæt he mid his agenum feore
mancynn alysde . . . , and *on þa/þæt gerad . . . þæt*, e.g. *LawIAs* 4
and *Or* 52. 32 *7 he Cirus Persea cyning hæfde þriddan dæl his firde*
beæftan him, on þæt gerad, gif ænig wære þe fyr fluge þe on ðæm
gefeohte wæs þonne to þæm folce þe þær beæftan wæs, þæt hine
mon sloge swa raðe swa mon hiora fiend wolde, where once again—
as its position shows; see §1978—*þæt* might introduce a noun
clause. On these two patterns, see Shearin 1903, pp. 67 and 76.

§2920. In clauses of result, Callaway (1933, pp. 12–13) records *on*
þa wisan þæt ' "in such wise that" ' in *BenR* 69. 7 *sy þeah seo leaf*
on ða wisan þæt þær seo foresæde bot fylige and *on þa wisan . . .*
þæt ' "in such wise . . . that" ' in *BenR* 65. 1 . . . *we þa geðafunga*
þæs drynces on þa wisan doð þæt þær næfre seo fyl be fullum ne
weorðe.

g. To *adverb 'too'* + *adjective/adverb* + (. . .) þæt

§2921. The nine examples of this pattern culled from Benham (pp. 220 and 227-8) and from Callaway (1933, p. 10) fall into three groups. First, there are three in which *þæt* introduces a clause which explains the preceding *an/seo tid*, viz. *HomU* 37. 236. 5 *and him ðuhte þonne seo tid to lang þæt he hit gehyrde and þærinne wære*, *HomU* 37. 237. 21 . . . *and hire þuhte seo tid to scort þæt heo ne moste gehyran ymbe Cristes þrowunge secgan*, and

Jul 712   Wæs an tid to læt
               þæt ic yfeldæda   ær gescomede,
               þenden gæst ond lic   geador siþedan
               onsund on earde.

§2922. Second, we have three examples in which the adv. *to* modifies an adjective and one in which it modifies the phrase *swiðe gestrongade*, viz. *Solil* 3. 19 *ac me þincð þath þeah, þæt þu si to unhal þæt ðu ne mage hit æall awritan* (where the *ne* could be called 'expletive'; see §§2039-46), *Bo* 23. 20 . . . *buton þu git to ful sy þæs þe þe læfed is, þ þe forðy wlatige*, *BlHom* 43. 22 *Se mæssepreost se þe bið to læt þæt he þæt deofol of men adrife* . . . , and *Or* 292. 6 . . . *for þon him geþuhte þæt þa þeoda þa hiora wiðerwinnan wæron wæren to swiðe gestrongade þæt hie mon leng ne mehte mid gefeohtum oferswiþan*. To these we can add

GenB 338   þa spræc se ofermoda cyning,   þe ær wæs engla scynost,
               hwitost on heofne   and his hearran leof,
               drihtne dyre,   oð hie to dole wurdon,
               þæt him for galscipe   god sylfa wearð
               mihtig on mode yrre,

if we take *dole* as nominative plural of the adjective. In these examples, the *þæt* clause is clearly consecutive. But I hesitate to erect *to* . . . *þæt* into a divided formula like *swa* . . . *þæt* because *to þæt* does not introduce consecutive clauses (§2925) whereas *swa þæt* frequently does (§2835) and because in MnE we would either use 'so that' for *þæt* or (at least in those examples in which both clauses have the same subject) would replace the *þæt* clause with an infinitive construction; see §1929.

§2923. Third, we have *Solil* 37. 1 *ne herast þu hi na to swiðe þæt ic hyre a ðe ma wilnige?* (misclassified by Benham, p. 220) and *CP* 135. 22 . . . *ðylæs hie gehefegien ðæs monnes mod ðe hi to suiðe lufað, ðæt he for ðære byrðenne gehefegad 7 ofersuiðed, ne sie besenced of ðæm ymestun to ðæm nioðemestum*, where in my opinion *þæt* means 'so that' and is not used in combination with *to suiðe*. This is in contrast to *Or* 292. 6 (§2922), where *swiðe* could be omitted without affecting the grammatical relationship of *to* and *gestrongade*.

h. To *preposition* + þæt?

§2924. Shearin (1903, p. 76) is followed by Mann (p. 36) in claiming that *to þæt* introduces clauses of purpose in *Solil* 26. 21, *Mart 2* 42. 7 . . . *ond het him beran wæter to, þæt he mihte onbergean, Mart 2* 66. 25 . . . *ond him brohtan þæt heafod to, þæt he gesege hulic þæt wære*, and *ÆLS* 34. 110 *þurh mine bene þe com þæs wynsuma bræð to, þæt þu wite heonanforð hwæs blod readaþ on rosan gelicnysse*. But, as I demonstrate by my punctuation, *to* in the last three examples is an adverb or separable prefix or . . . ; see §§1060-80. The same is true in the example from *Solil*, which I do not quote because there are other textual difficulties. But, however we resolve them, we can (I think) be certain that *ic cume* and *to* go together and that Jost's insertion of *þam* between *to* and *þæt*, accepted by both Endter and Carnicelli, is unnecessary.

§2925. Benham's other example (p. 220 but my §2923) of consecutive *to þæt* is not OE: *ChronE* 264. 12 (1137) *Me dide cnotted strenges abuton here hæued ⁊ uurythen to ð it gæde to þe hærnes.* Here *to* could be taken with *uurythen*. But Clark (1970, 55. 24) reports *it* for *to*.

j. Other *prepositions* + þæt

§2926. In final clauses Shearin (1903, pp. 76-7) notes *wiþ þæt* four times in *Lch*, e.g. *Lch* i. 224. 19 *Wiþ þ ðu nane yfele geancymas ðe ne ondræde genim þas ylcan wyrte carduum silfaticum on ærne mergen*, and perhaps—for, as he notes, *embe* may be an adverb independent of *þæt* conj.; cf. §2925—*embe þæt* in *John(WSCp)* 10. 39 and *HomU* 26. 136. 11 *and gyf hwylc man sy þæt ne cunne his pater noster and his credan, beo he swyðe geornlice embe þæt he hit leornige.*

§2927. Shearin (1903, p. 77) describes as 'hardly tenable' the view that the *þæt* clauses in such formulae were originally the direct objects of the prepositions. He explains them as the result of the blending of dem. *þæt* and conj. *þæt* in combinations like ☆*wiþ þæt þæt*; cf. *wiþ þæt . . . þæt* in *Solil* 68. 21 *and hie gelære þæt hy hi wið þæt warien þæt hy hær ne cumen*. This theory accords with the known facts that *wiþ* is found with the accusative—so too is *embe*[149] —and that conj. *þæt* is sometimes unexpressed in noun clauses (§§1981–90). Mann (p. 37) compares ME *for that*. But I doubt whether *for that* is the result of direct reduction of *for* + dat./instr. of dem. (+ (. . .) *þæt*) or of an analogical ☆*for þæt þæt*. According to *OED* (s.v.), *for that* conj. first appears *c.*1200 in Orm as *forr þatt* and 'for that that' in 1620—a little late to be relevant. But *for* conj. appears much earlier. Its occurrence in *GD(C)* 174. 29 is probably an error; MS *O* has *forðon*. But we find it in *ChronF* 130. 24 (995) *far* and in *ChronE* 251. 31 (1123) *for*. It seems more likely that *for that* is conj. *for* + *that* (see *OED*, s.v. *that* conj. II. 7), just as Orm's *ȝiff þatt* (*OED*, s.v. *if* conj. 5) must be *if* (< OE *gif*) + *that*. So *for that* is probably not relevant either.

9. CLAUSES OF PURPOSE INTRODUCED BY *ÞY LÆS (ÞE)*

§2928. There are in OE two ways of expressing negation in purpose clauses—by use of a negative or negatives in a clause introduced by one of the final connectives already discussed in §§2825–927 or by the use of the conjunction *þy læs (þe)*;[150] see §§2961–8. The sequence *þy læs (þe)* . . . adv. *ne* can occur when needed, e.g. (despite Shearin 1903, p. 95) *CP* 247. 14 *Eac sint to manianne ða halan ðæt hie Gode wilnigen to licianne ðe hwile ðe hie mægen, ðylæs hie eft ne mægen, ðonne hie willen*, Latin *Admonendi sunt ne placere Deo si cum possunt noluerint, cum voluerint sero non possint*. Shearin (1903, p. 95) is misleading about two other examples, viz. *Bede* 76. 24 . . . *buton ænigre ældenne is to gebeorenne 7 to gefremmenne, þy læs gif hwylc lytel ælding sy, þætte ne mægge gemeted beon se ðe alesed si* and *Mart 2* 210. 27 *heo wyscte þæt heo nanne æfter hyre ne forlete, þe læs, gif hyra hwylc wære hyre oferstealla, þæt se ne myhte on heofenum beon hyre efngemæcca*, when he claims that in both of them 'after a clause interjected after *ðe læs*, we find the construction resumed with the formula *ðæt . . . ne*'. In both, the negative *ne* is essential to the sense of the *þy læs*/*þe læs* clause. We could say that *þætte*/*þæt* resumed the construction or that it was superfluous. This is in marked contrast to *BlHom* 177. 31 *7 on ðas word ic becom þe*

[149] So also is *to*. Those who accept *to þæt* as a final conjunction—see §2924—can follow Shearin in explaining it in the same way as *wiþ þæt*.

[150] Small (1930, pp. 378–9) suggests that *þon læs þe* 'less than' ceased to be used in comparisons of inequality as *þy læs þe* became specialized in the sense of 'lest'—where it survived—whereas *þon ma þe* 'more than' remained, only to be superseded by *ma þonne*. See also Small 1926, pp. 302–3.

læs þe oðre wisan ænig man leoge, 7 þu ne wene þæt þu Iudea
leasungum gelyfan þurfe, where *þæt* has to be supplied before *þu*
ne wene, since the point is that Nero is *not* to think that he needs to
believe the lies of the Jews.

§2929. *þy læs*—the formula without an appended indeclinable
particle *þe*—'is distinctive of early usage' (Shearin 1903, p. 95). It is
the only form found in the early prose (Shearin (1903, p. 96) blames
the twelfth-century scribe for *ðy læst* in *Solil* 50. 3), in *BlHom* (apart
from *BlHom* 177. 31 (§2928), where *þe* can be taken as a personal
pronoun), and in the poetry, except for

Seasons 178   and we bebeodað   þurh beorn godes
                     þæt manna gehwilc   þe for moldan wunað
                     ær þam æreste   ures dryhtnes
                     efen feowertig daga   fæsten hewe
                     oþ þa nigoþan tid,   and he na bruce
                     flæsces oþþe fyrna,   þæ læs þe he fah wese.[151]

On the other hand, the form with appended *þe* 'is almost a sure
criterion of lateness' (Shearin 1903, pp. 95–6). It is the only form in
the *Catholic Homilies*. Yerkes (1976, p. 198) notes that MS *H* of
Gregory's *Dialogues* has *þe læs þe* four times where Wærferth used
þy læs, viz. *GD(H)* 35. 28, 50. 20, 80. 32, and 128. 14. We find *þe*
læs þe in *GD(H)* 59. 24, but *þe læs* in *GD(H)* 95. 20. These facts,
along with the comparison with Latin *quominus*, support Shearin's
conclusion (1903, p. 95) that the form without an appended *þe* 'is
the logical and the earlier one'. On the variations in the W-S Gospels,
see Shearin 1903, p. 96.

§2930. Variant spellings recorded in the prose for this earlier form
by Shearin (1903, p. 95)—with his number of occurrences in
brackets—are *þy/ðy læs* (166), *þe/ðe læs* (40), *þi/ði læs* (6), *ðe leas*
(1), and *þe les* (1). This list is not complete. I note *þi les* in *Gen(C)*
3. 22. There are probably others. In the poetry we find *þy/ðy/þe/þi*
læs. A few typical examples must suffice here: *Or* 168. 5 *7 eall his*
cynn mon ofslog, þy læs hit monn uferan dogore wræcce, oþþe ænig
oþer dorste eft swelc anginnan, Latin *Cognati omnes supplicio traditi:*
ne quis eum ejusdem familiae umquam aut imitari, aut ulcisci medi-
taretur, Bede 58. 20 *Warnode he him þy læs hie on hwylc hus to him*
ineodan, Latin *Cauerat enim ne in aliquam domum ad se introirent,*

---

[151] This poem was not available to Shearin. But he errs (1909, p. 246) in saying that *þy*
læs | þe in *Max i* 169 is a final conjunction; *þe* comes after the half-line division and intro-
duces an adjective clause. In *PPs* 118. 11, *ðe* is probably a personal pronoun; see § 2930. In
GuthB 1232 and *PPs* 113. 10, *þæt* is better taken as a demonstrative object of the verb.

Mark(WSCp) 14. 2 *Ða cwædon hi næs na on freolsdæge þe læs þæs folces gehlyd wurde*, Latin *dicebant enim non in die festo ne forte tumultus fieret populi*, *Luke(WSCp)* 12. 58 *do þ ðu beo fram him alysed þe læs* [*Li eaðemæg ł ðylæs*] *he þe sylle þam deman*, Latin *da operam liberari ab illo ne forte trahat te apud iudicem*, *Ps(P)* 2. 12 *Onfoð lare þy læs eow God yrre weorðe and þy læs ge wendon of rihtum wege*, Latin *Apprehendite disciplinam nequando irascatur Dominus et pereatis de via justa*,

PPs 118. 133   Gerece ðu me swylce,   þæt ic on rihtne weg
                 æfter þinre spræce   spedum gange,
                 þy læs min ænig unriht   ahwær wealde,

Latin *Gressus meos dirige secundum eloquium tuum; et non dominetur mei omnis injustitia*, *PPs* 68. 14 *Alys me of lame, þe læs ic weorþe lange fæst*, Latin *Eripe me de luto ut non inhæream*, and

PPs 118. 11   Forðon ic on minre heortan   hydde georne,
                 þæt ic þinre spræce   sped gehealde,
                 þy læs ðe ic gefremme   fyrene ænige,

where I take *þe* as a personal pronoun translating *tibi* in Latin *In corde meo abscondi eloquia tua ut non peccem tibi*.

§2931. Shearin (1903, pp. 96–7) records the occurrences in the prose of the formula with an appended *þe* as follows: *þe/ðe læs þe/ðe* (53), *þy/ðy læs þe/ðe* (44), *þi/ði læs þe/ðe* (13), *þe les þe* (1), *þi les þe* (1), *þæ læs þe* (1), *þi læs þæ* (1), *ðe læsse þe* (1), *þe læste* (3), and *læste* (2). I have made a few silent corrections here. On *Solil* 50. 3 *ðy læst*, see §2929. The fact that the form with the demonstrative *þy/ðy* or *þi/ði*—which Shearin (1903, p. 96) understandably calls 'the logical spelling'; see §§2934–5—occurs in eighty per cent of his examples without appended *þe* but in slightly less than fifty per cent (59 of 120) of those with it, is symptomatic of the decreasing importance of the instrumental as the formula evolved through the stages traced by Shearin (1903, p. 98):

1. *ðy (ðe, ði) læs* = Alfredian usage.
2. *ðe (ðy, ði) læs ðe* = Ælfrician usage.
3. *ðe læste* = *HomU* 47. 300. 27 and *BenRW* 63. 10 and 69. 27.
4. *læste* = *BenRW* 23. 24 and 31. 2.
5. 'lest'.

As noted in §2929, the only form with appended *þe* found in the poetry is *þæ læs þe* in *Seasons* 178.

§2932. A few typical examples from the prose of the formula with appended *þe* follow: *Matt(WSCp)* 25. 9 *Ða 7 swarudun þa gleawan 7 cwædun nese þe læs þe we 7 ge nabbon genoh*, Latin *responderunt prudentes dicentes ne forte non sufficiat nobis et uobis*, *ÆCHom* i. 124. 31 *Afyrsiað þone yfelan fram eow ðylæs ðe an wannhal scep ealle ða eowde besmite*, *Gen* 19. 15 *Aris 7 nym ðin wif 7 þine dohtra 7 far ðe heonon, ðy læs þe ðu losige samod mid þissere forscyldigan burhware*, Latin *Surge, tolle uxorem tuam, et duas filias quas habes: ne et tu pariter pereas in scelere ciuitatis*, and *HomU* 47. 300. 26 *ne nænne man man ne læte unbisceopod to lange þe læste him forðsið getimige*.

§2933. The verb in clauses introduced by *þy læs (þe)* is overwhelmingly a verb of full meaning in the subjunctive. 'Modal' verbs are rare; see §2972. The few aberrant indicatives are discussed in §2984.

§2934. *OED* (s.v. *lest* conj.) says 'OE. phrase *þy læs þe*, lit. "whereby less" = L. *quominus (þy* instrumental of the dem. and rel. pron. + *læs* "less" a. + *þe* relative particle)'. Shearin (1903, p. 94) says that in *ðy læs* '*læs* contains the negative idea, and *ðy* is used relatively with conjunctional force, the combination being exactly parallel to *quo minus* of the Latin'. There is a nice ambiguity here. Are we meant to infer that *þy læs*—which, as we have seen, is the earliest form—is a calque on *quominus*? The fact that all the examples of it cited by Shearin (1903, p. 138) occur in Latin-based texts may appear to lend support to the notion. Its distribution in the poetry —see Shearin 1909, p. 246, and Mitchell 1959, Appendix 'Purpose 3' —provides little obvious evidence against the suggestion, for *þy læs* occurs at the head of a clause only in poems based directly or indirectly on Latin sources except in

Beo 1917   sælde to sande   sidfæþme scip
               oncerbendum fæst,   þy læs hym yþa ðrym
               wudu wynsuman   forwrecan meahte.

But here, as Mann (p. 11) agrees, the two elements may still have their original functions 'by that/which . . . less'; cf. *Beo* 487 *ahte ic holdra þy læs, ‖ deorre duguðe, þe þa deað fornam*. But even if *þy læs* in *Beo* 1917 above does mean 'lest', it could, as it were, be a solitary Anglo-Saxon swallow overwhelmed by intruding cuckoos—*þy læs* based on Latin *quominus*. However, Mann (pp. 10–11 and 37–9) seems to accept a purely native origin from non-conjunctional *þy læs*—seen, for example, in *Or* 156. 22 . . . *buton þær þy læs ofslagen wære*, *ÆCHom* ii. 538. 6 *Ure Drihten foresæde þa toweardan frecednyssa þises losigendlican middaneardes, þæt hi ðy læs manna mod gedrefon, gif hi beoð cuðe on ær*, and *Beo* 487 above—to conjunctional *þy læs* in which *þy*—originally a demonstrative in a relative function 'by which', vital to the sense—eventually lost that function and dropped out to give MnE 'lest'. Such an origin has already been proposed for other conjunctions; see Mitchell, at press (*c*). Can we adjudicate?

§2935. The very marked preponderance of 'the logical spelling' *þy/ þi læs* in the formulae without appended *þe* noted by Shearin (1903, p. 95)—172 examples out of 214, which is eighty per cent—supports the instrumental origin of the first element, but is not evidence for imitation of Latin *quominus*. Nor is the equation '*þy læs* = *quominus*'; it may merely show that the Anglo-Saxons and the Romans sometimes thought along similar lines. But were they the same lines? Were they directed to the same end? Our immediate answer must be 'No', for the syntactical functions of *þy læs* and *quominus* do not overlap in any obvious way. *Ne* and *quominus* are both used after verbs of preventing, refusing, and the like, in classical Latin (GL, §§547-9); both 'are originally final, but the final sense is often effaced, especially in *quominus*' (GL, §547). This connection perhaps provides the faint possibility of inverted uses of *þy læs* for *quominus* in that Latin verbs of fearing take *ne* when the negative is wished and the positive feared (GL, §550) and OE verbs of fearing occasionally take *þy læs*, e.g. *Bede* 294. 25 . . . *þa ongon þæs cynelecan modes monn him ondrædan, þonne he to deaðe cumende wære 7 mid micle sare wæced þy læs he owiht unwyrþes oðþe ungerisnes dyde mid his muþe, oðþe mid oðerra lima styrenesse*. But I have found no examples of such inverted uses; the original of *Bede* 294. 25 has *ne*: Latin *Qui . . . timere coepit homo animi regalis ne ad mortem ueniens tanto adfectus dolore aliquid indignum suae personae uel ore proferret uel aliorum motu gereret membrorum*. *Quominus* is in fact uncommon in later Latin. On the evidence of Jones's *Concordance* it does not appear in Bede's *Historia*. Some of the standard dictionaries of medieval and ecclesiastical Latin make no mention of the word. None of them cites *quominus* as introducing clauses of purpose. Nor does Nunn (§§157-62). In view of this, it is hard to argue that *þy læs* gradually became an accepted calque on *quominus*; theoretically, there are few, if any, situations in which even the dreamiest scribe would be tempted to gloss the one by the other.

§2936. We must now of course ask whether any scribe actually did so—a vital question which seems never to have been asked. In §2930 we have seen *þy læs* translating *et non* (*PPs* 118. 133), *nequando*

(Ps(P) 2. 12), *ne (Or* 168. 5 and *Bede* 58. 20), *ne forte (Mark(WSCp)* 14. 2 and *Luke(WSCp)* 12. 58), and *ut non*, an ecclesiastical equivalent for *ne* in final clauses *(PPs* 68. 14 and 118. 11). To these can be added *quatenus*, which is used as a final conjunction in post-classical texts (Lewis and Short, s.v. *quatenus* F), e.g. *CP* 237. 21 and *CP* 363. 8 *Eac sint to manianne ða ðe on ðam beoð abisgode ðæt hie sibbe tiligað, ðæt hie ærest tilgen to kyðanne ðæm ungesceadwisum modum hu sio lufu beon scyle ðære inweardlican sibbe, ðylæs him æfter firste sio uterre sib derige*, Latin *Admonendi itaque sunt qui faciendae pacis studiis occupantur, ut pravorum mentibus prius amorem debeant internae pacis infundere, quatenus eis postmodum valeat exterior pax prodesse*. But *quominus* . . . ? As far as I can discover, there are no examples concealed in the *þy læs* clauses listed by Shearin (1903, pp. 138-9). I have found none elsewhere. So I am left to conclude either that *þy læs* was a gradual native development and the parallelism between *quominus* and *þy læs* is a matter of chance or—as would seem to me more likely—that its regular use in translated texts was due to an influential and momentarily inspired scholar and teacher who, seeking a gloss for Latin *ne* 'lest' and obviously unable to use OE *ne*, seized on the parallel between *þy læs*, which was already used at least adverbially (§2934), and *quominus* as the answer to his problem. In which event, *þy læs* is after all, to some extent at least, a Latin calque.

10. *WEALD*

§2937. *Weald þeah* occasionally appears in the prose as an adverb 'perhaps, may be'. Examples include *ÆCHom* ii. 340. 8 *Nyte ge ða micclan deopnysse Godes gerynu; weald þeah him beo alyfed gyt behreowsung* and *ÆCHom* ii. 466. 9 *þis godspel ðincð dysegum mannum sellic, ac we hit secgað swaðeah; weald ðeah hit sumum men licige*, in both of which I discard Thorpe's punctuation for that given in BT, s.v. *weald* adv. conj. See §3148.

§2938. Occasionally too we find *weald* followed by an indefinite, e.g. *ÆCHom* i. 6. 18 *Bið nu wislicor þæt gehwa ðis wite and cunne his geleafan, weald hwa ða micclan yrmðe gebidan sceole*, *WPol* 212. 6 *Bisceopum gebyreð þæt symle mid heom faran and mid heom wunian wel geþungene witan, huru sacerdhades, þæt hi wið rædan magan for Gode and for worulde and þæt heora gewitan beon on æghwylcne timan, weald hwæt heom tide*, and *WHom* 2. 62 *And ðy man sceal wacigean 7 warnian symle þæt man geara weorðe huru to ðam dome, weald hwænne he us to cyme* . . . , where *weald hwa*, *weald hwæt*, and *weald hwænne*, can be translated respectively 'in case/lest anyone, anything, any time'. On the analogy of these examples, BT (loc. cit.) suggests the insertion of *hwæt* after *weald* in *ÆCHom* i. 316. 23 *Namon ða to ræde, þæt him wærlicor wære, þæt hi sumne dæl heora landes wurðes æthæfdon, weald him getimode*, which would give 'in case/lest anything'.

§2939. Only in

And 1352   We ðe magon eaðe,   eorla leofost,
               æt þam secgplegan   selre gelæran
               ær ðu gegninga   guðe fremme,
               wiges woman,   weald hu ðe sæle
               æt þam gegnslege

do we find anything similar in the poetry. BT, GK, and ASPR, agree in translating *weald* as an imperative 'Decide/determine thou how it shall happen to thee'. But BTS and Brooks translate *weald hu* 'whatever', comparing the prose phrase *loca hu*, on which see §§3363-4. This example differs from all the others given in BT(S)—first in that, whereas *hwa, hwæt,* and *hwænne,* are used as indefinites, *hu* does not seem to be, and second in that the translation 'in case/lest in any way' would not make any sense in the context. A more accurate translation for *weald hu* would be 'however' and 'whoever, whatever, whenever', would be satisfactory translations for the examples cited in the previous section. This use of '-ever' provides a common element for all the examples known to me.

11. OTHER METHODS OF EXPRESSING PURPOSE AND RESULT

a. The infinitives expressing purpose

§2940. As pointed out in §§954 and 1535, the line of demarcation between the various uses of the infinitive is often a tenuous one. Thus, in *ÆHom* 6. 22 *nu for feawum dagum sohton þa Iudeiscan þe to stænenne* it is not clear whether *þe* is governed by *sohton* or by *to stænenne,* for its position allows either interpretation; see §3907 and Pope's penetrating note on the line. If we adopt the first view, we can say that the infinitive is one of specification or purpose; if we adopt the second, it can be the object of *sohton* or an infinitive of purpose. Again, I have hesitated in §949 to follow Callaway (1913, pp. 105-6) in classifying as final such examples as *LS* 23. 241 *ac gewuna he is to getacnigenne of þære sawla dædum* and *ÆCHom* i. 2. 24 . . . *buton þam bocum . . . þa synd to hæbbenne*; see Shearin

1903, p. 26. On similar problems of classification and terminology, see §§1552–4 and Callaway 1913, pp. 133 and 148 nn. 6 and 9. But despite all this, there is no doubt that the infinitive does express purpose in OE prose and poetry. Many of the dissertations on individual texts refer to this topic. But the major discussions are those by Shearin (1903, pp. 8–31, where there is some valuable comparative material, and 1909, pp. 235–9) and Callaway (1913, pp. 132–48).

§2941. Here, as in §§2817–24, we must ask the question 'whose purpose?' by distinguishing those examples in which the implied (or logical) subject of the infinitive is the same as that of the finite verb from those in which it is different. Callaway neglects this point. Visser (i, §623, and ii, §947) gives it desultory treatment. Shearin discusses it sensibly, although his lists (1903, pp. 22–6) contain many examples of misclassification. But we also have to distinguish the form of the infinitive. In practice, this boils down to asking whether we have the uninflected infinitive *beran* and the like or the inflected infinitive *to beranne/berenne*; here Callaway's discussion (1913, pp. 146–7) is the more valuable. Like Shearin (1903, p. 29) I have found no periphrastic perfect infinitives which express purpose and, like Callaway (1913, p. 147), no passive infinitives of purpose.

§2942. Let us take the form of the infinitive first. It is somewhat surprising that Visser could both cite Callaway as an authority (ii. 1020) and yet say that 'there are a few examples in Old English with a bare infinitive [of purpose]' (ii, §946), for Callaway (1913, p. 132) gives the following figures for final infinitives:

	Prose	Poetry
Uninflected infinitive	323	119
Inflected infinitive	526	15
Total	849	134

Callaway (1913, p. 146) glosses these figures: in the poetry the predominant final infinitive is the uninflected form after verbs of motion; in the prose the uninflected form can occur after verbs of motion and of giving, but the inflected infinitive is more common; many verbs have only the inflected infinitive; in early and late prose the inflected infinitive is the norm, except in the *Gospels* and the *Leechdoms*; 'the Latin original has much to do with whether or not the infinitive is inflected in Anglo-Saxon prose'; and finally, the few instances of the inflected infinitive in the poetry may also be the result of Latin influence. Shearin's observation (1903, p. 12) that most of the uninflected forms occur in earlier writings remains to be tested.

§2943. Here, as elsewhere, the question arises whether the infinitive —in both its forms—is always active or whether it can sometimes be passive. As I have pointed out in §923, I believe this question to be terminological: the infinitive is always active, but can often be conveniently translated as passive. In this, I agree with Shearin (1903, pp. 16 and 28-9) and Callaway (1913, pp. 132-3), both of whom have some valuable information to offer on the OE renderings of the various Latin infinitives.

§2944. The infinitive usually follows its verb—examples will readily be found in the sections which follow—but there are occasional exceptions, e.g. *Bede* 12. 7 *7 Mellitum 7 Iustum þa biscopas to bodigenne hider gecyrdon*, *Bede* 22. 18 *Ðæt Ceadwala Westseaxna cyning to gefulliane com to Rome*, *Lch* ii. 192. 16 . . . *þonne he slapan gan wille*, *HomU* 44. 288. 31 *me þyrste and ge me drincan ne sealdon*, and *GenA* 2264 *Heo þa fleon gewat || þrea and þeowdom*.

§2945. Like Shearin (1903, p. 29), I have noted no examples of the type 'He paid him not to do it'. A negated infinitive phrase of purpose either follows an already negated verb, e.g. *ÆCHom* i. 320. 5 *Se Hælend is ealles mancynnes dema, ac he ne com na to demenne mancynn, swa swa he sylf cwæð, ac to gehælenne*, or a positive infinitive phrase of purpose with which it is contrasted, e.g. *ÆCHom* ii. 488. 29 *We sind asende to gecigenne mancynn fram deaðe to life, na to scufenne fram life to deaðe*. *To* is usually repeated with the second and succeeding infinitives in co-ordinate groups, e.g. *Bede* 330. 18 . . . *to gebiddenne ge ælmessan to sellenne ge Gode asægdnesse to beranne þæs halgan laces*, *LawAfEl* 36 *Gif mon næbbe buton anfeald hrægl hine mid to wreonne 7 to werianne* . . . , and the two examples from *ÆCHom* just quoted. Exceptions in which we have an inflected infinitive followed by one uninflected infinitive or more can generally be explained as the result of separation, e.g. *Bede* 250. 18 *þa sende he Gearaman þone biscop, se wæs Trumheres æfterfylgend, in þa mægðe Eastseaxna to gereccenne þone gedwolan, 7 heo to soðfæstnesse geleafan eft gecegan*, or of mechanical glossing, e.g. *Luke(WSCp)* 1. 72 *mildheortnesse to wyrcænne mid urum fæderum 7 gemunan his halegan cyþnesse*, Latin *ad faciendam misericordiam cum patribus nostris et memorari testamenti sui sancti*. See further §924 and the references given there; Shearin 1903, pp. 30-1; and Callaway 1913, pp. 147-8.

§2946. For the expression of purpose, an uninflected or inflected infinitive can alternate with a phrase, e.g. *ÆCHom* ii. 340. 20 *Ne lufode he woruldlice æhta for his neode ana ac to dælenne eallum wædliendum*, or with a clause, e.g. *LS* 8. 48 *and ic com þæt ic me þe ætywde þurh þysne heort and for hine þe gehuntian and gefon* and *John(WSCp)* 12. 47 *Ne com ic middaneard to demanne ac þ ic gehæle middaneard.*

§2947. Writing of 'the prepositional [= inflected] infinitive phrase of purpose', Shearin (1903, pp. 21-6) observes that 'this logical abbreviation of the final clause by means of the phrase', as he calls it, 'is possible whenever the subject of this clause is co-incident in meaning with some element within the main clause; which element, in event of the abbreviation of the final clause, would become the logical subject of the infinitive'. (Elsewhere (1903, p. 101), he says that 'the term "logical subject" means . . . the agent of the action'.) There are (he goes on) six possible relationships between the principal clause and the 'doer', i.e. the performer of the action of the infinitive. First, the doer may be the subject of the main verb, which may be active, e.g. *Bede* 62. 14 *þa ongunnon monige dæghwamlice efstan 7 scyndan to gehyranne Godes word* and *ÆCHom* ii. 424. 18 *Decius ða gewende to oðrum burgum to tintregienne ða cristenan*, or passive, e.g. *Bede* 272. 24 . . . *þonon he wæs sended Ongolþeode Godes word to bodienne 7 to læranne* and *ÆCHom* i. 194. 28 . . . *þa se engel wearð asend fram Gode to ðam mædene to cyðenne Godes acennednysse þurh hi.* Second, the doer may be the object of the main verb, e.g. *Bede* 142. 22 *þa sende he hine godcunde lare to læranne in Eastengle* and *ÆCHom* i. 402. 29 *Se asende his sunu Titum to oferwinnenne ða earman Iudeiscan.* Third, the doer may appear in the dative in the principal clause, e.g. *Or* 296. 1 *7 for þæm þe hie geonge wæron, he hie betahte his twæm ealdormonnum to bewitanne* and *ÆCHom* ii. 190. 13 *þa forgeaf se Ælmihtiga God him and his ofspringe þone eard to bugienne þe is gehaten Iudealand.* Fourth, the doer may appear in the genitive in the principal clause, e.g. *Bo* 40. 15 *þ bið þonne cyninges andweorc 7 his tol mid to ricsianne* and *Luke(WSCp)* 20. 20 . . . *7 þ hig hine gesealdon þam ealdron to dome 7 to þæs deman anwalde to fordemanne.* Fifth, the doer may be governed by a preposition in the principal clause, e.g. *GD(C)* 104. 30 *7 þa þa þæt glæsfæt . . . to þam arwurþan fæder wæs gebroht . . . to bletsigenne.* . . . Shearin's sixth group contains main clauses with some element which is 'felt vaguely' as the doer and infinitives which are joined to nouns, e.g. *Bede* 232. 3 *7 þeah cwæð he, þætte þæt wære heora gewuna, from þæm he þæt gemet geleornade regollices þeodscipes, þætte þa onfongnan neowan stowe mynster to timbrenne oðþe cirican—þætte þa sceolde ærest mid gebedum 7 mid fæstenum Drihtne gehalgian*; to adjectives, e.g. *Bede* 410. 3 *Ða gecas him geferan, ða þe æghwæðer ge on hiora dædum ge on gelærednesse frome 7 scearpe wæron Godes word to bodienne 7 to lærenne*; or to adverbs, e.g. *ÆCHom* ii. 78. 14 . . . *nu ge habbað hwonlice to swincenne*. Shearin himself uses the verb 'fades' of the purpose element in these examples. Here we have a terminological rather than a syntactical problem.

§2948. Space does not permit a full consideration of the preferences of individual verbs for the uninflected and/or inflected infinitive. That this can be a matter of importance has been shown by my discussions of *Bede(T)* 344. 1 *Hwæðre þu meaht singan* in *NM* 66 (1965), 107-11, and *NM* 70 (1969), 369-80. Shearin (1903, pp. 9-31) offers examples and comments, but Callaway's classification (1913, pp. 132-48) is more valuable. First he treats active verb-forms. Here he distinguishes verbs which take only the uninflected final infinitive (1913, pp. 133-5)—they include *gengan, gewitan, gesittan, licgan, (a)biddan*; verbs which take either an uninflected or an inflected final infinitive (1913, pp. 135-43)—these include especially certain verbs of motion, e.g. *arisan, (a)sendan*, and *wendan*, and of offering and giving, e.g. *beodan, giefan*, and especially *sellan* (on which see also Shearin 1903, pp. 13-15 and 26-8, and Callaway 1913, p. 147); and verbs which take only the inflected final infinitive (1913, pp. 143-5)—'a very large number of verbs of such varied significations that it seems unwise to attempt to classify them', but among which are numbered *astigan, bindan, bringan, niman*, and *wunian*. For details of the distribution of the infinitives in the poetry, see Shearin 1909, pp. 235-9.

§2949. The infinitive of purpose is naturally less frequent after a passive verb. But when it does occur, the inflected form is more common. Typical examples are *BlHom* 157. 34 *7 nu syndon gesette þa apostolas inhlet æ hie bodian hire* and *ÆCHom* ii. 488. 29 *We sind asende to gecigenne mancynn fram deaðe to life*. See further Callaway 1913, pp. 145-6.

§2950. Callaway (1913, p. 148 n. 7) notes that in *LS* 14. 218 and *Gen* 22. 4 *þa on ðone ðriddan dæg, þa hi ða dune gesawon, ðær ðær hi to sceoldon to ofsleane Isaac* . . . , the final infinitive depends on an infinitive which has to be supplied after the 'modal' auxiliary.

§2951. Callaway (1913, pp. 148 n. 8 and 252–6) discusses the origin of the various Germanic usages of the infinitive of purpose. He attributes some to Latin and, for Gothic, to Greek influence, but regards others as native idioms. One of the latter is the uninflected infinitive of purpose after verbs of motion. Mann (*Archiv*, 187 (1950), 24) sees this as the origin of the final infinitive of modern speech.

b. The inflected infinitive expressing result

§2952. Callaway (1913, pp. 162–8) notes that the inflected infinitive may denote tendency or result after adjectives and verbs. With adjectives, it is sometimes difficult to decide whether the infinitive denotes purpose or specification; consider *BlHom* 223. 21 *To þæs mihtig he þonne wæs ælce untrumnesse to hælenne* . . . , *ÆLS* 25. 94 *Ic eom eald to hiwigenne*, *ÆCHom* i. 340. 24 . . . *þæt hi ne beoð ealles swa carfulle to beganne ða earfoðlican drohtnunge*, and *Dan* 283 *Metod alwihta, hwæt! þu eart mihtum swið* ‖ *niðas to nergenne*. With verbs, the difficulty is that of deciding whether the infinitive is the object of the finite verb or whether it expresses purpose or result; consider *CP* 263. 17 *ac mid ðam fostre ðære Godes lufan hie sculon up arisan* 7 *weaxan a ma* 7 *ma to lufigeanne ða godcundan weorc*, *BlHom* 165. 4 *forþon þe nænig mennisc tunge ne geneah þæs acendan engles godcund mægen to gesecgenne*, *ÆCHom* ii. 84. 15 *He gearcað urne godan willan to fultumigenne* (see §851 fn. 299), and *Phoen* 274 *Ðonne afysed bið* ‖ *agenne eard eft to secan*.

c. The present participle expressing purpose

§2953. Shearin found no examples of the present participle expressing purpose in the poetry (1909, p. 239) but recorded eleven examples in the prose (1903, pp. 32–3), with the observation that 'this is an extension of the common appositive participle of circumstance, i.e. manner or concomitant action, after verbs of motion, rarely after verbs of rest'; on this, see §§967–9. There is room for difference of opinion in the classification of individual examples, but these two are typical: *CP* 173. 1 . . . *gif he ðonne færð secende hwæt he sellan scyle* . . . and *ÆCHom* ii. 358. 5 . . . *þa ferde he to ðam wæle his lic secende*.

§2954. As has been pointed out in §§967-9, the spheres of the present participle and the infinitive often overlap. That both can express purpose is clear from a comparison of the examples in §2953 with *ÆCHom* ii. 428. 17 *He eode into Godes temple hine to gebiddenne. John(Li)* 1. 31 *cuom ic in uætre fulguande* ɫ *to fulguanne*, Latin *ueni ego in aqua baptizans*, is interesting in this respect. But both can also express manner; compare *LS* 14. 328 *And þa ure drihten him self com of heofonum to eorþan astigan* with *ÆCHom* ii. 14. 6 . . . *þæt se heahengel Gabrihel him com to fleogende* (see Shearin 1903, p. 13) and *Beo* 702 *Com on wanre niht* ‖ *scriðan sceadugenga* with

Beo 1972   . . . þæt ðær on worðig   wigendra hleo,
              lindgestealla   lifigende cwom,
              heaðolaces hal   to hofe gongan.

d. Prepositional phrases expressing purpose

§2955. Shearin (1903, pp. 33-54, and 1909, pp. 239-41) detects prepositional phrases which express purpose introduced by six different prepositions. The table which follows records them and the number of examples noted by Shearin.

Phrases introduced by	Prose	Poetry
To	358	90
For	70	
On	68	9
In	7	3
Ymbe	6	
Æfter	4	
Total number of examples	513	102

Typical examples include: (*to*) *ChronE* 13. 15 (449) *Hy ða sona sendon hider mare weored þam oðrum to fultume, ÆCHom* i. 28. 26 *We wyllað to trymminge eowres geleafan eow gereccan þæs Hælendes acennednysse*, and *Beo* 1829 *ic ðe þusenda þegna bringe,* ‖ *hæleþa to helpe*; (*for*) *Bede* 168. 28 *ac for leornunge haligra gewreota he wæs micelre tide in Ibernia Scotta ealonde wuniende, ÆCHom* i. 414. 25 *Be ðam is swutol þæt seo gesihð him wearð æteowod for oðra manna beterunge, na for his agenre*, and *ÆCHom* i. 328. 28 *Ne cepð nan man deorwyrðra reafa buton for ydelum gylpe, soðlice þæt he sy toforan oðrum mannum þurh his glencge geteald*, where the *for* phrase is parallel to, or explained by, the *þæt* clause; (*on*) *Or* 68. 13

Tarcuinius þa . . . aspon Tuscea cyning him on fultum, ÆCHom i.
510. 16 . . . *þæt hi beon on fultume his gecorenum*, and

El 1050   . . . siððan Elene heht   Eusebium
                 on rædgeþeaht,   Rome bisceop,
                 gefetian on fultum,   forðsnoterne,
                 hæleða gerædum   to þære halgan byrig;

(*in*) *Bede* 348. 22 *Ond seo tunge þe swa monig halwende word in
þæs scyppendes lof gesette . . .* and *GuthA* 136 *siþ þam frofre gæst* ||
in Guðlaces geoce gewunade; (*ymbe*) *ÆCHom* ii. 380. 24 *Herodes
cyning wolde, æfter Cristes upstige to heofenum, geswencan sume of
ðære gelaðunge, and sende werod ymbe þæt*; and (*æfter*) *Or* 154. 22
*þa sendon Tarentine ægwern æfter fultume þær hie him æniges
wendon.* For fuller discussions, more examples, and details of the
distribution of the various prepositions, see Shearin (loc. cit.).

e. Final and consecutive paratactic constructions

§2956. We have already seen in §§1690 and 1735 that purpose
may be expressed by means of sentences in asyndetic and syndetic
parataxis. But a few more examples will not be out of place. Clauses
with *willan* often express purpose, e.g. *John(WSCp)* 4. 7 *þa com þær
an wif of Samaria wolde wæter feccan*, where *Ru* and *Li* have an inflected infinitive and the Latin *haurire* (on this construction see
§1690), and *Matt(WSCp)* 25. 10 *Witodlice þa hig ferdun 7 woldon
bycgean þa com se brydguma*, where *Li* has *to bycganne, Ru bycgan*,
and the Latin *emere*. On this construction, see further Shearin (1903,
pp. 91-2 and 1909, p. 245) and Andrew (*SS*, pp. 87-8, and *Postscript*, p. 56).

§2957. Examples which will surprise some of today's grammatical
purists include *BlHom* 23. 13 . . . *þa he bæd þæt he moste faran 7
his fæder bebyrgean* '. . . that he might be allowed to go and [might
be allowed to] bury his father', *ÆCHom* i. 30. 28 *Hwæt ða hyrdas
þa him betweonan spræcon 'Uton faran to Bethleem, and geseon þæt
word þe us God æteowde'* 'Let us go and [let us] see . . .', and *And*
216 *Ðu scealt þa fore geferan ond þin feorh beran* || *in gramra gripe*.
These can be contrasted with

GuthB 1178   Fys æfter þon
                 þæt þu gesecge   sweostor minre,
                 þære leofestan,   on longne weg
                 to þam fægran gefean   forðsið minne,
                 on ecne eard,   ond hyre eac gecyð
                 wordum minum,   þæt ic me warnade

hyre onsyne   ealle þrage
in woruldlife,

where, remarks Behre (p. 105), 'the first part of the passage is almost
equivalent to a co-ordinate sentence of this type: "Hasten . . . and
tell . . .". This interpretation is borne out by the following imperative
gecyð. . . .' It is borne out in another way by the existence of examples in which OE þæt clauses of purpose represent Latin paratactic sentences, either with et (e.g. PPs 82. 4 and 118. 15) or without it
(e.g. PPs 139. 10).

§2958. Other examples in which a paratactic clause expresses purpose include Exod 33. 2 *7 ic sende minne engel beforan þe 7 adrife
ut Chananeum*, Latin *Et mittam praecursorem tui angelum et eiiciam
Chananaeum*, and Matt(WSCp) 18. 12 . . . *7 gæð 7 secþ þ an þe forwearð*, Latin *et uadit quaerere eam quae errauit*, where Li has *7
geongeð to soecenne ða ilca ðiu geduolade*. See further Shearin 1903,
pp. 12-13.

§2959. The result of an action may be stated in a following simple
sentence or clause, either without a co-ordinating adverb or conjunction, e.g. ÆCHom i. 380. 18 *Broðer, þu wære Gode gecoren ær ic,
ðe gedafnað þæt þu ðisne deofles ðen mid ðinum benum afylle* and
(despite Andrew, Postscript, pp. 74-5)

Beo 1567   bil eal ðurhwod
         fægne flæschoman;   heo on flet gecrong,
         sweord wæs swatig,   secg weorce gefeh,

or with one, e.g. ChronA 70. 5 (870) *Her rad se here ofer Mierce
innan East Engle 7 wintersetl namon æt þeodforda*, ChronA 126. 4
(993) . . . *7 him þær com togeanes Byrhtnoð ealdorman mid his
fyrde 7 him wið gefeaht 7 hy þone ealdorman þær ofslogon 7 wæl-
stowe geweald ahtan*,

Beo 523   Beot eal wið þe
         sunu Beanstanes   soðe gelæste.
         Ðonne wene ic to þe   wyrsan geþingea . . . ,

and

GenA 1010   Hwæt, befealdest þu   folmum þinum
             wraðum on wælbedd   wærfæstne rinc,
             broðor þinne,   and his blod to me
             cleopað and cigeð.

f. Swa ... [þæt]

§2960. Shearin (1909, p. 242) tells us that 'in Old English the adverbial conjunction of purpose is never omitted, as sometimes is the case in the cognate branches'. I have found no examples. But Benham, who specifically excludes from his consideration 'paratactic constructions of result' (p. 204), observes on p. 206 that 'to the rule that in OE prose the result clause is always bound to the main clause by a conjunction, there are but two exceptions'. These are *Bede* 144. 21 *Is ðæt sægd, ðæt in ða tid swa micel sib wære in Breotone æghwyder ymb, swa Eadwines rice wære, þeah þe an wiif wolde mid hire nicendum cilde, heo meahte gegan buton ælcere sceðenisse from sæ to sæ ofer eall þis ealond*, where the Latin has *Tanta autem eo tempore pax ... ut ...*, and *ÆCHom* i. 142. 12 *þa turtlan getacniað clænnysse: hi sind swa geworhte, gif hyra oðer oðerne forlyst, þonne ne secð seo cucu næfre hire oðerne gemacan.* To these might be added *Ch* 1536 *W* 50. 22 *7 ic hopyge to him swa godan 7 swa mildheortan he hit nylle sylf don . . .* , where Whitelock supplies [þ] before *he*. The Latin certainly supports the insertion of *ðæt* in *Bede* 144. 21, and similar insertions are justifiable in the other two examples. The alternative is to explain the absence of *þæt* as a genuine paratactic construction, the ancestor of MnE 'He's so clever, there's nothing he doesn't know'. In these examples, unlike those in §2859, *swa* can only be an adverb. It cannot be a conjunction. This is also true of such sentences in the poetry as *GenB* 252, *GenB* 673, and

GenB 655   Adam, frea min,   þis ofet is swa swete,
                 bliðe on breostum,   and þes boda sciene,
                 godes engel god,   ic on his gearwan geseo
                 þæt he is ærendsecg   uncres hearran,
                 hefoncyninges.

Here at least I am reluctant to assume scribal omission of *þæt*.

12. NEGATION

§2961. Here we are concerned with the negation of final and consecutive clauses. On negated infinitives of purpose see §2945. Where necessary, phrases of purpose can be negated by *na*, e.g. *ÆCHom* i. 414. 26 *... for oðra manna beterunge, na for his agenre.*

§2962. A clause of purpose can be negated in two ways. First, we have clauses introduced by *þy læs (þe)*. Such clauses, which are discussed in §§2928–36, can be negated when the sense demands; see §2928. Second, we have clauses introduced by the conjunctions discussed in §§2825-927 and negated by adv. *ne*, either alone or accompanied by one or more negative elements—adverbs, adjectives, or pronouns. Typical examples include (with *ne* immediately before the verb) *Bo* 40. 25 *Forþy ic wilnode andweorces þone anwald mid to reccenne, þ mine cræftas 7 anweald ne wurden forgitene 7 forholene, ÆCHom* i. 88. 2 *He ða his cempan to ðam slege genamode, and het heora ælcum fiftig scyllinga to sceatte syllan, þæt hi heora handa fram ðam blodes gyte ne wiðbrudon,* and

And 1613   Sende þa his bene   fore bearn godes,
                bæd haligne   helpe gefremman
                gumena geogoðe,   þe on geofene ær
                þurh flodes fæðm   feorh gesealdon,
                ðæt þa gastas,   gode orfeorme,
                in wita forwyrd,   wuldre bescyrede,
                in feonda geweald   gefered ne wurdan,

and (with *ne* and other negative elements) *CP* 75. 19 *Se reccere sceal bion simle clæne on his geðohte ðætte nan unclænnes hine ne besmite . . .* and *ÆLS* 1. 201 *. . . and hyre gedafnað þæt heo swa swa hlæfdige geornlice foresceawige hwæt heo gehwylcum lime bebeode to donne . . . þæt þær nan þing unþæslice ne gelympe on nanes limes þenunge.* From Shearin's examples from the prose (1903, pp. 93-4) and the poetry (1909, pp. 245-6, where he is far from accurate; see Mitchell 1959, pp. 372-4), and from my own collections, it would seem that negated final clauses of this type require *ne* immediately before the verb; cf. §§1627-9. Exceptions known to me are rare. We find *na* for *ne* in *ChronE* 205. 21 (1070) *7 þa munecas wiðstoden þ hi na mihton in cumen;* see §1618. In *Ps(A)* 12. 4 the glossator has put OE *ne* for Latin *ne* 'lest'. In *ÆGram* 2. 19 *ælcum men gebyrað þe ænigne godne cræft hæfð þæt he ðone do nytne oðrum mannum and befæste þæt pund þe him god befæste sumum oðrum men þæt godes feoh ne ætlicge and he beo lyðre þeowa gehaten and beo gebunden and geworpen into ðeostrum,* there is an anacoluthon of a sort. Is *ne* missing before *beo* and *beo*? In other words, did Ælfric forget that he started with *þæt . . . ne* and not with *þy læs þe*? Or are the clauses containing *beo* consecutive clauses of contingent result with unexpressed *þæt*? For the latter possibility, compare *PsFr* 50. 12 (§2803).

§2963. Shearin (1903, p. 98, and 1909, p. 246) claims that 'the purpose clause negatived by *læs* in the combination *ðy læs (ðe)* differs from that whose negative is *ne*, in that it denotes the purpose, not as a negative action or state, but as something feared or not desired'. I do not see the point of this. 'Lest' is a satisfactory translation for *þæt . . . ne* whenever the clause is taken as final. We find *þæt . . . ne* translating Latin *ne* in *PPs* 68. 23 and 105. 19 and translating *ut . . . non* in what may be final clauses but could be taken as consecutive clauses of contingent result in *PPs* 103. 33 and 118. 80. In *Luke* 21. 34, *WSCp* has *þe læs* where *Li* and *Ru* have *þte ne*; there are similar variations in *John* 5. 14 and 12. 42. I have found no evidence to support Shearin's distinction. He himself says (1903, p. 93) that 'the two methods differ but slightly . . . , one construction sometimes even running into the other'. Neither of the examples he quotes in my opinion illustrates this. In *CP* 461. 30, the *ðylæs* clause is governed by *ondræde* and the *ðætte . . . ne* clause is one of purpose. In *CP* 41. 2, the *ðylæs* clause is one of purpose, but that with *ðæt . . . ne* may express a contingent result rather than a purpose. In any event, the distinction between 'something feared or not desired' and 'a negative action or state' is, as I see it, not one between two conceptions of purpose, but between purpose and result.

§2964. Shearin (1909, p. 246) continues the statement quoted above with these words: 'Thus a *ðy læs (ðe)* clause tends to become a mere object-clause; this is actually the case in *Bede* 294. 25 [§2935], where it follows *ondrædan*.' This shading of final clauses into noun clauses can also be seen in *þæt* clauses, e.g. *Whale* 35, and in *þæt . . . ne* clauses, e.g. *Ex* 526. It does not occur in all *þy læs (þe)* clauses. There is certainly a close connection between final clauses and noun clauses; see §§1928 and 1938. But, in my opinion, there are two forms of the negative final clause, introduced respectively by *þæt . . . ne* and *þy læs (þe)*, both of which express 'something feared or not desired'.

§2965. An 'expletive' negative occasionally occurs in final clauses; see *Solil* 3. 19 (§2922) and *MCharm* 1. 64 (§2906). On *MSol* 449 see Menner's note to his lines 439–40.

§2966. There is nothing exceptional about the syntax of negative consecutive clauses. We find adv. *ne* alone, e.g. *CP* 3. 17 *Swæ feawa hiora wæron ðæt ic furðum anne anlepne ne mæg geðencean besuðan Temese ða ða ic to rice feng, ÆCHom* i. 66. 7 *and þær toeacan him weaxað untrumnyssa on his lichaman þæt he ne mæg ætes oððe wætes brucan*, and *ÆCHom* i. 140. 2 *Gif þonne hwylc wif to ðam unspedig wære þæt heo ðas ðing begytan ne mihte, þonne sceolde heo bringan twegen culfran-briddas, oððe twa turtlan*; adv. *ne* and other negative elements, e.g. *CP* 175. 23 . . . *on oðre wisan ða ðe sua aheardigað ðæt hi hit for nanum ege ne forlætað, ÆCHom* i. 540. 11

Sume hi sind swa micclum to Gode geðeodde þæt nane oðre him betwynan ne synd, ÆCHom i. 404. 11 . . . *and þa lafe ðæs hungres ofsloh se Romanisca here, and ða burh grundlunga towurpon, swa þæt ðær ne belaf stan ofer stane* . . . , and

Beo 565 ac on mergenne mecum wunde
       be yðlafe uppe lægon,
       sweordum aswefede, þæt syðþan na
       ymb brontne ford brimliðende
       lade ne letton;

and negative elements without adv. *ne* immediately before the verb, e.g. *GD* 206. 19 *7 swa ða in eallum þam wisum se bere hyrde þam bebode þæs Godes weres þæt he no to middes dæges ham com* . . . and *LS* 10. 153. 13 *and swa sarlice he wæs mid þam sare geswenced þæt he naðer þara ne gesittan ne standan mihte.* Further examples of negative consecutive clauses expressing actual and contingent results will be found in §§2905-10.

§2967. Benham (pp. 231-2) lists as particles 'giving negative force to consecutive clauses' *uneaðe* in examples like *ÆCHom* ii. 156. 25 *þa gestod hine swa micel lichamlic costung þæt he uneaðe þære lichamlican ontendnysse wiðstandan mihte* and *earfoðlice* in examples like *ÆCHom* i. 86. 13 *Him stod stincende steam of ðam muðe swa þæt earfoðlice ænig læce him mihte genealæcan.* But St. Benedict resisted the temptation—albeit *uneaðe*—and the doctors carried Herod to the hot baths—no doubt *earfoðlice.*

§2968. On negated *swa (. . .) (swa)* clauses see §§2864-70. It may be noted that in examples like *ÆCHom* i. 166. 9 *and he ða fæste feowertig daga and feowertig nihta, swa þæt he ne onbyrigde ætes ne wætes on eallum þam fyrste,* the negated *swa þæt* clause can be translated 'without tasting . . .' or 'not tasting . . .'; cf. §2868.

13. MOOD

a. Introductory remarks

§2969. Various writers, including especially Callaway (1933, *passim*), Behre (pp. 100-1 and 292-3), and Muxin (*UZLGU* 262, vyp. 50 (1958), 160-1), have contributed to the formulation of the general statement which follows. In clauses of purpose, which express the aim to which the action of the main clause is directed, the subjunctive is consistently used, e.g. *ÆCHom* i. 20. 34 *Ic gegaderige in to þe of deorcynne and of fugelcynne symble gemacan, þæt hi eft to fostre beon* and *ÆCHom* i. 34. 28 *He wæs mid wacum cild-claðum bewæfed, þæt he us forgeafe ða undeadlican tunecan, þe we forluron on ðæs frumsceapenan mannes forgægednysse.* In clauses of result, the indicative is used when the action of the subordinate clause is presented as actually taking place or as one event in a series of events following each other directly and dependent on each other, e.g. *ÆCHom* i. 132. 11 *Se ðe on ðisum andweardum life is wiðinnan ablend, swa þæt he næfð nan andgit ne hoga embe Godes beboda, he bið þonne eft wiðutan ablend, and ælces leohtes bedæled* and *ÆC Hom* i. 156. 35 *He ferde ðurh ða menniscnysse, swa þæt he wæs acenned, and ferde fram stowe to stowe, and dead þrowade, and of deaðe aras, and astah to heofenum.*[152] But when the result is presented as something contemplated or contingent, as a tendency, as an imaginary action and not as one event in a series of other events dependent on each other, the subjunctive is used, e.g. *ÆCHom* i. 508. 30 *Nis þeahhwæðere nan mann to ðam dyrstig þæt he on niht-licere tide binnan ðære cyrcan cuman durre, ac on dægrede* and (a good illustration of the imaginary) *ÆCHom* ii. 166. 3 *þa wurpon hi ða anlicnysse inn to heora kycenan, and færlice ða weard him eallum geðuht swilce fyr eode of ðære anlicnysse, swa þæt seo kycene eal forburne; ac hit næs swa him geðuht wæs, ac wæs þæs deofles dydrung.* Here, at any rate, OE usage was not influenced by the Latin use of the subjunctive in both final and consecutive clauses. Liggins (1970, p. 307) tells us that

while *CP* translates a Latin subjunctive by an OE subjunctive in over 60% of cases and *Bo* and *Sol* do so frequently, there is not one instance of this in *Or*. It might be argued that *Or* is simply carrying to extremes a preference for the indicative that is also very strong in *Bede*, but it is curious that *Or* has about half a dozen subjunctives for which there is no corresponding Latin, while *Bede* has no such cases.

My impression is that this is due, not to the fact that King Alfred had a greater reverence for the Latin subjunctive than did the translators of *Or* and *Bede*, but to differences in subject-matter. The predominantly narrative *Or* and *Bede* recount series of events in the past, which call for preterite indicatives in consecutive clauses. The philosophical texts are more likely to be concerned with contingent or imaginary results and so to contain a higher percentage of subjunctives. Four clauses in *Or* with the subjunctive which can be classified as consecutive all belong to this last group; they are the *þæt(te)*

---

[152] I do not accept Visser's formulation (ii, §877) that the indicative is used 'when the result is not intended, not desired, not aimed at, but purely automatic'. Here again Mann's work (pp. 3 and 40-9) is derivative and, since it adds little to what Shearin and Benham had to say, outmoded.

clauses beginning in *Or* 40. 28 (the first *þæt* clause), 84. 26, and
94. 31 (all with the present subjunctive), and *Or* 36. 28 (with the
preterite). So I will be surprised if further work does not confirm my
impression.

§2970. It is unnecessary to quote here more examples illustrating
these uses of the moods. Those seeking them will find them in my
discussions of the various conjunctions, in the authorities cited in
§§2802-4, and in Visser, ii, §§891-4. I have already mentioned in
Neophil. 49 (1965), 51-2, and in §§2803-4, two difficulties which
beset those attempting to classify clauses on the basis of the distinctions set out above, viz. the circularity of the argument and the
natural inability of modern scholars to agree on how to interpret
individual examples. The latter is documented by Visser (ii. 927-8).
But further discussion is necessary, with special reference to examples
in which different classification is possible. As usual, I avoid any detailed discussion of the 'nature' of the subjunctive. Those interested
should consult first Behre, pp. 100-17 and 292-312. If still interested, they can pursue the matter in the works of Hotz, Vogt, Glunz,
Cobb, and Mann. But they will do well to bear in mind Behre's comment (p. 106): 'in many cases, however, a clear distinction between
the different kinds of the subjunctive of volition as occurring in clauses
of purpose cannot be drawn without violence and hairsplitting'. Suit-
ably generalized, this might replace *Excelsior* on the banners of all
syntacticians of OE. On the possibility that the consecutive subjunctive in certain types of construction is of Latin and not of native
origin, see Callaway 1933, pp. 28-55 and 72-3.

b. The 'modal' auxiliaries

§2971. In the course of these discussions we will need to distinguish
between clauses with finite forms of verbs with full meaning and
finite forms of the 'modal' auxiliaries. A few points about the latter
must be made here.

§2972. I turn first to clauses of purpose. Here we must note that in
both prose and poetry, clauses introduced by *þy læs (þe)* rarely contain a finite form of a 'modal' auxiliary. Shearin (1903, pp. 98-9)
gives references for the prose to three examples with *magan*, including *ÆCHom* ii. 262. 20, and three with **sculan*, including *ÆCHom*
ii. 162. 33—less than two per cent of his 334 examples. I found
three in the poetry—*Beo* 1917 (but see §2934) and *And* 1145 with
magan and *Res* 51 with **motan*—less than seven per cent of my

forty-four examples (Mitchell 1959, Appendix 'Purpose 3'). Final clauses negated by *ne*, however, take 'modal' auxiliaries much more frequently; according to Shearin (1903, pp. 99 and 100) they do not differ significantly in this respect from positive final clauses. Those seeking fuller details in Shearin 1903, pp. 98-9 and 100-15, and Shearin 1909, pp. 246-7, are urged to compare carefully the figures he gives in different places for the same phenomenon. A brief examination of the significance of the various 'modal' auxiliaries in clauses of purpose and references to further discussions will be found in my §§2817-24.

§2973. In consecutive clauses, according to Benham (pp. 236-7), the 'so-called modal auxiliaries . . . are not real modal auxiliaries. . . . In general, the meanings of the several auxiliaries, as worked out by Shearin [1903, pp. 101 ff.], would be valid for the result clause; thus *magan* means *ability*; *motan, opportunity*; *sculan, obligation*; *willan, desire*; and these are used, in most cases, as *bona fide* verbs.' This subject is taken up by Standop; see pp. 30-7 (*magan*), 81-2 (**motan*), 103-4 (**sculan*), and 141 (*willan*). But here again, further discussion would impinge on the realm of the lexicographer.

§2974. Two brief inroads are, however, necessary if I am to keep the promise made in §2824. A consideration of the uses of the MnE verb 'may' inevitably raises the question whether OE *magan* is ever merely a circumlocution for the subjunctive. I agree with Standop (p. 36) that for consecutive clauses expressing actual result the question does not arise; when *magan* does occur in such clauses, as in *ÆCHom* i. 66. 7 *and þær toeacan him weaxað untrumnyssa on his lichaman, þæt he ne mæg ætes oððe wætes brucan*, it is a verb with full meaning. But the question does arise in final clauses or in consecutive clauses expressing a contemplated or contingent result (§2969). The example most cited here is probably

And 544   Nænig manna is
             under heofonhwealfe,   hæleða cynnes,
             ðætte areccan mæg   oððe rim wite
             hu ðrymlice,   þeoda baldor,
             gasta geocend,   þine gife dælest,

where Standop (p. 36 fn. 1) is inclined to see a genuine circumlocution. Brooks in his edition emends *mæg* to *mæge*, comparing

GuthB 890   Nænig hæleþa is
              þe areccan mæge   oþþe rim wite
              ealra þara wundra   þe he in worulde her
              þurh dryhtnes giefe   dugeþum gefremede

and observing that 'the emendation of MS *mæg* is certainly right, for there is no reason to change the mood', but Samuels (*RES* 14 (1963), 176) replies that 'the fact that *mæg* in itself expresses potentiality (whereas the indicative *wat* would not) provides adequate reason'. Another relevant example is

Jul 372   Ic hine þæs swiþe   synnum onæle
                    þæt he byrnende   from gebede swiceð,
                    stepeð stronglice,   staþolfæst ne mæg
                    fore leahtra lufan   lenge gewunian
                    in gebedstowe,

where *mæg* is parallel to *swiceð* and is certainly not a mere circumlocution for the subjunctive. But the last two examples do not necessarily decide for Brooks against Standop and Samuels. We may have in them and in *And* 544 a manifestation of the wide range of meanings spanned by *magan*, which range from that seen in

PPs 70. 7   Sy min muð and min mod   mægene gefylled,
                 þæt ic þin lof mæge   lustum singan
                 and wuldur þin   wide mærsian
                 and þe ealne dæg   æghwær herian,

Latin *repleatur os meum laudem tuam ut possim cantare gloriam tuam . . .* , where *magan* has the sense of *possum*, to

PPs 68. 23   Syn hiora eagan   eac adimmad,
                þæt hi geseon ne magon   syþþan awiht,

where *magon* + infinitive represents the simple subjunctive of Latin *Obscurentur oculi eorum, ne videant.*

§2975. That the answer to our question must be a personal one as far as final clauses are concerned is clear from a consideration of these examples and of those from the prose said by Shearin (1903, pp. 121-2) to be final clauses with indicative forms of *magan*. Shearin classifies *Bo* 105. 5 *Ac þær ic nu moste þin mod gefiðerigan mid þam fiðerum, þ ðu mihtest mid me fliogan, þonne miht þu ofersion ealle þas eorðlican þing* as final. Benham (p. 240) takes it as consecutive. Since I regard *mihtest* as an ambiguous form, I sit on the fence here. Shearin also classifies *GD* 264. 3 *þonne hwæðre se lichama . . . swa þeh gestandeþ 7 þurhwunað in þam ungeændedlican wite, þæt be þon mæg beon ongyten þæt þa þe mid gaste 7 mid lichaman gesyngiað butan soðre gecyrnesse, hi beoð a wuniendlice lifiende in helle . . .* as final. If Benham had classified it as consecutive, I would have agreed with him. Another example taken as final by Shearin and, tacitly, by Benham is *Bo* 132. 4 *Ic þe mæg eac*

reccan sum bispell be þæm þ þu hit meaht þe sweotolor ongitan.
Here I agree with both of them. Similar differences of opinion are
likely to arise if one considers the rest of the ten examples with
magan cited by Shearin (1903, pp. 121-2). So, having alerted the
reader to the existence of the problem, I leave open the question of
how to classify examples like *LS* 10. 162. 30 *forþon þæt gedafenað
þæt se gast beo gegearwod þæt ic mæg gode filian*, *Phoen* 341, and

And 859	We ðe, Andreas, eaðe gecyðað
	sið userne, þæt ðu sylfa miht
	ongitan gleawlice gastgehygdum

(which is numbered among the clauses taken by Shearin (1909,
pp. 247-8) as final)—with the warning that we have what in the cur-
rent vernacular would doubtless be called 'a chicken-and-egg situation': if these are clauses of purpose, the indicative forms of *magan*
can be circumlocutions for the subjunctive, and if the indicative
forms of *magan* can be circumlocutions for the subjunctive, these are
clauses of purpose. I cannot see how certainty is possible. Liggins
(1955, pp. 214-15) observes that in *BlHom* 147. 8 *Ond þa andswarode him seo halige Maria 7 wæs cweþende, 'Ic do a þine gife,
min Drihten, 7 ic þe bidde for þinum naman þæt þu gehwyrfe on me
ealle eaþmodnesse þinra beboda, forþon þe ic mæg don þine gife'*,
'the sense clearly suggests the idea of purpose rather than of explanation or of cause'. Why not the idea of result or even—see § 3056—
of time 'until'? See further Standop, pp. 37-41.

§ 2975a. This book was at press when Krzyszpień, 'The periphrastic
subjunctive with *magan* in Old English', *SAP* 11 (1980), 49-64, came
to my attention. This sensitive and often perceptive article gives
some more examples of pairs of sentences in which a subjunctive
form of a full verb and a subjunctive form of *magan* appear in what
seem to be the same or similar circumstances, e.g. *Ps(P)* 22. 8-9 and
Ps(B) 22. 6. It is marred by the author's apparently limited knowledge of OE (e.g., p. 57, the *gif* clause in *ÆHomM* 14. 72 is a dependent question, not a condition); by his unjustified faith in the
unambiguity for mood of ambiguous verb-forms (p. 52 *mihtan*, p. 53
mihton, and p. 62); by his acceptance of the simplistic distinction
between indicative and subjunctive which I reject in § 877 (p. 50 and
passim); by undue reliance on Visser, especially the latter's notion
of the 'modal preterite' (my § § 647-50) (p. 50 and *passim*); by his
use of a very limited corpus; by partial quotation (e.g., p. 53 *Or* 202.
18); and by what seems to me undue faith in his own reliability as
a native informant of OE. Krzyszpień (p. 50) writes: 'The subjunctive

mood was represented by a verbal inflection (the inflectional subjunctive) or by the use of certain verbs construed with the infinitive (the periphrastic subjunctive). The verbs which appeared in the periphrastic subjunctive were *sculan, willan, magan, motan, þurfan*, and a few more.' The first sentence must not be taken to imply that the inflexional subjunctive and the periphrastic subjunctive are identical in function in OE, as they are (in my use of the terms) in MnE, for Krzyszpień (p. 56; cf. pp. 51, 54, 55, 57, and 61) makes it clear that he believes the opposite to be true: 'The inflectional subjunctive expressed general non-fact modality. *Magan* in the periphrastic subjunctive expressed possibility.' This statement made the phrases 'not wholly (semantically) interchangeable' (pp. 53 and 61) rather surprising—when were they?—but I am in basic sympathy with it as far as *magan* is concerned, for it implies that *magan* was still something closer to a verb of full meaning than to a mere auxiliary. But its extension to the verbs other than *magan* (uncritically accepted by Krzyszpień 'after McLaughlin (1970: 263)') (p. 50 fn. 3) must await more detailed examination and perhaps clearer definition of the term 'periphrastic subjunctive'. The same is true of the long list of types of clause in which, it is claimed, 'the inflectional subjunctive did not alternate with the periphrastic subjunctive with *magan* in the OE period' (pp. 58-61); consider, *inter alia, Bo* 110. 15 (my §1680), *ÆHom* 26. 53 (my §1656), *ÆCHom* ii. 50. 23 (my §2766), and *Met* 19. 34 (my §2036). It follows that Krzyszpień's conclusions cannot be accepted as they stand without qualification. But equally they cannot be neglected, for they point the way for future workers, who will, however, continue to face the difficulty of finding criteria by which to determine the exact nuance of *magan* in any given example.

§2976. Whether *willan* is ever used in clauses of purpose is largely a terminological problem. We find preterite forms of *willan*—none of which, despite Shearin (1903, pp. 120-1), is unambiguously indicative—in *ÆCHom*, not only in examples with 'semi-subordination' (§1690), e.g. *ÆCHom* ii. 144. 7 *Se halga ða het him bringan sæd; wolde on ðam westene wæstmes tilian . . .* , and examples with syndetic parataxis, e.g. *ÆCHom* ii. 38. 25 *þaða Crist wæs þritig wintra, þa com he on ðisum dæge to Iohannes fulluhte, æt ðære ea þe is gehaten Iordanis, and wolde beon gefullod æt his handum*, but also in clauses introduced by *þæt*, e.g. *ÆCHom* i. 32. 5 . . . *ure Hælend . . . gemedemode hine sylfne þæt he wolde on ðisum dægðerlicum dæge, for middangeardes alysednysse beon lichamlice acenned of þam mædene Marian*; by *to ði/ðy þæt*, e.g. *ÆCHom* i. 322. 11 *Ic*

*com to ði þæt ic wolde sendan fyr on eorðan, and ic wylle þæt hit
byrne* and *ÆCHom* i. 382. 31 . . . *cwædon þæt hi comon fram
Hierusalem to ðy þæt hi woldon ðæra apostola lic bebyrian;* by *to
ði/ðy . . . þæt,* e.g. *ÆCHom* i. 82. 22 *ac to ði he com þæt he wolde
his heofenlice rice geleaffullum mannum forgyfan;* by *forðan ðe,* e.g.
ÆCHom i. 138. 4 *Lytel he wæs gesewen, forðan ðe he wolde gefeccan þa lytlan, and gebringan up to his rice* (*ÆCHom* ii. 40. 21,
with *forði ðe,* may be an example, but the second *wolde* can be
taken as parallel to the first); by *forðy þæt,* e.g. *ÆCHom* i. 82. 20
*þearflæs he syrwde ymbe Crist: ne com he forðy þæt he wolde his
eorðlice rice, oþþe æniges oðres cyninges mid riccetere him to geteon;
ac to ði he com þæt he wolde his heofenlice rice geleaffullum mannum forgyfan* (where we find two clauses introduced by different
formulae, one clause being negated, the other not); and by *forði . . .
þæt,* e.g. *ÆCHom* i. 304. 4 *þu eart Godes Sunu; forði ðu come þæt
ðu woldest us fordon.* (These last two are both exemplified in
ÆCHom ii. 534. 30 and 33.) Such examples are not peculiar to
ÆCHom. We find Latin *ut* clauses with the imperfect subjunctive
represented by clauses with preterite forms of *willan* introduced by
þæt, e.g. *Exod* 20. 20, *John(WSCp)* 10. 31 *Ða Iudeas namon stanas þ
hig woldon hyne torfian,* Latin *sustulerunt lapides Iudaei ut lapidarent eum* (where *Li* has *gestændon* and *Ru gistendun*), and the examples
I quote in *Neophil.* 52 (1968), 293; introduced by *to þon þæt,* e.g.
Or 126. 22 *7 siþþan he for to þæm hearge þe Egypti sædon þæt he
wære Amones heora godes, se wæs Iobeses sunu heora oþres godes,
to þon þæt he wolde beladian his modor Nectanebuses þæs drys, þe
mon sæde þæt heo hie wið forlege, 7 þæt he Alexandres fæder wære,*
Latin *Inde ad templum Jovis Ammonis pergit, ut ignominiam sibi
patris incerti et infamiam adulterae matris aboleret* (see further van
Dam, pp. 64–5, and Liggins 1970, p. 305); introduced by *for ðæm
þe,* e.g. *Or* 62. 32 *þis ic sprece nu for ðæm þe ic wolde þæt þa ongeaten . . . ,* Latin *Itaque haec ob hoc praecipue commemoranda
credidi ut intelligant hi . . .* (for more examples with grouped *for* formulae with *þe,* see Liggins 1955, pp. 45–6 and 130); and introduced
by *forðam . . . þe* and *forði . . . þe,* e.g. *Solil* 57. 12 *Forðam þu
woldest beon þe þu woldest lybban and forði woldest þu lybban þe
þu woldest witan,* Latin *esse vis, vivere et intelligere; sed esse ut vivas,
vivere ut intelligas.* Liggins (1955, p. 91) tells us that '*forþæm* is
sometimes followed by *wolde, woldon,* but all the examples I have
found primarily signify "wish, desire"; there are no clear-cut instances
of a purpose construction, as there are when the verb is introduced
by *forþæm þe*'. *CP* 47. 8 *Ðonne siendon monige ðe fleoð for eaðmodnesse anre, forðon hie noldon ðæt hie mon ahofe ofer ða ðe him*

beteran ðynceað ðonne hie selfe emphasizes the terminological nature of the problem; *forðon hie noldon ðæt* . . . can be translated 'because they did not wish that . . .' but represents *ne* 'lest' of the Latin *Et sunt nonnulli, qui ex sola humilitate refugiunt, ne eis, quibus se impares aestimant, praeferantur. Bo* 135. 1 *Oft hit eac gebyreð þ se yfla forlæt his yfel for sumes oðres yfles mannes andan, forðæm he wolde mid þy tælan þone oðerne þ he onscunode his þeawas*, where there is no direct Latin equivalent, perhaps comes even closer to being a 'clear-cut' instance. These OE constructions can represent other Latin final constructions, e.g. *Or* 148. 29 *Ac Antigones, se mid ungemete girnde anwalda ofer oþre, 7 to þæm fæstenne for þær Alexandres laf wæs 7 his sunu, 7 hie þær begeat, to ðon þæt he wolde þæt þa folc him þy swiþor to buge þe he hæfde hiera ealdhlafordes sunu on his gewealde*, Latin *Tum Antigonus ardens cupiditate dominandi* . . . , *CP* 403. 31 . . . *7 he ðara gedonena scylda eft gemyndgade, forðæmðe he wolde ðæt hi sceamode ðæt hie eft on ðære oðerre worulde wæren unclæne* . . . , Latin *quatenus pollui in futuris erubescant*, and *Bede* 216. 5 *Nese, cwæð he. Ne onfeng he his godum gitsiende ac forþon þe he wolde his sawle gehælan*, Latin *'Non' inquit 'propter auaritiam, sed propter saluandam eius animam suscepit'*. In the poetry we find *Dream* 33 *Geseah ic þa frean mancynnes* || *efstan elne mycle þæt he me wolde on gestigan. Dan* 188 might provide a negative example, but I prefer to take it as consecutive, expressing an actual result, rather than as final or consecutive expressing a tendency.

§2977. The pattern is also found with present forms of *willan*. But this is less frequent. Typical examples are *GD* 298. 7 *we comon hider þæt we willað sume þa broðra sændan in camphad of Gregories mynstre*, Latin *ad hoc venimus ut de monasterio Gregorii quosdam fratres in militiam mittamus, ÆCHom* i. 292. 15 *Nu eac on urum timan, gehwær þær halige men hi restað, æt heora deadum banum God wyrcð fela wundra, to ði þæt he wile folces geleafan mid þam wundrum getrymman*, and

Dream 103   He ða on heofenas astag.   Hider eft fundaþ
              on þysne middangeard   mancynn secan
              on domdæge   dryhten sylfa,
              ælmihtig god,   ond his englas mid,
              þæt he þonne wile deman,   se ah domes geweald,
              anra gehwylcum   swa he him ærur her
              on þyssum lænum   life geearnaþ

(on which see Mitchell 1968*c*, pp. 292-3).

§2978. The reader will have noticed one important fact about all these examples: both the principal or governing clause and the subordinate clause have the same subject. This is also true of the four examples cited by Liggins (1955, pp. 134-5), viz. *ÆCHom* i. 82. 20 (§2976), *ÆCHom* i. 168. 1, *ÆCHom* ii. 6. 24, and *ÆCHom* ii. 44. 17, which is described as final by Shearin (1903, p. 71), and of all the examples with *for* formulae which I discuss in §§3045, 3049, 3066, and 3069. *Dream* 33 (§2976) is not an exception, since *frean mancynnes* is the subject of the accusative and infinitive construction on which the *þæt* clause depends. On this, see further Standop (pp. 141-3) and Shearin (1903, p. 114), who rightly says that this is because '*willan*, in contradistinction to *sculan* and *motan*, marks the finality as a motive of action dependent upon the will of the purpose agent himself'. An apparent exception quoted by van Dam (p. 65) is *GD* 219. 11 *þa gesawon hi unfeor þanon ænne ofen inæledne se wæs gegearwod to þon þæt man wolde on bacan.* But here *man*—the actual subject of the *to þon þæt* clause—is the logical subject of the preceding adjective clause. In *BlHom* 113. 14 *þa ongan hine eft langian on his cyþþe, forþon þæt he wolde geseon eft ⁊ sceawian þa byrgenne*, *hine* is the logical subject of its clause and represents the same person as *he*.

§2979. What are we to call these clauses? Shearin (loc. cit. and 1909, p. 249) and Standop (pp. 141-3) regard them as final. Van Dam (pp. 64-6) suggests that examples like *Or* 126. 22 and *Or* 148. 29 (both quoted with their equivalents in §2976), and similar clauses involving *þencan*, e.g. *Or* 44. 29 *þa wurdon hiora wif swa sarige . . . þætte hie wæpna naman, to þon ðæt hie heora weras wrecan þohton*, can be described as causal. (Neither van Dam's example with *gelician* (*Or* 116. 4) nor his example with *gewilnian* (*GD(C)* 77. 20) has an infinitive in the relevant clause.) There is no doubt that in an example like *John(WSCp)* 10. 31 (§2976) *þ hig woldon hyne torfian* can be translated 'because they wished to stone him'. But the Latin equivalent *ut lapidarent* and the fact that *Li* and *Ru* have the preterite forms *gestændon* and *gistendun* suggest that the *þæt* clauses are more likely to be final than causal. Moreover, in my opinion, the evidence for *þæt* = 'because' except as an occasionally convenient translation is nil; see §§3118-27.

§2980. An argument in favour of taking the examples under discussion as clauses of purpose is perhaps to be found in the suggestion made by Standop (pp. 141-3) that this use of *willan* is an extension and a relic of the earlier but still current usages of *willan* in semi-subordination, as in *ÆCHom* ii. 144. 7 (§2976), and in syndetic paratactic constructions, as in *ÆCHom* ii. 38. 25 (§2976). It is interesting to compare this last example with the text of which it may be a reminiscence: *Matt(WSCp)* 3. 13 *þa com se Hælend fram Galilea to Iordane to Iohanne þ he hine fullode*, Latin *Tunc uenit Jesus a Galilaea in Iordanen ad Iohannem ut baptizaretur ab eo*, where the OE preterite suggests that the *þæt* clause is final, not causal. (The other gospels use different constructions.) But van Dam's comment (p. 65) that 'the change from the final to the causal signification is only partial and due to the use of the verbs of wishing or intending' is a useful reminder that the problem is terminological and that further discussion will not help us to decide how exactly to translate examples such as *Dream* 33 *Geseah ic þa frean mancynnes* || *efstan elne mycle þæt he me wolde on gestigan*—'in His wish to ascend on me' or 'because He wished to ascend on me' or 'so that He would ascend on me'?—or to decide how this example differs from *Dream* 40 *Gestah he on gealgan heanne,* || *modig on manigra gesyhðe, þa he wolde mancyn lysan*. I must leave the problem here, with the observation that the presence of ind. *willaþ* in the *þæt* clause in *GD* 298. 7 (§2977) warns us not to be too ready to conclude that there is *no* difference between the examples with *willan* and those with subjunctive forms of verbs of full meaning; on this, see Wilde, *Ang.* 63 (1939), 353. Those seeking further examples of clauses introduced by one of the conjunctions under discussion and containing a verb of volition or intention should see Shearin 1903, pp. 114–15; van Dam, pp. 70–1; and my discussions of these formulae (which include full references to Liggins 1955) in the sections I list in §2978.

c. Clauses of purpose with the indicative?

§2981. As I said in *NQ* 205 (1960), 273, I regard this as largely 'a pseudo-problem arising from different ways of looking at the same example'. I have discussed it—with a review of previous writings— in *Neophil.* 49 (1965), 51–5. The sections which follow, though complete in themselves, can be supplemented there.

§2982. Shearin's forty-eight examples from the prose (Shearin 1903, pp. 116–23) include *John(WSCp)* 20. 31 twice. I divide the remaining forty-seven into four groups: those with ambiguous or indicative forms of 'modal' verbs (twenty-three); those with *-est* forms of the second person preterite singular of weak verbs with full meaning, which—on the evidence of *Gen* 44. 21 *7 þu bude us þæt we hine læddan to þe þæt þu hine gesawe 7 wistest be þam þæt we* *sceaweras næron*—I do not accept as unambiguously indicative (eight); those with indicative forms of verbs of full meaning which are better taken as consecutive or which belong to my group B(i) in §2988 (eight), e.g. *BlHom* 231. 5 *æfter þon ic sende to þe Andreas þinne broþor, þæt he þe utalædeþ of þyssum carcerne*; and the remaining eight examples. Of these, only the first and fourth groups require discussion here.

§2983. Of the twenty-three examples with modal verb-forms, I eliminate seven with the ambiguous forms *sceoldest* (five) and *woldest* (two). The ten examples with forms of *magan* are discussed in §§2974-5. The remaining six examples are *GD* 298. 7 with *willaþ* (§§2977 and 2980); two with *ic sceal*, viz. *Nic* 496. 35 *ic eom iohannes þæs hehstan witega 7 ic eom cumen toforan hym þ ic his wegas gegearwian sceal* and *ÆCHom* ii. 14. 8 *Ic eom cumen to ðe, Danihel, to ði þæt ic sceal ðe tæcan*, which belong to my group B(i) (§2988); and three with *heo/hio mot*, viz. *Bo* 45. 28, where I am inclined to see a noun clause, and *Bo* 49. 22 and the similar *ÆCHom* ii. 378. 21 . . . *swa swa Ælmihtig Scyppend, þe ær gesette ðære sæ gemæru, þæt heo nateshwon ne mot middaneard ofergan*, which can be put in either my group A or my group B(i) in §2988, according to individual preference.

§2984. In the fourth group, *þæt* is a demonstrative qualifying *ylce* in *Lch* i. 348. 8. In *CP* 236. 7, *ðæt* introduces either a consecutive clause or a noun clause in apposition with *ðæm*. In *John* 20. 31 and *Luke* 8. 12 the manuscripts fluctuate between a final clause with the subjunctive and a consecutive clause with the indicative. This leaves four examples, one introduced by *þæt*—*GD* 315. 8, where Shearin (1903, p. 122) explains the ind. *geseoþ* in MS *C* as possibly 'due to attraction' without noting that MS *O* has the expected *geseon*—and three by *þy læs (þe)*. In *BlHom* 239. 8 *Cum nu mid us, forþon þe þu eart ure wealdend, þy læs wen is þæt hi us eft genimon* . . . , we could have had *þy læs wen sie* (which we have in *BlHom* 247. 2) but —as Shearin (1903, p. 122) says—'*wen* probably contains enough of optative meaning to make the combination *wen is* equivalent to *(hit) sie*'. In *Luke(WSCp)* 14. 29 *þe læs* is separated from its verb *agynnað* (Latin *incipiant*) by the verbs *legð* and *mæg . . . fullfremman* —which makes Shearin's idea of attraction plausible. The most intractable example is *LS* 34. 172 . . . *and þinon awyrgedan deofolgildan we næfre nellað offrian þy læs ðe we us sylfe gebringað on fylðe*. This is so aberrant that one must suspect scribal error—which is in a sense a form of attraction and might explain *Luke(WSCp)*

14. 29. It is noteworthy that the seven verbs which precede *gebringað* in *LS* 34. 172 and the four which follow it are all present indicative.

§2985. Shearin (1903, p. 83) suggests taking five adjective clauses with indicative verbs as clauses of purpose. Even his most convincing example—*ÆCHom* i. 78. 15 *of ðe cymð se Heretoga seðe gewylt and gewissað Israhela folc*, with which he compares *Matt* 2. 6 *ex te enim exiet dux qui reget populum meum Israhel*—does not convince me. But it is, I suppose, a matter of terminology.

§2986. The proposed examples from the poetry—which I list and discuss in *Neophil.* 49 (1965), 51-3—fall into three groups: those with ambiguous or indicative forms of 'modal' verbs; those which are better explained as noun clauses; and those which are better taken as consecutive or which belong to my group B(i) in §2988. Of these, only the first group—where I supplement Shearin's list (1909, pp. 249-50)—demands consideration here.

§2987. What is said in §§2974-5 about the prose examples with indicative forms of *magan* applies to those in the poetry—*And* 859, *Phoen* 344, and *Jul* 372. *PPs* 101. 21 can be disregarded as a crude translation. *ChristC* 1386, with the ambiguous form *ðu mostes*, can be taken as purpose or result. The same is true of the first *þæt* clause, with *þu moste*, in

ChristC 1460 Ic onfeng þin sar þæt þu moste gesælig
      mines eþelrices eadig neotan,
      ond þe mine deaðe deore gebohte
      þæt longe lif þæt þu on leohte siþþan,
      wlitig, womma leas, wunian mostes,

but the second, again with the ambiguous form *mostes*, must be purpose, for this is part of God's speech on the Day of Judgement to the evildoers who have not reached and will not reach that Light. The two examples with *mot*—*Phoen* 381 and *Met* 5. 42—are like those in the prose and can belong in group A or group B(i).

§2988. So I find myself in happy agreement with what I wrote in *Neophil.* 49 (1965), 54-5. There I accepted the second half of Shearin's statement—'Finally, we hope that the illustrations in the foregoing section have shown beyond doubt the existence of an indicative in the purpose clause, used to express the finality as an objective reality, or due to some peculiarity, of attraction, &c., in the immediate context' (1903, p. 123)—but claimed that the grounds for accepting the existence of an indicative expressing reality in a final clause are slender, indeed almost non-existent. The real difference between those who deny and those who affirm that final clauses can take the indicative is probably terminological, in that they are giving different expression to the basic position set out schematically below.

	Kind of Result	Mood
A	Actual Results which have taken, or are taking, place	Indicative
B	Results which have not yet taken place:	
	(i) those which are certain to happen or which the speaker thinks (or implies) are certain to happen	Indicative or Subjunctive, varying with the speaker
	(ii) those which are possible but not certain	Subjunctive
	(iii) those which are unlikely (or impossible)	Subjunctive

Looked at from one point of view, category B(i) may be described as consecutive, from another as final. The latter is the viewpoint of those who say that the indicative can occur in final clauses.

In my article, I went on to illustrate this by an examination of the attitudes of different scholars to *El* 930. Here I can make the point by drawing the reader's attention to *WHom* 19. 51 and *John(WSCp)* 17. 26 *7 ic him cyðde ðinne naman 7 gyt wylle cyþan þ seo lufu ðe þu me lufodest sy on him 7 ic eom on him*, Latin *et notum feci eis nomen tuum et notum faciam ut dilectio quia dilexisti me in ipsis sit et ego in ipsis* (where the OE translator has supplied the ind. *eom*)— in these examples Visser (ii. 862) no doubt meant to see a shift from modal to zero form, not 'from zero to modal form'—and by quoting two examples Visser does not mention, viz. *BlHom* 111. 27 *7 se man næfre toðon leof ne bið his nehmagum 7 his worldfreondum, ne heora nan hine to þæs swiþe ne lufað þæt he sona syþþan ne sy onscungend, seoþþan se lichoma 7 se gast gedælde beoþ, 7 þincð his neawist laþlico 7 unfæger* (where *sy* and *þincð* are parallel), and *ÆCHom* i. 410. 5 *þa deoflu æteowiað þære synfullan sawle ægðer ge hyre yfelan geðohtas, and ða derigendlican spræca, and ða manfullan dæda, and hi mid mænigfealdum ðreatungum geangsumiað, þæt heo on ðam forðsiðe oncnawe mid hwilcum feondum heo ymbset bið, and ðeah nan utfær ne gemet, hu heo ðam feondlicum gastum oðfleon mage* (where *oncnawe* and *gemet* are parallel). In these examples, we can see the attitude of the speaker or writer changing from hesitating expression of an intended purpose to an affirmation of what is or will in his opinion be a certain result, affirmation which may be minatory (*BlHom* 111. 27 and *ÆCHom* i. 410. 5) or triumphant (*WHom* 19. 51 and *John(WSCp)* 17. 26).

d. Purpose or result?

(1) *Introductory remarks*

§2989. In §2829, I gave reasons for my reluctance to accept Callaway's claim (1933, p. 17) that 'in Consecutive Clauses introduced by Single Particles, the Subjunctive is much more frequent than the Indicative' and spoke of the marked discrepancy between Callaway's figures and those of Benham. Callaway (1933, p. 17) found in his limited corpus of the prose 348 *þæt(te)* clauses with the subjunctive which he classified as consecutive. He says that in the same texts Benham found 141 *þæt(te)* clauses with the indicative. Yet Benham (pp. 232-3) says that he found 1,379 consecutive clauses with the indicative and 297 with the subjunctive. So Callaway's total of subjunctives in *þæt(te)* clauses in a limited corpus which includes both prose and poetry is greater than Benham's total of subjunctives in all the consecutive clauses he found in an almost comprehensive coverage of the prose. In contrast, Callaway (1933, p. 7) tells us that 'the Subjunctive is far less frequent than is the Indicative' in clauses introduced by 'the Correlative Particles of Subgroup A', viz. *swa (. . .) swa, swa (. . .) þæt(te), swilc (. . .) þæt(te)*, and the like. The table which follows uses Callaway's figures, but makes the important distinction between grouped and divided conjunctions which he failed to make. Since the purpose of the table is to compare *þæt(te), swa þæt(te)*, and *swa . . . þæt(te)*, I omit sixty-five examples of other grouped and divided conjunctions given by Callaway (1933, p. 6).

Conjunction	Subjunctive	Indicative	Total	Percentage of Subjunctives
þæt(te)	348	141	489	71. 2
swa þæt(te)	91	375	466	19. 5
swa . . . þæt(te)	206	319	525	39. 2
Totals	645	835	1480	43.6

This table, which may reflect the fact that *þæt(te)* and *swa . . . þæt(te)* are more likely to be followed by clauses containing a contingent or contemplated result than *swa þæt(te)*, throws a somewhat different light on things. But when we turn to Benham's figures we seem to be looking not under a different light but at a different landscape. Benham (pp. 232-7) gave only blanket figures for all conjunctions when he analysed his examples according to mood, but his percentage of subjunctives for the prose was only 16.8.

Mood	Verbs of full meaning	'Modal' Auxiliaries	Total
Indicative	1379	377	1756
Subjunctive	297	71	368
Totals	1676	448	2124

The discrepancy cannot be accounted for by the fact that Callaway's corpus included some poetry. Several statistical points can be made. Benham does not say what he does with ambiguous verb-forms, but Callaway's 698 examples from the prose include ninety ambiguous forms; see Callaway 1933, pp. 34 fn. 2 and 73–4. (I take up this point below.) Benham's total of 368 subjunctives includes 107 in texts not read by Callaway (Callaway 1933, pp. 26–7). The presumption then must be that where Benham found 261 subjunctives (368−107) which may include some ambiguous forms, Callaway found 698, including ninety ambiguous forms. Callaway (1933, p. 74) says that 'when all possible deductions shall have been made from my total for the consecutive subjunctive in Old English prose, the number remaining will be appreciably larger than that given by Dr. Benham and others'. To me the difference remains staggering.

§2990. The primary reason for this difference is the fact that classification is an extremely subjective business; here I agree with Callaway (1933, p. 4 and *passim*). The reader can test this for himself by a comparison of the Greek, Latin, Gothic, OE, and various later English, versions of *John* 9. 2 and by a consideration of the list of clauses with the subjunctive which Wülfing (ii, §462) took as consecutive; some contain modal verbs, some ambiguous verb-forms, some are noun clauses, some final. He must also consider the possibility that, since *þæt* regularly introduces final clauses and *swa þæt(te)* and *swa . . . þæt(te)* rarely if ever do, Callaway included in his total of consecutive *þæt* clauses with the subjunctive many clauses which are, or could be taken as, final clauses. He himself mentions this danger (1933, p. 17), with the comment that there is very little overlap between his examples and those of Shearin; see also Callaway 1933, p. 74. It is clear that the existence of this personal equation makes it a profitless task to attempt a detailed reconciliation of the figures given by Benham and Callaway. But some examination of how the discrepancies might have arisen will, I hope, prove fruitful to the investigator who pursues this topic in greater detail than is possible here.

(2) *Clauses with the subjunctive*

§2991. The possibility of different interpretations of clauses with an indicative verb-form has already been discussed in §§2981-8. Clauses with a subjunctive verb-form are another potential source of disagreement. As with other subordinate clauses (see the General Index), there is no automatic connection between the form of the principal clause and the mood of the verb of a final or consecutive clause; see §2997. But the presence of a 'volitional expression' (see §2391), of a negated indicative, or of a rhetorical question, in the principal clause is frequently associated with the expression of a contingent or contemplated result by means of a subjunctive in a following consecutive clause. Since final clauses in the same syntactical situation also have the subjunctive, the possibility of ambiguity arises.

§2992. We find what may be an unambiguous indicative after a volitional expression in

Husb 26   Ongin mere secan,   mæwes eþel,
                    onsite sænacan,   þæt þu suð heonan
                    ofer merelade   monnan findest,
                    þær se þeoden is   þin on wenum,

where, says Behre (pp. 103-4), it is used 'to emphasize the absolute certainty that the woman . . . will find her lover faithfully waiting for her'. But see §2803. Another possible example is *Lch* ii. 60. 4 *Wiþ heort wærce rudan gelm seoþ on ele 7 do alwan ane yntsan to smire mid þy þ stilð þam sare*, but *þ* is more likely to be a demonstrative subject than a conjunction. However, the subjunctive is the usual mood in such circumstances in both final and consecutive clauses. Sometimes there is no ambiguity. The context certifies that the first *þæt* clause in *ÆCHom* ii. 452. 34 *Se swicola deofol genam þæt wif him to gefylstan, þæt he ðone halgan wer ðurh hi geswice, swa swa he ær Adam þurh Euan beswac; ac se ylca God þe geðafode þæt he swa gecostnod wære, heold hine wið þæs deofles syrwungum, and wið his sawle lyre* is one of purpose and that in

MCharm 12. 11   Swa litel þu gewurþe   alswa linsetcorn,
                      and miccli lesse alswa anes handwurmes hupeban, and
                      alswa litel þu gewurþe þet þu nawiht gewurþe

we have a consecutive clause. The syntax may help us. In *And* 956, *PPs* 140. 5, and

PsFr 50. 12   Ne awyrp þu me,   wuldres ealdor,
               fram ðinre ansyne   æfre to feore,

> ne huru on weg aber   þone halgan gast,
> þæt he me færinga   fremde wyrðe,

Latin *Ne proicias me a facie tua, et spiritum sanctum tuum ne auferas a me*, the *þæt* clauses express a tendency or possible result the achievement of which is not desired. They do not express the speaker's purpose; this would require *þæt . . . ne* or *þy læs*. But the question arises: are subordinate clauses such as those in *ÆCHom* i. 604. 5 *Uton awurpan þeostra weorc, and beon ymbscrydde mid leohtes wæpnum, swa þæt we on dæge arwurðlice faron, And* 1182 *Gað fromlice* ‖ *þæt ge wiðerfeohtend wiges gehnægan*, and *And* 1332 *Gað fromlice* ‖ *ðæt ge guðfrecan gylp forbegan*, final or consecutive? To Krapp (*Andreas* (1906), glossary, s.v. *þæt* 3) and Behre (p. 110), they are final. To Benham (p. 234), who 'cannot agree with Delbrück' that they are final, and (to judge by his silence) Shearin, they are consecutive. Examples like *And* 956, *PPs* 140. 5, and *PsFr* 50. 12 above, show that it is possible to take them as consecutive. Behre's apparent certainty that they are final seems to me to reflect a failure in method. He finds that a negated indicative or a rhetorical question in the principal clause tends to be associated with a subjunctive in a subordinate adjective, temporal, or consecutive, clause. Why then, after discussing the influence of a volitional expression on the verb of adjective and temporal clauses (chapters v and vi), does he fail to do so for consecutive clauses (chapter xi)? His own comment (p. 100) allows us the choice and illustrates our dilemma: 'in clauses of purpose (final clauses) the subjunctive is used to express a volitional attitude towards a verbal activity conceived of as the intended result of a preceding action'. Hence it is possible to take

Beo 2804   se scel to gemyndum   minum leodum
                    heah hlifian   on Hronesnæsse,
                    þæt hit sæliðend   syððan hatan
                    Biowulfes biorh

as consecutive or final—my type B(ii) (§2988).

§2993. The mere presence of a negated indicative in the principal clause does not demand a subjunctive in a following consecutive clause. The negative of litotes provides exceptions in *Rim* 15 . . . *ne wæs me in healle gad*, ‖ *þæt þær rof weord rad* and, in asyndetic parataxis with a positive clause, in *Beo* 1519 and

Mald 117   Gehyrde ic þæt Eadweard   anne sloge
                    swiðe mid his swurde,   swenges ne wyrnde,
                    þæt him æt fotum feoll   fæge cempa.

These are actual results. But the subjunctive is used when the result is contingent, e.g.

Jul 55   Næfre þu þæs swiðlic   sar gegearwast
                 þurh hæstne nið   heardra wita,
                 þæt þu mec onwende   worda þissa,

and when the result is assumed but regarded as unattainable, e.g. *Beo* 1366 *No þæs frod leofað* || *gumena bearna, þæt þone grund wite.* A virtual negative too may be accompanied by a subjunctive, e.g.

Rid 60. 3   fea ænig wæs
                 monna cynnes,   þæt minne þær
                 on anæde   eard beheolde. . . .

So once again the question 'Purpose or result?' can arise. The context seems to me decisive for the former in

ChristC 1571   Ne biþ þæt sorga tid
                 leodum alyfed,   þæt þær læcedom
                 findan mote,   se þe nu his feore nyle
                 hælo strynan   þenden her leofað.

We can detect purpose or contingent result, but not actual result, in

And 301   Næbbe ic fæted gold   ne feohgestreon,
                 welan ne wiste   ne wira gespann,
                 landes ne locenra beaga,   þæt ic þe mæge lust ahwettan,
                 willan in worulde,   swa ðu worde becwist.

But in

JDay ii 107   þonne stedelease   steorran hreosað,
                 and seo sunne forswyrcð   sona on morgen,
                 ne se mona næfð   nanre mihte wiht,
                 þæt he þære nihte   genipu mæge flecgan,

an assumed but impossible result seems the only possibility.

§2994. Campbell (*RES* 7 (1956), 65 fn. 2) has given a concise and accurate statement of the situation which obtains when the principal clause contains a question. 'It may be noted that . . . a positive real question counts as positive, but a positive rhetorical question as virtually a negated statement: contrast

And 1343   Hwæt wearð eow swa rofum,   rincas mine,
                 lindgesteallan,   þæt eow swa lyt gespeow?

with

And 1372   Hwylc is þæs mihtig   ofer middangeard,
                 þæt he þe alyse   of leoðubendum,
                 manna cynnes,   ofer mine est?,

both clauses of result, but the former after a real, the latter after a rhetorical question.' In the first example we have an actual result, in the second one which is unreal or unattainable; see further Behre, p. 296. I have not been conscious of any ambiguities arising as a result of this difference; in *ÆCHom* ii. 432. 2 *La hwæt fremað ðære burhware þeah ðe þæt port beo trumlice on ælce healfe getimbrod, gif ðær bið an hwem open forlæten, þæt se onwinnenda here þurh ðam infær hæbbe?*, for example, we have a rhetorical question— answer 'Nothing!'—followed by the subjunctive of a contemplated result. But there may be such ambiguities.

§2995. Difficulties of classification do, however, sometimes arise in dependent speech. It is, for example, an open question whether the *to ðan þæt* clause is final or consecutive in *ÆCHom* i. 36. 30 *þæt tacen þe se engel ðam hyrdum sæde we sceolon symle on urum gemynde healdan, and þancian ðam Hælende þæt he gemedemode hine sylfne to ðan þæt he dælnimend wære ure deadlicnysse, mid menniscum flæsce befangen, and mid waclicum cildclaðum bewunden,* which should be compared with *ÆCHom* i. 32. 5 (§2976) and is further discussed in §2997. Behre (pp. 292–306) discusses the mood of verbs in consecutive clauses in dependent speech.

§2996. I turn now to sentences in which a positive statement is followed by a clause with a subjunctive verb. According to the simple rule discussed in §2803, this ought to certify the clause as final. But it does not always conclusively do so; consider

PPs 118. 31   Swa ic fæste ætfealh,   þæt ic forð heonun
                  þine gewitnysse   wel geheolde,

Latin *Adhaesi testimoniis tuis, Domine.* A few examples must serve to illustrate the problems of classification which arise. On *Bo* 57. 31 and *Met* 13. 73 see §2845. In §2835 I give my reasons for taking *ÆCHom* i. 596. 10 and *ÆCHom* ii. 252. 21 as final. I agree with Benham (p. 253) that in *ÆCHom* i. 574. 34, *ÆCHom* i. 164. 9 *Swa eac we beoð soðlice ungerade, gif we lufiað þa sceortan softnysse and ða hwilwendlican lustas to ðan swiðe, þæt hi us gebringan to ðam ecan pinungum,* and *ÆCHom* i. 318. 7 *Æfter ðære gebysnunge wurdon arærede muneclif mid þære gehealdsumnysse, þæt hi drohtnian on mynstre, be heora ealdres dihte, on clænnesse, and him beon heora æhta eallum gemæne, swa ða apostoli hit astealdon,* we have clauses of result. Shearin's failure to list these may mean that he agrees, but his work is not without omissions. With characteristic carelessness Benham lists *ÆCHom* ii. 258 19 *Ða bifode seo eorðe, and toburston stanas, þæt eal middaneard eft wurde astyred þurh*

Cristes ðrowunge to soðum geleafan, and ða heardheortan hæðenra ðeoda to heora Scyppende siððan gebigde among his consecutive *þæt* clauses (p. 241) but not among his consecutive clauses with the subjunctive (p. 253). Shearin (1903, p. 133) takes it as final. Here we can detect either the purpose of the Creator or the hoped-for result of his actions.

§ 2997. From his examination of the other Germanic languages, Callaway (1933, p. 67) concludes that the chief factor in their use of consecutive subjunctives is to be found in the contingent nature of the dependent consecutive clause and not in the nature of the governing clause. He reaches the same conclusion for OE. Callaway's book was published in 1933, Behre's in 1934. The former agrees in essence with the latter's comment (p. 292) that 'the negative or interrogative nature of the main clause . . . does not in itself cause the use of the subjunctive in the dependent clause' and extends this dictum (as Behre failed to do) to cover consecutive clauses which follow imperative main clauses. He again attacks the 'Erdmann–Bernhardt theory of mood-syntax' (Callaway 1933, pp. 28–35 and 72). But, as I have discussed this problem in some detail for temporal clauses (§§ 2610–25 and 2772), I do not propose to pursue it here. However, his conclusion that the consecutive subjunctive is due to the contingent nature of the dependent consecutive clause, while very often true, fails to recognize that the subjunctive may be used of an actual result, the truth of which is not denied. Behre (p. 304) puts it thus: 'The constitutive factor, then, that determines the use of the subjunctive in consecutive and relative clauses after negative and interrogative expressions is an attitude of meditation or reflection on the part of the speaker generally towards an assumed event, sometimes also towards a fact.' This may be illustrated by a consideration of

And 573   Hu mihte þæt gewyrðan   in werþeode,
                þæt ðu ne gehyrde   hælendes miht,
                gumena leofost,   hu he his gif cyðde
                geond woruld wide,   wealdendes bearn?,

where, as Behre (p. 298) puts it, 'Andreas expresses his surprise at the content of the *þæt*-clause but he does not deny its validity' and perhaps of *ÆCHom* i. 36. 30 (§ 2995), where the subjunctive might convey the speaker's surprise (either genuine or assumed for rhetorical purposes) at a result which certainly happened and which he believes to be true; cf. the first noun clause in the hymn

                It is a thing most wonderful,
                Almost too wonderful to be,

That God's own Son should come from Heaven
And die to save a child like me.

And yet I know that it is true. . . .

(3) *Clauses with an ambiguous form of a verb of full meaning*

§2998. These need not detain us long. It will suffice to point out that, while the context sometimes determines whether we have a clause of purpose or result, e.g. *Or* 34. 7 *7 he sæde þæt he of þæm drycræfte geleornode godcundne wisdom, þæt he þæs landes wæstm-bærnesse þara syfan geara ær beforan sæde, 7 þara opera syfan geara wædle þe þær æfter com* (result) and *CP* 233. 21 *7 icte ða his agne scylde mid ðæm æfste, ðæt he tiolode menn forlæran ðæt hie wurden eac forlorene sua he wæs* (result, then purpose), there is often room for difference of opinion. Thus Shearin (1903, p. 131) takes *Or* 38. 27 *Hwæðre God þa miclan Pharones menge gelytlode, 7 hyra ofermætan ofermetto genyðerode; 7 beforan Moyse 7 hys folce he ðone Readan Sæ on twelf wegas adrigde, þæt hi drigan fotan þæne sæ oferferdon* as a clause of purpose. But, although Benham (p. 240) is silent, it seems to me more natural to take it as a clause of result. On the other hand, Benham (p. 240) classifies the second *þæt* clause in *Or* 106. 11 *þæt hus hæfdon Romane to ðæm anum tacne geworht þæt on swelce healfe swelce hie þonne winnende beon woldan, swa suþ, swa norþ, swa east, swa west, þonne andydan hie þa duru þe on þa healfe open wæs, þæt hie be þæm wiston hwider hie sceoldon* as a clause of result. Shearin (1903, p. 131) is silent. At the risk of being the only man in step, I must say that this seems better taken as a clause of purpose. Here again what Quirk (p. 72) specifically called 'the bureaucratic matter of classification' is seen to depend on whether we look at the question from the point of view of the modern reader or someone else who lived after the action was completed, or from that of the initiator of the action.

(4) *Clauses with an ambiguous form of a 'modal' auxiliary*

§2999. The problem here is similar to that which arises with ambi-guous forms of verbs of full meaning. It can be sufficiently illustrated by reference to three examples with *magan*; for more see Benham, p. 210. In *ChronA* 11. 22 (418) *Her Romane gesamnodan ealle þa goldhord ðe on Brytene wæron 7 sume on eorðan behyddan þ heo nan man syððan findon ne mihton*, Shearin (1903, p. 139) detects purpose, Benham (pp. 209–10) result. The same two alternatives present themselves in *ÆCHom* ii. 156. 4 *þa aheng se munuc ane lytle bellan on ðam stanclude, þæt Benedictus mihte gehyran, þurh ðære*

bellan sweg, hwænne he his bigleofan þær feccan sceolde; forðan þe
se Romanus ne mihte him to gegan for ðam stanclude. The fact that in

Beo 1503   hring utan ymbbearh,
              þæt heo þone fyrdhom   ðurhfon ne mihte,
              locene leoðosyrcan   laþan fingrum

we can detect the purpose of the maker or of the wearer or even of
a personified coat-of-mail, an actual result, or a hoped-for result,
illustrates the terminological nature of the problem. Examples like
these, I suppose, can be placed in either my group B(i) or my group
B(ii); see §2988.

14. CLAUSE ORDER AND CO-ORDINATION

§3000. Benham (p. 255) offers us an 'Index of Result Clauses which
do not Immediately follow the Main Clause' which is so lacking in
discrimination that I have been able to illustrate from it almost all
the different phenomena discussed in the next three sections. Further
examples will be found in the sections in which I discuss the various
conjunctions.

§3001. Normally clauses of purpose and result immediately follow
the principal clause, e.g. *ChronE* 30. 23 (656) and *CP* 175. 1 *For
ðære ungelicnesse ðara hieremonna sculun beon ungelic ða word ðæs
lareowes, ðæt he hiene selfne geðeode to eallum his hieremonnum,*
or the governing subordinate clause on which they depend, e.g.
ChronD 170. 18 (1050) *Ulf p̄r wæs geset þam ƀrice to hyrde þe
Eadnoð hæfde ac he wæs syððan of adryfon forþan þe he ne gefremede naht biscoplices þæron swa þ us sceamað hit nu mare to
tellanne.* But—as Benham points out (p. 239) and sometimes succeeds in illustrating (p. 255)—a clause which is more closely linked
to the principal clause or to the governing subordinate clause may
intervene. This intervening clause is most commonly adjective, e.g.
Or 86. 23 and *Or* 38. 7 *þæt syfeðe wæs þæt þær com hagol se wæs
wið fyre gemenged, þæt he ægþer sloh ge ða menn ge ða nytenu.* But
other kinds of clause may intervene, e.g. (temporal) *Or* 136. 5 *Swa
egefull wæs Alexander þa þa he wæs on Indeum, on easteweardum
þissum middangearde, þætte þa from him ondredan þe wæron on
westeweardum,* (comparative) *Or* 90. 1 *Ac siþþan hit cristen wearð,
þæt helle fyr wæs siþþan geswiðrad, swa ealle ungetina wæron, þæt
hit nu is buton swelce tacnung þæs yfeles þe hit ær dyde,* (concessive
and others) *Or* 196. 16, (explanatory) *Bede* 240. 19 *þa wæs geworden ymb syx hund wintra 7 feower 7 syxtig æfter Drihtnes*

menniscnesse eclipsis solis, þæt is sunnan asprungennis, þæt heo sciman ne hæfde, and (parenthetic) *VSal 1* 262 *Ic sece mynne dryhten and la, hwæt hæbbe ic gedon, ic axie þe, þæt ic ne mot mynne dryhten habban?* In *ChronE* 37. 21 (675) *Đas landes ic gife Scē Peter eal swa freolice swa ic seolf hit ahte 7 swa þ nan min æfter-gengles þær nan þing of ne nime,* we have a comparative clause followed by a co-ordinated clause which may be taken as final or consecutive.

§ 3002. Benham not only fails to distinguish these situations from one another. He also confuses them with those in which a subordi-nate clause comes within the consecutive clause. Here we must distinguish first, examples in which the consecutive conjunction appears only once, e.g. *Bede* 322. 9 *Đa wæs heo fæstlice gehalad, þætte wundorlice gemete for openre wunde 7 geoniendre, mid þa heo bebyrged wæs, þa seo þynneste dolgswæð 7 seo læsseste æteawde*; second, those in which the conjunction is repeated in whole or in part—see further § 3003—e.g. *Bede* 378. 26 *Weox seo adl sticce-mælum, 7 sona on ðære ilcan niht hefigre gefremed wæs, swa ðæt, ða dæg com, þæt he uneaðe þurh hine sylfne ariisan oþþe gan mihte*; third, those in which both the conjunction and the subject of the clause are repeated, e.g. *Bede* 160. 25 and *Or* 84. 11 *Hu God þa mæstan ofermetto 7 þæt mæste angin on swa heanlice ofermetto geniðerade þæt se, se þe him ær geþuhte þæt him nan sæ wiþhabban ne mehte . . . þæt he eft wæs biddende anes lytles troges . . .* ; fourth, examples like *Or* 198. 15 *Swa lað wæs Pena folc Scipian þa he hie gefliemed hæfde, swa, þeh þe he hie sume wið feo gesealde, ðæt he þæt weorð nolde agan þæt him mon wið sealde, ac he hit oþrum monnum sealde,* where the concessive clause intervenes between the repeated *swa* and *þæt*; and fifth, a construction which Benham did not understand but which requires separate consideration.

§ 3003. This construction is seen in *Bo* 25. 5 *Feawe sint to þæm gesceadwise gif he wyrð on ungeðylde þ he ne wilnige þ his sælða weorðen onwende* and in *CP* 67. 20 *Đæt sindon ða ðe gehiera ð Godes word, 7 mid ðære geornfulnesse 7 mid ðære wilnunge ðisse worlde 7 hiere welena bið asmorod ðæt sæd Godes worda, ðeah hie upaspryttæn, ðæt hie ne moten fulgrowan ne wæstmbære weorðan.* Here, I believe, despite Benham (p. 255) and, for the *CP* example, the EETS translation, the clauses introduced by *gif* and *þeah* belong within the *þæt* clause and not to the principal clause of the sentence. This is demonstrated by a comparison of *GD(C)* 34. 1 *he wæs swiðe yfellic on his gegerelan 7 swa forsewenlic þeh þe hit gelumpe þæt him hwilc man þe hine ne cuþe ongen come 7 se þonne wære ge-greted þæt he forhogode togenes gretan*—another example cited by Benham (p. 255)—with *GD(H)* 34. 1 *soðlice he wæs swiðe waclic on his gewædum 7 swa forsewenlic þæt þeah hwilc man him ongean come þe hine ne cuðon* [sic] *7 he þone mid wordum gegrette, he wæs forsewen, þæt he næs ongean gegreted.* Benham (p. 221) claims that in *Bede* 274. 29 *Wæs he se cyning in þa tid bicumen in swa micle lufan þære Romaniscan cirican gesetenisse 7 þære apostolican, þæt gif he from þære untrymnesse gehæled wære, þæt he wolde to Rome feran* and *ÆLS* 8. 79 *Hat hi swa yfele and swa unclæne þæt gif ðu hwylcne wyrige þæt ðu gewisce him þæs þæt his lif beo gelic þinum laðum godum*, 'the fact that a conditional clause follows *ðæt* makes a repetition of *ðæt* a necessity'. This is not true. When a subordinate clause precedes a final or consecutive clause on which it is dependent, we find the same three arrangements we found when a subordinate clause precedes and is dependent on a noun clause; see §1978. They are first, *þæt* preceding the first clause, as in *GD(H)* 34. 1 above; second, *þæt* preceding the second clause, as in *GD(C)* 34. 1 above; and third, *þæt* preceding both the first and the second clause, as in *Bede* 274. 29 and *ÆLS* 8. 79 above and in *Bede* 160. 25 and *Or* 84. 11 (§3002), where the subject of the *þæt* clause is also repeated. Other examples of this last type—repetition or partial repetition of the final or consecutive conjunction—include *þætte . . . þæt* in *Bede* 270. 2 and *CP* 145. 24; *þæt ic . . . þæt ic* in *Bede* 486. 7; *swa . . . þætte . . . þæt* in *Bede* 268. 8; *swa ðætte . . . þte* in *Bo* 43. 19; *swa þætte . . . þæt* in *Bede* 142. 2; and *to þon þætte . . . þætte* in *Bede* 288. 3.

§3004. It remains now to ask whether final or consecutive clauses ever occupy initial position in the sentence. For consecutive clauses the answer, as far as I am aware, is 'No'; the nearest to it I have found are examples like *ÆCHom* ii. 418. 12 *To ðan swiðe ic geoffrige Gode soðe behreowsunge, þæt ic ealle mine bec, on ðam þe se dry-cræft onstod, awearp, and ic wiðsoc eallum deofles cræftum samod*, where the first element of a divided formula begins the principal clause, but the result clause follows. But very occasionally we find a clause of purpose—the term is certainly more appropriate here than 'a final clause'—in initial position under Latin influence. But *Ps(A)* 16. 4 *ðætte he ne sprece muð min wirc monna . . . ic heold weagas ða heardan*, Latin *ut non loquatur os meum opera hominum . . . ego custodiui uias duras*, hardly qualifies as idiomatic OE. *Bede* 2. 14 *7 þæt ðy læs tweoge hwæðer þis soð sy, ic cyðe hwanan me þas spell coman* also imitates the Latin. *Bede* 288. 3 *þære sweostor mægen þæt æfter þæs apostolis cwide in untrymnesse gefremed wære, wæs heo semninga gehrinen mid hefigre untrymnesse lichoman* has the subject of the purpose clause before the conjunction in a clumsy imitation of the Latin *Cuius ut uirtus, iuxta Apostolum, in infirmitate perficeretur, tacta est repente grauissimo corporis morbo.* The same holds for *Bede* 74. 13. Another example is *GD* 153. 26 *ac þæt se man mage swa fela of eorðan gefremman, þy com to eorðan of heofonum se scyppend heofones ⁊ eorðan, and þæt eac mage se lichama deman be þam gastlican þeawum, þæt wæs geeadmodod þa he þan men forgeaf, þa þa he wæs lichama geworden fram mannum,* Latin *Sed, ut tanta valeat homo de terra, caeli et terrae conditor in terram venit e caelo, adque, ut iudicare caro etiam de spiritibus possit, hoc ei largire dignatus est, factus pro hominibus Deus caro.* In *Bede* 72. 10 *Gif micel feornis siiðfætes betweohn ligeð, þætte bisceopas æþelice cuman ne magon, hwæðer mot biscop halgad beon buton oðera biscopa ondweardnesse?*, the clause of purpose is subordinate to the preceding *gif* clause.

§3005. The following examples will demonstrate that final or consecutive clauses may be placed side by side without any co-ordinating conjunction or may be co-ordinated by a conjunction such as *ond* or *ac*, with or without repetition of the conjunction: *þy læs . . . þy læs . . . ⁊* in *GD* 349. 6 *ac forþon us is to tilianne þæt . . . we gehealdan him sylfum ure mod mid strængðe . . . þy læs þonne þæt unnytte geþoht ⁊ þæt toflowene tobrece ure bene, þy læs seo idle bliss undercreope on urum mode ⁊ þonne seo sawl forleose þæt gestreon þære inbryrdnesse . . .* , Latin *ne . . . ne . . . et . . .* ; *ðætte ðurh ða mildheortnesse his arfæsðnesse ðæt . . . ⁊ eac . . . ⁊ ðætte . . . ne . . .* in *CP* 97. 22, where the first *ðætte* is repeated after a phrase by *ðæt*; *þæt . . . , þæt . . . ne . . . , ac þæt . . . and . . .* in *ÆCHom* i. 610. 15; and *þæt . . . and . . .* with a change of subject in *ÆCHom* ii. 262. 7 *Hwæt ða Iudei eodon to Pilate, bædon þæt he bude ða byrgene besettan mid wacelum weardum, þæt he ne wurde forstolen, and ðam folce gesæd, þæt he sylf aryse.* Space prevents multiplication of examples from the prose.

§3006. In the poetry, we find two clauses of purpose, each introduced by *þæt* with no intervening conjunction, in *El* 673. These clauses may be co-ordinate or the second may be dependent on the first. We have two result clauses in asyndetic parataxis in *Beo* 2575 and (with the second clause negated) in

Met 17. 28   Forðæm hine anæþelað   ælmihtig god,
      þæt he unæþele   a forð þanan
      wyrð on weorulde,   to wuldre ne cymð.

þæt is repeated after *and* in *PPs* 149. 8-9, where we have two purpose clauses. But it is not repeated in the second of two purpose clauses after *ond* in *ChristA* 261, or after *oþþe* in

Gifts 97   Nis nu ofer eorþan   ænig monna
                mode þæs cræftig,   ne þæs mægeneacen,
                þæt hi æfre anum   ealle weorþen
                gegearwade,   þy læs him gilp sceððe,
                oþþe fore þære mærþe   mod astige ... ,

or in the second of two result clauses after *ne* in *GuthA* 280, or after *ond* in

Rid 40. 8   ... heht mec wæccende   wunian longe,
                þæt ic ne slepe   siþþan æfre,
                ond mec semninga   slæp ofergongeþ,
                beoð eagan min ofestum betyned,

where a third result clause with no co-ordinating conjunction follows.

H. CAUSAL CLAUSES

1. INTRODUCTORY REMARKS

§3007. Some bibliographical observations are necessary here. It is a matter for regret that the 1955 London Ph.D. dissertation 'The Expression of Causal Relationship in Old English Prose' by Elizabeth M. Liggins has not been revised and printed. It is based on an almost complete reading of OE prose,[153] is sound in aim and method, and is successful in execution. My debt to it is apparent in the pages which follow; I acknowledge it with gratitude. The reader will find a convenient summary of Liggins's conclusions about causal conjunctions at her pages 204-10. J. van Dam's *The Causal Clause and Causal Prepositions in Early Old English Prose*, printed in 1957, was not, of course, available to Liggins but contains no mention of her work. I have referred to it where necessary. Since it is based on a limited corpus within the early prose, it supplements, but does not supersede, Liggins. Ernst Jäger's *Die Konjunktionen* 'for' *und* 'for that' *im Englischen* (Giessen, 1923) is short and far from reliable. For a useful survey of previous writings, including mention of works which, though not primarily concerned with the expression of cause in OE, deal with it incidentally, see Liggins 1955, pp. 10-16.

---

[153] On the evidence of her remarks (1955, pp. 51 and 53), Liggins uses the term 'Alfredian translations' (without the inverted commas) to embrace *CP, Or, Bo, Solil, Bede*, and *GD*. 'Alfred's two early translations' (1955, p. 96) are *CP* and *Bede*.

§3008. The word 'cause' is used here in a narrow grammatical sense, embracing both 'that which produces an effect; that which gives rise to any action, phenomenon, or condition' (*OED*, s.v. *cause* I. 1) and 'a fact, condition of matters, or consideration, moving a person to action; ground of action; reason for action, motive' (*OED*, s.v. *cause* I. 3). Cause in this sense is, of course, most frequently expressed in what formal grammarians classify as clauses of cause. As I use this term, it covers any clause 'which states the cause or reason for a consequence, the grounds for an assertion, or the definition of a remark made in the clause with which it is associated' (Liggins 1955, p. 8). For a discussion of the differing implications and emphasis involved in expressing an action and its cause by adverbs or by conjunctions introducing clauses which precede or which follow the principal clause, see Liggins 1955, pp. 193 ff.

§3009. Liggins (1955, p. 38) tells us that

in OE, as in NE, the clause introduced by the causal conjunction may serve to explain, or may be directly dependent on, almost any other element of the preceding member: a simple verb, pronoun, noun, adjective, or adverb, for example, a verbal notion (such as a verb + noun object), a negative or an interrogative idea.

References to 'a verbal concept in the principal clause' are most common; next in order of frequency are references to 'nouns, negatives, and adjectives' (Liggins 1955, p. 206). I am indebted to Liggins for some of the examples which follow: (a verb) *ChronA* 32. 5 (658) *he wæs þær iii gear on wrece, hæfde hine Penda adrifenne 7 rices benumenne forþon he his swostor anforlet* and *BlHom* 5. 5 *Heo wæs ful cweden næs æmetugu, forðon þe heo wæs mid gife gefylled*; (a noun) *Lch* ii. 210. 22 *ælc broþ is to forganne for þon þe hit biþ þindende 7 yfele wætan wyrcþ. ægru sint to forganne forþonþe hira wæte bið fæt 7 maran hæto wyrcð*; (an adjective, then a verb) *Or* 246. 23 *þa heo þæron gelegen wæs, þa het hio niman ipnalis þa nædran, 7 don to hiere earme, þæt hio hie abite; for þon þe hiere þuhte þæt hit on þæm lime unsarast wære, for þon þe þære nædran gecynd is þæt ælc uht þæs þe hio abitt scel his lif on slæpe geendian*; (a numeral) *ÆCHom* i. 188. 9 *Fif hlafas ðær wæron, and fif ðusend manna þær wæron gereordode; forðan ðe þæt Iudeisce folc wæs underðeodd Godes æ, ðe stod on fif bocum awriten*; (an adverb) *ÆCHom* ii. 120. 29 *Rihtlice hi sind Angle gehatene, forðan ðe hi engla wlite habbað*; (a verb + noun object) *LawAfEl* 2 *Ne minne noman ne cig ðu on idelnesse; forðon þe ðu ne bist unscyldig wið me gif ðu on idelnesse cigst minne noman*; (a negative) *Bo* 21. 10 *Eala, Wisdom, þu þe eart modor eallra mægena, ne mæg ic na wiðcweðan ne andsacigan þ þe þu me ær sædest, forþonþe hit is eall soð* and the first *forði ðe* clause in *ÆCHom* ii. 40. 21 *Crist wolde beon gefullod, na forði ðe him neod wære æniges fulluhtes, forði ðe he næfre nane synne ne geworhte*; (an interrogative) *ÆCHom* i. 278. 24 *Hwi swa? Forði þonne se sunu wyxð, þonne ealdað se fæder*; and (a causal clause) *Or* 17. 21 *þa cirdon hie up in on ða ea, for þæm hie ne dorston forþ bi þære ea siglan for unfriþe; for þæm ðæt land wæs eall gebun on oþre healfe þære eas* and the second *forði ðe* clause in *ÆCHom* ii. 40. 21, above.

§3010. The problem of the ambiguous adverb/conjunction arises with *nu* (§§3097-106) and with formulae introduced by *for*, where we find grouped formulae without *þe* (e.g. *forþon*), grouped formulae with *þe* (e.g. *forþon þe*), and divided formulae (e.g. *forþon . . . þe*). In *BlHom* 31. 14 *7 forþon ic þe ne fylge, forþon on þyssum þrim þu eart oforswiþed*, adv. *forþon* 'for this reason' or, as Bliss and Frantzen (*RES* 27 (1976), 399) put it, 'for the reason I am about to explain' points forward to conj. *forþon* 'because'. In *BlHom* 3. 17 *deofol þonne. . . beswac þone ærestan wifmon; forþon wæs se engel sprecende to ures Drihtnes meder . . .* , adv. *forþon* 'therefore' refers back to the preceding clause. The same is true of *forði* in *ÆCHom* i. 568. 19 *Soðlice he towende þa hæðenan godas, and hi forbærnde, forðan ðe hi næron godas, ac wæron manna handgeweorc, treowene and stænene, and he hi forði tobrytte*, where we have adv. *forði* contrasted with conj. *forðan ðe*. Such examples are typical; generally speaking, we can easily distinguish the adverb from the conjunction. But there are difficulties.

§3011. It must not be assumed that formulae with *þe* are always conjunctions and cannot be adverbs. Liggins (1955, pp. 197-8) gives examples of such formulae used adverbially, viz. *GD(C)* 67. 1 (MS *O* has *forþon*), *BlHom* 57. 3, 65. 12, and 229. 16, *ÆLS* 32. 267 (see §3013), and *ÆLS* 37. 92, disagreeing—rightly in my opinion —with the EETS translation 'because that' in the last. There are more, including three examples of *forþæm þe . . . forþæm þe* 'therefore . . . because', viz. *BlHom* 163. 35, *John(WSH)* 5. 16, and *John (WSH)* 10. 17, and one of *forþæm þe . . . forþæm þe* 'because . . . therefore', viz. *HomU* 37 (*H*) 235. 3—the last three of these are variants in late manuscripts of patterns in which the adverb is without *þe* (see Liggins 1955, pp. 66 and 70); *GD* 350. 7, where *forþon þe* (line 12) means 'therefore' or 'for that reason'; and *ÆCHom* i. 66. 12 *þonne færlice gewitt he of ðissere worulde, nacod and forscyldigod, synna ana mid him ferigende; forðan þe he sceal ece wite ðrowian.* All this goes to support Baker's observation (*Speculum*, 55 (1980), 25) that '*forðam (ðe)* is not a very stable conjunction'; cf. §3016. The fact that Morris translates *BlHom* 57. 3 *forþon þe* and *BlHom* 229. 16 *forðon þe* as 'wherefore' but *BlHom* 65. 12 *forþon þe* as 'therefore' displays in another form the problem of the ambiguous demonstrative/relative discussed in §§2109-21.[154]

§3012. 'It is occasionally difficult', says Liggins (1955, pp. 29-30), 'to decide whether an element such as *forþæm* should be taken as a conjunctive adverb or as a preposition + pronoun (= "because of that")'. ('Conjunctive adverb' is Liggins's term for words such as *forþæm* and *forþy* when they mean 'therefore' or 'hence'.) For me, this difficulty arises more than 'occasionally' in both prose and poetry, whether the formula occurs initially, e.g. *ÆCHom* i. 184. 3 and (with the element order VS) *ÆCHom* i. 16. 14; after *and*, e.g. *ÆCHom* i. 66. 28; medially, e.g. *ÆCHom* i. 96. 11; or in final position, e.g. *ÆCHom* ii. 438. 21. But I have to agree with Liggins when she concludes her sentence with the words 'but it makes little difference to the sense'.

§3013. What is perhaps a more serious difficulty is also noted by Liggins (1955, p. 29), viz. the existence of examples of a *for* formula 'in passages where it could be taken either as a conjunction or as a conjunctive adverb (= "therefore")'. She illustrates this remark with *BlHom* 41. 36 *forþon*, noting the inconsistency between Morris's punctuation of *BlHom* 41. 36-43. 7 and his translation (1955, p. 197), and with examples such as *Bo* 25. 24, *Bo* 65. 18, *ÆCHom* i. 48. 15, and *ÆCHom* i. 268. 29, in which 'the conjunction is followed immediately by the verb', observing that in such sentences 'there is a bare possibility that *forðy* is an adverb, but in every case the sense is better if it is regarded as an explanatory conjunction' (1955, pp. 123-4). There are examples in the poetry too in which a choice presents itself between 'for' and 'therefore' as a translation for a *for* formula without *þe*. Examples include *GenB* 729, *GenB* 770, and

ChristA 239   þu eart seo snyttro   þe þas sidan gesceaft
    mid þi waldende   worhtes ealle.
    Forþon nis ænig þæs horsc,   ne þæs hygecræftig,
    þe þin fromcyn mæge   fira bearnum
    sweotule geseþan.

See further Mitchell 1959, Appendix 'Cause 1'. Although (as I note in §3011) Liggins takes *for þan þe* as 'therefore' in *ÆLS* 32. 267

---

[154] Considerations of space often force me to content myself with references rather than quotations in this and the next two sections.

Crist geswutelaþ mannum . . . þæt he is ælmihtig god . . . þeah þe þa earman Iudei hine eallunge wiðsocen for þan þe hi synd awyrgede . . . , I am myself inclined to include it here as another ambiguous example; Skeat's 'because' is not, I think, impossible. For further discussion of the adverbial use of *for* formulae, see Liggins 1955, pp. 196-8, and on the interchangeability of the various *for* formulae and *þy* as adverbs, see Liggins 1955, pp. 201-2.

§3014. Another problem—one which persists into the English of today—is that of deciding whether a causal conjunction is co-ordinating or subordinating. Writing on MnE 'for', Haber (*American Speech*, 30 (1955), 151) observes that 'the only practical conclusion is that the conjunction has two uses, subordinating and co-ordinating, and that punctuation is of no significance in identifying either'. The same is true for OE. Van Dam (p. xii) remarks that 'owing to the subordinating character of *þe*, the group-conjunction *for þæm þe* was more used as a subordinating than as a coordinating link', thereby rightly implying that even the presence of *þe* is not sufficient to prove that the formula must be a subordinating conjunction: see further §§1858-9. But, as I have said in *NQ* 223 (1978), 394, I believe that Haber may have been guilty of an over-simplification. In my experience, there are times when even the intonation patterns of an utterance I hear spoken do not enable me to say firmly that *for* is co-ordinating rather than subordinating or vice versa. That the same difficulty may have existed in OE is suggested by a consideration of examples like *BlHom* 25. 22 *Wa eow þe nu hlihaþ, forþon ge eft wepað on ecnesse* and *BlHom* 25. 20 *Eadige beoþ þa þe nu wepað, forþon þe hi beoþ eft afrefrede.* I am encouraged in this belief by the fact that Liggins quite independently also holds it. Throughout her work, she recognizes the existence of examples of *for* formulae both with and without *þe* in which 'the meaning is either ambiguous or is somewhere between these two extremes' of 'true Reason' and 'Explanation', which I discuss in the next few sections (1955, p. 75); see in particular Liggins 1955, pp. 37, 75, 122, and 127. (These are the 'ambiguous' examples in the table in §3017.) Here again we feel the lack of intonation patterns and native informants, although (judging from the situation in MnE) even they would not help us to solve all our difficulties.

§3015. Liggins (1955, pp. 4-10) discusses this problem in some detail. She distinguishes clauses which give 'the cause or reason for an event'—these are introduced by conjunctions such as 'because' and causal *quia*—and 'those which amplify, explain or suggest the reason for, a statement'—usually introduced by 'for', *enim*, and the like—and calls them respectively 'clauses of true Reason (often described by grammarians as "subordinate")' and clauses of 'Explanation (often called "coordinate")'. She uses the term 'conjunct' to cover both these, 'to describe the clause which states the cause or reason for a consequence, the grounds for an assertion, or the definition of a remark made in the clause with which it is associated. To this other clause the usual term "principal" is applied.' She gives among her reasons the fact that element order, mood, and even clause order, cannot be decisive criteria in OE—the same is true of punctuation, the presence of a possible correlative, and (for the poetry) metre; on these see Mitchell 1959, pp. 430-2—and points out that in his *Grammar* Ælfric makes no attempt to distinguish 'coordinate' from 'subordinate' clauses and in his *Homilies* regularly uses formulae with *þe* where they can only be 'explanatory'. These things certainly underline the dilemma of the syntactician of OE. But, while I am aware of these distinctions and make them when it is possible to do so as they become relevant—see the Indexes—I have not adopted the term 'conjunct'.

§3016. Liggins quite rightly explored the possibility that 'clauses of true Reason' and 'Explanatory Clauses' were introduced by different conjunctions, but was forced to conclude (1955, p. 204) that none of the causal conjunctions she had discussed was used exclusively in one kind of clause or the other:

Nearly all of these conjunctions may be used to express either true Reason or Explanation. However, *forþæm þe* is used more often than *forþæm* to introduce a Reason, though in both cases the Explanatory uses far outnumber the others. *Forþy þe, forþæm þæt, forþy þæt* and *þy* are used chiefly at the head of clauses of Reason; on the other hand, *þæt* clauses generally contain an explanation or amplification of a preceding statement.

(On *þæt(te)*, see §§3118-27.) Jäger (p. 89) put forward the simplistic solution that in OE there was a sharp distinction between *forþæm* 'for' and *forþæm þe* 'because': 'in ae. Zeit waren *forþæm* = "denn" und *forþæm þe* = "weil" in ihrem syntaktischen Gebrauch scharf voneinander geschieden' ['in the OE period *forþæm* = "for" and *forþæm þe* = "because" were clearly separated from each other by their syntactic usage']. I reached the conclusion independently, and so agree with Liggins (1955, p. 73), that 'this is far from being the case'. A few typical exceptions follow. They include formulae with *þe* meaning 'for' in *CP* 304. 10 *We willað nu faran to ðære stowe ðe God us gehaten hæfð, ac far mid us, ðæt we ðe mægen wel don, forðæmðe God hæfð suiðe wel gehaten Israhela folce*, *ÆCHom* i. 6. 13

Ne sende se deofol ða fyr of heofenum, þeah ðe hit ufan come;
forðan þe he sylf næs on heofonum, syððan he for his modignysse of
aworpen wæs, and

Met 10. 63   þeah ge nu wenen   and wilnigen
                   þæt ge lange tid   libban moten,
                   hwæt iow æfre þy bet   bio oððe þince?
                   Forðæm þe nane forlet,   þeah hit lang ðince,
                   deað æfter dogorrime,   þonne he hæfð drihtnes leafe,[155]

and formulae without *þe* meaning 'because' in *Bede* 34. 31 *Mid þy ðe*
he geseah S̄c̄m̄ Albanum, þa wæs he sona yrre geworden, forþam he
mid his sylfes willum geþristade, þæt he hine sylfne on geweald
sealde swylcere frecednysse for þam cuman . . . , ByrM 30. 12 *Ðas*
þing we swa hwonlice her hrepiað on foreweardum worce, forðan we
hig þenceað oftor to hrepian 7 to gemunanne, and

Beo 1333   Heo þa fæhðe wræc,
                   þe þu gystran niht   Grendel cwealdest
                   þurh hæstne had   heardum clammum,
                   forþan he to lange   leode mine
                   wanode ond wyrde.

Jäger could have seen that he was wrong by consulting Wülfing, ii.
122-7 and 685, by noting the fact that the *for* formula with *þe* is
recorded only thirteen times in the poetry, and by considering variant readings such as those in *Chron* 658, where *ChronA* 32. 6 has *for-*
þon, ChronB forðon þe, and *ChronE* 33. 29 *forþan þ̄; Bede* 272. 32,
where MSS *T, B,* and *O,* have *forþon þe* and MS *Ca forðon;* and
CPPref 8, where MS *H* has *forðæm,* MSS *J* and *D forðon,* and MS *T*
for þæm þe. As Liggins (1955, p. 74) remarks, their existence—her
table (1955, p. 178) shows that there are 135 places in which there
are manuscript variations between *for* formulae with and without *þe*
—'would, alone, disprove Jäger's assertion'. The reader will have no

[155] I detect some confusion in Liggins here. She cites *Bo* 22. 5 *Hwæt, he is giet hal 7*
gesund, 7 hæfð ælces godes genog; forðon ðe ic wat þ̄ ðu auht ne forslawode þte þu þin
agen feorh for hine ne sealdest . . . and *ÆCHom* ii. 204. 34 *Witodlice ælc gesceaft is ydel-*
nysse underðeod, þæt is, awendedlicnesse, forðan ðe hi beoð awende fram brosnunge to un-
brosnunge as examples of *forþæm þe* expressing 'mere connection' and goes on to say that
'in 989 cases, the conjunction is simply a connective' (1955, p. 37). Yet these 989 examples
are listed under the heading 'Explan' in her table (1955, p. 39). She makes the same equation elsewhere. I cannot construe *forðon ðe* in *Bo* 22. 5 as 'for'—Sedgefield has 'and'—
and, while agreeing that Thorpe's 'for' is possible for *forðan ðe* in *ÆCHom* ii. 204. 34, I
would say that 'and' was also acceptable. However, as Liggins rightly stresses throughout
her thesis, such classifications are frequently a matter of personal interpretation. This was
my reason for not attempting in my D.Phil. thesis to distinguish those examples in the
poetry in which a *for* formula meant 'because' from those in which it meant 'for'. The letter
p after a reference in Appendix 'Cause 1' to that thesis (Mitchell 1959) merely indicates that
(in *Beowulf*) Klaeber and (elsewhere) the Columbia editors punctuate the *forþon* clause as
principal by separating it from the preceding clause with a semi-colon or a full stop and that
forþon seems to mean 'for' rather than 'therefore'.

difficulty in finding for himself more exceptions to Jäger's 'rule'. Those requiring further documentation will find it in van Dam, pp. 41, 45-8, and 53-4,[156] and Liggins 1955, pp. 173-7 and 204-5, where Liggins says of *for* formulae without *þe*, with *þe*, and with *þæt*, that 'most of them may be interchanged, either in various manuscripts or within the one manuscript of a single work'. For her discussion on variations within the one manuscript of a single work, see Liggins 1955, pp. 177-85, where she tells us that in Ælfric in particular the choice was governed by stylistic considerations, including sentence rhythm and the pronunciation of the following word. See also Baker, *Speculum*, 55 (1980), 25-6.

§3017. However, it could be that Jäger's error was the one made so often by Andrew, viz. that of erecting a tendency into a 'rule'. I base this observation on Liggins's figures for clauses which are introduced by the *for* formulae and which follow the principal clause. Those for *forþy/þi (þe)* are most striking. Of the formulae without *þe* eighty per cent (thirty-six examples out of forty-five) are 'explanatory' (Liggins 1955, p. 122). But of those with *þe* seventy-five per cent (twenty-five examples out of thirty-three) express 'true Reason' (Liggins 1955, p. 127). Her figures for *forþæm (þe)*—where *þæm* embraces *þam, þan,* and *þon*—are less striking. The 'explanatory' use is the predominant one with both formulae, but the percentages vary markedly. Of the formulae without *þe*, 79.2 per cent (1011 examples out of 1277) are 'explanatory' and only 10.3 per cent (132 examples out of 1277) express 'true Reason' (Liggins 1955, p. 75). For those with *þe*, the respective percentages are 55.7 per cent (989 examples out of 1776) 'explanatory' and twenty-six per cent (462 examples out of 1776) 'true Reason' (Liggins 1955, pp. 37 and 39). These figures, which are set out in tabular form below, suggest that there is probably something in Kivimaa's observation (p. 164) that 'the appending of *þe* seems to make for a closer tie to the main clause and its omission for a looser one, because causal clauses of explanation are not so intimately bound to the main clause as those of reason'. So perhaps Jäger expressed part of the truth. But Kivimaa's use of 'seems' is to be noted. Thus, when translating *Or* 294. 13 . . . *7 feng him self to þæm onwalde, for þon þe he ne mehte self habban þæs onwaldes noman, for þy he næs Romanisc*, it seems reasonable to take *for þon þe* as 'because' and *for þy* as 'for'. Yet in *Or* 138. 23 *Ac se gefea wearð swiþe raðe on heora mode to gedrefednesse*

---

[156] The fact that all the (nine) examples of *for þy þe* recorded by van Dam (p. 57) are 'subordinating' may reflect his limited corpus; Liggins (1955, pp. 127-8) says that there are seven 'Explanatory' examples elsewhere without giving specific references. But see §3011.

gecierred, þa hie gesawan þa deadan men swa þiclice to eorþan beran þe þær ær æt ham wæron; for þy þær wæs se micla moncwealm on þære tide, MS *C* has *for þon þe* for *L*'s *for þy*.

TABLE (based on Liggins 1955) giving numbers and percentages of clauses introduced by a *for* formula without a correlative which follow the principal clause

	'True Reason'	'Explanatory'	'Ambiguous' (§3014)	Total
Formulae without *þe*:				
forþæm/þam/þan/þon	132 (10.3%)	1011 (79.2%)	134	1277
forþy/þi	6 (13.3%)	36 (80%)	3	45
Formulae with *þe*:				
forþæm/þam/þan/þon þe	462 (26%)	989 (55.7%)	325	1776
forþy/þi þe	25 (75%)	7 (21%)	1	33

§3018. So, as the table demonstrates, there are many individual instances in which it is impossible to decide the exact nuance implied by a *for* formula, whether it has or does not have *þe*. This has been demonstrated by the variant readings and the examples quoted in §§3016-17 and by the fact that formulae with *þe* can be adverbial 'therefore' (§3011). Two other points are relevant. First, there are individual differences in the usage of authors; see Liggins 1955, *passim*, especially pp. 204-5 and 536-44. Second, there is the fact that formulae with and without *þe* can represent both Latin *quia/quod* and also *enim/nam*, as van Dam's table (p. 84) demonstrates:

	quia	*enim*	*nam*	*quod*
for þæm	95	31	—	13
for þæm þe	85	—	9	13
for þon	124	43	54	23
for þon þe	112	12	14	25

We have therefore to conclude that we cannot ascertain the function of one specific *for* formula on the basis of the presence or absence of *þe*.

§3019. It will, however, be convenient—though a glance at *OED*, s.v. *cause*, will show that a good many questions are begged here—to

divide causal clauses into three groups: those giving the accepted—
I avoid the word 'true' because of Liggins's use of the term 'clause of
true Reason'; see §3015—the suggested, and the rejected or denied,
cause or reason respectively. The accepted cause is the actual cause
or that thought or represented by the speaker to be such. A suggested
cause is one which is put forward by the speaker as a possible reason,
or as that advanced by others. It may, in reality, be the accepted
cause, but the speaker is not affirming that it is. A favourite example
with Latin grammarians is *Socrates accusatus est quod iuventutem
corrumperet* 'Socrates was accused on the ground that he corrupted
the youth'. A rejected or denied cause is one which is advanced and
denied by the speaker, e.g. 'He did this, not because he wanted to,
but because he had to'.

§3020. All rejected or denied causes are in a sense also suggested
causes. But I have found in OE no examples of suggested cause
exactly parallel to that about Socrates in §3019. Examples like *Bede*
56. 17 and *Bede* 216. 7, cited by van Dam (p. 81), and *ÆCHom* i.
82. 25—all of which are in conditional sentences—are not the
same. Nor is *CP* 341. 20 *Oðer is ðæt hwa for hreowsunge his synna
ælmessan selle, oðer is ðæt he forðy syngige 7 reafige ðy he tiohchie
ðæt he eft scyle mid ðy reaflace ælmessan gewyrcean*, also quoted by
van Dam (pp. 81-2). The incomplete sentence about the Virgin's
womb and Christ in *BlHom* 5. 15 [. . .] *þy þe he hine onfehþ, ne
beluceþ he hine no* merely asserts that the truth of the first statement does not certify the truth of the second. On this example see
also §3135.

§3021. There are no syntactical grounds for distinguishing what is
sometimes called an 'actual' cause, e.g. 'He is sitting in that room
because the light is on (and he wants to read)' from a so-called
'logical' cause, e.g. 'He is sitting in that room (and I know) because
the light is on'. Thus, *BlHom* 17. 30 *Rihtlic þæt wæs þæt se blinda
be ðæm wege sæte wædliende; forþon þe Drihten sylfa cwæþ, 'Ic
eom weg soðfæstnesse'; 7 se þe ne can þa beorhtnesse þæs ecan
leohtes, se bið blind* can be translated 'It was right and proper . . .
because . . .' ('actual' cause) or 'The blind man rightly sat . . . because
. . .' ('logical' cause).

§3022. I turn briefly to the question of Latin influence. Writing of
the early prose, van Dam (p. 84) remarks that even in the 'more
faithful translations hardly anything was found to show that the
Latin had a decisive influence on the Old English causal clause'.

Liggins (1955, pp. 172-3, 201, 208-10, and 533-6), covering prose of all periods, reaches much the same conclusion (p. 536): 'OE prose, then, suggests that the direct influence of Latin on the causal constructions was quite limited in its extent.' She makes two qualifications worthy of note here. The first (p. 533) is quite firm:

The influence of Latin on causal constructions in OE seems to be marked only in a few of the constructions without a finite verb. The most important of these are the participial constructions, the nominative and dative absolutes, the appositive participial phrases and the use of participles as adjectives or substantives.

The second (p. 534) is less so:

It may be that Latin originals sometimes influence the relative order of principal and conjunct clauses, since an OE translator is apt to repeat the order in the text before him, and also the tendency to invert the order of subject and verb in some contexts, but the evidence is not very clear.

I have found nothing to suggest that Latin influence was any stronger in the poetry.

§3023. To conclude these introductory remarks on causal clauses, I quote another statement from Liggins (1955, p. 536):

Some usages are restricted to a given context or to a given period, but the total impression is that there were no really significant changes in the methods of causal expression between Alfred's time and that of Ælfric and his followers. Such differences as there are seem to belong to the individual writer rather than to his period.

§3024. But the expression of cause in OE is not limited to causal clauses. It is found in other clauses and in expressions without finite verbs. Most obvious, perhaps, are temporal clauses, for *post hoc* is often *propter hoc*; see §2533. Liggins (1955, pp. 1-10 and 520 ff., and *passim*) adds others: clauses of purpose—'it often happens that the motive for an action is both its "cause" and its "purpose"' (p. 3); clauses of result—'if A is the cause of B, then B is the result of A' (p. 2); adjective clauses—'all the major and most of the minor types of relative constructions may be used with a superadded causal sense' (p. 399; see further van Dam, p. 84); modal clauses, including those in which '*swa* means both "since" and "in the way that"' (p. 335), those 'in which *swa* is associated with the comparative degree of an adverb or adjective' (p. 334), and proportional constructions involving *swa . . . swa* (pp. 344-9); clauses of concession, e.g. *ÆCHom* ii. 216. 23 *Gif hwam seo lar oflicige, ne yrsige he nateshwon wið us, ðeah ðe we Godes bebodu mannum geopenian*, where *þeah þe* retains its concessive force but also has 'shades of condition, cause and time' (pp. 387–8); and clauses of condition, e.g. *ÆCHom* i. 252. 21 *Gif ge cunnon, þa ðe yfele sind, syllan ða godnysse eowrum bearnum, hu micele swiðor wile eower Heofonlica Fæder forgyfan godne gast him biddendum*, where 'the conjunction [*gif*] has the force of NE "since"' (pp. 362–3).

§3025. Two paratactic clauses may also express a causal relationship. Liggins (1955, p. 9) compares 'I know it because he told me' with 'I know it. He told me', where 'the second member gives the reason for the fact stated in the first'. A relationship of cause and effect may also be expressed in two clauses joined by *and*. 'Usually', says Liggins (1955, p. 448), 'the fact or cause is stated in the first one and the consequence in the second, so that *and* is equivalent to NE "and therefore, and so". But there are also a fair number of cases in which the consequence is stated before the cause, and in which *and* then becomes equivalent to NE "for" or "because".' Clauses of the type 'He is in earnest; therefore/so/hence he will succeed' (Liggins 1955, p. 193) also occur.

§3026. Liggins (1955, p. 220) tells us that 'in almost all the examples to be discussed, the causal function is additional to the basic one expressing time, condition, and so on; very rarely has the original one been totally replaced by the causal' and warns us (1955, p. 218) that 'there is necessarily a fair degree of subjectivity in analysis of this kind'. But this—rightly—did not deter her and must not deter others from attempting such analysis. Both the various types of clauses so far mentioned and expressions without a finite verb which express cause will be discussed in more detail in the appropriate places; see the Indexes.

2. QUESTIONS DEMANDING A CAUSE, REASON, OR PURPOSE

§3027. Liggins (1955, p. 512) observes that 'often it is only the context which determines whether the question seeks information about the cause or the purpose of a fact. Sometimes either type of answer would be appropriate.' The question may, of course, be dependent or non-dependent except, perhaps, with combinations of *to* + dat./instr. of *hwæt* or with *hwæt* itself; see §3029. On the question 'cause or purpose?', see further van Dam, p. 34. The most common interrogatives are *hwi/hwy* and *for* + dat./instr. of *hwæt*. Van Dam (p. xi) found in the early prose fifty-eight examples of *for hwon*, twenty-four examples of *for* + other forms of *hwæt*, thirteen examples of *hwi/hwy*, and ten of *to* + dat./instr. of *hwæt*. (I can find only nine of these; see van Dam, pp. 34–5.) His three examples with *on* (pp. 32–3) can be dismissed; in all of them *hwam/hwon/hwy* is dependent on the phrase *gelang on* 'dependent on, consequent on'. Liggins's figures (1955, pp. 512–14) can be presented in tabular form:

Interrogative	Non-dependent question	Dependent question	Total
hwi (þonne)	152	45	197
forhwon	31	15	46
forhwi (þonne)	23	13	36
to hwi	13	0	13
to hwon/hwan/hwam	23	0	23
hwæt (þonne)	21	0	21

These figures appear to exclude examples of interrogative forms which, in Liggins's phrase (1955, p. 512), ' "correlate" with a causal clause', e.g. *CP* 25. 15 *Forðonðe nan cræft nis to læranne ðæm ðe hine ær geornlice ne leornode, forhwon beoð æfre suæ ðriste ða ungelæredan ðæt hi underfon ða heorde ðæs lariowdomes, ðonne se cræft ðæs lareowdomes bið cræft ealra cræfta?* (Liggins 1955, p. 71), *ByrM* 104. 11 *Hwi, la broðer, dest ðu þæt þæs monan yld byð on anre ylde on Kł. Aprelis 7 Mai, þænne þu hyt næfre swa gemetst on þam getele?*, and *ÆLS* 10. 236 *þa axode Titus þone eadigan apostol hwi he geþafode þæt heo swa lage on þam legerbedde þonne he oðre alefede ealle gehælde and heo ana læg swa* (Liggins 1955, p. 256). This may account for the discrepancies between van Dam's figures and hers. There is obviously room for further work here. It seems odd that van Dam found fifty-eight examples of *forhwon* in his five texts—*Bede, Chron, CP, GD*, and *Or*—all of which were read by Liggins, who records only forty-six. So too does the fact that *hwi/hwy* appears only thirteen times in those five texts when Liggins records a total of 197 examples. For references to more examples than I quote below, and for details of the distribution of the various forms, see van Dam, *passim*, and Liggins 1955, pp. 512–19, though the latter unfortunately does not give full references. Liggins also gives examples of variations between manuscripts, e.g. *GD* 88. 31, where MS *H* has *for hwi*, MS *C* *to hwon*, and MS *O* *for hwon*.

§3028. A few typical examples of these interrogatives will suffice: (with *hwi/hwy*) *Or* 134. 12 *þa wundrade Alexander hwy hit swa*

æmenne wære, John(WSCp) 20. 15 *Wif hwi wepst ðu?, ÆCHom* ii.
310. 1 *þa befran se arleasa casere, hwi he suwade,* and *GenB* 282
Hwy sceal ic æfter his hyldo ðeowian . . . ?; (with *forhwæm/for-*
hwam) GD(O) 227. 8 *þu gefera Coliuerte, for hwam aris þu swa ær?*
and *CP* 240. 16 *ðonne mon mæg ongietan of hwæm hit ærest com 7*
for hwæm; (with *forhwan/forhwon) Bede* 112. 10 *Forhwon ne recst*
þu us þone hwitan hlaf . . . ? and *GD* 288. 4 *7 hi ascodon for hwan*
þæt wære; and (with *forhwi/forhwy) CP* 423. 22 *Forhwy bið se syn-*
fulla onbryrd mid ðære hreowsunga 7 ne bið no ðy ryhtwisra . . . ?,
GD 242. 16 *þa wundrode se halga man for hwi hi swa acsodon . . . ,*
Coll 249 *Ic ahsige eow forhwi swa geornlice leorni ge?,* and *PPs* 113.
5 *Oððe þu, Iordanen, for hwi gengdest on bæcling?*

§3029. On the evidence provided by van Dam (pp. 34–5) and Liggins (see the table in §3027), the *to* formulae are used only in non-
dependent questions, e.g. *GD(C)* 227. 20 *To hwan wundrast þu,*
Petrus, for þissere wisan?, Bede 440. 8 *To hwon sitton ge her?,*
ÆCHom ii. 74. 35 *To hwi stande ge her ealne dæg ydele?,* and *Soul i*
17 . . . *to hwan drehtest ðu me . . . ?* Similarly, as the table in §3027
shows, Liggins records only non-dependent questions with *hwæt*
'why', e.g. *GD(H)* 40. 18 *hwæt wundrast þu, Petrus . . . ?* (MS *O* has
to hwan), ÆCHom ii. 164. 27 *Maledicte, non Benedicte, þu awyrigeda*
and na gebletsod, hwæt witst ðu me, hwi ehtst ðu min?, and *GenB*
278 *Hwæt sceal ic winnan?* My collections offer no examples of
dependent questions with these interrogatives.

§3030. Liggins (1955, pp. 514–15) also notes the use of *humeta,*
e.g. *ÆCHom* ii. 310. 2 *Eft hine axode se arleasa casere humeta he*
wolde his geogoðe amyrran; of *for hwilcum ðingum,* e.g. *ÆCHom* i.
424. 1 *For hwilcum ðingum neadað se deofol eow þæt ge cristene*
men to his biggengum ðreatniað?; and (in imitation of Latin) of the
formula *hwæt is þæt,* e.g. *Luke(WSCp)* 2. 49 *hwæt is þ gyt me*
sohton?, Latin *quid est quod me quaerebatis?,* and *GD(H)* 60. 6 . . .
nu lysteð me axian hwæt þæt sy þæt þa þa ure alysend ageaf gesihþe
twam blindum mannum, þa het he þæt hi hit nanum men ne asædon
. . . , Latin . . . *libet inquirere quidnam sit quod Redemptor noster. . . .*

§3031. As in MnE, a question may be answered by a causal clause
without an expressed principal clause, e.g. *Bo* 138. 8 *Ða cwæð ic:*
Hwy forlæte wit hi a þa ma? Ða cwæð he: Forðy þe folcisce men
secgað þ ælc reðu wyrd 7 unwynsumu sie yfel, ÆCHom i. 278. 24
Hwi swa? Forði þonne se sunu wyxð, þonne ealdað se fæder, and
Coll 141 *7 forhwi forlæst þu þa getemedon ætwindan fram þe?*

Forþam ic nelle fedan hig on sumera, forþamþe hig þearle etaþ. Liggins (1955, pp. 48-9, 93-4, 124, and 132) quotes more examples. We may also note here those rhetorical formulae in which the question is posed and answered, e.g. *Bo* 68. 9, *ÆCHom* ii. 464. 16, and *ÆC Hom* ii. 566. 31 *Hwi sind ða deadan slapende gecwedene, buton forðan ðe hi sceolon arisan geedcucode þurh ðone Ælmihtigan Scyppend?*, and the occasional appearance of the equivalent of the MnE formula 'I know not why', e.g. *LS* 8. 325 *þa we up comon þa næs ure modor mid us, nat ic forhwi.*

§3032. Finally, there are two problems of classification or terminology. Liggins (1955, pp. 516-17) classifies as dependent statement rather than dependent question clauses such as that introduced by *hwi* in *ÆCHom* i. 48. 9 *Se wisa Augustinus spræc ymbe ðas rædinge, and smeade hwi se halga cyðere Stephanus cwæde þæt he gesawe mannes bearn standan æt Godes swyðran, and nolde cweðan Godes bearn.* These, she says, 'are very similar to Indirect Questions, the difference lying in the meaning of the verb in the principal clause'. The difference is exquisite. She also suggests (1955, pp. 518-19) that in examples like *ÆCHom* i. 502. 16 *and he ða mid graman wearð astyred, hwi se fearr angenga his heorde forsawe* '*hwi* . . . is almost equivalent to NE "because" ' and is used 'to introduce an Adverbial Clause'. We could, I suppose, understand a verb or participle of asking or saying to introduce a question in this and the three other examples she cites, all of which (she points out) contain 'a notion of anger'. In view of the Latin *pro quo ualde sumus contristati, cum hic esset defunctus*, I prefer the reading of *Bede(Ca)* 248. 24 . . . *þ hi swiðe geunrotsade wæron forðon ðe he þær forðferan sceolde*, despite the readings of the other manuscripts: *T forhwon, B forhwam, C forhwon ðe*, and *O forhwon þe* (*þ* incompletely erased, reports Miller, to form *h*). But see Liggins 1955, pp. 119-20.

3. CLAUSES INTRODUCED BY *FOR*, ALONE AND IN COMBINATION

a. Introductory remarks

§3033. I begin by reminding the reader of two things. The first is that (apparent) combinations of *for* + dat./instr. of *se, seo, þæt* (+ (. . .) *þæt/þe*) are not always conjunctions; consider *Bede(T)* 298. 24 *For þæm Theodor biscop in Hrofesceastre Quichelm to biscope gehalgode*, Latin *Pro quo Theodorus in ciuitate Hrofi Cuichelmum consecrauit episcopum, Bede(T)* 376. 19 *Gegyrewað ðone lichoman*

mid neowum hræglum fore ðam ðe ge ðær on noman, Latin *'Noua'*
inquit 'indumenta corpori pro his quae tulistis circumdate' (where
both the sense and *fore* warn us that we do not have a causal conjunction), *Bede(O)* 384. 11 . . . *gif ic an his wundur asecge þ me an*
þara broðra sæde for þam 7 on þam þe hit gefremed wæs, Latin . . .
unum eius narro miraculum quod mihi unus e fratribus propter quos
et in quibus patratum est ipse narrauit, *Mark(WSCp)* 13. 20 . . . *ac*
for þam gecorenum þe he geceas he gescyrte þa dagas, and *ÆCHom*
ii. 260. 3 *Ða wælhreowan Iudei noldon geðafian, for ðam symbel-*
dæge, þæt hi swa hangodon cuce on ðam rodum, ac woldon hi ac-
wellan. . . . (On *BlHom* 63. 1, see Liggins 1955, p. 139.) The second
is that it is sometimes difficult to decide whether a particular example of the formula is an adverb, a co-ordinating conjunction,
a subordinating conjunction, or something in between; see §§1858,
2418, and 3014. On the origin of the *for* formulae, see §§2426 and
2912, and Mitchell, at press (*c*).

§3034. *For* alone is rare; see §3037. OE clauses of cause are most
frequently introduced by a *for* formula. This is true of eighty-six per
cent of the clauses in early prose examined by van Dam (p. 40). The
figures given by Liggins (1955, chapter ii) confirm this preponderance of *for* formulae in prose of all periods. It holds for the poetry
too; see Mitchell 1959, pp. 813–22.

§3035. The following spellings for the demonstrative element occur
in both prose and poetry, *þ* here representing both *þ* and *ð*: *þæm,*
þam, þan, þon, þy, and *þi*. Liggins has two groups, distinguishing the
first four from the last two. Van Dam has three: *þæm, þam*, and *þan*;
þon; *þy* and *þi*. Liggins's grouping makes it impossible for us to tell
whether *þon* is the most common spelling throughout OE prose, as it
is in early prose (van Dam, p. xii, and Table 1 below) and in the
poetry, where it is especially frequent in *PPs* and *Met* (Mitchell 1959,
p. 428 fn. 1). In the sections which follow, I discuss separately
grouped formulae without *þe* or *þæt*, grouped formulae with *þe* and
with *þæt*, and divided formulae. There is no point in attempting to
exemplify all the various spellings and combinations in all the various
functions of the *for* formulae; the variations are authorial or scribal
and have no syntactical significance. This is neatly illustrated by the
variations in *HomU* 26. 141. 4 . . . *stingað stranglic sar on his eagan,*
forðam, swa hwæt swa he unrihtes geseah, þæt wæs eall sylfwilles.
stingað hine scearplice on þone muð, forði, swa hwæt swa hine lyste
etan oððe drincan oððe on unnyt sprecan, eall he hit aræfnode.
stingað hine mid sorhlicum sare on his heortan, forðam þe on hyre ne

wunode arfæstnys ne mildheortnys ne godes lufu. Much valuable material on their distribution will be found in van Dam, where there is an index, and in Liggins 1955, where the table of contents has to serve as one. The possibility of authorial variation for stylistic reasons has been mentioned in §3016.

§3036. The tables which follow may, however, be of interest. Table 1 is based on van Dam's figures (pp. xi–xii, 11, 16–18, 41, 45, 49, 53, and 56–7) for *Bede, Chron* up to 901, *CP, GD,* and *Or.* Table 2 presents the figures given by Liggins (1955, pp. 36, 51, 62, 74, 96, 104, 120, 124, 127, and 131) for clauses in which the *for* formula is not used correlatively.

Table 1

Adverb		Conjunction		Conjunction	
for þæm	128	*for þæm*	197	*for þæm þe*	103
for þam	37	*for þam*	75	*for þam þe*	41
for þan	7	*for þan*	31	*for þan þe*	22
for þon	154	*for þon*	394	*for þon þe*	335
for þy/þi	38	*for þy*	5	*for þy/þi þe*	9

Table 2

Conjunction	Position in relation to governing clause			
	Before	Within	After	Total
for þæm/þam/þan/þon þe	61	3	1776	1840
for þæm/þam/þan/þon	25	3	1277	1305
for þy/þi þe	4		33	37
for þy/þi	1 [157]		45	46

With these observations and figures in mind, I turn now to discussion of the various conjunctions in which *for* appears.

b. For

§3037. *OED* (s.v. *for* B conj.) notes no examples of *for* as a causal conjunction before *c.*1150. Van Dam (pp. 40–1) finds earlier ME

---

[157] This is *Bede(B)* 118. 14, where MS *T* has *forðon þe.* Further comments on Table 2 will be found in §3198.

examples—the first is *ChronE* 251. 31 (1123)—and cites as OE examples *GD(C)* 174. 28 . . . *ac sume his wisan fyrwetgeornlice ic forgange 7 forlæte, for ic þæncende efste to þam dædum 7 wundrum oþra æþelra wera*, where MS *O* has *forðon*, and *ChronF* 130. 23 (995) *Ac þa hi to Rome coman, þa nolde se papa naht þ don, far hi ne brahtan nan gewrit*, which comes from a late addition described by Whitelock as 'spurious'. Liggins (1955, pp. 137-9 and 544) justifies her claim to have found earlier examples than seem hitherto to have been recorded by citing *Bede(B)* 102. 2, where the other manuscripts (*T, O,* and *Ca*) all have *mid þy*; the Hatton and Royal manuscript versions of *John* 15. 21 and *John* 19. 42, in both of which the Corpus manuscript has *forþam*; *HomU* 46. 292. 7, which occurs only in Lambeth MS 489, dated by Ker (p. xvii) 's. xi (3rd quarter)'; and (from BTS, p. 764) *Leof 32 . . . ac feng þa on his gebedo . . . for þær wæs an forehus æt þære cyrcan duru*, which 'is in a rough ugly hand, s. xi²' (Ker, p. 110). BTC (s.v. *for* conj.) adds examples from Bodley 343 and Cotton Vesp. D. xiv, both twelfth-century manuscripts. So *for* has only a shaky claim to being a causal conjunction in OE.

c. For *formulae without* þe *or* þæt

§3038. I recapitulate briefly here three points which have already been made about these formulae. First, they can be co-ordinating as well as subordinating (§§3014-15); cf. *CP* 91. 12 *Ðæt word ðære ðreaunge is cæg, forðæm hit oft anlycð 7 geopenað ða scylde ðe se him self ær nyste se hie ðurhteah, Or* 138. 23 *Ac se gefea wearð swiþe raðe on heora mode to gedrefednesse gecierred, þa hie gesawan þa deadan men swa þiclice to eorþan beran þe þær ær æt ham wæron; for þy þær wæs se micla moncwealm on þære tide, ÆCHom* ii. 242. 1 *Crist foresæde gefyrn, mid feawum wordum, his agene ðrowunge, ærðan ðe hit gewurde, forðan ealle ðing he eallunge wiste ærðan ðe ðeos woruld wurde gesceapen*, and *GuthA* 469 *Ealles þu þæs wite awunne; forþon þu hit onwendan ne meahtes*, where I would use 'for' in my translations, with *Or* 92. 5 *þæt wæs ærest for þæm þa Gallia hæfdon beseten Tusci þa burg, Or* 294. 13 . . . *7 feng him self to þæm onwalde, for þon þe he ne mehte self habban þæs onwaldes noman, for þy he næs Romanisc, LS* 34. 311 *and þa þa he him hearmian nolde for þi hit swa geweorðan sceolde, god ælmihtig him þa þæs geuðe . . .* , and

Beo 415   þa me þæt gelærdon   leode mine,
þa selestan,   snotere ceorlas,
þeoden Hroðgar,   þæt ic þe sohte,
forþan hie mægenes cræft   minne cuþon,

where I would use 'because'. But there are many 'ambiguous' examples; see §§3014-15.

§3039. Second, they express 'true Reason', i.e. mean 'because', less frequently than the formulae with *þe*; see §§3016-18. For further documentation, discussion, and illustration, of the shades of meaning of these formulae in the various texts, see van Dam, pp. 41-2, 49-51, and 56; Liggins 1955, pp. 74-8 and 120-4; Mitchell 1959, p. 433 and Appendix 'Cause 1'; and §§3081-9.

§3040. Third, when not correlative with a *for* formula or other adverb (phrase) used correlatively (see §§3072-80 and 3199), they normally follow their principal clause; see §3198 and the examples in §3038, which are typical. Of non-correlative clauses introduced by *for þæm/þam/þan/þon* in the prose, the proportion of those preceding the principal clause to those following it is, according to Liggins's figures (Table 2 in §3036), 1:51 compared with 1:29 for similar formulae with *þe*. For formulae with *þy/þi* the figures are without *þe* 1:45 and with *þe* 1:8. In most of the clauses which precede the principal clause, the *for* formula expresses 'true Reason'. Typical examples are *Bede* 2. 13 *forþon ðe* [pers. pron.] *God to cyninge geceas, þe gedafenað þine þeode to læranne, BlHom* 229. 18 *Min Drihten Hælend Crist, forðon we ealle forleton ure cneorisne ⁊ wæron þe fylgende, ⁊ þu eart ure ealra fultum, ða þe on þe gelyfað, beheald nu ⁊ geseoh hu þas men þinum ðeowe doþ*, and *LS* 7. 159 *þa forþam se sylfe Smaragdus wæs wlitig on ansyne . . . þonne besende se awyrgeda gast mænigfealde geþohtas on heora mod.* Liggins (1955, pp. 95-9 and 102-4) records none in Ælfric and observes (p. 102) that 'there are only three cases of a *forþæm* clause in First Position for which there are no apparent Latin sources. . . . This order of the clauses, then, does reflect a strong Latin influence, but it *may* also occur independently.' Examples from the poetry like

PPs 90. 14   Forðon he hyhte to me,   ic hine hraðe lyse,
                  niode hine scylde,   nu he cuðe naman minne,

Latin *Quoniam in me speravit, liberabo eum; protegam eum quoniam cognovit nomen meum*, also reveal the strength of Latin influence. On clause order, see further §§3198-9; on mood, see §§3174-9; and on clauses with a form of *willan*, see §§2976-80.

d. Grouped *for* formulae with *þe*

§3041. Here too I recapitulate those points which have already been made about these formulae. First, they 'may be used to suggest anything from a strong sense of causality . . . to that of mere connection' (Liggins 1955, p. 37); see §§3016-18 and consider *ÆCHom* ii. 520. 9 *Thomes ðrowunge we forlætað unawritene, forðan ðe heo wæs gefyrn awend of Ledene on Englisc on leoðwison* ('because'), *ÆCHom* i. 6. 13 *Ne sende se deofol ða fyr of heofenum, þeah ðe hit ufan come; forðan þe he sylf næs on heofonum, syððan he for his modignysse of aworpen wæs* ('for'), *ÆCHom* i. 198. 25 *Hu mæg þæt beon þæt ic cild hæbbe, forðan ðe ic nanes weres ne bruce?* ('seeing that'), and *ÆCHom* ii. 204. 34 (§3016 fn.). Second—not surprisingly in view of the presence of *þe*—they are subordinating, i.e. they express 'true Reason', more frequently than the formulae without *þe*. But, generally speaking, the 'explanatory' use is the prevailing one with both types of formula; for details see the table in §3017. Further documentation, discussion, and illustration, of these and the intermediate possibilities will be found in van Dam, pp. 45-8, 53-4, and 57, and Liggins 1955, pp. 36-40 and 127-32. What is interesting about Liggins's two discussions—especially in view of the fact that she appears to regard *þe* in all the divided *for* formulae as a variant of *þy/þi*—is the fact that in both of them she fails to state precisely what she thinks *þe* is and says nothing about the occasional examples in which the last element is *þy/þi* and which I mention in §3044. I take *þe* as a subordinating particle; see *Guide*, §169.

§3042. Third, like those without *þe, for* formulae with *þe* normally follow their principal clause when not used correlatively (§§3072-80); the examples quoted in §3041 are typical. For the comparative figures see §3040. It is also true for non-correlative formulae with *þe* —as it was for formulae without *þe* (§3040)—that clauses introduced by them which precede their principal clause more frequently express a strong idea of cause. According to Liggins (1955, pp. 51-2), the figures are 88.5 per cent—fifty-four of sixty-one examples— against only 26 per cent (§3017) for clauses introduced by *for þæm/ þam/þan/þon þe* which follow their principal clause. Typical examples are *Or* 24. 17 *7 for ðon þe sio sunne þær gæð near on setl þonne on oðrum lande, þær syndon lyðran wedera þonne on Brettannia* and *ÆCHom* i. 18. 13 *Forðan ðe ðu wære gehyrsum ðines wifes wordum, and min bebod forsawe, þu scealt mid earfoðnyssum þe metes tilian.* . . . In the remaining seven examples (11.5 per cent), the formula carries the weaker sense of 'since', according to Liggins; she cites *ÆCHom* ii. 80. 23 *And forðan þe seo onfangenes þæs rices is of Godes godnysse, rihtlice is her bæftan gecweden on endebyrdnysse þæs godspelles, 'La hu, ne mot ic don þæt ic wille?'* and goes on to remark (1955, pp. 52-3) that these initial clauses are more frequent in 'Alfredian' prose and in works closely based on Latin sources. On this latter point see further Liggins 1955, pp. 58 and 60-1. All of the four *for þy/þi þe* clauses which preceded their principal clause noted by Liggins (1955, pp. 131-2) expressed 'a strong Reason'; they are *Bo* 144. 1, *ChronE* 229. 32 (1094), *ChronE* 249. 1 (1119), and *ÆCHom* i. 340. 31 *and forði ðe hi dweligende fram heora Scyppende gewiton, hi willað geinnian ða æftran hinðe mid þam uferan gestreonum.*

§3043. There are only thirteen examples of formulae with *þe* in the poetry, viz. *Beo* 503; *Dan* 176 and 225; *ChristC* 1202; *Max i* 5; *PPs* 77. 24, 101. 12, and 137. 5; *Met* 10. 66 and 20. 195; *Men* 65; *LPr ii* 93; and

KtPs 16   Gelamp þæt him mon ansende   saula neriend,
               witgan mid wordum,   weorada dominus,
               and secgan het,   selfum gecyðan
               ymb his womdeda   waldendes doom,
               þæt se fruma wære   his feores sceldig,
               for ðam þe he Uriam het   aldre beneman,
               fromne ferdrinc   fere beserode,
               and him Bezabe   brohte to wife
               for gitsunga,   þe he godes eorre
               þurh his selfes weorc   sona anfunde.

The reasons for this scarcity are probably metrical.

§3044. There are occasional examples in which the last element of the formula is *þy*, e.g. *CP(C)* 338. 1 *ac forðyðy he his agnes ungemetlice breac*, where *CP(H)* 339. 2 has *forðyðe*. I take *þy* in such sentences to be an inverted spelling for *þe* rather than the causal conjunction. But see §§3063-4.

§3045. Liggins (1955, pp. 45-6 and 130) observes that 'while *wolde, woldon* (and *nolde, noldon*) are frequently used with *forþæm þe* in the general sense of "wished, desired", a clause of this type is sometimes equivalent to one of purpose' and gives examples. They include *Or* 62. 32 *þis ic sprece nu for ðæm þe ic wolde þæt þa ongeaten . . .* , Latin *Itaque haec ob hoc praecipue commemoranda credidi ut intelligant hi . . .* , *CP* 101. 6 *Ne cuæð he ðæt forðyðe he wolde his treowa 7 his geleafan forlætan suæ suæ hie, ac he wolde ætiewan his arfæsðnesse*, *CP* 403. 31 *. . . 7 he ðara gedonena scylda eft gemyndgade, forðæmðe he wolde ðæt hi sceamode ðæt hie eft on ðære oðerre worulde wæren unclæne*, Latin *. . . Dominus corruptis in hoc mundo mentibus transactas ad memoriam culpas revocat, quatenus pollui in futuris erubescant . . .* , *Bede* 216. 5 *Nese, cwæð he, ne onfeng he his*

godum gitsiende ac forþon þe he wolde his sawle gehælan, Latin
'*Non*' *inquit* '*propter auaritiam, sed propter saluandam eius animam
suscepit*', *ÆCHom* ii. 244. 27 *Æfter gereorde Crist bletsode husel,
forðan ðe he wolde ða ealdan æ ær gefyllan, and siððan ða niwan
gecyðnysse halwendlice onginnan*, and *HomU* 35. 220. 31 *and he
þæt dyde forþon þe he wolde þa get his mildheortnesse an mannum
gecyþan*. See further §§2976-80.

e. Grouped for *formulae with þæt*

§3046. In §§2912-13, I examine the differences between *for* formulae with *þe* and with *þæt* and conclude that Kivimaa's statement
(p. 157) is basically sound: 'The functions of the conjunctive phrases
with *for* can roughly be outlined so that in the texts that reflect
genuine OE usage, the combinations with *þe* express cause and those
with *þæt* purpose, except when *þæt* is apparently used for emphasis
in causal phrases, as in Ælfric's writings.' But emphasis is not the only
factor. Kivimaa (p. 165) herself admits that 'vacillation occurred'.
Van Dam (p. 74) sees 'the desire for variation for stylistic purposes'
in *CP* 263. 9 and *Or* 294. 12. Liggins (1955, pp. 117-18) notes that
such clauses can express 'explanation', e.g. *BlHom* 113. 14 *þa ongan
hine eft langian on his cyþþe, forþon þæt he wolde geseon eft 7
sceawian þa byrgenne*, although they more often express 'true
Reason', as in *BlHom* 47. 19 *7 gif þa lareowas þis nellaþ fæstlice
Godes folce bebeodan, þonne beoþ hi wiþ God swyþe scyldige, forþon þæt Godes folc sceal witon hu hi hi sylfe scyldan sceolan wiþ
deoflu*, and (pp. 179-80) cites such variations as that between *forði
. . . forði þæt* in *ÆCHom* i. 162. 25 *Se weig seðe læt to heofenan
rice is forði nearu and sticol, forði þæt we sceolon mid earfoðnysse
geearnian urne eðel* and *forði . . . forði þe* in *ÆCHom* i. 162. 35 *Se
weg seðe læt to forwyrde is forði brad and smeðe, forði þe unlustas
gebringað þone man to forwyrde* as examples of a writer's willingness to 'vary his conjunctions, apparently just for the sake of diversity'. But Shearin takes *ÆCHom* i. 162. 25 as final (1903, p. 71) and
—to judge from the silence on which Liggins (1955, p. 137) comments—*ÆCHom* i. 162. 35 as causal; on these examples see §§2914
and 3077. So I examine here the comparatively few clauses known to
me which are introduced by grouped *for* formulae with *þæt* and
which can or must be taken as causal. These can be divided into five
groups if I exclude the suspect passage from *Solil* discussed in §2916.

§3047. First, there are those which are suspect because other manuscripts have variant readings. Typical examples include *GD(O)* 304. 25

forþon þæt but *GD(C)* 304. 25 *forþon þe* and *ChronE* 81. 18 (887) *forðan þet* but *ChronA* 80. 22 (887) *forþæm*. For more see *Bo* 138. 10, *ChronE* 23. 21 (616), *ChronE* 33. 29 (658), and *Mark* 16. 14. On *HomU* 37. 239. 20 see §3054 fn.

§3048. Second, there are the examples in *ChronE* and *ChronF* for which there are no corresponding readings in other manuscripts. Liggins (1955, pp. 117-19) notes *for þan þet* or a variant thereof in *ChronE* 29. 11 (654), *ChronE* 115. 22 (963), and three times in the *ChronE* annal for 1066, viz. *ChronE* 199. 2, 199. 3, and 199. 8. All five are in Peterborough additions. She adds (1955, pp. 134-7) four examples of variants of *forþi þæt*—all late—viz. *ChronE* 53. 5 (777), *ChronE* 115. 27 (963), *ChronF* 130. 34 (995), and *ChronE* 245. 6 (1114); her other nine examples belong to the First and Second Peterborough Continuations.

§3049. The third group consists of examples with a present or past tense of *willan* in the causal clause. *CP* 251. 16 *Murcnað ðonne forðy ðæt he Gode nolde ðiowigan ða hwile ðe he meahte*, where we have *nolde*, is clearly causal, as the Latin shows: *Et tunc gemunt homines, quod Deo servire noluerunt*. . . . But what I regard as a terminological problem arises when the two clauses have the same subject and that introduced by the *for* formula has a positive form of *willan*, e.g. *Bo* 53. 25 *Sume þonne þa þe ðas welan wilniað, hi his wilniað forþam þæt hi woldean ðy maran anweald habban*, where there is no equivalent clause in the Latin, and *ÆCHom* ii. 44. 18 . . . *ac he com ofer Criste on culfran hiwe, forði þæt he wolde getacnian mid þam þæt Crist wæs on ðære menniscnysse swiðe liðe and unhearmgeorn*. The fact that Shearin (1903, p. 71) classifies the latter as final while Liggins (1955, p. 136) describes it as causal, even though 'the sense . . . is equivalent to that of a clause of purpose', illustrates the problem, which arises with other conjunctions and is discussed in §§2976-80.

§3050. Fourth, there are a few examples with a form of **sculan* in the causal clause, viz. *BlHom* 47. 19 (§3046); *HomU* 35. 213. 18 (so Liggins (1955, p. 117), but *forðon* may be the conjunction and *þæt Godes folc* a nominal group); and *ÆCHom* ii. 46. 28 *Hwi ðonne fullode Iohannes? Forði þæt he sceolde Crist fullian, seðe ne behofode nanre synne forgifenysse. Hwi fullode he a ma manna þonne Crist ænne? Forði þæt we ne sceoldon wenan þæt his fulluht wære swa god, þæt nan man ne moste beon on ðam gefullod buton Crist ana*, of which Liggins (1955, p. 136) says that 'from here it is an easy step to the use of *forði þæt* as a purely final conjunction', as in *ÆCHom* i. 474. 4 *þa cwæð se Hælend, þæt he nære for his agenum synnum, ne for his maga, blind geboren, ac forði þæt Godes wundor þurh hine geswutelod wære.* (On this last example see §2915.)

§3051. The last group consists of examples with *forþy/þi þæt* from Ælfric, who—if we exclude the examples from the late *Chronicle* cited in §3048—is the only OE writer to use this formula; see Liggins 1955, pp. 134-7.[158] They are *ÆCHom* ii. 46. 28 (§3050); *ÆCHom* i. 162. 25 (§2914); the examples with *wolde* cited in §2976; *ÆCHom* ii. 46. 23, where we have the indicative because the accepted cause is given; *ÆCHom* i. 82. 25, *ÆCHom* i. 296. 24 (§2914), and *ÆCHom* ii. 206. 7, where we have a subjunctive (equivalent) expressing a rejected cause; and *ÆCHom* i. 184. 29 *ac ðæs wundredon men, na forði þæt hit mare wundor wære, ac forði þæt hit wæs ungewunelic,* where we have first the accepted and then a rejected cause. 'In every case', says Liggins (1955, p. 134), 'the clause is one of Reason.' She attributes Ælfric's use of this formula to a desire for diversity; see §3046.

§3052. Liggins's table of Variant Constructions—table 6 (1955, p. 178)—confirms that the distinction between *for* formulae without and with *þe* and those with *þæt* was strictly observed in practice; it lists only two instances of causal clauses in which a *for* formula without *þe* or *þæt* varies with a formula with *þæt* and only seven instances of causal clauses in which a formula with *þe* varies with a formula with *þæt*.

§3053. As I said in §2915, the syntax of final clauses introduced by the *for* formulae differs from that of clauses expressing cause only in the fact that the former regularly have the subjunctive whereas in the latter the subjunctive is restricted to those clauses expressing a suggested or rejected—as opposed to an accepted—reason; consider *ÆCHom* i. 184. 29 (§3051) and see §§2969-99.

f. Other grouped formulae with for

§3054. These need only be listed. They include *þæt wæs . . . for þæm* in *Or* 92. 5 (Liggins 1955, p. 95); *þæt(te) is/bið/wæs (. . .) for þæm þe,* e.g. *Bo* 110. 17, *CP* 277. 14, and *Or* 106. 9 (Liggins 1955,

---

[158] It is perhaps convenient to note here that of the six examples of causal *forþy/þi . . . þæt* discussed in my §§3068-9, *Bo(B)* 107. 4 is suspect, *LS* 7. 121 was once attributed to Ælfric, and the remaining four are from Ælfric.

pp. 50-1); *þ wæs forðan þet* in *ChronE* 205. 11 (1070) (Liggins 1955, p. 119); *forþan ðe þæt* in *ÆLS*(B) 31. 1465, where MS *A* has *þæt* (Liggins 1955, p. 119[159]); *forð* in *GD(O)* 268. 11, where MS *C* has *forþon* (van Dam, p. 49 fn. 1); *for ðonne* in *Bede(Ca)* 80. 28, where MS *T* has *forþon* and MSS *B* and *O forðon*, and *for þonne* in *GD(C)* 267. 4, where MS *O* has *forþon* (ibid.); *forð þe* in *GD(O)* 264. 5 and *forþon þa* in *GD(O)* 154. 2, in both of which MS *C* has *forþon þe* (van Dam, p. 53 fn. 1); and *forð ðe* in *GD(O)* 264. 2, where MS *C* has *forðon ðe* (ibid.). Scribal error can reasonably be invoked to explain many, if not all, of these variations.

§3055. We find *for þe* in *GD(O)* 330. 7, where MS *C* has *forþon þe* (van Dam, p. 53 fn. 1), and in *John(WSB, C)* 15. 21, where the Corpus MS has *forþam* and Hatton and Royal have *for* (Liggins 1955, pp. 139-40). Liggins (ibid.) follows Schipper in reporting *for þe* in *Bede(B)* 128. 5, where MSS *T, O,* and *Ca,* have *mid þy.* Miller reports *for þi,* the manuscript itself has *forþi.* This makes me wonder all the more what grounds Liggins (ibid.) had for her remark that *for þe* 'seems to be a distinct form from *forþy*'.

§3056. Liggins (1955, p. 140) cites as a solitary example of causal *for þæt Solil* 10. 4 . . . *and cumað oððer grenu: wexað and growað and rip*[*i*]*að, for þat hy eft onginnað searian.* She is right—because of the sense and the ind. *onginnað*—to deny Wülfing's claim (ii. 156) that *for þat* introduces a clause of purpose. But a causal clause does not really give sense either. One would expect a conjunction meaning 'until' and I am inclined to see at the root of this reading a variant of *fort(e)* and/or *forþ þæt* 'until'; see §2760.

g. Divided for *formulae* with *þe or þy*

§3057. Here a word or group of words intervenes between *for* + demonstrative in a governing clause and *þe, þy,* or *þæt,* at the beginning of a clause which is, or can be taken as, causal, e.g. *on weg* in *ChronA* 90. 29 (897) *þa comon forðy on weg ðe ðara oþerra scipu asæton.* Occasionally the separating element is not an essential part of the grammatical sentence, e.g. *Or* 242. 32 'for þon', cwæð he, 'þe ic wat þæt nan swa god man ne leofað swa he is on þeosan life . . . .'. Occasionally it reinforces the prepositional formula, e.g. *CP* 147. 9 . . . *nalles forðæm anum ðe hie wilnigen ðæt hi mon synderlice*

---

[159] I omit Liggins's second example, *HomU* 37. 239. 20, since I take *þæt yfele geþanc* as neuter singular accusative. The neuter plural (as opposed to the masc. pl. *geþancas*) appears as *geþancu* in BT(S), s.v.

lufige . . . 'not only/merely because . . .' and *Or* 32. 4 *Ða manigfealdan wæstmas wæron for þam swiþost ðe Iordanis seo ea ælce geare þæt land middeweard oferfleow mid fotes þicce flode, 7 hit þonne mid ðam gedynged wearð* 'chiefly/especially because . . .'; cf. *Or* 17. 35 *Swiþost he for ðider, toeacan þæs landes sceawunge, for þæm horschwælum* and see Liggins 1955, pp. 148-9, for more such examples in *Or*. (Such reinforcing adverbs or adverb groups need not divide the formula; see *ChronA* 89. 31 (897), *LS* 23. 773, and *ÆCHom* i. 50. 27 . . . *and rihtlice swiðor forðan ðe heora arleasnysse fyligde se eca deað.* . . .) But normally it is an integral part of the sentence, as in *Or* 230. 12 *Næs na mid Romanum ær ne siþþan swa heard gefeoht swa þær wæs, for þon þe hie wurdon on ælce healfe utan befangen, 7 heora eac mæst for þon forwearþ þe hiora gemitting wæs on sondihtre dune, þæt hie for duste ne mehton geseon hu hi hi behealdan sceolden* (where, despite Liggins (1955, p. 149), *mæst* is not a superlative adverb, but the subject of *forwearþ*), *CP* 339. 1 *nis hit no gesæd ðæt he for ðy getæled wære ðy he oðre menn reafode, CP* 337. 21 *Ac forðæm hie cueðað ðas word ðe hie belucað hiera modes earan ongean ða godcundan lare, CP* 435. 20 *Forðæm wæs ðis gecweden ðe hit is swiðe gewunelic ðætte domeras 7 rice menn on setelum sitten, ChronA* 90. 29 (897) above, *BlHom* 17. 29 *7 forðon God to us niþer astag þe he wolde þæt we wæron upahafene to his godcundnesse,* and *WHom* 11. 146 *7 forðam hit wearð swa rædleas þe hit Godes beboda forgymde to swyðe.* Examples with *wolde* such as *BlHom* 17. 29 above shade into clauses of purpose; see §§ 2976-80. But generally these clauses express what Liggins (1955, p. 148) describes as 'strong Reason'. The *for* element usually appears medially in its clause, but may occur initially or immediately after initial *ond* or *ac*. These latter arrangements would seem to give extra emphasis. All three patterns are exemplified above. The only possible example in the poetry is

Phoen 368   Forþon he drusende   deað ne bisorgað,
               sare swyltcwale,   þe him symle wat
               æfter ligþræce   lif edniwe,
               feorh æfter fylle,   þonne fromlice
               þurh briddes had   gebreadad weorðeð
               eft of ascan,   edgeong weseð
               under swegles hleo.

But here *þe* may be a relative pronoun 'who' rather than part of a conjunction introducing a causal clause with an unexpressed subject. Similar difficulties occasionally arise in the prose. Thus Wülfing (i, § 296) takes *ðe he* in *CP* 27. 2 *Ac forðonðe nu eall se weorðscipe ðisse worolde is gecierred, Gode ðonc, to weorðscipe ðæm æwfæstam, ðæt ða sindon nu weorðoste ðe æwfæstoste sindon, forðon licet suiðe monig ðæt he æwfæsð lareow sie, ðe he wilnað micle woroldare habban* as relative 'who'. The EETS translation has 'because', but it is not clear whether this implies that *forðon . . . ðe* is a prepositional formula or whether, as van Dam (pp. 72-3) has it, '*forðon* is not a correlative to *ðe*, but to a preceding *forðonðe*'. 'We may', he goes on, 'perhaps, assume *þe* to be a causal connective here.'

§3058. This last remark leads us into another problem. Shearin (1903, pp. 69-70) reminds us that in divided formulae with *þæt* such as *forþæm . . . þæt* it is sometimes difficult to decide whether we have a divided final conjunction or whether the *for* element 'is merely an illative "therefore" within the main clause'. This difficulty does not arise with divided formulae with *þe* if we accept the view expressed in my *Guide* (§169) that in examples like *ChronA* 86. 27 (894) *7 he hi him eft ageaf forþæm þe hiora wæs oþer his godsunu . . .* and *ChronA* 90. 29 (897) (§3057), '*þe* warns us that the combination is a conjunction. We can call *þe* (if we wish) a subordinating particle.' For, if this is true, the *for* element is an integral part of the conjunction and cannot be 'merely an illative "therefore" within the main clause'. But the situation is quite different if *þe* can stand alone as a causal conjunction. On this point, van Dam (p. 74) writes 'Summing up I come to the conclusion that *þe* is not a full-blooded causal conjunction used alone.' But he goes on to say (p. 75) that in groups like *for þæm/þon/þy . . . þe* it is 'possible that *þe* is merely a weakened form of *þy*'—which does occur alone as a causal conjunction 'because'; see §§3063-4. So, if this last suggestion is true, it is misleading to speak of such combinations as 'divided prepositional formulae'. Is it true?

§3059. Van Dam separates what I have been calling 'divided formulae with *for*' into four groups. The fourth group consists of examples in which the last element is *þæt*; these are discussed in §§3067-70. Of the remaining three, the first is typified by *Or* 132. 13 *He þa Alexander hit swiþost for þæm angann þe he wolde þæt his mærþa wæren maran þonne Ercoles, þeh ðe he hie mid micle forlore þæs folces begeate*, in which van Dam (p. 49) speaks of *for þæm* as 'belonging to the main clause [and] functioning as an antecedent to *þe*'. He lists nine examples from *Or* with *for þæm/þam/þan . . . þe* (p. 49), one with *forþon . . . þe*, viz. *Or* 230. 14 *. . . 7 heora eac mæst for þon forwearþ þe hiora gemitting wæs on sondihtre dune, þæt hie for duste ne mehton geseon hu hi hi behealdan sceolden* (p. 51), but none with *for þy . . . þe* (pp. 56-7). In all ten examples, the final element in the formula (a word I must continue to use for want of a better) is *þe* or *ðe*. None has the spelling *þy/þi/ðy*.

§ 3060. The same is true of all the examples in his second group. This is typified by *Or* 188. 3 *Ac for þæm he geneðde swiþost ofer þone munt þe he wiste þæt Flamineus se consul wende þæt he buton sorge mehte on þæm wintersetle gewunian. . . .* In this group, van Dam (p. 75) suggests, 'the counter part of the causal adverb adjunct in the main clause was dropped before *þe*'. This appears to mean that *for þæm . . . for þæm þe* was an essential stage in the development of this pattern—which to me seems identical with that seen in the ten examples in his first group; see below. Here he includes thirteen examples (p. 75). (Different manuscripts are counted separately here only when the readings differ significantly.) They comprise eight with *for þæm/þam/þan . . . þe*, viz. *Or* 188. 3 above and seven from *CP*, including *CP(C)* 32. 6 *Forðæm we ðis feawum wordum sædon, þe we woldon gecyðan hu micel sio byrðen bið ðæs lareowdomes*; three with *forþon . . . þe*, viz. *GD(C)* 76. 23, *GD(C)* 303. 25, and *Or* 46. 2 *For þon hie dydon swa þe hie woldon þætte þa oþere wif wæren emsarige him . . .* ; and two with *forþy . . . þe*, viz. *GD(O)* 303. 25 and *ChronA* 90. 29 (897) (§ 3057). I repeat that in all twenty-three examples in these two groups the final element is *þe* or *ðe*.

§ 3061. But his third group consists of eight examples in which the final element in the formula is *þy, þi,* or *ðy*—not *þe* (pp. 52 and 78) —three with *for þæm/þam . . . þy*, viz. *Or* 76. 8, *GD(O)* 91. 18, and *CP* 220. 12 *Forðæm hiene swæ hrædlice sio gedrefednes utadrifð ðy hiene ðærinne ne belycð nan ege ðære lare wisdomes*; three with *for þon . . . þy*, viz. *GD(C)* 91. 18, *GD* 168. 26, and *CP(H)* 33. 6 *Forðon we ðiss feawum wordum sædon, ðy we woldon gecyðan hu micel sio byrðen bið ðæs lareowdomes*; and two with *forþy . . . þy*, viz. *CP* 341. 20 and *CP* 339. 1 . . . *nis hit no gesæd ðæt he for ðy getæled wære ðy he oðre menn reafode. . . .*

§ 3062. Before discussing van Dam's method of division, I must note that Liggins (1955, pp. 148-50) distinguishes only two groups, according to the spelling of the demonstrative element, viz. *for þæm/þam/þan/þon . . . þy* (thirty-two examples) and *for þy/þi . . . þy* (fifteen examples). These forty-seven examples include all except six of van Dam's and are made up as follows: all the examples in van Dam's first group (10); all the examples in his second group less *GD(C)* and *GD(O)* 303. 25 and *CP(C)* 32. 6 (10); all the examples in van Dam's third group except *GD(C)* and *GD(O)* 91. 18 and *GD* 168. 26 (5);

ChronB 90. 29 (897) (1); and from texts not in van Dam's corpus, thirteen from *Bo*, five from *Solil, BlHom* 17. 29 and *WHom* 11. 146 (both in §3057), and *HomU* 34 (*F*) 195. 9 (21). So Liggins made a distinction which is purely orthographic and of no syntactical significance—as manuscript variants like *GD(C)* 304. 1 *forþon . . . þe* but *GD(O)* 304. 1 *for ði . . . þe* and sequences like *Solil* 57. 12 *Forðam þu woldest beon þe þu woldest lybban and forði woldest þu lybban þe þu woldest witan* demonstrate—but failed to make another orthographic one which might be syntactically significant, that between those examples in which the final element is *þe/ðe* and those in which it is *þy/þi/ðy*. Seven of her forty-seven examples belong to the latter category, viz. *CP(H)* 33. 6, *CP* 220. 12, *CP* 339. 1, *CP* 341. 20, *Or* 76. 8, *Bo* 84. 12, and *Solil* 58. 2 *Forði ic wolde beon þi ic wolde lybban.* (The last two are not given by van Dam; see §3061.) To these we have to add the three examples from *GD* given by van Dam and cited in §3061. So, out of the fifty-three examples referred to by van Dam and Liggins, ten have *þy/þi/ðy* as the last element of the formula.

✕ §3063. Exactly what motivated Liggins here is not clear. She says (1955, p. 49) 'For *forþæm . . . þe* as correlatives, or members of different clauses, see below—12b' (viz. 1955, pp. 145-54). She tells us that 'the forms *þy* and *þe* seem to be used interchangeably as independent conjunctions' (p. 141). She then speaks (p. 145) of 'a special type of *þy* construction . . . in which the principal clause contains a *þy* comparative', quotes as examples *CP* 5. 24 . . . *7 woldon ðæt her ðy mara wisdom on londe wære ðy we ma geðeoda cuðon* and *CP* 207. 4 *Ðone scamleasan mon mæg ðy bet gebetan ðe hine mon suiður ðreað 7 sciend*, and then says that 'it is hard to know whether *þe* is a causal conjunction [see my §§3128-47, especially §3141] or a relative pronoun'. (Or an instrumental of comparison?) She then lists without discussion (pp. 147-8) ten examples with *þæs þy* + comparative + *þy/þe*. She then discusses the forty-seven examples listed in §3062 (pp. 148-50), but she does not ask what *þe* and *þy* are. However, the fact that she implies that in all forty-seven examples the final element is *þy* suggests that she had rejected the view that *þe* was ever the indeclinable particle. I cannot agree with her procedure here. The fact that one of *þe* and *þy* may sometimes be a variant of the other is demonstrated by examples like *CP(H)* 339. 2 *forðyðe* but *CP(C)* 338. 1 *forðyðy* and *CP(C)* 32. 6 *forðæm . . . þe* but *CP(H)* 33. 6 *forðon . . . ðy* and by variations like *Solil* 57. 12 *forði . . . þe* but *Solil* 58. 2 *Forði . . . þi*. But it was up to Liggins to demonstrate —not to assume—that they were interchangeable in these formulae and, if so, that *þe* was a variant of *þy* rather than that *þy* was a variant of *þe*, which the weight of numbers here (forty-three examples against ten, or eighty per cent)—and the fact that in contexts where we certainly have indeclinable *þe* we rarely find the spelling *þy*—would suggest was more likely.

§3064. There can be no doubt that in OE indeclinable *þe* and instr. sg. *þy* were separate words and that van Dam was right to make them the basis of a distinction. Theoretically there are three possible ways of explaining these formulae. We can say that *for þon . . . þe* represents only a divided form of *forþonþe* and that *þy* is an inverted spelling for *þe*. Or we can say that *forþonþe* has indeclinable *þe* and that *forþon . . . þe* is different in kind, with *þe* an inverted spelling for *þy* 'because'; cf. *forþon . . . forþonþe* and MnE 'for this reason . . . because'. (I dismiss the notion that, in *forþonþe*, *þe* always stands for *þy* 'because' and doubt whether it ever did.) Or we can say that in *forþon . . . þe*, *þe* was sometimes indeclinable *þe* and sometimes *þy* 'because'. I must say that I would be extremely reluctant to agree that *þe* in *forþon . . . þe* could never be the indeclinable particle. But since I do not see how certainty can be reached, I must leave the problem here.

§3065. Liggins was, however, right not to anticipate van Dam in distinguishing examples like *Or* 132. 13 (§3059) from those like *Or* 188. 3 (§3060). I can see neither the necessity nor the justification for van Dam's distinction between what I have called his first and second groups and regard the theory that in the first group *for þæm* functioned as an antecedent to *þe* (van Dam, p. 49) while in the second we originally had *forþæm . . . forþæmþe* (van Dam, p. 75) as most unlikely. I can see no reason for assuming that correlative patterns were an essential stage in the development of any grouped formulae and find it hard to accept the idea of two distinct origins for those with *for*.

§3066. There remain to be discussed those examples in which both clauses have the same subject and the verb of the causal clause is a form of *willan*. They include (with the last element *þy/þi*; see §3062) *CP* 33. 6 *Forðon we ðiss feawum wordum sædon, ðy we woldon gecyðan hu micel sio byrðen bið ðæs lareowdomes*, Latin *Haec itaque breviter diximus, ut quantum sit pondus regiminis monstraremus*, *Solil* 58. 2 *Forði ic wolde beon þi ic wolde lybban*, and *Bo* 84. 12 *Forðy ic hit þe secge eft þy ic nolde þ ðu wende þ se God þe fæder is and fruma eallra gesceafta, þ him ahwonan utan come his sio hea goodnes þe he full is*, Latin *Ne hunc rerum omnium patrem illud summum bonum quo plenus esse perhibetur uel extrinsecus accepisse uel ita naturaliter habere praesumas*, and (with the last element *þe*) *CP* 207. 21 *Forðæm he spræc ðas word ðe he wolde ðara scamleasna scylda tælende geopenian, 7 ðara scamfæstena giemelieste he wolde mid liðelicum wordum gedieglan*, Latin . . . *dicens . . . ut et illorum culpas increpatio dura detegeret et horum negligentiam mollior sermo velaret*, *Solil* 57. 12 *Forðam þu woldest beon þe þu woldest lybban and forði woldest þu lybban þe þu woldest witan*, and *Bo* 53. 28 *Manega sint þara þe forþi wilniað anwaldes þe hie woldon ormæte feoh gegaderian oððe eft þone hlisan heora naman hi wilniað þ hi gebrædan*, Latin . . . *uel qui potentiam seu pecuniae causa seu proferendi nominis appetunt.* Liggins (1955, pp. 148-50) notes fourteen such examples in her *forþæm . . . þy* group—*Or* 76. 8, where *nolde* is in the principal clause, should be eliminated—and four in her *forþy . . . þy* group (my §3062). I add here *GD(C)* 76. 23 *eac swylce manige men syndon þe forþon tiliað þæt hi god don þe hi willað gedwellan þa gife oðera manna weorces*, Latin *sunt namque nonnulli qui idcirco bona facere student ut gratiam alienae operationis obnubilent*, and *BlHom* 17. 29 *7 forðon God to us niþer astag þe he wolde þæt we wæron upahafene to his godcundnesse*. In my opinion all these examples in varying degrees shade into clauses of purpose; see §§2976-80. After examining them, with special reference to the Latin originals quoted above, I cannot see why Liggins (1955, p. 150) says of her four examples with *forþy . . . þy* that *wolde/nolde* 'in each case . . . has the sense of "wish" or "desire", and the expression is not equivalent to a final one in the way that several of those with *forþæm . . . þy . . . wolde* are'. The Latin equivalent of *Solil* 57. 12 above seems conclusive here: *esse vis, vivere et intelligere; sed esse ut vivas* [OE *forðam . . . þe*], *vivere ut intelligas* [OE *forði . . . þe*].

h. Divided for *formulae with* þæt

§3067. Like their grouped counterparts (§§3046-53), divided *for* formulae with *þæt* introduce final clauses more often than they introduce causal clauses, where the formulae with *þe* are preferred. On the divided formulae with *þæt* in final clauses see §§2911-16. Here I examine those sentences in which they introduce clauses which are, or can be taken as, causal. Three of the five groups which occur with grouped formulae with *þæt* (§§3046-51) are represented here. As with the divided formulae with *þe* or *þy*, the *for* element may occur medially in its clause, at the beginning, or immediately after initial *ond* or *ac.* The remarks made in §3053 about mood in grouped formulae with *þæt* are applicable here, *mutatis mutandis.*

§3068. First, we have three examples with variant readings in other manuscripts, viz. *Bo(B)* 107. 4 *ac forðy hi sint yfle þ hi hit ne metað,* where MS *C* has *þe; Or(C)* 246. 28 *7 hio for þæm dyde þæt hio nolde þæt hie mon drife beforan þæm triumphan . . . ,* where MS *L* has *þe;* and *HomU* 34 *(B)* 195. 9 *and forþan he deð þæt, þæt he wile, þæt þa earman iudeiscan men scylan wenan þæt he sy soð Crist,* where MS *F* has *þe.* Second, we have one example with *forþy . . . þæt* and a form of **sculan,* viz. *ÆHex* 490 *Ða forwyrnde him God ðæs inganges forðig* [MS *D forðy*] *to ðam lifes treowe ðæt we lybban ne sceoldon swylce earmingas on ecum lichaman. . . .*

§3069. The third group consists of those examples in which both clauses have the same subject and the verb of the causal clause is a form of *willan.* There are six with *for þæm/þam/þan/þon . . . þæt,* viz. (with *wolde) CP* 319. 7, where the Latin has *quatenus* 'so that, in order that' (a post-classical usage), *BlHom* 15. 34, and *BlHom* 29. 16 *7 forþon he þyder com þæt he wolde gecompian wiþ þone awerigdan gast;* (with *nolde) Or(C)* 246. 28 (§3068); (with *woldan) BlHom* 69. 11; and (with *wile) HomU* 34 *(B)* 195. 9 (§3068). On these see van Dam, pp. 70-1, and Liggins 1955, p. 165. They come close to being final clauses; see §§2976-80. The same is true of four examples with *forþy/þi . . . þæt,* viz. (with *woldest) ÆCHom* i. 304. 4 *þu eart Godes Sunu, forði ðu come þæt ðu woldest us fordon* and (with *wolde) LS* 7. 121, where (Liggins 1955, p. 164, reports) the Latin has *ideo . . . ut, ÆCHom* ii. 470. 13, and *ÆCHom* ii. 578. 34 *He hæfde getacnunge ures Hælendes Cristes, seðe forði astah of heofenum to ðisum middanearde, þæt he wolde mancynn gesibbian, and geðwærlæcan to þam heofenlicum werode,* which Shearin (1903, p. 71) actually classifies as final.

§3070. There remain four examples. Two examples with the indicative seem clearly causal, viz. *Bede(T)* 76. 31 *þæt is þonne gesegen gemeted fore intingan unforhæfdnisse anre, forþon, þonne heo ne willað ahabban from heora werum, þætte heo forhycgað fedan þa ðe heo cennað,* where *þætte* is supported by *þ* in MSS *B, O,* and *Ca,* and *CP(H)* 265. 7 *Se ðe for ðæm anum god deð ðæt he sumre ðreaunge yfel him ondrætt,* where MS *C* also has *ðæt* and the sequence *for ðæm anum . . . ðæt* is noteworthy (cf. §3057). Emendation would be hazardous here. Liggins (1955, p. 165) detects some similarity to the examples with *willan* in §3069 in *GD(C)* 76. 27 *ne hi na forþon*

*opre mæn feormiað þæt hi mycclum gyman hwæþer heom þæt god
sy þæt hi doð,* where MS *H* has *forþam þe.* Van Dam (pp. 52-3)
proposes *Or* 34. 17 as an example, but I suspect that the first *þæt*
clause is the object of *sæde.* Here again, we can conclude that the
statement by Kivimaa (p. 157) quoted in §3046 is basically sound.

j. For *formulae with a noun*

§3071. These formulae are too few in number, too inconsistent in
their use of *þe* or *þæt,* and too late in appearance, for me to be able
to believe that they were the original patterns and that the *for* formulae discussed above developed from them by omission of the
noun; see Mitchell, at press (*c*). Those known to me are *for ðam
þingum þe* in *LawEGu Prol* 2 and in *Bo(C)* 99. 11 *þ hi dydon for
þam ðingum þe hi woldon witan hu heah hit wære to ðæm heofone,*
where MS *B* has *for þam ðingum þ; for ðam intingan þe* in *ÆCHom*
i. 512. 6 *þa, for ðam intingan þe he cwæð 'Syle for me and for ðe',
wendon þa apostolas þæt Petrus wære fyrmest;* and *for ðam intingan
þæt* in *ÆCHom* ii. 534. 35 *Se ðe bodað for ðam intingan þæt he his
Drihtnes hæse and willan gefremme . . . ne derað him nan ðing on
ðam ecan eðele.* In none of these can *þe* be construed as a relative.
The same is true of *þæt* even if we disregard problems of concord.
Here we see again (I believe) *þe* as a subordinating particle, intrusion
of *þæt* into its domain in *Bo(B)* 99. 11 above, and the variation between *þe* and *þæt* already noted (§3046) as typical of Ælfric. For
more examples of these formulae, see Liggins 1955, pp. 477-8 and
483-4.

k. *Correlation*

§3072. As Liggins (1955, p. 532) points out, 'correlation is regularly found in each of the main classes of causal clause employing
a finite verb. It is most frequent with temporal/causals and condi-
tional/causals [see my §§3149-64], where the correlating element
nearly always carries concepts of both time and result, "then/there-
fore".' But it must not be assumed too readily that all sequences of
forþæm (þe) . . . forþæm (þe) and the like involve correlation. Liggins (1955, pp. 105-7) notes that it is sometimes difficult to decide
whether *forþæm* is equivalent to 'for' (either introducing an explanatory clause or serving as a weak introductory word), means 'therefore', or is an adverb correlative with a later clause of reason. Thus,
she suggests, in *Bo* 47. 4 *Ne wen ðu no þ ic to anwillice winne wið ða
wyrd; forðæm ic hit no self nauht ne ondræde, forþam hit oft*

gebyreð þ sio lease wyrd nauþer ne mæg þæm men don ne fultum ne eac nænne dem. Forþam hio nis nanes lofes wyrðe, forþam hio hire self gecyð þ heo nanwuht ne bið, all four examples of *forðæm/forþam* may mean 'for' or either or both pairs may be correlative. This gives four possible translations. Moreover, a slight change in Sedgefield's punctuation would make the second and third a correlative pair and open up new possibilities. Here the Latin does not help. But in *CP* 65. 19 *Ðonne is sio lytle nosu ðæt mon ne sie gescadwis; forðæm mid ðære nose we tosceadað ða stencas, forðam is sio nosu gereaht to gesceadwisnesse*, where *forðæm . . . forðam* might appear to be correlative, the Latin *Parvo autem naso est, qui ad tenendam mensuram discretionis idoneus non est. Naso quippe odores foetoresque discernimus. Recte ergo per nasum discretio exprimitur . . .* suggests the sequence 'for . . . therefore', which the EETS translation adopts. Liggins (1955, p. 107) lists other examples in which there is similar uncertainty. Van Dam's suggestion (p. 43) that in *CP* 101. 21, where we have the sequence *Forðæm . . . Forðæm . . . forðæm*, the second *Forðæm* means 'therefore', referring back to the previous argument, and 'is correlative in appearance only' is also supported by the Latin; it represents *Hinc*. In *BlHom* 101. 15, where Liggins (1955, pp. 64-5) prefers to take *forþon . . . forþon þe* as correlative but concedes that Morris's 'wherefore . . . for' is possible, I am not able to adjudicate.

§3073. Liggins's comment (1955, p. 64) on the *forþæm . . . forþæm þe* patterns can be extended to all correlative causal combinations: 'this construction could occur in almost any type of prose—translated or original, religious or secular'. But the actual combinations naturally vary with the context and the intention and preferences of the writer. For more details and more examples than space permits here, see van Dam (pp. 42-4, 47-9, 51-2, 54-5, and 57) and Liggins 1955 (pp. 63-73, 105-17, 124-7, and 132-3). In such examples, it is safe to assume that the form with *þe* is the conjunction.

✕ §3074. Van Dam (p. 79) says that 'when reading Old English texts, one gets the impression that correlatives to the various sorts of adverb clauses are used on a large scale'. I must confess that this was my own impression concerning causal clauses. The figures surprised me. Van Dam (p. 79) goes on: 'On actual count, however, the number of instances in which correlatives to causal clauses were found to be employed, appeared to be rather small, viz. 8 per cent (124 out of the total of 1536 clauses).' The table which follows confirms this scarcity. It is based on Liggins's figures. The totals for clauses without correlatives are drawn from Table 2 in §3036. Those for clauses with correlatives can be only approximate for the reasons given in §3072.

Conjunction	Examples without correlatives	Examples with correlatives	Percentage of examples with correlatives
forþæm/þam/þan/þon þe	1840	110	5.6
forþæm/þam/þan/þon	1305	58	4.3
forþy/þi þe	37	10	21.3
forþy/þi	46	14	23.3
Totals	3228	192	5.9

There is room for more work on the comparative frequency of correlative constructions in sentences involving the various types of subordinate clause. But see Mitchell, at press (c), where I give my reasons for disagreeing with some of the observations made by Erickson 1978.

§3075. This scarcity of correlative causal constructions in OE is not due to the influence of Latin, for correlation is more common in the OE translations than in the Latin originals. This is confirmed both by van Dam (p. 84)—'Of the total number of instances of causal correlative groups only 20 per cent had a correlative group in the Latin as well'—and by Liggins (1955, p. 532)—'Correlation in each group of constructions is found much more commonly in OE texts than in any of the Latin ones from which they are translated.'

✗ §3076. In the sections which follow, examples will be found which demonstrate that the principal clause may precede or follow a correlative causal clause; that the correlative adverb may stand at the head of its clause or within it; and that a correlative causal clause may express 'true Reason' or 'Explanation'. As Liggins (1955, p. 206) remarks, 'all but a few of the rare conjunctions may be used with or without correlating elements in the principal clause'. Space does not permit exemplification of all possible combinations of all adverbs and (all spellings of) all conjunctions; for this see the references given in §3073. The table which follows, also based on Liggins's figures, shows that in two-thirds (67.7 per cent) of correlative causal constructions, the principal clause precedes the causal clause. This figure agrees closely with that given by van Dam (p. 79): 'In approximately seventy per cent of the cases in which correlative groups were noted, the causal clause follows the main clause, which, indeed, is its usual position.'

Causal clauses with correlatives

Conjunction	Principal clause precedes causal clause	Causal clause precedes principal clause	Total
forþæm/þam/þan/þon þe	77	33	110
forþæm/þam/þan/þon	35	23	58
forþy/þi þe	5	5	10
forþy/þi	13	1	14
Totals	130	62	192

× §3077. I cite first some examples of correlative *for* formulae in which the principal clause precedes the causal clause: (with a conjunction without *þe*) *CP* 363. 4 *Forðæm he cwæð ða word, forðæm ða Saducie antsacodon ðære æriste æfter deaðe, Solil* 21. 14 *forði me ne sceamað nanwiht þeah ic mærre, forði ic wot þæt ic gyt wis ne eom, ByrM* 64. 18 *Bissextus ys forþon geciged, forþon bis ys twia 7 sextus ys se syxta, Met* 20. 181, and

Met 10. 35   Forþy ic cwæð þæs wisan   Welandes ban,
                forðy ængum ne mæg   eorðbuendra
                se cræft losian   þe him Crist onlænð,

and (with a conjunction with *þe*) *CP* 431. 11 (or does *forðy* mean 'therefore'?), *CP* 445. 22 *Forðæm he cwæð ðæt he forðy ne funde his weorc fulfremed beforan Gode, ða ðe he ær worhte, forðæmðe he ða ne worhte, ða ðe he ða wyrcean sceolde, Or* 50. 15 *For þon nis me þæs þearf, cwæð Orosius, to secgenne, for þon hit longsum is 7 eac monegum cuð, ÆCHom* i. 162. 35 *Se weg seðe læt to forwyrde is forði brad and smeðe, forði þe unlustas gebringað þone man to forwyrde, PPs* 101. 12, and

Met 20. 193   Forðy men habbæð   geond middangeard
                eorðgesceafta   ealla oferþungen,
                forðæm ðe hi habbað,   þæs ðe hi nabbað,
                þone ænne cræft   þe we ær nemdon.

Erickson (1978, p. 99) claims that 'Old English displays an unusual syntactic construction where a main clause adverbial (*forðon*) appears to anticipate the homophonous subordinator introducing a following subordinate clause'. I do not think 'unusual' is the right word; see Mitchell, at press (*c*).

§3078. Second, we have similar combinations in which the causal clause precedes the principal: (with a conjunction without *þe*) *CP*

401. 17 *Forðæm of ðæm gesinscipe weaxað eorðlice ymbhogan 7 sorga, forðæm se æðela ðioda lareow his hieremen to betran life spon, ðylæs hi mid eorðlicre sorge wurden gebundne*, ByrM 90. 8 7 *Februarius, forðon he ys se læsta 7 he hæfð twegra daga læs þonne þa oðre, forþon he forlæt eahta 7 feowertig tida*, and

GenB 309　　　　　　　　　　Forþon heo his dæd and word
　　　　　noldon weorðian,　forþon he heo on wyrse leoht
　　　　　under eorðan neoðan,　ællmihtig god,
　　　　　sette sigelease　　on þa sweartan helle

(where I would be inclined to take the subordinate *Forþon* clause *apo koinou* with what precedes and with what follows), and (with a conjunction with *þe*) GD 177. 22, GD 323. 18 *forþon þe hi burnon on þære unalyfdan lufe þæs gebrosniendan lichaman, hi forþon eac samod to lore wurdon in þam bryne 7 fulan stence*, Bo 63. 23 *Ac forþæmþe . . . forðy . . . 7 forðyþe . . . forðy*, and ÆLS 24. 142 *Forðan ðe þu rihtlice gelyfdest on þone ðe me asende, forðam ic eom asend to þe þæt ðu gesund beo*. This last pattern does not appear in the poetry.

§3079. Third, we have correlative sequences of one *for* formula, without or with *þe*, used as a conjunction, and an adverb other than a *for* formula. Once again space does not permit citation of all the combinations listed by van Dam and Liggins in the references given in §3073. The examples which follow are typical: (with adv. *þa*; see below) CP 233. 19 *Forðæmðe he hefonrice mid his agenre scylde forworhte, ða ofðuhte him ðætte menn wæron to ðæm gesceapene . . .* ; (with adv. *þonne*) Bede 36. 4 *Forðon ðe ðu þone mangengan 7 þone wiþfeohtend 7 þone forhycgend ura goda ðu me helan woldest, swyðor þonne minum ðegnum secgean, þonne wite ðu þæt þu scealt ðam ylcan wite onfon, ðe he geearnode . . .* and ÆCHom ii. 280. 4 *. . . þonne ðicge we his lichaman gebrædne to fyre, forðan ðe se Halga Gast com on fyres hiwe to ðam apostolum, on mislicum gereordum*; (with adv. *þy*) CP 435. 12 *Ðy ne wricð Dryhten no gelice ða gesiredan synne 7 ða færlice ðurhtogenan, forðæm sio gesirede syn bið ungelic eallum oðrum synnum*, GD(C) 91. 18 *forþon . . . þy*, GD(O) 330. 17 *þi . . . forðam* (MS C has *forþy . . . forþonþe*), ÆC Hom i. 248. 33 *þi he cwæð 'Na for freondrædene', forðan ðe nan man nære wyrðe ne þæs geleafan ne ðæs ecan lifes . . .* , and

KtPs 68　　　þy ic ðe mid benum　biddan wille
　　　　　lifes and lisse,　liohtes aldor,
　　　　　forðan ðu me uncuðe　eac ðan derne
　　　　　þinre snetera hord　selfa ontendes;

(with adv. *eornostlice*) *ÆCHom* ii. 574. 5 *Waciað eornostlice, forðan þe ge nyton þone dæg ne ða tid*; and finally (with adv. *nu*) *GD(C)* 60. 4, *ByrM* 132. 5 *ac forþan þe we witon þæt þas þing þincað clericum 7 uplendiscum preostum genoh mænigfealde, nu wille we ure spræce awendan to þam iungum munecum* . . . , and

GuthA 582

                      Nu þu in helle scealt
deope gedufan,   nales dryhtnes leoht
habban in heofonum,   heahgetimbru,
seld on swegle,   forþon þu synna to fela,
facna gefremedes   in flæschoman.

In

GenB 799

                            Nu wit hreowige magon
sorgian for þis siðe.   Forþon he unc self bebead
þæt wit unc wite   warian sceolden,
hearma mæstne.   Nu slit me hunger and þurst
bitre on breostum,   þæs wit begra ær
wæron orsorge   on ealle tid,

the *forþon* clause can be taken *apo koinou* with both *nu* clauses. We can extend Liggins's observation (1955, p. 63) about such adverbs when they are used correlatively with *forþæm þe* to those so used with all *for* formulae: 'These correlatives are, for the most part, either causal or temporal. The definiteness of the sense of time in the members of the second group varies a good deal.' Here it is instructive to compare *CP* 113. 14 *Forðy he ongeat ðæt he ma mehte ðonne ænig oðer, ða wende he ðæt eac mara wære*, where *ða* could be translated 'then' or 'therefore', with *Bo* 61. 21 *þa forseah se Catulus hine, forðy he þæran sittan sceolde*, where (as Liggins (1955, p. 126) puts it) 'the context makes it clear that *þa* = "therefore" and is almost devoid of temporal sense'.

§ 3080. The fourth and last group comprises examples in which an adverbial *for* formula is used correlatively with a different causal conjunction. Again a few typical examples must suffice: (with conj. *þa*) *Bede* 88. 20 *ac þa he feaht, forðon he wæs gehæfted* and *ÆLS* 31. 121 *Hwam twynað la forði þæt þæs geleaffullan weres wære se sige þa þa him wæs getiþod þæt he wæpenleas nære aworpen þam here?*; (with conj. *nu*) *GD(C)* 75. 11 *7 ic forþon sece hwær ic me gerestan scyle nu ic on his cæstre nane ne fand*, *ÆCHom* i. 278. 31 *Nu ðu gehyrst þæt seo beorhtnys is ealswa eald swa þæt fyr þe heo of cymð, geðafa nu forði þæt God mihte gestrynan ealswa eald Bearn, and ealswa ece swa he sylf is*, and

LPr ii 2

                       Forðam we clypiað to þe,
are biddað,   nu þu yþost miht
sawle alysan;

(with conj. *mid þy*)

ChristC 1425   Mid þy ic þe wolde cwealm afyrran,
             hat helle bealu,   þæt þu moste halig scinan
             eadig on þam ecan life,   forðon ic þæt earfeþe wonn;

and (with conj. *þæs þe*)

Soul i 152   Forþan me a langaþ,   leofost manna,
             on minum hige hearde,   þæs þe ic þe on þyssum hynðum wat
             wyrmum to wiste. . . .

l. Uses other than causal

(1) Adversative/concessive uses?

§3081. Here I am skating on what threatens to become the thin ice of semantics. So I do not propose to linger. Sweet's statement (EETS, OS 45, p. xl)—'fully endorse[d]' by van Dam (p. 11) and by me— is a convenient starting-point: 'There is evident difficulty in connecting the clauses of a long argument, arising from the paratactic nature of O.E. syntax, and consequent scarcity of particles and freedom in their use. Hence the monotonous repetition of such words as *ðonne* and *forðæm* in the most varied senses. . . .' We do not need to go as far as Glogauer (§11) in attributing a vague meaning like 'and' to *forþon* 'for that (reason)' in

GenA 1018   þu scealt geomor hweorfan,
             arleas of earde þinum,   swa þu Abele wurde
             to feorhbanan;   forþon þu flema scealt
             widlast wrecan,   winemagum lað.

But many scholars have claimed that *forþon* can mean 'however', 'but', 'and yet', or 'nevertheless'. On the meaning 'and', see §3016 fn.

§3082. The argument about these alleged meanings has centred chiefly on *The Seafarer*. Space does not permit me to rehearse the arguments. Those in favour of the view that 'adversative/concessive' *forþon* occurs in this poem include Daunt (*MLR* 13 (1918), 474-8); Bolton (*MP* 57 (1959-60), 260-2); and Quirk (pp. 58-61), who accepts Burnham's claim (p. 115) that in *ÆLS* 15. 166 *He wæs ærest gecoren eallra þæra godspellera ac he is forði se feorða forþam þe he sette þa feorðan boc*, '*forþi* has true concessive meaning . . . "but in spite of that" ("for all that", "nevertheless")'. But it could be an example of correlative *forþi* 'for the reason I am about to explain'; see §3010. Daunt includes other examples of 'adversative/concessive' *forþon* and both she and Bolton give references to further discussions. On the other hand, Timmer (*EStudies*, 24 (1942), 39-40), Gordon (*The Seafarer*, especially line 27 n., but see below), and Horgan (*RES* 30 (1979), 41-9), see *forþon* in *The Seafarer* as causal; see also Turville-Petre, *MÆ* 26 (1957), 58. A third group of scholars, however, find in this poem and elsewhere what has been variously described as a 'loose' or 'colourless' or 'neutral' use of *forþon* meaning something like 'truly', 'indeed', 'verily', 'now', 'as for that', or 'and so'. They include Lawrence (*JEGP* 4 (1902-3), 463-5); Klaeber (3, Glossary, s.v. *for-ðam*); Liggins (1955, pp. 213-14); Pope (*Magoun Festschrift*, pp. 168, 189 n. 11, and 191 n. 28); Campbell (*RES* 7 (1956), 67); Gordon (for *Sea* 27); and Blakeley (*Arch. L.* 8 (1956), 71-2), who (like Campbell; see § 3084) deals a fatal blow to the alleged evidence in favour of 'adversative/concessive' *forþon* from the glosses.

§ 3083. The use of *for* to signify hindrance has been noted by various authorities, including van Dam (p. 5), who quotes Sweet's comment (*Reader*, 8) on *ChronA* 84. 22 (894) *þa gegaderade Ælfred cyning his fierd 7 for þæt he gewicode betwuh þæm twam hergum, þær þær he niehst rymet hæfde for wudufæstenne ond for wæter- fæstenne*: 'the *for* in this passage seems to be used, as it frequently is, to signify *hindrance*'. But such examples cannot be used to justify 'adversative/concessive' interpretations of *forþon*. In the well-known 'He cannot see the wood for the trees', 'for' means 'because of', not 'in spite of'. This is true in all the OE examples cited by van Dam (p. 5). However, there is no doubt that OE *for* does occasionally mean 'in spite of', e.g. *Bo* 1. 3 . . . *swa swa he hit þa sweotolost 7 andgitfullicast gereccan mihte for þam mistlicum 7 manigfealdum weoruldbisgum þe hine oft ægðer ge on mode ge on lichoman bis- godan, LawAf* 5 *gif he for hungre libban mæge . . .* , and *ChronE* 136. 17 (1006) *Ac for eallum þissum se here ferde swa he sylf wolde*; this last is *OED*'s first quotation for this sense. See further Burnham (pp. 112-15); Quirk (p. 132); BTS, s.v. *for* III. 14; and *OED*, s.v. *for* A. VII. 23a, where we read that the sense 'in spite of, notwithstand- ing', is 'rare exc. in *for all, any,* with a sb.; also absol. *for all that,* etc.'. This last comment emphasizes the fact that this usage is no reason for insisting that *forþon* can mean 'however'. Equally, despite Campbell's independent endorsement (*RES* 7 (1956), 67)—'It is, however, to be doubted if the poet [of *The Seafarer*] would expect his audience to follow such an alternation between the normal mean- ing of the word and a highly abnormal one'—I remain unconvinced of the validity of Blakeley's claim (*Arch. L.* 8 (1956), 72) that 'Quirk's suggestion that *forðon* is sometimes causal, sometimes concessive, in the same text . . . is *a priori* highly unlikely.' There were intonation patterns and few modern readers will have difficulty in understanding the following sentence: '*For* all Blakeley's arguments, I do not agree, *for* "for" can be used in both senses in the same sentence.'

§3084. None the less, I do not find the case for 'adversative/concessive' *forþon* proven. I began this discussion by agreeing with a quotation from Henry Sweet. I end by agreeing with one from another magisterial figure, Alistair Campbell (*RES* 7 (1956), 67 and fn. 2):

> Formulae are apt to be misused by later wielders of a poetical tradition, and *forþon* might very probably become an almost meaningless introductory word. . . . Other evidence [outside *The Seafarer*] for concessive *forþon* is poor. The gloss *forþon uel hueþre* for *uero* contrasts two possible renderings of *uero* but does not equate them. Cases of *forþon* translating *autem* or *sed* reflect freedom of rendering. In the passages quoted by Burnham (p. 31), *forþon* is not truly correlative with *þeah*, but means 'for that reason'. Quirk has shown all possible instances in verse outside the *Seafarer* to be suspect.

(2) *Introducing noun clauses*

§3085. Liggins (1955, pp. 92–5, 131, and 215–16) discusses sentences in which a *for* formula without or with *þe* can be said to introduce a noun clause. Sometimes this is the result of mistranslation of Latin *quia* or *quoniam* introducing a noun clause, e.g. *Mark(WSCp)* 8. 17 *Hwæt þence ge forþam ge hlafas nabbað*, Latin *quid cogitatis quia panes non habetis*, and *Matt(WSCp)* 2. 23 . . . *þ wære gefylled þ gecweden wæs þurh ðone witegan for þam ðe he nazarenisc byð genemned*, Latin . . . *ut adimpleretur quod dictum est per prophetas quoniam nazareus uocabitur*, where *Ru* has *þte*. As Liggins (1955, pp. 94–5) observes, some of these examples are ambiguous. Thus, in *John(WSCp)* 4. 37 *on þyson is witodlice soð word forðam oþer is se ðe sæwþ oþer is se ðe ripþ*, Latin *in hoc enim est uerbum uerum quia alius est qui seminat et alius est qui metit*, where *Li* has *forðon ł þte*, *forðam* could mean 'for'.

§3086. There are, of course, both in OE and MnE, areas of overlap between noun clauses and causal clauses; see §1929. So it is no surprise to find *for* formulae instead of *þæt* after verbs of pitying, showing mercy, giving thanks, rejoicing, sorrowing, hoping, and the like. Examples include *LS* 23. 357 *Miltsa me abbud forðon ic gewilnode mid him to farenne* and *ÆHom* 6. 93 *Fæder, ic þancige þe for ðam ðe þu me gehyrdest*, in both of which a present-day translator could use 'that' or 'because'. See further Liggins 1955, pp. 92–3.

§3087. Both Gorrell (p. 351) and Liggins (1955, p. 216) discuss a group of examples from the nineteenth Blickling Homily (*St. Andrew*). Here we find noun clauses introduced by *for þon/ðon þe* after *witan* (*BlHom* 235. 13 and 243. 17; we can add *BlHom* 245. 9 *Nu ic wat, Drihten, forþon þæt þu ne forlete me*), after *gecyþan* (*BlHom* 237. 4), and after *cweþan* (*BlHom* 247. 2). There may be an example after *geseon* with *forþi* (*BlHom* 243. 33), but the text is corrupt. As Liggins (ibid.) observes, these 'may be due to a Latin text. This homily shows many peculiarities of style.'

(3) *The expression of time*

§3088. Van Dam (p. 47) cites two sentences in which *for þæm þe* denotes 'time when'—a usage not noted by Adams. I detect a causal element in the second, viz. *CP* 85. 5. But in *CP* 305. 1 *La ah ðeah-hwæðre se foreðancula wer, forðæmðe he spræc to ðæm upahæfenan, he bæd his fultumes, swelce him niedðerf wære, forðæmðe* does come close to meaning 'when'.

(4) *The expression of purpose*

§3089. Liggins (1955, p. 527) notes that 'an idea of purpose is usually strong in a causal clause containing a verb of "wishing" or "desiring" '. She instances *willan, nyllan, wilnian*, and *myntan*. On this see §§2976–80 and the General Index.

4. OTHER PREPOSITIONAL FORMULAE

a. *With* be

§3090. Liggins (1955, p. 168) records *be þam þæt* in *ÆLS* 26. 150 *Hit gewearð swa be þam þæt him wann on Penda Myrcena cyning.*

b. *With* of

§3091. *Bo(B)* 29. 4 has *of þam þe*, but this is probably a scribal error, since we find *Bo(C)* 29. 4 *forðæm þe* (Liggins 1955, p. 168). Flamme (p. 74) lists *of þon* among his causal conjunctions, but I have not yet discovered the reference he had in mind.

c. With on/in

§3092. Here there are first, examples with on *þon*/*þæm . . . þæt* in which the prepositional phrase anticipates the *þæt* clause but cannot be part of a divided causal formula, e.g. *Bede* 162. 32 *ond swiðe on þon sargedon, þæt heo þam lareowe onfon ne woldon, þe heo him to sendon*, *CP* 207. 3, and *BlHom* 215. 8 (Liggins 1955, p. 159); second, examples with on *þan*/*þæm þe* such as *CP* 123. 1, *Bo* 88. 27 *Ac hi dwoliað sume on ðæm þe hi wenað ðæt hi mægen habban full god 7 fulla gesælða on þisum andweardum godum*, *Luke(WSCp)* 10. 20, and *ÆLS* 1. 112, in which—according to Liggins (1955, p. 169)— 'the phrase has a defining function and is, indeed, equivalent to NE formal "in that" '; and third, examples with on/in *þon*/*þæm þæt*, e.g. *Bede(C)* 474. 17 *Ond he blissade in þon þæt he oðþæt in lichoman gehealden wæs oð þæt he geseah þa his geherend þone Eastordæg onfon*, where MS *B* has *on þam þæt*, *Bo* 146. 17 *Ac mest monna nu onhyreð nu neatum on þam þæt hi willniað woruldlusta swa swa netenu*, and *ApT* 4. 14 *and . . . he blissode on ðam þæt he his agenre dohtor wer wæs*. Liggins (1955, pp. 168-9) says that 'it may be that these should be classed with the three . . . in which on *(in) þon* anti- cipates a *þæt* clause, with the verb intervening', viz. those in the first group above. But she goes on: 'The existence of on *þan þe*, however, [the second group above] lends support to the idea that on *þæm þæt* may be a compound conjunction.' This seems to be contradicted by her comment (quoted above) on the examples with on *þan þe*. I pre- fer to believe that in all three groups the phrases retained much of their literal significance and had not fossilized into causal formulae. This is supported by the fact that I have cited all Liggins's examples and have found no more myself, and by a consideration of *Bo* 146. 17 above, where 'because' is not a possible translation of on *þam þæt*.

d. With þurh

§3093. Van Dam (pp. 76 and 84 fn. 1) 'noted only three examples of this causal group-conjunction. In each case it renders the Latin *per hoc*, so that Latin influence is possible.' His examples are *GD* 232. 2, *GD* 336. 23, and *Bede* 78. 7, all with *þurh þæt þe*. There are more outside his corpus, including *þurh þæt* in *WHom* 19. 71 *7 heora yldran me swa gegremedan þurh þæt hy noldan mine lage healdan*; *þurh þæt þe* in *ÆCHom* ii. 462. 34 and *WHom* 20(*EI*). 81; *þurh þæt . . . þe* in *WHom* 6. 11 *. . . þonne scealt þu ealra þæra sawla on domesdæg gescead agyldan þe þurh þæt losiað þe hy nabbað þa lare and ða mynegunge þe hy beðorfton* (imitated in *HomU* 47. 303. 31, below); *þurh þæt þæt* in *ÆCHom* ii. 284. 35 *Næron hi onlihte þurh þæt þæt hi Godes beboda gehyrdon*; the correlative pattern in *WHom* 20(*EI*).152 *And þurh þæt þe man swa deð þæt man eal hyrweð þæt man scolde heregian 7 to forð laðet þæt man scolde lufian, þurh þæt man gebringeð ealles to manege on yfelan geþance 7 on undæde* . . . ; and *þurh þæt* . . . *þæt* in *HomU* 47. 303. 31 . . . *þonne sceole ge eallra þæra sawla gescead witan and agildan on domes dæg þe þurh ðæt losiað þæt hi nabbað þa lare and þa mingunge þe hi beþorfton*. For more examples, see Liggins 1955, pp. 154, 166, and 357-8.

e. *With* to

§3094. Neither Shearin (1903, pp. 64-8, and 1909, p. 243) nor Benham (pp. 218-20 and 228-30) makes any mention of the use of formulae with *to* to introduce causal clauses. BTS (s.v. *se* V. 3) notes that *to þon þæt* is used 'with verbs of intention or desire governing an infinitive or a clause, where the action of the verb in the infinitive or clause is intended, *because*'. Both van Dam (p. 65) and Liggins (1955, pp. 169-70) comment on the mixture of final and causal significations in such sentences. I quote the latter: 'The signifcation of "*to þon þæt* + verb" is then almost equivalent to "in order that", but formally it constitutes a special type of causal construction, similar to the use of "*forþæm þe* + a verb of intention".' Liggins (ibid.) tells us that, of ten examples, six have forms of *willan*, e.g. *Or* 148. 29 *Ac Antigones* . . . *for þær Alexandres laf wæs 7 his sunu 7 hie þær begeat, to ðon þæt he wolde þæt þa folc him þy swiþor to buge þe he hæfde hiera ealdhlafordes sunu on his gewealde*; three have *þencan*, e.g. *Or* 44. 31 . . . *þætte* [*hie*] *wæpna naman, to þon ðæt hie heora weras wrecan þohton*; and one has *gelician*, viz. *Or* 116. 4 *þa geceas he him ane burg wið þone sæ, Bizantium wæs hatenu, to ðon þæt him gelicade þæt hie þær mehten betst frið binnan habban*. These categories cover all the BTS examples. Van Dam (pp. 65-6) adds more from *Or* and *GD* with *to þan/þon þæt*, including one with (*ge*)*wilnian*, viz. *GD(C)* 77. 20 *þa wæs he gelæded to þam Godes were to þan þæt he gewilnode 7 abæde him þa helpe þæs halgan mannes þingunga*, where MS *H* lacks *gewilnode* and has a final *þæt* clause. Liggins (1955, p. 170) gives from *ÆCHom* ten clauses whose verb is a form of *willan*, seven of which are introduced by *to þy þæt*, e.g. *ÆCHom* i. 322. 11 *Ic com to ði þæt ic wolde sendan fyr on eorðan*, and three with *to þy* . . . *þæt*, e.g. *ÆCHom* i. 82. 20 *ne com he forðy þæt he wolde his eorðlice rice* . . . *him to geteon; ac to ði he com þæt he wolde his heofenlice rice geleaffullum mannum forgyfan*.

This Ælfrician usage should be compared with that discussed in §§3051 and 3069. *Mutatis mutandis*, the BTS comment quoted above can be applied here.

§3095. Van Dam (p. 65) says that 'there is only one instance in which *to þon þætte* is causal without a verb of wishing or intending being employed', viz. *Bede* 316. 20. But here *to þon þætte* is an attempt to represent Latin *adeo ut*.

§3096. There are no examples known to me of *to þæs (þe)* introducing causal clauses. Williams and Mackie are right to take *to þæs* in *Max i* 35 *Dol biþ se þe his dryhten nat, to þæs oft cymeð deað unþinged* as an example of *to* + genitive marking the object to which motion takes place 'to that one/him'; see BT, s.v. *to* II.

5. NU

§3097. *Nu* serves as both adverb and conjunction. Used alone as an adverb of time 'now', it naturally refers to the present and is used with a present tense, e.g. *CPEp* 1 *Ðis is nu se wæterscipe*; with a perfect, e.g. *Beo* 375 *is his eafora nu* || *heard her cumen, sohte holdne wine*; or with a preterite functioning as a perfect, e.g.

PPs 94. 10 Nu ic feowertig folce þyssum
        wintra rimes wunade neah,
        aa and symble cwæð and eac swa oncneow,
        þæt hi on heortan hyge dysegedan,

where the OE preterites represent the perfects of the Latin *Quadraginta annis proximus fui generationi huic: et dixi: Semper hi errant corde*. *Þa*, not *nu*, is used when the reference is to a single completed act in the past. So in *Sat* 109 *Nu ic feran com, com* is to be construed as a perfect, and in *Sat* 106 emendation of *Nu* to *Iu* seems unavoidable. *Nu* also serves as an adverb of cause, both alone and correlative with conjunctions such as *nu*—the problem of the ambiguous adverb/conjunction then arises; see §2541—and the various *for* formulae. This usage is discussed in the sections which follow. The other functions of adverb, sometimes almost co-ordinating conjunction, *nu* are a matter for the lexicographer rather than the syntactician, but see (*inter alios*) BTS, s.v. *nu*; Schücking, pp. 122–5; and Quirk, pp. 67–8 and 115–16. *Nu* is also found in combination with other adverbs, e.g. *CP* 377. 21 *nu ðonne, ÆCHom* i. 462. 3 *nu tomerigen, ÆCHom* ii. 104. 22 *nu toniht, Beo* 2859 *nu gen, Beo* 956 *nu gyt, Beo* 426 *nu ða*, and *Beo* 602 *ungeara nu*.

§3098. As a subordinating conjunction, *nu* means 'now that, seeing that, since it is a fact that', and is causal rather than temporal, introducing 'the statement of a cause presumed to be familiar to both speaker and audience' (Liggins 1955, p. 296). Unlike *þa, þonne*, and other temporal conjunctions which are at times used causally, it does not seem to have a purely temporal sense; see §2591. But the temporal sense is more apparent in some sentences than in others; see Möllmer, p. 37, and compare *Bede* 70. 26 with *Bede* 234. 29, *ÆC Hom* ii. 288. 4 with *ÆCHom* ii. 98. 14 (Thorpe's 'while' seems to me unhappy) and *ÆCHom* ii. 332. 22 (§3099; Thorpe's 'when' must be taken to imply 'seeing that'), *Beo* 1474 with *KtPs* 31, and

El 701
          Ic þæt halige treo
   lustum cyðe,   nu ic hit leng ne mæg
   helan for hungre

with

El 632
   Hu mæg ic þæt findan   þæt swa fyrn gewearð
   wintra gangum?   Is nu worn sceacen,
   CC oððe ma   geteled rime.
   Ic ne mæg areccan,   nu ic þæt rim ne can.
   Is nu feala siðþan   forðgewitenra
   frodra ond godra   þe us fore wæron,
   gleawra gumena.

§3099. As van Dam (p. 61) writes,

the causal conjunction *nu*[1] is, of course, temporal in origin. As such it did not denote the actual present, but a starting-point in time. It indicated that the action stated in the sub-clause and which is the cause of the action mentioned in the main clause, has or had only just taken place. Thus, as the starting-point of a cause, it shifted its meaning from temporal to causal. Its genesis is exactly the same as that of the causal conjunction *since* in Modern English, which also developed its meaning from a starting-point in time.
    [1] Cp. Adams, pp. 61-62.

His third sentence rightly suggests that the verb of the *nu* clause refers to 'a state still continuing at the time when the action of the principal clause takes place' (Liggins 1955, p. 302). This, as Liggins (pp. 302-5) implies, is true not only when the verb of the *nu* clause is a 'periphrastic perfect', as in

ChristA 11
          Nu is þam weorce þearf
   þæt se cræftga cume   ond se cyning sylfa,
   ond þonne gebete,   nu gebrosnad is,
   hus under hrofe,

but when it is a present tense, e.g. *ÆCHom* ii. 472. 21 *La leof, sege me humeta canst ðu, nu ðu eart Ebreisc, Grecisc gereord, and Egyptisc, and eac Ethiopisc?*, a 'periphrastic present', e.g. *Bede* 348. 2 *Ne þinre forþfore swa neah is, nu þu þus rotlice 7 þus glædlice to us sprecende eart*, or a preterite serving as a perfect, e.g. *PPs* 90. 14 . . . *niode hine scylde, nu he cuðe naman minne*, Latin . . . *protegam eum, quoniam cognovit nomen meum*, and

PPs 117. 24   we eow æt godes huse   gearwe bletsiað,
                    nu us drihten god   deore onlyhte,

Latin . . . *benediximus vos de domo Domini: Deus Dominus et in-luxit nobis*. The equivalence between the OE preterites and the Latin perfects in the last two examples illustrates the general truth that the preterite after *nu* represents a perfect and should usually be so trans-lated; as Glogauer (p. 32) puts it, *nu* differs from other temporal/causal conjunctions in referring only to 'eine Handlung im Präsens oder eine Vollendung in der Gegenwart' ['an action in the present tense, or an action completed in the present']. So the Wrenn–CH translation of *Beo* 2247 *Heald þu nu, hruse, nu hæleð ne mostan,* ‖ *eorla æhte*—'Now do thou, O Earth, hold fast what heroes might not—the possessions of nobles'—would be more accurate if it read '. . . since heroes have not been allowed to . . .', with the *nu* clause perhaps shading into concession; cf. *Res* 25 (§3104). We have what are only apparent exceptions in *ÆCHom* ii. 332. 22 *Humeta rædað sume men ða leasan gesetnysse, ðe hi hatað Paulus gesihðe, nu he sylfe sæde þæt he ða digelan word gehyrde, þe nan eorðlic mann sprecan ne mot?*, for Paul's saying still holds—'he has said'—and Ælfric could have written *sægþ* for *sægde*, and in

ChristA 82   Huru treow in þe
          weorðlicu wunade,   nu þu wuldres þrym
          bosme gebære,   ond no gebrosnad wearð
          mægðhad se micla,

where we should read 'hast borne' and 'has not been destroyed' in Gollancz's translation 'Verily the faith that dwelt in thee was wor-shipful, since thou didst bear within thy bosom the flower of glory, and thy great maidenhood was not destroyed.'

§3100. Consequently, almost all possible combinations of tenses in the principal and causal clauses are to be found. For reasons of space, I set them out in diagrammatic form in the table which follows, with references to examples from my limited collections.

Tense of Subordinate clause	Tense of Principal clause		
	Present	Preterite	Perfect
Present	*Ex* 530 *JDay ii* 68 and 69	*ÆCHom* ii. 332. 25 *ÆLS* 5. 318	*Mald* 231
Preterite	*Ex* 278[160] *And* 317	*ChristA* 82	*Ex* 420 *GenB* 729
Perfect[161]	*GenB* 835 *ChristA* 11	No example recorded	*GenB* 504

§ 3101. As already noted, the problem of the ambiguous adverb/conjunction arises here. This has already been discussed (see the General Index) and need only be exemplified by quoting without punctuation a few passages containing *nu* which can be punctuated to give one or two sentences: *Or* 14. 5 *Nu hæbbe we awriten þære Asian suþdæl nu wille we fon to hire norðdæle*, *Or* 110. 9 *Nu ic þyses Alexandres her gemyndgade cwæð Orosius nu ic wille eac þæs maran Alexandres gemunende beon*, *ÆCHom* i. 252. 27 *Nu ge gleawe men nellað syllan eowrum cildum næddran for fisce nele eac ure Heofonlica Fæder us syllan þæs deofles geleaflæste*, *ÆCHom* i. 350. 21 *Efne nu ðu eart gehæled ne synga ðu heononforð*,

And 1300   Sleað synnigne   ofer seolfes muð
                 folces gewinnan   nu to feala reordaþ,

and

Sat 155   Nu ic eom dædum fah
                 gewundod mid wommum   sceal nu þysne wites clom
                 beoran beornende   in bæce minum
                 hat on helle   hyhtwillan leas.

The punctuation of the last example and of *Beo* 939 in the standard editions should be compared with that of *Beo* 2799. See further Liggins 1955, pp. 305–7, and Mitchell 1959, pp. 436–7, and compare *ÆCHom* i. 478. 1 with *ÆCHom* i. 586. 7.

§ 3102. Liggins (1955, p. 302) reports that *nu* causal clauses 'are relatively common only in Alfred's philosophical works, in the homilists and in Byrht [ByrM]' and gives details of the distribution of her

[160] Reading *nu* for *hu* in *Ex* 280 (after Tolkien).
[161] Liggins (1955, p. 304) records that of 160 causal *nu* clauses in the prose, 111 had a present tense, 33 a preterite = perfect tense, and 16 a 'periphrastic perfect', but does not give the figures for the verb of the principal clauses. There is room for more work here.

160 prose examples in a table (p. 303). They include fifty-eight examples in which *nu* introduces a causal clause in second position without a correlative adverb in the principal clause, e.g. *ÆCHom* i. 378. 6 *Untwylice þu lihst þæt þu God sy, nu ðu nast manna ge-ðohtas*—this construction 'is the most frequent and also the most general in its distribution' (Liggins 1955, p. 302)—and twenty-four with a causal clause in first position without an accompanying correlative adverb, e.g. *ÆCHom* i. 202. 6 *Nu ðu nylt gelyfan minum wordum, beo ðu dumb oðþæt þæt cild beo acenned*. Unfortunately, she fails to give full references. Liggins records no examples of a *nu* clause occurring within the principal clause in OE prose. *Beo* 2247 (§3099) is the only one in the poetry. Examples like *Or* 94. 16 *Ne wene ic, cwæð Orosius, nu ic longe spell hæbbe to secgenne, þæt ic hie on þisse bec geendian mæge, ÆCHom* i. 588. 1 *þe gedafenode, nu ðu manna dema eart, þæt þu oncneowe ðinne Deman*, and

Beo 1474   Geþenc nu, se mæra   maga Healfdenes,
                   snottra fengel,   nu ic eom siðes fus,
                   goldwine gumena,   hwæt wit geo spræcon . . . ,

do not strictly belong here.

§3103. The figures given by Liggins mean that almost half of her examples (78/160) of causal *nu* clauses in the prose are accompanied by a principal clause containing a correlative adverb and/or interrogative. The principal clause can come before the causal clause, e.g. *BlHom* 175. 12 *nu is min yfel twyfeald nu Paulus þæt ilce læreþ*, or after it, e.g. *LS* 8. 360 *Nu ic hæbbe eall þis gesæd swa hit gelamp, nu bidde ic ðe þurh þæt miccle mægen ures drihtnes þæt þu me secge hweðer þu ðis gecnawe*, where the element order suggests that the first *nu* is a conjunction. But see §3915. The adverb *nu* need not have first position in its clause, e.g. *Bo* 108. 3 *Ongit nu hu unmehtige þa yflan men bioð, nu hi ne magon cuman ðider*. . . . Liggins (1955, pp. 297-302) gives examples of conj. *nu* correlative with adverbs other than *nu*, including *forþon*, e.g. *GD(C)* 75. 11, *þonne*, e.g. *BlHom* 123. 1, and *nu ðonne*, e.g. *CP* 377. 21. Causal *nu* clauses can also be used with principal interrogative clauses in the prose, e.g. *Bo* 68. 9 . . . *forhwy* . . . *nu* . . . ?, *Bo* 38. 16 *Nu þonne nu* . . . *hwylce* . . . *þonne* . . . ?, *ÆCHom* i. 366. 13 *Nu* . . . *hu* . . . ?, and *ÆCHom* ii. 104. 16 *Hwæt do ic la, nu ic næbbe hwær ic mæge ealle mine wæstmas gegaderian?*

§3104. The table which follows gives comparative figures for prose and poetry. Those for the poetry must be read in the light of the problems of the ambiguous adverb/conjunction and of the *apo koinou* construction.

Position of *nu* clause	Prose (after Liggins)	Poetry
NO CORRELATION		
Subordinate clause		
follows	58	45
precedes	24	17
occurs within	0	1 (*Beo* 2247)
CORRELATION		
Subordinate clause follows a principal clause with		
adv. *nu*	17	12 (*Beo* 426, 1474, etc.)
other adverb	9	2 (*GuthA* 316, *LPr ii* 2)
interrogative	21	47	0
Subordinate clause precedes a principal clause with		
adv. *nu*	13	2 (*And* 644, *ChristB* 573)
other adverb	12[162]	0
interrogative	6	31	0
Apo koinou		1 (*Sat* 391)[163]
Doubtful examples	0	2 (*Ex* 280, *PPs* 117. 24)
Editors have *nu* principal clause for ambiguous adv./conj.[164]	0	21
Totals	160	103

The comparative scarcity of correlation in the poetry is noteworthy but not surprising. As in the prose, the correlative principal clause may precede the causal clause, e.g. *Beo* 426 and *ChristA* 11 (§3099), or follow it, e.g. *And* 644 and *ChristB* 573. We find correlation between *forðon/forðam* adv. and *nu* conj. in *GuthA* 316 and *LPr ii* 2. In

[162] Includes *CP* 405. 18. Liggins (1955, p. 298) misconstrues here.
[163] Other examples could perhaps be included here.
[164] It is only fair to say that Liggins (1955, *passim*) does recognize the existence of this problem.

Res 25   Nu þu const on mec
            firendæda fela,   feorma mec hwæþre,
            meotod, for þinre miltse,   þeah þe ic ma fremede
            grimra gylta   þonne me god lyfde,

the *nu* clause shades into concession. According to Adams (p. 61), the
same is true in *Bo* 80. 22 *Wundorlice cræfte þu hit hæfst gesceapen
þæt þ fyr ne forbærnð þ wæter 7 þa eorþan, nu hit gemenged is wið
ægðer.* See Quirk, pp. 67–8 and 115–16.

§3105. *Nu* clauses refer to the actual or accepted cause or, as Möllmer (p. 38) has it, to the 'offensichtlichen, bekannten Grund' ['obvious, well-known reason']; I have noted no instances of a suggested
or rejected cause. This accounts for the fact that conj. *nu* is followed
by the indicative or by an ambiguous form which must be so taken.
The only exceptions known to me are *BlHom* 163. 3, where there is
probably textual corruption (see Liggins 1955, p. 305), and *Az* 44,
where the corresponding passage in *Dan* 327 has *þæt* for *nu* and ind.
habbað for subj. *habban* (see Mitchell 1959, pp. 438–9). The indicative is the rule even when the principal clause contains an imperative,
e.g. *Beo* 1474 (imp. + pres. ind.), *Mald* 93 (imp. + 'periphrastic perfect'), and *GenA* 1916 (imp. + pret. ind. = perfect).

§3106. Liggins (1955, p. 308) notes that 'the most common of the
Latin constructions to be translated by a *nu*-construction is that with
si, in the sense of a fulfilled condition'. A typical example is *CP*
393. 8 *Hwa mæg ðonne æhta oððe anwaldes oððe weorðscipes
wilnian butan plio, nu se swelc plioh ðæron gefor, se ðe his no ne
wilnode?*, Latin *Quis ergo opes, quis potestatem, quis gloriam
quaerat innoxie, si et illi extiterunt noxia, qui haec habuit non quae-
sita?* See further van Dam, pp. 61–3, and note that for *nu* in *ÆLS
(A)* 31. 1406 *Hwæt bið be us synfullum nu se swicola deofol swa
mærne sacerd derian wolde?*, MS *B* has *gif.* For other Latin equivalents of, and other OE variants for, conj. *nu*, see Liggins 1955,
pp. 308–9.

6. *ONO*

§3107. This word, with its variant spellings, has been discussed by
Miller in the introduction to his *Bede* (pp. xxix–xxxiii), where he
describes it as 'belonging to Northumbria and Mercia, and not used in
the Saxon South' and says that 'it is clear . . . that *ono* never means
"if", though Bede has been quoted in support of this sense'. Liggins
(1955, p. 213) is in agreement, for she writes: 'Comparison with the
Latin and examination of the contexts in which it appears make it

clear that *ono* in *HE* [*Bede*] is a weak connective, and not a conditional conjunction—as Miller pointed out long ago.' As I note in
§3672, this is sound. Her reason for mentioning *ono* is presumably
that (as Miller shows) it sometimes translates Latin *ergo, igitur*, or
nam; see §§3166-7. So it is reasonable for van Dam (pp. 55-6) to
see *ono* as correlative to conj. *forðon þe* in *Bede* 70. 15, where *Ac
forðon þe . . . ono se* represents Latin *sed quia . . . qui*. Van Dam
(p. 63) makes two other points: first, that Miller contradicts himself
by translating *ono þætte* as 'if this' in *Bede* 76. 1, where the Latin
has *quod ergo* and *þætte* means 'that which', and second, that he
translates *ono he* as 'since he' in *Bede* 82. 11, where the OE has *Ono
he* for Latin *Qui enim*. (This example does not appear in Miller's
table, p. xxix.) In both Miller is wrong. We must conclude that *ono*,
which is not a conditional conjunction 'if', is not a causal one 'because' either.

7. *SWA*, ALONE AND IN COMBINATION

§3108. Another of the extensions to which the basically modal conjunction *swa* is liable is its use in a causal clause. QW (p. 101) rightly
draws our attention to the 'cause-equivalence in . . . *þa wearð he on
slæpe swa swa God wolde* "then he fell asleep just as (i.e. because)
God wished" '. We can compare the modern use of 'as' in the meaning 'since, because' and examples from the poetry like

Beo 350		Ic þæs wine Deniga,
	frean Scildinga	frinan wille,
	beaga bryttan,	swa þu bena eart,
	þeoden mærne	ymb þinne sið. . . .

For a fuller treatment of this topic, the reader is in the first instance
referred to Liggins (1955). She cites four examples of temporal/causal
swa 'as soon as', viz. *CP* 419. 10, *GD(C)* 46. 6, *Or* 172. 8, and *LS* 7.
89 *and swa he þone munuc geseah þa axode he hine to hwi he come*
(pp. 320-1). It is not clear to me why these four alone are chosen.
She distinguishes *swa (swa)* with a modal/causal function, instancing
ÆCHom i. 138. 33 *Seo eadige Maria ða geoffrode hire lac Gode mid
þam cilde, swa hit on Godes æ geset wæs* and *ÆCHom* i. 32. 1 *Ða
gecyrdon þa hyrdas ongean wuldrigende and herigende God on
eallum ðam ðingum þe hi gehyrdon and gesawon, swa swa him fram
þam engle gesæd wæs* (pp. 335-6), from *swa (swa)* with a causal
function, instancing *BlHom* 97. 12 *Forþon we sceolan weorðian þæt
halige sigetacen Cristes rode 7 æfter fylgeon 7 biddan ure synna
forgifnessa ealle æt somne, swa he for us ealle þrowade on ðære rode,*

BlHom 121. 14 *ah he þæt wolcn him beforan nam, swa he ealle gesceafta on his handa hafað*, and *ÆCHom* ii. 504. 16 *Ða cyrde Martinus ongean to Hilarium, swa swa he mid wope hine georne bæd, þæt he æfter ðam siðe hine gesecan sceolde* (pp. 337-41). The dividing-line here and in the other examples she cites is not always clear. She then discusses *swa* constructions of comparison and degree with a causal shade of meaning (pp. 341-55)—on these see my §§3262-300—and summarizes her findings on modal/causal connectives (pp. 358-9).

§3109. As she herself recognizes, there is bound to be much difference of opinion on the interpretation of individual examples. Thus she deliberately excludes from her lists examples such as *ChronE* 139. 16 (1009) *swa heora gewuna wæs* and *WHom* 20(*EI*). 190 *swa us þearf is* because they 'are used as parenthetical tags, with little real meaning' (p. 334 fn. 1). Some readers may think this more true of the second than of the first example. She classifies *swa swa* as a causal conjunction in *ÆCHom* i. 80. 8 *þa betealde he hine swiðe geaplice, swa swa he wæs snotorwyrde, to ðan swiðe, þæt se casere hine mid maran wurðmynte ongean to Iudeiscum rice æsende*, presumably in agreement with Thorpe's 'as he was so sagacious' (p. 338). But the translation 'clever talker as he was' seems to me a strong possibility. Typical of similar instances in the poetry is

ChristA 140
                      Se wæs æ bringend,
lara lædend,   þam longe his
hyhtan hidercyme,   swa him gehaten wæs,
þætte sunu meotudes   sylfa wolde
gefælsian   foldan mægðe,
swylce grundas eac   gæstes mægne
siþe gesecan,

which Ericson (1932, p. 62) classifies as causal, but which can readily be taken as comparative. Space does not permit further discussion here of a problem which often shades into the terminological. But see Glogauer, p. 35; Ericson 1932, *passim*; Andrew, *Postscript*, pp. 26-7; van Dam, p. 64; Liggins, loc. cit.; and Mitchell 1959, pp. 450-3. I discuss the possibility of taking *swa* in *Cæd* 3 as a causal conjunction in *NQ* 212 (1967), 203-4.

8. *SWA þÆT*

§3110. As Liggins (1955, p. 340) observes, 'causal *swa þæt* is used always in an explanatory sense = NE "in that" or "for" '. Typical examples include *Bede* 142. 2 *7 his þa neorran tide wæron wyrson þam ærran, swa þætte þy þeawe þe geo þa ealdan Samaritane dydon,*

þæt he wæs gesewen Criste þeowian 7 eac deofolgeldum, Bede
374. 9, *ÆLS* 32. 206, and *ÆCHom* i. 258. 26 *Crist is Godes Sunu,*
swa þæt se Fæder hine gestrynde of him sylfum, butan ælcere meder.
There are inevitably borderline examples. Liggins includes *Or* 288. 31
here, while Adams (p. 55) is inclined to see temporal *swa þæt* in
HomU 46. 293. 12. It would not be difficult to reverse these.

9. *SWELCE*

§3111. Neither BT nor its Supplements recognize *swelce* as a causal
conjunction. But Ælfric occasionally uses it to introduce what is
clearly a causal clause with a subjunctive verb. It introduces a clause
which explains why something did not happen in *ÆCHom* i. 82. 28
ac hit wære to hrædlic, gif he ða on cildcradole acweald wurde,
swilce ðonne his tocyme mancynne bediglod wære; here the subjunctive is consistent with the hypothetical nature of the whole sentence.
In all but one of the remaining examples (*ÆLS* 34. 287 (§3112)),
the *swelce* clause gives a rejected cause in a sentence which also expresses an accepted cause; on these concepts see §§3019-21. Examples
known to me are *ÆCHom* i. 262. 5 *We wendað us eastweard þonne*
we us gebiddað, forðan ðe ðanon arist seo heofen, na swilce on east-
dæle synderlice sy his wunung, where the accepted cause is expressed
first, and five in which it follows the rejected cause, viz. *ÆLS* 5. 17,
ÆCHom i. 8. 4 *Swa swa ælmihtig wyrhta, he wyrcð his weorc þurh*
his gecorenan, na swylce he behofige ures fultumes, ac þæt we ge-
earnion þæt ece lif þurh his weorces fremminge, ÆCHom i. 128. 29,
ÆCHom i. 366. 5, and (with correlative adv. *forþi*) *ÆCHom* i. 34. 23
Næs þæt cild forði gecweden hire frumcennede cild swilce heo oðer
siððan acende, ac forði þe Crist is frumcenned of manegum gastlicum
gebroðrum. Liggins includes all but one (*ÆCHom* i. 262. 5) of these
examples in the second of four groups in which *swelce* has 'at least
a partly causal function' and says that in them 'it is only concepts of
manner and of cause that are combined. Again an unreal supposition
is made, but this time it is specifically denied . . .' (Liggins 1955,
p. 355; see also Liggins 1960, pp. 461-2). This usage has much in
common with the idiom discussed in §§3370-81, in which comparative + hypothetical *swelce* 'as if' introduces clauses with a subjunctive verb.

§3112. Liggins's remaining groups (1955, pp. 355-7) have respectively three, one, and one, examples. Those in the first—*CP* 147. 9,
CP 151. 21, and *LS* 23. 461 (where we have *swilc*)—are said to
express unreal condition, combining the senses 'in the manner that'
and 'if (and because)'. In all of them, the EETS translation has 'as if'.

I agree. The solitary example in her third group is the exception noted in § 3111, viz. *ÆLS* 34. 287 *and Almachius wolde witan ymbe þa æhtan swylce heo wydewe wære.* Here I accept Liggins's verdict: '*swylce* is almost purely causal. I can see no reason for the subjunctive, as the clause states a definite fact. Presumably it is used here on the analogy of the subjunctive generally found with this connective.' Her fourth group appears to comprise only *CP* 133. 6 *Suelc ðæt folc bið, suelc bið se sacerd*, Latin *Et erit sicut populus, sic sacerdos.* The reason for distinguishing this from similar examples of comparative *swelc . . . swelc* (§ 2375) eludes me.

10. *ÞÆS, ÞÆS ÞE*, AND *ÞÆS . . . ÞE*

§ 3113. As a conjunction introducing a clause which gives or may be said to give a cause or reason, *þæs (þe)* has three possible sources. (I rule out Johnsen's inevitable suggestion of a 'local-demonstrative origin'; see *Ang.* 38 (1914), 100.) It may have arisen as a natural extension of temporal *þæs (þe)* discussed in §§ 2679-85, for it is easy to detect a blend of temporal and causal in examples like *Or* 184. 10 (see Adams, p. 200; van Dam, pp. 68-9; and Liggins 1955, p. 316), *Bede* 42. 3 *And þæs ðe þa seo costnung ðære ehtnesse gestilled wæs, þa wæron forðgongende þa cristenan men 7 ða geleafsuman, þa þe hi ær on ða frecnan tid þære ehtnysse on wudum 7 on westenum 7 scræfum hi hyddon 7 digledon*, and

GenA 2719   Sealde him to bote,   þæs þe he his bryd genam,
                gangende feoh   and glæd seolfor
                and weorcþeos.

In such examples the translation 'because' cannot be ruled out. Liggins (1955, pp. 316 and 321-2) adds more examples. They seem to me somewhat arbitrarily selected when I compare them with similar examples quoted by Adams but not by Liggins.

§ 3114. Sometimes *þæs (þe)* may be, or may have its origin in, a genitive governed by a verb or noun. In *Beo* 227 *Gode þancedon ‖ þæs þe him yþlade eaðe wurdon*, we could say that *þæs þe* is either the genitive of *þæt þe* introducing a noun clause or the genitive of dem. *þæt + þe* meaning literally 'for that [thing] namely'; see §§ 1958-9. Since Latin *quia* may introduce either a noun clause or a causal clause, *þæs* in *CP* 379. 24 *Waa me ðæs ic swigode*, Latin *Vae mihi quia tacui* (cited by van Dam, p. 68, and Liggins 1955, p. 167), may introduce a noun clause, with *þæs* for *þæt* under the influence of *Waa* and/or *swigode* (which can take either the accusative or the genitive)—compare *GD(C)* 24. 33 with *GD(H)* 24. 35 (both in

§ 1959)—or may be a reduced form of *þæs þe*, meaning 'for that' and so 'because'. Van Dam (p. 68) seems to hover between these two views when he describes *þæs* as 'a causal conjunction' and as 'a genitive dependent on *wa* to denote the cause of the distress'. The two explanations offered for *CP* 379. 24 are also possible for examples from the poetry like

El 961　　　　　　　　　　Gode þancode,
　　　wuldorcyninge,　　　þæs hire se willa gelamp
　　　þurh bearn godes　　　bega gehwæðres,
　　　ge æt þære gesyhðe　　þæs sigebeames,
　　　ge ðæs geleafan　　　þe hio swa leohte oncneow,
　　　wuldorfæste gife　　　in þæs weres breostum.

Examples like these must not be confused with those in which *þæs* *(þe)* is the genitive of the relative *þæt (þe)* 'that which, what' as in

Beo 1397　　　Ahleop ða se gomela,　Gode þancode,
　　　mihtigan Drihtne,　　þæs se man gespræc

and *ÆCHom* ii. 448. 19 *and ic ðearfum ne forwyrnde þæs ðe hi gyrndon*, where Thorpe rightly translates 'and I refused not to the poor that which they desired'. Van Dam (p. 68) makes this error when he takes *þæs þe* as causal in *Or* 21. 8 *7 swiðost ealle hys speda hy forspendað mid þan langan legere þæs deadan mannes inne, 7 þæs þe hy be þæm wegum alecgað, þe ða fremdan to ærnað, 7 nimað*; it means 'with what'. Thorpe similarly errs in translating *ÆCHom* ii. 528. 7 *þonne we biddað ongean ure agenre þearfe, þonne forwyrnð se mildheorta God us þæs ðe we ungesceadwislice biddað* 'When we pray against our own need, then the merciful God forewarns us that we pray indiscreetly'; the meaning is '. . . then God in His mercy denies us what we ask in our folly'. There are indeed ambiguous examples, e.g. *ÆCHom* ii. 422. 12 *Ic halsige ðe þæt ðu me do miltsunge ðæs ðe ic wið ðe agylte*—'because' or 'for that in which'?—and

Beo 1778　　　　　　　　þæs sig Metode þanc,
　　　ecean Dryhtne,　　þæs ðe ic on aldre gebad,
　　　þæt ic on þone hafelan　heorodreorigne
　　　ofer eald gewin　　eagum starige!

—'because' or, as Wrenn–CH has it, 'for what I have gained while still alive,—that with mine eyes I gaze upon this blood-stained head, the age-long struggling past!' Liggins (1955, p. 167) says of *HomU* 34. 204. 15 *hi scylon þonne þæs ece lean habban and he heom þonne on dæg luflice geþancað þæs ðe hy on life him rihte gehyrdon* that it is 'more likely that we have a compound conjunction rather than the genitive of a relative pronoun + *þe* clause'. I would rule out the latter interpretation as intolerably strained. On *Beo* 1748 see Mitchell 1959, pp. 443-4.

§3115. Third, causal *þæs (þe)* may have arisen as an extension of semi-adverbial uses of dem. *þæs* 'for that, *therefor, because of that' seen in a range of varying examples in *Bo* 36. 1 *hwelce cehhettunge ge woldan þæs habban 7 mid hwelce hleahtre ge woldon bion astered*, *BlHom* 13. 22 *7 we þæs gelefað* . . . 'we therefore believe . . .', *ÆCHom* ii. 480. 26 *Sy þæs Gode lof a on ecnysse, HomU* 34. 204. 15 (§3114), and

Beo 587   . . . þeah ðu þinum broðrum   to banan wurde,
                 heafodmægum;   þæs þu in helle scealt
                 werhðo dreogan,   þeah þin wit duge.

(For more such examples see Liggins 1955, pp. 199-200; Sorg, pp. 55-8; and Klaeber, 3, Glossary, s.v. *se*.) The conjunction would then mean literally 'for that (namely)'; consider

ChristC 1232   Ðonne bið gæsta dom   fore gode sceaden
                      wera cneorissum,   swa hi geworhtun ær,
                      þær bið on eadgum   eðgesyne
                      þreo tacen somod,   þæs þe hi hyra þeodnes wel
                      wordum ond weorcum   willan heoldon.

This seems to me the most likely origin for causal *þæs (þe)* in those examples from the poetry in which it is correlative with adverb *forþon*, e.g. *GenB* 302 *Forþon he sceolde grund gesecean* ‖ *heardes hellewites, þæs þe he wann wið heofnes waldend*,

Sat 483   Hæfdon forþon hatne grund,
                 þæs git ofergymdon   hælendes word,
                 æten þa egsan,

and possibly

Soul i 152 ˙   Forþan me a langaþ,   leofost manna,
                      on minum hige hearde,   þæs þe ic þe on þyssum hynðum wat
                      wyrmum to wiste . . . ,

though here too *þæs þe* may introduce a noun clause, since *langian* can take the genitive; in which *þæs (þe)* is correlative with adv. *þæs*, e.g.

Ex 49   Swa þæs fæsten dreah   fela missera,
               ealdwerige,   Egypta folc,
               þæs þe hie wideferð   wyrnan þohton
               Moyses magum,   gif hie metod lete,
               on langne lust   leofes siðes;

or in which it is used alone, e.g.

GenA 2309

> Ic þa wære forð
> soðe gelæste, þe ic þe sealde geo
> frofre to wedde, þæs þin ferhð bemearn,

El 1316

> Him bið engla weard
> milde ond bliðe, þæs ðe hie mana gehwylc
> forsawon, synna weorc, ond to suna metudes
> wordum cleopodon,

and

Sat 172

> Ðæs ic wolde of selde sunu meotodes,
> drihten adrifan, and agan me þæs dreames gewald,
> wuldres and wynne, me þær wyrse gelamp
> þonne ic to hihte agan moste,

the only example in which the editors place a causal *þæs (þe)* clause before its principal clause. I would prefer to regard *Sat* 163a–80a as a verse paragraph; see §3799. Two Ælfric examples—*ÆLS* 1. 55 *. . . and hi ealle swa þæh alotene beoð to þære eorðan weard and þider wilniað oððe þæs þe him lyst oððe þæs þe hi beþurfon . . .* and *ÆLS* 12. 56 *He wearð ða bebyrged and him læg on uppan fela byrðena eorðan binnon seofon nihton þæs ðe he forsoc þa feawa axan*—may belong here. Liggins (1955, p. 167) says that 'some notion of time survives in LS xii, but in LS i, the meaning is wholly causal'. I agree about *ÆLS* 1. 55. But in my opinion *þæs ðe* in *ÆLS* 12. 56 could be causal 'because' or temporal 'after', for the man's death occurred *on ðære wucan* (*ÆLS* 12. 51) in which he refused to accept the ashes on Ash Wednesday.

§3116. I have discussed all the examples of causal *þæs (þe)* in the prose proposed by van Dam and Liggins. There are more in the poetry; see Sorg, pp. 59–62, and (for a full list of examples) Mitchell 1959, Appendix 'Cause 5' and 'Cause 6'. Quirk (pp. 115–16) suggests a concessive interpretation for the *þæs* clauses in *ChristC* 1093 and *PPs* 77. 11.

§3117. Causal *þæs . . . þe* has not been noted in the prose. It occurs in the poetry in

Phoen 409

> þæs þa byre siþþan
> gyrne onguldon, þe hi þæt gyfl þegun
> ofer eces word,

Jud 5

> Hyre ðæs fæder on roderum
> torhtmod tiðe gefremede, þe heo ahte trumne geleafan
> a to ðam ælmihtigan,

and possibly in

Phoen 567   Me þæs wen næfre
                    forbirsteð in breostum,   ðe ic in brego engla
                    forðweardne gefean   fæste hæbbe.

But here *þæs* may be dependent on *wen*, with *ðe* 'because' or *ðe ic*
'I who'.

11. *þÆT(TE)*

a. Introductory remarks

§3118. Two points must be made before I embark on what is, for
both OE and MnE, largely a terminological problem. First, I feel—
and again the usage is deliberate—that examples from OE prose cannot legitimately be used to support the translation of *þæt* by 'because' in OE poetry, for in the prose the problems associated with
translating or paraphrasing Latin periods into OE led to the use of
clauses introduced by *þæt* in many contexts and functions which
were alien to the poetry. Second, in the poetry and, for the reason
just given, even more in the prose, *þæt* is a maid-of-all-work, with
a much wider range of uses than MnE 'that'; see §1929. In the words
of van Dam (p. 69), 'being practically devoid of meaning, it [*þæt*]
can introduce all sorts of clauses'. Liggins (1955, p. 163) writes:

Causal *þæt* in OE is much less specialized in its functions than NE causal *that*,
of which Jespersen [*MnEG* v. 389] says: '*That* chiefly serves to express the psychological reason or motive for a state of mind'. This is one of the important
senses of the OE form, but it serves, too, in many places where NE would use
'because', while in another group of examples it is equivalent to the compound
in that of formal or literary language, *since* or *for* of colloquial usage.

But since OE *þæt* is more widely used than MnE 'that', the fact that
it can often conveniently be translated by 'because' does not prove
that it was a causal conjunction. Thus, it is certainly convenient to
translate *þæt* as 'because' in *GenB* 393 *Ne magon we þæs wrace ge-
fremman,* || *geleanian him mid laðes wihte þæt he us hafað þæs
leohtes bescyrede* and in

GuthA 448   Treow wæs gecyþed,
                    þætte Guðlace   god leanode
                    ellen mid arum, þæt he ana gewon.

But when we consider

Beo 2101   Me þone wælræs   wine Scildunga
                    fættan golde   fela leanode,
                    manegum maðmum,   syððan mergen com,

where *þone wælræs*, the 'cause' of the reward, is the direct object of *leanian*, we see that the *þæt* clauses in *GenB* 393 and *GuthA* 448 may be noun clause objects of their verb (Jespersen's 'primaries') rather than adverb clauses of cause (Jespersen's 'tertiaries'). By a not unreasonable extension, we can say that *þæt* introduces a noun clause in *And* 275 *Bið ðe meorð wið god,* ‖ *þæt ðu us on lade liðe weorðe* instead of following *OED* (s.v. *that*, conj. II. 2(*b*)), where it is quoted as an example of *þæt* 'introducing a clause expressing the cause, ground, or reason of what is stated in the principal clause'. A similar line of argument holds for verbs and nouns expressing vengeance and punishment (§3124)—both are rewards of a sort (as *GenB* 393 above demonstrates)—and for verbs and nouns expressing emotion (§3124).[165] One last illustration must suffice. Morris translates *BlHom* 19. 4 *Smeagean we nu 7 þencan hwæt þæt tacnode þæt seo menigo styrde þæm blindan þæt he cleopode* 'Let us now consider and think what was denoted by the multitude that endeavoured to restrain the blind man from crying out'. It would be easy to translate the last *þæt* as 'because'. But I believe Morris's 'from' to be right here; cf. *BlHom* 15. 19 *7 swa hie him swyþor styrdon, swa he hludor cleopode.*[166] The sections which follow contain many more examples to demonstrate that a possible equivalence between OE *þæt* and MnE 'because' does not prove the former to be a causal conjunction. However, I have to admit that the problem is subjective as well as terminological. Two illustrations of this must suffice: van Dam's distress (p. 70) that 'neither Wülfing, nor Wright mention[s] *þæt* as a causal conjunction' and the table set out below, which speaks for itself.

Text	Number of causal *þæt* clauses according to	
	van Dam (p. 69)	Liggins (1970, pp. 304-5)
Or	5	22
Bede	6	12
CP	1	17

These are the only three texts for which they both give figures in the places cited.

[165] On this much discussed topic, see, *inter alios*, Nader, pp. 449-50; Kenyon, *JEGP* 13 (1914), 164-5; Glogauer, pp. 39-40; Behre, p. 308 and chapter viii; Liggins 1955, pp. 3, 94-5, 156-62, and 215-16; and Ericson, 'Noun Clauses in *because*', *Ang.* 61 (1937), 112-13.

[166] However, *BlHom* 15. 19 demonstrates that Morris's 'endeavoured to restrain' is wrong; they kept on restraining him, but without success. So *styran* does not necessarily mean 'to succeed in restraining'. This is an exact parallel to *wehte* in *Beo* 2854; see §872 and Mitchell 1975*a*, p. 16.

b. In the poetry

§3119. I have discussed most of the alleged examples of causal *þæt* in OE poetry in *Neophil.* 52 (1968), 292-9, where I claim that 'we must, I think, reject Wrenn's "in as much as" [for *þ* in *Beo* 1141]; the evidence for a causal use of *þæt* in Old English poetry is very slender'. I see no reason for setting aside this verdict. I did not discuss *Mald* 242 *Abreoðe his angin,* ‖ *þæt he her swa manigne man aflymde,* listed as causal by BTS (s.v. *þæt* IV), but here we have a noun clause in apposition with *angin.* A. S. Abbate, *Le Proposizioni introdotte dalla Congiunzione* þæt *nel* Beowulf (Naples, 1974), 127-8, offers six more examples. I would classify four of these as noun clauses (*Beo* 3129, *GenA* 2824 and 2920, and *Jud* 285), one as either noun or adjective with *þæt* 'what' (*Jud* 92), and one as result (*Dan* 28).

§3120. However, I must tie up one loose end in my article, where (pp. 295-6) I referred to

Beo 14   fyrenðearfe ongeat,
            þ hie ær drugon   aldorlease
            lange hwile

without explaining that in my opinion the manuscript *þ* is rightly resolved as *þæt* and introduces a noun clause which is the object of *ongeat.* It may be the only object, with *fyrenðearfe* the object of *drugon,* placed outside its clause; see §1920. Or it may be the second object, parallel to *fyrenðearfe,* with the latter understood as object of *drugon* (see §1969) or with *drugon* used intransitively or absolutely. (I am becoming increasingly unwilling to accept the argument that, because a verb usually or almost invariably appears with an object, it cannot be used intransitively or absolutely.) I cannot endorse Chambers's suggestion that *lange hwile* is the object of *drugon.*

c. In the prose

§3121. 'A *þæt* clause', says Liggins (1955, p. 157), 'is seldom a purely causal one.' I have claimed that it is never so in the poetry and would extend this claim to the prose if Liggins is using the word 'causal' here—as she does elsewhere (see my §3015)—in contrast to 'explanatory'; cf. her observation (1955, p. 204) that '*þæt* clauses generally contain an explanation or amplification of a preceding statement'. This is not true of an example like *Bede* 254. 22 *Ond hwæðre þis aræddon betweonum him, þæt he se abbud his latteow beon sceolde in Breotone, forþon þe he ær twiga þa dælas Gallia rices fore missenlecum intingum geferde 7 gesohte, 7 forþon þe him se weg þæs siðfætes genoh cuð wæs, 7 eac swylce þæt he wæs in his agnum geferscipe wel gemonnad*, where *þæt* is used (I suspect for reasons of euphony) to avoid a third *forþon þe*, or of *þæt* clauses like those in *ÆHom* 6. 338 . . . *þam Hælende . . . se þe sylfwilles com þæt he sweltan wolde* and *Dream* 33 *Geseah ic þa frean mancynnes* ‖ *efstan elne mycle þæt he me wolde on gestigan*, which contain a form of *willan* and which shade into clauses of purpose; see §§2976-80 and Liggins 1955, pp. 159-60. But in a broad sense, it is true of all other examples of 'causal' *þæt* clauses cited by van Dam (pp. 69-70) and by Liggins (1955, pp. 156-66), or otherwise known to me. Before I discuss the categories into which these remaining examples can be divided, it will be convenient to list them and to summarize some facts reported by Liggins.

§3122. She recorded 188 'causal' *þæt* clauses in second position. If we exclude 20 which contain a form of *willan* (see above), we have four groups: (a) 94 follow verbs, nouns, or adjectives, expressing emotion; (b) 5 follow verbs or nouns of revenge or punishment; (c) 4 are the equivalent of MnE 'not that . . .' or the like; and (d) the remainder (as I see it) are defining or 'explanatory' (Liggins 1955, pp. 156-62). In 56 of these 188 clauses the mood was indicative, in 114 ambiguous, and in 18 subjunctive. Twelve of the subjunctives follow verbs expressing emotion (Liggins 1955, pp. 160-2). On these, see Behre, pp. 232-3. (Liggins (1955, p. 161 fn. 1) finds his comments 'probably over-subtle' for OE prose. But I cannot accept the proposition that prose must be less subtle than poetry in its use of the subjunctive.) The remaining subjunctives express uncertainty, condition, or the like. None of them is comparable with the use of the subjunctive to express suggested or rejected cause.

§3123. Liggins (1955, p. 162) records only one 'causal' *þæt* 'in first position', viz. *Bede* 280. 15 *Forðon þa Bonefatius forðferde æfter seofontyne gearum his biscophada, þa gehalgode Theodor biscop after him þone Biise to biscope; ond þa gena bi him lifgendum, þæt he wæs bewered from þære biscopþegnunge mid hefigre untrymnesse, wæron twegen biscopas Ecce 7 Beadowine fore hine gecorene 7 gehalgode*, where the presence of *þæt* or *þ* in all manuscripts is testimony rather to the translator's failure to deal with the Latin *Quo adhuc superstite sed grauissima infirmitate ab administrando episcopatu prohibito, duo sunt pro illo, Aecci et Baduuini, electi et consecrati episcopi* and/or to the wide and ill-defined uses of *þæt* than to the existence of causal *þæt* 'because'. The only example of an inter-polated causal *þæt* clause she records (pp. 162-3) is *ÆLS(A)* 31. 1465 *Gif ge for minstres þingon and þæt he mid eow wæs hine habban willað, þonne wite ge þis* . . . , where I suspect scribal error; as I report in §3054, MS *B* has *forþan ðe þæt*.

§3124. Typical examples of the four categories listed in §3122 fol-low: (*a*) with verbs or nouns expressing an emotion or a mental state or attitude, *Bo* 126. 1 *oððe hwa ne wundrað þte sume tunglu habbað scyrtran hwyrft þonne sume habban* (in my opinion a noun clause; cf. *Bo* 126. 10 *Oððe hwa ne wundrað ðæs þ sume steorran gewitað under þa sæ*, where we have a noun clause in apposition with *ðæs*, and

Met 29. 93   Nis þæt nan wundor,   forðæm wuhta nan
          æfre ne meahte   elles wunian,
          gif hi eallmægene   hiora ordfruman
          ne þiowoden,   þeodne mærum,

where *forðæm* does mean 'because'), *CP* 3. 18 *Gode ælmihtegum sie ðonc ðætte we nu ænigne on stal habbað lareowa, ÆCHom* i. 430. 18 *Hælend Crist, ic ðancige ðe mid inweardre heortan þæt ic mot faran into ðinum rice, ÆCHom* i. 572. 6 *Min Drihten Hælend, sy ðe lof and wurðmynt þæt þu me gemundest, ÆHom* 4. 289 *Eadig is Maria þæt arwyrðe mæden, þæt heo Godes Sunu abær bliðe to mannum, HomU* 26. 140. 20 *wa me earmre, þæt ic æfre geboren sceolde wurðan* . . . , and

GenA 2216   þa wæs Sarran   sar on mode,
          þæt him Abrahame   ænig ne wearð
          þurh gebedscipe   bearn gemæne,
          freolic to frofre;

(*b*) with verbs or nouns expressing revenge or punishment, *Or* 160. 10 *þa Romane þæt geacsedan, þa sendon hie þider Genutius heora consul mid fultume, to þon þæt he an him gewræce þæt hie þa slogon 7 hiendon þe ealle Romane friþian woldon, ÆCHom* i. 402. 6 *Gregorius se trahtnere cwæð, þæt se Hælend beweope ðære ceastre toworpennysse, ðe gelamp æfter his ðrowunge, for ðære wrace heora mandæda, þæt hi ðone heofenlican Æðeling manfullice acwellan woldon*, and *GenB* 393 (§3118); (*c*) after a negative (cf. MnE 'not that') *GD(C)* 8. 31 *we witon þæt us eallum cuþ is þæt Marcus 7 Lucas writon þæt godspel nalæs þæt hi hit gesawon ac hi hit ge-leornodon, swa hi hit gehyrdon of Petres muðe 7 of Paules þæra apostola* (where I would be inclined to put marks of parenthesis be-fore *nalæs* and after *geleornodon* but MS *O* has . . . *nalæs no þi þe*

hig hit . . . and the reviser writes in *H* . . . *na for þy þe hig hit* . . .),
BlHom 19. 32 *Næs þæt na þæt he nyste hwæt se blinda wolde, se
ealle þing wat, 7 him leoht forgeaf; ah Drihten wile þæt hine mon
bidde, se þe ær geteod hæfde þæt he þon biddendan ece lif forgeafe*,
and *Bo* 13. 26 *næs hit no þ an þ* . . . (on which see §§1777–99).
Liggins's fourth example (1955, p. 160) is *CP* 109. 2, where the
ðæt clause is the object of *gefeon*, which is negated by *ne* . . . *na*. The
remaining use is (*d*) the defining or the 'explanatory'. We see this in
examples like *Or* 110. 26 *þa feng Philippus to Mæcedonia rice, 7 hit
ealle hwile on miclan pleo 7 on miclan earfeþan hæfde, þæt ægþer ge
him mon utane of oðrum londum an wann, ge eac þæt his agen folc
ymbe his feorh sierede* . . . and *ÆCHom* i. 114. 18 *Ne talige nan man
his yfelan dæda to Gode, ac talige ærest to þam deofle, þe mancyn
beswac, and to Adames forgægednysse; ac ðeah swiðost to him
sylfum, þæt him yfel gelicað, and ne licað god*. In *LS* 34. 296 *Hwær
syndon þa wiðersacan eowre lyðran magas þe min bebod forhogedon
þæt hi ðam wurðlicum godum nane lac ne offredon*, according to
Liggins (1955, p. 157), the *þæt* clause is 'one of cause or of weakened
result', with *þæt* meaning 'in that' or 'so that'. But the translation
'by not offering . . .' is more satisfactory. In all three, and many similar examples, *þæt* could be said to introduce a noun clause explaining
or defining the preceding statement. *BlHom* 31. 19 *Us is þonne to
geþencenne þæt we þas dæda þus gedone from Drihtne mid ealre
þoncunga 7 mærsunga hine herian 7 lufian, þæt se þe wæs ær eallum
worldum geteod 7 geendebyrd, wolde mid his Suna lichoman þysne
middangeard alysan fram deofles anwalde* may belong here. But the
þæt may be a second object of *herian* and *lufian*; cf. *ChronE* 138. 21
(1009) *Đa genam se Brihtric him to hundeahtatig scipa 7 þohte þ he
him myceles wordes wircean sceolde þ he Wulfnoð cuconne oððe
deadne begytan sceolde*, where Liggins translates the second *þ* as 'in
that', detecting 'a concept of manner', but where Whitelock suggests
that it introduces a clause which is the second object of *þohte*: '. . .
intending to make a big reputation for himself and to capture Wulf-
noth alive or dead'. Perhaps 'by capturing . . .' is a possible compromise.

§3125. None of these *þæt* clauses is 'causal' in the sense that—to
take one example selected entirely at random—the *forðan ðe* clause
in *ÆCHom* ii. 178. 16 *An subdiacon bæd þone halgan wer sumne
dæl eles to his bricum, forðan ðe hi ðicgað on ðam earde ele on
heora bigleofum swa swa we doð buteran* is causal. Liggins (1955,
p. 158), however, claims that some *þæt* clauses 'are undoubtedly adverbial clauses'. She first quotes *GD(C)* 57. 13 . . . *þa sæde he þam
ælmihtigan Gode mycele þancas þæt he ongæt þæt God hine in*

þære his wædle þa gyt wolde ma geswæncan 7 genyrwian, pointing
out that MS *H* reads . . . *þa þancode he swiðe Gode ælmihtigum,
forþam þe he oncneow þæt.* . . . She goes on (p. 158 and fn. 1):

As the last quotation shows, several verbs are constructed both with *þæt* and
with *forþæm/forþæm þe*, with no distinction in meaning. With the quotation
from AHom I, xxix. 430. 18 [= *ÆCHom* i. 430. 18 (my §3124)] compare also
John XI. 41: *fæder ic do þe þancas forþam þu gehyrdest* [*me*]. . . . It is just
possible that *forþam* in such cases does introduce a noun clause, but this seems
unlikely.

I would accept not only this argument but also its reverse: that it is
just possible that *þæt* in *GD(C)* 57. 13 and *ÆCHom* i. 430. 18 does
introduce a causal clause, but this seems unlikely. Here Liggins—
like BT, which (s.v. *þæt* IV. Introducing clauses expressing cause,
reason) cites *Matt(WSCp)* 16. 8 *þ* where *Li* has *forðon* and *Ru* has
forþon þ—is trapped in a terminological problem. Such variations
do not prove that *þæt* means 'because'. They merely demonstrate
that in some contexts OE *þæt* and *forþon (þe/þæt)* were interchangeable just as MnE 'that' and 'because' sometimes are.

d. Preceded by a correlative

§3126. Examples in which *þæt* is correlative with an adverb or
prepositional phrase fall into another category from those in which
þæt appears alone. On patterns like *forþy . . . þæt, forþæm . . . þæt,
forþon . . . þæt, for þæm anum . . . þæt, þy . . . þæt*, and *þurh þæt
. . . þæt*, see the Table of Contents of VII H and the Index of Words
and Phrases. Liggins (1955, p. 159) notes that *on þon . . . þæt* occurs
in *Bede* 162. 32 *ond swiðe on þon sargedon þæt heo þam lareowe
onfon ne woldon, þe heo him to sendon* and compares *CP* 207. 3 and
BlHom 215. 8.

§3127. On *þæt* introducing a clause of purpose expressing accepted
cause after a clause of rejected cause + *ac*, see §§3183 and 3189.

12. þE/þY, ALONE AND IN COMBINATION

a. Introductory remarks

§3128. As a causal adverb, *þy/þi*—in origin the neuter instrumental
of dem. *se*—is used in correlative constructions (see §§3137-43,
3144, and 3145-7) and alone, e.g. *Bo* 22. 26 *þy ic wundrige hwi ðu
ne mæge ongietan þ ðu eart nu git swiðe gesælig.* . . , *ÆCHom* i. 260.
28 *God is ure Fæder, þi we sceolon ealle beon gebroðru on Gode,*

ÆCHom i. 266. 10 *þi we sceolon gelomlice mid þam gastlican ge-reorde ure sawle geclænsian and getrymman*, and

Beo 2067   þy ic Heaðo-Beardna   hyldo ne telge,
                  dryhtsibbe dæl   Denum unfæcne,
                  freondscipe fæstne.

Liggins (1955, pp. 201-2) notes that adv. *þy/þi* serves the same functions as adverbial *for* formulae—she compares *HomU* 40. 273. 14 *ðy us is mycel þearf* . . . with *HomU* 26. 134. 21 *forði is ælcum men oferþearf* . . .—and lists the Latin words they translate. On these and other adverbs meaning 'therefore, accordingly', see Liggins 1955, pp. 193-201. The adverb is sometimes spelt *þe* in correlative constructions. But no one, I imagine, would argue that the indeclinable particle *þe* was used adverbially.

§3129. This happy certainty does not extend to the conjunctional uses. BT and GK recognize both the instrumental *þy* and the indeclinable particle *þe* as causal conjunctions. Liggins (1955, p. 141) is content to say that 'the forms *þy* and *þe* seem to be used interchangeably as independent constructions', though she does quote Benham (p. 223) 'This *ðe* is for *ðy*, instrumental. . . .' This interchangeability is demonstrated by variant readings such as *ChronD*'s *þe* for *þy* in *ChronA* 54. 4 (787) *7 þa se gerefa þærto rad 7 hie wolde drifan to þæs cyninges tune þy he nyste hwæt hie wæron*. But it does not prove that the indeclinable particle *þe* meant 'for' or 'because'. Kivimaa (p. 150) seems to imply that it did not: 'The originally instrumental *þe* . . . is interchangeable with *þy* as a causal conjunction. . . .' In §§3062-4, I asked—but could not answer— whether *þe* and *þy* in formulae such as *forþæm* . . . *þe* and *forþæm* . . . *þy* are respectively the indeclinable particle and the instrumental of dem. *þæt*, or whether *þe* is merely an inverted spelling for *þy*, or whether the reverse is true. The same question has to be asked when *þe* and *þy* are used as causal conjunctions alone and in combination with elements other than *for* formulae.

§3130. One can readily see how the instrumental *þy* could become a causal conjunction by a normal extension of (semi-)adverbial *þy* seen in *Beo* 2067 (§3128), possibly through the attested stage *þy þe*; compare the development of *forþon* and *þæs*. But it is rather more difficult to suggest a plausible line of development for *þe* indeclinable particle. The causal use of *þe* could be seen as an extension of the temporal use of *þe* 'when'. But whether *þe* does ever mean 'when' is dubious and even if it does, it is not established that it is *þe* indeclinable particle rather than a variant spelling of *þy*; see §§2594-6. Other possible origins for indeclinable *þe* 'for' or 'because' are even less plausible. It is unlikely to have arisen from a causal use of adjective clauses introduced by *þe* indeclinable relative + personal pronoun; on this see §3131. It is also unlikely to be a worn-down form of *þy* . . . indeclinable particle *þe* 'for that . . . namely' (see §3138) or of the formula *forþon* . . . indeclinable particle *þe* (see §§3057 (end)-64).

§3131. A few other points are relevant without being conclusive. Liggins (1955, p. 142) notes the existence of *þa* variants for what she sees as temporal/causal *þe* in *Bede(O, Ca)* 446. 24 . . . *awrat he æþele boc his þeode mid sinoþes bebode wið Brytta gedwolan, þa hi rihte Eastran ne weorþedon on heora tide* . . . , where MS *B* has *þe*, and in *Or* 2. 5. But in both of these contexts *þe hi* could mean 'who'. On the same page, Liggins agrees that *þe hy* could mean 'who' in *WHom (E)* 4. 82 *7 ðurh þæt wyrð mæst manna beswicen þe hy ne beoð swa wære ne swa wel gewarnode ær swa hy beðorfton*, but argues that MS *C*'s *forðam hi* establishes *þe* as a causal conjunction. I do not find her logic impeccable; in all three examples the manuscripts may offer different constructions. But even if we accept that they do not, *þe* could still be for *þy* 'for' or 'because'. (With the variations in *WHom* 4. 82, cf. *GD(C)* 32. 32 *forþon þe* but *GD(H)* 32. 31, where the reviser has *þe*.) Numerous examples could be cited in which the combination *þe* and personal pronoun is ambiguous. In *ÆCHom* ii. 266. 18 *þone timan hi heoldon him to Eastertide, seofon dagas mid micclum wurðmynte, ðe hi ahredde wurdon wið Pharao, and of ðam earde ferdon*, we can translate '. . . the time . . . when they . . .', '. . . the time . . . in which they . . .', or '. . . because they . . .'. In

PPs 65. 18   Drihten si gebletsad,   þe he ne dyde æfre
nymðe he mine bene   bealde gehyrde,
ne his milde mod   me dyde fremde,

þe reads quite well as a causal conjunction. But the Latin has *qui*. In

PPs 52. 6   Forþam manna ban   mihtig drihten
liste tosceadeð,   þa him liciað;
beoð þa gehyrwede   þe forhycggeað god,

þa (line 2) represents *qui* and *þe quoniam*. In

PPs 138. 17   Blodhreowe weras,   ge bebugað me,
þe þæt on geþohtum   þenceað cweðende . . . ,

þe represents *quia*. I am not claiming that these Latin equivalents are conclusive. Even if they were, our difficulty would remain. More such examples can be found in Mitchell 1959, p. 448. But I will end with a glance at *BlHom* 33. 32 *Ac on þæm wæs gecyþed þæt he wæs on anum hade twegra gecynda; he wæs soþ man, þy hine dorste deofol costian, swylce he wæs soþ God, þe him englas þegnedon.* Morris notes that 'in MS *y* is written in pale ink above the *e*' of *þe* and translates 'But in him was manifested that he was of two natures in one person—he was true man, therefore the devil dared to tempt him, he was also true God, for angels ministered unto him.' Here a series of questions arises. Is Morris's 'therefore . . . for' right? Is 'for . . . therefore' possible? Or are the two clauses parallel? If so, is the manuscript reading *þy . . . þe* right? Or should we follow the corrector's *þy . . . þy*? Or should the scribe have written *þe . . . þe*? If they are parallel, do we translate 'therefore . . . therefore', 'for . . . for', or read *þe hine . . . þe him* 'whom . . . whom'? Or are the two clauses not parallel? If so, which of the possible combinations do we accept? My answer to all these questions is 'I don't know'.

§3132. In the sections which follow, the status of *þe* is further discussed as it becomes relevant. Certainty is impossible. My own inclination, however, is to believe that when *þe* introduces a causal clause, it is a variant of *þy* and not the indeclinable particle.

b. þe and þy

§3133. As I have just said, I incline to the view that these two forms are both spellings for the neuter instrumental of *se* used as a causal conjunction; the fact that Liggins (1955, pp. 141–5) records only eleven examples of uncorrelated *þy* in all her texts excluding *Li* and *Ru* against twenty-six of uncorrelated *þe* does not prove that indeclinable *þe* means 'because'. Since van Dam (p. 77) records seven examples of causal *þy*, it would seem that he is talking of indeclinable *þe* at pp. 71–5, where, after an analysis of eight *þe* clauses, he comes to the florid but (I believe) basically sound conclusion 'that *þe* is not a full-blooded causal conjunction used alone. . . . It is only in example 8 that *þe* seems a causal conjunction without restrictions.' Example 8 is *GD* 330. 13 . . . *7 he hine þa þy na ne gemette þa þa he eft com to þam baðum, forþon se deacon mihte beon geclænsod þære synne æfter deaðe, forðon he ne gesyngode na mid hete ne mid niðe ac for þam gedwolan, þe he nyste hwæþer he woh dyde.* If the *þe* clause is causal, *þe* could be a form of *þy* meaning 'because' or 'in that' introducing a defining or explanatory cause; cf. *Bo* 32. 18 *þæs menniscan lifes gecynd is þ hi þy anan seon beforan eallum oðrum gesceaftum þy hi hie selfe ongiton hwæt hie send 7 hwonan hi send;*

7 þi hi send wyrsan þonne nytenu, þy hi nellað witan hwæt hi sint, oððe hwonan hi sint. But the Latin has . . . *sed iam praedictum Pascasium in loco eodem minime invenit. quia enim non malitia sed ignorantiae errore peccaverat purgari post mortem potuit a peccato.* So *þe* could mean 'by which', introducing an adjective clause.

§3134. Examples of causal *þe/þy* from the prose include *ChronA* 60. 15 (823) . . . *7 Cantware him to cirdon . . . þy hie from his mægum ær mid unryhte anidde wærun*; *Solil* 1. 5 *ne com ic naþer mid anre byrðene ham, þe me ne lyste ealne þane wude ham brengan gif ic hyne ealne aberan meihte*, where Visser (ii, §894) wrongly takes *lyste* as a present subjunctive; *CP* 233. 16, where *ðe bi him* represents Latin *De illo namque* and could be translated 'because/for concerning them' or 'concerning whom'; *GD(O)* 271. 5 *7 hi þa apostolas þe* [MS *C þa*] *forleton heora sawle to deaðe þy hy gelyfdon þæt heom gearu wære þære sawle lif æfter þæs lichaman deaðe*, where MS *C* has *þy þe* for *þy*; *GD* 216. 29, where MS *O* has *þy* but MS *C þy . . . þe*; *BlHom* 23. 35 *Eal þis he þrowode for ure lufan 7 hælo þy he wolde þæt we þæt heofenlice rice onfengon*; *BlHom* 69. 12 *He wæs eac se wyresta gitsere þe he gesealde wiþ feo heofeones Hlaford 7 ealles middangeardes*, where *þe he* may mean 'who'; and *John(WSCp)* 9. 16 *nis ðes man of Gode þe restedæg ne healt*, Latin *non est hic homo a deo quia sabbatum non custodit*, where *Li* and *Ru* have *forðon*. In all these examples and in all those known to me in verse and prose, the *þe/þy* clause follows its principal or governing clause. Liggins (1955, pp. 141-5) gives more examples from the prose. Typical of those in the poetry are *KtHy* 7 and *KtHy* 22 (both in §2184), where the element order suggests a causal interpretation,

GenA 2623   Hæleðum sægde
     þæt Sarra his   sweostor wære,
     Abraham wordum   (bearh his aldre),
     þy he wiste gearwe   þæt he winemaga,
     on folce lyt   freonda hæfde,

and, with the *ðy* clause expressing a rejected cause—a rare usage according to Liggins (1955, p. 144)—

WaldA 12   Nalles ic ðe, wine min,   wordum cide,
     ðy ic ðe gesawe   æt ðam sweordplegan
     ðurh edwitscype   æniges monnes
     wig forbugan   oððe on weal fleon,
     lice beorgan,   ðeah þe laðra fela
     ðinne byrnhomon   billum heowun,
     ac ðu symle furðor   feohtan sohtest,
     mæl ofer mearce. . . .

c. þy þe

§3135. This combination rarely introduces causal clauses. Liggins (1955, p. 154) notes three examples in which the *þy þe* clause follows the principal clause, viz. *ChronB*'s *þy þe* where *ChronA* 54. 4 (787) (§3129) has *þy* and *ChronD* has *þe*; *CP* 175. 9 *Ealle he gret mid anre honda ðy ðe he wile ðæt hi anne song singen*; and (expressing a rejected cause) *GD(O)* 8. 32 . . . *þæt Marcus 7 Lucas writon þæt godspel nalæs no þi þe hig hit gehyrdon ac hig hit geleornedon* . . . , where MS *C* has *nalæs þæt hi* and the revised version in MS *H na for þy þe hig*. Van Dam (p. 78) adds five more examples from *GD*. In all these the *þy þe* clause follows the principal clause. Three of them—*GD(C)* 152. 14, where MS *H* has *forþam þe*, *GD(C)* 239. 6, and *GD(C)* 249. 3—express rejected cause. We may add *Bo(B)* 91. 25 *þy þe* where MS *C* has *forðy þe*. The only possible example of a *þy þe* clause preceding the principal clause is *BlHom* 5. 15 *þy þe he hine onfehþ, ne beluceþ he hine no*. But this is suspect because of the gap in the manuscript immediately before *þy þe*. On this example see also §3020.

§3136. I have noted only two examples in the poetry, viz. *Res* 51, where *þy þe* may be a relative 'in which' or 'by which', and

Dan 83   Wolde þæt þa cnihtas cræft leornedon,
        þæt him snytro on sefan secgan mihte,
        nales ðy þe he þæt moste oððe gemunan wolde
        þæt he þara gifena gode þancode
        þe him þær to duguðe drihten scyrede,

where again we have a rejected reason.

d. Correlative patterns with a comparative of an adjective or adverb

§3137. Adverbial uses of *þy* + a comparative, e.g. *ÆCHom* i. 418. 4 . . . *and geoffra Gode þone ðe ðu getuge, þæt þu ðy orsorglicor become to ðam æðelan wulderbeage*, and of *þæs þe* + a comparative, e.g. *ÆCHom* ii. 20. 31 . . . *þæt mancynn wære þæs ðe geleaffulre and ðæs þe gewisre on hwæne hi sceoldon gelyfan* are well attested; see Liggins 1955, pp. 203-4, and my §§3243-50 and §§3334-59. Here we are concerned with sentences in which such expressions are followed by a clause introduced by *þe/þy*, but which do not conform to the pattern discussed in §§3243-50.

§3138. We must distinguish two types of examples—type A, in which both clauses have a comparative, e.g. *CP* 207. 4 *Ðone scamleasan mon mæg ðy bet gebetan ðe hine mon suiður ðreað 7 sciend* (on these see §3141) and

GenA 1324 þæt is syndrig cynn;
symle bið þy heardra   þe hit hreoh wæter,
swearte sæstreamas   swiðor beatað,

and type B, in which only the principal clause has a comparative, e.g. *Or* 148. 31 . . . *to ðon þæt he wolde þæt þa folc him þy swiþor to buge þe he hæfde hiera ealdhlafordes sunu on his gewealde* and

Beo 1432 Sumne Geata leod
of flanbogan   feores getwæfde,
yðgewinnes,   þæt him on aldre stod
herestræl hearda;   he on holme wæs
sundes þe sænra,   ðe hyne swylt fornam.

Adams (p. 27) says that in *Or* 148. 31 '*ðe* has a causal colouring, as *ða* often does, but the primary notion is that of time'. 'However', counters van Dam (p. 72), 'I take *þe* to be causal here'. Liggins (1955, p. 145) adds another interpretation: 'It is hard to know whether *þe* is a causal conjunction or a relative pronoun.' Although I am suspicious of the sequence *him . . . to* (see §1062) . . . *þe he* 'to him . . . who', I have to admit the possibility. Similarly, *ðe* in *Beo* 1432 could be translated 'when' or 'because' or (with *hine*) 'whom'. But since the action of the *ðe* clause in *Beo* 1432 is one which takes place by degrees, it is possible to describe the sequence *þe sænra ðe* as a correlative comparative construction, with *þe* as the instrumental and with *ðe* as either the indeclinable particle—'He was more slug-gish in swimming to that [extent], namely death was carrying him off'—or as the instrumental—'By that much he was more sluggish in swimming, by that much death had taken him off'. But see §3341. Small's note on this passage (1930, p. 369) is confused.

§3139. Other examples of my type B can be similarly explained, e.g. *CP* 220. 23 . . . *ðætte hit ðonne se ne wrece þe hit wat þe swiður þe he licet mildheortnesse 7 forgifnesse ðær ðær nan ne bið*, where the EETS translation reads '. . . that . . . he who knows may not punish it the more severely the more they stimulate [sic] humanity and forgiveness where none is'; *CP* 277. 24 (§3141); *ByrM* 70. 8 . . . *ac he mæg myclum fremian ealdum 7 iungum þæt hig þe wisran beon þe hig his fare cunnon*; *ByrM* 114. 28 *Him mæg beon þe glædre his heorte þe he sum þing herof undergyte*;

Rid 9. 9 Mec seo friþe mæg   fedde siþþan,
oþþæt ic aweox,   widdor meahte
siþas asettan.   Heo hæfde swæsra þy læs
suna ond dohtra,   þy heo swa dyde;

and

Mald 312   Hige sceal þe heardra, heorte þe cenre,
        mod sceal þe mare, þe ure mægen lytlað,

where Quirk (p. 117) detects a concessive element. The *þe* clause can
be taken as temporal and/or causal in all of these and as adjective in
some. I do not press the comparative interpretation in any; see again
§3341.

§3140. But *Or* 148. 31 (§3138), and other type B examples in
prose and poetry in which the action of the *þe* clause is not one
which can take place by degrees or in part, cannot be construed as
containing the correlative comparative construction. Such examples
include *Bo* 31. 10 *Wenst þu þ hi a ðy deorwyrðran seon þe hi to
þinre note gelænde wæran?*; the version of *Bede* 208. 23 offered in
MSS *O* and *Ca*, which is discussed by van Dam (p. 72); *ÆLS* 30. 385
. . . *and hi ealle gegadere wundrodon and blissodon for heora ge-
metinge and miccle þe bliðran þe hi oferwinnen hæfdon þa hæþenan*;
WHom 7. 127 *7 hit is ealles þe wyrse þe his ænig ende ne cymð æfre
to worulde*; *ChristB* 789; and

ChristC 1255 Ðonne hi þy geornor gode þonciað
       blædes ond blissa þe hy bu geseoð,
       þæt he hy generede from niðcwale
       ond eac forgeaf ece dreamas.

The temporal and/or causal interpretation is the only one possible
in some of these examples. Here, then, we have further evidence that
þe/þy can mean 'because'. Johnsen (*EStudien*, 44 (1911–12), 228)
quotes more examples, including three in which the subordinate
clause is introduced, not by *þe/þy*, but by a *for* formula, viz. *CP*
51. 5, *CP* 397. 30 *Forðæm bið sio scyld ðy hraðor gehæled, forðæmðe hio ne bið unliefedo*, and *WHom* 6. 205 *Ac Godd hine fordeþ
þe raþor, forðam þe he wile gebeorhgan þam ðe him sylfum syn
gecorene 7 gecweme*. In these only the causal interpretation is possible. On examples like *Bo* 62. 1 *forðæm ælces monnes yfel bið þy
openre gif he anwald hæfð*, see §3546.

§3141. Liggins (1955, pp. 145–7) lists twenty-five examples (excluding *Or* 148. 31) of 'causal' clauses with the pattern *þy* + comparative
+ *þe/þy* clause. Of these, three belong to my type A, viz. *CP* 5. 24
(§3341), *CP* 207. 4 (§3138), and *Bo* 63. 3 *gif þonne ænig mon a þe
unweorðra bið, þonne bið ælc dysig man þy unweorðra þe he mare
rice hæfð ælcum wisum men*. (On *Bo* 63. 1 and *CP* 429. 7 see below.)
She noted the existence of what I call types A and B but nevertheless

went on to write (p. 147): 'Benham (p. 224) lists as Clauses of Result
CP XXXI, 207. 4, ib. LV, 429. 8, Boeth XL, vii, 140. 31, but none of
the others. It is hard to see on what grounds he differentiates a passage such as CP XXXI [207. 4 (my §3138)] . . . from 7 hio bið
micle ðe ieðre to oferfeohtanne ðe hio self fieht wið hie selfe mid
oferspræce to fultome ðæm wiðfeohtende. (CP XXXVIII, 277. 24).'
Benham, careless as usual, certainly failed to include *CP* 5. 24 and *Bo*
63. 3 among his examples. But he was consistent in that he cited
only what he called 'correlative, progressive result clauses' (p. 222),
which he described as 'the progenitors of such modern periods as the
following . . . : "But *the* less blood he drew, *the* more he took of
treasure." Here there is a result, as it were, at every advance in the
degree of action in the first clause' (p. 222). (These remarks, actually
made of the pattern with *swa . . . swa*, are extended by Benham to
the *þe . . . þe* pattern at p. 223.) All his examples have a comparative
in both clauses except *CP* 429. 7 *Ac hie sint to manienne ðæt hi
ongieten ðæt hit bið se degla Godes dom ðæt hi eft ðy mare wite
hæbben ðe hi gere witon ðæt hi on ðweorh doð*, where the EETS
translation 'But they are to be admonished to understand that it is
the secret judgment of God, that they are afterwards to have the
more punishment the more accurately they know that they are doing
wrong' correctly reflects the Latin . . . *ut quo melius videt, eo
deterius pereat*. Liggins (1955, p. 146) rightly notes that we have a
similar failure on the part of a translator to represent one of the
Latin comparatives in *Bo* 63. 1 *Geðenc nu hwæðer ænig mon bio a
ðe unweorðra þe hine manige men forseon*, Latin *Nam si eo abiectior
est quo magis a pluribus quisque contemnitur*. . . . So Benham could
have included this example too. But the grounds on which he differentiates *CP* 207. 4 (§3138) and the like from *CP* 277. 24 above are
quite clear: he includes my type A examples (to which *CP* 429. 7
and *Bo* 63. 1 really belong) and excludes my type B examples. The
passage from Liggins (1955, p. 147) quoted above continues: 'Such
constructions are not purely causal—elements of manner, proportion and often of time are also important—but they are much more
closely linked to the causal relationship than to that of result. In
every case it is the statement of cause that is introduced by the conjunction.' As might now be expected, I accept this more readily for
examples of type B than for those of type A. On both types, see
further §§3334-46.

§3142. Examples with the pattern *þæs þe/þy* comparative (. . .)
þe/þy also occur. Most of them belong to type B, e.g. *CP* 231. 13,
GD 47. 8 . . . *se þe lufode þone ceorl þæs þe swiðor þe he hine*

forseah, and *ÆCHom* ii. 546. 30 *Witodlice hire lima lyre becom to eacnunge haligra mægna, forðan ðe heo hi gebysgode mid gebedum þæs ðe swiðor þe heo nan ðing elles don ne mihte*. But *CP* 435. 2 *Ac hi beoð ðæs ðe lator ðe hi oftor ymbðeahtiað* belongs to type A. That—*pace* Liggins (1955, p. 148)—is why Benham (p. 224) classified it as result. I have so far recorded no examples to parallel

El 955   Sefa wæs þe glædra
                  þæs þe heo gehyrde   þone hellesceaþan
                  oferswiðedne,   synna bryttan,

an example of type B with *þæs þe* meaning 'when' or 'because'. But it can be compared with the examples of what I have called types 2b and 2d in §3337. *þæs þe* cannot introduce a comparative clause because the action described is not one which can take place gradually.

§3143. On the constructions described above, see further §§3334–46 and 3355-9.

e. þy (. . .) þæt

§3144. These combinations too are not common. We find *þy þæt* introducing a rejected cause in *Solil* 70. 12 *Nat ic hyt na þy þæt ic hyt self gesawe ac forði þe hyt man me sæde*. This is the only example recorded by Liggins (1955, p. 156) or myself. Examples of *þy . . . þæt* include *Or* 21. 14 7 *þy þær licgað þa deadan men swa lange 7 ne fuliað þæt hy wyrcað þone cyle him on* (or does *swa lange . . . þæt* mean 'as long as'? See §2641); *GD(C)* 174. 2 where it introduces a rejected cause but is replaced by *þi . . . þe* in MS *H*; *GD(C)* 243. 11, where MS *O* has *þy . . . þe*; *Bo* 78. 18 *Eala cniht, þy þu eart gesælig þ þu hit swa ongiten hæfst*, where MS *B* reads *hwæt* for *þy*; *WHom(E)* 21. 14 where *WHom(I)* 21. 14 (§3145) agrees with the other manuscripts in reading *þy . . . þe*. In all these examples, *þæt* could be said to introduce a noun clause in apposition with and/or explaining *þy*.

f. Other correlative patterns

§3145. Correlative *þe/þy . . . þe/þy* occurs, but is not common. Typical examples include *ChronA* 62. 23 (836) . . . 7 *þy fultumode Beorhtric Offan þy he hæfde his dohtor him to cuene*, *GD* 216. 28 *ac he wæs fleonde þa woruldlican are 7 þæt þy dyde þe he nolde þæt he æfre ofer þæt in þysum life wære gesewen from þam mannum . . .*, *BlHom* 121. 11 *Nalas þæt wolcn þær þy forþ com þe ure*

Drihten þæs wolcnes fultomes þearfe hæfde æt þære upastignesse,
WHom(I) 21. 14 *Ac þy hit is þe wyrse wide on earde þe man oft*
herede þæt man scolde hyrwan, where MS *E* has *þy . . . þæt,* and
(the only such example in the poetry)

Beo 2638   Ðe he usic on herge geceas
          to ðyssum siðfate   sylfes willum,
          onmunde usic mærða,   ond me þas maðmas geaf,
          þe he usic garwigend   gode tealde,
          hwate helmberend. . . .

Liggins (1955, pp. 150–3) gives more examples from the prose. Not
every such sequence is necessarily correlative. Van Dam (p. 77) and
Liggins (p. 150) differ concerning *CP* 308. 4. Liggins (p. 151) takes
ðy . . . ðy as correlative in *CP* 33. 16 *Ne fleah he ðy rice ðy his ænig*
monn bet wyrðe wære. So too does Visser (ii, §894), comparing *Bo*
88. 4 *þy hi secað anwald . . . ðy hi wenaþ þ hit sie þ hehste good.*
Since *rice* is often used absolutely in the sense 'rule, dominion' and
since *fleon* used transitively takes the accusative, this is preferable
to explaining *ðy rice* as instrumental for dative on the analogy of
datives after *æt-/be-/oð-fleon.*

§3146. Patterns such as *forþon . . . þe* and *forþon . . . þy* have been
discussed in §§3057–66. Liggins (1955, p. 155) notes *forðy . . . þy*
þe in *ChronB,* where *ChronA* 62. 23 (836) (§3145) has *þy . . . þy,*
and *forðan . . . þy þe* in *HomU* 34. 206. 2 *and þonne sæde se diacon*
þæt þæt fyr cymð forðan ofer manna bearn, þy þe men gelefað to
hwon drihtnes sylfes ærendgewrites.

§3147. On *ðonan . . . ðe* in *CP* 73. 8, see §2594, Adams, pp. 27–8,
and Liggins 1955, pp. 153–4.

13. WEALD ÞEAH

§3148. Liggins (1955, p. 171) says that '*weald þeah* = "for perhaps" ' in *ÆCHom* ii. 466. 9 *þis godspel ðincð dysegum mannum*
sellic, ac we hit secgað swa ðeah, weald ðeah hit sumum men licige
(Thorpe's punctuation) and goes on to remark that 'the subjunctive
mood expresses the doubt in the speaker's mind, and is probably also
influenced by *þeah*'. The last observation is sound. But it is hard to
see why *ÆCHom* ii. 466. 9 is singled out from the other sentences
with *weald þeah* quoted by BT(S), s.v. *weald* adv. conj. I, in independent clauses, with *þeah*, 'perhaps, may be'. The reason may be—
weald þeah—Thorpe's punctuation and his translation 'seeing that
to some it may be pleasing'. See §2937.

14. OTHER TYPES OF CLAUSE EXPRESSING CAUSE

§3149. The point has frequently been made that my system of classification, in common with others, is Procrustean. So it is not surprising to find elements of cause in clauses which are formally classified as something else. Thus, Liggins detects elements of time, condition, manner, and cause, in *CP* 163. 10 *Ðonne bireð ælc lareow hlæd to ðæs monnes mode ðonne he him gecyðð hu sio byrðen wiexð 7 hefegað* (1955, p. 217) and 'a conditional/causal function, with a temporal suggestion also' in three examples with *þæt*, viz. *CP* 303. 3, *Bede* 394. 23, and *Bede(C, Ca, O)* 394. 25, where MS *T* has *þa* (p. 390). See further Adams (pp. 10–12) and Liggins (1955, pp. 1–5 and 217–21) and note the latter's observation (p. 220) that 'in almost all the examples to be discussed, the causal function is additional to the basic one expressing time, condition, and so on; very rarely has the original one been totally replaced by the causal'. For reasons of space, I must content myself here with a brief discussion of each type of subordinate clause in turn and with appropriate references for those who wish to go further.

§3150. Among the many difficulties in the classification of *þæt* clauses is that of deciding whether they are noun or cause. On this, see §§3118–25. The possibility of noun clauses introduced by *for* formulae is discussed in §§3085–7.

§3151. Liggins (1955, p. 398) quotes 'He who hesitates is lost' and 'She could not speak of it to her grandmother, who was too old' to illustrate the fact that both limiting and non-limiting adjective clauses may contain 'an idea of cause' and rightly observes that 'even when the idea of cause is quite strong, the clauses always remain primarily attributive'. The causal meaning is 'much more likely' to be found in limiting clauses and 'may vary from a statement of true Reason to one of vague Explanation' (p. 435). She carefully documents the use of the various relatives in this way: *se* and/or *þe* (pp. 399–405); indefinite relative pronouns with *swa, swylc*, and *loca* (pp. 405–12); local conjunctions (pp. 425–33; on these see §3153); and 'Conjunctive Adverb *þanon*' (pp. 433–4). She offers some general comments (pp. 412–25 and 434–7). A few examples follow to illustrate her conclusion (p. 399) that 'all the major and most of the minor types of relative constructions may be used with a superadded causal sense. The addition of this shade does not alter the construction in any way; the clue to its presence is to be found only in the context': (limiting clauses) *BlHom* 45. 6 *Se biscop sceal, þe wile onfon Godes mildheortnesse 7 his synna forgifnesse, þrafian þa mæssepreostas, mid lufe ge mid laþe, þæt hie healdan Godes æwe on riht*, ÆCHom ii. 556. 12 *Se ðe næfð, him bið ætbroden þæt þæt he hæfð*, and *Beo* 142 *heold hyne syðþan ‖ fyr ond fæstor se þæm feonde ætwand*, and (non-limiting clauses) *Bede* 198. 5 *þa frægn hine 7 ahsode his mæssepreost on his agen geðeode, þe se cyning ne cuðe ne his higen, for hwon he weope*, ÆCHom i. 270. 14 . . . *and we sceolon lufian and filigan urum Drihtne, seðe us læt to ðam ecan life*, and

Beo 1609   . . . ðonne forstes bend   Fæder onlæteð,
               onwindeð wælrapas,   se geweald hafað
               sæla ond mæla.

The response of readers to each individual example will inevitably vary. But a sentence like

Beo 703   Sceotend swæfon,
          þa þæt hornreced   healdan scoldon,
          ealle buton anum

provides a probably unnecessary reminder that not all adjective clauses express cause.

§3152. The close relationship which sometimes exists between these two types of clause was felt by some Anglo-Saxon translators, for van Dam (p. 84) found fifty-six examples in which 'the Latin has an attributive clause, which the translator felt to have causal force and translated accordingly'. His example is *Bede* 194. 14, where *forðon he* represents *qui*. But he goes on to note that this does not always happen and that 'the Latin does not appear to have influenced the use of causal conjunctions' in his texts. This agrees with Liggins's observation (1955, p. 399): 'In the close Latin translations, OE generally transmits in a mechanical fashion.'

§3153. The presence of a causal element in clauses introduced by *þær, þær þe*, or *þær þær*, has been detected by van Dam (p. 68: one example) and by Liggins (1955, pp. 425–8). This may be an extension of the use of *þær* in the idiomatic temporal sense 'when'; see §§2460–3. Typical examples include *CP* 129. 7 *Sua eac ðær ðæt heafod bið unhal eall ða limu bioð idelu, CP* 355. 3 . . . *7 mid ðæm ðu geearnode Godes irre, ðær ða godan weorc ær næren on ðe mette* (van Dam's example), ÆCHom i. 38. 12 *Ðas word geswuteliað þæt ðær wunað Godes sibb þær se goda willa bið*, ÆCHom ii. 104. 29, and *ÆCHom* ii. 104. 32 *Soðlice ðær ðær þin goldhord is, þær bið þin heorte*. For further discussion see §§2464–5. On *þær þe* in *Sat* 637, see §2456, and on causal/conditional *þær*, §3621.

§3154. Liggins (1955, pp. 429-30) detects a causal element in the clauses introduced by *swa hwær swa* in *Matt(WSCp)* 24. 28 *Swa hwær swa hold byþ þæder beoð earnas gegaderude*, Latin *Ubicumque fuerit corpus illuc congregabuntur aquilae*; by *þider* in *Or* 236. 17 *7 raðe þæs þe þa senatus gehierdon þæt Marius to Rome nealæcte, hie ealle ut aflugon on Creca lond æfter Sillan 7 æfter Pompeiuse, þider hi þa mid firde gefaren wæron*; and by *þonon ðe* in *ÆCHom* ii. 132. 5 . . . *and þu ðonon on idelum wuldre befealle wiðinnan, þonon ðe ðu wiðutan on wurðmynte ahafen bist*. She sees *þanon* as an ambiguous adverb/conjunction in examples like *BlHom* 237. 30 *þanon wæs geworden* . . . (pp. 433-4) and *ðonone* as an adverb 'therefore' in *CP* 289. 3 . . . *ðonne wierð gehnescad ðonone sio ðreaung ðæs anwaldes* (p. 200).

§3155. *Post hoc propter hoc* is often true. So it is not surprising that, as Liggins (1955, p. 330) puts it in her summary, 'most of the expressions indicating action either subsequent [sc. prior; see my §2530] to or simultaneous with that in the principal clause may also carry a pronounced causal signification'. On *þa* and *þonne*, see below. For the rest, I must content myself with references to the discussions by Liggins and others: *þonecan þe* (Liggins 1955, p. 281); *mid* formulae (Liggins 1955, pp. 281-95; Liggins 1970, p. 300; van Dam, pp. 57-61[167] and 71; Visser, ii, §894; and Kivimaa, p. 165); *nu* (Liggins 1955, pp. 296-309, and my §§2591-3); *siþþan* (Liggins 1955, pp. 310-15, and my §§2666-78); *æfter* formulae (Liggins 1955, p. 200—*æfter þon* means 'accordingly' in *BlHom* 81. 27— and pp. 315-16, and Liggins 1970, p. 300); *þæs þe* (Liggins 1955, p. 316, and my §§2679-85); combinations involving *sona* and *hraþe* (Liggins 1955, pp. 317-22); *swa lange swa* and *swa oft swa* (Liggins 1955, pp. 322-4); *þa hwile þe* (Liggins 1955, pp. 324-5); and *þam timum þe* (Liggins 1955, p. 325).

§3156. Nor is it surprising that, as Liggins (1955, pp. 221-2) points out, the temporal conjunctions which most often express cause are *þa (þa)* and *þonne*. The former is discussed by van Dam (pp. 66-8) and Liggins (1955, pp. 222-49, and 1970, p. 300) and in my §2579. Typical examples of causal *þa* include *Or* 218. 9 *Se ilca consul gedyde eallum Romanum þa bismerlecestan dæd, þa he aspon of Sciþþium DC monna to him his geþoftena* . . . 'in that'; *Bede* 88. 20 *ac þa he feaht forðon he wæs gehæfted* 'as'; and *ÆCHom* i. 86. 19 *þaða he mid swiðlicum luste his lifes gewilnode, þa het he hine*

---

[167] But *mid þæm þæt* in examples like *ChronA* 90. 2 (897) might be, not a formula, but a prepositional phrase with an appositive, explanatory *þæt* clause.

ferigan ofer ða ea Iordanen, ðærþær wæron gehæfde hate baðu, þe wæron halwende gecwedene adligendum lichaman 'as'. I discuss *CP* 5. 5—where the EETS translation wrongly gives 'if' for *ða ða*—in *NQ* 208 (1963), 327.

§3157. On *þonne*, see van Dam, p. 76, Liggins 1955, pp. 249-80, and my §§2566 and 2587. Typical examples include *CP* 25. 16 . . . *forhwon beoð æfre suæ ðriste ða ungelæredan ðæt hi underfon ða heorde ðæs lariowdomes, ðonne se cræft ðæs lareowdomes bið cræft ealra cræfta?* 'seeing that'; *ÆCHom* i. 592. 11 *Witodlice mannes ege is smice gelic and hrædlice, þonne he astyred bið, fordwinð* 'because' (but 'if' would do equally well); and *Coll* 229 *Hwilc eower ne notaþ cræfte minon, þonne hus 7 mistlice fata 7 scypa eow eallum ic wyrce?*, Latin *Quis uestrum non utitur arte mea, cum domos et diuersa uasa et naues omnibus fabrico?* There is no automatic association between the subjunctive mood and the presence of an element of causality in *þonne* clauses; see §2619.

§3158. Liggins (1955, pp. 220-1) reminds us that 'conjunctive adverbs as well as conjunctions may carry this duality of meaning—for example, *þonne* and *þa*, which so often mean "then and therefore", just as NE "then" may do'. She discusses the causal use of these two adverbs, and of *nu, nu þonne, nu forþi, siþþan*, and *æfter þæm* (1955, pp. 325-30).

§3159. The existence of a relationship between cause and purpose and between cause and result has been noted in §3024. These relationships have already been discussed in the appropriate sections; see the Indexes. In *BlHom* 137. 6 Morris translates adv. *toðon* as 'therefore'. Liggins (1955, p. 200) suggests that it may have been wrongly inserted under the influence of *BlHom* 137. 4 . . . *toðon frome 7 toðon anrode*.

§3160. An element of cause can frequently be detected in clauses of comparison introduced by *swa (swa), swa . . . swa*, and *(þæs) þe . . . þe*. Again, the reader is referred to the Indexes.

§3161. Burnham (p. 2) observes that

the concessive sentence may be represented by the formula, linguistically though not mathematically true, $a-b = a$, in which b has a positive value. It is evident that this relation, like the conditional, has affinities with that of cause. The concession—the notion subtracted, as it were, from the main proposition—may often be looked upon as a blocked or inoperative cause or reason. The view, the reason, the circumstance is admitted, but the opposite of its natural consequence is asserted.

I have already discussed aspects of this problem in §§3024 and 3081-4. The reader wishing to pursue the matter should consult Burnham, pp. 1-4 and 112-15; Quirk, pp. 7-8 and 115-16; and Liggins 1955, pp. 387-8.

§3162. In the discussions just mentioned, Burnham, Quirk, and Liggins, refer to the fact that, in Burnham's words (p. 2), 'Old English, like other languages, reflects in its idioms the close relationship between the notions of concession, condition, and cause'. We read at Mather, p. 1, that 'the conditional construction is often regarded as a variety of the causal construction'. Behre (p. 131), citing *CP* 32. 1 *forðæm gif he on ðæm wel deð, he hæfð ðæs god lean*, observes that '*gif (þær)*-clauses represent together with the main clause a cause and effect relation'. Liggins (1955, pp. 360-2 and 396-7) discusses the 'causal/conditional' relationship in more detail, with examples (pp. 362-95). She concludes (p. 396) that 'the principal ways of expressing a conditional idea in OE are all regularly used with an added causal signification, and may even become almost wholly causal in their meaning'. Her findings concerning *gif, buton*, and *nemne*, are discussed here. On the nineteen examples in which she detects 'causal/conditional *þær*' (1955, pp. 388-90), see §3621. On causal elements in other conditional constructions, see Liggins 1955, pp. 383-8, 390-1, and 394-5, and my Indexes.

§3163. Liggins (1955, pp. 362-83) distinguishes two types of *gif* clauses which express cause. First, she records (1955, p. 362) twenty-one examples

in which *gif* has a purely causal sense. It introduces the statement of a *fact*, either still existing at the time when the statement is made, or else, more rarely, a historical one. It is undisputed, and is presumed to be accepted by both speaker and audience (that is to say, the conjunction has the force of NE 'since'). The conjunct clause in every case stands in First Position. . . .

These are 'conceded' conditions; see §3543. Her examples include *ÆCHom* i. 252. 21 *Gif ge cunnon, þa ðe yfele sind, syllan ða godnysse eowrum bearnum, hu micele swiðor wile eower Heofonlica Fæder forgyfan godne gast him biddendum* and *ÆCHom* ii. 418. 24 *Gif se mildheorta God ðe god wæs þaða ðu yfel wære, hu miccle swiðor bið he ðe welwyllende, gif ðu yfeles geswicst, and hine mid godum weorcum gegladast.* She then lists a much larger number of examples of 'conditional/causal *gif*', with the comment that 'from the viewpoint of grammar, the formula "If (and because) A, therefore B" applies to the ideal and the unfulfilled conditions just as it does to the real' (1955, p. 365). So her examples include (my sequence here is grammatical, not historical) *ÆCHom* i. 472. 6 *Gif he rihtwis bið, he hæfð þonne maran geðincðe þurh his brocunge, gif he geðyldig bið, CP* 43. 4 *Fed ðonne min sceap, gif ðu me lufige, LawAf* 58 *Gif se midlesta finger sie ofaslegen, sio bot bið xii scill., ChronA* 48. 17 (755) *7 þa gebead he him hiera agenne dom feos 7 londes gif hie him þæs rices uþon*, and *BlHom* 233. 21 *Gif þis gebod eow wære geseald fram eowrum Drihtne, astigað hider mid gefean on min scip.* Liggins's method of presenting her results—by the number of examples in each text without specific references—is such that I have been unable to identify any of her examples of a rejected or imaginary condition with the preterite subjunctive in both clauses, although she specifically states (1955, pp. 365 and 379) that there are some.

§3164. She also distinguishes two types of 'causal/conditional clauses with *buton*' (1955, pp. 391–4), viz. those in which 'the clause is equivalent to a negative conditional "if not . . . therefore (not) . . ." ', e.g. *HomU* 36. 231. 14 *and ic sende hæðen folc ofer eow, þe eow ofnimað eowre æhte and eower lif and eowere wif and cild, butan ge þa teoðunge syllan to godes cyrican for minum lufan*, and those in which *buton (þæt)* 'combines the functions of a pair of conjugations [*sic*], one exceptive and one causal, "unless because" ', e.g. *LawVIAs* 12. 1 . . . *þæt man nænne gingran mann ne sloge þonne xv wintre man buton he hine werian wolde oððe fleoge 7 on hand gan nolde*, where 'unless' seems to offer an adequate translation, and (her only example with *buton þæt*) *Bo* 59. 24 *Hwi bið elles ælce dæg swelc seofung 7 swelce geflitu 7 gemot 7 domas, buton þ ælc bit þæs reaflaces þe him on genumen bið, oððe eft oðres gitsað?*, where the Latin has *nisi quod*. Again, space forbids further discussion. She finds 'causal/conditional *nemne*' only in *Bede(O)* 160. 16 . . . *ne he on horses hricge cuman wolde, nemne hwilc mare nyd abædde*, where MS *B* has *buton* and MS *Ca* has *nemne* with *butan* written above (1955, p. 394).

15. PARATAXIS

a. Asyndetic parataxis

§3165. Liggins (1955, pp. 438–47) offers an excellent discussion of causal asyndetic parataxis. One example from each of her main categories must suffice. We find the effect stated first followed by the cause in *ÆCHom* ii. 388. 23 *Ðaða Drihten ðam scipe genealæhte, ða wurdon hi afyrhte, wendon þæt hit sum gedwimor wære*; the cause expressed first in *ÆCHom* ii. 394. 1 *Drihten, ic losige: help min*; an explanatory clause second in *Mark(WSCp)* 6. 48 *7 he geseah hi on rewette swincende him wæs wiðerweard wind*, Latin *et uidens eos laborantes in remigando erat enim uentus contrarius*; and a parenthetic explanatory clause in *LS* 23. 122 *ænne oððe twegen on þam mynstre hi forleton. næs na to þam þæt hi þa begytanan gestreon heoldon—næs þær swilces nan þincg—ac þæt hi þæt gebedhus butan þam godcundan symbelnyssum ne forleton*. Liggins examines these types carefully, with reference to Latin originals and variant readings. See also van Dam, pp. 80-1, and for the poetry Schaar, pp. 153-72.

b. Syndetic parataxis

§3166. Some aspects of this topic have already been discussed. Liggins's term 'conjunctive adverbs' (1955, pp. 193-5) embraces all adverbs which can be used in the meaning 'therefore, hence'. These include *for* formulae (see §§3011-13); *eornostlice*, e.g. *GD(H)* 63. 13 *eornostlice swa micele swyðor is to ondrædeanne rihtwisra manna yrre*, where MSS *C* and *O* have *forþon* and the Latin *ergo*; *ono*, e.g. *Bede* 76. 33 *Ono þas wiif, þa ðe heora bearn of unrihtum gewunum oðrum to fedenne sellað, nemne seo clæsnunge tiid forð-geleore, ne sceolon heo heora werum gemengde beon*, where the Latin has *itaque*; and *witodlice*, e.g. *Matt(WSCp)* 12. 28 *Gyf ic soþlice on godes gaste awurpe deoflu, witodlice on eow becymð godes rice*, where *Li* has *cuðlice ł forðon*, *Ru þonne ł cuþlice*, and the Latin *igitur*. On the last three, see van Dam, pp. 63 and 79, and Liggins 1955, p. 199. The remainder have been discussed elsewhere; see the Indexes. Liggins (1955, pp. 193-204) gives a full list.

§3167. We have already seen (§§1858 and 3011-15) that a *for* formula can mean 'for' ('explanatory conjunction') as well as 'therefore' ('conjunctive adverb'). The same is true of *þy*; see §3128. So it is perhaps no surprise to find Liggins (1955, p. 212) writing: 'The Gospels sometimes render *enim*, *nam* and (occasionally) *uero* by *soþlice* or *witodlice*, which then function as loose connectives in just the same way that *forþæm*, for instance, does in similar contexts.' Examples include *GD(H)* 76. 14 *soðlice ne wene ic na, þæt þes wer wære gelustfullod on arfæstnysse weorke . . .*, where MSS *C* and *O* have *forþon* and the Latin *namque*, and *Mark(WSCp)* 1. 38 *þa cwæð he fare we on gehende tunas 7 ceastra þ ic ðar bodige. Witodlice to ðam ic com*, where *Li* and *Ru* have *forðon/forþon* and the Latin *enim*. *Ac* and *ono* are similarly used; see §§1770 and 3107 respectively. Liggins (1955, p. 171) tells us that *ac, soþlice, witodlice*, and *ono*, 'are used to introduce explanatory clauses, but never true causal ones'.

§3168. The lexicographers have much work to do with *eornostlice, soðlice, witodlice*, and the like. When I consider the great variety of Latin words they translate (see BT(S), s.vv.) and when I read Ælfric *De Coniunctione (ÆGram* 257. 15-266. 8), I do not envy them.

§3169. It remains now to consider 'causal' *and* clauses. This topic has already been mentioned in §§1735-7, with reference to Maisenhelder's work, and in §3025. But Liggins's discussion (1955, pp. 447-57) is comprehensive and scholarly. Space permits only a brief summary and grateful acknowledgement. She first discusses sentences in which the *effect* is stated in the first of two clauses joined by *and* (pp. 448-52). Typical examples are *Or* 80. 19 *Ac gesette þa men on ænne truman þe mon hiora mægas ær on ðæm londe slog, 7 wiste þæt hie woldon geornfulran beon þære wrace þonne opere men* and *ÆCHom* ii. 500. 21 (§1735). Her conclusion (p. 452) is that 'when the statement of the consequence precedes that of the fact, the only real difference between a pair of clauses connected by *and* and a similar pair whose connection is asyndetic seems to be a stronger sense of relation in the former case'.

§3170. She then turns to sentences in which the *cause* is stated in the first of two clauses joined by *and*, e.g. *Bede* 132. 22 *þa oncneow he hit sona sweotole 7 wæs swiðe forht geworden 7 him to fotum feoll* and *Bede* 298. 9 *7 mid þy he tu ger rice hæfde 7 cyning wæs, þa wæs he inbryrded mid lufan þæs uplecan rices 7 þæt eorðlice forlet in þæs ilcan biscopes tid, 7 to Rome ferde 7 þær his lif geendade* . . . (pp. 452-6). In most of her examples, the verbs refer to time past. She contrasts this pattern with those in which the cause is stated in the first of two clauses in asyndetic parataxis, as in *ÆCHom* i. 432. 13 *Ypolitus gebysmrað eowre stengas; swingað hine mid gepiledum swipum* (pp. 452-3):

But when the cause or fact is stated first, the difference between the two constructions is a more complex one. In an asyndetic connection, the fact stated is often a repeated or continuous one, the existence of which causes, or makes desirable, the action stated in the second clause (the consequence). . . .

When a pair of independent clauses are connected by *and* in a causal relationship, the second is likely to state an event which is caused by and is also subsequent to the perfective action stated in the first. *And* has the double sense of 'and then/and therefore'.

She then summarizes her findings (pp. 456-7).

§3171. Two examples perhaps deserve special mention. Morris translates *BlHom* 53. 6 7 *he* 'and because he'. There is a relationship of cause and effect, but the OE sentence is clumsy and anacoluthic. Van Dam's discussion (pp. 80-1) of *ChronA* 20. 1 (584) may be incomplete; the death of Cuþa can be seen as the cause of all the subsequent acts of Ceawlin, including his anger and his return home.

16. CAUSAL EXPRESSIONS WITHOUT A FINITE VERB

§3172. Here again, I content myself largely with a summary of Liggins's comprehensive treatment (1955, pp. 458-511). She begins by citing three nominative absolute constructions, viz. *BlHom* 247. 8, *LS* 23. 685, which 'renders a Latin . . . nominative absolute', and a third which 'renders a Latin ablative absolute', viz. *LS* 23. 610 *Ac þas þincg ealle þus oncnawenne, far ham mid sibbe*, Latin *His omnibus acceptis . . .* , and adds that 'it looks as though this construction was a definite imitation, and was not regarded as good OE prose idiom' (pp. 458-9). She then discusses dative absolutes such as *Matt (WSCp)* 13. 6 *Soþlice upsprungenre sunnan hig adruwudon 7 forscruncon*, Latin *Sole autem orto aestuauerunt* (pp. 459-63). Here she endorses for 'causal' dative absolutes the general conclusion reached by Callaway (1889, p. 30), writing 'At least in its causal use, it seems safe to say that this idiom is not a natural OE one, but is very strongly influenced by Latin, and is, in fact, almost confined to contexts where that influence is a direct one' (p. 460); see §§3825-31. An element of cause is to be detected in phrases with present participles, e.g. *ÆCHom* ii. 134. 15 *Hwæt ða Cuðberhtus þa gyt mid his plegan forð arn, oðþæt his lareow mid biterum tearum dreoriglice wepende, ealra ðæra cildra plegan færlice gestilde*, and with second participles, e.g. *ÆCHom* ii. 246. 15 *Hi ða mid þam worde wendon underbæc, feallende to eorðan, mid fyrhte fornumene* (Liggins 1955, pp. 463-7; see also van Dam, p. 63). Liggins's two examples of uninflected 'causal' infinitives follow verbs of emotion (p. 468). Both are quoted by Callaway (1913, p. 160); see §959. Her only example of an inflected 'causal' infinitive (ibid.) is not listed by Callaway (1913, p. 161): *Or* 220. 8 *Hwæþer Romane hit witen nu ænegum men to secganne, hwæt hiera folces on Ispanium on feawum gearum forwurde?* But it does not differ essentially from his examples, which follow expressions of fear, loathing, regret, and shame. Liggins's next category (pp. 469-71) comprises participles used as nouns or adjectives. Two examples must suffice: *ÆCHom* i. 498. 22 *Ælc synn and tal bið forgifen behreowsigendum mannum* and *CP* 9. 17 *Ðætte unlærede ne dyrren underfon lariowdom*.

§3173. Liggins now turns her attention to 'causal' expressions without verbs. They are appositive constructions, e.g. ÆCHom i. 588. 28 *Egeas cwæð, 'Ic wundrige ðe, snoterne wer, þæt ðu ðyssere lare fylian wylt . . .'* (1955, pp. 471-2); adjectives and nouns, e.g. *ChronA* 101. 10 (921) *7 þa eft swiðe raþe æfter þam hie foron eft ut mid stælherge nihtes 7 comon on ungearwe men 7 genomon unlytel ægþer ge on mannum ge on ierfe* and *ÆCHom* i. 6. 5 *þa ðe his leasungum gelyfað, þam he arað and hi habbað syððan þa ecan susle to edleane heora gedwyldes* (pp. 472-3); oblique cases of the noun, with the case itself having the causal function, as in *CP* 111. 25 . . . *ond ða wunderlice dome gewearð ðæt he geearnode mid his agne inngeðonce ðone pytt ðe he on aworpen wearð*, or with the case determined by the noun's governing word, e.g. *ÆCHom* i. 136. 11 *And he wæs þa bliðe þæs behates*, though I do not see clearly how this differs from *ÆCHom* i. 6. 5 above, except (as Liggins's classification implies) that in one the genitive depends on an adjective and in the other on a noun (pp. 474-7); and nouns meaning cause, e.g. *ÆCHom* i. 484. 13 *and wæs seo læsse synn intinga þære maran* (pp. 477-8). She concludes with a detailed discussion on the use of prepositional phrases to express cause (pp. 479-509; see also van Dam, pp. 1-39) and a summary (pp. 509-11), in the course of which she says: '*For* is the only preposition which is regularly used in an almost purely causal sense' (p. 511).

17. MOOD

§3174. According to QW (p. 100) 'causal clauses contain indicative verbs'; so also Pinsker, p. 182. Similar or indeed even more sweeping assertions are quoted and rightly condemned by Visser (ii, §894). As we shall see in §§3176-7, the subjunctive is the regular mood in clauses expressing a rejected or denied reason. The normal mood in both prose and poetry in clauses which state the actual cause is the indicative; see Liggins 1955, pp. 45, 57, 90-1, 100, 118, 126, and 529. (Examples will be readily found in the preceding discussions.) This is true even when the principal clause contains an imperative, a subjunctive, a form of **sculan*, a rhetorical question, or a negative which refers to the principal clause. Only the last category needs further discussion here; for the rest, see Liggins 1955, pp. 152-3 and 529-32, and Mitchell 1959, pp. 434 and 438-9.

§3175. Van Dam (p. 82) asserts that the subjunctive in the first causal clause in *Or* 98. 29 *Æfter þeosan gewinne gewearð þætte Perse gebudan frið eallum Creca folce, næs na for þæm þe hie him ænigra goda uþen, ac for þæm þe hie wunnon on Egypti, þæt hie mosten for him þy bet þæm gewinne fullgongan* is due to its 'being dependent on a negative main clause', whereas 'the indicative in the second causal clause . . . is dependent on a positive main clause'. This is wrong. There is one principal or rather 'governing' clause, i.e. the *þætte* clause, and that is not negated. The distinction is between a negated causal clause expressing rejected or denied reason and a not-negated causal clause expressing actual reason; see §§3180–5. Van Dam's error is clearly seen when we consider examples in which a negated principal clause is followed by an indicative, e.g. *CP* 129. 13 *Forðy ne magon ða hieremenn begietan ðæt leoht ðære soðfæst-nesse, forðæm ðonne sio giornfulnes eorðlicra ðinga abisgað ðæt ꝫgit, ꝫ ablent ðæs modes eagan mid ðære costunga ðæm folce . . . ,* *ÆCHom* i. 4. 18 . . . *ac his tima ne bið na langsum, forþan þe Godes grama hine fordeð,* and *El* 635 *Ic ne mæg areccan, nu ic þæt rim ne can.* Liggins's figures for the prose (1960, p. 461) are decisive. Of 680 causal clauses associated with a negative principal clause, 511 had the indicative and 169 an ambiguous form. There was not one unambiguous subjunctive. This last remark holds for the poetry. 'It seems certain, then,' as Liggins (ibid.) remarks, 'that the mere presence of a negative in the principal clause is not relevant.'

§3176. *For* formulae introducing final clauses naturally take the subjunctive; see the General Index and Liggins 1955, p. 118. But there are certain contexts in which a clause expressing an actual reason *may* have the subjunctive. We can start from a table based on figures given by Liggins (1960, pp. 457–8) for her fifty-three causal clauses in the prose with unambiguous subjunctives.

Number	Reason for subjunctive	Number of examples	References
1.	A conditional construction	6	van Dam, pp. 81–2; Liggins 1955, pp. 67, 88, and 161–2.
2.	A final construction	1	Liggins 1955, pp. 43 and 89–90. But cf. her Table (1955, p. 187).
3.	Dependent speech	9	van Dam, p. 82; Liggins 1955, pp. 42–3, 89, 126, and 161.
4.	Causal clause introduced by defining *þæt*	15	Liggins (1955, p. 187) shows 18 examples.
5.	Rejected or denied reason	15	§§3180–94
6.	No convincing explanation	7	Liggins 1955, pp. 89–90 and 185–92.

Liggins gives the figure as 52 (1955, p. 185) and as 53 (1955, p. 207). She notes (1955, pp. 185, 207, and 209) that subjunctives are more common in 'Alfredian' prose; see her tables showing distribution by texts (1955, p. 186) and distribution according to associated constructions (p. 187).

§3177. Typical examples of these subjunctives include (1) *CP* 297. 20 *Se ðe ðonne sua forbygð ðone wielm 7 ðone onræs his hatheortnesse, forðæmðe hine mon slea mid liðelicre andsuare, ðonne bið his unðeaw ofslægen butan ælcre niedðrafunga* and *ÆCHom* i. 248. 33 *þi he cwæð, 'Na for freondrædene', forðan ðe nan man nære wyrðe ne þæs geleafan ne ðæs ecan lifes, gif Godes mildheortnys nære ðe mare ofer manncynne*; (2) *CP* 85. 5 *Se ðonne tacnað ðæt eall ðætte ðæs sacerdes ondgit ðurhfaran mæge, sie ymb ða hefonlican lufan, næs ymbe idelne gilp, ðylæs him losige ðæt heofenlice ondgit, forðæmðe he sie gehæfted mid ðæm luste his selfes heringe*; (3) *Bo* 90. 2 *Hu ne sædon we þe ær þ þis andwearde lif þe we her wilniað nære no þ hehste good, forðæm hit wære mislic 7 on swa manigfeald todæled . . . ?, Bede* 56. 17, and *Bede* 210. 15; and (4) *CP* 129. 2 *7 sua hit gebyreð, ðonne he fægnað ðæt he sie abisgod mid woroldðingum, ðæt he ne conn oðre læran ða godcundan wisan ðe he læran scolde*. On (5) see §§3180–94. Hard-to-explain examples (6) include *CP* 209. 21, where the influence of a final construction is possible, and *Solil* 30. 14 *To þam þrim is godes fultumes ðerf, forðam man naþer ne ðat god ne nane dæd don ne mæge, buton hys fultume*, where Endter follows Holthausen in emending *mæge* to *mæg*. Liggins (1955, p. 185) notes that five of the seven occur in *CP* and suggests the possibility of Latin influence, 'perhaps more general than specific'. For further discussion of all these types see the references given in the table above. But (with the caveat noted in §3193) I agree with Liggins's observation (1955, p. 192): 'For each of the constructions in which subjunctives are found, there are also other examples where the indicative is used, and usually these are more numerous. The "denied reason" is the only one where the indicative is the exception and the subjunctive the rule.' This point is illustrated by the fact that MS *B* has *wæs* for the last *wære* in *Bede(O)* 460. 31 . . . *7 þær on bead þæt hi æninga gedyden, þæt Willfrið wære onfongen on his bysceopscire: forþon þe he hire unrihtlice benumen wære* and by a comparison of *Solil* 63. 31 . . . *and cwæðan þæt hit forði wilnige þæt to witanne þæt ær us wæs, forði hit simle wære syððan god þone forman man gesceapen hafde* with *Solil* 64. 3 *And ic wene þæt hyt wille cweðan to þe þæt hyt forði þæt wite þæt hyt hær gesihð and gehyrð, forði hyt her is on ðisse weurulde*.

§3178. All the causal clauses in the poetry refer to an actual cause and have an indicative or an ambiguous verb-form except for the four examples of rejected cause discussed in §3192; two examples of clauses which are clearly not subordinate, viz. *Exhort* 58 *Forþam þu sylf ongyte*, where some editors emend to imp. *ongyt*, and *PPs* 54. 19, where neither *forðon* nor the subjunctive *geseon* seems to have a direct Latin equivalent; and

Az 44   Gecyð cræft ond meaht,   nu þec Caldeas
               ond eac fela folca   gefregen habban . . .

where

Dan 327   Gecyð cræft and miht   þæt þa Caldeas
               and folca fela   gefrigen habbað . . .

has a *þæt* clause with the indicative.

§3179. The time-reference of causal clauses may be to the present, e.g. *ÆCHom* i. 16. 20 *ne mæg he nane gesceafta gescyppan, forðan ðe he nis na Scyppend* and *PPs* 53. 6; to the future, e.g. *ÆCHom* i. 14. 1 *ne hrepa þu þæs treowes wæstm, forþan ðe þu bist deadlic* and *Soul i* 157; or to the past. Here *for* formulae have two functions. Like *nu*, they may refer to an act or series of acts completed (and therefore often to a state) in the present, e.g. *ÆCHom* i. 8. 25 *he is ordfruma, forði þe he wæs æfre; he is ende butan ælcere geendunge, forðan þe he bið æfre ungeendod*, where I would translate *wæs* 'has been', and *PPs* 90. 14 *Forðon he hyhte to me, ic hine hraðe lyse . . .*, where *hyhte* represents Latin *speravit*. But they may also refer to a completed act or series of acts or to a state in the past, e.g. *ÆC Hom* i. 14. 31 *and [God] gehalgode þone seofoðan dæg, forðan ðe he on ðam dæge his weorc geendode*, *ÆCHom* i. 30. 5 *þa ferde Ioseph . . . forðan ðe he wæs of Dauides mægðe*, and *And* 526. *Or* 17. 35 *Swiþost he for ðider, toeacan þæs landes sceawunge, for þæm horschwælum, for ðæm hie habbað swiþe æþele ban on hiora toþum . . .* and *ÆCHom* i. 18. 13 *Forðan ðe ðu wære gehyrsum ðines wifes wordum, and min bebod forsawe, þu scealt mid earfoðnyssum þe metes tilian . . .* are sufficient to demonstrate that here (as elsewhere) there is no rigid 'sequence of tenses'; see §§859–64.

18. NEGATION AND THE EXPRESSION OF REJECTED OR DENIED CAUSE

§3180. The uses of negatives *within* clauses of accepted, suggested, and rejected or denied, cause do not differ from those of negatives in other clauses described in §§1595–632; consider *ÆCHom* i. 52. 35

. . . *eal he hit forlyst, forðan ðe se apostol Paulus ne bið geligenod
. . .* , *ÆCHom* ii. 404. 24 *Warniað eow georne wið swilcum licceterum,
forðan þe hi ne sind na scep,* and the second *forði ðe* clause in *ÆC
Hom* ii. 40. 21 (§3182). What concern us here are the syntactical
patterns by which a rejected reason is expressed, either alone or
along with an accepted reason. There are marked similarities between
OE and MnE here, but one important difference: in OE, when the
rejected cause is expressed in a clause, the verb of that clause is in the
subjunctive.

§3181. Let us begin with those sentences in which a rejected cause
and the accepted cause are expressed by two contrasting clauses in
that order, both introduced by causal conjunctions. In both OE and
MnE, we have type A, in which the negative is in its logical position
immediately before the clause giving the rejected reason, e.g. 'He did
it, not because he had to, but because he wanted to' and *ÆCHom* i.
184. 29 *ac ðæs wundredon men, na forði þæt hit mare wundor wære,
ac forði þæt hit wæs ungewunelic.* Other OE examples include *Or*
24. 25 . . . *næs na for ðam þe* . . . *ac for ðam þe* . . . and *Or* 98. 30
. . . *næs na for þæm þe* . . . *ac for þæm þe* . . . (in both of which *næs*
is the adverb, not *ne* + *wæs*). Type B also belongs here. In this pattern, the negative is illogically attached to the verb of the main clause,
e.g. 'He did not do it because he had to, but because he wanted to'
and *CP* 401. 11 *ne cwæð he ðeah no ðæt ðæt* ['that which'] *he
cwæð forðæmðe he gesinscipe tælde, ac forðæmðe he wolde ða sorga
aweg adrifan ðisses middangeardes.* . . . Other examples (neither with
exactly the same conjunction in both clauses) are *BlHom* 39. 20 *Ne
bæd he no þæs forþon þe him þæs ænig þearf wære, ac forþon he
wolde ægþær ge ofer heofenum, ge ofer eorþan, us his miltse ge-
cyþon* and *ÆCHom* i. 34. 23 *Næs þæt cild forði gecweden hire
frumcennede cild swilce heo oðer siððan acende, ac forði þe Crist is
frumcenned of manegum gastlicum gebroðrum.* Care must be taken
to distinguish this type from examples in which the negative properly
belongs to the verb of the principal clause, e.g. 'He did not come, because his car broke down' and *ÆCHom* ii. 18. 11 *ne þeahhwæðere
we ne magon hi ealle gereccan, forði na þæt an þæt halige witegan be
him witegodon, ac eac swilce hæðene men setton on heora bocum be
eallum ðisum ðingum þe we nu beforan eow ræddon.* In *Solil* 70. 12
*Nat ic hyt na þy þæt ic hyt self gesawe, ac forði þe hyt man me
sæde, na* can be construed as reinforcing the negative *nat* (type B; cf.
BlHom 39. 20, just quoted) or as negating the *þy þæt* clause (a conflation of types A and B). The point is exquisite; in either event we
logically need [*wat*] before *forði þe*.

§3182. But the second clause need not have a subordinating conjunction. So we have, corresponding to type A, type C. (Here I part company with Liggins (1960, p. 457), for she does not recognize this type.) Examples include 'He did it, not because he wanted to, but he had to' and *ÆCHom* i. 128. 29 *Drihten wundrode þæs hundredes ealdres geleafan, na swilce he hine ær ne cuðe, seðe ealle ðing wat, ac he geswutelode mannum his geleafan mid herunge þam þe he wundorlic wæs.* See also *Or* 74. 35 . . . *nales na for þæm þe . . . ac . . .*, *ÆCHom* i. 82. 26 . . . *na forði þæt . . . ac . . .* (where the subjunctive in the *ac* clause is conditional), *ÆCHom* i. 366. 6 . . . *na swilce . . . ac*, and *ÆCHom* ii. 40. 21 . . . *na forði ðe . . . ac.* Type D corresponds to type B, e.g. 'He did not do it because he had to, but he wanted to' and *ÆCHom* ii. 206. 7 *Ne gereste he hine forði þæt he werig wære . . . ac he geswac ða his weorces.* See also *CP* 33. 16 *Ne fleah he ðy rice ðy his ænig monn bet wyrðe wære, ac he wolde us ða bisene astellan, ðæt we his to suiðe ne gitseden* and *BlHom* 121. 11. In *BlHom* 69. 9 *Ne cwæþ he þæt na forþon þe him wære ænig gemynd þearfendra manna ah he wæs gitsere, na* could reinforce *ne* (type C) or could negate the *forþon þe* clause (a conflation of types C and D); cf. *Solil* 70. 12 (§3181).

§3183. Occasionally a final clause with a subjunctive verb follows *ac* instead of a clause giving the actual reason, e.g. (type A) *ÆCHom* i. 8. 4 *Swa swa ælmihtig wyrhta, he wyrcð his weorc þurh his gecorenan, na swylce he behofige ures fultumes, ac þæt we geearnion þæt ece lif þurh his weorces fremminge* and *ÆCHom* i. 296. 25 . . . *na forði þæt . . . ac to ði þæt . . .* , and (type B) *ÆCHom* i. 82. 20 *ne com he forðy þæt he wolde his eorðlice rice, oþþe æniges oðres cyninges mid riccetere him to geteon; ac to ði he com þæt he wolde his heofenlice rice geleaffullum mannum forgyfan* and *ÆCHom* i. 82. 24 . . . *to ðy þæt . . . ac þæt. . . .*

§3184. We find . . . *na þæt . . . ac . . .* in two examples of type C, viz. *ÆCHom* i. 298. 28, where *þæt* can hardly be translated 'because', and *ÆCHom* i. 222. 8, where it can, and a type A example with . . . *na þæt . . . ac forði* in *ÆCHom* i. 390. 30, where Thorpe's translation seems to me to represent the original more accurately than that offered by Andrew (*SS*, §79).

§3185. I have so far noted no OE examples of type E, seen in 'He did it because he wanted to, not because he had to'. But see §3190.

§3186. We find *ac* followed by a phrase rather than a clause giving the accepted cause in *John(WSCp)* 7. 22 *Forðy Moyses eow sealde ymbsnydenysse næs na forþi þe heo of Moyse sy ac of fæderon* (on this sentence see Liggins 1955, p. 131). The sequence . . . *na swilce* . . . *na ðurh . . . ac þurh . . .* in *ÆCHom* i. 262. 5 is noteworthy.

§3187. In all the examples so far cited, a clause expressing a rejected cause is followed by a clause or phrase introduced by *ac* in which the true reason is stated. We have only the clause of rejected reason after *ði . . . þe* in *Solil* 70. 8 *nat ic no ði hwa þa burh timbrede þe ic self hyt gesawe* and in *CP* 304. 16, where 'a clause introduced by *la ah ðeahhwæðre* follows some lines later, though there is no direct grammatical link' (Liggins 1960, p. 458).

§3188. But, as we see from *ÆCHom* i. 262. 5 (§3186), the rejected cause, like the accepted one, can be expressed by something other than a clause. Thus we find prepositional phrases followed by a clause preceded by *ac* in the equivalent of type A in *ÆCHom* i. 2. 18 . . . *na þurh gebylde mycelre lare ac forþan þe . . .* ; of type B in *Bede(B)* 216. 5 *Nese, cwæð he, ne onfeng he his godum for gytsunge* [MS *T gitsiende*] *ac forðon þe he wolde his sawle gehælan*; and of type C in *ÆCHom* i. 388. 31 *Paulus ehte cristenra manna, na mid niðe, . . . ac he wæs midspreca and bewerigend þære ealdan æ. . . . Solil* 16. 17 *ne lufige ic hi na forði ac forðam þe hi men sint* can be seen as type B or as another example of conflation of types A and B.

§3189. Here too we find final clauses with the subjunctive rather than clauses expressing the actual reason, e.g. (with two *for* phrases and then the clause; type B) *ÆCHom* i. 474. 4 *þa cwæð se Hælend, þæt he nære for his agenum synnum, ne for his maga, blind geboren, ac forði þæt Godes wundor þurh hine geswutelod wære*, (type B) *ÆCHom* ii. 324. 10, and (type B) *ÆCHom* ii. 452. 22 *Ne geðafode God þis to forwyrde þam eadigan were ac þæt he wære to bysne eallum geleaffullum mannum.*

§3190. There are also examples in which neither the rejected nor the accepted cause is expressed in a clause, e.g. (type B) *ÆCHom* ii. 340. 20 *Ne lufode he woruldlice æhta for his neode ana ac to dælenne eallum wædliendum* and (type E; see §3185) *ÆCHom* ii. 342. 34 *and eft, ðonne þu utfærst betwux mannum, far for heora sawla hælu, na for woruldlicum gestreonum.*

§3191. Three sentences from *Cura Pastoralis* said by Liggins (1960, pp. 458-9) to contain a clause of 'denied reason' followed by the 'true reason' give me difficulty. In *CP* 109. 2 the meaning seems rather that the second reason is a better one than the first. In *CP* 457. 28 it is that there are better reasons than the two given. The third is *CP* 147. 9, where I take . . . *nalles forðæm anum ðe . . . ac swelce . . .* as '. . . not only/merely because . . . but also [because] . . .', despite Liggins (1960, p. 459) and the EETS translation 'not merely because . . . but as if'; see §3057. The fact that the causal clauses are in dependent speech and are subordinate to a final clause explains the subjunctive mood.

§3192. There are only four examples of rejected cause in OE poetry. Three have ambiguous verb-forms, viz. *Dan* 85 . . . *nalles ðy þe*, with no actual cause expressed; *Dan* 529 . . . *nalles þy . . . ac . . .* (type C); and *GuthA* 150 . . . *nales þy . . . ac* (type C, with *þæt lond* demonstrative + noun). The fourth has the subjunctive of rejected cause: *WaldA* 12 (§3134). I prefer this—the first of two explanations proposed by Behre (pp. 307-8)—to his second, viz. that 'the use of the subjunctive . . . may also be connected with the employment of the subjunctive in certain *þæt*-clauses after verbs of saying', since I do not accept *þy* as a conjunction which introduces noun clauses. The point verges, I agree, on the terminological. But the existence of the three other examples cited here favours the causal explanation. The failure of Behre and of the editors Dickins and Norman to discuss these three examples illustrates the danger of working without full collections. On *WaldA* 12, see further Liggins 1955, pp. 190-1, and 1960, pp. 459-60, and Mitchell 1959, pp. 460-2.

§3193. Liggins (1955, pp. 44-5 and 191, and 1960, pp. 458-9 and 461) cites *CP* 327. 7 as the sole example in which a clause expressing a 'denied reason' has the indicative. I believe that the sequence *beoð . . . beoð . . . beoð . . . beoð* provides us with sufficient grounds for making what I would call the obligatory emendation of the second *beoð* to *beon*. I discuss this at greater length in *NQ* 208 (1963), 327-8.

§3194. Those wishing to pursue this use of the subjunctive, and its nature, should see in the first instance Wülfing, ii. 126; Behre, pp. 306-8; Liggins 1955, pp. 42-5, 128-31, 135, 152-3, 156, 160, 185-92, and 529-32; and Liggins 1960, pp. 457-61.

19. ARRANGEMENT OF CLAUSES

§3195. Correlation has already been discussed in the appropriate sections; see my Table of Contents. Liggins (1955, *passim*) gives a much fuller treatment for each individual conjunction.

§3196. As with most other conjunctions which introduce adverb clauses, a causal conjunction is not usually repeated in the second of two co-ordinate clauses, e.g. *ÆCHom* i. 50. 25 and *John(WSCp)* 17. 7-8 *Nu hi gecneowon þ ealle þa þing þe þu me sealdest synd of ðe forþam ic sealde him þa word ðe ðu sealdest me 7 hig under-fengon 7 oncneowon soðlice þ ic eom of þe 7 hig gelyfdon þ þu me sendest*, where the Latin has . . . *quia* . . . *et* . . . *et* . . . *et*. . . . But it can be, e.g. *GD(C)* 46. 12 and *John(WSCp)* 2. 24-5 *Se hælend ne geswutelode hine sylfne him forðam he cuðe hi ealle 7 forþam him næs nan þearf þ ænig man sæde gewitnesse be men*, where the Latin has . . . *eo quod* . . . *et quia*. . . . A second conjunction is, of course, obligatory when the second causal clause is subordinate to the first, as in *GD* 330. 13 (§3133).

§3197. When another clause is interpolated into a causal clause, the causal conjunction is not repeated, e.g. *CP* 209. 21 . . . *ðonne magon we hi sua raðosð to ryhte gecierran ðæt we him sume opene scylde, ðe ær ðurhtogen wære, healfunga oðwieten, ðæt hie forðæm scamige, forðæm of ðære scylde ðe he hine ðonne bereccan ne mæge, he on-giete ða he ðonne deð*. . . . Van Dam (pp. 43-4) draws our attention to the remarkable sequence *forðæm* . . . *nu* in *CP* 261. 22.

§3198. I turn now to clause order. 'Explanatory causal clauses', says Liggins (1955, p. 526), '. . . by their very nature, must follow the statement they seek to explain.' But clauses of 'true Reason'—crudely speaking, those in which the conjunction can be translated 'because'; see §3015—may precede or follow the principal or governing clause; see Liggins 1955, pp. 205-6. When such a clause precedes, 'the stress placed upon the reason is stronger . . . than it is when the order of the clauses is reversed' (Liggins 1955, p. 526). Van Dam (pp. 82-3) records that in his corpus 88 per cent of causal clauses followed the principal clause, 9.5 per cent preceded it, and 2.5 per cent were interpolated in it. Liggins (1955, *passim*) makes clause order part of her system of classification and is therefore a mine of information on the topic. I can consider here only some salient features. I give her figures for *for* formulae which are not used correlatively in Table 2 in §3036; in almost 97 per cent (3131/3228) the causal clause follows the principal clause. The causal clause pre-cedes the principal clause in ninety-one examples—Liggins includes here *ÆCHom* ii. 62. 6, where the words *God cwæð, Ic swor þurh me sylfne* introduce the relevant sequence, which is in non-dependent speech; *CP* 305. 1 and *HomU* 21. 2. 4, where a noun subject before the conjunction is repeated by a pronoun after it; and *Bede* 432. 21, where *Ac ðu þonne* precedes the *forðon* clause and the subject is repeated in the principal clause (Liggins 1955, pp. 62 and 104)— and is interpolated in six, viz. (without *þe*) *Bede(T)* 196. 25, *Bo* 92. 22, *John(WSCþ)* 13. 29—on this example see §3803—and (with *þe*) *Bede(B)* 196. 25, *Bede* 432. 3, and *ÆLS* 16. 60 *Eft Helias se æðela witega forðan þe he wan wið unrihtwisnysse wearð on heofenlicum cræte to heofonum ahafen*; see Liggins 1955, pp. 62-3 and 104-5. We may also note here that a *for* formula with *þe* precedes its principal clause more often than one without *þe* (see Table 2 in §3036 and Liggins 1955, p. 206); that causal clauses preceding their principal clause are more common in 'Alfredian translations' (see §3007 fn.) than anywhere else (Liggins 1955, p. 209); and that Waterhouse (1978, p. 438) tells us that in *ÆLS* 'it is the causal clause which is most consistent in its behaviour, in that it is almost always in final position, whether in a Fore-and-Aft [e.g. Sp | P | Sp] or a Both Following arrangement. It is also the type of clause which is found in a majority of cases in the one-to-two construction.' On this see §§1906 and 1911.

§3199. Clauses involving correlation demand separate treatment. When two *for* formulae are correlated, the principal clause precedes the causal clause in 80 out of 97 examples (82. 5 per cent); these figures are based on Liggins 1955, pp. 63-70 and 107-8. The corresponding figures for all *for* formulae used as conjunctions with any correlative adverb whatever are 130 out of 192 examples (67.7 per cent); for details see §3076. So van Dam (p. 82) exaggerates: 'postposition of the causal clause is also the rule in those cases where the main clause opens with a correlative causal adverb'. On this see further §§3072-80 and Mitchell, at press (*c*).

§3200. On clause order when cause is expressed paratactically, see §§3165-71. On clause order when clauses of other types are used with an element of cause, see the appropriate sections in this work and in Liggins 1955.

§3201. Those intending further work on this subject will find it fruitful to pursue the suggestions and hints given by Liggins (1955, *passim*). Thus—to give only one example—she tells us in the course of her discussion on temporal/causal *þa(þa)* clauses (pp. 236-7) that 'on the whole, when the conjunct clause follows its principal, a preterite verb has the imperfect sense; when it precedes the principal, the preterite verb is perfect in meaning'. Her examples include the contrasting pair *ÆCHom* ii. 118. 13 *He wæs swiðe wacol on*

Godes bebodum, ðaða he sylf herigendlice leofode but *ÆCHom* ii.
486. 16 *Ðaða hi ðis dydon, ða forhtode ðæs cynges heorte*; see also
Liggins 1955, p. 331.

J. CLAUSES OF COMPARISON

1. INTRODUCTORY REMARKS

§3202. I use the term 'clause of comparison' or 'comparative clause'
to describe any clause which involves a comparison. The Report of
the Joint Committee (p. 17) distinguishes clauses of manner, e.g.
'Heaven does with us as we with torches do' from clauses of degree,
e.g. 'It is as long as it is broad', 'It is longer than it is broad', and
'Blood is thicker than water'. These can be distinguished in OE; cf.
Beo 400 *sume þær bidon,* ‖ *heaðoreaf heoldon, swa him se hearda
bebead* with *Beo* 593 . . . *gif þin hige wære,* ‖ *sefa swa searogrim, swa
þu self talast,*

Beo 1559		þæt wæs wæpna cyst,—
buton hit wæs mare	ðonne ænig mon oðer
to beadulace	ætberan meahte . . . ,

and *Beo* 469 *se wæs betera ðonne ic!* But, although *þonne* always
introduces a clause of degree, the distinction cannot always be made
with clauses involving *swa*. Thus, whether we classify

Met 22. 16		He ongit siððan
yfel and unnet	eal þæt he hæfde
on his incofan	æror lange
efne swa sweotole	swa he on þa sunnan mæg
eagum andweardum	on locian

as manner or degree depends on whether we ask ourselves 'How does
he see?' or 'How clearly does he see?' No syntactical differences
exist between clauses of manner and degree introduced by the same
conjunction. So the basis of my classification is the form of the introductory conjunction and of any elements with which it may be
correlative, not whether the clause is one of manner or degree. I do
not therefore concern myself with arguing whether we need follow
Popova in distinguishing, not only clauses of manner and degree, but
also a third class of comparative clause exemplified by *Mart 2* 142.
20 . . . *ond swa hine mon ma hirste, swa wæs he fægerra on ondwlitan.*[168] Such clauses, which have been traditionally described as

[168] O. A. Popova, *Učenye zapiski Dal'nevostočnogo Gosudarstvennogo universiteta*, 11
(jazykoznanie), Vladivostok (1968), 74–9. See also Kivimaa, p. 152 fn. 1.

clauses of degree—see, for example, Curme 1931, pp. 296-8—are discussed in §§3287-9.

§3203. Nor have I found it possible always to distinguish 'comparisons of equality', e.g. 'He is as tall as I am', from 'comparisons of inequality', e.g. 'He is taller than I am'. These categories too break down; consider 'He is not as tall as I am' and 'He is not taller than I am'. But my system of classification does in fact go as far towards making the distinctions discussed above as is possible without the intrusion of the personal element or other non-grammatical criteria. And it avoids unnecessary labelling.

§3204. Here again we find difficulties of interpretation and examples of the inevitable overlap in the function of clauses which are formally distinguished. Comparison may be expressed by what is grammatically an adjective clause, e.g. *PPs* 101. 24 *þu þonne byst se ilca se þu ær wære*; cf. also *Beo* 1231 ... *druncne dryhtguman doð swa ic bidde* with

Ex 558 wile nu gelæstan þæt he lange gehet
mid aðsware, engla drihten. . . .

On the ambiguity of some clauses introduced by *swelce*, see §2378. Consecutive elements have been detected in clauses introduced by *(eal)swa (swa), (swa) swa . . . swa, swelce . . . swelce, þæs* (alone and in combination), and *þy . . . þy*; see initially §2811. Elements of cause have been detected in clauses introduced by *(eal)swa swa* and *(swa) swa . . . swa* (§3024), by *swelce* (§§3111-12), and by *þæs*, alone and in combination (§§3113-17). Clauses with *þe/þy . . . þe/ þy*, in which elements of concession (Burnham, p. 86, and Quirk, p. 117) and condition (Jespersen, *A System of Clauses* (SPE Tract 44, 1926), 167) have also been detected, could be added; see Benham, pp. 223-4, and §§3334-46. Liggins (1955, pp. 334-59) discusses in some detail the use of modal connectives 'with an added causal meaning'. Quirk (pp. 108-12) discusses 'concessive-equivalent clauses of manner' with *swa*, noting that Burnham (p. 74) refers to *swa* 'as a true concessive conjunction'. I agree with him in rejecting this view; see §§3476-82. Clauses with *swa (swa)* indeed present many problems. Some are more easily resolved than others. Thus, combinations like *swa hraþe swa* and *swa lange swa* have been treated as temporal conjunctions. Whether *swa* in *ChronE* 136. 17 (1006) *Ac for eallum þissum se here ferde swa he sylf wolde* and *swa swa* in *ChronE* 133. 27 (1001) *7 þær him ferdon onbuton swa swa hi sylf woldon* mean '(just) as', 'wherever', or 'as far as', is more difficult to decide; see §§2489-93. See further the Index of Words and Conjunctions, s.v. *swa (swa)*.

2. COMPARISONS OF INEQUALITY EXPRESSED
WITH *þONNE*

a. Forms of þonne *and its origin*

§3205. The most common form of the comparative particle is *þonne/ðonne*. Manuscript variants include *þon* and *þone* in *Bede* 260. 18 and *than, ðon, þone*, and *thonne*, in *BDS* 2. *ChronE* 49. 19 (755) has *þone* where *ChronA* 48. 20 (755) has *þonne*. On *þon* in *Mald* 33 see Joly 1967, p. 21 fn. 36, and Robinson, *JEGP* 75 (1976), 26. I am unable to accept Joly's claim (1967, p. 22) that the reduced form *þon/þan* is of 'late appearance' in view of the examples cited by Small (1924, pp. 89-91) and of the *OED* comment quoted in §3207. Later forms include *þænne* (*Coll* 8) and *þanne* (*ChronE* 173. 4 (1048)).

§3206. Detailed discussion of the origin of the comparative conjunction *þonne* 'than' lies outside the scope of this work. For fuller exposition of the various theories than is possible here, see initially *OED*, s.v. 'than'; Small 1924, especially pp. 1-14 and 70-154; and Joly 1967, pp. 9-17. I shall content myself with the briefest summaries. First, '*than* is the old form of the adverb *then*' (Curme 1931, p. 274). Second, '*Than* (*then*), used as a comparative particle since OE . . . is originally a temporal adverb (OE *þonne, þanne*, Mod.E. *then*) used as a connective with a relative meaning ("when")' (Mustanoja, p. 283). Third, *than* is 'closely allied to (perhaps once identical with) A.S. *ðone*, acc. masc. of the demonst. pronoun' (Skeat, *Etymological Dictionary*, s.v. *than*; see also Adams, pp. 25-6). Fourth, there is the view that *þonne* is of local origin. This was advanced by Johnsen (*Ang.* 39 (1915-16), 104-6): '*þonne* is frequently used in Cart. [Charters] as a local-demonstrative adverb. It is an extension of *þon*, which belongs to the pronominal stem, by the suffix *-ne* < *-nai*'; by degrees it became an adverb of time and then a conjunction. Joly (1967, p. 11) quotes Partridge (*An Etymological Dictionary of English*): 'E[nglish] *than* probably at first "from that (place or point), from there".' Small (1924, pp. 95-100) makes a vigorous and successful attack on Johnsen's theory; 'thoroly convincing' is Sturtevant's verdict on the attack (*MLN* 40 (1925), 496). Small's own view (1924, p. 77) is this: 'In the English comparative particle *than* we have *a blending of concrete temporal succession with the abstract notion of contrast, to express the comparative relation*' (his italics). Or, as he puts it elsewhere (1924, p. 14), 'we have essentially an *adversative* relation expressed in terms of a *temporal* relation'. Spitzbardt (*Philologica Pragensia*, 2 (1959), 9–14), who makes no mention of Johnsen or Small, derives *than* from *þanne*, for which he claims a local origin, comparing *þanne* with *þanon* without actually deriving the former from the latter. The last theory to be mentioned—apart from Joly's, on which see below—is that advanced by Campbell (*OEG*, §709 and fn. 2):

§709. The i.s.n. *þon* and d.s.n. *þæm* are freely used in forming phrases, which are used as advs., and (with or without the particle *þe*) as conjunctions, e.g. *æfter þæm* (*þe*) after, *for þon* (*þe*) because. Note also *siþþan* after, i.e. *siþ* + *þon*, and the comparative uses of *þon* (1) as 'than' (usually *þonne*), and (2) in phrases like *þon ma* the more, where it interchanges with *þy* and *þe*.[2]

[2] Strictly *þon ma* is comparative 'more than some other already indicated', and is rarely used with resultative force 'more for a reason already indicated', *þe* (*þy*) *ma* is both comparative and resultative. Examples B-T, s.v. *ma*. [But see my §§3243–50.]

§3207. It is clear that one of the major disagreements is about which came first—*þan/þon* or *þanne/þonne*. The comment of *OED* (s.v. *than*) that 'already in the 8th c. OE *þanne* appears as *ðan, þan, than*' implies a reduction, whereas Small (1924, pp. 89–90) raises the possibility that 'than' may be 'a survival of the simpler and older form of the adverbial conjunction, *þan*' rather than 'merely an off-shoot of the longer form'. Joly (1967, p. 16), following Campbell, accepts that 'the relationship between instrumental *þon* and *þonne*, the comparative particle, can be provisionally admitted as a working hypothesis', but goes on to assert (1967, p. 17) that

since, as it has been suggested above, *þonne* cannot reasonably be derived from the temporal adverb (*þonne*), but must be related to the instrumental *þon*, one can only infer that the OE comparative particle has to be analysed as *þon* + *ne*, i.e. the instrumental to which is added a significant element whose presence is phonetically marked. My assumption is that this significant element is no other than the *negative particle* [his italics][169]

and (1967, p. 21) that

the optional use of negation finds an explanation in the fact that, in a comparative clause, negation is hardly a negative. It is commonly termed 'expletive' and

[169] Joly (1967, p. 12) complains that 'most scholars have made a fundamental error which consists in deriving *than* from *then*. ... This type of error is very common in linguistics.' I cannot accept his first sentence as final, but do not propose to argue. However, I will say that in my opinion Joly has made two errors very common among modern linguists who adopt the attitude that 'the main interest of this study, if any, is the technique of analysis I have adopted' (Joly 1967, p. 44). The first is that of embarking on a subject with inadequate knowledge (witness his failure to cite such relevant bibliographical items as Small 1924 and Small 1929 and his elementary errors in interpreting the two sentences discussed in §3207). The second is that of transforming the suggestion that something is (un)likely into the certainty that it has been proved right or wrong (witness his shift from 'it seems safer, at least provisionally' (1967, p. 12) and 'can be provisionally admitted as a working hypothesis' (p. 16) to 'cannot reasonably be ... but must be' (p. 17) and 'perfectly legitimate' (p. 32)).

sometimes 'expressive' negation. Its purpose is only to *signify the negative move-ment* which is implied in the mechanism of comparison. In reality it does not negate the verb of the clause. Therefore, on account of its instability, this type of negation tends to disappear. It has already been observed that Modern French uses both *que . . . ne* and *que.* OE generally seems to have favored the use of negation with the comparative conjunction, hence *þonne,* i.e. instrumental *þon* + negative *ne.* In spite of the early tendency of finals to be reduced, the form *þonne* kept its ground for several centuries.

I cannot pursue his theoretical arguments. But I can say that I know of no evidence for his assertion (1967, p. 21) that 'OE generally seems to have favoured the use of negation with the comparative conjunction' beyond the circular one that it is true if Joly's claim that *þonne = þon + ne* is true. The closest Joly comes to producing any examples is at 1967, p. 23. The only one from OE is *nan mihtigra þe nis,* which he takes from *Bo* 79. 10 *Eala, Dryhten, hu micel ⁊ hu wunderlic þu eart . . . forþam ðe nan mihtigra þe nis, ne nan þin gelica, ne þe nan neodþearf ne lærde towyrcanne þ þ ðu worhtest* and which he misconstrues: 'one might think that *þe nis* is due to a wrong division of syllables—*þe nis* standing for *þon is*—but it is equally right to assume, as I do, that this sequence of words has to be analysed as follows: conjunction (here the relative particle *þe*) + negated verb'. Here the negative is essential, not expletive, and, as Small (1929, p. 57) long ago pointed out, *þe* is dative of comparison 'no one is mightier than Thou'—an idiom of which Joly elsewhere (1967, p. 20) shows awareness. From here Joly advances to the equally astonishing claim that another of his examples—*The Owl and the Nightingale,* lines 21-2, *Bet þuȝte þe dreim þat he were ‖ Of harpe ⁊ pipe þan he nere*—'corroborates this analysis; *þe nis* is on a par with *þan he nere.* In the latter case, the *n* of *nere* cannot proceed from a wrong division of words, since the pronoun *he* separates the comparative particle from the verb. *Nere* is obviously the contracted negative form of subjunctive *were (ne were > nere*).' I can agree with the last sentence, but must point out that again the negative is essen-tial, not expletive, since the contrast is between *were* and *nere.* The remaining example (*The Owl and the Nightingale,* lines 563-4) involves the variants *þe* (MS *C*) and *þene* (MS *J*) and in my opinion proves nothing about OE *þonne.* I cannot see the relevance of the rest of the evidence Joly produces in alleged support of the proposi-tion *þonne = þon + ne.* The presence of an adversative relationship in OE clauses of comparison involving *þonne* is implicit in the theories that it derives from temporal *þonne* and cannot be used to establish even the possibility that an expletive negative was present in such clauses.

b. General considerations

§3208. The classification of comparisons of inequality is not easy. Behaghel (*DS* iii, §1273) distinguishes type A, in which the principal and the subordinate clause have a common conception, e.g. 'They are more wicked than he is'—common conception 'wickedness'—from type B. ii, those which contain a judgement, e.g. 'They die rather than that they surrender' (see §3209) and 'It is better that one man should die than that the world should perish'. This is not satisfactory. First, as Wilde (1939, p. 372) points out, all comparative clauses contain a judgement of some sort, with the exception of purely temporal clauses such as 'I go before he comes', which comprise Behaghel's type B. i. Second, sentences of type B. ii do in fact have a common element. Behaghel's two examples can be restated as 'For them death is more honourable than surrender' and 'The death of one man is more desirable than the destruction of the world'. So his two types give different linguistic expression to what is basically the pattern '*X* is better than *Y*', where 'better' represents Behaghel's 'gemeinsames Vorstellungsglied' ['link expressed in a common conception'].

§3209. In *DS* iii, §1281, Behaghel subdivides his type B. ii into two groups—first, sentences in which the principal clause as a whole is compared with a subordinate, e.g. 'One can more easily drive a camel through the eye of a needle than the soul of a rich man may come to Heaven' (an abbreviated version of *Heliand* 3299–304), and second, sentences in which the comparison is between two parallel subordinate clauses, e.g. 'It is better [that] one man should die for the people than [that] the whole people should perish.' His example 'Sie sterben lieber, als daß sie sich ergeben' (literally translated in §3208) certainly conforms to the first type. But the idiomatic equivalent in MnE is 'They die rather than surrender', where the comparison is really between the ideas expressed in the two verbs: 'For them death is more honourable than surrender'. So it may be fruitful to approach this problem by asking which grammatical elements of the sentence express the ideas which are to be compared.

§3210. It is less easy to answer this question than it looks. In the last two examples quoted, the answer is that they are the same—parallel subordinate clauses and parallel verbs. We may compare respectively *ÆCHom* i. 178. 34 *forði læsse pleoh bið þam cristenum men þæt he flæsces bruce þonne he on ðissere halgan tide wifes bruce*, where the absence of *þæt* after *þonne* is idiomatic (§3232), and *CP* 26. 18 . . . *ac mid hira agenre gewilnunge hi bioð onbærnde, þæt hi gereafiað swæ heane lareowdom swiður ðonne hi hine geearnigen.* In both of these, the subject is repeated in the *ðonne* clause. Other elements may be compared, e.g. two subjects in *Or* 66. 25 *Ac þa cyningas þe æfter Romuluse ricsedon wæron forcuðran 7 eargran þonne he wære* and two genitives in *ÆCHom* i. 146. 14 *forðon þe mare wæs hyre modes þrowung þonne wære hire lichaman.* In these and other such examples discussed in §§3215–16 and 3232–7, the two elements between which the comparison is made are grammatically the same and are specifically stated. The 'contracted' comparative clauses in which the verb of the *þonne* clause is not expressed belong here, e.g. *ÆCHom* i. 10. 3 *Maran cyððe habbað englas to Gode þonne men*, where both the sense and the syntax certify that *men* is nominative plural, not dative singular—that would have required repetition of the preposition, as in *ÆCHom* ii. 550. 13 *On ðam twam pundum is mare getacnung þonne on ðam fif pundum sy* —and *ÆCHom* i. 128. 19 *Wel wat gehwa þæt cyning hæfð maran mihte þonne ænig hundredes ealdor.* On these see §§3217–18.

§3211. In our next group, the elements compared are both specifically stated but are grammatically different, e.g. *ÆCHom* ii. 362. 18 *Beo ælc man underðeod mihtigran men ðonne he sylf sy*, where an adjective + noun in the dative is compared with the nom. sg. pers. pron. *he*, and *ÆCHom* ii. 154. 28 *Ac Benedictus gewilnode swiðor to ðoligenne earfoðnyssa and geswinc for Gode, þonne he cepte woruldlice herunga, oððe þises lifes hlisan*, where an inflected infinitive is compared with a noun clause with idiomatic non-expression of *þæt* (§3232) and the direct objects are also compared; see §§3216 and 3228. More examples will be found in §§3219 and 3228–31.

§3212. I turn finally to those examples in which (as it seems to me) the second of the two elements between which the comparison is made is implied, not stated. This is obviously so in sentences like *ÆCHom* ii. 408. 33 *Hwæt is fulre ðonne meox? and swaðeah, gif ðu his wel notast, hwæt bið wæstmbærre?*, where we mentally add *ðonne meox*. But I am also inclined to see 'ellipsis' or non-expression (see §§3858–61) in examples like *ÆCHom* ii. 42. 15 *Hu mihte beon mare gecyðnys be Criste þonne ðær gedon wæs?*, where *seo gecyðnys þe* is implied after *þonne*. Both these patterns are discussed in §§3220–1.

c. *Positive degree* + *þonne*

§3213. This construction occurs in direct imitation of the Latin in

PPs 117. 8   God ys on dryhten   georne to þenceanne,
            þonne on mannan wese   mod to treowianne.
    9   God ys on dryhten   georne to hyhtanne,
            þonne on ealdormen   ahwær to treowianne,

Latin *Bonum est confidere in Domino quam confidere in homine. Bonum est sperare in Domino quam sperare in principibus.* Bright (*MLN* 27 (1912), 181-3) shows that this 'false idiom' occurred in the Greek of the Septuagint as a result of misunderstanding of the Hebrew and spread from there into the Latin and translations based thereon. So the Lindisfarne gloss shows a reverence first for the sacred text and then for OE idiom in *Matt(Li)* 18. 9 *god ł betra ðe is an ege in lif ingeonga ðon tuoe ego hæbbe gesende in tintergo fyres,* Latin *bonum tibi est uno oculo in uitam intrare quam duos oculos habentem mitti in gehennam ignis.* In

PPs 83. 10   Ic me þæs wyrce   and wel ceose,
            þæt ic hean gange   on hus godes,
            þonne ic on fyrenfulra   folce eardige,

þonne represents Latin *magis quam.*

§3214. Bright (ibid.) reviews and dismisses the other possible examples. He is right to do so, despite Lehmann (*Studies for Einar Haugen* (Mouton, 1972), 323-30), and does so acceptably for *Ex* 373 (see Lucas's note); for *El* 646 (see Gradon's note); for *Alex* 26. 9 7 *he swiðe þæs londes fæstenum truwode þonne his gefeohte 7 gewinne* (although he fails to point out that the Latin *magis quam* supports the emendation of *swiðe* to *swiðor*); and for all the other examples he mentions apart from the notorious *Beo* 69, which is no longer relevant because of Robinson's successful defence of the manuscript reading; see my §46.

d. *Sentences with a principal clause and a* þonne *clause of comparison*

(1) *in which the same elements are compared*

§3215. Here we are concerned with sentences in which the two elements compared are grammatically the same and are specifically stated; see §3210. Some typical examples follow, with the grammatical nature of the compared elements in brackets: (subjects) *Or* 66. 25

(§3210), *ÆCHom* i. 358. 27 *Cuð is gehwilcum snoterum mannum þæt seo ealde æ wæs eaðelicre þonne Cristes Gesetnys sy*, and

Rid 40. 60   swylce ic eom wraþre   þonne wermod sy,
         þe her on hyrstum   heasewe stondeþ;

(genitive objects) *Bo* 5. 19 *Hu se scop sang þ ma manna fægnodon dysiges folces gedwolan þonne hie fægnedon soþra spella*; (indirect objects) *Or* 120. 27 *7 þær Romane swiþost for þæm besierede wæron þe him þæt land uncuþre wæs þonne hit Somnitum wære*; (complements) *Bede* 260. 16 *þa gehadode he sumne mon, se wæs ma in ciriclecum þeodscipum 7 in lifes bylwitnesse gelæred, þon he from wære in worulde þingum, þæs noma wæs Putta* and *GD* 180. 8 . . . *heo wende þæt hit ma wære bysmrung þonne efensargung*; (verb or verb groups) *Bede* 236. 18 . . . *þæt þær micle ma moncynnes adronc on þam wætre þonne mid sweorde ofslegen wære, ÆCHom* i. 602. 1 *ure hæl is gehendre þonne we gelyfdon, GenB* 825 *hit þe þeah wyrs ne mæg* ‖ *on þinum hyge hreowan þonne hit me æt heortan deð*, and (with what is for MnE a superfluous pronoun subject after *þonne*)

Met 21. 25   ac hi swiðor get
         monna gehwelces   modes eagan
         ablendað on breostum,   þonne hi hi beorhtran gedon;[170]

and (adverbs and/or adverbial expressions) *Or* 40. 24 . . . *þæt þeos world sy nu wyrse on ðysan cristendome þonne hio ær on þæm hæþenscype wære* and *ÆCHom* i. 618. 6 *þonne bið seo sunne be seofonfealdum beorhtre þonne heo nu sy*—in these two examples, the tense of the verbs alone would be sufficient to sustain the comparison; cf. *Bo* 11. 9 *Ac þeah þu nu fyr seo ðonne þu wære* . . . , where *ær* is implicit in *wære*—*Or* 24. 26 . . . *for ðan þe he brycð swiðor on ðone suðdæl þonne he do on þone norðdæl, ÆCHom* ii. 550. 13 (§3210), and *ÆCHom* i. 340. 17 *Ic secge eow, mare bliss bið on heofonum be anum synfullan men, gif he his synna mid dædbote behreowsað, ðonne sy be nigon and hundnigontig rihtwisum ðe nanre behreowsunge ne behofiað*. The first of two elements which are compared may be unexpressed or implied, e.g. *CP* 61. 12 . . . *7 his breosð sien simle onhielde for arfæstnesse to forgiefnesse, næfre ðeah suiðor ðonne hit gedafenlic sie for ryhtwisnesse* and *ÆC Hom* i. 2. 12 *Ic Ælfric munuc and mæssepreost, swa þeah waccre þonne swilcum hadum gebyrige, wearð asend*. . . . So too may the second; see §§3220-1. For examples in which two clauses are compared, see §§3232-8.

---

[170] Quirk's suggestion (pp. 114 and 118) that *þonne* here introduces a 'concessive-equivalent temporal member' in my opinion makes nonsense of the sentence. Cf. rather MnE 'rather than that'. (On [*þæt*] see §3232.)

§3216. Two distinct grammatical elements may be involved in both sides of the comparison, e.g. *Or* 24. 27 *7 sio hæte hæfð genumen þæs suðdæles mare þonne se cyle þæs norðdæles hæbbe, ÆCHom* i. 306. 15 *þa gastlican wundra sind maran þonne þa lichamlican wæron, ÆCHom* i. 498. 5 *Swa bið eac se digla deað ðære sawle eaþelicor to aræenne, þe on geðafunge digelice syngað, þonne synd ða openan leahtras to gehælenne, ÆCHom* i. 236. 11 *Nu is geðuht þæt him sy sumera ðinga eaðelicor to aræenne ðone deadan of ðam duste, þonne him wære to wyrcenne ealle gesceafta of nahte*, where we have comparisons between the two inflected infinitives and the verbs *sy* and *wære*, and

Dan 631   Gewat þa earmsceapen   eft siðian,
                 nacod nydgenga,   nið geðafian,
                 wundorlic wræcca   and wæda leas,
                 mætra on modgeðanc,   to mancynne,
                 ðonne gumena weard   in gylpe wæs.

ÆCHom ii. 154. 28 (§3211) also belongs here, combining as it does two distinct patterns.

(2) with no expressed verb

§3217. The examples under discussion here are those 'contracted' comparative clauses in which the verb of the *þonne* clause is not expressed, such as MnE 'Blood is thicker than water'. A few typical examples will suffice, the compared elements being named in brackets: (subjects) *Bede* 136. 27 *Hwa mæg þa nu eað . . . to bysene oðerra monna gerisenlecor toweorpan þonne ic seolfa . . . ?, ÆCHom* i. 96. 15 *Witodlice se fyrenfulla bið earmra ðonne ænig nyten*, and *Beo* 469 *se wæs betera ðonne ic*; (objects of various kinds) *ÆCHom* i. 132. 5 *Ða sind Godes bearn gecigede, þe hine lufiað swiðor þonne þisne middangeard, ÆCHom* i. 452. 18 *. . . ac hi cwædon þæt hi uðon ðæra laca þam undeadlican Cyninge, ðe hi swa mihtelice generede, micele bet ðonne ðam deadlican cwellere, ÆCHom* i. 424. 3 *Gif hit riht sy þæt we to deoflum us gebiddon swiðor þonne to ðam Ælmihtigan Gode . . . , Beo* 1138 *he to gyrnwræce ‖ swiðor þohte þonne to sælade*, and

ChristC 1394   Fæcnum feonde   furþor hyrdes,
                  sceþþendum scaþan,   þonne þinum scyppende . . . ;

(adverbs or adverbial expressions) *ÆCHom* i. 102. 20 *Is hwæðere æfter gecynde on gesceapennysse ælc lichamlice gesceaft ðe eorðe acenð fulre and mægenfæstre on fullum monan þonne on gewanedum, ÆCHom* i. 486. 31 *Ac se wisa Salomon cwæð, þæt selre wære to wunigenne mid leon and dracan þonne mid yfelan wife and oferspræcum,*

ÆCHom i. 534. 1 *He leofode on mynstre for neode swiðor þonne for beterunge*, and *Beo* 1579 . . . *oftor micle ðonne on ænne sið*; and (other elements) *ÆCHom* i. 332. 3 *þes cwyde is swiðor to ondrædenne þonne to trahtnigenne*, *ÆCHom* i. 594. 20 *and ic sceal his rode sigor swiðor wiscan ðonne ondrædan*, and

Jul 413   Ic þære sawle ma
          geornor gyme   ymb þæs gæstes forwyrd
          þonne þæs lichoman. . . .

In *Rid* 23. 7 . . . *ic beo lengre þonne ær*, the comparison is between present time *ic beo* [*nu*] and past time [*ic wæs*] *ær*.

§3218. As in the last pattern discussed, we find examples in which two different grammatical elements are involved on both sides of the comparison, e.g. *ÆCHom* i. 96. 5 *Be ðysum ðinge ge habbað oft gehyred, ac us is acumendlicere eower gebelh, þonne þæs Ælmihtigan Godes grama* and

Beo 677   No ic me an herewæsmun   hnagran talige
          guþgeweorca,   þonne Grendel hine.

Three are involved in *ÆCHom* i. 432. 25 *We wilniað mid urum hlaforde clænlice sweltan swiðor ðonne unclænlice mid eow lybban.*

(3) *in which different elements are compared*

§3219. But, as I have pointed out in §3211, the compared ideas are not always expressed by means of the same grammatical element. Thus we find a comparison between object and subject in *Or* 70. 1 . . . *7 him gesetton hirran ladteow þonne hiera consul wære*, *ÆCHom* i. 290. 22 *He wolde don Crist læssan þonne he is, ChristC* 988 *þær bið wundra ma* ǁ *þonne hit ænig on mode mæge aþencan*, and

Beo 247   Næfre ic maran geseah
          eorla ofer eorþan,   ðonne is eower sum,
          secg on searwum.

In *ÆCHom* i. 118. 26 . . . *and ðurh modignysse, ðaða he wolde beon betera ðonne hine se Ælmihtiga Scyppend gesceop*, we have a comparison involving the subject of one construction and the object of another; contrast *ÆCHom* i. 10. 32 . . . *þaða he wolde mid modignysse beon betera þonne he gesceapen wæs*. The subject accusative of an accusative and infinitive is compared with the nominative subject of a verb in *ÆCHom* i. 8. 2 *For wel fela ic wat on þisum earde gelæredran þonne ic sy* and in

Met 22. 21   and he eac ongit   his ingeþonc
          leohtre and berhtre   þonne se leoma sie
          sunnan on sumera. . . .

ÆCHom ii. 362. 18 *Beo ælc man underðeod mihtigran men ðonne he sylf sy* (see §3211) will conclude this list of examples. For those in which the second of the two compared elements is a clause, see §§3228-31.

(4) *with non-expression of the second compared element*

§3220. As I have noted in §3212, two patterns belong here. The first is that seen in *ÆCHom* i. 284. 5 *forðan swa hwæt swa læsse bið þonne God, þæt ne bið na God; þæt þæt lator bið, þæt hæfð anginn, ac God næfð nan anginn*, where *þonne God*, expressed after *læsse bið*, has to be supplied after *lator bið*. More examples of this type will be found in §§183-6, where I discuss the so-called 'comparative absolute'. See also, *inter alia*, *ÆCHom* i. 88. 28, 130. 10, and 228. 27, and *ÆCHom* ii. 48. 17, 440. 21, and 440. 26.

§3221. The second pattern comprises those sentences in which, as I read them, an antecedent and a relative or a relative for the same antecedent must be supplied after *þonne* to make the comparison logically complete. Typical examples of this type, which is noted by Grossmann (p. 8) and by Anklam (p. 8), include *Bede* 284. 15 *Wæs seo beorhtnes þæs onsendan leohtes mara, þon sunnan leoht bið æt middan dæge*, where the comparison is between the *brightness* of the two lights; *Or* 86. 7 and *Or* 118. 15; *Or* 86. 3 *þeh ic ær sæde þæt we to helle sceolden, þeh ne geortriewe ic na Gode þæt he us ne mæge gescildan to beteran tidun þonne we nu on sint* '. . . to better times than [those which] we are now in'; *ÆCHom* i. 94. 24 *ac hi ne dorston nænne oðerne naman Criste gescyppan þonne se heahengel him gesette* '. . . than [that which] . . .'; *ÆCHom* i. 390. 34 and *ÆCHom* ii. 218. 25; and sentences in which the implication is that the first of the two compared elements is the greatest example of its kind which could be envisaged and in which we can supply '[any which]', e.g. *ÆCHom* ii. 586. 35 . . . *and seo gastlice cwen, Godes gelaðung, oðe gehwilc halig sawul, ðonne heo cymð to þære heofenlican Hierusalem, þonne gesihð heo micele maran mærðe and wuldor ðonne hire ær on life ðurh witegan oððe apostolum gecydd wære* and

ChristB 838   Ðær biþ oðywed   egsa mara
               þonne from frumgesceape   gefrægen wurde
               æfre on eorðan.

These last two examples, with their preterite subjunctives, invite comparison with examples like *WHom* 18. 20 *And þæt wæs þæt mæreste hus þe on eorðan geworht wurde* discussed in §2403. This implication is not present in all those examples in which we can supply '[any which]'; consider *ÆCHom* i. 608. 25 . . . *and heora ofðriccednyss on eorðan gelamp swiðor þonne we on ealdum bocum rædað*, where we have pres. ind. *rædað*. In *BlHom* 79. 7 *þa he þa geseah þæt hie nænige bote ne hreowe don noldan, ah hie for þon heora yfelum þurhwunedon, Drihten þa sende on hie maran wræce þonne æfre ær ænigu oþru gelumpe, buton Sodomwarum anum*, where we have pret. subj. *gelumpe* and Morris, supplying rel. pron. 'that', translates '. . . more vengeance than any other that ever before happened, except upon the people of Sodom alone', the *buton* phrase describes a greater vengeance.

e. Mood in þonne *clauses of comparison*

§3222. We can begin by saying that when the principal clause is positive, the verb of the *þonne* clause is more likely to be subjunctive, and that when the principal clause is negative, the verb of the *þonne* clause is more likely to be indicative. In his Oxford lectures Alistair Campbell was wont to point out that in this, *þonne* clauses resembled *ær* clauses; see §§2731-42. But these are merely tendencies. There is no 'rule'. The figures for the poetry illustrate this.

The principal clause is	The verb of the *þonne* clause is				
	Pres. Ind.	Pret. Ind.	Pres. Subj.	Pret. Subj.	Ambiguous
Negative	3	1	3	0	8
Positive	0	3	17	7	22

My own samplings for the prose reveal very similar tendencies in both early and late prose, including the marked predominance of positive principal clauses followed by *þonne* clauses with the present or preterite subjunctive. But complete statistics remain to be established; it is perhaps worth noting that Small did not attempt a descriptive syntax of OE comparative clauses with *þonne* in *The Comparison of Inequality* (Small 1924).[171]

§3223. Some typical examples from the prose follow: (negative principal clause + indicative) *Or* 86. 3 (§3221) and *ÆCHom* i. 356. 6 *Betwux wifa bearnum ne aras nan mærra man ðonne is Iohannes se*

---

[171] The work he mentions at Small 1930, p. 380, does not seem to have appeared. That mentioned at Small 1930, p. 380 fn. 8, is presumably Callaway 1931. Visser (ii, §889) gives examples of both indicative and subjunctive in *þonne* clauses, but fails to mention the distinction discussed above.

Fulluhtere (present tense), and *ÆCHom* i. 104. 5 *ac we ne hrepodon þone traht na swiðor þonne to ðæs dæges wurðmynte belamp* and *ChronE* 151. 4 (1016) *næs nan mare unræd gered þonne se wæs* (preterite tense); (negative principal clause + subjunctive) *CP* 61. 13 *. . . næfre ðeah suiðor ðonne hit gedafenlic sie for ryhtwisnesse* and *Solil* 48. 18 *nis nanwiht wyrse on ðam men þonne wene he þæt he si þæs wyrðe þe he nis* (present tense; I have so far recorded no examples with the preterite subjunctive in either prose or poetry); (positive principal clause + indicative) *Bede* 284. 15 (§3221) and *ÆCHom* i. 16. 14 *forði is se man betera, gif he gode geðihð, þonne ealle ða nytenu sindon* (present tense), and *CP* 421. 3 *ðonne bið hit fulre ðonne hit ær wæs* and *ÆCHom* i. 10. 32 *. . . þaða he wolde mid modignysse beon betera þonne he gesceapen wæs* (preterite tense); and (positive principal clause + subjunctive) *Or* 86. 7 *7 nu sume men secgað þæt þa beteran wæren þonne nu sien* and *ÆCHom* i. 8. 2 *For wel fela ic wat on þisum earde gelæredran þonne ic sy* (present tense), and *Or* 40. 24 *. . . þa þe secgað þæt þeos world sy nu wyrse on ðysan cristendome þonne hio ær on þæm hæþenscype wære* and *ÆCHom* i. 356. 28 *Iohannes wæs hraðor mannum cuð þurh his mærlican drohtnunga þonne Crist wære* (preterite tense).

§3224. Examples from the poetry with a positive principal clause + subjunctive include (present tense)

Rid 40. 23   Ic eom on stence   strengre micle
            þonne ricels   oþþe rose sy

and

Beo 1384   Ne sorga, snotor guma!   Selre bið æghwæm
            þæt he his freond wrece   þonne he fela murne,

and (preterite tense) *Dan* 247 and

ChristB 838   Ðær biþ oðywed   egsa mara
            þonne from frumgesceape   gefrægen wurde
            æfre on eorðan.

The examples of other combinations are (positive + present indicative) none; (positive + preterite indicative) *GenA* 961, *Dan* 631, and

ChristC 1489   Nu is swærra mid mec   þinra synna rod
            þe ic unwillum   on beom gefæstnad,
            þonne seo oþer wæs   þe ic ær gestag . . . ;

(negative + present indicative) *GenB* 825, *Az* 85 (but see Small 1930, p. 383 fn. 12, and Small 1926, p. 304), and

Beo 247   Næfre ic maran geseah
        eorla ofer eorþan   ðonne is eower sum,
        secg on searwum;

(negative + preterite indicative)

GuthB 1057   Wyrd ne meahte
                  in fægum leng   feorg gehealdan,
                  deore frætwe,   þonne him gedemed wæs;

(negative + present subjunctive) *Ex* 427, *GuthA* 384, and

BDS(Dg) 1   For þam nedfere   næni wyrþeþ
                  þances snotera   þonne him þearf sy
                  to gehicgenne   ær his heonengange . . . ;

and (negative + preterite subjunctive) none.

§3225. Various statements have been made on the subject of mood in comparative clauses introduced by *þonne*. Hotz (p. 70) is diffi- cult to follow when he asserts that

when the result of comparison between the activities, resp. of measurement over against each other, turns out to be such, that the subject-matter of the main sentence is quantitatively or qualitatively superior to that subject-matter which furnished the measure of comparison, the relatively lesser value of the latter finds an eloquent expression by the subj. mood; f. i.:—

Ic eom on stence strengre [*micle*] *þonne ricels oðде rose sy* [*þe sva aenlice*] *on eorдan tyrf vynlic veaxeд*. Räts. 41, 24. . . . If the comparative of the adj. or the adv. thus standing in the main sentence, be negatived, there will no longer exist superiority of the main activity over the other; then, the relation being that of equality (or perhaps of inferiority), the subj. is not wanted:—Aelfr., de Nov. Test. 12, 21 *Crist sylf cveд be him, þät ne come nateshvon betvux vifa bearnum nan maerra man, þonne he väs*.

If the comparative be a so-called comparative of inferiority, the indic. like- wise comes in.

This theory is difficult to interpret—is *uncuþre* in *Or* 120. 27 *7 þær Romane swiþost for þæm besierede wæron þe him þæt land uncuþre wæs þonne hit Somnitum wære* to be taken as meaning more *uncuþ* or less *cuþ*?—and, like the others, does not always work. Behaghel (*DS* iii. 625 ff.), supported by Wilde (1939, p. 373), advances much the same view as that expressed in the following statement by Camp- bell (*RES* 7 (1956), 65 fn. 2), which reflects the general tendencies noted above: 'comparative clauses with *þonne* . . . take the subjunc- tive only after a positive indicative principal clause . . . for the pur- poses of these rules, a positive real question counts as positive, but a positive rhetorical question as virtually a negated statement'. Both Campbell and Behaghel believe in the existence of a 'rule'. Campbell (ibid.) explains exceptions in which a negative principal clause is followed by a subjunctive as 'largely due to the use of familiar sentence-patterns in positions not syntactically justified', while to

Behaghel (*DS* iii. 626) 'Widersprüche gegen diese Regel im An. und Ae., insbesondere das Auftreten des Ind. bei positivem Hauptsatz sind nicht anders zu beurteilen als die entsprechenden Verhältnisse im Mhd., nämlich als Auflösungen der alten Regel.'[172] Whether this 'old rule' was ever completely observed is impossible to say. It certainly was not in OE, as Hotz (p. 71) knew and as we have seen above.

§3226. Small (1924, p. 3) attempts to explain what he recognizes are tendencies, not 'rules': 'when the main clause is negative the indicative usually occurs, *because the sense of the subordinate clause describes an actual fact or occurrence*' [his italics]. I do not find this either plausible or illuminating. I cannot see that the 'actuality' differs in any of the following MnE variations 'He is stronger/not weaker than I am' and 'He is weaker/not stronger than I am' or in any of these OE sentences: *ÆCHom* ii. 550. 13 *On ðam twam pundum is mare getacnung þonne on ðam fif pundum sy* but *ÆCHom* i. 220. 25 *Ac we habbað nu micele maran endebyrdnysse þære Cristes bec gesæd þonne ðis dægðerlice godspel behæfð* and *ÆCHom* i. 356. 6 (§3223); and *ÆCHom* ii. 584. 23 *Mare is þin wisdom and ðin weorc þonne se hlisa wære þe ic gehyrde* but *ÆCHom* i. 118. 26 . . . *ðaða he wolde beon betera ðonne hine se Ælmihtiga Scyppend gesceop* and *ÆCHom* i. 104. 5 (§3223). It is clear that the subjunctive does not necessarily imply that the content of the *þonne* clause is false, uncertain, or impossible. Small (1924, p. 3) also tells us that 'in AS. and in Gothic the mode of the comparative clause is governed by the *sense* or *meaning* of the clause and has nothing to do with the fact that the clause is one of *comparison*'. This is probably true as far as it goes. But neither it nor his later comment on it (Small 1930, pp. 379-80) accounts for the variations in mood in what appear to a modern reader to be similar situations.

§3227. Behre (pp. 270-7) attempts a psychological explanation. In general, the indicative is used when 'the content of the dependent clause is presented directly to the hearer . . . to record a fact without any implication as to the speaker's attitude of mind' (p. 276), whereas (p. 277)

to sum up our results: the subjunctive in clauses introduced by the comparative particle *þonne* is of a volitional nature. After an affirmative main clause the volitional subjunctive is generally concessive in character, whereas after a negative main clause it may be optative, hortative, preceptive, or concessive.

[172] 'Examples contradicting this rule in ON and OE, especially the occurrence of the indicative with a positive main clause, should be regarded no differently from the corresponding examples in MHG, that is, as denials of the old rule.'

This, like many such explanations, is circular. It does not explain why the content of the *þonne* clause is sometimes presented objectively, but is sometimes coloured by the speaker's or writer's attitude. The explanation for this is lost with the minds of those who produced the various sentences. There I must leave it—for the time being at least.

f. Sentences with a principal clause and a non-comparative subordinate clause governed by þonne

§3228. This pattern is not very common. Usually the second clause is a noun clause with idiomatic absence of conj. *þæt* after *þonne*; see §3232. The nature of the element with which this clause is contrasted varies widely. Examples include (with a noun) *ÆCHom* ii. 522. 7 *Næfð nan man maran lufe þonne he sylle his sawle for his freondum* and

Ex 406   He þæt gecyðde   . . .
                þæt he him lifdagas   leofran ne wisse
                þonne he hyrde   heofoncyninge;

(with an interrogative) *CP* 43. 10 *Hwæt is ðonne betere ða hwile ðe we libben, ðonne we ures flæsces lustum ne libben, ac ðæs bebodum ðe for us dead wæs ⁊ eft aras?*; (with a negative pronoun) *Solil* 4. 4 *nat ic þonne nanwiht betere þonne þu ðe gebidde*; (with a verb) *CP* 27. 18 . . . *ac mid hira agenre gewilnunge hie bioð onbærnede, ðæt hie gereafiað sua heane lariowdom suiðor ðonne hi hine geearnien*; (with an inflected infinitive) *ÆCHom* ii. 154. 28 (§3211), where I disagree with Thorpe, who appears to see a comparison between *gewilnode*—rather than *to ðoligenne*—and *he cepte*; (with a passive infinitive) *Bede* 294. 10 *þonon monegum wæs gesewen ⁊ oft cweden, þætte swelces modes wer ma gedafonade beon to biscope gehalgad, þonne cyning wære*; and (with a phrase) *LawAf* 32 *Gif mon folcleasunge gewyrce ⁊ hio on hine geresp weorðe, mid nanum leohtran ðinge gebete þonne him mon aceorfe þa tungon of*. To these we can add *ÆCHom* ii. 146. 27 . . . *and ðe is leofre on ðisum wacum scræfum ðonne ðu on healle healic biscop sitte*, where the comparison seems to be between an unexpressed infinitive *beon* (or *sittan*) and the noun clause.

§3229. Exceptionally, we find *þæt* expressed after *þonne* in *ÆC Hom* ii. 368. 14 *Hwæt mæg beon mare bliss to gehyrenne þonne þæt we moton wunian mid þæs Ælmihtigan Godes Suna on his heofenlicum ðrymme ecelice . . . ?* In

Rid 40. 58   Ic eom on goman   gena swetra
                  þonne þu beobread   blende mid hunige,

þonne may seem to represent *þonne þonne* 'than when/if', but again
we probably have unexpressed *þæt*. So I prefer to supply mentally
þæt rather than *þonne* in

PPs 118. 9   On hwan mæg se iunga   on godne weg
                  rihtran þe rædran   ræd gemittan,
                  þonne he þine wisan   word gehealde?,

Latin *In quo corrigit iunior viam suam? in custodiendo sermones
tuos.*

§3230. We also find sentences in which the contrast is between a
personal pronoun and an antecedent + an adjective clause, e.g.
ÆCHom ii. 78. 16 . . . *forðan ðe hi gewitað to heofenan rice hrædlic-
or þonne ða ðe fram cildhade Gode þeowodon*; compare *ÆCHom*
ii. 538. 8 *Eaðelicor we forberað þa frecednyssa ðe we witon on ær,
þonne ða ðe us færlice becumað*, which exemplifies the pattern discussed in §3236.

§3231. The mood in the subordinate clauses governed by *þonne* in
examples of this pattern is determined by the context and by the
rules appropriate to the type of clause involved; see the Indexes.

g. Sentences with a principal clause and two non-comparative clauses linked by þonne

(1) Noun clauses

§3232. The most common form of this pattern is that in which two
noun clauses are compared. All such examples known to me, with
the exception of those quoted in §3235, share the following characteristics: the noun clauses contain two possible or hypothetical
actions or situations which are being weighed; consequently the verbs
have subjunctive forms or ambiguous forms which are to be taken as
subjunctive (see Behre, pp. 272–3); the conj. *þæt* is unexpressed in
accordance with OE idiom (see §§3210 and 3211); and the principal clause is positive—here my observations agree with those of
Behaghel (*DS* iii, §1281). The last characteristic is, I think, understandable, since a positive preference is being expressed for the first
alternative. If we read ☆*Him nære swa ðeah na wyrse* . . . in *ÆCHom*
ii. 480. 8 *Him wære swa ðeah betere þæt he forburne þonne he
ætburste*, the issue would remain open.

§3233. Typical examples from the prose include *Or* 82. 28, *Or* 174. 25, and *Or* 210. 22 *Æfter þæm þe ðæt gedon wæs, hie cwædon þæt him leofre wære þæt hie mid þære byrig ætgædere forwurdon þonne hie mon butan him towurpe*; *BlHom* 33. 22 and *BlHom* 101. 23 *Eac we magon geþencean þæt þæt hefigre is, þæt man mid mandædum 7 mid synnum him sylfum geearnige edwit, þonne mon mid godum 7 soþfæstum dædum geearnige him þa ecean ræste æfter þisse worlde*; *Ch* 1445, *Ch* 1446, and *Ch* 1447 *þa cwæð Æðelstan þ him leofre wære þ hit to fyre oððe flode gewurde þonne he hit æfre gebide*; and *ÆCHom* i. 178. 34 *forði læsse pleoh bið þam cristenum men þæt he flæsces bruce, þonne he on ðissere halgan tide wifes bruce* and *ÆCHom* ii. 244. 20 *ac hit is anfealdlice gecweden þæt him betere wære þæt he næfre nære ðonne he yfele wære.*

§3234. There are four such examples in the poetry, viz. *PPs* 83. 10, where *þonne* = *magis quam*, *PPs* 118. 72, *Beo* 1384 *Selre bið æghwæm,* ‖ *þæt he his freond wrece, þonne he fela murne*, and

Mald 31		and eow betere is
	þæt ge þisne garræs	mid gafole forgyldon,
	þon we swa hearde	hilde dælon.

§3235. As noted in §3232, the mood in the examples so far cited is subjunctive or subjunctive equivalent because two possibilities or hypotheses are being compared. But in *ÆCHom* i. 226. 14 *Mare wundor wæs, þæt he of deaðe aras, þonne he cucu of ðære rode abræce. Mare miht wæs, þæt he ðone dead mid his æriste tobræc, þonne he his lif geheolde, of ðære rode astigende*, Ælfric is contrasting facts (as he and I see them) with accepted impossibilities; hence the contrast between the indicatives and the subjunctives. In *ÆC Hom* i. 184. 26 *Mare wundor is þæt God Ælmihtig ælce dæg fet ealne middangeard, and gewissað þa godan, þonne þæt wundor wære, þæt he þa gefylde fif ðusend manna mid fif hlafum*, the comparison is between two facts. The subjunctive *wære* is not unexpected after *þonne*; see §§3222-7.

(2) *Antecedent + adjective clause*

✕ §3236. It will suffice to cite a few examples of this pattern: *ÆC Hom* i. 300. 34, *ÆCHom* ii. 538. 8 (§3230), *ÆCHom* ii. 554. 27, *ÆCHom* ii. 94. 5 *Sind swa ðeah miccle ma ðæra þe be heora agenum lustum lybban willað, þonne ðæra þe ðysre deopnysse cepan*—cf. *ÆCHom* i. 536. 22 *Micele ma is þæra manna þe lybbað be agenum lustum, ðonne þæra sy þe heora lifes ðeawas æfter Godes bebodum gerihtlæcað*, where the verb *sy* '[there] is' is expressed after *þonne*

—and *ÆCHom* ii. 544. 9 . . . *and se ðe his mod gewylt is betera ðonne se ðe burh oferwinð*. These invite comparison with the examples in §3221, where we have non-expression or non-repetition of the antecedent and/or relative. On the fluctuations of mood in these examples, see §§3222-7.

(3) *Clauses of condition*

§3237. Here we are concerned with three difficult examples from the poetry, viz. *JDay i* 73, *Soul i* 76 (§3415), and the corresponding *Soul ii* 71. For reasons of space, I must refer the reader to my discussion of these in Mitchell 1959, pp. 485-6.

(4) *Non-expression of the second compared element*

§3238. We find here occasional examples similar to those discussed in §§3220-1, in which both *ponne* and the second compared element —here a clause—have to be or can be supplied from the context. In *ÆCHom* i. 528. 21 *Witodlice ge geseoð pæt gehwam sceamað, gif he gelaðod bið to woruldlicum gyftum, pæt he waclice gescryd cume to pære scortan blisse; ac micele mare sceamu bið pam ðe mid horium reafe cymð to Godes gyftum, pæt he for his fulum gyrelan fram pære ecan blisse ascofen beo into ecum peostrum*, we can supply *ponne pam ðe waclice gescryd cymð to woruldlicum gyftum*. In *ÆCHom* ii. 440. 17 *Martha wæs geornful hu heo mihte God fedan; Maria hogode swiðor hu heo mihte, purh Godes lare, hire sawle gereordigan*, we can supply *ponne Martha*, with *hogode swiðor* meaning 'took stronger/ better thought', or *ponne hu heo mihte God fedan*, with *swiðor* meaning 'rather'. In *ÆCHom* i. 482. 26 *peah hwæðere gif we hwær unwærlice swerion, and se að us geneadige to wyrsan dæde, ponne bið us rædlicor pæt we ðone maran gylt forbugon, and ðone að wið God gebetan*, the sense is that it is better to avoid the great guilt than to commit it.

3. *þE* 'THAN'?

§3239. Does indeclinable *þe* ever mean 'than'? I give in §§3243-50 reasons for rejecting the view that it carries this sense in *þon ma þe* and combinations like it. Here we are concerned with the possibility that *þe* means 'than' in other contexts. Small (1930, p. 382 fn. 10) has no doubt about the answer:

The two or three times in all the Old English literature when *þe* is clearly a writing for *þonne* are undoubtedly scribal errors (cf. *MLN* 41, 302, n. 2). I doubt if anyone, in view of the vast number of occurrences of *þonne* as the particle of comparison in OE, would maintain that these two or three chance writings in late MSS indicate an idiomatic use of the relative particle as a free substitute for the conjunction of inequality. From a recent reading of all the extant OE writings I am convinced that the particle, *þe*, never at any time embraced the meaning or function of the subordinate conjunction of comparison, *þonne*.

I accept the general verdict that *þe* never served 'as a free substitute' for *þonne* 'than', but disagree with some of the details of Small's argument.

§3240. The proposed examples (with the exception of *Bo* 79. 10, dismissed in §3207, and of *CP* 319. 18 and *ÆCHom* i. 154. 16, both of which are cited by *OED*, s.v. *The, particle* 1. b., but belong with the examples discussed in §§3243-50) all involve compound numerals formed by subtraction and the use of *læs* or *wana*; see §§ 573-6. In those involving *læs* we can distinguish two types. Type A is exemplified in *ChronE* 27. 30 (641) *7 he rixode twa læs xxx geara* and *ChronE* 27. 33 (643) . . . *se wæs biscop an læs xx wintra 7 ii monðas 7 xxi daga*. Small's first explanation of these (1926, p. 302 fn. 2) was that 'the comparative particle is omitted altogether' and that they 'may be due to careless copying of manuscripts'. Type B is seen in *ChronA* 91. 28 (901) *7 he heold þæt rice oþrum healfum læs þe xxx wintra* and *BlHom* 215. 34 *Ða he þa hæfde twæm læs þe twentig wintra* . . . , where Small (ibid.) saw *þe* as 'probably a scribal error for the regular *þonne* or *þanne*. Compare *ibid.* 1048 [*ChronE* 173. 4] *ma þanne xx.*' I suppose that Small's purpose in introducing this last example—it reads *ChronE* 173. 3 (1048) . . . *7 ofslogon ægðer ge wiðinnan ge wiðutan ma þanne xx manna*—was to establish a type C as the original which gave type B by scribal miswriting of *þe* for *þonne* and type A by scribal omission of *þe* or *þonne*. A closer and more relevant parallel for his argument would have been *ChronA* 91. 19 (897) *þy ilcan sumera forwearð no læs þonne xx scipa*. But neither of these provides a secure basis for comparison, for they are not compound numerals and there are to the best of my knowledge no numerals of the pattern *☆an læs þonne xx* 'nineteen'. This reinforces my own feeling that type A represents the original form of these numerals. Examples of this type invite comparison with Latin numerals and may be calques on them; note *ÆGram* 287. 6 *Man cweð eac undeuiginti, an læs twentig, duodeuiginti, twam læs twentig, duodetriginta, twam læs þrittig et cetera*. I am further strengthened in this belief by the fact that Small (1929, pp. 74-9)—contradicting himself without apparently realizing it—explained the two examples of type A above and others like them 'as examples of the case-construction' in which a comparative + the dative expressed comparison, as in *Bo* 79. 10

. . . *forþam ðe nan mihtigra þe nis* (§3207); see §§1358-64. So the smaller numerals represent the dative of measure 'by *x* (years)'; the larger numerals *y* 'are *indeclinable* nouns standing in the *dative relation* to the preceding comparatives' (Small 1929, p. 76); and the whole phrase means literally 'less than *y* by *x* (years)'. Of the truth of this explanation, he claims (1929, p. 74), 'there can be no doubt'. I agree and in conclusion quote part of his exposition (1929, p. 77):

Some would explain the syntax of all the above examples containing *læs* as if that word had become a stereotyped quasi-preposition equivalent to *minus* even in OE, thus, *Chronicle* 27, A.D. 641, E: Ond he rixode twa læs XXX geara = 'And he ruled thirty years less two'. The *NED* (s.v. *less*, A. I. 4) cites three of the OE occurrences as examples of this prepositional use. To attribute this idiom to OE, however, is quite wrong. The word order in all the OE examples is decidedly against it [but see my §3242 fn.], and *læs* retained its true comparative force to the end of the period. There is not a single example of anything like 'thirty less two' for 'twenty-eight' in OE; it is always 'two less thirty', etc., in which the case relationship of *thirty* plainly answers to the comparative force of *less*, and in which *minus* cannot be substituted for the latter.

§3241. Small does not explain type B examples in the light of this second theory, but his handling of examples with *wana þe* (my §3242) suggests that he would have shared the view I expound below. If we accept type A as the original—as we now seem bound to do—we must reject the view that *þe* in type B means 'than' and explain it as an intrusion. It could, I suppose, be seen as a form of the instr. *þy* serving to express comparison 'than that' (see §3245), with the larger numeral *y* in apposition. But I am more inclined to explain it as indeclinable *þe* inserted with some idea of making a connection which seemed necessary because the numerals which followed *læs* were indeclinable and/or because the dative of comparison was dying out and was therefore not recognized. We could perhaps suggest an analogy with *þon ma þe* and the like (§§3243-50) or—less likely, since the forms with *þe* are later, not earlier (§2929)—with *þy læs þe* 'lest'. Such confusion is not unknown in OE; see, for example, §3246. This is not the same as the explanation advanced by Joly (1967, p. 15 fn. 19): 'In fact, the use of *þe* (the relative particle) instead of *þonne* (the comparative particle) is due to an identity of function: both help to *coordinate* sentences.' This view arises from the same basic misconception as led Joly to misinterpret *Bo* 79. 10 (§3207) and assigns a definite role to *þe* in type B examples, whereas I regard it as an accidental and erroneous intrusion.

§3242. The idiom with *wan, wana* is different. The word is an adjective 'wanting, lacking', generally indeclinable and taking either the

genitive of what is missing, e.g. *BlHom* 17. 36 *wite he þæt he biδ
wana þæs ecan leohtes*, or *of* + dative, e.g. *ÆGram* 202. 10 *desum,
ic eom wana of δam getele*. All the examples known to me involve
the numeral *an* and in all but one we find the genitive *anes* dependent on *wana*; cf. *BlHom* 17. 36 above. So *Bede(Ca)* 252. 9 *anes
wona xx wintra* means 'twenty winters lacking one'.[173] The exception is *ChronE* 119. 8 (972) *7 he wæs þa ana wana xxx wintra*,
where, as Rissanen (p. 33) points out, MS *E*'s *ana* and MS *D*'s *ane*
may be 'caused by the gradual levelling and loss of OE case endings'.
We can take *Bede(Ca)* 252. 9 *anes wona xx wintra* as exemplifying
our type A here. In *Bede(B)* 252. 9 *an læs δe twentig wintra*, we have
type B with *læs* (§3240). But in *Bede(O)* 252. 9 *anes wana þe xx
wintra* and *Bede(T)* 252. 9 *anes won δe twentig wintra*, we have type
B with *wana*. Small (1929, p. 75 fn. 1) sees *þe* in examples like the
last two as the result of a change by which *wana* was apprehended as
a preposition or possibly even as a subordinating conjunction rather
than as an adjective—'lacking' > 'lacking from' > 'from'. 'The
change . . . was sometimes indicated, and probably bridged over, by
the addition of one of the particles *of* or *þe*, as for example, *Ælfric's
Grammar* (Zupitza) 202. 11: Ic eom *wana of* δam getele. *Andreas*
1040: Anes *wana þe* fiftig.' Again, I am in agreement with the basic
proposition that *þe* in these examples is an accidental and erroneous
intrusion.

4. þON/þY/þE + A COMPARATIVE + þE = A COMPARATIVE + þONNE

§3243. The authority on this construction is G. W. Small. His first
discussion (Small 1926) is supplemented by his longer treatment
(Small 1930), where he gives a necessary warning against confusing
the pattern under discussion with apparently similar constructions
(1930, pp. 369-70)—they include particularly those expressing
proportion (§§3287-9 and 3334-46)—and cites sixty examples of
it from the prose and all seven from the poetry (1930, pp. 370-7)—
his *Lch* ii. 352. 3 is *MCharm* 7. 12. Typical examples—which demonstrate that 'this locution is not necessarily an indivisible syntactic
unit' (Joly 1967, p. 14)—include *Bo* 46. 18 . . . *ne hine mon ne
mæg þon eδ on him geniman δe mon mæg þa sunnan awendan of
hiere stede, Bo* 126. 12 *Ac hio ne biδ þeah þy near þære sæ δe hio
biδ on midne dæg, ÆCHom* i. 154. 16 (§3362), *ÆCHom* i. 212. 23

---

[173] This, of course, invalidates Small's argument (my §3240) that the element-order in
all the OE examples is against explaining *twa læs xxx geara* as 'thirty years less two'. But it
does not, in my opinion, invalidate his conclusion.

and sealdon us bysne þæt we ne sceolon, for nanum ehtnyssum oððe earfoðnyssum, urne geleafan forlætan, and fram Criste bugan, ðe ma ðe hi dydon, ÆCHom ii. 318. 28 *ðe ma ðe* (an example missed by Small), *HomU* 35. 206. 14 *ac men him nellað gelefan þe ma þe heo Noe dydon,*

Whale 78　　　　　　　　　　　nagon hwyrft ne swice,
　　　　　　　utsiþ æfre,　　þa þær in cumað,
　　　　　　　þon ma þe þa fiscas　　faraðlacende
　　　　　　　of þæs hwæles fenge　　hweorfan motan,

and

Met 20. 179　　　. . . þæt hire þy læsse　　on ðæm lytlan ne bið
　　　　　　　anum fingre　　þe hire on eallum bið
　　　　　　　þæm lichoman.

We also find 'contracted' comparative clauses in which the verb is unexpressed, e.g. *Bo* 111. 17 *7 se þe hiora welt ne myrnð nauþer ne friend ne fiend þe ma þe wedende hund*, *CP* 215. 13 . . . *ðæt hi hira selfra ne agon ðy mare geweald ðe oðerra monna*, *CP* 319. 18, *Æ Gram* 253. 4 *and hi næfre ne ateoriað on naðrum getele þe ma þe on casum*, *Dan* 263 *Næs him se sweg to sorge ðon ma þe sunnan scima*, and

Met 28. 37　　　Ne bið hio on æfen　　ne on ærmorgen
　　　　　　　merestreame þe near　　ðe on midne dæg,

and two sentences in which something has to be supplied in the comparative clause, viz. *Mart 2* 214. 9 . . . *ond het þone cnyht lædan on þæt hus ond het fif mædenu swyðe geglengede gangan on þæt hus. þa onhylde se halga cnyht hys ansyne on dune ond nolde hig na geseon þe ma þe fif næddran crupon on þæt hus* '. . . and desired to gaze upon them no more than [he would have desired to gaze if] five serpents had crept into the house' and *Mart 2* 218. 7 *þa cwæð heo 'nis me þynes weales hæmed næfre þe leofre þe me nædre to-slyte'* 'Then she said "Intercourse with your servant is not more pleasing to me than [that or (*Small 1930, p. 376*) the sensation would be if] a serpent should tear me apart".'

§3244. Some statistics culled from Small 1930, pp. 377–81, follow. The comparative may be that of an adjective (eight examples, including *Mart 2* 218. 7 and *Met* 20. 179, both in §3243) or an adverb (fifty-nine examples, including the remainder in §3243; of these, forty-nine have *ma*). The first element is *þon* in sixteen examples, *þy* in six, and *þe* in forty-five. There is no distinction of function; these forms are interchangeable here, as they often are elsewhere in OE.

Small 'is led to believe that the form *þon* was the first to enter the first part of the construction . . . the other forms of the demonstrative having been attracted into it'. The verb of the comparative clause is expressed thirty-eight times and has to be understood twenty-nine times. The nature of the principal clause and the mood of the verb in the comparative clause will be considered below.

§3245. The idiom consists of two parts, the division coming after the comparative. The first part, Small (1930, p. 381) reminds us, 'exists as a separate idiom and has a wide-spread use in all periods of English down to the present day with cognate forms in all the other Germanic languages'. Fowler (*Modern English Usage* (1st edn.), s.v. *the* 5) gives a masterly account of the idiom in MnE. Typical OE examples include

Beo 2275   He gesecean sceall
                  hord on hrusan,   þær he hæðen gold
                  warað wintrum frod;   ne byð him wihte ðy sel,

El 94   þa þæt leoht gewat,
                  up siðode,   ond se ar somed,
                  on clænra gemang.   Cyning wæs þy bliðra
                  ond þe sorgleasra,   secga aldor,
                  on fyrhðsefan,   þurh þa fægeran gesyhð,

and

Brun 44   Gelpan ne þorfte
                  beorn blandenfeax   bilgeslehtes,
                  eald inwidda,   ne Anlaf þy ma.

More, including some from the prose, will be found in Small 1926, pp. 303–7.[174] The three quoted above have been selected for their relevance to Small's penetrating comment (1926, p. 305): 'If one should ask in these examples, "Better than what?" "Happier than what?" "More than what?" one would find that the idiom invariably points back to some condition or fact previously mentioned or *plainly understood*' [his italics]. The answer to these questions is—according to Small's theory, which I accept—the instr. *þon/þy/þe* meaning 'than that' or 'than before', and so respectively (*Beo* 2275) 'than in the previously-described state of being, without gold'; (*El* 94) 'than in the previously-described state of fear'; and (*Brun* 44) 'than the previously-mentioned Costontinus'. Small (1926, p. 304)

---

[174] Small's list is far from complete. We can add from *ÆCHom* the following: *ÆCHom* i. 4. 7, 224. 6, 250. 1, 278. 27, 334. 5 and 6, 380. 28, 406. 34, 418. 5, 556. 27 and 29; and *ÆCHom* ii. 462. 23, 538. 7 and 11.

rejects the two solutions proposed by Delbrück for *El* 94 and by
other writers for other examples. He rules out both the proposal that
þon/þy/þe is the instrumental of measure—'to translate *þy bliðra*
and *þe sorgleasra* as "happier and more carefree *by that much*" gives
no meaning to the context because there is no previous measure to
be referred to that could serve as the antecedent of measure, and *þy*
(or *þe*) is useless without an antecedent'—and the proposal that it is
the instrumental of means—' "happier by that means" is clearly out
of the question here, since the phrase, *þurh þa fægeran gesyhð*, covers
that aspect of the situation fully and explicitly'. Some scholars
would appear to want it both ways; thus the Wrenn–CH translation
of *Beo* 2277b is 'and not be one whit the better for it'. Small (1926,
p. 305) concludes that 'the context must be the guide, and many of
these occurrences before the comparative, by referring back to a fact
or condition previously mentioned as the *basis for comparison*, serve
to complete the formula of comparison and are in fact, *instrumentals
of comparison*'. In his later treatment of the first part of the formula
(1930, pp. 384–8), he replaces this tentative statement with a justifiably firm one: 'In the opinion of the writer the form *the* immediately before the comparative *never*, from OE to PE, means "by that
much". It always in that position refers to a condition or object
previously named or understood, and is functionally a true case of
comparison, meaning not "*by* that", but "*than* that" or "*than* before". . . .' I agree, subject to the reservations about *no þy ær* made
in §1801 and to the comments made in §3341 about the *þy/þe . . .
þy/þe* patterns. *Lch* ii. 254. 9 *gif hit* [*blod*] *swiþe read sie oþþe won
þonne bið hit þy þe swiþor to lætanne. gif hit clæne oþþe hluttor sie
læt þy þe læsse*, which he translates 'quite literally, "If the blood be
very red or dark, then it is to be let for that reason more abundantly
than usual; if it be clean or clear then because of that, let less *than
before*" ', is very apposite here, for 'the two instrumental forms
constitute a challenge to the translators who habitually use *the*
before the comparative in the sense of *cause* or *measure*' (Small
1930, pp. 384–5).

§3246. The rejection of these two proposals rules out those explanations of the full formula which take the first *þy/þon/þe* as an
instrumental of means (or cause) or of measure and the second as
'than'. Small argues convincingly against this (1926, p. 312, and
1930, pp. 381–2):

In the opinion of the present writer this view is not tenable after a close study of
the construction in its varying context. . . . Moreover, the forcing of the relative
particle, *þe*, into the function and meaning of the subordinate conjunction of

inequality, *þonne*, 'than', is unwarranted by usage outside of our particular construction (1930, p. 381).

The fact that there is a hard core of examples in which we have the instrumental + a comparative + *þonne* (not *þe*)—(with the verb after *þonne* expressed) *Or* 260. 28 *He hæfde giet þe ma unþeawa þonne his eam hæfde ær Gaius, ÆLS* 12. 106, *HomU* 27. 146. 19, *Met* 14. 9, and possibly *Az* 85 (see §3224), and (with the verb after *þonne* unexpressed)

Beo 503   forþon þe he ne uþe,   þæt ænig oðer man
                   æfre mærða þon ma   middangeardes
                   gehede under heofenum þonne he sylfa,

Soul i 52, and the corresponding *Soul ii* 49—is not (I believe) proof that *þe* and *þonne* are interchangeable, but rather demonstrates that even in OE there were writers who could be posthumously convicted of having offended against an Anglo-Saxon equivalent of Fowler's dictum (*Modern English Usage* (1st edn.), s.v. *the* 5) that 'good writers do not, and bad writers do, allow themselves a *than* after a comparative that has *the* before it'. Small (1930, p. 383 fn. 12) explains these as blendings due to the intervention of some other part of the sentence between the two parts of the construction with *þe*, as a result of which the speaker 'loses the connection somewhat and falls back unnecessarily on the regular *þonne* construction'. Scribal error is (I believe) responsible for *HomU(B)* 37. 242. 12 *þe ma þonne*, where MS *H* has *na ma þe*. Either *na ma þonne* or *þe ma þe* would be more acceptable than the two manuscript readings, if I am right in believing that the construction condemned by Fowler was not syntactically sound in OE either.

§3247. The explanation advocated by Small and preferred by myself depends on our acceptance of the already stated proposition that the first element is an instrumental of comparison meaning 'than that' or 'than before'.[175] After a review of the evidence for such an instrumental (1926, pp. 307-9), Small concludes that 'we may, perhaps, go as far as to say that in the complex syncretism of forms associated with the instrumental case in Germanic, there was a survival

---

[175] Small (1930, p. 386) says that Fowler's conclusion (*Modern English Usage* (1st edn.), s.v. *the* 5)—reached as it was without reference to earlier forms of the construction—'is precisely the same as that favored above', viz. that the first element is the instrumental of comparison and not that of means or measure. 'Precisely' is not quite the word. Fowler explicitly says that the original meaning of *the* is 'in the single type *by that* (i.e. *thereby* or *on that account*, or sometimes *by so much* or *by that amount*)'. What is significant is the statement by Fowler quoted in §3246. This is strong support for Small's proposition that the final *þe* in the full formula does not mean 'than'. His phrase 'precisely the same' could justly be used of what is implied in that statement.

of an Indo-European instrumental of comparison'. He discusses this
usage at length elsewhere (1929, pp. 89-96), where (in a passage
quoted in §3261) he notes its restriction to the demonstrative pronoun *se, seo, þæt*, in negative sentences. To this first element is
added the indeclinable particle *þe* to indicate a subordinate relationship, just as it does in formulae like *forþam þe*; see §§2424-30 and
3041 and Small 1930, pp. 382-3. The following exposition, given by
Small (1926, pp. 312-13), which refers to *Dan* 263 and *Met* 28. 37
(both in §3243), is illuminating:

we may take the following particle, *þe*, in one of its established functions of
introducing substantive clauses. This, in my opinion, gives the true syntactical
analysis of our idiom and reveals the basic meaning: *Daniel* 264,—'To them the
roaring flame was no more harmful *than this* (*næs þon ma*), namely, (*þe*) sunshine,' or, 'than this, namely, what sunshine is.' *Metres of Boethius* 28, 36,—
'Neither in the evening nor at dawn is it (the sun) nearer to the sea than this
(*þe near*), namely, (*þe*) its distance at noon,' or, 'what it is at noon.' Thus, the
demonstrative pronoun and the relative particle, *þon . . . þe, þy . . . þe*, or *þe
. . . þe*, are together equivalent to the comparative particle, *than* (*þonne*); however, the function of comparison lies not in the relative particle but in the preceding demonstrative pronoun, *þon* (*þy, þe*), functioning as an instrumental of
comparison.

§3248. 'The sixty-seven examples of this subordinate conjunction',
says Small (1930, p. 377), 'all follow main clauses that are colored
with *doubt* or *negation*'; so too does *ÆCHom* ii. 318. 28 (§3243).
In fact they all follow negative main clauses except that in *Bo* 25. 18
wið þas ic wat þu wilt higian þon ær þe ðu hine ongitest, which is not
really on all fours with the other examples, since *þon ær þe* means
'before'; see Small 1930, p. 390 fn. 24. So we can confidently accept
Small's other formulation (1930, p. 381) that the formula is 'a variant
means of expressing inequality in negative sentences', a rare alternative to the comparative with *þonne* and to the dative of comparison
and one whose distribution is restricted to negative sentences; see
Small 1930, p. 377.

§3249. Of the thirty-eight expressed verbs, twenty-eight are indicative (so too *ÆCHom* ii. 318. 28), eight are ambiguous, and two—
those in *Bo* 138. 15 and *MCharm* 7. 13 *ne ace þe þon ma þe eorþan
on eare ace*—are subjunctive referring to what is hypothetical or uncertain. There is therefore no mechanical rule that a negated principal
clause must be followed by an indicative in the comparative clause.

§3250. It is appropriate that the last words should be those of
Small: 'the *influence of Latin* upon our construction is shown to

have been nothing at all' (1930, p. 378) and a longer comment (1930, pp. 380-1):

> Our idiom seems to have *flourished principally in the prose*, if the extant writings are truly representative, and impresses one as having originated in racy colloquial speech. By the time of Alfred it had become frequent in the written language, but was apparently too colloquial to enter extensively into the more conservative poetical writings. This locution was not formed through necessity but as a variant means of expressing inequality in negative sentences. It represents a play upon the resources of language, perhaps the kind of capricious syntactical experiment that bobs up continually in the living speech. There was nothing foreign about the idiom; it had its vogue and died as a purely English experiment.

Those requiring further assurance or more details should consult Small 1930 and Small 1926 and the references cited there. I give my testimony for what it is worth: I think Small's theory is right.

5. OTHER METHODS OF EXPRESSING COMPARISONS OF INEQUALITY

a. Ac

§3251. *Ac* comes close to meaning 'than' in

Beo 134

                                Næs hit lengra fyrst
        ac ymb ane niht   eft gefremede
        morðbeala mare,

where Gehse (pp. 38-9) detects a mixture of comparative and adversative constructions. There may be more such examples. I have to admit that I have not been on the lookout for them.

b. *Ær conjunction, alone and in combination*

§3252. For examples in which this conjunction means 'with greater probability than' or 'rather than', see §§2721 and 2724. In the latter, an element of wish or purpose is necessary, as in *ÆCHom* ii. 308. 9 *Alexander papa, ic sece ærest æt þe, þæt þu me ardlice secge hwæt se intinga sy þæt ge wyllað sweltan sylfwilles for Criste, ærðan ðe ge æfre his geleafan wiðsacan.* In

Beo 1368

        Ðeah þe hæðstapa   hundum geswenced,
        heorot hornum trum   holtwudu sece,
        feorran geflymed,   ær he feorh seleð,
        aldor on ofre,   ær he in wille,
        hafelan beorgan;   nis þæt heoru stow!,

I prefer Wrenn–CH's purely temporal 'sooner than' to Talbot Donaldson's 'rather . . . than', which to me implies a weighing of alternatives;
the instinctive reaction of the unthinking stag emphasizes the horror
of the mere and so underlines Beowulf's courage.

c. Butan *and* nemne

§3253. *Butan* and *nemne* sometimes come close to meaning 'than'
after a negative principal clause or after a rhetorical question containing a comparative, e.g. *ÆCHom* i. 498. 1 *forðan ðe he ne geðafode
þæt ðæra ma manna inne wære, buton se fæder, and seo modor, and
his ðry leorningcnihtas, ÆCHom* ii. 116. 4 . . . *and ða Iudeiscan ne
hedað na mare buton ðære stæflican gereccednysse, WHom(EI)* 20.
127 . . . *7 la, hwæt is ænig oðer on eallum þam gelimpum butan
Godes yrre ofer þas þeode, swutol 7 gesæne?*, and

And 662
                    Næs þær folces ma
      on siðfate,   sinra leoda,
      nemne ellefne   orettmæcgas,
      geteled tireadige.

On the status of *butan* and *nemne* in these and similar sentences, see
§§3629–31 and 3649–50.

d. Oþer (. . .) oþer

§3254. The correlative use of *oþer (. . .) oþer* in the sense 'one . . .
(an)other' or 'other than' needs merely to be recorded; examples include *CP* 31. 6 *Ðeah ðæt folc ðyrste ðære lare, hie hie ne magon
drincan, ac hio bið gedrefed midðamðe ða lareowas oðer doð oðer
hie lærað* and *ÆCHom* ii. 574. 1 *Drihten ne oncnæwð hi, forðan ðe
hi sind oðre, oþre hi wæron.*

e. Ne *and* na?

§3255. The first use of these words, and of *nor*, for 'than' are recorded in the period *c.*1375–1400; see *OED*, s.vv., and Joly 1967,
pp. 24–30. I have found no OE examples.

f. Prepositions

§3256. A comparison of inequality may be expressed by a comparative + a prepositional phrase, e.g.

Beo 1282
                          Wæs se gryre læssa
      efne swa micle,   swa bið mægþa cræft,

wiggryre wifes   be wæpnedmen,
þonne heoru bunden,   hamere geþruen,
sweord swate fah   swin ofer helme
ecgum dyhtig   andweard scireð,

where strict grammar would require ☆*be wæpnedmannes*, and *GD(H)* 151. 23 . . . *þa þe þenceað þæt hi beon be dæle beteran toforan oðrum mannum*, where MS *C* has . . . *þa þe þæncað þæt hi syn sylfe ma gode þonne oðre men*. On *ma gode* see §189.

§3257. Visser (i, §275) notes that the type 'taller than him', where 'than' has to be construed as a (quasi-)preposition, does not occur before the sixteenth century 'apart from the isolated instance' in *Matt (Li)* 3. 11 *ðe ðe soðlice æfter mec tocymende* ɫ *toword is strongra ðon mec* ɫ *ðon ic is*, Latin *qui autem post me uenturus est fortior me est*. Here the translator first made an ungrammatical attempt to render Latin *fortior me*—unlike the scribe of *Ru*, who wrote *me strængra*—and then produced the same grammatical alternative as the translator of *WSCp*, who wrote *strengra þonne ic*. This 'isolated instance' is an example of unidiomatic literalness, not a straw in the wind.

§3258. On *butan* and *nemne*, see §§3629–31 and 3649–50.

§3259. The usual translation of Latin *super*, as in *Ps* 50. 8 *lauabis me et super niuem dealbabor*, is *ofer*, as in *KtPs* 75 *and eac ofer snawe self scinende*, but the comparative + *þonne* sometimes occurs, as in *Ps(P)* 50. 8 *and aðweah me þæt ic sy hwitra þonne snaw*. See Small 1924, p. 29, and 1929, pp. 47–9.

g. The genitive, dative, and instrumental, cases

§3260. Nader's suggestion (1882, p. 5) that in *CP* 4. 13 *Ure ieldran* we have a genitive of comparison 'older [ones] than we' was rightly rejected by Wülfing (i, §245) and by Small (1929, p. 86). Wülfing's own suggestion (i, §10a) that the genitive of comparison appears in *Bo* 71. 21 *Gif þu þe wilt don manegra beteran 7 weorðran, þonne scealt þu þe lætan anes wyrsan*, Latin *Dignitatibus fulgere uelis? Danti supplicabis et qui praeire ceteros honore cupis, poscendi humilitate uilesces*, was in its turn rightly rejected by Small (1929, pp. 84–6), who—quoting *CP* 4. 13, above, and *Mald* 276 *þa his betera leg*—saw in *manegra* and *anes* genitives of possession 'the better and superior of many' and 'the inferior (underling) of one person'. Small (1929, pp. 84–8), after discussing more suggested examples from OE and 'other Germanic dialects', sums up:

We may, therefore, quite reasonably conclude that the *genitive* came into use with comparatives whenever the comparatives left the function of an adjective and assumed that of a noun. This in itself eliminates once and for all the possibility as well as the necessity of interpreting such a genitive as the case of comparison.

I agree. But Small left one riddle behind. After quoting *GD(C)* 266. 22 *Hwæt hafað ma se snottra man þam dysigan . . . ?*, Latin *Quid habet amplius sapiens stulto* [or, in some manuscripts, *a stulto*]. . . *?*, he notes that MS *O* has *þæs dysgan* and remarks (1929, p. 66 fn. 1) 'This use of the genitive instead of the dative is only sporadic, being found occasionally in the glosses.' He then refers the reader to the discussion I have just summarized. But there he remains silent about *GD* 266. 22. We must, I suppose, convict the *O* scribe of error here.

§3261. On the dative of comparison see §§1358-64 and, on the instrumental of comparison, which is limited to the demonstrative pronoun *se, seo, þæt,* in negative sentences, §§3243-50. But Small (1929, p. 96) is worth quoting here:

The traces of a case of comparison that we find in the demonstrative forms are thus classed as the *instrumental of comparison* in OE, although different conditions may warrant a different terminology in the other Germanic dialects. One recognizes, however, that this variation upon the case of comparison has something of a stereotyped quality about it; its very limitation to the demonstrative pronoun shows that it was not a free and versatile usage. The further limitation of this instrumental of comparison to negative sentences forces us to conclude that it is not to be placed beside the dative as a *conscious* method of expressing the comparison of inequality in the recorded period of OE speech.

6. COMPARATIVE CLAUSES INTRODUCED BY *SWA*, ALONE AND IN COMBINATION

a. Introductory remarks

§3262. The etymology of *swa* is a difficult question; see *OED*, s.v. *so*, Ericson 1932, pp. 82-5, and Nummenmaa, p. 17. Johnsen (*Ang.* 38 (1914), 97-8) is out of step in postulating that 'the original sense and function of *swa* was also that of a local-demonstrative adverb'. *Swa* is well established in OE as both an adverb and a conjunction. In my opinion the latter derived from the former; see §1688. Nummenmaa (pp. 17-20) offers a summary of both these uses; see also my Index of Words and Phrases.

§3263. The main adverbial use of *swa* is that of comparison, including degree and manner; see §3202. It may modify an adjective, e.g.

ÆCHom i. 88. 23 *swa gehende*; a participle, e.g. *ÆCHom* i. 222. 33 *swa gehiwod*; an adjective + a noun, e.g. *ÆCHom* i. 52. 22 *swa miccles lareowes geleafan*; an adverb, e.g. *ÆCHom* ii. 128. 26 *swa hrædlice*; an adverb + an adjective, e.g. *ÆCHom* ii. 128. 5 *swa miccle mare*; or a verb, e.g. *ÆCHom* i. 572. 29 *And hi swa dydon* and (in final position) *ÆCHom* i. 64. 3 *Hi dydon swa* and *ÆCHom* ii. 322. 17 *Swilce . . . þam rihtwisum ætbredað his rihtwisnysse swa*. In these (and other) functions it may be replaced by *þæs* or *þus*; see the standard dictionaries, Ericson 1932, p. 38, and Sorg, pp. 53–5. *Swa* is used in adverbial combinations such as *ÆCHom* i. 286. 24 *ealswa* (see Jost, *Ang.* 51 (1927), 96–7) and *ÆCHom* ii. 222. 33 *swa ðeah* (see Ericson 1932, pp. 33–6) and as part of a conjunction, e.g. *ÆC Hom* i. 86. 25 *swa þæt*; see the Index of Words and Phrases. Johnsen (*Ang.* 38 (1914), 97–8) records examples of a local-demonstrative use in the Charters, e.g. *Ch* 1165 *Of Wiþelesshete to þe hagan æt Mimfelda. Sua of Mimfelde to þare greten wich.* . . . Ericson (whose work cannot be accepted without checking) notes that in *Bede* 352. 13 *swa* represents Latin *iam* (1932, p. 21); cites examples from *Bede* of what he calls 'the Pepysean, "And *so* to bed" ', including *Bede* 44. 19 *7 swa mid mycele sige ham foran*, where the Latin has *sicque* (1932, pp. 74–5); and records adv. *swa* in correlation with various temporal conjunctions, e.g. *Or* 188. 8 *Mid þæm þe . . . swa*, which he renders '*When . . . then*' (1932, pp. 75–6); see further §2695. I discuss problems associated with initial *swa* in §§3267–70. For a fuller catalogue of the adverbial uses of *swa*, see Ericson 1932, pp. 21–3, 27–32, and 38–42, and BT(S, C).

§3264. Two difficult questions demand mention. First, adverbial *swa* may refer back, as in *ÆCHom* i. 222. 33 *Rihtlice wæs se bydel Cristes æristes swa gehiwod*, or forward, as in *ÆCHom* i. 240. 32 *He flyhð forðan ðe he is hyra, and na hyrde, swilce hit swa gecweden sy, Ne mæg se standan ongean fræcednyssa þæra sceapa, seðe ne gymð þæra sceapa mid lufe*. . . . On the relevance of this to the punctuation and meaning of some passages in the poetry, see Mitchell 1968*b*, pp. 175–8; Chambers (ed.), *Widsith*, pp. 133 and 206–7; Dunning and Bliss, pp. 30–6; and Irving, *Ang.* 90 (1972), 322.

§3265. Second, Nummenmaa (p. 18) observes that 'in connection with some verbs the adverb of manner *swa* may obtain the character of a quasi-object (cf. ModE *he did so*) or of a quasi-predicate (cf. ModE *it is so*)'; cf. Ericson 1932, pp. 22–3. This formulation, which is perhaps based on translations such as *le* or *es* for 'so' rather than on the English idiom itself, has its dangers. I give my reasons for insisting that *swa* is not—and should not be called—a pronoun in §§2379-82. So, while I find myself more in sympathy with Visser when he says of *Met* 11. 102 *gif hit meahte swa* that 'it is doubtful whether this *swa* was apprehended as an object' (i, §557) than when he says that in *Rid* 29. 6 *gif hit swa meahte* 'it is doubtful whether the word *swa*, functioning as a complement to *meahte*, should be looked upon as an object or as an adverbial adjunct' (i, §573), I would dismiss entirely the notion that *swa* could be the object; I cannot imagine how anyone could describe *swa* as the subject of the passive equivalent of *ÆCHom* ii. 46. 18 *ne deð seo culfre na swa.*

§3266. The basis of my classification of the comparative uses of *swa* conjunction is the form of the introductory conjunction and of any elements with which it may be correlative, not whether the clause is one of manner or degree; see §§3202-4. For uses other than the comparative, see §§3319-22.

b. Swa *adverb or conjunction?*

§3267. As with *þa, þonne,* and other words which are used as both adverbs and conjunctions, the problem of the ambiguous adverb/ conjunction arises with initial *swa*. (It is perhaps worth reminding the reader that these terms are not used in the sense in which Ælfric employs *conivnctiones* and *adverbia* in *ÆGram* 265. 11-266. 8.) Ericson (1932, p. 19) says that *swa* in the initial position is 'normally . . . an adverb of manner. Frequently, however, it takes over the sense of a resultant adverb ("therefore") [see further Ericson 1932, pp. 76-7], or it may serve as a mere transitional link between clauses or at the head of a sentence. In such examples, the modal signification is so low that the *swa* approximates "and".' For reasons which will become apparent, it is necessary to distinguish initial *swa* in positive clauses from initial *swa* in negative clauses; Ericson intended his remark to apply only to the former.

§3268. These indeed present few problems in the prose. *Swa* is clearly adverbial in *ÆCHom* i. 60. 33 *Ydel bið se læcedom þe ne mæg ðone untruman gehælan; swa bið eac ydel seo lar ðe ne gehælð ðære sawle leahtras and unðeawas,* with order VS; in *ÆCHom* ii. 42. 1 . . . *and ðu siððan . . . beo æt minum handum gefullod þurh ðone Halgan Gast: swa wit sceolon gefyllan ealle rihtwisnysse,* with order SV; and even in *ÆCHom* i. 182. 16 *Ða genam se Hælend þa fif hlafas, and bletsode, and tobræc, and todælde betwux ðam sittendum: swa gelice eac þa fixas todælde; and hi ealle genoh hæfdon*, with order adv. OV. Sometimes *swa* can be read as a con-junction rather than an adverb; consider (with order VS) *ÆCHom* i. 12. 12 and *ÆCHom* i. 182. 13, and (with order SV) *ÆCHom* i. 156. 21. But to take *swa* as a conjunction in such passages creates awk-ward sentences and seems to me strained, almost perverse. I think the same about Ericson's suggestion (1932, p. 19 fn. 17) that *swa swa* in *BlHom* 79. 1 is a conjunction, not (as Morris took it) an adverb.

§3269. Turning to the poetry, we find Cook—in his glossary to *Christ*, s.v. *swa* adv.—observing that 'the adv. and the conj. cannot always be discriminated with certainty'. There are certainly no syn-tactical guides. The context sometimes decides, e.g. in

Beo 1534   Swa sceal man don,
               þonne he æt guðe   gegan þenceð
               longsumne lof;   na ymb his lif cearað,

but often fails; consider

Brun 5   Bordweal clufan,
               heowan heaþolinde   hamora lafan,
               afaran Eadweardes,   swa him geæþele wæs
               from cneomægum,

where Campbell prefers a semi-colon to the ASPR comma after *Eadweardes*; in *Cæd* 5, on which see Mitchell 1967*b*, pp. 203-4, and Stanley, *Poetica* (Tokyo), 2 (1974), 15-16; and in other passages dis-cussed in Mitchell 1959, pp. 489-90. Small (*MLN* 49 (1934), 538) says that 'we shall be closer to the true syntax if we interpret all these examples from the poetry paratactically as simply "thus", "and thus", or "in this way" '. I sympathize with this view. But here, as in all situations when a choice exists between parataxis and hypotaxis, the decision must be a personal one.

§3270. As is clear from his citation of

Beo 1138   he to gyrnwræce
               swiðor þohte   þonne to sælade,
               gif he torngemot   þurhteon mihte,
               þæt he Eotena bearn   irne gemunde.
               Swa he ne forwyrnde   weorodrædende,
               þonne him Hunlafing   hildeleoman,
               billa selest   on bearm dyde;
               þæs wæron mid Eotenum   ecge cuðe

(where Ericson (1930, pp. 159 and 164-5) follows Kemp Malone in translating *swa* as 'since'), Small intended the observation I have just quoted to apply to negative as well as positive clauses introduced by

swa. Ericson's conclusion (1930, p. 175) is directly contrary to that
of Small. For he says (1930, p. 175): 'Since, then, in this collection
of representative cases, there is not a single clear case of adverbial
(non-conjunctive) *swa* in the initial position, one may with safety
conclude that the appearance of *swa* at the head of a negative clause
is *prima facie* evidence of its conjunctive character.' I reject this
view. One cannot 'with safety conclude' anything from a 'collection
of representative cases', even when it is based on 'the whole body of
Old English poetry, as well as . . . a substantial and representative
portion of the prose' (1930, p. 174); consider *ÆCHom* ii. 590. 3
*Gold, and seolfor, and deorwurðe stanas beoð on fyre afandode, ac
hi ne beoð swa ðeah mid ðam fyre fornumene. Swa eac ða ðe habbað
gode weorc ne þoliað nane pinunge on þam bradum fyre þe ofergæð
ealne middaneard . . .* , which is outside Ericson's corpus but offers
a clear example of adv. *swa* introducing a negative clause, and compare *swa* in

GenB 287   Frynd synd hie mine georne,
            holde on hyra hygesceaftum.   Ic mæg hyra hearra wesan,
            rædan on þis rice.   Swa me þæt riht ne þinceð,
            þæt ic oleccan   awiht þurfe
            gode æfter gode ænegum,

taken by Ericson (1930, pp. 168-9) as causal 'since', with *swa* in

GenB 507   Ic gehyrde hine þine dæd and word
            lofian on his leohte   and ymb þin lif sprecan.
            Swa þu læstan scealt   þæt on þis land hider
            his bodan bringað,

taken by Ericson (1932, p. 20) as an adverb. *Beo* 1138 has been
much discussed. The suggestion by Brady (*ASE* 8 (1979), 99-100)
that it provides another example of the construction discussed in
§§2861-3 is an attractive one. But I can see no reason for Ericson's
insistence that *swa* in *Beo* 1142 cannot be an adverb: if, as seems
generally agreed (see, *inter alios*, Small 1924, pp. 125, 148, and 154),
the adverbial use of *swa* preceded its use as a conjunction, it is difficult to see why a negative should be avoided after *swa* adverb but
accepted after *swa* conjunction. Further work would, I believe, produce more exceptions in the prose. But in my opinion it is unlikely
to alter the conclusion reached by Dobbie in his excellent discussion
of the problem in his note on *Beo* 1142-5: 'Thus, while we must
agree with Malone's statement that negative clauses with initial adverbial *swa* are rare, we cannot accept Ericson's conclusion that they do
not exist.'

c. Clauses introduced by swa, swa swa, eal(l)swa, and efne swa, with no correlative

§3271. Nothing very exciting here. The distinction is not syntactical. It is a matter of emphasis and/or personal taste which is preferred among these and *þæs (þe)*. Thus, on the evidence of Ericson (1932, pp. 10-11 and 13), *Bede, Or,* and *BlHom,* prefer *swa,* with *Bede* offering nineteen instances of *swa/swa swa* variation. According to Jost (*RES* 10 (1959), 77) '*eallswa* is so rare that in all Ælfric's works I found two instances only'; for these, see §3275. But, he goes on, Wulfstan 'uses *swa, swa swa,* and *eallswa* almost indifferently. Only to introduce quotations he has *eallswa* with hardly an exception.' On these points see further Jost, *Ang.* 51 (1927), 90-2, and Baker, *Speculum,* 55 (1980), 24.

§3272. A clause introduced by *swa (swa)* is not necessarily comparative or modal. It may, for example, shade into the temporal (see Blake's note on *Phoen* 41 and 322, and my §§2692-6) or the causal (see von Schaubert in *Philologica,* pp. 33-4, but Blake's note on *Phoen* 36, and my §§3108-9). See further §§3319-22 and the Index of Words and Phrases.

§3273. Comparative clauses introduced by *swa* include *Bede* 50. 15 . . . *þæt yfell wræc come ofer ða wiþcorenan, swa on þam ende þara wisena sweotolice ætywed is,* where the Latin has *sicut; ÆCHom* i. 18. 2 *Nis hit na swa ðu segst* (rare in Ælfric; see Jost, *Ang.* 51 (1927), 89-90, and Pope, *Ælfric,* i. 102-3); *Gen* 18. 5 *Do swa þu spræce,* where the Latin has *ut;*

GenB 681

	Hit nis wuhte gelic
elles on eorðan,	buton swa þes ar sægeð,
þæt hit gegnunga	from gode come;

and

ChristA 15

	nu sceal liffrea
þone wergan heap	wraþum ahreddan,
earme from egsan,	swa he oft dyde.

For references to more examples see Ericson 1932, pp. 9-12.

§3274. With *swa swa* we have *Bede(O)* 108. 29 *Se þridda wæs, swa swa we ær cwædon, Æþelbyrht Cantwara cyning,* where MS *Ca* has *swa swa,* MSS *T* and *B swa,* and the Latin *ut; ÆCHom* i. 24. 35 *and hit weox swa swa oðre cild doð, buton synne anum* (the usual arrangement in Ælfric when a principal clause without correlative precedes the comparative clause; see Jost, *Ang.* 51 (1927), 88); *ÆCHom* i.

80. 8 *þa betealde he hine swiðe geaplice, swa swa he wæs snotor-*
wyrde, to ðan swiðe, þæt se casere hine mid maran wurðmynte
ongean to Iudeiscum rice asende (Thorpe and Sweet, *R*. 15, 71. 46,
mislead here by failing to insert a comma after *snotorwyrde*); *Gen*
16. 2 *Abram ða dyde swa swa him dihte Sarai*; and

Met 12. 26   and ðu awyrtwalast   of gewitlocan
                 leasa gesælða,   swa swa londes ceorl
                 of his æcere lycð   yfel weod monig.

Ericson (1932, pp. 12-15) gives references to more examples. But his
claim (1932, p. 12) that in *ÆLet* 4. 648 *7 he swutelice sæde on his*
gesetnisse be Cristes acennednisse, swa swa he com to mannum
feowerhund geara 7 hundnigontig geara fram Darie ðam cininge, swa
swa is 'an interrogative adverb: "how" ' is presumably based on
L'isle's mistaken translation 'And therein he spake plainly of Christs
birth: How hee should come to mankinde. . . .' But that would require
subj. *come*; the ind. *com* requires some such translation as 'as indeed
he did come . . .'. His other example, *Cæd* 5, can also be dismissed;
see §3269.

§3275. For *eal(l)swa* conj. I offer the following examples: *GD(C)*
119. 4 *7 þær onfeng his bigleofan, eall swa his gewuna wæs ær, of*
þæs Godes mannes handa; the two instances noted by Jost in Ælfric,
viz. *ÆLet* 1. 20 . . . *ac, ealswa we ær sædon, on sumum mædene* and
ÆHex 376 *Sume menn wendon ðæt ðeos woruld wære æfre buton*
ælcum anginne eall swa heo nu is (see Jost, *Ang*. 51 (1927), 90-1);
Gen 41. 17 *Witodlice Pharao rehte Iosepe þa swefn þe hine mætte,*
eal swa hit her bufan awriten is; and

JDay ii 1   Hwæt! Ic ana sæt   innan bearwe,
               mid helme beþeht,   holte tomiddes,
               þær þa wæterburnan   swegdon and urnon
               on middan gehæge,   eal swa ic secge.

Ericson (1932, pp. 30-1) lists more examples.

§3276. We find *efne/emne swa* in *GD(C)* 118. 30 and 139. 10 . . .
þa geecte he þær to þæt word 'þines muðes', emne swa he openlice
cwæde . . . (in both of which MS *H* has *swilce*); in *BlHom* 219. 30
and 221. 29; in

Beo 1570   Lixte se leoma,   leoht inne stod,
              efne swa of hefene   hadre scineð
              rodores candel;

and in other examples listed by Ericson 1932, pp. 32-3.

§3277. In the last two combinations, we sometimes find *swa* doubled, e.g. *Ch* 342 *suo al se, Ch* 1219 *also so*, and *GD(C)* 86. 7 *efne swa swa.*

§3278. In these clauses the verb usually has the indicative mood; see §§3295-300.

d. *Correlative* swa (swa) . . . swa (swa): *general comments*

§3279. Three types of sentence involving correlative *swa (swa)* . . . *swa (swa)* can conveniently be distinguished. First, there are those in which the first *swa* qualifies an adjective, an adjective + a noun, or an adverb, e.g. *BlHom* 79. 27 *Wæs þæt wite swa strang swa Godes geþeld ær mycel wæs*; second, those with the comparative of adjectives or adverbs; and third, those in which a comparison is made between the actions or states described in two clauses introduced by *swa (swa)*, e.g. *BlHom* 31. 36 *swa þonne beoþ þa synfullan genyþerade mid heora ordfruman swa he genyþerad wearþ*. These are discussed in turn in the sections which follow. The usual mood is the indicative; see §§3295-300.

§3280. On *swa* . . . *swa* 'either . . . or', see §§1825-6; on *swa hwæþer swa*, §§1826 and 2363-73. Both are exemplified in *ÆLS* 17. 254 *and þæt is seo æ þæt god forgylt ælcum menn be his gewyrhtum ægðer ge on þysre worulde ge on þære toweardan, swa god swa yfel, swa hwæðer swa he begæð*. The combination *swa hu swa* is found, e.g. *ÆCHom* ii. 326. 29 *Begen hi sind men on middanearde acennede and hi habbað æt Gode swa hu swa hi geearniað* and *ÆCHom* i. 588. 28 *Ic wundrige ðe snoterne wer, þæt ðu ðyssere lare fylian wylt, swa hu swa hit gewurde, sylfwilles oððe neadunge, þæt he on rode gefæstnod wære*. On other combinations with *swa . . . swa*, such as *swa hwæt swa, swa sona swa*, and *swa wide swa*, see the Index of Words and Phrases.

e. *Combinations of* swa + *an adjective (+ a noun)/adverb* + *(. . .)* swa

§3281. Typical examples of these comparisons, which are traditionally called clauses of degree, include *Or* 254. 29 *þa wearð Tiberius Romanum swa wrað 7 swa heard swa he him ær wæs milde 7 ieþe, Or* 17. 11 *þa wæs he swa feor norþ swa þa hwælhuntan firrest faraþ, ÆCHom* i. 162. 1 *Swa micel he hæfde swa he rohte, ÆCHom* i. 58. 5 *He wæs Cristes moddrian sunu, and he hine lufode synderlice; na swa micclum for ðære mæglican sibbe swa for ðære clænnysse his ansundan mægðhades, ÆLS* 1. 79 *Nis nanum menn on ðisum deadlican life libbendum nanes þinges swa mycel neod swa him biþ þæt he cunne þonne ælmihtigan god mid geleafan,* and *Beo* 593 . . . *gif þin hige wære,* ‖ *sefa swa searogrim, swa þu self talast.* Jost (*Ang.* 51 (1927), 88–9) suggests that *swa . . . swa* is the rule in Ælfric's writings in combinations of this sort, but notes the existence of exceptions. *ÆCHom* i. 76. 13 *He gewat swa freoh fram deaðes sarnysse, of ðisum andweardan life, swa swa he wæs ælfremed fram lichamlicere gewemmednysse* can be added to his list. Ericson (1932, pp. 42–6) lists more examples.

§3282. The first two elements are sometimes repeated, both by Ælfric, e.g. *ÆCHom* i. 94. 1 and *ÆCHom* i. 84. 10 *Ne mihte se manfulla ehtere mid nanre ðenunge þam lytlingum swa micclum fremian, swa micclum swa he him fremode mid ðære reðan ehtnysse hatunge,* and by other writers; see Ericson 1932, pp. 44 and 46.

§3283. Ericson (1932, p. 46, and 1931, p. 18) notes examples in which the second *swa* is replaced by a relative pronoun; they include *Bede(T)* 266. 33 *þæt wæs swa soðlice mid dæd gefylled swa him to cweden wæs,* where MS *B* has *þ* for the second *swa,* and *ÆJudgEp* 415. 30 . . . *þonne sende he him to swa fela eoroda ðe mihton gebigan þæt mennisc him to. . . .* Other variations include *swa eac . . . swa* (*Bede* 48. 25), *eall swa . . . swa swa* (*Judg* 15. 19), *efne swa . . . swa* (*Met* 22. 19), and *emne swa . . . swa* (*And* 333). For further examples of these and similar variations, see Ericson 1932, pp. 43–4 and 46.

§3284. The second *swa* is sometimes doubled, as in *ÆCHom* i. 76. 13 (§3281) and *Judg* 15. 19 (§3283). It may be repeated, as in *Or* 142. 5 *Swa oft swa Galli wið Romanum wunnan, swa wurdon Romane gecnysede.* Ericson (1932, p. 42) offers some examples in which 'a regular modal clause appears to be a defective form of such a comparison'. I take all these as examples of the *swa (swa)* comparison discussed in §§3271–8 and see no reason for postulating an absent correlative *swa.* His two alleged examples of *swiðe . . . swa (swa)* (1932, p. 44) belong there too. But examples of certain formulae with only one *swa* can be found in §3289.

§3285. *ÆLS* 26. 172 *Se earm wearþ geled arwurðlice on scrine of seolfre asmiþod . on sancte petres mynstre binnan bebban byrig . be þære sæ strande . and lið þær swa andsund swa he of aslagen wæs,* where the EETS translation reads '. . . and lieth there as sound as when it was cut off', might appear to offer some support to the suggestion that *swa* in *Wan* 43 means 'as when'; see §2608. But it seems to me a clear example of comparison, '. . . and lies there as sound as it was cut off [sound]'.

§3286. Like *þonne* clauses, which are also traditionally called clauses of degree, *swa* clauses of this type follow the principal clause. Examples like *Or* 142. 5 (§3284), *Or* 274. 10 *swa longe swa seo ehtnes wæs þara cristenra monna, swa longe him wæs ungemetlic moncwealm getenge* . . . , and *GD* 325. 21 . . . *ac swa swyþe swa he wæs full þære uncyste, swa swyðe he wæs mid oferhygdum onblawen 7 mid woruldspedum* (see Ericson 1932, p. 46), are exceptions if we take *swa oft swa*, *swa longe swa*, and *swa swyþe swa*, as compound conjunctions. But if we do that, we could argue that they no longer introduced clauses of degree, but had become fossilized into compound conjunctions. So the problem becomes terminological.

f. Swa . . . swa *and the comparative of adjectives or adverbs*

§3287. This pattern occurs only in the prose and takes two forms. The first and most common is that in which both the first and second *swa* are accompanied by the comparative of an adjective (+ a noun) or of an adverb. Here we can distinguish examples without a verb after the second *swa*, e.g. *Or* 18. 29 *7 þæt byne land is easteweard bradost 7 symle swa norðor swa smælre*, *Exod* 19. 19 *7 ðære byman sweg weox, swa leng swa swyðor*, and the familiar *WHom(EI)* 20. 8 . . . *7 þy hit is on worolde aa swa leng swa wyrse*, from those with a verb after the second *swa*, e.g. *Or* 20. 22 *7 þa kyningas, 7 þa oðre heahðungene men, swa micle lencg swa hi maran speda habbað, hwilum healf gear þæt hi beoð unforbærned, 7 licgað bufan eorðan on hyra husum*, *Exod* 1. 12 *Swa hi swiðor wæron geswencte, swa wæron hi swiðor gemenifylde 7 weoxon*, and (with *þe* before the second comparative) *WHom* 15. 56 and *WHom* 14. 51 *And æfre swa he eadmodlicor þæt deð, swa him God ælmihtig þe raðer gemiltsað*. Johnsen (*EStudien*, 44 (1911-12), 236) describes the last two as examples of 'contamination'. Variations of the latter type include examples with the second *swa* repeated, e.g. *Bede* 136. 14 *Forþon swa micle swa ic geornlicor on þam bigange þæt sylfe soð sohte, swa ic hit læs mette* and *BlHom* 95. 31 *7 swa myccle swa þæs mannes miht beo mare, 7 he biþ weligra on þisse worlde, swa him þonne se uplica Dema mare tosecþ* . . . , and with the second *swa* and other elements repeated, e.g. *Or* 182. 25 *þonne is wen, swa micle swiðor swa he þencð þæt he hit adwæsce, þæt he hit swa micle swiðor ontydre, GD* 330. 24 *soðlice swa myccle swyþor swa nealæcende is þeos 7wearde woruld to ende, swa myccle ma eac seo towearde woruld mid hire nealæcunge geneahhe byð gecyþed . . .* , and *GD* 335. 21 . . . *þæt hi þonne acnawan þæt hi sylfe sculon beon swa myccle ma gyldende þære godcundan gife in ecnesse, swa myccle ma swa hi geseoþ oðra yflu beon witnode in ecnesse. . . .* Both Wærferth and the reviser of *GD* use this last type and variants of it, such as *GD(C)* 41. 15 . . . *swa myccle ma . . . swa myccle . . . rumor 7 wid-dor . . .* , repeating the first *swa*; MS *H* has . . . *swa mycele swyðor . . . swa micele swa . . . widdor. . . .* Ericson (1932, p. 58) lists more examples. Most of those from *GD* which he lists among the examples without repetition of the second *swa* (1932, p. 57) should have appeared among those with such repetition (p. 58). The subordinate clause usually precedes the principal clause, e.g. *Bede* 136. 14, *GD* 330. 24, and *Exod* 1. 12 (all quoted above), but the principal clause may precede, either in part, e.g. *Or* 20. 22, or in full, e.g. *GD* 335. 21 (both quoted above).

§3288. Ericson (1932, p. 58) includes as the second (and less common) form of the pattern under discussion that in which only one *swa* has a comparative. Examples include *CP* 191. 9 *Forðæm him is suiðe micel ðearf ðæt he sua micle wærlicor hine healde wið scylda swa he gere witan mæg ðæt he no ana ne forwierð . . .* , *Or* 38. 18 *swa swyðe swa hi ær Moyse 7 hys folce þæs utfæreldes wyrndon, swa micle hy wæron geornran þæt hi him fram fulgen, BenR* 138. 23 . . . *þa butan tweon swa micele eaðelicor and sel drohtniaþ swa hy stiþlice afedde wæron,* and *GD(H)* 130. 3 *7 swa micele swyðor sceamiende ongan his gylt bewepan, swa micele swa he ongeat hine sylfne æfweardne agyltan on gesihðe þæs fæder Benedictes,* where MS *C* has *swa myccle ma . . . swa mycclum swa . . . ma.* The principal clause may precede the subordinate clause, as in *CP* 191. 9, *BenR* 138. 23, and *GD(H)* 130. 3, or follow it, as in *Or* 38. 18.

§3289. Ericson (1932, pp. 55–8), comparing this use of correlative *swa* with that of *þy* discussed in §§3243–50, sees the antecedent of the former in the use of 'single *swa* . . . between two adverbs of the comparative degree or positives with intensive quality'. His examples include (with the second element positive and no verb after *swa*) *Beo* 1853 *Me þin modsefa* ‖ *licað leng swa wel, leofa Beowulf*; (with two comparatives and no verb after *swa*)

GenA 988   Of ðam twige siððan
       ludon laðwende   leng swa swiðor
       reðe wæstme,

which is the only example in the poetry in which *swa* is used between two comparatives to indicate correlation;[176] and (with two comparatives and a verb after *swa*) *BlHom* 121. 36 *Hwæt we witon þæt æghwylcum men biþ leofre swa he hæbbe holdra freonda ma*. With *GenA* 988 we may compare *Lch* ii. 34. 15 *7 beþe þa eagan on þam baþe betere swa oftor*.

g. Other comparisons involving two clauses introduced by swa (swa)

§3290. Here we have to do with what are traditionally called clauses of manner; the Joint Committee's example (p. 17) is 'Heaven does with us *as we with torches do*', which can (for our purposes) be re-phrased 'as we with torches do, so Heaven does with us'. Both patterns occur in OE.

§3291. We find, with the subordinate clause first 'as . . . so', the following arrangements: *swa . . . swa*, e.g. *BlHom* 57. 10 *swa se lichoma buton mete 7 drence leofian ne mæg, swa þonne seo saul, gif heo ne bið mid Godes worde feded gastlice, hungre 7 þurste heo bið cwelmed* and

ChristA 85   Swa eal manna bearn
              sorgum sawað,   swa eft ripað,
              cennað to cwealme;

swa swa . . . swa, e.g. *Bede* 164. 15 *þa he þa biscophade onfongen hæfde, swa swa he ær mid þa metgunge þæs gesceades funden hæfde, swa he æfter fæce mid oðrum gastlicum mægenum gefrætwed æteawde* and *ÆLS* 1. 205 *Swa swa God ælmihtig oferstihð ealle gesceafta, swa oferstihð seo sawul ealle lichamlice gesceafta; swa swa . . . swa eac*, e.g. *ÆCHom* i. 40. 19 *Swa swa anra gehwilc manna wunað on sawle and on lichaman an mann, swa eac Crist wunað on godcundnysse and menniscnysse, on anum hade an Crist*; *efne swa . . . swa*, e.g.

Alms 5   Efne swa he mid wætre   þone weallendan
              leg adwæsce,   þæt he leng ne mæg
              blac byrnende   burgum sceððan,
              swa he mid ælmessan   ealle toscufeð
              synna wunde,   sawla lacnað;

---

[176] *Beo* 1282 (§3256), where strict grammar would require ☆*be wæpnedmannes* in line 1284b, is not an example, for *læssa* has to be understood with the second clause; *efne swa micle swa* belongs with the examples discussed in §§3281–6. This sentence is discussed by Gehse, p. 35.

ealswa . . . swa, e.g. *WHom* 7. 97 . . . *forðam ealswa þa godan habbað ece lif on myrhðe, swa habbað þa yfelan 7 þa forwyrhtan ece lif on yrmðe;* and other variations such as *swa . . . swa eac swylce* and *ealswa . . . swa eac* exemplified by Ericson (1932, pp. 52–3). Jost (*Ang.* 51 (1927), 88) states that *swa swa . . . swa (eac),* not *swa . . . swa,* is the norm in Ælfric when the subordinate clause precedes.

§ 3292. When the principal clause precedes the subordinate 'so . . . as', we find (with adverb *swa* in initial position) *swa . . . swa,* e.g. *BlHom* 31. 36 *swa þonne beoþ þa synfullan genyþerade mid heora ordfruman swa he genyþerad wearþ, GD* 233. 28 *swa hit is swa þu sægst,* and

LPr ii 39   Swa þin heahsetl is   heah and mære,
                   fæger and wurðlic,   swa þin fæder worhte,
                   æþele and ece,   þar ðu on sittest
                   on sinre swiðran healf;

swa . . . swa swa, e.g. *ÆCHom* ii. 446. 31 *Swa stod se deofol on Godes gesihðe swa swa deð se blinda on sunnan* (here again Ælfric prefers *swa swa*); and *swa . . . ealswa,* e.g. *Ch — R* 194. 7 *swa he nu dagum Breotanrices fægran iglandes Eadwearde cyncge sealde 7 geuþe ealswa he æror geara his magum dyde.* But *swa* 'so' need not have initial position in its clause, e.g. (with *. . . swa . . . swa*) *Bede* 126. 18 *Ond he lustlice hine onfeng 7 him geheht þæt he swa don wolde swa he hine bæd* and

PPs 118. 85   Me manwyrhtan   manige on spellum
                  sægdon soðlice;   na ic hit swa oncneow,
                  swa hit þin æ hafað,   ece dryhten;

(with *. . . swa . . . swa swa*) *GD* 185. 27 *ac he wolde cunnian hwæþer hit swa wære swa swa he ær secgan gehyrde* and *ÆLS* 26. 74 . . . *and sylf swa leofode swa swa he lærde oðre* (see Jost, *Ang.* 51 (1927), 88–9, for more examples from Ælfric); (with *. . . eac swa . . . swa swa*), *Bede* 290. 29 *7 eac swa wæs swa swa heo bæd;* and (with *. . . eac swa ealswa*) *HomU* 29. 173. 7 *ute don eac swa ealswa hi dydon.* Ericson (1932, pp. 53–4) quotes other combinations such as *swa eac . . . swa* and lists more examples. But I do not include here, as he does, examples with *swa swa,* such as *Gen* 16. 2 *Abram ða dyde swa swa him dihte Sarai* (on these see §§ 3271–8), or with adv. *swa* used independently of conj. *swa,* such as *Gen* 43. 11 *Gyf ge nyde swa don sceolon, doþ swa ge willon.*

§ 3293. Ælfric sometimes chooses to express this type of comparison paratactically; consider *ÆCHom* i. 492. 4 *Se cniht wæs ancenned sunu his meder, swa bið eac gehwilc cristen man gastlice ðære halgan gelaðunge sunu, seo is ure ealra modor . . . , ÆCHom* ii. 582. 17 *On eorðlicere cyrcan lið stan ofer stane, and ælc berð oðerne, swa eac on Godes geleaðunge, þa geleaffullan ælc hylt his æftergengan up, þurh lare and geðylde* . . . , and perhaps *ÆCHom* i. 300. 33 *Ðæra apostola tweonung be Cristes æriste næs na swa swiðe heora ungeleaffulnys, ac wæs ure trumnys.*

§3294. Problems of punctuation sometimes arise in the poetry. Thus, if the ASPR stop after *ælmihtig* is replaced by a comma in

ChristA 330   ond efne swa þec gemette,   meahtum gehrodene,
                     clæne ond gecorene,   Crist ælmihtig.
                     Swa ðe æfter him   engla þeoden
                     eft unmæle   ælces þinges
                     lioþucægan bileac,   lifes brytta,

the passage can be translated 'As Christ found you spotless . . . so he left you undefiled'. See also *Met* 5. 12–23 and *Phoen* 646–61, which is discussed by Schaar, pp. 89–91.

h. *Mood in the* swa *clauses already discussed*

§3295.The prevailing mood in the *swa* clauses discussed in §§3262–94 is the indicative. Small's statement (1924, p. 3) that 'the mode of the comparative clause is governed by the *sense* or *meaning* of the clause and has nothing to do with the fact that the clause is one of *comparison* [his italics]' is applicable here. Visser (ii, §§887–8) offers a limited collection of examples which confuses the various types of *swa* clauses which I distinguish. As I have full figures for the poetry (see Mitchell 1959, pp. 496–8 and 521–3), I start with a summary of the position therein. We find the subjunctive in six examples in the poetry, including

Jul 87   Dem þu hi to deaþe,   gif þe gedafen þince,
                swa to life læt,   swa þe leofre sy

(where the first *swa* means 'or') and *El* 541 *Do swa þe þynce*, and the indicative in at least eleven (the 'at least' reflects the existence of the ambiguous adverb/conjunction), including

And 332   Farað nu geond ealle   eorðan sceatas
                emne swa wide   swa wæter bebugeð,
                oððe stedewangas   stræte gelicgaþ

and

MCharm 8. 11   Beo ge swa gemindige   mines godes,
                   swa bið manna gehwilc   metes and eþeles.

So Behre's rule about '*swa (swylce)*-clauses connected with a main clause containing an expression of volition' (pp. 277–8) would be nearer the truth if it started 'the subjunctive may be used . . .' rather than 'the subjunctive is used . . . to denote an attitude of volition towards the content of the dependent clause, an attitude that is manifested in the main clause, too, by another expression of volition (an imperative or a volitional subjunctive)'. Campbell (*RES* 7 (1956), 65) did not go as far as Behre when he spoke of 'perhaps the most far-reaching rule of OE syntax—viz. that . . . *swa* clauses . . . take the subjunctive when the principal clause contains an imperative, a subjunctive, or a negated indicative'.

§3296. However, I found in the poetry no *swa* clauses with the subjunctive after a negated indicative in the principal clause; the verb-forms are either indicative, as in

Met 13. 73   Nis nu ofer eorðan   ænegu gesceaft
    þe ne hwearfige,   swa swa hweol deð,
    on hire selfre

and

Met 31. 8   nabbað hi æt fiðrum fultum,   ne magon hi mid fotum gangan,
    eorðan brucan,   swa him eaden wæs,

or ambiguous. Rhetorical questions too are followed by the indicative, e.g.

And 190   Hu mæg ic, dryhten min,   ofer deop gelad
    fore gefremman   on feorne weg
    swa hrædlice,   heofona scyppend,
    wuldres waldend,   swa ðu worde becwist?,

or by an ambiguous form, never by the subjunctive.

§3297. So the indicative is the norm. The strength of the preference for the indicative is revealed by a consideration of

Beo 590   Secge ic þe to soðe,   sunu Ecglafes,
    þæt næfre Grendel swa fela   gryra gefremede,
    atol æglæca   ealdre þinum,
    hynðo on Heorote,   gif þin hige wære,
    sefa swa searogrim,   swa þu self talast

and

Met 28. 44   Hwa þegna ne mæge
    eac wafian   ælces stiorran,
    hwy hi ne scinen   scirum wederum
    beforan ðære sunnan,   swa hi symle doð

middelnihtum   wið þone monan foran,
hadrum heofone?,

where the indicatives *talast* and *doð* triumph over an impressive array of subjunctives, negatives, and (for *doð*) a rhetorical question.

§3298. Understandably (I hope) I do not have full figures for the prose. But the evidence I have suggests that the situation there is the same as it is in the poetry. The subjunctive is found after a volitional expression, e.g. *Lch* ii. 62. 2 *gedrinc swa hates swa þin blod sie scenc fulne do swa þonne þe þearf sie*, *BlHom* 61. 28 *Deme ge nu swa swa ge willon þæt eow sy eft gedemed* . . . , *Ch* 1500 . . . 7 *ðæt wiorð gedæle fore hiora gastas suæ ælmeslice 7 suæ rehtlice suæ he him seolfa on his wisdome geleornie*, *Ch* 1471 *þænne ga þis foresprecene land into Xp̄es cyricean mid mete 7 mid mannan eal swa hit stande*, and *Ch* 1512 7 *gange syððan into þære stowe swa gewered swa hit stande mid mete 7 mid mannum*, and after a dependent command or wish, e.g. *BlHom* 47. 35 7 *him bebeodan þæt hi Godes domas on riht healdan, þa Godes þeowas heora tidsangas 7 heora cyricean mid rihte healdan, 7 þa læwedan swa him mid rihte tobelimpe*. In *LawIne* 7 *Gif hwa stalie swa his wif nyte 7 his bearn, geselle lx scill. to wite*, a conditional clause precedes and a jussive subjunctive follows the *swa* clause. But the indicative also occurs after volitional expressions, e.g. *Ch* 1526 *And lete men stonden so mikel so ic þeron fond*, *Ch* 1486 7 *æfter hiræ dege gange hit into sc̄a Marian stowæ into Beorcingan æalswa hit stænt mid mæte 7 mid mannum*, and *Ch* 1455 R 128. 6 7 *æfter hys dæge gange þ land into sc̄e Augustine swa gewerud swa hyt þonne byð*, and after a dependent command or wish, e.g. *Ch* 1519 *and ic wille after þe forwarde þæt ic and Eadwine and Wlfric after mine time fon to alkere þinge þe min ower is þer on tune buton so mikel so ic an into þe kirke*. (These indicative examples date from *c.*942-51 (*Ch* 1526) to *c.*1052-66 (*Ch* 1519).)

§3299. We find the indicative rather than the subjunctive in *swa* clauses after a principal clause with a negated indicative, e.g. *BlHom* 45. 2 *þa wæs him forgolden æfter his agenum gewyrhtum. 7 her sægþ on þyssum bocum, þæt þæm biscopum þe her on worlde syndon, swyþe gelice gegange þæm biscope þe Paulus on þære fyrenan helle geseah, gif hi nellaþ healdan Godes æwe, swa swa him haligu gewreotu bebeodaþ*, *ÆCHom* i. 80. 24 *and þaþa hi his cenningstowe geaxodon, þa gewendon hi wið þæs cildes, and noldon ðone reðan cwellere eft gecyrran, swa swa he het*, *WHom(EI)* 20. 34 7 *gedwolgoda þenan ne dear man misbeodan on ænige wisan mid hæþenum leodum, swa swa man Godes þeowum nu deð to wide* . . . , and *Coll* 99 *Ic ne mæg swa fela swa ic mæg gesyllan.* I have not as yet found an example in which a subjunctive follows a negated indicative.

§3300. Despite such variations in mood as those seen in *Bo* 122. 9 *7 wenð þ ælcum men sie swa swa him si 7 ælcum men ðince swa swa him þincð*, *BlHom* 95. 31 *7 swa myccle swa þæs mannes miht beo mare, 7 he biþ weligra on þisse worlde, swa him þonne se uplica Dema mare tosecþ*, *Lch* ii. 90. 11 *7 sele þam seocan men drincan swa he nyte swa þu scealt þa opre ætas 7 drincan sellan*, and *Ch* 1422 *Ða gewearþ hi þæt se Æþeling sealde þam hyrede xx punda wið þam lande ælswa hit stod mid mete 7 mid mannon 7 mid ællon þingon 7 bruce his dæg 7 ofer his dæg eode þ land eft into ðære halgan stowe mid mete 7 mid mannon 7 mid eallum þingum swa swa hit ðonne wære*, the prevailing mood in the *swa* clauses discussed in §§3262–94 is the indicative. The subjunctives which do occur can usually be explained as due to the presence of an element of volition, hypothesis, or uncertainty, about an event in the future or the future-in-the-past. But the 'rules' quoted above are far from universal in their application. Indeed, to the best of my present knowledge, the one concerning a negated indicative is invalid.

j. Anlic/(un)gelic + swa

§3301. These constructions, which are to be distinguished from those with *anlice/(un)gelice (þe)* described in §§3371–2, are discussed by Ericson (1932, pp. 37–8) and Mitchell (1959, pp. 514–16). They occur in the prose, e.g. *Bede* 318. 30 *Ond þa, gelice swa swa heo bebead, nales in oðre stowe butan in middum hire hiwum æfter endebyrdnesse, þe heo geleorde, in treowenre þryh wæs bebyrged* and *BlHom* 17. 3 . . . *he him gehet his æriste swa he þa mid soðe gefylde, gelice swa he ær þa þrowunge dyde*, but are more conveniently illustrated from the poetry.

§3302. We find *anlic/gelic* used adjectivally governing a dative of comparison in

PPs 85. 7   Nis þe goda ænig   on gumrice
ahwær efne gelic,   ece drihten . . .

and

PPs 143. 15   Wærun heora dohtru   deore gesette
and ymb frætwum   utan gegyrede,
efne anlicast   æþelum temple.

In

Dan 345   þa wæs on þam ofne,   þær se engel becwom,
                    windig and wynsum,   wedere gelicost
                    þonne hit on sumeres tid   sended weorðeð
                    dropena drearung   on dæges hwile,
                    wearmlic wolcna scur

and

Phoen 424   Is þon gelicast,   þæs þe us leorneras
                    wordum secgað,   ond writu cyþað,
                    þisses fugles gefær,   þonne frod ofgiefeð
                    eard ond eþel,   ond geealdad bið,

the dat. *wedere* and the instr. *þon* are elaborated by a temporal *þonne* clause, while in

Dan 273   Him þær on ofne   owiht ne derede,
                    ac wæs þær inne   ealles gelicost
                    efne þonne on sumera   sunne scineð,
                    and deaw dryge   on dæge weorðeð,
                    winde geondsawen

and

Sat 149   Ealle we syndon   ungelice
                    þonne þe we iu in heofonum   hæfdon ærror
                    wlite and weorðmynt,

gelicost and *ungelice* directly govern a temporal *þonne* clause.

§3303. Similar stages can be traced with *swa* clauses. In

PPs 88. 32   bið him weorðlic setl
                    on minre gesihðe   sunnan anlic
                    and swa mona   meahte on heofenum,
                    þe is ece gewita   æhwær getreowe,

the adj. *anlic* governs a dative of comparison. The *swa* clause is probably independent, but (it might be argued on the analogy of the examples with *þonne* clauses quoted in §3302) could be parallel to *sunnan* and dependent on *anlic*; see below. The Latin *et sedes eius sicut sol in conspectu meo, et sicut luna perfecta in aeternum, et testes in caelo fidelis* is inconclusive. In

And 501   Is þon geliccost   swa he on landsceare
                    stille stande,   þær hine storm ne mæg,
                    wind awecgan . . .

and

ChristB 850   Nu is þon gelicost   swa we on laguflode
                    ofer cald wæter   ceolum liðan

geond sidne sæ,   sundhengestum,
flodwudu fergen,

gelic(c)ost governs the instrumental of the demonstrative followed by a *swa* clause. Finally, we have examples in which the *swa* is directly dependent on a form of *anlic/gelic*. Examples include (with a verb in the *swa* clause)

ChristB 782   Is þam dome neah
              þæt we gelice sceolon   leanum hleotan,
              swa we widefeorh   weorcum hlodun
              geond sidne grund,

PPs 123. 6   Wærun ure sawla   samod anlice
              niþa generede,   swa swa neodspearuwa
              of grames huntan   gryne losige,

and perhaps *PPs* 88. 32, above; and (with *swa* clauses without verbs followed by *swa* clauses with verbs)

PPs 82. 10   Sete hi nu, min god,   samod anlice
              swa se wægnes hweol   oþþe windes healm,
              and swa færincga   fyr wudu byrneð,
              oððe swa lig freteð   lungre morhæð

and

PPs 91. 11   Se soðfæsta   samed anlicast
              beorht on blædum   bloweð swa palma,
              and swa Libanes beorh   lideð and groweð.

§ 3304. The inclusion of *PPs* 88. 32 (§ 3303) in this last group must, however, be doubtful because it is (as far as I have observed) the only example in which the form of *anlic/gelic* preceding the *swa* must be adjectival. In all the others, it is either adverbial, e.g. the two prose instances cited in § 3301,

PPs 147. 5   He snaw sendeð   samed anlice
              swa þu wulle flys   wolcnum bringe,
              and þone toweorpeð   wide swa æscean,

and *ChristB* 782 (here I go along with Ericson (1932, p. 37); *gelice* does not agree with *leanum* and can scarcely be construed with *we*), or ambiguous, e.g. *And* 501 and *PPs* 123. 6 (both in § 3303).

§ 3305. The prevailing mood in these clauses is the indicative, but the subjunctive occurs when an element of hypothesis is involved and *swa* approaches the sense of MnE 'as if', e.g. *ChristB* 850 and *PPs* 123. 6 (both in § 3303). On this see further § § 3370-81.

k. Swa + *a superlative* + *a form of* magan

§3306. This idiom is most common in the legal codes; in legal documents such as wills, charters, and (we can add here) the prescriptive passages of Wulfstan's sermons; and in the *Leechdoms*. Elsewhere in the prose its occurrence seems sporadic. In the poetry it occurs most often in the *Metres*. Ericson (1932, pp. 47–8) addresses himself to it. But he is perhaps at his most casual here and what he writes can be disregarded except as a confused collection of examples.

§3307. The simple form of the construction (type A) is that seen in *Bede* 116. 4 *7 sona in eallum þingum þære cirican eahtum 7 godum freoðode 7 fultemede, swa he fyrmest meahte, Lch* ii. 34. 10 *do on þ eage swa he hatost mæge, ÆLS* 1. 169 *forðan þe seo sawul is gesælig ðe þonne scyppend lufað . . . and him fremian wile swa heo fyrmest mæge, WHom* 2. 69 *Leofan men, utan . . . lufian God over ealle oðre þing 7 his willan wyrcan swa we geornost magan, ChronE* 159. 18 (1036) *7 Godwine eorl 7 ealle þa yldestan menn on West Seaxon lagon ongean swa hi lengest mihton,* and

Met 27. 28

	þæt is, þæt he lufige
godra gehwilcne	swa he geornost mæge,
mildsige yflum,	swa we ær spræcon.

Here we have *swa* + the superlative of an adjective or adverb x + a subjunctive or ambiguous form of *magan*, with the infinitive to be supplied from (the verb of) the main clause, in the sense 'as x as possible' (usually with a positive governing clause, but see *HomS* 16. 62 (§3309)); cf. the Latin *Caesar quam aequissimo loco potest castra communit* and . . . *non eos praetereant horae constitutae, sed ut possunt agant sibi,* the original of *BenR* 78. 9 *and hig na forgiman þa gesettan tida, ac ælcne tidsang gefyllan, swa hig betst magon.* We occasionally find *swa swa,* e.g. *ÆLet* 6. 231 (§3311) and *Ch* 1507 *7 ic wille þa menn þe þa land habbað, þa word gelæstan þe on mines fæder yrfegewrite standað swa swa hy fyrmest magon.* In *Or* 260. 30 . . . *7 bebead his agnum monnum þæt hie simle gegripen þæs licgendan feos swa hie mæst mehten,* we must either take *mæst* as an adjective governing the partitive genitive *þæs licgendan feos,* despite BT (s.v. *mæst* adv.), or gloss this as the sole example of *(ge)gripan* + genitive.

§3308. I have noted three variations of this pattern. (There may be more; there is room for work here.) First (type B), the finite form of *magan* may govern an expressed infinitive (+ object), e.g. *Lch* ii.

124. 20 . . . *þonne lege on swa þu hatost mæge aræfnan; Lch* ii. 130.
5 *þonne on morgen forlæt blod of earme oððe of sweoran swa mæst
aræfnan mæge; LawIAsProl; WHom* 8c. 142 *And æfre swa þæt cild
raðost ænig ðing specan mæge, tæce man him sona ealra þinga ærest
pater noster 7 credan* (here *swa . . . raðost* shades into 'as soon as',
but with the subj. *mæge*); *Beo* 3159 and *And* 1229 (both in §3310);
and (with the swa clause governed by *buton* and unusual element
order for the metre)

Met 8. 15   Hwæt, hi firenlusta   frece ne wæron,
            buton swa hi meahton   gemetlicost
            ða gecynd began   þe him Crist gesceop. . . .

§3309. The second variation (type C) is that in which we find *swa*
+ the positive degree of an adjective or adverb before the *swa* of type
A. Sometimes this adjective or adverb is the same as that in the
superlative, e.g. *LawVIIIAtr* 43. 1 *7 utan God lufian innewerdre
heortan 7 Godes laga giman swa wel swa we betst magon* and two
examples very like it, viz. *LawVAtr* 35 and *LawVIAtr* 3. 1; *Lch* ii.
50. 15 . . . *hafa on muþe swa hat swa þu hatost mæge; Lch* ii. 124. 6
. . . *stæppe on swa hat swa he hatost mæge; Ch* 1538 . . . *7 dælon hi
þ heafodbotl him betweonan swa rihte swa hi rihtlicost magon* . . . ;
and possibly *HomS* 16. 62 . . . *þæt hi hit sylfe ærest ne don and eac
oðre swa feala, swa hi mæst mægon, oferdrenceað.* In these, the first
swa element seems superfluous in that its non-expression would leave
us with what I have called type A. So it is possible that type C was
the original and that type A represents a later shortening. Examples
like *Ch* 1487 *ic wæs þinum fæder swa gehyrsum swa ic fyrmest
myhte*, in which the positive and superlative elements are different
and in which non-expression of the first would alter the sense, might
give support to this idea. The same could be said of *ChronA* 158. 5
(1031) and *LawIVEg* 2. 1 (both in §3310).

§3310. The third variation (type D) combines types B and C, i.e.
swa + the positive degree of an adjective or adverb before the simple
pattern and an infinitive after it. Examples include *BlHom* 125. 21
*7 is sin hwyrfel on wilewisan geworht swa fægre 7 swa weorþlice
swa hit men on eorþan fægrost 7 weorþlicost geþencean meahton,
GD(C)* 212. 23 . . . *oð þæt he gehreas in ða dene, seo wæs under þam
munte swa feor ofdune swa man geseon mihte feorst* [MS *O fyrrest*],
and *Ch* 1538 . . . *and æfre ælce geare ealle gemænelice ane feorme
into Baðum swa gode swa hi bezte þurhteon magon. ChronA* 158. 5
(1031) . . . *beo an scip flotigende swa neh þan lande swa hit nyxt
mæge . . .* and *LawIVEg* 2. 1 *7 ic wille þæt woruldgerihta mid*

Denum standan be swa godum lagum, swa hy betste geceosan mægen
belong here in the sense that the same word appears in both positive
and superlative degrees. But they differ from the previous three in
that the first *swa* element gives extra information—viz. *þan lande*
and *lagum*—which is essential to the sense. (I do not myself regard
ofdune in *GD(C)* 212. 23 above as essential to the sense, but admit
the possibility of including this example here rather than above.) So
they, like *Ch* 1487 (§3309), could be used to support the suggestion
that the forms of the idiom with *swa . . . swa* (types C and D) may
have been the originals and that types A and B derived from them by
non-expression of the *swa* + positive adjective/adverb when it was
tautologic. One trouble with this theory is that the supporting examples with non-tautologic first *swa* element are (as far as I know
now) rare and late—*LawIVEg* 962–3, Will of Ælfhelm 975–1016 (so
Whitelock), and *Chron* 1031—whereas examples of the other types
are more numerous and date from the early monuments. Another
difficulty which future workers in this field may find relevant is this.
In those examples of types C and D which have a positive form of an
adjective (rather than of an adverb), there is at least a presumption
that the superlative element is also an adjective. (Can *bezte* in *Ch*
1538 and *betste* in *LawIVEg* 2. 1—both type D above—be anything else?) Yet, so far as I am aware, no examples of types A and B
have been produced in which the superlative element must be an
adjective. *Or* 260. 30 has been discussed in §3307. In

Beo 3159   . . . ond betimbredon   on tyn dagum
                      beadurofes becn,   bronda lafe
                      wealle beworhton,   swa hyt weorðlicost
                      foresnotre men   findan mihton,

we can construe *hyt weorðlicost* as accusative singular neuter referring to *becn*. But Klaeber glosses *weorðlicost* as an adverb, without
(as far as I can observe) explaining the reference of *hyt*. This passage
invites comparison with

And 1229   Heton þa lædan   ofer landsceare,
                      ðragmælum teon,   torngeniðlan,
                      swa hie hit frecnost   findan meahton,

where Brooks notes that '*hit* refers back to the fem. *landsceare*' and
appears to gloss *frecnost* as an adjective. This is certainly possible.
But if we explain the reference of *hyt* and *hit* as general rather than
specific, it is also possible to take both superlatives as adverbs; as
noted above, BT takes *mæst* in *Or* 260. 30 as an adverb. I must leave
the question open. But we cannot (I think) argue that, because types

A and B normally have the superlative of an adverb, they cannot have the superlative of an adjective.

§3311. With the verb *magan* a difference in mood can be detected only in the present singular. Here the subjunctive is the usual form and can occur whether the principal clause contains a volitional expression or not; compare *Lch* ii. 34. 10 and *Met* 27. 28 with *ÆLS* 1. 169 (all in §3307). We can, I think, reasonably interpret most of the present plural forms as subjunctive too. That the subjunctive should be the prevailing mood in the present is not surprising. The nature of the texts involved (§3306) means that many of the examples of this idiom follow a principal clause containing a volitional expression and that the reference is to a contemplated or wished-for event in the future. There are, however, a few examples with the indicative. We find *mæg* following *sceal* in *LawEpiscInscr* 3 *He sceal beon symle ymbe some 7 ymbe sibbe, swa he geornost mæg*, but following a principal clause without a volitional expression as defined in §2391 in *ÆLet* 6. 231 *Ðæt is on gastlicum andgite, se ðe godes bebodu nele nu gefyllan, swa swa he fyrmest mæg* (both type A) and

PPs 74. 2   Ic þin wundur eall   wræclic sæcge,
                     swa ic fæstlicast mæg   befon wordum
                     and eac soð   symble deme

(type B). It is hard to see any reason for all the differences in mood in these three examples and the three listed above.

§3312. As already noted, the preterite forms of *magan* are ambiguous for mood. So we have no means of determining whether *meahte* in *ChronE* 135. 30 (1004) *7 he þa gegaderode his fyrde diglice swa he swyðost muhte* is indicative, reflecting the fact that from the point of view of the reporter and/or writer the reference is to the past, or subjunctive, reflecting the attitude of the performer contemplating an act still to be completed.

l. Swa + *a superlative* + *a verb other than* magan

§3313. This construction—of which Ericson (1932, pp. 47-8) makes no mention after his introductory hint 'Verbs like *magan* . . .' apart from a reference to *LawIIIAtr* 1 (§3315)—differs from that just discussed in both meaning and in the fact that, since none of the verbs which I have noted in the *swa* clause can govern an infinitive, types B and D cannot occur. Most of the examples belong to type A. Many of these have the present subjunctive *sie/sy* after a volitional expression, e.g. *Ch* 1188 *7 he brytnie swæ higum mæst red sie 7 ðæm sawlum soelest*; after a dependent command or wish, e.g. *Ch* 1510 *Ic bebeode on Godes noman ðæt mon agefe ðæt lond Inn higum to heora beode him to brucanne on ece ærfe swæ him liofast sie*; or after an inflected infinitive which could (it seems to me) be interpreted as expressing a command or wish, e.g. *Ch − R* 144. 12 *. . . 7 æfter lyfe to atenne swa hym leofæst sy*, *Ch* 1275 *. . . to hæbbenne 7 to brucenne swa him sælest sie*, and (with *swa . . . swa*) *Ch* 1510 *. . . all on æce ærfe to brucanne ge minne dei ge æfter swæ to ationne swæ me mest red 7 liofast sie*. But we find the indicative *bið/byð* in a formula which Wulfstan uses at the end of at least three of his homilies, viz. *WHom* 2. 71, 3. 78, and 7a. 47 *þonne geleanað he hit us swa us leofost byð*, where he is making a firm statement, not expressing a command or wish.

§3314. A similar contrast presents itself between examples with the pret. subj. *wære*, e.g. *Ch* 1200 *. . . ac hia hit atuge yfter hira dege swe hit him boem rehtlicast 7 elmestlicast were* and *Ch* 1465 *. . . þ he moste ateon þ land æt Apoldre swa him sylfan leofast wære*, in both of which we can detect an element of volition and a time-reference to the future-in-the-past, and those with the pret. ind. *wæs*, e.g. *PPs* 80. 12 *Ac hi lifian het lustum heortena ‖ swa him leofust wæs* and

Met 20. 9

	þu þysne middangeard
from fruman ærest	forð oð ende
tidum totældes,	swa hit getæsost wæs,
endebyrdes . . . ,	

in which we have simple statements about the past.

§3315. There are a few examples with other verbs. In *Ch* 1503 *. . . þ ic moste be godes leafe 7 be his geunnan minre are 7 minra æhta swa me mæst ræd þuhte* (type A), and *Ch* 1454 *7 bæd 7 het þ hi scioldon Wynflæde 7 Leofwine swa rihtlice geseman swa him æfre rihtlicost þuhte* (type C), *þuhte* can, on the analogy of the examples with *wære* in §3314, be taken as preterite subjunctive, whereas in *LawIIIAtr* 1 *Ðæt is: þæt his grið stande swa forð swa hit fyrmest stod on his yldrena dagum* (type C), *stod* is indicative and seems to refer to an acknowledged truth in the past. The pres. ind. *singað* conveys a strong sense of actuality in *HomU* 27. 143. 9 *ealle we habbað ænne heofonlicne fæder, þæt is god sylfa, and þæt we swuteliað swa oft swa we oftost pater noster singað* (type C), in contrast to the pres. subj. *geceosen* in a dependent wish in *LawIVEg* 12 *þonne wille ic þæt stande mid Denum swa gode laga swa hy betste geceosen* (a type C example in which the first *swa* element contains the essential *laga* and therefore cannot be left unexpressed without affecting the sense). Further study of these type A and type C constructions may throw light on the problem discussed in §3310.

m. Contracted comparative clauses introduced by swa, alone and in combination

§3316. We are not concerned here with sentences in which a *swa* clause of comparison is implied, but not expressed, after *swa* adv. of degree. Ericson (1932, pp. 38–42) cites MnE 'I never saw *so* many toads (i.e. "as there are here")' and, among his many OE examples, *Bede* 178. 32 . . . *in þære stowe* . . . *þær his hors swa hraðe gehæled wæs, Num* 11. 15 . . . *þæt ic ne sy mid swa miclum yfele geswenct,* and

Beo 590 Secge ic þe to soðe, sunu Ecglafes,
      þæt næfre Grendel swa fela gryra gefremede. . . .

We may add *Lch* ii. 124. 18 . . . *lege on swa hat.* . . . Contracted comparative clauses are (in the words of Onions, p. 64) those in which 'part . . . is . . . omitted, leaving only sufficient to indicate the person or thing with which the comparison is made'. (I prefer 'unexpressed'; see §§1572 and 3859.) As the examples which follow demonstrate, various elements may be compared, including noun and pronoun subjects and objects, participles, adverbs, and phrases.

§3317. There are two basic patterns which Ericson (1932, pp. 15–17) failed to distinguish. The first is that in which we have, in Ericson's words, '*swa* as a conjunctive adverb in an ellipsis, often rendered by "like"', as in MnE 'You shall eat grass like/as an ox'. His '*swa*' embraces not only *swa* alone, as in *BlHom* 109. 36 . . . *biþ þonne se flæschoma ascyred swa glæs, BlHom* 207. 19 *7 gelomlice ða stanas swa of oðrum clife stæðhlyplice ut sceoredon, LS* 35. 253 . . . *forþon he cwæð þæt man sceolde þeowian his hlaforde swa his drihtne,* and

Beo 642 þa wæs eft swa ær inne on healle
      þryðword sprecen, ðeod on sælum,
      sigefolca sweg;

but also *swa swa,* e.g. *ÆCHom* ii. 434. 2 . . . *and þu etst gærs swa swa oxa, ÆCHom* ii. 322. 18 *Forði hi fornimð helle fyr swa swa ceaf, and heora wyrtruma bið swa swa windige ysla, ÆCHom* i. 550. 5 . . . *forðan þe hi synd, æfter þæs apostolican cwyde, 'Swa swa naht hæbbende, and ealle ðing geagnigende', ÆGenPref* 70 . . . *7 he spræc to him eallum ðrym swa swa to anum,* and

PPs 121. 3   Hierusalem,   geara ðu wære
swa swa cymlic   ceaster getimbred,
þær syndon dælas   on sylfre hire;

and combinations such as *eal(l)swa,* e.g.

MCharm 12. 8   Clinge þu   alswa col on heorþe,
scring þu   alswa scerne awage,
and weorne   alswa weter on anbre,

and *efne swa,* e.g. *HomU* 21. 5. 8 . . . *ac wenað þæt se man scyle deadlice swyltan efne swa nyten.*

§3318. The second pattern is that seen in MnE 'He's as drunk as a lord'. In OE we find *swa . . . swa,* e.g. *ÆCHom* i. 442. 32 . . . *ðus befrinende, 'Hwæt is ðeos ðe her astihð swilce arisende dægrima, swa wlitig swa mona, swa gecoren swa sunne, and swa egeslic swa fyrdtruma?', ÆCHom* i. 382. 10 *ne eom ic wyrðe þæt ic swa hangige swa min Drihten,* and

ChristC 1229   þær hy arasade   reotað ond beofiað
fore frean forhte,   swa fule swa gæt,
unsyfre folc,   arna ne wenað;

swa . . . swa swa, e.g. the first clause in *ÆHex* 135 *Ðæt lyft is swa heah swa swa ða heofonlican wolcnu and eac eal swa brad swa swa ðære eorðan bradnyss;* and combinations such as *eal(l)swa . . . swa,* e.g. *ÆLS* 29. 159 . . . *þæt þa wundra gebigdon þa wiðerrædan hæðenan to þæs hælendes geleafan eallswa swiðe swa his bodung, eal(l)swa . . . swa swa,* e.g. the second clause in *ÆHex* 135 above, and *eal(l)swa . . . eal(l)swa,* e.g. *ÆCHom* i. 260. 23 *Eallswa bealdlice mot se ðeowa clypigan God him to fæder ealswa se cyning.* The examples quoted demonstrate that the element between the two *swas* may be an adjective or participle, an adverb, or a verb. They also demonstrate that Ælfric's usage varied; see Jost, *Ang.* 51 (1927), 94–5. For more examples see Ericson 1932, pp. 15–17, and on *swelce swa* see §3325.

n. Other uses of swa

§3319. On *(swa . . .) swa* '(either . . .) or' see §§1825–6. On the use of *swa* introducing negative clauses or sentences, see §§1924, 2861–3, 3267–70, and 3476–80.

§3320. Peltola, in an article which deserves the attention of lexi-cographers (*NM* 60 (1959), 156–73), distinguishes the 'similative' use of *swa (swa)*, as in *ÆCHom* i. 274. 6 *Se ðe þe mundað swa swa fæder, he bið swylce he ðin heafod sy*, from its 'identifying' func-tion. I have discussed the former in §§3316–18 under the heading 'contracted comparative clauses introduced by *swa*'. Peltola divides the latter into two groups, each of which is further subdivided into two. The first group comprises 'substantival *swa*-phrases'. These con-sist of *swa (swa)* + a noun, either alone or appropriately qualified, and are divided into 'appositional' and 'predicative'. The 'apposi-tional' *swa* phrase 'does not refer to the Predicate, but to the total meaning of the sentence. It can often be replaced by a subordinate clause indicating a causal relation. The relationship of identification is generally between the *swa*-phrase and the Subject.' Peltola's ex-amples include *Bede* 206. 5 *Ac ic, swa swa soðsagal stærwritere, þa þing, þe be him oððe þurh hine gewordene wæron, ic awrat, 7 þa þing þe herunge wyrðe wæron, ic herede*, Latin *quasi uerax histori-cus*, and *ÆCHom* i. 432. 1 *þæt ic dyde na swa swa dry ac swa swa cristen*. The 'predicative' *swa* phrase is 'closely associated with the Predicate verb and qualifies it in the manner of an adverbial phrase. The relationship of identification may concern the Subject, the Object, or any other substantival adjunct of the verb.' Peltola's examples include *ÆCHom* ii. 462. 4 *Witodlice se ðe is þæra æhta ðeow, he ðeowað him swa swa hlaforde, and se ðe is þæra æhta hlaford, he dælð hi swa swa hlaford*. But the line between the two is sometimes a fine one; consider *ÆLS* 27. 195 *He dælde þa his eahta ealle on ælmyssan and on clænnysse leofode swa swa Cristes ðegen*, in which (as Peltola observes) '*swa swa Cristes ðegen* may mean: 1. "because he was Christ's servant", 2. "in the capacity of Christ's servant" '. The 'appositional' form of this construction is, according to Peltola, more common than the 'predicative', in place of which we often find simple apposition or predication; phrases with *to, on*, and *for*; subordinate clauses; and phrases of other kinds.

§3321. The reverse is true with 'adjectival' *swa* phrases, which con-sist of *swa (swa)* + an adjective. Here the 'appositional' type, seen in *Bede* 80. 7 *Forþon, mid þy seo æ monig þing bewereð to etanne, swa swa unclæne . . .* , Latin *Nam cum multa lex uelut inmunda mandu-care prohibeat . . .* , is less common, Peltola tells us, than the 'predi-cative', seen in *ÆCHom* i. 474. 1 *Sume menn beoð geuntrumode for Godes tacnum, swa swa Crist cwæð be sumum blindan men, ðaða his leorningcnihtas hine axodon, for hwæs synnum se mann wurde swa blind acenned*. Again, the difficulty of distinguishing the two types arises; Peltola cites in illustration *ÆCHom* i. 454. 16 *To ðyssere becom Godes apostol Bartholomeus, and eode into ðam temple to ðam deofolgylde Astaroð, and swa swa ælðeodig ðær wunade*, where *swa swa ælðeodig* may mean ' "since he was a foreigner" ' or ' "(in the role of) a foreigner" '. But, he goes on, 'the appositional and predicative use of adjectives without *swa* is commoner'. For more examples of all types, and for discussion of these and other means of expressing identity, and of the origin of the identifying use of *swa*, see Peltola, loc. cit. On the presence of a causal element in some of them, see also Liggins 1955, pp. 343–4.

§3322. There are occasional examples in which *swa* adv. or conj. may be used in the asseverative sense, as in MnE 'So help me God' and 'As God is my helper, I shall keep my promise'. These include *VSal* 1. 234 *Swa me se sylfa dryhten lybbe, þam wyrestan deaðe þu scealt sweltan, VSal* 1. 253, *LawSwer(B)* 8 *Hu se sceal swerigean ðe mid oðre on gewitnesse standeð. On ealmihtiges Godes naman, swa ic her N on soðre gewitnosse stande, unabeden 7 ungeboht to, swa ic hit minum egum oferseah 7 minum earum oferhyrde, þæt þæt ic him mid secge, ApT* 30. 26 *Nim nu, lareow Apolloni, swa hit þe ne mislicyge, and bring þinum lærincgmædene,*

Beo 435   ic þæt þonne forhicge,   swa me Higelac sie,
min mondrihten   modes bliðe,
þæt ic sweord bere   oþðe sidne scyld,
geolorand to guþe . . . ,

and

Jul 80   Ic þæt geswerge   þurh soð godu,
swa ic are æt him   æfre finde,
oþþe, þeoden, æt þe   þine hyldu
winburgum in,   gif þas word sind soþ,
monna leofast,   þe þu me sagast,
þæt ic hy ne sparige,   ac on spild giefe,
þeoden mæra,   þe to gewealde.

For more possible examples, see Ericson 1932, pp. 80–1, and Mitchell 1959, pp. 350 and 617, where I note that at least some of these sentences can be otherwise explained. Here it is appropriate to quote the sound observation made by Small in his review of Ericson 1932 (*MLN* 49 (1934), 538):

The form *swa* embraces so many subtle gradations of meaning and function in OE texts that one may often choose among several possible interpretations. Dr. Ericson in his analyses has often permitted himself to be influenced by the Middle and Modern English development of *swa* constructions, thus adopting an historical point of view. But there are cases in which a more conservative interpretation can be justified and, in the present reviewer's opinion, would be preferred.

For a full list of uses of *swa*, see the Index of Words and Phrases.

7. *SWELC/SWELCE* ALONE AND IN COMBINATION

a. Swelce *indefinite or adverb/conjunction?*

§3323. The fact that the adverb/conjunction *swelce* is identical in form with the instrumental singular masculine and neuter, the accusative singular feminine, and the nominative and accusative plural, of the indefinite *swelc* sometimes gives rise to problems of classification without ever obscuring the meaning. When the forms are different, the difficulty does not arise, e.g. *ÆLS* 31. 1249 *and þær com gesewenlice eall swylc oþer swer ufan of heofonum and þone oþerne tosloh*, where (as Jost, *Ang.* 51 (1927), 96, points out) Skeat's 'as it were another pillar' is wrong; the meaning is 'a second such pillar, in all respects similar'. But, whereas the lack of agreement in *ChronE* 136. 3 (1005) *Her on þyssum geare wæs se mycla hungor geond Angelcynn swilce nan man ær ne gemunde swa grimne* means that *swilce* is a conjunction, it can be either a conjunction or an indefinite taking its number from *swelcerra manna* in *Or* 68. 25 *þa he ðæt secgean nolde, þa acsedon hie hine hu fela þær swelcerra manna wære swelce he wæs; compare ÆLS* 32. 259 (§3324), *ÆCHom* ii. 428. 22 (§3325), and *BlHom* 33. 7 and *CP(C)* 100. 6 (both in §3327). For further examples see §§2378 and 3327 and, on *Rim* 23 *swylce eorþe ol*, Macrae-Gibson, *NM* 74 (1973), 77–8. However, I have to confess that I do not follow the logic of Jost's remark (*Ang.* 51 (1927), 93) that 'die Übereinstimmung von *swylc*, resp. *swylce* mit *seinem* [my italics] Beziehungswort verbietet es, in diesem Wort etwas anderes als ein adjektivisches Pronomen zu sehen' ['the agreement of *swylc* or *swylce* with *its* [my italics] antecedent does not permit it to be regarded as anything other than an adjectival pronoun']. I can see that if *swelce* does not agree with a *potential* antecedent, it is the conjunction. But I do not see why the fact that it *appears* to agree means that it must be the indefinite. The problem is further complicated by examples like *BlHom* 59. 28 *Eal swylce seo lange mettrumnes biþ þæs seocan mannes, þonne hine god forlætan nele eþelice lifian, ne he þeah swyltan ne mote, 7 swa þeah hwæþere oþ þone deaþ he hine tintregaþ, swylc is þæt lif þysses middangeardes* and a prose passage from *MCharm* 1. 45 *Ðonne þæt eall sie gedon, þonne nime man uncuþ sæd æt ælmesmannum and selle him twa swylc, swylce man æt him nime, and gegaderie ealle his sulhgeteogo togædere*, in which we appear to have conj. *swylce* co-ordinate, as it were, with indefinite *swylc*.

b. Indefinite swelc (. . .) (swelc)

§3324. On *swelc* 'such as, whatever' used alone combining both antecedent and relative, see §2374. On *swelc . . . swelc* in the sense of Latin *talis . . . qualis* and MnE 'such . . . as', see §2375 and *Ang*. 51 (1927), 93, where Jost observes that the absence from his Ælfric collections of sg. *swelc . . . swelc* used as an 'adjektivisches Pronomen'—the plural appears, for example, in *ÆLS* 32. 259 *Nis angelcynn bedæled drihtnes halgena þonne on Englalanda licgaþ swilce halgan swylce þæs halga cyning is and Cuþberht se eadiga and sancte Æþeldryð . . . and eac hire swustor ansunde on lichaman*—is probably a matter of chance. *CP* 133. 6 below certainly qualifies, as do *LawVAs* 1. 1 . . . *sece swylcne hlaford on þa gewitnesse swylcne he wille* and similar examples quoted in §2375. But, like Jost, I have noted none in Ælfric, though we do find *ÆCHom* i. 32. 11 . . . *forðan ðe næfre næs swilc sibb ær þam fyrste on middangearde, swilc swa wæs on his gebyrde tide, ÆCHom* ii. 162. 24 . . . *þæt he ðone cwelmbæran hlaf aweg bære and on swilcere stowe awurpe ðær hine nan man findan ne mihte*, and *ÆCHom* i. 454. 18 *On ðam deofolgylde wunade swilc deofol ðe to mannum þurh ða anlicnysse spræc* . . . , and the like, on which patterns see §2377. So Jost is probably right about 'chance'. However, it is a delicate point whether in *ÆLS* 32. 259 above *swylce* is a plural pronoun agreeing with *swilce* and *ansunde* (as Jost takes it) or a conjunction (as the singular verb in *þæs halga cyning is* might suggest); compare *Or* 68. 25 (§3323) and see §2378. Liggins (1955, p. 357) detects an element of cause in *CP* 133. 6 *Suelc þæt folc bið, suelc bið se sacerd*; see §3112.

c. Indefinite swelc + (. . .) swa

§3325. Combinations of indefinite *swelc* with *swa* are used correlatively in the meaning 'such . . . as' and vary in both function and meaning between Latin *talis . . . qualis, tantus . . . quantus*, and *tot . . . quot*, reflecting the fact that OE *swelc*, like MnE 'such', is somewhat vague in meaning. Thus, in *Lch* ii. 116. 11 *drince þisne drenc nigon niht 7 þicge swilcne mete swa he wille*, there may be a comparison with the kind of food he does not want or with the amount of food he would normally eat or with the maximum amount of food he could eat. The examples which follow will serve to illustrate the variety of combinations possible: *ÆCHom* ii. 192. 34 *þæt eahtoðe wite wæs, þæt gærstapan ofereodon eall þæt land swilce swa næfre ærðan næron, ne eft næfre ne gewurðað*; *Lch* ii. 42. 19 . . . *genim eorðgeallan grenes seaw oþþe hunan seaw oþþe wermodes seaw, swilc þara an swa þu wille*; *Lch* ii. 116. 11 above; *Lch* ii. 84. 4 *genim beanmela oþþe ætena oððe beres oþþe swilces meluwes swa þe þince*; *ÆCHom* ii. 348. 24 *me is alyfed eft to lybbenne mid mannum, na swaþeah swilcum life swa ic ær leofode*; *ÆCHom* i. 52. 23 *Uton lufian ure gebroðra on Godes gelaðunge mid swilcum mode swa swa ðes cyðere þa lufode his fynd* (Thorpe 'with such affection as that with which . . .'); *ÆCHom* i. 32. 11 (§3324);

Soul i 138

	Eala, min dryhten,
þær ic þe moste	mid me lædan,
þæt wyt englas	ealle gesawon,
heofona wuldor,	swylc swa ðu me ær her scrife!;

and

Dan 61

Gestrudan gestreona	under stanhliðum,
swilc eall swa þa eorlas	agan sceoldon.

Contracted *swa* clauses also occur, e.g. *ÆCHom* ii. 162. 17 . . . *Florentinus, se wolde habban swilcne hlisan swa Benedictus ac he nolde herigendlice lybban*. *ÆCHom* ii. 428. 22 *Ic ne eom swilce swa oðre men* may belong here, with *swilce* taking its number from *oðre men*. But *swilce* may be a conjunction; cf. *Or* 68. 25 (§3323). For more examples see Jost, *Ang.* 51 (1927), 93 and 96.

§3326. Both clauses may require the same case, e.g. *ÆCHom* i. 52. 23, *ÆCHom* ii. 348. 24, and *Dan* 62 (all in §3325), or a different one, e.g. nominative/accusative in *ÆCHom* i. 360. 34 *Se witega hine het stemn, forðan ðe he forestop Criste, ðe is Word gehaten: na swilc word swa menn sprecað, ac he is ðæs Fæder Wisdom, and word bið wisdomes geswutelung*; genitive/nominative in *Lch* ii. 84. 4 (§3325); and genitive/accusative in

Beo 2231

	þær wæs swylcra fela
in ðam eorðhuse	ærgestreona,
swa hy on geardagum	gumena nathwylc,
eormenlafe	æðelan cynnes,
þanchycgende	þær gehydde,
deore maðmas.	

Since *brucan* can govern the accusative as well as the genitive and the dative, *ÆCHom* i. 450. 1 *and he mid þam worde him bead swylce lac swa he sylf breac* can be placed in the first group.

d. Swelce

§3327. In many examples, it is impossible to decide whether *swelce* is an indefinite or a conjunction; see §3323. We can detect unambiguous conj. *swelce = swa (swa)* introducing comparative clauses in examples like *Bo* 91. 1 . . . *þ nan þing ne bið swilce hit wæs, ChronE* 136. 3 (1005) (§3323), *Beo* 756 *ne wæs his drohtoð þær* || *swylce he on ealderdagum ær gemette*, and in contracted examples like *Matt (WSCp)* 10. 25 . . . *þ he sy swylce hys lareow 7 þeow swylce hys hlafurd* and *El* 802 *Ða of ðære stowe steam up aras* || *swylce rec under radorum*; see also §2378. But I have found few convincingly unambiguous instances of conj. *swelce* and have been unable to supplement them from the lists of alleged examples given by BT(S), s.v. *swilce*, and by Jost, *Ang.* 51 (1927), 93-4. Rightly or wrongly, I do not regard as unambiguous those in which *swelce* might be an indefinite taking its number from a plural element in one of the two clauses, e.g. *BlHom* 33. 7 *Cuþ is þæt se awyrgda gast is heafod ealra unrihtwisra dæda, swylce unrihtwise syndon deofles leomo* and *CP(C)* 100. 6 *Ðonne ic wæs mid Iudeum ic wæs swelce hie*, where (to underline the point) MS *H* has *suelc*—compare again *Or* 68. 25 (§3323)—and those in which *swelce* is or could be an adverb 'likewise, also', e.g. *BlHom* 33. 33 *he wæs soþ man, þy hine dorste deofol costian, swylce he wæs soþ God, þe him englas þegnedon* (here I agree with Morris, not with Jost) and

Prec 54	Seldan snottor guma sorgleas blissað,
	swylce dol seldon drymeð sorgful
	ymb his forðgesceaft, nefne he fæhþe wite,

where Gollancz translates 'just as', but 'likewise' is certainly possible.

§3328. This scarcity of unambiguous examples holds for the works of Ælfric. Indeed, the question arises whether Ælfric ever uses *swelce* to introduce a comparative clause or whether it is always to be translated 'as if', a usage exemplified in *ÆCHom* ii. 256. 27 . . . *swilce he cwæde* . . . 'as if he had said . . .' and discussed in §§3370-81. Jost (*Ang.* 51 (1927), 93) proposes as an example *ÆLet* 4. 495 *An ys Parabole, þæt ys bigspellboc, na swilce ge secgað ac wisdomes bigspell.* Pope (*Ælfric*, i. 102 fn. 5) rightly objects. But it is not necessary to follow him in postulating ellipsis of *swa*; on *swelc* alone meaning 'such as', see §2374.[177] We can, however, with one slight reservation discussed below, follow Pope when he observes (*Ælfric*,

[177] Potter (*RES* 4 (1953), 366) is, I believe, guilty of a similar error in his criticism of Timmer's note on *Jud* 65.

i. 102-3) that in Ælfric 'when *swylce* introduces a clause of manner, it regularly means "as if" and the verb is in the subjunctive. When it introduces an adverbial phrase the meaning is still "as if"; and even when it introduces a noun there is usually a stronger sense than with *swa swa* that the likeness is fanciful or inexact.' See further his glossary, s.v. *swilce, swylce*, conj., and cf. Jost, *Ang.* 51 (1927), 95-6. But despite Pope's note on the passage, I would add to his examples *ÆHom* 29. 4 *Mannum is eac to witenne þæt manega drymenn maciað menigfealde dydrunga þurh deofles cræft, swa swa wisceras oft doð, and bedydriað menn swilce hi soðlice swylc þing don, ac hyt is swaþeah dydrung mid deofles cræfte*, translating 'as if they were actually doing such things'. Here the idiomatic pres. subj. *don* (§§3378-9) and Skeat's 'as if' give the vital clues. We may compare *ÆCHom* ii. 140. 14 *Hwæt se swicola feond hi swiðe bedydrode, swilce ðær sum hus soðlice forburne, brastligende mid brandum, gedwymorlice swaðeah.*

§3329. A striking illustration of Pope's statement (my §3328) is to be found in *ÆCHom* i. 222. 30 *His wlite wæs swilce liget and his reaf swa hwit swa snaw.* But—and here is the slight reservation—what is the point of the variation *swa . . . swa, swa . . . swa*, but *swa . . . swilce*, in *ÆCHom* i. 516. 13 *Gif hwilc sibling þe bið swa deorwurðe swa ðin eage, and oðer swa behefe swa ðin hand, and sum swa geðensum swilce ðin agen fot . . .* ? Is Jost (loc. cit.) right when he says that *ÆCHom* i. 46. 4 *þa beheoldon ða hine ðe on þam geðeahte sæton, and gesawon his nebwlite swylce sumes engles ansyne* can be translated either 'wie das Gesicht eines Engels ist' ['as is the countenance of an angel'] or 'wie wenn es das Gesicht eines Engels wäre' ['as if it were the countenance of an angel']? The dilemma is neatly illustrated by the fact that Thorpe's translation of *ÆCHom* i. 614. 17 *Swa is ðisum middangearde: æt fruman he wæs ðeonde swylce on geogoðhade, he wæs on lichamlicere hælðe growende, and on speda genihtsumnysse fætt, langsum on life, stille on langsumere sibbe; ac he is nu mid ylde ofsett, swylce mid gelomlæcendum hefigtymnyssum to deaðe geðread* has 'as' for the first *swylce* and 'as it were' for the second. We might similarly ask whether Pope's distinction can be extended to non-Ælfrician texts and whether there is any special significance in the use of *swilce* instead of *swa* in examples like *BlHom* 21. 25 *7 þonne seo sawl hie gedæleþ wiþ þone lichoman, hwylc biþ he þonne buton swylce stan oþþe treow?, And* 88, and

GuthB 1309   *Eal þæt beacen wæs*
        ymb þæt halge hus,   heofonlic leoma,
        from foldan up   swylce fyren tor

> ryht aræred   oð rodera hrof,
> gesewen under swegle,   sunnan beorhtra,
> æþeltungla wlite.

There is room for more work here.

e. Swelce (. . .) swa

§3330. The use of this combination as a conjunction is seen in

Dream 90   Hwæt, me þa geweorðode   wuldres ealdor
ofer holmwudu,   heofonrices weard,
swylce swa he his modor eac,   Marian sylfe,
ælmihtig god   for ealle menn
geweorðode   ofer eall wifa cynn,

where I follow Dickins and Ross; in

GuthB 1273   Swylce on sumeres tid
stincað on stowum   staþelum fæste
wynnum æfter wongum   wyrta geblowene,
hunigflowende,   swa þæs halgan wæs
ondlongne dæg   oþ æfen forð
oroð up hlæden;

and in *Rid* 15. 3 *Me on bæce standað* || *her swylce swe on hleorum*, where the form and sense suggest that *swylce* is unlikely to be an indefinite. But, despite Ericson (1932, p. 37), it is not a conjunction in *Josh* 2. 12 and *HomU* 34. 195. 22. The rest of Ericson's examples are also doubtful. The meaning is 'as if' in *Bede* 134. 24 and (I suspect) in *LawAfEl* 13. Ericson's *Cr* 92 is probably *Dream* 90, above. *Swylce* in *PPs* 77. 27 is adverbial and *swylc* in *PPs* 147. 6 is best taken as an indefinite. I have recorded no more examples. However, Friend (*MLN* 69 (1954), 385-7) takes *Beo* 1142 *swa* . . . 1146 *swylce* as correlative 'as . . . in like manner'.

f. Swelc + a superlative + a form of magan

§3331. This combination occurs in

Beo 2867   . . . þonne he on ealubence   oft gesealde
healsittendum   helm ond byrnan,
þeoden his þegnum,   swylce he þrydlicost
ower feor oððe neah   findan meahte. . . .

g. Swelc + a superlative + a verb other than magan

§3332. What appears to be an example of this combination occurs in *Ch* 1275 . . . *ðet is Cuðred dux 7 Wulfriðe his wife 7 anan man þerto suil him liofost sio.* . . .

h. Mood

§3333. *Mutatis mutandis*, the remarks made about the corresponding types of *swa* clauses are applicable here. The indicative is the prevailing mood except when *swelce* + the subjunctive carries the sense 'as if'.

8. CONSTRUCTIONS INVOLVING *þY/þON/þE* AND A COMPARATIVE

§3334. The origin and development of the modern constructions with 'the' and the comparative—which have been discussed by Johnsen, *EStudien*, 44 (1911-12), 212-39; Christophersen, pp. 115-17; Fowler, *Modern English Usage* (1st edn.), s.v. *the* 5 and 6; id., *The King's English* (3rd edn.), pp. 78-82; and others—are topics outside the scope of this work. But much that has been written reveals ignorance of, or failure to refer to, the OE constructions. Thus, Christophersen (p. 116) complains that 'Johnsen, from whose materials I have chiefly drawn my information, does not seem to have realised the historical connection between the two types of construction, the single and the double *the*.' He in his turn does not seem to have realized that there are more than two constructions. So I list here the OE comparative constructions with *þe*, some of which have already been discussed.

§3335. I begin by excluding as special developments the idiom seen in *HomU* 35. 206. 14 *ac men him nellað gelefan þe ma þe heo Noe dydon . . .* , in which *þe ma þe* follows a negative and means 'more than', and the isolated examples of this sort in which *þonne* appears in place of *þe* after the comparative, e.g. *HomU* 37. 242. 10 *. . . þæt hy nyton þa tid hwænne we of þysum earman life gewitan sceolon þe ma þonne se þeof wat. . . .* These are discussed in §§3243-50. The remaining constructions can be divided into five types, the last two of which I have not as yet encountered in OE.

§3336. Type 1 is the OE equivalent of MnE 'I am (much/none) the better (for taking those pills)'. It consists of instr. *þy/þon/þe* + a comparative and, as in MnE, can follow a negative, e.g. *CP* 143. 9 *. . . 7 he nyle hie arasian ðylæs hira lufu aslacige 7 he him ðe wirs licige*, *CP* 97. 6 *. . . he bið nohte ðon læs mid ðære besmiten*, and *ÆCHom* ii. 462. 22 *. . . we gelyfað þæt he gegæð Gode buton he þe swiðor forscyldgod wære*, or not, e.g. *Or* 100. 15 *Ic scæl eac þy lator Romana istoria asecgan þe ic angunnen hæfde* and *CP* 313. 2 *7 for* ðære ilcan eaðmodnesse he ofermodgað innan micle ðy hefelicor; can be accompanied by an explanatory phrase, e.g. *CP* 423. 20 *Forðæm wæs sanctus Paulus gecostod . . . ðæt he ongeate his synna 7 forðæm wære ðy strangra on godum weorcum*, *CP* 339. 25 . . . *ðæt hie for ðæm godan hlisan ðy forcuðran ne weorðen*, and *WHom* 5. 108 *And eal hit forwurde gyf God ne gescyrte þæs þeodscaðan lifdagas þe raþor ðurh his mihta*; or can be reinforced by an intensifying adverb, e.g. *CP* 97. 6 and 313. 2, both quoted above. This formula is the first half of the constructions mentioned in the previous section and is discussed with them in §§3243-50. But I remind the reader of my agreement—as qualified in §3245—with Small's view (1930, p. 384): 'In the opinion of the writer the form *the* immediately before the comparative *never*, from OE to PE, means "by that much". It always in that position refers to a condition or object previously named or understood, and is functionally a true case of comparison, meaning not "*by* that", but "*than* that" or "*than* before". . . .' This view is contrary to that expressed by Johnsen (*EStudien*, 44 (1911-12), 212-13)—'*the* = *þy* properly means *by that*'—but is accepted by Christophersen (p. 115), who observes that the function of *þon/þy/þe* here was 'to indicate the basis or standard used, the starting-point in the comparison'.

§3337. In type 2, a principal clause containing a formula of type 1 is accompanied by a subordinate clause without a comparative adjective or adverb. The most common pattern (type 2a) is that with a *þe* clause; on this see below. The remaining patterns need only be described and exemplified: type 2b, with a causal clause introduced by a *for* formula, e.g. *CP* 397. 30 *Forðæm bið sio scyld ðy hraðor gehæled forðæmðe hio ne bið unliefedo* and *WHom* 6. 205 *Ac Godd hine fordeþ þe raþor, forðam þe he wile gebeorhgan þam ðe him sylfum syn gecorene 7 gecweme*; type 2c, with a conditional clause, e.g. *CP* 397. 6 *forðæmðe he mæg micle ðy ieð adreogan ða tionan ðe him oðre men doð, gif he wile gemunan ða ðe he oðrum monnum deð*, *ÆCHom* ii. 538. 7 . . . *þæt hi ðy læs manna mod gedrefon gif hi beoð cuðe on ær*, and *ÆCHom* ii. 538. 11 *gif ðu unwær bist, þu bist ðe swiðor geswenct*; and type 2d, with a temporal clause, e.g. *CP* 433. 25 . . . *ðara godena monna, ða sculon ongietan ða costunga 7 ðæt gefeoht, ærðæmðe hit cume, ðæt hi mægen ðy fæstor gestondan, ðonne hit cume?* and *Bo* 23. 13 *Eall hie us þyncað þy leohtran ða hwile þe þa oncras fæste bioð*.

§3338. Type 2a may be exemplified by

Mald 312   Hige sceal þe heardra,   heorte þe cenre,
               mod sceal þe mare,   þe ure mægen lytlað,

where, since the action of the *þe* clause is one which can take place
by degrees or in part, we may claim to have a correlative comparative
construction '. . . (according/in proportion) as our strength dimin-
ishes'. This type has of necessity been discussed among causal constructions in §§3137-43, where it forms a sub-group of type B and
is contrasted with type 3 below, which there features as type A. In
that discussion it was agreed that *þe ure mægen lytlað* could be a
temporal or causal clause 'when . . .' or 'because . . .'. Sometimes *þe*
may be said to introduce an adjective clause, e.g.

MSol 243   Bald bið se ðe onbyregeð   boca cræftes;
                symle bið ðe wisra   ðe hira geweald hafað,

where we have to assume an unexpressed subject if we wish to take
the *ðe* clause as one of comparison. On such difficulties see further
Small 1926, p. 302 fn. 1, and my §§3138-40, where I point out
that the correlative comparative construction without a second comparative (called type 2a here, type B in §3138) is not to be found in
those examples in which the action of the *þe* clause is not one which
can take place by degrees or in part, e.g.

ChristC 1255   Ðonne hi þy geornor   gode þonciað
                blædes ond blissa   þe hy bu geseoð,
                þæt he hy generede   from niðcwale
                ond eac forgeaf   ece dreamas.

In examples of type 2a, the subordinate clause follows its principal
or governing clause.

§3339. I turn now to type 3, in which both clauses have a comparative and the subordinate clause again follows its principal or governing clause, e.g. the well-known *CP* 5. 24 . . . *7 woldon ðæt her ðy
mara wisdom on londe wære ðy we ma geðeoda cuðon, Bo* 138. 20,
Bo 140. 31 below, and

Met 12. 18   Swa þincð anra gehwæm   eorðbuendra
                sio soðe gesælð   symle ðe betere
                and þy wynsumre,   þe he wita ma,
                heardra henða,   her adreogeð.

More examples will be found in §§3138-41, where I called this
construction type A. Here too *þe/þy* could be said to introduce
a temporal 'when' clause, a causal 'because' clause, or a correlative
comparative clause '(in proportion/according) as'. The fact that the
first *þon/þy/þe* is immediately followed by its comparative, whereas
the second *þy/þe* is (as far as I have observed) always separated from
its comparative by some other element(s) of the clause—e.g. the

subject in *CP* 5. 24 above but the subject and the object in *Bo* 140. 31 *þa men habbað simle freodom þy maran þe hi heora mod near godcundum ðingum lætað, 7 habbað þæs þy læssan friodom þe hi hiora modes willan near þisse weoruldare lætað*—makes it impossible to claim that the second clause *must* be one of correlative comparison. Hence arise arguments about the nature of the second *þy/þe*, already discussed for causal clauses in §§3063-4 and discussed again here in §3341: do we have indeclinable particle *þe* or instr. *þy*, and is it used in a causal or comparative function?

§3340. What I call types 4 and 5 are, as far as I know, not represented in OE with correlative *þy/þe . . . þy/þe*. But they are exemplified by the first and second examples respectively in *OED*'s note s.v. *the* adv. 2: 'The relative clause usually comes first, e.g. "The more one has, the more one wants"; but the order may be reversed, as "One wants the more, the more one has"; and in either order the comparative in the relative clause is sometimes followed by *that*, e.g. "the more that one has".' The only OE example given by *OED* —it is silent s.v. *thy* adv.—is *CP* 5. 24, quoted in §3339 as an example of type 3. Like other type 3 examples, it differs from the *OED* example of type 4 in two ways: first, the second *þe* is separated from its comparative and does not immediately precede it, and, second, the principal clause precedes the subordinate clause, whereas in type 4—the more common MnE type—the reverse is true. Type 3 and type 5 have the order of clauses in common, but still differ in separation against non-separation of *þe/the* and the comparative.

§3341. What is the connection between these types? The general assumption seems to be that types 2a and 3 are extensions of type 1. I regard this as reasonable, with the proviso that type 3 is quite likely to have arisen directly from type 1, but could be an extension of type 2a. Christophersen (p. 116) takes the view that types 2a and 3 are related—'the explanatory *þe*-clause might incidentally contain a comparative'; that in both types the first *þe* is instrumental and the second a 'conjunction' (i.e. the indeclinable *þe*) in the sense 'according as' rather than, as Johnsen (*EStudien*, 44 (1911–12), 228) has it, 'because'; and that 'though elsewhere displaced by the particle *that*, the conjunction was here preserved because a parallelism was established between the two *þe*'s, the latter being now put directly before the comparative. This, to my mind, is clearly the origin of the modern *the . . . the* phrase.' So type 4 (Christophersen does not cite examples of type 5) is a 'continuation' of types 2a and/or 3. This does not feel right to me and I find it hard to envisage the process without documentation from ME and eMnE. Here the vital question is the status of the second *þe/the*. Most scholars would, I think, agree with Christophersen (p. 115) that in types 4 and 5 both *þe/the*s are instrumental: 'from a historical point of view, *the* is not the article, but the demonstrative pronoun functioning as a primary in *the worse for drink* and *the more the merrier*'. If this is so and if the second *þe* in OE examples of types 2a and 3 is the indeclinable particle, as Christophersen (p. 116) asserts (see above), then it is hard to see how Christophersen can be right in thinking that types 4 and 5 have their origins in types 2a and 3, even if we agree with his comment (p. 116) that 'with the passage of time, the first (demonstrative) *þy(þe)* became shortened and unaccented and thus coincided in sound with the conjunction'. So we can see how there may have emerged, by a sort of 'popular etymology' and misunderstanding of the original idiom—in which the first *þy/þe* was 'a true case of comparison' (§3336) and the second introduced a temporal or causal or adjective clause (§§3938-9)—the view that both the first and the second *þy/þe* were in origin instrumentals expressing degree. Such a view would perhaps most naturally have first arisen in those apparently correlative *þy/þe . . . þy/þe* patterns with two comparatives in which the action of the subordinate clause is one which takes place by degrees and spread from there. It may even have been a factor in the development of types 4 and 5 (§3340), which are not represented in my OE collections.

§3342. At this stage it will be fruitful to examine in terms of the types established above the patterns found in the *swa (. . . swa)* clauses involving a comparative discussed in §§3287-9. The closest we come to examples of type 1 seems to be the pattern seen in *GenA* 989 *leng swa swiðor* (quoted in full in §3289) and *Lch* ii. 34. 15 *7 beþe þa eagan on þam baþe betere swa oftor*. But these are not really type 1, since they have two comparatives. Indeed, the first can be expanded to a type 4—'the longer (time they grew), the greater (they were)'—and the second to a type 5—'(it will be) the better, the oftener (one bathes it)'. Type 2a can be detected in *CP* 191. 9 *Forðæm him is suiðe micel ðearf ðæt he sua micle wærlicor hine healde wið scylda swa he gere witan mæg ðæt he no ana ne forwierð, ðonne he oðrum yfele bisene steleð*, where the governing *swa* clause precedes the subordinate *swa* clause. But we also find sentences like *Or* 38. 18 *swa swyðe swa hi ær Moyse 7 hys folce þæs utfæreldes wyrndon, swa micle hy wæron geornran þæt hi him fram fulgen*, where the subordinate clause comes first—an arrangement which has not been recorded, and would seem impossible, with

þy/þe . . . þy/þe. We find examples of type 3 with *swa . . . swa*, e.g.
GD 335. 21 and *Or* 20. 22 (both in §3287). In the former, all of the
governing clause precedes the subordinate *swa* clause. In the latter,
part of it does so. But here too the subordinate *swa* clause may come
first, e.g. *CP* 103. 18 *7 sua micle sua hio estelicor of dune astigeð,
sua hio ieðelicor up astigeð*. Future workers may find this difference
in the clause arrangements possible with *þy/þe . . . þy/þe* and with
swa . . . swa significant. They may also find it significant that examples
like *Or* 18. 29 *7 symle swa norðor swa smælre* and *WHom(EI)* 20. 8
swa leng swa wyrse correspond to MnE 'the more the merrier' and
can therefore be called contracted examples of type 4. I have as yet
recorded no corresponding type 4 examples with verbs and no OE
examples at all of type 5 with *swa . . . swa*. I do not have full statistics. But Christophersen (p. 116) is probably right when he suggests
that *swa . . . swa* predominates over *þy/þe . . . þy/þe* in types 2a and
3. With type 1, *þy/þe* seems more common than *swa*.

§3343. Future workers on the subsequent history of constructions
with *swa (. . . swa)* and *þy/þe (. . . þy/þe)* will need to take into
account the differences between the various types which have already
been discussed. Johnsen (*EStudien*, 44 (1911-12), 233-4) did notice
the separation of the second *þe* and its comparative in OE types 2a
and 3, but his statement that 'in correlation *the* is in the first instance
a relative in the second a demonstrative'—cf. Fowler, *The King's
English* (3rd edn.), 79—is true only of examples of type 4, in which
the subordinate clause comes first, and not of examples of types 2a,
3, or 5, in which the governing clause precedes it.

§3344. Future workers will also need to examine the possibility
that MnE usage is sometimes the result of a blending of constructions
with *swa* and constructions with *þy/þe*. One can perhaps see the
beginning of such blends in examples with *swa . . . swa* and a type 1
þe pattern in the principal clause, e.g. *WHom* 14. 51 (§3287) and
WHom 15. 56 *7 æfre, swa he hine sylfne swyðor geeadmed on his
dædbote, swa byð his dædbot Gode andfengre, 7 Godes mildheort-
nes him micle þe gearwre*—in these two examples the subordinate
clause has a comparative without *þe*—and in *ÆTemp* 12. 26 *Ælc
ðing swa hit ðe fyrr bið swa hit ðe læsse ðincð*, where we have two
correlative *swa* clauses, with type 1 *þe* patterns in each clause. There
is room for a full diachronic investigation here. Anyone attempting
it should not overlook Nummenmaa, pp. 115-17, or Johnsen's useful collection of examples in *EStudien*, 44 (1911-12), 212-39.

§3345. On mood, it will suffice to say that clauses with *þy/þe (. . . þy/þe)* and a comparative have the indicative unless one or more of the factors noted in §§3295-300 produces a subjunctive; for typical examples see *ByrM* 70. 8 and 114. 28 (both in §3139).

§3346. *Mutatis mutandis*, what has been written above is applicable to those examples discussed in §§3355-9 in which *þæs* precedes the first *þy/þe*.

9. *þÆS (þE)*

a. Introductory remarks

§3347. Here we are concerned with comparative uses of *þæs (þe)*. For other uses of *þæs (þe)*, *þæs . . . þe*, and *þæs . . . þæt*, see the Index of Words and Phrases.

§3348. We have already seen in §1141 that *þæs* is sometimes used for *swa* in the poetry, e.g. *Sea* 39 *Forþon nis þæs modwlonc mon ofer eorþan* || *ne his gifena þæs god . . .* and *Beo* 1366 *No þæs frod leofað* || *gumena bearna þæt þone grund wite*, but that usages such as *Bo(C)* 75. 4 *þæs welig þ* are less common in the prose; indeed MS *B* has *swa welig þ*. This adverbial use of *þæs* is demonstrative in origin. The use of *þæs (þe)* as a conjunction may be an extension of the adverbial use or of the pronominal use; cf. *Phoen* 567 *Me þæs wen næfre* || *forbirsteð in breostum . . .* with *Beo* 271 *ne sceal þær dyrne sum* || *wesan, þæs ic wene* 'according to/from what' and

Beo 381   Hine halig God
          for arstafum   us onsende,
          to West-Denum,   þæs ic wen hæbbe,
          wið Grendles gryre—

Wrenn notes that in *Beo* 272 '*þæs* is gen. of respect, or instrum. gen. = "according to that (which)", or "from what" ' and translates *Beo* 383*b* ' "as I confidently expect"—lit. "from what I have expectation" '. But see §3351.

§3349. Here again we must consider whether *þe* is the indeclinable particle or a form of the instrumental *þy*. Examples like *Bo* 58. 29 *Nese la nese; næs ic næfre git nane hwile swa emnes modes, þæs þe ic gemunan mæge, þ ic eallunga wære orsorg . . .* , rendered by BT (s.v. *se* V (2)(b)) '. . . from what, as far as', suggest that it is the indeclinable particle. I must confess that the idea that it was anything

else had not entered my head until I saw Kivimaa's observation
(p. 153) that 'a third common use of *þæs þe* is in comparisons,
e.g. *CP* 123. 18 *Sio wund bið ðæs ðe wierse ⁊ ðy mare. þe* here
would seem instrumental in origin.' I agree that *þe* is instrumental in
CP 123. 18. But the status of *þæs* is doubtful. I do not know whether
Kivimaa merely chose an unfortunate example—*CP* 123. 18 belongs
with the type 1 examples discussed in my §3336—or whether she
meant to imply that *þe* was instrumental in all examples of *þæs þe*
used as a comparative conjunction. So two questions have to be
answered: first, can *þe* be instrumental in *Bo* 58. 29 and the like?
and second, is *þæs þe* in examples like *CP* 123. 18 a combination or
is *þæs* an adverb independent of *þe* expressing cause or some other
relationship? We can best answer these questions by analysing the
various *þæs þe* comparative constructions in OE.

b. þæs (þe) *conjunction 'as'*

§3350. As Wülfing (i. 381) rightly observes, *þæs þe* serves in *Bede*
as a translation of Latin *ut* in various meanings, e.g. *Bede* 86. 18 *þæs
þe ic demo*, Latin *ut arbitror*, and *Bede* 88. 23 *þæs þe swa to
cweðenne sy*, Latin *ut ita dixerim*. Similar examples are to be found
elsewhere, e.g. *Bo* 54. 27 *ðæs ðe him ðincð*, *BlHom* 37. 13 *þæs þe
we magon* (on this type, see §3353), *HomU* 21. 4. 12 *þæs þe we
sylfe wistan ful georne*, and *WHom* 6. 133 *þæs ðe bec secgað*. Sometimes it is not clear whether we have the conjunction or a relative;
see §3353 and Wülfing, i, §28b. As far as I have observed, *þæs* does
not appear in the sense 'as' in the prose and *þæs þe* is avoided by
Ælfric in favour of *swa swa*. Examples like *ÆHom* 10. 144 *ac hi
mihton blissian on mode þæs ðe swiðor . . .* belong in §3356.

§3351. Both *þæs* and *þæs þe* appear as conjunctions 'as' in the
poetry or at least can be so taken. Typical examples include *Beo*
272 *þæs ic wene* and *Beo* 383 *þæs ic wen hæbbe* (but both these
could be genitive demonstratives governed by *wen(e)*); *And* 687
þæs we gefrægen habbað; and *GenA* 1239 *þæs þe bec cweðaþ* and
And 472 *þæs ðe me þynceð*. Wülfing (i. 381-2), Schücking (pp.
35-6), and Sorg (pp. 64-7), offer more examples. However, I have
the overwhelming impression that *þæs (þe)* is much less common
than *swa (swa)*.

§3352. This impression is strengthened by the fact that I have so
far recorded only one example of *þæs þe* + a superlative + a form
of *magan*, viz.

Beo 1349   Ðæra oðer wæs,
           þæs þe hie gewislicost   gewitan meahton,
           idese onlicnes,

which may be compared with the more common pattern with *swa* discussed in §§3306–12.

§3353. But it is worthy of note that a considerable minority of clauses introduced by *þæs þe* 'as' have a form of the verb *magan*, e.g. *BlHom* 37. 11 . . . *ah we sceolan on þas tid þas feawan dagas on for-hæfdnesse lifgean, urne lichoman 7 ure heortan clænsian from yflum geþohtum þæs þe we magon.* The literal sense is probably 'to that (extent) namely . . .' and so 'as we can'. Morris's translation is 'as much as we are able', which seems to imply 'as best we can'. Other such examples include *Bo* 58. 29 (§3349), *Ps(P)* 10. 3 *For þam hi wilniað þæs þe hi magon þæt hi toweorpen þæt God geteohhad hæfð to wyrcanne*, Latin *Quoniam quae perfecisti destruxerunt*, *Law VAtr* 23 7 *æghwylc unriht aweorpe man georne of þysan earde þæs þe man gedon mæge*, and (I would suggest, despite Thorpe's '. . . and ever teach rightly what they may know by the outer senses') *ÆC Hom* ii. 550. 19 . . . *þæt hi, mid onbryrdnysse þæs upplican eðles, syllað gode bysne oðrum geleaffullum, and symle tæcað riht þæs ðe hi magon tocnawan be ðam yttrum andgitum, þeah ðe hi ne cunnon ða incundan deopnysse Godes lare asmeagan.*

§3354. I end with two observations. First, the answer to the first question asked in §3349 is this: I do not see how *þe* in the construc-tions so far discussed can be the instrumental. I conclude that it is the indeclinable particle *þe* and that its original function may some-times have been that of a general subordinate 'namely' (see the com-ment on *BlHom* 37. 11 in §3353), sometimes that of a relative (see the comment on *Bo* 58. 29 in §3349). Second, as with similar *swa (swa)* clauses (§§3295–300), the mood of the verb in the *þæs (þe)* clause is indicative unless some special factor intervenes, e.g. the jussive subjunctive in *Law VAtr* 23 (§3353) and the note of (simu-lated) doubt or uncertainty in *Bo* 58. 29 (§3349); see §§2025–6 and 3296, where I note that I have as yet found no examples of *swa (swa)* clauses of this type in which a negated indicative in the princi-pal clause is followed by a subjunctive.

c. *þæs + instrumental þy/þe + a comparative*

§3355. Our problem here is whether *þæs* is an addition to and inde-pendent of the formulae discussed in §§3334–46—as is suggested by the variations *ðæs ðe . . . ðy . . . ðe* in *CP* 123. 17 *Ond suaðeah oft sio wund bið ðæs ðe wierse 7 ðy mare, gif hio bið unwærlice gewriðen, 7 him bið ðæt sar ðe gefredre, gif sio wund bið to ungemetlice fæste gewriðen* and *ðæs ðe . . . ðy . . . ðy* in *CP* 131. 16 . . . *ðæt he wære ðæs ðe freorra to ongietanne ða dieglan 7 ða gæstlican ðing, ðæt he meahte ðæt folc ðy wislicor 7 ðy rædlicor læran*—or whether it is an integral part of it—as BT's heading (s.v. *se* V) '*ðæs ðe* . . . with comparatives' seems to imply. That the first explanation is acceptable in theory is established by Johnsen's demonstration (*EStudien*, 44 (1911-12), 213, 217-18, and 222) that *þy/þe* + a comparative is frequently intensified by an adverb or a pronominal form used adverbially; examples not cited in §3336 include *Bo* 23. 12 *micle þy eð* and (perhaps more to the point) causal *forðæm* in *CP* 423. 21 *forðæm . . . ðy strangra*. The likelihood of the second— that gen. *þæs* and instr. *þy/þe* 'than that' or 'than before' (§3336) could function together as one combination—is in my opinion remote. However, since both possibilities are represented in the quoted translations of the examples which appear in the next sections—the first by the use of a MnE equivalent for *þæs* (I have italicized these) and the second (if I may argue *ex silentio*) by the absence of such an equivalent—it remains for me to establish that the first works in practice.

§3356. In favour of my proposition is the fact that examples with *þæs* (which have already been mentioned briefly in §§3137 and 3355) can be divided into the same types as those without it discussed in §§3334-46. We find type 1 in *CP* 131. 16 (§3355) (EETS 'the more leisure'); *Matt(WSCp)* 20. 31 *þa clypodon hig þæs ðe ma*, Latin *at illi magis clamabant*, and *Mark(WSCp)* 10. 26 *Hi þæs ðe ma betwux him wundredon*, Latin *qui magis admirabantur*, in both of which *Li* has *suiðor* and *Ru swiðor/-ur*; *ÆCHom* ii. 20. 31 . . . *þæt mancynn wære þæs ðe geleaffulre and ðæs þe gewisre on hwæne hi sceoldon gelyfan* (Thorpe 'the more believing, and the more certain'); and *ÆCHom* ii. 370. 17 *Nu behofige ge ðæs þe swiðor þæs boclican frofres* (Thorpe '*so much the more*').

§3357. Examples of type 2a include *CP* 215. 1 *ðæt hie wenden ðæt hie ðæs ðe untælwyrðran wæren ðe hie wendon ðæt he nyste hira leohtmodnesse 7 hira unfæsðradnesse* (Latin *tanto . . . quanto*, EETS 'the less culpable'); *CP* 231. 13 *Ðæs ðy wyrse wite hie sculon habban on ende ðe him licað ðæt mon wel doo* . . . (EETS 'The worse punishment'); *ÆCHom* i. 490. 13 *and ðæs þe wyrsan þe we hi lufiað* (Thorpe 'and the worse that we love them'); and *GD* 47. 8 and

ÆCHom ii. 546. 30 (Thorpe 'the more as she could do nothing else') (both in §3142). I have recorded no examples of type 2b, but type 2c appears in *CP* 123. 17 (§3355) (EETS 'aggravated') and type 2d in *ÆCHom* i. 156. 19 *He hrymde ðæs ðe swiðor, oð þæt se Hælend his stemne gehyrde, and hine gehælde* (Thorpe '*so much* the louder') and *ÆCHom* i. 478. 10 . . . *þæt hit wære geðuht þæs ðe mare ge-mynd þæs fæder, ðaða se sunu, his yrfenuma, wæs geciged þæs fæder naman* (Thorpe 'the greater remembrance').

§3358. Type 3 (with two comparatives) can be exemplified by *Bo* 141. 2 *7 habbað þæs þy læssan friodom þe hi hiora modes willan near þisse weoruldare lætað* (Sedgefield 'no freedom') and *CP* 435. 2 *Ac hi beoð ðæs ðe lator ðe hi oftor ymbðeahtiað* (EETS 'the later' but Small (1930, p. 369) '*that much* the later'). I have recorded no examples of types 4 and 5.

§3359. Are there any examples in which *þæs* cannot be explained as an independent adverb? In my opinion, the answer is 'No'. But I must leave it to the reader to make up his own mind. The translation 'so much/that much' is available in them all. In some, the recapitulatory causal sense 'therefore' is also possible, e.g. *CP* 131. 16 (§3355), *Bo* 141. 2 (§3358), and *ÆCHom* i. 156. 19 (§3357). In others, anticipatory *þæs* 'for that (reason to be given)' would fit, e.g. *ÆCHom* i. 490. 13 (§3357), which could be translated literally 'for that the worse namely/because we love them'. If we accept—as I believe we are bound to do—that *ðæs* in examples like *ðæs ðe swiðor* is an independent adverb, then all the sentences cited here contain examples of one of the types discussed in §§3334–46. The fact that they can be divided into the same types, share the same characteristics, raise the same difficulties, and are amenable to the same solutions, in my opinion confirms this diagnosis.

10. OTHER WAYS OF EXPRESSING COMPARISONS OF EQUALITY

a. Hu *with two comparatives*

§3360. With examples like *Lch* ii. 34. 16 *betere swa oftor* and *GenA* 989 *leng swa swiðor*, discussed in §3289, we may compare *Ps(A)* 37. 8 *a hu lenge swiðu[r]*, Latin *usquequaq:, GuthA* 20 . . . *ac him bið lenge hu sel*, and

GuthA 136   Feond wæs geflymed;   siþ þam frofre gæst
                        in Guðlaces   geoce gewunade,

lufade hine ond lærde   lenge hu geornor,
þæt him leofedan   londes wynne,
bold on beorhge.

b. Gelice . . . gelice

§3361. I interpret *gelice . . . gelice* in *ÆCHom* i. 504. 31 *Hwæt ða hæðenan ða forhtmode fleames cepton, and gelice hi wurdon mid þam fyrenum flanum ofscotene, gelice mid þæra cristenra wæpnum hindan ofsette, oðþæt hi heora burh Neapolim samcuce gesohton* as correlative 'just as . . . so'. Thorpe has 'at the same time that'.

§3362. For other uses of *gelic(e)*, alone and in combination, see the Index of Words and Phrases. *ÆCHom* i. 154. 16 *þeos woruld, þeah ðe heo myrige hwiltidum geðuht sy, nis heo hwæðere ðe geliccre ðære ecan worulde, þe is sum cweartern leohtum dæge* is an example of the formula discussed in §§3243–50.

c. Loc(a) hu '(just) as, however'

§3363. In this formula, we must construe *loc(a)* as an imperative governing a dependent question or exclamation; cf. *loc(a) hwa/hwæt/hwæþer/hwelc* 'whoever/whatever/whichever' (§2383); *loc(a) hwær* 'wherever' and *loc(a) hwider* 'withersoever' (§2502); and *loc(a) hwænne* 'whenever' (§2779). Examples include *ÆLS* 4. 261 *And gif he þurh his drycræft þæt fyr adwescan mæg, gewitna hi ealle loca hu þu wylle*; *ÆCHom* i. 474. 24 *Se ðe geuntrumod beo, bidde his hæle æt his Drihtne, and geðyldelice þa swingla forbere, loc hu lange se soða læce hit foresceawige, and ne beceapige na ðurh ænigne deofles cræft mid his sawle ðæs lichaman gesundfulnysse*, where Thorpe has *forbere; loc* and translates *loc* as 'let him behold'; and *ByrM* 156. 15 *7 loca hu eald se mona beo þy dæge, swa fela daga tell þu fram Martius monðes ende upweard . . .* , where Liggins (1955, pp. 354–5) detects an element of cause.

§3364. There is room for more work on the formulae consisting of *loc(a)* + an interrogative. They seem to occur in later rather than in earlier texts. As far as I have observed, the prevailing mood in clauses introduced by them is the present subjunctive. One's first inclination is to say that this is due to the influence of the imp. *loc(a)*. But further examination shows that most examples of the formulae introduce clauses subordinate to a principal clause which itself contains a volitional expression. This is true of the three examples in §3363 and of others such as *ÆCHom* ii. 576. 10 *Bide me loce hwæs ðu wille and ic ðe sylle, Josh* 2. 19 7 *loce hwa ut gange, licge he ofslagen,* and *John(WSCp)* 8. 7 *Loca hwylc eower si synleas wurpe ærest stan on hi.* In *HomU* 46. 294. 24 *ac man ah . . . mid eadmodnysse hlystan loca hwæt þa lareowas heom þær to godes lage tæcan* and *HomU* 46. 294. 32 *and loca hwa þære mihte age, he mot gehæftne man alysan, ah* and *mot* might be said to supply an element of command or wish, while the absence of any such idea might explain the ind. *bið* after *loca hwonne* in *HomU* 34. 199. 16 *loca hwonne þara godes þegna Enoh and Elias tima cumen bið, þæt heora bodung geendod bið, þæt wilde deor þe of ðære neowelnesse up cymð, feohteð togeanes heom.* . . . A principal clause with a preterite verb is followed by the ambiguous *woldon* in *ChronE* 139. 18 (1009) *ac þeahhweðere hi ferdon loc hu hi woldon.* Sentences like *Matt(WSCp)* 21. 20 7 *his leorningcnihtas wundrodon 7 cwædon loca nu hu hrædlice þ fictreow forscranc* and *John(WSCp)* 11. 36 7 *þa Iudeas cwædon loca nu hu he hyne lufode,* Latin *dixerunt ergo Iudaei ecce quomodo amabat eum,* are not examples; cf. *ÆGram* 231. 5 *Demonstrativa synd æteowigendlice. en, efne oðõe loca nu, her hit is; en, adest episcopus, efne, her is se bisceop; ealswa, ecce: ecce, uenit rex, efne nu, her cymð se cyning.* The passage beginning *ChronA* 158. 3 (1031) . . . *swa þ loc whenne þ flod byð ealra hehst* . . . is part of an unfinished sentence. The corresponding passage in *Ch* 959 begins . . . *swa þ ðonne hit bið full flod* and ends with a principal clause containing a jussive subjunctive. This is another demonstration that the subjunctive is not obligatory in a clause subordinate to such a principal clause (see the General Index). But it can occur when no such element is present; cf. *ByrM* 60. 4 *loca hwylce hig beoð, beoð swa fela concurrentes* with *ByrM* 46. 18 *þises circules gewuna ys oðõe ryne þæt loca hwylce concurrentes beon on þam geare þe byð bissextus, þæt þa wæron fif wintrum ær.* . . . See further §3461.

d. The dative case

§3365. On the dative case expressing comparison, see §§1358-64.

e. Non-prepositional phrases

§3366. QW (p. 100) notes that for the expression of 'the modal relation (manner, attendant circumstances, comparison) . . . we also find participial and absolute expressions: *he ealle woruldcara awearp from his heortan, nanes þinges wilnigende* "he cast away all thoughts of the world from his heart, desiring nothing", *upahafenum handum langlice bæd* "with upraised hands (he) prayed long" '. Whether phrases like *upahafenum handum* should be called 'absolute' is discussed in §§3810-11.

f. Prepositional phrases

§3367. Modal relationships of varying kinds can be expressed by prepositional phrases. A full catalogue is a matter for the lexicographer but typical examples include (with *for*) *Bo* 56. 10 *nis hit nan cyn þ mon ðæt for nauht telle, Bo* 116. 29 *Eala þ hit is micel cræft þæs modes for þone lichoman, ÆLS* 8. 103 *Crist me is for hæle*, and

Met 10. 7   Higesnotrum mæg
          eaðe ðincan   þæt þeos eorðe sie
          eall for ðæt oðer   unigmet lytel;

(with *on*) *ÆCHom* ii. 210. 29 *Lamb we offriað on Godes lace, ÆC Hom* i. 322. 19 . . . *he wæs æteowod on culfran and on fyre*, and *ÆCHom* ii. 182. 23 . . . *seo wæs fram cildhade Gode gehalgod, on mægðhade him ðeowigende*; (with *to*) *ÆCHom* ii. 522. 31 *Ne nimð se hlaford his ðeowan him to rædboran* . . . and *ÆCHom* ii. 430. 17 *Gif he sum hus Gode arærð, hwæt mæg þæt to wiðmetennysse þære healican heofenan, and ðære ecan wununge þe God him gearcað on his rice, to edleane þæs lytlan huses?* (cf. *ÆCHom* ii. 456. 13 *Ic eom lame wiðmeten and yslum and axum geanlicod*); and (with *wiþ*) *Bo* 29. 3 *þeah hi Godes gesceaftes sien, ne sint hi no wið eow to metanne, forðæm þe oþer twega oððe hit nan god nis for eow selfe, oððe þeah forlytel god wið eow to metane* and *ÆCHom* i. 584. 10 *Hwæt is ænig lac wið þisum willan* . . . ? See further Peltola, *NM* 60 (1959), 165-6.

g. Prepositional conjunctions

§3368. Comparison can also be expressed by the use of prepositional conjunctions. Typical examples include (with *æfter*) *Bede* 60. 28 *Æfter þon þe heo lærdon, heo sylfe þurh all lifdon*; (with *be*) *ÆCHom* i. 418. 13 *Nim nu ure cyrcan maðmas, and dæl cristenum mannum, be ðan ðe ðe gewyrð* and (with a parallel *swa swa* clause) *ÆCHom* i. 242. 22 *Gif se lareow wel tæce and yfele bysnige, doð swa swa he tæcð, and na be ðam þe he bysnað* (see Kivimaa, pp. 152-3); (with *on*) *ÆCHom* ii. 322. 3 *Eow bið ameten swa swa ge amæton, on ðam ylcan gemete ðe ge mannum doð* (where we again have a parallel *swa*

swa clause); and (with *to*) *Ch* 877b *þa getæhton ealle þ* [MS *Hi þa*] *witan þe þær wæron ge gehadode ge læwide þam cynge ealle Wulboldes ære 7 hine silfne to þam þe se cynge wolde swa to life swa to deaþe* (where Robertson translates '. . . to be disposed of as the king desired . . .') and *BlHom* 123. 22 *þes Hælend þe nu up on þysne heofon from eow astag, oþþe ahafen wæs, he eft cymeþ on domes dæg to þæm gemete þe ge hiene nu gesawon on heofen astigendne*, which may be compared with *Acts* 1. 11 *Hic Iesus . . . sic veniet quemadmodum vidistis eum euntem in caelum*.

h. *þe* '*as*'?

§3369. Despite the similarity of examples like

And 970

	Wolde ic eow on ðon
þurh bliðne hige	bysne onstellan,
swa on ellþeode	ywed wyrðeð,

Rid 33. 9

Is min modor	mægða cynnes
þæs deorestan,	þæt is dohtor min
eacen up liden,	swa þæt is ældum cuþ,
firum on folce . . . ,	

and

GenA 899

. . .	oðþæt ic fracoðlice
feondræs gefremede,	fæhðe geworhte,
and þa reafode,	swa hit riht ne wæs,
beam on bearwe	and þa blæda æt,

I take *þe* not as a conjunction 'as' but as a relative particle in

Beo 2135

Ic ða ðæs wælmes,	þe is wide cuð,
grimne gryrelicne	grundhyrde fond

and

Mald 189

he gehleop þone eoh	þe ahte his hlaford,
on þam gerædum	þe hit riht ne wæs.

In the latter, we can follow Gordon's '. . . on those trappings which it was not right (to mount on)' or take *þe hit* together, translating 'which was not right'. On the use of the translation '(according/in proportion) as' for the *þe* (? = *þy* instr.) which follows the comparative in examples like *Beo* 1435 *he on holme wæs* || *sundes þe sænra ðe hyne swylt fornam*, see Small 1930, p. 369; Christophersen, p. 116; and §§3137–43 and 3338.

11. COMPARATIVE CLAUSES INVOLVING A HYPOTHESIS

§3370. These clauses are introduced by a conjunction which can be translated 'as if' and have the subjunctive when the verb is expressed. A list of the conjunctions I have noted in the prose follows, with a reference to at least one example. *Swa* and *swelc(e)* occur alone and in combination, either with one another or with *efne*: *swa*, e.g. *Bede* 402. 12 *þa wæs ic sona swa ic of hefgum slæpe aweht wære* (where *sona* and *swa* are completely independent of one another) and *BlHom* 135. 33 *þæs wordes andgit is swa mon cwepe þingere oþþe frefrend*; *(efne) swa swa*, e.g. *Or* 104. 21 *On þæm dagum wæs Alexander geboren on Crecum swa swa an micel yst come ofer ealne middangeard* and *BlHom* 81. 18 *Hie cwædon, 'hæl us on þon hehstan', efne swa swa hie openlice cwædon, 'Hæl us on eorþan, þu þe godcund mægen hafast on heofenum'*; *swa . . . swa*, e.g. *Bede* 218. 25 *þa wæs he meted swa unsceðed swa he in þa ilcan tid of þissum leohte gelæded wære*; *(efne) swelce*, e.g. *Or* 2. 23 *Hu Romanum wearð an wundor opiewed swelce se heofon burne*, *CP* 45. 3 . . . *ðæt is ðæt hine tæle ðæs folces gesomnung emne suelce hie him on ðæt nebb spæten*, *ÆCHom* ii. 382. 9 *Petrus ða him filigde and ðuhte him swilce hit swefen wære* (no more a 'noun clause' than *swa* is a pronoun? Cf. §3407), and *ApT* 34. 11 *And Arcestrates . . . hine lædde ham mid him, na swilce he cuma wære ac swilce he his aðum wære*; *swa . . . swelce*, e.g. *Or* 92. 29 *þa þa iermingas þe þær to lafe wurdon ut of þæm holan crupon þe heo on lutedan, swa bewopene swelce hie of operre worolde come . . .* , *ÆCHom* i. 390. 14 *Se ðe eow hrepað, hit me bið swa egle swylce he hreppe ða seo mines eagan*, and *ÆCHom* ii. 102. 11 *þa ælmessan þe of reaflace beoð gesealde sind Gode swa gecweme, swilce hwa acwelle oðres mannes cild, and bringe ðam fæder þæt heafod to lace*; *swelc swa*, e.g. *Bede(O)* 134. 26 . . . *swylc swa þu æt swæsendum sitte* (where MS *Ca* has *swa gelic swa*); and *swelce . . . swa*, e.g. *LS* 23. 415 *Ac swilce me hwilc strang meniu ongean stode þæt me þone ingang beluce, swa me seo færlice godes wracu þa duru bewerede*. To these we may add phrases such as *eal þæt sylfe swylce* 'exactly as if' in *WHom* 8c. 126 *And ðeah þæt cild to ðam geong sy þæt hit specan ne mæge, þonne hit man fullað, his freonda forspæc forstent him eal þæt sylfe swylce hit sylf spæce* (cf. *WHom* 13. 28 *eal þæt ylce þe* in a similar formula) and the combinations involving forms of *anlic* and *gelic* discussed in the next section. Contracted clauses of this type also occur, e.g. *ÆCHom* i. 6. 6 *Se arleasa deð þæt fyr cymð ufan swilce of heofonum on manna gesihðe* and *ÆCHom* i. 60. 18 *Drusiana þa aras swilce of slæpe awreht*. On these, see §3329. We may also note the infinitive of purpose in *Bede* 270. 4 . . . *swa he lyft onstyrge ond his hond swa swa us to sleanne beotiende æteaweð* . . . 'as if to strike us'.

§ 3371. In

Met 20. 166   Hwæt, hi þeah eorðlices   auht ne haldeð,
                         is þeah efneðe   up and of dune
                         to feallanne   foldan ðisse,
                         þæm anlicost   þe on æge bið,
                         gioleca on middan,   glideð hwæðre
                         æg ymbutan,

we have rel. pron. *þe* 'most like to that which is in an egg' and the ind. *bið*, certifying that no hypothesis is involved. But in the formulae listed below, all of which carry the sense 'as if' and introduce a clause with a subjunctive verb, *þe* appears in its subordinating function, 'namely'; see § 2428. They include *anlicost þe* (*Bo* 122. 1); *þam gelice þe* (*Lch* i. 108. 9); *gelicost þæm þe* (*Or* 214. 4); *ðæm gelicost ðe* (*Bo* 104. 16); *þam gelicost . . . þe* (*Or* 142. 12 and *HomU* 21. 2. 18); *geliccost þon þe* (*ThCap* 1 29); *þon gelicost þe* (*BlHom* 203. 35); and *þæs licost . . . þe* (*Or* 150. 31), where—since *licost* can govern only the dative—*þæs* is an adverb 'so, thus' (§ 3348). To save space, I quote only two examples in full, viz. *CP* 397. 28 *Ða he spræc gelicost ðæm ðe hit hwelchwugu syn wære ða he cwæð ðæt he hit forgiefan wolde 7 geðafian*, EETS 'He spoke very much as if it were a sin . . .', and (with a contracted clause) *Lch* ii. 230. 25 . . . *7 dropeteð blod swa þon gelicost þe tobrocen fæt.*

§ 3372. The combination *gelice 7* occurs four times in *Or*, but has not been recorded elsewhere. In *Or* 230. 26 . . . *for þon þe elpendes hyd wile drincan wætan gelice 7 spynge deð*, it means '(like) as' and takes the present indicative. But in *Or* 74. 23 (§ 3378), *Or* 92. 15 *Gelice 7 mon mæd mawe hie wæron þa burg hergende 7 sleande buton ælcre ware*, Latin *quasi aridam segetem succidit*, and *Or* 112. 29 (wrongly included by Wülfing (ii, § 466) among the *CP* examples), it means 'as if', Latin *quasi*, and has a verb which is (to be taken as) preterite subjunctive. The following sentences may throw some light on this apparently curious use of *7/ond*: *LawIICn* 51. 1 *Ne byð na gelic þæt man wið swustor gehæme 7 hit wære feorr sibb*, *LawIICn* 76. 2 . . . *þæt [cild] þa gitseras letan efenscyldig 7 hit gewittig wære*, and *LawAf* 52 . . . *þæt biþ gelic 7 eagan bot.*

§ 3373. Formulae with *swa* and *swelce* used in conjunction with a form of *anlic/gelic*, present less difficulty than those with *7*. They include *efne þon gelicost swa swa* (*Bede* 292. 31 . . . *heo þa freo on hire fota gongum bliðe ham hweorfende wæs, efne þon gelicost, swa swa heo to ðon þæt wilwendlice leoht an forlete), onlicost suelce* (*CP* 105. 12), *onlicost . . . swelce* (*Or* 140. 10), *gelic þam swylce* (*WHom* 3. 44), *gelice þon swylce* (*GD(C)* 85. 7; MS *H* has *swylce* alone), *efne þæm gelicost swylce* (*BlHom* 221. 14), *þam gelicost swilce* (*Solil* 48. 5), and *þam gelicost . . . swylce* (*HomU* 35. 213. 14 *and nu doð men þam gelicost syððan swylce hit wære idel spell and unsoð*). We find contracted clauses here too, e.g. *GD(C)* 4. 26 . . . *þone hit lufade þær gelice swilce lifes ingang* (MS *H* too has *gelice swilce*).

§3374. I have recorded *anlicost hu* only in

PPs 106. 26   Gedrefede þa   deope syndan,
                  hearde onhrerede   her anlicast,
                  hu druncen hwylc   gedwæs spyrige.

§3375. Certain points can be made about the distribution of these conjunctions in the various prose texts. *Bede* prefers *swa (swa)*, Ælfric (almost) without exception *swelce*; see §§3328-9. 'Alfredian' texts other than *Bede* tend to choose *swelce* rather than *swa*. *Gelice 7* has been recorded only in *Orosius*. On these preferences see further Jost, *Ang.* 51 (1927), 96; Bately, *Ang.* 88 (1970), 448-9; and Visser, ii, §890. The last, like Wülfing (ii. 162-5) and Ericson (1932, pp. 17-18 and 44), offers more examples.

§3376. We find the following conjunctions in the poetry: *swa*, e.g. *ChristC* 1376 *Onginneð sylf cweðan* ‖ *swa he to anum sprece* and *Wan* 95 *Hu seo þrag gewat,* ‖ *genap under nihthelm, swa heo no wære; swelce*, e.g.

Whale 8   Is þæs hiw gelic   hreofum stane,
             swylce worie   bi wædes ofre,
             sondbeorgum ymbseald,   særyrica mæst . . .

and *Finn* 35 *Swurdleoma stod,* ‖ *swylce eal Finnsburuh fyrenu wære; þon gelicost swa*, e.g.

ChristB 850   Nu is þon gelicost   swa we on laguflode
                 ofer cald wæter   ceolum liðan
                 geond sidne sæ,   sundhengestum,
                 flodwudu fergen;

þon anlicast swa, e.g.

PPs 89. 4   For þinum eagum, ece drihten,
               þusend wintra bið   þon anlicast,
               swa geostran dæg   gegan wære;

and *emne þon gelicost . . . þe* in

GenA 1941   ...   and hine fægre heold,
þeawfæst and geþyldig   on þam þeodscipe,
emne þon gelicost,   lara gemyndig,
þe he ne cuðe   hwæt þa cynn dydon.

A full list of examples in the poetry is given in Mitchell 1959, Appendix 'Comp 7'.

§3377. Three possible examples of *swa (swa)* contracted clauses present themselves in the poetry: *PPs* 70. 10 (*swa swa*), *PPs* 108. 28 (*swa* = Latin *sicut*), and

ChristC 1281   Beoð þa syngan flæsc
scandum þurhwaden   swa þæt scire glæs,
þæt mon yþæst mæg   eall þurhwlitan,

which Ericson (1932, p. 18) translates '*as if* clear glass'. But 'like' would do as well. Hypothesis is not necessarily involved in any of these three examples. On this problem see §§3328-9 and note GK's uncertainty about *PPs* 117. 12, which it lists s.v. *swa adv. und conj.* 6. *wie* and 8. *gleich als ob, wie wenn.*

§3378. The mood in comparative clauses involving hypothesis is not unexpectedly the subjunctive; in Behre's words (p. 284), 'in clauses introduced by *swa (swylce)* "as if" the subjunctive is used to denote an attitude of reflection on the part of the speaker towards the content of the dependent clause. The basis of this use of the subjunctive is the subjunctive of conditionality. . . .' Thus, we have the subj. *reste* after *swa* 'as if' but the ind. *weorð* after *swa* 'as' in

PPs 77. 65   þa wearð aweaht   wealdend drihten,
swa he slæpende   softe reste
oððe swa weorð man   wine druncen.

(Men do get drunk, but God never sleeps.) But one important difference must be noted between these clauses and OE conditional clauses when they both refer to a hypothetical state in the present: the preterite subjunctive is the rule in conditional clauses, e.g. *Bo* 28. 8 (§3602) and *ÆLS* 1. 86 . . . *and seo sawl nis na of godes agenum gecynde. Gif heo wære of godes gecynde genumen, witodlice ne mihte heo singian*, whereas the present subjunctive is the rule in comparative clauses involving a hypothesis, e.g. *CP* 275. 9 *Hu, ne bið he ðonne swelce he sie his slaga, ðonne he hine mæg gehælan 7 nyle?* and *ÆCHom* i. 390. 14 (§3370). When the hypothetical state is in the past, both types of clause have the preterite subjunctive.

The contrast in the tense of 'as if' clauses is apparent in *Or* 74. 23 *Nu seo burg swelc is, þe ær wæs ealra weorca fæstast 7 wunderlecast 7 mærast, gelice 7 heo wære to bisene asteald eallum middangearde, 7 eac swelce heo self sprecende sie to eallum moncynne, 7 cweþe. . . .* The reader will find more supporting examples in the preceding sections. Of the nine examples referred to but not quoted in §3371, the first seven have the present subjunctive, the last two the preterite. Despite Jost (*Ang.* 51 (1927), 92 fn. 1) *ÆLS* 25. 312 *Đas cumað to us swylce hi cenran syndon* is not an exception; as Pope (*Ælfric*, i. 102 fn. 5) notes, *syndon* is a subjunctive form in Ælfric. *ByrM* 96. 3 *Se ðe his agene spræce awyrt, he wyrcð barbarismum; swylce he cweðe þu sot þær he sceolde cweðan þu sott* is another example with the present subjunctive, with *sceolde* apparently used of the present, as 'should' is in MnE.

§3379. The general rule, then, is that in combinations of a governing clause and a comparative clause expressing hypothesis, the 'as if' clause has the present subjunctive when the governing clause refers to the present but the preterite subjunctive when the governing clause refers to the past. (The mood of the governing clause of course depends on the context.) Or, to put it in another way: *as far as I now know*, the preterite subjunctive never refers to a present state in OE, as it does in MnE sentences like 'He's running as if he were tired'; OE would require the equivalent of 'He's running as if he be tired'. The second formulation is better than the first, for it covers sentences in which the preterite subjunctive is the equivalent of a MnE pluperfect, e.g.

Wife 23	eft is onhworfen
is nu * * *	swa hit no wære
freondscipe uncer	

'. . . as if it had never been' and *ÆCHom* i. 514. 11 *þæt is, Se ðe witegan, oððe sumne rihtwisne Godes ðeow underfehð, and him for Godes lufon bigwiste foresceawað, þonne hæfð he swa micele mede his cystignysse æt Gode, swilce he him sylf witega wære, oþþe rihtwis Godes þeow* '. . . will have . . . as if he himself had been . . .'. The reference of the latter is to the future life; cf. *Matt* 10. 41. Thorpe's 'as if he himself were . . .' is wrong.

§3380. The fact that we have been speaking of 'comparative clauses involving an hypothesis' and that Gildersleeve and Lodge (§602) call the Latin equivalent 'conditional sentences of comparison' does not certify the correctness of the analysis accepted by Mather (p. 53) and

Fowler (*Modern English Usage* (1st edn.), s.v. *as* 4) that 'He runs as if he were tired' was once 'He runs as he would run if he were tired'. The history of the construction in English, including the difference in tense just described and the now archaic use of 'as' in such sentences as Coleridge's 'He looks as he had seen a ghost', suggests that the conjunction 'as if' did not arise from suppression of a comparative clause. I believe—to put it in simple terms—that in OE the comparison is expressed by the conjunction and the hypothesis by the subjunctive verb. Thus, *ChristC* 1376 *Onginneð sylf cweðan* || *swa he to anum sprece* originally meant 'He will begin to speak: so he may speak to one person' or 'as he may speak to one person' and

PPs 78. 3   Hi þara bearna blod   on byrig leton
                 swa man gute wæter   ymb Hierusalem

originally meant 'They have shed the blood of their children in the city: thus a man might pour water around Jerusalem' or 'as a man might pour water around Jerusalem'. Such interpretations may seem strange to us and we have not the means of knowing whether they would have seemed sensible to an Anglo-Saxon. But they make sense in most (if not all) of the OE 'as if' clauses, including the noteworthy *ChronC* 168. 35 (1049) . . . *7 ridon þa to Bosanham eall swa hi sceoldon to Sandwic*. They invite comparison with MnE 'as it were' and similar examples cited by *OED*, s.v. *as* 9. They are in accord with Mather's observation (p. 54) that 'to my feeling the modal idea is much stronger than the conditional in such sentences'. And they may be said to demonstrate the first stage in what Behre (p. 282) described as 'the sense-change of *swa*, so that it comes to mean no longer "in the same way as" but "in the same way as if" '.

§3381. On Ælfric's use of *swelce* + the subjunctive to express a rejected cause, which may have been an extension of *swelce* + the subjunctive 'as (if)', see §3111.

12. MOOD

§3382. On the uses of the moods in the various types of comparative clauses discussed above, see my Table of Contents and the appropriate sections.

13. ARRANGEMENT OF CLAUSES

§3383. Correlation has already been discussed in the appropriate sections; see the Table of Contents. I have nothing particular to say

about the use of comparative clauses in co-ordination except that it
is not common. One can compare something to two or three different things in the same sentence if the fancy takes one. But it is not
done very often. Typical OE examples include (with asyndetic parataxis) *ÆCHom* ii. 322. 3 (§3368), and (with syndetic parataxis)
ÆCHom i. 242. 22 (§3368), *PPs* 77. 65 (§3378),

And 332   Farað nu geond ealle   eorðan sceatas
                   emne swa wide   swa wæter bebugeð,
                   oððe stedewangas   stræte gelicgaþ,

and (with *swa* repeated)

PPs 82. 10   Sete hi nu, min god,   samod anlice
                   swa se wægnes hweol   oþþe windes healm,
                   and swa færincga   fyr wudu byrneð,
                   oððe swa lig freteð   lungre morhæð.

§3384. By their nature *þonne* clauses and other clauses expressing
inequality follow the principal clause. So too do clauses with *swa* +
adjective (+ noun)/adverb + *swa*, clauses with *þy* + a comparative
+ *þy*, and comparative clauses involving a hypothesis. Clauses with
swa + a comparative + *swa* may precede or follow the principal
clause. When two clauses are compared, the comparative clause may
precede or follow the principal clause; see the relevant sections and
Jost, *Ang.* 51 (1927), 87-97.

§3385. Waterhouse (1978, p. 438) notes that in *ÆLS* 'the modal is
very likely to be a formulaic-type line-filler, inserted to complete the
line and provide the alliteration in the B half-line', as in *ÆLS* 19. 241
and *ÆLS* 13. 47 *Ælc rihtwis man hæfde swa swa we rædað on
bocum.* . . . Clauses of this type may also occur within the principal
clause, e.g.

ChristB 468   Hæfde þa gefylled,   swa ær biforan sungon,
                   witgena word   geond woruld innan
                   þurh his þrowinga.

K. CONCESSIVE CLAUSES

1. INTRODUCTORY REMARKS

§3386. The nature of the concessive relationship has been well discussed by Quirk, who gives a summary of previous views on the subject (pp. 4–10) and a review of previous writings on concessive clauses

in OE (pp. 10–13); his work was reviewed by Campbell (*RES* 7 (1956), 64–8), myself (*MÆ* 25 (1956), 36–40), and others. Collinson's 'Tradition and Divergence in the Syntax of some Western Languages' (*TPS* 1959, pp. 1–13) appeared after Quirk's book.

§3387. In essence, it can be said that an adverb clause of concession contains a proposition in spite of which the truth of the principal clause is asserted, e.g. 'I'll come to thee by moonlight, though hell should bar the way'. 'Old English, like other languages,' observed Burnham (p. 2), 'reflects in its idioms the close relationship between the notions of concession, condition, and cause.' A concessive clause differs from a causal clause in that the opposite of the expected result is asserted: in the words of Burnham (p. 2), 'the concession— the notion subtracted, as it were, from the main proposition—may often be looked upon as a blocked or inoperative cause or reason'. Burnham (p. 2) goes on to observe that 'the close relation between the concessive and the conditional idea is shown by the frequency with which conditional particles are adapted to concessive use'. In both, 'the main proposition is thought of as *conditioned* by the subordinate' (Burnham, p. 1). But it can be said that a conditional clause is often the antithesis of a concessive clause, for in a conditional sentence the truth of the main clause is dependent on the truth of the subordinate clause, e.g. 'I'll come if I can'.

§3388. We find concession shading into cause in *ÆCHom* ii. 216. 23 (§3024) and in *Bo* 64. 29 *Hwelc gesceadwis mon mihte cwepan þ he a ðy weorðra wære þeah he hine weorðode?* and its equivalent

Met 15. 13   Ðeah hine se dysega   do to cyninge,
hu mæg þæt gesceadwis   scealc gereccan
þæt he him ðy selra   sie oððe þince?

Conversely, we find cause shading into concession in *BlHom* 5. 16 *þy þe he hine onfehþ, ne belucep he hine no* and in

Res 25   Nu þu const on mec
firendæda fela,   feorma mec hwæþre,
meotod, for þinre miltse,   þeah þe ic ma fremede
grimra gylta   þonne me god lyfde.

See further Burnham, p. 3, and Quirk, pp. 7–8 and 115–16.

§3389. The often close relationship between time and cause (§2533) is reflected in the fact that Liggins (1955, pp. 387–8) detects 'shades of condition, cause and time' in examples like *CP* 101. 11 *Ðeah we nu ofer ure mæð ðencen 7 smeagean, ðæt we dooð for Gode; ðonne*

we hit eft gemetlæcað, ðonne doð we ðæt for eow, where the variation *Ðeah . . . ðonne* is noteworthy, and *ÆLS* 18. 257 *ða feollan ealle
on cneowum, biddende þone witegan mid bifigendre heortan þæt he
hi ne forbærnde ðeah ðe hi heora ærende abudon*. . . . Conversely,
Shearin (*MLN* 26 (1911), 257) detects a 'temporal-concessive' *þa*
clause in *John(WSCp)* 21. 11 . . . *7 ða hyra swa fæla wæs, næs þ net
tobrocen*, where the Latin has *cum*.

§3390. But how frequently are 'conditional particles . . . adapted
to concessive use' in OE (Burnham, p. 2)? I accept Burnham's own
verdict (p. 92): 'the spontaneous use of *gif* in a concessive sense is
rare; where the word is truly concessive, it is usually influenced by
Latin *si*.' (On *si* 'even if, although, albeit', see Lewis and Short, s.v.
si I. B. 5.) Possible examples of concessive *gif* cited by Mather
(pp. 21-2), Wülfing (ii. 151), and Burnham (pp. 80-5), include
CP 337. 20 *Gif we nauht ðæs ne dooð ðe us mon mid goode leanian
ðyrfe, ne do we eac nan woh ðe us mon fore tælan ðurfe* (but the
EETS translation has 'if'), *ÆCHom* i. 350. 2, and *ÆCHom* ii. 322.
10 *þis sæde Drihten, and gif eowere synna wæron wolcnreade ær
ðan, hi beoð scinende on snawes hwitnysse* (cf. *Isa* 1. 18 *Si fuerint
peccata vestra ut coccinum, quasi nix dealbabuntur*), where I agree
with Burnham (pp. 83-4) that *and* is continuative rather than intensive. Quirk speaks of 'a rare concessive use of *gif*' (p. 7), but admits
only one example from the poetry as 'certain' (pp. 88-90), viz.

GenB 661   Gif þu him heodæg wuht   hearmes gespræce,
                 he forgifð hit þeah,   gif wit him geongordom
                 læstan willað.

Campbell (*RES* 7 (1956), 67) accepts that this is concessive, but
underlines Quirk's warning that an example from *GenB* is not a guide
to OE usage. I myself can see a case for taking *gif* in *GenB* 661 as
conditional, despite the following *þeah*. But the combination is in
effect concessive. We may compare examples like *BenR* 53. 14 *Gif he
þænne eft for his unðeawum utfærð oþþe adræfed bið, he þeah sy
onfangen oð þan þriddan siðe*, Latin *Quod si denuo exierit, usque
tertio ita recipiatur*, of which Burnham (p. 82) says: 'the *gif*-clause
must, in my judgment, be regarded as having a double use. It is seen
first as a condition: "take the case when." As, however, it refers to
an exceptional case, the writer views it also as a concession, and adds
an adversative.'

§3391. Burnham (p. 92) continues her verdict on the relationship
between concession and condition in OE with the words 'The tendency

of Old English is rather to employ *ðeah* in a conditional sense.' This is tersely contradicted by Campbell (*RES* 7 (1956), 66 fn. 2): 'There is no evidence that *þeah* can be used for *gif*.' Here he accepted Quirk's verdict (p. 38) that in the poetry 'there is not a single example of *þeah* that can be said with certainty to be deliberately conditional', but rejected his two prose examples, viz. *Or* 21. 15—on this see §3421—and *LawIICn(A)* 72. 1 *And gif se bonda, ær he dead wære, beclypad wære, þonne andwirdan þa erfenumen, swa he sylf sceolde, þeah he lif hafde*, Latin *Si autem uir ante mortem proclamatus de talibus fuit, oportet ut eius heredes secundum iusticiam respondeant, sicut ipse deberet si uiueret*, suggested by Liebermann (*Laws* II, s.v. *þeah* II(3)) and by Burnham (p. 33) and accepted by Quirk (p. 38), but translated by Campbell (loc. cit.) thus: '. . . let the heirs answer, as the man would have to do himself, even though he were alive.' I would agree with Liebermann, Burnham, and Quirk, translating 'if he were alive' in the belief that the translator should have written *gif* for Latin *si*. Here we may note *John(WSCp)* 10. 38 *Gif ic wyrce mines fæder weorc 7 gif ge me nellað gelyfan, gelyfað þam weorcum*, Latin *Si autem facio et si mihi non uultis credere operibus credite*, where *Li* has *gif . . . gif* ł *ðæh*, an example of *gif/þeah* fluctuation which predates those from Laȝamon's *Brut* referred to by Quirk (p. 90). *LawIICn* 75, proposed by Liebermann (loc. cit.), probably belongs here too; MS *G* has *þe*[*ah*] *. . . oððon gif*, MS *B* *ðeah . . . oððon gyf*, and MS *A* *þeah þe . . . oððe gif*, for Latin *Si . . . aut si.*

§3392. Other examples from the prose have been proposed: (by Mather, p. 52) *Mark(WSCp)* 7. 26 and *HomU* 34. 198. 18, in both of which the Latin original has *si*, and (by Waterhouse 1978, p. 295) *ÆLS* 31. 743 *þeah ðu earming woldest on þisum endnextan timan manna ehtnysse geswican and þine dæda behreowsian, ic on god truwode þæt ic þe mildsunge behete*, which is based on the Latin of Sulpitius Severus *si tu ipse miserabilis ab hominum infestatione desisteres . . .* (J. E. Cross, private communication, 1979). On the last see §3674.

§3393. Quirk (p. 38) makes no mention of *Met* 22. 43, which (despite Glogauer, pp. 41-2) seems clearly concessive, and takes as concessive

PPs 61. 11   þeah þe eow wealan to   wearnum flowen,
nyllan ge eow on heortan þa   hige staðelian,

Latin *Divitiae si affluant, nolite cor apponere*, where AV *Ps* 62. 10 reads 'If riches increase, set not your heart upon them'. I find it hard

to adjudicate, but would refer to my comment on *LawIICn(A)* 72. 1
(§3391). We must bear in mind these examples and those discussed
in §3421, when we read Quirk's cautious conclusion (p. 39): 'The
conditional function of *þeah* must therefore be said to be extremely
rare in OE and probably not in evidence at all in the poetry.' Space
prevents further documentation. But see Mather, pp. 21-2 and 52;
Burnham, pp. 1-3, 33-4, and 80-5; Brouwer, *Neophil.* 3 (1917),
258-61; Quirk, pp. 6-7, 38-9, 42-3, and 88-90; Horn, p. 221;
Mitchell 1959, pp. 548 and 618; and §§3421 and 3434.

§3394. There are other problems. Quirk comments on 'the notional
closeness of concession to exception' (p. 7) and on the similarities
and differences between the concessive and the adversative relations
(pp. 4-5 and 8-9); on these see §§3641-6, 3656-8, and 3515-24.
But I end this discussion by quoting Quirk (p. 6; his italics): 'Perhaps the most satisfactory statement to use as a working guide is
simply that *the concessive relation may be said to exist between two
parts of an utterance when one part is surprising in view of the other.*'

§3395. We have seen that in a concessive sentence the truth of the
main clause is asserted, despite the proposition contained in the subordinate clause. But the truth of the subordinate clause is not always
asserted. If we consider the sentence *Ruat caelum, fiat voluntas tua*,
we find four possibilities: the heavens are in fact falling (actual fact
conceded); the heavens are not falling, but are assumed to be for the
purpose of the argument (assumed fact conceded); the heavens have
not yet fallen, but may do so (hypothesis of possibility); and the
heavens have not fallen and are not expected to do so (hypothesis
contrary to fact). But these distinctions cannot always be made; as
Burnham says (p. 3), 'the broader division between fact and hypothesis is . . . much more readily grasped and more fundamental'. It is
more readily grasped in MnE, where the mood of the verb is decisive
—cf. 'Though she is rich, she is not happy' with 'Though she may be
the richest woman in the world, she is not happy'—than it is in OE,
where the subjunctive is the prevailing mood in *þeah (þe)* clauses. The
context sometimes enables us to distinguish concessions of fact, e.g.

Beo 202   Ðone siðfæt him   snotere ceorlas
                   lythwon logon, þeah he him leof wære,

from concessions involving possibility or hypothesis, e.g.

Beo 2029   Oft seldan hwær
                   æfter leodhryre   lytle hwile
                   bongar bugeð,   þeah seo bryd duge!

But it too frequently fails; consider *Beo* 588 *þæs þu in helle scealt* ‖ *werhðo dreogan, þeah þin wit duge*—'shrewd though you are' or 'shrewd though you may be'?—and

Jul 494
                  Ic asecgan ne mæg,
    þeah ic gesitte   sumerlongne dæg,
    eal þa earfeþu   þe ic ær ond siþ
    gefremede to facne—

'and I might' or 'but I won't'? So little would be gained by attempting to classify OE concessive clauses according to the nature of the concession; consider *BlHom* 65. 9 *Witodlice þa æfstigan men, 7 þa tælendan, þeh hi syn þæs morþres scyldige, hi hit him to nanre synne ne gelyfaþ; þa æfstigan, þeah hi syn deaþes scyldige, hie heora scylda ne ongytaþ; forþon þe hie næfre forgifenesse æt Gode ne biddaþ*, where Morris translates '. . . though they be guilty of murder . . . though they are worthy of death . . .', and *ÆCHom* i. 26. 25 *þeah ðe eal mennisc wære gegaderod, ne mihton hi ealle hine acwellan, gif he sylf nolde*, where what is conceded may be viewed as something possible under God or as something impossible.

§3396. A formal classification has therefore been adopted. Concessive expressions have been divided into kinds and then classified according to the introductory conjunction. Three kinds have been described by Burnham (p. 4):

The simple concession contains a fact or notion *in spite of* which the main proposition stands. The disjunctive or alternative concession introduces mutually exclusive possibilities, in spite of *either of which* the proposition is maintained. But this is often only a more emphatic substitute for the former method. 'Whether I come or not'—though it may be logically analyzed into 'if I come, or though I do not come'—is often simply equivalent to 'though I do not come.' The indefinite concession generalizes the situation: the main proposition is asserted *in spite of any* possibility—*no matter what* the case may be.

On the validity of the last category see §§3438-9. We might, however, add that a disjunctive concession may also be a substitute for an 'indefinite concession'; cf. 'Whether it is summer or winter, he has a cold shower every morning' with 'No matter what the season, he has a cold shower every morning' and see Quirk, p. 91. To these three, Quirk (pp. 9 and 36-7) adds the 'even' concession, e.g. 'A man might walk unharmed throughout the realm—even laden with gold', and the 'elliptical' concession, e.g. 'Love ceases not, though prophecies do', that is 'though much ceases, for example prophecies'; see §§3421 and 3423-4.

§3397. In his review of Quirk (*RES* 7 (1956), 64–8), Campbell rightly noted that 'the nature of his material . . . is threefold. (1) There are clauses (e.g. those with *hwæþre*, and most with *þeah*) which are grammatically concessive and concessive in sense. (2) Many clauses are not grammatically concessive, but have another grammatical function, but in their context convey a concessive idea.' These include not only causal clauses (see §§3388–9), but also adjective clauses, clauses of place, time, and comparison, and principal clauses before *ac* clauses. '(3) Some clauses are introduced by a conjunction substituted for the one which would be normally used. This device is clearly an OE. rhetorical figure, i.e. a use of language in a manner not obvious or ordinary (Quintilian ix. 1. 4).' Campbell (ibid., pp. 65–6) says that 'the chief instances in Quirk's field' are (*a*) 'the concessive use of the *ond* clause'; (*b*) 'noun clauses with *þeah* for *þæt*'; (*c*) 'clauses in which the concessive force of *þeah* is much reduced or entirely absent'; and (*d*) 'clauses in which *þeah* has a pregnant force, "even though"'. See §§3399–406, 3430, and 3515 for (1); §§3459–75 and 3516–24 for (2); §§3516–24 for (3*a*); §§3407–15 for (3*b*); and §§3422 and 3421 for (3*c*) and (3*d*).

§3398. Burnham (p. 126) says that 'the independence of the native idiom is marked'—an observation which somewhat too strongly contradicts the concessive clause in the same sentence: 'Though there is considerable Latin influence upon the concessive expression of Old English. . . .' We should perhaps read 'some Latin influence'. Quirk (pp. 41–3) notes that the poets too are not greatly influenced by Latin. Regrettably, both Burnham and Quirk failed to give full references to all the examples they recorded.

2. *ÞEAH (ÞE)*

a. þeah (þe) *introducing simple concessive clauses*

§3399. *þeah* (with its variant spellings with initial *ð* and medial *æ*, *æa*, and *e*) is used as an adversative adverb 'however' and also as a concessive conjunction 'although', and so takes its place among the ambiguous adverb/conjunctions. But in practice there is rarely any real difficulty. Thus, the mood of *nesan* and (if we take it as a verb) of *geferan* is decisive for the conjunction in

And 514   Hwilum us on yðum   earfoðlice
                  gesæleð on sæwe,   þeh we sið nesan,
                  frecne geferan.

One difficult example is

ChristC 1418   þa ic sylf gestag,
    maga in modor,   þeah wæs hyre mægdenhad
    æghwæs onwalg,

where neither the mood (see §3425) nor the order VS (cf. *Met*
13. 39 and see §§3922-8) is decisive. But even here, the sense is
little affected.

§3400. Collinson (*TPS* 1959, p. 10) says that 'a remoter connection
with the coordinators is observed in the common Germanic adverb
and conjunction **þauh* (E. *though*, G. *doch* etc.), if it consists of an
adversative particle represented by Skt. *tu* with PG *-uh* (Lat. *-que*
in *atque, neque*)'. Burnham (p. 12) adds to the list of cognates Goth.
þau, OHG *doh*, OS *thoh*, and ON *þó*. Since both OHG *doh* and OS
thoh can mean 'although', Small (1924, p. 153) errs in claiming that
'English is alone in making this particle a subordinate conjunction
with concessive meaning.'

§3401. It is probable that the adverbial use came first and that the
conjunction *þeah* developed from it through the intermediate stage
þeah þe; see Horn, pp. 213-14 and 217-18, and Mann, *Archiv.* 197
(1960-1), 20. Burnham (p. 14) reports that 'the only conclusion
demonstrable from the prose texts of Old English is that in the
period known to us the two forms interchange. But . . . we may well
infer the evolution: *ðeah* adv. > *ðeah ðe* > *ðeah* cj.; though we cannot detect the process.' Her evidence (pp. 13-14) includes *þeah* in
the early laws, e.g. *LawIne* 6. 4 *7 þeah hit sie on middum felda
gefohten, cxx scill. to wite sie agifen*; alternation of *þeah* and *þeah
þe* in the same text, e.g. *Or* 38. 17 *7 þeah þæt folc nolde ær Gode
abugan, hy hwæðre þa hyra unðances him gehyrsume wæron* but
Or 66. 30 . . . *7 his suna geþafode þæt he læg mid Latinus wife,
Lucrettie hatte, Brutuses sweostor, þa heo on firde wæron, ðeh þe
hie Romana bremuste wæron to ðæm cyninge*, *BlHom* 21. 6 *Hwæt
we witon þonne se mon bið blind, þeah he mycel age 7 feala fægeres,
þæt him bið mycel daru, gif he hit geseon ne mæg* but *BlHom* 95. 9
*þonne geseoþ ealle gesceafta ures Drihtnes mihte, þeah þe hie nu
mennisce men oncnawan nellan ne ongytan*, and (with both in one
sentence) *HomU* 21. 2. 7 *ac Adam se æresta man ne þorfte he na
tweogan, þeah ðe he ut adrifen wære of neorxnawonges gefean and
ðeah he hit ne gesawe, þa he gemunde swa þeah þæt ylce þæt he ær
geseah* . . . ; and Ælfric's not unexpected preference for *þeah þe*, e.g.
ÆCHom i. 26. 25 (§3395), where (as far as I have observed) Wulfstan

prefers *þeah* (cf. Kivimaa, p. 46 fn. 4). Burnham's failure to give any statistics for *þeah (þe)* clauses in the prose is to some extent remedied for the 'Alfredian' texts by Liggins (1970, p. 309), where she corrects some of the figures given by Kivimaa, pp. 153-4:

A systematic examination of the complete texts of *Or, Bo* and *Sol* and samplings from various parts of *CP* gave the following results:

	Or	*CP*	*Bo*	*Sol*
þeah	52	51	152	45
þeah þe	41	5	5	1

However, study of the distribution shows that the mere totals for *Or* are somewhat misleading, for the earlier books prefer *þeah* to *þeah þe* (35:12) and in III, viii-V the simple form is less common than the compound (17:29). Book VI has only *þeah* (5:0). [This gives 57 for *þeah*.]

The predominance of *þeah* in this table is noteworthy. See Baker (*Speculum*, 55 (1980), 24-6) on the usage in some later texts. There is room for more work here.

§3402. The poetry shows similar fluctuations. We find *þeah* in

GenA 1037   Ne þearft ðu þe ondrædan   deaðes brogan,
                  feorhcwealm nu giet,   þeah þu from scyle
                  freomagum feor   fah gewitan

but *þeah þe* in

GenA 952   No hwæðre ælmihtig   ealra wolde
                  Adame and Euan   arna ofteon,
                  fæder æt frymðe,   þeah þe hie him from swice. . . .

Both appear in

Beo 679   forþan ic hine sweorde   swebban nelle,
                  aldre beneotan,   þeah ic eal mæge;
                  nat he þara goda,   þæt he me ongean slea,
                  rand geheawe,   þeah ðe he rof sie
                  niþgeweorca.

In these examples with *þe* the possibility of elision of *e* before *h* may arise. *PPs* shows a marked preference for *þeah þe*, e.g.

PPs 146.11   Nafast ðu to manna   mægene willan,
                  ne þe on þinum selegescotum   swiðe licað,
                  þeah þe weras wyrcean   wræst on eorðan,

but *þeah* occurs in

PPs 138.13   Nis min ban wið þe   deope behyded,
                  þæt þu wislice   worhtest on diglum,
                  þeh min lichama   lytle ðrage
                  on niðerdælum   eorðan wunige.

Conversely, *Met* prefers *þeah*, e.g.

Met 7. 34   . . . grundweal gearone;   se toglidan ne þearf,
                   þeah hit wecge wind   woruldearfoða
                   oððe ymbhogena   ormete ren . . . ,

but has *þeah þe* in

Met 7.50   . . .   and hine singale
                   gemen gæle,   þonne him grimme on
                   woruldsælða wind   wraðe blaweð,
                   þeah þe hine ealneg   se ymbhoga
                   ðyssa woruldsælða   wraðe drecce.

GenB has only *þeah*; cf. OS *thoh*. The one example of *þeah þe* noted
by Quirk (p. 22) in *El* is presumably

El 81   Ne ondræd þu ðe,
          ðeah þe elþeodige   egesan hwopan,
          heardre hilde.

It may be one; cf. *Ex* 448 for *hwopan* without a dative of the person
threatened. But *þe* could be the personal pronoun; cf. *GuthA* 190.
For fuller details of the distribution in the poetry, see Quirk, pp. 21–3,
and Mitchell 1959, Appendix 'Conc 1' and 'Conc 2'. Quirk (pp. 39–40)
rightly examined these variations to see if they had any significance,
but—as Campbell (*RES* 7 (1956), 66) says—'it is not surprising that
Quirk (pp. 39–40) is unable to establish a distinction between *þeah*
in conjunctival function and *þeah þe*, for here *þe* is not a sense-bearing
word, but a particle indicating that the preceding word is a conjunction, not an adverb'. This lack of distinction is well brought out in
HomU 21. 2. 7 (§3401) and *Beo* 679 above. For the possibility that
metrical considerations may influence the choice between *þeah* and
þeah þe, see §2287.

§3403. Burnham (pp. 21–2) notes that 'the *ðeah*-clause is sometimes periphrastically introduced', e.g. *Bede* 124. 13 *Nales þæt sona
þæt innstæpe 7 ungeþeahtenlice þæm gerynum onfon wolde þæs
Cristenan geleafan, þeah þe þæt wære, þæt ofer þæt deofolgeldum
ne þeowode, seoðþan he hine to Cristes þeowdome gehatenne hæfde*,
where the Latin has *quamuis*, Miller translates 'though the fact was,
that . . .', and (says Burnham) 'the construction serves . . . to give
weight and impressiveness to the statement of the *ðeah*-clause'. In
some other examples, including *ÆCHom* i. 242. 20 *Ge sceolon beon
geornfulle to eower agenre ðearfe, þeah hit swa getimige þæt se
lareow gimeleas beo* . . . , 'the intention is, apparently, to emphasize the remoteness or deplorableness of the idea contained in the

concessive clause'. They have in common the idea of emphasis. This may also be achieved by correlation and reinforcement; see §§3528-35.

§3404. The subordinating conjunction stands at the head of its clause. The only OE examples known to me of the MnE type in which an adjective or adverb precedes 'though' are those recorded by Burnham (pp. 18-19) and Quirk (pp. 23-4), viz. the difficult *Solil* 26. 21 *uncuð þehṭ ic wære, ðonun cume* [*ic*] *to* [*þam*] *þ ic hine mæge sweotolor geseon* (see Carnicelli's note, pp. 64-5) and

Rid 48. 1   Ic gefrægn for hæleþum   hring endean,
                torhtne butan tungan,   tila þeah he hlude
                stefne ne cirmde,   strongum wordum.

§3405. It is generally supposed that *þeah þe* is always a conjunction. Thorpe's punctuation of *ÆCHom* i. 286. 1 *Oðer ðing deð seo hætu, and oðer seo beorhtnys; and ðeah ðe hi ne magon beon to-twæmde: belimpð, hwæðere ðeah, seo hæðung to ðære hætan, and seo onlihting belimpð to ðære beorhtnysse* misleadingly suggests to modern readers that he took *ðeah ðe* as an adverb. This would give sense. But he translates it 'though', with *ðeah ðe* correlative with *hwæðere ðeah*. This seems right to me.

§3406. The prevailing mood in *þeah (þe)* clauses is the subjunctive; see §§3425-9. On the arrangement of such clauses within the sentence, see §§3528-40.

b. Clauses with þeah (þe) for þæt

§3407. Quirk (p. 116) and Campbell (*RES* 7 (1956), 66) report that clauses of this sort are found in prose only. The exceptions are apparent rather than real; see §3415. Burnham (p. 125) remarks that 'the ðeah-clause, while retaining its concessive force, may be substantive'. Campbell (loc. cit.) speaks of 'noun clauses with *þeah* for *þæt*'. I do not object to these terms, but do without them to avoid terminological arguments. Those who do object should note that *þeah (þe)* clauses occasionally occur in what would seem to be apposition with *hit*, e.g. *ÆLS* 2. 160 *Ic wene þæt hit ne sy unrihtwisnysse ætforan gode þeah ðe þu wifes bruce and blysse on life* and *ÆLS* 31. 1080 *. . . and cwæð þæt hit ne sceolde his munuchade derian þeah þe he hire frofres and fultumes bruce*, and should ponder Burnham's comments (p. 27) on *CP* 333. 8.

§3408. Wülfing's suggestion (ii. 86) that this use of *þeah (þe)* is the result of confusion is rightly rejected by Horn (p. 222). Campbell (loc. cit.) makes a characteristically original and perceptive point when he observes that these clauses 'originally . . . would imply that the clause denoted something contrary to expectation . . .'. This is perfectly illustrated by the two examples quoted in §3407, where (I suggest) Ælfric deliberately used *þeah þe* to warn his audience that the saint is being tempted to commit sin. The rest of Campbell's sentence reads '. . . then they would become used for mere variety of expression'. Without native informants, it is impossible to prove or disprove this. But in my opinion all the examples cited below can be seen as expressing something contrary to expectation or, we may add, hope.

§3409. The examples now to be considered can be divided into three groups. Mention has already been made in §1960 of the first, viz. the use of *þeah (þe)* after verbs or nouns meaning 'wonder'. Burnham (p. 33) tells us that 'the usual translation for *si* after negative and interrogative expressions like *quid mirum* or *non mirum est* is *ðeah'. Gif* may also appear after words meaning 'wonder', e.g. *ÆCHom* i. 286. 26 (§1960). But *þeah (þe)* is more common in my collections; typical examples include (after a negative principal clause) *Bede* 178. 11 *Ne þæt swiðe to wundrienne is, þeah þe in þære stowe his deaðes untrume hælo onfenge . . .* , CP 275. 12 *Nis hit nan wundor, ðeah he swugie 7 bide his timan*, and (after an exclamatory or interrogative principal clause) *ÆCHom* ii. 186. 9 *Hwilc wundor wæs, ðeah se halga wer ealne middaneard ætforan him gesawe. . . .* Burnham does not specifically state that examples of *þeah (þe)* for *þæt* after words meaning 'wonder' are restricted to these two contexts. But she cites none to the contrary. Nor does Horn (pp. 222–3), nor Wülfing (ii. 86), apart from *Solil* 33. 13, of which Wülfing was rightly suspicious; see the editions.

§3410. Burnham (p. 33) says that '*ðeah* is the usual particle' after words meaning 'wonder'. But as 'the *ðeah*-clause, the most frequently used concessive construction, is . . . not represented by a list of references' because it is not among 'those forms of clause which seemed to me to repay such study' (Burnham, p. 133), and as my own collections are not complete, I have not the references for checking whether *þeah (þe)* is restricted to the two contexts mentioned in §3409 or for ascertaining the extent to which *þæt, þeah*, and *gif*, overlap; see §1960. There are certainly examples of words meaning 'wonder' governing a *þæt* clause after both negative and positive principal clauses, e.g. (negative) *Bo* 126. 1 *oððe hwa ne wun-dra ð þte sume tunglu habbað scyrtran hwyrft þonne sume habban* and

Met 28. 49   Hwæt, nu hæleða fela
              swelces and swelces   swiðe wundrað,
              and ne wundriað   þætte wuhta gehwilc,
              men and netenu,   micelne habbað
              and unnetne   andan betweoh him,
              swiðe singalne,

and (positive) *ÆCHom* i. 226. 14 (§ 1960) and

Beo 771   þa wæs wundor micel,   þæt se winsele
              wiðhæfde heaþodeorum,   þæt he on hrusan ne feol,
              fæger foldbold.

There is room for more work here.

§ 3411. The second group of clauses with *þeah (þe)* for *þæt* occurs with words meaning 'profit, benefit', e.g. *BlHom* 55. 4 *Hu nyt bið þæm men þeh he geornlice gehyre þa word þæs halgan godspelles gif he þa nel on his heortan habban 7 healdan . . . ?; ÆCHom* ii. 432. 2 *La hwæt fremað ðære burhware þeah ðe þæt port beo trumlice on ælce healfe getimbrod, gif ðær bið an hwem open forlæten, þæt se onwinnenda here þurh ðam infær hæbbe?; Mark(WSCp)* 8. 36 *Hwæt fremað men ðeah he eallne middaneard gestryne 7 do his sawle for-wyrd?*, where the Latin has *si* and *Li gif ł ðæh; Matt(WSCp)* 16. 26, which is a variant version of the same saying of Jesus, with *gyf* where *Mark* has *7; Luke(WSCp)* 9. 25, *ThCap* 2 (Sauer) 345. 16, and *HomS* 16. 130—further variations of the same sentence, with *7, and*, and *and*, respectively, not *gif*; and, finally, yet another variation which demonstrates the equivalence of a rhetorical question and a negated statement, viz. *ThCap 1* (Sauer) 345. 17 *Ure Drihten cwæð þ þam men nawiht ne forstode þeah he ealne middaneard gestrinde gif he his sawle forleosan wolde.*

§ 3412. But here too we also find *gif*, e.g. *LawRect* 10. 1 *Gyf he mare geearnian mæig, him bið sylfum fremu* and (with appositive *hit*) *Lch* iii. 224. 7 *gyf se wæta byð mare ðonne þ fyr þonne fremað hit* (cf. . . . *þær þær . . . hyt* in *ThCap 1* (Sauer) 371. 8), and *þæt*, e.g. *ÆCHom* ii. 402. 2 *þeah ðe þe man bere mete toforan, hwonlice ðe fremað þæt ðu hine geseo, buton ðu his onbyrige, ÆLS* 25. 829 *. . . forðan þe him fremað swiðor þæt þa ungesewenlican fynd beon oferswyðde þonne ða gesewenlican*, and the second sentence in *CP(C)* 332. 8 *Hwæt forstent ænegum men, ðeah he gemangige ðæt* *he ealne ðisne middangeard age, gif he his saule forspildeð? Swelce sio Soðfæstnes openlice sæde: Hwelc fremu bið men ðæt hie ge- striene eall ðæt him ymbutan sie, gif he forliest ðæt him oninnan bið. . . .* This last example is important for three reasons: first, it is a variant of *Mark(WSCp)* 8. 36 (§3411); second, it is followed by a paraphrase with *ðæt* instead of *ðeah* after a rhetorical question; and third, the alternative version in *CP(H)* 333. 8 (on which see Burnham, p. 27) has the pronoun *ðæt* before *ðeah* in what seems to be an appositive function; cf. §3407. The Latin has *si* in both clauses.

§3413. The third group of clauses with *þeah (þe)* for *þæt* consists of those which depend on words expressing emotions other than wonder. They include (with *gebelgan*) *Solil* 35. 18 *ne gebelg þu þe wið me, þeah ic þe frasige and ðin fandige*; (with *ondrædan*) *CP* 371. 25, where the Latin has an infinitive (Burnham, p. 27);[178] (with *forðencan*) *Solil* 31. 3; (with *ofþyncan*) *Ps(P)* 36. 1; (with *seofian*) *Solil* 48. 11; and (with *unrotsian*) *Solil* 32. 6 *Hwæt, ic wene þæt nan man ne si to þam dysig þæt he forði unrotsige þeah he ne mage þas sunnan . . . geseon.* In all these, a negative expression precedes the *þeah (þe)* clause. Only full collections will enable us to discover whether *þeah (þe)* occurs only after a negative. But we do find *þæt* after a negative, e.g. *CP* 107. 16 . . . *7 eft wið ða wiðerweardan ne ondræde he ðæt he begonge his ryhtwisnesse.* . . . BTS, s.v. *for- þencan*, offers us another apparent example, viz. '*Ne scealt þu þe forðencan þæt þu fulraðe ne mæge becuman to ðam ðe ðe ðu wilnast, Solil. H.* 30. 20.' But both Endter and Carnicelli report *þeað*, not *þæt*, the latter with the note '*þeað þu* < *þeah þu* shows consonant assimilation'. BTS is quoting from Hargrove, who also reports *þeað* but emends to *þæt*.

§3414. In the prose, then, I have found *þeah (þe)* for *þæt* in clauses expressing wonder which follow a negative expression or a rhetorical question or exclamation; in clauses dependent on words meaning 'benefit, profit' which follow a rhetorical question or a negative ex- pression; and in clauses expressing emotions other than wonder which follow a negative expression. But, as noted above, other con- junctions may occur in these contexts. Further work is needed here; there may be more examples like the two quoted in §3407, which do not altogether conform to the above patterns.

---

[178] In *CP* 213. 17, the *ðeah* clause is in co-ordination with the two preceding *for* phrases. Liggins (1955, pp. 387–8) includes this among the examples in which *þeah (þe)* clauses 'also have shades of condition, cause and time'.

§3415. Four examples from the poetry remain to be considered. In two, the idea of benefit is present in a principal clause which is not a rhetorical question or a negative statement. They are

Soul i 76 Forðan þe wære selre swiðe mycle
   þonne þe wæron ealle eorðan speda,
   (butan þu hie gedælde dryhtne sylfum),
   þær ðu wurde æt frymðe fugel oððe fisc on sæ,
   oððe on eorðan neat ætes tilode,
   feldgangende feoh butan snyttro,
   oððe on westenne wildra deora
   þæt wyrreste, þær swa god wolde,
   ge þeah ðu wære wyrma cynna
   þæt grimmeste, þær swa god wolde,
   þonne ðu æfre on moldan man gewurde
   oððe æfre fulwihte onfon sceolde

and the corresponding *Soul ii* 71. The clause introduced by *þær* 'if' in *Soul i* 79 is parallel to that introduced by *þeah* in *Soul i* 84. Both could be replaced by *þæt* introducing noun clause subjects of *wære selre*. Perhaps the poet was not entirely in control of this long period. The *þeah þe* clause in

PPs 146. 11 Nafast ðu to manna mægene willan,
   ne þe on þinum selegescotum swiðe licað,
   þeah þe weras wyrcean wræst on eorðan,

for which there is no equivalent in the Latin, can be taken as concessive rather than as a noun clause subject of *licað*; see Mitchell 1959, p. 536. An apparent example of *þeah þe* for *þæt* in *PPs* is due to the sporadic failure of the translator to render correctly the Latin idiom by which 'in imitation of Heb. the verb *jurare* may be followed by *si* to express a strong negative, and by *nisi* to express a strong affirmative' (Nunn, p. 65). He correctly translated *si* by *þæt ... ne* in

PPs 88. 32 Ic æne swor að on halgum,
   þæt ic Dauide dæda ne leoge,
   þæt on ecnesse his agen cynn
   wunað on wicum,

Latin *Semel iuravi in sancto meo, si David mentiar.* But in

PPs 131. 2 Swa ic æt frymðe geswor ferhðe wið drihten
   and gehat gehet, he geheold teala
   wið Iacobes god þone mæran,
  3 þeah þe ic on mines huses hyld gegange
   oþþe selegesceot þænne swæs wese
   oððe on min restbedd ricene gestige,
  4 Gif ic minum eagum unne slæpes,
   oþþe minum breawum beode hnappunga,
   oþþe ic on þunwange þriste gereste ... ,

where the Latin *Ps* 131. 2-5 has *Sicut iuravit . . . Si introiero . . . ; si ascendero . . . ; si dedero . . .*, he offers first *þeah þe* and then *gif* for *si*. In *PPs* 94. 11, too, he rendered *si* by *gif*. See further my comments in *MÆ* 25 (1956), 40.

c. þeah (þe) *introducing dependent nexus questions*

§3416. As noted in §2089, *þeah (þe)* may mean 'whether', introducing dependent nexus questions. In my collections, it occurs most frequently after *nytan*. The only example in the poetry belongs here, viz.

GenB 531	Nat þeah þu mid ligenum fare
þurh dyrne geþanc	þe þu drihtnes eart
boda of heofnum;	

see Quirk, p. 39.[179] This is also the only example known to me in which two alternatives are expressed after *nytan þeah (þe)*. The apparent change of mood—*fare* is presumably subjunctive—is noteworthy, but we have seen similar changes in the second of two clauses in dependent speech elsewhere, for example in §1947.

§3417. In all the recorded prose examples, a negative alternative is implied. They include *Bo* 64. 9 *Ic nat þeah ðu wene þæt hi on hiora agenre cyððe ealne weg mægen; Bo* 107. 25 *Ic nat ðeah þe elles hwæt ðince; Solil* 20. 8 *Ic nat þeah hym þuhte þæt hym beþorften þæt hi his mare wiston* (where Wülfing (ii. 172) and others unnecessarily supplied *gif* after *þeah*); *Solil* 48. 2 *þonne ic nat þeah me licie . . .* (wrongly emended in Endter's edition); *LS* 18. 134. 614 *nat ic þeah heo beo beswicen þurh þæs engles hiw*; and *Josh* 9. 7 *We nyton ðeah ge wunion her on neawyste hwær . . .*; for further examples, see Burnham, p. 34. But we also find *hwæþer*, e.g. in the sequences *Solil* 20. 7 *Forðam ic nat hweðer him genoh þuhte . . . Ic nat þeah hym þuhte . . .* and *Ch* 1507 *H* 18. 25 *7 ic nat naht gewislice hwæðer þæs feos swa micel is, ne ic nat þeah his mare sy*, in which we have two alternatives, each with an implied negative.

§3418. The occasional examples of *þeah (þe)* clauses after a negated form of *rec(c)an* 'to care' present a terminological problem. They include *CP* 179. 9 *. . . 7 ne reccað ðeah menn wenen ðæt hie yfel don*, Latin *. . . et tamen quibusdam factis publice mala de se opinari*

---

[179] Despite Klaeber, I reject the idea that we have an example of a dependent nexus question introduced by *þeah* after *gemunde* in *Beo* 1129; see Klaeber, 3, note to *Beo* 1129b-30, and Mitchell 1959, p. 53.

permittunt; *Ps(P)* 9. 33 *Ne recþ God þeah ic þus do*, Latin *Non re-
quiret Deus*; and *Mark(Ru)* 4. 38 *ne reces ðu ðah we deade sie*,
Latin *non ad te pertinet quia perimus*. On the analogy of examples
like the last two quoted in §3417, *CP* 195. 6, and *CP* 145. 20 . . .
*ðonne hie ne recceað hwæðer mon hie selfe synderlice 7 ungemet-
lice lufige*, we can describe them as dependent questions. But we also
find negated forms of *rec(c)an* introducing *þæt* clauses in *Mark(Li)*
4. 38 *ne reces ðu þ we deado sie* (Latin *quia*) and *LibSc* 25. 3 *ne na
recð se ealda feond þæt he eorþlice afyrre fram us ac þæt he soþe
lufe on us slea* (Latin *ut . . . ut*); see further Horn, pp. 222-3. On the
analogy of these, we could call them dependent statements. I have
found no examples with *gif* comparable to MnE 'I don't care if . . .'.

§3419. I have recorded two *þeah (þe)* clauses after *uncuþ*, viz. *Solil*
50. 9 *uncuð þæah me syððan scamige* . . . and *ÆLS* 18. 119 *Clypiað
git hluddor uncuð þeah þe he slæpe*. . . . Burnham's comment (p. 34)
on the latter—'The meaning is evidently "perhaps"; one may compare "Who knows whether?" '—gains added point when we compare 3 *Kgs* 18. 27 *Clamate voce majore, deus enim est, et forsitan
loquitur, aut in diversorio est, aut in itinere, aut certe dormit*. . . .

§3420. What Burnham (p. 34) calls 'the singular phrase *weald ðeah*
[which] also means "perhaps" ' has been mentioned in §2937,
where *ÆCHom* ii. 340. 8 and ii. 466. 9 are quoted. Other examples
include *Nic(A)* 488. 27 *weald þeah we hyne gemetan magon*, *Nic(A)*
488. 33 *weald þeah se gast 7 we hyne gemetan moton* (where *Nic(B)*
489. 34 reads *weald þeh ðe gast habbe þone helend gelæht*), and
Josh 9. 7 *weald ðeah eower eard us gesceote*. BT includes three of
these examples s.v. 'weald; *adv. conj.* I. in independent clauses, *with
þeah, perhaps, may be*'. Burnham (p. 34) says that 'whether it
[*weald*] is to be explained as originally noun or verb cannot be determined'. Since the prevailing mood in the *þeah (þe)* clauses discussed
here is the subjunctive, the fact that all the examples cited above
have subjunctive or ambiguous verb-forms perhaps slightly inclines
the scale in favour of the idea that originally *þeah* introduced a
dependent question, with *weald* possibly an imperative rather than
a noun; cf. *And* 1352, discussed in §2939. On *weald* 'lest' see §2938.

d. þeah (þe) *'even though'*

§3421. Campbell (*RES* 7 (1956), 66 and fn. 2) uses the formula
'clauses in which *þeah* has a pregnant force, "even though", and
stands for *þeah + furðum* or some other such expression' to cover

Met 14. 1　　　Hwæt bið ðæm welegan　　woruldgitsere
　　　　　　　　on his mode ðe bet,　　þeah he micel age
　　　　　　　　goldes and gimma . . . ,

Beo 1368　　　Ðeah þe hæðstapa　　hundum geswenced,
　　　　　　　　heorot hornum trum　　holtwudu sece,
　　　　　　　　feorran geflymed,　　ær he feorh seleð,
　　　　　　　　aldor on ofre,　　ær he in wille,
　　　　　　　　hafelan beorgan,

and similar examples from the poetry cited by Quirk (pp. 37–8). A possible example from the prose is *Or* 21. 15 *7 þeah man asette twegen fætels full ealað oððe wæteres, hy gedoð þæt ægþer bið ofer-froren, sam hit sy sumor sam winter,* translated by Campbell (loc. cit.) 'and even though you put down two vessels, they so work that one is frozen'. Here Campbell denies Quirk's conditional interpreta-tion (p. 38 fn. 3), with the words 'There is no evidence that *þeah* can be used for *gif*.' But the more I ponder examples like *ÆCHom* i. 394. 5 *þeah hwa forlæte micele æhta and ne forlæt ða gitsunge, ne forlæt he ealle ðing* (where *hwa* introduces an element of hypothesis), *ÆC Hom* i. 618. 26 *þeah ðe gyt wære oðer þusend geara to ðam dæge, nære hit langsum,* and *ÆCHom* i. 618. 30, the more I fluctuate be-tween the translations 'even though', 'even if', and 'if', for *þeah (þe)* in these and similar examples. I am not alone in this; consider BT's heading s.v. *þeah* II (2) 'in hypothetical clauses, *though, if, even if*', and the distinction between '*even if*' and '*if even, if only*' made in BTS, s.v. *þeah* II 2(*a*) and (*β*).

e. *Clauses in which the concessive force of* þeah (þe) *is much reduced or entirely absent*

§3422. Campbell (*RES* 7 (1956), 66) uses this formula to describe some examples from the poetry in which, according to Quirk (p. 39), *þeah (þe)* is 'used weakly or plainly without concessive feeling'. The reader should ponder the proposed examples for himself, considering all the time whether it is the context or *þeah (þe)* which guides him.

f. þeah (þe) *introducing 'elliptical concessions'*

§3423. 'Elliptical concessions' where *þeah (þe)* is the equivalent of 'though it may be conceded that' are discussed by Behaghel (*DS* iii, §1422) and Quirk (pp. 36–7); see also Burnham (p. 4) and Brouwer, *Neophil.* 3 (1917), 258–61. Typical examples include *Solil* 61. 17 *Honorius is swiðe god, þeah his feder betere were* and *ÆCHom* ii.

142. 10 *Ða wiste Cuðberhtus eal be ðam wife, and wolde þurh hine sylfne sona hi geneosian; forðan ðe heo ærðon eawfæst leofode, ðeah ðe se unsið hire swa gelumpe*, both quoted by Burnham (p. 33) as examples of concessive clauses 'loose in connection' to the principal clause; *Az* 42 *Fyl nu þa frumspræce, þeah þe user fea lifgen*, quoted by Quirk, p. 37; and

Met 24. 44　　　　Gif ðu weorðest　　on wege rihtum
　　　　　　　　　up to ðæm earde,　þæt is æðele stow,
　　　　　　　　　ðeah ðu hi nu geta　forgiten hæbbe,

quoted by Behre (p. 123) with this comment: 'The sentence is probably contracted: "that is a noble place (sc. which you should know or remember), though you have until now forgotten it." ' So *Solil* 61. 17 might mean something like 'Honorius is very good (and ranks high among good men), although his father was better'; *ÆCHom* ii. 142. 10 '. . . because she had previously lived piously (and therefore deserved better fortune), though misfortune had so come upon her'; and *Az* 42 'Fulfil now the ancient promise (which we still want to see fulfilled), though few of us are living'.

§3424. Quirk (pp. 135–6) notes that 'we find this phenomenon among the concessions formed with . . . *hwæðere* . . . , zero relating element . . . , concessive-equivalent relative members . . . , and other constructions. It seems more than usually common with *ac*. . . .'

g. *Mood and tense in* þeah (þe) *clauses*

§3425. '*þeah* takes the subjunctive in subordinate clauses by rule, and quite independently of the reality of the concession.' The number of exceptions to Campbell's dictum (*RES* 7 (1956), 65) is small in both the prose and the poetry. As Burnham (p. 25) puts it, 'the strongest statement, then, that we can make is that the indicative *may* appear after *ðeah*, but exceptionally in both earlier and later texts'. The truth of Burnham's further comment (p. 25) that 'Old English did not mark by mode the distinction between fact and supposition introduced by *ðeah*' can be illustrated by comparing *ÆC Hom* i. 20. 4 *heo is ece, and næfre ne geendað, þeah se lichama geendige, þe sceal eft þurh Godes mihte arisan to ecere wununge*, *ÆCHom* i. 82. 33 *Ne forseah Crist his geongan cempan, ðeah ðe he lichamlice on heora slege andwerd nære*, and

Beo 1830　　　　　　　　　Ic on Higelace wat,
　　　　　　　Geata dryhten,　þeah ðe he geong sy,
　　　　　　　folces hyrde,　þæt he mec fremman wile
　　　　　　　wordum ond weorcum,

all of which concede accepted facts (negatively expressed in *ÆCHom* i. 82. 33), with *ÆCHom* i. 6. 16 *Ne eac se wælhreowa Antecrist næfð þa mihte þæt he heofenlic fyr asendan mæge, ðeah þe he þurh deofles cræft hit swa gehiwige, ÆCHom* i. 26. 25 *þeah ðe eal mennisc wære gegaderod, ne mihton hi ealle hine acwellan, gif he sylf nolde*, and

Sat 515   Næs nan þæs stronglic   stan gefæstnod,
              þeah he wære mid irne   eall ymbfangen,
              þæt mihte þam miclan   mægne wiðhabban,

in which a hypothesis is conceded, and with *ÆCHom* i. 72. 12 *þa cwæð se apostol, 'þeah þu me attor sylle, þurh Godes naman hit me ne derað'* and *Beo* 588 *þæs þu in helle scealt* ‖ *werhðo dreogan, þeah þin wit duge*, where, in the light of the context, the issue seems to me open. Quirk (p. 40) puts it tellingly:

. . . beyond stating that there is no evidence of the indicative being used for 'unreal' concessions there is little that we can say. In Beo 202 we read, 'Men did not blame him for going, *though he was dear to them*'; in 2160, 'He would not give them to his son, *though he was loyal to him*'; in 2466, 'He could not persecute the warrior, *though he was hateful to him*.' In the first two cases we have the subjunctive, in the third the indicative; he would be bold who asserted that this indicative deliberately matched the 'reality' of the concession.

§3426. In the poetry, where I disregard *Jul* 490 and (now) *Husb* 39 as corrupt, I find that of 210 simple concessive clauses introduced by *þeah (þe)*, 118 have the subjunctive, 85 an ambiguous form, and 7 the indicative. (Quirk's figures (pp. 28–34) differ slightly; see Mitchell 1959, Appendix 'Conc 1' and 'Conc 2'.) The seven with the indicative are (with the present tense) *Soul i* 135 (which rests on an emendation and is without a parallel in *Soul ii*),

GenB 733   Swa þu his sorge ne þearft
            beran on þinum breostum,   þær þu gebunden ligst,
            murnan on mode,   þæt her men bun
            þone hean heofon,   þeah wit hearmas nu,
            þreaweorc þoliað,

and

Rid 95. 10   þeah nu ælda bearn
            londbuendra   lastas mine
            swiþe secað,   ic swaþe hwilum
            mine bemiþe   monna gehwylcum,

and (with the preterite tense)

Beo 1612   Ne nom he in þæm wicum,   Weder-Geata leod,
            maðmæhta ma,   þeh he þær monige geseah,

Beo 2466   No ðy ær he þone heaðorinc   hatian ne meahte
                  laðum dædum,   þeah him leof ne wæs,

Met 29. 51   ligeð him behindan
                  hefig hrusan dæl,   þeah hit hwilan ær
                  eorðe sio cealde   oninnan hire
                  heold and hydde   haliges meahtum,

and *ChristC* 1418 (§3399), where *þeah* may be an adverb. All of
these concede something which is real or a fact. *GenB* 733, *Beo* 1612,
and *Beo* 2466, are accompanied by a negated principal clause, the
remainder by a positive principal clause.

§3427. Exact figures for the prose are not yet available. My own
collections are incomplete. Burnham (pp. 23-5) says that of 693
þeah (þe) clauses from 'a selection of representative texts' only ten
have 'certain indicatives', but failed to give references and was unable
to supply them in response to a personal letter. With the exception
of *BlHom* 33. 8 (see below), those which I have been able to trace
either have ambiguous forms, e.g. *nahtest* in *Bo* 31. 9 *7 swælce hi
woldan bion þeah þu hi næfre nahtest* and the examples with *synd*
which I wrongly accepted as unambiguous indicatives in *Neophil.* 49
(1965), 47-8 (see §651), or are contradicted by another, usually
better, manuscript, e.g. the three examples (against Burnham's two)
from *ÆTemp* which I discussed in the same article, where I pronounced this verdict: 'the indicatives in these *þeah* clauses can, from
the point of view of an Anglo-Saxon Fowler, be dismissed as late bar-
barisms to be resisted at all costs'. Five of Burnham's examples
remain untraced—one each from *Bede, Solil, BenR, ÆLS*, and
Napier's collection of homilies. The possibility is strong that some at
least of these have ambiguous forms. This is certainly true of all the
þeah (þe) clauses listed as having indicative verbs by Wülfing (ii,
§459), including the examples from *Bede* and *Solil*. So far, however,
the only unambiguous indicative known to me in the prose is *BlHom*
33. 8 *forþon nis þæt nan wundor þeah se hea cyning 7 se eca drihten
hine sylfne let lædon on þa hean dune. . . .* This example, with the
pret. ind. *let* in a *þeah* clause following *nan wundor*, presents a striking contrast with *BlHom* 33. 12 *Nis þæt to wundrigenne þeah þe he
wære costod . . .* , with its pret. subj. *wære*. Full prose collections
will almost certainly produce some simple concessive *þeah (þe)*
clauses with unambiguous indicatives. But these will not render invalid the conclusions of Burnham and Campbell quoted in §3425.
Those examples of indicatives already cited from the prose and
poetry all occur in concessions of fact. So I have no reason to change

the conclusion I reached in *Neophil.* 49 (1965), 48: 'The sporadic indicatives are departures from the norm which represent the beginnings of the process which led to the modern preference for the indicative in "though"-clauses which concede a fact.'

§3428. This overwhelming preference for the subjunctive means that there is no question of any possible influence from a volitional expression or a negated indicative in the principal clause. The use and nature of the subjunctive has been much discussed. Quirk (pp. 28-9) offers cogent criticism of the work of previous writers. For reference to more discussions, see Mitchell 1959, pp. 567-9. To these may be added Muxin, *UZLGU* 262, vyp. 50 (1958), 159-60. Quirk (p. 34) concludes 'that the indicative . . . is a very rare and sporadic feature and that those scholars who deny the inherently subjunctive character of dependent *þeah*-members are giving grossly undue prominence to the irregular'. This is the main reason for my reluctance to accept Onions's tentative suggestion that *þeh* be read for the second *þe* in

Mald 189　　　he gehleop þone eoh　　þe ahte his hlaford,
　　　　　　　　on þam gerædum　　þe hit riht ne wæs;

see §§2180, 2231, 2249, and 3486-7, and Mitchell 1965*b*, p. 48. The arguments I deploy in the last against emendation are equally telling in favour of the acceptance by Endter and Carnicelli of Jost's emendation of *þe* to *þeh* and *weron* to *were* to produce *Solil* 69. 1 *Ac þa goodan nellað heora yflum freondum arian, forðam hy nellað heora yfeles geswican, ðe ma þe Habraham wolde þam welegan arian, þeh he hys ægnes kinnes were*, where the subjunctive in Hargrove's *þe he hys ægnes kinnes were* puzzled Burnham (p. 94).

§3429. As in OE generally, the tenses of the verbs in concessive sentences depend on the actual time relationship and not on any artificial 'sequence of tenses'; see §§859-64. So examples like *Bo* 76. 9 *7 he bið anfeald untodæled þeah he ær on mænig tonemned wære* need cause no surprise. The reference of the present subjunctive in a concessive clause can be to the present, e.g. *ApT* 24. 5 *Ðeah ðu stille sy and unrot, þeah ic þine æðelborennesse on ðe geseo*, or to the future, e.g. *LS* 23. 619 *forðon witodlice þeah þu ær wille faran ahwyder, þu ne miht*. That of the preterite subjunctive is usually to the past, e.g. *ÆCHom* i. 6. 13 *Ne sende se deofol ða fyr of heofenum, þeah ðe hit ufan come*, but may be to the future-in-the-past, e.g. *ÆLS* 27. 176 *Nu synd þa Iudeiscan and se sceamlease læwa Cristes deaðes scyldige þe syrwdon be him, þeah þe hit us become to ecere alysednysse*.

3. OTHER WORDS OR PHRASES WHICH MAY
INTRODUCE SIMPLE CONCESSIVE CLAUSES

a. Hwæðere

§3430. Burnham (pp. 17–18) suggests that *hwæðere* is used as a conjunction 'though' in *Bede* 52. 27, where she has reservations, and in
ÆCHom i. 158. 12, where she suggests that Ælfric may have been
guilty of 'careless construction'. In both sentences *hwæðere* can be
explained as an adverb.

b. Swa

§3431. See §§ 1924, 2861–3, and 3476–82.

c. Swa þeah (þe/þæt)

§3432. The most convincing example of *swa þeah* introducing a concessive clause is *ÆCHom* i. 2. 12 *Ic Ælfric munuc and mæssepreost,*
swa þeah waccre þonne swilcum hadum gebyrige, wearð asend on
Æþelredes dæge cyninges fram Ælfeage biscope . . . , where the verb
is unexpressed. Burnham (pp. 16–17) and Quirk (p. 21) quote and
discuss other possible instances. But in all of them, either *swa* or
þeah or *swa þeah* can be taken as an adverb.

d. (Swa) þeah hwæðere

§3433. Burnham (p. 18) sees the possibility of a concessive conjunction 'though' in *þeah hwæðere* in *ÆCHom* i. 152. 27 and in *swa þeah*
hwæðere in *LS* 23. 284. Here again an adverbial interpretation is
acceptable.

4. DISJUNCTIVE OR ALTERNATIVE CONCESSIVE
CLAUSES INTRODUCED BY *SAM . . . SAM, SWA . . . SWA,*
OR *þEAH (þE) . . . OþþE*

§3434. Burnham (pp. 35–43) prefers 'disjunctive', Quirk (pp. 83–7)
prefers 'alternative', as a term to describe a concession which 'introduces mutually exclusive possibilities, in spite of *either of which* the
proposition is maintained' (Burnham, p. 4) or a concession which
'makes a specific attempt to remove in advance all possible threats to
the validity of the utterance to which it is related . . . "Please come,
wet or dry" ' (Quirk, p. 83). Here we are concerned with sentences in

which these alternatives are expressed in clauses introduced by con-junctions, including the pattern *þeah (þe) . . . oþþe*, which neither Burnham nor Quirk admits. For disjunctive concessions expressed in clauses without conjunctions, see §§3443-8. Whether the individual clauses which combine to make up the disjunctive concessive con-struction should be described as concessive or conditional remains a matter of dispute; see Quirk, p. 84. Such concessions may also be expressed by words and/or phrases; see §§3502-5. Quirk (pp. 83-4) gives a useful discussion and bibliography, to which can be added Nusser, pp. 185-96. Examples of this type often shade into 'indefi-nite concession'.

§3435. Burnham (p. 36) observes that

sam seems related to the series *som* (noun), *samod, samen, gesamnian*, and *same* (in the combination *swa same*). If this view is correct, the original use of the correlative probably is, 'the same in this case . . . the same in that'. . . . But this notion probably faded early into the more general one of connection, and the particle has no more specific meaning than correlative *swa . . . swa* in its conces-sive use, or than our comparable *whether . . . or*.

This last equation can be accepted without hesitation. Most of Burn-ham's thirteen examples of *sam . . . sam* 'whether . . . or' (pp. 35-7 and 133) are found in 'Alfredian' texts; they include *Or* 21. 15 (§3421), *Solil* 24. 8 *sam ic wylle, sam ic nelle, ic sceal secgan nide riht* (cf. *ÆCHom* i. 532. 6 *forðan þe we sceolon, wylle we nelle we, arisan . . .*), and, with three *sam* clauses, *Solil* 58. 16 *Sam he hine miclum lufige, sam he hine lytlum lufige, sam he hine mydlinga lufige, be þam dæle he lufað god þe he wisdom lufað*. From other texts she offers *BenR* 66. 14 *Sam hy fæsten sam hy ne fæsten, gif hit þonne beo seo tid æfengereordes, arisen hy . . .*—cf. *BenRGl* 74. 7 *7 forði on ælcere tide sit fæstenes sit gereordung . . .*, where the scribe has written Latin *sit* for OE *sie*, although the Latin has *Et ideo omni tempore sive jejunii sive prandii . . .*—and *Lch* i. 166. 9 *Eft wið wunda som hy syn of irenne som hy syn of stence oððe fram nædran, genim þysse ilcan wyrte. . . .* But Burnham's collections are not com-plete. From her own corpus she omits *Bo* 6. 25 *Hu ælc wyrd beoð god, sam heo mannum god þince, sam heo him yfel þince*, and there are examples elsewhere in the prose, e.g. *LibSc* 169. 12 *Se apostol sæde sam ge eornostlice etan sam ge drincan sam ge aht elles gedon ealle on wuldre godes doð*, Latin *Paulus apostolus dixit Siue ergo manducatis siue bibitis siue aliud quid facietis omnia in gloria dei facite*, but not in the poetry. I have so far found no unambiguous indicatives in *sam . . . sam* clauses; the subjunctive is the regular mood. On *sam . . . sam* with words and/or phrases, see §3505.

§3436. On *swa . . . swa* 'either . . . or' used alone or with a clause introduced by *swa* or *swa hwæþer swa*, see §§1825-6. My present collections contain no parallels to *Bede(T)* 412. 1 *Ah gong nu 7 saga him: swa he welle swa he ne wille, he sceal to Columban mynstre cuman*, Latin *At nunc uade et dic illi quia uelit nolit debet ad mona- steria Columbae uenire*, where all other manuscripts also have *swa . . . swa* except MS *B*, which reads *ac gang nu sege him wille he nelle he. . . .*

§3437. *þeah (þe)* sometimes introduces a series of clauses linked by *oþþe* which express mutually exclusive possibilities. For the prose it will suffice to quote *BlHom* 95. 12 *7 þonne hateþ Sanctus Michahel se heahengl blawan þa feower beman æt þissum feower endum mid- dangeardes, 7 awecceaþ ealle þa lichoman of deaþe, þeah þe hie ær eorþe bewrigen hæfde, oþþe on wætere adruncan, oþþe wildeor abiton, oþþe fuglas tobæron, oþþe fixas toslitan, oþþe on ænige wisan of þisse worlde gewiton ealle hie sceolan þonne arisan*, where the sequence introduced by *þeah þe* can be taken *apo koinou*. The only similar example in the poetry is

PPs 68. 31   Ic þam leofan gode   licie swyþor
                þonne æðele cealf,   þeah þe him upp aga
                horn on heafde   oððe hearde cleo,

where there is only one verb.

5. INDEFINITE CONCESSIVE CLAUSES?

§3438. What is described as the indefinite concession 'generalizes the situation: the main proposition is asserted *in spite of any* possi- bility—*no matter what* the case may be' (Burnham, p. 4) or, as Quirk (p. 91) puts it, 'is like the alternative in that it seeks to chal- lenge any attempt to deny the validity of the member to which it is related. But whereas the alternative type does this by specifying such wide limits as make denial impossible, the indefinite does it in a generalizing challenge which says that there are no limits.' In my opinion, however, there is no such thing as an indefinite concessive clause; this would require an OE conjunction ☆*swa þeah swa* and a MnE equivalent ☆'thoughever'. Indefiniteness is, it is true, sometimes read into a *þeah (þe)* clause. Thus, for *Beo* 2029 (§3395) we find the translation '. . . however good the bride may be' in Wrenn–CH. Beo- wulf is certainly describing what he thinks to be a general truth, but Wrenn's own 1953 translation '. . . though the bride . . . may be an outstanding one' or Donaldson's '. . . even though the bride is good'

in my opinion more nearly represents the OE syntax. For the Wrenn–
CH translation is not an indefinite concessive clause but, in Quirk's
terminology (p. 102), a 'concessive-equivalent' construction which
I would classify as an indefinite clause of degree (or manner); see
§§3467–75. The same holds for all the MnE examples quoted by
scholars such as Burnham (p. 4) and Quirk (pp. 91–4) to illustrate
indefinite concessions. Thus, '. . . no matter what the case may be',
'Whoever he were . . .', 'Whatever I've done . . .', and the like, are indefinite adjective clauses; '. . . wheresome'er he is' is an indefinite
clause of place; and clauses introduced by 'whenever' are indefinite
clauses of time.

§3439. *Mutatis mutandis*, this observation holds for all the alleged
OE 'indefinite concessions' distinguished by Burnham (pp. 51–65)
and Quirk (pp. 91–101). Campbell (*RES* 7 (1956), 65) made the
point clearly when pointing out that 'Quirk might have gained by
more preliminary clearance of the ground to clarify the nature of his
material':

Many clauses are not grammatically concessive, but have another grammatical
function, but in their context convey a concessive idea. This is well stated by
Quirk of concessive-equivalent clauses of manner (p. 108), but it would apply
to many other concessive-equivalents (e.g. relative, temporal, and local clauses,
and principal clauses before *ac* clauses).

All these indefinite 'concessive-equivalents' are discussed in §§3459–
75.

6. CONCESSIVE CLAUSES WITH NO CONJUNCTION
AND INITIAL VERB

a. Simple concessions

§3440. Inversion of the subject and verb in a simple clause can express a condition, e.g. 'Had he been here, it wouldn't have happened',
or an 'even though' concession, e.g. 'Had he been here, it would still
have happened'. I do not follow Quirk (p. 87) in using the term 'zero
subordinator'. If such clauses are subordinate in OE, the inversion
(and the subjunctive mood, when it occurs) can be seen as the means
of subordination. But, as we shall see (§3441), it is not certain that
they are subordinate. Curme (1931, p. 338) asserts that 'this form of
the concessive clause is unknown in Old English' and Burnham (p. 44)
comes close to agreeing: 'With a few apparent exceptions, all inverted
concessive clauses are disjunctive or distributive.' The only exceptions she mentions (pp. 44 and 60) are what I call indefinite clauses

of degree (or manner); see §§3467–75. So it is impossible to know
whether she had in mind examples like *ApT* 20. 23 *Ic swerige þurh
ða gemænan hælo þæt ic me næfre bet ne baðode þonne ic dide
todæg nat ic þurh hwilces iunges mannes þenunge*, which may be
compared with

Fates 109   Ic sceall feor heonan,
                   an elles forð,   eardes neosan,
                   sið asettan,   nat ic sylfa hwær,
                   of þisse worulde

and

Jul 699   Min sceal of lice
                   sawul on siðfæt,   nat ic sylfa hwider,
                   eardes uncyðgu.

But I would hesitate to call these concessive. The ind. *nat* may seem
to support me; but see §3442. So too may the fact that we also find
the order SV, e.g.

Beo 274   . . . þæt mid Scyldingum   sceaðona ic nat hwylc,
                   deogol dædhata   deorcum nihtum
                   eaweð þurh egsan   uncuðne nið. . . .

Presumably we have here a construction related to pron. *nathwylc*
but with different emphasis and with expression of the subject of
nat; cf.

ChristA 186   . . . þæt ic of þam torhtan   temple dryhtnes
                   onfeng freolice   fæmnan clæne,
                   womma lease,   ond nu gehwyrfed is
                   þurh nathwylces.

But there remains a possibility that the pron. *nathwylc* started life
as a paratactic concessive expression.

§3441. The two apparently convincing examples of the 'even though'
concession with VS in the poetry can both be taken as (something
approaching) principal clauses. The first, in which *wære* may be indicative or subjunctive, is *Soul i* 144 *Wære ðu on wædle, sealdest me
wilna geniht*. So this could be seen as an indicative question: 'Were
you in poverty?'; see §1644. The second, with the subj. *drince*, is
Sisam's reading (1953, p. 56) of

Seasons 206   drince he him þæt drofe,   duge hlutter þe
                   wæter of wege,   þæt is wuldres lar,

where the manuscript has *lare* correctly in line 204, but wrongly
(according to Sisam, my admiration for whom increases the more

deeply I probe his work) in line 207. Leslie (*JEGP* 52 (1953), 557–8) accepts MS *lare* in the latter, but does not explain why it is not nominative, which his translation would seem to demand. Sisam's translation is 'though he [the priest] should drink dirty (water), let the pure water which is divine doctrine do you good (*duge þe*)'. Leslie suggests 'let *him* drink the muddy water from the road, avail yourself of clear—that is the teaching of heaven'. We could combine Leslie's version of the first clause with Sisam's version of the second. The other solutions known to me demand drastic emendation.

§3442. The fact that the indicative occasionally occurs after *þeah (þe)* means that the indicative in *ApT* 20. 23, *Fates* 109, and *Jul* 699 (all in §3440), and that in the manuscript reading of

OrW 23　　　　　　　　　　　　Ic þe lungre sceal
　　　　　　meotudes mægensped　　maran gesecgan,
　　　　　　þonne þu hygecræftig　　in hreþre mæge
　　　　　　mode gegripan,　　is þin meaht forswiþ,

does not rule out a concessive interpretation. Quirk (p. 96) gives well-founded objections to Mackie's 'however great your ability' for *is þin meaht forswiþ*, but it could perhaps be translated '. . . though your ability is very great'. So there may be some plausibility in Thorpe's *eart ðu* for the manuscript *eart ðe* where ASPR has *ðe eart* in

GuthA 271　　　Ðu þæt gehatest　　þæt ðu ham on us
　　　　　　gegan wille,　　ðe eart godes yrming.

But see Quirk, pp. 104–5. Quirk (p. 88) provides evidence that the indicative sometimes occurs alongside the subjunctive in concessions of this type in MHG and MnE. The presence of the indicative in two challenge constructions from *Met* discussed in §3455 perhaps lends additional support to the proposition that the indicative might have occasionally occurred in simple inverted concessions in OE. See further Mitchell, *MÆ* 25 (1956), 37–8.

b. Disjunctive or alternative concessions

§3443. What can be called disjunctive or alternative concession with initial V(S) is well established in the later prose; see Burnham, pp. 44–50. Burnham (p. 49)—without being able to give any evidence —sees it as 'probably . . . an idiom of native growth' and goes on: 'The concessive use of such clauses would seem to be merely an extension of the conditional use. *Contrasted* conditions, in fact, amount to a disjunctive concession.' This is well illustrated by the sequence of imperatives *Ageot . . . Ageot . . . Geot ðu . . . , geot ðu . . .* in *ÆCHom* ii. 564. 12 *Ageot ele uppon wæter oðða on oðrum wætan, se ele flyt bufon. Ageot wæter uppon ðone ele, and se ele abrecð up and swimð bufon. Geot ðu ðone ele ær, geot ðu siððan, æfre he ofer-swið þone oðerne wætan.* No one, I imagine, would describe these imperative clauses as subordinate. Yet we must not assume that their intonation patterns were identical to those of the MnE equivalent.

§3444. Either the present subjunctive or the preterite subjunctive may introduce two contrasted clauses which can be described as con-ditional (see §3434) and which combine to form a 'disjunctive or alternative concession'. Here, as with the 'inverted conditions' dis-cussed in §§3678-83, the question arises: do we have parataxis with co-ordinate principal clauses, or hypotaxis with subordinate and principal clauses, or does the relationship fall somewhere between the two? *Mutatis mutandis*, the remarks made there apply here. So I do not repeat them. The difficulty is clearly illustrated in the much discussed sequence *sy . . . sy* in *Wife* 42-53, on which I can make no firm pronouncement.

§3445. Typical examples of disjunctive concessions include (with the present subjunctive) *ÆLS* 32. 81 . . . *þæt ic nelle abugan fram his biggengum æfre . . . swelte ic lybbe ic, ÆCHom* i. 532. 6 *forðan þe we sceolon, wylle we nelle we, arisan on ende þyssere worulde . . . , ÆCHom* i. 252. 14 *Getimige us tela on lichaman, getimige us untela, symle we sceolon þæs Gode ðancian, ÆCHom* ii. 10. 5 *þonne hwilc mæden mid luste weres bricð, þonne bið hire mægðhad æfre siððan adylegod, hæbbe heo cild næbbe heo,* and *ÆCHom* ii. 566. 33 *Beon ða mædenu snotere, beon hi stunte, ealle hi moton slapan on ðam gemænelicum deaðe,* and (with the preterite subjunctive) *ÆCHom* ii. 388. 19 *se brym hwoðerode under his fotswaðum, ac swa ðeah he hine bær, wolde he nolde he, ÆCHom* ii. 68. 7 *Petrus se apostol bead . . . þæt hi wæron heora hlaforde getreowe and holde, wære se hlaford good, wære he yfel,* and *ChronE* 245. 10 (1114) *⁊ se cyng þa bebead þone arcб þ he sceolde him læden to Cantwara byrig ⁊ blætson him to б, wolde he nolde he.* The last four examples cited by Visser (ii, §885) belong here. According to Burnham (p. 46), 'the parallel clauses may stand in any part of the sentence, though the initial posi-tion is exceptional'.

§3446. Variations include sentences in which more than two alter-natives are expressed by verbs, e.g. *Ch* 1047 *⁊ ic wille þæt ælc þara landa þe on mines fæder dæge læg into Xpes cyrcean wære hit kynges*

*gife, wære hit bisceopes, wære hit eorles, wære hit þegenas, eall ic
wille þæt ælces mannes gife stande*; sentences with more than one
verb but with other alternatives expressed with *oþþe/ouþer*, e.g.
ChronE 31. 27 (656) *And ic bidde ealle þa ða æfter me cumen, beon
hi mine sunes, beon hi mine breðre, ouþer kyningas þa æfter me
cumen, þ ure gyfe mote standen* . . . and *Ch* 959 . . . *7 eal þ ðe of
ðas healue þare middelsæ wurð gefunden 7 to Sandwic gebroht, bi
hit scrud, bi hit net oððe wæpne oððe isen, gold oððe seoluer, þ
healue dæl sceal beon ðare muneke*; sentences with only one verb
and *oþþe/oþer*, e.g. *LawIICn(G)* 83 . . . *si he Denisc oððe Englisc, beo
he his weres scyldig* . . . , where the other manuscripts have (in various
spellings) *sy he Denisc, sy he Englisc*, and *Ch* 1112 *And gif what sy
mid unlage out of þan bissopriche geydon, sy hit on londe oþer an
oððer þinge* . . . ; and sentences in which all remaining alternatives
are embraced in one indefinite adjective clause, e.g. *Bo* 63. 21 *Wære
se mon on swelcum lande swelce he wære þe hi ahte, ðonne wære his
wela 7 his weorðscipe mid him, LawICn* 3 . . . *sy hit þurh feohtlac,
si hit þurh reaflac, sig þurh þæt þe hit sy, Law VIIIAtr* 4, where a similar sequence ends with . . . *si þurh þæt þæt hit sy, ÆCHom* i. 318. 28
. . . *wæron hi Ebreisce, oððe Grecisce, oððe Romanisce, oððe Egyptisce, oððe swa hwilcere ðeode swa hi wæron þe ða lare gehyrdon,
HomU* 40. 271. 1 *And riht is, gif hwæt færlices on þeode becymð
(beon hit hereræsas, beon hit færcwealmas, beon hit miswyderu
oððon unwæstmas, beo swa hwæt swa hit beo) sece man þa bote aa
to gode sylfum*, and *ChronE* 36. 22 (675) . . . *beo he of Englelande
ouðer of hwilc oðer igland beo he.*

§3447. Like Burnham, I have recorded no examples from the early
prose. There are no certain examples in the poetry, unless we follow
Behre (p. 48) and Quirk (p. 86) in interpreting *secge* and *swige* in
ChristA 189 *Me nawþer deag,* || *secge ne swige* as finite verbs in the
first person singular present subjunctive. Cook suggested taking them
as nouns, explaining the first as a *hapax legomenon*. I lean towards
this view. Similar constructions with nouns are recorded in §§3502-3.
If they were verbs, we should expect ☆*secge ic swige ic*. On *Wife* 42,
see §3444.

§3448. The subjunctive is the rule in these clauses in OE. On the
usage in OHG and MHG, see Burnham, p. 46.

c. Indefinite concessions?

§3449. *Mutatis mutandis*, the reasons given in §§3438-9 lead me to
conclude that strictly speaking there are no indefinite concessive

clauses with the order VS. In my opinion, the Latin *Iuvenes et vir-gines, senes cum iunioribus, laudent nomen Domini* suggests that Behre (pp. 21, 46, and 48) was both confused and over-ingenious in his handling of

PPs 148. 12   Beon ge, hægestealdas   and glade fæmnan,
ealde and geonge   ealle ætsamne;
herian naman drihtnes   mid neodlofe.

For he describes it as 'the simple type' (p. 48) but says (p. 46) that 'I interpret the subjunctive of the first clause as concessive-generaliz-ing. . . . The clause by allowing or admitting two groups of alterna-tives . . . and summing up by an indefinite expression . . . emphasizes the general application of the exhortation expressed by the main clause.' I detect no concession.

§3450. Disjunctive concessions to which an indefinite adjective clause has been added (§3446) consist of two or more clauses. So too do the examples of the so-called 'challenge' or 'permissive' con-structions discussed in §§3451-6. They do not belong here.

7. THE PATTERNS *UNDERSTANDE SE þE CUNNE* AND *UNDERSTODE SE þE CUþE*

§3451. The basic pattern here consists of a subjunctive verb fol-lowed by an indefinite clause—which may be adjectival, local, or comparative—also with the subjunctive. The verbs may be present or preterite in tense. This pattern must not be confused with that seen in *ÆCHom* ii. 2. 17 *Ætforan ælcum cwyde we setton ða swutel-unge on Leden. mæg swa ðeah se ðe wile þa capitulas æfter ðære forespræce geendebyrdian*, which Thorpe (with a comma after *Leden* for the OE *punctus*) translates as '. . . though every one who will, may order the chapters according to the preface', but where (with a stop for Thorpe's comma) 'Everyone who will, may however . . .' would better reflect the fact that we have two independent state-ments. The pattern under consideration may itself occur in indepen-dent sentences, e.g. *Ch* 1487 . . . *7 æfter his dæge ga hyt for uncra begra sawle þider him leouest sy, Ex* 7 *Gehyre se ðe wille!*, and *Rid* 67. 15 *Secge se þe cunne,* ‖ *wisfæstra hwylc, hwæt seo wiht sy*, but is also found functioning as a subordinate 'concessive-equivalent' clause, e.g.

Beo 2764   Sinc eaðe mæg,
gold on grunde   gumcynnes gehwone
oferhigian,   hyde se ðe wylle!

and

Beo 1392　　　　Ic hit þe gehate:　　no he on helm losaþ,
　　　　　　　　　ne on foldan fæþm,　　ne on fyrgenholt,
　　　　　　　　　ne on gyfenes grund,　　ga þær he wille!

Visser (ii, §§862 and 884) fails to make this distinction. It is with the latter function we are concerned here. But there is sometimes room for difference of opinion, depending on how continuative one feels the construction to be. Thus I would be inclined to substitute a stop for Thorpe's comma in *ÆCHom* ii. 604. 20 *Be ðisum we habbað on oðre stowe awriten, ræde þæt se ðe wylle* and for Bethurum's comma in *WHom(BH)* 20. 77 *7 eall þæt is Gode lað, gelyfe se ðe wille.*

§3452. The patterns represented by *WHom(BH)* 20. 80 *understande se ðe wille* and *WHom* 17. 19 *understode se ðe cuðe* have been called 'hortatory' and 'permissive' (Burnham, p. 62) and 'challenge' or 'challenging' (Quirk, pp. 93-4, and Visser, ii, §862). But it is more important to begin by making a distinction which both Burnham (pp. 51-65) and Quirk (pp. 98-101) fail to make with sufficient clarity than by arguing about terminology. Burnham (p. 53) says that 'it is sometimes difficult . . . to decide whether or not a given indefinite clause has a concessive coloring'. It is less difficult if we make proper distinctions. Thus Burnham (p. 58) cites under the same heading *LawVIAs* 8. 4 *7 habban þa gerefscypas begen þa fullan spæce gemæne, si swa hwær swa hit sy, swa be norðan mearce swa be suðan,* which is a clear example of the 'permissive' formula, and *ÆGram* 277. 11 *þas synd gehatene praepositiones, forþan ðe hi beoð æfre foresette oðrum wordum, swa hwær swa hi beoð gefegede,* which is an indefinite clause of place. More such oppositions could be cited from her collections (pp. 51-61). She shows that she is aware of the distinction (pp. 62-3), but her failure to make it more explicitly means that her comments on these constructions (pp. 61-5) lack clarity. Quirk, who speaks dismissively of 'the bureaucratic matter of classification' (p. 72), similarly lumps these constructions together (pp. 98-101); the phrase 'variety of pattern' (p. 99) is not really adequate.

× §3453. Indefinite adjectival, local, temporal, and comparative, concessive-equivalent clauses are discussed in §§3459-75. Here I give examples of the concessive use of 'permissive' formulae. Examples with the present subjunctive include sentences with adjective clauses introduced by *seþe,* e.g. *Ch* 987 *7 ic nelle na geþafian þ man þam*

bisceope ænige unlage beode, beo gerefa se þe beo and *Beo* 2764
(§3451); by *þæt (þæt)*, e.g. *Bo* 112. 19 *wyrce hwa þ ðæt he wyrce
oððe do þ he do, a he hæfð þ þ he geearnað, ApT* 18. 5 *Gemiltsa me,
þu ealda man, sy þæt þu sy*, Latin *Miserere mei, quicunque es, senior,*
and *Exhort* 16 (§3455); by *swylc*, e.g. *LawIVAs* 6. 2c *7 sece swylce
socne swylce he sece, þæt he ne sy his feores wyrðe* . . . ; and by *swa
hwylc swa*, e.g. *WHom* 8(c). 43 *Do swa hwylc swa hit do, Godes
sylfes miht byð on þære dæde þurh halig geryne.* We also find examples with clauses of place introduced by *þær (þær)*, e.g. *BlHom*
129. 33 *for þon æghwylc man, sy þær eorðan þær he sy, þurh gode
dæda Gode lician sceal, 7 ælc man sceal his godan dæda ahebban, gif
he sceal god 7 medeme weorþan, ÆLS* 13. 66 . . . *man mot mærsian
his drihten and hine gebiddan, beo þær þær he beo*, and *Beo* 1392
(§2510); by *þanon þe*, e.g. *Ch* 959 and *VSal 1* 202 *Beo þanon þe he
beo, sig he cynyng æfter me*; and by *swa hwær swa*, e.g. *LawVIAs*
8. 4 (§3452). To these we may add comparative clauses with *swa
(swa)*, e.g. *LawGer* 5 *Swa sceal god scyrman his hlafordes healdan, do
ymbe his agen swa swa he wylle* and

Wan 11   Ic to soþe wat
              þæt biþ in eorle   indryhten þeaw,
              þæt he his ferðlocan fæste binde,
              healde his hordcofan, hycge swa he wille.

§3454. The examples with the preterite subjunctive demonstrate
the same types. Thus, we find sentences with adjective clauses introduced by *seþe*, e.g. *Or* 154. 18 . . . *7 cwædon þæt him wislecre
þuhte þæt hie ða ne forluren þe þær ut fore, hæfde bearn se þe
mehte* and *LawVIAs* 7 *dyde dæda se þe dyde þe ure ealra teonan
wræce, þæt we wæron ealle swa on anum freondscype*; by *swylc*, e.g.
Bo 64. 5 *ac simle him wolde þ fylgean 7 hi symle weorðe gedon,
wæron hi on swelcum lande swylce hi wæron*; and by *þe*, e.g. *ChronE*
217. 2 (1085) *7 þær him comon to his witan and ealle þa landsittende
men þe ahtes wæron ofer eall Engleland wæron þæs mannes men þe
hi wæron.* Clauses of place include (with *þær*) *Bo* 11. 19 *wære þer he
wære, simle he hæfde þone mid him* and (with *þider*) *Bede* 386. 1
*Caerde we usic ðider we cærde, gemaetton we usic æghwonon geliice
storme foresette 7 foretynde.* . . . With *swa (. . . swa)*, we find examples such as *LawIne* 43. 1 *ne ðearf he hiora ma geldan, wære hiora
swa fela swa hiora wære* and

PPs 93. 7   Sægdan and cwædan,   þæt ne gesawe
                    drihten æfre,   dyde swa he wolde,
                    ne þæt Iacobes god   ongitan cuðe.

In some of these examples at least, the formula has concessive flavour. Burnham (p. 58) remarks that 'the subordination becomes still more complete when, with the use of the preterit, all suggestion of permission is lost', citing *Ch* 1507 *H* 16. 17 *þa spræce wyt ymbe uncre bearn, þæt hy sumre are beþorftan, sælde unc on þam brocum swa unc sælde*, where the reference is to the future-in-the-past '. . . come what may'. But such a suggestion is not to be found in all the examples with the present tense and is not essential.

§ 3455. As already noted, the prevailing mood in both clauses of the formula is the subjunctive. There are occasional examples with an imperative in the first clause, e.g. *ÆCHom* ii. 436. 6 *Gif ðam þe ðu wille ðine sylene, ðis gewrit ic ðe gerecce* and

Exhort 16   Wyrc þæt þu wyrce,   word oððe dæda,
                   hafa metodes ege   on gemang symle.

An indicative occurs in the first clause in

Met 20. 26   Is ðæt micel gecynd
                   þines goodes,   þencð ymb se ðe wile,
                   forðon hit is eall an   ælces þincges,
                   þu and þæt ðin good

and in

Met 19. 1   Eala, þæt is hefig dysig,   hygeð ymbe se ðe wile,
                   and frecenlic   fira gehwilcum
                   þæt ða earman men   mid ealle gedwæleð. . . .

Quirk (p. 99) takes these as concessive. But they may be independent. The indicative appears in the second clause in

LPr ii 121   Sy swa þu silf wilt,   soðfæst dema,
                   we þe, engla god,   ealle heriað . . . ,

where I print the Grein–Wülker comma instead of the ASPR semi-colon after *dema*, explaining line 121 as concessive. The indicative *wilt* perhaps gives an indication of the poet's attitude to God. It is certainly not 'permissive'.

§ 3456. As Burnham (p. 40) notes, this pattern occasionally occurs in conjunction with *swa hwæþer swa/swæþer*, as in *CP* 85. 14, *CP* 451. 13, and *LawIIAs* 24 . . . *þonne onfo se his þe he hit ær ætbohte, beo he swa freoh swa ðeow, swa hweðer he sy.*

8. CONTRACTED CONCESSIVE CLAUSES

§ 3457. Examples in which the verb of the concessive clause is not expressed, e.g. 'Though still only thirteen, she's very sophisticated', are much less frequent in OE than in MnE. From the prose it will suffice to cite *ÆCHom* i. 2. 12 (§3432) and *ÆCHom* i. 94. 5 *ac gehwylce halgan andbidodon on Abrahames wununge buton tintregum, þeah on hellewite, oðþæt se Alysend com*. There are no certain examples of this sort in OE poetry. One possibility is

PPs 73. 19   Ne byð se eadmoda   æfre gecyrred,
              þeah þe wædla   and þearfa he wyle
              naman þinne   neode herian,

where the Latin has *Ne avertatur humilis factus confusus; pauper et inops laudabunt nomen tuum*. It is tempting to interpret

Met 11. 31   Swa hæfð geheaðærod   hefonrices weard
              mid his anwealde   ealle gescealfta,
              þæt hiora æghwilc   wið oðer winð,
              and þeah winnende   wreðiað fæste,
              æghwilc oðer   utan ymbclyppeð,
              þy læs hi toswifen

in this way. But the prose equivalent is *Bo* 49. 5 *Swa hæfð se ælmihtiga God geheaðorade ealle his gescefta mid his anwealde þæt heora ælc winð wið oðer, 7 þeah wræðeð oðer, þ hie ne moton toslupan*, where *þeah* is clearly an adverb modifying *wræðeð*. So in the metrical version it may be an adverb modifying *wreðiað* rather than a conjunction with *winnende*.

§3458. The difference between the adverb and the conjunction in examples such as these is perhaps exquisite. But it can sometimes be detected in OE, either through an inflexion, e.g. in *ÆLS* 37. 252 *ne mæg ic hine oferswiðan forðon swa deadne?*, where *dead* would be required for *swa* to be interpreted as a concessive conjunction (as is suggested by Burnham, p. 133), or through element order, e.g. *Met* 20. 229,

ChristA 209   Saga ecne þonc
              mærum meotodes sunu   þæt ic his modor gewearð,
              fæmne forð seþeah,

and similar examples referred to by Quirk (p. 36).

9. INDEFINITE 'CONCESSIVE-EQUIVALENT' CLAUSES

a. Introductory remarks

§3459. I have claimed in §§3438–9 and 3449–50 that none of the alleged examples of indefinite concessive clauses cited by various writers on the subject is properly speaking a concessive clause. In my

opinion, they are, in Quirk's terminology (p. 102), 'concessive-equivalent' adjective, local, temporal, or comparative, clauses. This is confirmed by the fact that, whereas the verb of a true concessive clause
is in the subjunctive mood, the mood of the verb of a 'concessive-
equivalent' clause is unaffected by the concessive element. Campbell
(*RES* 7 (1956), 65) puts it well:

þeah takes the subjunctive in subordinate clauses by rule, and quite independently of the reality of the concession. This Quirk clearly shows (p. 40), but
when he passes on to indefinite concessive relative and local clauses, he omits to
indicate that the syntax of these is unaffected by their being concessive. He even
(pp. 100-1) appears to regard the subjunctive of some passages (*Jul.* 87, *Gen.*
2723, *Ex.* 271, *And.* 223) as indicating their concessive meaning, although it is
in all these cases due to the fact that the principal clause contains an imperative
or (once, *Ex.* 271) a subjunctive.

Burnham is guilty of the same error; see, for example, pp. 56 and 59.
The reader will find clear illustrations of the truth of Campbell's
statement in the examples cited below. On patterns such as *understande se þe cunne* and *wære hiora swa fela swa hiora wære*, see
§§3451-6.

§3460. The subjective element in deciding whether or not a non-
concessive clause contains the idea of concession has been stressed by
Burnham (pp. 66-7 and 90-4) and by Quirk (pp. 91-4 and 102-3).
As Burnham (p. 66) says,

such clauses often indicate an attempt to say or suggest two things at once—
the concessive idea superadded to some other. Accordingly, the concessive
element may be more or less distinct in a given case, and classifications become
debatable. It is impossible to eliminate the personal equation altogether from
judgments upon these points.

This applies to all types of 'concessive-equivalent' clauses, whether
indefinite or not. Those seeking more examples than space permits
me to quote should consult the appropriate sections of Burnham,
Quirk, and Mitchell 1959.

§3461. To avoid unnecessary repetition, it may be said here that
Visser (ii. 910) with some plausibility detects 'the modality . . . of
concession and indefiniteness' in the clauses introduced by *loc(a)* +
an interrogative in examples like *Josh* 2. 19, *John(WSCp)* 8. 7, and
ÆLS 4. 261 (all in §§3363-4).

b. *Adjective clauses*

§3462. Typical examples of indefinite adjective clauses in which a
concessive element has been or may be detected follow, the presence

of such an element being contingent, as Quirk (p. 98) observes, on our being 'prepared to look upon the generalization as conveying a "no matter who" indifference': (with *se* or *seþe*) *Bede* 2. 7 *Forðon þis gewrit oððe hit god sagað be godum mannum, 7 se ðe hit gehyreþ, he onhyreþ þam, oððe hit yfel sagaþ be yfelum mannum, 7 se ðe hit gehyreð, he flyhð þæt 7 onscunaþ, LawAfEl* 13 *Se mon se ðe his gewealdes monnan ofslea, swelte se deaðe, LawAfEl* 14 *Se ðe slea his fæder oððe his modor, se sceal deaðe sweltan, ÆCHom* ii. 94. 8 *se ðe þis tobrece, bete swa him his scrift tæce,* and *Beo* 142 *heold hyne syðþan* || *fyr ond fæstor se þæm feonde ætwand,* and (with combinations involving *swa*) *Ch* 1508 *Ond swe hwylc mon swa ðet sio þet ðes londes bruce ofer minne deg on Cloppaham, þanne geselle he CC peninga eghwylce gere to Ceortesege for Elfredes sawle to feormfultume, ÆLS* 9. 92 *Ne miht þu gebigan minne willan to þe. Swa hwæt swa þu minum lichaman dest, ne mæg þæt belimpan to me,*

Beo 685   ...   ond siþðan witig God
          on swa hwæþere hond   halig Dryhten
          mærðo deme,   swa him gemet þince,

and

GenB 755   Swa hwæt swa wit her morðres þoliað,
          hit is nu Adame   eall forgolden
          mid hearran hete   and mid hæleða forlore,
          monnum mid morðes cwealme.

For more examples, see Visser, ii. 912.

§3463. Burnham (pp. 38–43) classifies as disjunctive concessions examples with *swa . . . swa . . . swa hwæþer swa/swæþer* and *swa hwæþer swa/swæþer . . . swa . . . swa* such as *Bo* 91. 19 *Nim ðonne swa wuda swa wyrt, swa hwæðer swa þu wille* and *ÆGram* 260. 12 *siue uir siue mulier, swa hwæþer swa hit sy swa wer swa wif* and provides a valuable series of variations. These come close to being indefinite 'concessive-equivalent' adjective clauses, as Burnham (pp. 41–2) recognizes:

The use of *swa . . . swa,* or an equivalent disjunctive, with the clause containing *swæðer* or *swa hwæðer swa* is so nearly uniform that I have thought it most true to the facts of Old English to treat concessions of this type as primarily disjunctive, instead of classing them with the indefinite concessions to be considered in another chapter.

She goes on to claim that 'it is apparently out of this elaborate disjunctive construction that the simpler use of the *swæðer*-clause alone developed'; her illustrative examples include *Bo* 67. 9 *swa hwæðer swa hi dydon, ne dohte him ða nawðer . . .* and *ÆGram* 123. 9 . . . *ac hi ne geendiað næfre on or, swa hwæðer swa hi getacniað.* Here too, as in § 2975, the problem is which comes first.

§ 3464. The only comparable examples in the poetry are

LPr ii 96   þonne bið egsa   geond ealle world,
                    þar man us tyhhað on dæg   twegen eardas,
                    drihtenes are   oððe deofles þeowet,
                    swa hwaðer we geearniað   her on life,
                    þa hwile þe ure mihta   mæste wæron,

where *oððe* is used in place of *swa . . . swa*, and those like

El 605   þe synt tu gearu,
            swa lif swa deað,   swa þe leofre bið
            to geceosanne,

where *hwæþer* is not used; on these see §§ 1825-6.

c. Clauses of place

§ 3465. Here again, the presence or otherwise of a concessive element depends on the extent to which each reader is prepared to find in any example the idea of 'no matter where'. Examples cited by Burnham (pp. 58-9) and Quirk (p. 101) include (with *þær*)

And 932   Wast nu þe gearwor
            þæt ic eaðe mæg   anra gehwylcne
            fremman ond fyrþran   freonda minra
            on landa gehwylc,   þær me leofost bið

and

GenA 2723   Wuna mid usic   and þe wic geceos
            on þissum lande   þær þe leofost sie,
            eðelstowe,   þe ic agan sceal;

(with *swa hwær swa*) *ÆGram* 277. 11 (§ 3452), *BenR* 31. 7 *and swa hwær swa he sy sittende, standende, oðþe gangende, onhnigenum heafde simle his gesyhða aduna on eorðan besette*, and

And 332   Farað nu geond ealle   eorðan sceatas
            emne swa wide   swa wæter bebugeð,
            oððe stedewangas   stræte gelicgaþ;

and (with *swa hwider swa*) *ÆAdmon 1* 34. 18 *Se eorðlica kempa bið æfre gearo and caf swa hwyder swa he faran sceal to gefeohte mid ðam kininge.* For more, see Visser, ii. 912.

d. Clauses of time

§3466. Burnham does not give any examples of temporal 'concessive-equivalent' clauses and Quirk (p. 92) says there are none in the poetry. However, in

Part 5   In swa hwylce tiid   swa ge mid treowe to me
              on hyge hweorfað,   ond ge hellfirena
              sweartra geswicað,   swa ic symle to eow
              mid siblufan   sona gecyrre
              þurh milde mod,

quoted by Quirk (p. 100), *in swa hwylce tiid swa* could be replaced by *þonne*. It is possible to detect a 'no matter when' indifference there and in examples like *Or* 184. 7 *Ac hit God wræc on him swa he ær ealneg dyde, swa oft swa hie mid monnum ofredan, þæt hie mid hiera cucum onguldon þæt hie ungyltige cwealdon, Bede* 342. 20 (§2562), *Ps(A)* 4. 1 *mid ðy ic gecede ðe ðu geherdes me*, Latin *cum inuocarem te exaudisti me, Ps(P)* 4. 1 *þonne ic cleopode to þe, þonne gehyrdest þu me*, and

GenA 1832   Saga þu, Sarra,   þæt þu sie sweostor min,
              lices mæge,   þonne þe leodweras
              fremde fricgen   hwæt sie freondlufu
              ellðeodigra   uncer twega,
              feorren cumenra.

e. Comparative clauses

§3467. Burnham (p. 59) cites *ÆCHom* i. 588. 28 *Ic wundrige ðe snoterne wer, þæt ðu ðyssere lare fylian wylt, swa hu swa hit ge-wurde, sylfwilles oððe neadunge, þæt he on rode gefæstnod wære.* Other clauses of manner into which the sense of 'no matter how' can be read include

El 541   Do swa þe þynce,
              fyrngidda frod,   gif ðu frugnen sie
              on wera corðre.

§3468. 'Concessive-equivalent' clauses of degree have given rise to much confusion. Burnham (pp. 59–61) fails to distinguish the two *Chron* examples in §3469 from examples like *LawIne* 43. 1 (§3454). Quirk's conception of 'indefinite concessions of degree' (pp. 94–8) —the existence of which I do not admit (§3459)—is far wider than Burnham's. This explains, in part at least, why 'the poetic material is startlingly different' (Quirk, p. 97) and means that many of his con-clusions must be dismissed; see Mitchell, *MÆ* 25 (1956), 38–9.

Clauses which in my opinion can conceivably be called even 'conces-sive-equivalent' indefinite clauses of degree are rare and fall into two groups. Both involve a negated verb and *swa* or *þæs* modifying an adjective or an adverb.

§3469. In examples of type (*a*), the negated verb occupies initial position and we have the order VS. I have not been able to add to the three examples of this type recorded by Burnham (pp. 59-61) and Quirk (pp. 94-8). Two of these occur in the prose. There seems to be general agreement that the last six words in *ChronE* 133. 28 (1001) . . . *ne him to ne dorste sciphere on sæ ne landfyrd, ne eodon hi swa feor up* express concession—'. . . went they never so far in-land' (Ashdown); '. . . however far inland they went' (Garmonsway); '. . . no matter how far inland they went' (Whitelock). Similar to this is *ChronE* 220. 15 (1086) *7 nan man ne dorste slean oðerne man, næfde he næfre swa mycel yfel gedon wið þone oðerne*. But neither the ambiguous verb-form *eodon/næfde* nor the element order demands that we interpret these as subordinate clauses; compare *ChronA* 89. 30 (897) *Næfde se here, Godes þonces, Angelcyn ealles forswiðe gebrocod*.

§3470. The only example in the poetry is

GenB 828   Gif ic waldendes   willan cuðe,
              hwæt ic his to hearmsceare   habban sceolde,
              ne gesawe þu no sniomor,   þeah me on sæ wadan
              hete heofones god   heonone nu þa,
              on flod faran,   nære he firnum þæs deop,
              merestream þæs micel,   þæt his o min mod getweode,
              ac ic to þam grunde genge,   gif ic godes meahte
              willan gewyrcean.

This differs from the two prose examples in two respects: first, as elsewhere in the poetry (§1141), we have *þæs* for *swa*, and second, we have an unambiguous subjunctive *nære*. But, as with the two prose examples, there is nothing in the mood of the verb nor in the element order to say that the *nære* clause must be subordinate rather than principal; compare

Max i 33   ne sy þæs magutimbres   gemet ofer eorþan,
              gif hi ne wanige   se þas woruld teode.

We must follow Timmer (*The Later Genesis*, p. 112) in saying that grammatically the *þæt* clause in *GenB* 828 is a noun clause object of *gesawe*. We can analyse the *nære* clause either as an independent parenthetical statement or as a subordinate clause with VS going

with the noun clause, even though it precedes *þæt*; on this see §1978.
If we did not have *ne gesawe þu no sniomor*, we could follow Braasch
(p. 128), Timmer (op. cit., p. 129), and Quirk (p. 97 fn. 7), and say
that the *þæt* clause is grammatically a clause of result—which, as
I show below, it is logically. Indeed, the *nære* clause comes close to
being used *apo koinou*; Klaeber (*Ang.* 49 (1925), 368) spoke of a
doubled relationship ('diese doppelte Beziehung'). Here we may
compare

Sat 515	Næs nan þæs stronglic	stan gefæstnod,
	þeah he wære mid irne	eall ymbfangen,
	þæt mihte þam miclan	mægne wiðhabban,

where the contents of the result clause introduced by *þæt* could have
been expressed in a principal clause preceding the clause introduced
by *Næs*. Quirk (p. 95) plausibly detects a concessive element in this
Næs clause and in the similar clauses in *Sea* 39 (§2906) (*Forþon nis
. . .*) and *Hell* 64 (§3474) (*. . . ne bið*), both of which are followed
by a consecutive *þæt* clause.

§3471. Clauses such as these have much in common with my type
(*a*), but are clearly principal clauses. So the first of the two questions
which arise in connection with *ChronE* 133. 28, *ChronE* 220. 15,
and *GenB* 828, is this: were clauses like the three clauses introduced
by negated verbs originally—and if so, did they remain—independent statements, subordinate clauses, or something in between? (On
the 'in between', see §2536 and Mitchell 1978*b*.) They could be
translated 'they did/might not go so far inland', 'he had/would not
have done so much evil', and 'the sea would not have been so fear-
fully deep', with the contents of the accompanying statement as the
implied result, viz. 'that the Anglo-Saxons dared oppose them', 'that
anybody dared slay him', and 'that I would doubt Him'. I cannot
answer this question.

§3472. The second question is this: can we say that the two ambiguous verbs *eodon* and *hæfde* in *ChronE* 133. 28 and 220. 15
respectively (both in §3469) are to be taken as subjunctive, on the
analogy of *nære* in the example from *GenB*? I cannot answer this
either. All I can do is to state the obvious—that no examples with
the order VS known to me have an unambiguous indicative; to point
out that, if we take them as independent clauses, there is no reason
why they must all have the same mood—*eodon* could be an indicative of simple statement (cf. the indicatives in *Sat* 515, *Sea* 39, and
Hell 64; see §3470) and *næfde* and *nære* could be subjunctives of

something hypothetical or uncertain; and to remind the reader of Campbell's statement quoted in §3459. Quirk's claim (p. 97) that 'the indefinite concession of degree' has a subjunctive verb in OE prose is based on Burnham's collections (pp. 59-61), which (as I have pointed out in §3468) include examples which I classify differently.

§3473. The indicative is the prevailing mood in examples of type (*b*), the pattern being negative + *(to) þæs* + adverb/adjective + an indicative verb. No examples of this type have, as far as I know, been recorded in the prose. This may account for the absence of examples with *swa*; see §1141. Let us start with the three most secure examples, viz. the clauses introduced respectively by *no*, *næfre*, and *næfre*, in

Beo 967   ic hine ne mihte,   þa Metod nolde,
                   ganges getwæman,   no ic him þæs georne ætfealh,
                   feorhgeniðlan,

MSol 146   Mæg simle se godes cwide   gumena gehwylcum
                   ealra feonda gehwane   fleondne gebrengan
                   ðurh mannes muð,   manfulra heap
                   sweartne geswencan,   næfre hie ðæs syllice
                   bleoum bregdað,

and (with *to þæs*)

MSol 68   He mæg ða saule   of siennihte
                  gefeccan under foldan,   næfre hie se feond to ðæs niðer
                  feterum gefæstnað.

Kock (*Ang.* 43 (1919), 304-5, and ibid. 46 (1922), 82-5) sees here a lost OE idiom, the equivalent of MnE 'however . . . ' or 'no matter how . . .'; he translates *Beo* 968b 'however eagerly I clung to him'. Klaeber (*Ang.* 50 (1926), 197) says that this example 'is perfectly clear and shows how such an idiom could arise. "I could not prevent him from getting away; [I pressed him hard, but] I did not press him so hard [that he had to stay in my power]." ' These examples differ from those of type (*a*), not only in element order, but also in having no accompanying statement which expresses the result. This must be inferred by the hearer or reader from the context.

§3474. These three examples have much in common with the *næfre* clause in

JDay i 109   Næfre mon þæs hlude   horn aþyteð
                   ne byman ablaweþ,   þæt ne sy seo beorhte stefn
                   ofer ealne middangeard   monnum hludre,
                   waldendes word

and with the *ne* clause in

Hell 64   ne bið he no þæs nearwe   under niðlocan
                   to þæs bitre gebunden   under bealuclommum,
                   þæt he þy yð ne mæge   ellen habban . . .

(Mackie's text), which are clearly principal clauses followed by a consecutive clause introduced by *þæt* and which are admitted by Quirk (p. 95) as 'indefinite concessions of degree'; with similar examples not cited by Quirk, such as *Beo* 1366 *No þæs frod leofað* || *gumena bearna, þæt þone grund wite*; and also with the rhetorical question in

And 1372   Hwylc is þæs mihtig   ofer middangeard,
                   þæt he þe alyse   of leoðubendum,
                   manna cynnes,   ofer mine est?,

which Quirk (p. 96) hesitates to admit. Klaeber's explanation accepts that examples of type (*b*) were originally simple statements—a possibility I have already envisaged for examples of type (*a*). There are no syntactical reasons for saying that examples of type (*b*) must be subordinate. Their verbs are indicative and final position of a verb in a clause which must be principal is well attested; consider *Beo* 202 and *Beo* 1 (§3944). Here I agree with Quirk (p. 97): 'indeed, there is little to indicate that these concessive members containing *þæs* (corresponding to *swa* in prose) involve grammatical dependence at all'. So the same question must be asked for type (*b*) as was asked for type (*a*): were they originally, and did they ever get beyond being, simple statements? Neither of these putative concessive expressions has survived as such. So it must remain uncertain whether they ever had any real existence as concessive constructions except in the minds of modern grammarians. All the OE examples could be independent clauses. If we reject Kock's *Rid* 31. 4 (*Ang.* 46 (1922), 83), which depends on an emendation not accepted by ASPR or Craig Williamson, they all follow the principal clause unless we accept Grundtvig's *þæs* for MS *þæm* in

Beo 1506   Bær þa seo brimwylf,   þa heo to botme com,
                   hringa þengel   to hofe sinum,
                   swa he ne mihte   —no he þæs modig wæs—
                   wæpna gewealdan . . . ,

which gives us a mid-clause example usually classified as type (*b*).[180] In 1959 (Mitchell 1959, p. 556), I argued that it was impossible to

[180] Kock's attempt (*Ang.* 43 (1919), 304–5) to find another example in *Beo* 2423 has not been generally accepted. The element order is different and we have *þon*, not *þæs*. Klaeber (*Ang.* 50 (1926), 197) suggested contamination. Kock's acceptance of *þon* here makes it hard to understand why he balked at *þæm* in *Beo* 1508b.

take this as an independent clause because the translation 'he was not brave enough for that' was inadmissible and we were therefore forced to translate 'no matter how brave he was'. I went on:

The existence of one example in which Kock's explanation of this syntactical pattern seems obligatory is a strong argument in favour of applying it to the remainder, where it always gives good sense. Further support is provided by the ON, OHG, and O Swedish, parallels adduced by Kock [loc. cit.]. Etymological *hapax legomena* have been admitted on slighter evidence than this.

I must now enter what is in essence a semantic caveat: some such translation as 'he was not in the mood/of a mind for that' would fit the context if *modig* could bear it.

§ 3475. Kock's explanation of these type (*b*) examples is not susceptible of final proof and has not been accepted by all. But it drew this accolade from Klaeber (*Ang.* 50 (1926), 197): 'It is one of his fine discoveries deserving to be accepted, though with a certain reservation as to details.'

10. *SWA (SWA)*

§ 3476. Like Wilde (1939, p. 331), Quirk (pp. 108-9) rightly insists that *swa* is not a true concessive conjunction (Burnham (p. 74) implies agreement) but 'always basically introduces a clause of manner and retains this function when the member is being used concessively' (Quirk, p. 108); cf. here the passage from Burnham quoted in § 2863. The fact that in these so-called simple concessive clauses after *swa* the prevailing mood is the indicative—in sharp contrast to *þeah (þe)*, with its overwhelming preference for the subjunctive—further illustrates the gap between the two types. Burnham (p. 26) says that the use of the indicative in these *swa* clauses 'adds, of course, to the difficulty of determining in doubtful cases whether *swa* is concessive or modal'. In my opinion, it is decisive for the latter.

§ 3477. The basic issues involved have already been discussed in §§ 2861-3. Here it remains to round off the discussion by asking whether there are any sentences in which *swa* must be taken as concessive. I begin with clauses which contain a negative. Burnham (pp. 14-16) asserts that in *Mart 5* 20. 27 *ond on fruman he þær wunade, swa he nænigne oðerne mon ne geseah*, the *swa* clause 'is plainly modal . . . "without seeing" '; that in *Mart 2* 208. 20 *þa het he hig belucan on byrnendum baðe on þæm heo wæs dæg ond nyht swa heo na ne geswætte*, 'the emphasis is on the contrast expressed . . . "yet" ' (but Herzfeld translates 'without sweating'); that in *Or*

206. 1 *þa Antiochus þæt gehierde, þa bæd he Scipian friþes, 7 him his sunu ham onsende, se wæs on his gewealde, swa he nyste hu he him to com*, 'swa appears as a conjunction clearly implying the concessive relation'; that in *Or* 296. 25 and *Or* 260. 17 . . . *þæt þær wæron XXX M ofslagen, 7 æt þæm geate oftredd, swa nan mon nyste hwonon sio wroht com*, 'it is not clear whether *swa* is equivalent to "yet" (with loose coördinate concession) or to "although" (with subordinate concessive clause)'; and that in *CP* 301. 24 . . . *ðæt is ðæt sume menn onderfoð eaðmodnesse hiw, sume ofermodnesse, sua sua hie nyton* (where Sweet has 'without knowing it') and *GD(C)* 61. 4 *ac þeh þæt hi nytte syn oðrum mannum, hi beoð full oft geypte swa hi nellað*, *swa* has 'a tinge of concessive meaning'. I am not alone in my failure to detect these distinctions; Liggins (1970, pp. 309-10), whose corpus did not include *Mart*, says that in the examples quoted above from *Or, CP*, and *GD*, 'the *swa*-clause . . . expresses a parenthetical comment rather than a real concession connected with the action of its principal clause'.

§3478. Burnham (pp. 14-15) also cites some examples from the poetry, distinguishing *swa* concessive 'although' in

GenB 390
                                             Hafað us god sylfa
        forswapen on þas sweartan mistas;   swa he us ne mæg ænige
                                        synne gestælan,
        þæt we him on þam lande lað gefremedon,   he hæfð us þeah
                                         þæs leohtes bescyrede,
        beworpen on ealra wita mæste

(where OS influence is possible; see Mitchell 1959, p. 545) from *swa* introducing 'a sort of weakened result-clause' in

And 260
        Him ða ondswarode   ælmihti god,
        swa þæt ne wiste,   se ðe þæs wordes bad,
        hwæt se manna wæs   meðelhegendra,
        þe he þær on waroðe   wiðþingode.

But these can be translated respectively 'without being able . . .' and 'without the suppliant knowing . . .'.[181]

§3479. All these examples—along with many others, such as

GenB 611
        þu meaht nu þe self geseon,   swa ic hit þe secgan ne þearf,
        Eue seo gode,   þæt þe is ungelic

[181] In *And* 260 *swa þæt* could introduce a result clause, 'in such a way that . . .'. Indeed, the fact that Burnham (p. 15) italicizes both *swa* and *þæt* must cast some doubt on how she construed the sentence. Krapp's suggestion that *swa* means 'as though' is wrong; see Brooks's note and Glogauer, p. 36. The latter points out the significance of a passage quoted by Krapp (1906 edition of *Andreas*, p. xxv): *we witon þæt ure drihten mid us wæs on þæm scipe and we hine ne ongeaton*.

wlite and wæstmas,   siððan þu minum wordum getruwodest,
læstes mine lare,

where the *swa* clause can be classified as one of comparison, concession, or result, and can be translated 'without my needing to tell you'
—illustrate that the distinctions are highly personal, 'somewhat ill-
defined' (Burnham, p. 14), and 'delicate and subjective' (Campbell,
RES 7 (1956), 67). This is strikingly reinforced by a comparison of
the number of 'concessive-equivalent' *swa* clauses detected in the
poetry by Ericson (1932, pp. 62-3) and Quirk (pp. 108-12); see
Campbell, loc. cit., and Mitchell 1959, p. 544. The discrepancy is
largely the result of Quirk's inclusion of examples like *GenA* 901 . . .
swa hit riht ne wæs; see §2861. More terminological complications
can be introduced. Ericson (1930, p. 162) writes that 'in Old English,
swa is sometimes used as . . . a pseudo-conjunction, in the sense of
"yet" '. On this possibility (which Quirk does not appear to have
considered), see Mitchell, *MÆ* 25 (1956), 37, and my §§2861 and
3482. On the applicability of the term 'semi-subordination' to examples of the type *swa he hit nyste*, see §§1923-4.

§3480. All this, and considerations of space, compel me to conclude
my discussion of clauses with *swa* + a negative + an indicative or
ambiguous verb without examining in detail all the proposed examples
of concessive *swa*. But the collections of Burnham (pp. 14-16 and
133), Ericson (1932, pp. 62-3), Quirk (pp. 108-12), and Mitchell
(1959, pp. 543-7), and my §§2857-70, do not include any examples
which contradict Quirk's observation (p. 108) that '*swa* is never an
autonomous concessive connective'. This verdict embraces *Beo* 1142;
see Brady, *ASE* 8 (1979), 99-100, and my §3270.

§3481. It also embraces the proposed examples in which *swa* introduces a positive clause. Burnham (p. 133) proposes *Matt(WSCp)*
23. 28, where *swa* represents Latin *sic*; (with '(?)') *BlHom* 97. 22,
where Morris plausibly translates 'thus'; *ByrM* 94. 1, where Crawford
has 'in the same way'; and *ÆLS* 37. 252 *ne mæg ic hine oferswiðan*
forðon swa deadne?, where Skeat ambiguously translates 'May I not
overcome him even when dead?' but *swa* is an adverb (§3458). Ericson (1932, p. 62) adds *GD(H)* 33. 22, translating *swa* 'although'. But
a comparison with *GD(C)* 33. 23 shows that this is wrong; *swa* . . .
þæt introduces a result clause 'so . . . that'.

§3482. Quirk (p. 110) implies that there are nine positive concessive-
equivalent clauses introduced by *swa* in the poetry. From the cryptic
clues he gives, I seem to have managed to identify eight of them.

I agree that none is primarily a concessive subordinate clause. They are *ChristC* 984 and *JDay i* 12 (place or comparison); *Beo* 1671, *ChristB* 453, and *PPs* 105. 26 (comparison); *Phoen* 41 (time); *PPs* 105. 33 (*swa . . . furðum* 'as soon as'); and *PPs* 61. 4 (where *swa* seems to represent Latin *verumtamen*). Ericson (1932, p. 63) adds *El* 494 (probably comparison, but see Mitchell 1959, pp. 546-7). Small (1924, p. 137) detects 'an adversative shade, approaching opposition, which may be translated by "although" ' in

LPr iii 19   Forgyf us, gumena weard,   gyltas and synna,
                      and ure leahtras alet,   lices wunda
                      and mandæda,   swa we mildum wið ðe,
                      ælmihtigum gode,   oft abylgeað.

This certainly merits comparison with the *þeah* clause in

El 511   Nu ðu meaht gehyran,   hæleð min se leofa,
                      hu arfæst is   ealles wealdend,
                      þeah we æbylgð wið hine   oft gewyrcen,
                      synna wunde. . . .

But *swa* could be an adverb introducing a parenthetic explanatory clause or a comparative conjunction 'as we . . .'. So our end is our beginning: *swa* is not 'a true concessive conjunction'.

11. OTHER 'CONCESSIVE-EQUIVALENT' CLAUSES

a. Introductory remarks

§3483. Whether or not a clause which is not formally concessive contains an implication of concession is very much a matter of personal judgement; see §3460. But such an implication can be detected in some adjective clauses and in adverb clauses of certain types. These are exemplified below. For a general discussion, with special reference to the possibility of Latin influence, see Burnham, pp. 90-4. To avoid unnecessary repetition, I will remind the reader that the mood of the verb of a 'concessive-equivalent' clause is unaffected by the concessive implication. Quirk's comment (p. 106) that in adjective clauses 'there is no evidence of the subjunctive being introduced because of the concessive function' can be extended to all such clauses. See also Burnham, pp. 93-4.

b. þæt *clauses*

§3484. Quirk's observation (p. 116) that 'there are four other substantive members introduced by *þæt* which may be thought to have some concessive force without "even" significance' confuses two kinds of clause. In

GenB 392 ...	he hæfð us þeah þæs leohtes bescyrede,
beworpen on ealra wita mæste.	Ne magon we þæs wrace ge-fremman,
geleanian him mid laðes wihte	þæt he us hafað þæs leohtes be-scyrede,

we have a noun clause in which the meaning of *þæt* hovers between 'that', 'because', and perhaps even 'although'. In the other three—*JDay ii* 141, *JDay ii* 242, and

ChristC 1396	Nu ic ða ealdan race anforlæte,
	hu þu æt ærestan yfle gehogdes,
	firenweorcum forlure þæt ic ðe to fremum sealde—

þæt means 'what'.

§3485. It is tempting to follow Ericson (1932, p. 63) in explaining as concessive the *swa þæt* clause in *ÆLet(L)* 4. 797 *Hig noldon na feohtan mid fægerum wordum anum, swa þæt hi wel spræcon 7 awendon þæt eft þe læs ðe him become se hefigtima cwyde.* . . . Indeed L'isle translates 'They would not fight with brave words only, how wel soever they spake, but took soon another course. . . .' But I suspect that the *swa þæt* clause is a blend of the explanatory and the consecutive. I cannot construe *þæt . . . þæt* as parallel demonstratives because I can think of no plausible explanation for the resulting *swa* clause.

c. Adjective clauses

§3486. Quirk (pp. 103-4 and 107) convincingly establishes that definite adjective clauses can express concession by comparing two passages in the prose Boethius with their metrical equivalent, viz. *Bo* 105. 20 *Ac gif þu æfre cymst on þone weg 7 to þære stowe þe ðu nu geot forgiten hafst, þonne wilt ðu cweþan* . . . but

Met 24. 44	Gif ðu weorðest on wege rihtum
	up to ðæm earde, þæt is æðele stow,
	ðeah ðu hi nu geta forgiten hæbbe,
	gif ðu æfre eft þær an cymest,
	ðonne wilt þu secgan and sona cweðan . . . ,

where we have respectively an adjective clause and a *þeah* clause, and *Bo* 14. 12 *þonne heo þonne swa gemenged wyrð mid ðan yþum, þonne wyrð heo swiðe hraðe ungladu, þeah heo ær gladu wære on to locienne* but

Met 5. 7   Swa oft smylte sæ   suðerne wind
græge glashlutre   grimme gedrefeð,
þonne hie gemengað   micla ysta,
onhrerað hronmere;   hrioh bið þonne
seo þe ær gladu   onsiene wæs,

where we have the reverse and *þe* cannot be emended to *þeh*; see §3428. The adjective clauses may be limiting, e.g. *Bo* 116. 26 *Hwæt, þa menn þe ðisum leasungum gelefdon, þeah wisston þ hio mid þam drycræfte ne mihte þara monna mod onwendan, þeah hio þa lichoman onwende*, or non-limiting, e.g. *ÆHomM* 11. 226 *Saul se cyning, þe syngode ongean god and hine swa gegremode þæt god cwæþ be him þæt him ofþuhte þæt he hine to cyninge gesette, næs na sona dead for his synnum swa þeah.* . . .

§3487. I follow Burnham's classification (pp. 67–73) in citing the following as typical examples: (with an adversative in the adjective clause) *Bede* 370. 16 *swa swa he sylf in ða ilcan tid monegum monnum mid his ðære gewunelican bilwitnesse diglum wordum openade 7 cyðde, þa mon hweðere æfter fæce sweotollice ongeotan mihte*, where *hweðere* represents Latin *tamen*, and *ÆLS* 25. 81; (with an adversative in the main clause) *Bo* 116. 26 and *ÆHomM* 11. 226, both in §3486; (with a demonstrative in the main clause) *Or* 74. 22 *Seo ilce burg Babylonia, seo ðe mæst wæs 7 ærest ealra burga, seo is nu læst 7 westast, ÆCHom* i. 138. 7 (§2122), and

PPs 117. 21   þone sylfan stan   þe hine swyðe ær
wyrhtan awurpan,   nu se geworden is
hwommona heagost;

and (without demonstrative or adversative but with an adverb or some other emphatic word or phrase to point the contrast) *ÆCHom* i. 332. 28 *forðan ðe ðæra wiðercorenra wite tiht for wel oft heora mod unnytwurðlice to lufe, swilce hi þonne lufian heora siblingas, ðe ær on life ne hi sylfe ne heora magas ne lufedon, Met* 5. 7 (§3486), and

El 930   . . . ond þec þonne sendeð   in þa sweartestan
ond þa wyrrestan   witebrogan,
þæt ðu, sarum forsoht,   wiðsæcest fæste
þone ahangnan cyning,   þam ðu hyrdest ær.

But, as Quirk (p. 105) notes, a reinforcing element is not essential; consider *CP* 147. 16 (§2147), *ÆCHom* i. 18. 21 *Ða deadan fell*

getacnodon þæt hi wæron ða deadlice þe mihton beon undeadlice,
gif hi heoldon þæt eaðelice Godes bebod,

Beo 2053   Nu her þara banena   byre nathwylces
                frætwum hremig   on flet gæð,
                morðres gylpeð,   ond þone maðþum byreð,
                þone þe ðu mid rihte   rædan sceoldest,

and

GenB 364   þæt me is sorga mæst,
              þæt Adam sceal,   þe wæs of eorðan geworht,
              minne stronglican   stol behealdan,
              wesan him on wynne. . . .

For further examples, see Burnham, pp. 67–73, and Quirk, pp. 103–8.

d. *Clauses of place*

§3488. See §§2466–7.

e. *Clauses of time*

§3489. An implication of concession has been detected in temporal clauses introduced by *þa, þonne, mid* formulae, *oð þæt,* and *syþþan.* Adams (p. 11) says that 'the ease with which the *ða*-clause brings two acts into the field of view is so great that *ða* occasionally seems to have a concessive force'. His examples are *Bede* 36. 32 . . . *tealde 7 wende þæt he mid swinglan sceolde þa beldu 7 þa anrednesse his heortan anescian, ða he mid wordum ne mihte,* Latin . . . *autumans se uerberibus, quam uerbis non poterat, cordis eius emollire constantiam,* and *John(WSCp)* 12. 37 *Ða he swa mycele tacn dyde beforan him, hi ne gelyfdon on hyne,* Latin *Cum autem tanta signa fecisset coram eis, non credebant in eum.* To these we may add *Or* 30. 21 *hio wæs wilniende mid gewinnum þæt hio hy oferswiðde, ða hio hit ðurhteon ne mihte,* Æ*CHom* i. 140. 9 *na þæt an þæt he wolde mann beon for us, ðaða he God wæs, ac eac swylce he wolde beon þearfa for us, ðaða he rice wæs,* and

GenA 2299   þa wearð Abrahame   Ismael geboren,
             efne þa he on worulde   wintra hæfde
             VI and LXXX.

§3490. Both Burnham (p. 77) and Small (1924, p. 75) cite *John (WSCp)* 4. 9 *Humeta bitst þu æt me drincan þonne ðu eart iudeisc,* Latin *quomodo tu iudaeus cum sis bibere a me poscis,* and *John (WSCp)* 7. 15 *Humeta cann þes stafas þonne he ne leornode,* Latin *quomodo hic litteras scit cum non dedicerit*, the latter observing that *þonne* may have 'a shade of meaning approaching concession, that may best be translated, "seeing that", "in view of the fact that" '. Other examples include *ÆCHom* i. 64. 33 *ac se ungesæliga gytsere wile mare habban þonne him genihtsumað, þonne he furðon orsorh ne bricð his genihtsumnysse* and

Met 5. 34   . . .   ne eft to waclice
        geortreowe   æniges godes,
        þonne þe for worulde   wiðerwearda mæsð
        þinga þreage   and þu ðe selfum
        swiðost onsitte,

but (despite Quirk, pp. 114 and 118) not

Met 21. 25   . . .   ac hi swiðor get
        monna gehwelces   modes eagan
        ablendað on breostum,   þonne hi hi beorhtran gedon,

where *þonne* means 'than', not 'when'; see §3215.

§3491. Other typical examples of what are described as 'concessive-equivalent' temporal clauses—either with or without adversatives and/or adverbs or other emphatic words or phrases to point the contrast—include (with a *mid* formula) *Bede* 80. 7 *Forþon, mid þy seo æ monig þing bewereð to etanne, swa swa unclæne, hwæðre in godspelle Drihten cwæð* . . . and *Bede* 454. 11 *þa þancode he him geornlice þære ærfæstnesse, þe he him forgifen hæfde, mid þy he ællþeodig wæs*; (with *oþþæt*)

Deor 38   Ahte ic fela wintra   folgað tilne,
        holdne hlaford,   oþþæt Heorrenda nu,
        leoðcræftig monn   londryht geþah,
        þæt me eorla hleo   ær gesealde

(so Quirk, p. 113, but Burnham offers no examples); and (with *syþþan*) *BlHom* 177. 30 *7 syþþan hie ðæt feoh onfengon, ne mihtan hie hweðre forswigian þæt þær geworden wæs.* On *nu* see §§3099, 3104, and 3493. For discussion and more examples, see Burnham, pp. 74–8; Quirk, pp. 112–14; and Campbell, *RES* 7 (1956), 67–8.

f. Clauses of cause

§3492. 'The close relationship between the notions of concession, condition, and cause' (Burnham, p. 2) has been discussed in §§3387–9.

§3493. Burnham's section on temporal clauses includes the following observation (p. 78): 'Although Adams (p. 61) regards *nu* as a causal conjunction in use, it is clearly temporal in origin, and I have accordingly placed it here.' With Quirk (pp. 112-13 and 115-16), I agree with Adams; see my §2591. 'Concessive-equivalent' *nu* clauses include *Bo* 68. 9 *Eala, wuldur þisse weorulde, ea, forhwy þe haten dysige men mid leasre stemne wuldor, nu ðu nane neart?* and

Met 17. 16   Hwy ge þonne æfre   ofer oðre men
                   ofermodigen   buton andweorce,
                   nu ge unæðelne   nænigne metað?

§3494. Quirk (pp. 115-16) also includes two *þæs* clauses, viz. *ChristC* 1090 and

PPs 77. 11   Effremes bearn   ærest ongunnan
                 of bogan stræle   bitere sendan,
                 þæs hi on wiges dæge   wendon æfter.

There is room for difference of opinion here.

g. Comparative clauses

§3495. On clauses introduced by *swa (swa)*, see §§3476-82.

§3496. Sentences in which two comparatives are balanced by means of *swa . . . swa* have been discussed in §§3287-9; they occur only in the prose. But, as Burnham (pp. 86-7) observes,

When the first clause gives a reason or circumstance naturally leading to a certain result, and the second gives the opposite result which actually does follow, we have concession. *Swa ic swyþor drince, swa me swyþor þyrsteð* (Dial. 116. 21) is a more emphatic way of saying, 'Although I drink, I thirst.' But a temporal element also is usually present in concessions of this sort; the opposition of two facts is stated not simply as existing, but as continuous. Thus the example just quoted might be paraphrased, 'In spite of my drinking more and more, I thirst more and more.'

Other examples include *Bede* 136. 14 *Forþon swa micle swa ic geornlicor on þam bigange þæt sylfe soð sohte, swa ic hit læs mette*, Latin . . . *quia uidelicet quanto studiosius in eo cultu ueritatem quaerebam, tanto minus inueniebam, Exod* 1. 12 *Swa hi swiðor wæron geswencte, swa wæron hi swiðor gemenifylde 7 weoxon*, Latin (with only one comparative) *Quantoque opprimebant eos, tanto magis multiplicabantur et crescebant*, and *ÆCHom* i. 268. 26 *Se goda man swa he swiðor afandod bið swa he rotra bið*. See further Burnham, pp. 85-8.

§3497. In the poetry, and occasionally in the prose, we find two comparatives balanced by means of *þy . . . þy*; see §3339. These sentences too may have a concessive implication. Burnham (p. 88) cites no prose examples except one from ME, viz. *ChronE* 266. 18 (1140) *oc æfre þe mare he iaf heom, þe wærse hi wæron him*. Quirk (p. 117) offers from the poetry three examples of the 'correlative comparative construction' which 'one can confidently regard as concessive'. The first of these, viz.

GenA 1324   þæt is syndrig cynn;
     symle bið þy heardra   þe hit hreoh wæter,
     swearte sæstreamas   swiðor beatað,

has a comparative in both clauses—my type 3 (§3339). The other two—*Rid* 47. 5 *Stælgiest ne wæs* ‖ *wihte þy gleawra, þe he þam wordum swealg* and *Mald* 312 (§3338)—have comparatives only in the principal clause and belong to my type 2a (§3338).

§3498. An implication of concession has also been detected in sentences involving *swa . . . swa* without a comparative. Examples from the prose cited by Burnham (pp. 88-90) include *Or* 152. 16 *. . . ac swa ealde swa hie þa wæron hie gefuhton* and *ÆLS* 9. 109 *Hwæt is se intinga þæt an þusend manna þe ne magon astyrian, swa unstrang swa ðu eart?* Quirk (p. 118) cites from the poetry four sentences with *efne/emne swa wide swa* in which the 'concession has the "even" meaning'; they include

And 332   Farað nu geond ealle   eorðan sceatas
            emne swa wide   swa wæter bebugeð,
            oððe stedewangas   stræte gelicgaþ

'. . . to the very limits to which . . .'.

h. Conditional clauses

§3499. 'The close relationship between the notions of concession, condition, and cause' (Burnham, p. 2) has been discussed in §§3387-94.

§3500. Quirk (pp. 62-3) discusses a number of examples in which *butan* 'was not autonomously concessive but occasionally *concessive-equivalent*, combining its exception function with a concessive one'. They include *Bo* 40. 8 *. . . ne ic ealles forswiðe ne girnde þisses eorðlican rices, buton tola ic wilnode þeah . . .* and (after a form of *nytan*) *Bo* 70. 26 *ic nat humeta, buton we witon þ hit unmennisclic dæd wæs* and (Holthausen's 1894 text)

Pha 4   Nat ic hit be wihte,   butan ic wene þus,
                 þæt þær screoda wære   gescyred rime
                 siex hundred godra   searohæbbendra,

for which J. R. R. Tolkien was wont to offer the translation 'I don't
really know, but I rather guess . . .'. On such examples, see further
§§3626 and 1773.

12. OTHER METHODS OF EXPRESSING CONCESSION

a. *Affirmation and negation*

§3501. Here it will suffice to quote Brouwer's statement (*Neophil.*
3 (1917), 259) that a spoken 'Yes' or 'No' can express concession:

> Et d'autre part, il y a lieu de remarquer que la concession peut se trouver à
> peu près partout. Telle principale peut, en tel moment, dans telles circonstances,
> dans la bouche d'un tel, exprimer une concession; un 'oui', un 'non' peuvent être,
> et sont souvent, éminemment 'concessifs', mais on reconnaîtra que la terminolo-
> gie grammaticale n'a rien à voir à des considérations de ce genre.[182]

This was no doubt true in OE.

b. *Co-ordinated words and phrases*

§3502. Phrases such as *Beo* 718 *ær ne siþðan* can be viewed as the
equivalent of an indefinite concession 'no matter when', but 'it may
be supposed that such a cliché as this has not always full concessive
feeling' (Quirk, p. 85). The following examples are typical: (with
ond) *Beo* 839 *feorran ond nean*; (with *(ne . . .) ne*) *Beo* 718, above,
and *Beo* 511 *ne leof ne lað*; (with *(oþþe . . .) oþþe*) *Beo* 2870 *ower
feor oððe neah* and *Jul* 335 *oþþe feor oþþe neah*; and (with *(ge . . .)
ge*) *ChristB* 846 *leofum ge laðum* and *Met* 9. 2 *ge neah ge feor*.

§3503. These examples—all from the poetry—refute Burnham's
observation (p. 123) that 'there are no concessions in Old English
corresponding to the familiar absolute phrase, "day or night"'. Full
collections may reveal some from the prose to supplement the few
expressions cited by Burnham (pp. 117 and 121) as approximating
to this MnE usage, e.g. *BenR* 13. 2 *ge þeow ge freoh* and *LS* 34. 277
læsse oþþe mare.

---

[182] 'And moreover, we may justifiably point out that concession can be found almost
anywhere. Any main clause can, at a given moment, in certain circumstances, from the lips
of a particular person, express a concession; a "yes", a "no", may be, and often are, emi-
nently "concessive", but it is obvious that grammatical terminology is not concerned with
considerations of this kind.'

§3504. On *swa* . . . *swa* 'either . . . or', as in *ÆGram* 260. 12 *siue uir siue mulier, swa hwæþer swa hit sy, swa wer swa wif*, see §§1825-6. This occurs in both prose and poetry.

§3505. Examples involving *sam (þe)* . . . *sam (þe)* occur only in the prose; they include *RegCGl* 707 . . . *sam gebroþrum sam eallum geleaffullum, RegCGl* 1177 . . . *sam þe hi sylfum, sam eallum æftergencgum hyra, LibSc* 189. 14 . . . *sam þe þeow sam þe frig*, and *LibSc* 226. 13 . . . *sam þe gecorenra to reste sam þe wiþercorenra to deaþe.*

c. Other words and phrases

§3506. Here considerations of space make it necessary for me to refer the reader to Burnham and Quirk. Quirk (pp. 119-20) gives a general discussion and exemplifies the concessive use of words as follows: adv. *mid þy*, e.g. *ChristC* 1425 (pp. 61-2); *gyt(a), gen(a)*, e.g. *Res* 117 (pp. 63-7); adv. *nu*, e.g. *Dan* 414 (pp. 67-8); adv. *þa* and *þonne*, e.g. *ChristC* 1497 and *PPs* 77. 37 (pp. 68-70; see also Small 1924, pp. 75-6); other words, e.g. *swylce* in *Rid* 40. 60 and interj. *huru* in *Hell* 15 (pp. 70-1); words with 'even' significance such as *efne* and *furþum*, e.g. *Met* 20. 154 and *ChronE* 140. 30 (1010) (pp. 123-6); *wiht*, e.g. *Beo* 1660 (pp. 126-31); and appositive nouns, adjectives, and participles, e.g. *ChronC* 100. 27 (916) *Her wæs Ecgbriht abbud unscyldig ofslegen* (pp. 120-3; see also Burnham, pp. 116-19). As Quirk's general discussion (pp. 119-20) suggests, lists such as these cannot be exhaustive.

§3507. Non-prepositional phrases with a concessive implication may be adverbial (see Burnham, pp. 121-2, and Campbell, *RES* 7 (1956), 68); appositional (see Quirk, pp. 120-1, and Callaway 1901, pp. 282-3); participial (see Quirk, pp. 122-3); or absolute, either with or without a participle (see Callaway 1889, p. 21; Burnham, pp. 119-21; and Quirk, p. 123).

§3508. I give my reasons for finding the case for concessive/adversative *forþon* not proven in §§3081-4. Yet—as in MnE; see *OED*, s.v. *for* A. VII. 23—*for* can introduce concessive phrases, usually with *eall*, e.g. *ÆCHom* i. 108. 22 *And ðeah þa heardheortan Iudei noldon for eallum ðam tacnum þone soðan Scyppend tocnawan* and *ChronE* 136. 17 (1006) *Ac for eallum þissum se here ferde swa he sylf wolde*, but occasionally without it, e.g. *GD* 219. 14 . . . *7 nallæs þæt an þæt*

*his lichama wæs gesund for þy fyre ac eac swylce ne mihton hi for-
bærnan nanra þinga his hrægles* and

GenA 2473   Onfoð þæm fæmnum,   lætað frið agon
                gistas mine,   þa ic for gode wille
                gemundbyrdan,   gif ic mot, for eow,

where *for eow* means 'against you' or 'despite you'. See further
Hupe, *Ang.* 12 (1889), 389–90; Burnham, pp. 112–15; and Quirk,
p. 132.

§3509. Phrases introduced by other prepositions may also contain
an implication of concession; see Burnham, pp. 109–12 and 116, and
Quirk, pp. 121–2.

d. Parataxis

§3510. I begin by noting the existence of three problems of classification or terminology. First, there is the difficulty of deciding
whether two juxtaposed clauses are in causal, adversative, or concessive, relationship. On this, see Quirk, pp. 50–4, 54–5, and 73–5, and
my §§1735–6 and 1772. Second, while I concede that it is not
always possible to say that the concessive element comes first or
second—consider the relationship between the two sentences in

Beo 856   Ðær wæs Beowulfes
           mærðo mæned;   monig oft gecwæð
           þætte suð ne norð   be sæm tweonum
           ofer eormengrund   oþer nænig
           under swegles begong   selra nære
           rondhæbbendra,   rices wyrðra.
           Ne hie huru winedrihten   wiht ne logon,
           glædne Hroðgar,   ac þæt wæs god cyning

and in MnE 'He scored five goals and he's only fourteen'—I believe
that the distinction can and therefore should sometimes be made.

§3511. Third, I find it both convenient and logical to distinguish
here six types of concessive parataxis: type (*a*), in which there is no
linking word; type (*b*), in which the linking word is an adverb; type
(*c*), in which it is what may be called a sentence adverb or a conjunction, e.g. *hwæþre*—see my §§1101–2; type (*d*), in which it is a
conjunction such as *ond* or *ac*; type (*e*), in which we have both a conjunction and an adverb; and type (*f*), in which we have both a conjunction such as *ond* and a word such as *hwæþre*. Types (*a*) and (*b*) can
be described as asyndetic, types (*d*), (*e*), and (*f*), as syndetic. I leave it

to the reader to decide about type (c). See further Quirk, pp. 72-3. Types (e) and (f) can be said to involve 'reinforcement'; see §§3528 and 3534. On sentences with conj. *ne* see §1834. On those involving correlation see §3533. On words meaning 'yet, nevertheless' in the works of Alfred and Ælfric, see Godden, *EStudies*, 61 (1980), 211-12.

§3512. Space permits little more than exemplification of these six types. Burnham (pp. 95-108) and Quirk (pp. 72-82) offer fuller discussions, with examples and comments on the relationship between Latin originals and OE translations. To clear the ground, I quote here a few examples to demonstrate that a concessive relationship may exist between a clause and a group of words without a finite verb which can be described as a contracted clause or as a phrase: type (a),

GenA 1933   þær folcstede   fægre wæron,
               men arlease,   metode laðe;

type (b),

GenB 486   Lytle hwile   sceolde he his lifes niotan,
               secan þonne landa   sweartost on fyre

and *Whale* 49 *He hafað oþre gecynd,* ‖ *wæterþisa wlonc, wrætlicran gien;*[183] type (c),

ChristA 209   Saga ecne þonc
               mærum meotodes sunu   þæt ic his modor gewearð,
               fæmne forð seþeah . . . ;

and type (d),

Jud 46   þær wæs eallgylden
               fleohnet fæger   ymbe þæs folctogan
               bed ahongen,   þæt se bealofulla
               mihte wlitan þurh,   wigena baldor,
               on æghwylcne   þe ðær inne com
               hæleða bearna,   ond on hyne nænig
               monna cynnes,   nymðe se modiga hwæne
               niðe rofra   him þe near hete
               rinca to rune gegangan.

§3513. I turn now to sentences in which two complete clauses are juxtaposed. I have not recorded any convincing examples of type (a) in the prose, with the possible exception of *Matt(WSCp)* 20. 23 *Witodlice gyt minne calic drincaþ; to sittanne on mine swiþran healfe . . . nys me inc to syllanne,* Latin *calicem quidem meum bibetis;*

---

[183] I follow BT in taking *gien(a)* and *giet(a)* as adverbs, thereby avoiding the erection of a seventh type involving words which may be adverbs or conjunctions (see *OED*, s.v. *yet*) or sentence adverbs (Onions, p. 17).

sedere autem ad dexteram meam . . . non est meum dare uobis, quoted
by Burnham (p. 103). Apart from this, the nearest Burnham gets is in
her observation (p. 108) that we have 'an example of the baldest
juxtaposition within a clause' in the ME *ChronE* 264. 29 (1137) *þa
ræueden hi 7 brendon alle the tunes ð wel þu myhtes faren all a dæis
fare sculdest thu neure finden man in tune sittende ne land tiled.*
This absence of recorded examples reflects the fact that asyndetic
parataxis is less common in the prose than in the poetry, where we
find (with the concessive element first)

And 505 　　　　　　　　Ðu eart seolfa geong,
wigendra hleo,　　nalas wintrum frod,
hafast þe on fyrhðe,　　faroðlacende,
eorles ondsware.　　Æghwylces canst
worda for worulde　　wislic andgit

and (with the concessive element second)

Beo 513 　　　　þær git eagorstream　　earmum þehton,
mæton merestræta,　　mundum brugdon,
glidon ofer garsecg;　　geofon yþum weol,
wintrys wylmum.

The fact that Quirk (p. 75) rebukes Glunz (p. 58) for classifying this
as concessive emphasizes the personal nature of such classifications.
Quirk (pp. 74-82) quotes and discusses many more examples from
the poetry without considering whether the concessive element
comes first or second—a point of special relevance to his analysis of
the element order in these sentences (pp. 78-80).

§3514. The concessive use of adverbs—my type (*b*)—has already
been mentioned in §§3501 and 3506. The following will serve as
examples: *Bede* 64. 10 *þæt halige gewrit þæt cyðeð þæt... þonne is
þeaw þæs apostolican seðles . . . ,* Latin *Sacra scriptura testatur . . .
Mos autem sedis apostolicae est . . . , BlHom* 175. 34 *Hit is seþe þes
dry Simon sagað þæt he sy; ðonne nis hit swa, ÆCHom* ii. 454. 15 *Hi
comon hine to gefrefrigenne, ða awendon hi heora frofer to edwite,*

ChristC 1496 　　. . . earm ic wæs on eðle þinum　　þæt þu wurde eadig on minum.
þa ðu þæs ealles　　ænigne þonc
þinum nergende　　nysses on mode,

and the second *nu* in

Dream 78 　　Nu ðu miht gehyran,　　hæleð min se leofa,
þæt ic bealuwara weorc　　gebiden hæbbe,
sarra sorga.　　Is nu sæl cumen
þæt me weorðiað　　wide ond side
menn ofer moldan. . . .

§3515. I turn now to type (c). It is in my opinion to be expected that when the second of two paratactic clauses contains an element such as *þeah* or *hwæþre* (or variants thereof), or a combination involving one or both of them (but not *ond* or *ac*), the concessive element will be the first, not the second, clause. As far as I have observed, this is true in OE. I do not find convincing the examples in which Burnham (pp. 98-9) thinks that the concessive element is the second clause—even *ÆCHom* i. 384. 22 *Godes gelaðung wurðað þisne dæg ðam mæran apostole Paule to wurðmynte, forðam ðe he is gecweden ealra ðeoda lareow: þurh soðfæste lare wæs ðeah hwæðere his martyrdom samod mid ðam eadigan Petre gefremmed* is dubious, despite Thorpe's '. . . though his martyrdom . . .', and so far I have recorded no unambiguous examples in the poetry. There is perhaps room for more work here. But it is no hard task to find examples in which the concessive element is the first clause. Consider (with *þeah*) *ÆCHom* ii. 346. 24, *Dan* 124, and *Met* 1. 26; (with *hwæþre*) *ÆC Hom* i. 18. 34 and *Beo* 2873; (with *þeah hwæþre*) *ÆCHom* i. 40. 24 and *MSol* 442; (with *swa þeah*) *ÆCHom* ii. 132. 1 and

Beo 2964   Hyne yrringa
            Wulf Wonreding   wæpne geræhte,
            þæt him for swenge   swat ædrum sprong
            forð under fexe.   Næs he forht swa ðeh,
            gomela Scilfing . . . ;

and (with *swa þeah hwæþre*) *ÆCHom* ii. 452. 20 *Drihten cwæð to ðan scuccan, Efne he is nu on ðinre handa, swa þeah hwæðere heald his sawle*. For more examples, see Burnham, pp. 98-9 and 103-4. On *hwæþre*, see Horn (*EStudien*, 70 (1936), 46-8) and Quirk (pp. 44-8).

§3516. Type (d) involves sentences in which two clauses are joined by *ond* or *ac*. Quirk (pp. 54-8) firmly establishes the concessive use of *ond*. He notes in particular that *ond* 'often corresponds to a more explicit sign in the original. Thus *ond* in Rid 40/18 corresponds to *rursus*, in 40/44 to *ecce tamen*, in 40/64 to a *cum*-clause' (p. 57) and points out that the Chronicle

provides particularly interesting material to show the interchangeability of *and* with other concessive elements. In E 755 . . . *7* corresponds to *7 þeah* in A; in F 887 *7* corresponds to *þeah* in A and E. In F 1016 we find *7* for *ac* in D and E; in D 1050 *7* for *ac* in C; in C 1065, E 1070 and E 1076 *7* for *ac* in D; in D 1050 *ac* is written over *7* [p. 57].

This rightly leads him to urge the retention of MS *7* instead of ASPR's *ac* in

Sat 405   Let þa up faran   eadige sawle,
                   Adames cyn,   ac ne moste Efe þa gyt
                   wlitan in wuldre   ær heo wordum cwæð . . .

and of MS *þe* instead of *þeh* (as proposed by Bright) in

And 629   Hwæt frinest ðu me,   frea leofesta,
                   wordum wrætlicum,   ond þe wyrda gehwære
                   þurh snyttra cræft   soð oncnawest?

§3517. But, as Campbell (*RES* 7 (1956), 66) points out, Quirk fails
to make the distinction between those sentences in which the concessive element is the first clause and those in which it is the second. We
find the concessive element first followed by a positive *ond* clause in
Ps(P) 49. 22 *Eall þis yfel þu dydest, and ic swugode and þolode*,
Matt(WSCp) 9. 37 *witodlice micel rip ys 7 feawa wyrhtyna*, Latin
messis quidem multa operarii autem pauci (with no verb after *and*),

GenB 418   . . .   þær geworht stondað
                   Adam and Eue   on eorðrice
                   mid welan bewunden,   and we synd aworpene hider
                   on þas deopan dalo

(where Kock (p. 90) translates *and* 'whereas'), and

GenB 810   Hwilum of heofnum   hate scineð,
                   blicð þeos beorhte sunne,   and wit her baru standað,
                   unwered wædo,

and followed by a negative *ond* clause in *Mark(WSCp)* 8. 18 *Eagan ge*
habbað 7 ne geseoð, 7 earan 7 ne gehyrað, Latin *oculos habentes*
non uidetis et aures habentes non auditis, the manuscript reading of
Sat 405 (§3516), and

GuthA 60   Sume him þæs hades   hlisan willað
                   wegan on wordum   ond þa weorc ne doð.

For more examples, see Burnham, pp. 100–6.

§3518. The following will serve as examples in which the *ond*
clause is the concessive element: *ChronA* 94. 5 (905) *þa ætsæton ða*
Centiscan þær beæftan ofer his bebod 7 seofon ærendracan he him
hæfde to asend, *BlHom* 143. 9 *To hwan ondrædeþ þeos halige Maria*
hire deaþ 7 mid hire syndan Godes apostolas 7 oþre þa þe hie beraþ
to hire æriste?, and *And* 629 (§3516). See further Burnham, pp. 95–7.

§3519. Quirk (pp. 48–9) rightly rebukes Burnham for her failure to
give an adequate treatment of concessive *ac* in the prose, but is in his

turn rebuked by Campbell (*RES* 7 (1956), 66–7) for 'his method of presenting his material'. As I point out in §1772, there is much work for the lexicographers to do on *ac*. However, it seems to me that the substitution of 'but' for 'and' in 'He scored five goals and he's only fourteen' (§3510) removes the possibility of taking the second clause as the concessive element; the emphasis is different if we read 'He's only fourteen, but he scored five goals'. This is, however, certainly a matter of feeling. So it is perhaps possible to take the *ac* clauses as the concessive elements in

Rid 39. 16   Ne hafað hio sawle ne feorh,   ac hio siþas sceal
                 geond þas wundorworuld   wide dreogan.
                 Ne hafaþ hio blod ne ban,   hwæþre bearnum wearð
                 geond þisne middangeard   mongum to frofre.
                 Næfre hio heofonum hran,   ne to helle mot,
                 ac hio sceal wideferh   wuldorcyninges
                 larum lifgan.

But, for the reasons advanced in §3515, I take the *Ne hafaþ* clause in line 18 as the concessive element and therefore think that the *Ne hafað* clause in line 16 and the *Næfre* clause in line 20 should be similarly explained. I agree with Quirk (p. 49) that *ac* clauses are 'notionally apodoses' and with the corollary (which he does not state) that the first clause is the concessive element; consider *Solil* 37. 8 *Ic gehyre nu þæt þu ne tiohhast nan wif to hæbbenne. Ac ic wolde witan hwæðer ðe nu gyt ægnig lufe oððe lust si ænigre hwem-nesse*, *Mark(WSCp)* 14. 38 *witodlice se gast is gearu ac þ flæsc is untrum*, Latin *Spiritus quidem promtus caro uero infirma*, *ChristC* 1565,

PPs 118. 143   Me costunga   cnysdan geneahhe,
                   and nearonessa   naman gelome;
                   ac ic þine bebodu   efnde and læste,
                   eac on minum mode   hi metegade georne,

and (with no verb with the *ac* element)

JDay ii 61   He mid lyt wordum   ac geleaffullum
                 his hæle begeat   and help recene. . . .

§3520. Quirk (pp. 49–50) notes that 'elliptical' concessions are frequent with *ac*; his examples include *JDay ii* 65 and *Or* 17. 27 *þa Beormas hæfdon swiþe wel gebud hira land, ac hie ne dorston þær on cuman*, where 'the real concession intended here seems to be, "Although they would have liked to see the B.'s land, because it was well cultivated, they did not dare to investigate." '

§3521. Type (*e*)—in which the conjunction is augmented by an adverb—is sufficiently exemplified by *Or* 206. 34 *þa þa Lapidus Mutius wæs consul, wolde seo strengeste þeod winnan on Romane, þe mon þa het Basterne, 7 nu hie mon hæt Hungerre, BlHom* 57. 18 *Manige men beoð heardre heortan þe þa godcundan lare gehyraþ, 7 him mon þa oft bodaþ 7 sægþ, 7 hi hi þonne agimeleasiað*, and

PPs 56. 8   Hi deopne seað   dulfon widne,
                    þær ic eagum   on locade,
                    and hi on ðone ylcan   eft gefeollan;

see further Burnham, p. 98, and Quirk, p. 56.

§3522. Examples of type (*f*) with *ond* include (with the concessive element first) *ChronA* 68. 20 (867) *7 hie late on geare to þam gecirdon þæt hie wiþ þone here winnende wærun, 7 hie þeah micle fierd gegadrodon, 7 þone here sohton æt Eoforwicceastre, BlHom* 93. 16 *7 þonne hit biþ æt sunnan setlgange 7 þeah hweþre nænig leoht ne æteoweþ, Beo* 2878 *ond . . . swa þeah*, and

PPs 113. 13   þa muð habbað,   and ne magon hwæþere
                      wiht hleoðrian   ne word sprecan,

and (with the concessive element second) *ChronA* 48. 29 (755) *7 he his feorh generede 7 þeah he wæs oft gewundad, BlHom* 23. 26 . . . *ne hie næfdan for him lamb to syllenne, ah twegen culfran briddas him genihtsumedan, 7 twegen turturan gemæccan; 7 hwæþere hie wæron of Dauides cynnes strynde, þæs rihtcynecynnes*, and possibly

El 716   Stopon þa to þære stowe   stiðhycgende
                 on þa dune up   ðe dryhten ær
                 ahangen wæs,   heofonrices weard,
                 godbearn on galgan,   ond hwæðre geare nyste,
                 hungre gehyned,   hwær sio halige rod
                 . . .   . . .
                 wunode wælreste.

Ælfric uses a variety of patterns, including *and ðeah* (*ÆCHom* i. 108. 22), *and . . . hwæðere* (*ÆCHom* i. 40. 28), *and swa ðeah* (*ÆC Hom* i. 8. 8), and *and þeah hwæðere* (*ÆCHom* i. 188. 5).

§3523. Quirk (p. 136) tells us that 'reinforcement of *ac* is unknown in OE verse'. Typical examples from the prose include *ÆCHom* i. 114. 20 . . . *ac ðeah* . . . , *ÆCHom* i. 188. 7 . . . *ac ðeah hwæðere* . . . , *ÆCHom* i. 230. 28 . . . *ac . . . hwæðere þeah*, and *ÆLet* 1. 100 *Manega sinoðas wæron syððan gehæfde ac þas feower syndon fyrmeste swa þeah*. The reinforcing element may occur in the first clause, e.g. *LS* 34. 184 *Ne ðincþ hit me þeah nan ræd ac ic eow læte unbeheafdod.*

§3524. In most of the examples so far cited of all these types, the concessive element has been co-ordinated with the principal clause of the sentence. But it may be co-ordinated with a subordinate clause. This is often an adjective clause, e.g. *John(WSCp)* 20. 29 *þa synt eadige þe ne gesawon 7 gelyfdon,* Latin *beati qui non uiderunt et crediderunt, HomU* 36. 231. 25 *and swa hwylc mæssepreost swa hæbbe þis gewrit and nelle cyðan godes folce, þonne cweð se hælend þæt his sawel wære awerged,* and possibly

PPs 88. 42   Hwylc is manna   þæt feores neote
                   and hwæþere on ende   deað ne gesceawige?

But such co-ordination is not restricted to adjective clauses; consider *VSal 1* 83 *Cum raðe and fulla me, þæt ic mæge myd ealre heortan on hyne gelyfan, forþon ic hyne næfre ne geseah and he me swa þeah halne gedyde* and *PPs* 88. 42 above, where *þæt* may introduce a clause of result (see §§2140-3), and see Burnham, pp. 106-8.

e. OE equivalents of 'without' or 'not' + a present participle

§3525. It has already been pointed out in §§2861-3 and 3476-80 that *swa* introducing negative clauses is often 'a rather characterless connective . . . , with the negative, corresponding to Modern English "without", "not being" ' (Burnham, p. 15). Other OE patterns which can express something approaching this idea include negated *ond* clauses, e.g. *Mark(WSCp)* 8. 18 (§3517) and

Beo 134   Næs hit lengra fyrst,
                   ac ymb ane niht   eft gefremede
                   morðbeala mare,   ond no mearn fore

(see further §3517); clauses introduced by *butan* or *nefne,* e.g. *ÆC Hom* i. 170. 12 *Hi moton ure afandian, ac hi ne moton us nydan to nanum yfle, buton we hit sylfe agenes willan don* . . . and

Beo 3053   . . . þæt ðam hringsele   hrinan ne moste
                   gumena ænig,   nefne God sylfa,
                   sigora Soðcyning   sealde þam ðe he wolde
                   —he is manna gehyld—   hord openian . . . ;

negated result clauses, e.g. *ÆCHom* i. 166. 9 . . . *and he ða fæste feowertig daga and feowertig nihta, swa þæt he ne onbyrigde ætes ne wætes on eallum þam fyrste* and

Beo 565 . . . ac on mergenne   mecum wunde
be yðlafe   uppe lægon,
sweordum aswefede,   þæt syðþan na
ymb brontne ford   brimliðende
lade ne letton

(see further §2966); negated participles, e.g. *Or* 250. 11 *For þære dæde wearþ Agustus swa sarig þæt he oft unwitende slog mid his heafde on þone wag*, *ÆCHom* ii. 176. 29 *þurh Benedictes gebedum him wæs se ungesewenlica draca æteowod, ðam ðe he ær filigde na geseonde*, *ÆCHom* ii. 32. 1 . . . *læg na swa ðeah cwacigende*, and

GenA 2648   Me sægde ær
þæt wif hire   wordum selfa
unfricgendum,   þæt heo Abrahames
sweostor wære

(see further Callaway 1901, p. 351, where we find a list of OE substitutes for the appositive participle); and prepositional phrases governed by *butan*, e.g. *Bede* 154. 4 *þa æt nyhstan cwom Eanfrið buton geþeahte*, *ÆCHom* i. 24. 24 . . . *and cydde hire þæt Godes Sunu sceolde beon acenned of hire, buton weres gemanan*, and

ChristA 37   þæt wæs geworden   butan weres frigum,
þæt þurh bearnes gebyrd   bryd eacen wearð.

§3526. Clauses with an initial negative also deserve mention here. They fall into the two inevitable groups—first, those introduced by a negated verb, e.g. (with the same subject) *PPs* 134. 17 . . . *and nose habbað, nawiht gestincað* and *PPs* 134. 18 *habbað fet swylce, ne magon feala gangan*, and (with a different subject)

Beo 2275   He gesecean sceall
hord on hrusan,   þær he hæðen gold
waroð wintrum frod;   ne byð him wihte ðy sel,

and second, those introduced by a conjunction or sentence adverb such as *ne*, *na*, *no*, or *nalles*, not immediately followed by a verb, e.g. *Bede* 160. 16 *Ferde he geond eall ge þurh mynsterstowe ge þurh folcstowe, ne he on horses hricge cuman wolde* and (with two examples)

Beo 1534   Swa sceal man don,
þonne he æt guðe   gegan þenceð
longsumne lof;   na ymb his lif cearað.
Gefeng þa be eaxle   —nalas for fæhðe mearn—
Guð-Geata leod   Grendles modor.

Both types occur in *PPs* 134. 17, *PPs* 134. 18, and

PPs 113. 15   Handa hi habbað,   ne hio hwæðere magon
gegrapian   godes awiht,
and fet habbað,   ne magon feala gangan.

Quirk (p. 77) rightly criticizes Andrew's suggestion (*SS*, pp. 66–7)
that *na/no* in examples of the second group is a scribal error for *ne*,
but himself falls into the old trap of confusing conj. *ne* 'nor' with
adv. *ne* 'not' when he quotes *Ic þa hine lange beseah ne ic hine
oncnawan mihte*—a sentence cited by Andrew (p. 66) without reference—as an example of 'concession without relating element'.

13. MOOD

§3527. This has been discussed for each type of clause. The subjunctive is the norm for true concessive clauses, whether the concession
is one of fact or not. Hotz (p. 65) quotes *Bo* 76. 12 *þeah nu God
anfeald sie 7 untodæled, swa swa he is, se mennisca gedwola hine
todæleð on mænig mid heora unnyttum wordum* and goes on: 'The
speaker evidently is conscious of the subj. taking away from the validity of the fact verified just before, and, in order to recall its being
a fact, he parenthetically inserts *swa swa he is*, availing himself just of
the strongly demonstrative character of *swa (svâ)* to set off the truth.'
I have found no evidence that the mood of the verbs of 'concessive-
equivalent' clauses is affected by the presence of a concessive idea or
implication.

14. ARRANGEMENT OF CLAUSES

a. Correlation

§3528. Quirk (pp. 14–19) distinguishes 'reinforcement' from 'correlation'. Reinforcement is 'the multiple signaling of the concessive
relation within a member' and 'is chiefly found in grammatically
nondependent members of a relationship', e.g. 'He went, *yet nevertheless* with regret'. Correlation 'on the other hand has to do with
linking different members in a concessive relation', e.g. '*Though* with
regret, he went *all the same*'. This seems clear enough until he confuses the issue by at least appearing to give 'Although he went, he
was nevertheless sorry' as an example first of correlation and then of
reinforcement (pp. 14–15). The distinction is a useful one, but needs
restating, for the two are not mutually exclusive.

§3529. First, let us consider correlation of a principal and a subordinate clause. This can take the form of a subordinating concessive conjunction correlative with a single concessive element which may be called a sentence adverb or a conjunction (§§1101–2), e.g. *Or* 38. 17 *7 þeah þæt folc nolde ær Gode abugan, hy hwæðre þa hyra unðances him gehyrsume wæron, ÆGram* 264. 13 *quamuis non roget, tamen uult habere, ðeah ðe he ne bidde, þeah he wyle habban, WHom* 1(b). 30 *7 ðeah þæt geweorðe . . . þeah we agan þearfe . . .* , and

Phoen 563   þeah min lic scyle
         on moldærne   molsnad weorþan
         wyrmum to willan,   swa þeah weoruda god
         æfter swylthwile   sawle alyseð . . . ;

of a subordinating concessive conjunction correlative with a negated comparative phrase (cf. MnE 'nevertheless'), e.g. *CP* 163. 18, *ÆCHom* i. 224. 5 *þeah man deadne mannan mid reafe bewinde, ne arist þæt reaf na ðe hraðor eft mid þam men*, and

Ex 259   Ne beoð ge þy forhtran,   þeah þe Faraon brohte
         sweordwigendra   side hergas,
         eorla unrim!;

or of a subordinating concessive conjunction correlative with a temporal or causal adverb, e.g. *Bo* 132. 2 *þeah he mæge sume his willan ongitan, þonne ne mæg he eallne* and

Beo 525   Ðonne wene ic to þe   wyrsan geþingea,
         ðeah þu heaðoræsa   gehwær dohte,
         grimre guðe. . . .

§3530. Second, we can speak of a combination of correlation and reinforcement when a subordinating concessive conjunction is correlative with two elements which may be said to reinforce one another, e.g. (with two sentence adverbs or conjunctions) *BenR* 119. 3 . . . *eac swylce þeah . . .* , *ÆCHom* ii. 56. 28 . . . *and þeah ðe . . . swa ðeah . . .* , and *ÆCHom* i. 286. 2 . . . *and ðeah ðe hi ne magon beon totwæmde, belimpð hwæðere ðeah seo hæðung to ðære hætan*; (with an adverb and a sentence adverb or conjunction) *HomU* 21. 2. 9 . . . *and ðeah he hit ne gesawe, þa he gemunde swa þeah þæt ylce þæt he ær geseah*; (with an adverb and a negated comparative phrase) *WHom* 8(c). 40 . . . *þeah he sylf ælc unriht dreoge on his life, ne byð seo þenung þæs na þe wyrse*; or (with two adverbs)

GenA 1037   Ne þearft ðu þe ondrædan   deaðes brogan,
         feorhcwealm nu giet,   þeah þu from scyle
         freomagum feor   fah gewitan.

§3531. Third comes reinforcement of the subordinating concessive conjunction. Burnham (p. 21) speaks of the use of *nu* after *þeah* (and other conjunctions) 'rather as a mere expletive than as an intensive' in examples like *Bo* 46. 30 *þeah ge nu wenen 7 wilnian þ ge lange libban scylan her on worulde, hwæt bið eow þonne þy bet?* and (with correlative *sua ðeah*) *CP* 41. 2 *Sua ðeah, ðeah ic nu ðis recce, næ tæle ic na micel weorc ne ryhtne anwald.* It is hard to be certain how colourless *nu* is in such examples, although it is clearly much more so there than in *Ps(P)* 22. 4 *þeah ic nu gange on midde þa sceade deaðes, ne ondræde ic me nan yfel.* Quirk (p. 16) suggests that *nu, gyt, nu geta,* and *ær*, serve as reinforcing elements to *þeah (þe)* in *Met* 22. 25, *Soul i* 135, *Bo* 24. 44, and *El* 1120, respectively.

§3532. The reinforcing function of *eall* is more certain than that of *nu.* Burnham (pp. 19-20) observes that

in the use of *eall* as a strengthening particle with *ðeah* we have the source of the modern conjunction *although*. This is only one of many cases where *eall*— which shades from its literal meaning, 'quite', 'altogether', to an intensive of the most general sort—serves to emphasize a word or phrase. The most common is the familiar *eal swa* in its various senses.

The beginnings of this usage can perhaps be seen in examples like *Bo* 106. 14 *7 ðeah he eall wille, he ne mæg gif he ðæs ðinges anwald næfð, ÆCHom* ii. 122. 11 *þa ne mihte se papa þæt geðafian, þeah ðe he eall wolde*, and

Beo 679   forþan ic hine sweorde   swebban nelle,
                   aldre beneotan,   þeah ic eal mæge.

I have found no OE examples of the type 'albeit'. For discussion of this question see, in addition to the standard grammars and dictionaries, Burnham, pp. 19-21; Horn, pp. 219-21; Bødtker 1908, pp. 45-6; Quirk, pp. 132-3; Mitchell 1959, pp. 542-3, and *MÆ* 25 (1956), 40; and Collinson, *TPS* 1959, p. 11.

§3533. I turn now to paratactic concessive expressions, i.e. those in which there is no subordinating conjunction. My fourth group contains examples involving correlation between non-dependent clauses, e.g. *Luke(WSCp)* 22. 22 *7 witodlice mannes sunu gæð æfter þam ðe him forestihtud wæs. þeah hwæðere wa þam men þe he þurh geseald bið* and

Met 15. 7   Hwæt, se feond swa ðeah
                   his diorlingas   duguðum stepte.
                   Ne mæg ic þeah gehycgan   hwy him on hige þorfte
                   a ðy sæl wesan;

for further examples see Burnham, p. 103, and Quirk, p. 19.

§3534. The last category to be considered is that in which one non-subordinating concessive word is reinforced by another, as in *Alex* 11. 9 *7 he sylfa þursti wæs se min þegn 7 hwæþre he swiðor mines feores 7 gesynto wilnade þonne his selfes* and *Rid* 39. 27 *ne hafað heo ænig lim, leofaþ efne seþeah.* For a fuller treatment of these, see §§3521-2.

§3535. The examples given above can be supplemented by reference to Burnham, pp. 18-21 and 28-32; Quirk, pp. 15-19; and Mitchell 1959, p. 549.

b. Clause order

§3536. The order of clauses in concessive sentences involving parataxis has already been discussed in §§3510-24. In both prose and poetry, the subordinate concessive clause may follow the principal clause, as in *BlHom* 21. 31 *7 bið þonne undeaþlic, þeah he ær deaþlic wære, Beo* 588 *þæs þu in helle scealt* || *werhðo dreogan, þeah þin wit duge,* and, with a strongly negative principal clause (see Quirk, p. 34),

Beo 2160   no ðy ær suna sinum   syllan wolde,
                   hwatum Heorowearde,   þeah he him hold wære,
                   breostgewædu;

precede it, as in *BlHom* 85. 27 *þeah hie ær þæs ecan lifes orwene wæron, hie synt nu swiþe bliþe* and

Beo 1368   Ðeah þe hæðstapa   hundum geswenced,
                   heorot hornum trum   holtwudu sece,
                   feorran geflymed,   ær he feorh seleð,
                   aldor on ofre,   ær he in wille,
                   hafelan beorgan;

or occur within it, e.g. *Bede* 102. 14 *ond þæt þridde, þæt ge Ongolþeode ætgædre mid us Drihtnes word bodige, all oðer þing ða ge doð, þeah heo ussum þeawum wiðerworde syn, we geþyldelice aræfnað* and

Jul 494   Ic asecgan ne mæg,
          þeah ic gesitte   sumerlongne dæg,
          eal þa earfeþu   þe ic ær ond siþ
          gefremede to facne. . . .

For more examples, see Burnham, pp. 26-30, and Quirk, pp. 17-18 and 26-8. On the order VS in the principal clause when it follows the subordinate clause, see Behaghel, *PBB* 53 (1929), 401-18.

§3537. When the principal clause contains a correlative concessive element, it normally follows the subordinate clause; for examples, see §§3529-31. Sentences like *Or 252. 1 Ic wille, cwæð Orosius, on foreweardre þisse seofeþan bec gereccean þæt hit þeh Godes bebod wæs, þeh hit strong wære, hu emnlice þa feower onwealdas þara feower heafedrica þisses middangeardes gestodon* are rare.

§3538. In my opinion, Quirk (pp. 26-8) places too much value on clause order as a criterion for punctuation in OE poetry; see Mitchell 1969a, pp. 78-81.

c. Co-ordination

§3539. For reasons of space, I restrict myself here to examples from the poetry. As with other types of clause, co-ordination may be achieved without connectives, e.g. *Jul* 191 and

Beo 1714   . . .   oþ þæt he ana hwearf,
            mære þeoden   mondreamum from,
            ðeah þe hine mihtig God   mægenes wynnum,
            eafeþum stepte,   ofer ealle men
            forð gefremede,

or with them, e.g. *GuthA* 299 *þeah . . . ond, GenB* 717 *þeah . . . ac,* and (with no verb after *oðða*)

PPs 68. 31   Ic þam leofan gode   licie swyþor
            þonne æðele cealf,   þeah þe him upp aga
            horn on heafde   oððe hearde cleo.

§3540. Repetition of the conjunction *þeah (þe)* is not usual, but may occur, e.g. in *Met* 10. 24, *Met* 14. 1, and *Met* 16. 8.

L. CONDITIONAL CLAUSES

1. INTRODUCTORY REMARKS

§3541. *OED* (s.v. *condition* I. 4 and 6) defines a conditional clause as one which expresses 'something that must exist or be present if something else is to be or take place; that on which anything else is contingent; a prerequisite'. The term traditionally applied to a conditional clause is 'protasis', the principal clause being called the 'apodosis'. Mather (p. 1) reminds us that while 'logically the apodosis is dependent upon the protasis, grammatically the relation is reversed'. For personal and pedagogic reasons, I accept the recommendation of the Joint Committee (p. 17) that the terms 'If-clause' and 'Then-clause' be substituted for 'protasis' and 'apodosis'. The terms are of general application and 'If-clause' does not certify that the OE clause under discussion is introduced by *gif*. Where necessary, I use terms such as '*gif* clause', '*butan* clause', or '*nefne* clause'. For some comments on the distribution of conditional sentences in the different OE texts, see Mather, pp. 78–81.

§3542. Various methods of classifying conditional sentences exist. Latin grammarians detect three types—A, the logical, e.g. *Si id credis, erras* and *Si id credidisti, errasti*; B, the ideal, e.g. *Si id credas, erres* and *Si id credas, erraveris*; and C, the unreal, e.g. *Si id crederes, errares* and *Si id credidisses, erravisses*; see GL, pp. 380–7. This system is not suitable for OE; see below. Mather (p. 24) adopts a five-fold classification:

First, must come the great class of simple or logical conditions with the indic. in both clauses.

Second, the conditions which with a mandatory apodosis have regularly the subj. in protasis. This class is so important for Anglo-Saxon that the erection of an especial category for it seems justified; and its logical nature suggests that it follow the simple condition immediately.

Third, the ideal condition which is regularly expressed by the pret. subj. in both clauses. As an appendix to this class the instances of the pres. subj. in protasis not included under class two may be appropriately collected.

Fourth, the unfulfilled or unreal condition, which takes the pret. subj. in both clauses.

Fifth, the exceptive condition, introduced by buton nemne, or nymðe, which has the subj. in protasis, forms appropriately a special class, though logically it is related sometimes to class three, sometimes to class one.

This classification hovers uneasily between the functional (e.g., the distinction between his third and fourth classes, which correspond to types B and C above) and the formal (e.g., the distinction between his first and second classes, both of which belong to type A above) and is not consistently applied in practice, e.g. 'the few cases where buton is used in an unreal condition . . . have been classed with the unreal or unfulfilled condition' (Mather, p. 43). So all the examples in Mather's fifth class belong to type A above.

§3543. Onions (pp. 57–62) distinguishes the 'open condition' (type A above) as class A, but groups types B and C above in his class B. He then distinguishes class C,

a third class of Conditional Sentences, in which the Principal Clause is like that of Class A (*i.e.* does not speak of what *would be* or *would have been*), but the

If-Clause marks the action as merely *contemplated* or *in prospect* and implies a certain *reserve* on the part of the speaker.

    If this *be* so, we are all at fault.

       [*Be* implies 'I do not say (or know) that it is'.]

. . .

    If it *were* so, it was a grievous fault.

       [*Were* implies 'I do not say (or know) that it was'.]

This class C seems to me a form of 'open condition'. Wood (pp. 355-6) differs from Onions in putting types A and B (§3542) together in opposition to type C and adds what he calls the 'conceded condition', in which 'the fact stated in the conditional clause is conceded in advance'. His examples include 'She is fifty if she's a day' and 'You say your father would object? If that is the case, I will not press the matter.' He goes on:

    We have, then, three stages of condition, ranging from doubt or uncertainty on the one hand, to certainty in one direction or another on the other hand, and exemplified respectively in the clauses *if that is the case* (it may or may not be), *if that is the case* (and it is), *if that were the case* (but it is not); even with open conditior. there are different degrees of doubt, extending from probability to near improbability.

Onions (p. 60) had already noted the existence of the 'conceded condition' in one of his 'Additional Remarks', but distinguished it from what we may call the 'denied condition':

    It is true that in some cases we say 'if' when the context shows that a *fact* is in our minds. 'If thy family is proud, mine, sir, is worthy' = 'Thy family is no doubt proud, but mine is worthy'. 'If Elizabeth was resolute for peace, England was resolute for war'. . . . Again in some cases the Conditional Sentence *as a whole* may suggest that the speaker does not believe the supposition to be true: *e.g.* 'If this is so, I'm a Dutchman', 'Do it if you dare'. But in all these cases the If-Clause itself suggests nothing as to the actual state of the case; any implication of reality or unreality which the sentence contains, is due to the sentence as a whole or to the context.

This last sentence is important. Wood's classification (pp. 357-8) of 'If you think that, you are wrong' as conceded depends on the assumption that the person addressed has just said 'I (do) think that' and his classification of 'If you feel cold, come nearer to the fire' as open assumes that the person addressed has not just said 'I (do) feel cold'. So we cannot classify the sentence 'If Andrée keeps on painting those pictures, she'll lose all her friends' until we know whether Andrée has in fact announced her intention of continuing to paint. This restriction also holds for what we might call 'denied conditions'. Thus, in Onions's first example 'If this is so, I'm a Dutchman', it is (presumably) clear that the speaker is not a Dutchman. But his second example, 'Do it if you dare', may be either denied or open, depending on the context; cf. *Beo* 1379 *sec gif þu dyrre!* (discussed by Behre (p. 134)[184]), where the condition turns out to be open, since Beowulf does in fact dare, even if (as seems unlikely) Hrothgar was suggesting that he would not.

§3544. In my previous writings, I have used the threefold A, B, C, classification described in §3542. I now propose to abandon it for three reasons: it is based on Latin and does not fit OE; Onions (pp. 57–62) used A, B, C, in a different way; and (I now believe) names are simpler. So I distinguish first, Conceded and Denied Conditions, in which the condition 'is accepted as being fulfilled and as applying to the matter in question' (Wood, p. 355) or as not being fulfilled; second, Open Conditions, 'where it is not stated whether the condition is or is not fulfilled and where neither possibility is therefore excluded' (loc. cit.)—these may have verbs in the present or preterite indicative or subjunctive, there being 'different degrees of doubt, extending from probability to near improbability' (Wood, p. 356); and third, Rejected or Imaginary Conditions, 'where a condition is stated which does not or cannot exist' (ibid., p. 355). This classification, I believe, conforms to the facts of OE and will help to avoid much barren discussion. Thus we will not need to argue whether *Bede* 374. 25 *þa sægdon hie ðæt 7 cyðdon Eadbyrhte heora biscope þæt him ðæt licede 7 leof wære, gif hit his willa wære* belongs to type A or type B (§3542)—i.e. whether the preterite subjunctives in dependent speech represent present subjunctives in non-dependent speech or present indicatives which have become preterite subjunctives; to decide what sort of open condition is represented in *Bede* 2. 11 *Gif se oðer nolde, hu wurð he elles gelæred?*—it seems to approach Onions's class C; or to argue whether *wyle* in *ÆLS* 1. 19 and *wære* in

MCharm 4. 20   Gif ðu wære on fell scoten   oððe wære on flæsc scoten
                     oððe wære on blod scoten
                     oððe wære on lið scoten,   næfre ne sy ðin lif atæsed

are indicative or subjunctive. No system of classification can cope with an example like *ÆCHom* ii. 200. 4 *Hit bið swiðe langsum, gif we ealle ðas getacnunga eow nu ætsomne gereccað, ac we willað*

---

[184] I have to admit that I do not always find Behre's observations on conditional sentences helpful. I do not really understand what he means by 'hypothetical periods' (p. 50) and would regard conditions with the indicative mood such as 'If there is lightning, thunder follows' as containing what Behre calls 'conditions beyond the scope of the speaker's control' (p. 51) and 'uncontrollable conditions' (pp. 51 and 138), which he expects to take the subjunctive. So I cannot follow his argument in these places.

nu sume eow geopenian, and sume eft on gelimplicere tide, which is
in form open but, as the *ac* clause shows, is in effect rejected.

§3545. The Then-clause may be a positive or negative statement or
hypothesis, an expression of volition, a question (rhetorical or otherwise), an exclamation (see Mather, pp. 27-9), or a subordinate clause.
It may be in non-dependent or in dependent speech. The possible
combinations of Then- and If-clauses in the different types of conditional sentences are analysed below. If the Then-clause is or contains an
expression of volition, the mood of the verb of the If-clause may be
affected; see §§3560-90 and 3595-7. Although the fact that the
governing clause is a rhetorical question, a negated statement, or a
clause of purpose, sometimes affects the mood of other subordinate
clauses (see the General Index), this does not seem to obtain in conditional sentences; consider *ÆCHom* i. 250. 7 *Hwilc fæder wile
syllan his cilde stan, gif hit hine hlafes bitt?*, *ÆCHom* i. 350. 9 *Gif se
rihtwisa gecyrð fram his rihtwisnysse, and begæð unrihtwisnysse arleaslice, ealle his rihtwisnysse ic forgyte; and gif se arleasa behreowsað
his arleasnysse, and begæð rihtwisnysse, ne gemune ic nanra his synna*,
and *ÆCHom* ii. 558. 1 *ðonne sceal se, þær ðær he mæg, earmum
ðingian to ðam rican þe he cyððe to hæfð, þy læs ðe he geniðerod
beo, gif he ðæs pundes rihtlice ne bricð.* However, there is room for
more work here. Conditional sentences in dependent speech present
special problems because of the possibility of a change in the tense
and/or the mood of the verbs and are therefore discussed separately
in §§3612-14.

§3546. The inevitable problems of classification arise. A *gif* clause
comes close to being the equivalent of a noun clause introduced by
þæt in sentences like *ÆCHom* i. 210. 9 *Godes myldheortnys is þæt
we untigede syndon; ac gif we rihtlice lybbað, þæt bið ægðer ge
Godes gifu ge eac ure agen geornfulnyss* and *ÆCHom* ii. 72. 3 *god we
tellað, gif we ðyssera gemyndige beoð, þe ge nu gehyred habbað.*
Here we may compare Mather's observation (p. 51) that in sentences
like *CP* 31. 16 *Se ðe ænigne ðissa ierminga besuicð, him wære betere
ðæt him wære sumu esulcweorn to ðæm suiran getiged, 7 sua
aworpen to sæs grunde* and *ÆCHom* ii. 480. 8 *Him wære swa ðeah
betere þæt he forburne þonne he ætburste*, we have examples which
demonstrate that 'a subject clause, introducing a purely hypothetical
or unreal idea, may be in a truly conditional relation to the verb of
which it is the logical subject'. See further §§1960 and 3624, Behre,
pp. 55-6, and Mitchell 1959, pp. 579-80. On the use of clauses intro-

duced by *gif* with words meaning 'wonder' and 'profit, benefit', see §§1960 and 3409-12. I have not recorded examples of *gif* clauses with the verbs of emotion discussed in §§3413-15. But examples like *CP* 31. 25 *forðæm gif he on ðæm wel deð, he hæfð ðæs god lean* (where the *gif* clause is, as it were, in apposition with *ðæs*) and *CP* 253. 7 *Gif ic ryhtwis wæs, ne ahof ic me no forðy* not only show that the line between noun clauses and conditional clauses is sometimes a fine one, but also help us to see why 'the conditional construction is often regarded as a variety of the causal construction' (Mather, p. 1). This last observation is also illuminated by a comparison of examples such as *CP* 397. 30 *Forðæm bið sio scyld ðy hraðor gehæled, forðæm ðe hio ne bið unliefedo* with examples like *CP* 81. 8 . . . *forðon sio stefn ðæs lariowes micle ðe ieðelicor ðurhfærð ða heortan ðæs gehirendes, gif he mid his ðeawum hi ðæron gefæsðnað*; see further Johnsen, *EStudien*, 44 (1911-12), 227-32, and my §§3162-4. I discuss the use in the *Paris Psalter* of OE *gif* to translate *si* in the formula *iurare si* expressing a strongly negative oath in §3415 and in *NM* 70 (1969), 81-4.

§3547. *Gif* may introduce a dependent nexus question, e.g. *ÆCHom* ii. 244. 6 *þa befran Iudas, gif he hit wære*; see §2084. But, as hinted there, it is sometimes difficult to decide whether we have a dependent question or a conditional clause, e.g. *ÆCHom* ii. 228. 20 *Smeaga nu gehwa on his mode, gif ðas beboda and oðre þillice habbað ænigne stede on his heortan, ðonne tocnæwð he hwæðer he is fram Gode*, where we can accept Thorpe's 'whether' for *gif* or can understand *þæt* before *þonne* (§1987); *ÆCHom* ii. 490. 30 and *ÆCHom* ii. 248. 16 *þa axode hine se ealdorbiscop, and mid aðe gehalsode, þæt he openlice sæde, gif he Godes Sunu soðlice wære*, where the difference is exquisite;

Beo 272   þu wast, gif hit is
         swa we soþlice   secgan hyrdon,
         þæt mid Scyldingum   sceaðona ic nat hwylc,
         deogol dædhata   deorcum nihtum
         eaweð þurh egsan   uncuðne nið,
         hynðu ond hrafyl,

on which see also §3714; and (with the odds on the conditional explanation; see §3555) *Rid* 32. 13 *Rece, gif þu cunne,* ‖ *wis worda gleaw, hwæt sio wiht sie*. But, despite the position of *sceawiað* (note the chiasmus), the *gif* clause in *ÆCHom* ii. 76. 29 *Mine gebroðra, behealdað eowere ðeawas, and gif ge gyt Godes wyrhtan sind, sceawiað* seems to me interrogative, with *gif* meaning 'whether'.

§3548. Behre (pp. 60-1) rightly observes 'that the subjunctive of conditionality has sometimes an emotional or optative tone'. He cites

Met 11. 96

	Eala, sigora god,
wære þis moncyn	miclum gesælig,
gif hiora modsefa	meahte weorðan
staðolfæst gereaht	þurh þa strongan meaht

and goes on: 'The optative element of the apodosis may be expressed thus: "Would that this mankind were so happy!" [With this, cf. my §1975.] The form of the apodosis is identical with that of an unrealizable wish.' As a result, some writers speak of the possibility of 'ellipsis' of a Then-clause in such examples as *ÆCHom* ii. 308. 15 *Eala gif ðu wære hund! Hund is sawulleas and on helle ne ðrowað*, *ÆCHom* i. 588. 17 *Eala gif ðu witan woldest þære halgan rode gerynu*, 'If only I had known!', and 'If that isn't the limit!'; see Mather, p. 22, and Wood, pp. 363-4. An alternative explanation of the origin of the idiom is that the independent wish is the earlier form from which the use in a conditional sentence developed. But see §3550. Editors sometimes differ in their punctuation of passages in which a clause can be explained as expressing either an independent wish or a condition. Thus Schaar (pp. 76-8) replaces the ASPR exclamation mark with a comma in

ChristC 1312

Eala, þær we nu magon	wraþe firene
geseon on ussum sawlum,	synna wunde,
mid lichoman	leahtra gehygdu,
eagum unclæne	ingeþoncas!
Ne þæt ænig mæg	oþrum gesecgan
mid hu micle elne	æghwylc wille
þurh ealle list	lifes tiligan,
feores forhtlice,	forð aðolian. . . .

This difficulty arises frequently when the clause in question begins with an imperative, a jussive subjunctive, or a preterite subjunctive; see §§3678-83.

§3549. Behre (pp. 140-1) gives two explanations for the nature of the subjunctive forms *wære* in

MCharm 4. 23   gif hit wære esa gescot   oððe hit wære ylfa gescot
            oððe hit wære hægtessan gescot,   nu ic wille ðin helpan

—'unrealizable wish' (p. 140), 'concessive' (p. 141)—but claims that 'the present tense [*wille*] is striking and seems to suggest omission of the proper apodosis, e.g. "it would make no difference" '. One cannot deny the possibility. But the difference in tense is not conclusive; cf. *Exod* 21. 29 and *ÆCHom* i. 236. 28 *Gif hwa alefed wære, oððe limleas on þissum life, he bið þonne swa hit awriten is.* . . . In conditional sentences, as elsewhere (see §§859-64), there is no rule of tense sequence; consider *Bo* 31. 8 *Gif hi nu gode sint 7 fægere, þonne wæron hi swa gesceapene* (where a present state is conditional upon a past event); *ÆCHom* i. 216. 8 *and ða þurh his un-scæððigan deað wurdon we alysede fram ðam ecan deaðe, gif we us sylfe ne forpærað* (where the intended result of a past action can be nullified by action in the future); *ÆCHom* i. 112. 19 *Ac eft seo miccle mildheortnys ures Drihtnes us alysde þurh his menniscnysse, gif we his bebodum mid ealre heortan gehyrsumiað* (where *alysde* is a perfect or future perfect); *Bede* 402. 24 (§3554) and *LS* 23. 779; *ÆCHom* ii. 322. 10 . . . *and gif eowere synna wæron wolcnreade ær ðan, hi beoð scinende on snawes hwitnysse* (where *beoð* has a future reference); and *ÆCHom* i. 56. 3 *ac gif hit is hefigtyme on ðyssere worulde, hit becymð to micelre mede on ðære toweardan* (where the time-references are respectively present and future).

§3550. Mann (*Archiv*, 197 (1960-1), 18-22) claims that both the use of OE *gif* as a conjunction introducing dependent questions 'whether' and as a conjunction introducing conditional clauses 'if' had their origin in an adverbial use in which *gif* or its ancestor had the meaning 'perhaps' and introduced a non-dependent question which was accompanied by a logically related but grammatically independent sentence. Thus, *John(WSCp)* 9. 25 *gif he synful is þ ic nat* originally meant 'Perhaps he is sinful? That I know not' and *Beo* 452 *Onsend Higelace, gif mec hild nime,* ‖ *beaduscruda betst* originally meant 'Send to Higelac the best of war-garments. Perhaps battle will take me off?' This stage, he admits, cannot be exemplified in the extant OE monuments. It would also conflict with the suggestion made in §3548 that its use in independent wishes may have been the origin of the use of *gif* in conditional sentences. But, as Mann points out (loc. cit.), the question of a wish can scarcely arise in *Beo* 452; see also Behre, p. 135. However, the two are perhaps not mutually exclusive and both are in conformity with the generally accepted view that parataxis preceded hypotaxis.

§3551. When conditional clauses introduced by *gif* and *þær* are negated, the principles laid down in §§1595-632 apply. Illustration would be superfluous. On *butan* and *nefne* 'if . . . not, unless', see §§3634-40 and 3652-5 respectively. On *gif* 'on condition that', see §§3659-60.

2. CONCEDED AND DENIED CONDITIONS

§3552. *Mutatis mutandis*, what is said about the syntax of open conditions in §§3556–601 applies to conceded and denied conditions with the same syntactical patterns. Indeed, as has already been noted, it is often difficult to decide which we have. Here we need do little more than recognize the existence in OE of conceded and denied conditions, and exemplify them.

§3553. The *gif* clause in what the context shows to be a conceded conditional sentence expresses—either positively or negatively—an accepted fact; see the quotation from Onions (p. 60) in §3543. Such conditions require the present or the preterite indicative. Behre's statement (p. 132) that 'the traditional view is erroneous, viz. that the indicative is used in the protasis of a hypothetical period to represent its content as real or as a fact' is to be taken, not as meaning that the indicative never serves this function—it does in conceded conditions—but as meaning that it does not always do so—it does not in open conditions. But BTS (s.v. *gif*) and many other works, including Sweet, *Pr.* 9, §94, certainly fall into the error condemned by Behre; see Visser, ii. 882, and my §3584.

§3554. Visser's examples of conceded condition or, as he has it (ii. 766 fn. 1), examples of 'non-conditional *gif* . . . [with] the meaning of "seeing that", "conceded that" ' include *Bo* 16. 30 *Swa eac gif þu þe selfne to anwalde þæm woruldsælðum gesealdest, hit is riht þæt þu eac hiora þeawum fulgonge* and *John(WSCp)* 13. 14 *Gif ic þwoh eowre fet ic þe eom eower lareow 7 eower hlaford ge sceolon þwean eower ælc oðres fet.* There can be no doubt about the second example in view of *John(WSCp)* 13. 12 *Syððan he hæfde hyra fet aþwogene. . . .* But I am inclined to see *Bo* 16. 30 as an open condition; cf. *Bo* 16. 28 *Hwæt, þu wast gif þu þines scipes segl ongean þone wind tobrædest, þ þu þonne lætæst eall eower færeld to ðæs windes dome* and *ÆCHom* i. 122. 23 *ac se inra mann, þæt is seo sawul, bið micele atelicor, gif heo mid mislicum leahtrum begripen bið,* in both of which the whole sentence expresses an accepted truth, but the *gif* clause does not express a conceded fact. What are perhaps more convincing examples are to be found (with positive *gif* clauses) in *Bede* 402. 24 *7 þæs mæssepreostes noman him næmde, from ðæm ic wiste þæt ic gefulwad wæs. Cwæð he se biscop: Gif ðu from þissum mæssepreoste gefulwad wære, þonne ne eart ðu fullfremedlice no on riht gefullwad* (Visser (ii. 815) is wrong), *CP* 43. 8 *Be ðam Paulus se apostol cuæð: Gif Crist for us eallum dead wæs, ðonne weorðað ealle menn deade, CP* 53. 8, *BlHom* 233. 20 (see § 3597), *LS* 23. 779, and *ÆCHom* i. 342. 13 *Be ðam is to smeagenne hu micclum se rihtwisa mid eadmodre heofunge God gegladige, gif se unrihtwisa mid soðre dædbote hine gegladian mæg,* and (with negative *gif* clauses) *Bo* 31. 2 *Gif ðonne þisse worulde wlites ⁊ wela to wilnienne nis, hwæt murcnast þu þonne æfter þam þe þu forlure . . . ?* and *ÆCHom* ii. 78. 12 *Gif ge noldon Gode lybban on cildhade, ne on geogoðe, gecyrrað nu huru ðinga on ylde to lifes wege, nu ge habbað hwonlice to swincenne.* In the sequence *gif . . . gif þonne* in examples like *CP* 43. 4 *Fed ðonne min sceap, gif ðu me lufige. Gif ðonne seo feding ðara sceapa bið ðære lufan tacen, hwi forcwið ðonne se ðe him God suelce cræftas giefð ðæt he ne fede his heorde . . . ?* and *ÆCHom* i. 306. 10 *Gif hwa bið geuntrumod on his anginne, and asolcen fram godre drohtnunge, gif hine hwa ðonne mid tihtinge and gebisnungum godra weorca getrymð and arærð, þonne bið hit swilce he sette his handa ofer untrumne and hine gehæle,* the first *gif* clause seems to be open but then to be conceded, as it were, for the sake of the argument.

§ 3555. I have not found the OE equivalent of Onions's first example of a denied condition 'If this is so, I'm a Dutchman'—☆*Gif þis swa bið, þonne eom ic Friesa.* As I have pointed out in § 3543, it is difficult to be sure about *Beo* 1379 *sec gif þu dyrre!,* an obvious equivalent of Onions's second example 'Do it if you dare', but like it ambiguous. However, the riddler is probably hoping, and may be implying, that his hearer will be unable to meet the challenge in *Rid* 32. 13 *Rece, gif þu cunne,* ‖ *wis worda gleaw, hwæt sio wiht sie* and

Rid 39. 28	Gif þu mæge reselan　　recene gesecgan
	soþum wordum,　　saga hwæt hio hatte;

cf.

Rid 55. 14	Nu me þisses gieddes
	ondsware ywe,　　se hine on mede
	wordum secgan　　hu se wudu hatte,

where, despite the difficulties, some such meaning as 'dares' or 'presumes' can reasonably be assigned to *mede*.

3. OPEN CONDITIONS INTRODUCED BY *GIF* WITH THE PRESENT TENSE IN BOTH CLAUSES

a. Indicative Then-clauses

§ 3556. The normal mood in *gif* clauses expressing open conditions with a present tense in both clauses and an indicative in the Then-clause is the indicative. In such sentences, 'there is no implication as to the fulfilment of the condition: they are quite colourless' (Onions, p. 60). Open conditions of this type appear in all periods of OE; Mather (pp. 83–4) offers a list. A few examples from Ælfric must suffice for the prose: (with reference to the immediate present) *ÆC Hom* i. 122. 11 *Drihten, gif þu wilt, ðu miht me geclænsian*; (with reference to the future) *ÆCHom* i. 420. 2 *Gif ðes bealdwyrda biscop acweald ne bið, siððan ne bið ure ege ondrædendlic*; (expressing an accepted truth) *ÆCHom* i. 52. 33 *Gif ge forgyfað, eow bið forgyfen*; (with a negated *gif* clause) *ÆCHom* i. 70. 28 *Gif ðonne eower godes miht þa halgan cyrcan towurpan ne mæg, ic towurpe eower tempel þurh ðæs Ælmihtigan Godes mihte*; (with a negated Then-clause) *ÆCHom* i. 160. 10 . . . *ne nan limn ne deð nan ðing, gif se lichama bið sawulleas*; and (with both clauses negated) *ÆCHom* i. 54. 4 *gif ic næbbe ða soðan lufe, ne fremað hit me nan ðing*. There is no evidence that a negated indicative in the Then-clause 'causes' a subjunctive in the *gif* clause.

§3557. But there are examples in which a Then-clause with a present indicative is accompanied by a *gif* clause with the present subjunctive. Prose examples include *Bede* 442. 9 *Ic seolfa cuðe sumne broðar, ðone ic wolde ðæt ic næfre cuðe, ðæs noman ic eac swylce genemnan mæg, gif ðæt owiht bryciæ*, *Bo* 30. 7 *Gif þu þonne þæt gemet habban wille 7 þa nydþearfe witan wille, þonne is þæt mete and drync*, *ÆCHom* i. 388. 29, 452. 24, 476. 4, and 482. 26, *ÆCHom* i. 532. 4 *Gif hwam twynige be æriste, þonne mæg he understandan on þisum godspelle, þæt þær bið soð ærist þær ðær beoð eagan and teð*, and *ÆCHom* ii. 306. 19 *Gif hwa elles secge, we sceotað to him*. The presence of *mæg* in the Then-clauses in *Bede* 442. 9 and *ÆCHom* i. 532. 4 does not explain the subjunctives; we find the indicative in *gif* clauses so accompanied in *ÆCHom* i. 4. 2, 4. 7, 556. 29, 576. 9, and 592. 28, and in *ÆCHom* ii. 406. 26 *Soðlice gif se man þurhwunað yfel, ne mæg he habban gode weorc; and gif se goda man ðurhwunað on his godnysse, ne mæg he yfele wæstmas forðbringan*.

§3558. In the poetry, a present indicative in the Then-clause is regularly accompanied by a present indicative in the *gif* clause, e.g. *Beo* 660 *Ne bið þe wilna gad, || gif þu þæt ellenweorc aldre gedigest* and

Jul 328
egesful ealdor,
gedon habbaþ.

Ne biþ us frea milde,
gif we yfles noht

Behre's comment (p. 134) that 'outside Group B [i.e. examples with the preterite tense, except for *Max i* 31 and *Met* 23. 1, on which see

§3604] . . . the subjunctive is rarely met with in a protasis connected with an apodosis not containing a volitional expression' was not intended to, and certainly does not, apply to the prose; see the examples quoted in §3557, which could easily be multiplied. (There is room for more work here.) But the exceptions in the poetry are few:

GenB 427   Gif hit eower ænig mæge
                gewendan mid wihte   þæt hie word godes
                lare forlæten,   sona hie him þe laðran beoð

(Behre, p. 136, detects 'an optative shade of meaning' in *mæge*); *MCharm* 2. 45 (since *magan* cannot express a wish; see §1013); *And* 70 (but see §3560); and

JDay ii 301   Hwæt mæg beon heardes   her on life,
                gif þu wille secgan   soð þæm ðe frineð . . . ?

(the only example in the poetry of a Then-clause consisting of a rhetorical question accompanied by a *gif* clause with the subjunctive; cf.

Seasons 195   Hwa mæg þyngian   þreale hwilcum
                wiþ his arwesan,   gyf he him ærur hæfð
                bitere onbolgen,   and þæs bote ne deð . . . ?

and see Mitchell 1959, p. 587). Neither rhetorical nor genuine questions 'cause' a subjunctive in an accompanying *gif* clause; consider *Gen* 18. 24 *Gyf on ðære byrig beoð fiftig rihtwisra manna sceolon hi ealle samod forwurþan, 7 ðu nelt arian þære stowe for þam fiftigum rihtwisum, gyf hi þær swa fela beoð?*, *Matt(WSCp)* 18. 12 *Hwæt ys eow geþuht gyf hwylc mann hæfð hund sceapa 7 him losað an of þam hu ne forlæt he þa nigon 7 hundnigontig on þam muntum . . . ?*,

GenA 2482   Wilt ðu, gif þu most,
                wesan usser her   aldordema,
                leodum lareow?,

and

Met 10. 68   Hwæt þonne hæbbe   hæleþa ænig,
                guma æt þæm gilpe,   gif hine gegripan mot
                se eca deað   æfter þissum worulde?,

where the subj. *hæbbe* is not volitional. On the variant readings in *Bo* 19. 11, see §3571.

§3559. I am unable to account for the exceptions which I have cited in §§3557–8 beyond speculating that they may be syntactical equivalents of 'inverted spellings' brought about by analogy with the fluctuations between the indicative and the subjunctive in *gif* clauses accompanied by a Then-clause containing a volitional expression (see §§3560–90), fluctuations which are also in my opinion likely to be analogical. These conclusions, which I reached independently, to some extent march with those of Kihlbom (pp. 263–4); see §3590. A different explanation has been put forward by Mattsson (*Kock Studies*, pp. 200–24). In his view, the examples of the present subjunctive that are recorded in conditional clauses in Germanic are relics from a period in which the present subjunctive had the meaning of unreality in the present, relics which could be used sporadically as stylistic variants of the present indicative. Mattsson's OE examples are sadly inadequate—the only *gif* clauses he cites have the subjunctive and are accompanied by Then-clauses with a volitional expression—and his whole argument seems to turn back on itself; see Kihlbom, *SN* 11 (1938–9), 257–60.

b. Then-clauses containing a 'volitional expression'

§3560. OE conditional sentences with a present indicative in the Then-clause (§§3556–9) are traditionally distinguished from those in which the *gif* clause is dependent on what is variously called a 'mandatory apodosis' (Mather, p. 24), a 'Vordersatz auffordernd-wünschend' (Wilde, p. 341), or 'an apodosis containing an expression of volition' (Behre, p. 132). Here, as elsewhere, I use Behre's term 'expression of volition' (p. 132) or 'volitional expression' (p. 134), which he defines as follows (p. 132):

1) an imperative, 2) a subjunctive of volition, 3) a *sceal*-construction, 4) an infinitive dependent on an expression of volition, 5) an expression of determination or intention with regard to the subject's own action. As examples: 1) *Saga, gif ðu cunne, on hwylcre þyssa þreora þeoden engla geþrowode þrymmes hyrde!* El. 857.—2) *Gyf hyt hwa gedo, ne gedige hit him næfre!* Charms 5 C: 13.— 3) *Gif her inne sy isenes dæl, hægtessan geweorc, hit sceal gemyltan.* Charms 2: 18.—4) *... bæd him for hungre hlafas wyrcan:* »gif þu swa micle mihte hæbbe.«) Sat. 674.—5) *... we him þa guð-getawa gyldan woldon, gif him þyslicu þearf gelumpe ...* Beow. 2637.

An example of (5) with the present tense appears to be

And 70　　　　Gif þin willa sie,　　wuldres aldor,
　　　　　　　　þæt me wærlogan　　wæpna ecgum,
　　　　　　　　sweordum, aswebban,　　ic beo sona gearu
　　　　　　　　to adreoganne　　þæt ðu, drihten min,
　　　　　　　　engla eadgifa,　　eðelleasum,
　　　　　　　　dugeða dædfruma,　　deman wille;

see Behre, p. 136, but note the indicatives in the *gif* clauses in *Beo* 1822 and

Jul 47   Gif þu soðne god
     lufast ond gelyfest,   ond his lof rærest,
     ongietest gæsta hleo,   ic beo gearo sona
     unwaclice   willan þines,

the only other examples with the same Then-clause in the poetry.

§3561. Then-clauses with a volitional expression, which are particularly common in legal codes, may have an expressed subject, e.g. *LawAf* 7. 1 *Gif he losige 7 hine mon eft gefo, forgielde he hine self a be his weregilde*, or an unexpressed one, e.g. *LawAf* 35 *Gif mon cierliscne mon gebinde unsynnigne, gebete mid x scill*; see Visser, i, §13, and my §1511.

§3562. The main problem peculiar to OE conditional sentences with a volitional expression in the Then-clause is the mood of the *gif* clause. On the basis of variations such as those in *CP* 31. 25 *forðæm gif he on ðæm wel deð, he hæfð ðæs god lean* but *CP* 357. 2 *Gif hio ðonne of oðres gewite, on ðæs oðres hio ðurhwunige*; in *ÆCHom* i. 56. 17 *We secgað eow Godes riht; healdað gif ge willon. Gif we hit forsuwiað, ne bið us geborgen* but *ÆCHom* i. 268. 19 *Gif he fealle, he eft astande*; in

Beo 445   Na þu minne þearft
     hafalan hydan,   ac he me habban wile
     dreore fahne,   gif mec deað nimeð

but

Beo 452   Onsend Higelace,   gif mec hild nime,
     beaduscruda betst,   þæt mine breost wereð . . . ;

and in

And 344   Gif ge syndon þegnas   þæs þe þrym ahof
     ofer middangeard,   swa ge me secgaþ,
     ond ge geheoldon þæt eow   se halga bead,
     þonne ic eow mid gefean   ferian wille
     ofer brimstreamas,   swa ge benan sint

but

And 417   Gif ðu þegn sie   þrymsittendes,
     wuldorcyninges,   swa ðu worde becwist,
     rece þa gerynu . . . ;

the following 'rule' is often established: 'the *gif* clause has the present indicative when the Then-clause has the present indicative, but the present subjunctive when the Then-clause has a volitional expression'. Before considering the validity of this, we may note that this problem has provoked a great many inaccurate statements. Sometimes these are the result of faulty observation, inadequate analysis, and poor method—Visser's almost complete failure (ii, §880) to quote the Then-clauses which accompany his *gif* clauses is remarkable in the light of his comments in ii, §860,[185] and leads him to the ambiguous and in the grammatical sense false remark that in the two examples from *Beowulf* quoted above 'the circumstances and situation were identical'. Sometimes they are the result of loose thinking —note Kihlbom's shift from 'almost exclusively' (*SN* 11 (1938-9), 257) to 'only' (ibid., pp. 259 and 261), her subsequent admission of 'exceptions in late OE prose' to the 'rule' which she modifies with these adverbs (ibid., p. 261, but see my §§3571-2), and her failure to note that both Behaghel (*DS* iii. 669-70) and Mattsson, whose article she attacked with some justice (see §3559), had quoted exceptions in other Germanic languages.

§3563. Behre's statement (p. 134) may be taken as a starting-point for our discussion: '. . . it is an indisputable fact that, if the apodosis contains an exhortation, wish, etc. addressed to others or an expression of determination with regard to the action of its subject, the subjunctive is found in the vast majority of cases. . . .' The fact that Behre does not use the blanket term 'an expression of volition' after the words 'if the apodosis contains' warns us that we must treat separately the five phenomena which Behre grouped under that term (my §3560). Let us start with the poetry, which was his main concern.

§3564. Here the subjunctive is the norm in *gif* clauses accompanied by a Then-clause containing an imperative, e.g. *Beo* 452 and *And* 417 (both in §3562); a jussive subjunctive, e.g.

---

[185] Visser makes the same mistake when comparing *Rid* 32. 13 with *Rid* 36. 12 (ii. 885) and when dealing with the mood of verbs in indefinite adjective clauses (ii, §876). For the same reason, the table and statistics for *gif* clauses presented by Wilde (pp. 338-40) are of little more than curiosity value. But he redeems himself later (pp. 341 ff.).

Again, Visser (ii. 886) observes that in *gif* clauses in *Juliana* there are twenty indicative or ambiguous verb-forms (his 'modally zero') against two subjunctives (his 'modally marked') viz. *þince* in *Jul* 87 and *weorþen* in *Jul* 335. My figures are twenty against three, counting *sin* in *Jul* 334 as subjunctive. What Visser fails to say is that these verbs occur in fifteen *gif* clauses; that in *Jul* 87 the Then-clause has an imperative and that in *Jul* 334 the Then-clause has two present subjunctives in dependent speech; that in *Jul* 201 we have *sceal* in the Then-clause and ind. *fylgest* in the *gif* clause; that in *Jul* 47 (§3560), *ic beo gearo sona* is accompanied by a *gif* clause with four indicatives; that in *Jul* 382 both verbs are ambiguous; and that in the remaining ten sentences, the verbs in the Then-clauses are indicative or ambiguous equivalents and the fourteen verbs in *gif* clauses are indicative. I have not analysed the figures he gives for Wulfstan. But I suspect the picture is similar. *Pace* Marino (*Mediaevalia*, 5 (1979), 1-2), all this shows how much detailed work remains to be done on OE.

PPs 94. 8 Gif ge to dæge drihtnes stefne
     holde gehyran, næfre ge heortan geþanc
     deorce forhyrden drihtnes willan

and *MCharm* 9. 13 *Gif hyt hwa gedo, ne gedige hit him næfre!*; or an unexpressed verb of command, e.g. *MCharm* 4. 6 *Ut lytel spere, gif her inne sie!* The subj. *durre* therefore supports Sisam's reading (p. 51) of

Seasons 168 Hige, synnig man, gyf þe susla weard
     costian durre, þonne he Crist dyde,
     wereda wulderfrean, womma leasne,
     ne mæg he þæs inne ahwæt scotian
     gif he myrcels næfþ manes æt egum,

where *þonne* represents Latin *sicut* and the ASPR version begins *Higesynnig man. . . .* The only exceptions with a present indicative in the *gif* clause are the easily understandable *mæg* after *mæge* in *Met* 23. 1 (see §3604) and possibly (if we compare *MCharm* 4. 6 and 4. 15, both in §3565)

Rid 11. 8   Wa him þæs þeawes,
     siþþan heah bringað horda deorast,
     gif hi unrædes ær ne geswicaþ.

On *Met* 10. 68, see §3558; on examples like *Vain* 77 (§1989) and *PPs* 65. 16 (§3595), where *gif* clauses have the preterite indicative, see §§3595–601. For a full list of examples, see Mitchell 1959, p. 843. So much, then, for Behre's groups A(1) and (2) (p. 132).

§3565. The situation is quite different when the Then-clause contains a form of **sculan* (Behre's group A(3)). Here the verb of the *gif* clause is indicative, as in

Beo 683   ac wit on niht sculon
     secge ofersittan, gif he gesecean dear
     wig ofer wæpen

(eleven definite examples; see Mitchell 1959, p. 843), or ambiguous, as in

MRune 2 Sceal ðeah manna gehwylc miclun hyt dælan
    gif he wile for drihtne domes hleotan

(three definite examples; see ibid.). The only definite example with the subjunctive is

MCharm 4. 18 Gif her inne sy isernes dæl,
     hægtessan geweorc, hit sceal gemyltan.

This can be explained as a repetition of the *gif* clauses in *MCharm* 4. 6 and 4. 15 *Ut, lytel spere, gif her inne sy!*; cf. *MCharm* 4. 12 *Ut,*

lytel spere, gif hit her inne sy! In *And* 1520, *gif* may introduce a
nexus question. Here Behre's preoccupation with the subjunctive has
betrayed him; his three examples (p. 150) are *MCharm* 4. 18 and two
gif clauses with preterite verb-forms in dependent speech—a construction he does not include among his 'expressions of volition'
(p. 132).

§3566. In Behre's group A(4) (p. 132), 'the apodosis contains . . .
an infinitive dependent on an expression of volition', as in

Sat 670   Brohte him to bearme   brade stanas,
                bæd him for hungre   hlafas wyrcan—
                'gif þu swa micle   mihte hæbbe'.

This, as *Sat* 670 and his other examples (p. 150) demonstrate, is a
clumsy way of saying that the *gif* clause is dependent on an accusative and infinitive after a verb of commanding. I can see no logical
justification for the inclusion of these examples and the exclusion of
gif clauses in dependent speech from Behre's definition (p. 132).
I agree with the latter decision. So I leave examples with the accusative and infinitive for discussion in §§3787-8. Behre (pp. 150-1)
further confuses the issue by including among examples of his group
A(5)—'the apodosis contains an expression of determination or intention with regard to the subject's action'—only *gif* clauses which
are in dependent speech and/or which express unfulfilled conditions.
All have preterite verb-forms. These I discuss below as they become
relevant. Behre (p. 151) adds as group 6 two examples in which 'the
volitional attitude is not clearly expressed in the apodosis', viz. *And*
70 (but see §3560) and *Rid* 4. 7 (but see §3624).

§3567. So the 'rule' for the poetry must be restated: in a conditional
sentence in which both clauses have verbs in the present tense, the
verb of the *gif* clause is indicative unless the Then-clause contains an
imperative or a jussive subjunctive. Then it can be subjunctive; cf. the
situation in clauses of time (§§2615-21). Some exceptions have
been discussed in §§3556-9. More will be found below.

§3568. Behre's phrase 'vast majority' (see my §3563) was not intended to apply to the prose, but it is capable of giving a misleading
impression about the general situation in OE. It is easy enough to
find examples in the prose which conform to Behre's 'rule' if we dismiss (as I do) his categories 4, 5, and 6, and if we exclude *willan*,
which—one would have thought—would very often function as an

'expression of volition', but which consistently goes with an indicative in an accompanying *gif* clause, e.g. *CP* 63. 3, *ÆCHom* i. 68. 24, and

Mald 36   Gyf þu þæt gerædest,   þe her ricost eart,

                 . . .   . . .

              we willaþ mid þam sceattum   us to scype gangan . . . ,

although there are the inevitable exceptions, e.g. *Bo* 89. 20 *Gif þonne hwelc mon mæge gesion þa birhtu þæs heofenlican leohtes . . . , þonne wile he cweðan . . .* , *ÆCHom* i. 388. 29 *We willað nu mid sumere scortre trahtnunge þas rædinge oferyrnan and geopenian, gif heo hwæt digles on hyre hæbbende sy*, and possibly

El 788   . . . swa ic þe, weroda wyn,   gif hit sie willa þin,
                 þurg þæt beorhte gesceap   biddan wille
                 þæt me þæt goldhord,   gasta scyppend,
                 geopenie,   þæt yldum wæs
                 lange behyded,

where, however, the *gif* clause probably belongs in the dependent desire (see §1978), since it is God's will that men pray.

§3569. Thus, we find (with an imperative) *CP* 43. 4 *Fed ðonne min sceap, gif ðu me lufige* and *ÆCHom* i. 170. 1 *Gif ðu Godes Sunu sy, sceot adun*; (with a jussive subjunctive) *CP* 323. 4 *Gif hwa ðenige, ðenige he suelce he hit of Godes mægene ðenige . . .* and *ÆCHom* i. 96. 1 *ac gif hit him dyslic þince, þonne cide he wið God*; (with *uton* + infinitive) *Solil* 46. 14 *Ac gyf unc swa þince, uton gebyddan unc hær dæglanges* and *HomU* 35. 209. 5 *utan frefrian ahwænede and hyrtan ormode, alysan gehæfte, gif us to þam onhagie*;[186] and (with a form of **sculan*) *CP* 367. 22 *Ac gif we wilnigen ðæt hie ðæs wos geswicen, ðonne sculon we hie ealra ðinga ærest 7 geornost læran ðæt hie ne wilnigen leasgielpes*, *ÆCHom* i. 156. 21, and *ÆC Hom* ii. 460. 12 *Gif ure ænigum sum ungelimp becume, ðonne sceole we beon gemyndige þises mæran weres*. . . . For more examples, see Wülfing, ii, §449, and Mather, pp. 31–3 and 85–6.

§3570. But, as in the poetry, Behre's rule works only very occasionally for Then-clauses containing a form of **sculan*. We find inexplicable variations in parallel sentences, e.g. *Lch* ii. 22. 3 *gif seo adl sie cumen of micelre hæto, þonne sceal man mid cealdum læcedomum lacnian . gif hio of cealdum intingan cymð, þonne sceal mon*

---

[186] I have recorded no examples from the poetry of *gif* clauses with a Then-clause containing *uton* + infinitive. But a principal clause with *uton* + infinitive is accompanied by a temporal clause with the present subjunctive in *PPs* 136. 7 (*oðþæt*) and in *ChristB* 771 and *Partridge* 12 (*þenden*).

mid hatum læcedomum lacnian, and numerous exceptions, including *Bede* 86. 16 *Gif þær þonne oðre seon, þe ða þegnunge gefyllan mægge, þonne sceal he hine eaðmodlice ahabban from onsægdnesse þæs halgan gerynes, þæs þe ic demo* (for more from 'Alfredian' texts see Wülfing, ii, §448) and the following typical examples from *ÆCHom*: *ÆCHom* i. 14. 12, 122. 35, 162. 27, 170. 15, 174. 33, 274. 9, 274. 12, 416. 20, 428. 28, 484. 6, 590. 2, and 594. 3, *ÆC Hom* ii. 282. 22, 324. 2 (cf. 324. 28), 374. 3, and *ÆCHom* ii. 278. 27 *and we sceolon mid biternysse soðre behreowsunge ure mod geclænsian, gif we willað Cristes lichaman ðicgan*. These can be paralleled from other texts. So Wülfing (ii, §449) was on firm ground when he omitted **sculan* from his list of phenomena which were accompanied by a subjunctive in a *gif* clause.

§3571. But, even apart from these variations, the number of breaches of both sorts—indicative where the 'rule' requires a subjunctive and subjunctive where it requires an indicative—is greater than Behre or any other scholar has recognized or has been willing to admit. We find variations between manuscripts, e.g. *Bo(C)* 19. 11 *Hu wilt þu nu andwyrdan þæm woruldsælðum gif hi cweðað to þe* . . . , where MS *B* has *cwðan*, and *Bo(C)* 114. 9 *Gif eac hwylc good man from gode gewit, þonne ne bið he þon ma fullice good gif he eallunga from gewit*, where MS *B* has . . . *gif he eallunga from gode gewite*; variations in glosses, e.g. *Matt(Li)* 6. 23 *gif uutedlice ego ðin unbliðe ł yfelwyrcende se ł byð all lichoma ðin ðiostrig bið*, where the Latin has *fuerit* . . . *erit*; variations in parallel *gif* clauses dependent on the same Then-clause, e.g. *Exod* 22. 7 *Gyf hwa befæste his feoh to hyrdnesse 7 hit man forstylð þam þe hit underfehð, gyf man þone þeof finde, gylde be twifealdon*; variations in co-ordinate clauses (despite Hotz, p. 58), e.g. *Lch* ii. 94. 23 *Gif mon mid treowe geslegen sie oððe mid stane oþþe byl on men gebersteð to þon dohlsealf gyþrife ontre gelodwyrt sigelhweorfa gecnuwa þa wyrta swiþe* . . . and *LawAbt* 3 *Gif cyning æt mannes ham drincæþ 7 ðær man lyswæs hwæt gedo, twibote gebete*; variations in parallel sentences, e.g. *Bo* 114. 7, *LawAbt* 10 *Gif man wið cyninges mægdenman geligeþ, L scillinga gebete*. [11] *Gif hio grindende þeowa sio, xxv scillinga gebete, ÆCHom* ii. 104. 1 *Teoh ðu forð renscuras, gif ðu miht, and gewætera ðine æceras. Gif ðu mage, do þæt sunne scine, þæt ðine æceras ripion, Exod* 1. 16 *gyf hit hisecyld biþ, ofsleaþ þæt, gyf hit mædencyld sy, healdað þæt, ApT* 24. 8 *Gif ðu for neode axsast æfter minum naman, ic secge þe ic hine forleas on sæ. Gif ðu wilt mine æðelborennesse witan, wite ðu þæt ic hig forlet on Tharsum*, and *Ch* 1483 *W* 6. 26 *gif he bern habben, þanne an ic hem, gif he non ne habbeþ* [Addit. MS *habben*] *þanne an ic it Athelfleð mine douh-ter* . . . ; variations in *gif* clauses with no Then-clause, e.g. *Lch* ii. 4. 7 *Læcedom gif mon blod hræce* but *Lch* ii. 6. 21 *Læcedomas gif mannes getawa beoþ sare oþþe aþundene*; and variations in 'formulae of polite address' (see Mather, pp. 22–3 and 34–5), e.g. *CP* 7. 6 *Forðy me ðyncð betre, gif iow swæ ðyncð* . . . but *Bede* 392. 32 *Ic wille 7 me leof is, gif ðu mæge.* For more breaches of the 'rule', see Hotz (pp. 56–7), Mather (pp. 86–7), and the late additions in *ChronE* 33. 15 (656) and 37. 23 (675).

§3572. The degree of inconsistency within different texts or groups of texts varies. I have space to consider only a few. Here again there is room for more work. Departures from the 'rule' in *gif* clauses accompanied by a Then-clause with an indicative, an imperative, or a jussive subjunctive, are not common in 'Alfredian' texts. A few have just been quoted. Others include (jussive subjunctive + indicative) *CP* 103. 9 *Gif hie ðonne giet ðær tueonað, gongen ðonne to ðæm halgan gewritum, CP(H)* 199. 7 *Ac gif he ðonne eallunge forberan ne mæg* . . . *ðonne sprecen hie ymbe his ða læstan unðeawas* . . . (but MS *C* has 198. 7 *Ac gif hie ðonne eallunga forberan ne mægen* . . .) and *Bede(T)* 64. 25 (but MS *B* has *syn* for *synd* and both forms can be regarded as ambiguous; cf. *Bede* 76. 19, where again there is manuscript variation between *syn* and *synd*); (imperative + depen-dent question + indicative) *Bo* 27. 18 *Geþenc nu hwæt þines agnes sie ealra ðissa woruldæhta 7 welena, oððe hwæt þu þæron age unandergildes, gif þu him sceadwislice æfter spyrest*; and (present indicative + subjunctive in *gif* clause) *Bede* 442. 9 and *Bo* 30. 7 (both in §3557).

§3573. Here, as with clauses introduced by *seþe* (see §§2397–8), the legal codes are markedly inconsistent and cry out for a complete study. In some, all jussive subjunctives—imperatives, as in *LawIne* 22, are rare—are accompanied by a subjunctive in the *gif* clause, e.g. I, II, and III, Eadmund (*LawIIEm* 1. 1 has two *gif* clauses—one with the subjunctive accompanying *wille ic* and one with the indica-tive in dependent speech) and I, II, and III, Eadgar.

§3574. As far as I have observed, there are no codes which have only the indicative in *gif* clauses accompanied by a jussive subjunc-tive. I Wilhelm seems to be the most consistent in its preference for the indicative. The table which follows gives the mood of the verbs in the conditional clauses in the OE and the Latin. All the Then-clauses in both languages have the subjunctive.

LawWl	Verb in *gif* clause	Verb in *si* clause
1	beclypað	compellet, *v.l.* compellat
1. 1	forsæcð	nolit, *v.l.* noluit
1. 2	beclypað	compellet, *v.l.* compellat
	byð	placeat
2. 1	byð	sit
	nelle	nolit
	mage	possit
2. 2	byð	fuerit
2. 3	nele	nolit
3. 1	beclypað	appellet, *v.l.* appellat
	wille	uelit
3. 2	durre	audeat

This table evokes the following comments: all the Latin verb-forms in *si* clauses in the base manuscript are unambiguously subjunctive except *fuerit* (perfect subjunctive or future perfect indicative); four variant readings in other Latin manuscripts substitute indicative forms; the only unambiguously subjunctive OE verb-form is *mage*; despite *OEG*, §768, *nelle, nele, wille*, and *wile*, may (I believe) all be indicative forms in the first and third person singular (see SB, §428); and finally, the compiler of the Anglo-Saxon code, with his preference for the indicative, shows a sturdy disregard for the Latin usage. Whether his preference for the indicative can be attributed to French influence is an obvious question. It seems unlikely. Jeannine Alton (private communication) has kindly provided me with an analysis of the *si* clauses in both manuscripts of Leis Willelme (Liebermann, i. 492–520). The approximate figures (there are a few difficult forms) for those *si* clauses which are not co-ordinate with a following clause are given in the accompanying table. (On the examples in which *si* is followed by two clauses in co-ordination, see §3588.)

Leis Willelme	*Si* clause subjunctive		*Si* clause indicative	
	MS *Hk*	MS *I*	MS *Hk*	MS *I*
Then-clause indicative	0	0	18	18
Then-clause subjunctive	6	7	8	17

There is thus a general predominance of the indicative in *si* clauses. But in those sentences in which the Then-clause has the subjunctive, the predominance of the indicative in *si* clauses is so far from overwhelming that we can virtually rule out the possibility that French influence lies behind the Anglo-Saxon I Wilhelm's preference for the indicative.

§3575. Some codes show a marked preference for a subjunctive *gif* clause when the Then-clause has a jussive subjunctive, e.g. those of Hloþhære and Eadric and of Ine. Viewed from our present point of view, Alfred's Laws fall into two distinct sections: *LawsAf* 1-43, where the subjunctive is overwhelmingly predominant—when accompanied by a jussive subjunctive, the indicative occurs only in *LawsAf* 12, 25, and 36—and *LawsAf* 44-77, where the subjunctive and the indicative are equally prominent in the same circumstances. But IV Eadgar, in marked contrast to I, II, and III, Eadgar (§3573) shows a marked preference for the indicative.

§3576. In the Laws of Æðelberht I find—*pace* Hotz (p. 57) and Mather (p. 12)—seventy-nine indicatives and seventeen subjunctives in *gif* clauses accompanied by a jussive subjunctive. Of these ninety-six forms, *weorþan* has thirty present indicative forms—*(ge)weorþeþ* 17, *(ge)weorþ* (see *OEG*, §201(1)) 12, *worðeþ* 1—but no subjunctives; the verb 'to be' has ten subjunctive forms but only two indicative, viz. *LawsAbt* 77 and 77. 1; *gedon, slean,* and *stelan,* have both indicative and subjunctive forms; *LawAbt* 79 has *wille, LawAbt* 80 *wile* (on these forms see §3574); and the remaining verbs have only indicative forms. The inconsistency extends to co-ordinate clauses governed by the same *gif* in *LawAbt* 3 (§3571); see §§3585 and 3718 for Hotz's observations (pp. 57-8) on such variations. Liebermann dates this code 601-4. But he dates the *Textus Roffensis* from which it is taken *c.*1120, a date confirmed by Ker (p. 443)—'compiled almost certainly in the time of Bishop Ernulf (1115-24)'. So is this an 'early' or a 'late' code? Mather (p. 12) takes it as early: 'If we may trust to the antiquity and reasonably faithful transmission, so far as syntax is concerned, by Alfred [why?] of Æðelbirht's Laws, circa 610, the indic. originally stood in such conditions and the subj. was just beginning to intrude at that time.' But Kihlbom (*SN* 11 (1938-9), 261) speaks of 'the Anglo-Saxon laws (Hotz, p. 57)' providing 'exceptions in late OE prose'. I return to this problem of mood variation in §3588.

§3577. A similar variety of constructions will be found in the laws set out in *Exod* 21 and 22. Typical examples include (indicative Then-clause + indicative) *Exod* 21. 19 *Gyf he arist ꝣ ut gæð mid his stafe, he bið unscyldig þe hine sloh*; (indicative Then-clause +

subjunctive) *Exod* 22. 2 *Gyf man ðeof gemete 7 he hus brece 7 hine man þær gewundie, se slaga bið unscyldig*; (jussive subjunctive Then-clause + subjunctive) *Exod* 21. 27 *Gyf he toð of aslea, læte hig frige*; (imperative Then-clause + subjunctive) *Exod* 22. 26 *Gyf ðu wed nime æt ðinum nextan, agyf him his reaf ær sunnan setlunge*; and (jussive subjunctive Then-clause + indicative) *Exod* 21. 2 *Gyf ðu Ebreiscne ðeow bigst, þeowige ðe syx gear 7 beo him freoh on ðam seofoðan.*

§3578. Again, eleven of the fourteen examples from the Gospels quoted by Visser (ii. 884) have the present tense. Six of them conform to the 'rule': *Matt* 5. 39 and 4. 3 (not 18. 3), and *Mark* 4. 23 and 7. 16 (imperative or jussive subjunctive + subjunctive); *Matt* 4. 9 and 5. 46 (indicative + indicative). But five offend against it: *Matt* 4. 6 and 18. 15, *Mark* 9. 47, and *John* 8. 39 and 14. 15 (imperative + indicative). His list is not complete; see Mather, p. 87.

§3579. Mather (pp. 79 and 86) reports that the *Blickling Homilies* and those in Napier's collection 'seldom admit an indic.' in a *gif* clause with 'a mandatory apodosis'.

§3580. I conclude this survey with Ælfric, who is a frequent offender against the 'rule', using both subjunctive and indicative in *gif* clauses with an accompanying imperative, e.g. *ÆCHom* i. 56. 17 *We secgað eow Godes riht; healdað gif ge willon* and *ÆCHom* ii. 256. 5 *Gif ðu Godes Sunu sy, ga of ðære rode* but *ÆCHom* i. 54. 17 *Gif ðu offrast ðine lac to Godes weofode, and þu þær gemyndig bist þæt ðin broðor hæfð sum ðing ongean ðe, forlæt ðærrihte ða lac ætforan ðam weofode* . . . and *ÆCHom* ii. 294. 3 *Gif ge willað beon se dæg þe ic worhte, lybbað þonne rihtlice* . . . , and with an accompanying jussive subjunctive, e.g. *ÆCHom* i. 96. 1 *ac gif hit him dyslic þince, þonne cide he wið God* and *ÆCHom* ii. 48. 33 *Gif se lareow riht tæce, do gehwa swa swa he tæcð* but *ÆCHom* i. 124. 33 *Gif his hreofla bið godigende, þæt is gif he yfeles geswicð, and his ðeawas ðurh Godes ege gerihtlæcð, he hæbbe wununge betwux cristenum mannum* and *ÆCHom* ii. 488. 6 *and beo siððan Godes grama ofer us gif we æfre to hæðenum gylde bugað*. For more such *gif* clauses with the indicative, from Ælfric and elsewhere, see Mather, pp. 31–3 and 86–7.

§3581. We now see from our consideration of adjective clauses (§§2391–8), temporal clauses (§§2610–21), and conditional clauses, that blanket terms such as 'expressions of volition' are unserviceable.

Gif clauses containing forms of **sculan* and of *willan* or formulae such as *ic beo sona gearu* have a subjunctive rarely, not regularly. With an imperative or a jussive subjunctive in the Then-clause, the 'rule' adumbrated in §3562 obtains much more regularly. But the extent to which it is valid has been greatly exaggerated. Too many previous writers seem to have taken it almost for granted without establishing the facts; they were more concerned with discussing one or both of these questions: Which was the original mood in such conditional sentences? What is the nature of the subjunctive in the *gif* clause? I do not attempt to answer either of them, but cannot avoid a few comments which will, I hope, be of use to future workers.

§3582. Mather appears to contradict himself on the first question. As already noted in §3576, he argued that the preponderance of indicatives in the Laws of Æðelberht established the indicative as the earlier idiom (p. 12). But, both earlier in his book (p. 8) and later (pp. 30 and 79), he attributed the indicative to Latin influence— Behre (p. 134) accepts this—and argued (p. 30) that 'the better texts show a preponderance of the subj., abundantly large to establish it as the better idiom'. This would seem to imply that the subjunctive was the original mood and the indicative the intruder, sometimes perhaps under Latin influence and sometimes as part of the native development by which the indicative became the norm in MnE. This in turn would mean that the preponderance of indicatives in Æðelberht's code—for which Liebermann offers no corresponding Latin—and in that of I Wilhelm—which, as we have seen in §3574, is in this respect at any rate independent of the Latin—represents a later, not an earlier, stage. More work is needed here both on OE and on its Germanic cognates.

§3583. I turn now to the second question—the nature of the subjunctive in a *gif* clause accompanied by an imperative, a jussive subjunctive, or one of the other phenomena discussed above. Until the facts are established—and, in Mather's immortal words (p. 7), 'there is a certain humble satisfaction even in an unintelligent knowledge of the facts'—I can find no enthusiasm for a long discussion about the nature of the subjunctive in these *gif* clauses or for a searching enquiry into the minds of those who did and those who did not use them. Anyone who can summon up the necessary enthusiasm will find plenty of material, much of which either reveals ignorance of, or suppresses the number of exceptions to, the 'rule'. Some of the main protagonists are mentioned below. Numerous references to others will be found in their works; see also Mitchell 1959, pp. 587–91. I content myself here with brief comments on the main theories.

§3584. BTS (s.v. *gif*), struggling desperately to maintain the proposition that the present indicative denotes certainty, reality, or truth, whereas the present subjunctive implies uncertainty or hypothesis, observes of *Matt(WSCp)* 4. 3 *Gyf þu godes sunu sy cweð þ þas stanas to hlafe gewurðon*, Latin *Si filius dei es dic ut lapides isti panes fiant*, and *Matt(WSCp)* 4. 6 *Gyf þu godes sunu eart asend þe þonne nyðer*, Latin *Si filius dei es mitte te deorsum*, that 'perhaps the different renderings of the same Latin words are intended to mark a change in the speaker's mind. . . . But sometimes the distinction seems not very clearly marked.' It certainly escaped the man who wrote *BlHom* 27. 5 *Gif þu sie Godes sunu cweþ þæt þa stanas to hlafum geweorþan* and *BlHom* 27. 10 *Gif þu sy Godes sunu send þe nyþer of þisse heanesse*. This view has been criticized and/or rejected by Mather (pp. 6-12),[187] Behre (pp. 131-2), Muxin (*UZLGU* 262, vyp. 50 (1958), 158-9), and Visser (ii. 882), but is still purveyed by some of the standard primers, e.g. QW (pp. 83-4). We can reject it, with the qualification made in §3553.

§3585. Hotz (p. 57) advanced the theory that these *gif*-clause subjunctives were due to 'an external law . . . of symmetry', but came close to contradicting himself when he asserted (pp. 57-8) that in examples like *Exod(L)* 21. 28 *Gif oxa hnite wer oððe wif 7 hig deade beoð, si he mid stanum oftorforod* and *Exod* 22. 7 *Gyf hwa befæste his feoh to hyrdnesse 7 hit man forstylð þam þe hit underfehð, gyf man þone þeof finde, gylde be twifealdon* the variation in mood is used 'to set off a condition from a subordinate one. . . . It seems not to matter, whether the subj. be nearest to the optat. or imperative, or not, provided that the indic. alternate with the subj.' (On this claim, see §3718.) Mather (pp. 8-9) criticizes the idea that this use of the subjunctive is 'wholly mechanical and irrational', pointing out that *butan* clauses—not considered by Hotz—are not susceptible to the 'law of symmetry', since they regularly have the subjunctive even when the Then-clause has the indicative, as it usually does. This theory of 'symmetry' or 'mood-attraction' was opposed by Behre (pp. 133-4)—though scarcely 'disproved'; cf. his pp. 136-7 —and by Kihlbom (*SN* 11 (1938-9), 258), who gives references to the main discussions.

§3586. Behre (p. 137) and Kihlbom (*SN* 11 (1938-9), 257-8 and 264-6) discuss the theory advanced by Delbrück and Vogt—Kihlbom again gives the references—that the subjunctive under discus-

---

[187] As I point out in my unpublished MA thesis, pp. 359-65 (for details see §2678 fn.), Mather's argument here seems to me somewhat confused.

sion is one of conditionality or potentiality. Neither regards it as satisfactory. (But note Behre's comments on 'potentiality' and 'unreality' (pp. 51 and 60).) However, Mann (*Archiv*, 197 (1960-1), 21) bluntly asserts that 'dieser Optativ ist potential'.

§3587. Other writers have glanced at the idea that the subjunctive is due to the adhortative or advisory nature of the Then-clause; see Mather (pp. 8-12)—'the subj. in such clauses is then rather adhortative, at least in origin, than potential or hypothetical'—Glunz (pp. 38-47 and 74-6), and Muxin (*UZLGU* 262, vyp. 50 (1958), 158-9). The view is 'denied' by Behre (pp. 141-3) and by Kihlbom (*SN* 11 (1938-9), 260-1 and 264).

§3588. Kihlbom (*SN* 11 (1938-9), 264) accepts Behre's conclusions for his group A examples (my §§3564-6 and 3589): 'The only explanation which can be reconciled with and fully covers all the facts of the case, both the early state of things and the later history, is that suggested by Behre who on the basis of the OE usage regards these subjunctives as *volitional-meditative*.' But I have to say that nothing said by Behre himself or by those he condemns can explain to me the variations between the indicative and the subjunctive in *gif* clauses accompanied by an imperative or a jussive subjunctive, which I cite above from many sources, including the Laws of Æðelberht and *Exod* 21 and 22. Any competent psychiatrist would be tempted to diagnose schizophrenia in those responsible for these variations if Behre (p. 134) is right—'It stands to reason, therefore, that we should search for the explanation of the subjunctive in conditional clauses connected with a volitional apodosis in the mental attitude reflected by the volitional expression of the apodosis'—and to agree with Visser (ii. 886) who, after citing numerous variations like that seen in *Luke(WSCp)* 10. 6 *And gyf þar beoð sybbe bearn reste þar eower sib gif hit elles sy heo sy to eow gecyrred*, says: 'It is hardly conceivable that this should have to do with the attitude of the speaker towards the realisation of what is referred to in the *if*-clause'; cf. here Liggins 1955, pp. 271-9. But the problem is not confined to OE, as a comparison of the following examples will show: *LawAbt* 3 *Gif cyning æt mannes ham drincæþ 7 ðær man lyswæs hwæt gedo, twibote gebete* (indicative + subjunctive in *gif* clause, subjunctive in Then-clause); *Exod* 22. 10 *Gyf hwa befæste his nyxtan ænig nyten 7 hit bið dead oþþe gelewed oþþe ætbroden 7 hit nan man ne gesyhð*, [11.] *Sylle him aþ 7 ne nyde hine to gylde* (subjunctive + indicative + indicative in *gif* clause, subjunctive in Then-clause); *LeisWl(Hk)* 2. 3 *E cil francs hom ki ad e sache e soche e toll e tem e infangentheof, se il est enplaidé e il seit mis en forfeit el cunté, afert a l'os le vescunte en Denelahe xl ores* (indicative + subjunctive in *se* clause, indicative in Then-clause); *LeisWl(Hk)* 10 *Si hom fait plaie en auter e il deive faire les amendes, primereinement lui rende sien lecheof* (indicative + subjunctive in *si* clause, subjunctive in Then-clause); *LeisWl(Hk)* 20. 2a *E s'il fust desaparaillé, qu'il n'oust cheval ne armes, fuste quite par C sol* (subjunctive + subjunctive in *si* clause, subjunctive in Then-clause); and MnFr *S'il vient et que je le voie, je lui dirai. . . .*

§3589. And so we wind to Behre's theory but, unlike the weariest river, not safe. As I have already noted (§3543 fn.), I cannot follow some of Behre's arguments. But he sums up the difference in meaning between an indicative and a subjunctive Then-clause thus (p. 51):

The former is presented to the hearer in a first-hand and direct manner without any implication as to the speaker's mental attitude towards its realization or reality. The latter is presented to the hearer not first-hand and direct but as having been submitted to the reflection and meditation of the speaker with regard to its realization or reality. The latter has often an emotional or optative tone.

On the moods in *gif* clauses, where he distinguishes group A, e.g.

Jul 87   Dem þu hi to deaþe,   gif þe gedafen þince,
              swa to life læt,   swa þe leofre sy,

from group B, which includes examples like *Met* 23. 1 (§3604) as well as those with the preterite subjunctive discussed in my §§3606–11, he concludes (p. 141):

To sum up, the subjunctive as met with in *gif (þær)*-clauses is used to express either a volitional-meditative (Group A) or a meditative-volitional (emotional) (Group B) attitude towards the realization or reality of the dependent clause. In either case the subjunctive has reference to an assumed event. From this it does not follow, as has often been maintained, that the subjunctive of the protasis of a conditional period has simply the function of representing the content of the conditional clause as assumed. All clauses of condition, including those in the indicative, express something as assumed. But the indicative is used in the protasis to present an assumed event to the judgment of the hearer in a first-hand and direct manner without any implication as to the speaker's mental attitude, whereas the subjunctive is used to express a volitional or meditative attitude towards the assumed event expressed by the protasis.

To this we must add his rider (p. 135) that 'in most cases the volitional (optative) subjunctive, as occurring in a protasis connected with a volitional apodosis, has a concessive aspect'. I postpone discussion of Behre's group B to §§3606-11, with the confession that the more I ponder the exquisite distinction between 'volitional-meditative' and 'meditative-volitional', the more confused I become.

§3590. So I conclude that, if the alleged distinction was ever fully established, it was already moribund in OE. Here I agree with Visser (ii. 885):

It seems a fair conjecture that, however rigidly in pre-historic Old English the use of the modally marked form may have been determined by the speaker's attitude towards the realisation of the activity or state in the *if*-clause, in the existing Old English documents there was a tendency to consider the modality of the conditional clause already sufficiently expressed by the conjunction—as it actually was in the numerous cases in which only one form of the verb was available (e.g. 'gif ic smeage'; 'gif ic smeade'; 'gif þu ride' (preterite); 'gif he wolde'; 'gif he dyde'; 'gif he fremede')—and that consequently the additional signalling of this modality by a special form of the verb was felt as redundant. (This tendency may have been stronger in the spoken language, but this is not provable.)

Hence we would have the situation that some writers used the indicative and subjunctive more or less consistently according to the 'rule', that some tended to use only the indicative, and that some used the two moods almost haphazardly. We might compare the situation which I postulate in §800 for the passive auxiliaries *wesan* and *weorþan* and might consider the status of MnE 'If that is/be true . . .' and 'If he was/were here . . .'. I must leave this discussion here. Those wishing to go further should consult Kihlbom (*SN* 11 (1938-9), 261-6), who pursues it into later stages of English. Mather (p. 7) is persuaded that the use of the present subjunctive which we have been discussing is not 'fortuitous and irrational'. Dr Johnson, it will be remembered, put a notably contrary point of view which has some relevance here: 'It may be reasonably imagined that what is so much in the power of men as language will very often be capriciously conducted.'

c. Other examples

§3591. I discuss in §§3603-4 a few conditional sentences which, while having the present tense in both clauses, do not conform to either of the patterns already discussed.

4. OPEN CONDITIONS INTRODUCED BY *GIF* WITH THE PRETERITE TENSE IN BOTH CLAUSES

a. Examples with the preterite indicative or an ambiguous equivalent

§3592. Here we may quote as typical *CP* 253. 7 *Gif ic ryhtwis wæs, ne ahof ic me no forðy* (arguably a conceded condition), *LS* 23. 135

ac gif heora hwilc operne feorran geseah wið his weard, he sona of þam siðfæte beah, ÆCHom ii. 392. 10 *Gif min fot aslad, Drihten, ðin mildheortnys geheolp me,* and

Rid 42. 3   hwitloc anfeng
          wlanc under wædum,   gif þæs weorces speow,
          fæmne fyllo.

In the last three examples *gif* could be translated 'whenever' without undue distortion.

§3593. Sentences such as the following, which have an indicative in one clause and an ambiguous form in the other, can reasonably be taken as open: *Bede* 162. 4 *7 gif þæt wæs, þæt hwæþere seldon gelomp, þæt he to cyninges simble gelaþad wære, eode he in mid ane oððe mid twam his preosta,* ÆCHom i. 332. 4 *Ðam rican wæs forgolden mid ðam hwilwendlicum spedum, gif he hwæt to gode gefremode; and ðam ðearfan wæs forgolden mid ðære yrmðe, gif he hwæt to yfle gefremode, Ex* 240, and

Met 1. 25   Wæs gehwæðeres waa.
          þeah wæs magorinca   mod mid Grecum
          gif hi leodfruman   læstan dorsten.

So too can some sentences with ambiguous verb-forms in both clauses, e.g. *Bede* 162. 12 *Ond he þes biscop ricum monnum no for are ne for ege næfre forswigian nolde, gif heo on hwon agylton, ac he mid heardre þrea hiæ onspræc 7 heo gebette* (note Miller's 'when they did anything wrong'), ÆCHom i. 80. 7 *þa gewende he to Rome, be ðæs caseres hæse, þæt he hine betealde, gif he mihte. þa betealde he hine swiðe geaplice . . .* , ÆCHom i. 534. 3 *He nahte geðyld gif hine hwa to goddre drohtnunge tihte,* and

PPs 68. 11   Gif ic mine gewæda   on witehrægl
           cyme cyrde,   cwædan hi syþþan,
           þæt ic him wæfersyn   wære eallum.

Mather (pp. 84–5) gives references to more examples, but the reader will need to examine each one for himself.

b. Some difficult examples

§3594. Problems of classification, however, do sometimes arise when both clauses have ambiguous forms. In *Or* 86. 10 *gif hie þonne soð ne sædon, þonne næron naþer gode ne þa, ne nu,* we probably have an open condition, with indicative-equivalent verb-forms, rather than an imaginary condition, with subjunctive equivalents. The fact that Edmund was subsequently killed suggests that the condition is open in *ÆLS* 32. 79 *ac ic wolde swiðor sweltan gif ic þorfte for minum agenum earde*. In *ÆLS* 26. 249 *Nu ic sceall geendian earmlicum deaþe and to helle faran for fracodum dædum, nu wolde ic gebetan gif ic abidan moste and to gode gecyrran*, the speaker's *ic sceall* suggests that he regards his desire as remote or impossible. Yet in fact, the man *syððan leofode lange on wurulde and gewende to gode* (*ÆLS* 26. 265). 'To God all things are possible.' In *ÆCHom* ii. 88. 18 *Hwa wolde me æfre gelyfan, gif ic wolde gereccan þæt ðornas getacnodon welan, ðonne ðornas priciað, and ða welan gelustfulliað? Ac swa ðeah hi sind untwylice ðornas . . .* , the remote *wolde* forms are for rhetorical purposes. One can see why Mather (pp. 33–4) grouped it among his examples of 'the ideal or purely hypothetical condition'. But, as we see, Ælfric goes on to fulfil the condition. In *ÆLet* 4. 1007 *ða ge mihton rædan 7 eow aræman on þam, gif ge holde wæron eowrum agenum sawlum*, it is unlikely that Ælfric was implying uncertainty or impossibility; we can compare

And 478

Wolde ic freondscipe,
þeoden þrymfæst,   þinne, gif ic mehte,
begitan godne,

where *wolde* and *mehte* express politeness, not uncertainty, or, as Behre puts it (p. 139), 'an attitude of modesty or reserve on the part of the speaker'. He interprets these ambiguous forms as ('moderative') subjunctives. He could be right; cf. *ÆCHom* i. 40. 26 *We mihton eow secgan ane lytle bysne, gif hit to waclic nære: sceawa nu on anum æge . . .* , where the subj. *nære* suggests remoteness or impossibility but Ælfric goes on to give his little comparison. The last example here is

GenB 409

Gif ic ænegum þægne   þeodenmadmas
geara forgeafe,   þenden we on þan godan rice
gesælige sæton   and hæfdon ure setla geweald,
þonne he me na on leofran tid   leanum ne meahte
mine gife gyldan . . . ,

where Behre (pp. 139–40) detects 'a feigned attitude of modesty' on Satan's part. A conceded condition is presented as remote or uncertain. I see here two implications: 'Of course I did!' and 'Somebody had better!' (Campbell (*RES* 10 (1959), 187) has a different explanation. This is one of the rare occasions on which I disagree with him.)

5. OPEN CONDITIONS INTRODUCED BY *GIF* WITH THE PRETERITE TENSE IN ONE CLAUSE, THE PRESENT IN THE OTHER

a. The Then-clause contains a 'volitional expression'

§3595. Here it seems best to start with some examples and then to draw some morals. So I present *LawIne(E)* 49. 1 *Gif hie þonne þær næren oftor þonne æne, geselle scill. se agenfrigea . . .* and *LawIne(E)* 49. 2 *Gif hi ðær tuwa wæren, geselle twegen scill.* (in these both MSS H and B have *næron* and *wæron* respectively); *Bo(C)* 75. 21 *Gif þu nu ænigne mon cuðe þara þe hæfde ælces þinces anwald 7 ælcne weorðscipe hæfde, swa forð þ he na maran ne ðorfte, geþenc nu hu weorðlic 7 hu foremærlic þe wolde se man þincan* (here Sedgefield fails to report that MS B has *cuþest*); *ÆCHom* ii. 144. 15 *Gif se Ælmihtiga eow ðises geuðe, brucað þæra wæstma, and me ne biddað. Gif he ðonne eow ðises ne getiðode, gewitað aweg, wælhreowe fugelas, to eowrum eðele, of ðisum iglande*; *Exod(B)* 21. 29 *Gyf se oxa hnitol wære for dæge oððe for twam 7 hi hit his hlaforde cyddon 7 he hine belucan nolde 7 he wer oððe wif ofhnit, oftorfie man ðone oxan mid stanum 7 ofslea ðone hlaford* (here MS L has *hnite*); *Exod* 21. 36 *Gyf se oxa hnitol wæs 7 se hlaford hine ne heold, gilde oxan mid oxan 7 hæbbe him ðone deadan*;

MCharm 4. 20   Gif ðu wære on fell scoten   oððe wære on flæsc scoten
                 oððe wære on blod scoten
                 oððe wære on lið scoten,   næfre ne sy ðin lif atæsed;
                 gif hit wære esa gescot   oððe hit wære ylfa gescot
                 oððe hit wære hægtessan gescot,   nu ic wille ðin helpan;

and

PPs 65. 16   Gif ic me unrihtes oncneow   awiht on heortan,
                  ne wite me þæt,   wealdend drihten.

§3596. Here we may note first, that the preterite sometimes functions as a simple past tense (as in *LawIne(E)* 49. 1 and 49. 2), sometimes serves as a perfect (e.g. *ÆCHom* ii. 144. 15), and sometimes can be taken either way (e.g. *MCharm* 4. 20); second, that in conditional sentences containing an imperative or a jussive subjunctive the *gif* clauses do not always have the subjunctive; and third, that in the second conditional sentence in *MCharm* 4. 20, *ic wille* (not normally regarded as a 'volitional expression') is accompanied by a *gif* clause with three subjunctive verb-forms. On these last two points compare §§3564 and 3568. The reader will observe inconsistencies within the same sentences and texts similar to those exemplified in §§3571–80.

§3597. A few examples deserve special comment. In *BlHom* 247. 1 *Gif eow swa lice þuhte, utan gangan on þissum carcerne and hine ut forlætan*, where Morris translates 'If it so please you . . .', the pret. *þuhte* may be polite; cf. 'If it should so please you . . .'. In *BlHom* 233. 20 *Drihten him to cwæð, 'Gif þis gebod eow wære geseald fram eowrum Drihtne, astigað hider mid gefean on min scip'*, we can without blasphemy assume that Christ, who had himself given this command, was testing Andrew—possibly in a semi-humorous way. The *Andreas* poet puts it straightforwardly:

And 343   Him þa ondswarode   ece dryhten:
                'Gif ge syndon þegnas   þæs þe þrym ahof
                ofer middangeard,   swa ge me secgaþ,
                ond ge geheoldon þæt eow   se halga bead,
                þonne ic eow mid gefean   ferian wille
                ofer brimstreamas,   swa ge benan sint.'

Finally, Mather (p. 38) suggests the possibility of 'ellipsis' of an imperative 'remember' in *HomS* 40. 260. 2 *gif þu wene, þæt hit þin bocland sy, þæt þu on eardast, and on agene æht geseald, hit þonne wæron mine wæter, þa þe on heofenum wæron, þonne ic mine gife eorðwarum dælde.*

b. The Then-clause contains a present indicative

(1) The *gif clause contains a preterite indicative or an ambiguous equivalent*

§3598. Examples with a preterite indicative in the *gif* clause include *Bo* 32. 30 *Gif hit ær scandlic wæs, ne bið hit no ðy fægerre* and

PPs 103. 27   Gif þu þine ansyne fram him   æfre awendest,
                   þonne hi gedrefde   deope weorðað.

§3599. We find ambiguous indicative equivalents in one or both clauses in *ÆCHom* i. 268. 30 *. . . oðþæt he færð of ðisum life to ðam ecan wite, gif he ær geswican nolde, þaþa he mihte and moste, ÆCHom* i. 556. 2 *and gif hi min ehton, þonne ehtað hi eac eower* (where *ehtað* means 'will persecute'), *ÆCHom* ii. 452. 31 *Gif we god underfengon of Godes handa, hwi ne sceole we eac yfel underfon?, ÆCHom* i. 598. 5 *Gif ðu to ði come þæt þu me alyse, nelle ic beon alysed lybbende heonon, MSol* 30, and

GenB 661   Gif þu him heodæg wuht   hearmes gespræce,
                he forgifð hit þeah,   gif wit him geongordom
                læstan willað.

(2) *The* gif *clause contains a preterite subjunctive*

§3600. The only example of this pattern I have recorded is *ÆCHom* i. 236. 28 *Gif hwa alefed wære, oððe limleas on þissum life, he bið þonne swa hit awriten is, þæt 'Ealle ða þe to Godes rice gebyrigað, nabbað naðor ne womm ne awyrdnysse on heora lichaman.'* But cf. *MCharm* 4. 23 (§§3549 and 3595).

c. *Some difficult examples*

§3601. The examples which follow demonstrate that the type of conditional sentence under discussion is not limited to the patterns treated in §§3595–600. Mather (pp. 84–5) gives more references, but they have to be checked. I will content myself with quoting *Bede* 2. 11 *Gif se oðer nolde, hu wurð he elles gelæred?* (Miller 'If your hearer be reluctant . . .'); *Bede* 102. 18 *Gif he nu for us arisan ne wolde, micle ma gif we him underþeodde beoð, he us eac for noht gehygeð*; *Or* 214. 22 *þæt wæs siþþan Crist geboren wæs þæt we wæron of ælcum þeowdome aliesde 7 of ælcum ege, gif we him fulgongan willaþ*; *ÆCHom* i. 36. 1 *Se Godes Sunu wæs on his gesthuse genyrwed, þæt he us rume wununge on heofonan rice forgife, gif we his willan gehyrsumiað* (where Thorpe mistranslates the pres. subj. *forgife* as 'might give'); *ÆCHom* i. 232. 33 *þisne anweald forgeaf Crist þam apostolum and eallum bisceopum, gif hi hit on riht healdað* (where *forgeaf* can be translated 'has given');

Met 10. 1   Gif nu hæleða hwone   hlisan lyste,
            unnytne gelp   agan wille,
            þonne ic hine wolde   wordum biddan
            þæt he hine æghwonon utan   ymbeþohte,
            sweotole ymbsawe,   suð, east and west . . .

(where *wolde* seems to qualify as a 'volitional expression'; cf. §3596); and

Met 25. 22   Gif mon ðonne wolde   him awindan of
            þæs cynegerelan   claða gehwilcne,
            and him þonne oftion   ðara ðegnunga
            and þæs anwaldes   ðe he ær hæfde,
            ðonne meaht ðu gesion   þæt he bið swiðe gelic
            sumum ðara gumena   þe him geornost nu
            mid ðegnungum   ðringað ymbeutan

(where one might expect an imaginary condition with ☆*ðonne meahte ðu gesion*).

6. REJECTED OR IMAGINARY CONDITIONS INTRODUCED BY *GIF*

a. Introductory remarks

§3602. In §3544 I accept the definition given by Wood (p. 355) of rejected or imaginary conditions as occurring 'where a condition is stated which does not or cannot exist' and give my reasons for adopting these terms. But problems of classification inevitably remain. Thus, we can argue whether we have open or imaginary condition in *Bo* 28. 8 *Gif nu eall þises middaneardes wela come to anum men, hu ne wæren þonne ealle oþre men wædlan buton him anum?* (where common sense suggests the latter) or in *MCharm* 4. 20 (§3595); whether we have open or rejected condition in *WHom* 7. 99 *Ðam yrmingan wære micle betere, gif hit beon mihte, þæt hi swa deade wæron* . . . and

Rid 29. 5   walde hyre on þære byrig   bur atimbran
        searwum asettan,   gif hit swa meahte;

or rejected or imaginary conditions in *Bo* 33. 8 *Gif þu nu wære wegferend 7 hæfdest micel gold on ðe 7 þu þonne become on þiofscole, þonne ne wendes þu þe þines feores, ÆCHom* ii. 140. 17 *þa wolde þæt folc þæt fyr adwæscan gif hit ænig wæta wanian mihte, Bo* 50. 3 and the corresponding

Met 11. 96   Eala, sigora god,
        wære þis moncyn   miclum gesælig,
        gif hiora modsefa   meahte weorðan
        staðolfæst gereaht   þurh þa strongan meaht,
        and geendebyrd,   swa swa oðra sint
        woruldgesceafta.   Wære hit, la, þonne
        murge mid monnum,   gif hit meahte swa

(where it is not clear whether the speaker is lamenting that such happiness is unattainable in the present or is reminding us that it can be attained in the future), and

Ex 411   Up aræmde   Abraham þa;
        se eorl wolde slean   eaferan sinne
        unweaxenne,   ecgum reodan
        magan mid mece,   gif hine metod lete

(where Abraham believed that God would permit the sacrifice of Isaac until God prohibited it). But such difficulties must not deter us from recognizing that the distinctions are real or from attempting to exemplify the various types. The examples given below may be supplemented from Mather (pp. 39-40 and 88), Wilde (pp. 343-4), a sometimes muddled Visser (ii, §§815, 861, and 880 at p. 891); and Mitchell 1959, p. 844.

b. Sentences in which both clauses have the present indicative

§3603. We can agree with Mather (p. 41) that we have in *Gen* 13. 16 *gyf ænig man mæg geriman ðære eorðan dust, þonne mæg he eac swylce geriman þinne ofspring* 'a condition universally recognized as contrary to fact. . . . Logically such a condition must be classed with the unfulfilled.' *ÆCHom* i. 4. 2 *Manega lease Cristas cumað on minum naman, cweðende, 'Ic eom Crist', and wyrcað fela tacna and wundra, to bepæcenne mancynn, and eac swylce þa gecorenan men, gif hit gewurþan mæg* does not belong here. The deception of the faithful is only too possible. The Authorized Version of *Matt* 24. 24 '. . . if it were possible' is (I have heard it said) 'probably an instance of the influence of Calvinistic bias'.

c. Sentences in which both clauses have the present subjunctive

§3604. I have so far recorded no such examples from the prose. Two from the poetry which are discussed by Behre (p. 138) deserve consideration. The first is

Met 23. 1   Sie ðæt la on eorðan   ælces ðinges
gesælig mon,   gif he gesion mæge
þone hlutrestan   heofontorhtan stream,
æðelne æwelm   ælces goodes,
and of him selfum   ðone sweartan mist,
modes þiostro,   mæg aweorpan,

which he translates 'Lo, he would be on earth in everything a blessed man, if he could see the clearest heavenly stream'. Some may see a jussive subjunctive 'Let him be' in *Sie*. Behre says that 'we may infer from the context that the protasis is unrealizable'. This is arguable. The ind. *mæg* is probably due to the waning of whatever influence led the writer to use the subj. *mæge*. The corresponding prose is *Bo* 101. 19 *Gesælig bið se mon þe mæg geseon þone hluttran æwellm þæs hehstan godes, 7 of him selfum aweorpan mæg þa þiostro his modes*. The Latin has

Metre iii. 12   Felix qui potuit boni
Fontem uisere lucidum. . . .

However, that Behre's view is possible is attested by the second example,

Max i 31   Umbor yceð,   þa æradl nimeð;
              þy weorþeð on foldan swa fela   fira cynnes,
              ne sy þæs magutimbres   gemet ofer eorþan,
              gif hi ne wanige   se þas woruld teode,

which seems to state the idea of Malthus rather clearly and to carry the implication 'but He does'.

d. Sentences containing a preterite indicative

§3605. Visser (ii, §819) offers examples of what he calls 'the modal preterite' in OE rejected conditions, e.g. *ApT* 32. 7 *Eala lareow, gif ðu me lufodest, þu hit besorgodest.* I have given in §§647-50 my reasons for doubting whether this term—which he contrasts with what is 'traditionally, the subjunctive' (ii, §812)—has any place in an *Old English Syntax*. My doubts are not diminished by the fact that all the preterite forms Visser cites are ambiguous ones which are to be taken as preterite subjunctives except that in *Ps(B)* 7. 5, where the indicative *ageald* represents Latin *reddidi*. Other versions have the indicative (e.g. *A, F*) or the subjunctive (e.g. *K*). See Nunn, §171. In *BlHom* 23. 15 *agælde* is present subjunctive. On *GenB* 641 and on *Beo* 1655 see §§649 and 3654 respectively.

e. Sentences in which both clauses have the preterite subjunctive or an ambiguous equivalent

(1) *Mood*

§3606. Some writers have agreed with Behre (p. 53) that the preterite subjunctive 'was first used to denote unreality with reference to past time only, then also with reference to present and future time'; see, *inter alios*, Behre (pp. 50-6 and 138-41) and Mattsson (*Kock Studies*, pp. 211-24). Visser (ii, §860) misquotes and seems to misunderstand Behre's statement (p. 54) that 'the use of the present of the subjunctive as the means of expressing conditionality in independent sentences is obsolescent in the historical records of OE'. I assume from his examples (my §3604), although I am not certain, that Behre meant that in the extant OE monuments the present subjunctive is rare in what I call rejected and imaginary conditions. It is certainly true that in sentences expressing such conditions the preterite subjunctive is the rule in both prose and poetry. Examples follow in the relevant sections.

§3607. But it is appropriate to remind the reader that (as pointed out in §1681) unreality in OE is timeless; unlike Latin and MnE,

OE does not distinguish grammatically between unreality in the past, present, or future, although the reference of a preterite subjunctive can be made specific by the use of an adverb, e.g. *Bo* 28. 8 (§3602) and *Matt(WSCp)* 11. 21 *forþam gyf on Tyro 7 Sydone wærun gedone þa mægnu þe gedone synt on eow, gefyrn hi dydun dædbote on hæran 7 on axan.* The context usually resolves the difficulty when the distinction is important, e.g. in *ÆCHom* i. 130. 5 *Drihten, gif ðu her andwerd nære, nære ure broðer forðfaren* and many of the examples quoted in the sections which follow. But sometimes this very timelessness has its advantages, e.g. in *ÆLS* 27. 181 *Swa milde is se hælend þæt he miltsian wolde his agenum slagum gif hi gecyrran woldon and biddan his miltsunge swa swa heora mænig dyde swa swa se hundredes ealdor* . . . , where the ambiguous *woldon* offers us the choice of 'was willing', 'would be willing', and 'would have been willing', and

El 776　　　　　　　　　　　　gif he þin nære
　　　　　sunu synna leas,　　　　næfre he soðra swa feala
　　　　　in woruldrice　　　　wundra gefremede
　　　　　dogorgerimum,

where *gif he . . . nære* means both 'if He had not been' and 'if He were not'.

(2) *Rejected conditions*

§3608. I begin with a series of examples from Ælfric in which the preterite subjunctive or its equivalent refers to the past but which illustrate different combinations of positive and negative clauses: (both clauses positive) *ÆCHom* i. 82. 28 *ac hit wære to hrædlic gif he ða on cildcradole acweald wurde* and *ÆCHom* i. 142. 26 *Sprecan he mihte gif he wolde*; (the *gif* clause negated) *ÆCHom* ii. 246. 29 *Swa fela ðusend engla mihton eaðe bewerian Crist wið ðam unmannum, mid heofenlicum wæpnum, gif he ðrowian nolde sylfwilles for us*; (the Then-clause negated) *ÆCHom* ii. 324. 23 *gif we hit forsuwian dorston, ne sæde we hit eow*; (both clauses negated) *ÆCHom* i. 52. 1 *Witodlice næfde Godes gelaðung Paulum to lareowe, gif se halga martyr Stephanus swa ne bæde, ÆCHom* i. 150. 7 *He nære na man geðuht gif he mannes life ne lyfode*, and *ÆCHom* i. 168. 1 *ac he ne dorste Cristes fandian, gif him alyfed nære*; (two co-ordinate *gif* clauses, one positive, one negated) *ÆCHom* i. 18. 23 *Ne þorfte Adam ne eal mancynn þe him siððan ofacom næfre deaðes onbyrian, gif þæt treow moste standan ungehrepod, and his nan man ne onbyrigde*; and (the Then-clause a rhetorical question) *ÆCHom* i. 320. 7 *Gif he ða wolde deman mancynn, ðaða he ærest to middangearde com, hwa wurde þonne gehealden?* Examples from other texts in which both clauses refer to the past include *Or* 186. 23 . . . *þa com him ðær ongean Scipio se consul, 7 ðær frecenlice gewundod wearð, 7 eac ofslagen wære, gif his sunu his ne gehulpe* and

GenB 784   næfdon on þam lande þa giet
          sælða gesetena,   ne hie sorge wiht
          weorces wiston,   ac hie wel meahton
          libban on þam lande,   gif hie wolden lare godes
          forweard fremman.

§3609. Now I offer from various sources a selection of examples with other time-references. First, there are those in which, as Mather (p. 40) puts it, 'the condition is unfulfilled in present or in future time; or the relation is a general one and consequently the time is not specified', e.g. *Bede* 134. 18 *Hwæt ic wat, gif ure godo ænige mihte hæfdon, þonne woldan hie me ma fultumian, forþon ic him geornlicor þeodde 7 hyrde* (we may perhaps have here dependent speech with unexpressed conj. *þæt*), *Bo* 37. 28 *Gif se anweald ðonne of his agenre gecynde 7 his agnes gewealdes god wære, ne underfenge he næfre þa yfelan ac þa godan, ÆCHom* i. 404. 27 *Gif þu wistest hwæt þe toweard is, þonne weope ðu mid me, ÆCHom* ii. 46. 19 *Mare we mihton sprecan be ðære.culfran gecynde gif hit to langsum nære, Luke(WSCp)* 7. 39 *Gyf þe man witega wære witodlice he wiste hwæt 7 hwylc þis wif wære þe his æthrinþ þ heo synful is*, and

Met 20. 100   Eorðe sio cealde
          brengð wæstma fela   wundorlicra,
          forðæm hio mid þæm wætere   weorðað geþawened.
          Gif þæt nære,   þonne hio wære
          fordrugod to duste   and todrifen siððan
          wide mid winde. . . .

§3610. Second, there are those in which the time-references of the clauses are different, e.g. *Or* 122. 11 *Hwæt, ge witon þæt ge giet todæge wæron Somnitum þeowe, gif ge him ne alugen iowra wedd 7 eowre aþas þe ge him sealdon, BlHom* 33. 36 *Weorþian we forþon Drihtnes godcundnesse, gif he nære soþ God ofer ealle gesceafta, na him englas ne þegnodon* (where *nære* means both 'had not been' and 'were not'; cf. *El* 776 in §3607), *ÆLS* 1. 87 *Gif heo wære of godes gecynde genumen, witodlice ne mihte heo singian, ÆCHom* i. 276. 18 *Gif he ongunne and anginn hæfde, butan tweon ne mihte he beon Ælmihtig God, ÆCHom* i. 328. 24, and

Mald 193   ac wendon fram þam wige   and þone wudu sohton,
          flugon on þæt fæsten   and hyra feore burgon,

and manna ma   þonne hit ænig mæð wære,
gyf hi þa geearnunga   ealle gemundon
þe he him to duguþe   gedon hæfde,

where an action in the past merits perpetual disapproval.

(3) *Imaginary conditions*

§3611. Satisfying examples of what Mather (p. 33) calls 'the ideal or purely hypothetical condition' are less easy to find. The following seem to fill the bill in that, while they are in a sense impossible, they represent situations imagined for the sake of argument which cannot be said to be rejected: *Bo* 35. 30 *Gif ge nu gesawan hwelce mus þ wære hlaford ofer oðre mys, 7 sette him domas, 7 nedde hie æfter gafole, hu wunderlic wolde eow ðæt þincan; hwelce cehhettunge ge woldan þæs habban, 7 mid hwelce hleahtre ge woldon bion astered,* *Bo* 75. 21 (two examples), *Bo* 142. 2 *Hu wolde þe nu lician gif hwilc swiðe rice cyning wære 7 næfde nænne freone mon on eallum his rice ac wæren ealle þiowe?*, *CP* 113. 24 *Ac ðæt mennisce mod bið oft upahafen, ðeah hit mid nane anwalde ne sie underled; ac hu micle ma wenstu ðæt hit wolde, gif ða wlenca 7 se anwald ðær wære to gemenged!*, *ÆCHom* ii. 454. 22 *Iob cwæð, Eala gif mine synna and min yrmð, þe ic ðolige, wæron awegene on anre wægan, þonne wæron hi swærran gesewene ðonne sandcorn on sæ*, and perhaps *GenB* 834 *ac ic to þam grunde genge, gif ic godes meahte || willan gewyrcean*, which seems to me the only possible example of an imaginary conditional sentence in the poetry—there may be room for disagreement here—but which could be taken as an open condition expressing a genuine possibility; cf. *ÆCHom* i. 212. 25 *Menig man is cristen geteald on sibbe, þe wolde swiðe hraðe wiðsacan Criste, gif him man bude þæt man bead þam martyrum*, where it would be interesting to know exactly what nuance Ælfric had in mind. In conclusion I draw attention to the sequence... *gif hwa bið swa scearpsiene... gif þonne hwa wære swa scearpsiene...* in *Bo* 72. 30.

7. THE CLASSIFICATION OF CONDITIONAL SENTENCES WITH *GIF* IN DEPENDENT SPEECH

§3612. While, as already noted in §2100, there is no rule in OE that a subordinate clause in dependent speech has the subjunctive, changes from present to preterite tense and from indicative to subjunctive mood may occur. Such changes, however, can affect only conceded and denied conditions or open conditions, since it is to these that the present tense and the indicative mood are essentially restricted; the mood and tense in (for example) *ÆCHom* i. 220. 9 *We cweðað nu, gif hwa his lic forstæle, nolde he hine unscrydan, forðan ðe stalu ne lufað nane yldinge, ÆCHom* i. 224. 35 *þa lareowas cwædon, þæt ða aræredan menn næron soðlice gewitan Cristes æristes, gif hi næron ecelice arærde*, and in

Beo 590   Secge ic þe to soðe,   sunu Ecglafes,
    þæt næfre Grendel swa fela   gryra gefremede,
    atol æglæca   ealdre þinum,
    hynðo on Heorote,   gif þin hige wære,
    sefa swa searogrim,   swa þu self talast,

would have been the same in non-dependent speech. So we have an open condition in *ÆCHom* ii. 2. 10 *Ic gesette on twam bocum þa gereccednysse ðe ic awende, forðan ðe ic ðohte þæt hit wære læsse æðryt to gehyrenne, gif man ða ane boc ræt on anes geares ymbryne, and ða oðre on ðam æftran geare*; a conceded condition, 'seeing that he did not exist', in *ÆLS* 1. 67 *Æft gif hwylc gewytleas man wenð þæt he hine sylfne geworhte, þonne axie we hu he mihte hine sylfne gewyrcean gif he ær nes*; and (I think) an open condition in *ÆCHom* i. 246. 16 *He ferde, and bodode, þæt him wæs Godes grama onsigende, gif hi to Gode bugan noldon*, where it seems better to believe that the warning was couched in real terms than to take *wæs onsigende* as an equivalent for *onsige* 'would descend'.

§3613. Two main difficulties arise from the possibility of changes in mood and tense in dependent speech. The first is that of deciding whether we have a conceded or open condition on the one hand or a rejected or imaginary condition on the other. The second is that, when we have decided that we have an open condition, it is often uncertain how remote it was (or would have been) in non-dependent speech. Both these difficulties are seen in *ÆCHom* i. 82. 12 . . . *ðohte gif he hi ealle ofsloge, þæt se an ne ætburste þe he sohte*. Christ did escape. So from Ælfric's point of view, it is a rejected condition. But Herod's thought might have been the equivalent of 'If I kill them all, he whom I seek will not escape' or a less confident 'If I were to kill them all, he whom I seek would not escape'. Since Beowulf did not lose his life in the fight with Grendel's mother, we can see the condition as a rejected one in

Beo 1474   Geþenc nu, se mæra   maga Healfdenes,
    snottra fengel,   nu ic eom siðes fus,
    goldwine gumena,   hwæt wit geo spræcon,
    gif ic æt þearfe   þinre scolde
    aldre linnan,   þæt ðu me a wære
    forðgewitenum   on fæder stæle.

But did Hrothgar say 'If you lose your life, I will take the place of a father . . .' or 'If you were to lose your life, I would take the place of a father'? And if the latter, was he thinking 'but of course you won't' or 'and you might'? Does *Bede* 374. 25 *þa sægdon hie ðæt 7 cyðdon Eadbyrhte heora biscope þæt him ðæt licede 7 leof wære, gif hit his willa wære, ða geðafode he þæt heora geðeahte* . . . imply 'if it is your will' or 'if it were your will'? *Beo* 2633 (§3687) and the changes in tense and mood in *ÆCHom* i. 124. 5-14 are of interest here. See further Gorrell, pp. 459 and 465-6.

§3614. The context sometimes helps, e.g. *ÆCHom* i. 108. 5 *ac he wolde þæt ða Iudeiscan boceras ða witegunge be ðam ræddon, and swa his cenningstowe geswutelodon, þæt hi gehealdene wæron, gif hi woldon mid þan tungelwitegum hi to Criste gebiddan: gif hi þonne noldon, þæt hi wurdon mid þære geswutelunge geniðerode*, where the two alternatives of an open condition are spelt out. However, care must be taken with sequences such as *ÆCHom* i. 134. 13-23, *ÆCHom* i. 138. 34-140. 5, and *ÆCHom* i. 124. 5 *Seo ealde æ bebead þæt gehwilc hreoflig man gecome to þam sacerde, and se sacerd sceolde hine fram mannum ascirian, gif he soðlice hreoflig wære. Gif he nære swutelice hreoflig, wære ðonne be his dome clæne geteald*, where the sentence beginning *Gif he nære* . . . is an open condition dependent on *bebead*. On *Vain* 77 and *Met* 25. 30, see §3714.

8. *ÞÆR* 'IF'

§3615. Here, as with *gif*, it is important to distinguish conceded and open conditions from rejected and imaginary conditions. Meroney's treatment of 'Old English *ðær* "if" ' (*JEGP* 41 (1942), 201-9)— with its useful list of examples—is much weakened by his failure to do this.

§3616. Despite Wilde (see my §3621), *þær* undoubtedly means 'if' in rejected and imaginary conditions in both prose and poetry. Thus, we find parallel clauses introduced by *þær* and *gif* in *Bo(B)* 105. 5 *Ac þær ic nu moste þin mod gefiðerigan mid þam fiðerum, þ ðu mihtest mid me fliogan, þonne miht þu ofersion ealle þas eorðlican þing. Gif þu mihtest þe fligon ofer þam rodore, þonne mihtest þu gesion þa wolcnu under þe* . . . (where I take *miht* as an error for *mihte*; cf. *Bo* 95. 32 in §3619). We also find variations between manuscripts, e.g. *Matt(Ru)* 23. 30 *7 cwæþað þær we wærun on dagum fædra ure ne wærun we foeran eora in blodgyte uitgana*, where *Li* and both W-S versions have *gif* for Latin *si*, and *VercHom* 1. 22, where Förster reports one manuscript with *gif*, two with *þær*, and one with *gif* on an erasure of *þær*. However, I am inclined to take *þær . . . to* as adverbial in *CP* 217. 21 *forðæm, gif se weobud ufan hol nære 7 ðær wind to come, ðonne tostencte he ða lac*; cf. *þær . . . on* in *Lch* i. 398. 1 *Her ys seo bot hu ðu meaht þine æceras betan gif hi nellaþ wel wexan oþþe þær hwilc ungedefe þing on gedon bið*, which I discuss in §3623.

§3617. I now quote some typical examples of rejected and imaginary conditions introduced by *þær* to demonstrate that *þær* can translate both *si* and, with the aid of negatives, *nisi* and that the time-references of the clauses can vary as they do with similar conditions introduced by *gif* (see §§3602-11). Imaginary conditions include *Bo* 105. 5 (§3616); *Bo* 100. 3 *þær yfel auht wære, þonne meahte hit God wyrcan; forðy hit is nauht* (a statement which earns the rebuke from Boethius that *Me þincð þ ðu me dwelle 7 dydre, swa mon cild deð* and which also illustrates the not uncommon sequence *þær . . . þonne*; cf. *gif . . . þonne* (§§3719-21)); and

Soul i 76   Forðan þe wære selre   swiðe mycle
           þonne þe wæron ealle   eorðan speda,
           (butan þu hie gedælde   dryhtne sylfum),
           þær ðu wurde æt frymðe fugel   oððe fisc on sæ,
           oððe on eorðan neat   ætes tilode,
           feldgangende   feoh butan snyttro,
           oððe on westenne   wildra deora
           þæt wyrreste,   þær swa god wolde,
           ge þeah ðu wære   wyrma cynna
           þæt grimmeste,   þær swa god wolde,
           þonne ðu æfre on moldan   man gewurde
           oððe æfre fulwihte   onfon sceolde.

Rejected conditions include *Or* 68. 19 *Æfter þæm Porsenna 7 Tarcuinius þa cyningas ymbsæton Romeburg, 7 hie eac begeaton, þær Mutius nære, an monn of ðære byrig: he hi mid his wordum geegsade*, Latin *. . . et nisi hostem Mucius constanti urendae manus patientia permovisset . . .* , and *Or* 88. 4 *. . . 7 þær wurdon mid hungre acwealde, þær heora þa ne gehulpe þa þær æt ham wæron* (in these examples, the time-reference is to the past); *CP* 415. 7 *Ðær we us selfum demden, ðonne ne demde us no God*, 1 *Cor* 11. 31 *Quod si nosmetipsos diiudicaremus, non utique iudicaremur* (here, despite EETS 'When we judged ourselves, God judged us not', the reference is timeless; *NEB* has 'But if we examined ourselves, we should not thus fall under judgement'); *KtPs* 50. 120 and, despite the ind. *est* in

Ps 118. 92 *Nisi quod lex tua meditatio mea est, tunc forte periissem in humilitate mea,*

PPs 118. 92   þær me þin æ   an ne hulpe,
                   ðe ic on mode   minum hæfde,
                   þonne ic wende   on woruldlife,
                   þæt ic on minum eadmedum   eall forwurde

(here the reference is to a continuing state); and

Beo 2729   Nu ic suna minum   syllan wolde
                  guðgewædu,   þær me gifeðe swa
                  ænig yrfeweard   æfter wurde
                  lice gelenge

(here the two clauses refer to the present and the past respectively). For more examples, see Wülfing, ii, §451; Mather, pp. 40-1; Meroney, *JEGP* 41 (1942), 201-5; Visser, ii. 894-5; and Mitchell 1959, p. 845. No examples have been found in Ælfric or Wulfstan. For the suggestion that the usage is colloquial rather than literary, see Mather, pp. 79-80. On *Beo* 2570 and *Sat* 106 see Meroney, *JEGP* 41 (1942), 205-9.

§3618. The only example with *þær þe*, so far as I know, is *Verc Hom* 6. 88 *þær ðe þis God ne wære, nænige þinga ura goda on hyra onsyne gefeollon*, Latin *Nisi hic deus esset deorum nostrorum, dii nostri coram eo in facies suas minime cecidissent.*

§3619. In rejected and imaginary conditions, both clauses have the preterite subjunctive. Visser (ii. 894) misleadingly speaks of 'modally zero' forms (his term for 'indicative' or 'non-subjunctive'; see my §601) in *Beo* 794 (see §3622) and in *Bo(B)* 95. 32 *þær þu gemyndest þa word þe ic þe sæde on þære forman bec, þonne miht þu be þam wordum genog sweotole ongitan þ þ ðu ær sædest þ ðu nysstest*, where *gemyndest* is an ambiguous form and *miht* is an error for *mihte*, the form preferred by the scribe of MS *B* to *meahte*, which (Junius reports) MS *C* had in this passage. Space does not permit me to deal here with the indicatives *fornam* in *PPs* 80. 13, *bicwom* in *ChristC* 1105, and *ateah* in *ChristC* 1493. I discussed these in Mitchell 1959, pp. 601-3, but am now inclined to see in them 'suppressed apodoses'; see my discussion of *Beo* 1657 *wæs* in §3654, and note Campbell's comment (*RES* 7 (1956), 68)—in disagreement, which I do not completely share (*wolde* could be ambiguous in form), with Quirk (p. 115)—that *þær* in *ChristC* 1494 introduces 'an unfulfilled condition'. Full collections may reveal more examples in which the Then-clause of a rejected condition has the preterite indicative. But we can avoid one in *VercHom* 4. 252 if we insert the words in square brackets from MS *Q* to give us the Then-clause of a rejected condition: *VercHom* 4. 252 *Næs me næfre gyt in him ieðe to wunianne, nihtes fyrst ne dæges fyrst; ne ieðlice næs ic ane nihtes fyrst ne dæges on him[; nihtes ne dæges ic in him wunode] þær ic wiste hu ic ut fulge.*

§3620. Rejected and imaginary conditions introduced by *þær* and unrealized or impossible wishes such as *Bo* 110. 15 *Eala, ðær hi ne meahton, Met* 8. 39, and *Deut (Lambeth 427)* 32. 29—these and similar examples are quoted in §1680—are so alike that the temptation is strong to postulate a common origin or to suggest that one is the derivative of the other. Meroney (*JEGP* 41 (1942), 204), who does not sufficiently distinguish the two constructions, includes the three sentences cited above among 'four unmistakable instances of anacoluthon'. (The fourth is *ChristC* 1312; see §3623.) This implies that the conditional sentence came first. I agree that this is possible, but do not share Meroney's confidence that it must be so. The well-known

GenB 368   Wa la, ahte ic minra handa geweald
              and moste ane tid   ute weorðan,
              wesan ane winterstunde,   þonne ic mid þys werode—

may represent a half-way stage between an independent wish (see §1680) and a conditional sentence, but does not tell us which, if either, came first.

§3621. We must now ask whether *þær* can introduce conceded or open conditions. This may be little more than a terminological problem. We have already seen that *þonne* 'when' develops both a causal and a conditional equivalence (§§2587, 3156-8, and 3695) and it should be no surprise that *þær* in examples like *CP* 129. 7 *Sua eac ðær ðæt heafod bið unhal eall ða limu bioð idelu, ðeah hie hal sien* . . . and

Beo 1834   . . . ond þe to geoce   garholt bere,
              mægenes fultum,   þær ðe bið manna þearf

can be seen as shading into a temporal (§§2460-3 and Mather, p. 52), causal (§3153), or even conditional, function. If these are conditional clauses, they are conceded or open conditions. But in both of them *þær* can be translated as 'where'. The same is true of two of the nineteen examples which Liggins (1955, pp. 388-90) mentions in the course of her discussion of what she calls 'causal/

conditional' *þær* clauses, viz. *Bo(C)* 71. 17 . . . *7 þær hit þe wexð, þonne wanað hit oþrum?*—where both the present indicatives and MS *B*'s *þær þær* incline me to accept Liggins's own suggestion that *þær* 'is probably local rather than conditional'—and *LawIICn* 72 *7 þær se bonda sæt uncwydd 7 unbecrafod, sitte þæt wif 7 þa cild on þam ylcan unbesacen*—where I do not understand why Liggins says that *þær* 'may be used in a *metaphorically* local sense' [my italics]. For such examples we can sympathize with Wilde's claim (p. 367) that *þær* is purely local:

> Ohne Zweifel hat die Konjunktion *þær* rein lokalen Charakter. Sie bedeutet 'da, dort'. Die Tatsache, daß die Sätze konditionalen Sinn haben, berechtigt noch nicht zu der Zuordnung zu den Konditionalsätzen; denn dann müßten auch viele Sätze mit *þa hwile þe* zu dieser Kategorie gezählt werden. Es ergibt sich also bei diesen *þær*-Sätzen die Tatsache, daß eine lokale Konjunktion einen konditionalen Satz einleitet, eine Tatsache, die wir schon vielfach bei den Temporalsätzen beobachtet haben.[188]

But this is obviously untrue in rejected or imaginary conditions and in unrealized or impossible wishes; we cannot translate *þær* as 'where' in *Or* 68. 19 (§3617) or in

Met 8. 39 Eala, þær hit wurde oððe wolde god
      þæt on eorðan nu ussa tida
      geond þas widan weoruld wæren æghwæs
      swelce under sunnan.

The same is true of the remaining seventeen of Liggins's nineteen examples of 'causal/conditional' *þær* clauses (1955, pp. 388–90); all are rejected or imaginary conditions with a preterite subjunctive or an equivalent ambiguous form in which *þær* cannot be translated 'where' or 'because'. Although I can see that *Or* 90. 26 *7 hie þa hrædlice beforan heora feondum forweorþan sceoldon, þær hie ða burg ne abræcen mid þæm cræfte þe þa scondlicost wæs* . . . implies that they remained alive because they captured the city, I do not understand the principle on which this *þær* clause is included among the 'causal/conditional' while *Or* 68. 19 (§3617) is not; Porsenna and Tarquin failed to capture Rome because Mutius was there.

§3622. We have no evidence on which to argue whether *þær* in examples like *Or* 68. 19 and *Met* 8. 39 is of different origin from *þær*

---

[188] 'There is no doubt that the conjunction *þær* has a purely locative character. It signifies "there, in that place". The fact that the clauses have conditional sense does not of itself justify their inclusion as conditional clauses; for then one would have to include many *þa hwile þe* clauses in this category. The conclusion one can draw from these *þær* clauses is that a locative conjunction introduces a conditional clause, a fact we have already frequently observed with temporal clauses.'

in examples like *CP* 129. 7 and *Beo* 1834 (all in §3621). But it is tempting to suggest that *þær* + the preterite subjunctive or an equivalent ambiguous form introduces a conditional clause expressing rejected or imaginary condition and that *þær* + any other verb-form introduces a conditional-equivalent local clause, i.e. that it can be translated 'if' but that 'where' gives adequate sense. Such a suggestion cannot, of course, help us to decide whether ambiguous forms such as *meahte* in

Beo 762　　　Mynte se mæra,　þær he meahte swa,
　　　　　　　widre gewindan　ond on weg þanon
　　　　　　　fleon on fenhopu

or *wolde* in

Met 25. 64　　Sceal ðonne nede　nearwe gebugan
　　　　　　　to ðara hlaforda　hæftedome,
　　　　　　　þe he hine eallunga ær　underþiodde.
　　　　　　　Ðæt is wyrse get,　þæt he winnan nyle
　　　　　　　wið ðæm anwalde　ænige stunde;
　　　　　　　þær he wolde a　winnan onginnan,
　　　　　　　and þonne on ðæm gewinne　þurhwunian forð,
　　　　　　　þonne næfde he　nane scylde,
　　　　　　　ðeah he oferwunnen　weorðan sceolde

are indicative or subjunctive. In this last example, we learn from the context and from *Bo* 112. 10 *þær he hit a anginnan wolde, 7 þonne on þam gewinne þurhwunian ne mihte, þonne næfde he his nane scylde* that *wolde* is subjunctive in a *þær* clause expressing a rejected condition 'if he were willing . . .'. In *Beo* 762, the fact that Grendel did get away, albeit mortally wounded, might enable us to decide for Wrenn–CH's 'wheresoever he could' or for Swanton's 'whenever he could' and against Klaeber's 'in case that, if'. If so, *meahte* is indicative.

Beo 794　　　　　　　　　þær genehost brægd
　　　　　　　eorl Beowulfes　ealde lafe,
　　　　　　　wolde freadrihtnes　feorh ealgian,
　　　　　　　mæres þeodnes,　ðær hie meahton swa

is more difficult. We are told that the retainers had no chance; hence, no doubt, the agreement between Wrenn–CH 'if they could', Swanton 'if they could', and Klaeber 'in case that, if'. But they did not know. So from their point of view 'wheresoever they could' or Donaldson's 'however they might' could perhaps be justified. Such difficulties are a reflection, not on the theory but on the OE verb system. They are compounded when the *þær* clause is in dependent speech, with its possibilities of changes in tense and/or mood; consider *Bede*

28. 19 *Ða geþafedon hi ðære arednesse, 7 him wif sealdon, þæt ðær seo wise on tweon cyme, þæt hi ðonne ma of þam wifcynne him cyning curan þonne of þam wæpnedcynne*, Latin . . . *ea solum condicione dare consenserunt, ut ubi res ueniret in dubium, magis de feminea regum prosapia quam de masculina regem sibi eligerent*— note the verb *cyme* (Miller reports no variants) and Latin *ubi*—and

GenB 386   . . . and þæt wiste eac   weroda drihten,
                    þæt sceolde unc Adame   yfele gewurðan
                    ymb þæt heofonrice,   þær ic ahte minra handa geweald—

does *þær* mean 'wherever' (open) or 'if' (rejected; a subordinate devil did the tempting)? On such problems, see further §§3612-14.

§3623. The possibility that full collections may reveal *þær* examples like *Max i* 31, where the present subjunctive after *gif* expresses a rejected condition (see §3604), warns us against embracing too enthusiastically the distinction suggested in §3622. So too does the notorious

ChristC 1312   Eala, þær we nu magon   wraþe firene
                       geseon on ussum sawlum,   synna wunde,
                       mid lichoman   leahtra gehygdu,
                       eagum unclæne   ingeþoncas!
                       Ne þæt ænig mæg   oþrum gesecgan
                       mid hu micle elne   æghwylc wille
                       þurh ealle list   lifes tiligan,
                       feores forhtlice,   forð aðolian,
                       synrust þwean   ond hine sylfne þrean. . . .

The ASPR punctuation (given here) implies that *magon* is a present subjunctive expressing an impossible wish; cf. *Max i* 31. But I am inclined to take the *þær* clause as conditional, with a comma after *ingeþoncas*—see Schaar, pp. 76-8—and to interpret both *magon* and *mæg* as indicatives. So interpreted, *ChristC* 1312 is to be classed with the equally exceptional *Gen* 13. 16; see §3603. The preference of Rushworth *Matthew* for *þær* where the other versions have *gif* in examples like *Matt(Ru)* 24. 24 . . . *swa þ in gedwolan sien gelædde monigra þær þ beon mæge ge þa gecorenan geta* (see §3603) also tells against my suggestion. However, consideration of a few typical examples in which *þær* 'if' has been detected in clauses without a preterite subjunctive or its equivalent suggests that it can be taken as a reasonable working principle. It would probably have had Wülfing's support—'Auch dieses Fügewort kommt nur mit dem Konjunktiv vor' ['This conjunction, too, occurs only with the subjunctive'] (ii, §451)—and that of Meroney—'Apparent and borderline cases, on closer inspection, nearly always qualify as instances of ðær "where". Like the clearcut examples these questionable ones also dwindle out before Ælfric's time' (*JEGP* 41 (1942), 202). Such examples include *Conf 1* 337 *Gif man ofslea mannan on folcgefeohte oððe for nyde, þær he his hlafordes ceap werige, fæste xl nihta*; *LawIIIAtr* 13. 2 7 *þæt dom stande þar þegenas sammæle beon; gif hig sacan, stande þæt hig VIII secgað*, Latin *Et iudicium stet ubi taini consenserint; si dissideant, stet quod ipsi octo dicent*; and *LawIIIAtr* 13. 3, where the Latin also has *ubi*. In *Lch* i. 398. 1 (§3616), *þær* is probably better taken as part of the adverbial combination *þær . . . on* than as a conjunction. In *Conf 3* IV. 23 *Gif hwylc man mid arwan deor ofsceote . . . 7 þær hund oððe wulf oððe fox oððe bera on befangen hæbbe . . . ne abite his nan cristen man*, Latin *Si quis sagitta percusserit cervum . . . et forsitan ex eo lupus, ursus, canis aut vulpes gustaverit, nemo manducet, þær* also seems to me an adverb, either representing *forsitan* or forming a combination with *on*, as in the previous example.

§3624. I have found no *þær* clauses in the poetry which must be taken as conceded or open conditions. Some possible examples have already been discussed in §3621. In those which follow, *þær* can be translated 'where', shading variously into 'when', 'because', or even 'if':

GuthA 344	Swa sceal oretta	a in his mode
	gode compian,	ond his gæst beran
	oft on ondan	þam þe eahtan wile
	sawla gehwylcre	þær he gesælan mæg,

| Jul 364 | þær ic hine finde | ferð staþelian |
| | to godes willan, | ic beo geara sona . . . , |

and

ChristB 751		Is us þearf micel
	þæt we mid heortan	hælo secen,
	þær we mid gæste	georne gelyfað
	þæt þæt hælobearn	heonan up stige
	mid usse lichoman,	lifgende god.

In

ChristB 840		þær bið æghwylcum
	synwyrcendra	on þa snudan tid
	leofra micle	þonne eall þeos læne gesceaft,
	þær he hine sylfne	on þam sigeþreate
	behydan mæge . . . ,

where Ettmüller and Cook emended *þær* to *þæt*, and in

| Rid 4. 7 | | Wearm lim |
| | gebundenne bæg | hwilum bersteð, |

seþeah biþ on þonce   þegne minum,
medwisum men,   me þæt sylfe,
þær wiht wite   ond wordum min
on sped mæge   spel gesecgan,

where Craig Williamson (whose punctuation I follow) takes *þær* as 'if' on the authority of *Guide*, §179, we may have *þær* introducing a noun-equivalent clause; see §§1960 and 3546 and compare the use of *þæt* in *Mald* 32 with that of *gif* in *MSol* 33 and of *þær* in *Soul i* 79.

§3625. So, while I am not prepared to lay it down as a 'rule' that *þær* 'if' does not introduce conceded or open conditions, I would recommend that editors intending so to gloss it give careful consideration to all the other possibilities adumbrated above before finally committing themselves.

9. *BUTAN*

a. *Introductory remarks*

§3626. *Butan*—the variant spellings of which include *buta, buten, bute, buton, butun,* and *boten*—is, of course, the ancestor of the MnE adversative conjunction 'but'. However, it is arguable whether it had acquired that function in OE; see §1773. It occasionally serves as an adverb meaning 'outside' as opposed to 'inside', e.g. *ChronA* 68. 24 (867) *7 þær was ungemetlic wæl geslægen Norþanhymbra, sume binnan, sume butan,* or as an adverb meaning 'without', e.g. *CP* 293. 17 . . . *ða iersigendan ðonne him to getioð ðæt ðætte hie eaðe butan bion meahton*, Latin . . . *isti autem etiam quae tolerentur important* (or is *butan* a postposition governing the acc. *ðætte*?), *CP* 57. 18 *Hu mæg he ðonne ðæt lof 7 ðone gilp fleon ðonne he onahæfen bið, se his ær wilnode ða he butan wæs?*, Latin *Nescit laudem, cum suppetit, fugere, qui ad hanc didicit, cum deesset, anhelare*, and *Bo* 82. 30 . . . *7 þeah ne bið ealles butan.*

§3627. It also serves as a preposition with the dative or (less frequently) the accusative in various senses, including 'outside', e.g. *ChronA* 88. 10 (894) . . . *7 þa men ofslogon þe hie foran forridan mehton butan geweorce* and *GD* 198. 10 . . . *he awearp þæt lic ut buton þone weall*; 'without', e.g. *Bede* 154. 4 *þa æt nyhstan cwom Eanfrið buton geþeahte* . . . and *ChristB* 599 . . . *þonc butan ende*; and 'except', e.g. *Or* 178. 30 . . . *7 þær ealle ofslagene wæron buton feawum*,

Beo 703   Sceotend swæfon,
                    þa þæt hornreced   healdan scoldon,
                    ealle buton anum,

HomU 37. 238. 27 . . . *þeah hit ne sy butan feorðan dæl anes hlafes*,
and

Dan 570   . . . *þæt þu ne gemyndgast   æfter mandreame,
                    ne gewittes wast   butan wildeora þeaw.*

For more examples see Wülfing, ii, §§ 1042-7.

§ 3628. Kivimaa tells us that '*buton* and *buton þæt* were, for the most part, differentiated in meaning: the former generally meant "unless", the latter "except that". But occasionally the meanings were reversed' (p. 154); that *þæt* in *buton þæt* 'is conjunctival in nature' (p. 163); and that 'the fact that *buton* in conjunctive use is originally the adverb and not the preposition is confirmed by the form *þæt* itself: the preposition *buton* generally took the dative, rarely the accusative, and if *buton* had been prepositional, **buton þæm* would certainly have occurred as the more natural form' (p. 163). I disagree twice. First, I have not construed *butan þæt* as 'unless' except in examples in the Psalters such as *Ps(F)* 118. 92 *buton þæt æ ðin smeaung min is þonne wenunga ic forwurde on eadmodnysse min*, Latin *Nisi quod lex tua meditatio mea est tunc forte periissem in humilitate mea*, where *nisi quod* and *buton þæt* can be translated 'unless' but have the literal meaning 'except that, save only that'.[189] Second, her last argument seems to me relevant only if *þæt* is taken to be a pronoun; as I have shown in § 1958, I am reluctant to believe that the conj. *þæt* was declinable. But I am equally reluctant to believe that *þæt* in *buton þæt* is a pronoun. We have *butan* governing dem. *ðam* in *Gen* 9. 3 *7 eal ðæt ðe styrað 7 leofað beo eow to mete, swa swa growende wyrta ic hi betæce ealle eow,* [4.] *Butan ðam anum ðæt ge flæsc mid blode ne eton* 'except that alone/only, that . . .'[190] and *butan* governing dem. *þæt* in *BlHom* 101. 4 . . . *7 þær*

[189] Such glosses have little, if any, syntactical significance. In *Ps(ACDEJK)* 118. 92 we have *nymþe þæt* and in *Ps(BL)* 118. 92 *nymþe þætte*. *Ps(I)* 118. 92 has *butan ł nymþe forðan þe*. (I have not recorded the variant spellings of *nymþe*.) There is room for more work here; the works cited by Flasdieck at *Ang.* 69 (1950), 138, are not always complete and/or accurate. See further § 3652 and the variants of *Ps(C)* 93. 17 *nymþe forþon = nisi quia* reported by Wildhagen.

[190] I am inclined to suspect that *butan þæm/ðæm þæt* lies behind *butan þæm/ðæm þe* in *Or* 28. 28 . . . *oð he hæfde ealle Asiam on his geweald genyd suð fram þæm Readan Sæ 7 swa norð oþ þone sæ þe man hæt Euxinus; butan þæm þe he eac oftrædlice for mid miclum gefeohtum on Sciððie þa norðland* and *Or* 90. 25 and to compare it with *butan ðam anum ðæt* in *Gen* 9. 4; cf. § 1957. Despite BTS (s.v. *butan* A. I. (4)), *Or* 28. 28 is not comparable with *ChronA* 72. 11 (871), on which see § 3644.

noht elles ne wunað, buton þæt an þæt se þe gesælig bið mæg hine
sylfne be þære bysene læran . . . 'except that alone/only, that . . .'.
But in each of these examples we also have conj. *þæt* introducing
a noun clause.[191] Varnhagen (pp. 8-9) sees such examples as these
as an intermediate stage in the development of the conjunctional use
of *butan* and *butan þæt*. I doubt this. Indeed, at the moment I am
reluctant to accept that *butan þæt* is ever a conjunction in the sense
that combinations like *to þam þæt* (§2892) and perhaps *gyf þæt* in
HomU 44. 284. 9 (§3671) are conjunctions. My present feeling is that
in examples like *LibSc* 1. 1 *drihten segð on godspelle maran soþe lufe*
nan mann hæfþ butan þæt sawle his alecge æghwylc for freondum
his, Latin *Dominus dicit in euuangelio maiorem caritatem nemo*
habet quam ut animam suam ponat quis pro amicis suis, and in *Matt*
(WSCp) 5. 13 *gyf þ sealt awyrð on þam þe hit gesylt bið hit ne mæg*
syððan to nahte buton þ hit sy ut aworpen, Latin *si sal euanuerit in*
quo sallietur ad nihilum ualet ultra nisi ut mittatur foras, *þæt* (which
in both examples translates *ut*) introduces a noun clause governed by
butan; that in examples like *Bede* 446. 1 *Ða wæs æfter seofon hund*
wintra 7 fif wintrum æfter þære Dryhtenlican menniscnesse þæt
Ealdfrið Norþanhymbra cyning forðferde ymb twentig wintra his
rices, butan an ne wæs þa gena gefylled, Latin *Anno dominicae in-*
carnationis DCCV Aldfrid rex Nordanhymbrorum defunctus est,
anno regni sui uicesimo necdum impleto, *butan* alone does not mean
'except that' but that we have a noun clause with unexpressed *þæt*
(cf. §§3228-31) governed by *butan*; and that therefore, in

GenA 1400　　　þam æt niehstan　　　wæs nan to gedale,
　　　　　　　　nymþe heof wæs ahafen　　　on þa hean lyft,
　　　　　　　　þa se egorhere　　　eorðan tuddor
　　　　　　　　eall acwealde,　　　buton þæt earce bord
　　　　　　　　heold heofona frea,　　　þa hine halig god
　　　　　　　　ece upp forlet　　　edmodne flod
　　　　　　　　streamum stigan,　　　stiðferhð cyning,

þæt can be either a conjunction or a demonstrative with *bord*
(§1321). I propose to describe these as clauses governed by *butan*
'except'; they are further discussed in §§3641-6.

§3629. But here we must ask this question: What is the status of
butan in the examples just quoted and in others like them? Varnhagen proposed 'the general rule' (p. 13)—to which he was forced to

---

[191] Glosses such as *Ps(F)* 118. 92, above, and those which follow do not contradict this
statement: *Ps(K)* 123. 1 and 123. 2 *butan þæt* for *nisi quia*, *Ps(I)* 123. 1 and 123. 2 *butan*
forþan þe for *nisi quia*, *Ps(C)* 123. 1 *nymðe þæt* for *nisi quod*, *Ps(C)* 123. 2 *nymþe forþon*
for *nisi quia*.

admit a few exceptions even in his limited corpus (p. 14)—'that in affirmative sentences with the idea of generality *butan* is mostly to be regarded as preposition; that in negative sentences however it is to be taken as conjunction'. I see no reason for accepting this. We have already seen prep. *butan* 'without' in negative sentences in *HomU* 37. 238. 27 and in *Dan* 570 (both in §3627). To these exceptions to the second half of Varnhagen's rule may be added *Mark(WSCp)* 12. 32 . . . *þ an god is 7 nis oðer butan him*, Latin . . . *quia unus est et non est alius praeter eum*, and examples with rhetorical questions demanding a negative answer, e.g. *Ps(P)* 17. 30 *Hwylc ys God butan uran Gode? oððe hwylc Drihten butan urum Drihtne?*, and *ÆCHom* i. 48. 23 *Hwa mæg beon rihtlice geciged mannes Bearn, buton Criste anum . . . ?*

§3630. *Butan* is clearly a conjunction introducing a contracted conditional clause when it has the nominative both before and after it. Such examples occur, not only in negative sentences—e.g. *Luke (WSCp)* 17. 18, *Luke(WSCp)* 18. 19 *nis nan man god buton god ana*, Latin *nemo bonus nisi solus deus*, *ÆCHom* i. 372. 24 . . . *þæt nan God nys buton ðu ana*, and

Phoen 357   þæt ne wat ænig
        monna cynnes,   butan meotod ana,
        hu þa wisan sind   wundorlice,
        fæger fyrngesceap,   ymb þæs fugles gebyrd—

and in rhetorical questions demanding a negative answer—e.g. *BlHom* 11.19, *Ps(P)* 13. 11 *Hwa arist elles of Syon to þæm þæt he sylle Israelum hælo, butan þu, Drihten, . . . ?*, *ÆCHom* ii. 544. 23 *Hwæt is se calic þe Crist dranc buton seo ðrowung þe he for mancynne ðrowade?*, and *ChristB* 694 *Hwæt sindan þa ǁ gimmas swa scyne buton god sylfa?*—but also in positive sentences in which there is a negative implication, e.g. *ÆCHom* i. 110. 11 *Gewite ðis gedwyld fram geleaffullum heortum, þæt ænig gewyrd sy, buton se Ælmihtiga Scyppend, seðe ælcum men foresceawað lif be his geearnungum.* I would include among such exceptions to the first half of Varnhagen's rule examples like *ChronA* 98. 29 (918) *þa slog hie mon æt ægþrum cirre, þæt hira feawa on weg comon, buton þa ane þe þær ut æt swummon to þam scipum* and

Met 4. 51   þonne ic wat þætte wile   woruldmen tweogan
               geond foldan sceat   buton fea ane,

where, although *þa ane* and *fea ane* could be accusative, it seems more natural to take them as nominative, as does Varnhagen himself for *Met* 4. 51 (p. 14). Here we may compare *ÆCHom* i. 406. 13, *ÆC Hom* ii. 238. 22 and 24, *ÆCHom* ii. 238. 35 *Hwa is lif buton Crist?*, and

Met 28. 18   Hwa is on weorulde   þæt ne wafige,
                   buton þa ane   þe hit ær wisson . . . ?,

in all of which a word or phrase which can be nominative or accusative is more naturally taken as nominative, as the second half of Varnhagen's rule would require.

§3631. In examples like *BlHom* 213. 19 . . . *eal he þæt for Godes lufan sealde buton ðone dæghwamlican andleofan anne þe he nede big lifgean sceolde, El* 538, and

Beo 1612   Ne nom he in þæm wicum,   Weder-Geata leod,
                  maðmæhta ma,   þeh he þær monige geseah,
                  buton þone hafelan   ond þa hilt somod
                  since fage,

and *ÆCHom* ii. 48. 2 *Næs nanum men forgifen þæt he moste habban oððe gecweðan his agen fulluht buton Iohanne anum* and

Pan 15   Se is æghwam freond,
                  duguða estig,   butan dracan anum,
                  þam he in ealle tid   ondwrað leofaþ
                  þurh yfla gehwylc   þe he geæfnan mæg,

where we have either an accusative or a dative both before and after *butan*, it is arguable whether we have a preposition or a conjunction. I would be reluctant to call Varnhagen's rule into use here. Perhaps this difficulty is at the root of the difference of opinion between Mossé and Whitelock discussed by Joly (1967, p. 30), who notes that Mossé saw *butan* in *WHom(EI)* 20. 127 *7 la, hwæt is ænig oðer on eallum þam gelimpum butan Godes yrre ofer þas þeode, swutol 7 gesæne?* as the equivalent of *þonne* 'than', whereas Whitelock glossed it as 'except'. What Joly does not say is that Whitelock explained it as a preposition with the dative. But, since *yrre* could equally well be nominative, it could be a conjunction. The same terminological problem arises in other examples in which *butan* comes close to meaning 'than'; see §3253. The reader will, I hope, pardon me if I give such difficulties as a reason for not pursuing the question whether *butan* is a preposition or a conjunction when it is followed by a genitive, as in

JDay ii 203   ne bið þær ansyn gesewen   ænigre wihte,
                  butan þara cwelra   þe cwylmað ða earman

(where one could (I suppose) argue whether the unexpressed *ansyn* after *butan* on which *þara cwelra* depends is nominative (as I believe) or accusative) or when it governs a clause in such examples as those discussed in §3628. Future workers should note Pope's observation (*Ælfric*, ii. 839): 'Some scribes have a tendency to spell the prep. *butan* and the conj. *buton*, but there is no general rule.' (Cf. Flasdieck, *Ang.* 69 (1950), 140 fn. 38.) And there are manuscript variations: *LawAfEl(E)* 36 has *buton* where the other manuscripts have *butan*.

§3632. *Butan* 'except' may also govern infinitives, adverbial expressions, and prepositional phrases. We find a subject infinitive in *ÆCHom* i. 490. 9 *Hwæt is lange lybban buton lange swincan?*; object infinitives in *ÆCHom* i. 476. 17 *Hwæt wylle we endemenn ðyssere worulde . . . buton herian urne Drihten and eadmodlice biddan . . .* ; qualifying infinitives in *LawAfEl* 36 *Gif mon næbbe buton anfeald hrægl hine mid to wreonne 7 to werianne . . .* ; and an accusative and infinitive in *Sea* 18 *þær ic ne gehyrde butan hlimman sæ.* Examples of adverbial expressions include *Or* 92. 36 *7 næron on hie hergende buton þrie dagas*, *Bede* 318. 15 *Ond seldon in hatum baðum heo baðian wolde, buton þam hyhstan symbelnessum 7 tidum æt Eastran 7 æt Pentecosten 7 þy twelftan dege ofer Geochol*, and

El 659   . . .   ond þis næfre
           þurh æniges mannes   muð gehyrdon
           hæleðum cyðan,   butan her nu ða.

There are prepositional phrases in *Bede* 138. 2 *Forðon þam biscope heora halignesse ne wæs alyfed, þæt he moste wæpen wegan, ne elcor buton on myran ridan*, *BlHom* 21. 21 *Hwæt gelyfeþ se lichoma butan þurh þa sawle?*, *ÆCHom* i. 114. 29 *forðan þe nan man ne bið gehealden buton þurh gife Hælendes Cristes* (see Jespersen, *Neg.*, pp. 136-7), and *ÆCHom* i. 616. 29 *þa rihtwisan nahwar syððan ne wuniað buton mid Gode on heofonan rice, and ða arleasan nahwar buton mid deofle on helle suslum.* Here too I hesitate to pronounce on the status of *butan*. On the possibility of an adversative use of *butan* in OE, see §1773.

§3633. In §3628 I have spoken of clauses governed by *butan* 'except', e.g. *BlHom* 39. 28 *Hwæt mænde he þonne elles, buton þæt we gefyllon þæs þearfan wambe mid urum godum?* In contrast to these, I distinguish clauses introduced by *butan* 'unless, if . . . not', e.g. *BlHom* 101. 6 . . . *þæt hie sceolan æfter þæm wlencum ece edwit þrowian, buton him seo soþe hreow gefultmige.* I avoid the term 'exceptive' because it is used to embrace both these types by Varnhagen (pp. 9-11), who distinguishes them, and by Behre (pp. 144-8), who does not.

b. Clauses introduced by butan *conjunction 'if . . . not, unless'*

§3634. *Butan* is frequently used as a conjunction in the sense 'un-less' or 'if . . . not'. Despite Kivimaa (p. 154), I have not recorded *butan þæt* in this sense; see §§3628. In MnE we can have Unless-clauses containing a negative when the implication or emphasis makes this preferable to a positive clause introduced by 'if', e.g. 'It will be a good thesis, unless he doesn't finish it'. So far I have noted no such examples in OE. Most grammars state or imply that MnE 'if . . . not' and 'unless' are equivalent in meaning and therefore inter-changeable. This is generally true, e.g. 'I shall not go if you do not/ unless you come with me', and 'The horse will run if it does not rain/ unless it rains'. Such examples can easily be paralleled in OE; con-sider *ÆCHom* ii. 422. 21 *Gif ðu ðe hraðor ne gewitst fram Iacobe, and buton ðu wyrige Cristes naman, þu scealt beon beheafdod samod mid him, LawIIAs* 20. 6 *Gif he nylle hit geþafian, leton hine licgan buton he opwinde, ÆCHom* i. 332. 34 *forðan ðe se ðearfa nære fullice gewrecen on ðam rican, gif he on his wite hine ne oncneowe; and eft nære his wite fulfremed on ðam fyre, buton he ða ylcan pinunga his siblingum gewende,* and *Matt(WSCp)* 24. 22 *⁊ buton þa dagas gescyrte wærun, nære nan mann hal gewordyn,* where *Ru* begins *⁊ þær ne wære scynde þa dagas.* . . . There are, however, in MnE some examples in which we would perhaps hesitate to replace 'if . . . not' by 'unless'. Conceded conditions may belong here; see §3636 fn. Examples proposed and discussed by Wood (pp. 360–1) include 'You should see a doctor if you are not well' and 'If you don't at first succeed, try again'. I must leave it to others to examine the validity of his methods and the exact significance of such hesitations. But I have noted a few such examples in OE, including *Bede* 78. 32 *Gif þonne for micelre arwyrðnesse hwylc mon ne geþyrstgað onfon, se is to herienne; ac gif he onfehð, nis he to demenne, CP* 25. 18, *CP* 83. 19 *Gif ðonne mid nanum ðissa ne bið onwæced his inngeðonc, ðonne bið hit swutul ðæt he bið suiðe gerisenlice besuapen mid swiðe wlitige oferbrædelse on bæm sculdrum, Met* 25. 29 *gif he wyrsa ne bið, ne wene ic his na beteran,* and

Max ii 43   Ides sceal dyrne cræfte,
    fæmne hire freond gesecean,   gif heo nelle on folce geþeon
    þæt hi man beagum gebicge.

However, I have not detected any syntactical difference between the two groups in either OE or MnE.

§3635. Behre (p. 144) distinguishes 'exceptive clauses connected with an affirmative main clause' from 'exceptive clauses connected with a negative main clause'. (On the term 'exceptive', see my §3633.) Mather (pp. 13–14 and 41–2) seems to make the same distinction when he separates *butan* clauses which state 'a true exception', e.g. *ÆCHom* ii. 2. 22 *Micel yfel deð se ðe leas writ, buton he hit gerihte* —'the formula is: a thing will happen, except under certain conditions'—from *butan* clauses which state 'an indispensable condition', e.g. (with a negative Then-clause) *ÆCHom* i. 170. 14 *We ne beoð na fulfremede buton we beon afandode* and (with a rhetorical question expecting a negative answer) *ÆCHom* i. 184. 19 *Hwæt mihte seo godnys ana, buton ðær wære miht mid þære godnysse?*—'the formula is: This will not happen, unless this happen'.[192] I do not find these distinctions significant; indeed I am not sure that I understand them. Would *ÆCHom* ii. 2. 22 above be very different if it began ☆*Micel god ne deð se ðe leas writ . . .*? Would *Bo* 103. 20 . . . *ðonne forlyst he eall his ærran good, buton he hit eft gebete*, which Mather (p. 14)—possibly by mistake—includes among his examples of 'indispensable condition', require different classification if it read ☆. . . *ðonne næfð he . . .*? Would the two *gif* clauses in *Bede* 78. 32 (§3634) reverse their classification if the sentence read ☆*Gif þonne for micelre arwyrðnesse hwylc mon fæsteð þære halgan gemænsumnesse, se is to herienne; ac gif he ne fæsteð, nis he to demenne*? I am inclined to answer 'No' to all these questions. This attitude was confirmed by my consideration of Behre's discussion (pp. 144–8). But, whatever the theoretical validity of the distinction, it finds no grammatical expression in the syntax of OE *butan* clauses.

§3636. *Gif* clauses which regularly take the indicative retain that mood even when the verb is negated: *Bede* 78. 32 (§3634), *CP* 69. 17 *Ðurh ðone æpl ðæs eagan mon mæg geseon, gif him ðæt fleah on ne gæð, gif hine ðonne ðæt fleah mid ealle ofergæð, ðonne ne mæg he noht geseon, ÆCHom* i. 420. 2 *Gif ðes bealdwyrda biscop acweald ne bið, siððan ne bið ure ege ondrædendlic* and *ÆCHom* i. 420. 32 *Lucille, gif ðu gelyfst on Hælend Crist, he onliht ðine eagan*, and *Jul* 119. However, with *butan* 'unless, if . . . not', the regular mood is the subjunctive, both in open conditions and in rejected or imaginary conditions, irrespective of the mood and tense of the verb of the governing clause and of whether or not the sentence is in dependent speech.[193] The examples which follow may be supplemented from Wülfing, ii, §450; Mather, p. 88; Visser, ii, §881; and

---

[192] It is perhaps worth noting that examples like *Or* 21. 12 *7 gyf þar man an ban findeð unforbærned, hi hit sceolan miclum gebetan* are not the equivalent of either.

[193] I have not classified any *butan* clauses as conceded. If we have an open condition in 'If you do not agree with him, you are wrong', we can replace 'If . . . not' with 'Unless'. Can we do so if the condition is conceded?

Mitchell 1959, pp. 846 and 848. The reader will notice the variety of temporal relationships which exist between the Then-clause and the *butan* clause. Behre (pp. 144-8) offers comments on the differing nature of the subjunctive in a variety of *butan* clauses.

§3637. *Butan* clauses with the present subjunctive normally express open condition. (*Max i* 31, discussed in §3604, restrains me from replacing 'normally' with 'regularly' or 'always', although I have found no examples of rejected or imaginary condition with *butan* + the present subjunctive.) Those with the preterite subjunctive may express open condition. Examples not already quoted include *Or* 210. 19, *Bo* 35. 10 *Forþampe se anwald næfre ne bið good buton se god sie þe hine hæbbe, LawAfEl* 25 *Gif he siððan æfter sunnan upgonge þis deð, he bið mansleges scyldig 7 he ðonne self swelte, buton he nieddæda wære, BlHom* 175. 14 *þonne forþon ne mæg þin rice leng stondan, buton þu heora forwyrde þe geornor þence, ÆCHom* i. 260. 24 *Ealle we sind gelice ætforan Gode, buton hwa oðerne mid godum weorcum forðeo* (cf.

Mald 70   Ne mihte hyra ænig   oþrum derian,
                   buton hwa þurh flanes flyht   fyl gename),

WHom 7. 110 *Ne wyrð þær bedihlad þæt dihlyste geþanc þe æni man æfre geðohte, buton hit ær geandet 7 gebet wære*, and

And 185   Nu bið fore þreo niht   þæt he on þære þeode sceal
                   fore hæðenra   handgewinne
                   þurh gares gripe   gast onsendan,
                   ellorfusne,   butan ðu ær cyme.

To these can be added *ÆCHom* i. 212. 12 *þonne gif he mid deofles weorcum hine sylfne bebint, ðonne ne mæg he mid his agenre mihte hine unbindan, buton se Ælmihtiga God mid strangre handa his mildheortnysse hine unbinde* (with its suppressed apodosis ☆7 *bið gebunden*), *ÆCHom* i. 476. 4 *ac þæt he tælð to unalyfedlicere wiglunge, gif hwa ða wyrta on him becnitte, buton he hi to ðam dolge gelecge* (where the subj. *becnitte* is unusual), *HomU* 35. 205. 19 *and næs ænig word þæt ænig man on hine funde butan hit wære eall soð þæt þæt he sæde* (a complicated way of saying 'He spoke no word unless it was true', but see Mather, p. 43); and

GenB 241   Stod his handgeweorc
                    somod on sande,   nyston sorga wiht
                    to begrornianne,   butan heo godes willan
                    lengest læsten

(see Mitchell, *NM* 70 (1969), 70-2, and Vickrey, *NM* 71 (1970), 191-2).

§3638. Wülfing (ii, §450) observes that *butan* 'if . . . not, unless' by nature does not take the indicative. The variations in *Matt* 12. 29—*WSCp* . . . *buton he gebinde ærest þone strangan 7 þonne hys hus bereafige*; *Li* . . . *buta* . . . *gebinde* . . . *genimeð ł gehrypes*; *Ru* . . . *nymþe* . . . *gebindaþ* . . . *tobregdeþ*—do not shake the conclusion. The only real exception known to Mather (pp. 14-15 and 43) and to me is late: *HomU* 35. 216. 14 *forþon hiom sænd god on micelne brogan, fyr and hungor, butan hio to godes geleafan ær gecyrran willaþ*. On *Or* 292. 15 see §3646.

§3639. There are no unambiguous examples of rejected or imaginary conditions introduced by *butan* in the poetry; on *Beo* 963, see §3640. Those in the prose include *CP* 441. 32 *Forðæm, buton he ðæt woh ær towurpe ne meahte he noht nytwyrðlice ðæt ryht getimbran; forðæm, buton he of his hieremonna mode ða ðornas ðære idlan lufan ær upatuge, unnyt he plantode on hi ða word ðære halgan lare*, *ÆCHom* i. 26. 29, *ÆCHom* i. 174. 20 *Buton se deofol gesawe þæt Crist man wære, ne gecostnode he hine; and buton he soð God wære, noldon ða englas him ðenian*, *ÆCHom* i. 184. 19, *ÆCHom* i. 332. 35, *ÆCHom* ii. 40. 19, and *ApT* 40. 20 *Buton þes man me þone first forgeafe þæt ic me to Gode gebæde, þonne ne become ic to þissere are*, Latin *Nisi iste ad testandum deum horarum . . . spacium tribuisset mihi, modo vestra pietas non defendisset*.

§3640. Here, as elsewhere, it is important to note the effects on mood and tense which result from the use of dependent speech. Thus we have the preterite subjunctive in an open condition referring to the future in *ÆCHom* i. 72. 10 . . . *and cwæð þæt he nolde gelyfan buton Iohannes attor drunce, and þurh Godes mihte ðone cwelmbæran drenc oferswiðde* and in a rejected condition referring to the past in *ÆCHom* i. 216. 4 *We habbað oft gesæd, and git secgað, þæt Cristes rihtwisnys is swa micel, þæt he nolde niman mancyn neadunga of ðam deofle, buton he hit forwyrhte* and in *ÆCHom* i. 440. 27. But I am not sure which we have in

Beo 963   Ic hine hrædlice   heardan clammum
        on wælbedde   wriþan þohte,
        þæt he for mundgripe   minum scolde
        licgean lifbysig,   butan his lic swice.

Did Beowulf say to himself at the time of the fight 'If his body does not escape, he will have to struggle for his life' or is he looking back with regret 'If his body had not escaped, he would have had to struggle for his life'? See further §§3612-14.

c. Clauses governed by butan 'except'

§3641. In §3628 I give my reasons for taking *þæt* as a conjunction introducing a noun clause in examples like *CP* 249. 16 *Oððe hwæt is ure weorðscipe on ðissum eorðlicum lichoman buton ðæt we sint gesceapene æfter ðære biesene ures Scippendes?*, *Or* 268. 26 *he wæs swiþe yfel monn ealra þeawa, buton þæt he wæs cene 7 oft feaht anwig*, *BlHom* 39. 28 *Hwæt mænde he þonne elles, buton þæt we gefyllon þæs þearfan wambe mid urum godum?*, *ÆLS* 31. 1355 *Ne gedafnað cristenum menn buton þæt he on duste swelte*, *ÆCHom* i. 186. 6 *Ne gæð na mare to metinge buton þæt þu hit geseo and herige* (Mather, p. 58, takes this as a clause of purpose), *ÆCHom* ii. 76. 7 *Hwæt is to cweðenne, þæt nan man us to ðam wingearde ne gehyrde, buton þæt nan man us ne bodade lifes weig?*, *ChronE* 215. 15 (1083) *Hwæt magon we secgean buton þ hi scotedon swiðe 7 þa oðre ða dura bræcon þær adune . . .* , and

Met 9. 18   Næs þæt herlic dæd,
          þæt hine swelces gamenes   gilpan lyste,
          þa he ne earnade   elles wuhte,
          buton þæt he wolde   ofer werðiode
          his anes huru anwald cyðan;

for taking the same view with regard to *þæt* in the combination *buton ðam anum þæt* in *ÆCHom* ii. 448. 33 *Efne nu ealle ða ðing ðe he ah sindon on ðinre handa, buton ðam anum þæt ðu on him sylfum ðine hand ne astrecce* and to the second *þæt* in examples like *BlHom* 147. 15 *7 næfde heo noht on hire buton þæt an þæt heo hæfde mennisce onlicnesse*; and for construing as a noun clause with unexpressed *þæt*, the clause which follows *butan* in examples like *Or* 17. 4 *ac hit is eal weste, buton on feawum stowum styccemælum wiciað Finnas . . .* , *ÆCHom* ii. 374. 16 *hwæt deð he ðonne buton bitt and hine beladað?* 'What does he then do except pray and excuse himself?', where it seems better to understand [*þæt he*] than to regard *bitt* and *beladað* as governed directly by *butan, CEdg* 10, and

Beo 1559   þæt wæs wæpna cyst,—
          buton hit wæs mare   ðonne ænig mon oðer
          to beadulace   ætberan meahte,
          god ond geatolic,   giganta geweorc.

On *GenA* 1400 see §3628. In the same section I explain my unwillingness to decide whether *butan* in such examples is a conjunction or a preposition and my resulting adoption of the formula 'clauses governed by *butan* "except" '. On variations of mood, see §§2016–38.

§3642. The reader will have seen from the examples in §3641 that the noun clauses governed by *butan* may serve as subject, as in *ÆLS* 31. 1355, or object, as in *ChronE* 215. 15 (1083); may be in apposition with a demonstrative, as in *Gen* 9. 4 (not quoted) and *BlHom* 147. 15; or may seem to be completely dependent on *butan* itself, as in *Or* 17. 4. In *Bo* 8. 18 (not quoted) it is arguable whether *ic wat* is parenthetic or governs the following *þ* clause; cf. Sedgefield's punctuation with that of Mather (p. 58). In

GenB 681   Hit nis wuhte gelic
                elles on eorðan,   buton swa þes ar sægeð,
                þæt hit gegnunga   from gode come,

buton may govern the *swa* clause and *sægeð* the *þæt* clause, or the *swa* clause may be parenthetic, with *buton* governing the *þæt* clause. It is perhaps also possible that the poet meant to say 'unless, as this messenger says, it came from God' and that *þæt* is a mistaken insertion under the influence of *sægeð*.

§3643. Adverb clauses governed by *butan* also seem to be completely dependent upon it. They include clauses of place, e.g. *Or* 17. 28 *Ac þara Terfinna land wæs eal weste buton ðær huntan gewicodon, oþþe fisceras, oþþe fugeleras*; clauses of time, e.g. *CP* 399. 3 *7 ðeah ne bioð na gemengde buton ðonne hi wilniað bearn to gestrienanne*, *ÆCHom* ii. 568. 16 *Hwæt is 'on middre nihte' buton þonne ðu nast and þu his ne wenst?*, *Men* 29, and

Sat 387   Him beforan fereð   fægere leoht
                þonne we æfre ær   eagum gesawon,
                buton þa we mid englum   uppe wæron;

clauses of purpose, e.g. *John(WSCp)* 10. 10 *þeof ne cymð buton þ he stele 7 slea 7 fordo*, Latin *nisi ut*; causal clauses, e.g. *CP* 423. 22 and *ÆCHom* ii. 566. 31 *Hwi sind ða deadan slapende gecwedene, buton forðan ðe hi sceolon arisan geedcucode þurh ðone Ælmihtigan Scyppend?*; and clauses of comparison, e.g. (with *swa* 'as') *ChronA* 90. 18 (897) *næron nawðer ne on Fresisc gescæpene ne on Denisc, bute swa him selfum ðuhte þæt hie nytwyrðoste beon meahten* and possibly *GenB* 681 (see §3642), (with *swa . . . swa* 'as . . . as') *ÆC Hom* i. 154. 15 *. . . ne we his na mare ne cunnon buton swa micel swa we ðurh Cristes lare on bocum rædað*, (with *swa* + a superlative)

Met 8. 15   Hwæt, hi firenlusta   frece ne wæron,
                buton swa hi meahton   gemetlicost
                ða gecynd began   þe him Crist gesceop . . . ,

and (with *swilce* 'as if') *ÆCHom* ii. 36. 11 *þonne he bitt þæt God þone oðerne fordon sceole, hwæt deð he ðonne buton swilce he deme, and God slea?* In *BlHom* 227. 13 *ne gedafenað Cristenan men þæt he elles do butan swa he efne on axan 7 on duste licge*, the subj. *licge* is parallel to the subj. *do*, which is appropriate in this noun clause, and therefore does not certify that *swa* means 'as if'. *þæt* for *swa* would give good OE. Perhaps *swa* is an adverb 'thus' rather than a conjunction 'as'. I have recorded no examples in which *butan* governs a clause of result, of concession, or (not surprisingly) of condition.

§3644. *Butan* can also govern either an adjective clause or the antecedent of an adjective clause. *Num* 23. 12 *Balaam cwæð ða: Cwyst ðu, mæg ic oþer sprecan buton ðæt Drihten het?*, where *ðæt* means 'what(ever)' and *buton ðæt* translates *nisi quod*, provides a clear example of the first phenomenon. The second is more easily exemplified: *CP* 457. 21 *Hwæðres ðonne ðara yfela is betere ær to tilianne, buton swæðres swæðer frecenlicre is?*, *ChronA* 72. 11 (871) *7 þæs geares wurdon viiii folcgefeoht gefohten wiþ þone here on þy cynerice be suþan Temese butan þam þe him Ælfred þæs cyninges broþur 7 anlipig aldormon 7 cyninges þegnas oft rade onridon þe mon na ne rimde, BlHom* 185. 8 . . . *ne magan þær nænige oþre men onfon, buton þa ane þe mid clænum geleafan hie to þæm gegearwiaþ, ÆLS* 27. 179, *ÆCHom* ii. 414. 10 *and nis nan oðer Godes Sunu buton se ðe fram Iudeum on rode ahangen wæs*, where Thorpe's 'save him who' misrepresents the OE idiom, and *ÆCHom* ii. 492. 19 . . . *þæt ge nænne oðerne ne wurðion eow to Gode buton þone ðe we bodiað*, where Thorpe's 'but him whom' is acceptable. In the last two examples, the adjective clauses refer to a specific antecedent, Christ. It is a terminological problem whether in examples like *ÆCHom* ii. 392. 5 *Ne bið nan man trum ðurh God, buton se ðe hine undergyt untrumne þurh hine sylfne*, where the adjective clause refers to anyone whom the cap fits and where Thorpe's 'except him who' is inaccurate, belong to the first or second group. I have no means of deciding whether *buton se ðe* means 'save he who' or 'except whoever'; see §2204 and cf. *buton þa þe* in *BlHom* 103. 14 *Nis þæt þonne nænig man þæt þurfe þone deopan grund þæs hatan leges 7 þæs heardan leges gesecean, buton þa þe heora sylfra ræd on ofergeotolnesse Godes beboda forlætað.*

§3645. Behre's failure in his discussion of mood in *butan* clauses (pp. 146-7) to distinguish clauses introduced by *butan* 'unless' from clauses governed by *butan* 'except' leads him into modal fenlands where we need not venture. The mood in Except-clauses is not affected by the presence of *butan* but is determined by the type of clause which follows it. Mather (p. 15), writing forty years before Behre, expressed this important truth: 'The verb in the indic. is properly not introduced by buton but by the following conjunction.' The same, of course, is true of any subjunctives which occur after *butan* 'except', e.g. those in the clause of purpose in *John(WSCp)* 10. 10 (§3643).

§3646. A few inconclusive comments follow on the status of *butan* when it governs a clause. Mather (pp. 43(2) and 15) saw it as a conjunction: 'In most of these cases we have merely a contracted clause, which leaves the proper verb of buton to be supplied from the context.' This would mean that in *Or* 292. 15 *Se wære wierðe ealra Romana onwaldes for his monigfealdum duguðum, buton þæt he þa wiþ his hlaford won for oðra monna lare, buton þæt* is the equivalent of 'unless [it had been] that' rather than of 'except [prep.] that'. Similarly the combination *buton se ðe* in *ÆCHom* ii. 414. 10 and *ÆCHom* ii. 392. 5 (both in §3644) should be interpreted as 'unless [it is] he who'; as I have pointed out there, Thorpe's 'save him who' and 'except him who' misrepresent the OE idiom. Again, the combination *buton þone ðe* in *ÆCHom* ii. 492. 19 (§3644) would mean 'unless [you worship] him who'. Such interpretations are a counter to the possible argument that *butan* must be a preposition because, if it were a conjunction, it ought to affect the mood of an indicative verb in the clause which follows it. But the possibility that it is a preposition should not be dismissed too lightly; see, in addition to §§3629-31, Onions, p. 104; Jespersen, *Ess.*, pp. 350 and 352-3; and Johnsen and Jespersen, *EStudien*, 46 (1912-13), 7-8 and 330-2 respectively. There is room for further work here. I conclude by remarking that I have the impression that clauses governed by *butan* are less common with positive principal clauses than with principal clauses containing negatives or rhetorical questions.

10. *NYMþE*

a. *Introductory remarks*

§3647. There is general acceptance of Flasdieck's verdict (*Ang.* 69 (1950), 140) that '*nympe, nemne* is one of the best known Anglianisms'. Mather (*MLN* 9 (1894), 77) suggests that 'the fact that *buton* is found with *nemne* from the first is, perhaps, proof that the form was old, and that its tenth century use was archaistic. The fact that the word is found in no form in Middle English tends to strengthen this conclusion.' Flasdieck (loc. cit.) reports that 'by far the most common forms in OE prose are *nympe* and *nemne*'. Hence I use *nympe*. Other variant spellings include *næfne, næmne, nefne, nempe, nimpe, nymne, nymppe*, and forms with *ð* for *þ*; for fuller details, see Flasdieck, *Ang.* 69 (1950), 135-71.[194] *Nympe* has much in common with *butan*. In *Ps(I)* 118. 92 *butan ł nymðe forðan þe* glosses *nisi quod*. We find *nymðe* glossed *butan* in *Bede(Ca)* 78. 24 and *buton* in *Sat* 18. The variation *Bede(T)* 78. 1 *nemne* but *Bede(T)* 78. 3 *butan* is shared (apart from differences in spelling) by MSS *B, O*, and *Ca*; cf. *BlHom* 223. 36 *Ne gehyrde nænig man on his muþe oht elles nefne Cristes lof 7 nytte spræce, ne on his heortan buton arfæstnesse 7 mildheortnesse 7 sibbe. Nemne* in *GD(C)* 54. 8 is replaced by *buton* in MS *H*. We find *nemne buton* 'except' in *BlHom* 19. 22 and *nympe • bute* 'unless' in *Ch* 813. *Nympe* shares most of the functions already described for *butan* in §§3626-46. On its use as a conjunction 'unless, if not' introducing clauses and as a conjunction 'except' governing clauses, see §§3652-5 and 3656-8. Its other uses are described here. Indeed, *nympe* raises so many of the problems already discussed concerning *butan* that it was tempting to treat them together. But, for the sake of clarity, I keep them separate, comparing and contrasting them when necessary.

§3648. There are spasmodic examples in *Ps(E)* of *nympe* glossing Latin conj. *neque*, e.g. *Ps(E)* 80. 10 and 130. 1 (three examples). The subsequent disappearance of the word makes it impossible to say whether this denotes a trend or is merely an individual idiosyncrasy. The dictionaries and grammars do not recognize *nympe* as an adverb. We find the glosses *nam: soðes ł nymðe* in *Ps(I)* 118. 24 and *numquid: nimðe* in *PsCa(E)* 5. 8. *Nemne* can be translated 'only' in *Lch* ii. 202. 17 *7 þonne hie ælcra drincan willen, drincan hie nemne wæter*. But a comparison with *Bede* 78. 23 *Ond hwæt elles is to secenne wið þæm hungre nemne ondlifen, wið þurst drync, wið hæto celnis . . . ?* (where *ondlifen* is probably nominative and *nemne* a conjunction), *BlHom* 223. 36 (§3647) (where *lof* and *spræce* are accusative), and

Sat 334   Nabbað he to hyhte   nymþe cyle and fyr,
                 wean and witu   and wyrma þreat,
                 dracan and næddran   and þone dimman ham,

suggests that in *Lch* ii. 202. 17, above, we have a negated sentence without *ne* immediately before the verb (§1627), that *nemne* means

---

[194] Not all the lists offered by the scholars whom Flasdieck cites are complete and/or accurate. See also Mather, p. 80, and Flasdieck, *Ang.* 70 (1951), 46.

'except', and that *wæter* is an accusative object of *drincan*. Whether *nymþe* in the examples in which it is followed by an accusative, when that would be the appropriate case if *nymþe* were not there, is a preposition or a conjunction, I do not know. But I have found no certain examples of *nymþe* preposition with the accusative in prose or poetry, and the dictionaries and grammars are silent on this point. However, since *nymþe* preposition + dative is so far established only by

Beo 1080

                    Wig ealle fornam
    Finnes þegnas   nemne feaum anum,
    þæt he ne mehte   on þæm meðelstede
    wig Hengeste   wiht gefeohtan . . . ,

full collections may establish *nymþe* as a preposition with the accusative.

§3649. Like *butan* (§3630), *nymþe* is clearly a conjunction introducing a contracted conditional clause when it has the nominative both before and after it, 'the verb of the second clause being the same as that in the first, and not expressed . . .' (BT, s.v. *nefne*, *nemne* II). GK's observation (s.v. *nefne* 2, præp.) that 'gewöhnlich aber steht durch Attraktion, wie bei unserem *außer*, statt des Dativs der Kasus, der außerdem die Satzkonstruktion erfordert' ['but usually, as with the German conjunction *außer*, the case which the construction would otherwise require occurs by attraction instead of the dative']—the examples include

Beo 1933

    nænig þæt dorste   deor geneþan
    swæsra gesiða,   nefne sinfrea,
    þæt hire an dæges   eagum starede

and

Rim 77

    oþþæt beoþ þa ban   gebrosnad on an
    ond æt nyhstan nan   nefne se neda tan
    balawun her gehloten—

seems to me to overwork the concept of attraction.[195] In most of the examples known to me, the principal clause is either a negated statement, e.g. *LS* 3. 239 *nes nefre in his muðe nymðe crist nymðe mildheortnis* and *Rim* 77, above, or a rhetorical question demanding a negative answer, e.g. *Bede* 78. 23 (§3648) and *Sat* 17 *Hwa is þæt*

---

[195] The GK articles on *butan*, *nefne*, and *nemðe*, contain inconsistencies; cf., for example, the treatment of *buton* in *Beo* 1614 with that of *nefne* in *Beo* 2151.

ðe cunne || *orðonc clene nymðe ece god?* But there is a positive principal clause followed by *nymðe fea ane* in

GenA 2133   Eaforan syndon deade,
            folcgesiðas,   nymðe fea ane,
            þe me mid sceoldon   mearce healdan.

These three patterns are also found with *butan*; see §3630.

§3650. As already noted, difficulties similar to those encountered in deciding whether *butan* is a preposition or a conjunction arise with *nymþe*. Much that is said in §§3629-31 concerning *butan* applies here. The major difference is that, since *butan* is established as a preposition with the accusative and *nymþe* is not (§3648), we must await the full collections before arguing whether *nymþe* can be a preposition in examples like *BlHom* 223. 36 (§3647) and *Beo* 2150 *ic lyt hafo* || *heafodmaga nefne, Hygelac, ðec* (here the principal clause is a virtual negative), in which it is preceded and followed by the accusative. The presumption for the moment must be that it is a conjunction. The same is true in examples in which the form following *nymþe* can be either nominative or accusative, e.g. *GenA* 2133 and

And 662   Næs þær folces ma
            on siðfate,   sinra leoda,
            nemne ellefne   orettmæcgas,
            geteled tireadige.

In examples such as

Rid 25. 1   Ic eom wunderlicu wiht,   wifum on hyhte,
            neahbuendum nyt;   nængum sceþþe
            burgsittendra,   nymþe bonan anum,

in which *nymþe* is preceded and followed by a dative, it can be either a preposition or a conjunction. Examples with genitives have to be treated individually. In *Bede* 384. 22 . . . *ne we us nohtes elles wendon naemne deaðes seolfes*, where *deaðes seolfes* is a genitive object of *wendon*, and in

Beo 2532   Nis þæt eower sið,
            ne gemet mannes,   nefne min anes,
            þæt he wið aglæcean   eofoðo dæle,
            eorlscype efne,

where *min anes* depends on the nominative *gemet*, we have contracted clauses introduced by the conjunction. Until *nymþe* is established as a preposition with the accusative, the same must be presumed for

BlHom 161. 6 *forþon þe we gehyrdon . . . þæt næniges Godes haligra gebyrd . . . ciricean ne mærsiaþ nemþe Cristes sylfes 7 þyses Iohannes,* where we understand accusative *gebyrd* after *nemþe*.

§3651. Like *butan, nymþe* 'except' governs prepositional phrases, e.g. *Bede* 278. 11 *Se feorða is: þætte munecas ne leoren of stowe to oðerre, ne of mynstre to oðrum, nemne þurh leafnesse his agnes abbudes* and

Sea 44   Ne biþ him to hearpan hyge   ne to hringþege,
              ne to wife wyn   ne to worulde hyht,
              ne ymbe owiht elles,   nefne ymb yða gewealc. . . .

Butan is also recorded governing infinitives and adverbial expressions; see §3632. My present collections do not include similar examples with *nymþe*.

b. Clauses introduced by nymþe conjunction 'if. . . not, unless'

§3652. Like *butan, nymþe* is used as a conjunction 'if . . . not, unless'; note the variation in the conditional conjunctions in *Ch* 98 *gif heo þ nyllen syn heo þonne amansumade from dælneomencge liceman 7 blodes usses drihtnes hælendes Cristes • 7 from alre neweste geleafulra syn heo asceadene 7 asyndrade nymðe heo hit her mid þingonge bote gebete. Mutatis mutandis*, the remarks made in §3634 about the interchangeability of 'if . . . not' and 'unless' apply here. But I do not know why Behre (p. 147) uses the word 'almost' when he writes that in

Beo 1055   . . .   swa he hyra ma wolde,
                 nefne him witig God   wyrd forstode
                 ond ðæs mannes mod

'the exceptive clause *nefne forstode* is almost equivalent to *gif ne forstode*'. The following combinations can be translated 'unless' but both the OE and its Latin equivalent have the literal meaning 'except that, save only that': *Ps(C)* 123. 1 *nymðe þæt = nisi quod* (*PPs* 123. 1 *nymþe*); *Ps(L)* 118. 92 *nymþe þætte = nisi quod* (*PPs* 118. 92 *þær . . . ne*); *Ps(L)* 123. 2 *nimþe forþan = nisi quia, Ps(C)* 123. 2 *nymþe forþon = nisi quia* (*Ps(F)* 123. 2 *buton forðon, Ps(I)* 123. 2 *butan forþan þe, PPs* 123. 1 line 3 *nymþe*). In *Ps(E)* 93. 17 *nimðe = nisi quia*. See further §3628.

§3653. Conditional clauses introduced by *nymþe* conjunction 'if . . . not, unless' may accompany positive Then-clauses, e.g. *Bede*

86. 1 ... *þæt is, þæt he þa synne þæs geþohtes mid tearum aþwea,* 7 *nemne ær þæt fyr þære costunge gewitee, þæt he hine scyldigne ongete swa swa oð æfentiid, Ch* 98 (§3652), *LawGrið* 15 ... *he bið feorhscyldig, nimþe se cyng alyfan wille þæt man wergylde alysan mote,* and

Dan 143   Ge sweltað deaðe,   nymþe ic dom wite
                   soðan swefnes,   þæs min sefa myndgað,

or negative Then-clauses, e.g. *Bede* 76. 33 *Ono þas wiif, þa ðe heora bearn of unrihtum gewunum oðrum to fedenne sellað, nemne seo clæsnunge tiid forðgeleore, ne sceolon heo heora werum gemengde beon, Bede* 220. 25 *Ne hine mon on oðre wisan his bene tygþian wolde, nemne he Cristes geleafan onfenge mid þa ðeode, þe he cyning ofer wæs, Ch* 333 *R*20. 18, and

Jul 108   Næfre ic þæs þeodnes   þafian wille
                   mægrædenne,   nemne he mægna god
                   geornor bigonge   þonne he gen dyde. . . .

As with *butan* (§3635), there is no syntactical distinction between the two. The rhetorical question is the equivalent of a negated statement in *GD* 221. 8 *hwanon furðor beoð halige men sigorfæste, nymðe hi campian* 7 *feohtan wið þam searwum þæs ealdan feondes?* Apart from *Beo* 1055, the examples so far cited are open conditions. The regular mood is the present or preterite subjunctive as appropriate. Behre's remarks (p. 147) about

Phoen 259   No he foddor þigeð,
                   mete on moldan,   nemne meledeawes
                   dæl gebyrge,   se dreoseð oft
                   æt middre nihte

seem to assume that here *nemne* cannot mean 'unless'. We have the present indicative in

Max i 105   ham cymeð, gif he hal leofað,   nefne him holm gestyreð,
                   mere hafað mundum   mægðegsan wyn

(here I adopt the punctuation I suggested in *Neophil.* 49 (1965), 157). The expected subjunctive occurs in

Max i 183   Idle hond æmetlan geneah tæfles monnes,   þonne teoselum
                                                                         weorpeð,
                   seldan in sidum ceole,   nefne he under segle yrne

(again the punctuation is mine; see *RES* 15 (1964), 130). Behre (p. 147) appears to believe that the indicative is a relic of an earlier usage, but it could be explained as a late intrusion, foreshadowing the modern usage.

§3654. Examples of rejected or imaginary conditions introduced by *nymþe* include, in addition to *Beo* 1055 (§3652), *Ps(E)* 93. 17 *Nimðe me drihten demæe usser gefultumed fegere æt þeærfe weninga min saul sohte helle*, Latin *Nisi quia dominus adiuvasset me paulominus habitaverat in inferno anima mea*, its metrical equivalent

PPs 93. 15   Nymðe me drihten,　　dema usser,
                 gefultumede　　fægere æt þearfe,
                 wenincga min sawl　　sohte helle,

and

Beo 1550   Hæfde ða forsiðod　　sunu Ecgþeowes
                 under gynne grund,　　Geata cempa,
                 nemne him heaðobyrne　　helpe gefremede,
                 herenet hearde,——　　ond halig God
                 geweold wigsigor;　　witig Drihten,
                 rodera Rædend　　hit on ryht gesced
                 yðelice,　　syþðan he eft astod,

where we can supply ☆*ond halig God geweolde wigsigor* after line 1553a. In view of the examples of rejected or imaginary conditions introduced by other conjunctions, the expected mood in both clauses is the preterite subjunctive. However, the indicative sometimes occurs in one or other of the clauses. It appears under Latin influence in the Psalter glosses; see Nunn, §171. Thus, in *Ps(E)* 93. 17 and *PPs* 93. 15 above, *sohte* represents *habitaverat*, which is rendered by *eardade* in *Ps(A)* 93. 17 and by *eardode* in *Ps(CD)* 93. 17. But *Ps(K)* 93. 17 has *butan forðā gefylsteð me lytle eardude on helle sawel min*, Latin *Nisi quia dominus adiuuit me paulominus habitasset in inferno anima mea*. See further the different renderings of *Ps* 123. 1, 2 and *Ps* 126. 1. We have a special case of what can be described as a 'suppressed apodosis' —☆*ond wære getwæfed*—before *nymðe* in

Beo 1655   Ic þæt unsofte　　ealdre gedigde,
                 wigge under wætere,　　weorc geneþde
                 earfoðlice;　　ætrihte wæs
                 guð getwæfed,　　nymðe mec God scylde

and, if we accept the emendation *næfne* or *næfne he* for *næs he*, in *Beo* 3074; cf. such MnE sentences as 'And in Wessex the outlook was well nigh hopeless, were it not that the King never gave up hope' and 'Don Antonio de Noronha was very nearly decapitated by one of the Arabs, had not Albuquerque warded off the blow with his shield'. See further Mitchell 1959, pp. 602 fn. 1, 613-15, and 885, and Mitchell, at press (*b*).

§3655. The difficulty of deciding whether we have open or rejected conditions in some examples in dependent speech, already noted with *butan* (§3640), arises here too. I leave the reader to decide which we have in *Alex* 36. 14 . . . *þ ic wolde gewitan hweþer sio segen soð wære þe me mon ær be þon sægde þ þær nænig mon ingan mehte 7 eft gesund æfter þon beon nymþe he mid asegendnisseum ineode in þ scræf* and in

Beo 778   þæs ne wendon ær   witan Scyldinga,
                  þæt hit a mid gemete   manna ænig
                  betlic ond banfag   tobrecan meahte,
                  listum tolucan,   nymþe liges fæþm
                  swulge on swaþule.

c. *Clauses governed by* nymþe *'except'*

§3656. The formula adopted in the heading reflects my unwillingness to decide whether *nymþe* is a conjunction or a preposition governing a clause in examples like *GD(C)* 54. 7 . . . *hwæt magon we ærest ongytan nemne þæt þa þe mycelre geearnunge beoð mid drihtene, hwilum hi magon begytan þa þing þe heom ær teohhode næron?* (where MS *H* has *buton*) and *GD* 336. 1 *hwæt elles forþon is þæt, þæt hit sy to gebiddane for þam feondum, nymðe þæt se apostol cwæð þæt God heom sylle dædbote to ongytanne þa soþfæstnesse . . . ?*—in these I take *þæt* as a conjunction introducing a noun clause; see §3641—or in examples like *Bede* 182. 23 *Ða wæs geworden þætte þære seolfan neahte þa brohton ban ute awunedon, nemne mon geteld ofer abrædde* and *Bede* 462. 6 *7 he þær læg IIII dagas 7 IIII niht swa swa dead mon, nemne ðynre eðunge anre ætwyde þæt he lifes wæs*—here I take the clauses following *nymþe* as noun clauses with unexpressed *þæt*; see §3641. The reasons for this unwillingness are given in §§3629-31, where the same difficulties are discussed in relation to *butan*.

§3657. *Nymþe þæt* does not occur in the poetry. But *nymþe* governs a clause with unexpressed *þæt* in

Beo 1351   oðer earmsceapen
              on weres wæstmum   wræclastas træd,
              næfne he wæs mara   þonne ænig man oðer

and in *GenA* 1400 (§3628). Mather (p. 43), accepting *-st* added to *byrgde* above the line in the Junius manuscript, would take as an example of this kind

GenA 876   For hwon wast þu wean   and wrihst sceome,
                     gesyhst sorge,   and þin sylf þecest
                     lic mid leafum,   sagast lifceare
                     hean hygegeomor,   þæt þe sie hrægles þearf,
                     nymþe ðu æppel   ænne byrgde
                     of ðam wudubeame   þe ic þe wordum forbead?

But *byrgde(st)* can be taken as an ambiguous but subjunctive form and, despite Mather's 'There is hardly any conditional force in the *nymþe* clause', 'unless' or 'if . . . not' gives better sense than his 'except (that)'.

§3658. Clauses governed by *nymþe* 'except' do not necessarily have the subjunctive, but take the mood appropriate to them. As with *butan* 'except' (§§3643-4), they are not necessarily noun clauses; thus we have a clause of comparison in *Ch* 1500 . . . *7 ða sprece nænig mon uferran dogor on nænge oðre halfe oncærrende sie nymne suæ þis gewrit hafað*. On *Bede* 280. 1 see Mather, p. 57. Here, as with *butan* (§3646), I have the impression that positive principal clauses are less common than those containing negatives or rhetorical questions.

11. 'ON CONDITION THAT'

a. Introductory remarks

§3659. Wood (pp. 358-9) makes a distinction between MnE 'on condition that' and 'provided that' which in my opinion does not always hold. Thus, *gif* in *Bede* 28. 14 *Gif ge þæt secan wyllaþ, þonne magon ge þær eardungstowe habban* can bear both senses (the order of the clauses is significant in MnE) and *wið þan þæt* in *ÆCHom* i. 56. 10 *Menigfealde earfoðnyssa and hospas wolde gehwa eaðelice forberan wið þan þæt he moste sumum rican men to bearne geteald beon* . . . can mean 'so that', 'on condition that', or 'provided that'. But lexicographers should perhaps explore it. They should also note the closeness between purpose and the idea of 'on condition that' apparent in the last example; consider *Bede* 50. 29 *7 him Bryttas sealdan 7 geafan eardungstowe betwih him þæt hi for sibbe 7 hælo heora eðles campodon 7 wunnon wið heora feondum*, where Miller has '. . . on condition of . . .', and see Shearin 1903, p. 74.

b. Single word conjunctions

§3660. *Gif* can mean 'on condition that', e.g. *ÆCHom* i. 232. 33 *þisne anweald forgeaf Crist þam apostolum and eallum bisceopum, gif hi hit on riht healdað* and

GenB 641   ac he þeoda gehwam
                    hefonrice forgeaf,   halig drihten,
                    widbradne welan,   gif hie þone wæstm an
                    lætan wolden   þe þæt laðe treow
                    on his bogum bær,   bitre gefylled.

Butan and *nymþe* cannot of course be directly translated as 'on condition that'. But the clauses they introduce can sometimes carry that implication. Thus, Miller translates *Bede* 220. 25 *Ne hine mon on oðre wisan his bene tygþian wolde, nemne he Cristes geleafan onfenge mid þa ðeode, þe he cyning ofer wæs* 'His prayer was only granted on condition of his receiving the faith of Christ, along with the people under his rule'. The *butan* clause in *WHom* 7. 110 (§3637) could be similarly interpreted. Klaeber (*Archiv*, 191 (1954–5), 218, and 3, glossary, s.v. *þæt*) assigns conditional value 'provided that' to the second *þæt* in

Beo 1096   Fin Hengeste
                    elne unflitme   aðum benemde,
                    þæt he þa wealafe   weotena dome
                    arum heolde,   þæt ðær ænig mon
                    wordum ne worcum   wære ne bræce . . . ,

asking 'How could Finn solemnly declare that nobody would break the treaty?' But he offers no parallel. *Bede* 50. 29 (§3659) suggests the possibility that here too we have a clause of purpose 'so that . . .'. But it could also be taken as a prospective but not intended result 'in such a way that . . .'. In *Or* 210. 19 *Ac hit Scipia nolde him aliefan wið nanum oþrum þinge butan hie him ealle hiera wæpeno ageafen, 7 þa burg forleten, 7 þæt nan ne sæte hiere X milum neah, þæt* could express an intended result. But 'provided that' gives good sense. There is room for more work here. On *swa* see §3673.

c. Prepositional combinations without nouns

§3661. The preposition *wiþ* can carry the sense 'in consideration of, in return for', e.g. *Or* 210. 19 (§3660) and *BlHom* 69. 13 . . . *he gesealde wiþ feo heofeones Hlaford 7 ealles middangeardes*. So it is not surprising that prepositional combinations containing a demonstrative introduced by *wiþ* come to have the sense 'on condition that'. It is impossible to say whether these combinations became fossilized as conjunctions or whether the components retained their literal meanings; see §2606 and compare *CP* 329. 15 *Gehieren ða reaferas, ða ðe higiað wið ðæs ðæt hie willað oðre menn bereafian* . . . with *Bo* 25. 18 *wið þas ic wat þu wilt higian.* The examples which follow seem to me consistent with either view.

§3662. The pattern with *þe* occurs in *Bede* 54. 3 . . . *7 ecne þeowdom geheton, wiðþon þe him mon andlifne forgefe,* ÆLS 12. 117 . . . *nolde he syllan ealle his æhta* . . . *wið þan þe he libban moste* . . . ?, possibly *Lch* iii. 92. 10, *ChronE* 145. 6 (1014) . . . *7 cwæð þæt he heom hold hlaford beon wolde* . . . *wið þam þe hi ealle anrædlice buton swicdome to him gecyrdon,* and *HomU* 31. 181. 18 . . . *and þeowemen þa ðrig dagas beon weorces gefreode wið ciricsocne and wið ðam þe hi þæt fæsten þe lustlicor gefæstan* (where Napier has a comma between *ðam* and *þe*). Examples with *þæt* include *CP* 255. 8 *Hu micle suiðor sculon we ðonne beon gehiersume ðæm ðe ure gæsta Fæder bið wið ðæm ðæt we moten libban on ecnesse!* (which approaches causal 'seeing that'; cf. *CP* 255. 2 *Ac hwelc wite sceal us ðonne to hefig ðyncan ðære godcundan ðreaunga wið ðæm ðe we mægen geearnian ðone hefonlican eðel,* where the EETS translation has '. . . in comparison with our meriting . . .'), *ÆCHom* i. 56. 10 (§3659), and *ÆLS* 12. 100 *Mænig welig man is on ðyssere worulde þe wolde mycelne scet. and ungerim feos syllan wið þam gif he hit gebicgan mihte. þæt he her for worulde lybban moste butan eallum geswyncum æfre ungeendod* (where the elements are divided, there is a *punctus* before *þæt,* and *hit* might refer to *þam* and/or to the *þæt* clause).

§3663. The only possible example known to me in the poetry is

JDay ii 301   Hwæt mæg beon heardes   her on life,
                gif þu wille secgan   soð þæm ðe frineð,
                wið þam þu mote   gemang þam werode
                eardian unbleoh   on ecnesse . . . ?,

where we could put a colon after *wið þam* and take what follows as non-dependent speech. However, Lumby translates:

    What of hardship can there be here in life,
    If thou wilt say sooth to him that asketh thee,
    To set against this, that thou mayest, among that host,
    Live unchanging through eternity . . . ?

and Höser (§115) also postulates unexpressed *þæt* but offers a causal interpretation.

§3664. The close relationship between this type of condition and the idea of purpose, already noted in §3659, may lie behind the prevalence of the subjunctive mood in the examples known to me.

§3665. It is, however, difficult to take as formulaic *wiþ þon gif*, so far recorded only in *Lch*; the elements are to be taken separately in *ÆLS* 12. 100 (§3662). Examples include *Lch* ii. 48. 28 *Wiþ þon gif mannes muð sar sie, genim betonican . . .* ; cf. *Lch* ii. 50. 10 *Wið toþwærce gif wyrm ete, genim eald holen leaf. . . .* Such combinations may be independent introductory phrases. Liggins (1955, p. 391) detects an element of cause in examples such as *Lch* ii. 154. 2 *Eft wiþ þon stande on heafde, aslea him mon fela scearpena on þam scancan, þonne gewit ut þ atter þurh þa scearpan* and the like. In *Lch* iii. 86. 11 *Eft sona wd wið gif þeo ylca adle cilde egelic on geogeþe . . .* , we obviously have corruption.

§3666. In *Ch* 1376 *þæt is ðonne þet se biscop 7 se hired him sealdon xïi hida landes æt Mordune þe his yldran heora æftergengan to ði betehtan þet hi ælce geare of ðan lande geformædon . . . , to ði . . . þet* seems to mean 'on condition that'. But again there is an element of purpose.

d. *Combinations involving nouns*

§3667. Space does not permit citation of all the recorded patterns, which may be grouped or divided. The most common nouns are *gerad* (usually neuter but occasionally feminine; see BTS, s.v.) and —not in ME only, as Visser (ii. 890) asserts—*for(e)w(e)ard, forwyrd* (despite BT(S), s.vv., apparently neuter in these combinations). So we find *on þ gerad þe* (*Ch* 1487), *on þ gerad þ* (*ChronE* 110. 35 (945)), *on þ gerad . . . þ* (*Ch* 1420); *on þa gerad þe* (*Ch* 385), *on ða gerad ðæt* (*Ch* 1285), *on þa gerad . . . þ* (*Ch* 1299)—in these three examples, *þa* may be accusative plural neuter or accusative singular feminine; *to ðæm gerade ðæt* (*Rec* 6. 5), *to þam gerade . . . þe* (*Ch* 1446); *to þam forewearde þ* (*Ch* 981), *to þam forwyrdan þ* (*Ch* 1465), *on þ forwyrd þ* (*Ch* 1465), and *into þat forwarde þat* (*Ch* 1519). Other nouns include *red* (*Ch* 1483) and *(ge)ræden* (*ÆCHom* i. 56. 7 and *Ch* 1507). I have recorded two nouns without prepositions, viz. *aredness* in *Bede* 28. 19, 58. 13, and 274. 9 . . . *ðære arædnisse toætecedre þæt heo eac swylce for hine se ðe him þa stowe gesealde, a þa stondendan munecas þær to Drihtne cleopodon*— Mather (p. 54) detects dative absolutes in the first two—and *cost* in *Ch* 939 *getiðode he ðæs . . . þæs costes ðe heo þis gelæste. . . .* The verb of the subordinate clause is subjunctive or an ambiguous equivalent, perhaps reflecting a close relationship to purpose; see Shearin 1903, p. 76. In *Ch* 1362 *7 ic gean him þæs worðiges æt Bryneshamme . . . on þ ilce gerad þe þis oðer is*, where we have the indicative, *þe* introduces an adjective clause.

12. OTHER CONDITIONAL CONJUNCTIONS

a. And *'if'?*

§3668. Here we are concerned, not with OE equivalents of MnE sentences such as 'Laugh and the world laughs with you' = 'If you laugh, the world laughs with you'—I discuss these in §3691—but with whether there are in OE any precursors of ME and eMnE 'and, an' = 'if', first recorded by *OED*, s.v. *and* conj. C. 1, in Laȝamon's *Brut* 8313 *And þu hit nult ileuen . . . ich hit wulle trousien* and 3524 *Help him nou an þou miht*, where the verbs are indicative, and in *Havelok* 2861 *And þou wile my conseil tro,* || *Ful wel shal ich with þe do*, where the verb is subjunctive. (Similar fluctuations are apparent in the OE sentences quoted below.) Visser (ii. 888) states firmly 'Not in Old English'. Suggested examples include *HomU* 36. 229. 22 and 231. 11 (Wülfing, *Ang. B.* 12 (1901), 89; in these, *and* can, I think, mean 'and'); *Exod* 4. 23 (Einenkel, cited by Hart, *MLN* 17 (1902), 231; the tenses suggest that *and* represents *et* in Crawford's Latin text, but Trautmann (*Ang.* 42 (1918), 129) quotes a different Latin version with *siquidem* and AV has 'and if'); *ÆHomM* 8. 409 *Swa is eac on lichaman se læssa man betere, swa swa Zacheus wæs, mid gesundfulnysse, þonne se unhala beo and hæbbe on his wæstme Golian mycelnysse, þæs gramlican entes* (Hart, loc. cit.; 'even if he has . . .' would give good sense, but the literal MnE equivalent could be '—and let him have . . .'. This example is comparable with *ÆHom* 15. 52 *and se ðe bote underfehð, and he beo syððan hræðe þæs of life, he sceal to reste gewiss . . .* , on which see §3670); *ÆHom* 15. 1 (where we can follow Pope's note on *ÆHom* 15. 52—'and . . . approaches "if", but the sequence can perhaps better be regarded as elliptical'—or can take *and* as 'and', introducing a co-ordinate noun(-equivalent) clause); *Rid* 15. 9 (where Trautmann, loc. cit., withdraws his emendation of *ond* to *gif* in favour of *ond* = 'if' but where I independently reached—and so agree with—the solution proposed by Craig Williamson: that *gif . . . ond* = *gif . . . ond* [*gif*]; cf. *Bo* 83. 28 (§3675)); and

Jul 376   Swa ic brogan to
   laðne gelæde þam þe ic lifes ofonn,

> leohtes geleafan,   ond he larum wile
> þurh modes myne   minum hyran,
> synne fremman,   he siþþan sceal
> godra gumcysta   geasne hweorfan

(Hart, loc. cit.; Strunk and ASPR agree that *ond* means *gif*; Woolf's comment reads: '*ond*. An unusual use of the co-ordinating conjunction in the sense of "if".' But we could take *Swa ic . . . gelæde . . .* and *he . . . wile . . .* as parallel clauses joined by *ond* 'and' and begin a new sentence after *Jul* 380a.)

§3669. Liggins (1955, pp. 385–7) rejects the two examples from *HomU* 36 (§3668), but proposes seven more examples—all of them in my opinion equally dubious: *Bede(B)* 408. 26, where all other manuscripts have *gif* for Latin *si*; *ChronE* 36. 19 (675), a late interpolation where 'and' gives good sense and 'if' would in my opinion misrepresent the syntax of the original; *Matt(WSCp)* 26. 15 and *Mark(WSCp)* 8. 36, in both of which *7* represents Latin *et*; *Luke (WSCp)* 9. 25 *Hwæt fremað ænegum men þeah he ealne middaneard on æht begite 7 hyne sylfne forspille and his forwyrd wyrce?*, where the sequence *7 . . . and* represents Latin *autem . . . et*; *ÆCHom* ii. 104. 10 *On idel swincð se ðe gold hordað and nat hwam he hit gegaderað*, where the absence of an expressed subject is natural after *and* 'and', but would contrast strangely with the expressed subjects in the eight *gif* clauses in *ÆCHom* ii. 102. 29–104. 8 if *and* meant 'if'; and *ÆCHom* ii. 410. 10 *Hwæt fremað þe þæt ðin cyst stande ful mid godum, and ðin ingehyd beo æmtig ælces godes?*, where *and* merely introduces a co-ordinate noun clause dependent on *þæt*, just as in *Mark(WSCp)* 8. 36 and *Luke(WSCp)* 9. 25 it introduces a co-ordinate noun(-equivalent) clause dependent on the preceding *ðeah/þeah*.

§3670. So each of the proposed examples of OE *and* 'if' can be explained away—more or less convincingly. They may derive some support from one another, but can draw none from those with *gelice ond* 'as if', discussed in §3372. More work is necessary here. Anyone attempting it will have to bear in mind one factor which, as far as I know, has not yet been mentioned, viz. the relative order of the two clauses. The alleged conditional clause can with certainty be said to follow its principal clause in all but three of the OE examples cited in §§3668–9. On *ÆHom* 15. 52 see below. The others are *ChronE* 36. 19 (675), where in my opinion *and* cannot mean 'if',[196] and *Jul* 376. Here, if *ond* does mean 'if', the clause it introduces can

---

[196] It is true that it is written in full as *and* and not abbreviated to *7*, which is the normal form. But we find *And* 'and' in the same late addition at *ChronE* 35. 34 and 36. 7.

be taken with either the preceding or the following clause, or *apo koinou* with both. If a choice had to be made, I would link it with the clause which follows. But in most of the ME examples, the conditional clause introduced by *an, and* precedes its principal clause. The earliest ME example with the conditional clause in second position cited by *OED* is '1250 *Lay.* 3524 *Help him nou an þou miht.*' *MED* does not record one until 'c1400 (c1378) *PPl.B* (Ld) 2.132'. A study of the context shows that initial *And* means 'And', not 'If', in both sentences in *ÆCHom* i. 252. 30 *And ðu nelt syllan ðinum bearne þrowend for æge, nele eac God us syllan orwenysse for hihte. And ðu nelt ðinum bearne syllan stan for hlafe, nele eac God us syllan heardheortnysse for soðre lufe*; note the indicatives *nelt*. But it also shows how *and* might have acquired the meaning 'if', as does a study of some of the other sentences already discussed. The closest OE example I have noticed to the ME pattern is *ÆHom* 15. 52 (§3668), where we have the subjunctive in an *and* clause which precedes a principal clause. Pope in his glossary speaks of this as 'an apparent instance of the conditional *and*, meaning *if*, with subjunctive' and offers an admirable note with which I shall conclude my discussion: '52. *and he beo syððan hræðe þæs of life*, almost "even if he die very soon afterwards". The conditional idea is indicated by the subjunctive, but we are at least very close to the familiar Middle English use of *and* as "if" or "even if".'

b. Gif þæt?

§3671. Mann (*Archiv*, 197 (1960–1), 22) agrees with *OED* (s.v. *if* I. 5) that the combination 'if that' first occurs in *Orrmulum* in the form *ȝiff þatt*. Geoghegan (p. 41) proposes as an example *Ch* 1483 . . . *ic an þat lond at Lauenham mine douhter childe gif þat god wille þat heo ani haueð*. This cannot be ruled out, but the first *þat* may be a demonstrative anticipating the following *þat* clause. The same explanation is less likely in *HomU* 44. 284. 9 *gyf þæt þonne hwylc mon sy þæt him on his mode to earfoðe þince, þæt he on ælce tid swa forwernedlice lyfige, tylige he þonne huru þæt he þis fæsten selost afæste* . . . , but even here remains a possibility.

c. Ono 'if'?

§3672. BT's gloss '*ono* "if"' is presumably cancelled by BTS's stark comment (s.v.) 'See Bd. M. 1. xxix', which directs us to Miller's observation (EETS, OS 95, p. xxxi) that '*ono* never means "if", though Bede has been quoted in support of this sense'. I have found nothing which contradicts Miller, despite Visser (ii. 766 fn. 1 and 882 fn. 1). See further §3107.

d. Swa 'if', 'provided that'?

§3673. *Swa* is sometimes translated 'if' or 'provided that', but usually some other interpretation is available. Proposed examples include *Bo* 130. 19 (Mather, p. 53; clearly comparative); *Ch* 1211 *þa gyt heo ne moste landes brucan ær hire frynd fundon æt Eadwearde cyncge þæt he him [Godan] þæt land forbead swa he æniges brucan wolde; 7 he hit swa alet* (Mather, p. 53; Sweet (*R.* 8) and Harmer translate *swa* as 'if'. But I have a feeling that the relationship could be vaguely consecutive; see §§2857–8); *ApT* 10. 3 *Swa ðu gesund sy, sege me for hwilcum intingum þeos ceaster wunige on swa micclum heafe and wope*, Latin *Si valeas . . .* , and *ApT* 30. 26 *Nim nu, lareow Apolloni, swa hit þe ne mislicyge . . .* , Latin *Tolle, magister Apolloni, praeter iniuriam tuam . . .* (Visser, ii. 894; here we may have the asseverative use of *swa* seen in *Beo* 435, *Jul* 80, and MnE 'So help me God' (§2857)); *GenB* 552 and 574 (Glogauer, p. 37, and Girvan, *MÆ* 18 (1949), 73; here *swa* can mean 'when' or 'because'); *El* 589 (Mather, p. 53, and Glogauer, p. 37; here *swa* can mean 'as' or 'because'); *GenB* 509 (Girvan, loc. cit.; here *swa* can be the adverb 'thus'); and

And 1284   Ic gelyfe to ðe,   min liffruma,
               þæt ðu mildheort me   for þinum mægenspedum,
               nerigend fira,   næfre wille,
               ece ælmihtig,   anforlætan,
               swa ic þæt gefremme,   þenden feorh leofað,
               min on moldan,   þæt ic, meotud, þinum
               larum leofwendum   lyt geswice

(Mather, p. 53; Krapp and Gordon suggest 'likewise'). See further Mitchell 1959, pp. 616–17. Glogauer's semantic equation '*swa* : *gif*?' is therefore tentative, as his question-mark suggests. But it may gain support from some of the cited examples.

e. þeah (þe)?

§3674. The existence of a close relationship between concession and condition cannot be denied. Wood (p. 363) finds 'condition + concession' in MnE 'If you don't care what the neighbours think, I do.' Mather (pp. 21–2), citing among other examples *ÆCHom* ii. 322. 10 *. . . and gif eowere synna wæron wolcnreade ær ðan, hi beoð scinende on snawes hwitnysse*, tells us that 'a formal condition may have an adversative sense and therefore belong properly to the concessive construction'. But see §3390. Liggins (1955, pp. 387-8) detects 'an adversative/conditional/causal function' in the *and* clauses which follow *þeah (þe)* in *LawIIAtr* 2. 1 and *ÆCHom* ii. 430. 9 *þeah ðe hwa micel to gode gedo, and siððan mid gylpe ætforan Gode his weldæda gerime, þonne beoð hi Gode swa gecweme swa him wæron þæs gylpendan sunderhalgan.* The EETS translation gives 'if' for both *Ðeah* and the first *ðonne* in *CP* 101. 11 *Ðeah we nu ofer ure mæð ðencen 7 smeagean, ðæt we dooð for Gode; ðonne we hit eft gemetlæcað, ðonne doð we ðæt for eow.* Liggins (ibid.) detects 'shades of condition, cause and time' in this *ðeah* clause and in other examples, including the *ðeah ðe* clause in *ÆCHom* ii. 216. 23 *Gif hwam seo lar oflicige, ne yrsige he nateshwon wið us, ðeah ðe we Godes bebodu mannum geopenian; forðan ðe he cwæð. . . .* But I hesitate to ascribe a conditional sense to *þeah (þe)*. The prose examples suggested by Quirk (pp. 38-9) have been convincingly explained as concessive by Campbell (*RES* 7 (1956), 66 fn. 2). Morris's translation of the *þeah* clause in *BlHom* 47. 10 *Ne ablinnan we, manna bearn, þæt we . . . mid Cristes rode tacne us gebletsian. þonne flyhþ þæt deofol fram us; forþon him biþ mara broga þonne ænigum men sy, þeah hi mon slea mid sweorde wiþ þæs heafdes* is 'if one were about to strike off his head'. But it can be construed as a noun(-equivalent) clause; see §1960. Skeat offers the translation 'if' for *þeah* in *ÆLS* 31. 743 *þeah ðu earming woldest on þisum endnextan timan manna ehtnysse geswican and þine dæda behreowsian, ic on god truwode þæt ic þe mildsunge behete.* But the point may be that, no matter how late the repentance, God *is* merciful. Glogauer (pp. 41-2) suggests *Met* 22. 45, where *þeah* can reasonably be taken as concessive, and *PPs* 131. 3, where we have a literal translation of the Latin idiom in which a verb of swearing with *si* expresses a strong negative oath. See further the Index of Words and Phrases; Mather, p. 52; Burnham, pp. 33-4; Quirk, pp. 38 and 42; and Mitchell 1959, p. 618.

13. CONTRACTED CONDITIONAL SENTENCES

§3675. I have found no contracted conditional clauses like that in MnE 'This is serious, if true' introduced by *gif* in either OE prose or poetry. In *Bo* 83. 28 *forðæm gif hit swa nære, þonne nære he þ þ he gehaten is; oððe ænig þing ær wære oððe æltæwre, þonne wære þ betere þonne he*, MnE idiom would require the equivalent of *oððe gif*. On contracted *butan* and *nymþe* clauses, see §§3630 and 3649.

§3676. As Mather (p. 59) observes, that 'ellipsis is very rare' in which 'a complete clause must be supplied from the context to complete the sense of the conditional sentence. Ellipsis is practically always of the apodosis; for an apodosis is grammatically complete by itself and suggests no other member.' His examples (p. 61) include *BlHom* 69. 16 *Symle ge habbaþ þearfan* [to whom you may do good] *gif ge willaþ teala don, ah ge nabbaþ me symle* and, 'with an interrupted construction', *ÆCHom* ii. 428. 21 *Huru gif he cwæde þæt he nære sumum oðrum mannum gelic,—ac he cwæð, 'Ic ne eom swilce swa oðre men'*. In *ÆCHom* ii. 204. 3 and ii. 204. 4 we have *gif* clauses without their principal clauses. These are contractions of *Luke* 11. 20 and *Matt* 12. 28 respectively. A principal clause can also be supplied in *Bo* 30. 7 *Gif þu þonne þæt gemet habban wille, 7 þa nydþearfe witan wille, þonne is þæt mete and drync 7 claðas 7 tol to swelcum cræfte swelce þu cunne þ þe is gecynde . . .*—Mather (pp. 59-60) suggests 'some such apodosis as "know that", "I tell you", "you may learn" or the like . . . , upon which the apparent apodosis depends' —and in examples like *ÆCHom* ii. 308. 15 *Eala gif ðu wære hund!*; see §3548. The equivalent of MnE 'If they avoid what they love', 'If he shares the burden of his riches with the poor', 'If you learn this lesson', and 'If he had done this', are implied in the independent sentences which precede the *þonne* clause in *CP* 441. 13, *ÆCHom* i. 254. 32, *El* 526, and *GenB* 258; cf. §3693.

§3677. In

Rid 43. 4   Gif him arlice
                    esne þenað   se þe agan sceal
                    on þam siðfate,   hy gesunde æt ham
                    findað witode him   wiste ond blisse;
                    cnosles unrim   care, gif se esne
                    his hlaforde   hyreð yfle . . .

(Craig Williamson's punctuation), the second *gif* clause depends on [*ac hy findað*] *cnosles unrim care*. On *GenB* 368, see §3682.

14. CONDITIONAL CLAUSES WITH NO CONJUNCTION AND INITIAL VERB

§3678. Here we are concerned with the 'inverted conditional clauses' seen in patterns like MnE 'Were he here, . . .', 'Did he but know it, . . .', 'Had I but plenty of money, . . .', and 'Should he come, . . .'. The inversion of verb and subject, the subjunctive 'were'—the 'modal preterite' (Visser, ii, §812) or Jespersen's 'imaginative' preterite (*MnEG* iv. 112 ff.); see §647—and the intonation of the spoken sentences, certify that these are subordinate clauses. The present tense is not used in such constructions in MnE except in fossilized expressions like 'Be he alive (or) be he dead, . . .' or in sentences in which an imperative has the force of a condition, e.g. 'Wait a moment (and) I'll come down'. Both these phenomena occur in OE. The former, discussed in §§3443–8, is seen in *ÆCHom* ii. 10. 5 *þonne hwilc mæden mid luste weres bricð, þonne bið hire mægðhad æfre siððan adylegod, hæbbe heo cild næbbe heo*, where two contrasted clauses with subjunctive verbs, which can be described as conditional, combine to form a disjunctive or alternative concession. The latter is seen in examples like *BlHom* 103. 1 *Gecyrraþ to me, þonne gecyrre ic to eow, CP* 395. 34 *Berað eowre byrðenna gemænelice betwux iow, ðonne gefylle ge Godes æ*, Latin *Invicem onera vestra portate, et sic adimplebitis legem Christi, Luke(WSCp)* 6. 37 *Nelle ge deman 7 ge ne beoð demede. Nelle ge genyðerian 7 ge ne beoð genyþerude. Forgyfaþ 7 eow byð forgyfen*, where the Latin has *et* three times, and *MCharm* 4. 5 *Scyld ðu ðe nu, þu ðysne nið genesan mote*; see further §3691. These exemplify what Behre (p. 142) calls 'the use of the imperative or the subjunctive to form a protasis-equivalent'.

§3679. The intonation patterns show that in MnE examples with the imperative we have two paratactic sentences, whereas in 'Be he alive (or) be he dead, . . .' we have subordinate clauses. We can perhaps guess that the OE imperative clauses are also paratactic. But when we turn to OE examples with the present subjunctive, the lack of intonation patterns creates uncertainty. In a MnE utterance like 'Let's try it. Then we'll know', we clearly have parataxis. But this is comparable with examples like *HomU* 25. 129. 10 and *WHom* 13. 103 *Utan andettan ure synna urum scriftan þa hwile þe we magan 7 motan, 7 betan 7 a geswican 7 don to gode swa mycel swa we mæst magan. þonne beorge we us sylfum wið ece wite, 7 geearniað us heofona rice*, and not with examples like *ÆCHom* ii. 10. 5 (§3678) or with examples of a pattern which does not occur in MnE but is seen in the following: (with one clause with an initial subjunctive verb followed by a clause with no linking conjunction or adverb) *ÆCHom* i. 160. 8 *Gewite seo sawul ut, ne mæg se muð clypian, þeah ðe he gynige*; (with one clause with an initial subjunctive verb followed by a clause introduced by a co-ordinating conjunction or an adverb) *ÆCHom* i. 160. 5 *Gewite þæt ungesewenlice ut, þonne fylð adune þæt gesewenlice*; (with two clauses with an initial subjunctive verb followed by a clause with a co-ordinating conjunction or adverb) *ÆCHom* ii. 92. 1 *Hæbbe se mann heardheortnysse and unge-wyldelic mod, and næbbe ða soðan lufe and anrædnysse, þonne forsearað swiðe hraðe þæt halige sæd on his heortan*; and (with a clause with an initial subjunctive verb preceded by what can be taken

as a principal clause), *Law VIIIAtr* 39 *And git mæg ðeah bot cuman,
wille hit man georne on eornost aginnan.* Other examples conforming
to one of these patterns include *BlHom* 13. 6 and 13. 24; those from
WPol quoted by Visser (ii, §882); *ÆCHom* i. 178. 23 (or is *do*
imperative singular—cf. *Bo* 42. 4—rather than first person plural
subjunctive, as the context allows?); *ÆCHom* i. 256. 13 *Gif rice wif,
and earm acennað togædere, gangon hi aweig, nast ðu hwæðer bið
þæs rican wifan cild, hwæðer þæs earman*, where I take *gangon hi
aweig apo koinou*; and *WHom* 18. 135 . . . *forðam ne bið hit naht,
beo ðær ænig tweonung.* Mather (p. 26), comparing *gewurðe hit* in
HomU 47. 305. 4 *and hit bið to menigfeald, gewurðe hit þriddan
siðe, and mid ealle misdon, gewurðe hit feorðan siðe* with the immediately following *gif* clause in *HomU* 47. 305. 6 *and, gif hit oftur
gewyrð, nyte we hu þæt faran mæg*, says that 'such collocations of
the subj. and indic. go far to prove that the subj. is formal and not
logical in such inverted clauses'. I cannot agree with this. *Mutatis
mutandis*, Behre's comment (p. 142) that in *HomU* 25. 129. 10 *ac
uton don, swa us þearf is, beon ymbe þa bote, geswican unrihtes and
gebugan to rihte, þonne geearnige we, gif we þæt willað, sona godes
mildse* we have an example 'in which the condition expressed by the
"adhortative" *uton* is repeated in the form of a clause of condition
with *willan* in the indicative' seems nearer the mark. The subjunctive
would be out of place after *gif* in *HomU* 47. 305. 6 and the indic.
gewyrð for the subj. *gewurðe* would make nonsense of *HomU* 47.
305. 4. Alistair Campbell was wont to say in his lectures that 'real
condition may be expressed by inversion with the present subjunctive'. His examples were *ÆCHom* i. 160. 5 and i. 160. 8, both quoted
above. Liggins (1955, p. 383) detects a causal element in these two
sentences and in *Law VIIIAtr* 39, also quoted above, and gives further
examples.

§3680. But the question posed in §3444 recurs: are these clauses
with initial present subjunctives principal clauses or subordinate
clauses or does the relationship fall somewhere between the two?
There is in my opinion no doubt that we can explain all the examples
mentioned above as in one way or another paratactic. If we follow
Mather (p. 26) in taking *geseo* as indicative in *LS* 34. 275 *and ic eac
þæt sylfe wat, geseo we ænigne mann þe georne hine sylfne to urum
godum bugan wylle eall þæt he ær agylte læsse oþþe mare, we lætað
hit of gemynde swilce hit næfre ne gewurde*, we should (I think) say
that it introduces a question, not an inverted conditional clause (see
§3693); compare 1 *Cor* 7. 27 (AV) 'Art thou bound unto a wife?
seek not to be loosed. Art thou loosed from a wife? seek not a wife.'

But it could be taken as a jussive subjunctive; compare *Or* 182. 16 and *Or* 182. 19 *Ahsige þonne eft hu longe sio sibb gestode: þonne wæs þæt an gear*, Latin *Quandiu? anno uno* and §3691. One of these two explanations is applicable to all the examples cited in §3679. So we may have or we may originally have had two independent clauses, one expressing a wish or command, or asking a question, the other making a statement dependent on the fulfilment of the wish or command, or containing a reply to the question. See further Behaghel, *DS* iii, §1285, and Behre, pp. 142-4. Such a view is in accordance with the general theory that parataxis preceded hypotaxis. But, since I can at the moment see no means of determining what stage these OE examples represent, I propose to leave the question open.

§3681. I am reluctant to agree that the present indicative could introduce an inverted conditional clause in an example like *LS* 34. 275 (§3680), despite the possibility that the indicative might occasionally have occurred in simple inverted concessions; see §3442. Behaghel (*DS* iii, §1285) offers a few examples from other Germanic languages which, in his opinion, have their origin in non-dependent questions. The few possible examples in OE poetry can be taken as either non-dependent questions or principal clauses making a statement. They are

Jul 401
                    Ic þæs wealles geat
      ontyne þurh teonan;   bið se torr þyrel,
      ingong geopenad,   þonne ic ærest him
      þurh eargfare   in onsende
      in breostsefan   bitre geþoncas . . .

(reported by Mather, p. 26, after Mätzner; *þonne* could mean either 'when' or 'then');

Deor 28
      Siteð sorgcearig,   sælum bidæled,
      on sefan sweorceð,   sylfum þinceð
      þæt sy endeleas   earfoða dæl

(taken as conditional by Schücking and Kemp Malone; see the ASPR note); and

Beo 1735
      Wunað he on wiste,   no hine wiht dweleð
      adl ne yldo,   ne him inwitsorh
      on sefan sweorceð . . .

('If he dwells in prosperity . . .' would give good sense, but E. G. Stanley (private communication) is rightly reluctant to take it so in view of examples like *Beo* 375, 471, and 476, where we have VS in what cannot be conditional clauses).

§3682. So far, then, we have not been able to prove that the inverted conditional clause existed in OE. We turn now to the OE equivalents of the MnE examples with 'were' or the 'modal preterite' quoted in §3678. The only possible example in the poetry—

GenB 368   Wa la, ahte ic minra handa geweald
　　　　　　and moste ane tid　　ute weorðan,
　　　　　　wesan ane winterstunde,　　þonne ic mid þys werode—

could be an unrealized or impossible wish; cf. §3620. The few possible examples I have so far recorded in the prose fall into four groups. In the first, *nære* is followed by a *þæt* clause: *ChronD* 111. 16 (943) *7 he hy gewyldan meahte, nære þ hi on niht ut ne ætburston of þære byrig*; *WHom* 13. 44 *Ealle we scoldan forweorðan ecan deaðe, nære þæt Crist for us deað þrowode*; and *ByrM* 104. 29 *Nære þæt se mona wære on anre ylde on kl. Aprelis 7 on kl. Mai, þonne gelumpe þe mycel gedwyld.* . . . The second is typified by *ÆCHom* i. 94. 33 *Eaðe mihte þes cwyde beon læwedum mannum bediglod, nære seo gastlice getacning* and *ÆLS* 11. 328 *Næron swa manega martyras, nære seo mycele ehtnyss.* (Here, as in *ÆCHom* ii. 330. 2, *John(WSCp)* 15. 24, *Met* 11. 97, *Met* 11. 101, and elsewhere, the principal clause has the order VS. Cf. the examples from *Beo* referred to in §3681.) According to Behaghel (*DS* iii, §1285), examples of this sort go back to sentences containing non-dependent wishes. The plausibility of this is to some extent confirmed by *GenB* 368, above. However, I find it hard to argue that in the prose examples so far cited in this section, the clauses introduced by *nære* express either non-dependent wishes or questions.

§3683. The third group consists of *Bo* 23. 10 *Eala, wæran þa ancras swa trume 7 swa ðurhwuniende, ge for Gode ge for worulde, swa swa þu segst; þonne mihte we micle þy eð geþolian swa hwæt earfoþnessa swa us on become*, the only example I have so far recorded which is comparable with ME *But were she sauf, hit were no fors of me* and MnE 'Were Richelieu dead, his power were mine', and of *HomU* 38. 243. 20 *ac wolde man geswican þara mandæda, þonne godade hit sona*. But in these, as in *GenB* 368 (§3682), we may have unrealized or impossible wishes. *ÆCHom* ii. 294. 31 may belong here. Thorpe takes *wurde* and *towurpe* as present subjunctives, translating 'Let our strength be renewed, then will we cast down this idol'; cf. §3682. But they could be preterite, expressing an unrealized or impossible wish. The fourth group has so far only *HomS* 40. 258. 1 . . . *ac, sceolde se min þearfa aswæman æt þinre handa, noldest þu geþencan, hwa hit þe sealde*, which can be compared with MnE 'Should he come, you would soon know the truth'. This and the five examples with *nære* in the first two groups are the best evidence I so far have for the existence of inverted conditional clauses in OE. In their comparative lateness and the absence of firm examples with *nære* or *wære* from the poetry, they are comparable with OE inverted concessions, which 'are not found in the earlier prose' (Burnham, p. 48) and are not firmly attested in the poetry; see §§3440-50. See further Behaghel, *PBB* 53 (1929), 401-18. Here I must leave the problem.

15. CONDITIONAL SENTENCES IN DEPENDENT SPEECH

§3684. The effects of their use in dependent speech on the mood and tense of conditional sentences has already been discussed briefly in connection with *gif* (§§3612-14), *þær* (§3622), *butan* (§3640), and *nymþe* (§3655). The points made there were that these changes can affect only conceded or open conditions, since the regular mood in rejected or imaginary conditions is the preterite subjunctive, and that the main difficulties arise when we try to decide which of these we have or, if the condition is open, how remote it was in non-dependent speech. A full treatment of conditional sentences in dependent speech cannot be attempted here. Wülfing (ii, §449) is a useful source of examples. Mather (pp. 62-70) gives examples of all sequences of tenses and moods and includes sentences in which the conditional clause is dependent on a clause of purpose or result. But he wrote before Gorrell's study of dependent speech, which, in addition to offering more examples to supplement those which follow (pp. 458-66), noted some important tendencies (pp. 465-6):

In indirect conditional sentences after verbs in the present tense there is a noticeable tendency to retain the indicative in the protasis, especially if the governing verb is usually followed by this mood; and often, when the regular subjunctive is used in the apodosis, there is a seeming independence of expression and an almost complete retention of the direct construction in the protasis. On the contrary, when the tense of the governing verb is past, the subjunctive is very consistently employed in the protasis after verbs of all kinds. These separate tendencies are, I think, to be explained by the peculiar characters of the two tenses. In the present tense there is a nearer approach to direct narration in which the logical conditional sentence has always the indicative in the protasis, and in many cases the event narrated is presented as actually taking place before the eye. The past tense on the other hand has not this picturesque quality; the transition to direct discourse is not so easy or frequent; and, as the hypothetical statement contained in the protasis is made at a time remote from the vivid present and often with regard to an action in the future, there is naturally a strong entrance of the moments of uncertainty and unreality; hence arises the predominant use of the subjunctive in conditional sentences after a verb in past time.

On the position of the *gif* clause in relation to the conj. *þæt*, see §1978.

§3685. It is natural and logical that normally the present tense will be found in conceded or open conditional sentences when the verb introducing the dependent speech is in the present tense; we cannot tell whether we have non-dependent speech or dependent speech with unexpressed *þæt* in *ÆCHom* i. 18. 2 . . . *ac God wat genoh geare, gif ge of ðam treowe geetað, þonne beoð eowere eagan geopenode.* . . . The mood is usually explicable in terms of the particular construction employed. Thus, we have indicatives in dependent statement in *ÆCHom* i. 528. 21 *Witodlice ge geseoð þæt gehwam sceamað, gif he gelaðod bið to woruldlicum gyftum* . . . and in dependent question in *CP* 53. 10 *Ðær bufan is geteald hwelc he beon sceal, gif he untælwierðe bið*, but subjunctives in *ÆCHom* i. 8. 9 and

Jul 332   þonne he onsendeð   geond sidne grund
                  þegnas of þystrum,   hateð þræce ræran,
                  gif we gemette sin   on moldwege,
                  oþþe feor oþþe neah   fundne weorþen,
                  þæt hi usic binden   ond in bælwylme
                  suslum swingen.

But there are variations. We have *sie ł bið* in the *gif* clause in *Mark (Li)* 12. 19, where the Latin has *si . . . fuerit*. The subjunctive appears under the influence of *wenan* in *Bo* 60. 12 and of *cweþan* in *LawAf* 42. 5; cf. the indicatives in *LawAf* 42. 6. We have pres. subj. *beon* in the Then-clause in *ÆCHom* ii. 316. 20 *Micel mildheortnys þæs Metodan Drihtnes, þæt we beon gecigede swa gesæliglice ures Scyppendes frynd, gif we his hæse gefyllað, we ðe næron wurðe beon his wealas gecigde, and we habbað swilce geðincðe þurh ða gehyrsumnysse*, where Ælfric does not wish to presume. Thorpe takes *and we habbað . . .* as part of the dependent speech. This is not essential, but is certainly possible in the light of examples like *ÆCHom* i. 292. 23 *ac gif se man æfter his fulluhte aslide, we gelyfað þæt he mæge beon gehealden, gif he his synna mid wope behreowsiað, and be lareowa tæcunge hi gebet*, where both *gif* clauses—one with the subjunctive and one with two indicatives—belong in the dependent speech; compare *LawIIEm* 1. 1. The Then-clause has the present subjunctive, the *gif* clause the present indicative, in *CP* 407. 15 and *ÆCHom* i. 342. 13 *Be ðam is to smeagenne hu micclum se rihtwisa mid eadmodre heofunge God gegladige, gif se unrihtwisa mid soðre dædbote hine gegladian mæg*. Some of these examples illustrate what Mather (p. 62)—referring to 'dependent constructions in present time'— called 'a tendency to isolate the conditional clause, the verb of which

often remains as in direct discourse, unaffected by the change of
mood in the apodosis'. But again we must bear in mind that there is
no automatic rule that subordinate clauses in dependent speech have
the subjunctive; see §2100 and consider *Bo* 127. 7 *swa swa mon on
ealdspellum sægð þ an nædre wære þe hæfde nigon heafdu, 7 symle
gif mon anra hwelc of aslog, þonne weoxon þær siofon on ðæm
anum heafde.*

§3686. But, when the sense demands, one or both of the clauses in
a conditional sentence governed by a verb in the present or perfect
tense can be in the preterite. Both clauses are naturally in the preterite subjunctive in rejected or imaginary conditions, e.g. *Or* 122. 11
*Hwæt, ge witon þæt ge giet todæge wæron Somnitum þeowe, gif ge
him ne alugen iowra wedd 7 eowre aþas þe ge him sealdon* and *ÆC
Hom* i. 216. 4 *We habbað oft gesæd, and git secgað, þæt Cristes
rihtwisnys is swa micel, þæt he nolde niman mancyn neadunga of
ðam deofle, buton he hit forwyrhte.* In conceded or open conditions,
we find both clauses in the preterite indicative in

Met 26. 42   Cuð is wide
              þæt on ða tide   þeoda æghwilc
              hæfdon heora hlaford   for ðone hehstan god,
              and weorðodon   swa swa wuldres cining,
              gif he to ðæm rice wæs   on rihte boren,

where the indicatives refer to actions which were in the past at the
time of writing. We find a Then-clause in the present tense accompanied by a *gif* clause in the preterite in *ÆCHom* i. 256. 20 *Oðer is
þæt hwa rice beo, gif his yldran him æhta becwædon,* which is followed immediately by *oðer is, gif hwa þurh gytsunge rice gewurðe,*
where the *gif* clause may have the present or the preterite (= perfect)
subjunctive. So far I have recorded the reverse—Then-clause preterite tense, *gif* clause present—only in sentences with the introductory
verb in the preterite; see §3688.

§3687. When the verb introducing the dependent speech is in the
preterite, the conditional sentence normally and naturally has preterite verb-forms, not only in rejected or imaginary conditions, where
again the preterite subjunctive is obviously the rule, e.g. *ÆCHom* i.
224. 35 (§3612), but also in conceded or open conditions. In these,
the preterite indicative may occur in either or both clauses, e.g. *Or*
19. 12 *þyder he cwæð þæt man mihte geseglian on anum monðe
gyf man on niht wicode 7 ælce dæge hæfde ambyrne wind, Bede*
268. 15 *sægde he—gif he æt leorninga sæte oððe elles hwæt dyde,
gif semninga mare blæd windes astah, þæt he sona instæpe Drihtnes*

mildheortnesse gecegde 7 þa miltse bæd monna cynne, and *ÆCHom* i. 246. 16, quoted and discussed in §3612. But what would in non-dependent speech have been verbs in the present tense with a future reference appear in dependent speech as preterite subjunctives referring to the future-in-the-past, e.g. *Bo* 103. 8 *7 sæde gif he hine under bæc besawe þ he sceolde forlætan þæt wif* and

Beo 2633   Ic ðæt mæl geman,   þær we medu þegun,
þonne we geheton   ussum hlaforde
in biorsele,   ðe us ðas beagas geaf,
þæt we him ða guðgetawa   gyldan woldon,
gif him þyslicu   þearf gelumpe,
helmas ond heard sweord.

For further examples and discussion of sentences in which all the verbs are in the preterite, see Mather, pp. 67–9, and the sections cited in §3684.

§3688. What Alistair Campbell in his lectures called 'a failure to adjust the time' in subordinate clauses in dependent speech introduced by a verb in the preterite is exemplified in *Matt(WSCp)* 22. 24 (= *Mark* 12. 19 and *Luke* 20. 28), *ÆCHom* i. 494. 15, *ÆCHom* ii. 248. 5, and *ÆCHom* ii. 2. 10 *Ic gesette on twam bocum þa gereccednysse ðe ic awende, forðan ðe ic ðohte þæt hit wære læsse æðryt to gehyrenne, gif man ða ane boc ræt on anes geares ymbryne, and ða oðre on ðam æftran geare.* (Despite Mather (p. 68), the two subjunctives *foo* and *sciele* in *CP* 59. 9 are not dependent on *cwædon*. So this is not an example.) This phenomenon is not restricted to dependent speech; consider *ÆCHom* i. 36. 1 *Se Godes Sunu wæs on his gesthuse genyrwed, þæt he us rume wununge on heofonan rice forgife, gif we his willan gehyrsumiað.*

§3689. I must content myself with brief comments on sentences containing conditional clauses with conjunctions other than *gif* in dependent speech. *þær* introduces a rejected condition in *Bo* 51. 6 (where the conditional clause precedes *ic wat ðæt*) and in *CP* 305. 18 *Ac ðæm anstræcum is to cyðanne, ðær hie ne wenden ðæt hie selfe beteran 7 wisran wæren ðonne oðre menn, ðæt hie ne læten hiera geðeaht 7 hiera wenan sua feor beforan ealra oðerra monna wenan.* The difficulty of deciding whether *þær* ever introduces conceded or open conditions has been illustrated in §3622 by two examples in dependent speech, viz. *Bede* 28. 19 and *GenB* 386.

§3690. *Butan* and *nymþe* regularly take the subjunctive. So interest here is restricted to the problems discussed in §3684 and to examples in which we have variations of tense, e.g. *CP* 9. 5 and *ÆCHom* i. 26. 16 *and cwæð þæt nan man ne mæg beon gehealden, buton he rihtlice on God gelyfe, and he beo gefullod, and his geleafan mid godum weorcum geglenge*, or (exceptionally) of mood, e.g. *ÆCHom* i. 14. 6 *Nast þu na þæt ic eom þin Hlaford and þæt þu eart min þeowa, buton þu do þæt ic þe hate, and forgang þæt ic þe forbeode*, where the imp. *forgang* may mark a transition to non-dependent speech.

16. PARATAXIS

§3691. In examples like *Matt(WSCp)* 7. 7 *Biddaþ 7 eow bið geseald. Seceaþ 7 ge hit findaþ. Cnuciað 7 eow biþ ontyned*, Latin *Petite et dabitur uobis quaerite et inuenietis pulsate et aperietur uobis, Matt (WSCp)* 8. 8, *Luke(WSCp)* 6. 37 (§3678), *ÆCHom* ii. 346. 16 *Do well on eallum ðinum life, and we siððan æfter ðinum weldædum bliðne ðe eft genimað to us*, and *PPs* 68. 32 . . . *seceað drihten and eower sawl leofað*, Latin *Quaerite Dominum et vivet anima vestra*, we have an imperative sentence followed by a co-ordinate *ond* clause expressing the result which will follow if the command or injunction is executed. These can be seen as the equivalent of a conditional sentence. In MnE examples of this sort, the initial verb cannot always be interpreted as an imperative; compare *Matt* 7. 7 'Ask, and it shall be given you; seek, and ye shall find; knock, and it shall be opened unto you' with 'Spare the rod and spoil the child' and see further Visser, i, §26, and Wood, pp. 359–60. In MnE, 'and' can be replaced by 'then', e.g. 'Be good. Then you can go', or can be unexpressed, e.g. 'Come to me. You'll be safe'. So too in OE, e.g. (with *þonne*) *CP* 395. 34 (§3678), where *ðonne* represents Latin *et*; *Bo* 42. 4, where the sequence *Do nu . . . þonne meaht þu . . .* renders a Latin conditional sentence (Mather, p. 27); *HomU* 40. 272. 13; and *PPs* 118. 117 *Gefultuma me fæste; ðonne beo ic fægere hal . . .* , Latin *Adiuva me, et salvus ero*; and (without *ond*) *Lch* ii. 68. 10, *Lch* ii. 228. 19 *Eft lege dweorgedwostlan gecowene on þone nafolan, sona gestilleþ*, and *MCharm* 4. 5 (§3678). For more examples involving asyndetic parataxis, see §1705.

§3692. Mather (p. 60) points out that '*oððe* or *elles* introducing a clause, which is not a mere alternative, are [*sic*] equivalent logically to a negative protasis formed from the immediately preceding statement. They are often used to introduce a clause expressing the result of the non-fulfilment of a command.' Typical examples are *ÆCHom* i. 424. 21 *Geoffra ðine lac urum godum, oððe þu bist mid eallum*

ðisum pinungtolum getintregod and *ÆCHom* i. 462. 31 . . . *and forði
ic sprece ðe he me het; elles ic ne dorste on his andwerdnysse sprecan,
ne furðon ure ealdor.* See further Liggins 1955, pp. 394-5.

§3693. On examples like *CP* 321. 11 *Hwy sculon hie ðonne beon
forðæm upahæfene 7 aðundene on hira mode? Him wære ðonne
micel ðearf ðæt hie leten Godes ege hie geeaðmedan*, where the first
sentence implies a conditional clause—'If they were to be proud and
inflated, then it would be very necessary . . .'—see §3676. But it is
not necessary to assume 'ellipsis'. Thus, the relationship may be one
of question and answer in both the OE and the Latin versions of *Or*
182. 16 *Ac frine hie mon ponne æfter hu monegum wintrum sio sibb
gewurde pæs pe hie æst unsibbe wið monegum folcum hæfdon:
ponne is pæt æfter L wintra 7 feower hundum. Ahsige ponne eft hu
longe sio sibb gestode: ponne wæs pæt an gear*, Latin *Et hoc post
quantum temporis? post annos quadringentos et quadraginta. Quandiu? anno uno*; see Mather, p. 60. But see also my §3680.

17. OTHER CONSTRUCTIONS WHICH MAY EXPRESS CONDITION

§3694. According to Mather (p. 46), 'no construction affords a better example of the vicissitudes of form and of meaning than the
conditional sentence in its many points of contact with other constructions'. On variations between *pæt, gif, pær*, and *peah*, in what
can be described as noun clauses, see §1960 and Mather, p. 51.
Shearin (1903, p. 90) sees 'purpose blending with condition' in *LS*
23. 732 *and he geornlice mid his eagena scearpnyssum hawigende
ge on pa swiðran healfe ge on pa wynstran swa swa se gleawesta
hunta gif he pær mihte pæs sweteste wildeor gegripan*—but *gif* may
introduce a dependent question; see §2059—and in *Bede* 408. 25
and 414. 17 *Cuomon hio to Ealdseaxna mægðe, gif wen wære pæt hi
pær ænige purh heora lare Criste begytan mihte*, where *gif wen wære
pæt* represents Latin *si forte*. On 'condition expressing purpose',
see further Mather, pp. 58-9, and §3659. The overlap between condition and place has been discussed in §3621, between condition and
cause in §§3162-4, and between condition and concession in §3674.
On *swa, swelce* 'as if', see §§3370-80.

§3695. The fact that clauses of time often express the idea of cause
has been noted in §§3155-7. They may also shade into condition.
This is particularly true of *ponne* clauses. As an adverb, *ponne* is frequently used in correlation with *gif*; see §§2571 and 3719-21. The

small semantic distinction between *gif* 'if' and *þonne* 'whenever' is apparent in pairs like *ÆCHom* ii. 210. 34 *Turtlan we offriað, gif we on clænnysse wuniað. þeorfe hlafas we bringað Gode to lace, ðonne we buton yfelnysse beorman on ðeorfnysse syfernysse and soðfæstnysse farað*; see §2587. *Notes 2* is a fruitful source of such variations. Mather (p. 51) notes that in *Bede* 82. 25 and 86. 11 *mid þy* translates *cum*. But it may be added that in very similar contexts *cum* is translated by *þonne* in *Bede* 86. 7 and *gif* translates *si* in *Bede* 86. 14 and *sin* in *Bede* 86. 19. These variations underline the closeness of 'whenever' and 'if', of *cum* and *si* (see GL, §583), and of *þonne* and *gif*; see further Adams, p. 62, and §§2587 and 2565. On the possibility of conditional *þa*, see §2579.

§3696. Mather (pp. 49 and 50-1) notes that *nu* occasionally translates Latin *si*, e.g. *Or* 58. 25 *Nu he þara læssena rica reccend is, hu micle swiþor wene we þæt he ofer þa maran sie, þe on swa unmetlican onwealdun ricsedon!*, Latin *Si autem . . .* , and *Matt(WSCp)* 7. 11 *Eornustlice nu ge þe yfle synt cunnun gode sylena eowrum bearnum syllan, mycle ma eower fæder þe on heofenum ys syleþ god þam þe hyne biddað*, Latin *Si ergo uos cum sitis mali nostis bona dare filiis uestris . . .* , and that *ær*, alone or in combination with *þam (þe)*, sometimes approaches the sense of *butan*, e.g. *CP* 331. 19 *He gesihð ðone welan ðe he wilnað, 7 he ne geliefð ðæs grines ðe he mid gebrogden wyrð, ærðon he hit gefrede*.

§3697. On temporal/conditional clauses, see further Mather, pp. 48-51 and 79, and the references given in Mitchell 1959, p. 581 fnn. 3, 4, and 5.

§3698. *Butan* and *nymþe* may introduce phrases which express condition; see §§3629-32 and 3649-51. They may also govern clauses, e.g. a clause of purpose in *Bo* 20. 24 *Forþam se deað ne cymð to nanum oðrum ðingum butan þ he þ lif afyrre*; see Shearin 1903, pp. 90-1, and my §§3641-6 and 3656-8. Despite Mather (pp. 54-5), *ðære* in *CP* 345. 15 *Seceað sibbe 7 god to eallum mannum; butan ðære ne mæg nan man God gesion* (Latin *sine qua*) and *þam* in *ÆC Hom* i. 134. 1 *Geleafa is ealra mægena fyrmest; buton þam ne mæg nan man Gode lician* are not unambiguous relatives; they could be demonstratives.

§3699. Mather (p. 47) begins his discussion of the 'relative condition' by citing Goodwin, *Syntax of the Moods and Tenses of the Greek Verb*, pp. 197-8: 'A relative with an indefinite antecedent gives a conditional force to the clause in which it stands, and is called a conditional relative.' Mather goes on to say that in OE 'the introducing relative is usually se ðe or swa hwa (hwylc) swa'. That these relatives are often the equivalent of *si quis* is illustrated by *CP* 53. 7 *Se ðe biscephade gewilnað, god weorc he gewilnað*, Latin *Si quis episcopatum desiderat, bonum opus desiderat*, and by a comparison of *ÆCHom* ii. 588. 23 *Swa hwa swa* . . . with 1 *Cor* 3. 12-13 *si quis* (both in §2372). Note also *CP* 335. 11 *Hwæt se ðonne unryhtlice talað, se ðe talað ðæt he sie unscyldig gif he ða good ðe us God teo gemanan sealde, him synderlice ægnað*, Latin *Incassum ergo se innocentes putant, qui commune Dei munus sibi privatum vindicant*, where *gif he* translates *qui*. For more such examples see Mather, pp. 47-8. Consider also *ÆCHom* i. 156. 1-9, where we have *Se man þe* . . . *ac gif he* . . . *Gif he* . . . *Se ðe* . . . *Swa hwa swa* . . . , for reasons which may be stylistic, but cannot be semantic; *ÆCHom* ii. 208. 19, where three co-ordinate *se ðe* clauses are 'correlative' with *þonne* in the principal clause; the variations between *gyf* and *se ðe* in *Exod* 21; and *Beo* 142 *heold hyne syðþan* ‖ *fyr ond fæstor se þæm feonde ætwand* and

GenB 481   Sceolde on wite a
                     mid swate and mid sorgum   siððan libban,
                     swa hwa swa gebyrgde   þæs on þam beame geweox,

in both of which we could have had a conditional clause.

§3700. The use of an adjective clause instead of a conditional clause sometimes involves anacoluthon in OE; see §§2213 (*se* + *þe*) and 2372 (*swa hwa swa*). Liebermann (*Archiv*, 118 (1907), 384) sees the opposite—a *gyf* clause where the sense requires an adjective clause —in the addition *gyf he cyninges man sy* in *LawIEm(B)* 3.

§3701. In many of the examples in which a *se þe* clause is the equivalent of a *gif* clause, it is accompanied by a principal clause containing a 'volitional expression'. That the subjunctive is not the rule in either *se þe* clauses or *gif* clauses in such contexts has been demonstrated in §§2391-8 and 3560-90. More exceptions will be found in the indefinite adjective clauses in *BlHom* 17. 35, *ÆCHom* i. 156. 6, and *Exod* 21. 12 and 22. 14.

§3702. In all the examples so far cited, the adjective clause has been the equivalent of an open condition. Gorrell (p. 462) cites *ÆCHom* ii. 338. 33 *Se awyrigeda gast andwyrde, God gecwæð, þæt ælc synn ðe nære ofer eorðan gebet, sceolde beon on ðissere worulde gedemed* as one illustration of his statement that in dependent speech 'examples are occasionally found of adjectival and other subordinate clauses, that play the part of a protasis; the preterite subjunctive is regularly employed' and translates 'if it were not atoned for it should be judged'. This is not to be taken as implying that the condition would have been a rejected or an imaginary one in non-dependent speech; see §§3612-14.

18. MOOD: CONCLUDING REMARKS

§3703. The mood of the verbs in the various types of conditional sentences, including the influence of a principal clause containing a volitional expression, has been discussed for each type in turn. Space does not permit a summary here; even the most simple statement—that conceded and open conditions have the present or preterite indicative and rejected and imaginary conditions the preterite subjunctive—requires the qualifications given in the relevant sections. For details see the Table of Contents and the Indexes. A summary of the use of the moods and tenses in conditional sentences in the poetry will be found in Mitchell 1959, pp. 630-3.

§3704. As far as I have observed, the presence of a negated indicative or a rhetorical question in the principal clause has no effect on the mood of the verb of an accompanying conditional clause.

§3705. Those wishing to examine the nature and origin of the subjunctive in conditional sentences should consult, *inter alios*, Behre, pp. 50-6 and 131-48; Mattsson, *Kock Studies*, pp. 200-24; Liggins 1955, pp. 276-81; and the references given by these writers and by Mitchell 1959, p. 590 fn. 3. It may perhaps be noted here that the fact that in OE clauses introduced by *swa* or *swelce* 'as if'—on which see §§3370-80—we find the present subjunctive when the reference is to the present, e.g. *BlHom* 135. 33 *þæs wordes andgit is swa mon cwepe þingere oþþe frefrend* '. . . as if one said/were to say . . .', is one of the main planks in Mattsson's argument (pp. 215-17) that the present subjunctive could express unreality in the present. But see §3559.

§3706. Having discussed the difficulty created by ambiguous verb-forms, Mather (p. 5) goes on: 'A second difficulty is that of determining the exact significance of those verbs, such as sculan and willan, which are moving towards an auxiliary and modal significance. I find instances where their modal significance is unquestionable, but in general agree with Lüttgens that they retain their independent value ever [*sic*; ?'even'] in Late West-Saxon.' A full study of the use of the 'modal' auxiliaries in OE conditional sentences, not possible here because of limitations of space, may well throw valuable light on their subsequent development. Anyone pursuing such a study should consult initially Behre, pp. 56-61, and Wilde, pp. 338-52.

19. CLAUSE ORDER

§3707. *Gif* clauses regularly precede a principal clause which contains correlative *þonne*. Clauses introduced by *butan* and *nymþe* tend to follow the principal clause, but may precede it, e.g. (with *butan*) *CP* 153. 3 (§3720) and *ÆCHom* ii. 230. 4 *Buton Drihten ða burh gehealde, on ydel waciað þa hyrdas ðe hi healdað*, and (see §3714) *Bede* 52. 21 *Cyðdon him openlice 7 sædon, butan hi him maran andlyfne sealdon, þæt hi woldan him sylfe niman 7 hergian, þær hi hit findan mihton*. For examples with *nymþe*, see §3654. The comments which follow must be read with these statements in mind.

§3708. When there is only one conditional clause, it may immediately precede the principal clause, e.g. *ÆCHom* i. 14. 12 *Gif ðu þonne ðis lytle bebod tobrecst, þu scealt deaðe sweltan*; immediately follow it, e.g. *ÆCHom* i. 86. 32 *ac ic mæg habban arwurðfulle licðenunge of heofigendre menigu, gif ge willað minum bebodum gehyrsumian*; occur within it, e.g. *ÆCHom* ii. 436. 21 *ac ge magon be ðison, gif ge wyllað, micel understandan* and (with the subject of the principal clause repeated—an arrangement not uncommon in Ælfric but not restricted to him; see *BlHom* 57. 10) *ÆCHom* i. 102. 22, i. 160. 11, and i. 168. 32 *swa eac seo sawul, gif heo næfð þa halgan lare, heo bið þonne weornigende and mægenleas*; separate the principal clause from a clause which is an essential part of it (P | Sc | Sp), e.g. *ÆCHom* i. 16. 14 *forði is se man betera, gif he gode geðihð, þonne ealle ða nytenu sindon*; or (in the poetry at any rate[197]) be used *apo koinou*, e.g. *Jul* 328 (see Meritt, p. 51) and

Vain 44   Nu þu cunnan meaht,
             gif þu þyslicne   þegn gemittest
             wunian in wicum,   wite þe be þissum
             feawum forðspellum   þæt þæt biþ feondes bearn
             flæsce bifongen,   hafað fræte lif,
             grundfusne gæst   gode orfeormne,
             wuldorcyninge.

---

[197] I have recorded no such examples in the prose. But their existence would not surprise me; see §§3800-3.

I am not certain that the form *gemittest* certifies that the *gif* clause cannot accompany the clause with imp. *wite*; see §§3564 and 3571-80.

§3709. These alternatives allow conditional sentences to be arranged in parallel, e.g. *ÆCHom* i. 96. 7 *Gif ge willað æfter menniscum gesceade lybban, þonne sind ge gastlice ymbsnidene; gif ge þonne eowere galnysse underþeodde beoð, þonne beo ge swa se witega cwæð . . .*, or in chiasmus, e.g. *ÆCHom* ii. 534. 11 *Seo sibb, þe se Godes bydel bodað, wunað on ðam huse, gif ðær bið sibbe bearn; gif ðær nan ne bið, seo sib gecyrð eft to ðam bydele* and

El 776   . . .   (gif he þin nære
                  sunu synna leas,   næfre he soðra swa feala
                  in woruldrice   wundra gefremede
                  dogorgerimum;   no ðu of deaðe hine
                  swa þrymlice,   þeoda wealdend,
                  aweahte for weorodum, gif he in wuldre þin
                  þurh ða beorhtan   bearn ne være). . . .

Ælfric sometimes combines both arrangements; consider the passage with five *gif* clauses which begins at *ÆCHom* i. 488. 32.

§3710. When a sentence contains two conditional clauses, three arrangements are possible: both may precede or follow the principal or governing clause or they may be separated by it. The 'both first' arrangement appears in *ÆCHom* i. 306. 10 *Gif hwa bið geuntrumod on his anginne, and asolcen fram godre drohtnunge, gif hine hwa ðonne mid tihtinge and gebisnungum godra weorca getrymð and arærð, þonne bið hit swilce he sette his handa ofer untrumne and hine gehæle* and *ÆCHom* i. 472. 2 *Gif se synfulla bið gebrocod for his unrihtwisnysse, þonne gif he mid geðylde his Drihten herað, and his miltsunge bitt, he bið ðonne aðwogen fram his synnum ðurh ða untrumnysse, swa swa horig hrægl þurh sapan.* In these two sentences, both conditions must be fulfilled before the principal clause obtains. So *þonne* is in a sense equivalent to *and* and the two *gif* clauses can be taken as co-ordinate in the pattern Sp + Sp | P. (Whether the co-ordination is asyndetic or syndetic depends on whether we think of *þonne* as an 'adverb' or a 'sentence adverb'; see §§1101-2.) I fluctuate between this analysis and the pattern Sc | Sp | P.

§3711. We find both clauses following the principal clause in *ÆCHom* i. 476. 4 *ac þæt he tælð to unalyfedlicere wiglunge, gif hwa ða wyrta on him becnitte, buton he hi to ðam dolge gelecge*, where I hesitate between P | Sp | Sc and P | Sp + Sp, and *ÆCHom* ii. 276. 35 *Micel god*

biδ cristenum mannum þæt hi gelome to husle gan, gif hi unscæδδig-
nysse on heora heortan beraδ to δam weofode, gif hi ne beoδ mid
leahtrum ofsette, where the *gif* clauses seem to say the same thing in
different words and my analysis is therefore P | Sp + Sp.

§3712. Examples with the principal clause in the middle include
ÆCHom i. 212. 12 *þonne gif he mid deofles weorcum hine sylfne*
bebint, δonne ne mæg he mid his agenre mihte hine unbindan, buton
se Ælmihtiga God mid strangre handa his mildheortnysse hine un-
binde (Sp | P | Sc) and *ÆCHom* ii. 538. 10 *Gif δe man scotaδ to, þu*
gescyltst δe, gif þu hit gesihst, where the analysis Sp | P | Sc is the first
to present itself; the first *gif* clause is the referent of *hit* in the second.
But if both *gif* clauses preceded the principal clause, we could have
Sp + Sp | P. The same rearrangement could give Sp + Sp | P in *ÆCHom*
i. 472. 6 *Gif he rihtwis biδ, he hæfδ þonne maran geδincδe þurh his*
brocunge, gif he geδyldig biδ. But is this Sc | P | Sp or Sp | P | Sp or
Sp | P | Sc?

§3713. There are, of course, numerous other possible arrangements,
e.g. *CP* 31. 25 *forδæm gif he on δæm wel deδ, he hæfδ δæs god lean,*
gif he yfle deδ, læsse wite he δrowaδ on helle, gif he ana δider cymδ,
δonne he do, gif he oδerne mid him δider bringδ and *ÆCHom* ii.
218. 16 *Swa sceolon eac cristene men δa eahta heafodleahtras mid*
heora werodum ealle oferwinnan, gif hi æfre sceolon to δam eδele
becuman, δe him on frymδe se Heofenlica Fæder gemynte, gif hi his
bebodum bliδelice gehyrsumiaδ. But space does not permit further
analysis. See Mather, pp. 44-5, 71-2, and (for comments on variations in element order within the clauses in different arrangements of
conditional sentences) 72-7; Behaghel, *PBB* 53 (1929), 401-18; and
(for summaries of her conclusions concerning the length and placing
of *gif* clauses in Ælfric's *Lives of the Saints*) Waterhouse 1978, pp.
289-90 and 295-6.

§3714. In accordance with OE idiom (§1978), a conditional clause
which precedes its principal clause is normally placed before the *þæt*
when the sentence is in dependent speech, e.g. *Bede* 102. 20 *þa se*
Godes wer Scs Agustinus is sægd þæt he beotigende forecwæde, gif
heo sibbe mid Godes monnum onfon ne wolden, þæt heo wæren un-
sibbe 7 gefeoht from heora feondum onfonde and *Met* 25. 30. Sometimes it is not clear whether the conditional clause is part of the
dependent speech or not, e.g. *Ex* 558, *Jul* 80 and 119, *Beo* 272
(here *gif* may mean 'whether'; see §3547), and

Beo 1845   Wen ic talige,
                    gif þæt gegangeð,   þæt ðe gar nymeð,
                    hild heorugrimme   Hreþles eaferan,
                    adl oþðe iren   ealdor ðinne,
                    folces hyrde,   ond þu þin feorh hafast,
                    þæt þe Sæ-Geatas   selran næbben
                    to geceosenne   cyning ænigne . . .

—'If it happens . . . I shall count it probable . . .' or 'I count it probable that, if it happens . . .'? But such ambiguities are largely grammatical and sometimes, at any rate, the conditional clause may be
used *apo koinou*. Unexpressed *þæt* occasionally occurs, e.g. *John
(WSCp)* 21. 25 *Witodlice oðre manega þing synt þe se hælend worhte
gif ða ealle awritene wæron ic wene ne mihte þes middaneard ealle
þa bec befon*, where the Latin has an accusative and infinitive, and
Vain 77 (§1989).

20. CO-ORDINATION

§3715. Clauses of condition occur in both asyndetic and syndetic
co-ordination. Examples of the former include (with the subordinating conjunction not repeated)

Rid 20. 24   Me bið forð witod,   gif ic frean hyre,
                    guþe fremme,   swa ic gien dyde
                    minum þeodne on þonc,   þæt ic þolian sceal
                    bearngestreona

and (with the subordinating conjunction repeated) *Bede* 102. 18 *Gif
he nu for us arisan ne wolde, micle ma gif we him underþeodde beoð,
he us eac for noht gehygeð* (note the change of tense) and *PPs* 88.
28–30. For some possible examples of this pattern see §3710.

§3716. Examples of syndetic parataxis include (with the subordinating conjunction not repeated) *ÆCHom* i. 6. 24 (*and*), *ÆCHom* ii.
452. 5 (*oþþe*), and

Met 4. 49   Gif ðu nu, waldend, ne wilt   wirde steoran,
                    ac on selfwille   sigan lætest,
                    þonne ic wat . . .

(*ac*), and (with the subordinating conjunction repeated) *ÆCHom* i.
222. 2 (*and*) and *ÆCHom* i. 112. 5 *þonne wære seo rihtwisnys
awæged, gif he hi neadunge to his ðeowte gebigde, oððe gif he hi to
yfelnysse bescufe* (*oððe*). In *ÆCHom* i. 412. 2 exclamatory *þæt is*
links two *gif* clauses. In *Bo* 83. 28 *forðæm gif hit swa nære, þonne
nære he þ þ he gehaten is; oððe ænig þing ær wære oððe æltæwre,*

þonne wære þ betere þonne he, one might have expected *gif* to be repeated after *oðð e*; cf. *Rid* 15. 9 (§3668).

§3717. Both types may occur in the same sentence; see for example
ÆCHom i. 306. 10, *Jul* 47, and *Jul* 119. Clauses introduced by different conditional conjunctions can of course be co-ordinate, e.g.
ÆCHom ii. 422. 21 *Gif ðu ðe hraðor ne gewitst fram Iacobe, and
buton ðu wyrige Cristes naman, þu scealt beon beheafdod samod
mid him.*

§3718. Hotz (pp. 57–8) quotes *Exod(L)* 21. 28 *Gif oxa hnite wer
oðð e wif 7 hig deade beoð, si he mid stanum oftorforod*, Latin *Si
bos cornu percusserit uirum aut mulierem, et mortui fuerint, lapidi-
bus obruetur*, to demonstrate 'how the selfsame documents [the
Laws] avail themselves of moods to set off a condition from a subordinate one. . . . Anglo-Saxon thus likes to mark the different order
of the conditions; Latin does not reflect it by the moods. It seems
not to matter, whether the subj. be nearest to the optat. or imperative, or not, provided that the indic. alternate with the subj.'; note
here *LawAbt* 3 *Gif cyning æt mannes ham drincæþ, 7 ðær man
lyswæs hwæt gedo, twibote gebete.* Mather (pp. 44–5) accepts this
'rule' as one which is based on legal texts and so 'hardly correspond[s]
to the usage of literary prose', observing that the change 'is found
rarely' and citing *Bede(T)* 268. 15 *sægde he—gif he æt leorninga
sæte oðð e elles hwæt dyde, gif semninga mare blæd windes astah,
þæt he sona instæpe Drihtnes mildheortnesse gecegde 7 þa miltse
bæd monna cynne.* But MS *O* has *sæt.* In view of this variation and
of those recorded in §§3576 and 3585, I am reluctant to believe in
the existence of Hotz's 'variation' as a grammatical principle. *Vain*
77 (§1989) does not in my opinion exemplify it.

21. CORRELATION

§3719. As already noted in §3707, *gif* clauses regularly precede
a principal clause which contains *þonne*, the regular correlative
adverb. The variety of arrangements possible can be illustrated from
ÆCHom. We find, *inter alia, gif . . . þonne . . .* in *ÆCHom* i. 72. 30
*ac gif ðu ðas deadan sceaðan on ðines Godes naman arærst, þonne
bið min heorte geclænsod fram ælcere twynunge; þonne gif . . .
þonne . . .* in *ÆCHom* i. 178. 21 *þonne, gif we teoðiað þas gearlican
dagas, þonne beoð þær six and ðritig teoðingdagas*; and *gif* pronoun
subject *þonne . . . þonne . . .* in *ÆCHom* i. 54. 22 *Gif ðu ðonne
þinum cristenum breðer deredest, þonne hæfð he sum ðing ongean*

ðe, and þu scealt be Godes tæcunge hine gegladian, ær ðu ðine lac
geoffrige. We also find adv. þonne in the gif clause but not in the
principal clause, e.g. ÆCHom i. 54. 24 Gif ðonne se cristena mann,
þe ðin broðor is, ðe ahwar geyfelode, þæt ðu scealt miltsigende for-
gifan. A gif clause can of course have first place without adv. þonne
in either clause, e.g. ÆCHom i. 170. 1 (§3569) and ÆCHom i. 68.
24 and gif man oðrum miltsað, hu micele swiðor wile God miltsian
and arian mannum his handgeweorce! The varying arrangements in
the passages beginning at ÆCHom i. 52. 27, ÆCHom i. 96. 7, and
ÆCHom i. 140. 33, will repay study.

§3720. The correlative adv. þonne can accompany other conjunctions, e.g. þær in Or 214. 5 and CP 415. 7 Ðær we us selfum demden,
ðonne ne demde us no God, and butan in CP 153. 3 Forðæm buton
he ðone timan aredige ðæs læcedomes ðonne bið hit swutol ðæt se
lacnigenda forliesð ðone cræft his læcedomes and possibly Bo 103. 17.

§3721. In the poetry, we find, inter alia, gif . . . ðonne . . . in Met
24. 28 and gif mon ðonne . . . and him þonne . . . ðonne . . . in Met
25. 22. Adv. þonne occurs in the gif clause but not in the principal
clause in Beo 1836, and we find an initial gif clause without adv.
þonne in either clause in Beo 1826. We have adv. þa . . . conj. þær
. . . in PPs 105. 19 and adv. þonne . . . conj. gif . . . in Beo 525.
Whether these can be described as correlative is arguable. Adv. þonne
may be correlative with a conditional clause with no conjunction and
element order VS in GenB 368. But see §3682.

M. THE ACCUSATIVE/NOMINATIVE/DATIVE AND INFINITIVE

1. INTRODUCTORY REMARKS

a. Terminology

§3722. The construction seen in Thales Milesius aquam dixit esse
initium rerum and ÆCHom i. 20. 18 and he lætt hi habban agenne
cyre is traditionally known as the accusative and infinitive. Visser's
objection (iii, §2056) that this 'cannot pass muster since it wrongly
suggests the existence of "accusative" forms in Middle and Modern
English' is no bar to its use in a work concerned with OE. Kageyama
(p. 166) objects that it 'is misleading, for there are verbs that require
the dative case in the object'. I meet this point by discussing the two
separately, unlike Visser (iii, §2059). Kageyama adopted the term

'object + infinitive', although Visser (ibid.) had already said that this 'is not wholly acceptable on account of its failing to express that the word that is the object is at the same time a subject'. In reply to this, one can say that it cannot be taken for granted that 'the word that is . . . a subject' is always an object; see §§3734–40. This is a reason for not accepting Visser's VOSI/VOSING/VOSP (iii, §2055), standing for verb + object/subject + infinitive/present participle/second participle. So it is not merely intractable obstinacy which leads me to cling to 'accusative and infinitive', 'accusative and present participle', and 'accusative and second participle'. On the 'nominative and infinitive' and the 'dative and infinitive', see §§3779–81 and 3782–6 respectively.

b. Classification of the governing verbs

§3723. Zeitlin (chapter III) adopts a fourfold classification of verbs which govern the accusative and infinitive construction: first, verbs of expressed or implied causation, including verbs of causing, of advising, etc., of allowing and preventing, of commanding, of requesting, and of creating, choosing, appointing, etc.; second, verbs of sense perception; third, verbs denoting a mental action—he observes (p. 78) that 'the dividing line between verbs of sense and mental perception is not one which can be precisely marked';[198] and fourth, verbs of declaration. Callaway's fivefold classification (1913, p. 107) varies only in separating verbs of commanding from verbs of causing and permitting. But he could not fit *habban* and *todælan* into any of these groups (1913, p. 108) and it is not clear exactly where the 'verbs of Inclination and Will' (1913, p. 122) belong; he puts them in a separate class at pp. 41–3. Visser (iii, §2066), who was also concerned with ME and MnE, distinguished eleven categories, with the warning that even 'this categorisation is not ideal: there is too much overlapping and too many verbs are ambivalent or polysemic'. His categories are: the verb *have*, and verbs of physical perception, of causing, of inducing and forcing, of allowing and hindering, of wishing, of liking and disliking, of commanding and forbidding, of mental perception, of teaching, and of saying and declaring. Despite the surface variations, we can detect a basic agreement among these systems.[199] I do not propose to attempt another. Those wishing to do

---

[198] Kageyama (p. 169) claims to have found a difference. But his observation (p. 166) that the verbs under discussion 'according to Callaway (1913) and Visser (1973) . . . are roughly classified into four categories' and his translation (p. 168) of *Matt(WSCp)* 4. 19 *7 ic do þ gyt beoð manna fisceras* as 'I make that it be men's fish' do not exactly engender confidence in his work.

[199] Macháček (1965, pp. 110–31) offers a different classification which I find confusing; for example, he places *gebeodan* (p. 111) in a different class from *beodan* and *be-/for-beodan*

so should consult, in addition to Callaway (1913, pp. 107-26) and
Visser (iii, §§2066-81), the following: (on *hatan*) Gorrell (pp. 375-7),
Callaway (1913, pp. 204-5), Royster (1918, pp. 82-4 and 89-93—
Royster sees *hatan* as causative as well as mandatory), Fröhlich (pp.
100-1), and Zuck (pp. 17-18); (on verbs of causing) Callaway (1913,
pp. 205-6) and Royster (1918, *passim*, and 1922, *passim*); (on verbs
of physical perception) Gorrell (pp. 475-6), Callaway (1913, p. 206),
Penttilä (pp. 48-9), Stewart (1976, *passim*), and Ogura (1979, pp.
19-20); (on verbs of mental perception) Gorrell (pp. 475-6), Callaway (1913, pp. 206-8), Fröhlich (p. 101), Ono (*passim*), and Stewart
(1976, p. 48 n. 3); (on verbs of declaring) Callaway (1913, p. 208)
and Ogura (1979, pp. 20-1); and (for more examples) Wülfing (ii,
§§482-3) and Scheler (pp. 93-8). More work is needed on the frequency of the various forms of the accusative and infinitive construction (see §3724) and of the alternative constructions (see §§3727-
33) after the various verbs.

c. The infinitives

§3724. The accusative and infinitive appears with the following infinitives: the infinitive in *-(i)an* (§§3745-7); the inflected infinitive
with *to* (§§3748-51); *beon/wesan* + the present participle (§3752);
and *beon/wesan/weorþan* + the second participle—the passive infinitive (§§3753-4). On the relationship between the accusative and
the infinitive, see §§3734-40.

d. The functions of the accusative and infinitive

§3725. As in Latin, the accusative and infinitive may serve as the
object of a verb (§§3745-76) or as the subject of an impersonal verb
(§§3777-8). I have found no examples of its use in exclamations,
the third of the functions detected in Latin by GL (§343. 2).

§3726. The accusative and infinitive may express a dependent statement, e.g. *GD* 203. 25 *hwæt! ic la acsie þe, hwæt cweþe wit þis beon
. . . ?* (where I give Hecht's punctuation, but the question may be
dependent rather than non-dependent) and *ÆCHom* i. 48. 17 *forði
gemunde swiðe gedafenlice þæt godcunde gewrit, mannes Sunu
standan æt Godes swiðran to gescyndenne þæra Iudeiscra ungeleaf-
fulnysse*, or a dependent desire, e.g. *Ps(P)* 41. 9 *On dæg bebead God
his mildheortnesse cuman to me* and *ÆLS* 4. 141 *Hwæt þa Martianus
het his manfullan cwelleras þone halgan beatan mid heardum saglum.*

(pp. 125-6) and separates *cweðan* (p. 111) from *secgan* (p. 124). Stewart (1973, pp. 59-60)
refines Callaway's classification.

e. Other constructions with the same or a similar function

§3727. Visser (iii, §§2057-65) lists and discusses eight constructions which he describes as 'more or less kindred' to the accusative
and infinitive. Four of these—represented respectively by MnE 'Let
we (he, I) go', 'I depended on him to come', 'I wanted for him to go',
and 'Look at her enter' (see Stoffel, *Archiv*, 62 (1879), 209-16, and
Zeitlin, p. 117)—have not been recorded in OE. Indeed, some of
them are scarcely acceptable MnE. The remaining four are discussed
below. To these may be added the double accusative (§§3766-76),
including the accusative and present participle (§3769) and the accusative and second participle (§3770).

§3728. The first of the four remaining types is the *þæt* clause,
which may express a dependent statement, e.g. *ÆCHom* i. 80. 5 *Nu
secgað wyrdwriteras þæt Herodes betwux ðisum wearð gewreged to
þam Romaniscan casere* and *Ps(P)* 28. 8 *Drihten us gedyde, þæt we
moston buian æfter þam folce* (on *þæt* clauses after causative verbs
see further Royster 1922, pp. 354-6), or a dependent desire, e.g.
ÆCHom i. 176. 30 *Cweð to ðysum stanum þæt hi beon to hlafum
awende* and *GD(C)* 78. 18 . . . *he þa bebead þæt man þam halgan
were þæt ilce hors eft bringan sceolde*, where *GD(H)* 78. 17 has . . .
þa geteohhode he hit to forgifenne þam ylcan halgan were, which
may mean 'then he assigned for giving' or (as we see from *GD(H)*
83. 9) 'then he resolved to give it'. On *þæt* clauses see further §§1929
and 1962-75. Whether the accusative and infinitive and the *þæt*
clause are synonymous constructions—a question raised in various
forms by Gorrell (pp. 376-7), Royster (1922, pp. 344-5), Phillipps
(*EStudies*, 35 (1954), 17-20), Macháček (1965, p. 110), and Stewart
(1976, p. 43 and n. 39)—cannot be discussed here. But compare
ÆCHom ii. 398. 28 with *ÆCHom* ii. 398. 30 and note the examples
discussed in §3732.

§3729. BT (s.v. *þæt* conj. I(2a)) speaks of *þæt* 'introducing substantive clauses . . . where the subject of the clause is omitted, and the
clause taken with the accusative of the main clause is equivalent to
the accusative and infinitive construction'. With the exception of *Bo*
35. 30 (§3738 fn.), the cited examples combine a noun clause and
an adjective clause. Typical are (with an indicative in the *þæt* clause)
Bo 38. 4 . . . *þe mon gesihð þ stronglic weorc wyrcð* and *ÆCHom* i.
234. 2 *þam mannum he sceal don synna forgifenysse, þe he gesihð
þæt beoð onbryrde ðurh Godes gife*, and (with a subjunctive) *Bo*
51. 29 . . . *atio . . . ealle þa weod þe he gesio þ þam æcerum derigen*

and *LawVIAs* 1. 1 . . . *þæt man ne sparige nanan þeof . . . þone þe
we on folcriht geaxian þæt ful sy*. See further §1980. *LawAf* 5. 5 *Se
ðe stalað on Sunnanniht oððe on Gehhol . . . : ðara gehwelc we
willað sie twybote, swa on Lenctenfæsten* may belong here. But the
absence of *þæt* suggests that *we willað* may be parenthetic, with *sie*
as a jussive subjunctive.

§3730. Visser (iii, §2059) exemplifies the second remaining type
with MnE 'I made him that he fell' and 'He forbade me that I should
speak', which would be more commonly expressed today as 'I made
him fall' (but not ☆'I made that he fell') and 'He forbade that I should
speak' (without what seems to me the tautologic 'me') or 'He forbade
me to speak'. Here see §§1929 and 1969. Visser's OE examples include some with the subject of the *þæt* clause appearing in the principal clause in the accusative, e.g. *Or* 204. 30 *Ac hiene Hannibal aspon
þæt he þæt gewin leng ne ongan*, *LS* 34. 59 . . . *and þa cristenan
nyddon þæt hi mid heom deofle on hand gangan sceoldon*, and *Alex*
34. 15 *þa het ic eallne þone here þ he to swæsendum sæte 7 mete
þigde*, and some with it in the dative, e.g. *Mark(WSCp)* 10. 48 *þa
budon him manega þ he suwode* and *WHom* 4. 37 *Leofan men, God
geþafað þam deofle Antecriste þæt he mot ehtan godra manna. . . .*
I cannot say to what extent, if any, these pronouns were felt as tautologic in OE, where *hatan* may take a bare infinitive, an accusative and
infinitive, a *þæt* clause, or a pronoun in the accusative and a *þæt*
clause; see §§679-80 and 3737. I can compare *ÆCHom* i. 588. 28
(§1969), *John(WSCp)* 5. 42 (§3737), and *Matt(AV)* 25. 24 'Lord,
I knew thee that thou art an hard man.' Beyond that, I can only
speculate.

§3731. Visser (iii, §2060) records no OE examples of the third
remaining type, 'I commanded him that (he) to go'. The closest
I have seen are *BlHom* 217. 19 *þa he þa Sanctus Martinus þæt geseah,
þæt þa oðre broðor ealle swa unrote ymb þæt lic utan stondan . . .*
and *ÆLS* 4. 323 *Geþafa þæt min modor me gespræcan and sume
þreo niht on minum ræde beon*, where the verbs of the principal
clause have no noun/personal pronoun object. Scribal error may be
involved here—*stondan* for *stodan*? and omission of *mihte* or infinitive forms for *gespræce* (= *gesprece*) and *beo*? The other two examples
cited by Callaway (1913, p. 126 n. 4) also lack the object. But in
them the apparent infinitive may be taken as subjunctive or explained
as the result of Latin influence.

§3732. The fourth remaining type (Visser, iii, §2061) combines
(*a*) a *þæt* clause and (*b*) an accusative and infinitive. These elements

occur in the order (*a*) (*b*) in his solitary OE example, *Or* 106. 22 . . .
*siþþan gelicade eallum folcum þæt hie Romanum underþieded wære,
7 hiora æ to behealdanne.* We may have a (*b*) (*a*) example in *ÆLS*
32. 52 *Nu het he þe dælan þine digelan goldhordas . . . and þu beo
his underkyning.* But in the absence of *þæt*, we may have a change
from dependent to non-dependent speech. See also *ÆCHom* ii.
106. 19, and *Dan* 541 and Farrell's note thereon.

§3733. Royster (1922, pp. 354-6) notes that 'an object plus a *to*-
prepositional phrase' may express causation, e.g. *John(WSCp)* 10. 33
. . . *forþam þe þu eart man and wyrcst þe to gode.*

f. The functions of the accusative and of the infinitive

§3734. Behind the seemingly innocent question 'What function or
functions does the accusative perform?', there lies a jungle of contradictory opinions. Is it the object of the governing verb, or the subject
of the infinitive, or both, or neither? Are the accusative and the infinitive separate units or do they combine to form a single conception? Are the answers necessarily the same for all examples, whatever
the governing verb? Zeitlin's chapter I offers a 'History of Theories'
up to 1908; see also Callaway 1913, pp. 241-8. After reading this
and some of the subsequent literature, I have some sympathy with
Royster's observation (1922, p. 335 fn. 32) that 'for the interests of
this study no good can come of attempting to determine whether the
accusative noun is the object of *don* or the subject of the infinitive'
in *BlHom* 239. 15 *And þone eadigan Matheum he gedyde gangan.* . . .
Nevertheless, even though time and space do not permit a full safari,
I propose to lead the reader into the jungle.

§3735. Stewart (1976, pp. 34-5) says that 'what we have going on'
in *Beo* 2604 *geseah his mondryhten ‖ under heregriman hat þrowian*
'is, roughly, all of the following: He saw his band of retainers. He saw
suffering. His band of retainers suffered/were suffering.' On the other
hand 'what is going on' in *Or* 44. 13 *Heton him þeh þæt andwyrde
secgan*—which she translates 'They ordered him to be told the
answer anyhow'—'is simply: They ordered something. He was told
the answer.' But a more literal translation—'However, they ordered
[someone] to tell him the answer'; see §3755—seems to me to
reveal other elements: someone must have been ordered to do the
telling and someone must have done so. Callaway (1913, p. 204)
seems to adopt a reverse position from that of Stewart when he
speaks of 'the looser union between infinitive and accusative after

these two groups of verbs [verbs of commanding and of causing and permitting] than after other groups, as after verbs of mental perception'. Müller-Hilmer, quoted by Wülfing (ii. 182), sees the accusative and the infinitive merged into one concept after *gefrignan* and *gehyran*, but as two separate objects after *hatan, lætan*, and verbs of perception—among which Callaway (1913, p. 108) includes *gefrignan* and *gehyran*. Zeitlin seems sometimes to agree with Stewart, sometimes to disagree not only with Stewart but also with himself. We read (Zeitlin, p. 108) that

> in some cases, as after *hatan* and *biddan*, the two elements were apparently felt as separate objects of the main verb, though they were loosely united by the logical relation of subject and predicate. But after verbs of direct causation it is impossible thus to analyze the component parts of the locution. In a sentence like 'he caused *him to work*,' *him* cannot be construed as independently the object of *caused* but must be considered as associated with the infinitive and forming with it a single objective conception dependent on the verb of the main clause. The tendency to dissociate the accusative from the main verb and to attach it to the infinitive is even stronger in those instances in which the latter element has a passive force. In 'he ordered *the army to be sent*,' *army* is manifestly not the direct object of the command, but rather *the sending of the army*.

We also read that 'when I say "he sees *a man walking*", I do not mean that he sees *a man* or that he sees *walking*, but only that he sees *a walking man*' (Zeitlin, p. 109) and that after verbs of causation we have 'a construction in which accusative and infinitive were at first separately dependent on the main verb' (ibid., p. 39). So far, then, there does seem to be a general consensus that there exist the two classes distinguished by Bock (1931, p. 217): first, those in which the accusative is directly dependent on the governing verb, and the infinitive and the governing verb are also directly related—according to Bock, the presence or absence of *to* with the infinitive denotes a different degree of closeness in this relationship—and second, those in which the accusative and the infinitive form a united group dependent on the governing verb. But there is no consensus about which verbs govern which form of the construction. To complicate matters further, Bock (1931, pp. 221-6) goes on to make a threefold distinction in OE: first, verbs of compelling, enticing, hindering, inducing, urging, and the like, to which the nominal object is more closely attached than the infinitive and in which the infinitive has preserved its original function of expressing purpose, e.g. *Bede* 54. 30 . . . *ðæt he sende Agustinum 7 oðre monige munecas . . . bodian Godes word Ongolþeode* and *Mark(WSCp)* 3. 14 7 *he hi asende godspell to bodigenne* (but see §3740); second, verbs such as *hatan, biddan, bebeodan, lætan, seon*, and *hieran*, after which the accusative and infinitive are syntactical additions of equal value and to which they are equally closely attached—as we shall see in §§3755-61, the 'subject accusative' (§3737) need not be expressed after these verbs, e.g. *ÆCHom* i. 88. 6 (§3736); and third, verbs of saying and thinking, after which the accusative and infinitive form a unit which is directly dependent on the governing verb.

§3736. Now hopelessly lost, I propose to consider the functions of the accusative in the accusative and infinitive construction. Callaway (1913, p. 107) speaks of 'the predicative infinitive with accusative subject'. If we accept this, then we can say that *ealne þone here* in *Or* 202. 7 *7 ealne þone here he het mid þæm scipum þonan wendan* and *hi* in *ÆCHom* i. 28. 7 . . . *and het hi faran geond ealne middangeard* are respectively the subjects of *wendan* and *faran*. (Examples like *ÆCHom* i. 88. 6 . . . *þa het he his agenne sunu Antipatrem arleaslice acwellan, toeacan þam twam þe he ær acwealde*, where Antipater is the victim, not the slayer, present a special problem; see §§3762-5.) We can also say that the accusative and infinitive usually has a subject different from that of its governing verb, e.g. *Or* 202. 7 and *ÆCHom* i. 28. 7 above, *Bede* 128. 15 . . . *þa geseah he semninga on midre niht sumne mon wið his gongan, ÆCHom* i. 234. 13 . . . *þaða Crist hine arisan het, ÆCHom* i. 20. 18 (§3722), and

Beo 784	. . .	anra gehwylcum
	þara þe of wealle	*wop gehyrdon,*
	gryreleoð galan	*Godes andsacan,*
	sigeleasne sang,	*sar wanigean*
	helle hæfton.	

This is perhaps not surprising in view of the nature of the verbs which take the construction; see §3723. One rarely if ever commands or causes oneself to do something. But the subjects may be the same when the meaning of the governing verb permits and the sense requires, e.g. (with *gehatan* 'to promise') *Bede* 122. 33 . . . *7 geheht hine sylfne deofolgildum wiðsacan* and *Bede* 316. 28 . . . *Drihtnes . . . se ðe hine gehatende wæs mid us eac wunian aa oð weorulde ende*—this verb has a wide variety of constructions (see BTS s.v. *gehatan* IV); (with *gemunan* 'to remember') *Bede* 322. 19 and *GD* 281. 9 *be þon eac ic geman me sylfne secgan* . . . ; (with *geseon* 'to see') *Bede* 80. 32 . . . *seðe hine gesiið hefigadne beon þurh yfelnesse unrehtes willan*; and (with *hyhtan* 'to hope') *LS* 23. 556 *forðon þe ic to soðan gehihte me ætstandan.* . . . Examples like *Bede* 378. 22 *þa he arisende wæs, þa gefelde he his lichoman healfne dæl from þæm heafde oð þa fet mid þa aðle geslægene beon, þe Grecas nemnað paralysis, 7 we cweðað lyftadl* almost belong here.

§3737. However, the use of the word 'subject' in this context has not achieved universal acceptance. Zeitlin (p. 7) reports that Bopp objected to it because the accusative is the subject only logically and not grammatically. But one has to have some term to distinguish *his þegnas* from *hine* (the object of the infinitive) in *Bede* 34. 25 *Ða het he hraðe his þegnas hine secan*. Grimm (*Deutsche Grammatik* (1837), iv) seems to deny the status of 'subject' to accusatives which follow verbs of commanding (p. 114) and of causing and permitting (pp. 117, 118-19, and 120). He distinguishes genuine ('echte und unzweideutige') accusative and infinitives, e.g. OHG *ih weiz in waltan*, from apparent examples like OHG *ih pat in queman*, in which (he says) the accusative belongs to *pat*, not to *queman*; he analyses these as respectively *ih weiz, daz er weltit* (NHG *ich weiß, daß er waltet* 'I know that he rules') and *ih pat in, daz er quâmi* (NHG *ich bat ihn, daß er käme* 'I order him that he come'). But he recognizes the existence of doubtful examples with verbs of physical perception such as *hören* 'to hear' and *sehen* 'to see', e.g. *ich sehe dich brennen*, which (he says) can mean either *ich sehe dich, wie du brennst* or *ich sehe, daß du brennst* (pp. 113-14). More work is necessary before this distinction can be accepted for OE. Part of it may take the form of establishing the relative frequency of the constructions with and without a noun/pronoun object after verbs of mental perception—compare *John(WSCp)* 5. 42 *Ac ic gecneow eow þ ge nabbaþ godes lufe on eow*, Latin *sed cognoui uos quia dilectionem dei non habetis in uobis*, where *Li* and *Ru* have *iuih* and *iowih* for *uos*, with *Luke (WSCp)* 4. 34 *ic wat þ ðu eart godes halega*, Latin *scio te qui sis sanctus dei*, where *Li* has *ðec ðuðe* for *te qui* and *Ru* lacks the verse —of physical perception—compare

Met 24. 55   Gif ðe ðonne æfre   eft geweorðeð
                 þæt ðu wilt oððe most   weorolde ðiostro
                 eft fandian,   ðu meaht eaðe gesion
                 unrihtwise   eorðan cyningas
                 and þa ofermodan   oðre rican
                 ðe þis werige folc   wyrst tuciað,
                 þæt hi symle bioð   swiðe earme,
                 unmehtige   ælces ðinges,
                 emne ða ilcan   þe þis earme folc
                 sume hwile nu   swiðost ondrædæð

with the corresponding prose *Bo* 105. 24 *Ic wat þeah, gif þe æfre gewyrð þ ðu wilt oððe most eft fandian þara þiostra þisse worulde, þonne gesihst þu nu þa unrihtwisan cyningas 7 ealle þa ofermodan rican bion swiðe unmihtige 7 swiðe earme wreccan, þa ilcan þe þis earme folc nu heardost ondræt*—and of commanding—compare

Bede 388. 10 . . . *ða heht he his geferan, ðæt hio sohton sumne earmne ðearfan* and *Ps(P)* 49. 5 *And he cleopað to þæm heofone, hæt hine þæt he hine fealde swa swa boc* with *Ch* 1432 . . . *7 heht þæt he cuome to him.* The noun/pronoun object is not uncommon after *hatan*, e.g. *Ps(P)* 49. 5, above, *biddan*, e.g. *ÆCHom* i. 70. 5 (§1969), and the like. Examples like *John(WSCp)* 5. 42, above, *Met* 24. 55, above, *ÆCHom* ii. 452. 14 (§1969), and *ÆCHom* i. 588. 28 (§1969), are perhaps less common. But the fact that they exist makes me reluctant to accept without further investigation that the conditions laid down by Grimm (*Deutsche Grammatik* (1837), iv. 114) for a 'true' accusative and infinitive occur only in combinations of an accusative and an infinitive after verbs of mental perception or of declaring (ibid., pp. 114-24, but see Callaway 1913, pp. 107 and 241-5):

> Überall nun, wo ein *im Satz ausgedrückter Acc.* nicht zum herschenden Verbo, sondern zu dem abhängigen Inf. dergestalt gehört, daß er bei Auffassung des ganzen in zwei Sätze den Nom. des zweiten, abhängigen Satzes gebildet haben würde, ist die Construction des *Accusativs mit dem Infinitiv* vorhanden. Jenes ih weiz in waltan zerlegt sich in die beiden Sätze: ih weiz, daz er weltit. Auch die Phrase ih pat in queman ist zerlegbar in ih pat in, daz er quâmi, gewährt aber keinen Acc. mit dem Inf., weil nach geschehner Auflösung das in noch bei pat verbleibt.[200]

However, I hope that after a comparison of *BlHom* 145. 8 . . . *þæt ge geseon þæt þeos eadige Maria sy geceged to deaþe* with *Bede* 34. 15 *And mid þy ðe he hine þa geseah on singalum gebedum 7 wæccum dæges 7 nihtes beon abysgadne* . . . and of *Ch* 1432, above, with *GD* 10. 4 *Hu man het Æquitium cuman to Rome*, and after a consideration of *GenB* 499 *þa het he me on þysne sið faran,* ‖ *het þæt þu þisses ofætes æte*, we can agree that it is not unreasonable to use the term 'subject accusative' of *hine* in *Bede* 34. 15, of *Æquitium* in *GD* 10. 4, and of *me* in *GenB* 499.

§3738. At any rate, I for one am prepared to agree with Visser (iii, §§2169-70) that in *ÆCHom* i. 72. 14 *þu scealt ærest oðerne geseon drincan*, *oðerne* can be described as the subject of *drincan*. But Visser

---

[200] 'The *accusative with infinitive* construction is present wherever an accusative *expressed in the sentence* belongs not to the main verb but to the dependent infinitive, so that if one were to construe the sentence as two separate phrases, it would become the subject of the second, dependent phrase. Thus the above example, OHG *ih weiz in waltan* can be analysed into the two phrases *ih weiz, daz er weltit*. Although the sentence *ih pat in queman* can likewise be analysed into *ih pat in, daz er quâmi*, it does not constitute an accusative with infinitive, because the *in* remains with the *pat* even after the sentence has been divided into its two phrases.'

also sees it as the object of *geseon*. Now Kageyama (p. 169) observes that he has 'not been able to find surface manifestations like . . . ☆*I saw her that she went*'. If there were none, we might argue on the analogy of *BlHom* 145. 8 (§3737) and similar examples quoted by BTS, s.v. *geseon* IV, that *oðerne* is unlikely to be the object of *geseon* because the corresponding construction with a *þæt* clause would be ☆*þu scealt ærest geseon þæt oðer drincþ*—cf. 'You shall see another man drinking'—rather than ☆*þu scealt ærest oðerne geseon þæt he drincþ*—cf. 'You shall see another man, you shall see a drinking'. But the fact that we have noted one firm example with *geseon*, viz. *Met* 24. 55 (§3737),[201] where the prose version has an accusative and infinitive, suggests to me the possibility that the Anglo-Saxons could 'see a man, see a drinking' as well as being able to 'see a man drinking'. So for those verbs at any rate which can take *þæt* clauses with or without its subject appearing as the object of the governing verb—they include not only *hatan* and *geseon* (§3737) but also verbs of wondering (§1969) and of persuading and compelling (§3730)—the view that the accusative of the accusative and infinitive can be both the object of the governing verb and the subject of the infinitive seems an acceptable possibility. Whether it must hold for all verbs which take the accusative and infinitive must remain a matter for debate. Despite Visser (iii, §2056), I do not see any sense in which 'my dear wife' in 'I hate my dear wife to have to listen to such nonsense' can have any 'object-character' in relation to 'hate'. The same seems to be true, *mutatis mutandis*, of OE sentences like *Bede* 340. 19 *7 hire sægde ealra heora modur Hilde abbudissan þa of worulde geleoran* and *ÆCHom* i. 590. 25 . . . *þæt ðu wenst me for tintregum ðe geopenian ða godcundan gerynu*. The terms 'VOSI' and 'object + infinitive', which neglects the subject function, are both objectionable in that they assume that the accusative always serves as object of the governing verb. The term 'accusative and infinitive' does not, for 'accusative', which describes the form of a word, is not synonymous with 'object', which describes a function. But I do have to agree with Visser's observation (ibid.) that 'a cursory examination of a number of VOSI-combinations reveals that, semantically, a uniform interpretation is out of the question'. The same, I imagine, would be true of a careful examination.

---

[201] *Bo* 35. 30 *Gif ge nu gesawan hwelce mus þ̄ wære hlaford ofer oðre mys* . . . may be another. Since *mus* is feminine, BT is probably right in taking *þ̄* as a conjunction (s.v. *þæt* conj. I(2a)). If so, the *þ̄* clause has an unexpressed subject. The other possibility—that *þ̄* is a relative pronoun with lack of concord—seems less likely; see §§2139–40. Since *geðanc* can be masculine, *he* in *ÆCHom* i. 390. 4 (§1969) might refer to *geðanc* rather than to *his*, so giving another example. But it seems strained.

§3739. To ask whether the infinitive is predicative or objective (Callaway 1913, p. 241) is another way of asking the question we have been discussing. It is predicative when it forms a unit with the accusative, objective when it is independently governed by the verb of the principal clause.

§3740. I cannot end this discussion without adding a complication of my own making. Callaway (1913, p. 139), followed by Bock (1931, p. 221), takes *bodian* in *Bede* 54. 30 (§3735) as an infinitive expressing purpose, whereas Callaway (1913, p. 109) classifies *blætsian* in *ÆLS* 12. 69 *þa sume dæg bæd he þone bisceop Ælfeh blætsian his ful* as a 'predicative infinitive with accusative subject'. The description of *þone biscop Ælfeh* as the accusative object of *bæd* and as the subject of *blætsian* can, no doubt, be justified by the existence, in both prose and poetry, of numerous examples like

Jul 278   Swa ic þe, bilwitne,   biddan wille
                 þæt þu me gecyðe,   cyninga wuldor,
                 þrymmes hyrde,   hwæt þes þegn sy,

where *þe* is the accusative object of *biddan* and *þu* is the subject of *gecyðe*. But in view of examples of what are usually called clauses of purpose like *Or* 294. 17, *LawAfEl(H)* 49. 4, and

Jul 325   þonne he usic sendeð   þæt we soðfæstra
                 þurh misgedwield   mod oncyrren,

where *usic* is the accusative object of *sendeð* and *we* the subject of *oncyrren*, one could argue for a similar interpretation of *Bede* 54. 30, viz. that *Agustinum* is the accusative object of *sende* and the subject of *bodian*. Here I propose to abandon the reader in the jungle (§3734).

g. The origin of the accusative and infinitive and its spread in English

§3741. The origin of the accusative and infinitive is another much-discussed topic; see Zeitlin (pp. 1–12), Callaway (1913, pp. 203–4 and 241–8), and Behaghel (*DS* ii. 325–6). Again the theories seem to conflict. Zeitlin (pp. 10–11) and Callaway favour what Callaway (1913, p. 203) calls 'the theory first suggested by Curtius and later amplified by Professors Brugmann and Delbrück'. Zeitlin (pp. 10–11) states it thus:

The whole matter is made very plain by Brugmann and Delbrück. The infinitive was originally a dative noun of action, used to express purpose. The action of the infinitive did not at first need to have a distinct subject; its subject might be that of the main verb or a dative or accusative dependent upon the main verb. This forms the basis of our construction. In time the accusative, which originally belonged to the transitive verb, was attracted to the infinitive as its subject— a confusion of syntactical relations which was produced, partly, by analogy to dependent clauses with a distinct subject (cf. 'I saw *him flee*' with 'I saw *that he fled*'). Later, verbs which were never associated with an accusative object assimilated the construction.

Zeitlin also notes that 'from a brief survey it appears that a number of the Indo-Germanic languages at a very early period in their history possessed the construction of an accusative with infinitive in its simplest and most limited form after verbs of causation' (p. 39)— contrast Behaghel's comment (*DS* ii, §724) that the accusative and infinitive is not 'Indo-Germanic' because 'Indo-Germanic' possessed no infinitive—that 'all [early] Germanic languages employ the accusative with infinitive commonly after verbs of causation and of sense perception, and quite frequently after verbs of mental perception' (p. 40), and that 'the accusative with infinitive after verbs of declaration is found in Old English only in translated documents in imitation of the Latin original' (p. 99). In GL (§527 n. 3) we read that 'the use of the Acc. and Inf. with *verba declarandi* is an outgrowth of the use after verbs of Creation (423), just as in English "I declare him to be", is an extension of "I make him to be", in which Acc. and Inf. have each its proper force'. (On this last clause, cf. §§3734–40.) Brugmann's two examples in the passage quoted by Callaway (1913, p. 203) are introduced by a verb of causing and by a verb of commanding respectively. Behaghel (*DS* ii, §724) says of the accusative and infinitive that its origin presumably lies in those usages in which the accusative is the direct object of the finite verb, as with *hören* and *sehen*. It is difficult to find consistency in all this or to reconcile it with Grimm's refusal to accept that the accusative and infinitive after verbs of causing and commanding is genuine ('echt') (my §3737). Callaway (1913, p. 242) says that we have 'what Grimm called the "genuine" accusative and infinitive construction' after verbs of mental perception and of declaring. Gorrell (p. 475) says that this 'genuine' construction is 'very rare' in OE and gives one example after *wenan* and one after *gemunan*. It is not clear whether he thought that the examples he goes on to cite after verbs of perception (pp. 475-6) are 'genuine' or not. There is room for more work here.

§3742. More work is also necessary before it can be decided whether Visser's observations (iii, §2056) that 'the number of verbs in early Old English occurring in the VOSI is comparatively small' and that 'in later Old English the idiom spread with striking rapidity' are compatible with Callaway's statements that 'the uninflected infinitive active as the quasi-predicate of an accusative subject, in object clauses . . . is common in Anglo-Saxon prose, early and late, and in Anglo-Saxon poetry' (1913, p. 107); that examples with an inflected infinitive 'occur in the prose texts only' (1913, p. 118); and that of the fifty-two examples with a passive infinitive, only two (both with *lætan*) are found in the poetry (1913, p. 120).

§3743. The extent to which the accusative and infinitive in OE is the result of Latin influence has been much discussed. Gorrell (p. 476) says that 'with the exception of the infinitive after *hatan*, there is here an obvious departure from the general Anglo-Saxon usage, for the construction can be regarded in no other light than a slavish imitation of a Latin original'. Callaway considerably modifies this observation. He finds it difficult to be sure about the sporadic examples with the inflected infinitive, but says that it 'is highly probable' that the use of the passive infinitive 'is due to Latin influence' and that 'it is evident, therefore, not only that the idiom was not native to Anglo-Saxon, but also that it was never naturalized therein' (1913, pp. 213-14). However, of the *-(i)an* infinitive, Callaway (1913, p. 208) concludes:

> To sum up the matter as a whole, the predicative infinitive with accusative subject is probably native with: (1) certain verbs of Commanding (*bebeodan, biddan,* and *hatan*); (2) certain verbs of Causing and Permitting (*lætan* and its compounds, *alætan* and *forlætan*); (3) certain verbs of Sense Perception (*hieran* and *seon*, and their compounds); (4) certain verbs of Mental Perception (*afindan, findan, gefrignan, gehyhtan, gemetan, gemittan, gewitan, onfindan,* and *witan*).
>
> It is probably due more or less to foreign (Latin) influence with: (1) this verb of Commanding, *forbeodan*; (2) certain verbs of Causing and Permitting (*biegan* [*began*], *don, gedon, geðafian, geðolian, geunnan,* and *niedan*); (3) certain verbs of Sense Perception (*gefelan, gehawian, sceawian*); (4) certain verbs of Mental Perception (*æteawan, eowan, gecyðan, gehatan, geliefan, gemunan, getriewan, læran, ongietan, tellan,* and *wenan*); (5) all the verbs of Declaring represented (*cweðan, foresecgan, ondettan,* and *secgan*).
>
> Its origin is indeterminable with: (1) this verb of Sense Perception, *behealdan*; (2) certain verbs of Mental Perception (*geacsian* and *tali(g)an*); (3) with certain Other Verbs (*habban* and *todælan*).
>
> In the large, the foregoing result tallies with the conclusion reached by previous students of the construction.

Callaway (1913, pp. 209-13) and Scheler (pp. 92-100) discuss the work of these earlier writers. On the accusative and infinitive in other Germanic languages, see Callaway 1913, pp. 241-8.

§3744. On the accusative and infinitive in ME and MnE, see (*inter alios*) Gorrell (p. 475), Zeitlin (*passim*, especially pp. 113 and 167-8;

his aim was to test what he claimed was 'the prevalent notion concerning the construction, that it is of fifteenth century origin and
due to Latin influence, [which] is indorsed by such scholars as
Professor Jespersen' (p. v)), Callaway (1913, pp. 209–13), Bock
(1931, pp. 217–19, 248 n. 11, and *passim*), and Visser (iii, §2056).

2. THE ACCUSATIVE AND INFINITIVE AS OBJECT

a. The uninflected infinitive in -(i)an

§3745. This is the most common infinitive in this construction.
Callaway (1913, p. 107) says that 'the uninflected infinitive active as
the quasi-predicate of an accusative subject, in object clauses, is found
about 1512 times in Anglo-Saxon'. In §§3762–5 I give my reasons
for supporting his use of the word 'active' with reference to examples
like *ÆCHom* ii. 422. 28 . . . *and se apostol abæd him wæter beran*,
in which *him* refers back to *se apostol* and it is not specified who is
to carry the water or (to anticipate my discussion) the subject accusative of the infinitive is not expressed. Here I am concerned with
examples in which it is. They occur in early and late prose and in the
poetry. As they do not present much difficulty, I propose to give
a few typical examples and to comment briefly on one or two exceptional patterns.

§3746. Following Callaway's classification (my §3723), we find
after verbs of commanding (with a transitive infinitive) *ÆLS* 4. 141
(§3726) and the first two infinitives in

Mald 2   Het þa hyssa hwæne   hors forlætan,
              feor afysan,   and forð gangan,

and (with an intransitive infinitive) *GD* 10. 4 (§3737), *ÆCHom* ii.
476. 22, where we have a divided subject accusative, and *gangan* in
Mald 2, above; after verbs of causing and permitting (with a transitive
infinitive) *ÆCHom* i. 20. 18 (§3722) and *Beo* 3166 *forleton eorla
gestreon eorðan healdan*, and (with an intransitive infinitive) *BlHom*
239. 15 (§3734) and *And* 835 . . . *oðþæt dryhten forlet dægcandelle
‖ scire scinan*; after verbs of sense perception (with a transitive infinitive) *ÆCHom* ii. 508. 15 . . . *þa ofseah he feorran ða hæðenan ferian
an lic to eorðan* and

El 240   Ne hyrde ic sið ne ær
              on egstreame   idese lædan,
              on merestræte,   mægen fægerre,

and (with an intransitive infinitive) *Bede* 128. 15 (§3736) and *Beo* 2604 (§3735); after verbs of mental perception (with a transitive infinitive) *ÆCHom* i. 590. 25 (§3738) and

Beo 2694   Ða ic æt þearfe gefrægn   þeodcyninges
andlongne eorl   ellen cyðan,
cræft ond cenðu,

and (with an intransitive infinitive) *ÆCHom* i. 48. 17 (§3726) and *Beo* 118 *Fand þa ðær inne æþelinga gedriht* ‖ *swefan æfter symble*; and after verbs of declaring—of which there are few examples—(with a transitive infinitive) *Bede* 122. 33 (§3736) and *Bede* 394. 25 *Bæd ic eac ætgædre mid hiene, 7 eac swylce mec gehet wedlum ælmessan sellan*, and (with an intransitive infinitive) *Bede* 340. 19 (§3738) and *GD* 203. 25 (§3726). For more examples, see Callaway 1913, pp. 107-18, and Visser, iii, §§2066-82, where the inflected infinitive is also included.

§3747. Occasionally the subject accusative has to be understood from a preceding clause, e.g. *hi ealle* in *ÆCHom* i. 12. 3 *and* [*se Ælmihtiga Scyppend*] *hi ealle adræfde of heofenan rices myrhðe and let befeallan on þæt ece fyr . . . , ealla gesceafta* in

Met 29. 82   Ealla gesceafta   on his ærendo
hionane he sendeð,   hæt eft cuman,

and *me* in

Mald 29   Me sendon to þe   sæmen snelle,
heton ðe secgan   þæt þu most sendan raðe
beagas wið gebeorge.

b. The inflected infinitive

§3748. I start by making what seems to be the obvious point that in *ÆCHom* i. 378. 35 . . . *ac Hælend Crist of heofonum me spræc to and sende me to bodigenne his lare eallum ðeodum*, we have an acc. pers. pron. *me* object of *sende* followed by an inflected infinitive expressing purpose and not an accusative and infinitive; see Callaway 1913, pp. 139-40. But see §3740 and consider the effect of substituting *lærde* for *sende* in the example just cited. This, as I have hinted in §§1548-51, is not the only problem of classification which arises here. Callaway (1913, p. 119) lists among his examples of the accusative and inflected infinitive *BlHom* 131. 32 *Halig frofre Gast . . . se eow ealle þa þing læreþ to donne, þe ic eow foresægde þæt ge don sceoldon æfter minum upstige, ÆGenPref* 104 *ac Crist sylf 7 his apostolas us tæhton ægðer to healdenne*, and (with the bracketed comment 'or final?') *LS* 23. 75 . . . *and us gerecce þa weorc to begangenne þe him licige*. In all of these, the alleged accusatives—*eow, us*, and *us*—could be dative. Yet elsewhere (1913, pp. 37-9) he quotes as examples of 'the objective infinitive' *Bo* 79. 17 . . . *ne þe nan neodþearf ne lærde to wyrcanne þ þ ðu worhtest, ÆCHom* ii. 216. 21 *þus tæhte Crist on ðære Niwan Gecyðnysse eallum cristenum mannum to donne*, and (with the bracketed comment 'or final?') *WHom* 6. 62 *þæt wæs þæt an scyp þe Godd sylf gedihte Noe to wyrcanne*, where *þe* and *Noe* could be accusative or dative, but *eallum cristenum mannum* is dative. Now, when they mean 'to teach, guide, direct s.o. to do s.t.', *(ge)dihtan* and *(ge)reccan* seem to take the dative of the person, *læran* the dative or accusative, and *tæcan* the dative, apart from the dubious *hi* in *ÆLS* 30. 94; see BTS, s.v. *tæcan* V. So I am unable to understand the basis for Callaway's distinction. A fine line divides *ÆCHom* ii. 316. 19 . . . *gif ge wyrcende beoð ða ðincg ðe ic bebeode eow to gehealdenne* (Callaway 1913, p. 45, 'objective infinitive') and *Luke(WSCp)* 11. 42 *þas þing eow gebyrede to donne* (ibid., p. 128, 'predicative infinitive with dative subject') from *Ps(P)* 41. 9 (§3726) (ibid., p. 108, 'predicative infinitive [uninflected] with accusative subject') and *Bede* 100. 28 . . . *þæt he Cristes geoc bere 7 eow lære to beorenne* (ibid., p. 119, 'predicative infinitive [inflected] with accusative subject'). See further §§3782-6, where the dative and infinitive is discussed.

§3749. Callaway is, of course, aware of the problem both in other Germanic languages (1913, p. 248) and in OE; see, for example, his comments on whether *us* and *me* respectively are accusative or dative in *Or* 126. 31 *Genoh sweotollice us gedyde nu to witanne Alexander hwelce þa hæðnan godas sindon to weorþianne* (1913, p. 118) and in *Matt(WSCp)* 8. 21 and *Luke(WSCp)* 9. 59 (1913, p. 125 n. 1). But, if we exclude *ÆLS* 31. 980 (§3767) by taking *licgenne* as an error for *licgende* or *licgendne*, we find that of the fourteen examples of accusative and inflected infinitive recorded by Callaway (1913, pp. 118-19) seven have as the 'accusative' subject one of the pronouns *me, us*, or *eow*, which can also be dative; two are not OE, but ME, belonging to the First Continuation of the Peterborough Chronicle, where *ðone* can be said to have replaced the dative (Clark 1970, p. liii); one (*Bede(T)* 334. 16) is rendered slightly dubious by *Ca*'s variant *hire underðeoddan* for *hire underþeodde*; and two with unambiguous accusatives—*Bede* 226. 26 *In þæm he gesomnode micel weorod Cristes þeowa, 7 heo lærde to healdanne regollices liifes þeodscipe* and *Bede* 472. 6 . . . *7 ðara þinga, ðe he oðre lærde to donne, he sylfa wæs se wilsumesta fylgend 7 læstend*—are governed by *læran*, which can take either the accusative or the dative of the person taught. The remaining two examples are *GD* 10. 22 *Hu Bonefatius foresæde to sweltenne þone cimbalgliwere* (repeated at *GD* 61. 20), which represents the Latin *Quomodo idem episcopus Bonefacius moriturum predixit cimbalarium*—both are the work of one man; see Yerkes, pp. 101-11—and *Luke(WSCp)* 1. 73, where *hyne us to syllenne* represents Latin *daturum se nobis*. In both of these the inflected infinitive denotes futurity. This is a meagre harvest. See Callaway's summing-up (1913, pp. 119-20 and 213), which includes the observation that 'the foregoing statistics make clear that the predicative infinitive with accusative subject is normally uninflected in Anglo-Saxon'.

§3750. No one has produced evidence to controvert this. None of the examples of the inflected infinitive cited by Gorrell (p. 475) has a possible subject. Scheler (pp. 97-8) has a few examples from *Li* and/or *Ru* where *WSCp* has the uninflected infinitive. Perhaps the most interesting is *Mark* 1. 34: *WSCp 7 hi sprecan ne let, Li 7 nalde leta spreca hie ł ne lefde hie to spreccanne, Ru 7 ne let him sprecan* (note the dat. *him*), Latin *Et non sinebat loqui ea*. Like Callaway, I have found no examples of the accusative and inflected infinitive in the poetry.

§3751. One last point. We find a variety of possible subjects for inflected infinitives in *ÆCHom*, including examples with no possible subject expressed, e.g. *ÆCHom* i. 218. 30 *Circlice ðeawas forbeodað to secgenne ænig spel on þam þrym swigdagum*; with a dative, e.g. *ÆCHom* ii. 344. 28 *Boda nu eallum mannum dædbote to donne*; with a dative or accusative, e.g. *ÆCHom* i. 308. 13 *ac Crist us forbead þæt hundum to syllanne*; and with an accusative, e.g. *ÆCHom* i. 604. 14 *Swa swa dæges leoht forwyrnð gehwilcne to gefremmenne þæt þæt seo niht geðafað*, which Callaway (1913, p. 40) oddly classifies as an 'objective infinitive' and which continues *swa eac soðfæstnysse ingehyd, þæt is, geðoht ures Drihtnes willan, us ne geðafað mandæda to gefremmenne*.

c. Beon + *the present participle*

§3752. All the examples known to me except *Bede* 190. 29, below, are quoted by Visser (iii, §2172). They are *Or* 42. 32 *þonne þa Lapithe gesawon Thesali þæt folc of hiora horsum beon feohtende wið hie* . . . , *Bede* 352. 9 *Mid þy he ða gehyrde þone mæssepreost gewitan in Hiibernia 7 þær forðferende beon* . . . , and the three sentences from *Bede* in which Callaway (1913, p. 125 n. 2) detects 'a kind of future infinitive active', viz. *Bede* 406. 21, 430. 24, and 190. 29 *Ic for soð wat, þæt þæt nis minre gegearnunge, þæt ic yldenne onfo to lifigenne, oðþo ne getreowe me onfoende beon* . . . , Latin *Verum noui non hoc esse meriti mei, ut indutias uiuendi uel accipiam uel me accepturum esse confidam.* . . . Visser adds *LS* 11. 24. 14 *7 do me dælnymende beon þære ecen myrhðe.* I am inclined to see *dælnymende* as a noun governing a phrase in the genitive 'a partaker of that eternal joy'. On inflexion, see § 1439.

d. Beon/wesan/(ge)weorþan + *the second participle*

§ 3753. Despite Stewart (1973, pp. 66 and 68 n. 22), the OE passive infinitive (§ 3724) is occasionally used in the accusative and infinitive —a construction which, according to Callaway (1913, pp. 213–14), was in all probability 'due to Latin influence', 'was not native' to OE, and 'was never naturalized therein'. The infinitive is usually *beon*, but *wesan/weosan* occurs occasionally. The only example I have so far recorded with *(ge)weorþan* is

GuthB 1259   . . .   nelle ic lætan þe
                 æfre unrotne   æfter ealdorlege
                 meðne modseocne   minre geweorðan,
                 soden sorgwælmum.

The following will serve to illustrate the construction and to demonstrate that the participle may be inflected or uninflected: (with verbs of commanding) *Bede* 14. 13 *Ðætte Cantwara cyning Erconbyrht bebead deofolgyld beon toworpene* and *GD* 194. 17 *þa het he þysne biscop beon gelæded to þære stowe* . . . ; (with verbs of causing and permitting) *BlHom* 33. 9 . . . *se eca Drihten . . . se hine sylfne forlet from deofles leomum 7 from yflum mannum beon on rode ahangenne, GuthB* 1259, above, and *GenB* 2196 *Ne læt þu þin ferhð wesan* ‖ *sorgum asæled*—these are the only two examples so far recorded in the poetry; (with verbs of sense perception) *Bede* 24. 3 *Ðæt ongean þam oðer, to deaðe becumende, geseah him fram deoflum tobrohte beon ða boc his agenra synna*; (with verbs of mental perception) *Bede* 340. 14 *Ða onget heo ge in þæm swefne ge on hire modes gesyhðe hire æteawed weosan, þætte heo geseah* and *LS* 23. 484 *Ða ic þas stemne gehyrde and for minum þingum ongeat beon geclypode, ic wepende spræc* . . . ; and (with verbs of declaring) *Bede* 64. 21 *þas drohtunge 7 þis liif þu scealt gesettan, þætte in fruman þære acennendan cirican wæs ussum fædrum, in þæm nænig heora, of þam þe heo ahton, owiht his beon onsundrad cwæð, ac him eallum wæron eall gemæno.*

§3754. For more examples see Wülfing, ii, §483; Callaway 1913, pp. 120-4; Scheler, pp. 94-6; and Visser, iii, §§2166-7, 2174, and 2183. On the construction in other Germanic languages, see Callaway 1913, pp. 246-7.

e. *The pattern* ☆se apostol bebead wæter beran/to berenne

§3755. Here we are concerned, not with examples like *ÆCHom* i. 12. 3 (§3747), but with sentences in which an infinitive of a transitive verb—usually that in *-(i)an*, but sometimes the inflected infinitive—is accompanied by an accusative or an accusative group which, in translation at any rate, can be taken either as its object 'The apostle ordered [someone] to bring water' or as its subject 'The apostle ordered water to be brought'. Typical examples (with an uninflected infinitive, chosen because they have a Latin original with a passive infinitive) are *Bede* 388. 20 *Ða bebead se biscop ðeosne to him lædan*, Latin *Hunc ergo adduci praecepit episcopus*, and *LS* 14. 286 *Ða wærð se gerefa swiðe eorre . . . and bæd þære fæmne fet and handan tosomne gebindon and innen þone weallende cetel gesetton*, Latin *Tunc iubet praefectus . . . ligari manus et pedes beatae Margaretae et ibi eam mortificari*, and (with an inflected infinitive) *ÆLS* 25. 88 *forðan þe Moyses forbead swyn to etenne* and *HomU* 46. 296. 3 (§3757).

§3756. Let us begin by stating what this pattern is not. It is not the construction seen in *Bede* 34. 25 *Ða het he hraðe his þegnas hine secan 7 acsian*, where the infinitive of a transitive verb has an accusative subject and an accusative object, or in *Or* 202. 7 *7 ealne þone here he het mid þæm scipum þonan wendan*, where the infinitive is intransitive and the accusative group is its subject. It cannot be equated with 'the objective infinitive' as described by Callaway (1913, pp. 28-72). Here, while rightly and disarmingly stressing the difficulties of classification (pp. 30-1), Callaway has lumped together at least six different constructions: first, those under discussion here, e.g. *ÆCHom* i. 58. 26 *se het afyllan ane cyfe mid weallendum ele* (p. 32); second, examples like *Or* 288. 11 *Raðe þæs he gesealde Ualente his breðer healf his rice. 7 he het oflsean Percopiosus, þe þa ricsian wolde, 7 monege oðre mid him*, Latin *Qui postea fratrem suum Valentem participem fecit imperii, et Procopium tyrannum pluresque satellites ejus occidit*, and *CP* 227. 25 . . . *7 eft innan hira burgum fæste belocene ðurh hiera giemelieste hie lætað gebindan . . . ?*, Latin *. . . sed per negligentiam postmodum intra urbis claustra capiuntur?*, where (as the Latin suggests here and I have noted in §§679-80) *hatan* and *lætan* can be said to function almost as auxiliaries (pp. 32-3); third, examples which I would agree exemplify 'the objective infinitive', e.g. *LS* 34. 255 *. . . þa halgan ðe he ealre worulde furðor onwreon gemynte* and *ÆLS* 6. 126 *. . . and se hæfde gemynt mynster to arærenne*, in which the governing verb and the infinitive have the same subject and the accusatives *ðe* and *mynster* can only be the object of the respective infinitives (p. 47); fourth, examples of the dative and infinitive discussed in §§3782-6, e.g. *CP* 451. 28 *. . . ða ða he sumum liefde to ðicgganne ðætte he nolde ðæt hi ealle ðigden* and (since *bebeodan* does not take the accusative of the person) *Bede* 410. 33 *. . . þa ðing ðe ic bebead him to secganne* (pp. 37 and 45); fifth, examples like *ÆLS* 9. 90 *. . . gif þu me unwilles gewemman nu dest*, which I would take as an accusative and infinitive, a possibility admitted by Callaway (p. 33); and sixth, examples like *Matt(WSCp)* 8. 21 *Drihten, alyfe me ærest to farenne 7 bebyrigean minne fæder*, which, since *alyfan* can take either the accusative or dative of the person, may belong to either the fourth or the fifth group (pp. 46-7).

§3757. Now let us have some examples which demonstrate what the construction is. Its essential feature is that the performer of the action (§1936) is not specified, either because his identity was obvious or because it was a matter of indifference. When old King Cole called for his pipe, did his hereditary pipebearer or the nearest serving man leap to obey? Sometimes the modern reader will be able to identify the performer(s), sometimes he will not; cf. here the situation with *man* (§§363-8). (Nagucka (*SAP* 11 (1980), 35) has independently and acceptably made this point: 'It seems that the sentences with *hatan* 2 ["order, bid, command"] without its object are permissible in Old English only in cases when the circumstances are not ambiguous or obscure.') I begin with some examples after verbs of commanding and the like, which comprise the largest group: *Or* 54. 31 *Het hiene þa niman 7 ðæron bescufan* (no identifiable agent); *Bede* 344. 20 *þa heht heo gesomnian ealle þa gelæredestan men 7 þa leorneras 7 him ondweardum het secgan þæt swefn, 7 þæt leoð singan* (where *gesomnian* can be transitive or intransitive and where Cædmon can be identified as the relater and the singer); *ÆCHom* ii. 420. 34 *swa þæt an sunderhalga geband þone apostol, and hine gelædde to þæs cynges domerne Herodes, se wæs þæs ealdan Herodes suna sunu; and he het hine ða beheafdian* (where the Pharisee and the executioner may or may not be the same man); *ÆCHom* ii. 422. 25 *Abiathar ða het cnucian his muð* (no identifiable agent); *ÆCHom* ii. 40. 9 (where the command is directed to the Jewish people, there are six infinitives, the first accusative *lamb* is repeated twice, and the last infinitive is accompanied by a *gif* clause); *ÆCHom* ii. 182. 17 *Min Drihten, ne beheald þu mine synna ac geleafan ðises mannes, se ðe bitt aræran his sunu* (where, judging from the context, the father could be addressing his prayer to Benedict and/or to the Lord, unless we take *se* alone as the relative—cf. *ÆCHom* ii. 182. 23 *seo*—and *ðe* as the 2nd pers. pron. 'Thee' = *Min Drihten*); *HomU* 46. 296. 3 *ac wite ge . . . þæt ic æfre fram frymðe bebead þone drihtenlican dæg to healdenne* (*ge*); *Dan* 241 *Hreohmod wæs se hæðena þeoden, het hie hraðe bærnan* (where the *esnas mænige* of *Dan* 243 are obviously involved but may not have been the direct recipients of the command); and *And* 1272 *Heton ut hræðe æðeling lædan* (no identifiable agent).

§3758. Other examples include those in which the infinitive takes a double accusative, e.g. *Bede* 344. 34 *7 heht hine læran þæt getæl þæs halgan stæres 7 spelles* (where *hine* (Cædmon) is the pupil, not the teacher) and *Or* 120. 32 *. . . se æþeling . . . het ascian þone cyning his fæder, þe þær æt ham wæs, hwæþer him leofre wære . . .* (where the King is the source of the information)—such sentences must not be confused with those containing the accusative and infinitive construction discussed in §§3745-7—and those which contain a dative object of the infinitive or of a preposition, e.g. *Or* 290. 31 *. . . 7 him siþþan het gearian* (where *him* is the direct object of *gearian*); *ÆCHom* ii. 422. 28 *. . . and se apostol abæd him wæter beran* and *Beo* 198 *Het him yðlidan ‖ godne gegyrwan* (in both of which *him* refers to the subject of the finite verb and denotes the beneficiary of the action); and *ÆCHom* i. 592. 22 *. . . ða on dægrede sende Egeas to ðam cwearterne, and het him lædan to þone halgan apostol* (where *him* refers to *Egeas* and is in some way or other (§§1076-8) related to *to*)—such sentences must not be confused with those containing the dative and infinitive construction discussed in §§3782-6.

§3759. The construction under discussion is not limited to verbs of commanding and the like. Examples after verbs of causing and permitting include *GD* 341. 36 *. . . gif hi letað hi selfe bebyrgan on haligre stowe* (where self-burial is certainly not involved); *CP* 349. 12 *læt inc geseman ær ðu ðin lac bringe* (where, as *Matt(WSCp)* 5. 25 *Beo þu onbugende þinum wiðerwinnan hraðe þa hwile þe ðu eart* *on wege mid him . . .* and *Luke(WSCp) 12. 58 Đonne þu gæst on wege mid þinum wiðerwinnan to hwylcum ealdre do þ ðu beo fram him alysed* suggest and the imp. *læt* confirms, the onus is on *ðu*); *BlHom 33. 9 7 se eca Drihten hine sylfne let lædon on þa hean dune* (cf. *BlHom 33. 2 . . . se godspellere cwæþ þæt Hælend wære læded from deofle . . . on þone hean munt); ÆCHom* i. 150. 26 . . . *þæt we sceolon on ðisum dæge beran ure leoht to cyrcan, and lætan hi ðær bletsian* (where some hearers may have known which priest was to officiate); and *Whale 65 læteð hine beswican þurh swetne stenc, ‖ leasne willan* (where the devil traps the sinner).

§3760. After verbs of sense perception we find (with *(ge)hyran)* *ÆCHom* i. 284. 10 *þonne ðu gehyrst nemnan þone Fæder, þonne understenst ðu þæt he hæfð Sunu, ÆCHom* ii. 350. 12 *þa þohte ic þæt þæt wære seo hell, þe ic oft on life ymbe secgan gehyrde,* and *El 659* (§3761), and (with *(ge)seon) Or 138. 25 . . . þa hie gesawan þa deadan men swa þiclice to eorþan beran þe þær ær æt ham wæron, ÆCHom* ii. 184. 16 . . . *and geseah ðære ylcan mynecene his sweoster sawle lædan to heofenan,* and

Dream 4   þuhte me þæt ic gesawe   syllicre treow
              on lyft lædan,   leohte bewunden,
              beama beorhtost.

§3761. Callaway does not mention verbs of mental perception in his discussion (1913, pp. 29–30), but here belong *Beo 74 Đa ic wide gefrægn weorc gebannan ‖ manigre mægþe . . .* and *And 1093 Đa ic lungre gefrægn leode tosomne ‖ burgwaru bannan,* both of which he cites under that heading among his 'objective infinitives' (1913, p. 35). Since he elsewhere lists *findan* among the verbs of mental perception (1913, p. 115), we can perhaps add

El 1251   Ic þæs wuldres treowes
              oft, nales æne,   hæfde ingemynd
              ær ic þæt wundor   onwrigen hæfde
              ymb þone beorhtan beam,   swa ic on bocum fand,
              wyrda gangum,   on gewritum cyðan
              be ðam sigebeacne,

where I cannot accept Kennedy's 'to make it known' (apparently expressing purpose); cf.

El 659   . . .   ond þis næfre
              þurh æniges mannes   muð gehyrdon
              hæleðum cyðan,   butan her nu ða.

For more examples after the various groups of verbs, see Wülfing, ii. 191–2; Callaway 1913, pp. 28–72; and Visser, iii, §1195.

§3762. What is the status of the infinitive in this pattern? In my *Guide* I wrote of the accusative and infinitive in general:

§161 This construction, well known in Latin, e.g. *Solon furere se simulavit* 'Solon pretended to be mad', and in MnE, e.g. 'I know him to be dead', is also an OE idiom. The subject accusative may be expressed, as in

> Het þa hyssa hwæne   hors forlætan,
>   feor afysan,   and forð gangan

'He ordered each of the warriors to release his horse and drive it away, and to go forth', but is often left unexpressed, as in *ꝺ ðe cyðan hate* lit. 'I order [someone] to make known to you . . .', and *he het hie hon on heam gealgum* lit. 'he ordered [someone] to hang them on the high gallows' (where *hie* is the object of *hon*). In the last two examples, the subject accusative is not expressed, either because everybody knows or because nobody cares who is to perform the action. In these, it is very convenient to translate the infinitives *cyðan* and *hon* as if they were passive— 'I order you to be told' (or '. . . that you be told . . .') and 'he ordered them to be hanged'. Much time has been spent in idle controversy over the question whether these infinitives were actually passive; what is important is that, when the subject accusative of the accusative and infinitive is not expressed, the active infinitive can usually be *translated* as a passive.

Here I clearly stated that for OE the term 'accusative and infinitive' embraced two patterns—one with a subject accusative expressed and one with no subject accusative expressed—and by the use of the phrase 'subject accusative' at least implied that in my opinion the *-(i)an* infinitive was active in both. However, Stewart (1973, p. 57) now tells us that 'there *is* something in Old English that must be considered a passive (non-active) infinitive'—the reference here is not to the analytic passive infinitive (§3724), for Stewart (ibid.) misleadingly says that 'morphologically there is but one infinitive, the active infinitive'; Knuth (*Neophil.* 51 (1967), 421) is guilty of the same lax exposition. So I am reluctantly compelled to indulge in 'idle controversy' about whether the *-(i)an* infinitive was comprehended now as active, now as passive, by the Anglo-Saxons. The problem is not restricted to this construction; see §§923, 938–43, and 2943, and Bock 1931, pp. 201 ff. Wülfing (ii. 191) and Knuth (loc. cit.) suggest that the infinitive can have both functions. Zeitlin (p. 44), Callaway (1913, pp. 29–30, and 107), Bock (loc. cit.), and Zuck (p. 17), disagree. It is hard to tell which side of the fence QW (p. 81) favours: 'A passive infinitive was usually expressed with the active form.' Stewart (1973, p. 67) either contradicts herself or misrepresents Callaway: 'In effect, our analysis simply elaborates the view taken by Callaway that the Old English objective infinitive contains two opposite meanings while remaining "active in sense as in form".'

§3763. QW (loc. cit.), Knuth (loc. cit.), and Stewart (1973, pp. 58–9), all speak of the 'ambiguity' of the accusative and infinitive construction. According to Stewart, the conditions for such ambiguity are that the infinitive verb must be transitive and take the same case as the governing verb—presumably the accusative!—and that the accusative 'must be animate or inanimate in such a way as to qualify as either subject or object' of the infinitive. The first two of these conditions always hold in the construction under discussion here and the third often does. Stewart (1973, pp. 57-8) says that 'in the absence of context' it is possible to translate '*Se cyning het his sunu ofslean* (*Orosius* 52. 24)' as 'The king ordered his son to kill' and complains that my 'rule of thumb [as set out in *Guide*, §161 (§3762)] . . . filters out *a priori*' this translation. It was meant to. Such a translation is clearly impossible. The passage reads *Or* 52. 23 *7 hu se cyning het his sunu ofslean, 7 hiene siþþan þæm fæder to mete gegierwan*, which Stewart would presumably translate as 'and how the King ordered his son to slay and then prepare himself as food for his father'—'in the absence of context'. I do not know what the point of these games is, but as far as I am concerned one might as well argue that, if one disregards the meaning of the words, *ChronE* 220. 16 (1086) *7 gif hwilc carlman hæmde wið wimman hire unðances . sona he forleas þa limu þe he mid pleagode* demonstrates William the Conqueror's anxiety to stamp out lesbianism. I do not think that Stewart has understood what I said.[202] It seems remarkable to me that a student of linguistics could detect ambiguity between two translations, one of which is sense and one of which is nonsense, or could believe that any normal hearer or reader of OE would have had difficulty in automatically solving alleged ambiguities of this kind. Stewart (1973, p. 57) complains that I imply that 'it is really a problem of translation—a problem that . . . can be solved almost automatically'. As a non-native reader of OE, I am proud to say that I am now able to solve this question 'almost automatically' and that §161

---

[202] Stewart (1973, *passim*) also misunderstood Visser's remarks (iii, §1195) as well as unfairly truncating them. Visser knew that there were two constructions; compare his iii, §1195, with his iii, §§2055-81. But he did to some extent invite the misunderstanding by careless expression, for neither 'He commanded to build a bridge' nor 'He commanded a bridge to build' is an acceptable English sentence. His point was—and in this he was right —that the respective order of the infinitive and the accusative is no guide to the function of the accusative; cf. Gorrell, pp. 375-6, and Callaway 1913, pp. 30 and 126 n. 8. Thus, we find what must be subject accusatives following the infinitive in *Or* 162. 6 (twice), *ÆLS* 1. 146 (two subjects joined by *and*), *Beo* 785, and *GenB* 438. Conversely, an accusative object may precede the infinitive, e.g. *Bede* 34. 25, *Bede* 344. 21 *7 þæt leoð singan, ÆLS* 4. 141, *Beo* 785, *Ex* 215, and *And* 1614. Hence the ambiguity in *Bede* 344. 20 (§3757). In

Beo 785   . . . þara þe of wealle   wop gehyrdon,
                  gryreleoð galan   Godes andsacan,

the object precedes *galan* and the subject follows it. The context and meaning remove the possibility of ambiguity. I have as yet noted no OE examples in which this is not so. But see GL, p. 331, remark 5, on the possibility in Latin.

of my *Guide* was intended to help others to do the same. I would stake my last *sceatt* that no Anglo-Saxon ever thought for one moment that *sunu* was the subject of *ofslean* in *Or* 52. 23 or would have been unable to cope with what Stewart (1973, p. 61) calls 'the somewhat untidy accumulation of linguistic elements'.

§3764. But the Anglo-Saxons would have been confronted by what I would call intolerable ambiguities if the infinitive in *-(i)an* had been indifferently active or passive. *Gen* 20. 11 . . . *7 þæt hi wyllað me ofslean* could have meant ☆'and that they are willing to be slain for me'. Since *fultumian* occurs with the personal passive (§851) and *derian* with the accusative (§1092), *CP* 233. 8 *7 sio womb sceal fulteman ðæm hondum* could have meant ☆'and the belly has to be helped by the hands' (§1367) and *Ps(K)* 104. 14 *na he let man derian him* ☆'he did not let anyone be injured for them'. Such examples could be multiplied. Other arguments against the 'dual voice' view are that it is theoretically unlikely and that, if it is true, it is hard to explain why the analytic passive infinitive was developed at all. The mere fact that Latin passive infinitives are often represented by OE *-(i)an* infinitives does not certify that the latter are passive. In *Bede* 118. 8 *heht his þegnas hine selfne beran ongean þæm fyre*, the active infinitive *beran* represents *efferri* of the Latin . . . *iussit se obuiam saeuientibus et huc illucque uolantibus ignium globis efferri*; cf. *Bede* 388. 20 *Ða bebead se biscop ðeosne to him lædan*, Latin *Hunc ergo adduci praecepit episcopus*. In *Bede* 172. 8 *ond swelce eac mid his ealdorlicnesse bebead, þæt feowertiglice fæsten healden beon ær Eastrum bi witerædenne*, the analytic passive infinitive—developed largely, if not exclusively, under Latin influence (§3753)—represents *obseruari* of Latin . . . *simul et ieiunium quadraginta dierum obseruari principali auctoritate praecepit*. We can say that an idiomatic alternative for *Bede* 388. 20 would be ☆*Ða bebead se biscop þæt man ðeosne to him lædde*, whereas *Bede* 172. 8 could be rendered ☆*ond . . . bebead þæt þæt feowertiglice fæsten healden wære* . . . ; cf. here Fröhlich, pp. 67–8, and Yoshino, pp. 284–5, though I do not accept all the latter's statements. Here the two constructions for *Bede* 172. 8 exemplify the new analytic constructions which were to triumph, whereas those for *Bede* 388. 20 represent constructions which were dying.

§3765. And so I return to §161 of my *Guide*. Knuth (*Neophil*. 51 (1967), 421) decreed that it 'should be re-written'. After this discussion, I prefer to leave it as it stands. I believe that the construction in which 'the subject accusative is not expressed' was a construction of ancient lineage known in Greek (Moore, §259), in Latin (GL, pp. 330-1), and in the Germanic languages (Callaway 1913, p. 30; Frary, pp. 7-8; Visser, iii, §1195; *et alii*). I do not believe that any native speaker of English would think of 'tell' in 'I heard tell that . . .' as passive and am given to understand that the same is true of *grüßen* in *Er läßt grüßen* . . . for native speakers of German. We might perhaps detect the same attitude towards *gretan* in Alfred when he wrote *CP* 3. 1 *Ælfred kyning hateð gretan Wærferð biscep* if *hateð* is an auxiliary (§§679-80) or if *hateð gretan* is a Latin calque (Smithers, *EGS* 1 (1947-8), 111-12). Callaway (1913, p. 30) observed that 'in a word, the possibility of the passive interpretation of these infinitives is not denied; but it is contended that the active interpretation is more consonant with all the facts so far discovered as to the infinitive, and is truer to the genius of Anglo-Saxon and of the Germanic languages in general'. I myself remain reluctant to admit that 'the possibility of the passive interpretation of these infinitives' ever existed for native speakers of OE.

   f. The patterns ☆He geseah þone cyning hræw/deadne/
   ofslægenne/steorfend(n)e

§3766. Many verbs which can govern a *þæt* clause and an accusative and infinitive are also found with the double accusative constructions exemplified in the heading. So we find *GD(H)* 78. 13 *þa þa se ilca þegen geseah þæt his hors wæs awended fram his wodnysse* . . . ; *GD(C)* 97. 14 *þa þa he geseah his fostormoder wepan* . . . and *GD(C)* 171. 19 . . . *þa geseah he Germanes sawle þæs biscopes Capuane þære cæstre in fyrenum clywene fram ænglum beon borne in þone heofon*; *ÆCHom* ii. 108. 24 *La leof, hwænne gesawe we ðe hungrine oððe ðurstine oððe cuman* . . . ?; *GD(H)* 46. 9 . . . *se ceorl geseah Constantium lytelne 7 forsewenlicne*; *GD(C)* 97. 11 . . . *forþon þe heo geseah tobrocen þæt fæt þe heo ær to læne onfeng*; and *GD* 335. 25 . . . *gif hi nellaþ gebiddan for heora feondum þa þe hi geseoþ þonne þær bærnende*, where the pres. ptc. *bærnende* corresponds to the inf. *ardere* in the Latin . . . *si pro inimicis suis quos tunc ardere viderint non orabunt*. As Visser (iii, §2147) reminds us, the passive form of the last construction is seen in *Bede* 324. 20 *ontimber* . . . *wæs gesegen up cumende*.

§3767. In the patterns under discussion, the second accusative is probably better described as 'predicative' than as 'appositive' (§§975-81, 986-8, and 1083). I have found no nouns or adjectives which do not carry an inflexion when one is appropriate. But the participles need not be inflected; see §§1438-9 and compare *GD* 250. 3 . . . *se bodode me þone ylcan wer forðferedne* with *Mark(WSCp)* 7. 30 *And þa heo on hyre hus eode heo gemette . . . þone deofol ut gan*, where *ut gan* renders *exisse*, and *GD(H)* 24. 32 *7 he þone þeof þær on hege hangiendne funde* with *GD(C)* 24. 31 *7 he þone þeof þær hangiende funde*. So, despite Callaway (1913, p. 126 n. 5) *licgenne* in *ÆLS* 31. 980 *þa comon his geferan and fundon hine licgenne on blodigum limum* is not an inflected infinitive without *to*, but an error for *licgende* or *licgendne*.

§3768. QW (p. 86) notes that the infinitive is used 'with verbs of motion, rest, and observation, often with durative aspect' and cites '*geseah . . . standan twegen . . . wepan*' and *Beo* 1516 *fyrleoht geseah*, || *blacne leoman beorhte scinan*, offering the translations 'saw two standing weeping' and '. . . saw a bright light shining'. The evidence is contextual. Stewart (1976, p. 36) says that 'in Modern English as well as in Old English the objective infinitive with verbs of physical perception is ambiguous with regard to aspect'. This statement too is consistent with the situation in MnE but may derive some support from the fact that the accusative and present participle construction came into OE late and under Latin influence; see §3769. A similar ambiguity between 'perfective' and 'durative aspect' (QW, p. 80) inheres in MnE sentences like 'Percy saw the window broken by the thieves' (Visser, iii, §2113). As far as we are concerned today, the same is true for OE.

§3769. Callaway (1913, p. 228) sums up his discussion of the construction with the present participle—the so-called VOSING—thus:

> When we consider, then, that the predicative use of the present participle with full verbal power is practically unknown in Anglo-Saxon poetry; that it very rarely occurs in Early West Saxon, and then usually in translating a Latin predicate participle; that it is very rare also in the more original prose; but that it is frequent in Late West Saxon, especially in the *Gospels* and in Ælfric, and that of the 80 examples in the *Gospels* all but two are in direct translation of Latin predicate participles;—when we consider all this, the conclusion seems irresistible that this predicative use of the present participle was not a native Anglo-Saxon idiom, but was imported from the Latin, chiefly through the instrumentality of Ælfric and of the translator(s) of the *Gospels*.

This is one of his reasons for rejecting the proposition that 'this predicative use of the participle (and, also, of the adjective and of the noun) had much to do with the origin of the predicative infinitive with accusative subject' (1913, p. 124). Space forbids my pursuing this argument. But see Callaway 1913, pp. 211-13, and Zeitlin's

review of Callaway's work (*JEGP* 13 (1914), 479-82), in which Zeitlin shows that, because he failed to make himself clear, Callaway
misunderstood him by assuming that he was referring to the present
participle as well as to the second participle in the discussion which
Callaway attacked. On the construction with the present participle,
see further Callaway 1913, pp. 225-30, and 1918, pp. 179-80;
Matsunami 1966*b*, pp. 49-54 and 57-8; Visser, iii, §§2083-99; and
Stewart 1976.

§3770. The construction with the second participle (VOSP) has not
attracted as much attention as that with the present participle and
there is room for more work. I have, for example, no record of any
discussion of its origin. It might seem a natural extension of the
predicative use of nouns and adjectives (§1083). But the same could
have been said of the use of the present participle until Callaway
presented the findings I have just quoted. The construction with the
second participle is not, I think, as uncommon as Visser's treatment
(iii, §§2111-12) might be taken to imply; see Callaway 1913,
pp. 122-4, and Visser, i, §§646-75, and iii, §§2111-30, but note
Matsunami 1958, pp. 175 and 178.

§3771. Zeitlin (p. 66) speaks of 'the parallel locution in which some
predicate other than an infinitive—an adjective, adverb, participle or
prepositional phrase—is employed with the accusative . . . most frequently after verbs of sense and mental perception . . .' and goes on:
'It is obvious that there is no essential syntactical difference . . . and
that it is often possible to employ the two locutions interchangeably.'
I would, I think, have written 'semantic' rather than 'syntactical' in
the last sentence. But the interchangeability of the constructions distinguished in §3766 can readily be demonstrated: *ÆCHom* i. 18. 29
ac God hine let frigne but *ÆCHom* ii. 416. 28 . . . *and læt hine gan
frigne*; *Bede* 214. 12 *þa geseah he ænne of þæm þreom ænglum . . .
foregongende in þone leg þæs fyres todælan* (where *todælan* may
express purpose), *BlHom* 177. 15 . . . *7 mon geseah hine blinde
onlyhtende 7 hreofe clænsian 7 laman gelacnian . . .* , *BlHom* 237.
22 *and he geseah þone eadigan Matheus ænne sitton singende*, and
ÆCHom i. 66. 35 *Ic geseah þa englas, þe eower gymdon, dreorige
wepan, and ða awyrigedan sceoccan blissigende on eowerum forwyrde* (for more such variations, see Callaway 1913, pp. 125-6, and
Visser, iii. 2343); *ÆCHom* i. 46. 31 *Efne ic geseo heofenas opene
and mannes Sunu standende æt Godes swiðran*, *ÆCHom* i. 62. 25
. . . *and gesawon heora ðeowan mid godewebbe gefreatewode and on
woruldlicum wuldre scinende*, and *ÆCHom* i. 608. 23 *Sume ðas*

tacna we gesawon gefremmede, sume we ondrædað us towearde; *ÆC Hom* i. 64. 17 . . . *þæt he do his ðeowan rice for worulde, genihtsume on welan, and unwiðmetenlice scinan*; *GD(C)* 169. 6 . . . *he geseah þære ylcan his swuster sawle utgangende of hire lichaman in culfran ansyne 7 þæt heo gesohte heofones deogolnesse* but *GD(H)* 169. 6 . . . *he geseah þære ylcan his swustor sawle ut agane of hyre lichaman 7 on culfran hiwe gesecean þæs heofones digolnysse*; and *Mark (WSCp)* 9. 32 *7 hi adredon hine ahsiende* but *Mark(Li)* 9. 32 *7 ondreardon hine þ hia gefrugno* for Latin *et timebant eum interrogare*. To these may be added examples like *ÆCHom* i. 426. 29 *Laurentie, ic geseo Godes engel standende ætforan ðe mid handclaðe, and wipað ðine swatigan limu*, *ÆCHom* i. 538. 14, *ÆCHom* i. 598. 16, *ÆCHom* ii. 340. 32, and *ÆCHom* ii. 136. 9 *Eft se halga Cuðberhtus . . . geseah heofonas opene and englas gelæddon Aidanes biscopes sawle . . . into ðære heofonlican myrhðe*, in which the concluding finite verb may be in a noun clause with unexpressed *þæt* or in non-dependent narrative after a transition like those discussed in §§1945-9. The constructions with an adverb or a prepositional phrase to which Zeitlin refers are perhaps exemplified in *Bede* 102. 31 . . . *þa geseah he Æðelfrið se cyning heora sacerdas 7 biscopas 7 munecas sundor stondan ungewæpnade in geheldran stowe. . . .* But it would be a bold man who asserted categorically that the adverb, the infinitive, the second participle, and the prepositional phrase, were all directly dependent on *geseah* and independent of one another.

§3772. One last problem, already mentioned in §988, remains, viz. whether the constructions set out in my heading are of independent origin from the accusative and infinitive constructions in which the inf. *beon/wesan* is accompanied by the same elements, or whether one arose from the other by 'omission' or 'insertion' of *beon/wesan*. Finality—if it be possible—must await detailed study of the distribution of the various constructions. The present state of our knowledge is starkly revealed by a comparison of Visser's confusing statement (iii, §2174) about the constructions with the second participle—'. . . in Old English the patterns with and without *to be* de [*sic*] not seem to occur with different frequencies. In Old, Middle and earlier Modern English the number of structures with *to be* is overwhelming', where the second 'Old' appears to be an error—and that of Macháček (1969, p. 129)—'No instances with *to be* are found here and the adjective or participle agrees in case with the preceeding [*sic*] object', an observation which (judging from the context, where nouns are also mentioned) seems to have general OE reference. I can at least demonstrate from *Bede* that it does not, for we

find (with a noun) *Bede* 82. 4 *ne tellað we synne weosan gesinscipe*
—see also *GD* 181. 24 and *HomU* 21. 2. 1; (with an adjective) *Bede*
6. 13 . . . *bæd hine cristenne beon* and *Bede* 84. 16 . . . *ær þon Dauit
ondete heo fram wiifum clæne beon*; (with a present participle) *Bede*
190. 29 and *Bede* 352. 9, both in §3752; and (with a second participle) *Bede* 378. 22 . . . *þa gefelde he his lichoman healfne dæl
from þæm heafde oð þa fet mid þa aðle geslægene beon* . . . and
Bede 386. 8 *Mid þy he þa us eac sceawode 7 geseah in gewinne 7 in
ormodnesse gesette beon.* . . .

§3773. Nader (1880, §30) supplied *wesan* with the adj. *bliðne* in
Beo 617 *bæd hine bliðne æt þære beorþege* and Ardern (p. xxxix)
saw 'the Infin. *wesan* suppressed' in *Mald* 24 *þær he his heorðwerod
holdost wiste*. The same could be said of examples with nouns such
as *LawIIAs* 20. 8 . . . *þæt he hine flyman nyste*. Visser (i, §646) objected on the grounds that the construction without the infinitive
was widely used in OE and that there are examples such as *CP* 277.
15 . . . *suelce he . . . sua nacodne hine selfne eowige* and *John(WSCp)*
13. 13 *Ge clypiað me lareow 7 drihten* in which the infinitive cannot
be supplied.

§3774. Writing of the construction with the present participle,
Visser (iii, §2172) remarks: 'In later English *to be* is often dropped.
. . . The idiom is strikingly frequent in Old English.' It is not clear
whether the last sentence refers to the idiom with the infinitive, as in
Or 42. 32 (§3752), or to that without it, e.g. *Or* 92. 9 *þa gesawan
hie Romana ærendracan on hie feohtende mid þæm burgwarum*—
'extremely common in Old English', says Visser (iii, §2084). It ought
to refer to the latter, on the evidence of my collections, in which
examples like *Or* 42. 32 are not common. The presumption from
Visser's first sentence above is that the construction with the infinitive came first and *beon/wesan* was then dropped. But here too there
are examples in which the infinitive cannot be supplied, e.g. *Bo*
20. 31 . . . *hwonne hi ðe sorgiendne forlæten* and *Beo* 372 *Ic hine
cuðe cnihtwesende*.

§3775. Yet Visser (iii, §§2112 and 2174) seems to imply that of
the constructions with the second participle, that without *beon/
wesan* came first, for he observes (§2112) that from OE on, 'colliga-
tions with *to be* + past participle . . . begin to establish themselves
alongside of the shorter cluster. . . . This *expansion* [my italics] into
a two-verb cluster is perhaps due to a tendency to express explicitly
the passival connotation, and in some cases also the non-completedness

of the action referred to by the past participle.' But here once again there are constructions with the double accusative in which *beon/wesan* cannot be supplied, e.g. those with *habban* (see §988), perhaps *ÆLS* 5. 357 *Tiburtius gemette ænne mann afeallene þæt he his heafod tobræc* (but compare *Bede* 386. 1), and *ÆCHom* ii. 416. 27 *alys ðu hine nu fram deoflum gehæftne.*

§3776. Zeitlin (p. 110) remarked of the constructions with a noun, adjective, or second participle, after verbs of declaration that 'the practical identity of the two locutions is illustrated by the fact that it is possible to convert every non-infinitive predicate into an infinitive by the introduction of the copula "to be" '. (On the exclusion of the present participle, see Zeitlin, *JEGP* 13 (1914), 481-2.) But since, as we have seen, this is not true of all examples in which we have two accusatives, it does not establish the *original* 'identity of the two locutions'; see further Callaway 1913, pp. 211-13, and Royster 1922, pp. 336-7. We almost certainly need to supply *beon* in *Coll* 7 *Wille beswungen on leornunge?*, Latin *Uultis flagellari in discendo?* But a comparison with *Coll* 8 *Leofre ys us beon beswungen for lare þænne hit ne cunnan*, Latin *Carius est nobis flagellari pro doctrina quam nescire*, suggests scribal omission. The insertion of *wesan* in *Beo* 991 *Ða wæs haten hreþe Heort innanweard || folmum gefrætwod* has often been suggested. But see Visser (*EStudies*, 35 (1954), 116-20) and Royster (1918, p. 89 fn. 28), both of whom disallow [*wesan*] and defend the manuscript reading. However, even a flock of such examples would not demand that we insert *beon/wesan* in those examples cited above in which it does not appear. I must leave the matter here, citing Royster's warning (1922, p. 336 fn. 41) that

there is no evidence whatever, nor is there any reason, for claiming priority for the construction with the *be*-infinitive. The appearance of the logically full construction in Middle English seems an addition rather than a restoration. The logically complete construction, here or elsewhere, is not necessarily earlier than the logically eliptical [*sic*] construction,

and expressing my willingness to extend to all the constructions under discussion Callaway's comment (1913, pp. 122-3) on those with the second participle:

We find, too, what may be considered an elliptical passive infinitive with accusative subject, made up of an accusative noun and of a past participle after an active transitive verb; and the infinitive (*beon* or *wesan*) is understood, or, at least, it may be considered as being understood . . . in most, if not all, of the instances the supplying of the infinitive is a matter of taste rather than of necessity. . . .

3. THE ACCUSATIVE AND INFINITIVE AS SUBJECT

§3777. The accusative and infinitive may serve as the subject of a Latin sentence when the predicate is a noun or neuter adjective, an impersonal verb, or an abstract phrase, e.g. *Facinus est vincire civem Romanum* and *Legem brevem esse oportet*; see GL, §535. Zeitlin (p. 167) says that 'this construction is not found at all in Old English'. However, writers before and after him have rightly recognized its existence; see the references given by Callaway (1913, p. 124). Typical of the examples given by Callaway are (with an active infinitive) *Matt(WSCp)* 3. 15 *þus unc gedafnað ealle rihtwisnesse gefyllan*, Latin *sic enim decet nos implere omnem iustitiam*, where *Li* has *suæ forðon gedæfnad is us þ we gefylle alle soðfæstnisse* and *Ru nu forðon ðe þus we sculon gefyllan æghwilce soþfæstnisse*, and *Matt (WSCp)* 17. 10 *hwæt secgeað þa boceras . þ gebyrige ærest cuman heliam*, and (with a passive infinitive) *Mark(WSCp)* 13. 10 *Ærest gebyrað beon þ godspel gebodud*.

§3778. Both Callaway (1913, pp. 124-5 and 245-6) and Scheler (p. 99) agree—against Stoffel (*Studies in English, Written and Spoken* (Zutphen, 1894), 54) and Zeitlin (p. 167)—that the construction is of Latin, not native, origin and occurs for the most part in translations only.

4. THE NOMINATIVE AND INFINITIVE

§3779. This name is sometimes given to a construction recorded in Greek and Latin by which the accusative subject of an infinitive appears as the nominative subject of passive verbs of saying, showing, believing, and perceiving, e.g. *Traditur Homerus caecus fuisse*; see Moore, §259, and GL, pp. 331 n. 2 and 332. A similar construction appears occasionally in OE, usually (it would seem) under Latin influence. Those least likely to be Latin-based among the twenty recorded examples are *ChronE* 235. 13 (1100) (§3780) and (if we follow Callaway 1913, p. 59)

Ex 43   Wæron hleahtorsmiðum   handa belocene,
           alyfed laðsið   leode gretan.

But here *laðsið* is probably the subject of [*wæs*] *alyfed*, with *gretan* an explanatory or a final infinitive.

§3780. Wülfing (ii. 190-1), followed by Scheler (p. 101), records six examples from *Bede*. Callaway (1913, pp. 59-60) added fourteen more, including four with an inflected infinitive. I would not accept all of them, but space does not permit detailed discussion here. Those I would accept include (with an infinitive in -*(i)an*) *Bede* 424. 2 . . . *forðon þe ic soðlice from deaðe aaras 7 eam eft forlæten mid monnum liifgan*, Latin . . . *quia iam uere surrexi a morte qua tenebar, et apud homines sum iterum uiuere permissus* and *ChronE* 235. 13 (1100) *7 to þam Pentecosten wæs gesewen innan Barrucscire æt anan tune blod weallan of eorþan* (Callaway compares *Or* 162. 6 . . . *þæt mon geseah weallan blod of eorþan*); (with an inflected infinitive) *Bede* 412. 28 *Ða ðæt se Godes wer Ecgbrihte geseah, ðæt he ne wæs forlæten, þeodum godcunde lare to bodienne* and *Lev* 11. 6 *Hara 7 swyn synd forbodene to æthrinene*; and (with a passive infinitive) *Bede* 78. 3 . . . *heo wæron bewered heora weorum gemengde beon* and *GD* 203. 21 . . . *an þing wæs þæt gesewen wæs on him tælwyrðe beon, þæt full oft swa mycclu blis in him wæs gesægenu beon.* . . .

§3781. A question of terminology arises. I shall allow Callaway (1913, p. 59) to pose it and to pronounce judgement:

At times the Modern English *John told me the story* is, in the passive, rendered, unhappily I think, by *I was told the story by John*, in which latter the direct object, *story*, of the active is illogically retained in the passive. This objective in the passive construction is by not a few grammarians called 'the retained objective,'—an awkward name, but, despite his objurgatory remarks thereon, not inferior, I think, to that proposed by Professor C. Alphonso Smith, 'the objective by position.' Similarly, at times, an active infinitive is found as the retained object of a few passive verbs which, when active, take a dative and an accusative as objects or an accusative and an infinitive as an objective phrase. This construction with the infinitive after passive verbs is by many, especially in Germany, called, not 'the retained objective,' but 'the nominative with the infinitive.' Both terms seem to me infelicitous, but, as I am unable to suggest a good substitute, I adopt the former as the less objectionable of the two.

5. THE DATIVE AND INFINITIVE

§3782. There is no doubt that the OE constructions to be discussed under this heading exist. The main difficulty is what to call them. The first of the two patterns to concern us is seen in *Luke(WSCp)* 4. 43 *soðlice me gedafænað oðrum ceastrum godes rice bodian*, *Mark (WSCp)* 9. 47 *betere þe is mid anum eagan gan on godes rice þonne twa eagan hæbbende sy aworpen on helle fyr*, and (with an inflected infinitive) *Matt(WSCp)* 17. 4 *Drihten, god ys us her to beonne* and *Luke(WSCp)* 11. 42 *þas þing eow gebyrede to donne*. Here we can take the infinitives as the subjects of the impersonal verbs and the

pronouns *me, þe, us*, and *eow*, as governed by the finite verbs. Or we
can take the pronouns as the subjects of the infinitives; I do not
think the element order in *Luke(WSCp)* 4. 43 or *Luke(WSCp)* 11. 42
a fatal objection to this view. As I have noted in §3748, the fact that
me, þe, us, and *eow*, can be either accusative or dative raises a difficulty which, for OE at any rate, cannot be brushed aside as easily as
it is by Kageyama (p. 166). The presumption is that these forms are
to be taken as dative in the quoted examples; cf. *Luke(WSCp)* 24. 26
hu ne gebyrede criste þas þing þoligean, where *WSH* also has *criste*
but *Li* and *Ru crist*, and *Matt(WSCp)* 19. 24 *7 eft ic eow secge þ
eaðelicre byð þam olfende to ganne þurh nædle eage þonne se welega
on heofona rice ga.*

§3783. If we take these pronouns as dative and if we accept the
proposition that they are the subjects of the infinitives, we have
a dative and infinitive construction comparable with the accusative
and infinitive. This is not as far-fetched as might at first seem. We
note that in *Matt(WSCp)* 18. 9 *Betere þe ys mid anum eage on life
to ganne þonne þu si mid twam asend on helle fyr, þe . . . to ganne*
before *þonne* is paralleled by *þonne þu si* after it—on the absence of
þæt, see §3232; that we have a similar pattern with the uninflected
infinitive and unexpressed *þu* in *Mark(WSCp)* 9. 47 (§3782); and
that in *Mark(WSCp)* 9. 43 and 9. 45, and in *Matt(WSCp)* 18. 8 *Betere
þe ys þ þu ga wanhal oþþe healt to life þonne þu hæbbe twa handa 7
twegen fet 7 sy on ece fyr asend*, we have *þe* in the principal clause
followed by two contrasted noun clauses with subject *þu*, the second
with unexpressed *þæt*. So *þe* can be seen as the subject of its infinitive in *Matt(WSCp)* 18. 9 and *Mark(WSCp)* 9. 47.

§3784. I turn now to the second pattern. Callaway (1913, p. 129)
says: 'So far as I have been able to discover, the phrase, "the dative
with infinitive", in the sense assigned to it by Grimm, is confined in
the grammars to the dative with infinitive after impersonal verbs . . .'.
Callaway, who opposes the use of the term, goes on 'But, if the phrase
is to be used at all, I do not see why it should not be used with reference, also, to the dative after certain personal verbs.' I agree. For me,
the conclusion that a dative pronoun or noun can be described as the
subject of an infinitive emerges from my consideration of some examples in which it accompanies 'personal' verbs. I invite the reader to
compare *ÆCHom* i. 416. 4 *Ða færlice het he his gesihum* [sic] *ðone
biscop mid his preostum samod geandwerdian* with *ÆLS* 4. 141
*Hwæt þa Martianus het his manfullan cwelleras þone halgan beatan
mid heardum saglum* (classified as an accusative and infinitive by

Callaway (1913, p. 110))—especially in the light of the series *Ch* 1432 . . . *7 heht þæt he cuome to him, Alex* 34. 15 *þa het ic eallne þone here þ he to swæsendum sæte,* and *Mark(WSCp)* 10. 48 *þa budon him manega þ he suwode*—and to compare

GenB 958   het þam sinhiwum   sæs and eorðan
               tuddorteondra   teohha gehwilcre
               to woruldnytte   wæstmas fedan

with

Jud 52   . . .   nymðe se modiga hwæne
               niðe rofra   him þe near hete
               rinca to rune gegangan

(classified as accusative and infinitive by Callaway (1913, p. 109))— especially in the light of the series *GenB* 500 . . . *het þæt þu þisses ofætes æte, Sat* 721 . . . *swa hine se mihtiga het* ‖ *þæt þurh sinne cræft susle amæte,* and

PPs 104. 9   . . . and gleawlice   Iacobe bead,
               þæt awa to feore   Israheles cyn
               his gewitnesse   wel geheolde,

where *Iacobe* is dative; cf. *PPs* 104. 19 *se goda Iacob.*

§3785. Callaway (1913, p. 131) sums up his discussion of what he calls 'the predicative infinitive with dative subject' thus:

In a word, I doubt whether we have a genuine dative-with-infinitive construction in Anglo-Saxon, that is, a predicative infinitive with dative subject substantially equivalent to a predicative infinitive with accusative subject, after either impersonal or personal verbs. Normally, after the former class of verbs the infinitive is subjective, and after the latter class the infinitive is objective; and after both the dative depends on the chief verb. In a few sporadic cases, almost exclusively in Late West Saxon, after a few personal verbs like *don* and *lætan,* we do have an uninflected predicative infinitive whose subject is dative in form, but probably by that time the distinction between the accusative forms (*hine* and *hie*) and the dative form (*him*) had broken down to such an extent that *him* was felt as an accusative. And once possibly (after *hieran*) we may have an inflected infinitive used predicatively with a dative; if so, the inflected infinitive is probably due to the gerundive in the Latin original.[203]

However, Callaway's position seems to me inconsistent. He says that '*gebyrian* "to happen", "to be fitting", and *gedafenian,* "to be fitting", are followed by both the accusative with an infinitive and the dative with an infinitive' (1913, p. 129 fn. 1). But we must accept that he refuses the status of 'genuine dative-with-infinitive construction',

[203] The example with *hieran* is *GD* 221. 24 . . . *þæt se ylca deofol . . . him hyrde þa scos of to donne.*

not only to dative examples with these verbs, but also to *Luke(WSCp)* 4. 43 *soðlice me gedafænað oðrum ceastrum godes rice bodian,* though he says (1913, p. 127) that this 'may be accusative and infinitive'. Yet he classifies *Luke(WSCp)* 13. 33 *Ðeah hwæðere me gebyreþ todæg 7 tomorhgen 7 þy æfteran dæge gan* as an accusative and infinitive, with the question 'or is *me* dative and *gan* subjective?' (1913, p. 124). I cannot really see why such a fundamental syntactical distinction should hinge merely on whether one interprets an ambiguous form like *me* as accusative or dative; note Visser's comment (iii, §2056): 'It is clear that, because in such utterances as "he bebead faran" it was not indicated explicitly who it was that was "beboden faran", there arose a tendency to supply this deficiency by inserting a (pro)noun before the infinitive while giving it the form going with the preceding verb', i.e. a dative or an accusative as appropriate. Nor does it seem logical that such a distinction should be made between different versions of the same sentence because one has the accusative and another the dative. Yet this seems to be Callaway's position; cf. his treatment of the two versions of *Luke(WSCp)* 24. 26 (§3782) which have acc. *crist* with that of the two versions with dat. *criste* (1913, pp. 124 and 127; his figures of 'three' and 'one' are wrong, according to Skeat's versions). Presumably the same distinction exists for Callaway (p. 127) between the London MS version of *LS* 10. 125. 64 . . . *swa þonne gedafenað þam men* [MS *þe*] *gelice þurh six daga fæsten þone gast gefrætwian* . . . and that of the Vercelli MS, which reads *þane man*. I believe that Callaway himself (1913, pp. 129–30, and elsewhere) came close to recognizing what I see as his inconsistency. Obviously the constructions I have discussed are not identical. But in both of them the person represented by the dative is the (potential) performer of the action of the infinitive and so the dative can be described, in some sense at least, as the subject of the infinitive.

§3786. There is obviously a lot more to be said; see initially Callaway 1913, pp. 127–31, 214, and 248–52; Callaway 1918, pp. 143–55; and Scheler, pp. 98–9. But I must leave this problem here, with the rueful confession first, that I am now somewhat more sympathetic to Carlton's description (1970, p. 99) of *him* as 'subject of gerund' in *Ch* 1510 *Ic bebeode . . . ðæt mon agefe ðæt lond Inn higum to heora beode him to brucanne* than I was in *MÆ* 40 (1971), 183, and second, that perhaps I brought all this on my own head by extending the definition of the accusative and infinitive in §§3734–40.

6. CLAUSES SUBORDINATE TO AN ACCUSATIVE AND INFINITIVE

§3787. A noun, adjective, or adverb, clause may be subordinate to an accusative and infinitive, e.g. *GD(C)* 137. 7 . . . *to þan þæt he ge-cyðde hine sylfne cunnan hwylce wæren Godes gestihtunge* . . . , *GD(H)* 137. 7 . . . *þæt he ætywde hine sylfne cunnan þa þing þe syndon Godes gestihtunge, BlHom* 21. 29 *oþþæt Drihten* . . . *hateþ þa eorþan eft agifan þæt heo ær onfeng, ÆCHom* ii. 510. 34 *þa bestang se halga his hand him on muð, het hine ceowan mid scearpum toðum his liðegan fingras, gif him alyfed wære,*

Seasons 25　　　We þæt gehyrdon　　hæleþa mænige
　　　　　　　　on bocstafum　　breman and writan,
　　　　　　　　þæt hie fæstenu　　feower heoldon,

and

And 364　　　Ða reordode　　rice þeoden,
　　　　　　　　ece ælmihtig,　　heht his engel gan,
　　　　　　　　mærne maguþegn,　　ond mete syllan,
　　　　　　　　frefran feasceafte　　ofer flodes wylm,
　　　　　　　　þæt hie þe eað mihton　　ofer yða geþring
　　　　　　　　drohtaþ adreogan.

The inf. *cweoðan* introduces direct speech in *Bede* 400. 17 . . . *þa geherde ic þone bisscop me on bæclinge mid geomrunge cweoðan: Eala; hwæt ðu me micel yfel ⁊ lað dest mid þinre ærninge.*

§3788. *Mutatis mutandis*, such clauses follow the rules applicable to subordinate clauses in dependent speech and may display the same peculiarities. Thus, we find a transition from an accusative and infinitive to the actual words of the speaker in

Sat 670　　　Brohte him to bearme　　brade stanas,
　　　　　　　　bæd him for hungre　　hlafas wyrcan—
　　　　　　　　gif þu swa micle　　mihte hæbbe

and a *gif* clause which may be taken *apo koinou* with *hateð* and the *þæt* clause in

Jul 332　　　þonne he onsendeð　　geond sidne grund
　　　　　　　　þegnas of þystrum,　　hateð þræce ræran,
　　　　　　　　gif we gemette sin　　on moldwege,
　　　　　　　　oþþe feor oþþe neah　　fundne weorþen,
　　　　　　　　þæt hi usic binden　　ond in bælwylme
　　　　　　　　suslum swingen.

These are the only examples in Behre's group A(4), which I discuss in §3566. On the mood of the verbs in the *gif* clauses in them and in *El* 1002, see (*mutatis mutandis*) §§3612-14.

VIII

OTHER SENTENCE ELEMENTS AND PROBLEMS

A. THE *APO KOINOU* AND RELATED CONSTRUCTIONS

1. INTRODUCTORY REMARKS

§3789. Meritt, to whom I express gratitude for a book which has coloured my thinking and my feeling for over twenty-five years, says (p. 3) that 'the use of the form "apo koinou" with Latin spelling, rather than with Greek spelling, seems increasingly desirable'. I became a believer in its necessity as the result of an unrevealed mishap in a printing house which made me speak of ἄραξ λεγόμενα when the proof which left my hands read ἄπαξ (*RES* 15 (1964), 137).

§3790. My attempt to define *apo koinou* consists almost entirely of quotations from Meritt. 'In general the term applies to that feature of language wherein it seems necessary to understand a word twice although it is expressed but once' (p. 3). 'It is a kind of verbal economy: a word or closely related group of words, expressed but a single time, serves at once a twofold grammatical construction' (p. 7). After an analysis of previous work on the topic, Meritt produced the following 'definition . . . as a working basis' (p. 16):

> ἀπὸ κοινοῦ is a syntactical construction in which a word or closely related group of words, occurring between two portions of discourse, contains an idea which completes the thought of the first part, to which it is grammatically related, at once supplies the thought essential to the following part, to which it may also be grammatically related, and is not felt to belong more closely with the first part than with the second.

At pp. 17–18 he added the following:

> Constructions are not considered ἀπὸ κοινοῦ if the word which would have to serve in common must serve two cases, one of which is different in form from the word as it appears; nor if it is distinctly more closely related to the preceding part of the sentence; nor if the second part is so subordinate in idea that a carrying over of thought is not essential.

But he was acutely aware of the inevitable difficulties. He tells us (p. 16) that 'it is not always possible to draw hard and fast rules about a phase of syntax, and in some cases the including of a construction in the category of ἀπὸ κοινοῦ or its exclusion therefrom is a matter of degree and not of clear-cut distinction' and later (p. 88) makes a state-ment about OHG which carries with it a general warning: 'Too much stress should not be laid on the assumption that these constructions were always enunciated with a pause between the two parts. The rhythm of the sentence must vary with the context, and not all asyndetic constructions are cast in the same mould.' As a result of these difficulties, I detect myself perhaps more than occasionally using the term *apo koinou* in the simpler and wider definition with which this section begins, for example, in my discussion of *Phoen* 583-654 (*Pope Studies*, p. 261 n. 4).

§3791. But, as well as difficulties, there are benefits. In Meritt's masterly words (p. 4),

the recognition of ἀπὸ κοινοῦ in the older languages is of value in a number of ways. It enables one to understand text as it stands without feeling that some-thing has been omitted which must be editorially supplied. And applying to a somewhat similar tendency it eliminates some unnecessary punctuation which occasionally gives to an early Germanic poem a halting quality with which it was not actually afflicted. It makes unnecessary certain grammatical exceptions, such as holding a usually transitive verb to be intransitive because its apparent object is also object of another verb. Quite the opposite from being a burdensome bit of linguistic paraphernalia for the student, it helps to bring home to him the realization that the dull printed page before him was once the spoken word as ready on the tongue of man as is his own.

§3792. The reader must consult Meritt for a full discussion of this construction. I content myself with mentioning the salient features of its use in OE. On those sentences in which the second part of a possible *apo koinou* is an 'attributive construction' (Meritt, pp. 18-19), as in MnE 'There is a man below wants to speak to you', see §§2304-12. On examples like

Beo 1180   Ic minne can
          glædne Hroþulf,   þæt he þa geogoðe wile
          arum healdan

(Meritt, p. 14), see §1969.

2. IN THE POETRY

§3793. Meritt (pp. 20-1) points out that in the poetry the common element or *koinon* may fill a half-line, which may be the first, e.g. *Phoen* 186 ... *suþan bliceð ǁ wedercondel wearm weorodum lyhteð*, or the second, e.g. *Beo* 1013 *Bugon þa to bence blædagande ǁ fylle gefægon*; 'may rarely occupy a half-line along with the first part of the construction', e.g.

Beo 513   þær git eagorstream   earmum þehton
                 mæton merestræta   mundum brugdon,

where *merestræta* is the common element; or 'may occupy a half-line along with the second part of the construction', e.g.

Rim 9   þa wæs wæstmum aweaht   world onspreht
                 under roderum areaht   rædmægne oferþeaht,

where the common element is *world*. Apart from examples in which it is a clause (§§3796-9), the *koinon* rarely occupies more than a half-line in OE. But see *PPs* 118. 52 (Meritt, p. 35) and *El* 741 (Meritt, p. 47). As far as I have noticed, Meritt offers no examples from OE in which the *koinon* occupies two full half-lines unless it is a clause. Of the type represented by *Beo* 513, Meritt (p. 20) says: 'Here one must decide between ἀπὸ κοινοῦ and asyndeton.' Despite his careful analysis of the four patterns, I am left with the uneasy feeling that this comment is applicable to at least some of the examples of the other three patterns. But this is a matter of feeling and terminology on which the reader must make his own decision.

§3794. Typical examples cited by Meritt (pp. 52-3) in which a *koinon* which is or contains a noun (equivalent) occupies a half-line include those in which it is nominative, e.g. *Phoen* 186 and *Beo* 1013 (both in §3793); accusative, e.g.

Met 27. 2   . . .   swa swa mereflodes
                 yþa hrerað   iscalde sæ
                 wecggað for winde?;

genitive, e.g.

Beo 1043   Ond ða Beowulfe   bega gehwæþres
                 eodor Ingwina   onweald geteah
                 wicga ond wæpna   het hine wel brucan;

and dative, e.g.

Beo 2167   . . . nealles inwitnet   oðrum bregdon
                 dyrnum cræfte   deað renian
                 hondgesteallan.

The *koinon* may also be a verb, e.g.

Beo 1730   . . . seleð him on eþle   eorþan wynne
                 to healdanne   hleoburh wera

and perhaps (but see Meritt, pp. 31–2)

PPs 137. 2   Eac ic þin tempel   tidum weorðige
                  þæt halige hus   holde mode . . . ;

or an adjective, e.g.

PPs 102. 14   . . . beoð mannes dagas   mawenum hege
                  æghwær anlice   eorðan blostman
                  swa his lifdagas   læne syndan.

Meritt also adds

Met 11. 33   . . . þæt hiora æghwilc   wið oðer winð,
                  and þeah winnende   wreðiað fæste
                  æghwilc oðer   utan ymbclyppeð,

in which two pronouns *æghwilc* and *oðer* serve as subject and object respectively to the two verbs, and two examples in which the *koinon* serves as both a subject and an object, viz.

Wan 51   . . . þonne maga gemynd   mod geondhweorfeð
                  greteð gliwstafum   georne geondsceawað
                  secga geseldan   swimmað eft on weg . . . ,

where *secga geseldan* serves as object of *geondsceawað* and subject of *swimmað*,[1] and

PPs 71. 15   He lyfað leodum,   him byð lungre seald
                  of Arabia gold   eorlas lædað,

where *gold* is both subject of *byð* and object of *lædað*. Meritt (pp. 20–36) offers more such examples. Not all will command acceptance; for example, some will prefer to keep the manuscript reading in *Beo* 1020 and there are other possible interpretations of *Beo* 1807. But there is much of value for editors to harvest, including Meritt's distinction (p. 34) between examples in which 'each of the two parts contributes toward the expression of one general idea or to the description of one particular event or situation', e.g.

Beo 2117   þa wæs eft hraðe
                  gearo gyrnwræce   Grendeles modor
                  siðode sorhfull,

and those in which 'the construction expresses two different ideas, often two actions, the second of which temporally follows the first', e.g.

Beo 2575   Hond up abræd
                  Geata dryhten   gryrefahne sloh
                  incge-lafe. . . .

---

[1] I regret that, in *RES* 31 (1980), 396 and 406, I failed by an oversight to say that Meritt had put forward this explanation of *secga geseldan* when I reported that some of my Oxford pupils had produced it independently.

§3795. *Beo* 513 (§3793) is the only OE example cited by Meritt (pp. 36-8) of a possible *koinon* standing in a half-line with the first part of the construction, but *Beo* 1431 *bearhtm ongeaton,* || *guðhorn galan* (Meritt, p. 14) might belong. Examples in which the *koinon* occupies a half-line along with the second part of the construction are more numerous. Meritt's examples (pp. 38-49 and 52-3) include those in which the *koinon* is a verb, e.g. *Beo* 1357 *Hie dygel lond* || *warigeað wulfhleoþu*; a nominative noun, e.g. *Rim* 9 (§3793); an accusative noun, e.g. *Phoen* 188 . . . *ðonne on þam telgum timbran onginneð* || *nest gearwian* and *Mald* 62 *Het þa bord beran beornas gangan*, where the ASPR comma after *beran* suggests an alternative interpretation; a genitive noun (no OE examples); a dative noun, e.g. *Jul* 142 *Het hi þa swingan susle þreagan*; an adjective, e.g. *Beo* 753 *he on mode wearð* || *forht on ferhðe*; and an adverb, e.g. *Met* 4. 17 *geara gehwelce he gongan sceal* || *beforan feran*. Meritt (p. 49) concludes his remarks with the observation that in OE poetry one finds both

constructions which seem rather awkwardly abrupt and constructions which allow a fairly free transition of thought from the first part to the second. It has been said that variation is the very soul of Old English poetical style. This variation in all Old Germanic verse at times forced upon itself the construction ἀπὸ κοινοῦ, which at times was more skillfully used as a ready link for two expressions.

§3796. We now turn our attention to sequences in which a principal clause may be taken *apo koinou*. Meritt (pp. 49-52), while noting that the *koinon* may be a principal clause and citing (after Behaghel) '*Heliand* 1065 *ef thu sis godes sunu be hwi ni hetis thu ef thu giwald haƀes?*' (a telescoped version of *Heliand* 1064-6), offers no OE examples. But this is the situation in sentences of what I call type Ba 2 with the pattern Sp | P | Sp; see §1906. The reluctance of editors to allow initial subordinate clauses in the poetry (§§2448-9 and 2536-8 and Mitchell 1980a, pp. 401-4) means that possible examples are sometimes concealed or not apparent; consider the principal clauses (beginning) in *Beo* 232, 1607, 1647, and 2713, the effect of changing Klaeber's semi-colon into a comma in

Beo 2715

	Ða se æðeling giong
þæt he bi wealle	wishycgende
gesæt on sesse;	seah on enta geweorc,
hu ða stanbogan	stapulum fæste
ece eorðreced	innan healde,

and the effect of Andrew's removal of the semi-colons in *Beo* 3040 and 3041 (*Postscript*, p. 103). Yet occasionally an example is admitted. One is the *syððan* clause in

Beo 2069   Ic sceal forð sprecan
        gen ymbe Grendel,   þæt ðu geare cunne,
        sinces brytta,   to hwan syððan wearð
        hondræs hæleða.   Syððan heofones gim
        glad ofer grundas,   gæst yrre cwom,
        eatol æfengrom   user neosan,
        ðær we gesunde   sæl weardodon.

But it too can be taken *apo koinou*; see §3797.

§3797. Nader (*Ang.* 11 (1888-9), 450-3) cited a series of examples in which a concessive clause can be construed with both the preceding and the following clause. They include the *ðeah þe* clauses in *Beo* 1716 (p. 453, where he used the term *apo koinou*) and in *Beo* 1927 (p. 451). Schücking (§40) noted that the same could be said of the *þeah* clause in *Beo* 203 and of the *syððan* clauses in *Beo* 1775 and *Beo* 2069 (§3796), but did not agree that they should be called *apo koinou*. The mere fact that they can be taken together, he argued, does not prove that the speaker actually linked them by his intonation. But the inevitable fact that we cannot prove that he did, does not prove that he did not. The only proof of *apo koinou* usage, he claimed, would be if the sense of both sentences was incomplete without the subordinate clause. I do not see the relevance of this to examples like the four cited above, to the *þeah* clauses in *And* 271 and

And 474   Ic wille þe,
        eorl unforcuð,   anre nu gena
        bene biddan,   þeah ic þe beaga lyt,
        sincweorðunga,   syllan mihte,
        fætedsinces.   Wolde ic freondscipe,
        þeoden þrymfæst,   þinne, gif ic mehte,
        begitan godne,

or to the *syððan* clauses in *Beo* 2943 and

Beo 1233   Wyrd ne cuþon,
        geosceaft grimme,   swa hit agangen wearð
        eorla manegum,   syþðan æfen cwom,
        ond him Hroþgar gewat   to hofe sinum,
        rice to ræste.   Reced weardode
        unrim eorla,   swa hie oft ær dydon.

In all these examples, the subordinate clause can be taken with the preceding or the following sentence, yet the sense of both sentences is complete without the subordinate clause—which does not prove that the latter stands alone or does not exist.

§3798. Concessive clauses are frequently found in a position where they can be taken *apo koinou*; see, in addition to Nader and Schücking

(§3797), Quirk, pp. 75-7, and Mitchell 1969*a*, pp. 78-81. This is also true of temporal clauses. We find, in addition to *syððan* (§3797), *ær* in *Wan* 69 (Mitchell 1980*a*, p. 407), *þa* in *Beo* 1467 and *Mald* 165 (§2536 and Mitchell 1980*a*, pp. 407 and 412), and *þonne* in

ChristC 944

          Halge sawle
 mid hyra frean farað, þonne folca weard
 þurh egsan þrea eorðan mægðe
 sylfa geseceð. Weorþeð geond sidne grund
 hlud gehyred heofonbyman stefn. . . .

In ASPR we read

Rid 15. 9 . . .   ond ic bide þær
  mid geoguðcnosle, hwonne gæst cume
  to durum minum, him biþ deað witod.

Craig Williamson (*Rid* 13. 10) begins a new sentence with *Hwonne*, remarking that 'the syntax is simplified considerably by taking *Hwonne* as an adverb meaning "when", introducing what Mitchell calls an "adverb clause of time" '. I would prefer to take the *hwonne* clause *apo koinou*, with the comment that usages such as this would have influenced the transition of *hwonne* from an interrogative to a temporal conjunction; see §§2775-83. A subordinate clause need not be involved, as the cited discussions will reveal. Thus, in *Beo* 967-73 the sequence could be paraphrased 'Although I could not stop him going . . . he left his hand. . . . Although he left his hand . . . he bought no respite.'

§3799. There is room for more work on these and other types of clause. On *þæt* in *GenB* 833, see Mitchell 1980*a*, p. 408. On *ðæs* 'because' in *Sat* 172, see §3115. *Beo* 418 *forþan hie mægenes cræft minne cuþon* gives the reason for the action described in *Beo* 415-17, while *Beo* 419-24a explains how they knew. In *Beo* 679 *forþan* means 'therefore' in relation to the preceding clause and 'for the reason I am about to explain' in relation to what follows. The *nu* clause in *Beo* 2799 can be taken both with what precedes and with what follows. So too can the *gif* clauses in *Beo* 1182, *Beo* 1481, and

Jul 328

        Ne biþ us frea milde,
  egesful ealdor, gif we yfles noht
  gedon habbaþ; ne durran we siþþan
  for his onsyne ower geferan.

On the *gif* clause in *GenA* 2414, see Mitchell 1959, pp. 51-2. Meritt (p. 51) quotes *Jul* 328 to illustrate his observation that

in spite of the possible diffuseness of the koinon, these clause constructions do have features of ἀπὸ κοινοῦ. While the instances where a dependent clause stands between two independent clauses need not be considered in the category of ἀπὸ κοινοῦ, since here it is not essential to take an element in common, yet at times one may strongly have the impression that this dependent clause was felt to be closely attached to the preceding and following parts.

I agree. But I would add in conclusion that the treatment of such subordinate clauses is more than a terminological problem. It is a matter which affects our fundamental attitude to the punctuation and so to the method of reading OE poetry. Or, to put the question in another way, is the unit of OE poetry the MnE sentence or the OE verse paragraph? See Mitchell 1980a, pp. 395-412.

3. IN THE PROSE

§3800. To Meritt (p. 81) 'it appears that the construction ἀπὸ κοινοῦ is very rare in prose'. His OE examples (pp. 84-5) are *Or* 96. 10 *Æfter þæm Læcedemonie gecuron him to ladteowe Ircclidis wæs haten*, *ChronE* 225. 17 (1090) *Se cyng wæs smægende hu he mihte wrecon his broðer Rodbeard swiðost swencean*, and a third in which the possibility of asyndeton arises, viz. *Bede* 216. 1 *Ða genom se engel sona þone mon wearp eft in þæt fyr*, Latin *Quem angelus sanctus statim adprehendens in ignem reiecit*; here 'there is no definite way of determining whether an object is to be used twice grammatically or used once and implied once'. For more such examples see §1576. It must be a matter of opinion whether it is appropriate to use the term *apo koinou* of examples such as *Bede* 216. 1; *GD(C)* 41. 9 ... *þæt anra gehwilces biscopes mod byþ forhergod 7 todrifeþ full oft seo þicnes þara woruldlicra ymbhogena*, Latin ... *quod uniuscuiusque praesulis mentem curarum densitas devastat*, where *mod* is first a subject and then a direct object; *ÆCHom* i. 26. 3 *þa siððan geceas he him leorningcnihtas, ærest twelf þa we hata ð apostolas*, where *geceas* governs two independent objects; *ÆCHom* i. 16. 31 *He com ða on næddran hiwe to þam twam mannum, ærest to ðam wife, and hire to cwæ ð ...* , where both the *to-* phrases depend on *com*; and *ÆC Hom* ii. 150. 22 *Ða gesæt he æt mysan micclum onbryrd he beseah to heofonum*, where *micclum onbryrd* can go with both clauses.

§3801. As I have pointed out in §§3796 and 3799, Meritt recognized the possibility that a clause could serve as a *koinon* in OE poetry. He did not extend this to the prose. But here too we have principal clauses in sentences with the pattern Sp | P | Sp, e.g. *ÆCHom* i. 26. 25 and the similar examples quoted in §1906. Such sentences exist in MnE and present no problems beyond that of terminology.

§3802. But difficulties do arise. I have suggested elsewhere (Mitchell 1980*a*, pp. 388-95) that it is wrong to assume that OE and MnE share identical sentence structures in the prose; that to use only MnE marks of punctuation for OE prose can lead to distortion of the syntax and the flow of an OE prose sentence or paragraph; and that the possibility of an *apo koinou* use of an antecedent and an adjective clause or adjective clauses arises in a passage from MS CCCC 162. I am encouraged in these beliefs by the fact that Waterhouse (1978, pp. 36 and 227) quite independently mentions the possibility of an *apo koinou* usage of *ÆLS* 31. 612 *þa ða he him wið spræc* and of the *þa þa/ða* clauses in examples like *ÆLS* 31. 474 *þysum weorce wæs sum oþer gelic þa þa he eac towearp sum oðer hæþengild . þa sloh sum hæþen man to þam halgan were* and *ÆLS* 27. 106 *Wearð þa godes wundor on þam weorcstanum þa ða se casere com mid eadmodnysse to . þa to eodon ða stanas . and geopenode þæt get* (Skeat's punctuation; it would be instructive to compare the various manuscripts).

§3803. As in the poetry, such examples are not restricted to temporal clauses; consider the causal clauses in *CP* 433. 13 *7 sio niht getacnað ða ðistro ðære blindnesse urre tidernesse. Forðæmðe nan mon ne mæg on niht gesion hu neah him hwelc frecenes sie, him is ðearf ðæt he hæbbe his sweord be his hype* and *ÆCHom* i. 38. 13 *Eornostlice mancynn hæfde ungeþwærnysse to englum ær Drihtnes acennednysse; forðan ðe we wæron þurh synna ælfremede fram Gode; þa wurde we eac ælfremede fram his englum getealde*; and the concessive clause in *ÆLS* 31. 121 *Hwam twynað la forði þæt þæs geleaffullan weres wære . se sige . þa þa him wæs getiþod þæt he wæpenleas nære aworpen þam here . þeah þe se arfæsta drihten eaþe mihte gehealdan andsundne his cempan . He ætbræd þæt gefeoht . þæt furðon næron gewemmede Martines gesihþa on oðra manna deaðe* (see Waterhouse 1978, p. 108). In the OE version of *John* (WSCp) 13. 29 *Sume wendon forþam Iudas hæfde scrin þ se hælend hit cwæde be him . . .* , the *forþam* clause can be taken with the dependent speech; see §1978 and cf. *And* 271 (Mitchell 1969*a*, p. 80). On conditional clauses see §3708. There is room for more work here. What is at stake is how we should read OE prose texts and how we should punctuate them for the different categories of present-day readers; see again Mitchell 1980*a*, pp. 388-95.

B. ABSOLUTE CONSTRUCTIONS

1. DATIVE/INSTRUMENTAL

a. What is an 'absolute'?

§3804. Our first problem is the word 'absolute'.[2] Callaway (1889, p. 2) notes that 'the absolute participle is in general easily distinguished from the appositive participle by the fact that the latter has no distinct subject of its own, but agrees with the subject of the verb or with a word in regimen, as in: In illo die exiens Jesus de domo, sedebat secus mare, Mat. 13. 1, etc.' But he admits that the two are sometimes difficult to distinguish. In common with most scholars, he also found it difficult to define the absolute construction (pp. 1-2):

A loosely paraphrased definition, restrictive enough for the present purpose, may be stated as follows: when to a substantive not the subject of a verb and dependent upon no other word in the sentence (noun, adjective, verb, or preposition) a participle is joined as its predicate, a clause is formed that modifies the verbal predicate of the sentence and denotes an accompanying circumstance, as in: Urbe expugnata imperator rediit. From its apparent grammatical independence, this has been denominated an absolute clause, though, as Hoffmann thinks (l. c. p. 783), incorrectly; since the clause stands in close relationship to the rest of the sentence, the absolute substantive differing, in fact, from the simple substantival modifier of a verb only by the annexation thereto of a predicative participle (Delbrück,[1] p. 42). It is with the participle so used that we have to do, here designated, as usual, the absolute participle.

[1] Delbrück, B.: Ablativ, Localis, Instrumentalis im Altindischen, Lateinischen, Griechischen u. Deutschen. Berlin, 1867.

Kellner (§409) described this definition as 'correct': 'To us the construction as exhibited in the above instances is really *absolute*, i.e. detached from all the members of the sentence.' However, he went on (§410): 'But originally there was no such a thing as an absolute participle. What we look upon as such was simply a very freely used case implying at first instrumental meaning, then including by degrees also cause and time.' (Cf. here GL's observations (§409) about 'the so-called Ablative Absolute'.) Visser presumably meant his definition of 'the absolute past participle construction' (ii, §1150) to embrace similar constructions with the present participle (ii, §1014): 'In this kind of Old English construction the person or thing denoted by the (pro)noun which forms a syntactical unit with the past participle is not identical with the person or thing denoted by the subject of the

[2] I acknowledge here my debt to J. A. Harvie, University of Otago, Dunedin, N.Z., for stimulus received from conversations and letters. His work has now borne fruit in 'Dative Absolutism in Perspective', *Melbourne Slavonic Studies*, 13 (1980 for 1978), 40-50.

main syntactical unit.' Nunn (p. 23) adds the words 'or object' after 'the subject' in a similar definition of the ablative absolute in Ecc. Lat.; for GL's further addition of a 'dependent case' see below. According to Matsunami (1966*a*, p. 318) 'a participle is . . . *independent* (or *absolute*) when its subject is grammatically independent of the rest of the sentence'. Nunn (p. 22) says that the construction is called absolute 'because it is independent of, or loosed from (*absolutus*), the main structure of the sentence'. Yet such definitions do not fit the facts. As we have seen, Callaway (1889, p. 1) speaks of 'apparent grammatical independence'. According to GL (§410, remark 3), 'as a rule, the Abl. Abs. can stand only when it is not identical with the subject, object, or dependent case of the verbal predicate. . . . This rule is frequently violated at all periods of the language, for the purpose either of emphasis or of stylistic effect.' Nunn (p. 23) exemplifies similar 'ungrammatical use of the Abl. Absolute' and Visser (ii. 1075) gives OE 'examples of quasi-absolute constructions' which violate the rule; on these, see §3808. 'Amid such complexities' (Callaway 1889, p. 1), it may be profitable to ask what sort of 'independence' of the principal clause is actually present in the OE constructions designated as absolute by the various writers on the subject.

§3805. Callaway was right to warn us (my §3804) that there is sometimes room for difference of opinion about the classification of individual examples. We can find instances in his own work, including *BenR* 31. 8 *onhnigenum heafde*, Latin *inclinato . . . capite*, where Callaway (1889, p. 10) sees either a dative absolute or a dative of manner, and *ÆCHom* i. 362. 10 . . . *he gearcað þone weig cumendum Gode* . . . , where Callaway (ibid.) admits the possibility of Thorpe's '. . . prepares the way for the coming God . . .'. It will suffice to add *GD(C)* 135. 6 *7 þa gehældum þam preoste he bebead* . . . and *GD(H)* 135. 5 *him þa gehæledum he bebead* . . . , which Tilley (p. 81) lists among his absolutes but which may exemplify the dative of person after *bebead*; *ApT* 12. 27 . . . *hwæt dest ðu þus gedrefedum mode on þisum lande?*, Latin . . . *quid ita in his locis turbata mente versaris?*, of which Chase (*MLN* 8 (1893), 244) said 'this may be an attributive use of the participle, *gedrefedum*, with *mode*, a dative of manner'; and *Luke(WSCp)* 9. 34, on which see §3808 fn. Such difficulties are understandable; unless the sentence is nonsense, there must inevitably be some connection between an absolute and the clause to which it refers—temporal, causal, or the like; see §3824. In practice, several different relationships or degrees of independence can be detected in the OE 'absolutes' listed by the grammarians.

§3806. First, there are those in which the two elements which make up the sentence have no person or thing in common, e.g. *Inita aestate ad exercitum venit, GD* 201. 25 *7 þa gewordenum ærmergenne he het beran mid him þone suflmete* ..., Latin *facto autem mane, fecit deferri pulmentum* ..., *ÆCHom* i. 566. 6 *þa geendodum dagum þære freolstide com seo sæ færlice swegende*, and possibly *ÆCHom* i. 508. 1 *Ac gað eow into ðære cyrcan unforhtlice, and me ætstandendum geneosiað þa stowe æfter gewunan mid gebedum*, though here we may have a comitative dative.

§3807. Second, we have those examples in which the same person or thing is involved logically, but not grammatically, in both elements, e.g. *Urbe expugnata imperator rediit* (the general and his troops captured the city), *GD(C)* 69. 15 *þa gesewenum þam wundre seo moder wæs onbryrded* ..., Latin *quo viso miraculo, conpuncta mater ipsa iam coepit agere* ... (the mother beheld the wonder), *GD(H)* 133. 1 *ðysum wordum þa gehyredum se cyning wearð swiðe þearle ablycged*, Latin *quibus auditis* (*GD(C)* 133. 1 has *þa se cyng þas word hæfde gehered* ...), and *ÆCHom* i. 340. 5 *Ðæra sceapa hlaford com ham, afundenum sceape* (Thorpe, 'The master of the sheep came home, having found [his] sheep'). That these examples exist because of the absence of a perfect participle active of transitive verbs in Latin and in OE is neatly illustrated by *ÆCHom* i. 546. 21 *Ðyses mædenes gebysnungum and fotswaðum fyligde ungerim heap mægðhades manna on clænnysse þurhwunigende, forlætenum giftum, to ðam heofonlicum brydguman Criste geþeodende mid anrædum mode* ... and by a comparison of *Matt(WSCp)* 8. 34 *7 þa þa hig hyne gesawun* and *Matt(Ru)* 8. 34 *7 geseende hine*, both of which represent Latin *et uiso eo*.

§3808. Then there are two groups in which the same person or thing is involved, not only logically but also grammatically, in both elements. So we have, third, a group which embraces what Visser (ii. 1075) calls 'quasi-absolute constructions (viz. such in which the person referred to by the (pro)noun in the dative is identical with that denoted by the (pro)noun functioning as the subject of the main syntactical unit)', as in *Neque illum me vivo corrumpi sinam*. Here belong the examples cited by Visser (ibid.); *Or* 34. 1 ... *þæt, him ða ondrædendum þæm gebroðrum, hy genamon Ioseph* ... , where I take *him* as reflexive dative (§3829);[3] four examples from *Orosius*

---

[3] *Luke(WSCp)* 9. 34 *7 hi ondredon him gangende on þ genip* is taken by Callaway (1889, p. 13) as containing a ' "crude" absolute participle', i.e. 'a weathered uninflected form' (ibid., p. 2), no doubt on the strength of the Latin *et timuerunt intrantibus illis in nubem*. But *him* could be reflexive dative and *gangende* nominative. Von Schaubert (p. 124) independently reached this last conclusion.

with the present participle of *ofþyncan* which are cited by Callaway (1889, p. 8) and seen as causal by Liggins (1955, p. 462), viz. *Or* 52. 17, 80. 22, 112. 26—in these there is no expressed pronoun subject for the impersonal verb—and *Or* 244. 16 *Hit þa eallum þæm senatum ofþyncendum 7 þæm consulum þæt he heora ealdan gesetnessa tobrecan wolde, ahleopon þa ealle 7 hiene mid heora metseacsum ofsticedon inne on heora gemotærne*—in which *hit* anticipates the *þæt* clause and seems to be an ungrammatical subject for the dative participle of the impersonal verb, and *eallum þæm senatum* is taken up by *ealle* (see further § 3821); *GD(H)* 170. 29 *7 þa . . . him ut lociendum geseah he ufan onsended leoht afligean ealle þa nihtlican þystru*, Latin *subito . . . respiciens vidit fusam lucem desuper cunctas noctis tenebras exfugasse*, but cf. *GD(C)* 170. 33 *7 þa . . . he wæs forð lociende 7 geseah . . .*; *ChronE* 55. 28 (792); and *Luke(WSCp)* 6. 48 *Soðlice gewordenum flode hit fleow into þam huse*, Latin *inundatione autem facta inlisum est flumen domui illi*. To these can, I think, be added the only clear-cut OE example I have recorded in which the (pro)noun in the dative refers to the accusative object of the principal clause, viz. *Mark(WSCp)* 6. 41 *7 fif hlafum 7 twam fixum onfangenum he on heofon locode 7 hi bletsode 7 þa hlafas bræc . . .*, Latin *et acceptis quinque panibus et duobus piscibus intuens in caelum benedixit et fregit panes. . . .* (As far as the OE subject *he*, we have an example of the second group above.) We may compare *Matt* 8. 23 *Et ascendente eo in nauicula secuti sunt eum discipuli eius*, where all the OE versions have two finite verbs except for *Li*'s *7 ofstigende hine ł ða he ofstag*. Here, as in the Latin of *Matt* 8. 34 (§ 3807) and 9. 27, where the OE versions again have either finite verbs or active present participles, the (pro)noun in the ablative refers to the object—unexpressed in *Matt* 8. 34 —of the governing clause. In *Luke(WSCp)* 17. 7 *Hwylc eower hæfþ eregendne þeow oððe scep læsgendne þam of þam æcere gehworfenum he him sona segð ga 7 site*, Latin *Quis autem uestrum habens seruum arantem aut pascentem qui regresso de agro dicet illi statim transi recumbe*, the active participles *gehworfenum* and *regresso* could be taken with *him* and *illi* respectively rather than as absolute. Examples like *Bede* 220. 16 *Ond him forðferdum Itthamar gehalgode Damianum for hine, se wæs of Suðseaxna cynne cumen* and *Bede* 14. 28 *Ðætte forðferdum Paulino þam biscope Ithamar for him æt Hrofeceastre biscopsetle onfeng*, in which the (pro)noun in the dative refers to the object of the prep. *for*, are also uncommon; cf. *Mark(WSCp)* 5. 2. I have found none in which the dative refers to a dependent case without a preposition, apart from *Matt(WSCp)* 10. 1 (§ 3809), *Matt (WSCp)* 16. 12, and *Luke(WSCp)* 9. 37.

§3809. Fourth, we have examples in which a possessive or a genitive of a personal pronoun in the 'absolute' construction refers to a person or thing in the governing clause. This is seen at its simplest in examples like *GD* 187. 23, *GD(C)* 85. 1, *GD(H)* 85. 1 *soðlice þa geendodre his bene he aras* . . . , Latin *expleta autem praece surrexit*, and *GD* 193. 1 *7 þa forlætenum hire agnum streame eall seo ea wæs him fylgende*, Latin *Quem, relicto alveo proprio, tota fluminis aqua secuta est*. More complicated manifestations appear in *Bede* 266. 18 *7 heo onfongenre his bletsunge swiðe unrote ut from him eodon*, Latin *atque illi percepta eius benedictione iam multum tristes exissent*, where *heo* received his blessing—compare the second pattern (§3807)—and went out from him, and in *Matt(WSCp)* 10. 1 *And tosomne gecigydum hys twelf leorningcnihtun, he sealde him unclænra gasta anweald*, Latin *Et conuocatis duodecim discipulis suis dedit illis potestatem spiritum inmundorum*, where *leorningcnihtun* refers to *him*—compare the third pattern (§3808)—and *hys* to *he*.

§3810. Those sentences in which a dative phrase refers to a part or parts of the body or to the dress or equipment of the subject of the governing clause, some of which have already been quoted, require separate treatment. The simplest type is that seen in the almost formulaic phrases in *Bede* 292. 27 *7 mid þy heo þær longe gebegdum cneom hire gebæd* . . . , Latin *cum ibidem diutius flexis genibus oraret* . . . , *ÆCHom* ii. 360. 7 *Se Hælend cwæð to his Fæder, up ahafenum eagum to heofenum* . . . , Latin *Subleuatis Iesus oculis in coelum dixit* . . . , and *ÆCHom* i. 74. 26 . . . *and astrehtum handum to Gode clypode*, Latin . . . *eleuatis manibus*. . . . Such phrases are classified as absolute by Callaway (1889, *passim*), Ahlgren (pp. 184-5), QW (pp. 66 and 98), and Visser (ii, §1151). There are variations. An adjective may replace the participle, e.g. *Bede* 340. 7 *þa geseah heo openum eagum*, Latin *apertisque oculis*, *ÆCHom* i. 90. 26 *Abraham hine astrehte eallum limum to eorðan*, *Luke(WSCp)* 23. 23 *And hig astodon 7 mycelre stefne bædon þ he wære ahangen*, Latin *uocibus magnis*, and (possibly) *ÆCHom* ii. 326. 6 *and heora fæder feoll foredum swyran* . . . and *ÆLS* 5. 379 *Hwæt ða Tiburtius bealdlice eode ofer ða byrnendan gleda unforbærnedum fotum*. I have, however, recorded no examples with noun + noun, as in the Latin *Caesare duce* and *Bede* 412. 31 *ducibus angelis*, where the OE has *Bede* 340. 20 *mid engla þreatum*. (Scheler, p. 71, here misquotes the Latin and wrongly gives *Bede* 340. 12 = Latin 412. 23 as the OE equivalent.) A possessive (or a genitive of a personal pronoun) or a demonstrative may accompany the dative noun, e.g. *GD(C)* 118. 26 *þa se hræfn untyndum his muþe 7 apenedum his fiþerum ongan yrnan ymb þone ylcan hlaf* and *GD* 247. 3 . . . *swa þæt heo toborstenum þam innoðum swulte for þam mægne þære halgan rode.* A preposition may govern the dative phrase, e.g. *ÆCHom* i. 372. 19 *Se Godes apostol ða genealæhte ðam lice mid aðenedum earmum* and *GD(H)* 118. 22 *se hrefn þa mid openum muðe 7 mid aþenedum fiðerum ongann yrnan . . . ymbutan þone ylcan hlaf*; these supplement Visser, ii. 1274. *Mark(WSCp)* 6. 5 does not belong here, despite Visser, ii. 1275.

§3811. The examples with prepositions seem to me clearly comitative or modal datives, datives of attendant circumstances or manner; compare them with *GD* 276. 15 *heo . . . wolde gewitan mid hire earum æt his nosþyrlum hweþer ænig liflic oroð him þa gyt inne wære* and see Mustanoja, pp. 116-17. The same is true of those with adjectives; compare *ÆCHom* ii. 516. 18 *Ða wearð he geuntrumod eallum lymum* with *ChronA* 46. 28 (755) *7 þa geascode he þone cyning lytle werode on wifcyþþe on Merantune* and consider the effect of reading *gelytlodum/-e* for *lytle* in the last example. In view of this, the 'absolute' status of examples of the type *astrehtum handum*—and even that of some of the other types discussed above —must be in doubt. Note here the remarks made by Delbrück and Kellner cited in §3804; consider *Bede* 12. 14 *Ðæt se papa Bonefatius þone ylcan cyning onsendum gewritum wæs trymmende to rihtum geleafan,* which Wülfing (i. 140) takes as a dative of means and Callaway (1889, p. 7) as a dative absolute, a possibility which Wülfing concedes; note the similar doubts about *ÆCHom* ii. 578. 20 *gebigedum cneowum* and *Bede* 186. 21 *Æfter ðissum wæs æfterfylgendre tide sum cneoht . . .* voiced by Scheler (p. 79); attempt to classify the various dative and prepositional phrases in *ÆCHom* i. 222. 10 and in *ÆCHom* i. 230. 12-18; and finally, see Ahlgren, pp. 192-5, and consider the following series: *ÆCHom* ii. 30. 19 . . . *and gemette ealle hire bearn mid ormætre cwylminge cwacigende eallum limum, ÆCHom* ii. 20. 2 . . . *and het gebindan ða cnihtas handum and fotum, John(WSCp)* 11. 44 *7 sona stop forð se ðe dead wæs gebunden handan 7 fotan, ÆLS* 21. 174 *and heo arn to cyrcan to þam arwurðan halgan gebundenum handum,* and *GD* 219. 21 . . . *forþon þa þry cnihtas wæron aworpene in þæt fyr gebundenum heora fotum 7 handum.* Here I must leave the reader to decide for himself which of the types distinguished above can properly be called 'absolute'. Visser (ii. 1278) offers a bibliography, to which can be added Wrenn, *MLR* 25 (1930), 188-90; Shimomiya, *Gengogaku Ronsō,* Tokyo, 4 (1963), 41-58; and Phillipps, *NM* 67 (1966), 282-90.

§3812. The status of certain prepositional phrases which do not concern parts of the body and the like also remains to be established. Callaway (1889, pp. 18 and 1 fn. 3) 'denies an absolute use to the participles preceded by *at* in Gothic and by *be* in A.S.', such as *Bede* 42. 13 . . . *Constantinus se be Diocletiane lyfgendum Gallia rice 7 Ispania heold*, where the reference is not to the subject of the governing clause and the Latin . . . *Constantius qui uiuente Diocletiano Galliam Hispaniamque regebat* has an ablative absolute, and *Bede* 106. 17 *Æfter Agustini fyligde in biscophade Laurentius, þone he forðon bi him lifigendum gehalgode*, where the reference is to the subject of the governing clause and the Latin *Successit Augustino in episcopatum Laurentius, quem ipse idcirco adhuc uiuens ordinauerat* has an appositive participle. Callaway (1889, pp. 42-4) views this pattern as an alternative method of rendering the Latin ablative absolute; cites more examples, including five from the poetry, viz. *Beo* 2665, *Ex* 324, *GuthB* 1234, *Jul* 133, and *Husb* 52; and says that 'the participle after *be* . . . is not absolute, but attributive: it does not predicate an action, but describes a state'. He finds confirmation of this view in the appearance of participles and adjectives in the attributive position before a noun, e.g. *HomU* 40. 269. 23 *be lifiendre cwenan*, *LawIne(B)* 17 *Be forstolenum flæsce*, and *LawIICn* 53 *be cwicum ceorle*. This argument carries little weight, for the noun follows the participle in most of the combinations which Callaway takes as absolute; see §3823. Scheler (pp. 79 and 81) agrees that they are not absolute, arguing that they are native constructions—Ahlgren (p. 184) is less sure about this—in which the participle is presumably appositive. The view that they are absolute has been adopted by Grimm and others (Callaway 1889, p. 43); by BTS, s.v. *be* III (28) —in apparent contradiction of what is said in BTS s.v. *be* II (3) (*a*); by Kellner (§411), as I understand him; by Visser (ii, §1014); and by Matsunami (1966*b*, pp. 71-2). Here, as with the next pattern, it is more important to recognize the existence of the construction than to give it a name.

§3813. Visser (ii. 1271) cites three examples with *æfter* in which the prepositional group is used 'to make the implicit relation between the absolute past participle and the noun forming a syntactical unit with it explicit': *Bede* 280. 21 *Æfter ðissum nales micelre tide forðaurnenre* . . . , Latin *Non multo post haec elapso tempore* . . . , which does not conform to his definition, since *æfter* governs only *ðissum*; *BlHom* 145. 22 *Æfter þyssum wordum gefylde, þa wæs Maria arisende 7 wæs utgangende of hire huse* . . . , on which see §3833; and *HomU* 36. 227. 18 *and æfter eallum þissum swa ge-*

wordenum. . . . We can add *ÆCHom* i. 354. 8 *æfter gewunnenum sige* . . . and *ÆCHom* i. 544. 9 *Æfter ablunnenre ehtnysse reðra cynega and ealdormanna.* . . . There may be more examples. One suspects Latin influence. But of the Latin sources of the last four examples (details of which J. E. Cross has privately communicated), only one has a comparable phrase. This is *Et post conpleta oratione [Maria] regressa est in domum et sic discubuit super lectum suum*, which is actually the equivalent of *BlHom* 145. 24 *þa þis gebed wæs gefylled þa wæs heo eft gangende on hire hus 7 heo þa wæs hleonigende ofer hire ræste.* The OE adapter omits some material here, but *BlHom* 145. 22 may represent *Et cum haec dixisset* or (perhaps more likely) *Haec omnia dicente beato Petro.* This apparent independence of Latin in at least three examples raises the possibility that the idiom was, if not native, at least naturalized. So too does the fact that Ælfric uses it. Yet *Or* 50. 27 *Ær þæm þe Romeburg getimbred wære lxiiiigum wintra* represents *Anno ante Urbem conditam lxiiii* and *Or* 100. 17 *Æfter þæm þe Romeburg getimbred wæs iii hunde wintra 7 lxxvi* represents *Anno ab Urbe condita ccclxxvi*; here the translator of *Orosius* did not use it when he had every reason to do so. More work is needed. But we do not, I think, have to follow Visser in taking these participles as absolute. They may be attributive; cf. §3812.

§3814. Callaway (1889, p. 51) writes:

Though seemingly frequent in some of the closer Anglo-Saxon translations from the Latin, the absolute participle occurs there chiefly in certain favorite phrases. In the freer translations the absolute participle is less frequent, is found mostly in certain collocations, and, moreover, wavers between an absolute and an attributive use. In the more independent literature the absolute participle is practically unknown. Hence the absolute construction is not an organic idiom of the Anglo-Saxon language.

There is general agreement that absolute constructions are most common in prose texts closely based on Latin originals, viz. *Bede, GD* (where, as Yerkes (pp. 325-9) shows, the reviser adds more absolutes than he leaves out), *BenR* and *BenRGl*, and the Gospels; see Callaway 1889, pp. 5-15, Callaway 1918, pp. 1-44, and Visser, ii. 1073 and 1261. Liggins (1955, pp. 459-61) notes that those absolutes which express cause in both *Bede* and *Chron* tend to occur in set formulae. Scheler (pp. 74-5) makes the same point about other absolutes. But a study of the distribution, the frequency, and the Latin equivalents, of the various OE patterns distinguished in the preceding sections may well throw new light on the origin of the OE absolute constructions and on the validity or otherwise of Callaway's last sentence above; see further §§3825–31.

§3815. Callaway (1889, pp. 15–16 and 29) records two dative absolute constructions in OE poetry, both of which lack a direct Latin original but, he suggests, may have been the indirect result of Latin influence. They are

GenA 1584   Hie þa raðe stopon,
          heora andwlitan   in bewrigenum
          under loðum listum . . .

and (with a doubtful reading; see below)

Rid 59. 12   Ne mæg þære bene
          æniges monnes   ungefullodre
          godes ealdorburg   gæst gesecan,
          rodera ceastre.

The first was accepted by Grein, Hofer (Ang. 7 (1884), 383), and Holthausen. But Krapp (ASPR note on GenA 1585) says 'Perhaps it would be better to emend to bewrigene.' Of the second, Craig Williamson (note on his Rid 57) says that the reading ungefullodre 'unfulfilled' for MS ungafol lodre (ASPR reports ungaful lodre) is accepted by all major editors, but notes Cosijn's preference for ungefullodra 'of the unbaptized'. It was, I presume, these uncertainties which led Matsunami (1966b, p. 71) to observe that 'there is no authentic dative absolute in all the range of OE poetry'.

b. The patterns

§3816. However we define an 'absolute', the dative is the most common case in OE. But the instrumental does occur, e.g. Bede 42. 1 fulfremede compe, sometimes with agreement (where possible) between the elements, e.g. Bede 262. 19 ðy uplican dome stihtigende, sometimes with a mixture of dative and instrumental forms, e.g. Bede 176. 23 togeteledum þy geare þe . . . and GD(C) 169. 19 ðy gedonum, where MS H has ðysum gedonum. On the evidence of the authorities listed in §3822, the instrumental is rare outside Bede. But, despite Callaway (1889, p. 2), it can be seen in both demonstratives and participles.

§3817. The simplest and perhaps most common pattern comprises a present or second participle and a noun, or a pronoun, or an indefinite (§241). Examples include Bede 184. 7 æfterfylgendre tide,

Latin *tempore sequente*, *Bede* 202. 14 *swapendum windum*, Latin *ventis ferentibus* . . . , and *ÆCHom* ii. 262. 13 *oferswiðdum deaðe*; *ChronA* 56. 12 (797) *Gode fultomiendum*, *Exod* 22. 3 *sunnan scinendre*, Latin *orto sole*, and *ChronA* 18. 2 (560) *Idan forðgefarenum* (a late interpolation); *Bede* 340. 20 *hyre geseondre*, Latin *se aspectante*, and *ÆCHom* i. 296. 1 *him on locigendum*; and *Bede* 284. 20 *eallum geseondum*, Latin *uidentibus cunctis*.

§3818. Visser (ii, §1150) makes the following statement:

When the past participle is the form of an intransitive verb ('him forðferdum'), the accompanying (pro)noun functions as a subject; when it is the form of a transitive verb ('Forlorenum þam irene'), the accompanying (pro)noun is virtually an object. In a number of cases, however, this dichotomy is not possible, since the border-line between transitivity and intransitivity is often very vague.

One proviso at least is necessary here: that in *GD(C)* 114. 2 *swa þa forlorenum þam irene he arn* the absolute could as easily be replaced by ✱*þa þæt iren forloren wæs* as by ✱*þa he þæt iren forleas*.

§3819. Callaway (1889, p. 21) notes that 'the subject of the absolute participle is sometimes omitted, chiefly in glosses'. His examples include *ChronE* 55. 28 (792) *7 Osred þe wæs Norþanhymbra cining æfter wræcsiðe ham cumenum gelæht wæs*, where the 'omitted' subject is the same as that of the principal clause; *BlHom* 245. 30 *And þus cweþende, fyren wolc astah of heofenum*, where *cweþende* may be nominative referring to *BlHom* 245. 27 *Se haliga Andreas þa cwæð*; *Luke(WSCp)* 24. 47, where . . . *agynnendum fram hierusalem* translates Latin . . . *incipientibus ab hierosolyma*; and *BenRGl* 11. 7 *fultumiendum*, Latin *adiuvante domino*.

§3820. Absolute constructions can occur in subordinate clauses, e.g. *GD* 207. 17 . . . *swa þæt afuliendum lichaman hi mid ealle forwurdon* and *Exod* 22. 3 *Gyf he sunnan scinendre ðæt deð* . . . , and (as we have already seen) can contain more than two words. Possible additions include demonstratives, possessives, and qualifiers of various kinds, e.g. *GD(C)* 35. 17 *þa lærendum þam preostum*, *Bede* 266. 18 *onfongenre his bletsunge*, *GD* 185. 12 *þa gehyredre þære his stemne*, *GD* 191. 24 *7 þa gecwedenum þyses witedomes wordum*, *Bede* 310. 22 *ond foregesettum þæm swiðe halgum godspellum*, *Bede* 464. 14 *him eallum fultumiendum*, and *Mark(WSCp)* 14. 17 . . . *him twelfum mid him* [18.] *sittendum 7 etendum*; negative *ne*, e.g. *Bede* 270. 35 *ne weotendum oððo ne gemændum þæm heordum þære stowe* and *Mark(WSCp)* 12. 20 *na læfedum sæde*; other adverbs, e.g. *þa* in the last three examples quoted from *GD*—Tilley (p. 79) notes this as a characteristic of Wærferth's style—*þær* in *Bede* 16. 30 *him þær forðferendum*, and *þa* and *eft* in *Bede* 472. 21 *þa gelyfendum eft Angelfolcum*; a prepositional phrase, e.g. *Bede* 310. 21 *ætgædre mid hine sittendum oðrum biscopum*; an object for the participle, e.g. *Bede* 448. 11 *þyssum monnum þone bysceophad þeniendum* and *ÆCHom* i. 310. 10, below; an element in co-ordination, e.g. *Bede* 270. 35 and *Mark(WSCp)* 14. 17, both quoted above, *GD(C)* 65. 8, and *ÆCHom* i. 310. 10 *Drihtne samod wyrcendum and ða spræce getrymmendum mid æfterfyligendum tacnum*—on this see Callaway 1889, p. 21 n. (3); a subject clause 'in imitation of the Latin original' (Callaway 1889, p. 21 n. (6)) in *BenRGl* 39. 12 and 45. 5; an object clause, e.g. *Or* 52. 17 *Se þa, mid ðon þe he geweox, him þa ofþyncendum 7 ðæm Perseum þæt hie on his eames anwalde wæron 7 on þara Meða, ac hie gewin uphofan*; an adjective clause, e.g. *HomU* 34. 201. 17 *eallum þam geleaffullum mannum þe ðær neah wæron on lociendum*; and an adverbial clause, e.g. *GD* 276. 15 *tolysdum þam limum swylce he dead wære* and *ÆCHom* ii. 260. 23 *geendodum weorcum swa swa he sylf wolde*. Callaway (1889, p. 21 n. (4)) points out that 'occasionally the A.S. absolute clause is incorrectly joined to the chief sentence by a conjunction'. His examples include *Or* 52. 17, above, where both *Se* and *ac* are superfluous, and *Matt(WSCp)* 17. 5 *Him þa gyt sprecendum 7 soþlice þa beorht wolcn hig oferscean*, where *7* is unnecessary. For examples governed by a preposition, see §§3811 and 3812.

§3821. Four examples with impersonal verbs are cited in §3808. All of them approach the anacoluthic; compare *Or* 244. 16 (§3808) with *Or* 232. 21 *Hit wæs þa swiþe ofþyncende þam oþrum consulum, Pompeiuse 7 Caton*. So the construction would not seem to be a natural idiom.

§3822. Those seeking more examples of dative/instrumental absolutes will find them in Callaway 1889, *passim*; Tilley, pp. 79–84; Wülfing, i, §§95 and 132; Scheler, pp. 70–8; and Visser, ii, §§1014 and 1150–1. Chase (*MLN* 8 (1893), 243–5) analyses the forty-four Latin ablative absolutes which are translated in the OE version of *ApT* and finds that only six are rendered by an absolute construction. I cannot understand why Helming (*MLN* 45 (1930), 175–8) calls her article 'The Absolute Participle in the *Apollonius of Tyre*'. She takes cognizance of only one of the six absolutes noted by Chase, whose article she does not mention.

§3823. There is room for more work on the relative order of the elements. Ahlgren (p. 184), whose examples are confined to those involving parts of the body, says that 'at first the participle generally preceded the noun, but later on it was frequently placed after the noun'. The only OE example he gives of the latter order is *Mark(Li)* 10. 17 *cneuo beged*, Latin *genu flexo*. My own impression is that the participle usually follows pronouns and indefinites—note *Bede* 284. 20 *eallum geseondum*, Latin *uidentibus cunctis*—but that, while the order noun + participle occasionally occurs in texts of all periods, there was a marked preference for the order participle + noun. An examination of those examples for which a Latin original has been traced suggests that there was also a strong tendency to follow its order. Confirmatory examples will be found above. Examples in which the Latin has noun + participle, the OE participle + noun, include *Bede* 184. 7 and 202. 14 (§3817), *Bede* 232. 22 *forðgongendre tide*, Latin *tempore autem procedente*, and *Mark(WSCp)* 1. 40 *gebigedum cneowum*, Latin *genu flexo*. But the reverse change is also attested, e.g. *Bede* 472. 30 *sumre neowre gefe lihtendre*, Latin *noua quadam relucente gratia*, *BenR* 10. 5 *Gode fultumigendum*, Latin *adiuvante Domino*, *BenR* 133. 16 *Gode fultumiendum*, Latin *adiuvante Christo* (but cf. *BenRGl* 118. 13 *fylstendum criste* and *ApT* 18. 18 *fultumiendum Gode*, Latin *deo favente* (but cf. *ApT* 14. 23 *gefultumigend Gode*, Latin *favente deo*)).

c. The functions

§3824. The functions of the dative absolute have been discussed by Callaway (1889, pp. 19-21) and Visser (ii. 1261-4). They include (in order of decreasing frequency) the expression of time, either contemporaneous with the action of the main verb, e.g. *ÆCHom* i. 294. 31 *þa mid þære bletsunge ferde he to heofonum, him on locigendum*, or prior to it, e.g. *ÆCHom* ii. 260. 23 *and on ðam seofoðan dæge hine sylfne gereste, geendodum weorcum* (see further Callaway, loc. cit.); of attendant circumstances or manner, e.g. *GD* 254. 36 *7 up arærdum þam sweorde swa wið þæs heofones se earm stod . . .*, *BenRGl* 10. 5 *Gode gefultumiandum* (cf. *BenR* 9. 7 *mid Godes fultume*), and *ÆCHom* i. 50. 30 *Stephanus soðlice gebigedum cneowum bæd þæt he Saulum alysde*; of cause, e.g. *GD* 247. 3 (§3810) and *ÆCHom* ii. 262. 11 *ac Crist aras . . . oferswiðdum deaðe* (see further Liggins 1955, pp. 459-62); of condition, e.g. *Bede* 176. 22 *Hæfde Oswald . . . nigon gear rice, togeteledum þy geare þe seo wildeorlice arleasnis Bretta cyninges . . . onscuniendlic wæs*; and of concession, e.g. *ÆCHom* i. 230. 12 *Nu cwyð eft se halga Gregorius þæt Cristes lichama com inn, beclysedum durum*. Callaway (loc. cit.) adds purpose, his sole example being *BenRGl* 71. 11, where *gehealdanra* appears to represent Latin *servata in omnibus parcitate*. The corresponding passage is *BenR* 64. 4 . . . *þæt forhæfednes . . . simble gehealden sy*.

d. Origin

§3825. Callaway (1889, pp. 36–46 and 51–2) offers a valuable treatment of 'the variety of methods available in A.S. for expressing the notions usually indicated by an absolute participial clause in other languages' (p. 36). They include subordinate and co-ordinate clauses, appositive nouns and participles, complementary adjectives, adverbs, infinitives, nouns in the dative (either alone or qualified by an adjective or participle), and prepositional phrases.[4] This tendency of OE to render the Latin ablative absolute by some construction other than an absolute, which is confirmed by Chase (my §3822) and by others, led Callaway (1889, p. 47) to the verdict that 'we have in A.S. an oligometochic language and in Greek and Latin polymetochic languages'. Callaway (1889, pp. 46–51 and 52) takes this to be the result of the failure of OE to naturalize the absolute participle and examines what he believes to be the effect on OE style of the substitution for an absolute of a prepositional phrase—'compact and at times felicitous' (p. 49)—of a co-ordinated finite verb—'monotonous; the sentence drags' (p. 49) . . . 'unwieldy . . . incapable of delicate shading' (p. 50)—or of a dependent sentence—'brevity and compactness are impossible; the sentence must be slow in movement and somewhat cumbersome' (p. 50). He concludes (p. 52): 'The language stood in sore need of a more flexible instrument for the notation of subordinate conceptions, of such an instrument as the absolute dative seemed capable of becoming but never became.'

§3826. Helming (my §3822) is less enthusiastic about the stylistic merits of participial constructions, urging that in *ApT* 'the independent statements of the Old English version . . . lend vigor and directness to the narrative' (p. 176) and suggesting that 'the use or non-use of the participial phrase seems to be a matter of temperament' (p. 177). We can, I think, agree that it is a question of taste whether one is (like Callaway) philometochic or (like Helming) misometochic. The problem is perhaps related to that of parataxis and hypotaxis (§§1683–9) and is one which students of OE style may find worth pursuing. But it must lead us to ask whether the facts stated by

---

[4] Amati (*passim*) gives for each of the four Gospels a list of Latin ablative absolutes (and of Latin constructions involving gerundives, infinitives, and participles not used absolutely) which are translated by clauses introduced by OE conjunctions.

Callaway (1889, p. 51) in the paragraph I quote in §3814 justify his conclusion that 'the absolute construction is not an organic idiom of the Anglo-Saxon language . . . was borrowed from the Latin . . . remained an alien to the last . . . was never naturalized in Anglo-Saxon' (p. 51) and that 'it failed to commend itself to our forefathers and never acquired a real hold in their language' (p. 30).

§3827. As Callaway (1889, pp. 22-4) points out, some early writers —including Grimm, Koch, Mätzner, and Owen—accepted, with varying degrees of commitment, the view that the absolute construction was a native Germanic idiom and was therefore native to OE. But Callaway lists others who preferred the view that the OE dative absolute was borrowed from Latin; among them were Erdmann, Hofer, Flamme, Einenkel, and possibly Napier. Callaway then discusses the question 'Which, then, of these two theories is to be adopted?' (pp. 24-31) and, as we have seen, reaches the answer that in OE it was a Latin borrowing. He held the same view for the Germanic languages in general (1889, pp. 31-6, and 1918, pp. 13-25). Many later scholars have accepted this conclusion, which Callaway repeated (1918, pp. 43-4), with the qualification that 'a secondary influence of native origin' was at work in the expressions with the prepositions *mið* (Nb.) or *be* (W-S) and possibly in those with a noun in the dative of the person interested plus a participle in the dative: Ahlgren (p. 184), Kellner (§410), Liggins (1955, pp. 460 and 533-4, and 1970, p. 315), Mossé (1945, §158(5)), Onions (§61c), QW (§111), and Terasawa (pp. 131-2).

§3828. Yet there have been uncommitted voices since Callaway wrote, including those of Wülfing (i. 147), Hirt (see Matsunami 1958, pp. 179-80, and Zadorožny 1974, p. 348), and Sweet (*Pr.* 8, p. 41): 'A past participle with a noun in the instrumental dative is used like the ablative absolute in Latin.' (Davis (*Pr.* 9, p. 47), in a reworded statement, has 'in imitation of' instead of 'like'.) There have even been dissentient voices. Scheler (pp. 80-1) expressed some reservation. Von Schaubert was not prepared to dismiss completely the possibility of some degree of native origin for her nominative and accusative absolutes (p. 181); see §3844. Visser (ii. 1261) also voiced doubts:

It is strange that no grammarian has as yet pointed out the improbability that authors like King Ælfred and Wærferth, when writing their translations, which were evidently in the first place, if not exclusively, meant for people who could not read Latin, should use a language profusely sprinkled with constructions unintelligible for their readers, and in this way consciously impair the clarity of their diction. So much is certain that Ælfric would not have used the absolute construction if it had a foreign tinge about it, since, in his Preface to *Genesis* (p. 24) he explicitly states that anyone who wants to translate Latin into English 'sceal gefadian hit swa þæt þæt Englisc hæbbe his agene wisan; elles hit biþ swiðe gedwolsum to rædenne þam þe þæs Ledenes wisan ne can.' The absolute construction, moreover, already occurs in the earliest part of the originally native O. E. Chronicle: anno 560, '*Idan forðgefarenum*'.

I had two reservations when I first read this: that *ChronA* 18. 2 (560) *Idan forðgefarenum* is a late addition and that the early translators may have had a greater reverence for the *form* of the Latin original than did Ælfric. Terasawa (pp. 131-2), reviewing Visser, offers a possible but perhaps not decisive counter to Visser's quotation from Ælfric—'But those people who did not know Latin might be more educated than we now suppose.' One of the four reasons Terasawa (ibid.) gives for his belief in Latin influence is this: 'There was a receptive factor for the Latin ablative absolute construction, since in OE the dative case absorbed some functions of the ablative case in Latin.' As we shall see, his countryman Matsunami draws a somewhat different conclusion from what appears to be the same point (1966*a*, p. 317): 'For example, it is now a truism to say that the dative absolute in OE originated in imitation of the Latin ablative absolute, but one very often overlooks the fact that the OE construction in the dative has basically something to be expanded into an absolute construction . . .'; see further Matsunami 1966*b*, pp. 71-2. Other dissenters will appear below.

§3829. Space does not permit a full rehearsal of the evidence for the contradictory views of native or Latin origin. But a few general considerations present themselves. First, one cannot pretend that no OE dative absolute is the direct result of imitation of Latin. Second, one must admit that there are, even in texts directly dependent on a Latin original, absolutes which are not paralleled in the Latin, e.g. *Gen* 14. 16 *gewunnenum sige* and *Or* 34. 1 *him ða ondrædendum þæm gebroðrum*, which represents the Latin appositive participle in *Or* 33. 29 *fratres veriti* (§3808); for more such examples see Callaway 1889, p. 21 nn. (1) and (2). Third, the fact that no OE examples like *Caesare duce* have so far been recorded—there is room for more work on the OE treatment of this pattern—might suggest that there was a native construction involving participles but that the combination of two nouns seemed unnatural. Fourth, as Scheler (p. 79) points out, the boundary between dative absolutes and adverbial datives—which, I suppose, are accepted as native—is a fine one, especially when it comes to constructions involving parts of the body;

see §§3810-11. Kellner (§410) and Onions (§61c) come close to hinting that two constructions, one native and one foreign, had been conflated. Even Callaway (1918, p. 44) spoke of 'a secondary influence of native origin'.

§3830. These are straws in the wind which suggest to me that it has perhaps been too easily assumed that the absolute construction had no native roots at all. Visser (ii. 1261) saw another; see my §3828. Matsunami (1966a, p. 316) claims that

Callaway is so ready to admit the superiority of Latin over OE whenever it is possible that, when he compares an OE translation with its Latin original, and finds a parallel passage between these two, he invariably concludes that the OE counterpart is an imitation of the Latin original pattern, and never asks himself how and why such and such a construction is syntactically possible in OE, even if it is coined after Latin

and goes on to say (pp. 316-17) of what he calls 'the native syntactic traits, together with the native syntactic trend' that 'there would be no grammatical borrowing without them, and foreign influence would not work independently of them in any way'. Dančev (1969, pp. 58-9) after quoting Visser (ii. 1261) says: 'It is obvious that no unequivocal decision concerning the origin of this construction seems possible, yet Visser's tacit admission that it may after all represent a native pattern seems plausible.' The figures given by Chase for *ApT* (my §3822) can be taken to demonstrate either that the foreign absolute construction 'failed to commend itself' and so 'remained an alien' to the author (Callaway 1889, pp. 30 and 51) or that the author did not like the native absolute construction. Callaway's attitude is that OE did not have an absolute construction of its own and that writers did not like it and so naturally did not regularly imitate it. One could, I suppose, reply with a question: If OE did have an absolute construction of its own, but native speakers and writers did not like it, what would be more natural than that it should appear only in translated texts and even there only spasmodically?

§3831. I cannot pursue this problem here. What is required is a much closer analysis, according to the classification suggested in §§3804-13, of the absolute constructions which do occur in OE, of the Latin absolutes which are rendered by OE absolutes, and of those which are not. Here I agree with Matsunami (1966b, p. 67): 'so far the formative process of the dative absolute has not been examined sufficiently'. He himself has some suggestive observations (1966b, pp. 71-4). Nothing may come of this. But it should, I believe, be done. If the verdict goes against Callaway, historians of later English may find it necessary to qualify the excellent 'Historical Note on the Absolute Participial Construction' given by Onions (§61c).

2. NOMINATIVE/ACCUSATIVE

§3832. Callaway (1889, pp. 2-3), after noting that in OE 'the normal absolute case is the dative' and that 'a few examples occur . . . of an absolute instrumental', went on to say that

instances occur, chiefly in the later MSS, of what may be termed a 'crude'[2] form of the absolute participle; by which it is meant that the participle shows a weathered, uninflected form that cannot be assigned to any definite case. That the participle is not a nominative or an instrumental is evident from the fact that the earlier MSS give the participle in the dative where the later ones show a 'crude' form, and that where we have but one MS the subject of the 'crude' participle is still a dative. The participle, then, while 'crude' in form, represents a dative of the earlier, unweathered stage of the language.

[2] The term is borrowed from Logeman, who uses it in his Rule of St. Benet (p. xxxix), though with a wider application than is here given to it.

His examples (pp. 6 and 12-14) include *Bede(Ca)* 38. 12 *eallum utagangende*, Latin *cunctis . . . egressis*, where MS *B* has *eallum utagangendum*; *Matt(WSH)* 17. 5 *hym . . . sprecende*, Latin *eo loquente*, where MS *Cp* has *him . . . sprecendum* but *sprecende* could be described as instrumental (§§3816 and 3837); and *Mark(WSH)* 5. 40 *ealle ut adrifene*, Latin *eiectis omnibus*, where MS *Cp* has *eallum ut adrifenum*. He offers more (1889, pp. 5-15). I presume his failure to cite *BlHom* 245. 3 *Đus gebiddende þam halgan Andrea, Drihtnes stefn wæs geworden on Ebreisc* was due to an oversight. On these 'crude' forms see further §3837. Callaway continued (p. 3): 'Lastly, it must be said that no clear example of an absolute participle in any other case than those mentioned occurs in Anglo-Saxon.' He apologetically qualified this later by admitting the existence of some nominative and accusative absolutes in *Gospels(Li)*, but insisted that both constructions were 'unknown in (the) West-Saxon' (1918, pp. 35 and 26). This verdict stood, as far as I know almost unchallenged, until von Schaubert began her work. Schrader (p. 20) saw an accusative absolute of age ('des Alters') in *ÆCHom* ii. 298. 6 *and [Philippus] gewat siððan, seofon and hundeahtatig geara, to ðam lifigendan Drihtne* (Schrader's punctuation). Thorpe omitted the commas, translating '. . . after eighty-seven years'. This seems right to me, though I have found no other examples of *siþþan* preposition. Ardern (§24e) saw the accusative used '?As Absolute case' in *CP*

9. 3 . . . *ne ða boc from ðæm mynstre: uncuð hu longe ðær swæ gelærede biscepas sien. . . .* There are two oddities about this: first, that I have always read it as [*hit is*] *uncuð* . . . , and second, that von Schaubert did not include this in her lists of examples (pp. 126-9); see §§ 3843 and 3874.

§ 3833. After some preliminary skirmishes (see her p. 8 fn. 7), von Schaubert produced her substantive work in 1954. It was on the whole favourably reviewed and subsequent writers, such as Visser (ii. 1075-6 and 1259-60) and Scheler (pp. 81-6), draw on it. The discussion which space permits here is short, follows von Schaubert in not treating the two cases in isolation, and cannot do justice to her discussions. Future editors must not neglect them. However, the more I study her work, the more convinced I become that she has not said the last word. She has not altogether escaped the besetting sins of the special investigator, viz. an eagerness to detect one's quarry in places where it is not and a tendency to indulge in special pleading to prove that it is; see below, *passim*. She is sometimes guilty of errors of interpretation. Thus, she blunders badly by taking *æfter* as a temporal conjunction, with *gefylde* as a finite verb, in *BlHom* 145. 22 *Æfter þyssum wordum gefylde, þa wæs Maria arisende* (pp. 123-4); see § 3813. (The first four words, J. E. Cross tells me, are an addition by the OE writer.) More work is needed on Callaway's 'crude' participles and on the alleged influence of Irish monks and their Gaul-derived Latin; see §§ 3832 and 3844 respectively. Keller's comment (*EStudies*, 38 (1957), 117) that 'at least $\frac{4}{5}$ of the abs. acc. are fixed formulas while the nominative construction is marked by greater freedom' is worth probing. Von Schaubert could have made it easier for her readers to understand that certain patterns recur in the examples which she interprets as nominative and/or accusative absolutes. And she is, in my opinion, far too ready to classify such examples as 'certain' or 'sure'—her word is 'sicher'. As Reed (*MLQ* 17 (1956), 175)—with unintentional irony—put it, 'happily enough, such efforts to lay the material on a Procrustean bed are strikingly fortunate'. Keller's review (*EStudies*, 38 (1957), 116) contained these words: 'And while many of the individual instances are undoubtedly open to different interpretations the whole bulk of material here gathered together is formidable evidence.'

§ 3834. In an attempt to answer the question 'Evidence for what?', I begin with a Table.

TABLE of nominative and/or accusative absolutes
listed by von Schaubert (pp. 126–9)

Text	Certain			Totals	Possible			Totals
	Nom.	Nom. or acc.	Acc.		Nom.	Nom. or acc.	Acc.	
Mart	1			1	1			1
BlHom	5	2	2	9				
CP	1		1	2				
Bede		3		3	1		1	2
VercHom						1		1
Gospels(Li)	11	11	20	42	2	4	1	7
Gospels(Ru)	9	3	8	20	1			1
RitGl		3	18	21		1		1
LS 23	4	1		5				
ÆCHom	1			1				
ÆLS		2		2				
BenRGl	1	3[5]	2	6				
BenR					1			1
RegCGl		1		1				
Gospels(WS)							1	1
Prose Totals	33	29	51	113	6	6	3	15
Poetry	12	6[5]	2	20	3			3
Hymns and Psalters	8	2[5]	1	11				
Grand Totals	53	37	54	144	9	6	3	18

§3835. These examples come largely from texts of Anglian origin or texts with Anglian elements; see §3844. The majority represent Latin ablative absolutes; see §3844. They perform the same functions in the sentence as OE dative/instrumental absolutes; see §3824, Callaway 1918, pp. 39–42, von Schaubert, pp. 171–2, and Liggins 1955, pp. 458–9 (my §3172). Lack of space makes it impossible for me to discuss them all.

§3836. Of the 144 examples which von Schaubert (pp. 126–9) classified as 'certain' ('sichere Fälle'), 62 come from Gospel glosses, 28 from other glosses, and 11 from glosses to Hymns and Psalters which

[5] These figures each include one example classified by von Schaubert as accusative or nominative.

von Schaubert, for a reason which escapes me, classifed as 'poetry'. Some indeed do seem 'certain'. They include (with a nominative absolute in OE) *BenRGl* 118. 5 . . . *mid rihtum rine we becumende to urum scyppende*, Latin . . . *ut recto cursu perveniamus ad creatorem nostrum*, where von Schaubert (p. 71) offers a cogent objection to Callaway's emendation (1889, pp. 14–15); (with a singular nominative absolute in the Latin and OE equivalents which could be nominative or accusative) *Ps(A)* 114. 5 *haldende cild dryhten geeaðmodad ic eam*, Latin *custodiens paruulos dominus humiliatus sum* (on this ambiguity of the ending -*e* in present participles, see § 1439); (with two OE pronouns, one nominative and one accusative, plus a present participle in -*e*, representing a Latin ablative absolute) *Matt(Li)* 6. 3 ðu ł ðeh . . . *wyrcende*, Latin *te . . . faciente*, and *Mark(Li)* 5. 35 *hine* ł *he sprecende*, Latin *eo loquente*, where *WSCp* has *him . . . sprecendum* and *Ru he sprecende*; (with OE plural forms which inevitably can be either nominative or accusative) *Ps(A)* 118. 157 (§ 3844), where the Latin has a nominative absolute, *Mark(Li)* 3. 23 7 *efne geceigdo ða ilco* ł *miððy geceigd weron ða ilco*, Latin *conuocatis eis*, where a clause is given as an alternative rendering for the Latin ablative absolute, and *PsCa* 6. 12. 2 *liomu tolesde*, where the Latin has an accusative absolute *artus solutos*; (with OE forms which might be nominative or accusative, singular or plural) *Matt(Li)* 27. 29 *cnew gebeged*, Latin *genu flexu*; (with OE ðec plus a present participle in -*e* representing a Latin ablative absolute) *DurRitGl* 103 ðec *scildende*, Latin *te protegente*, and the similar examples from the same text quoted by von Schaubert (p. 110); and (with OE hine plus a present participle in -*e* representing a Latin ablative absolute) *Matt(Li)* 9. 18 ðas hine *sprecende*, Latin *haec illo loquente*, where the other versions have a *þa* clause with pret. sg. *spræc*, and *John(Li)* 8. 30 ðas hine *spreccende* ł *miððy he uæs sprecende*, Latin *haec illo loquente*, where again the glossator offers a clause as an alternative. But others seem less certain. They include, not only the nine from Gospel glosses and the one from *DurRitGl* which von Schaubert lists as 'possible', but also some which she calls 'certain'. Thus, I agree that the OE participles are nominative in *Matt(Ru)* 2. 21 *he arisende soþlice iosep genom þone cneht*, Latin *qui surgens accepit puerum*, and in *Matt(Ru)* 8. 10 *geherende he þa hælend wundriende wæs*, Latin *audiens autem Iesus miratus est*. But are they absolute? See von Schaubert, pp. 98–9 and 170–1, but my § 3838. Again, I do not know what justifies her claim (pp. 119–20) that *bewende* in *Luke(WSCp)* 9. 55 *And hine bewende he hig þreade* and the variant *bewend* in *WSB* and *WSC* are accusatives; one might expect ☆*bewendne*. *WSH* has 7 *he bewente hine* 7 *hyo þreatede* for the Latin *et conuersus increpauit illos*. So *bewende* might be a preterite. This

is not an isolated instance. Indeed, von Schaubert's attitude to forms
of both the present and second participles demands consideration.

§3837. In her discussion (pp. 120-6) of Callaway's 'crude forms'
(my §3832), where she accepts Callaway's explanation for the examples from *Gospels(WSH)* but asserts that the rest of his examples
demand a different appraisal, von Schaubert seems to me somewhat
inconsistent. She calls in scribal error to explain examples which include *Bede(B)* 310. 21 *ætgædere mid hine sittende oðrum bisceopum,*
Luke(Ru) 8. 45 *ne sæccende ðonne allum*, Latin *negantibus autem*
omnibus, where *Li* has *onsæccendum ðonne allum*, and *ChronE*
225. 15 (1090) *Ðissum þus gedon*. She admits *-e* as an alternative for
dat. *-um* in *Bede(T)* 288. 14 *hwelcum teonde, Mark(Ru)* 14. 43 *him*
sprecende, Latin *eo loquente*, and *ChronE* 218. 35 (1086) and 222.
13 (1086) *Ðis(s)um þus gedone*. Here see §3816. I have already rejected her explanation of *BlHom* 145. 22 (§3833). It must in my
opinion be a matter of individual interpretation whether in *Matt(Ru)*
28. 13 *us slepende*, Latin *nobis dormientibus*, we have an accusative
-e or a dative *-e* for *-um*; *WSCp* has *ða we slepun* and *Li us slependum*.
A consideration of examples like *Mark(Li)* 3. 35 *hine ł he sprecende*,
Latin *eo loquente, Mark(Li)* 14. 43 *him ł hine sprecende*, Latin *eo*
loquente, and *Matt(Li)* 12. 46 *hine ł he spræcc ł spræcend*, Latin *eo*
loquente, suggests to me that sometimes at any rate the glossator
may have been glossing each word in turn rather than the Latin construction as a whole. If so, the OE pronouns and participles had little
if any real case significance. This is not carelessness, but merely a
natural way of doing it; see §§1777-81. Thus, in *Matt(Li)* 9. 27 *7*
geongende ł ða geeode ðona ðe hælend, Latin *Et transeunte inde*
Iesu, we cannot be sure whether *geongende* is an isolated form or
a nominative with *ðe hælend*, parallel to *ða geeode*, even though we
have to admit that the glossator sometimes gives two complete constructions as alternatives, e.g. *Mark(Li)* 3. 23 and *John(Li)* 8. 30; see
§3836. (Von Schaubert (pp. 168-9) sees examples like these two as
a concession by the glossator to the W-S literary koine. One is perhaps entitled to ask why this concession was not extended to other
Northumbrian constructions and indeed forms. To Callaway (1918,
p. 34), their existence 'further attests the ungenuineness of the
absolute construction'.) Von Schaubert (p. 54) quotes from Callaway
(1918, pp. 1-2) the following passage, which can be compared with
his 1889 statement (my §3832): 'At times, . . . , the form of substantive or of participle (occasionally of both) is indefinite; and we have
what may be termed "crude" forms of substantive or of participle
(or of both); that is, a weathered form that cannot with certainty be

assigned to any definite case, but that usually represents an unweathered dative-instrumental.' But later she is content with the
phrase 'a weathered form that cannot with certainty be assigned to
any definite case' (p. 121) as a definition of a 'crude' form. This at
any rate does not do justice to what Callaway said (1889, pp. 2-3,
and 1918, pp. 1-2). Space does not permit fuller consideration of the
points made by von Schaubert (*passim*, especially pp. 120-6 and
165-70). But I conclude with four observations. First, I do not
believe that the notion of crude forms can be completely dismissed.
It is at least consistent with the general reduction in inflexional endings. Second, I do believe that, while Callaway's suggestion (1918,
p. 36) that in the nominative absolute 'the nominative is due to
contamination, or, better, to the mixture of two constructions'—
'the glossator wavering in his rendering of the absolute participle of
the Latin between a finite verb, which requires a nominative as its
subject, and an absolute participle, which requires an oblique case'
(ibid., p. 38)—is certainly not true for all examples, it may well hold
for at least some of the examples in the glosses, to which it was of
course restricted. Third, it is a pity that Callaway (1918, pp. 26-30)
did not leave well alone after citing six other constructions in which
Northumbrian preferred the accusative where West-Saxon had the
dative and then saying that 'there seems to have been an interchange
of the accusative and the dative in Northumbrian that is unknown in
West-Saxon; of which interchange the accusative absolute offers the
most striking illustration'. This clearly did not imply accusative/
dative syncretism in the personal pronouns, of which there is no
mention in *OEG*, §§569 fn. 1 and 702-3. But he then went on to
talk loosely of syncretism elsewhere and so laid himself open to a
just rebuke by von Schaubert (pp. 165-7). Fourth, Callaway (1918,
p. 1) says that in *Li* 'we find . . . the accusative and, apparently, the
nominative used absolutely'. Von Schaubert (*passim*) agrees and
extends this verdict to the other glosses cited in the Table in §3834.
This view depends on the assumption that the glossator was consciously rendering a Latin absolute construction into OE or was
deliberately imitating one, that he was not glossing piecemeal or
mechanically putting down a remembered formula. I am not convinced that this has been proven. So at the moment I would submit
that the glosses cannot be used to support the proposition that either
the nominative absolute or the accusative absolute was idiomatic or
natural in OE speech or writing.

§3838. Here we must leave the glosses; for more on them, see Callaway 1918, pp. 25-39 and 40, and von Schaubert, pp. 49-59, 62-3,

71, 77–100, 104–5, and 109–26. When we eliminate the examples von Schaubert found in them, we are left with twenty-three 'certain' and five 'possible' examples from the prose texts and twenty 'certain' and three 'possible' from the poetry. Seven of those from the prose —three from *LS* 23, two from *BlHom*, and two from *ÆLS* 31—do seem convincing: two nominative absolutes, both of which follow the Latin source, viz. *LS* 23. 672 and 685 *Zosimus wundrigende . . . heo ongann of þam wættrum clypigan* (von Schaubert, pp. 62–3); two nominative or accusative absolutes for which no Latin source has yet been found, viz. *BlHom* 31. 19 and, with uninflected *gecweden*, *BlHom* 247. 8 *And þa gecweden þæt wæter oflan* (von Schaubert, pp. 63–4); and three nominative or accusative absolutes which represent a Latin ablative absolute, viz. *LS* 23. 610 *Ac þas þincg ealle þus oncnawenne far ham mid sibbe* and two from MS Bodley 343 in which the Cotton manuscript printed by Skeat has a dative absolute, viz. *ÆLS(B)* 31. 455 and 505 (von Schaubert, pp. 53, 55–6, and 59). Six more—three from *BlHom*, two from *LS* 23, and one from *Mart 2*—produce problems of terminology rather than interpretation. In *BlHom* 245. 30 *And þus cweþende fyren wolc astah of heofonum*, where *cweþende* refers to *BlHom* 245. 27 *Se haliga Andreas . . .* , we have what I would call an unattached or dangling participle rather than an absolute (Callaway 1889, p. 10, and von Schaubert, p. 64); cf. 'Walking down the street, the church came into view.' In the other five, I detect an OE appositive participle and a tautologic nominative pronoun; cf. *BlHom* 245. 23 *Mid þi [þe] he þus cwæð, se eadiga Andreas . . .* and Visser, ii. 1076. They are *Mart 2(B)* 84. 18 (von Schaubert, p. 59, but note the variant readings); *BlHom* 245. 7 and 16, both of which read *Se haliga Andreas þa lociende he geseah* (von Schaubert, pp. 64–5); *LS* 23. 549 (von Schaubert, p. 61); and, with a tautologic *and* unless we emend to *gehyr(e)de*, *LS* 23. 586 *Zosimus þa witodlice gehyrende þæt heo þæra haligra boca cwydas forðbrohte . . . and he hire to cwæð . . .* (von Schaubert, p. 60). These are comparable with *Matt(Ru)* 2. 21 and 8. 10; see §3836. But, despite von Schaubert (pp. 170–1) and Quirk (*Speculum*, 31 (1956), 214), I would not call them 'absolutes'.

§3839. Seven examples I cannot rate as 'certain' for the reasons given (the page numbers refer to von Schaubert): *CP* 93. 6 (pp. 65–6: a possible anacoluthon); *CP* 101. 13 (pp. 105–6: here we have evidence that *astigan*, like *oferstigan*, can take an accusative); *BlHom* 23. 2 (p. 74: I refuse to believe that *send* is not for *synd* 'are'); *BlHom* 115. 30 (pp. 107–8: in view of *BlHom* 123. 10, I suspect that *ahof on* lies behind MS *ahafen*); *BlHom* 179. 33 (pp. 106–7: the

Latin supports the emendation suggested in Morris's *Glossary*); *BlHom* 245. 9 (p. 57: the presence of prep. *on*); and *ÆCHom* i. 338. 5 (pp. 72-3: this could be described as a loosely appositional and summarizing use of a familiar formula). The remaining three examples are from *Bede*. Even if we accept von Schaubert's interpretation of *Bede* 140. 11 (pp. 69-71) against that of Miller, what she takes as an accusative absolute must be construed as the object of *aðwog*. But it makes an awkward sentence and *timbrede* seems unlikely to be a participle. The Latin has no absolute. In *Bede* 302. 27 von Schaubert (pp. 66-7) prefers the reading of MS *T weaxende*, although the other manuscripts have *wæcende* for Latin *inuadens*. In the third, I see sense in the original reading of *O*, viz. *Bede(O)* 318. 18 *7 þonne heo ærest þurh hyre þegnunge 7 hyre þinenna þa oþre Cristes þeowas þa þe þær wæron onþwegene wæron, þonne wolde heo eallra nyhst hi baþian 7 þwean*, taking the first *heo* as a tautologic nominative plural, as von Schaubert (pp. 68-9) suggests, but retaining the first *wæron*, now struck through, to avoid the awkward absolute.

§3840. No new point of principle emerges from a study of von Schaubert's five 'possible' prose examples; again the numbers refer to her pages. Two resemble *LS* 23. 586 (§3838), viz. *Bede* 450. 20 (p. 76) and *Mart 1* 8. 19 (pp. 76-7: here Herzfeld's emendation is simple and satisfying). Emendation is also possible in *VercHom* 2. 86 (pp. 75-6: von Schaubert's reading seems to have a superfluous *7*). In *Bede* 480. 18, MS *C* has a dative absolute. Von Schaubert's claim (pp. 108-9) for priority for the readings of *B* and *Ca*, which can be interpreted as accusative absolutes, seems special pleading. All manuscripts seem to have a superfluous *7*. In *BenR* 47. 12 (pp. 60-1), we have an anacoluthon, a clumsy change from pl. *hy* to sg. *gehwylc*, easily understandable in view of the Latin.

§3841. Von Schaubert's three 'possible' examples in the poetry— I exclude her examples from glosses; see my §3836—are *Beo* 31, *GenA* 2482a, and *Ex* 501a. All are familiar cruces. My general view concerning her twenty 'certain' examples (pp. 126-7, 8-49, and 100-4) is that her enthusiasm overcame her discretion; cf. here the comments of Keller (*EStudies*, 38 (1957), 116-17), Matsunami (1966b, pp. 67-71), and Quirk (*Speculum*, 31 (1956), 214). Those on which I am most ready to bestow the label 'certain' are *Jul* 412a, where some emend *mod* to *mode*, and *KtPs* 51, which is not Anglian (Ker, pp. 268-9, and my §3844) and which, despite von Schaubert (p. 127), could be nominative or accusative. We could get around these by supplying present subjunctive forms of a copula verb to give parenthetic exclamatory wishes. There is no justification for such a solution. However, 'ellipsis' of a preterite form of a copula verb is possible in *Beo* 2035, *GenA* 183a (so Callaway 1889, p. 17), and *Dan* 475a; on this see §3865. I see straightforward examples of nominative variation with a verb understood from a preceding clause in *GuthA* 743b (Roberts does not mention von Schaubert here or at *GuthB* 1038a (§3842)), *Phoen* 79a–80a, and *Rid* 53. 3a.

§3842. The ASPR punctuation offers a satisfactory non-absolute explanation for *GenB* 319b–20a ([*man*] from *GenB* 318a); *El* 1134b–35a ([*wæs*] from *El* 1131b); *GuthB* 1038a (*dæg* an 'endingless locative' (*OEG*, §572), *scripende* attributive (Callaway 1889, p. 18)); *Rim* 9b and *Ruin* 5a–6a (parallel participles); *Rid* 56. 3a (appositional variant of expressed object. Craig Williamson does not mention von Schaubert here or at *Rid* 53. 3a (§3841)); *KtPs* 97a (reinterpretation of manuscript reading. Despite Matsunami's strictures (1966a, pp. 315–16), Callaway (1889, p. 18) was on the right track here); and *Beo* 2106a and *And* 915a (compounds). A compound *waldendwyrhtan* is acceptable in *Ruin* 7 (Robinson, *NM* 67 (1966), 363).

§3843. If we accept *Beo* 936a *wea widscofen* as parenthetic, we can supply *wæs*; cf. §3865. But the emendation *gehwylcum* gives an appositional explanation of the preceding sentence; cf. *CP* 9. 3 (§3832) and *Beo* 1343a. I am not satisfied with any of the explanations of *GenA* 869 and suspect corruption. Here I shudder to think what A. E. Housman would have said of Keller's comment (*EStudies*, 38 (1957), 117): 'Her interpretations sound particularly attractive as no textual emendations are necessary.' Von Schaubert's ingenious tenacity in defence of manuscript readings in both prose and poetry ranks high among her faults.

§3844. Von Schaubert (pp. 130–58 and 158–65) discusses the dialect of her examples and confirms Callaway's view (my §3832) that nominative and accusative absolutes are not idiomatic in West-Saxon, arguing that they are confined to texts of Anglian origin or to texts with an Anglian element. Scheler (pp. 86–8 and p. 131 n. 328) and Gneuss (*Hymnar und Hymnen im englischen Mittelalter* (Tübingen, 1968), 161–3) offer qualifications in respect of certain manuscripts. Callaway (1918, p. 43) saw the examples in *Gospels(Li)* not as 'a native Northumbrian idiom, but . . . due to Latin influence'. All his accusative absolutes and nine of his ten nominative absolutes represent a Latin ablative absolute (pp. 34 and 36). So it was not unreasonable for him to claim that 'the absolute construction is due to the Latin influence' (p. 34). But he sought the explanation for the case, not in Latin but in OE, attributing the use of the accusative to a Northumbrian preference for it rather than for the dative (my §3837) and the use of the nominative to a mixture of two constructions (my §3837). Von Schaubert's discussion of her examples (pp. 170-81) results in the cautious conclusion that, while the possibility of native development cannot be ruled out, the probability of Latin influence must not be lost sight of. But why, she asks (p. 182), would it occur only in Anglian if it were a native development? She does not find psychological or stylistic reasons satisfying; but see Scheler, pp. 86-7. Her own suggestion (pp. 182-8) is that the Anglian predilection for nominative and accusative absolutes was the result of the influence of Irish monks who got from Gaul a Latin in which these constructions were widespread. Keller (*EStudies*, 38 (1957), 118) is attracted by this idea but argues that it would 'definitely point to Latin influence in the formation of the construction. This is a point the author does not make.' One of the reasons for this failure may be the fact that the percentage of nominative and accusative absolutes in the relevant Latin material is comparatively small. Callaway (1918, pp. 34 and 36) reports that the Latin has no examples relevant for *Gospels(Li)*. Von Schaubert's own figures show that of the 102 Latin absolutes which she says are represented by OE nominative or accusative absolutes, 17 are nominative or accusative and 85 ablative, i.e. one in six or 16.6 per cent. This gives her 12 per cent of her total—17 of 141. (I can only presume that this last figure excludes the three examples noted in my §3836 fn.) For the details see von Schaubert, pp. 170-1. Of these seventeen examples the most interesting to me is *Ps(A)* 118. 157 *monge oehtende mec 7 swencende mec from cyðnissum ðinum ic ne onhaelde* (von Schaubert, pp. 50-1). The absolutes here represent the Latin of the Roman Psalter *Multi persequentes me et tribulantes me a testimoniis tuis non declinaui*. But the Gallican Psalter has two co-ordinate clauses! It reads *Multi qui persecuntur me et tribulant me a testimoniis tuis non declinaui*. The OE version of this in *Ps(K)* 118. 157 *monige þa ehttende min 7 swencende me of cyþnesse þinum na ic ahylde* does not suggest marked grammatical alertness on the part of the glossator.

§3845. I can spare neither the time nor the space for the further work which is so obviously necessary here. It would be idle to deny that some OE nominative and accusative absolutes are direct renderings of Latin equivalents. But I would say that the evidence so far presented does not argue for Latin originals riddled with nominative and accusative absolutes. Indeed, it is arguable that it is not incompatible with

Callaway's notion that, while the use of an absolute construction is due to Latin influence, the reasons for the use of the nominative and accusative must sometimes be sought in the mind of the OE glossator or writer.

3. GENITIVE?

§3846. The only two proposed OE genitive absolutes known to me —*ChronD* 137. 4 (1006) *7 þær onbidedon beotra gylpa* and *Ch* 1447 . . . *7 wende Æðelstan hine eft into Sunnanbyrg ungebetra þinga*—were both dismissed by Callaway (1889, pp. 8-9), who classified them as genitives of manner. The latter, which Callaway saw as 'more nearly approaching an absolute clause' was revived by Carlton (1970, pp. 86-7 and 159), who translated 'things (being) unatoned'. Robertson proposed 'without making amends'. I believe Callaway to be right about this example; see my §§1391-4. For the former, Plummer, in his note on the passage, followed Earle, with the translation 'out of mere bravado', despite Callaway's rejection of Earle's comment that 'it is a genuine Saxon idiom = *out of insolent bravado*. It is a sort of genitive absolute . . .', and, referring to Callaway's view that the absolute participle in OE is 'a mere exotic imported from the Latin', said that 'this is certainly true of the dative absolute. I do not think it is true of the genitive absolute.' Both Garmonsway and Whitelock agree that *beotra gylpa* is the genitive object of *onbidedon*, the former translating 'and there awaited the great things that had been threatened'. This is clearly right. On the evidence available to me, I conclude that the genitive absolute had no existence in OE.

C. OTHER INDEPENDENT ELEMENTS

1. INTERJECTIONS AND THE NOMINATIVE OF DIRECT ADDRESS

§3847. These may be used alone or in combination, e.g. *Coll* 34 *Hig! Hig! micel gedeorf ys hyt, Coll* 35 *Geleof, micel gedeorf hit ys, Coll* 37 *Gea, leof, ic hæbbe*, and *Coll* 44 *Eala, hlaford min, micel ic gedeorfe*. Initial position is not obligatory, e.g. *ÆCHom* ii. 104. 16 *Hwæt do ic la, nu ic næbbe hwær ic mæge ealle mine wæstmas gegaderian?* and *Coll* 1 *We cildra biddaþ þe, eala lareow, þæt þu tæce us sprecan. . . .* For fuller discussion of these topics see §§1234-9 and 1242-7.

2. PARENTHESES

§3848. PG's definition of a parenthesis is 'a word or expression interpolated in a sentence (between commas, dashes, etc.) without being essential or necessary for the grammatical completeness of the sentence'. This is imprecise; in the sentence of forty-two words beginning *ÆCHom* i. 2. 12 *Ic Ælfric . . .* , only *Ic . . . wearð asend* are 'essential or necessary for the grammatical completeness of the sentence'. Krapp (1905, p. 33) says that he has included in his examination of 'the parenthetic exclamation in Old English poetry' 'only real parentheses, that is, sentences which are inserted as independent additions between the syntactical elements of other sentences'. Andrew (*Postscript*, pp. 63-5) is even more precise:

In the first place, it seems obvious that, since the parenthesised clause is fenced off at both ends, it should be a self-contained principal sentence. . . . In the second place, it also seems obvious that the parenthesis must definitely interrupt the main sentence . . . and not stand in a possible syntactical relation to it. . . . It seems to be a necessary corollary of the second rule that the parenthesis should not interrupt the main sentence unduly, i.e. to the extent of causing the hearers to lose the thread of it.

Three qualifications are necessary. First, 'a self-contained principal sentence' may embrace a complex sentence, e.g.

Beo 1002   No þæt yðe byð
      to befleonne   —fremme se þe wille—
      ac gesecan sceal. . . .

Second, the idea of grammatical independence is, I believe, the key one. But it must not be interpreted as admitting sentences which are in asyndetic parataxis and not in parenthesis, e.g. (as Krapp 1905, p. 33, notes) *bord up ahof* in *Ex* 253 or *holm gerymed* in

Ex 283   Wegas syndon dryge
      haswe herestræta,   holm gerymed,
      ealde staðolas.

Third, Anglo-Saxon hearers were trained to oral delivery and so would be less likely 'to lose the thread' than modern scholars might suspect; see Krapp 1905, p. 37, and Mitchell 1963a, p. 128. Thus, I have suggested that *Beo* 323b-27a could be parenthetic (Mitchell 1980a, p. 406) and Andrew himself glances at the possibility of a twelve-line parenthesis in *Beo* 1573-84 (*Postscript*, p. 66) but describes it as 'more than doubtful'. I agree about this particular example, where I see *Beo* 1588b-90a as a possible parenthesis (Mitchell 1980a, p. 406). But we must not be too cavalier in dismissing the possibility of longish parentheses in the poetry.

§3849. The parenthetic use in the prose of such expressions as *ic cwæþ/cwæþ he* has already been illustrated in §1949. Other verbs can be similarly used, e.g. *ÆCHom* ii. 310. 6 *Beorh ðe, ic bidde, and forlæt ðone biscop, ÆLS* 31. 1085 *Sege me, ic þe axige, gif þu æfre wære oððe on gefeohte oþþe on ænigum truman?*, and *ÆCHom* i. 2. 17 *þa bearn me on mode, ic truwige þurh Godes gife, þæt ic ðas boc of Ledenum gereorde to Engliscre spræce awende*; cf. *ÆC Hom* ii. 594. 22 . . . *we truwiað þurh Godes diht*, which is an after-thought which ends the sentence. The extra-metrical *cweþ he* in *Finn* 24 *Sigeferþ is min nama, cweþ he, ic eom Secgena leod* is described in Dickins's note as 'the only instance in AS. [poetry] of the parenthetical "said he", so common in Hildebrand and the Heliand'. The repeated phrase *Salomon/Saturnus cwæð* in *MSol* is extra-metrical but not parenthetical.

§3850. The formula *swelce he cwæde* appears as a translation of what Nevanlinna (*NM* 75 (1974), 570) calls 'hypothetical parenthetic expressions with *dicere*'. She discusses and illustrates the Latin and OE constructions (pp. 570-1). Her examples include *CP* 71. 12 *Ne gegripe eow næfre nan costung buton menniscu. Suelce he openlice cuæde: Mennisclic is ðæt mon on his mode costunga ðrowige on ðæm luste yfles weorces*, Latin . . . *ac si aperte diceret* . . . , *CP* 61. 22 . . . *suelce him mon to cueðe* . . . , Latin . . . *quasi specialiter dicitur* . . . , and *ÆCHom* i. 222. 27 . . . *swilce he swa cwæde*, Latin . . . *ac si aperte dicat*. But it is doubtful whether the expression meets the test of complete grammatical independence.

§3851. The same is true of the naming constructions discussed in §§1473-81, e.g. (in the prose) *Or* 70. 8 and *ÆCHom* ii. 96. 19 (both in §1475; on the status of *his* in the latter, see Mitchell 1980*a*, pp. 389-90) and (in the poetry) *Beo* 102 and

Beo 1455   Næs þæt þonne mætost   mægenfultuma,
                      þæt him on ðearfe lah   ðyle Hroðgares;
                      wæs þæm hæftmece   Hrunting nama;
                      þæt wæs an foran   ealdgestreona,

in both of which Andrew (*Postscript*, p. 65) detects a parenthesis.

§3852. I suspect that further work may reveal more parentheses as defined by Krapp and by Andrew (my §3848) in the prose than have so far been recorded. Thus, of the three examples of parenthetical adversative clauses noted by Burnham (p. 99), one is from Ælfric's alliterative prose, viz. *ÆLS* 21. 266 *wæs swaðeah unscyldig*, and the other two are from *LS* 34 (*Seven Sleepers*), viz. 233 *hæfde mid him þeah eaþelicne fodan* and 491 *þeah na swiðe embe þæt ne smeade* (or is this a subordinate clause?). See further Liggins 1970, p. 310. However, parentheses are certainly more characteristic of the poetry.

§3853. Schücking (pp. 135-9), Krapp (1905, pp. 33-5), and Andrew (*Postscript*, pp. 63-6), all give lists of examples from *Beowulf*. According to Krapp (p. 35) 'there can hardly be any question that to place an exclamatory parenthesis in the first half-line, at least in the earlier periods, was felt to be bad style'. Krapp (p. 34) regards *Beo* 3056a—*he is manna gehyld*—as 'the only one certain example' in *Beowulf* but 'probably a late addition'; he is loath to accept *Beo* 2778a and *Beo* 3115a. This point is worth pursuing.

§3854. A comparison of the three lists reveals how personal is the idea of what constitutes a parenthesis. Schücking and Krapp both include *Beo* 1422b —*folc to sægon*—, which Andrew excludes. Krapp admits *Beo* 18b —*blæd wide sprang*—, which Schücking excludes and Andrew suspects. Schücking admits *Beo* 1746b —*him bebeorgan ne con*—, which Krapp excludes and Andrew specifically disallows. Only Andrew admits *Beo* 102 and 1457 (my §3851). Krapp documents editorial disagreement about certain passages. Schücking records marked disagreement between himself and Sarrazin. None of these writers mentions *Beo* 2297b-9a (Mitchell 1980*a*, p. 406, but §3865). Such differences of opinion are relevant to my suggestion (Mitchell 1980*a*, pp. 405-6) that marks of broken parenthesis (−− . . . −−) be used to indicate possible parentheses.

§3855. Schücking (pp. 135-9) divides his parentheses into six groups, according to their function. First, there are those which come between a word meaning 'to speak' and the beginning of the speech. These can describe the speaker's appearance or mood, e.g. *Beo* 405b —*on him byrne scan . . .*— and *Beo* 2043b —*him bið grim sefa*—; give new information about him, e.g. *Beo* 348b —*þæt wæs Wendla leod . . .*—; or direct our attention to the audience, e.g. *Beo* 1699b —*swigedon ealle*—. The remaining five groups, which are not connected with verbs of speaking, perform the following functions: tell us something about a character, e.g. *Beo* 1537b —*nalas for fæhðe mearn*—; introduce a digressive consideration, e.g. *Beo* 1003b —*fremme se þe wille*—; describe another event going on (more or less) contemporaneously, e.g. *Beo* 1317b —*healwudu dynede*—; give the cause of the action being described, e.g. *Beo* 423b —*wean ahsodon*— (cf. here Schaar's discussion (pp. 153-72) of 'causal parataxis'); or may merely act as a line-filler, e.g. *Beo* 55b —*fæder ellor hwearf, ǁ aldor of earde*—, which follows close on the long description of Scyld's departure in *Beo* 26–52.

§3856. I am inclined to see the *swa* clause in

GenA 1564   . . .   and him selfa sceaf
                reaf of lice   swa gerysne ne wæs
                læg þa limnacod

as *apo koinou* rather than parenthetical. But see Liggins 1970, p. 310, and Quirk, p. 111.

§3857. More work is needed here. Anyone embarking on it should note that Krapp (1905, pp. 33–7) gives what he apparently intended to be a complete list of parentheses in the more important (or familiar) OE poems. Inevitably there is room for difference of opinion, but not with his observation (p. 37) that 'it may be said, in conclusion, that the parenthetic exclamatory sentence is a consistently used and persistent element of the Old English poetic style . . .'.

D. 'ELLIPSIS' OR IDIOMATIC NON-EXPRESSION OF SENTENCE ELEMENTS

1. INTRODUCTORY REMARKS

§3858. I have been reluctant to use the time-dishonoured term 'ellipsis' because of my uncertainty about the meaning it might convey and because of the laxness with which it has been defined. Guest (*TPS* 1844, p. 217), who observed that 'an ellipsis is commonly said to be the omission of some word or words *necessary* to the construction of a sentence' but who, as we shall see, qualified this definition, went on to remark that 'the mischiefs arising from indefinite terms may perhaps be less than those which result from definitions so loose and general'. Most definitions of 'ellipsis' include the word 'omission' or 'omit' and seem capable of covering everything from the syntactical devices of skilled stylists to the ungrammatical ramblings of the illiterate, from idiomatic non-expression or non-repetition of a word or phrase to unheeding carelessness by those who know no better. Guest (ibid.) inclined to the second of these two alternatives: 'It might perhaps be more satisfactory to call it a defective mode of expression, substituted for and originating in one more perfect.' The *OED* definition almost embraces both: 'The omission of one or more

words in a sentence, which would be needed to complete the grammatical construction or fully to express the sense.' Gowers (*Modern
English Usage*, 2nd edn.) did not improve Fowler's article on ellipsis
by adding the sentence '*Ellipsis* means the omission from a sentence
of words needed to complete the construction or the sense.' Other
writers, while clinging to 'omission' or 'omit', have not agreed that
'ellipsis' implies a failure to express the sense. They include Fowler
himself (ibid.); Onions (p. 4): 'Ellipsis plays a great part in English.
In poetical and rhetorical language it often lends dignity and impressiveness, with something of an archaic flavour; to colloquial speech
it gives precision and brevity, and saves time and trouble'; and Pei
and Gaynor: 'ellipsis: (1) The omission of a word or words considered essential for grammatical completeness, but not for the con-
veyance of the intended meaning'. This is better; failure to say what
one means deserves condemnation, not shrouding under a technical
term—even if it be 'anacoluthia'.

§3859. But even in the last definition the word 'omission' remains
—with its implication that something was or should have been
there; the word 'essential' carries a similar implication; and the word
'considered' raises the question 'by whom?'—by native speakers or
by grammarians? It is still a definition which excludes the possibility
that the non-expression of words or phrases was in itself idiomatic
and produced a construction different from that which would have
existed or did exist in similar sentences in which 'ellipsis' as defined
by Pei and Gaynor had not occurred. Thus Gowers (ibid.)—unlike
Fowler—followed Onions (§64) in speaking of 'omission' of a relative pronoun in sentences like 'This is the book I am reading' and
'There's somebody at the door wants to see you'. There is at least the
possibility that we have to do with different constructions. So my
sympathies are with Bosker (*Neophil.* 31 (1947), 32): 'Latin influence and logic are also responsible for the *ellipsis-mania*, of which
several instances are found even in the works of grammarians of high
repute.' He gives an impressive list of 'guilty' writers on MnE. To
provide one for OE would be a simple task. Thus, I prefer to avoid
the term 'ellipsis' in connection with the non-expression of conj.
þæt in noun clauses (§§1981–91); of antecedents or relative pronouns (§§2302–37); and of a subject accusative in examples like
ÆCHom i. 380. 8 *Hat nu aræran ænne heahne torr* (§§3755–65;
here I agree with Visser, iii, §1195). More examples are inevitably
cited below. But it will be more profitable to consider (as best we
can in our limited space and in the absence of much or any colloquial OE) the extent to which OE anticipated MnE in idiomatic

non-expression of words or phrases thought by grammarians to be 'necessary' for the grammatical completeness of a sentence.

§3860. Quirk and others (1972, pp. 536–50) avoid 'omission' and 'omit' in this definition—'in a strict sense of ellipsis, words are ellipted only if they are uniquely recoverable, ie there is no doubt as to what words are to be supplied, and it is possible to add the recovered words to the sentence'—but use them in their discussion. In practice, they extend the definition given above to include 'ellipsis dependent on linguistic context' (e.g. 'I'm happy if you are'); 'ellipsis not dependent on linguistic context' (e.g. 'Want a drink?', 'Looks like rain', 'See you later', and similar manifestations of 'familiar style'); and various forms of 'weak ellipsis'.

§3861. An analysis of some of the quoted examples suggests that this distinction between 'ellipsis' dependent and not dependent 'on linguistic context' is not completely satisfactory. If I burst into a noisy party and shout 'Anybody need a lift?' or 'Want a drink?' (Quirk and others, pp. 548 and 545), I can hope for intelligible replies. So these can be called examples of 'ellipsis . . . not dependent on the adjacent linguistic context for their interpretation' (ibid., p. 544). (So too, I suppose, can examples like *ÆCHom* ii. 204. 2 . . . *swa swa Crist on his godspelle cwæð* 'Gif ic, on Godes fingre, *deofla adræfe*'; . . . . But these are a special case; see §3676.) But if I go into a room and say 'Sounds fine to me'—What does?—or 'Want some?'—[You] singular or plural? Some what? (ibid., pp. 546 and 547)—I can expect at best blank looks. These seem to me 'dependent on linguistic context'. The same is true of 'Too weak?' in 'Why can't he get up? Too weak?' (ibid., p. 548). For OE at any rate, I prefer a syntactical distinction based on whether or not a full understanding of the 'ellipsis' demands the presence of another clause or sentence. The term 'echo constructions' (Brown 1970, p. 77) points to the vital difference between the two basic types, viz. that in those which necessarily involve two clauses or sentences, the unexpressed element(s) would, if expressed, echo an element which precedes or follows. It need not be the same form of that element (Quirk and others 1972, p. 536), e.g. 'She rarely sings, so I don't think she will tonight', and 'Why isn't he here today? Car still not working?' (ibid., pp. 536 and 548), *Solil* 38. 7 *Ic beþearf* . . .—*þæs æac wilnige and nede sceal* (where we can supply *wilnian* as well as *ic*), *CP* 165. 20 . . . *ðonne se reða reccere ongiett ðæt he his hieremonna mod suiður gedrefed hæfð ðonne he scolde* (where again we can understand an infinitive), and similarly *Solil* 58. 22

... *þeah ðu swa micel nyte swa ðu woldest* (cf. *Solil* 57. 16 ... *þeah* [*þu*] *eall nyte þæt ðu witan woldest*). Those contemplating further work on 'ellipsis' in OE should see Kohonen 1978, pp. 186–90.

2. NON-EXPRESSION OF AN ELEMENT OR OF ELEMENTS WHICH CANNOT BE SUPPLIED FROM ANOTHER EXPRESSED CLAUSE OR SENTENCE

§3862. The absence or scarcity of colloquial OE means that it is difficult to find OE parallels for such familiar expressions as 'Looks like rain', 'Looking for anybody?', 'Anything the matter?', and 'John done his homework?' (Quirk and others 1972, pp. 544–8), which can be ascribed 'to subaudibility rather than to ellipsis' (ibid., p. 545). If we had been within earshot of Beowulf during Breca's speech we might well have heard mutterings such as *'Mare beor!'*, *'Dysig!'*, and *'Scealt beon scoten!'* So a study specifically devoted to the syntax of OE direct speech as defined in §1935 might well be fruitful here. Patterns like '(There) Appears to be a big crowd outside' are idiomatic but not elliptical in OE, e.g. *Or* 90. 19 *On þæm dagum wæs an burg in Affrica* ... ; see §1496. 'I must away' is easily paralleled, e.g. *Or* 286. 20 ... *þæt he nyste hwær he ut sceolde*; see §1007. *CP* 11. 21 *Hu se lareow sceal beon clæne on his mode* seems more natural to our ears than *CP* 13. 20 *Ðætte on oðre wisan sint to manianne weras, on oðre wiif.* We find non-expression of a personal pronoun subject with imperatives and jussive subjunctives (§§879–919; I would not follow Pinsker (pp. 130–1) in speaking of 'ellipsis' here) and in other contexts (§§1503–16). We find non-expression of subject *hit*—hardly comparable with ' 's raining'—in some impersonal constructions (§§1031–5). None of these provides real parallels to the MnE examples quoted above.

§3863. Non-expression of inf. *beon/wesan* with full meaning appears where it would not be possible in MnE in *Beo* 1783, 2091, 2255, and 2659, and in

Mald 312   Hige sceal þe heardra,   heorte þe cenre,
mod sceal þe mare,   þe ure mægen lytlað

(on the absence of *sceal* in *Mald* 312b see §1532) and possibly

Beo 2363   Nealles Hetware   hremge þorfton
feðewiges,   þe him foran ongean
linde bæron;   lyt eft becwom
fram þam hildfrecan   hames niosan!

But in the latter we could supply *gangan* or the like (§1007) or, taking the non-expression as cataphoric (Quirk and others 1972, p. 537), *becuman* from *becwom*; cf. *Beo* 1855. Despite Klaeber's note, there is no need to assume 'omission of *wesan*' in *Beo* 617 ... *bæd hine bliðne æt þære beorþege*; see §§3772-6. But it can be understood to give an accusative and infinitive; Visser (i, §231 fn. 2) seems to have missed the point here. *CP* 291. 21 ... *buton ðæt he ongeat Titum hwene monðwærran 7 geðyldigran ðonne he sceolde, 7 Timotheus he ongeat hatheortran ðonne he sceolde?* does not seem conclusive either way.

✕ §3864. Non-expression of a finite form of *beon/wesan* appears in four examples from *Ps(B)* cited by Visser (i, §231); in

Beo 3062   Wundur hwar þonne
     eorl ellenrof   ende gefere
     lifgesceafta,   þonne leng ne mæg
     mon mid his magum   meduseld buan

(cf. 'No wonder he's late'); according to Klaeber in

Beo 2262   Næs hearpan wyn,
     gomen gleobeames,   ne god hafoc
     geond sæl swingeð . . . ;

and in a subordinate clause in

Sat 698   Wite þu eac, awyrgda,   hu wid and sid
     helheoðo dreorig,   and mid hondum amet.

Visser (i, §231) suggests that 'it is no doubt semantic "emptiness" which caused the copula *to be* to be omitted' in such examples, and notes that in MnE its ' "omission" has practically become confined to such exclamatory phrases as "Happy the man who . . ."; "Fine old oak this!"; "Who so reckless . . . ?" ' See §§1533 and 1673 for more examples.

✕ §3865. It is, I suppose, examples of this sort which encourage scholars to postulate 'ellipsis' of the verb 'to be' elsewhere. As noted in §§3843 and 3841, 'ellipsis' of a preterite form *wæs/wæron* has been suggested for *Beo* 936a, 1343a, and 2035—Klaeber (3, glossary, s.v. *eom*) describes these three as 'loosely joined elliptic clauses' with 'omission of wesan'—and *GenA* 183a (Callaway 1889, p. 17). Other possible examples are *Dan* 475a (§3841) and *Beo* 2297b-8a (see Mitchell 1968c, p. 297, but Mitchell 1980a, p. 406). On *Beo* 936a and 1343a, see §3843. If we assume 'ellipsis', *Beo* 2035 need not be parenthetical, but would be if *him* in *Beo* 2036a were taken to refer to *he* in *Beo* 2034a; *Beo* 2297b–8a could be, and *GenA* 183a, below, and *Dan* 475a must be, parenthetical. Von Schaubert (pp. 126-7) lists three of these four among her nominative or nominative/accusative absolutes; the exception is *Beo* 2297b–8a. It is fair to point out that, while there are a few fairly convincing examples of nominative absolutes in the poetry (§3841), the existence of parentheses with 'ellipsis' of *wæs/wæron* cannot be established except by circular argument. Perhaps our problem approaches the terminological. But I would be guilty of inconsistency if I refused to admit the possibility that von Schaubert (pp. 11-14) is right in insisting that the parenthesis in

GenA 181   . . .   ac him brego engla
     of lice ateah   liodende ban
     —wer unwundod—   of þam worhte god
     freolice fæmnan

represents a different construction from that in

Beo 2777   Bill ær gescod
     —ecg wæs iren—   ealdhlafordes
     þam ðara maðma   mundbora wæs
     longe hwile. . . .

3. NON-EXPRESSION IN A SUBORDINATE CLAUSE OF AN ELEMENT OR OF ELEMENTS WHICH CAN BE SUPPLIED FROM THE PRINCIPAL CLAUSE

§3866. I cannot illustrate here the full range of possibilities or attempt a detailed comparison with MnE. Typical examples involving adverb clauses include *ÆCHom* i. 96. 15 *Witodlice se fyrenfulla bið earmra ðonne ænig nyten*, *ÆCHom* ii. 434. 2 *and þu etst gærs, swa swa oxa*, and *ÆCHom* i. 382. 10 *ne eom ic wyrðe þæt ic swa hangige swa min Drihten*; *ÆCHom* i. 358. 27 *Cuð is gehwilcum snoterum mannum, þæt seo ealde æ wæs eaðelicre þonne Cristes gesetnys sy*; *ÆCHom* i. 94. 5 *ac gehwylce halgan andbidodon on Abrahames wununge buton tintregum, þeah on hellewite* (where *þeah* may mean 'though' or 'yet'); *CP* 277. 7 . . . *ðonne hit flowan ne mot ðider hit wolde*; *Solil* 61. 20 *hi ic wille wyrðian swa swa man worldhlaford sceal*; and *CP* 281. 23 . . . *ðonne we nellað hwæthwugu nytwyrðes don ðonne ðonne we magon*. . . . For more examples, see the General Index, under 'Non-expression'. All these patterns can be paralleled in MnE.

§3867. The frequent absence of distinction between nominative and accusative forms (§9) means that OE parallels can also be found for the ambiguous pattern seen in MnE 'He loves the dog more than his wife' (Quirk and others 1972, pp. 769-70), e.g. *Solil* 17. 16 *Woldest cunnan god swa swa Alippius*—though here and, one suspects, in most MnE examples, the ambiguity does not exist in the full context. However, the existence of some case distinctions means that OE examples are not always ambiguous even out of context, e.g. *ÆCHom* i. 132. 5 *Ða sind Godes bearn gecigede þe hine lufiað swiðor þonne þisne middangeard*, where Thorpe's 'They are called children of God who love him more than this world' allows us to supply either 'they do' (rightly) or 'does' (wrongly).

§3868. On non-expression of conj. *þæt* in noun clauses, see §§1981-91. On possible non-expression in accusative and infinitive constructions, see §§3755-65 (accusative subject) and 3772-6 (*beon/wesan*). On apparent absence of an antecedent or a relative pronoun, see §§2302-37. Despite Pinsker (pp. 130-1), I would not speak of 'ellipsis' in the pattern x *wæs gehaten*; see §1475.

4. NON-EXPRESSION OF AN ELEMENT OR OF ELEMENTS WHICH CAN BE SUPPLIED FROM A CO-ORDINATE CLAUSE

§3869. Again, space limits my exemplification. Future workers should use the table given by Quirk and others (1972, pp. 572-3) but should note that it does not include all the possibilities cited in their index, s.v. *ellipsis*. In OE, as in MnE, the phenomenon occurs in sentences with or without a co-ordinating conjunction. Here too the unexpressed elements may differ in form.

§3870. Elements not expressed may consist of one word, e.g. (the subject) *CP* 7. 24 . . . *ic hie on Englisc awende and to ælcum biscepstole on minum rice wille ane onsendan* and *Bo* 115. 21 *Ða gestod hine heah weder 7 stormsæ. Wearð þa fordrifen on an iglond* . . . ; (the object) *CP* 187. 5 . . . *sua se læce grapað 7 stracað 7 hyt* ['hides'] *his seax 7 hwæt* ['whets']; (a noun in a prepositional phrase) *Solil* 18. 3 *wost þu þonne* . . . *on hwilcum tungle he nu is oððe on hwilce he ðanon geð?*; (an element governing a genitive), *Coll* 302 *7 win nys drenc cilda ne dysgra, ac ealdra 7 wisra* (complement), *CP* 307. 9 *Ne sece ic no minne willan, ac mines Fæder* (object), and *CP* 291. 6 *Forðæm us ætiede se halga Gæsð ægðer ge on culfran onlicnesse ge on fyres* (noun governed by a preposition); (an infinitive) *Solil* 58. 1 *þa þreo ðing ic wat and þa ðreo ðing ic wolde*; and (a finite form of a verb) *Solil* 46. 5 . . . *hawie þonne on steorran and on monan, ðonne on ðere sunnan scyman.* To these may be added the analytic passive in *CP* 163. 23 *Ðurh ða pannan is getacnod se wielm ðæs modes, 7 ðurh ðæt isern ðæt mægen ðara ðreatunga* and the combination of *sint* and the inflected infinitive in *CP* 179. 15 *On oðre wisan sint to manianne weras, on oðre wif.*

§3871. Two or more elements may be unexpressed, as in *CP* 285. 1 . . . *ðonne ðynceað him sumu weorc suiðe hefug, sumu suiðe unwærlico, CP* 275. 9 . . . *ðonne he hine mæg gehælan 7 nyle, CP* 39. 11 *We magon monnum bemiðan urne geðonc 7 urne willan, ac we ne magon Gode, CP* 459. 18 . . . *ðy ic sceal sellan eow giet mioloc drincan, nalles flæsc etan, CP* 445. 10 *Ðæt scip wile hwilum stigan ongean ðone stream ac hit ne mæg,* and *CP* 441. 4 *On oðre wisan sint to manienne ða ðe nan god ne onginnað; on oðre ða ðe hit onginnað, 7 no ne geendiað.* See also *Solil* 16. 22, *CP* 31. 18, *CP* 301. 24, and *CP* 461. 22.

§3872. For more examples, see Brown 1970, pp. 77–9; Gardner, p. 36; and Shannon, pp. 15–16 and 39–40.

5. NON-EXPRESSION IN DIALOGUE OF AN ELEMENT OR OF ELEMENTS WHICH CAN BE SUPPLIED FROM A STATEMENT OR QUESTION BY ANOTHER SPEAKER

§3873. A few examples will demonstrate that this form of compression occurred in OE. I have little doubt that it was an inherited tendency, even though the examples from *Coll* are Latin-based: *ÆC Hom* i. 256. 1 *Hwæt sind þa ðe us biddað? Earme men, and tiddre, and deadlice. Æt hwam biddað hi? Æt earmum mannum, and tiddrum, and deadlicum. Butan þam æhtum, gelice sind þa þe ðær biddað, and ða ðe hi ætbiddað; Coll* 48 *Ys þæs* [= *þes*] *of þinum geferum? Gea, he ys. Canst þu ænig þing? Ænne cræft ic cann. Hwylcne? Hunta ic eom. Hwæs? Cincges; Coll* 96 *Hwær cypst þu fixas þine? On ceastre. Hwa bigþ hi? Ceasterwara;* and *Coll* 298 *7 hwæt drincst þu? Ealu, gif ic hæbbe, oþþe wæter gif ic næbbe ealu.* See further §3031.

§3874. Similar compressions can be found when an OE writer is, as it were, having a dialogue with himself for didactic or rhetorical purposes, e.g. *ÆCHom* i. 320. 2 *Hwi ofer Criste on culfran hiwe?*; see §1666. If *CP* 9. 3 (§3832) and *Beo* 936a and 1343a (§3843) are accepted as examples of non-expression of *hit/þæt is/wæs,* they could perhaps be included here.

6. 'WEAK ELLIPSIS'

§3875. MnE examples of so-called 'weak ellipsis' cited by Quirk and others (1972, pp. 540-4) and the OE equivalents of such examples can usually be regarded as different constructions from those of which they are alleged to be reductions. They include 'Houses *(which are) owned by absentee landlords* will be confiscated', *Bede* 210. 23 *Wæs fæger mynster getimbred in wuda*, and *ÆLS* 5. 357 *Tiburtius gemette ænne mann afeallene*; 'They sell cars *(that are) for handicapped drivers*', *Bede* 246. 18 *Nom he twegen biscopas of Bretta ðeode*, and *ÆCHom* i. 194. 12 *þa witegunga be Cristes acennednysse and be ðære eadigan Marian mægðhade sindon swiðe menigfealdlice on ðære ealdan æ gesette*; and '*The poor (people)* need more help', *CP* 271. 9 *On oðre wisan sint to monianne ða suiðe suigean*, and *ÆCHom* ii. 442. 14 . . . *we sceolon ða hungrian fedan*.

§3876. OE parallels of a sort exist for the so-called 'supplementing' clauses, as in 'I caught the train—*just*' (ibid., p. 543), e.g. *Bede* 140. 30 *Wæs Rædwald his fæder geo geara in Cent gelæred in þa gerynu Cristes geleafan, ac holinga* and *Ps(P)* 2. 11 . . . *blissiað on Gode and ðeah mid ege*, and 'appended' clauses, as in 'He is playful, *even mischievous*' (ibid., p. 544), e.g. *Ps(P)* 24. 6 *þa scylda mines iugoðhades ne gemun þu, Drihten, ne huru þa þe ic ungewisses geworhte, Coll* 104 *Hwilon ic do, ac seldon*, and *Coll* 295 *Ic bruce hwilon þisum mettum . . . mid syfernysse, swa swa dafnað munuce, næs mid oferhropse*.

§3877. Examples of 'weak ellipsis' such as 'He's drunk, AND I CLAIM THAT *because I saw him staggering*', which may be considered 'as involving semantic implication rather than ellipsis' (ibid., pp. 549-50), may be compared with those cited in §3676 and with *BlHom* 17. 30, quoted in §3021 as an example of 'logical' cause.

E. ANACOLUTHIA

§3878. Like every other language, OE inevitably had to suffer writers and, though I cannot produce evidence, speakers who were occasionally guilty of anacoluthia, defined by *OED* as 'a want of grammatical sequence; the passing from one construction to another before the former is completed'. So there survives an occasional undoubted anacoluthon—'an instance of anacoluthia, a phrase or series of words in which it appears' (*OED*). Sweet (ed.) (*CP*, p. xli) remarked that 'another result of the difficulty in reproducing the sense of the original is the use of anacoluthons, which are very frequent in the Pastoral'. His examples were *CP* 99. 17, *CP* 101. 15 (see §3880 fn.), *CP* 107. 20, *CP* 103. 3 *7 symle ymb ðæt ðe hine ðonne tueode, ðonne orn he eft innto ðæm temple*, and the well-known *CP* 3. 1 *Ælfred kyning hateð gretan Wærferð biscep . . . 7 ðe cyðan hate ðæt me com swiðe oft on gemynd . . .* , which cannot be blamed directly on the Latin and may have been deliberate. Other examples include *Or* 10. 19, *BlHom* 65. 4, *BlHom* 191. 36 (see Gorrell, p. 397), and *ÆCHom* i. 502. 29 *Wite ðu gewislice þæt se mann ðe mid his agenre flan ofscoten wæs, þæt hit is mid minum willan gedon* (see §3883). Liggins (1955, p. 104) rightly suggests that anacoluthia may explain the superfluous *þæt* in the three extant manuscripts of *Bede* 150. 31. But it may have been an early scribe rather than the translator who lost track of the sentence.

§3879. However, the purpose of these sections is not so much to convict the Anglo-Saxons of anacoluthia as to remove the suspicion that they were habitual offenders who regularly broke the rules of their own language. I have already (§§1893–6) suggested that what may seem to modern readers tautologic (and perhaps at times even anacoluthic) anticipatory and recapitulatory pronouns and correlative adverbs reflected the paratactic origin of OE and, in translated texts, 'the difficulty of expressing and defining abstract ideas in a language unused to theological and metaphysical subtleties' (Sweet (ed.), *CP*, p. xl). I still see no reason for departing from this view and do not think that such constructions should be called anacoluthic.

§3880. The point can be illustrated by a consideration of some examples of recapitulatory pronouns. If we dismiss as idiomatic the construction seen in *Or* 24. 21 *Nu hæbbe we gesæd ymbe ealle Europe landgemæro hu hi tolicgað* (§2067), we will find that most of the examples which contain what may seem to modern readers anacoluthic personal or (less often) demonstrative pronouns referring to uninflected proper nouns fall into one of three main groups: first, that in which the pronoun—and also the noun—is nominative, e.g. *Or* 24. 16 *Igbernia þæt we Scotland hatað hit is . . .* , *Or* 26. 4 *Tribulitania sio þiod þe man oðre naman hæt Arzuges hio hæfð . . .* , *Or* 26. 11, and *Or* 26. 29 *Cipros þæt igland hit lið;*[6] second, those in which it is genitive, e.g. *Or* 12. 19 *Nilus seo ea hire æwielme is . . .* ,

---

[6] *CP* 101. 15, which is anacoluthic as punctuated by Sweet (see his edition of *CP*, p. xli), might belong here if repunctuated with a comma after *slæpte*. The Latin seems to me to allow this interpretation.

Or 8. 10 . . . *ðær Asia 7 Europe hiera landgemircu togædre licgað,*
and *Or* 8. 28 *Affrica 7 Asia hiera landgemircu onginnað* . . .—note
this stop-gap for the group genitive; and third, those in which it is
dative, e.g. *Or* 12. 16, *Or* 24. 7, *Or* 26. 16 *Mauritania, hyre is be
eastan Numedia* . . . , and *Or* 26. 20 *Mauritania þe man oþre naman
hæt Tingetana be eastan hyre is Malua sio ea* (that *hire/hyre* here is
dative is attested by such examples as *Or* 24. 13 *þonne is be suðan
him* . . . and by those which follow), *Or* 26. 32 *Creto þæt igland him
is be eastan se sæ* . . . , *Or* 28. 18 *Corsica him is Romeburh be eastan,*
and *Or* 28. 21 *Balearis þa tu igland him is be norðan Affrica.* To
these may be added *Or* 22. 22 *þa land þe man hæt Gallia Bellica,
be eastan þæm is sio ea* . . . (not an exact parallel, but relevant).

§3881. We can say of those with a pronoun in the nominative either
that the pronoun is tautologic (§§246 and 317) or that the proper
noun is what is called a 'dangling subject' or 'nominativus pendens'
or, as Visser (i, §76) prefers, an 'anacoluthic subject'. But I am inclined to agree with Closs (p. 104) that such examples should not 'be
considered cases of anacoluthon'. Can we extend this verdict, as
Closs does, to those examples with a pronoun in the genitive or
dative? I believe so. Here it would be dangerous to say that the pronoun is tautologic, for it tells us the case of the proper noun, although
we may note that the translator did without a pronoun in *Or* 8. 23
Se westsuþende Europe landgemirce is. . . . Bock (1887, p. 20)—not
unreasonably—tried to explain such examples as *Or* 8. 10 and 12. 19
(both in §3880) as due to Alfred's [*sic*] reluctance to produce an
OE genitive for foreign proper nouns. But Wülfing (i, §251) saw the
obvious objection to this, that in *Or* 12. 19 the translator could have
written ☆*Nilus þære ea æwielme is* . . . or—my own alternative—
☆*Se æwielme þære ea (þe mon hæt) Nilus is.* . . . I would extend this
to examples with the dative by suggesting ☆*Creto þæm iglande is be
eastan se sæ* for *Or* 26. 32 (§3880) and ☆*Balearis þæm twæm iglandum
is be norðan Affrica* for *Or* 28. 21 (§3880). Even ☆*Corsican is Romeburh be eastan* would have been possible for *Or* 28. 18 (§3880),
which is immediately preceded by . . . *7 be norðan Corsica þæt
igland.* However, I suspect that in all these examples the proper
noun was a sort of equivalent of a modern heading and that *Or*
12. 19 would have sounded something like *Nilus seo ea: hire
æwielme is* . . . ; similarly (without a pronoun) *Or* 10. 6 *Asia: ongen
ðæm middeldæle on þæm eastende þær ligeð se muþa* . . . ; and so
on for all the examples cited above.

§3882. It is perhaps strange that Visser (i, §76) did not include any
of these among his ten OE examples of 'the anacoluthic subject'.

(There are more such examples in Laws and elsewhere; I cannot list them all.) In *CP* 33. 12 *Se se ðe ealne ðone wisdom ðara uferrenna gæsta oferstigð 7 ær worolde ricsode on hefenum, hit is awriten on ðæm godspelle, Iudeas comon 7 woldon hine don niedenga to cyninge*, we have a definite adjective clause referring to *Crist* with an antecedent *se* which refers to the 'postcedent' *hine*. Without the first *se* this would not qualify as anacoluthic, for we would have the *'seþe* relative; we could compare *Or* 98. 2 . . . *þætte þa þe ær ute oþra ðeoda anwalda girndon, him þa god þuhte þær hie mehten hie selfe æt ham wið ðeowdom bewerian*, where the adjective clause refers to *Or* 96. 36 *Læcedemonie* and the *him* to *'þa þe*, and the five examples now to be discussed.

§3883. Visser's other nine examples are all indefinite, referring to any individual who falls into the specified category and not to a particular individual or proper noun. Five of them can be construed as containing an indefinite *'seþe* adjective clause with the relative pronoun as subject followed by a 'postcedent' personal or demonstrative pronoun in a case other than the nominative, viz. *LawAf* 5. 5 *Se ðe stalað on Sunnanniht . . . ðara gehwelc we willað sie twybote . . .* ; *LawIIAs* 9 *Se ðe yrfe befo, nemne him mon V men his neahgebura*; *LawVIAs* 1. 2 *7 se þe ðeof dearnunga feormige . . . do him man þæt ilce*; *LawVIAs* 1. 3 *7 se ðe mid þeofe stande 7 mid feohte, lecge hine man mid þam þeofe*; and *Ps(P)* 33. 10 *ac þa þe God seceað, ne aspringeð him nan good*. I would not call these five anacoluthic. But the replacement of the indefinite adjective clause by a conditional clause would remove any possibility of an anacoluthon; cf. *BlHom* 53. 2, *ÆCHom* ii. 528. 9, *ÆCHom* i. 502. 29 (§3878), and the examples I cite in §2213—all of which Visser could have added to his ten.

§3884. This remedy is not available in the remaining four, viz. *LawIne* 33 (§3885), *LawIne(E)* 37 *Se cirlisca mon se ðe oft betygen wære ðiefðe . . . slea him mon hond of oððe fot*, *WHom* 18. 37 *Witodlice ælc þæra þe cyrican rihtlice secð . . . God gehyreð his bena*, and Visser's only example from the poetry

Max i 161   Wærleas mon ond wonhydig,
                    ætrenmod ond ungetreow,
                    þæs ne gymeð god.

§3885. However, in all nine we could regard the initial nominative —noun, adjective clause, or antecedent + adjective clause—as comparable with a modern heading; cf. §3881. So we could read *Law Ine(E)* 33 *Cyninges horswealh: se ðe him mæge geærendian, ðæs wergield bið cc scill.* Here again, I am reluctant to use the word 'anacoluthic'; we may be dealing with an OE idiom which has not survived. As Visser (i, §76) says 'In Pres.D. English the construction is avoided.'

§3886. The same reluctance possesses me when I consider other sentences or constructions which may perhaps seem loose or undesirable to modern readers. We may include here the loose use of modal and auxiliary verbs in *Cura Pastoralis* (Sweet (ed.), pp. xl–xli). Liggins (1955, pp. 103–4), referring to BTS, s.v. *and* II, plausibly explains superfluous *7/ond* in *Bede* 258. 13 and 304. 32 and superfluous *ac* in *Bede* 70. 26 as scribal. If we do not assume scribal omission of initial *þa* in *BlHom* 69. 20 *þæt Iudisce folc þa wiste þæt Hælend com to Lazares ham foran þa þyder,* and if we reject (as I believe we must) the idea that *þa wiste* means 'who knew', the construction is paratactic rather than anacoluthic. The variations between co-ordinated defining *þæt* clauses and a series of infinitives in *ÆCHom* i. 584. 4; between an accusative and infinitive construction and *þu beo* in *ÆLS* 32. 52 (§3732); and between the two objects of *geseah* in *ÆCHom* ii. 136. 9 *Eft se halga Cuðberhtus . . . geseah heofonas opene and englas gelæddon Aidanes biscopes sawle . . . into ðære heofonlican myrhðe* (see §3771); are all explicable in terms of accepted OE idioms. There seems little point in pursuing more (possible) examples of anacoluthia, though some will be found by reference to the General Index.

IX

ELEMENT ORDER

A. INTRODUCTORY REMARKS

§3887. I have adopted the term 'element order' as more accurate than the traditional 'word order' because the former refers to clause elements such as 'subject', 'verb', and 'object', and not to individual words such as 'He', 'kissed', and 'her'. But 'word order' will of necessity appear in many quotations.

§3888. The symbols used in this chapter are explained in the list of Symbols involving letters. S, C, and O, embrace qualifiers such as the genitives in *ÆCHom* i. 48. 33 *Ealra gecorenra halgena deað*, *ÆCHom* i. 30. 17 *se Godes engel*, and the unusual *Beo* 524 *sunu Beanstanes*. Adv. covers an adverb, an adverb group, or a combination thereof. We have SvVO in *ÆCHom* i. 22. 10 *Ic wylle settan min wedd. . . .*

§3889. Nickel (*NM* 73 (1972), 266) observes that 'the myth according to which an entirely free use can be made of the former [word order] in Old English was in part destroyed some time ago'. It dies hard; in 1973, Visser (iii. 1991 fn. 1) was able to write that '. . . the word order in Old English was so free that serious offences against it were not easily perpetrable'. Element order is no doubt more free in OE than it is in MnE. So it is vital that future workers distinguish those arrangements which are possible today from those which are not; see Mitchell 1964*b*, *passim*. This is not always easy; see Mitchell 1964*b*, p. 121 fn. 1, p. 133 fn. 1, p. 135 fn. 3, p. 137, and p. 138 fn. 1. But in both OE and MnE there are acceptable and unacceptable patterns; sentences like ☆*ic þisne buton ofslea and dracan swurde stafe* (cf. *ÆHom* 21. 441) are no more possible than sentences like ☆'I this without will kill and dragon sword staff', and one could not write the equivalent of *Tantus eos honos prosequitur amicorum*. Yet Visser is not the last or the only offender. Unnecessarily sweeping assertions continue to appear. Traugott (p. 107) makes two when she speaks of 'the obligatory shift of pronoun objects to preverbal position' in her type 1 order—'Subject (Auxiliary) Verb (Object)'. On the second of these quotations, see Mitchell 1964*b*, p. 121 fn. 1. On the first, see Mitchell 1964*b*, p. 124 fn. 1, and 1966, p. 90; note that

Farr (p. 14) says that 'the normal word-order of the Refl. Dat. is:
(1) Subject + *Refl. Dat.* + verb + object. (2) Subject + verb + *Refl.
Dat.* + object'—see my §3907; and consider such examples as
ÆCHom i. 12. 20 *ac God ne gesceop hine na to deofle*, *ÆCHom* i.
36. 32 . . . *and þancian ðam Hælende þæt he gemedemode hine
sylfne* . . . , *ÆCHom* i. 174. 8 *to him anum we sceolon us gebiddan*
(cf. *ÆCHom* i. 174. 4 and 10), *ÆCHom* i. 174. 31 *Deofol tiht us to
yfele*, *ÆCHom* i. 176. 28 . . . *mid þam ylcan Crist oferswiðde hine*,
and *ÆCHom* i. 176. 31 *þurh idel wuldor he fandode his* (cf. *ÆC
Hom* i. 176. 33). Misunderstandings which should long ago have disappeared persist. Without giving references, Kohonen (1976, pp. 181
and 185) claims to have found in *ÆCHom* i three clauses introduced
by 'negation particle *ne*' with order SV. But see §1602 and Mitchell
1966, p. 88. The time is, I believe, more than ripe for a critical survey of the present state of knowledge about OE element order, followed by a full descriptive syntax; see Mitchell 1966, p. 97. I cannot
attempt the task here. Anyone attempting it will need to take cognizance of both individual preferences or eccentricities—e.g., the
high proportion of subordinate clauses with verb in final position in
Orosius (Liggins 1970, p. 317) and the reluctance of the author of
VercHom 1 to begin a sentence with a subject except when translating Latin (D. Scragg, private communication)—and of the 'text-
linguistic approach' adopted by Kohonen (1976, pp. 176–7), in
which 'clauses are seen as part of the context, textual and situational,
their task being to transmit their share of the information of the
whole text' and which examines the 'relationship between what is
being said and what has already been said' (ibid.). To some extent,
at any rate, this is another way of saying that speakers and writers
deliberately vary the order for pedagogic, rhetorical, or stylistic,
purposes. Examples include *ÆCHom* i. 144. 29–33, where *towyrpð*
occurs four times in three different positions; the variation in *ÆC
Hom* i. 486. 30 *Hwæt is betwux fyðerfotum reðre þonne leo? oððe
hwæt is wælhreowre betwux næddercynne ðonne draca?*; and the
contrasted use of chiasmus and parallelism in *ÆCHom* i. 50. 25–
52. 6. Future workers will also need to distinguish the four types of
clauses distinguished (with their subdivisions) in Mitchell 1964*b*—
simple sentences and principal clauses (1) which do not begin with
ond, ac, ne, or a similar conjunction or with adv. *ne*, with an adverb
other than *ne*, or with an adverb phrase; (2) which begin with *ond,
ac, ne*, or a similar conjunction, the effects of which have too often
been overlooked (see the Index of Words and Phrases and Mitchell
1964*b*, pp. 117–19, and 1966, pp. 87–8); (3) which begin with adv.
ne, with an adverb other than *ne*, or with an adverb phrase; and

(4) subordinate clauses—and to extend to all these types of clauses the observations made by Liggins (1970, p. 317) about subordinate clauses:

A proper analysis of the word order would consider each type of subordinate clause separately, its position in the structure of the whole sentence, the possibility of Latin influence, the length of the sentence, the rhythm of the clause and of the sentence, the question of emphasis, and so on. I have not attempted any of this, though think it probable that it would prove most fruitful.

Other considerations include the comparative length of the various elements; 'the tendency to begin the clause with a given element that links it to the preceding context' (Kohonen 1976, p. 182); and 'the principle of end-weight' which accounted for the fact that frequently in *ÆCHom* i 'the end-position was occupied by longer and thus heavier adverbial elements, without regard to the givenness of the object or complement' (Kohonen 1976, p. 192). So a comparison of the positions of OE adverbs and adverb groups with those in MnE (Quirk and others 1972, chapters 5 and 6) suggests itself; see §3942. And so on. . . .

§3890. Here, however, space does not permit more than a summary of the basic facts; some observations about certain difficulties which arise or have been manufactured; and some bibliographical comments. For all topics other than element order, I have tried to read all the 'literature' which seems to me relevant and likely to be of value. But here I have had to surrender to the bulk of material. Those seeking a bibliography should consult Bacquet, pp. 32-43 (critical survey of previous writings) and 763-6 (select bibliography), and Kohonen (1978, pp. 203-18). Works not mentioned in either of these—some either published after Kohonen or dealing with poetry, which was not the concern of either writer—include: J. Aitchison, *TPS* 1979, pp. 43-65; Andrew, *Postscript*; M. C. Butler (see *YWES* 57 (1976), 15); W. M. Canale (see *DAI* 39 (1978), 2223-A); J. M. de la Cruz, *Studia Anglica Posnaniensia*, 8 (1976), 3-43; T. Dahl, *Form and Function Studies in Old and Middle English Syntax* (Copenhagen, 1936); T. P. Dolan, *MP* 74 (1977), 305-10; N. J. Engberg (see *DAI* 31 (1970), 1249-A); H. Fujiwara, *Collected Papers on Word Order and Infinitive in English* (Gakushuin, 1977); S. H. Goldman (see *DAI* 31 (1971), 5382-A); A. Grad, *Slavistična Revija*, VIII. Letnik, 1-2, Linguistica (1955), 11-27; G. Hübener, *PBB* 45 (1920-1), 85-102; W. P. Lehmann (see *OEN* 8. 1 (1975), 15, and *YWES* 57 (1976), 15); G. S. Metes (see *DAI* 33 (1973), 3621-A); T. Olszewska (see *OEN* 7. 1 (1973), 15); D. T. Ordeman, *JEGP* 31 (1932), 228-33; M. H. Roberts, *JEGP* 35 (1936), 466-81; W. Schlachter, *Zur Stellung des Adverbs im Germanischen* (Palæstra, 200) (1935); K. Schneider, *Die Stellungstypen des finiten Verbs im urgermanischen Haupt- und Nebensatz* (Heidelberg, 1938); T. A. Snegireva, 'Porjadok slov kak sredstvo svjazi meždu samostojatel'nymi predloženijami v drevne-anglijskij period', *Učenye zapiski Xabarovskogo pedagogičeskogo instituta*, 8 (1962), 139-201; D. A. Schmidt, 'A History of Inversion in English' (Ohio State University diss., 1981); and R. P. Stockwell in *Mechanisms of Syntactic Change*, ed. Charles N. Li (Austin and London, 1977), 291-314. Future workers will clearly neglect at their peril the evidence of syntactic glosses; see Robinson 1973 and a review by the same author in *Speculum*, 52 (1977), 680-1. Space also precludes detailed reference to the discussions on element order in the standard grammars or in the monographs on the various constructions and on the syntax of individual texts. More references to works which deal with the position of one particular element will be found in the appropriate sections.

§3891. It would no doubt be helpful to our studies if we had an answer to the question posed by Miller in 'Indo-European: VSO, SOV, SVO, or all three?' (*Lingua*, 37 (1975), 31-52). But I cannot pursue this much-disputed topic here. Nor can I pursue this suggestion by Nickel (*IF* 72 (1967), 267 fn. 16):

   A note on the problem of OE. word order may not be out of place here. Despite all assertions to the contrary I believe that there is something like a basic order of elements in the OE. verb phrase. By 'basic' I do not mean 'most frequent'. The basic order of elements is that from which all the other arrangements can be derived most economically. O. E. E. Closs in her study of OE. syntax (A Grammar of Alfred's Orosius, Berkeley Diss. 1964) more or less took the structure of the Modern English verb phrase as basic. It could quite easily be shown that this is inadequate for OE. A more adequate parallel is that of Modern German, where the various sentence patterns can most economically be derived from the order of subordinate clauses and infinitive constructions (for a discussion see M. Bierwisch, Grammatik des deutschen Verbs, Studia Grammatica II, Berlin 1966). This can quite profitably be adapted to account for the situation in OE. Cf.:

> þeah he him leof wære
> ða he þone [*sic*] cyning sohte
> for þæm he þær sittan ne mehton.
> wilnað biscophad to underfonne
> ongan fyrene to fremman.

The basic order would then be roughly

> (Time) (Loc) (Obj$_i$) (Obj$_d$) MV + Aux.

I am not sure whether the subject of the active form of 'can be derived' is intended to be 'modern scholars' or 'speakers of Anglo-

Saxon'. But I do believe that OE element order can be studied profitably even though these riddles have not been resolved. Indeed, I doubt whether such resolution is possible.

§3892. Campbell (1970, p. 94) says that the three clause types I characterize as SV, S . . . V, and VS, are

> the foundation of the prose of all Germanic nations, so we cannot doubt that they were an ancient heritage, preserved from generation to generation in popular speech. Yet in Old English prose they are much obscured, and I would suggest that the reason for this at least in part is that the new art of prose was influenced at its inception by the old-established art of verse.

He holds that it is 'frequent for the old tendency of verse to assert itself, so that the verb is drawn into the position before the first stress', as in *Beo* 997 *Wæs þæt beorhte bold* (p. 95), and that this explains 'two of the three major difficulties in Old English prose word-order' (p. 96), viz. initial V in principal clauses or simple sentences with a noun subject, as in *Or* 34. 25 *Wæs se hunger on þæs cyninges dagum on Egyptum* (see further §§3930–3), and the order VS in clauses introduced by *ond, ac,* and the like, and in subordinate clauses, e.g. *Or* 164. 18 *7 wæron þa men todon dysige þæt hie wendon . . .* and *Matt(WSCp)* 8. 18 *Ða geseah se hælend mycle menigeo ymbutan hyne . . .*, Latin *uidens autem Iesus turbas multas circum se. . . .* In each pattern, says Campbell (pp. 95 and 96), analogical extensions occurred in clauses with pronoun subjects, e.g. *Or* 118. 6 *Wæs þæt micel wundor þæt swa micel here . . . fleah* and *Or* 14. 26 *Nu hæbbe we scortlice gesæd ymbe Asia londgemæro . . .*, which he translates 'Now that we have briefly told . . .'. On this pattern, see §3101.

§3893. The third difficulty is 'the very imperfect establishment' of VS in principal clauses which do not begin with the subject (p. 96). We see this in the variation between VS and S(. . .)V, not only after adverbs such as *Her* (§3929) and prepositional phrases such as *Be ðæm* (§3929), but even after *þær, þa,* and *þonne* (§3922). According to Campbell (p. 96),

> the reason for this imperfect introduction of demonstrative order is not clear. Its more regular observance after *þa, þonne,* and *þær* is no doubt due to the fact that these three adverbs were identical in form with particularly common conjunctions, and avoidance of ambiguity was accordingly very desirable where they were concerned.

But the conflict is perhaps illustrated by the variants *Or(L)* 284. 33 *. . . , þa he gefor . . .* but *Or(C)* 284. 33 *. . . , þa gefor he . . .* , in what is a principal clause. Such ambiguity arises, of course, only in clauses introduced by an ambiguous adverb/conjunction and, as Campbell clearly implied—see my §2536—and confirmed in conversation (1964), only in the written language. In his words (p. 95), 'the new prose, with its need for precision, had to develop a more rigid distinction' between Adv.VS and Adv.S(. . .)V. Comparative studies to determine whether the three tendencies detected by Campbell in OE are apparent in the other Germanic languages would be of value here; see Campbell 1970, pp. 97-8.

§3894. The sections which follow assume a knowledge of my remarks about the frequent lack of distinction in OE between nominative and accusative forms (§9) and of the possibility that 'the element order SVO was already to some degree established as a grammatical device in OE' (§10). Important cross-references are given; these can be supplemented from the Indexes. The variety of orders displayed provides a salutary warning against the dangers of relying on element order to decide whether a particular clause is principal or subordinate, and in my opinion is something approaching proof that the intonation patterns of OE must have differed from those of MnE.

B. IN NON-DEPENDENT QUESTIONS AND EXCLAMATIONS

§3895. As in MnE, non-dependent nexus questions (both positive and negative) usually have either VS or vSV; see §1644. But in nexus questions introduced by hwæþer, we find SV or S . . . V; see §§ 1652-9. In x-questions, the normal arrangement is Interrog. VS. The variations are described in §§1661-70.

§3896. On non-dependent exclamations, see §1671. Dependent questions and exclamations by definition occur only in subordinate clauses and have the appropriate order.

C. IN NON-DEPENDENT COMMANDS AND WISHES

§3897. Although the usual patterns are V(S)—the subject is usually unexpressed in positive commands, expressed in negative—initial S is found; see §§879-900. On sentences which begin with the object, an adverb (phrase), a clause, or with ond, ac, or ne, see §§902-10.

§3898. Unrealized or impossible wishes are usually expressed by gif or þær and the preterite subjunctive. VS is rare. See §§1675-81.

§3899. Dependent commands and wishes occur in subordinate clauses and have the appropriate order.

D. IN NON-DEPENDENT STATEMENTS AND SUBORDINATE CLAUSES

1. INTRODUCTORY REMARKS

§3900. The early annals of the *Chronicle* show the three basic OE element orders in characteristic positions: SV in a principal clause, e.g. *ChronA* 4. 26 (1) *Octauianus ricsode lvi wintra*; S . . . V after *ond*, e.g. *ChronA* 4. 29 (2) *7 þa cild on Bethlem ofslægene wærun*, and in a subordinate clause, e.g. *ChronA* 6. 20 (46). . . *seþe Iacobum ofslog*; and VS after an adverb, e.g. *ChronA* 4. 31 (3) *Her swealt Herodus*. Unfortunately, it is not as simple as that. First, it is sometimes difficult to decide which order we have. Second, each of the three orders can appear in each of the four situations distinguished above. So it is convenient for me to draw the reader's attention now to the fact that in my discussions of these three orders, my examples come indifferently from clauses of these four types. Comments on relative frequency appear when appropriate and possible.

§3901. I have not found it helpful to give these orders names. The symbols SV, S . . . V, and VS, mark the basic divisions simply and clearly, but are not precise enough. Attempts to make them so end in confusion. Thus, the examples which follow under (*a*) and (*b*) could all be described as S . . . V: (*a*) *ÆCHom* ii. 334. 27 *Hi ða sungon*, *ÆCHom* i. 4. 16 *And se gesewenlica deofol þonne wyrcð ungerima wundra*, *ÆCHom* i. 204. 8 . . . *gif he mid þam gewitendlicum gestreonum beceapað him þæt ece lif*, and *ApT* 40. 1 *Hi ða ealle anre stæfne cwædon*; (*b*) *ÆCHom* i. 136. 32 . . . *ærðam ðe he Crist gesawe* and *ÆCHom* i. 134. 18 . . . *gif hit hysecild wære*. Again, the examples which follow under (*c*) and (*d*) could all be described as S . . . V . . . : (*c*) *ÆCHom* i. 2. 30 . . . *swa swa ure Drihten on his godspelle cwæð to his leorningcnihtum* and *ÆCHom* i. 4. 12 . . . *þe for heora mandædum siððan ecelice þrowiað on ðære sweartan helle*; (*d*) *ÆCHom* i. 312. 34 . . . *gif we gemyndige beoð Cristes bebodum and ðæra apostola lare*, *ÆCHom* i. 30. 33 . . . *þe him gesæd wæs be ðam cilde*, and *ÆCHom* ii. 556. 17 . . . *se ðe ða soðan lufe næfð to Gode and to mannum*. Yet it is obvious that the examples under (*a*) and (*c*) differ in kind from those under (*b*) and (*d*) and that the difference is that the (*a*) and (*c*) arrangements are possible in

MnE—sometimes perhaps with a minor variation in the position of an adverb, e.g. *ecelice* in *ÆCHom* i. 4. 12, or with some other alteration, e.g. 'himself' for *him* in *ÆCHom* i. 204. 8—whereas the (*b*) and (*d*) arrangements would be impossible today. The essential difference is that SV covers clauses in which S and V can be separated by elements such as adverbs or phrases, whereas in S . . . V the separating element must be or must include a noun object, a noun or adjective complement, a participle, an infinitive, or the like. Further definition is attempted in the appropriate sections below.

§3902. Examples remain which defy classification, e.g. *ÆCHom* i. 10. 33 . . . *þæt he mihte beon þam Ælmihtigum Gode gelic, ÆCHom* i. 346. 34 *and sume mid oferstigendre wurðfulnysse ðam oðrum sind foresette, ÆCHom* ii. 32. 31 . . . *þær heo lytle ær cwacigende stod*, and *ApT* 40. 12 *Ðæt forscildgode wif þa eallum limon abifode.* But these are a warning to the over-enthusiastic statistician rather than a real problem.

2. SV IN THE PROSE

§3903. Patterns with undivided SV which are possible in MnE include (with initial subject) *ÆCHom* i. 10. 5 *He gesceop gesceafta, ÆCHom* i. 174. 31 *Deofol tiht us to yfele, ÆCHom* i. 242. 26 *ic lufige hi and hi lufiað me*; (with an initial adverbial element) *ÆC Hom* i. 10. 5 *þurh his wisdom he geworhte ealle þing* and *ÆCHom* i. 8. 4 *Swa swa ælmihtig wyrhta he wyrcð his weorc*; and (with an initial conjunction) *ÆCHom* i. 18. 11 *and hi wæron ða nacode, ÆCHom* i. 10. 5 . . . *þaða he wolde*, and *ÆCHom* i. 28. 30 . . . *þæt on ðam timan se Romanisca casere Octauianus sette gebann.* An adverb (group) sometimes occupies a position which would not be quite 'right' in MnE, e.g. *ÆCHom* i. 2. 16 *his gebyrd and goodnys sind gehwær cuþe* and *ÆCHom* i. 16. 12 *and he worhte ða þone man mid his handum.*

§3904. In both OE and MnE, other elements can precede SV to give a special nuance or emphasis, e.g. (a complement) *ÆCHom* i. 84. 1 *Gesælige hi wurdon geborene* and *ÆCHom* i. 138. 3 *Lytel he wæs ðær gesewen*; (an indirect object) *ÆCHom* i. 26. 12, *ÆCHom* i. 276. 4, *ÆCHom* i. 118. 4 *þam acennedan cyninge we bringað gold*, and *ÆCHom* i. 24. 16 *And þyssere mægðe God sealde and gesette æ*; (a direct noun object) e.g. *ÆCHom* i. 14. 27 *Ealle gesceafta . . . God gesceop . . . , ÆCHom* i. 42. 30 *Ðyllice word Maria heold aræfnigende on hire heortan, ÆCHom* i. 86. 15 *Fela ðæra læca he acwealde*,

ÆCHom i. 276. 1 *Englas he worhte*, and *ÆCHom* i. 456. 26 *Ealle ðing he foresceawað and wat, and ealra ðeoda gereord he cann*; and (a direct pronoun object) *ÆCHom* i. 76. 6 *þe we heriað, ÆCHom* i. 68. 26 *þæt þæt we mid gitsigendum eagum agylton, þæt we nu mid wependum eagum bereowsiað*, and *ÆCHom* i. 42. 1 . . . *þæt hi man sceolde mid stanum oftorfian* (a special case on which see § 3937).

§3905. In those quoted examples in which the direct object has first position (OSV), not even momentary ambiguity is possible; S and O are distinguishable not only by the context but also by case and/or number or gender (*hire* in *ÆCHom* i. 42. 30). This is true in the majority of OSV examples, as far as I have observed. But since SOV is found in principal clauses (§3914), the context is sometimes the sole but sufficient guide, e.g. *ÆCHom* i. 44. 18 *Đas seofon hi gecuron, ÆCHom* i. 544. 33 *Deoflu hi oferswyðdon*, and *LS* 34. 55 *and hi ða hæþenan men þonne hi cristene men ahwær fundon, hi hi ut drifon* (where the ambiguity is purely morphological), and possibly *ÆCHom* i. 402. 12 *Feowertig geara fyrst Godes mildheortnys forlet ðam wælhreowum ceastergewarum to behreowsunge heora mandæda* (where *mildheortnys* could be an inverted spelling for the accusative; see *OEG*, §592(*f*), and *ÆLS* 2. 160). The absence of any real SOV/OSV ambiguity is not surprising. The problem would be resolved in spoken prose by intonation. Its presence in writing would be a reflection on the author.

§3906. In OE, as in MnE, an adverb (element) can intervene between S and V; see further Mitchell 1966, pp. 90-1. Examples include *ÆCHom* i. 12. 28 *And God þa geworhte ænne mannan of lame, ÆCHom* i. 2. 24 . . . *ðe Ælfred cyning snoterlice awende, ÆHomM* 8. 156 *And heo swa geefenlæcð hire weres meder, ÆCHom* i. 204. 8 . . . *gif he mid þam gewitendlicum gestreonum beceapað him þæt ece lif*, and (perhaps not quite 'right' today) *ÆCHom* i. 12. 11 *ac hi æfre beoð ymbe þæt an.*

§3907. There are, however, patterns which are to be accepted as OE variants of SV but which are not possible in MnE. Here we must note particularly first, the idiomatic position of adv. *ne* 'not' immediately before V, e.g. *ÆCHom* i. 42. 5 *ac he næs* and (with a now-tautologic additional negative) *ÆCHom* i. 4. 18 *ac his tima ne bið na langsum* —on this, see §§1603-13—and second, the intervention of a pronoun object or of pronoun objects, direct and/or indirect, between S and V. This is regular, but not compulsory; see §3889 and Mitchell 1966, pp. 90 and 95. Typical examples include *ÆCHom* i. 122. 14

He hit gecwæð, ÆCHom i. 10. 18 *God hi gesceop ealle gode, ÆC Hom* i. 8. 10 . . . *þæt he hi geornlice gerihte, ÆCHom* i. 596. 19 *Æfter ðisum wordum he hine unscrydde, ÆCHom* ii. 450. 23 *Drihten me forgeaf ða æhta and Drihten hi me eft benam, ÆCHom* i. 30. 18 *efne ic eow bodige micelne gefean, ÆCHom* i. 372. 10 *Cucenne we hine forbærnað,* and *ÆCHom* ii. 182. 20 *and se halga wer hine betæhte ansundne his fæder.* The fact that another accusative element follows V in *ÆCHom* i. 10. 18, i. 30. 18, and ii. 182. 20, is for me proof that they are variants of SV, not examples of S . . . V. This establishes the possibility that the others may also be variants of SV. Certainty is, of course, impossible; hence the vital importance of distinguishing noun and pronoun objects—still not understood by all.

§3908. Except of course for adv. *ne,* e.g. *CP* 31. 7 *hie hie ne magon drincan* and *Solil* 16. 13 *Ic hi ne lufige,* the position of an adverb (element) in relation to the pronoun object varies; note *ÆCHom* i. 8. 10 and ii. 450. 23 (both in §3907), *ÆCHom* i. 12. 32 *God þa hine gebrohte cn neorxnawange, ÆCHom* ii. 32. 30 *þæt folc ða mid micelre fægnunge and singalre herunge hi gelæddon to ðære stowe, ÆCHom* i. 6. 17 . . . *ðeah þe he þurh deofles cræft hit swa gehiwige,* and *ÆCHom* ii. 394. 17 *ac þæt wif hine hrepode synderlice mid geleafan.* To Campbell (1970, pp. 96-7), the intervention of adverb and/or pronoun between S and V 'again recalls the language of verse'.

§3909. We turn now to patterns with verbal periphrases, symbolically SvV. Patterns idiomatic in both OE and MnE include *ÆCHom* i. 20. 27 *Ic wylle fordon eal mancynn . . . ac ic wylle gehealdan þe ænne, ÆCHom* i. 28. 12 *He hæfð gerymed rihtwisum mannum infær to his rice, ÆHom* 4. 165 . . . *for ðan ðe he is gehaten Godes hand on bocum,* and *ÆCHom* i. 18. 15 *and seo eorðe þe is awyriged on þinum weorce.* Adverb elements can intervene between the auxiliary and the participle or infinitive, e.g. *ÆCHom* i. 44. 30 *þæt folc wearð ða micclum astyred* and (perhaps not quite 'right' in MnE) *ÆCHom* i. 56. 27 *Ælc lof bið on ende gesungen.* Examples like the latter complicate the production of statistics; see Mitchell 1964*b*, p. 121 fn. 1, and consider *ÆCHom* i. 8. 26 . . . *forðan þe he bið æfre ungeendod.*

§3910. Intervention by other elements produces patterns which are certainly not acceptable in MnE but which equally certainly do not fall with OE examples of S . . . V, which requires S(. . .)Vv (§3913). We find (with accusative noun and pronoun objects) *ÆCHom* i. 10. 28 *Ðaða hi ealle hæfdon þysne ræd betwux him gefæstnod . . .* and *ÆCHom* i. 4. 26 *ac he ne mæg nænne gehælan . . .* ; (with indirect

object) *ÆCHom* i. 12. 34 *and hi ealle beoð þe betæhte*; (with complement) *ÆCHom* i. 358. 11 *He is Wisdom gehaten. . . . He is Word gecweden*; and (with adverb element) *ÆCHom* i. 10. 28, above, and
ÆCHom i. 14. 24 *. . . forðan ðe heo is of hire were genumen*. The list
could be extended. S and v can be separated by an adverb (element),
e.g. *ÆCHom* i. 20. 6 *Adam þa wæs wunigende on þisum life mid
geswince* and *ÆCHom* i. 160. 16 *. . . þær þær heo æfre bið on
pinungum wunigende*, where *æfre* is perhaps not quite 'right' for
MnE and *on pinungum* is certainly not. The initial infinitive in *ÆC
Hom* i. 142. 26 *Sprecan he mihte, gif he wolde* is emphatic: 'He
could certainly have spoken if he had wanted to'.

3. S . . . V IN THE PROSE

§3911. We turn now to S . . . V. For unambiguous examples of this
pattern, the intervening element must be or must include a noun
object (direct or indirect), a complement (noun or adjective), or the
participle or infinitive of a verbal paraphrase (S(. . .)Vv). This order
—sometimes called 'subordinate'—is common in clauses introduced
by *ond, ac,* or conj. *ne*, e.g. *ÆCHom* i. 14. 15 *and Adam him eallum
naman gesceop, ÆCHom* ii. 122. 21 *ac eal folc ðone eadigan Gregor-
ium to ðære geðincðe anmodlice geceas,* and *ÆCHom* ii. 94. 33 *. . .
ne heora nan gerefscipe oððe mangunge ne drife* (where Thorpe's
Ne is misleading; see §§1839–41), and in subordinate clauses, e.g.
ÆCHom i. 14. 17 *. . . þæt þes man ana beo, ÆCHom* i. 18. 12 *. . .
hwi he his bebod tobræce, ÆCHom* i. 2. 20 *. . . þe ungelærede menn
þurh heora bilewitnysse to micclum wisdome tealdon,* and *ÆCHom*
i. 4. 5 *. . . butan se Ælmihtiga God ða dagas gescyrte.*

§3912. S . . . V . . . also occurs. The additional element need not be
adverbial, e.g. *ÆCHom* i. 20. 7 *and he and his wif ða bearn gestryndon,
ægðer ge suna ge dohtra,* but most commonly is, e.g. *ÆCHom* i.
28. 17 *and he ðonne ða manfullan deofle betæcð into ðam ecan fyre
helle susle, ÆCHom* i. 4. 33 *. . . þæt hi wel wyrðe beoð þære deoflican
ehtnysse, ÆCHom* i. 36. 14, and *ÆCHom* ii. 556. 17 *se ðe ða soðan
lufe næfð to Gode and to mannum.* On the position of *þonne* in
ÆCHom i. 28. 17 and of *wel* in *ÆCHom* i. 4. 33, compare §3901.
For further variations after *ond* and *ac*, see §§1719–32 and 1753–66.

§3913. With periphrastic verb-forms, the patterns which belong here
are S(. . .)Vv and S(. . .)Vv . . . , e.g. *ÆCHom* i. 14. 22 *. . . hu heo
hatan sceolde, ÆCHom* i. 6. 13 *. . . þe hit him cyðan sceolde, ÆCHom*
ii. 6. 8 *. . . ðaða we forwyrhte wæron, ÆCHom* i. 14. 15 *. . . ðaða he*

hi gesceapene hæfde, ÆCHom i. 82. 28 . . . *gif he ða on cildcradole acweald wurde, swilce ðonnę his tocyme mancynne bediglod wære, ÆCHom* i. 12. 4 . . . *þe him gegearcod wæs for heora ofermettum, ÆCHom* i. 30. 33 . . . *þe him gesæd wæs be ðam cilde,* and *ÆCHom* i. 34. 2 . . . *þæt ælc synderlice be him sylfum cennan sceolde on ðære byrig þe he to hyrde.*

§3914. All the examples of S . . . V so far quoted have been in clauses introduced by *ond, ac,* or conj. *ne,* or in subordinate clauses. But it must be stressed that S . . . V and at least some of its variants —more work is needed here—are found in principal clauses and simple sentences, both in those which are introduced by an adverb element other than *ne* and in those which are not so introduced. Sentences like *CP* 239. 15 *Ðæt gesuinc hira agenra welena hie geðrycð,* with Spron.OV, do not belong here; see §3907. Examples which do, include *Or* 44. 22 *Hi þa þæt lond forleton, Or* 68. 30 *he ðæt setl* 7 *þæt gewin mid ealle forlet, Or* 112. 15 *He hwæðre þa burg gewann, Or* 116. 16 *He þa his here on tu todælde, Or* 206. 29 *On ðære ilcan tide Hannibal his agnum willum hine selfne mid atre acwealde, ÆCHom* i. 50. 17 (§3916), *ÆCHom* i. 50. 30 and i. 88. 2 (both in §11), *ÆCHom* i. 72. 17 *ic unforhtmod ðæs drences onfo, ÆCHom* i. 544. 27 *þa on westenum wunigende woruldlice estas and gælsan mid strecum mode and stiðum life fortrædon,* and *ÆCHom* ii. 138. 20 *Ic ðinum gedwylde dearnunge miltsige.* These are all S . . . V. We have S . . . V . . . in *ÆCHom* i. 74. 6 *Hi ða begen þone apostol gesohton, his miltsunge biddende* and perhaps in *ÆCHom* i. 426. 9 *Ic on mines Drihtnes naman nateshwon ne forhtige for ðinum tintregum.* But I am inclined to place the last example in limbo; see §3902. Andrew's comment (*SS,* p. 53) on a group of four sentences which includes *Bede* 260. 5 *ic lustlice from þære þegnunge gewite* and *ÆCHom* ii. 96. 30 *He symle on his legere Gode ðancode* reads 'This is evidently the ancestor of the ModE order'. This refers only to the position of the adverb.

§3915. There are also examples of S(. . .)Vv(. . .) in the clauses now under discussion. They include *CP* 255. 22 *Baloham ðonne fulgeorne feran wolde, Or* 110. 6 *he mid eallum his mægene wið Romane winnan angan, Or* 76. 27 *Hio mid þæm healfan dæle beforan þæm cyninge farende wæs, Or* 58. 16 *hit God siþþan longsumlice wrecende wæs, ærest on him selfum,* 7 *siþþan on his bearnum . . . , Or* 86. 29 *Sona æfter þæm ealle heora þeowas wið þa hlafordas winnende wæron . . . ,* and other examples with a present participle cited by Bacquet, p. 628. So it was in my opinion unnecessary for Andrew

(*SS*, pp. 58-9) to explain away *Or* 56. 14 *Læcedemoniæ 7 Mesiane, Creca leode, him betweonum winnende wæron xx wintra* and *ÆCHom* ii. 334. 9 *Ða ðry englas gelicere beorhtnysse scinende wæron*. The existence of examples of S(. . .)Vv(. . .) in these sentences means that we cannot use element order to classify as principal or subordinate the *nu* clause in *Or* 74. 26 *Nu ic þuss gehroren eam 7 aweg gewiten, hwæt, ge magan on me ongietan 7 oncnawan þæt ge nanuht mid eow nabbað fæstes ne stronges þætte þurhwunigean mæge.*

§3916. Bacquet (pp. 617-29 and 645-6) cites more examples. But many of them are irrelevant because they are in clauses introduced by *ond, ac*, or conj. *ne*, and/or because they have pronoun objects. Bacquet regards sentences with a final verb as emphatic ('marqué'). Campbell (*RES* 15 (1964), 193) says that their 'emphatic nature is not certain'. I agree; see Mitchell 1966, p. 88, where I suggest that they might be explained as part of the 'traces de l'ancien système germanique' (Bacquet, p. 691). Campbell (1970, pp. 96-7), comparing *ÆCHom* i. 50. 17 *Ða reðan Iudei wedende þone halgan stændon* with *Beo* 7 *he þæs frofre gebad*, saw here too the possibility of 'contacts between the language of prose and verse'.

4. VS IN THE PROSE

§3917. Failure to distinguish patterns with initial V/v from those in which some element precedes V/v and the indiscriminate lumping together of the latter irrespective of the nature of that element have vitiated much previous work here; see Mitchell 1964*b*, pp. 117-18, and 1966, pp. 93-4. Even Kohonen, who recognizes this (1976, p. 181 and *passim*), gives blanket figures for main clauses introduced by 'some adverbial modifier or object or complement' in his Concluding Remarks (p. 193). In the periphrastic forms, we find both vSV and vVS; compare *ÆCHom* i. 92. 16 *Sarai wæs his wif gehaten* with *ÆCHom* i. 76. 16 *Manna wæs gehaten se heofenlica mete*. To save space, these patterns are subsumed under VS in the sections which follow, except when it is desirable to make the distinctions.

✕ §3918. Sentences or principal clauses with OVS include those with a direct noun or pronoun object cited in §10 and those with an indirect object or dative of interest, e.g. *ÆCHom* i. 86. 5 *Him wæs metes micel lust, ÆCHom* i. 86. 13 *Him stod stincende steam of ðam muðe, ÆCHom* i. 144. 24 *Ðam ungeleaffullum mannum com Crist to hryre, ÆCHom* ii. 384. 8, and *ÆCHom* i. 58. 19 *Witodlice ðisum leofan leorningcnihte befæste se Hælend his modor*. In §3907

I asserted that Spron.OV could be an idiomatic variation of SVO. I hesitate to apply an analogical argument here; see §3929. Examples with CVS include the two examples in §3917, *ÆCHom* i. 88. 10 *þyllic wæs Herodes forðsið*, *ÆCHom* i. 176. 9 *Ungewiss com se deofol to Criste*, and *ÆCHom* i. 238. 24 *God hyrde wæs Petrus and god wæs Paulus and gode wæron ða apostoli*. These orders can also occur after *ond* and *ac*, e.g. the sentences quoted in §1722, *ÆCHom* i. 180. 9 *ac þæt fæsten tælð God*, *ÆCHom* ii. 64. 15 *and hine astyrode se awyrigeda gast fram Gode*, *ÆCHom* i. 180. 32 *and him filigde micel menigu*, and (we can perhaps add) *ÆCHom* ii. 528. 6 *ac him næs þære bene getiðod*, where *þære bene* is the logical subject. So element order cannot tell us whether we have principal or subordinate clauses in the clause which immediately follows *getiðod* in the last example (*ÆCHom* ii. 528. 6 . . . *getiðod, forðan ðe him fremede to ecere hælþe seo hwilwende ehtnys*), in *ÆCHom* i. 50. 27 *and rihtlice swiðor, forðan ðe heora arleasnysse fyligde se eca deað, and þæt ece lif fyligde his deaðe* (note the chiasmus), and in *ÆCHom* i. 310. 2 *þæt rihtlice is gecweden, þæt he sæte æfter his upstige, forðan ðe deman gedafnað setl*, or whether *þam* is demonstrative or relative in *ÆCHom* ii. 542. 5 *Ic soðlice sylle eow muð and wisdom, þam ne magon wiðstandan ne wiðcweðan ealle eowere wiðerwinnan*.

§3919. But I have not found any real ambiguity of meaning arising from the use of these patterns. The context, even without the aid of inflexions and/or intonation, is in my experience usually decisive. See again §10. Kohonen (1976, pp. 187–90) reports that in *ÆCHom* i initial objects almost all contained given or known information and that the choice between OVS and OSV depended on the length and weight of the subject—OVS when it was long, OSV when it was a pronoun or some other 'rhythmically light one-word subject'.

§3920. Some of these variations of SVO/C are possible today for the achievement of special effects, e.g. adjectiveCVS in *ÆCHom* ii. 314. 20 *Manega sind beboda mannum gesette* 'Many are the commandments appointed for men', and *ÆCHom* i. 88. 10 (§3918) 'Such was Herod's death', and possibly examples like *ÆCHom* i. 406. 26 *Him ða to genealæhton blinde and healte* 'To Him then drew near the blind and the lame'. Some linger on as archaisms; cf. *CP* 3. 18 *Gode ælmihtegum sie ðonc* with 'To God be the glory'. Some would be impossible today. These include nounCVS in *ÆCHom* i. 76. 16 (§3917) and *ÆCHom* i. 92. 16 (§3917); nounOVS in *ÆC Hom* i. 310. 2 (§3918); and even pron.OVS in *ChronE* 79. 24 (885) *7 hine ofsloh an eofor*, where—such is the strength of the SVO pattern today—'and him slew a boar' would be taken by most people as SVO, with 'him' an error for 'he'.

§3921. Other nominal elements may occur initially, e.g. the genitive group in *ÆCHom* i. 44. 13 *þæra diacona wæs se forma Stephanus*, MnE 'Of these deacons the first was Stephen', not '. . . was the first . . .'.

§3922. The frequency of VS is greatest in simple sentences and principal clauses introduced by the ambiguous adverb/conjunctions *þær, þanon, þider, þa*, and *þonne*. With these words, it serves in the prose as a useful, but not infallible, guide in answering the question 'Principal clause or subordinate?' For even after these words the absence of the order VS does not certify—either in the prose or, still less, in the poetry—that they are not used as adverbs. Thus, we find SV in *ChronA* 88. 27 (895) *Ða þy ylcan gere onforan winter þa Deniscan þe on Meresige sæton tugon hira scipu up on Temese* and *ÆCHom* i. 12. 5 *þa sona þa nigon werod þe ðær to lafe wæron, bugon to heora Scyppende* (cf. *ÆCHom* i. 508. 7 *Hi ða sona þæs on merigen ðider mid heora offrungum bliðe comon*). In such examples, the intervention of other elements may be responsible for SV; cf. *ÆCHom* i. 414. 7. *þa on ðære ylcan tide þe he geendian sceolde, ða beseah he up*, where the repetition of *ða* probably ensured VS. But *þa* is immediately followed by S in *GD(C)* 142. 11 *mid þy þe he þa flascan gehylde, þa wæs þær hraðe sumu nædre ut gangende. þa se forecwedena cniht Exhilaratus for þære nædran þe he on ðam wine gemette, aforhtode 7 him swiþe ondred þæt yfel þe he him sylf gedyde*, Latin *cum flasconem inclinassit, de eo protinus serpens egressus est. tunc praedictus Exhilaratus puer, per hoc quod in vino repperit, expavit malum quod fecit*, where *GD(H)* 142. 12 has *se forecwedena cniht Exilaratus þa aforhtode*. . . . For other (possible) examples after *þær, þa*, and *þonne*, and for fuller discussion, see §§2518-26 and 2543-54. Whether in such examples as *Bede* 166. 28 *þa com he ærest upp in Westseaxum 7 heo þær hæðne gemette, þa ðuhte him nyttre 7 betre þæt* . . . we can translate *þa com he* as 'When he came' is another difficult question; see §§2544-6. But, despite the difficulties, editors of prose texts should not disregard too easily the rule of thumb that after *þær, þanon, þider, þa*, and *þonne*, clauses with SV or S . . . V are likely to be subordinate; consider *ChronA* 84. 33 (894) (§2553) and *ChronA* 62. 17 (835) *þa he þæt hierde 7 mid fierde ferde 7 him wiþ feaht æt Hengestdune*, where MS *B* has what I take to be a proper reading: *Ða he þ hyrde. þa ferde he þider mid fyrde*. . . .

§3923. Both Campbell (*RES* 15 (1964), 192-3) and I (Mitchell 1966, pp. 93-4) agree that VS after *þa* and *þonne* is not an emphatic order ('marqué'), as Bacquet (pp. 596-617) claims, but is the norm —though not the 'rule'—after these words when they are adverbs. I do not understand what distinction Bacquet can have had in mind when he said that *þa/þonne* VS is 'marqué', but that *þa/þonne* SV can embody 'le mode emphatique' (p. 599).

§3924. In negated principal clauses or simple sentences, we find *þa* and *þonne* in both initial position, e.g. *Bo* 107. 10 *ðonne ne gelyfð he nanes soðes, Bo* 127. 12 *þa ne meahte he geþencan . . . , CP* 69. 19 *ðonne ne mæg he noht geseon,* and *Deut* 1. 26 *Ða noldon ge faran,* and following initial *Ne* + verb, e.g. *Bo* 33. 23 *Næron þa welige hamas ne mistlice swotmettas ne drincas,* (with unexpressed subject) *Bo* 55. 26 *Nyton þonne nan herre good . . . ,* and *ÆCHom* i. 6. 13 *Ne sende se deofol ða fyr of heofenum, þeah ðe hit ufan come.* More work is needed to establish the relative frequency of these patterns, to discover whether one is more common with periphrastic verb-forms and/or with noun subjects (here see Bacquet, p. 644 fn. 1), and to examine their semantic implications. *Ða* in *Deut* 1. 26, above, is as it were resumptive, '(And) then', referring to the next stage in the action, whereas *ða* in *ÆCHom* i. 6. 13 means rather 'When he did that', referring to a specific action in the past, or (to use a modern cliché) 'at that point in time'.

§3925. With other ambiguous adverb/conjunctions, 'exceptions' with Adv.SV or Adv.S . . . V are in varying degrees almost the 'rule'. Andrew (*SS,* §35) suggests that as adverbs 'such words as *ær, forðam, nu, siððan, swa, þeah*' are normally followed by SV and that 'it is no doubt the desire to avoid ambiguity' which accounts for the occasional use of VS in the principal clause of a correlative pair. This is in my experience sound. But I would not follow Andrew in restricting VS to principal clauses or S . . . V to subordinate clauses after these words or (the implied corollary) in believing that VS certifies that these words are adverbs and S . . . V that they are conjunctions.

§3926. We have VS after *nu* in what are clearly principal clauses in *ÆCHom* i. 8. 9 *Nu bidde ic . . .* and *ÆCHom* i. 16. 19 *Nu cwædon gedwolmen. . . .* But in *ÆCHom* i. 478. 1 *Nu hæbbe ge oft gehyred be his mæran drohtnunge and be his ðenunge, nu wylle we embe ðises godspelles trahtnunge sume swutelunge eow gereccan,* the first clause may be subordinate; see §3101. We have SV in principal clauses in *ÆCHom* i. 56. 34 *nu todæg hi underfengon Stephanum* and *ÆCHom* i. 64. 26 *nu ge ondrædað eow deoflu*. But in *ÆCHom* i. 38. 34 *Nu we sind getealde Godes ceastergewaran and englum gelice uton forði hogian þæt leahtras us ne totwæmon fram ðisum micclum wurðmynte, forði* and the exhortation may suggest to a modern reader that the preceding *nu* with SV is subordinate; see Andrew, *SS*, §36, and *ÆCHom* i. 66. 29. I have already recorded S . . . V in clauses which can be taken as subordinate, e.g. *Bede* 348. 2 (§3099) and *ÆCHom* i. 588. 1 (§3102). But the *nu* clause in *ÆCHom* i. 56. 30 *nu todæg se æðela cempa Stephanus, fram lichamlicere wununge gewitende, sigefæst to heofenum ferde* is certainly not subordinate and contains an order which I am strongly tempted to describe as S . . . V.

§3927. Similar fluctuations and ambiguities occur with *ær*, e.g. *ÆCHom* ii. 252. 34 *ær hi sind gebundene ær hi beon geborene*, where the mood alone is decisive, but *ÆCHom* ii. 166. 18 *ac ær se ærendraca mihte to ðam gebroðrum becuman, ær hæfde se deofol towend þone weall*; with *forþon (þe)* (for examples see §§3033 and 3072); with *siþþan*, e.g. *ÆCHom* i. 72. 21 (§2669) and *ÆCHom* i. 460. 24 *Se awyrigeda deofol, siððan he ðone frumsceapenan mann beswac, syððan he hæfde anweald on ungelyfedum mannum* . . . but *ÆCHom* i. 304. 29 *syððan se geleafa sprang geond ealne middangeard, siððan geswicon ða wundra*; with *swa* (see §§3267–70); and with *þeah*, e.g. *ÆGram* 264. 13 *quamuis non roget, tamen uult habere, ðeah ðe he ne bidde þeah he wyle habban . tamen uult, ðeah he wyle* but *CP* 49. 11 *ðeah heo an tu tefleowe, ðeah wæs sio æspryng sio soðe lufu.*

§3928. A full survey of other variations when V immediately follows an ambiguous adverb/conjunction cannot be attempted here. In *NQ* 222 (1977), 2–11, Stanley argues convincingly that *Or* 20. 11 *7 þonne benimð Wisle Ilfing hire naman* should be translated 'And then the Ilfing makes off with the Vistula's name', but regrets his inability 'to find an ideal parallel, i.e. using a subject hemmed in by objects on either side, and all three nouns, and on top of that an adverbial beginning of the sentence immediately followed by the verb'. I too have found no ideal parallel, but can adduce in partial support *ÆCHom* i. 34. 5 . . . *swa eac nu us cyðað lareowas Cristes gebann*, where the first object is a pronoun and therefore can precede the verb, and *VercHom(V)* 1. 104 *Ða sende he Crist Anna gebundenne to Caifan.* We may have Adv.VOS in *Cæd(M)* 1; see §1515. In *Beo* 377 we have Adv.VOSO, but the first O is a pronoun, the second a clause in apposition with it.

§3929. When the clause is introduced by an element—single word, prepositional or non-prepositional phrase, or clause—which cannot be a conjunction, there is no possibility that it can be subordinate. So it is not surprising to find fluctuations in element order. A few examples will suffice: *ChronE* 95. 1 (906) *Her gefestnode Eadward cyng for neode frið* but *ChronE* 95. 3 (910) *Her Englehere 7 Dene gefuhton æt Teotanheale* and *ChronE* 75. 7 (876) *Her hine bestæl se here into Wærham*, which I believe to be an example of OVS rather than a variation of VS (cf. §§3918-20); *ChronA* 90. 11 (897) *þy ilcan geare drehton þa hergas . . . WestSeaxna lond, ÆCHom* i. 56. 28 *Mine gebroðra, gyrstandæg gemedemode ure Drihten hine sylfne*, and *ÆLS* 21. 290 *Hwilon wacodon menn . . .* but *Or* 226. 17 *Ac þære ilcan niht þe mon on dæg hæfde þa burg mid stacum gemearcod, swa swa hie hie þa wyrcean woldon, wulfas atugan þa stacan up* and *ÆC Hom* ii. 286. 25 *Oðrum dagum þu underfenge me on minum limum, gyrstandæg þu underfenge me on me sylfum*; *CP* 37. 15 *Bi ðam cuæð Salomonn se snottra* but *CP* 43. 8 *Be ðam Paulus se apostol cuæð*; *ÆCHom* i. 122. 16 *On gastlicum andgite getacnode þes hreoflia man eal mancyn* but *ÆCHom* i. 80. 4 *Of Egypta lande ic geclypode minne sunu*; *ÆCHom* ii. 286. 23 *Eft on þære ylcan nihte cwæð se Hælend . . .* but *ÆCHom* i. 56. 5 *Witodlice þurh ðines feondes lufe þu bist Godes freond* and *ÆCHom* i. 128. 12 *Gyrstandæg ofer midne dæg hine forlet se fefor* (this too is unlikely to be a variation of VS); and *ÆCHom* i. 334. 20 *Gif hi forseoð Moyses æ and ðæra witegena bodunga, nellað hi gelyfan, þeah hwa of deaðe arise* but *ÆCHom* ii. 322. 11 *Gif ge me gehyrað, ge etað þære eorðan god; gif ge me geyrsiað, eow fornimð min swurd*. Examples such as *ÆCHom* i. 334. 20 illustrate what Campbell (*RES* 15 (1964), 192) calls 'the general tendency to invert subject and verb in principal clauses if the subject has not the first place, so that the verb remains in the second place'. But it is obviously no more than a tendency.

§3930. We turn now to simple sentences and principal clauses in the prose which have initial V. Positive examples with VS include idiomatic substitutes for MnE 'There is/was . . .', e.g. *ÆCHom* i. 280. 26 *Is forþi þonne an Fæder, ÆCHom* i. 386. 17 *Wæs ða sum Godes ðegen binnan ðære byrig*, and (after *and*) *ÆLS* 32. 179 *and wæs swylce an seolcen þræd embe his swuran*; sentences with a verb of saying, e.g. *Bede* 70. 3 *Cwæð he, BlHom* 19. 17 *Cwæþ se godspellere*, and *ÆCHom* ii. 508. 26 *cwæð þeah heora an*;[1] and sentences with an

---

[1] There is room for more work here. See Andrew, *SS,* §58; Bacquet, p. 591; Robinson 1973, p. 474; and my §1949. Andrew (ibid.) says that 'Ælfric always has He cwæð.' I have noted no examples in *ÆCHom* of sentences beginning *Cwæð he*.

impersonal verb + a noun clause subject where MnE would begin with 'It ...', e.g. *ÆCHom* i. 6. 18 *Bið nu wislicor þæt gehwa ðis wite.*

§3931. I would not regard the order VS as conveying emphasis in any of these examples, even though Bacquet (p. 588) appears to imply that it does in *Or* 142. 13 and 212. 25 ... *cwæð he*.... I agree with Andrew (*SS*, §58) that *he* is unstressed in *Bede* 194. 6 *Wæs he Osrices sunu. ... Wæs he seofon winter Dera cyning. ... Wæs he se mon æfest 7 arfæst....* But I find it hard to understand how Bacquet (pp. 585-96) knew that the order VS is emphatic ('marqué') in examples like *Bo* 86. 10 *Is þis la wundorlic 7 wynsum 7 gesceadwislic spell þ ðu nu sægst* (though *la* may imply emphasis), *Or* 90. 12, and *Or* 118. 6 *Wæs þæt micel wundor þæt swa micel here for þæs cynges fielle fleah* (so also Andrew, *SS*, §58), and *CP* 467. 31 *Is hit lytel tweo ðæt ðæs wæterscipes welsprynge is on hefonrice.* Why are these sentences more emphatic than *Or* 21. 10 *7 þæt is mid Estum þeaw þæt þær sceal ælces geðeodes man beon forbærned, Bede* 164. 27 *þæt is wundor to cweðanne, Bede* 166. 11 *þæt eac swa æfter þam willan his bletsunge geworden wæs,* and *CP* 467. 28 *Ðis is nu se wæterscipe ðe us wereda God to frofre gehet foldbuendum?*

§3932. I have the same difficulty with the examples with a noun subject which Bacquet (ibid.) lists among his examples of the first type of 'la déclarative marquée'. I disregard here all those sentences which begin with anything other than V/v, including adverbial elements, subordinate clauses, and clauses introduced by *ond, ac,* and the like; see Campbell, *RES* 15 (1964), 192, and Mitchell 1966, p. 93. With Bacquet (p. 587), I exclude sentences with no expressed subject, such as *ÆCHom* i. 28. 5 *Com þa to his apostolum* and *ÆC Hom* i. 80. 14 *Sende ða his cwelleras*; on these see §§1690-8. But I have no means of knowing whether or not initial V imparts special emphasis to those which survive these tests, such as *Bo* 135. 25 *Healdað þa tunglu þa ealdan sibbe þe hi on gesceapne wæron, Or* 34. 25 *Wæs se hunger on þæs cyninges dagum on Egyptum þe mon hæt Amoses,* where the Latin has *Fuit itaque haec fames magna ...,* and *Bo* 10. 19 *Sittað manfulle on heahsetlum.*[2] Nor do I know how QW (p. 94) can make the distinction suggested in the following passage: 'V in initial position, in some cases for special declarative effect (*Wæs hit þa on ælce wisan hefig tyma* "It was then in every

---

[2] Examples such as these certify that *gehyraþ* in *BlHom* 19. 19 *Gehyraþ we nu þæt seo mennisce gecynd biþ a færende* could be indicative. Despite Visser (ii, §844), I do not believe it is an imperative; see Mitchell 1979b, pp. 538-9. But it could be a scribal error for *Gehyran*; see *BlHom* 19. 10 and cf. *BlHom* 21. 33.

way a grievous time", *Gegrette þa guma operne* "Then the one man saluted the other"), in other cases apparently because individual writers were fond of this style (it is especially common, for instance, in the Ælfredian Bede and in some of the poetry).' I can see that there may be some degree of emphasis in examples like *ÆCHom* i. 18. 8 *Wearð þeah þæt wif ða forspanen þurh ðæs deofles lare* and *ÆCHom* i. 102. 20 *Is hwæðere æfter gecynde on gesceapennysse ælc lichamlice gesceaft ðe eorðe acenð fulre and mægenfæstre on fullum monan þonne on gewanedum.* But whether it is due to the element order or to the presence of *þeah* or *hwæðere* I cannot tell. Similarly, I do not know how to decide whether examples with vS(. . .)V such as *ChronA* 84. 31 (894) *hæfde se cyning his fierd on tu tonumen* and *ChronA* 86. 16 (894) *wæs Hæsten þa þær cumen mid his herge* are emphatic or not. I do not reject emphasis as an explanation for at least some of the quoted examples. I just do not know how to test it.

§3933. There are other possible factors. We have already noted QW's mention of personal preference (§3932) and Campbell's suggestion about the influence of the verse tendency to place the verb before the first stress, originally with noun subjects and then analogically with pronoun subjects (§3892). Stylistic considerations—balance, rhythm, a desire for chiasmus—may sometimes play a part. I am also attracted by Fred C. Robinson's suggestion (private communication) that initial V often seems to mark a turning-point, a transition, or a change of pace, in the prose—just as a new paragraph does in MnE prose; consider, for example, *ÆCHom* i. 44. 20 *Weox ða dæghwonlice Godes bodung* and *ÆCHom* i. 50. 32 *Wearð ða Stephanes ben fram Gode gehyred*; cf. Kohonen's observations (1976, p. 187 fn. 1).

§3934. The order VS also occurs after *ond* and similar conjunctions and in subordinate clauses. In *Bo* 103. 21 *Her endað nu sio þridde boc Boeties 7 onginneð sio fiorðe*, apparently regarded by Bacquet (p. 591) as emphatic, I detect the influence of *Her* in both clauses. We have the equivalent of MnE 'and there will be' in *ÆCHom* i. 2. 29 *and beoð fela frecednyssa on mancynne.* Of *Or* 164. 18 *7 wæron þa men toðon dysige þæt hie wendon*—another of Bacquet's examples (p. 594)—Campbell (*RES* 15 (1964), 192) writes: 'It has already been pointed out that *ond* clauses are subordinate. This curious inversion in them may perhaps be regarded as emphatic, but clauses with it should be classified as exhibiting a variation on the basic order of the subordinate clause.[4]' Campbell's footnote 4 begins 'They are frequent with other conjunctions as well as *ond*.' I cite a few typical examples: *ÆCHom* i. 30. 1 . . . *gebann þæt wære on gewritum asett eall ymbhwyrft*, *ÆCHom* i. 110. 6 . . . *þæt wæron sume gedwolmen* '. . . that there were . . .', *ÆCHom* i. 50. 35 . . . *hu micclum fremige þære soðan lufe gebed*, and *ÆCHom* i. 38. 5 . . . *þy læs ðe wære geþuht anes engles ealdordom to hwonlic to swa micelre bodunge*, where *ðe* cannot be the personal pronoun. VS also occurs in clauses which can reasonably be taken as adjective, e.g. *ÆCHom* i. 352. 14 *Cristes fulluht he bodade toweard eallum geleaffullum, on ðam is synna forgyfenys þurh ðone Halgan Gast* and *ÆCHom* ii. 562. 25 *Ðeos andwerde gelaðung, þe underfehð yfele and gode, is wiðmeten ðam tyn mædenum, ðæra wæron fif stunte and fif snotere*; the unambiguous relative *on ðære þe* in *ÆCHom* i. 592. 34 *Ne belaf nan ceaster on eallum ðisum earde on ðære þe næron ure goda templa forlætene* seems to me to clinch the possibility, even though the verb is negated. With Campbell (above), I hesitate to regard these as emphatic. See also §3892.

§3935. We must now consider sentences with a negated initial verb. In these, adv. *ne* must precede the verb, as in *ÆCHom* i. 592. 34, above, 'Not one city has remained', 'No city has remained', 'There has remained no city', or 'There has not remained one city', *ÆCHom* ii. 350. 14 *Nis þis wite seo hell þe ðu wenst*, *ÆCHom* i. 82. 20 *ne com he* . . . , and (with v . . . V) *ChronA* 89. 30 (897) *Næfde se here, Godes þonces, Angelcyn ealles forswiðe gebrocad*, *ÆCHom* i. 40. 18 *Næs þæt word to flæsce awend*, and *ÆLS* 21. 424 *Ne mage we awritan ne mid wordum asecgan ealle þa wundra*. This *ne* VS arrangement is more common than Spron.O *ne* V, as in *Solil* 16. 13 *Ic hi ne lufige*, or S *ne* VO, as in *ÆCHom* ii. 110. 33 *He ne andwyrde ðam wife æt fruman*, on which see §1599. However, as Campbell puts it (*RES* 15 (1964), 191), Bacquet (pp. 127–34 and 629–44) 'chooses in the teeth of the statistics to regard the type *He hine ne geseah* as normal, and the ordinary *Ne geseah he hine* as emphatic. This is an improbable view, and M. Bacquet's case for it is built upon a misapprehension.' Campbell (pp. 191 and 192) and I (Mitchell 1966, pp. 91–2) give the same reasons for rejecting it. There is room for more work here. Anyone attempting it will need to take cognizance of the criticisms of Bacquet just referred to; to distinguish examples with noun subjects from those with pronoun subjects (this despite Bacquet, p. 66 fn. 2) and those with noun objects from those with pronoun objects (I have found few nounS and few pron.O in sentences with initial S); and to consider the question of stress. This last point is raised by Andrew (*SS*, §72) and by Bacquet (for example, in his comments on *Solil* 16. 5 on p. 630). But the difficulties of deciding on the stress pattern of any individual OE sentence—one of my constant themes—can be illustrated by reference to *CP* 63. 4 *Ne mæg ic ðæt ærendigean: ic ne eom him sua hiwcuð*, where what emphasis there is seems to me to fall on *ðæt* and *hiwcuð* and where I find it hard to believe that the difference in order signals that the first clause is emphatic, the second not, as Bacquet's theory would require.

§3936. It has become clear that there has been much discussion about the reason for, and the effect of, placing V before S in the various patterns described above. In the absence of intonation patterns and native informants, I must leave the problem here. Those wishing to give it further consideration will need to pay special attention to three works already much mentioned: Bacquet, pp. 585-646 (despite my almost complete disagreement with him), Campbell 1970, and Kohonen, 1976. They will also find that Snegireva (my §3890) has some valuable comments and suggestions about VS, including the following: it is used to contrast with the other orders; to link sentences, especially in oral narratives; to introduce new facts or a new train of thought; to change the emphasis; or to narrate a dynamic sequence of events by developing the narrative from stage to stage. Cf. §3933.

E. THE RELATIVE ORDER OF ELEMENTS OTHER THAN S AND V

§3937. Here too there is room for more of the detailed descriptive work in both prose and poetry which is made possible by *A Microfiche Concordance to Old English*. Andrew (*SS*, §§56-71) is always stimulating but sometimes wrong. Bacquet, despite his faults, must be consulted; see Campbell, *RES* 15 (1964), 190. However, full documentation is not possible here. But the sort of problems which await solution can be illustrated by the fact that as yet I have recorded no examples of indefinite *man* 'one' beginning a sentence; BT (s.v.) has two apparent examples but suppresses 7 in both. *Man* frequently occupies first position after *ond* and *ac*, after a subordinating conjunction, and after a non-nominative relative pronoun; note that it immediately follows *þær* in both the correlative clauses in *ChronE* 142. 6 (1011) *þær man mihte þa geseon earmðe þær man ær geseah blisse.* . . . But a pronoun object often intervenes, as in *ÆCHom* ii. 24. 22 *ac him man lede onuppan his agene tunecan*. On this see Smith, p. 242; Traugott, p. 109; Bacquet, p. 391 and *passim*; and

Campbell, *RES* 15 (1964), 192 fn. 1. Again, Andrew (*SS*, §66) argues that there can be 'no . . . justification' for *BlHom* 7. 7 *and on eallum monna cynne þe him hine ondrædað* 'which occurs more than once . . . this may be a scribal error for Ða þe hine him ondrædað'. This is not the pattern discussed in §2186 and I sense that he is wrong, for the reflexive *him* seems to go naturally with the subject *þe*—not *ða þe*, as Andrew reports. But I lack the evidence to demonstrate it. For more such difficulties see §§3940-3.

§3938. The position of complements and of direct and indirect objects has been discussed in this chapter. The following list covers only the major topics pursued in this book but can be supplemented from the Indexes: the breaking-up of groups joined by *ond, ac, ne*, and the like (§§1464-72); the order of appositional elements (§§1459-63); the relative order of noun qualifiers and of elements which modify them (§§142-80); the position of the attributive genitive (§§1304-30); the arrangement of compound numerals (§§555-60 and 569); the relative order of the elements in periphrastic verb-forms involving second participles in perfect tenses (§§702-43) and in the passive voice (§§757-8), present participles (§§682-701), infinitives (§§962-4), and 'modal' verbs (§§997-9); the position of negatives (§§1595-632); the position and stress of adverbs (§§ 1592-4 and 3942); pre-position and post-position of words traditionally called 'prepositions' (§§1060-80, Mitchell 1978*a*, and Mitchell 1980*b*); and interjections in initial, medial, or final, position (§§1234-9).

§3939. Co-ordinating conjunctions such as *ond* and *ac*, subordinating conjunctions, and relative pronouns, appear at the beginning of their clause. Occasionally material which properly belongs to a subordinate clause precedes it; see §1920. Occasionally material which belongs to the principal clause is placed in a subordinate clause; see §1921a. On clause order see §§1897-922.

§3940. To conclude this discussion, I offer the comments promised in §3937 on more difficulties which await solution. Objects have been discussed in §§1565-80. It is noticeable that pron.O tends to precede nounO, whether direct or indirect, e.g. *ÆLS* 32. 5 *swa swa Eadmundes swurdbora hit rehte Æþelstane cynincge, ÆCHom* i. 56. 17 *We secgað eow Godes riht, ÆCHom* ii. 450. 23 *Drihten me forgeaf ða æhta, ÆCHom* i. 478. 26 *and forgeaf hi his breðer Herode*, and *ÆCHom* i. 480. 16 *and cyðað him þa ðing þe ge gesawon and gehyrdon*. But when both the direct and indirect objects are nouns, their relative position varies; compare *ÆCHom* i. 482. 15 *God sylf forbyt ælcne að cristenum mannum* with *ÆCHom* i. 42. 27 *Godes heahengel Gabrihel bodode Marian ðæs Hælendes tocyme, ÆCHom* i. 124. 12 *and geopenian his digelnysse ðam gastlican læce* with *ÆCHom* i. 22. 22 *and sealde ælcum men þe ðær wæs synderlice spræce,* and *ÆCHom* i. 36. 8 *and se engel cydde Cristes acennednysse hyrdemannum* with *ÆCHom* i. 480. 13 *and wodum mannum gewitt forgeaf.*

§3941. The relative percentages in different prose texts of vV and Vv in principal, co-ordinate, and subordinate, clauses can be of value in determining authorship; see Liggins (1970, pp. 312–13) on 'Alfredian' texts and Baker (*Speculum,* 55 (1980), 27–8, 32, and 36) on the Byrhtferth canon. But I doubt whether such statistics will help with the dating of texts or will throw much light on the rate at which Vv was disappearing in OE. Baker's study has shown that marked variation can occur in texts of similar date and provenance. It is impossible to disentangle the strength of such factors as age, conservatism, pedagogic influence, and stylistic preference, on individual writers. But more analysis of periphrastic verb-forms with three elements, as in *ÆCHom* i. 262. 12 . . . *sceal* . . . *beon* . . . *gemyngod,* is necessary before we can be sure which patterns do not occur; see, for example, §758 and Traugott, p. 109. Bliss (*ASE* 9 (1980), 178–9) has suggested that 'there are a number of constraints controlling the word order in clauses containing an auxiliary and a verbal ['an infinitive or past participle' (his p. 158)]; there are also a number of tendencies which, while they cannot be said to control the word order, none the less make one word order preferable to another'. As Bliss (p. 179) remarks, his paper, which is based on *Beowulf,* opens up 'some obvious fields for further study'.

§3942. As noted already (for example in §§3903 and 3909), adverbs and adverb elements, including prepositional and non-prepositional phrases, occur in positions which are unidiomatic in MnE. To what extent, if any, the reverse is true, I do not know. Here the possibility of a detailed comparison of the positions occupied by these elements in OE, its Germanic cognates, and MnE, presents itself; anyone attempting it should not forget the work of Schlachter (Palaestra, 200 (1935)) and of Roberts (*JEGP* 35 (1936), 466–81). But, as far as I have observed, OE does not have fixed rules of precedence; compare *ÆCHom* i. 36. 35 *þa færlice* . . . with *ÆCHom* i. 40. 31 *Hrædlice ða* . . . , consider *ÆCHom* i. 28. 20 *and mid micelre gymene forbugað unrihtwysnysse, and geearniað mid godum weorcum þæt ece lif mid Gode* . . . , and note the different relative positions of the elements of time, manner, and place, in *ÆCHom* i. 28. 3 *and aras of deaðe mid þam micclum werede on þam þriddan dæge his þrowunge,* *ÆCHom* i. 28. 9 *Drihten ða on ðam feowerteogoðan dæge his æristes astah to heofenum, ætforan heora ealra gesihðe, mid þam ylcan lichaman þe he on þrowode,* and *ÆCHom* i. 28. 14 *Witodlice he cymð on ende þyssere worulde mid micclum mægenþrymme on wolcnum.*

§3943. Finally, it must be said that the extent to which the usage of poetry differs from that of prose, in the arrangement not only of S and V but also in that of other elements, remains to be established.

F. PROBLEMS PECULIAR TO THE POETRY

§3944. Here again a critical review of the work so far done is badly needed; I can but scratch the surface. I begin by reminding the reader that the three basic element orders already described occur in the poetry in both principal and subordinate clauses; that they are certainly even less help in poetry than in prose for solving the problem of the ambiguous principal/subordinate clause (see Andrew, *SS*, §§92-6, and Mitchell 1968*b*, pp. 190-1, and §2560); and that we find the order S . . . V in the first three principal clauses in *Beowulf*, viz.

Beo 1   Hwæt, we Gardena   in geardagum,
              þeodcyninga   þrym gefrunon,

Beo 4   Oft Scyld Scefing   sceaþena þreatum,
              monegum mægþum   meodosetla ofteah,

and *Beo* 7 (§3916), and in the first subordinate clause, viz. *Beo* 3 *hu ða æþelingas ellen fremedon!* Yet real ambiguity rarely arises. Occasionally it is difficult for the modern reader or hearer to decide whether the order is SOV or OSV, e.g. in *Finn* 18 and *Mald* 304; see §11. Even the context does not help in these examples, whereas in *Beo* 652 *Gegrette þa guma oþerne,* ‖ *Hroðgar Beowulf* the context and the parallelism tell us that *Hroðgar* is the subject. In the ambiguous examples, we tend to rely on our modern instinct that the subject comes first. However, we should perhaps remember here that OSV is still possible in MnE at least with a pronoun subject—'These seven they chose'—and perhaps even with a noun subject—'Such men the emperors honoured'—where SOV is not. On SVO or OVS in *GenA* 2887b, see §10 and Mitchell 1975*a*, pp. 13-14.

§3945. We must not think that element order in the poetry is more chaotic than that in the prose; it is subject to metrical and other considerations which either do not arise, or which play a less prominent part, in the prose. QW (§146) tells us that 'in the poetry as a whole there is great variety in the disposing of S, O, and V, and it is easier to speak of the word-order in any one poem than in OE poetry as such'. There is, I suppose, something in this, though I do not know of comparative work along these lines. Indeed, one could make much the same point about individual prose texts. In any event, such differences must not be emphasized at the expense of what Alistair Campbell (Lecture Notes)—while admitting that individual poets had personal peculiarities—called 'the unity of technique' in the major OE poems. The phenomena seen in *Beowulf* by Klaeber (3, p. xciv) could be paralleled from most of those poems:

> In the matter of word-order the outstanding feature is the predominance, according to ancient Germanic rule, of the end-position of the verb both in dependent and, in a somewhat less degree, independent clauses, as exemplified in the very first lines of the poem. The opposite order: verb – subject is not infrequently found to mark a distinct advance in the narrative (the more restful normal order being more properly adapted to description or presentation of situations and minor narrative links) or to intimate in a vague, general way a connection of the sentence with the preceding one, such as might be expressed more definitely by 'and,' (negatively) 'nor,' 'so,' 'indeed,' 'for,' 'however.' Besides, any part of the sentence may appear in the emphatic head-position, whereby the author is enabled to give effective syntactical prominence to the most important elements. . . .

But there are limits. I am not alone in regarding as impossible the sentence perpetrated by Wrenn and perpetuated by Bolton in what they print as

Beo 1068   Finnes eaferum,   ða hie se fær begeat,
                     hæleð Healf-Dena,   Hnæf Scyldinga,
                     in Fres-wæle   feallan scolde.

§3946. There are many considerations which future workers on element order in the poetry will find relevant. They obviously include the metrical patterns, the rules governing alliteration, the priorities accorded to the various parts of speech in the allotment of stress, and the effects of the choice of one part of speech or form of expression rather than another. (On the last, see Clemoes in Calder 1979, pp. 156-7.) Campbell (Lecture Notes) affirms that the authors of the major OE poems all showed 'the same respect for the natural laws of stress, the same ingenious avoidance of these by the device of interception, the same infinite variety in avoiding monotony in parallelism'. But there may be profit in investigating the extent to which individual poets practised 'interception', i.e. separation of syntactical units—including those joined by *ond, ac*, and the like—by the medial or end caesura, or by speech material, or by both (on this see §§149-57 and 175-7 and my discussion concerning 'enjambment of sense' in Mitchell 1980*a*, pp. 408-10), and in examining the similarities and differences in their use of parallelism and chiasmus.

§3947. Finally, there is Kuhn's 'Law of sentence particles'. I cannot better Campbell's explanation (1970, p. 94):

In Old English poetry, as in early Germanic poetry generally, the opening of the clause was governed by the law of sentence-particles observed in recent times by Hans Kuhn.[5] This law is simply that unaccented elements which are not proclitic or enclitic to accented elements in a clause must be placed either before the first stress, or between the first and the second stress of their clause.[6] Once the second stress is passed, these elements will receive a stress if they are used.[7] They are, principally, finite verbs, adverbs, conjunctions, and pronouns. They are contrasted with prepositions, articles,[8] and grammatical endings, which are proclitic or enclitic to the accented elements of their clause. The two positions in which sentence-particles are used may be illustrated by two half-lines of *Maldon*: 106 *Wæs on eorþan cyrm*; 126 *Wæl feol on eorðan*. Here we see an unaccented finite verb used before the first stress (106) and between the first and second stress (126). Further on than this it would be placed under accent. If a clause has two or more sentence-particles, they must be grouped together in one or other of the permitted positions, not divided between them, *e.g. Beow.* 269 *Wes þu us larena god*; *id.* 316 *Mæl is me to feran. Mal.* 106 *Wæs on eorþan cyrm*, illustrates a further limitation. If the position before the first stress of a clause is used at all, it must contain a sentence-particle. Clauses opening with a sentence-particle before the first stress alone or with an element (generally article or preposition) enclitic to the first stress are innumerable, *e.g. Beow.* 4 *Oft Scyld Scefing*; *id.* 915 *hine fyren onwod*; *id.* 997 *Wæs þæt beorhte bold*. But we seldom find in the position before the first stress material enclitic to that stress alone. Exceptions in Old English are almost all with forms of *se, e.g. Beow.* 107 *þone cwealm gewræc, id.* 1110 *Æt þæm ade wæs*.

[5]   Kuhn's views are put forward fully in 'Zur Wortstellung und -Betonung im Altgermanischen', *Beiträge zur Geschichte der deutschen Sprache und Literatur* lix (1933), 1-109.
[6]   I pass over certain licences allowed in the structure of clause openings of the metrical form A3 in the Sievers system, as they do not affect the points discussed in this paper.
[7]   And so, by definition, they cease to be sentence-particles.
[8]   Including possessives and indefinite adjectives of quantity (*manig, nænig, fela, etc.*).

This law is regularly invoked by critics of OE poetry. Thus, there has been much argument about the respective merits of the ASPR punctuation of

Sea 6   . . .   þær mec oft bigeat
                nearo nihtwaco   æt nacan stefnan,
            þonne he be clifum cnossað.   Calde geþrungen
            wæron mine fet,   forste gebunden,
            caldum clommum, . . .

and

Sea 18   þær ic ne gehyrde   butan hlimman sæ,
                     iscaldne wæg.   Hwilum ylfete song
                     dyde ic me to gomene,   ganetes hleoþor
                     ond huilpan sweg   fore hleahtor wera,
                     mæw singende   fore medodrince

(Sweet, *R*. 15, agrees in the position of the full stops) in contrast with that in Sweet, *R*. 8, where a full stop follows *geþrungen* and a colon follows *song* instead of the full stops after *cnossað* and *wæg*. It has been urged in favour of Sweet, *R*. 8, that in both places its punctuation avoids what are called 'breaches' of the 'law', whereas the ASPR punctuation involves such breaches. I myself would avoid the argument by taking *calde geþrungen* and *gebunden apo koinou* in the first passage and *hwilum ylfete song* and *dyde ic me to gomene apo koinou* in the second, thereby creating what I believe the poet intended—verse paragraphs; see Mitchell 1980*a*, p. 408. Presumably such *apo koinou* arrangements would also involve 'breaches' of Kuhn's 'law'. If this is so, it seems to me a reason for questioning the validity of Kuhn's 'law' rather than for rejecting the *apo koinou* interpretations. Kuhn's 'law' in fact seems to me to involve circular argument and/or to assume what it proves. It seems to presuppose that modern punctuation can accurately, completely, and faithfully, reflect the intonation patterns of OE poetry. Can it be described as a scientific or logical procedure to erect a 'law' and to sweep away exceptions by describing them as 'breaches' when those 'breaches' involve OE as idiomatic as the 'correct' forms? Why (if I may be pardoned a petulant aside) is Andrew pilloried and Kuhn canonized? I do not seek to dismiss Kuhn's 'law' completely. I have, for example, accepted in §2350 the argument that Andrew (*Postscript*, §§66 and 154-6) is wrong when he suggests that certain pronouns in *Beowulf* should be eliminated as scribal insertions; they conform to Kuhn's 'law' and it might be reasonable to expect 'errors' if scribes had inserted them. But it is interesting to note that all Campbell's examples are half-lines. It is when the rule is extended beyond the half-line that it often makes me read OE poetry in a way which I find unnatural. Kuhn's Law has become an accepted—indeed almost unquestioned —part of the impedimenta of critics of OE poetry. In my opinion, the time is ripe for a critical reappraisal, at least of the doctrine of the 'verse clause'.

G. DEVELOPMENTS IN THE OE PERIOD

§3948. As pointed out in §§3891-3, we would be on firmer ground here if we knew more about the origin of the three basic element orders. But at least two problems are entangled. The first involves the stylistic developments from the prose of Alfred's reign—sometimes stiff and unwieldy but often very powerful—to that of Ælfric, Wulf-stan, and the later *Chronicle*—more flexible, more controlled, more varied, but in my opinion rarely (if ever) reaching such heights as those attained by the *Orosius* translator in the opening lines of II. ii (*Or* 64. 20-66. 12). I cannot pursue this topic here.

§3949. Second, there are the developments which can now be seen as heralding the modern predominance of the SV order. From the discussion so far, it is clear that element order cannot be regarded as a final arbiter when the ambiguous principal/subordinate clause pre-sents itself in either OE prose or poetry. Even the pattern *þa* [conj.] S(. . .)V, *þa* [adv.] VS in the prose, which remains the safest guide, is not infallible; see §§2543-54. The situation is that already in OE the nominative and accusative distinction has disappeared in many inflexional classes (§9); that distinctive forms of the orders SV and S . . . V, while not completely interchangeable, occur in both princi-pal and subordinate clauses—see the various tables given in Kohonen 1976; and that there are many sentences in which the distinction, if not completely lost, is at least so blurred that we can reasonably con-clude that it must have lost any syntactical significance it may once have had. The following sequences are illuminating: *ÆCHom* i. 50. 29 *Saulus heold ðæra leasra gewitena reaf, and heora mod to þære stæninge geornlice tihte. Stephanus soðlice gebigedum cneowum Drihten bæd þæt he Saulum alysde*; *ÆCHom* i. 598. 32 *Uton nu biddan ðone Ælmihtigan Wealdend, þæt his eadiga apostol ure ðingere beo, swa swa he wunode his gelaðunge bydel*; and three clauses after the same compound conjunction, viz. *ÆCHom* i. 90. 13 *Æfter þan ðe wæron gefyllede ehta dagas Drihtnes acennednysse* . . . , *ÆCHom* ii. 244. 35 *Æfter ðan ðe ic arise of deaðe gesund* . . . , and *ÆCHom* i. 478. 14 . . . *æfter ðam ðe he ða cild acwealde for Cristes acenned-nysse.*

§3950. It is obvious that some reduction in the frequency of the S . . . V and VS orders must have accompanied the loss of inflexions; the greater the levelling of inflexions, the greater the need for SV. It is also obvious that SV did not become predominant in the OE period. Exactly when it did remains a matter of dispute and is a problem which lies outside the scope of this work. Relevant discussions include Mitchell 1964*b*, Mitchell 1966, pp. 95-7, Kohonen 1976, and Dolan, *MP* 74 (1977), 305-10. The importance of comparative studies for establishing the strength in OE of these and other well-known tendencies can be gauged by reference to Yerkes 1976, *passim*, and to D. M. Horgan (*ASE* 9 (1980), 213-21)—note (*inter alia*) her comments on the increased use of prepositions, on the tendency of the verb to move away from final position, and on the occasional use of 'modal' auxiliaries instead of subjunctive forms, in two later manuscripts (*T* and *U*) of *Cura Pastoralis*. But I would be inclined to be firmer than Amos (p. 139): 'The use of the position of the verb with respect to the subject as a criterion for dating Old English literature seems unpromising'; note *GD(C)* 79. 14 *⁊ ic þa acsode hine swiðe geornlice hwæt he wære* but *GD(H)* 79. 14 *⁊ ic þa geornlice hine axode hwanone he wære*.

§3951. Wise after the event, we can now see that the triumph of SV was inevitable before Norman influence began. Future workers may be able to document this change more accurately. I conclude by reminding my readers of the 'Englishness' of OE syntax. They may care to test this for themselves by reading aloud, without regard to the inflexions and in the exact order of the OE, their own translation of the well-known opening paragraph of Ælfric's Life of Edmund (*ÆLS* 32) and by counting the resulting number of ambiguities and of arrangements impossible in MnE.

X

SOME PROBLEMS RELATED TO THE POETRY

A. INTRODUCTORY REMARKS

§3952. I must start this chapter by bringing together several discussions which reflect my continuing unwillingness to accept many of the shibboleths which (as I see it) beset the criticism of OE poetry today.

§3953. Given our ignorance of intonation patterns, our lack of native informants, and the marked divergence of the various theories —including the inability of scholars even to agree whether the half-lines of OE poetry are or are not isochronous—I believe that critics are prone to place too much faith in whatever metrical theory they happen to accept. See §2780; consider the implications of Brooks's note on *And* 857 in relation to Bliss 1962, §5; and note that Cable (*JEGP* 69 (1970), 81-8), who accuses Andrew and Bliss of using 'unprovable assumptions' by 'assigning metrical stress to words on the basis of their grammatical category', bases his own paper on the statement quoted in my §2558—which in my opinion contains unprovable assumptions about both metre and syntax.

§3954. For the reasons given in §3947, I believe that there is need for a reconsideration of Kuhn's Law, with special reference to the concept of the 'verse-clause'. Anyone attempting the task should ponder carefully the implications of Stanley's remark (*CB*, p. 120): 'Though there are exceptions, the vast majority of clusters of three or more unstressed syllables come in the position between the last stress of a half-line and the first stress of the following half-line', and of the comments which follow it.

§3955. While not suggesting that OE poets knew only parataxis (§1896), I believe that some modern critics accept too easily the proposition that OE poetry is essentially hypotactic; see §2445 and Mitchell 1980a, pp. 398-9 and *passim*. In contrast, I note with wry amusement the willingness of the same critics to accept what I call 'thematic parataxis', i.e. parataxis on a higher level, in the larger context of the poem. Two brief illustrations from *Beowulf* must serve. In

Beo 81

                    Sele hlifade
heah ond horngeap;   heaðowylma bad,
laðan liges;   ne wæs hit lenge þa gen,
þæt se ecghete   aþumsweoran
æfter wælniðe   wæcnan scolde,

it is generally accepted that the first sentence describes the effect—the burning of Heorot—and the second the cause—hostility between father- and son-in-law. I do not dispute this. I merely observe that it is paratactically expressed. My second illustration involves the question of whether Hrothulf—unlike Beowulf—was a traitor. I do not wish to argue the case for or against this view. But I think it true to say that, if the poet did say that Hrothulf was a traitor, he said it paratactically. For the notion depends on this sequence: (i) a statement that Heorot was filled with friends when Beowulf was there (*Beo* 1013-19); (ii) the telling of the story of treachery and vengeance at Finnesburh (*Beo* 1068-159); (iii) a statement that the peace between Hrothgar and Hrothulf was still unbroken (*Beo* 1162-5). The poet does not specifically link these. He merely places them one after another, as the dictionary definition of parataxis has it. The connection can be made by a reader. But it is not essential to do so. It is hard to see what Hrothulf, already co-ruler with Hrothgar, had to gain by treachery. The impact of the poem is not weakened if it is held that he—like Beowulf—remained loyal.

§3956. For the reasons given in Mitchell 1980*a*, pp. 395-412, I believe that it is wrong to use modern punctuation for OE poetry. It often splits up the verse paragraph which I believe to be the unit of that poetry and imposes unnecessary decisions on editors. I am encouraged in this belief by the recent discovery in Alistair Campbell's Lecture Notes of the following observation: 'In ASPR punctuation quite ruins the superb simile *Phoen* 424-42, which is a continuous paragraph.' On this problem, see further §§1879-82.

§3957. In an important article which I carelessly overlooked until March 1981, Pilch (*Language and Style*, 3 (1970), 51-61) argues convincingly that 'in terms of Latin School Grammar, the syntactic interpretation of Old English texts is either wrong or unrewarding' (p. 61). I do not agree with all the details of his syntactical analyses of *Beo* 256-7 or of *Res* 78-89. But he offers two conclusions with which I am in complete agreement because I have reached them independently (Mitchell 1980*a*): that modern punctuation is a tool

unsuitable for editors of OE poems and that 'recursive' linkage (p. 59)
—which has much in common with what I call the *apo koinou* construction—occurs frequently in OE poetry. However, I quarrel most
strenuously with his observation (p. 60) concerning what he calls
'syntactic interpretation or *syntactic recognition'*: 'Given an appropriate statement of the syntax, it can be done by computer.' As the
result of both prejudice and experience, I detect great danger here:
see my Introduction. Future syntacticians of OE will have to take
care that they do not spend happy years programming a computer to
produce detailed analyses of OE texts only to find themselves in
complete agreement with the computer when it tells them what they
have told it. At their present stages of development at any rate, the
brain of the scholar is both more speedy and more sensitive for OE
syntactical analysis than any computer.

§3958. Inevitably the scepticism revealed in the preceding sections
colours my thinking. I do not expect everything I say here to be
accepted. But I believe that it deserves to be taken seriously and
hope that it will be.

B. THE RELATIONSHIP BETWEEN METRICAL AND SYNTACTICAL UNITS

§3959. It is an accepted commonplace that the language of OE
poetry is made up of a selection of ordinary prose patterns. This can
be expressed in different words by saying that there is in OE poetry
a tendency for the smaller syntactical units to occupy a line or half-
line and so to coincide with the metrical units; see Lehmann 1956,
pp. 32-4, where *Finn* 2-12 is cited as an example. *El* 157-65 is
another. But separation of related elements can be achieved by interception or enjambment of sense (see §3946), as in *Beo* 418 *forþan
hie mægenes cræft | minne cuþon* and

Beo 1703   Blæd is aræred
                   geond widwegas,   wine min Beowulf,
              ðin ofer þeoda gehwylce,

where the separation of *Blæd* and *ðin* gives dramatic emphasis, 'Fame
. . . thy fame'. That such separation is possible renders dubious (I believe) Phoenix's endorsement (p. 21) of the idea that the presence of
the mid-line caesura after *se mæra* in *Beo* 1474 *Geþenc nu, se mæra |
maga Healfdenes* certifies that *se mæra* is not attributive, but independent, and the corollary that *maga Healfdenes* must be in apposition

with it. On the other hand, I sometimes find myself questioning editorial line divisions, wondering (for example) whether *swelce* in

GenB 712   ac wende þæt heo hyldo   heofoncyninges
                worhte mid þam wordum   þe heo þam were swelce
                tacen oðiewde   and treowe gehet

and *his* in

Phoen 266   feorh bið niwe,
                geong, geofona ful,   þonne he of greote his
                lic leoþucræftig,   þæt ær lig fornom,
                somnað, swoles lafe,   . . .

should be placed at the beginning of the next line; see further
Mitchell 1959, pp. 647-8. My brief discussions of this problem in
§§149-57, Mitchell 1978*a*, pp. 253-5, and Mitchell 1980*a*, pp. 408-
10, are not definitive. There is room for more work here.

§3960. The same is true when we ask where clauses begin. Kuhn's
Law and my comments thereon (§3947) are relevant here. Fakun-
diny (p. 134) suggests that 'the Anglo-Saxon poets apparently preferred beginning new clauses with the off-verse'. On this see (*inter
alia*) §2537. But there is no rule that the beginning of a clause must
coincide with the beginning of a (half-)line; consider the noun clause
in *Beo* 92 *cwæð þæt se Ælmihtiga* | *eorðan worhte* and the adverb
clauses in *Beo* 1487 . . . *beaga bryttan,* | *breac þonne moste, GenA*
1153 *swealt þa he hæfde,* || *frod fyrnwita,* | *v and nigonhund,* and
Rid 73. 1 *Ic on wonge aweox,* | *wunode þær mec feddon* || *hruse ond
heofonwolcn.* Adjective clauses may also be preceded in the same
half-line by another element, e.g. (an antecedent) *Az* 141 *ealle þa þe
onhrerað* | *hreo wægas,* (a noun object) *JDay ii* 302 *gif þu wille
secgan* | *soð þæm ðe frineð,* and (a verb) *Beo* 1003—*fremme se þe
wille*—. Are these exceptions to Stanley's dictum (*CB*, p. 119) that
'the beginning of phrases, clauses and sentences must coincide with
the beginning of metrical phrases: a break within a half-line is not
tolerated'? The observations by Raw (p. 100) seem relevant here.

§3961. The syntactic structure of OE poetic formulae has been
investigated by W. A. O'Neil (for the elegiac poetry) and by G. L.
Gattiker (for *Beowulf*) in unpublished Wisconsin dissertations which
are listed and summarized by Cassidy (*Magoun Festschrift*, pp. 75-
85). He reports that from their texts emerged 'rather remarkable
results; for it turns out that Old English verse is built upon only
twenty-five syntactic patterns, six of which are noun-centered and
nine verb-centered frames of frequent occurrence, five adjective-

centered and five adverb-centered frames of less common occurrence, and five other minor types' (p. 78). This certainly would be remarkable if it were true—and not merely because Cassidy's list seems to total thirty patterns. Following Greenfield (*Journal of English Literary History*, 34 (1967), 148-50), I cite from Cassidy (p. 79) one of these patterns:

3] The N_1N_2 frame: a stressed noun in the genitive case qualifies another stressed noun or a nominal; the latter can be in any case:

> wuldres wealdend   [17a]
> sceaþena þreatum   [4b]
> þær wæs madma fela   [36b]

It has stressed or unstressed beginnings, hence may be realized through any of the verse types. It may be reversed, the genitive noun then following the other:

> Geata dryhten   [2991b]
> dryhten Geata   [2402a].

But this pattern—like the others—is not homogeneous, for the examples differ, not only in metre, but also in syntax. Greenfield (ibid., p. 149) puts these objections tellingly:

Cassidy claims that the notion of the syntactic frame should give us 'a firmer concept of the formula.' *Au contraire*: the idea of the formula as '*a group of words which is regularly employed under the same metrical conditions to express a given essential idea*' disintegrates almost entirely, not only because of the flexibility the frames allow the poet in the choice of *verbal* phrases and their own flexibility in regard to grammatical inversion (e.g., AN or NA; or N_1N_2 or N_2N_1) and verse types (most can occur in any of the five major Sievers categories), but because of their own 'non-fixity' with respect to the syntactic relations they enjoy in their own half-lines, or in the contexts of their own sentence structures.

Another of Cassidy's pupils, D. C. Green, continued along the same lines in his unpublished Wisconsin dissertation, 'The Syntax of the Poetic Formula in a Cross-section of Old English Poetry' (1967), and in *CHum.* 6 (1971), 85-93, using the computer and taking as his corpus some 6,200 lines of OE poetry. He added one syntactic frame to those distinguished above and claimed (p. 91) that 'these findings tend to confirm the usefulness of the syntactic frame theory'. But they are, of course, open to the same criticisms as those of O'Neil and Gattiker.

§3962. The fact that the analyses so far made have been insufficiently selective does not necessarily mean that this line of enquiry should not be pursued; more refined and meaningful subdivisions may well emerge. Future workers will need to study carefully the articles by Cassidy and Greenfield, and the stimulating thesis by Debra Doyle listed in the Postscript to my Select Bibliography. They will also need to consider carefully the extent to which such analysis is likely to founder on the 'infinite variety' achieved by the poets.

§3963. Other points worthy of consideration include the effects produced by the repetition of formulae—see Robinson 1979, pp. 144-5, and Monnin, *EStudies*, 60 (1979), 352-3—and their misuse. Here Campbell (Lecture Notes) identified offences against sense, e.g. in *Jul* 27, where *hine fyrwet bræc*, proper only to surprise or curiosity, is used to describe the love or desire of Heliseus for Juliana; against grammar, e.g. in *And* 303, where the genitive *landes ne locenra beaga*, appropriate after a numeral or a word expressing quantity, is used as a direct object of *Næbbe ic* in a succession of accusative objects (but see now Schabram 1981); against metre, e.g. in *And* 914 *Wes ðu, Andreas, hal!*, where *Andreas* does not alliterate as *Hroðgar* does in *Beo* 407 *Wæs þu, Hroðgar, hal*; and against sentence-structure, e.g. in *El* 462, where the formula *ageaf ondsware*, Campbell argued, offends against Kuhn's Law—in contrast to what he saw as its correct use in *El* 455 (but see §3947).

C. OTHER DIFFERENCES BETWEEN THE SYNTAX OF PROSE AND POETRY

§3964. Considerations of space demand that this discussion be largely supplementary and that the reader consult the Indexes for many of the differences in the syntax of prose and poetry which have already been discussed. Some of those which help to achieve compression and to give the poetry its characteristic texture are mentioned below. On element order see §§3944-7. A few others perhaps deserve mention here. I have recorded no examples in the prose like *Beo* 524 *sunu Beanstanes*. The pattern seen in *Mart 2* 100. 5 *drihtnes broðor*, which represents Latin *frater domini*, is the norm in OE prose and, of course, in MnE. We see in *Beo* 40 *him on bearme . . .* a common verse variant for the pattern seen in *Beo* 380 *on his mundgripe*. The use of adjectives as nouns, e.g. *Beo* 1397 *se gomela* and *Beo* 1595 *gomele ymb godne*, and of adjectives where modern speakers would tend to use adverbs, e.g. *Beo* 496 *Scop hwilum sang ‖ hador on Heorote* (cf. *Beo* 1571 . . . *hadre scineð ‖ rodores candel*) has been noted by Klaeber (3, p. xcii). So too has the use of weak forms of the adjective in places where it is not syntactically justified, e.g. *Beo* 2105 *gomela Scilding*; see §114.

§3965. There is less piling up of negatives in the poetry than in the prose; see §§1603-13. Klaeber (3, p. xciv) states: 'Both as a dialectal and a chronological test the mode of expressing negation has been carefully studied with the gratifying result of establishing *Beowulf* as an Anglian poem of about 725 A.D.' This is a reference to the work of Einenkel in *Ang.* 35 (1912), 187-248 and 401-24. I do not believe Klaeber's claim.

§3966. Pope (*Ælfric*, i. 107) accepts that Skeat was 'essentially right' when he 'emphasized the very loose and prosaic character of the rhythms' of Ælfric's alliterative prose. It is clear that the so-called 'half-lines' of the prose have more unstressed syllables than the poetry. McIntosh, in his 'Wulfstan's Prose' (*PBA* 35 (1949), 109-42), gives the following figures (p. 120): *Beowulf* varies from 4 to 6, averaging just under 5; *Sermo Lupi* varies normally from 5 to 7, averaging a little over 6; and, according to Pope's figures (*Ælfric*, i. 115), Ælfric's later homilies average just over 6. The difference may seem trifling, but it has one important syntactic effect on the poetry: it reduces the number of prop words, or grammar words, used and means that some are preferred to others. Thus, non-metrical conjunctions are avoided. *Swa* is often preferred to combinations like *swa hwær swa*; see §§2489-93 and GK, s.v. *swa. þa hwile þe* occurs only seven times in the poetry—4 in *Mald*, 1 in *DAlf*, 1 in *LPr ii*, 1 in *MCharm*—and *þa hwile* only in *JDay ii*; see §2629. The preferred word is *þenden*, which is not recorded in ME and which is glossed in the Junius MS (*GenB* 245) by *þa hwile*.

§3967. The absence of prop-words is reflected in the marked tendency to apposition in the poetry—Andrew (*SS*, p. 91) shows that in contrast the *Bede* translator depends almost entirely on relative clauses—and in the frequent use of asyndetic parataxis. Both these are illustrated in *Mald* 113 (§3973). See further Robinson 1979.

§3968. Compression is also achieved by the use of participles and phrases instead of clauses. More common in the poetry than in the prose are datives of comparison (§§1358-64) and (it seems to me) clauses with unexpressed personal pronoun subjects and objects. Lehmann and Tabusa (*The Alliterations of the Beowulf* (Austin, 1958), 8-9) remind us that 'its language is virtually nominal'. Their report of Simons's analysis of that part of the vocabulary of *Beowulf* beginning with *b* shows that almost 100 per cent of nouns, adjectives, adverbs, and forms of *begen*, carry stress and alliteration; that almost 60 per cent of non-finite verb-forms carry stress and alliteration, compared with less than 30 per cent of finite verb-forms; and that no forms of *beon* and no prepositions carry stress and alliteration.

Much the same holds for the late poem *Maldon*. The texture and syntactical pattern of this and other 'traditional' OE poems are quite different from those of Ælfric's alliterative prose; see §§3972-5.

§3969. OE poets could, of course, use verbal alliteration. A striking example is to be found in *Beo* 739-49, where the gruesome fleshliness of Grendel's meal is starkly brought out by the alliterating transitive verbs. Here we may recall that Shakespeare achieved some of his greatest effects by the use of transitive verbs and verbs of action.

§3970. We might expect that there would be fewer prepositions and more case-forms in the poetry than in the prose. I suspect that this may be so. But I am not able to demonstrate it and do not claim it. There is room for more work here. But a random check will confirm that prepositions are well established in the poetry.

§3971. The lines of classical OE poetry are not always end-stopped; clauses or sentences or verse paragraphs often begin in mid-line. I have spoken elsewhere (Mitchell 1980a, pp. 409-10) of what I call 'the excitement of the momentary riddle' exemplified in

Mald 7   . . . he let him þa of handon   leofne fleogan
             hafoc wið þæs holtes   and to þære hilde stop,

which (I suggest) probably presented itself to its Anglo-Saxon hearers in some such way as this: '. . . he let from him then from hands the dear one fly—hawk towards the wood . . .'. Today, I believe, we often miss this enjambment and this excitement by reading the poetry instead of hearing it recited or by hearing it recited too fast—a criticism of modern renderings often made by J. R. R. Tolkien. Slow and deliberate reading is also necessary for at least three other reasons. First, we need time to analyse the nominal compounds and their significance, for example *flodwudu, sundhengestas*, and *yðmearas*, in *ChristB* 850 (§3972). Second, we need time for the proper realization of the time-reference of simple tense- and mood-forms, e.g.

Beo 960   Uþe ic swiþor
             þæt ðu hine selfne   geseon moste,
             feond on frætewum   fylwerigne!;

see §2008. Third, we need time for recollection of hints given by the poet; consider *scriþað* in *Beo* 162 *men ne cunnon* ‖ *hwyder helrunan* | *hwyrftum scriþað* in relation to *scriðan* in

Beo 648   siððan hie sunnan leoht   geseon meahton,
                    oþ ðe nipende   niht ofer ealle,
                    scaduhelma gesceapu   scriðan cwoman
                    wan under wolcnum

and in *Beo* 702 *Com on wanre niht* ǁ *scriðan sceadugenga*. Grendel—
a mysterious creature of hell—is both a demon *and* a shadowgoer.
I am sure that Anglo-Saxon listeners too needed time and were given
time for such analyses.

D. ÆLFRIC'S ALLITERATIVE PROSE

§3972. In the course of an article entitled 'Ælfric' (*CB*, pp. 202-3),
Clemoes—one of the masters of Ælfrician criticism—says that
when Ælfric 'adopted a formally conceived rhythmical basis for his
prose', his 'creative step, I believe, was to divorce the rhythm and
alliteration of Old English poetry from its traditional vocabulary and
syntax and to associate them with the vocabulary and syntax of
prose'. He illustrates this with this (his own) arrangement of

ÆAdmon 1 42. 5   We wæron unþancwurðe   and wendon us fram Criste,
                    ac he us gesohte,   swa þæt he sylf nyðer astah
                    of his heofenlican settle   on swa mycelre eaðmodnysse
                    þæt he man wearð for us   on middanearde akenned.
                    And se læg on cildclaðum   se þe belycð on his handa
                    ealle þas eorðan   swa swa ælmihtig god.
                    And se þe heofenas gehealdeð   næfde hamas on worulde,
                    ne hwyder he ahylde   his heafod on life.
                    And se wæs hafenleas for us   se þe hæfð ealle þing,
                    þæt he us gewelgode   on his eceum welum.

A comparison of this with

ChristB 850   Nu is þon gelicost   swa we on laguflode
                    ofer cald wæter   ceolum liðan
                    geond sidne sæ,   sundhengestum,
                    flodwudu fergen.   Is þæt frecne stream
                    yða ofermæta   þe we her on lacað
                    geond þas wacan woruld,   windge holmas
                    ofer deop gelad.   Wæs se drohtað strong
                    ærþon we to londe   geliden hæfdon
                    ofer hreone hrycg.   þa us help bicwom,
                    þæt us to hælo   hyþe gelædde,
                    godes gæstsunu,   ond us giefe sealde
                    þæt we oncnawan magun   ofer ceoles bord
                    hwær we sælan sceolon   sundhengestas,
                    ealde yðmearas,   ancrum fæste

provides an excellent illustration of one of his points. In *ChristB* 850 we have two words recorded only in that passage, viz. *sundhengest* and *flodwudu*; one word recorded only there and in *Whale* 49, viz. *yðmearas*; and one word which is common in the poetry and appears occasionally in glosses, viz. *laguflod*. These four are poetic compounds. In the Ælfric passage, there are no such words. I was tempted to think I had found one in *hafenleas* '*harbour-lacking, haven-lacking', a sense which would fit the *Christ* passage and even that passage in Ælfric's *MidLent Sunday Sermon* (*ÆCHom* i. 182. 25-184. 4) which compares this present world with the sea. But *hafenleas* in Ælfric regularly means 'having-lacking, possession-lacking'. So in these passages Cynewulf's poetry retains 'its traditional vocabulary', while Ælfric's prose rejects it or at least lacks it. Here it is interesting to note Godden's observation (*EStudies*, 61 (1980), 217-19) that the word *metod* 'was deliberately dropped' by Ælfric, who 'clearly . . . had second thoughts about the use of poetic words'. Indeed, Godden comes close to suggesting that Ælfric was so unfamiliar with the 'traditional honorific phrase' *Metoda Drihten* 'Lord of fates' that he thought that *metoda* was weak singular masculine.

§3973. But there are numerous passages in OE poetry where the 'traditional vocabulary' is lacking. One, also from Cynewulf, must suffice:

ChristB 547 Ðæt is wel cweden, swa gewritu secgað,
        þæt him albeorhte englas togeanes
        in þa halgan tid heapum cwoman,
        sigan on swegle. þa wæs symbla mæst
        geworden in wuldre. Wel þæt gedafenað
        þæt to þære blisse, beorhte gewerede,
        in þæs þeodnes burg þegnas cwoman,
        weorud wlitescyne. Gesegon wilcuman
        on heahsetle heofones waldend,
        folca feorhgiefan, frætwum ealles waldend
        middangeardes ond mægenþrymmes.

It would be easy to multiply examples. A fruitful source would be the uninspired poetry of the *Paris Psalter*. Here we have poetry which had already divorced itself from 'its traditional vocabulary' and so had already taken part of what Clemoes describes as 'Ælfric's creative step'. Indeed, Clemoes almost admits this (*CB*, pp. 202-3): 'I am not suggesting that there was any direct link between Ælfric's prose and the Paris Psalter's metrical version of the psalms, but I think that there is little doubt that Ælfric derived his basic rhythmical scheme from poetry of this kind.' This is not what I would call 'traditional' OE poetry. We can see this if we compare Clemoes's illustrative passage

PPs 105. 18   Godes hi forgeaton,   þe hi of gramra ær
                   feonda folmum   frecne generede,
                   þe on Egyptum   æðele wundar
                   and on Chananea   cymu worhte
                   and recene wundur   on þam Readan Sæ

with *Beo* 702-21, a passage which contains what must, I think, be accepted as a Christian reference. (I regret that lack of space prevents my quoting this and the other four passages from *Beowulf* listed in this section.) The *Beowulf* passage and the two passages from *ChristB* have in common, against Ælfric and the *PPs* verse, mid-line beginnings of sentences. But, as I see it, even the two *ChristB* passages lack what I regard as one of the essentials of good OE poetry—that repetition with variation and advance which is seen in

Mald 113   Wund wearð Wulfmær,   wælræste geceas,
                  Byrhtnoðes mæg;   he mid billum wearð,
                  his swuster sunu,   swiðe forheawen

and is discussed in Mitchell 1980a, pp. 410-11. The two *ChristB* passages are to me closer in feeling to prose, even allowing for the 'traditional' poetic vocabulary in the first. I agree that we get complex sentences in *Beowulf*, e.g. *Beo* 1180-7, where we have the more usual 'loose' sentence-structure with the principal clause first—this indeed can be described as the norm in OE prose and poetry—and *Beo* 1822-30, where we have the 'periodic' structure with a subordinate clause first. Stanley (*CB*, p. 121) cites the last passage and *Beo* 1368-72 as examples which 'show that the poet's complexity of utterance is premeditated'. These passages, however, 'feel' different from the *ChristB* passages. The Ælfric passage and the *PPs* verse 'feel' even more different. The gaps are still wider when we consider passages like *Beo* 739-49 and

Dream 39   Ongyrede hine þa geong hæleð,   (þæt wæs god ælmihtig),
                  strang ond stiðmod.   Gestah he on gealgan heanne,
                  modig on manigra gesyhðe,   þa he wolde mancyn lysan.
                  Bifode ic þa me se beorn ymbclypte.   Ne dorste ic hwæðre bugan
                                                                    to eorðan,
                  feallan to foldan sceatum,   ac ic sceolde fæste standan.
                  Rod wæs ic aræred.   Ahof ic ricne cyning,
                  heofona hlaford,   hyldan me ne dorste.
                  þurhdrifan hi me mid deorcan næglum.   On me syndon þa dolg
                                                                    gesiene,
                  opene inwidhlemmas.   Ne dorste ic hira nænigum sceððan.
                  Bysmeredon hie unc butu ætgædere.   Eall ic wæs mid blode be-
                                                                    stemed,
                  begoten of þæs guman sidan,   siððan he hæfde his gast onsended.

Similar contrasts between the paratactic style of these last two passages and the hypotactic style of those from *ChristB* are, of course,
apparent in *The Dream of the Rood* itself and give rise to speculation
about the possibility of different authorship by members of the so-
called 'Cædmonian' and 'Cynewulfian' schools respectively. The fact
that any good poet has more than one style at his command and so
can respond differently to varying demands is obvious from the *Beowulf* examples cited. But it does not seem to enter the calculations
of some critics.

§3974. There is, of course, prosaic poetry. Indeed, I sometimes
wonder what Cynewulf would have lost if he had written in prose.
There is also, of course, poetic prose. To me, Ælfric's alliterative
prose is good prose, not bad poetry; see Mitchell 1980*a*, pp. 392–3,
where I suggest that sometimes, at any rate, the sweep of the prose
sentence rather than the demands of the alliterative line dictated the
pointing in *ÆLS*. So I agree with another master of Ælfrician criticism, Pope (*Ælfric*, i. 105):

> The term 'rhythmical prose' as applied to Ælfric's compositions must be under-
> stood to refer to a loosely metrical form resembling in basic structural principles
> the alliterative verse of the Old English poets, but differing markedly in the
> character and range of its rhythms as in strictness of alliterative practice, and
> altogether distinct in diction, rhetoric, and tone. It is better regarded as a mildly
> ornamental, rhythmically ordered prose than as a debased, pedestrian poetry.

But I do not agree with his decision to print this prose in verse lines,
which to my ear break up good prose into Hudibrastic-type rhythms
and make it read like bad poetry; see Mitchell 1980*a*, p. 389. So I have
come to think that the statement by Clemoes with which I began is
unnecessary and perhaps even misleading. Good OE poetry, like any
good poetry, is (in the words of Coleridge) made up of 'the *best*
words in the best order'—the vocabulary of poetry and the syntax
of poetry. I can see how you can 'divorce the . . . alliteration of Old
English poetry from its traditional vocabulary and syntax' and say
'I will have alliterative prose'. I agree that, in Pope's words (ibid.),
'so far as we know Ælfric invented the form'. But in what sense can
anyone 'divorce the rhythm . . . of Old English poetry from its traditional vocabulary and syntax'? Take away the words and the way
they are arranged and you have taken away the rhythm—and the
poetry.

§3975. I sometimes accuse myself of making a mere debating point
when I say this. But I do not really believe that this is so. The arrangement of two two-stress phrases into an alliterating unit exists in

Ælfric—with such significant differences (§3966 and Pope, *Ælfric*, i. 123-31) that I am reluctant to call it 'the . . . alliteration of Old English poetry'. The half-line rhythms are different—whether we follow Sievers, Heusler, Pope, or any other theoretician of OE metre. There is a higher proportion of unaccented syllables. The texture is quite different. These facts, and a reading of Pope's discussion (*Ælfric*, i. 105-36), dispel for me the notion that we have in Ælfric 'the rhythm of Old English poetry'. It is my belief that Clemoes's description of Ælfric's prose would have been even better than it is without the sentence with which I began. His next sentence reads: 'To do so, he retained only as much of the rhythm and alliteration of poetry as could be subordinated to the grammatical structure of a normal prose sentence.' I can find some of the alliteration. But none of the rhythm.

E. SOME PATHS WORTH PURSUING

§3976. I can but mention a few. They include: the extent to which syntactic, metrical, and alliterative, patterns can serve as a test of style and as a guide to the recognition of the characteristics of individual writers (see, for example, Le Page, *JEGP* 58 (1959), 434-41, and Green, *CHum.* 6 (1971), 91-3); the use of variation (see Mitchell 1980a, pp. 410-11, and the articles by Stanley and Robinson cited there); the interrelation of syntax, metre, and rhythm (see Shippey, chapter 4, and Raw, chapter 7); and the value of the study of syntax and element order for the appreciation of poetic effect. Examples of the last include Stanley's comments on the *Beowulf* poet's use of 'additive and annexive' syntax (*CB*, pp. 120-2); Shippey's analysis of different types of clauses in *Beowulf* (p. 38); and Greenfield's analysis of the 'one sentence' in *Wan* 19-29a (*NM* 64 (1963), 373-8), which understandably does not mention the 1969 edition of Dunning and Bliss, whose 'one sentence' is *Wan* 15-29a.

XI

AFTERWORD

§ 3977. The sections which follow are the results of afterthought while I was preparing the Indexes. Each of them is specifically linked to an earlier section in Chapters I–X. All such sections are preceded by the symbol × .

§ 3978. In § 42, please add at end:

For the possibility that a prepositional phrase may be accompanied by an uninflected parallel with the preposition not repeated, see § 3998.

§ 3978a. In § 84, please delete *ÆHom* 11. 153 and the comment thereon.

§ 3979. In § 88, please add to fn. 16:

PsCa6 6. 24 is quoted from Sweet (ed.), *The Oldest English Texts*, p. 408. However, on the evidence of Kuhn, Hoad's revision of Sweet's *A Second Anglo-Saxon Reader*, and the *Microfiche Concordance*, *bið* should read *bioð*. We therefore have a plural subject with a plural verb, as the Latin might have led me to expect. On the evidence of the Latin *et mouerunt caput, heafod* is singular in *Ps(F)* 21. 8 *7 hrysedon heora heafod* (where *Ps(K)*—*inter alia*—lacks *heora*); cf. *Matt(Ru)* 27. 39 *heora heafud*, Latin *capita sua*. But we cannot be sure and, even if we could, this would not be real evidence for OE usage. So *CP* 139. 16 *Ðæt feax ðonne on hira heafde* . . . will have to serve as a replacement for *PsCa6* 6. 24.

§ 3979a. In § 718, please note that, as the result of a tardily detected scribal error by the author, who wrote *areaht* for *areahte, Met* 8. 1 is misplaced. It should be in line 4 among the examples with accusative object and *inflected* participle.

§ 3980. In § 851 fn. 219, please add after the first sentence:

However, I think the literal translation would be 'he prepares our good will [for him] to help'; see § § 925-7.

§3980a. In §872, please add at end:

I would make a similar point concerning Tolkien's comment on *Finn* 18 *styrode*: 'In any case the sense is in all probability that Guthere restrained (was restraining, attempted to restrain— a sense often implied by the OE past tense) Garulf from thrusting his precious person forward' (J. R. R. Tolkien, *Finn and Hengest: The Fragment and the Episode*, ed. Alan Bliss (London, 1982), 87). I remain unable to accept an 'imperfective aspect' in OE and reluctant to take the step from 'was/were' + present participle to 'attempted/tried' + infinitive as a rendering for simple preterite forms.

§3981. In §894, please add at end:

I translate *MCharm* 6. 19: 'I sell/am selling it, you sell it!' Unlike Grendon, I cannot accept Cockayne's version—*Lch* iii. 69. 9 'I it sell, ‖ Or it have sold'—because I know of no evidence for *ge* 'or', though it can mean 'and' (§1741); because, even if *bebicgan* were the infinitive and not present subjunctive plural, it could not carry a causative sense or serve as a perfect; and because the second participle 'sold' would be *beboht.*

§3982. In §1009, please add at end:

But a warning is necessary against the dangers of too easily assuming that the apparently identical are in fact identical. Thus, in *ChronE* 143. 6 (1012) *Đa bugon to þam cyninge of þam here xlv scipa. 7 him beheton þet hi woldon þisne eard healdan. 7 he hi fedan scolde 7 scrydan, hi woldon* probably represents a spoken *We willaþ* (or its Danish equivalent) and *scolde* still carries its full sense of obligation.

§3983. In §1062, please add at end:

See further Hiltunen, *NM* 83 (1982), Papers on English Philology read at the symposium arranged by the Modern Language Society at Tvärminne on 26-8 November 1981, 23-37, and the same author's 1981 Oxford D.Phil. thesis referred to in fn. 1 of his article.

§3984. At §1219, please add at end:

Two other interesting examples are quoted by BT, s.v. *hu-hwega.* *Bede* 240. 22 *hu hugu ymb þa teogðan tid dæges*, Latin *hora circiter decima diei*, shows *ymb* used of a particular point of time; cf. *Mark (Li)* 6. 48 above. In *Lch* ii. 280. 16 *æfter þære blodlæse huhwega ymb iii niht, ymb* (I believe) means 'after' and *huhwega* 'about'.

§3984a. In §1286, please add at end:

But I would stress again the terminological nature of a classification so open to personal interpretation. Thus, on my final reading of the proofs, I *could* see a sense in which the eyes in *Lch* ii. 26. 6 above have mistiness.

§3985. In §1324, please add after the third sentence:

(In *ÆCHom* i. 84. 12, it is possible to take *ehtnysse*, not *hatunge*, as the governing noun and to translate 'with the fierce persecution of hatred'; cf. *ÆCHom* i. 84. 14 (§1313).)

§3986. In §1470, please add in the middle before 'The alleged parallel . . .':

Plummer's 'antique construction' derives little real support from the examples of non-agreeing parallels cited in §§42(8), 44(3), 1441, and 3998.

§3987. In §1797, please add after the first sentence:

(The pattern in which the second *þæt* is a relative pronoun and *þæt an (. . .) þæt* can be translated either 'only what' or 'that only which' (see §1781) also deserves mention here.)

§3987a. In §1845, please add before the last sentence:

But even in statements, it is not decisive in examples like the second clause in *ÆCHom* ii. 46. 18. However, my answer to the question in line 5 of this section is an almost unqualified 'No'. I concede the possibility that, since VS can occur at the beginning of principal clauses containing positive statements (§§3930-4), it cannot be claimed categorically that initial *ne* in a clause of this sort which is followed by a co-ordinate *ne* clause, as in *ÆCHom* i. 572. 2, must be the adverb and not the conjunction. But the infrequency of VS and the overwhelming regularity of *ne* VS in principal clauses containing statements (§3935) suggests to me that it is little more than a theoretical possibility that the first *ne* in *ÆCHom* i. 572. 2 is the conjunction, whether it is supposed to be there alone, in its own right, or by coalescence of *ne* + *ne*.

§3988. In §1878, please add after the fifth sentence:

To these three articles should be added a fourth by the same author: G. G. Alekseeva, ['On the variants and varieties of complex sentences with consubordination in Old English'], *Vestnik Leningradskogo Universiteta*, series 8 (1981), vyp. 2, 75–80, in which we are offered an alternative classification to that adopted here—five structural models, each with variants—and some figures on the relative frequency of the various patterns, again in a limited corpus.

§3989. In §1880, please add at end:

But I am becoming increasingly convinced of the validity and the importance of my observation in *RES* 31 (1980), 412, that 'I should be inclined to err on the side of light rather than heavy stopping', especially in the poetry. There I should also like to see the disappearance of pre-emptive and/or misleading titles such as *The Wanderer, Wulf and Eadwacer*, and *The Dream of the Rood*.

§3990. In §1930 fn., please add at end:

This comment by Robinson is also (I now see) relevant to the sentence in the middle of §1930 which begins 'The argument . . .', although it will be noted that *ða* and *ðis* have no syntactical functions in common and that the use of *ð* for both *ðis* and *ðæt* is not established.

§3991. In §1978, please add at end:

If the first *þæt* is a conjunction, the second means 'what'; see §§ 2126-8. If it is a demonstrative, the second means 'which'; see §§2124 and 2129.

§3991a. In §2134, please add at the end:

Of the two possible plural examples cited, *PPs* 121. 1 is the more difficult to explain away. In *Or* 256. 11 *þæt* 'who' gives sense, with *þa* as adv. 'then' or dem. 'those their sins' (§107). We could explain *þæt* as a tautology imported under the influence of *cwæð* to introduce what was wrongly taken as a noun clause. However, *Or* 256. 11 is perhaps best subsumed under (*b*) in §3124. For more possible plural examples see §2136.

§3991b. In §2159, please add at end:

I have, however, to confess that even now I have not eliminated all traces of the earlier classification. Thus the following examples cited as *seþe* really belong to type 3(*b*): *Jul* 1 (§2261) and *CP* 7. 6 and *ÆCHom* i. 114. 6 (both in §2281). In all three, the *se* element has the same form but would be accusative in the principal clause, nominative in the adjective clause.

§3992. In §2184, please add at end:

For an interesting variety of constructions involving *þu þe*, including sentences containing adjective clauses in both asyndetic and syndetic parataxis, see *Bo* 10. 1-27. However, please note that the comment which follows *PPs* 122. 1 applies to all three examples.

§3993. In §2836, please add in the appropriate places the text of two passages of which the reference alone is given:

ÆCHom i. 268. 1 *Is hwæðere getæht, æfter Godes gesetnysse, þæt wise men sceolon settan steore dysigum mannum, swa þæt hi þæt dysig and ða unðeawas alecgan, and þeah ðone man lufigan swa swa agenne broðor* and *ÆCHom* i. 604. 29 *Na on forligerbeddum and on unclænnyssum, ac beo arwyrðe sinscipe betwux gelyfedum mannum, swa þæt furðon nan forliger ne unclænnyss ne sy genemned on Godes gelaðunge; na on geflite and andan.*

§3994. In §3063, please add after the sixth sentence:

These ten examples with *þæs þy* + comparative + *þy/þe* all belong to either type 2a or type 3 of what I classify as comparative clauses; see §§3357-8, where four of them are quoted, viz. *CP* 231. 13 and *ÆCHom* i. 490. 13 (§3357) and *Bo* 141. 2 and *CP* 435. 2 (§3358). I do not understand why Liggins singled out these ten for special treatment. See further §§3355-9 and cf. §3142.

§3994a. In the tables in §§3074 and 3076, *for* should be printed as a separate word.

§3994b. In §3077, *Or* 50. 15 (line 14) should precede *Solil* 21. 14 (line 4).

§3995. In §3236, please add at end:

In *ÆCHom* ii. 538. 8 (§3230), *þa frecednyssa* is the antecedent for both limiting clauses if we take *ða ðe* as a relative. In

ChristC 1489   Nu is swærra mid mec   þinra synna rod
                    þe ic unwillum   on beom gefæstnad,
                    þonne seo oþer wæs   þe ic ær gestag,
                    willum minum,

the contrast is between two combinations of an antecedent + a limiting clause. In *ÆCHom* ii. 544. 9 above, *se ðe* means 'whoever' or 'he who'; see §2204. Whether we take *miccle ma* or *ðæra . . . ðæra* as the antecedent(s) in *ÆCHom* ii. 94. 5 above is a nice point of terminology. On the general problem compare §3221.

§3996. In §3453, please add after the second sentence:

The only type not represented in §§3453-4 is the permissive formula with a temporal clause such as ✩*man mot mærsian his drihten, bidde þonne he bidde* (cf. *ÆLS* 13. 66 in §3453) and ✩*cærde we usic þonne we cærde* . . . (cf. *Bede* 386. 1 in §3454). Like Quirk, I have found no examples in the poetry. Neither Wülfing (ii, §420) nor Burnham (pp. 59-65) records any in the prose. I can think of no reason why the pattern should not exist and suspect that the full collections will reveal examples; cf. §3466.

§3997. In §3864, please add at end:

There appears to be another OE example in *MCharm* 6. 15 *Criste, ic sæde, þis gecyþed!*, translated in ASPR as 'By Christ, I said, this has been made known!' I assume that 'By Christ' is intended to express agency, not blasphemy, but would prefer 'To Christ . . .'; see §§ 1371-8.

§3998. In §3865, please add at end:

However, *wer unwundod* could be an uninflected appositional variant of *of lice*, just as *lacende lig* in

Dan 473   We gesawon
          þæt he wið cwealme gebearh   cnihtum on ofne,
          lacende lig,   þam þe his lof bæron

could parallel either *wið cwealme* or *on ofne*; see §§42(8) and 1173.

§3999. In §3918, please add immediately after 'here' in the third sentence:

by suggesting that *ÆCHom* i. 86. 5 and *ÆCHom* i. 86. 13, both quoted above, display a variation of the order VS seen in *ÆCHom* i. 386. 17 (§3930).

§4000. I shall bring this Afterword to its conclusion by expressing the wish that I had given more cross-references in chapters I–X, especially to other discussions of specific passages from prose and poetry —I have tried to rectify this in the Indexes—and by observing that there is no Index of Persons listing the names of nineteenth- and twentieth-century scholars whose work is discussed in the course of this book. As I point out in my Select Bibliography, not all such writers on Old English syntax have received mention. Since I aim at giving as complete a coverage as is possible in *A Critical Bibliography of Writings on Old English Syntax*, now in progress, and since that work will contain an Index of Authors and Reviewers, referring not only to itself but also to this work, I have judged it premature to include an incomplete index here.

CONCLUSION

AS the time draws near for me to write *Finis*, I am more conscious of the work that I have not done than of the work that I have done. Even in those areas into which I have ventured, I have often left tracks—*stige nearwe, enge anpaðas*—rather than signposted highways. But it is not given to human beings to achieve perfection. If I had not adopted James Murray's attitude—'Continually I have to say "This is not right but we cannot spend another minute over it; it must go as it is"' (quoted by Robinson, *The Yale Review* (Autumn, 1977), 99)—I should have found myself at the age of sixty-two in the dilemma of Dr Strong as described by Charles Dickens (*David Copperfield*, chapter 16):

Adams our head-boy, who had a turn for mathematics, had made a calculation, I was informed, of the time this Dictionary would take in completing, on the Doctor's plan, and at the Doctor's rate of going. He considered that it might be done in one thousand six hundred and forty-nine years, counting from the Doctor's last, or sixty-second, birthday.

But I should like to have had another twenty years. I could then have verified yet again all quotations and references; checked all my OE quotations against the manuscript(s) rather than against the editions; made sure that, when I quote a Latin original, it is as far as is known that most likely to have been the source of the OE in question; examined more closely the possibility of the existence of Latin originals for those passages where I do not quote one; re-checked the statistics which I have produced from the work of earlier scholars; rethought and if necessary corrected my criticisms of other workers; removed the repetitions which became apparent only when I was inserting cross-references or compiling the Indexes, e.g. my discussion of *Beo* 917 in both §1686 and §2536 and of *weald þeah* in both §2937 and §3148; studied with the aid of the microfiche concordance more—if not all—of the examples, certain and doubtful, of each phenomenon; eliminated more of my inevitable errors; and produced and used a more consistent and acceptable system of punctuation and capitalization for OE prose and poetry. Or perhaps I should say that I could have made a start on these tasks.

I might also have been able to give more consideration to topics such as these: Latin influences on OE syntax (this is certainly now worth a monograph); syntactical glossing (the value of the study of this has been convincingly demonstrated by Robinson; see my §3890); the development of OE prose style (see §1896); syntactical tests for date and authorship (see, in addition to the references given in §§1896 fnn. and 1922, Baker (*Speculum*, 55 (1980), 22-37), Bately (*The Old English Orosius* (EETS, ss 6 (1980)), pp. lxxiii-lxxxvi), and Amos); the nature and extent of the debt which Wulfstan owed Ælfric; the syntactical peculiarities of different periods and genres; the possibility of dialectal variants in syntax; problems affecting the poetry (see my chapter X, especially §3976); and the way in which developments during the OE period point forward to later developments in the English language (here I am glad to note that the comparison between the language of MSS *C* and *O* and of MS *H* of Gregory's *Dialogues* suggested by Kruisinga (*EStudies*, 8 (1926), 48-9) has now been carried out; see Yerkes). Readers will doubtless be able to supplement this catalogue.

Those working on these topics and on OE syntax in general should consult (*inter alios*) the following: Kruisinga, *EStudies*, 8 (1926), 44-9; Small, *PMLA* 51 (1936), 1-7; Quirk, pp. 1-4; Liggins 1955, pp. 16-35; Terasawa, pp. 125-8; Utley, *NM* 73 (1972), 456-61; Rydén, *An Introduction to the Historical Study of English Syntax* (Stockholm Studies in English, 51 (1979)); and my Introduction, especially the passage from Royston quoted there.

The influence of French on the syntax of English is outside my brief. However, Bailey and Maroldt ('The French Lineage of English', *Langues en contact—Pidgins—Creoles—Languages in Contact*, ed. J. M. Meisel (Tübingen, 1977), 21-53) seem to me guilty of both over-simplification and exaggeration in their assessment of that influence. One of the prevailing impressions I have as a result of my work is what I once described as 'the "Englishness" of English syntax'; see Mitchell 1959, pp. xxx-xxxi. With the book at press (October, 1982), I am happy to find myself in agreement with the fundamental conclusions (though not with all the terminology or all the details) of Poussa's important article on 'The evolution of early standard English' (*SAP* 14 (1982), 69-85):

> It is argued that the fundamental changes which took place between standard literary OE and Chancery Standard English: loss of grammatical gender, extreme simplification of inflexions and borrowing of form-words and common lexical words, may be ascribed to a creolization with Old Scandinavian during the OE period. The Midland creole dialect could have stabilized as a spoken lingua franca in the reign of Knut. Its non-appearance in literature was due initially to the prestige of the OE literary standard. The influence of French to be seen in ME texts is less fundamental: mainly loanwords. Most of the French influence on syntax and word-formation probably came in during the standardization of

the English written language, through the habits of scribes who were accustomed to writing standard Latin and French.

But now I must stop, albeit at the risk of publication in 1984—a contingency which not even George Orwell's nightmares encompassed. To those who follow, I wish the same happiness as my long involvement with Old English has given me; the encouragement of *geferan* like Tom Dobson, Sarah Ogilvie-Thomson, and Fred Robinson; the privilege of personal contact with scholars like Alistair Campbell and Angus Cameron; the support of a wife like Mollie; and a belief in a sustaining God.

þenc be þæm wyrhtan þisse bec hwilum in þinum gebedum ond be hire þe hine wreþede ond be eallum þara þe þæron swuncon.

FINIS

INDEXES

THERE are three Indexes—the General Index, the Index of Words and Phrases, and the Index of Passages Particularly Discussed. References are to section numbers except when p(p). precedes the number. Volume I contains the General Index to §§1–1925, Volume II the complete General Index and the other two Indexes. Footnote numbers are given only when there is more than one footnote to the section cited. For the reason given in §4000, there is no Index of Persons containing the names of nineteenth- and twentieth-century scholars whose work is referred to in the course of this book. For Ælfric, Cynewulf, Wulfstan, and other OE writers, see the General Index. The word-by-word system of alphabetization has been used.

In the General Index, the head word is the (primary) noun, e.g. 'pronouns, personal', 'vowels, unstressed', and 'phrases, prepositional', except when that arrangement seemed perverse, pedantic, or misleading, e.g. 'element order', 'linguistic facts', and 'literary considerations'. For reasons of space, the number of cross-references is limited. Thus, the various functions of the periphrastic forms with present participles discussed in §§685–94 are not given separate entries and entries such as 'conjunctions, co-ordinating' must be used in conjunction with those under *and, ac, oþþe,* and the like, in the Index of Words and Phrases. For the same reason, there is no entry 'syntax, differences between Old English and Modern English'. The reader seeking such information should find it by referring to the phenomenon in which he is interested; thus, the entry 'pronouns, anaphoric' will lead him to §71. Cross-references such as that in §174 are not included. Entries under such items as 'sentences', both 'simple' and 'complex'; 'speech', both 'dependent' and 'non-dependent'; and 'clauses', 'principal', 'co-ordinate', and 'subordinate'; are necessarily highly selective, for many syntactical phenomena can occur in all these units. Entries involving square brackets, such as (s.v. 'case') *'see also* [case], concord' indicate that the reader is to search within the entry 'case'; contrast (also s.v. 'case') 'accusative *see* case, accusative', which refers to the separate entry 'case, accusative'.

The General Index must be treated as a supplement to the Contents. Thus, under 'concord' the reader is referred to '1–47 *see* Contents' and under 'agreement' to 'concord'. This explains why the General Index does not contain such entries as 'concords, the basic OE 25–47' or 'agreement between subject and predicate 26–39', but does contain the entries 'predicate, agreement with subject 26–39' and 'subject(s), agreement with predicate 26–39'. So it is imperative that invitations to '*see* Contents' be accepted, even though the penalty for non-acceptance is less severe than that described in Luke 14. 24. The Contents can also be used to advantage in entries which consist merely of figures, especially those in which there are no section numbers distinguished by italic type or accompanied by the words '*see* Contents' and/or '*especially*' to denote that the sections so distinguished serve as a useful introduction to the topic in question. Thus, under 'poetry, OE, usages', no discussions on nouns (§§54–96 in the Contents) are listed, whereas concord (§§1–47) and adjectives (§§97–219) attract entries. Again, the entry under 'adjectives, inflexions, strong and weak forms' directs the reader first to the main discussion ('97–141 *see* Contents') and then to the use of one or both of these forms in the nominative of address (§§1245-7), as subject (§1484), and in poetry (§3964). Further references to their use in poetry will be found in the entries 'poetry, OE, syntax influenced by metre and/or alliteration' (§139) and 'poetry, OE, usages' (§§105, 114, 122, 127, and 134).

Similar use can, of course, be made of the Index of Words and Phrases, which also embraces prefixes such as *ge-* and endings such as *-an, -en, -on*, and *-un*, but is not exhaustive and does not include references to items mentioned merely by way of illustration, such as *se wisdom*, Ælfric, and the like, in §54. The criterion is that the mention must be of syntactical significance, for example the fact that the endings cited above are not distinctive for mood (§22) and that *syn* and *syndon* can be both indicative and subjunctive (§2). References to such items as *freos* in *Dan* 66 (§62) and *hryre* in *Wan* 7 (§65), in which the use of a particular form in a particular context is in question, will be found through the Index of Passages Particularly Discussed.

The Index of Passages Particularly Discussed is intended to contain references both to *OES* and to all my articles and reviews up to December 1983, including those at press and in progress. But it is occasionally difficult to decide when a passage has been 'particularly' discussed. My criterion has been this: 'particular' discussion means that I have thrown, or have attempted to throw, some light (however dim) on the interpretation of the passage cited. Sometimes the case is clear—for inclusion *CP* 304. 6, for exclusion *CP* 304. 19 (on these two, see Mitchell 1979*a*, pp. 39-40) and the seven examples from Visser i, §323, discussed at Mitchell 1979*b*, pp. 541-2. Where there is doubt, e.g. *Alex* 14. 1 and *Bede* 480. 21 (on these two, see §486 and Mitchell 1972, p. 230, and 1979*a*, pp. 43-4), I have generally included the reference.

Having been sternly advised that 'anyone can write the book but only the author can write the indexes', I have forced myself to do so. I am entirely responsible for the Index of Words and Phrases and for the Index of Passages Particularly Discussed. The General Index has been edited from my draft by Jennifer Speake, whose patient and skilful assistance I gratefully acknowledge. I also thank Vera Keep for characteristic concern above the call of duty in offering, at the setting stage, suggestions about the layout of the General Index which have made it much easier to use, and Martin Garrett for careful help with the checking of the other two Indexes. I have tried to make the Indexes helpful rather than burdensome, selective rather than overwhelming, by attempting to ensure that the headings are the meaningful ones and that the sections included are those which contain significant discussion or reference. Some of the omissions are therefore deliberate. Others are the unintended result of 'a wobbling of the mental knees' which afflicted me as I approached the finishing line of what proved to be a longer race than I expected at the start. Those failings which remain are my responsibility. I can only crave indulgence both from the reader who finds that too much has been included and from the reader who finds that too much has been omitted, at the same time expressing the hope that somehow or other both will find what they seek.

GENERAL INDEX

clauses of purpose and result 2802-3006 *see*
Contents
    classification or terminology 1928-9,
      1938, 1952, 1977, 2139-43, 2238,
      2480, 2641, 2745, 2748, 2766, 2797,
      2802-936 *passim*, 2962-4, 2969-99,
      3001, 3046, 3050, 3053, 3066, 3067,
      3069, 3470, 3660
    expressing time 2608-9, 2827-8
    order 1925, 3000-4
clauses of result 2802-3006 *see* Contents
    expressing cause 3024, 3159
    none governed by *butan* 3643
    influence on mood of subordinate clause
      2618, 2641, 3684
    (plu)perfect periphrases in 705
    with antecedent *swelc* 2377
clauses of time 2530-801 *see* Contents
    adjective 2461, 2573, 2582
    in *apo koinou* 3796-8, 3802-3
    none recorded in challenge or permissive
      constructions 3996
    classification or terminology 1938, 2049,
      2052, 2055, 2302, 2480, 2481, 2530-
      5, 2573, 2593, 2597, 2609, 2641,
      2681-2, 2694, 2703, 2745, 2775-83,
      2797, 2827-8, 2862, 2873, 2918,
      2975, 3110, 3130-1, 3144, 3338-9,
      3493
    in comparative constructions 3337
    continuative 2739-40, 2753-4
    contracted 2719
    expressing cause, *see* cause
    expressing concession, *see* concession
    expressing condition, *see* condition
    expressing purpose, *see* purpose
    expressing result, *see* result
    expressing wishes 3252
    frequentative 2562-72 *passim*, 2582-90
      passim, 2789-96
    governed by *butan* 3643
    introduced by *þær (þær)* 2460-3
    order, *see* clause order
clauses, *þæt*:
    more common than MnE 'that' clauses
      1929
    vary with (accusative and) infinitives 668,
      966, 1929, 1992-3, 3886
    vary with participles 1929
    vary with verbal nouns 1929
collective expressions:
    an in 545
    cardinal numeral subjects 562, 564
    introduced by exclamatory *þæt* 2136
    see also nouns, collective
comitative relationship:
    expressed by dative case 1412-13, 3811

expressed by *mid* 818-19, 1413, 1501-2
comma(s), inverted, OE equivalents 327,
    1941, 2016
command(s):
    dependent, *see* desires, dependent
    expressed by inflected infinitive 3313
    expressed by passive voice 881
    non-dependent 879-919 *see* Contents,
      1645, 1671, 1675-82; ~, expressed
      by impersonal verbs 898; ~, expressed
      by present indicative 617
    see also infinitives, uninflected
comparative(s):
    absolute 183-6, 3220
    of adjectives, genitive with 1332, 1335-
      7; ~, as nouns 135
    of adjectives or adverbs, in comparisons
      of inequality 3205-53, 3384
    of adjectives or adverbs, with *hu* 3360;
      ~, with *swa*, alone and in combina-
      tion 3262-322 *see* Contents, 3384;
      ~, with *swelce*, alone and in combi-
      nation 3323-33; ~, with *þæs þe/þy*
      ... *þe/þy* 3063, 3142-3, 3160, 3347-
      59, 3384, 3994; ~, with *þe/þy* ... *þe/*
      þy 2106, 2594-5, 3063, 3137-43,
      3243-50, 3334-59, 3384
    conjunctions containing 2431, 2661,
      2666, 2717, 2728
comparison:
    adjectives 101, 104, 128, 135, 181-91
      see Contents
    adverbs 1107
    clauses of, *see* clauses of comparison
    expressed in adjective clauses 3204
    expressed by genitive case 1336-7, 3260
    expressed by parataxis 1735, 1864, 3293
    expressed by phrases 3256-9, 3366-7
    expressed by *swa/swelce (...) oþer* 513-
      16
    expressed by *þonne* 'than' clauses 1358-
      64 *passim*, 3205-38
    expressing extent or degree 1146
    indefinites not compared 379
    of inequality, expressed by *þonne* 'than'
      clauses 1358-64 *passim*, 3205-38;
      ~, expressed by dative/instrumental
      case, *see* case, dative, of comparison
    one element unexpressed 3212, 3215,
      3220-1, 3228, 3238, 3316-18,
      3320-1
    participles, *see* participles
    periphrastic 189
    see also comparatives; superlatives
complement 1581-8 *see* Contents
    adjectives as (part) 33-8, 1582
    adverbs as 1585

expressed by parataxis 617, 882, 1695, 1705, 1735, 3678-83, 3691-3

expressed by participles 1435

genitive of 1389

imaginary, *see* [conditions], rejected

negated, expressed by *swa* + negated verb 'without . . . , not . . .' 3525

open 3543-4, 3556-601 *see* Contents, 3612-14, 3615, 3621, 3624-5, 3636-7, 3653, 3655, 3684-7, 3689, 3702, 3703

rejected or imaginary 1631, 1843, 2571, 3544, 3602-11 *see* Contents, 3613, 3615-23, 3636-7, 3639, 3654-5, 3684, 3686-7, 3689, 3702, 3703

see also hypothesis

'conjunct', term explained 3015

conjunction(s) 1229-33 *see* Contents

  adversative 1685, 1752-805 *see* Contents, 1736, 1738

  alternative 1685, 1806-31 *see* Contents, 3280, 3319, 3434-7, *see also* alternatives

  æfter alone not one 3833

  classification or terminology 571, 924, 1229, 1662, 1685, 1739, 1744, 1806-31 *passim*, 1832-57 *passim*, 1858-60, 1872-5, 2151-2, 2195, 2377-8, 2419-20, 2422, 2424-31 *passim*, 2606, 3204, 3323-8, 3350, 3369, 3626-33, 3646, 3647-51, 3826, *see also* adverb/conjunctions, the ambiguous

  containing a comparative 2431, 2661, 2666, 2717, 2728

  co-ordinating 741, 1709-862 *see* Contents; ~, influence on element order (often overlooked) 1078, 1685, 1729-31, 1753, 3889, 3911-14, 3916, 3934, 3946; ~, repetition of elements after 166; ~, to be distinguished from sentence adverbs 1101; ~, *see also* co-ordination; parataxis

  cumulative 1685, 1709-51 *see* Contents

  divided, term explained 1230

  doubling 1889, 1895, 2424, 2450-5, 2489-90, 2521, 2525, 2539, 2546, 2575, 2583-4, 2718, 2858, 3277, 3279, 3284

  grouped, term explained 1230

  illative 1685, 1858-61, 1862, *see also* cause; clauses, explanatory

  (references to) lists of 1231 fn., 1232-3, 1775-6, 1861, 1862, 1931, 2416-20, 3054-5, 3126, 3182, 3196-7, *see also* Contents, *especially* 2437-3721

  negative co-ordinating 1832-57 *see* Contents

non-expression, of *swa* 2366-7, 2483; ~, of *þæt* 1981-91, 2928, 2960, 3210-11, 3215 fn., 3228, 3232, 3609, 3628, 3641, 3656-7, 3663, 3685, 3714, 3732, 3771, 3783, 3886

non-prepositional, sometimes difficult to distinguish from (antecedent and) relative pronoun 2152, 3114; ~, with nouns, *see* formulae, non-prepositional; ~, term explained 1230, 2419; ~, *see also, in the Index of Words and Phrases, those listed in* 1232

non-repetition 1788, 1790, 1808, 1976-80, 2529, (2801), 3002-3, 3005-6, 3182, 3196-7, 3284, 3287-8, 3540, 3668, 3715-16

origin 1157, 1230, 1233, 1956, 1980, 2107, 2152 fn., 2420, 2421-32, 2532, 2594 fn., 2628, 2639, 2646, 2661, 2666, 2682-3, 2696, 2698, 2701, 2712, 2716-17, 2728, 2747, 2755-6, 2758, 2799 fn., 2815-16, 2828, 2892, 2895, 2909-10, 2927, 2934-6, 3060, 3065, 3071, 3113-15, 3128-32, 3133, 3206-7, 3243-50, 3262, 3287, 3309-10, 3334-44, 3348-9, 3380, 3400-1, 3550; ~, *see also* adverbs, origin; parataxis, did it precede hypotaxis?

prepositional, correlation 1888 and fn.; ~, formation 1157, 1230, 1233, 2420; ~, term explained 1230, 2420; ~, with nouns, *see* formulae, prepositional; ~, *see also, in the Index of Words and Phrases, those listed in* 1233

repetition or resumption by different conjunctions 1960, 2066, 2842, 2928, 3121, 3181, 3389, 3417

simple, term explained 1230

sona 'as soon as' 2702

subordinating, preceded by material belonging to subordinate clause 1920-1, 3404; ~, *þe* not always a sign 1859, 1885, 1889, 2424, 3011, 3072-3, 3405; ~, *see also* clauses, subordinate *and references to Contents there given*; interrogatives; *Index of Words and Phrases*

þa, see Index of Words and Phrases

þa continuative 2544, 2546, 2554

þæt, more widely used than MnE 'that' 1929, 3118; ~, oblique cases 318

þe 'than' 573-4, 3239-42, 3243-50

see also adverb/conjunctions; clauses; phrases

consecutive, *see* result

in groups with (possibly) compound
verbs 1062, 1076-9
non-expression 567
(non-)repetition 41, 166, 337, 569, *see
also* pronouns, tautologic
and/or possessives qualifying nouns 103-
12, 118-22, 126-7, *see also* [demon-
stratives], alternating
qualitative, unnecessary category 2882
with relative pronouns 2153-79 *see*
Contents, 2201-25 *see* Contents
sum as 401
with *sum* 404-16
two qualifying a noun 104
þa, see Index of Words and Phrases
see also antecedents; articles, definite;
demonstrative/relatives, the ambiguous; qualifiers
Deor, usages 476
dependent:
    term discussed 52, 239-41
    uses, *see* clauses, subordinate; qualifiers;
    *and under the individual parts of
    speech*
descriptive or limiting, difficulty of distinguishing 1449-50, 1462, 2271-83
see also clauses, adjective
desires:
    dependent 1929, 1937-8, 1951-2046
    see Contents; ~, equivalent of accu-
    sative and infinitive 3726, 3728-9,
    3730-1; ~, element order 3899; ~,
    without principal clause 1974-5,
    3564; ~, *see also* speech, dependent
    non-dependent, *see* commands, non-
    dependent; element order; wishes,
    non-dependent
dialects, syntactical variations 63, 66, 68
    and fn., 109, 381, 388, 440, 441 and
    fn., 447 fn., 552 fn., 664 fn., 762 fn.,
    773, 1125, 1130, 1179, 1193, 1195,
    1222, 2184, 3107, 3647, 3835,
    3837, 3844
dialogue, non-expression of elements 3873-4
Dialogues of Gregory, *see* Gregory's *Dialogues*
distributive:
    dative 415 n. 3
    indefinites 432-3, 459
    numerals 584-6
Dream of the Rood, usages 1922 fn., 3973
Durham Ritual Gloss, usages 63, 66, 68,
1179

EF(F), Nickel's abbreviation 681
element order 3887-951 *see* Contents
    absolute constructions 3812, 3823
    accusative and infinitive 3763 fn.

adjectives, *see* qualifiers
adverbs and adverb phrases 703, 986,
1103, 1113, 1138, 1592-3, 1921
ambiguity in or from 1645, 1647, 1671,
2525
an, position 529, 537-8, 540
apposition 1445-8, 1459-63
'backwards pronominalization' 247
basic orders described 1078, 3889,
3892, 3900-1
bibliography 3890
classification or terminology 3887-94,
3900-2, 3909, 3914, 3917, *see also*
ambiguity
clauses, co-ordinate, *see* conjunctions,
co-ordinating, influence
clauses, principal, *see* clauses, principal,
material; clauses, subordinate, material; element order, patterns, S . . . V;
element order, patterns, VS
clauses, subordinate 1078, 1933, 3900-
36, *see also* clauses, principal, material;
clauses, subordinate, material; element
order, patterns, VS; ~, varieties, *see
following individual named clauses*: ~,
adjective 2110, *see also* antecedents;
~, causal 3012, 3015, 3057, 3134; ~,
of comparison 3240-2, 3267-70,
3292, 3340; ~, of concession 3399,
3440-50, 3458; ~, of condition 3440,
3444, 3713; ~, noun, position of
conjunction *þæt* 1978-80, 3003,
3803; ~, of place 2458-9, 2514-28
passim; ~, of purpose and result
3002-3, 3005-6; ~, of time 2530
collective noun subjects 80-1
combinations involving infinitives 920-
71 *see* Contents
complements 1588
conjunctions, co-ordinating, influence,
see conjunctions, co-ordinating
dative and infinitive 3782
demonstratives 143-57
desires, dependent 3899; ~, non-dependent 879, 880a, 883-910, 913-19,
1078, 1680, 3897-8
elements other than SV 3937-43
essential distinctions 3889, 3900-1,
3907, 3935
exclamations, dependent 3896
exclamations, non-dependent 1078,
1671, 3896
genitive (groups) 113, 143-4, 147, 149,
348, 1303, 1304-30, 1334, 3921,
3938, 3964
groups with a (possibly) compound verb
1060-80 *passim*

extraposition 44(3), 1429 and fn., 1441, 1448, 2294

fact:
    expressed by *beon/wesan* 658-9, 662
    expressed by indicative mood 877, *see also* mood, indicative
    expressed by subjunctive mood 877, *see also* mood, subjunctive
    see also truth, universal
final, *see* purpose
formulae:
    with *for*, classification or terminology 2911-16, 3033-89 *passim*, 3167
    non-prepositional, with noun, introducing clauses of time 2152, 2425, 2561, 2573, 2607, 2644, 2686, 2784-8, *see also Index of Words and Phrases s.v. 'þa hwile (. . .) (þe/þæt)'*; ~, ~, 'on condition that' 3667; ~, *see also* conjunctions, non-prepositional
    poetic, oral-formulaic theory 1922 fn.; ~, syntactic structure 3961-2; ~, unthinking or mechanical use 376, 1182, 1523, 3084, 3385, 3855, 3963
    'of polite address' 3571
    prepositional, infrequently correlative 1888 and fn.; ~, formation 1157, 1230, 1233, 2420; ~, not always fossilized 1781, 2152, 2600, 2604, 2892, 2911, 3011, 3033, 3092, 3155 fn., 3661; ~, with noun, introducing causal clauses 3071; ~, ~, introducing clauses of comparison 3368; ~, ~, 'on condition that' 3667; ~, ~, introducing clauses of purpose or result 2919-20; ~, ~, introducing clauses of time 2597-8, 2644, 2663-5, 2729-30, 2759-60; ~, must be distinguished from relative combinations containing preposition + demonstrative (antecedent) + (. . .) þe/þæt 1781, 2152, 2600, 2604, 2892, 2911, 3011, 3033, 3092, 3155 fn., 3661; ~, term explained 1230
    in prose, *see* sentences, in prose
fractions 578-80
French, influence on English 189 fn., 801, 811, 1193, 1202 and fn., 2043 fn., 3574, 3951, Conclusion
futurity:
    expressed by *beon/wesan* + inflected infinitive 945-8
    expressed by infinitives 945-8, 3749, 3752
    expressed by present tenses, *see* tenses

    expressed by present tenses of *beon/wesan* 652, 657-64
    expressed by present tenses of subjunctive 1676, 2000, 2740
    expressed by present tenses of *weorþan* 672
    expressed by preterite tenses of subjunctive 2007
    expressed by **sculan* or *willan* + infinitive 947, 1023-4, 1997
    see also tenses, future perfect
futurity-in-the-past, *see* mood, subjunctive, preterite

gender 55-71, *see* Contents
    agreement of antecedent and pronoun 45-7, 2291, 2338, 2356-8, 2681-2, *see also* pronouns, relative, concord
    agreement of noun/pronoun and appositive element 43
    agreement of noun/pronoun and attributive element 40
    agreement of subject and adjective/participle 33-8
    agreement of subject and complement 39, 323
    changes in nouns 62-5, 68
    concord, lack of 38, 63-5, 66-8, 69-71, 551
    distinctions in OE 3, 55-61
    distinctions survive in adjectives, participles, and pronouns 66-8
    feminine or neuter forms used referring to male and female 38, 551
    loss in OE 62-8
    non-repetition of *se* with nouns of different gender 337
    nouns with more than one 62-5, 2595
    subject, 'empty' 1964
    syntactical criterion 65, 67, 256
    see also concord; sex v. gender
Genesis A and/or *B*, usages, Introduction fn., 476, 878, 2536-7, 3470
Germanic languages, influence on English 188 fn., 259, 1796-9
glosses, syntactical 1158a, 1899 fn., 3890
Glosses, usages 63, 64 fn., 66, 68, 109-12, 225, 290, 360, 527, 555, 628, 765, 770, 780, 865, 878, 1014-15, 1152, 1158a, 1179, 1188, 1195, 1202, 1231 fn. 293, 1236, 1364, 1384, 1424, 1479, 1494, 1677, 1940, 1997, 2501, 2503, 2507, 2839, 2929, 2942, 3578, 3623, 3628 and fnn. 189 and 191, 3654, 3769, 3814, 3825 fn., 3832, 3836-7, 3841, 3844
Gospels, usages, *see* Glosses, usages

infinitives, perfect:
do not express purpose 2941
with *habban* 922
infinitives, uninflected:
and inflected, difference in functions
955, 970-1, 996-7, 1029, 2948
normal in passive infinitives, *see* infinitives, passive
normal with 'modal' verbs other than
agan 996
immediately preceded by *ne* 916a
with 'modal' verbs expressing command,
wish, or the like 917-18
inflexions, *see* ambiguity, inflexions; case,
dative, uninflected; concord; *and
under the individual parts of speech*
informants, native, absence of, Foreword,
Introduction, 273-4, 315, 329, 349,
475, 690, 1376-7, 1430, 1462, 1635,
1671, 1996, 2080, 2423, 2500, 2507,
2545, 2777, 2782, 2975a, 3014,
3408, 3936, 3953
instrument:
or agent 802-33a *passim*; ~, or cause,
expressed by prepositional phrases
812, 813, 817, 818, 833a
expressed by case forms, *see* case, dative;
case, genitive
expressed by compounds 803
expression of 762, 802-33a *see* Contents,
1228, 1365-70, 1372; ~, methods
summarized 803, 1228
term explained 802
see also agent
intensification 1146
see also adverbs; aspect; stress and/or
emphasis
interception in poetry 149-57, 175-7, 3946,
3959
interjections 1146, 1234-9 *see* Contents,
1242, 1648, 1667, 1671, 1858, 3847
classification or terminology 1234-6
(references to) lists of 1234 fn., 1238-9
is *uton* one? 916-16a
interrogatives 346-60 *see* Contents, 1147-
50, 3027-32
is *ac* one? 2806 fn. 134
an with 531, 535
case in dependent speech 2061
distinguished from relative adverbs and
conjunctions 1150, 2049-55, 2385,
2494-507, 2743, 2775-83
distinguished from relative pronouns
359, 521, 1150, 2049-55, 2385
genitive case with 1299
in groups with (possibly) compound
verbs 1062, 1076-9

oblique cases of *hwæt* 353
non-expression 2072-7
(non-)repetition 1868-9, 2072-7
with prepositions 1062, 1079
with same form as indefinites 379
intonation patterns in OE unknown,
Introduction, 11, 315, 386, 690,
887-8, 1146, 1309, 1430, 1462,
1497, 1645, 1647, 1671, 1686, 1718,
1881, 1885, 1895, 2059, 2109-10,
2118, 2122, 2156-7, 2160-2, 2246,
2253, 2272, 2279, 2283, 2284-6,
2423, 2445, 2544-5, 2782, 2804,
3014, 3083, 3443, 3501, 3678-9,
3797, 3881, 3885, 3889, 3893, 3894,
3905, 3919, 3936, 3953
see also informants, native, absence of;
stress and/or emphasis
introductory *þær* 754, 1491-7, 2439 fn.,
2553, 3862
substitutes for 3930

Judith, usages 792
Juliana, usages 476, 3562 fn.
juxtaposition, *see* parataxis

Kuhn's law 1846, 1881, 2350, 2541, 2545,
3947, 3954, 3960, 3963

Latin:
grammar, the basis for my syntactical
approach, Foreword, Introduction
influence 33 fn., 108, 109-12, 137, 172,
183, 188 fn., 189 fn., 190, 225, 244,
264 fn., 281, 310, 390a fn., 396 and
fn. 99, 410, 415 n. 3, 438, 447 fn.
117, 516, 523, 527, 555, 603 fn.,
628, 668, 689-90, 695-701, 724,
741 and fn. 182, 744, 751 fn. 184,
762 fn., 765, 768-76, 779-80, 792-4,
814, 827, 830, 917, 920, 922, 927,
928-9, 934, 938, 942, 944, 945-7,
958, 980, 984, 1038, 1192, 1201-2,
1205, 1207, 1219, 1226, 1227, 1347,
1363-4, 1424, 1436, 1461, 1463,
1477, 1479, 1496, 1537 and fn.,
1602, 1653-4, 1660, 1676, 1677,
1777-99 *passim*, 1805, 1841, 1843,
1854, 1922 fn., 1929, 1950, 1957,
1960, 1972-4, 1978, 2033, 2039,
2052-3, 2055, 2114, 2137, 2143,
2182, 2184, 2196, 2238, 2245, 2288
fn., 2297, 2391, 2442, 2446 and fn.,
2474, 2491, 2499, 2522, 2524, 2526,
2537, 2541, 2544-5, 2549, 2550,
2558, 2564, 2579, 2601, 2612-13,
2623, 2661, 2669-70, 2693, 2715,

Latin, influence (*cont.*)
    2737, 2768, 2770-1, 2776, 2800,
    2804 fn., 2806 and fnn., 2825-6,
    2832, 2839 fn., 2869, 2929, 2934-6,
    2942-3, 2945, 2951, 2969-70, 2976,
    3004, 3018, 3022, 3030, 3040, 3042,
    3066, 3072, 3075, 3085, 3087, 3093,
    3095, 3099, 3106, 3107, 3114, 3118,
    3123, 3128, 3131, 3141, 3152, 3164,
    3165-8, 3172, 3177, 3213-14, 3240,
    3250, 3257, 3350, 3390, 3392, 3398,
    3415, 3483, 3487, 3512, 3544, 3574,
    3582, 3584, 3654, 3674, 3699, 3731,
    3743, 3744, 3749, 3753, 3764, 3768,
    3769, 3778, 3779, 3812-15, 3820-3,
    3825-31, 3832-45 *passim*, 3846,
    3859, 3873, 3878, 3889
  of Irish monks derived from Gaul 3833,
    3844
  originals, attitude of OE writers to 773,
    3828, 3830, 3837; ~, not always a
    safe guide 689-90, 747, 934, 938,
    1885
  texts, editions of, *see* Select Bibliography
Laws, usages 290, 376, 792, 1223, 2242,
    2397-8, 2763, 3306, 3401, 3561,
    3573-7, 3582, 3588, 3718, 3882
Leechdoms, usages 2763, 2942, 3306, 3665
lexicography, problems in OE 68, 218, 314,
    422, 435 and fn., 442, 474-5, 481,
    494, 652, 673, 678, 823, 833a, 852,
    870, 1009, 1014, 1018, 1043, 1080,
    1091, 1124, 1139, 1151, 1189-90,
    1226, 1751, 1769, 1772, 1999, 2036,
    2367 fn., 2674, 2973, 3097, 3168,
    3320, 3367, 3474, 3519, 3659
Liber Scintillarum, usages 1364
Lichtenheld's test 36, 114, 122, 134, 336
'lilies of the field' construction, *see* subjects
    of noun clauses, appearance
limiting, *see* descriptive or limiting
'linguistic facts', Introduction
linguistics, modern, Introduction
lists of examples, *see* (references to) lists
    under individual parts of speech
'literary considerations', Introduction
loan words, discussed in *OEG* chapter X,
    54

Maldon, usages 792, 2538, 3968
manner:
  adverbs 1134, 1136 fn. 264
  clauses 3202, *see also* clauses of com-
    parison
  expressed in absolute constructions 3805,
    3811, 3824
  expressed by dative case, *see* case, dative

    expressed by genitive case 1389, 1391-
      2, 1393, 3846
    expressed by infinitives 959, 1553, 2954
    expressed by participles 1435, 2954
    see also comparison
  means:
    expressed by participles 1435
    expression of, *see* instrument
Menologium, usages 251, 570, 1218
metre:
    influence on syntax, *see* poetry, OE, syn-
      tax influenced by metre and/or alli-
      teration
    syntactical criterion 235, 1594, 1885,
      2111, 2160, 2446, 2556-8, 2669,
      2780, 3015, 3953
    see also poetry, OE
Metres of Boethius, usages 441, 1363, 2851,
    3306, 3402
Microfiche Concordance to Old English, A,
    Introduction; Conclusion
Middle English, when did it begin? 15
'modal preterite', *see* tense
modal relationships, *see* manner
'modal' verbs, *see* verbs, 'modal', auxiliary
modifiers:
    adjective 1103, 1590, 1592
    clause 1103
    sentence 1101-3, 1137, 1590
    verb 1103
    word 1101-3, 1137
    see also adverbs; phrases, non-preposi-
      tional; phrases, prepositional; *and
      under the individual types of adverb
      clause*
mood 874-919 *see* Contents
    clauses, principal, influences on 876
    clauses, subordinate, in accusative and
      infinitive 2509, 2767, 2769, 3787-8;
      ~, in dependent speech, *see* speech,
      dependent; ~, influences on 876, *see
      also* clauses, principal, influence *and
      the cross-references there given*; ~,
      adjective 2030, 2386-415 *see* Con-
      tents, 2434, 2512, 2732; ~, adverb
      2433-6; ~, causal 2915-16, 3015,
      3051, 3053, 3067, 3105, 3111-12,
      3122, 3148, 3157, 3174-9, 3180-
      94; ~, of comparison 2434, 2512,
      2732, 3221, 3222-7, 3231, 3232,
      3235, 3249, 3278-9, 3295-300,
      3305, 3307, 3308, 3311, 3328, 3333,
      3345, 3354, 3364, 3370-2, 3378-81,
      3382, 3705; ~, of concession 2016,
      3395, 3399, 3406, 3416, 3420,
      3425-9, 3435, 3440-9, 3451-6,
      3459, 3468-75, 3476, 3483, 3527;

~, of condition 2016, 2434, 2512, 2732, 3163, 3378, 3542, 3543 fn., 3544-5, 3548-9, 3553, 3556-614 *passim*, 3619, 3622-3, 3636-8, 3640, 3645, 3653-4, 3658, 3664, 3667, 3668, 3670, 3678-83, 3684-90, 3703-6, 3718, 3788; ~, noun, *see* speech dependent, mood; ~, of place 2434, 2484, 2487, 2508-13, 2732; ~, of purpose and/or result 2014, 2016, 2434, 2512, 2732, 2803-4, 2808, 2810, 2825-939 *passim*, 2969-99 *see* Contents, 3053, 3067; ~, of time 2016, 2100, 2434, 2512, 2540, 2562-72 *passim*, 2581, 2610-25, 2648-53, 2687-90, 2713-15, 2731-42, 2761-74, 2775-83, 2787, 2796, 3569 fn.

in dependent speech, *see* speech, dependent

in direct speech 1981-91

distinctions in OE 7, 21-2, 600(2), 601-1a, 874

imperative, *see* mood, imperative

indicative, *see* mood, indicative

influence of superlative as (part of) antecedent 2403

scribal imprecision may produce an unexpected mood 601

sequence 876

simple forms, time reference in poetry 3971

subjunctive, *see* mood, subjunctive

syntactical criterion 359, 1872, 1874, 1885, 2016-17, 2034-5, 2054, 2238, 2540, 2657, 2760, 2803-4, 2808, 2810, 2825-56 *passim*, 2857, 3440-1, 3470, 3476, 3927

mood, imperative 879-919 *see* Contents, 2003

basic OE paradigm 1096

in dependent speech 1949, 1993, 2003, 2957

expressing condition, *see* condition

(references to) lists of examples 880-80a

OE patterns listed 600(3), 601-1a, 883, 885-6, 1096

is there a first person paradigm? 885 fn., 886

is there a third person paradigm? 897, 899, 901

present indicative almost equivalent 617

in principal clause, influence 2027, 2030, 2096, 2391-400, 2434, 2508-9, 2512, 2611-21, 2649-50, 2687, 2714, 2732, 2763, 2765, 2769, 2779, 2803,

2819, 2877, 2997, 3105, 3174, 3295, 3363-4, 3455, 3459, 3548, 3560-90 *passim*, 3595-7

and/or subjunctive in non-dependent commands, wishes, and the like 875-919 (*see initially* 911-12), 1675

in subordinate clause 3443, 3690

mood, indicative 875-8 *see* Contents

forms 600(2), 601-1a

does not always indicate certainty, reality, or fact 877, 2000, 2025, 2080, 2085, 2094, 3553, 3584

in non-dependent speech 1639, 1643-70 *passim*, 1672

present 613-30 *see* Contents

preterite 632-44 *see* Contents

in purpose clauses 2981-8

mood, subjunctive 875-919 *see* Contents

of 'antecedent action', unhelpful term 2688

does not always express the false, the uncertain, the impossible 877, 2025, 3226

forms 600(2), 601-1a, 883, 885 fn., 910

expressed by 'modal' auxiliary and infinitive, *see* verbs, 'modal', auxiliary

expressing condition, *see* condition

and/or imperative in non-dependent commands, wishes, and the like 875-919 (*see initially* 911-12), 1675

jussive, expressing condition, *see* condition; ~, patterns listed 910; ~, term explained 883

nature, topic not always pursued 878

in non-dependent questions 1643-70 *passim*

first person singular not used in commands and wishes 883-4, 1675

present, functions 631; ~, expressing future 1676, 2000, 2740; ~, expressing a possible wish for the future with *gif* 1676; ~, expressing unreality in present 3559, 3705

preterite, functions 645-6; ~, referring to future 2007; ~, referring to future-in-the-past 646, 683, 1116, 1681, 2000, 2002-3, 2006-7, 2032, 2411, 2413, 2565, 2582, 2625, 2630, 2651-2, 2687, 2714, 2731, 2736, 2739, 2763, 2766-7, 2808, 2825, 3300, 3314, 3429, 3454, 3687; ~, timeless when expressing the unrealized or unreal 1676, 1679-81, 2008, 2907, 3606-7, 3612-14, 3640, *see also* unreality

in principal clause, influence 2027, 2030, 2096, 2391-8, 2399-400, 2434,

mood, subjunctive (*cont.*)
    2508-9, 2512, 2611-21, 2649-50,
    2687, 2689, 2714-15, 2732, 2763,
    2765, 2769, 2819, 2877, 3157, 3174,
    3295, 3297-8, 3300, 3354, 3364,
    3451-6, 3459, 3548, 3560-90 *passim*,
    3595-7
    'prospective' 2000
    sign of subordination 2016-17, 2034-5
    'temporal', misleading term 2614
morphology, OE, room for more work 2,
    15, 36, 68
motion and rest, ideas viewed differently in
    OE 1121-2, 1177, 1381, 1386, 2450
multiplication, formation of numerals by 572
multiplicatives 581-3

names:
    foreign, with genitive or dative of perso-
    nal pronouns or with possessives 298
    and fn., 1442, 2119, 3880-1; ~, un-
    inflected 1188, 1217, 1252, 1437
    place, inflexions 1481
    proper, in apposition 1451, 1461-3; ~,
    with dual pronouns 257
naming constructions 1252, 1473-81, 1697,
    2305
    classification or terminology 1476-7
    concord 1473-81
    in parenthesis 3851
necessity:
    expressed by *beon/wesan* + inflected
    infinitive 934-44
    expressed by *habban* + inflected infini-
    tive 950-3
    see also case, dative; obligation; verbs,
    'modal', auxiliary
negation 1595-632 *see* Contents, 1832-
    57 *see* Contents
    adverb *ne* before verb not essential in
    a negated clause 1607, 1614-30, *see*
    also [negation], multiple
    adverb *ne* if expressed must be immedi-
    ately before verb 907, 1677-8, 1832,
    1845, 3526, 3907-8, 3935
    adverb *swa* introducing negative princi-
    pal clauses 3267, 3270, 3319, *see*
    also [negation], conjunction *swa* +
    negated verb
    adverbs 1126-33, 1146, 1595-632 *see*
    Contents
    of alternatives 1756-64, 1832-57
    an in expressions of 526
    ænig in negative(-equivalent) sentences
    384, 1607, 1609-12
    classification or terminology 1133,
    1596-7, 1761, *see also Index of*

Words and Phrases s.v. 'ne, adverb or
    conjunction?'
clauses, subordinate, special uses 1598,
    1932, *see also* [negation], expletive
    negatives; ~, causal 3180-94; ~, of
    condition 3551, 3554, 3556, 3608,
    3617, 3629-30, 3634, 3636, *see also*
    3626-46 (*butan*) and 3647-58
    (*nymþe*); ~, of purpose 2928-36,
    2961-5; ~, of result 2966-8
conjunction *and* + negated verb 'without
    . . . , not . . .' 3525-6
conjunction *swa* + negated verb 'without
    . . . , not . . .' 1924, 2861-3, 2870,
    2968, 3476-80, 3525, *see also* [nega-
    tion], adverb *swa*
conjunction *þon ma þe* only with negated
    principal clauses 3247-50
contraction of adverb *ne* 1129-31, 1761
contraction of conjunction *ne* 1845 fn.
    27
direct and indirect 1133
element order 907, 1595-632 *passim*,
    1677-8, 1832-57 *passim*, 3180-94,
    3526, 3907-8, 3911, 3914, 3916,
    3924, 3934-5, 3987a
expletive negatives 2039-46, 2906, 2922,
    2965, 3207
expressed by *to* 'too' 1142-3
expressing concession 3501
implied or virtual 1133, 1142-3, 1631-
    2, 1762, 1764, 1830, 2083, 2405,
    2993, 3417, 3630, 3650, *see also*
    clauses, negative(-equivalent); ques-
    tions, non-dependent, rhetorical
indefinites 436-46 *see* Contents
infinitives of purpose 2945
multiple 1595-6, 1603-13, 2039-40,
    2042, 2044; ~, less common in
    poetry 3965; ~, not essential 1599-
    602, 1607, 1614-30, 1677, 1784,
    1792 fn., 1832, 1854, 3907
non-dependent command or wish 879-
    919 *passim*, 1645, 1675-81
non-dependent question 1640-70 *pas-*
    sim, 1870
non-dependent statement 1638, 1645
phrases of purpose 2961
present participles negated 'without . . . ,
    not . . .' 3525
in principal clause, influence 1595, 1981,
    1999, 2027-30, 2039, 2045, 2097,
    2140, 2396, 2399, 2404-9, 2434,
    2508, 2511-12, 2622, 2690, 2720,
    2731-42, 2766, 2768, 2877-8, 2906,
    2908, 2991-3, 2997, 3009, 3122,
    3124, 3174-5, 3222-7, 3247-50,

3253, 3261, 3295-7, 3299-300, 3335-6, 3354, 3409-11, 3413-14, 3418, 3426, 3428, 3468-75, 3545, 3556, 3608, 3629-30, 3635, 3646, 3649, 3653, 3658, 3704

sentence and word 1133, 1596-7, 1761

separation of verb and prefix by *ne* 1073

suffixes 1133, 1632

types 1133, 1596-7

word and sentence 1133, 1596-7, 1761

see also adverbs of denial; clauses of comparison with *þon ma þe*; clauses, negative(-equivalent); condition, denied; condition, negated; indefinites

'neutralization' 63, 68

nexus-questions, *see* questions

nominative and infinitive 957-8, 3779-81

non-expression 3858-77 *passim*

   see also under the individual parts of speech or sentence elements

non-inflexion, in parallel expressions, *see* concord, lack of

   see also under the individual parts of speech or sentence elements

non-repetition 3858-77 *passim*

   see also under the individual parts of speech or sentence elements

Notes 2, usages 3695

nouns 54-96 *see* Contents

   adjectives as 51, 106, 132-5, 1298, 3964

   agent 685, 690, 694, 700, 701, 974, 1929

   agreement of appositive elements 43-4

   agreement of attributive elements 40-2

   an (+ adjective +) 534-5

   attributive use 99

   collective, with *an* 545; ~, concord 78-86, 424, 432 fn. 113, 433, 1437, 1440, 1502, 1508, 2351-2; ~, with *sum* 405-6, 410; ~, *see also* clause order; collective expressions; element order

   comparatives and superlatives as 135

   as complement 1582

   compound, 54, 1290; ~, divided in poetry by an adjective 158; ~, expressing instrument 803; ~, *see also Guide*, §137

   co-ordinate with noun clauses 2068

   with dative case 1355-64

   with demonstratives, *see* demonstratives

   of emotion 3118, 3122, 3124, 3413-14

   endings sometimes distinctive for gender 61-6

   expressing cause 3172-3

   genitive case, functional equivalents 1344

with genitive case 270, 1273, 1280-330 *see* Contents

in groups with (possibly) compound verbs 1062, 1076-9

with infinitives 925-7, 971, 1929, 2788, 2947, 3632

inflexions, ambiguity or lack of 2, 8, 9, 11, 12-13, 14-15, 49, 61, 63, 65 and fn., 66, 228, 1038, 1217, 1220-2, 1252, 1324, 1341, 1390, 1421, 1423, 1437, 1473-4, *see also* ambiguity

in naming constructions 1473-81

(non-)expression of *se* with 333-5

in (non-)prepositional formulae, *see* formulae, (non-)prepositional

(non-)repetition 95-6, 166, 174, 299, 316, 358, 501, 556, 567, 1155, 1329-30, 3870

participles as, *see* participles

of possession, discussed 303; ~, qualifiers of 303-10

with possessives, *see* possessives

with possessives and *self* 483-6

with prepositional phrases 1158-60

with prepositions 1060-80 *passim*

of profit or benefit 3411-12, 3414-15, 3546

proper 92, 2249, 2257, *see also* names

of revenge and punishment 3118, 3122, 3124

of rewarding 3118

self as 477, 483

as subject/object of infinitives 937-44

and verb combinations, rection 1082, 1088

verbal, interchange with *þæt* clauses 1929, *see also* nouns, agent

of wonder 1960-1, 3409-10, 3414, 3546

see also absolute constructions; accusative and noun; antecedents; gender; qualifiers

number 72-93 *see* Contents

   agreement, antecedent and relative pronoun 2338, 2342-55; ~, complement and verb 323-7; ~, subject and adjective/participle 33-8; ~, subject and verb 26-32, 428-31, 3979; ~, sundry elements 39, 40, 43, 45

   changes caused by ambiguous pronoun forms, *see* pronouns, ambiguity

   distinctions in OE 5, 9, 18-20, 600(2) and (3)

   dual 5, 28, 72, 88 fn. 15, 89, 257-9, 415(3), 601(4), 881, 1709

   idiom *on heora bedde* 'in their beds' 87-91

infinitive as 931, 954-5, 971, 999, 1090, 1548-51, (1566), 3632

infinitive as direct object of 'modal' verbs 999

inner or internal 1258

non-expression 1570-9 *passim*, 2143, 3808, 3870, 3968

(non-)repetition 1570-9, 3870

noun clauses as 1090, 1566, 1892, 1954, 1962, 1966-70, 2065, 3642

outer or external 1258

possessive as 299

pronouns often precede *man* 3937

pronouns often precede noun objects 3940

of reflexive verbs 1052

second participles alone do not take one 984

split 1466, 1468

term discussed 39 fn., 602-6, 608, 1565

see also subject/object; voice, passive

obligation:

expressed by *agan* 932-3

expressed by *beon/wesan* + inflected infinitive 932-3, 934-44, 945

expressed by *habban* + inflected infinitive 950-3

expressed by **sculan* 933

see also case, dative; necessity; verbs, 'modal', auxiliary

Old English:

archaic or primitive 109-12, 117-20, 122, 139-40, 225, 232, 290-3, 336, 372-5, 527, 540, 697, 1226-7, 1347, 1780, 1796, 1799, 2198, 2635, 2909

colloquial, Introduction, 275 fn., 302, 312, 668, 1211, 1234 fn., 2242, 2601, 2661, 2816, 3250, 3617, 3859, 3862, 3878, 3892-3, *see also* intonation patterns

limited corpus, Introduction

how long did it last? 15

an oligometochic language? 973, 3825-6

spoken, *see* intonation patterns; Old English, colloquial

syntax, *see* syntax, OE

texts, *see* texts, OE

omission, term avoided 150,6, 1572, 2302, 3858-60

see also (non-)expression *and* (non-)repetition *under the individual elements or parts of speech*

Orosius, usages 109, 141, 419, 423, 428-9, 463, 690 fn., 691, 764, 786, 799, 1110 fn., 1185-6, 1424, 1493, 1784, 1819-20, 1881, 1922, 1949, 2147, 2562, 2659, 2679, 2736, 2751, 2763,

2810 fn., 2899, 2969, 3027, 3271, 3372, 3375, 3401, 3813, 3881, 3889, 3948

paragraph:

unit of OE prose 1881

verse, unit of OE poetry 1881, 3115, 3799, 3947, 3956

parallelism:

lack of concord, *see* concord, lack of

in poetry, *see* poetry, OE

parataxis 1683-875 *see* Contents

adversative 1685, 1705, 1736, 1738, 1752-805 *see* Contents

alternative 1806-31, 1863-7, *see also* alternatives

annulling 1768, 1771-2

antithetic 1767, 1772

asyndetic, *see* parataxis, asyndetic

'causal' (Schaar) 3855

classification or terminology—parataxis and/or hypotaxis 1683-6, 1693, 1697, 1767-72, 1814-15, 1817-24, 1826, 1832-57, 1858, 1879-925 *passim*, 2192 fn., 2444-9, 2539-60, 2694, 2702, 2858-9, 2861-3, 2911, 2913, 2918, 3014-18, 3351, 3440-4, 3451, 3457-8, 3470-1, 3474, 3477-80, 3482, 3510-11, 3616, 3620, 3623, 3680-3, *see also* adverb/conjunctions, ambiguous; demonstrative/relatives, ambiguous

continuative 1768-9

contrastive 1767, 1772

correlation a possible relic 3879

cumulative 1712-51 *see* Contents

expressing cause, *see* cause

expressing comparison 1735, 1864, 3293

expressing concession, *see* concession

expressing condition, *see* condition

expressing purpose 1690, 1693, 1735, 2956-8

expressing result, *see* result

expressing time, *see* time

or hypotaxis, too simple a question 1686, 1879, 2122, 2536, 2546, 2553, 2702, 2754, 3014, 3033, 3444, 3471, 3680, 3955

did it precede hypotaxis? 1688, 1894-5, 2296-7, 2422, 2431, 2537, 2628, 2815, 2828, 2875, 2884, 2889, 3081, 3270, 3401, 3548-50, 3620, 3680-3, 3879

mood, factors affecting 876

naming constructions 1474-5, 1697

negative 1595-632 *see* Contents, 1832-57 *see* Contents

participles, present:

with *beon/wesan* in accusative and infinitive 3724, 3752

in double accusative constructions 3766–76

functions 101, 683–94, 700, 974–82, 1556

negated 'without . . . , not . . .' 3525

not used with a passive sense 694, 756

vary with finite verbs 1558, 1692, 1713

vary with preposition + noun in *-ing,* *-ung* 981

in periphrastic verb forms 682–701 *see* Contents

participles, second:

in double accusative constructions 3766–76

general functions 984–9, 1556

functions in periphrastic passive 23–4, 762–81, 834 fn., 857

functions in periphrastic (plu)perfect 23–4, 724–33, 734–42, 984, 1005

functions change in periphrastic (plu)-perfect with *habban* 728, 984

in passive infinitives with uninflected and inflected infinitives 3753

intransitive verbs, time reference 23, 777–81

non-repetition in periphrastic passive 757

in periphrastic forms, passive 744–858 *see* Contents; ~, perfect 702–43 *see* Contents

transitive verbs, time reference 23, 728 fn., 735, 768–76, 781

two in passive periphrases 754

with verbs other than *beon/wesan* and *weorþan* 36, 743, 748, 800 fn., 985

voice 23–4, 728, 734–5, 984

partitive relationship, *see* apposition, partitive; case, genitive, *of* phrases; case, genitive, partitive; clauses, adjective, partitive

parts of speech:

in absolute constructions 3810–11, 3816–18, 3820–1, 3823, 3829

as antecedents 2249–51, 2252–70

in apposition 1428–63 *see* Contents

element order, *see* element order; *and under the individual parts of speech*

expressing concession 3506

governing causal clauses 3009

governing noun clauses 1951–4, 1962–75, 2056–8

introducing noun clauses 1956–61, 2047, 2059–63

as *koinon* 3793–5

listed and discussed but not defined 48–53

as nominative complement 1582–3

non-expression or (non-)repetition 3858–77 *passim, see also under the individual parts of speech*

as object 1566

overlap in form 50–2

in parataxis 1683–875 *passim*

as subject 1482–97

see also ambiguity, inflexions; *the individual parts of speech listed in* §48; *the Index of Words and Phrases*

performer, term discussed 1936, 1995 and fn.

periodicals, system of reference, *see* Select Bibliography

permissive constructions, *see* challenge or permissive constructions

person:

concord, antecedent and relative pronoun 2338–9, 2359–62; ~, subject-verb 26

denoted by genitive of noun 1274

distinctions in OE 4, 17, 600(2)

in dependent speech 1944–8, 1981–91 *passim,* 2048

in direct speech 1981–91

in represented speech 1945

personal constructions, term discussed 1025

phrases:

absolute 3804–46 *see* Contents; ~, noun + noun not yet recorded in OE 3810, 3829

adjective 1151–228 *see* Contents, 1240–379 *see* Contents, 1413, 1500, 3321

adverb 1151–228 *see* Contents, 1380–427 *see* Contents, 1500, 1589, *see also* [phrases] expressing . . . ; ~, initial, effect on element order, *see* adverbs, in initial position; ~, position, *see* adverbs, position

appositive, *see* apposition

case, *see* phrases, non-prepositional

classification or terminology 1413, 1500, 3320–1, 3804–15

explanatory 3336

expressing cause, *see* cause

expressing comparison 3256–9, 3366–7

expressing concession, *see* concession

expressing purpose 1160, 2946, 2955, 2961

expressing time 592–3

extra-metrical in poetry 3849

noun, *see* phrases, non-prepositional

non-prepositional, *see* phrases, non-prepositional

predicate (*cont.*)
    predicative use, adjectives and/or parti-
        ciples 128-9, 698-9, 701, 835, 837,
        975-8, 985, 1556; ~, indefinites 379,
        450; ~, infinitives 971; ~, *manig*
        415(4); ~, numerals 415(3); ~, pos-
        sessive 299
    or subject 348
    see also complements; objects
predicative, *see* predicate
prefixes:
    expressing instrument 803
    inseparable 1060-80 *passim*
    negative 1133, 1632
    separable 1060-80 *passim*
    see also aspect; *and under individual pre-*
        fixes in Index of Words and Phrases
pre-position, term discussed 1062, 1151
prepositional adverbs, *see* adverbs, preposi-
    tional
prepositional formulae, *see* formulae, prepo-
    sitional
prepositions 1151-228 *see* Contents
    with adverbs 1060-80 *passim*, 1155, 2458
    some also serve as adverb/conjunctions
        1157
    with antecedents and/or relative pro-
        nouns 1060-80 *passim*, 2161, 2180,
        2190, 2231-48 *see* Contents
    case endings replaced by 2, 8, 13
    case rection 1151-228 *see* Contents,
        1263, 1343, 1379
    changes in use of cases with 1222-8
    classification or terminology 216, 571,
        924, 1060-80, 1151, 1154, 1177,
        1739, 3626-33, 3646, 3647-51
    expressing agent or instrument, originally
        expressed idea of accompaniment,
        cause, place, space, or origin 808,
        810, 812, 813-17, 819, 821-3, 824,
        833a
    in expressions of reciprocity 280
    governing different cases in the same
        sentence 1173, 1177, 1183, 1186,
        1207, 1218, 1222, 1441
    governing reflexive pronouns 266, 269-
        71
    increase in frequency of use in OE period,
        Introduction, 1223-8, 3950
    with inflected infinitives 964
    with interrogatives 1062, 1079
    (references to) lists of 1152-3, 1156 fn.,
        1177-8
    in naming constructions 1479-81
    (non-)repetition 166, 555, 569, 1170-6,
        2235, 3210, 3978, 3998
    with nouns 1060-80 *passim*, 1158-60

in poetry, less used 3970; ~, no stress
    or alliteration 3968
with pronouns 1060-80 *passim*, 1155
is *sibþan* one? 3832
translator's choice affected by Latin
    original 762 fn.
use avoids ambiguity 1282
use by glossators to mark case 1158a
use in formation of adverbs and con-
    junctions 1157, 1230, 1233, 2420
variation in rection, *see* case, concord;
    the individual cases
with verbs 1060-80 *passim*, 1167-9,
    see also phrases, prepositional
see also accusative and infinitive; phrases,
    prepositional; *and under individual*
    prepositions in Index of Words and
    Phrases
'preterite, modal', *see* tense
prohibition, non-dependent, *see* clauses,
    negative(-equivalent); command, non-
    dependent
promises, *see* desires; wishes
'pronominalization, backwards' 247
'pronoun/adjectives', term rejected 239-41
pronouns 239-521 *see* Contents
    agreement with antecedent 45-7, 2303,
        2338-62 *see* Contents
    agreement with appositive elements 43-4
    agreement with attributive elements
        40-2
    ambiguity of or caused by forms 9, 11 fn.,
        12, 77 and fn. 10, 242, 255-6, 263,
        320-1, 345, 1027, 1038, 1220-1,
        1361, 1521, 2354, 3748-9, 3782-3,
        3785, *see also* ambiguity
    anaphoric, with *man* 377; ~, non-agree-
        ment in gender 69-71, 314; ~, *se* as
        316-17, 330
    anticipatory 1445-6, 1459, 1486-8,
        1503, 1892-5, 1954, 1963-7, 3359,
        3808, 3838, 3879, 3882-5, *see also*
        [pronouns], tautologic
    classification or terminology 239-42,
        271-4, 348, 378, 408, 432, 444, 455,
        457, 461, 484, 489-91, 1662, 1744,
        1806-31 *passim*, 1832-57 *passim*,
        1872-5, 2377-8, 3350, 3369; ~, *þe*
        relative or personal pronoun 2245-8,
        2930; ~, *see also* clauses, adjective,
        classification; demonstrative/relatives,
        the ambiguous
    as complement 1583
    dative of possession 304-10, 338
    demonstrative, *see* demonstratives
    element order 2180-200 *passim*
    gender 66-8

governed by prepositions 1060-80 *passim*, 1155

governing genitive 1273, 1280-330 *see* Contents

with infinitives 925-7, 971

negative 1832-57 *passim, see also* negation

personal, *see* pronouns, personal

possessive, *see* possessives

with prepositional phrases 1162-4

recapitulatory 246, 298, 317, 1442, 1447-8, 1454, 1459, 1489-90, 1503, 1537, 1571, 1665, 1893-5, 1916, 2119, 3215, 3359, 3838, 3879-81, *see also* [pronouns], tautologic

reflexive, *see* pronouns, reflexive

relative, *see* pronouns, relative

as subject 1482, 1485-90, 1599

as subject/object of infinitives 937-44

swa not one 1139, 1567, 2379-82, 3265

tautologic, a relic of parataxis 1893-5, 3879-81; ~, Andrew's 'otiose' personal pronouns in parataxis 1702, 1715; ~, *see also* antecedents, repetition;demonstratives, (non-)repetition; [pronouns], anticipatory;[pronouns], recapitulatory

þær not one 1155 fn.

see also element order

pronouns, personal 243-64 *see* Contents

alternating with demonstratives or possessives 303-10, 320-1, 338, 344, 1274, *see also* demonstratives and/or possessives

circumlocutions for 250

concord, *see* antecedents; gender

dative + *self* 487-91

expressing reciprocity 279-82

genitive, alternating with inflected forms of possessive 301; ~, first and second person used independently 300, 1275-6; ~, inflected as if a possessive 486 fn.; ~, with *self* 483-6, 1276

governing prepositional phrases 1163

in groups with (possibly) compound verbs 1062, 1076-9

in idiom *on heora bedde* 87-91

non-expression 244-5, 256, 2209, 3968

with ordinal numeral and *self* 479

'otiose' in parataxis 1702, 1715

referring to a 'postcedent' 247

with relative pronouns 2180-200 *see* Contents, 2201-25 *see* Contents, 2332, 3131, 3134, 3138, *see also* pronouns, classification or terminology, *þe*

with *sum* 402-3, 406

summary of uses 246-9

with vocative expressions 1242-3, 1247

see also antecedents

pronouns, reflexive 265-78 *see* Contents

classification or terminology 275-6

in commands, wishes, and the like 885, 889, 891, 917

dative, element order 3889, 3937

possessives as 297

self as 472-500 *passim*

self not always reflexive 275-6, 475, 478, 481, 487, 499-500

pronouns, relative 520-1, 2103-385 *see* Contents

classification or terminology 2152, 3114, *see also* demonstrative/relatives, the ambiguous; formulae, prepositional; interrogatives

compound, origin 2169-70; ~, term explained 2155-63

concord 46, 1178 fn. 269, 1180, 1498, 2123, 2124, 2131, 2134-44, 2240, 2303, 2338-62, 2476, 2681-2, 2878, 2886, 3738 fn., *see also* antecedents; gender

sometimes difficult to distinguish from non-prepositional conjunctions, *see* conjunctions, non-prepositional

distinguished from interrogatives 359, 521, 1150, 2049-55, 2385

or antecedents, doubling or repetition of (part of) 2122, 2124, 2129, 2148-9, 2164-5, 2192-3, 2208

with *eall, see Index of Words and Phrases s.v. 'eall'*

with genitive case 1301

governing prepositional phrases 1164

in groups with (possibly) compound verbs 1062, 1076-9

indefinite, *see* clauses, adjective, indefinite

introducing clauses of place 2474-5

(references to) lists of 520-1, 1931, 2108 fn.

(non-)expression 2302-37 *see* Contents, 3992

non-repetition 2148, 2188-9, *see also* [pronouns, relative], or antecedents

other than *se* and *þe* 2363-83, 2385

with personal pronouns, *see* pronouns, personal

with prepositions, *see* prepositions; ~, must be distinguished from prepositional formulae, *see* formulae, prepositional

repetition, *see* [pronouns, relative], or antecedents

pronouns, relative (*cont.*)
  replacing *swa* 3283
  þa, see Index of Words and Phrases s.v.;
    see also antecedents; demonstrative/
    relatives, the ambiguous
prose, OE:
  insecurity of early writers 317, 1472,
    1893-6, 3878-9
  sentence not always unit, *see* sentence
  sentence patterns used unthinkingly or
    mechanically 2732, 3225
  syntactical differences from poetry 3944-
    7, 3952-76 *passim, see also* poetry,
    OE, usages
Psalter, Paris, usages 36 fn., 64 fn., 815,
    1677, 2114, 2301, 2825, 3402, 3415,
    3546, 3973
Psalters, usages, *see* Glosses, usages
'pseudo-splits' 1467
punctuation, Introduction, 1671, 1691,
    1694, 1698, 1699-700, 1703, 1712,
    1717, 1718, 1724, 1840-1, 1859,
    1879-82, 1885, 1898 fn., 1899 fn.,
    1923, 1941, 2092, 2109, 2112, 2115,
    2161, 2272, 2274, 2279, 2283, 2285,
    2288, 2290, 2310, 2424, 2445-8,
    2453, 2462, 2466, 2469, 2522-3,
    2536-8, 2544, 2548, 2554, 2559,
    2601 fn., 2669, 2692, 2706, 2805 fn.,
    2851 fn., 2884, 3013-15, 3016 fn.
    155, 3072, 3101, 3148, 3264, 3269,
    3274, 3294, 3538, 3548, 3624, 3642,
    3653, 3662-3, 3726, 3789-803 *pas-
    sim*, 3842, 3848, 3854, 3880 fn.,
    3881, 3885, 3947, 3956-7, 3971,
    3974, 3989
  Andrew describes a 'curious superstition',
    see clause order
  manuscript, not a syntactical criterion
    1879-82
purpose:
  (expressed in) clauses, *see* clauses of pur-
    pose
  expressed in absolute constructions
    3824
  expressed in adjective clauses 2806,
    2808, 2985
  expressed in causal clauses 2812, 2911-
    16, 2976-80, 3045, 3049-50, 3053,
    3057, 3066, 3067, 3069, 3089, 3094
  expressed in clauses of concession 2812
  expressed in clauses of condition 2812,
    3659, 3664, 3666-7, 3694
  expressed in *swa* clauses 2857-70
  expressed in clauses of time 2687-8,
    2721, 2724, 2748, 2767-8, 2810 and
    fn., 3252

expressed in dependent speech 2001,
    2094
expressed by *for* phrases 1187
expressed by genitive case 1293
expressed by infinitives 946, 949, 954-5,
    959, 966, 968, 971, 1552-4, 2940-
    51, 3370, 3735, 3748, 3761, 3779
expressed by parataxis 1690, 1693, 1735,
    2956-8
expressed by participles 1435, 2953-4
expressed by phrases 1160, 2946, 2955,
    2961
shades into 'on condition that' 3659,
    3664, 3667

qualifiers 1-593 *see* Contents
  agreement with noun or pronoun 40-2
  of complement 1582, 1587
  element order, relative to modifying ele-
    ments 142-80; ~, relative to nouns
    102-27, 159-74, 986, 1499, 1561-
    4, 2364; ~, relative to one another
    143-58, 159
  infinitives, *see* adjectives, with infinitives
  non-inflexion of, *see* concord, lack of
  of object 1566
  post-position 126-7, 159-77, 295,
    1561-4
  splitting 1466, 1499, 2296, *see also*
    speech material(s)
  of subject 1498-502
  see also adjectives; articles; case, genitive;
    demonstratives; indefinites; interroga-
    tives; numerals; participles; possessives
quantity, adverbs of 1135-46
'quasi-impersonal', term not used 1025, 1043
questions:
  classification or terminology 348, 354,
    357, 1645, 1647, 1652, 1658-9,
    1662, 1670-2, 1869, 1872-5, 2017,
    2047-8, 2049-55, 2063, 2069, 2385,
    2494-507, 2775-83, 3363, 3726; ~,
    question or clause of condition 2059,
    3678-83, 3691-4
  demanding a cause, reason, or purpose
    3027-32
  dependent 1953, 2047-99 *see* Contents,
    3363; ~, element order 3896; ~, *see
    also* [questions], nexus; [questions],
    x-; *Index of Words and Phrases s.v.
    'loc(a)'*
  introduced by interrogative adverbs
    1147-50
  nexus, dependent 2047-82 *see* Contents,
    2083-90, 3416-20, 3547; ~, non-
    dependent 1640, 1643-60, 1870-1,
    1872-5

non-dependent 1640-70, 1671, 1868-75, 3895; ~, contracted 1666, 3873-4; ~, non-rhetorical in principal clause, influence 2027, 2029-30, 2404-9, 2766, 2994, 2997, 3009, 3103, 3409, 3545, 3558, 3704; ~, (plu)perfect periphrases in 705; ~, *see also* [questions], nexus; [questions], rhetorical; [questions], *x*-rhetorical, non-dependent 384, 1146, 1641, 1655, 2140-3, 2362, 3031, 3629-30; ~, ~, equivalent to negated statements 1631, 3225, 3411, 3474; ~, ~, in principal clause, influence 2140, 2399, 2404-9, 2622, 2690, 2738, 2767, 2877-8, 2991-2, 2994, 2997, 3174, 3253, 3296-7, 3411-12, 3414, 3545, 3558, 3608, 3630, 3635, 3646, 3649, 3653, 3658

x-, dependent 2047-82 *see* Contents, 2090, 2091-9; ~, non-dependent 1640, 1661-70, 1868-9, 1872-5

reality, *see* fact
recapitulation:
  of *don* by finite verbs 666
  see also pronouns, recapitulatory
reciprocity 279-88 *see* Contents, 459, 1508
rection, verbal, *see* verbs, rection
reflexive, *see* case, accusative; case, dative; case, genitive; possessives; pronouns, reflexive; verbs, reflexive constructions
reinforcement 1738, 1755, 3487, 3491, 3508, 3511, 3523, 3528-35
repetition:
  of verbs avoided by use of *don* 665
  expressing extent or degree 1146
  see also non-repetition *under the individual parts of speech or sentence elements*
reporter(s), term discussed 1936
requests, *see* desires; wishes
rest and motion, ideas viewed differently in OE, *see* motion and rest
result:
  (expressed by) clauses, *see* clauses of result
  expressed in adjective clauses 2807, 2809
  expressed in clauses of comparison 2811, 3141-2, 3204
  expressed in *swa* clauses 2857-70
  expressed in clauses of time 2745-7, 2797, 2810 and fn.
  expressed by genitive case 1293, 1389
  expressed by infinitive 959, 2952

expressed by parataxis 617, 1735, 1738, 1769, 2331, 2959, 2960
negated, expressed by *swa* + negated verb 'without . . . , not . . .' 2861-3, 3477-80, 3525
rhythm 889, 891, 914, 1032, 1201, 1430, 1462, 1507, 1712, 1730, 2161, 2200, 2285, 2424, 2525-6, 2550, 2554, 3790, 3889, 3919, 3933, 3966, 3976
  of poetry differs from that of Ælfric's alliterative prose 3966, 3972-5
Russian, transliteration, *see Select Bibliography*

St. Chad, usages 110-12
Scandinavian languages, influence on English 801, 1225 fn. 288, 1306, 1981, 2304 fn. 70
scribal imprecision, may produce unexpected mood 601
Seafarer, usages 3082
semi-subordination 626, 1690-7, 1713, 1923-4, 2976, 2980, 3477-80, 3525
sentence apposition 1458
sentence elements, *see* elements, sentence
'sentence modifiers' 1101-3, 1137, 1590
sentence structure 1146, 1876-925 *see* Contents, 2537, 3973
  as test of authorship 1922
  variations express extent or degree 1146
  see also adverb/conjunctions, the ambiguous; demonstrative/relatives, the ambiguous
sentences:
  'abstract', *see* 'abstract'
  as antecedents or 'postcedents' 342, 1490, 2125, 2249, 2267-9
  as complements 1585
  complex 1876-925 *see* Contents, 3988; ~, in dependent speech 1978-80; ~, term explained 1876
  compound, term avoided 1685
  'concrete' 653-64, 783, 784 fn. 200
  cumulative, *see* sentences, loose
  as *koinon* 3793, 3796, 3798-9, 3801
  loose or cumulative 1897-922 *passim*, 3973
  loose structure normal in prose and poetry 1898-900, 3973
  multiple, term avoided 1633, 1685, 1718, 1877
  in parataxis 1683-875 *passim*
  in parenthesis 3848-52
  periodic 1897-922 *passim*, 3973
  in poetry, do poets prefer them to begin with an off-verse? 3960; ~, clauses

sentences (*cont.*)

need not begin at beginning of (half-) line 3960, 3971, 3973

in prose, sentence patterns used unthinkingly or mechanically 2732, 3225

simple 1240–682 *see* Contents; ~, classification or terminology 1633–4; ~, elements 1240–632 *see* Contents; ~, types 1633–82 *see* Contents; ~, *see also* parataxis

structure, *see* sentence structure

type, effect on element order 3889

not always unit of OE prose and poetry 1633, 1879, 1881, *see also* paragraph, verse

separation of syntactically related elements, *see* groups, splitting

sequence of moods 876

sequence of tenses, *see* tenses, sequence

sex v. gender, conflicts in agreement 25, 47, 55, 68, 69–71, 292, 484, 486, 2178, 2356, 2358

SF(F), Nickel's abbreviation 681

short titles of OE texts, II, pp. xl–xlv

sign, Tironian, *see* positura

'similitative' *swa (swa)* 3316–18, 3320

Slavonic languages, transliteration, *see Select Bibliography*

Soliloquies, usages 691, 1363, 1930 fn., 2969, 3401

speaker, term discussed 1936

speech, dependent 1935–2102 *see* Contents

accusative and infinitive equivalent of 1929, 3726, 3728–32, 3738

classification or terminology 1935–50 *passim*

clause order, *see* clause order

element order, *see* element order

mood 1936, 1942–8, 1981–91 *passim*, 1992–2038, 2043, 2048, 2072, 2078–82, 2083–99 *passim*, 2434, 2877–8

merging into non-dependent speech 1945–7, 2022, 2037–8, 2040, 3732, 3771, 3788

sequence of tenses 859–64

subordinate clauses in, *see* accusative and infinitive; clauses, subordinate

tense 637, 1939–49, 1981–91 *passim*, 2018, 2032, 2034, 2048, 2072

verbal periphrases in 703 fn., 771 and fn.

not an expression of volition 2391, 2615

see also clauses, noun

speech, direct 703 fn., 1635–6, 1935–50, 1981–91, 3862

classification or terminology 1935–50 *passim*

element order 1981–91

tense 1981–91

speech material(s), qualifying elements separated from noun by 149–57, 175–7, 234, 295

see also qualifiers, splitting

speech, non-dependent 859–64, 1635, 1935–50, 1981–91, 1993–4, 2003, 2021, 2022, 2037–8, 2040, 2048, 2072, 2078

classification or terminology 875, 877, 880a, 881, 885 fn., 887, 1645, 1647–8, 1671, 1935–50 *passim*; ~, dependent or non-dependent 354, 1652, 1658–9, 1670, 1672, 2017, 2048, 2069, 3684–5, 3714, 3726

mood, *see* mood

transition of dependent speech or accusative and infinitive to 1945–7, 2022, 2037–8, 2040, 3732, 3771, 3788

verbal periphrases in 771 and fn.

speech, represented 1668, 1945, 1984, 1991

classification or terminology 1935–50 *passim*

splitting of groups, *see* groups, splitting of

statement(s):

dependent 1937–8, 1951–2046, *see* Contents; ~, accusative and infinitive equivalent of 3726, 3728–9, 3730, 3732, 3738; ~, *see also* speech, dependent

negated equivalent to non-dependent rhetorical questions, *see* questions, rhetorical

non-dependent 1638–9, 1645, 1647, 1671, 3900–36; ~, element order 1638, 3900–36

statistics:

element order, difficulty of producing 3902, 3909, 3914, 3917

use, Introduction, 750

stress and/or emphasis 220, 233, 315, 320, 328–9, 341, 409 fn. 102, 475–6, 478, 481, 483, 491, 518, 523–4, 558, 604, 793, 1146, 1309, 1472, 1486–7, 1497, 1508, 1594, 1606, 1710, 1712, 1730, 1733, 1857, 1881, 1965, 2110, 2122, 2131, 2155, 2167, 2169–70, 2178, 2200, 2246, 2285, 2343, 2349, 2545, 2556, 2558, 2833, 2847–52, 3046, 3198, 3403, 3889, 3910, 3916, 3923, 3931–6, 3946, 3968

see also intonation patterns; poetry, OE, stress

style 172, 317, 686, 793, 962–4, 1146, 1303, 1315, 1347, 1436, 1462, 1472, 1507, 1508, 1531, 1561, 1578, 1593, 1603 fn., 1606, 1638, 1663, 1687, 1704, 1857, 1878, 1881, 1893–6,

of physical action or 'affections', used in impersonal constructions 1032, 1037

of pleasing or displeasing 1082

of possessing and ruling 1053, 1082

of preventing and hindering 3723, 3735

of promising, see desires; wishes

of refusing 1086

of remembering or forgetting 1082

of rejoicing 3086

of rest, idea of motion sometimes inherent 1122; ~, see also [verbs] of motion and/or rest

of revenge and punishment 3118, 3122, 3124

of rewarding 3118

of saying, see [verbs] of speaking

of seeming 985

of sense perception, see [verbs] of physical action

of serving or resisting 1082

of shame 3172

of sorrowing 3086, 3172

of speaking 1690, 1901 fn., 1949, 1982, 2019 and fn., 2056, 2093, 3723, 3735, 3930; ~, in impersonal constructions 1037; ~, in periphrases with present participle 691; ~, with prepositions 1210, 1228; ~, in semi-subordination 1690

of teaching 3723

of thanking 1086, 3086

of thinking, see [verbs] of mental activity

of wishing 3723

of wondering 1960-1, 3409-10, 3414, 3546, 3738

see also individual verbs in the Index of Words and Phrases; list of verbal rections (§§1091-2)

verbs, transitive (use):

in absolute constructions 3818

auxiliaries beon/wesan and weorþan in passive, habban in (plu)perfect 734, see also verbs, auxiliary; verbs, periphrastic (plu)perfect; voice, passive rection 1255-6

lack perfect participle active 3807

in periphrastic (plu)perfect 702-4, 705-21, 723-33, 734-5, 743, 868

with prepositional adverbs 1065-71

used reflexively 1053-7

term discussed 602-6, 843, 1065 fn.

'transitive verb' sometimes shorthand for 'verb used transitively' 606

see also participles, second

'verbal', Bliss's term 599

verbal rection, see verbs, rection

'verbal substitution', Antipova's term 1527 fn., see also 665

Vercelli Homilies, usages 3889

vocabulary:

of poetry 3964-75 passim; ~, differs from that of Ælfric's alliterative prose 3972-5

grammar words less common in poetry 3966-7

voice:

active, see voice, active

active infinitive with verb in passive 957

distinctions in OE 7, 600(1)

infinitives, see infinitives

'medial' 1053

participles, second, see participles

passive, see voice, passive

voice, active 594-1099, see Contents

impersonal constructions 1036-43

voice, passive 600(1), 744-858 see Contents

auxiliary beon/wesan 600(1), 673, 734-5, 748-801, 1099

auxiliary weorþan 600(1), 673, 734-5, 748-801, 1099

in clause governing purpose clause 2821, 2823

cognate object becomes subject of periphrasis 754

with dative of interest 1351, 1372

'double passive group' 754

formed from double accusative 835-7, 1083

impersonal 834-58, 1030, 1044, 1045-51, 1485, 1965 and fn.; ~, formal subject hit not used 1485; ~, or indirect, term explained 749; ~, used in OE when verb does not take accusative object in active voice 834, 840, 843-7, 848-58 see Contents (for possible exceptions see 851 and fnn.; for apparent exceptions see 856-8)

infinitives, see infinitives, passive

with infinitives 2949

infinitive in accusative and infinitive 751-4, 761, 988, 3724, 3742-3, 3753-4, 3764, 3776, 3777, 3780

man + active form a substitute 369

periphrases with present participles not used with a passive sense 694

periphrastic 744-858 see Contents; ~, expressing action or state 724-42, 749, 766-7, 768 fn., 786-801, 806; ~, expressing command or wish 881; ~, with lætan 680; ~, non-repetition of participle 757; ~, patterns with verbs which govern only one accusative

INDEX OF WORDS AND PHRASES

THE keywords are arranged in alphabetical order, with *æ* following *a* and *þ* replacing *ð* and following *t*. The prefix *ge-* is ignored, e.g. *gehwa* will be found under *h* and *(ge)tiþian* under *t*. Unless there is some special reason to the contrary, a nominative form embraces all inflected forms of a noun, adjective, or pronoun, and an uninflected infinitive all forms of a verb. In combinations such as *to þæm (. . .) (þe/þæt)*, *þæm* represents all forms of dat. and inst. sg. neut. of *se*.

Space has not permitted full cross-referencing of spelling variants such as *hwanan, hwanon, hwonan, hwonon*, and the like. Although I sin in the good company of the Anglo-Saxon scribes and although no serious inconvenience for the reader is involved, I now regret the inconsistency in spelling which has produced such variations as *hwelc/hwilc* and *æghwilc/æghwylc* in the text. The time for amendment is past.

This Index does not contain references to words and phrases listed only in the following sections:

192–219 (adjectives)
1091–2 (verbs)
1177–8 (prepositions)
1231–3 (conjunctions)
1238–9 (interjections)

or in (the collections referred to in) those sections which appear in the General Index under the following headings:

adjectives, (references to) lists of
adverbs, (references to) lists of
conjunctions, (references to) lists of
interjections, (references to) lists of
prepositions, (references to) lists of
verbs, (references to) lists of.

The entries under *loc(a)*, *swa*, and *weald*, are not cross-referenced.

giet(a), *see* gien(a)

gif 376, 418, 421, 1676, 1679-81, 1890, 1916 fn., 1925, 1960, 1975 fn. 16, 1978, 2059, 2084, 2086, 2140, 2422, 2424, 2571, 2608, 2812, 2975a, 3003-4, 3024, 3162-3, 3390-1, 3409-12, 3415, 3417, 3418, 3422, 3541, 3546-7, 3550-1, 3553-4, 3556-614 *see Contents*, 3616-17, 3623-4, 3634, 3659-60, 3665, 3668, 3679, 3684-8, 3694-5, 3699-701, 3707-16, 3719, 3787-8, 3799, 3898

gif þæt 2424, 3628, 3671

gifeþe 1952

God Ælmihtig 137, 172

(ge)gripan 3307

growan 691

-gum 553

habban 24, 638, 641, 644, 670, 674, 702-4, 705-43, 868, 886, 922, 950-3, 971, 984, 988, 2499, 3723, 3743, 3775

-had 61

hafenleas 3972

ham 1381, 1386, 1418

(ge)hatan 375, 679-80, 746, 955, 1473-7, 1951 fn., 2305, 3723, 3730, 3735, 3736, 3737, 3738, 3743, 3756-7, 3764

gehaten 1474-5

hatte/hatton 7, 600(1), 746, 1473 and fn., 1475 and fn.

gehawian 3743

he (*all forms, both numbers*) 143, 239, 242, 250, 255-6, 259, 263-4, 275-7, 288-90, 292, 298, 303-10, 1274-5, 2114, 2116. *See also* hit

heafod 3979

healf 226, 578-9

healsian 1951

helpan 849, 883

heonan 1121

her 313 fn., 1076, 1079, 1121, 3893, 3929, 3934

hider 1121-2, 2515

hit 47(1), 47(3), 69-71, 749, 841, 936, 1025-6, 1031-5, 1047, 1485-90, 1506-7, 1510, 1516, 1539, 1546, 1892, 1960, 1963-5, 2064, 3407, 3412

hleotan 2056

hraþe 2601, 2691, 2695, 2701, 2707-11, 3155

hrædlice 2601, 2691, 2707, 2709, 2710

hreowan 1952

hu 347, 1148, 1648, 1672, 1938, 1961, 1972, 2062-3, 2939, 3360

huhwego 590, 3984

hulic 346

humeta 1148, 2062, 3030

hund 553, 556-60

huru 1862, 3506

hwa/hwæt 6, 240-1, 261, 346, 348-54, 356 fn., 359, 360, 378, 417-18, 519, 521, 936, 1148, 1299, 1647, 2049-54, 2060, 2063, 2274, 2363 and fn. 75, 2385, 2938-9, 3027, 3029-30, 3421. *See also* for hwæm; to hwæm; to hwæs

gehwa/gehwæt 285, 447-9, 459, 465-6, 519, 2263

hwanon 1124, 1148, 2062, 2494-5, 2499, 2501, 2504

hwær 1079, 1148, 2049, 2055, 2062, 2385, 2442, 2494-507, 2783

gehwær 2515

hwæt *interjection* 1237, 1647, 2547 fn.

hwæt is þæt? 3030

hwæt *pronoun, see* hwa/hwæt

hwæt . . . þæt 354

hwæthwugu 378, 419

hwæþer 346, 355, 435, 936, 1662, 1872-5, 2059, 2086 fn., 2363

gehwæþer 447, 451

hwæþer (. . .) þe (. . . þe) 1643, 1652-60, 1871, 1872-5, 2059, 2086-7, 3417, 3895

hwæþer (. . .) (oþþe) . . . oþþe 1875, 2086

(ge)hwæþere (þeah) 1890, 3397, 3424, 3430, 3487, 3511, 3515, 3522, 3523, 3932. *See also* swa þeah

hwelc 125, 346, 354, 356-9, 378, 420-3, 519, 521, 1972, 2049-54, 2060, 2274, 2363, 2377, 2385, 3030

gehwelc 125, 285, 347, 447-9, 459, 463, 467-9, 519, 2254, 2263, 2346, 2399-402

hwelchwugu 378, 423, 519

hwene *adverb* 1135

hwider 1124, 1148, 2062, 2442, 2494-5, 2499, 2501, 2504

hwilum . . . hwilum 1232, 1830, 1866

hwonne 1148, 1150, 1938, 2049, 2052, 2055, 2062, 2385, 2507, 2608, 2612, 2743, 2762, 2775-83, 2938-9, 3798

hwonne ær 2712, 2778 and fn.

hwy 1148, 2055, 2062, 3027, 3032

hycgan 1952

(ge)hyhtan 3736, 3743

hyngrian 1038

(ge)hyran 886, 2020, 3735, 3743, 3760, 3785 and fn.

hyrde ic 1750

-i 8

-iaþ, *see* -aþ, -eþ

ic (*all forms, three numbers*) 239, 243, 251-2, 253, 258, 261, 282, 289, 296, 300-1, 403, 747, 1274. *See also* min

nahte þon læs 1805

nahwæþer/naþor/nawþer 284, 415, 436, 443-4

nahwæþer/naþor/nawþer na/ne . . . na/ne 1847-51

nalæs 1620. *See also* nealles

nalles, *see* nealles

nama 1475, 1478-80

nan 415, 436-42, 519, 1128 and fn., 1162, 1332, 1595, 1610, 1612, 1629, 2254, 2263, 2346

nanþing 378

nanwuht, *see* naht

nat ic forhwi 3031

nathwa/nathwæt 378, 380

nathwilc 378, 380, 3440

nawiht, *see* naht

næfre 909, 1609, 1625, 1627, 1629

nænig 145, 381, 415, 436-42, 517 fn., 1128 and fn., 1595, 1609-12, 1627, 1629, 2254, 2263

nænig hwil 2699, 2760

næn(i)ge þinga 1128, 1611, 1625

næs *adverb* 1620 and fn., 3181. *See also* nealles

næs = ne wæs 1620 fn., 1761, 3181

ne *adverb* 883, 899, 907, 909 fn. 1, 916, 916a, 1073, 1128, 1597 fn., 1599-602, 1603-13, 1620-1, 1625, 1626, 1627-30, 1638, 1677-8, 1709 fn., 1726, 1756-64, 1779, 1832-57 *passim*, 1870, 2039-46, 2804, 2825, 2861-3, 2865-6, 2868-70, 2922, 2928, 2962-4, 2966, 2972, 3820, 3889, 3907-8, 3935

ne *adverb or conjunction?* 907, 1596-7, 1677, 1832, 1839-46, 1854-5, 2936, 3526

ne *conjunction* 166, 876, 890, 904-10, 1329, 1465, 1526-7, 1597 fn., 1602, 1627, 1629, 1677, 1832-57 *passim*, 1910, 2328, 2842, 3006, 3255, 3889, 3897, 3911, 3914, 3916, 3938

ne . . . ne 1832-57 *passim*, 3502-3

-ne 49-50, 63, 68, 1439

neah 216, 1420

nealles 1128, 1617, 1620-4, 1627, 1629, 1756-64, 1777-99 *passim*, 3526

nealles þæt an . . . ac (. . .) (eac) (swylce) 1783-4

nean 1122

nefne/nemne 1925, 3162, 3164, 3253, 3258, 3525, 3541, 3551, 3647-58 *see Contents*, 3660, 3690, 3698, 3707

nefne butan 3647

nefne forþon (þe) 3628 fnn. 189 and 191, 3647, 3652

nefne þæt(te) 3628 fnn. 189 and 191, 3652, 3657

neotan 2179

neoþan 1124

nese 1126

-nes(s) 61

ni 1129, 1596, 1603

nic 'not I' 243

niedan 872, 3743

niht(es) 1400 and fn., 1423, 2682

niman 1210 and fn. 279, 2948

niþer(e)/niþor 1124

no, *see* na

genog/genoh 97 fn. 23, 125, 241, 1135

noht, *see* naht

norþan 1123

'not' 1630

'not only . . . but (also)' 1777-99

nu 663, 862, 902, 909, 1120, 1860, 1885, 1888, 2418, 2423, 2536, 2539, 2541, 2561, 2591-3, 2784, 3010, 3079-80, 3097-106, 3155, 3158, 3179, 3491, 3493, 3506, 3514, 3531-2, 3696, 3799, 3925-6

nu gieta 3531

nu (. . .) þa 614, 2569

nu (. . .) þæt 2592-3, 2784 and fn. 126

*genugan 991 fn.

nyllan 917, 2306

nymþe, *see* nefne

nytan 2059, 2862, 3416, 3500

nyten 24

o 'ever' 1128

of 396 and fnn. 99 and 100, 409-16, 432, 437-8, 522, 550, 807, 813, 821-3, 830, 833, 1122, 1162, 1199-203, 1223, 1305-6, 1324, 1326, 1371, 2240, 2242, 2664, 3091, 3242

of hwæm 1149

of þæm dæge þe 2760

of þæm þe 3091

of- 870

ofdune 1124

ofer 1122, 3259

ofercuman 1404, 1406

ofergan 1404-5

oferstigan 3839

ofteon 847, 857-8

ofþyncan 3413, 3808

on, *see* in

-on, *see* -an

on an 2701

on forman 592

on his dagum þe 2644

on þa/þæt gerad . . . þæt 2919

on þa wisan (. . .) þæt 2920

on þæm dagum þe 2644

wiht 3506

willan 917, 919, 947, 990-1024 *passim*, 1690, 1923, 1985, 1997-8, 2007, 2010-12, 2015, 2018, 2081, 2415, 2509, 2535, 2818, 2824, 2900, 2911, 2914, 2956, 2973, 2975a, 2976-80, 2983, 3045, 3049, 3057, 3066, 3069, 3089, 3094, 3121, 3568, 3574, 3576, 3581, 3594, 3596, 3601, 3607, 3619, 3622, 3679, 3706, 3982

willende 993

(ge)wilnian 751 fn. 185, 955, 1342, 2979, 3089, 3094

gewis(s) 378, 432 fn. 111

(ge)witan 'to go' 2948

(ge)witan 'to know' 883, 919, 991 fn., 1011, 1018, 1441, 1952, 1985-6, 1987 fn., 2018, 2056, 2097, 2179, 3087, 3743

witodlice 1861-2, 1991, 3166-8

wiþ 831-2, 2755 fn. 123, 2760, 2926-7, 3367, 3661

wiþ þæm (þæt/þe) 2606, 2891, 2917, 3659, 3661-3

wiþ þæs (þæt) 2478, 2891, 2917, 3661

wiþ þæt (. . .) (þæt) 2426, 2606, 2891, 2917, 2926, 2927 and fn.

wiþ þon gif 3665

wiþ . . . weard(es) 1217

wiþsacan 2040

geworden 674, 778

writan 841, 857

wunian 691, 2948

wuton, *see* uton

ymb(e) 590, 807, 833a, 1218-19, 2926-7, 2955, 3984

ymbe þæt 2926-7

yþmearas 3972

INDEX OF PASSAGES
PARTICULARLY DISCUSSED

A. POETRY

B. PROSE